Lecture Notes in Computer Science 3784

Jianhua Tao Tieniu Tan
Rosalind W. Picard (Eds.)

Affective Computing and Intelligent Interaction

First International Conference, ACII 2005
Beijing, China, October 22-24, 2005
Proceedings

Volume Editors

Jianhua Tao
Tieniu Tan
Chinese Academy of Sciences
National Laboratory of Pattern Recognition
Beijing, P.O. Box 2728, China 100080
E-mail: {jhtao,tnt}@nlpr.ia.ac.cn

Rosalind W. Picard
MIT Media Lab
20 Ames Street, Cambridge, MA 02139, USA
E-mail: picard@media.mit.edu

Library of Congress Control Number: 2005934588

CR Subject Classification (1998): I.4, I.5, I.3, H.5.1-3, I.2.10, J.4, K.3

ISSN 0302-9743
ISBN-10 3-540-29621-2 Springer Berlin Heidelberg New York
ISBN-13 978-3-540-29621-8 Springer Berlin Heidelberg New York

Springer is a part of Springer Science+Business Media

springeronline.com

Printed in Germany

Typesetting: Camera-ready by author, data conversion by Scientific Publishing Services, Chennai, India
Printed on acid-free paper SPIN: 11573548 06/3142 5 4 3 2 1 0

Preface

This volume contains the proceedings of the 1st International Conference on Affective Computing and Intelligent Interaction (ACII 2005) held in Beijing, China, on 22–24 October 2005.

Traditionally, the machine end of human–machine interaction has been very passive, and certainly has had no means of recognizing or expressing affective information. But without the ability to process such information, computers cannot be expected to communicate with humans in a natural way. The ability to recognize and express affect is one of the most important features of human beings. We therefore expect that computers will eventually have to have the ability to process affect and to interact with human users in ways that are similar to those in which humans interact with each other. Affective computing and intelligent interaction is a key emerging technology that focuses on myriad aspects of the recognition, understanding, and expression of affective and emotional states by computers. The topic is currently a highly active research area and is receiving increasing attention. This strong interest is driven by a wide spectrum of promising applications such as virtual reality, network games, smart surveillance, perceptual interfaces, etc.

Affective computing and intelligent interaction is a multidisciplinary topic, involving psychology, cognitive science, physiology and computer science. ACII 2005 provided a forum for scientists and engineers to exchange their technical results and experiences in this fast-moving and exciting field. A total of 45 oral papers and 82 poster papers included in this volume were selected from 205 contributions submitted by researchers worldwide. The papers collected here cover a wide range of topics, such as facial expression recognition, face animation, emotional speech synthesis, intelligent agent, and virtual reality. We wish to thank the members of the Program Committee for their efforts in reviewing all these papers under tight time constraints, the members of the Organizing Committee for their careful and professional work on the logistics of the conference, and all authors for submitting their high-quality work to ACII 2005. Last but not least, the cooperation of Springer as the publisher of this volume is gratefully acknowledged.

We hope that readers find this volume a useful reference on affective computing and intelligent interaction.

August 2005

Conference Chairs: Tieniu Tan, Rosalind Picard
Program Committee Chairs: Jianhua Tao,
Nick Campbell, Andrew Ortony

Preface

This volume contains the proceedings of the 1st International Conference on Affective Computing and Intelligent Interaction (ACII 2005) held in Beijing, China, on 22–24 October 2005.

Traditionally, the machine end of human–machine interaction has been very [illegible]

[illegible]

Organization

ACII 2005 was organized by the National Laboratory of Pattern Recognition, Institute of Automation, Chinese Academy of Sciences. The conference webpage is located at http://www.affectivecomputing.org/2005/index.htm

Conference Chair

Tieniu Tan (Chinese Academy of Sciences, China)
Rosalind W. Picard (MIT, USA)

Program Committee

Chair:	Andrew Ortony (USA)	Nick Campbell (Japan)
	Jianhua Tao (China)	
Members:	Ruth Aylett (UK)	Gerard Bailly (France)
	Joseph Bates (USA)	Niels Ole Bernsen (Denmark)
	Lianhong Cai (China)	Lola Canamero (UK)
	Guozhong Dai (China)	Darryl Davis (UK)
	Dylan Evans (UK)	Xiaolan Fu (China)
	Björn Granström (Sweden)	Jon Gratch (USA)
	Wael Hamza (USA)	Keikichi Hirose (Japan)
	David House (Sweden)	Kristina Höök (Sweden)
	Thomas S. Huang (USA)	Stefanos Kollias (Greece)
	Aijun Li (China)	Henry Lieberman (USA)
	Christine Lisetti (France)	Jean-Claude Martin (France)
	Cindy Mason (USA)	Dominic Massaro (USA)
	Elmar Nöth (Germany)	Ana Paiva (Portugal)
	Zhigeng Pan (China)	Maja Pantic (Netherlands)
	Catherine Pelachaud (France)	Paolo Petta (Austria)
	Helmut Prendinger (Japan)	Fiorella de Rosis (Italy)
	Mark Steedman (UK)	Oliviero Stock (Italy)
	Mark Tatham (UK)	Thomas Wehrle (Switzerland)
	Chung-Hsien Wu (Taiwan)	Guangyou Xu (China)
	Yaser Yacoob (USA)	

Organizing Committee

Coordinator Chair	Jianhua Tao	
Technical Program Co-chairs	Zengfu Wang	Zhiliang Wang
	Hongxun Yao	Li Zhao
Publicity Co-chairs	Xiaolan Fu	Aijun Li
	Zhigeng Pan	Dongyi Chen

Publication Chair	Hoffmann Alfred	
Local Arrangement Co-chairs	Yiqiang Chen	Zhengxin Sun
Financial Chair	Wei Zhao	

Sponsored By

Nokia Ltd., China
Siemens Ltd., China

Supported By

International Speech Communication Association
National Natural Science Foundation of China
Chinese Association of Automation
China Society of Image and Graphics
China Computer Federation
National High-Tech Research and Development Program

Table of Contents

Affective Face and Gesture Processing

Affective Speech Processing

Evaluation of Affective Expressivity

Affective Database, Annotation and Tools

Psychology and Cognition of Affect

Affective Interaction and Systems and Applications

Gesture-Based Affective Computing on Motion Capture Data

Asha Kapur[2], Ajay Kapur[1], Naznin Virji-Babul[1], George Tzanetakis[1], and Peter F. Driessen[1]

[1] University of Victoria,
Victoria, British Columbia, Canada
{ajay, peter}@ece.uvic.ca, naznin@dsrf.org, gtzan@cs.uvic.ca
[2] Wake Forest University, School of Medicine,
North Carolina, United States
akapur@wfubmc.edu

Abstract. This paper presents research using full body skeletal movements captured using video-based sensor technology developed by Vicon Motion Systems, to train a machine to identify different human emotions. The Vicon system uses a series of 6 cameras to capture lightweight markers placed on various points of the body in 3D space, and digitizes movement into x, y, and z displacement data. Gestural data from five subjects was collected depicting four emotions: sadness, joy, anger, and fear. Experimental results with different machine learning techniques show that automatic classification of this data ranges from 84% to 92% depending on how it is calculated. In order to put these automatic classification results into perspective a user study on the human perception of the same data was conducted with average classification accuracy of 93%.

1 Introduction

Detecting and recognizing biological motion is an essential aspect of human evolutionary survival. The visual-perceptual system is extremely sensitive to the implicitly coherent structure revealed through biological movement. Humans have the ability to extract emotional content from non-verbal human interaction, facial expressions and body gestures. Training a machine to recognize human emotion is far more challenging and is an active field of research generally referred to as affective computing. Advances in this area will have significant impact on human-computer interactive interfaces and applications.

Imagine online learning systems which sense if a student is confused and re-explain a concept with further examples [1]. Imagine global positioning systems in cars re-routing drivers to less crowded, safer streets when they sense frustration or anger [2]. Imagine lawyers using laptops in the court room to analyze emotional behavior content from witnesses. Imagine audiovisual alarms activating when security guards, train conductors, surgeons or even nuclear power plant workers are bored or not paying attention [3]. These possible scenarios are indicative examples of what motivates researchers in this emerging field.

Currently there are two main approaches to affective computing: Audio-based techniques to determine emotion from spoken word are described for example in

J. Tao, T. Tan, and R.W. Picard (Eds.): ACII 2005, LNCS 3784, pp. 1 – 7, 2005.

[4,5,6] and video-based techniques that examine and classify facial expressions are described in [7,8,9]. More advanced systems are multi-modal and use a variety of microphones, video cameras as well as other sensors to enlighten the machine with richer signals from the human [10,11,12]. The above list of references is representative of existing work and not exhaustive. For more details on the evolution and future of affective computing as well as more complete lists of references readers are pointed to papers [3,13].

In the review of the literature as briefly discussed above, almost all systems focus on emotion recognition based on audio or facial expression data. Most researchers do not analyze the full skeletal movements of the human body, with the exception of [14] that uses custom-built sensor systems such as a "Conductor's Jacket", glove, and respiratory sports bra for data acquisition of selected human body movements. Others have used motion capture systems for affective computing experiments with different methods to our own [15, 16]. Research by [17,18] present experiments which confirm that body movements and postures do contain emotional data. Our team has designed a system that uses the VICON[1] motion capturing system to obtain gestural data from the entire body to identify different types of emotion.

In this paper we will first describe the VICON motion capturing system and how it is used to collect data for our experiments. Using the collected data we show results of training automatic emotion classifiers using different machine learning algorithms. These results are compared with a user study of human perception of the same data.

2 Motion Capture System

In this section we will describe how the VICON motion system captures body movement and the method in which the data was collected for the experiments.

2.1 Vicon Motion Systems

The Vicon Motion System is designed to track human or other movement in a room-size space. Spheres covered with reflective tape, known as markers, are placed on visual reference points on different parts of the human body. The VICON system consists of 6 cameras and is designed to track and reconstruct these markers in 3-dimensional space. When a marker is seen by one of the cameras, it will appear in the camera's view as a series of highly illuminated pixels in comparison to the background. During capture the coordinates of all the markers in each camera's view are stored in a data-station. The VICON system then links the correct positions of each marker together to form continuous trajectories, which represent the paths that each marker has taken throughout the capture and thus how the subject has moved over time. At least three of the cameras must view a marker for the point to be captured. Therefore to obtain continuous signals interpolation is used to fill in the gaps [19].

2.2 Data Collection

Markers were placed at 14 reference points on five different subjects (2 of which were professional dancers). The subjects were asked to enact four basic emotions using

[1] http://www.vicon.com (May 2005).

their body movements. No specific instructions for how these emotions should be enacted were given resulting in a variety of different interpretations. The basic emotions used were sadness, joy, anger, and fear. The VICON system measured the trajectories of each subject's movement in 3D space at a sampling rate of 120 Hz. Each subject performed 25 times each emotion for a length of 10 seconds. We manually labeled the reference points of the body throughout the window of movement and filled missing data points by interpolation. A database of 500 raw data files with continuous x, y, and z-coordinates of each of the 14 reference points was created. This database was used to extract features for the machine learning analysis described in section 4. Figure 1 shows a screenshot of the data capturing process.

Data collection involving psychology and perception is challenging and its validity is frequently questioned. Although arguably in acting out these emotions the subject's cognitive processes might be different than the emotion depicted, it turns out that the data is consistently perceived correctly even when abstracted as described in the next section. In addition, since the choice of movements was done freely by the subjects we can stipulate that their motions are analogous to the actual display of these emotions. Even though this way of depicting emotions might be exaggerated it is perceptually salient and its variability provides an interesting challenge to affective computing.

Fig. 1. Screenshot of the data capturing process. The dots on the screen correspond to the markers taped onto the human body.

3 Human Perception

A user study to examine human perception of the motion-capture data was performed in order to provide context for machine learning experiments, as well as to validate the collected data. A subset of 40 randomly ordered files from the database, with an equal proportion of each emotion and subject, were presented to each subject as point light displays. In these point light displays, only the 14 marker points are present (without stick figure lines) and the movement of the subject's emotion for a 10 second period is portrayed. Point light displays were used as they directly correspond to the data provided to the automatic classifiers and their perception is not affected by other semantic cues such as facial expressions.

A group of 10 subjects were tested in classification of these 40 point light displays. A confusion matrix from results of this experiment is shown in Table 1. An average recognition rate of 93% was achieved. It is worth noting that watching a series of 14 moving points humans can accurately identify different human emotions! This is probably achieved by looking at the dynamics and statistics of the motion parameters, which is what we use for features in the automatic system.

Table 1. Confusion matrix of human perception of 40 point light displays portraying 4 different emotions. Average recognition rate is 93%.

Sad	Joy	Anger	Fear	← Classified As
95	0	2	3	***Sad***
0	99	1	0	***Joy***
1	12	87	0	***Anger***
0	2	7	91	***Fear***

4 Machine Learning Experiments

From the human perception experiment described in section 3, it can be seen that motion-capturing preserves the information necessary for identifying emotional content. The next step was to see if machine learning algorithms could be trained on appropriate features to correctly classify the motion-capture data into the 4 emotions. This section describes the feature extraction process followed by experiments with a variety of machine learning algorithms.

4.1 Feature Extraction

After the raw data is exported from the VICON system, as described in section 2.2, feature extraction algorithms are run using a custom built MATLAB program for importing VICON data and extracting features. After experimentation the following dynamics of motion features were selected for training the classifiers. There were 14 markers, each represented as a point in 3D space, $v = [x,y,z]$, where x, y, z are the Cartesian coordinates of the marker's position. In addition, for each point the velocity (first derivative of position) dv/dt and acceleration (second derivative) d^2v/dt^2 were calculated. As we are mainly interested in the dynamics of the motion over larger time scales, we consider the mean values of velocity and acceleration and the standard deviation values of position, velocity and acceleration. The means and standard deviations are calculated over the length of 10-second duration of each emotion depicted. Although it is likely that alternative feature sets could be designed, the classification experiments described in the next section show that the proposed features provide enough information for quite accurate classification results.

4.2 Machine Emotion Recognition Experiments

Five different classifiers were used in the machine learning experiments: a *logistic regression,* a *naïve bayes* with a single multidimensional Gaussian distribution modeling each class, a *decision tree classifier* based on the C4.5 algorithm, a *multi-layer perceptron backpropogation artificial neural network,* and a *support vector machine* trained using the Sequential Minimal Optimization (SMO). More details about these classifiers can be found in [20]. Experiments were performed using *Weka* [20], a tool for data mining with a collection of various machine learning algorithms.

The column labeled "All" on Table 2 shows the classification accuracy obtained using 10-fold cross-validation on all the features from all the subjects and corresponds to a "subject-independent" emotion recognition system. The column labeled

"Subject" shows the means and standard deviations of classification accuracy for each subject separately using 10-fold cross-validation and corresponds to a "subject-specific" emotion recognition system. The last column labeled "Leave One Out" corresponds to the means and standard deviations of classification accuracy obtained by training using 4 subjects and leaving one out for testing.

Table 2. Recognition results for 5 different classifiers

Classifier	All	Subject	Leave One Out
Logistic	85.6 %	88.2%+-12.7%	72.8%+-12.9%
Naive Bayes	66.2 %	85.2% +- 8.8%	62.2%+-10.1%
Decision Tree (J48)	86.4 %	88.2% +- 9.7%	79.4%+-13.1%
Multilayer Perceptron	91.2 %	92.8%+-5.7%	84.6%+-12.1%
SMO	91.8 %	92.6%+-7.8%	83.6%+-15.4%

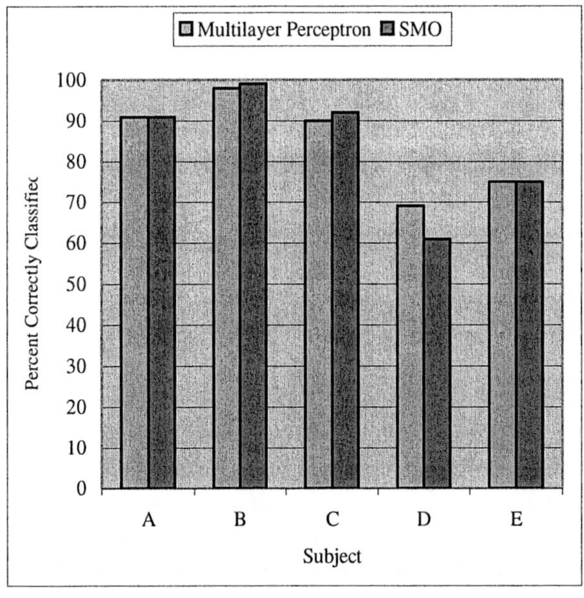

Fig. 2. Graph showing "Leave One Out" classification results for each subject using multi-player perceptron and support vector machine learning classifiers

As can be seen in Figure 2 there is considerable variation in classification accuracy based on which subject is left out. One observation is that the subjects who were professional dancers had a large repertoire of movements for each emotion making them good choices for the training set but poor for the testing set. As a consequence a professional dancer would be better if only one subject can be used to train a motion-based emotion recognition system.

Table 3. Confusion matrix for "subject independent" experiment using support vector machine classifier

Sad	Joy	Anger	Fear	← Classified As
114	0	2	9	***Sad***
0	120	4	1	***Joy***
2	3	117	3	***Anger***
10	3	4	108	***Fear***

Table 3 shows a confusion matrix for "subject independent" using the SMO classifier. As can be seen comparing the confusion matrix for human perception and automatic classification there is no correlation between the confusion errors indicating that even though computer algorithms are capable of detecting emotions they make different types of mistakes than humans.

In all the experiments the support vector machine and the multiplayer perceptron achieve the best classification results. It should be noted that training was significantly faster for the support vector machine.

5 Conclusions and Future Work

We have presented a system for machine emotion recognition using full body skeletal movements acquired by the VICON motion capture system. We validated our data by testing human perception of the point light displays. We found that humans achieved a recognition rate of 93% when shown a 10 second clip. From our machine learning experiments it is clear that a machine achieves a recognition rate of 84% to 92% depending on how it is calculated. SMO support vector machine and multiplayer perceptron neural network proved to be the most effective classifiers.

There are many directions for future work. We are exploring the use of different feature extraction techniques. We also are collecting larger databases of subjects including more intricate detail of facial expression and hand movements. Increasing the number of emotions our system classifies to include disgust, surprise, anticipation and confusion are planned upgrades in the near future. We are moving toward a real-time multimodal system that analyzes data from microphones, video cameras, and the VICON motion sensors and outputs a meaningful auditory response.

References

1. Kapoor, S. Mota, and R.W. Picard, 'Towards a Learning Companion that Recognizes Affect," *Proc. Emotional and Intelligent II: The Tangled Knot of Social Cognition, AAAI Fall Symposium*, North Falmouth, MA, November 2001.
2. R. Fernandez and R. W. Picard, "Modeling Driver's Speech under Stress," *Proc. ISCA Workshop on Speech and Emotions*, Belfast, 2000.
3. M. Pantic, "Toward an Affect-Sensitve Multimodal Human-Computer Interaction," *Proc of the IEEE.* vol. 91, no. 9, September 2003.
4. B.S. Kang, C.H. Han, S. T. Lee, D. H. Youn, and C. Lee, "Speaker dependent emotion recognition using speech signals," *Proc ICSLP,* pp. 383-386. 2000.

5. R. Cowie, E. Douglas-Cowie, N. Tsapatsoulis, G. Votsis, S. Kollias, W. Fellenz, and J. G. Taylor, "Emotion recognition in human-computer interaction," *IEEE Signal Processing Mag.*, vol 18, pp. 32-80, January 2001.
6. D. Ververidis, C. Kotropoulos, and I. Pitas, "Automatic Emotional Speech Classification," *Proc ICASSP,* pp. 593-596. 2004.
7. D. J. Schiano, S. M. Ehrlich, K. Rahardja, and K. Sheridan, "Face to interface: Facial affect in human and machine," *Proc CHI,* pp 193-200, 2000.
8. I.Essa and A. Pentland, "Coding analysis interpretation recognition of facial expressions," *IEEE Trans. Pattern Anal. Machine Intell.*, vol. 19, pp 757-763, 1997.
9. M.J. Blackand Y. Yacoob, "Recognizing facial expressions in image sequences using local parameterized models of image motion," *Int. J. Conmput. Vis.,* vol. 25, no. 1, pp 23-48, 1997.
10. Chen, L.S., Huang, T. S., Miyasato T., and Nakatsu R., "Multimodal Human Emotion/Expression Recognition," *Proc Third International Conference on Automatic Face and Gesture Recognition.* Nara, Japan, 1998.
11. L.C. De Silva, T. Miyasato, and R. Nakatsu, "Facial emotion recognition using multimodal information," *Proc FG,* pp. 332-335, 2000.
12. Y. Yoshitomi, S. Kim, T. Kawano, and T. Kitazoe, "Effect of sensor fusion for recognition of emotional states using voice, face image and thermal image of face," *Proc. ROMAN,* pp. 178-183, 2000.
13. Picard, R. W. "Towards Computers that Recognize and Respond to User Emotions." *IBM System Journal*, vol 39, pp.705-719, 2001.
14. R. W. Picard and J. Healey, "Affective Wearables," *Personal Technologies,* vol. 1, no. 4, pp. 231-240, 1997.
15. F. E, Pollick, H. Paterson, A. Bruderlin, and A. J. Sanford, "Perceiving affect from arm movement." *Cognition*, **82**. B51-B61, 2001.
16. Vines, M. M. Wanderley, C. Krumhansl, R. Nuzzo, and D. Levitin. "Performance Gestures of Musicians: What Structural and Emotional Information do they Convey?", *Gesture-Based Communication in Human-Computer Interaction - 5th International Gesture Workshop,* Genova, Italy. 2003.
17. H.G. Wallbott. "Bodily expression of emotion." *European Journal of Social Psychology* vol. 28, pp. 879-896, 1998.
18. M. DeMeijer. "The contribution of general features of body movement to the attribution of emotions." *Journal of Nonverbal Behavior.* vol. 13, pp. 247-268. 1989.
19. A. Woolard, *Vicon 512 User Manual,* Vicon Motion Systems, Tustin CA, January 1999
20. H. Ian, E. Frank, and M. Kaufmann, *Data Mining: Practical machine learning tools with Java implementations.* San Francisco, 2000.

Expression Recognition Using Elastic Graph Matching

Yujia Cao[1,2], Wenming Zheng[1,2], Li Zhao[1,2], and Cairong Zhou[2]

[1] Research Center for Learning Science, Southeast University, Nanjing 210096, China
[2] Department of Radio Engineering, Southeast University, Nanjing 210096, China
yujia_cao@seu.edu.cn

Abstract. In this paper, we proposed a facial expression recognition method based on the elastic graph matching (EGM) approach.The EGM approach is widely considered very effective due to it's robustness against face position and lighting variations. Among all the feature extraction methods which have been used with the EGM, we choose Gabor wavelet transform according to its good performance. In order to effectively represent the facial expression information, we choose the fiducial points from the local areas where the distortion caused by expression is obvious. The better performance of the proposed method is confirmed by the JAFFE facial expression database, compared to the some previous works. We can achieve the average expression recognition rate as high as 93.4%. Moreover, we can get face recognition result simultaneously in our experiment.

1 Introduction

Facial expression plays an important role in our daily face-to-face communication. Research on facial expression has already had a long history in the psychological field. In 1971, the famous psychologist Ekman defined six basic expressions: anger, disgust, fear, happy, sad and surprise [1]. This classification method is universal to ages, sex and race, therefore had been widely used in most of the facial expression related works. After 1980s, as the computer technology develops, facial expression analyse becomes more and more popular in pattern recognition and artificial intelligence field [2]. Many techniques are applied to facial expression recognition in recent years, for example: principal component analysis (PCA) [7],[10], Gabor wavelets [10],[17], neural network [8], Hidden Markov Models (HMM) [12], Point Distribute Model (PDM)[9], optical flow [11],[13], facial action coding system (FACS) [14], and so on. In this paper, we will propose a facial expression recognition method based on the elastic graph matching (EGM) approach.

The EGM method was first proposed by Lades et al. [3] and applied to face recognition. The original elastic graph is a rectangular lattice. Gabor wavelet transform is used for feature extraction. Based on the work of Lades et al, Wiskott [4] extracted more than one feature vectors on one fiducial point and called it elastic bunch graph (EBG). It is a net with fiducial points selected more wisely from the face image. Faces with large rotation angle and different size are also taken into consideration. In order to avoid the computational cost caused by the Gabor wavelet transform, Constantine [20] and Kun Ma [19] use morphological feature vectors and

J. Tao, T. Tan, and R.W. Picard (Eds.): ACII 2005, LNCS 3784, pp. 8 – 15, 2005.

discrete wavelet graph to do the elastic graph matching. But they can't get performance as good as the Gabor wavelet. The EGM method with Gabor wavelet features is widely considered very effective due to it's robustness against face position and lighting variations. That is because both the algorithm and the Gabor kernel have some endurance to translation, distortion, rotation, and scaling.

In consideration of the particularity of facial expression recognition task, the fiducial points (nodes of the elastic graph) are defined wisely in our approach. They are put in the local areas where the information of expression is rich. Experiment is designed on the standard facial expression database JAFFE. At the same time of expression recognition, we can get person recognition result simultaneously in our experiment.

2 Gabor Feature Extraction

2.1 Gabor Kernels

The two-dimension Gabor wavelet kernels have the characteristics similar to the mammalian cortical simple cells [5]. They have been found particularly suitable for extracting the local features, therefore are used widely for image analysis. The Gabor kernels take the form of a plane wave restricted by a Gaussian envelop function [3]:

$$\psi(\vec{x}) = \frac{\vec{k}^2}{\sigma^2}\exp(-\frac{\vec{k}^2\vec{x}^2}{2\sigma^2})\left[\exp(i\vec{k}\vec{x}) - \exp(-\frac{\sigma^2}{2})\right] \tag{1}$$

where $\vec{x}$ refers to the location of a given pixel $\vec{x}$ = (i, j); $\boldsymbol{\sigma}$ is a parameter which controls the width of the Gaussian ($\sigma = 2\pi$ in our experiment). The second exponent in the bracket makes the kernel DC-free, so they are robust against average brightness changes. The Gabor kernels are used at five frequencies index v=0,…,4, and eight orientations index μ=0,…,7, which is determined by vector $\vec{k}$:

$$\vec{k} = \begin{pmatrix} k_x \\ k_y \end{pmatrix} = \begin{pmatrix} k_v \cos\varphi_\mu \\ k_v \sin\varphi_\mu \end{pmatrix}, k_v = 2^{-\frac{v+2}{2}\pi}, \varphi_\mu = \mu\frac{\pi}{8} \tag{2}$$

2.2 Wavelet Transform

A wavelet transform is defined as a convolution of an image with the Gabor kernels:

$$C(\vec{x}) = \int \psi(\vec{x} - \vec{x}')I(\vec{x}')d^2\vec{x}' \tag{3}$$

In order to accelerate the computation, we can complete the convolution by the Fast Fourier Transform (FFT) and inverse Fast Fourier Transform (IFFT):

$$C(\vec{x}) = F^{-1}\{F\{\psi(\vec{x})\}F\{I(\vec{x})\}\} \tag{4}$$

Where F and F^{-1} refers to FFT and IFFT, respectively. The convolution result is called wavelet transform coefficients [4].

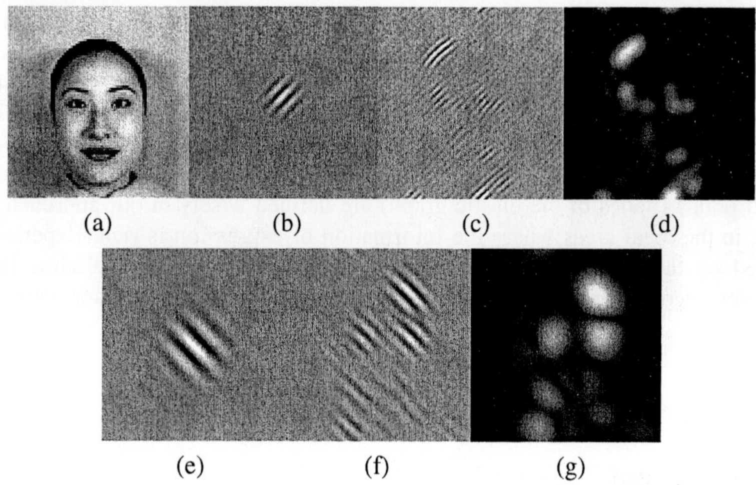

Fig. 1. (a) original image (b) The real part of Gabor kernels at v=2, u=2 (c),(d) the real part and the magnitude of wavelet transform coefficients (e) The real part of Gabor kernels at v=4, u=6 (f),(g) the real part and the magnitude of wavelet transform coefficients

From Fig.1, we can see that the wavelet transform coefficients are relatively small if the grey value in the image changes gently. When the kernel meets the edges in the image, the real part (and the imaginary part) of the coefficient oscillates (with frequency decided by μ), the magnitude grows. The response is especially strong if the direction of the edge and the kernel is identical. If the fiducial points are defined along edges, the real part changes remarkably even within several pixels, however, the magnitude provide a smooth peak [3]. So the magnitude of Gabor wavelet transform coefficients will be used for feature representation.

2.3 Feature Extraction

Applying the convolution with all possible $\vec{k}$, we obtain 40 complex coefficients at one image pixel $\vec{x}$. A vector is set up with the magnitude of these coefficients and is called a jet (5). A set of jets taken from the same fiducial point in different images is called a bunch.

$$\vec{J} = \{abs\{C_i(\vec{x}_0)\}\},\ i = 1,\ldots,40 \tag{5}$$

Distortions caused by facial expressions always occur on some specific areas, e.g. the eyebrow, the upper and lower eyelid, the mouth, the cheek, the chin and the area around the nose. In order to extract features effectively, we define fiducial points at these specific areas (Fig2 (a)), but ignore the forehead, the hair and the face profile [4]. With this development, we can get better performance with less fiducial points, therefore accelerates the matching process.

Some points are connected together to form some metric structure (Fig2 (b)). After extracting one jet at each point, an elastic graph is generated. When matching, the sub graphs (eye model, nose model, mouth model et. al) are allowed to move respectively. If we extract one bunch at each fiducial point, an EBG can be set up (Fig2 (c)).

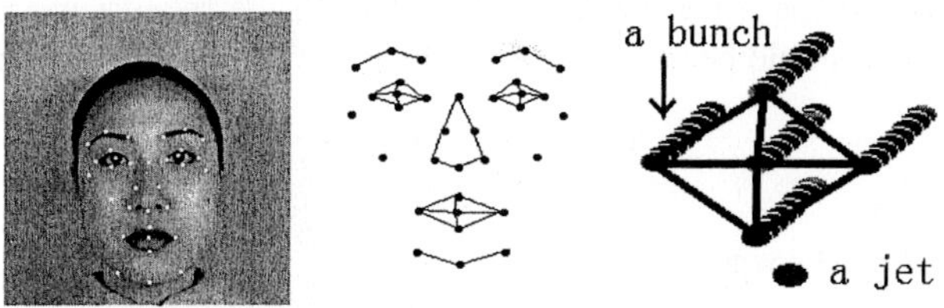

Fig. 2. (a) fiducial points (b) an elastic graph (c) a part of EBG

3 Elastic Graph Matching

As the elastic graph is already generated, we will design a coarse-to-fine process, which guides the elastic graph to match the face. The matching process will be controlled by some similarity functions which are related to the jets and the metric structure.

3.1 The Similarity Function

The similarity function between two jets is defined as:

$$S(\vec{J},\vec{J}')=\frac{<\vec{J},\vec{J}'>}{\|\vec{J}\|\cdot\|\vec{J}'\|} \tag{6}$$

Suppose that G and G' are two elastic graphs, each has N fiducial points. The jets similarity is defined as follows:

$$S_j=\frac{1}{N}\sum_{i=1}^{N}S(\vec{J}_i,\vec{J}_i'),\quad \vec{J}_i\in G,\vec{J}_i'\in G' \tag{7}$$

J_i and J_i' refers to a jet extracted from the i th fiducial point in G and G', respectively. The value of S_j is between -1 and 1. More similar the two model graphs are, the closer S_j is to 1.

The metric structure similarity is defined as:

$$S_e=\frac{1}{E}\sum_{i=1}^{E}|d_i-d_i'| \tag{8}$$

$$\text{where, } d_i=\|\vec{e}_i\|,\vec{e}_i\in \mathrm{G}\ ,\ d_i'=\|\vec{e}_i'\|,\vec{e}_i'\in \mathrm{G}' \tag{9}$$

E is the total number of edges in the elastic graph. $\vec{e}_i$ and $\vec{e}_i$ represents the i th edge in G and G', respectively. d_i and d_i' refer to the length of $\vec{e}_i$ and $\vec{e}_i$. The value of S_e is positive. The greater the difference between two elastic graphs is, the greater the value is. We define a parameter λ to determine the relative weight of jets and metric structure. It should be negative. Then there comes the total similarity function:

$$S_{total} = S_j + \lambda S_e \tag{10}$$

3.2 The Matching Process

The elastic graph matching will be completed from coarse to fine. The matching procedure we designed has the following three stages:

Stage 1: We use the model graph as a whole, which means that the relative positions of fiducial points are not allowed to change. Only S_j is used to calculate the similarity. The elastic graph goes through the whole test image with a step of 8 pixels, searching for a position which has the maximum S_j, then searches in a 9×9 square area around the position with a step of 2 pixels and find the best fitting position again. At the end of this stage, the elastic graph is approximately put on the face.

Stage 2: We match the sub graphs separately. For each sub model, check the ± 1, ± 2, ± 3 position in the x and y dimensions, respectively. At each position, try three different size and $\pm 5°$ rotation. In order to prevent the sub graphs from departing too far away from their original positions and maintain the general shape of the elastic graph, the metric structure is also taken into consideration. Therefore, S_{total} is used to measure the similarity. After this stage, the elastic graph has already matched the face, but still need some refined adjustment.

Stage 3: In order to further enhance the matching precision, each fiducial point moves in a 3×3 square area, scanning for a better fitting position. S_{total} is still used to control the displacements. Some matching results are shown in Fig. 3.

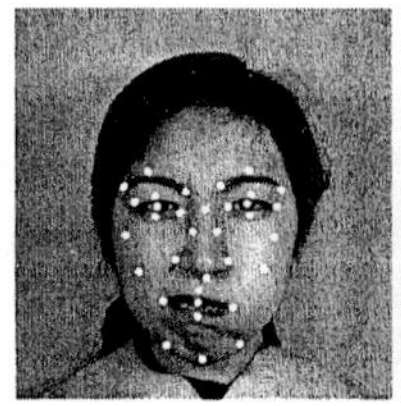 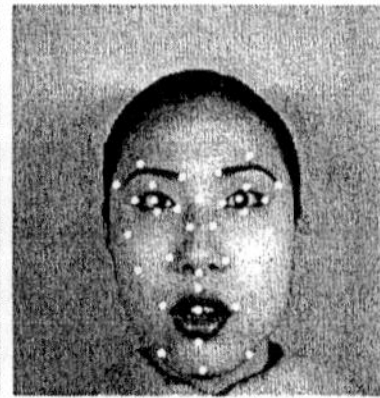  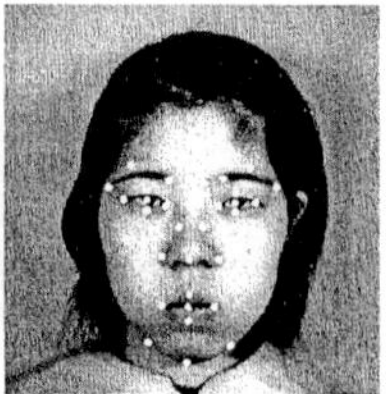

Fig. 3. Some matching results

4 Experiments and Results

The JAFFE database [6] contains 213 images of Japanese women. There are 10 people in the database; each person has 7 expressions (6 basic expressions and neutral face). The image size is 256×256. The faces are all frontal but the illumination intensity is not the same.

The training process has two tasks: 1) Use all the neutral faces to generate an average elastic graph. It will be used for matching a test image. 2) For each expression, use 1/3 training images to generate an EBG. The remaining 2/3 images will be used for testing.

When a test image is input, we firstly use the average elastic graph to do the matching (the process is described in 3.2). When the elastic graph has matched the face precisely, we calculate its graph similarity with the 6 EBGs. The graph similarity function is defined as (11). It is an average of M S_{total} in one EBG. The expression (EBG) with the maximum similarity is identified to be the recognition result. Therefore, a test image is recognized correctly if the EGB of the correct expression yields the highest graph similarity.

$$S_g = \frac{1}{M}\sum_{n=1}^{M}\left[\frac{1}{N}\sum_{i=1}^{N} S\left(\vec{J}_{ni}, \vec{J}_{ni}^{(k)}\right) + \frac{\lambda}{E}\sum_{j=1}^{E} | d_{nj} - d_{nj}^{(k)} |\right], \quad k = 1,\ldots,6 \tag{11}$$

We can also identify the person in the test image to be the one with the maximum S_{total} in the best matching EBG. In this way, we realize the expression recognition and the person recognition simultaneously.

We use the cross-validation technique [21] to yield an average recognition rate (the same experiment procedure was repeated three times). The results are shown in Table1-3. According to the results, we can see that the recognition rate of 'Surprise' and 'Happy' is high, that is because these expressions cause obvious distortion on the face. The muscle movement of the other four expressions is relatively week, therefore they are harder to recognize. We also notice that the person with distinct expression is easy to recognize.

Table 1. Expression average recognition results

Expression	Anger	Disgust	Fear	Happy	Sad	Surprise
Number of test images	20	19	22	21	21	20
Correct recognition	18	16	20	21	20	20
Recognition rate	90.0%	84.2%	90.9%	100%	95.2%	100.0%
Average recognition rate	93.4%					

Table 2. Person average recognition results

person	1	2	3	4	5	6	7	8	9	10
Test images number	14	13	13	11	12	12	11	12	12	13
Correct number	12	13	13	10	10	11	10	11	10	12
Average correct recognition rate: 91.1%										

Table 3. Total results

Total number of test images	Expression √ Person √	Expression × Person ×	Expression × Person √	Expression √ Person ×
123	109	5	3	6

Table 4. Comparison with previous work

Method	Training image ratio	Test image ratio	Recognition rate
LBP+Coarse-to-Fine classification in[15]	8/9	1/9	77%
HLAC+ Fisher weight maps in [16]	8/9	1/9	69.4%
Wavelet +PCA+LDA in [17]	8/9	1/9	75%
	9/10	1/10	92%
Multi-Layer Perceptron in [18]	9/10	1/10	90.1%
Our elastic graph matching method	1/3	2/3	93.4%

We compare our work to some previous work with different methods on the same database. Though the numbers of training images are different, all these recognition results are gained with the cross- validation technique. So they are still comparable. The result (Table 4) shows that the proposed approach achieve higher recognition rate with fewer test images.

5 Conclusion and Future Work

We proposed a facial expression recognition approach based on the elastic graph matching method. Experiment on the JAFFE database shows the performance of our approach. The average recognition rate is 93.4%, which is higher than previous work on the same database. The highest single expression recognition rate reaches 100%.

In the future, we need more studies to test the performance of our approach on images with more challenging variations, such as side lighting, profile faces and glasses. We will try other feature extraction method in aim of accelerate the matching process. If the facial expression recognition technology can be combined with psychology judgement, the performance will be essentially improved to reach the practical applying level.

Acknowledgment

This work was supported in part by the Jiangsu nature science foundations under grants BK2005407.

References

1. P.Ekman, W.V.Friesen, Constants across cultures in the face and emotion, J.Personality Social Psychol. 17 (2) (1971) 124-129.
2. B. Fasel, Juergen Luettinb Automatic facial expression analysis: a survey Pattern Recognition 36 (2003) 259-275

3. Martin Lades et al, Distortion Invariant Object Recognition in the Dynamic Link Architecture, IEEE Trans. Computers, vol. 42, no. 3, March 1993
4. Laurenz Wiskott, Jean-Marc Fellous et al, Face Recognition by Elastic Bunch Graph Matching, IEEE Trans. Pattern Analysis and Machine Intelligence, vol. 19, no. 7, July 1997
5. D.A.Pollen, and S.F.Ronner, Visual Cortical Neurons as Localized Spatial Frequency Filters, IEEE Systems, Man, and Cybernetics, vol.13, no.5, pp.907-916, Sept.-Oct. 1983.
6. Michael J. Lyons, Shigeru Akamatsu et al, Coding Facial Expressions with Gabor Wavelets, Proceedings, Third IEEE International Conference on Automatic Face and Gesture Recognition, April 14-16 1998, Nara Japan, IEEE Computer Society, pp.200-205.
7. Andrew J. Calder, A, Mike Burton, Paul Miller, Andrew W. Young. A Principal Component Analysis of Facial Expressions Vision research 41(2001) 1179-1208
8. C. Lisetti, D. Rumelhart, Facial expression recognition using a neural network, Proceeding of the 11th International Flairs Conference, AAAI Press, New York, 1998
9. C. Huang, Y, Huang, Facial expression recognition using model-based feature extraction and action parameters classification, J. Visual Commun. Image Representation 8(3) (1997) 278-290
10. M. Dailey, G. Cottrell, PCA Gabor for expression recognition, Institution UCSD, Number CS-629, 1999
11. K. Mase, A. Pentland, Recognition of expression from optical flow, IEICE Trans. E 74 (10) (1991) 3474-3483.
12. Ira Cohen, Ashutosh Garg, Thomas S. Huang, Emotion Recognition from Facial Expressions using Multilevel HMM, http://citeseer.ist.psu.edu/502003.html
13. Y. Yacoob, L.S. Davis, Recognition human facial expression from long image sequences using optical flow, IEEE Trans.PAMI, 18(6) (1996) 636－642
14. P. Ekman, E. Rosenberg, J. Hager, Facial action coding system affect interpretation database(FACSAID), www.yahoo.com
15. Xiaoyi Feng, Facial Expression Recognition Based on Local Binary Patterns and Coarse-to-Fine Classification, Proceedings of the Fourth International Conference on Computer and Information Technology (CIT'04)
16. Yusuke Shinohara and Nobuyuki Otsu, Facial Expression Recognition Using Fisher Weight Maps, Proceedings of the Sixth IEEE International Conference on Automatic Face and Gesture Recognition (FGR'04)
17. Michael J. Lyons, Julien Budynek, and Shigeru Akamatsu, Automatic Classification of Single Facial Images, IEEE Trans.PAMI, vol. 21, no. 12, DECEMBER 1999
18. Zhengyou Zhang et al. Comparison Between Geometry-Based and Gabor-Wavelets-Based Facial Expression Recognition Using Multi-Layer Perceptron Automatic Face and Gesture Recognition, 1998. Proceedings. Third IEEE International Conference on 14-16 April 1998 Page(s):454 - 459
19. Kun Ma and Xiaoou Tang, Discrete Wavelet Face Graph Matching, Image Processing, 2001. Proceedings. 2001 International Conference on Volume 2, 7-10 Oct. 2001 Page(s):217 - 220 vol.2
20. Constantine L. Kotropoulos, Anastasios Tefas et al, Frontal Face Authentication Using Discriminating Grids with Morphological Feature Vectors, IEEE Trans. Multimedia, vol. 2, no. 1, March 2000
21. C. Bishop. Neural Networks for Pattern Recognition.Clarendon Press, Oxford, 1995.

The Bunch-Active Shape Model*

Jingcai Fan, Hongxun Yao, Wen Gao, Yazhou Liu, and Xin Liu**

School of Computer Science and Technology,
Harbin Institute of Technology, Harbin, China
{jcfan, yhx, yzliu}@vilab.hit.edu.cn,
wgao@jdl.ac.cn, xin_liu@hit.edu.cn

Abstract. Active Shape Model (ASM) is one of the most powerful statistical tools for face image alignment. In this paper, we propose a novel method, called Bunch-Active Shape Model (Bunch-ASM), based on the standard ASM, to automatically locate facial feature points in Face Recognition. In Bunch-ASM, eyes are localized by a face detector and the matching strategy used in Elastic Bunch Graph Matching (EBGM) is introduced. Experimental results prove that the Bunch-ASM performs much better than the standard ASM and the ASM with iris-refinement.

1 Introduction

Face recognition, as one of the most important techniques of biometric authentication, has received significant attention recently for its wide potential applications, such as public security, law enforcement, information security and financial security, etc., as stated by Wenyi Zhao et al [1]. But the FRVT2000 [2] shows that practical face recognition system is still a great challenge. One of the bottlenecks comes from face alignment. S.Shan et al [3] proved that alignment error would influence the last recognition accuracy greatly.

A variety of approaches have been proposed to deal with the face alignment problem over the past 20 years. Kass et al [4] introduced Active Contour Models (ACM), an energy minimization approach; Cootes et al proposed Active Shape Model (ASM) [5] and later Active Appearance Model (AAM) [6], which have been proven to be the most powerful tools in this field. Yet, as further research shows [7,8,9], the ASM can achieve good performance only when the object or structure class is fairly consistent in shape and intensity appearance. Besides, the Mahalanobis distance used in ASM brings inherent error since the mean shape can not cover the variations of local feature vectors. AAM may give a quite good match to image texture, but when the target image and background vary significantly, it is still unable to locate feature landmarks accurately. Furthermore, both the training process and the searching procedure of AAM are quite complex and slow. Among other methods, Wiskott et al [10] constructed a

* Partially supported by NSFC under contract No. 60332010.

** Corresponding author.

J. Tao, T. Tan, and R.W. Picard (Eds.): ACII 2005, LNCS 3784, pp. 16–23, 2005.

stack-like structure, called Face Bunch Graph. Through the iterating distortion of the graph, this Elastic Bunch Graph Matching (EBGM) algorithm can tolerate a certain degree of pose and expression changes and demonstrate a successful result. However, since this method is Gabor feature based, its time-consuming nodes searching process confines its further progress.

On account of all above, in our work, we represent a novel local matching strategy, called Bunch-ASM, to avoid the inherent error in standard ASM brought by the Mahalanobis distance. Besides, the approach of Wei Wang et al [9] is introduced to initialize the active shape, which has been proved that the location results are more accurate than that of the standard ASM. Experimental results show that the Bunch-ASM proposed in this paper performs much better without increasing much time than ASM.

The remaining part of the paper is organized as follows: In Sec. 2, the standard Active Shape Model is briefly reviewed, and Sec. 3 represents in detail the Bunch-ASM. The experimental results are described in Sec. 4, and Sec. 5 is a short conclusion with an outline of the future work.

2 The Standard Active Shape Model

ASM is definitely one of the most popular approaches for the shape detecting. It allows for considerable variability but still specific to the class of objects or structure they intend to represent.

The ASM depends on a set of points which are thought capable and sufficient to represent objects or image structures, such as the boundary, internal features etc. Given a set of annotated images, the manually labeled landmark points in each image can be represented as a vector:

$$\overrightarrow{X} = (x_0, y_0, x_1, y_1, \cdots, x_{n-1}, y_{n-1})^T \quad . \tag{1}$$

After aligning these vectors by changing the pose (scaling, rotating, and translating) of shapes, Principle Component Analysis [11] is applied to get a set of orthogonal basis $\overrightarrow{P}$ with corresponding eigenvalue $\overrightarrow{b}$. Then:

$$\overrightarrow{X} \approx \overline{x} + \overrightarrow{P}\overrightarrow{b} \quad . \tag{2}$$

where $\overline{x}$ is the mean shape. Meanwhile, Cootes et al [5] used a normalized derivative local texture models, called profile, to updated the position of each landmark depending on Mahalanobis distance between the local texture of each landmark, called the searching profile g_s, and the mean model profile $\overline{g}$. The Mahalanobis distance can be denoted as:

$$f\left(g_s\right) = \left(g_s - \overline{g}\right)^{\mathrm{T}} C_{\mathrm{g}}^{-1} \left(g_s - \overline{g}\right) \quad . \tag{3}$$

where C_{g} is the covariance matrix of the normalized derivative profiles.

3 The Bunch-Active Shape Model

In the standard ASM, the local matching strategy is to calculate the Mahalanobis distance between the profile of each target landmark and that of the mean shape, and then pick up the point whose distance is the smallest upon the local searching profile. As analyzed in Sec. 3.1, the matching strategy would bring inherent error. In this section, we will detailed introduce the Bunch-ASM proposed in this paper.

3.1 Variations of the Profiles

In standard ASM, the calculating Mahalanobis distance is very fast since only the mean shape is needed, instead of all the training set. But the mean shape brings the inherent error because the profiles of the corresponding feature points vary a lot with different face images, as is shown in Fig. 1. We can easily conclude from the Fig. 1 that the profile of the landmark varies greatly with different faces, thus if we use the mean profile of this feature point, inevitable error is brought in.

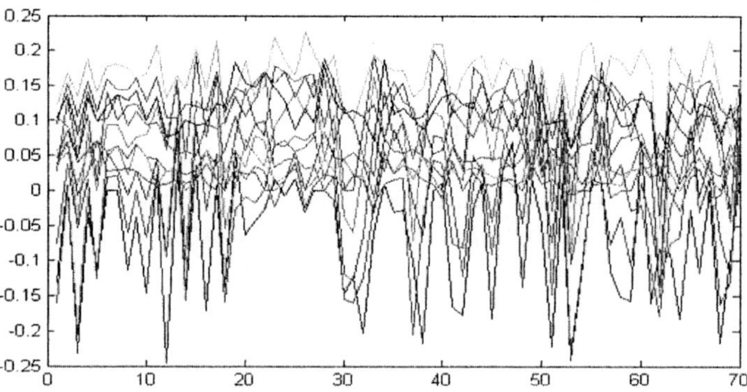

Fig. 1. The variation of the profile of the first landmark in ASM. The value of each dimension of the profile and the face number are represented at the y and x coordinates. And the twelve curves denote the variations of the twelve dimensions in the profile vector, respectively.

3.2 Establishing the Profile Bunch Graph (PBG)

As illuminated above in Sec. 3.1, the mean shape brings unavoidable error because of the great variation of the corresponding profiles. So, in this paper, we build a stack-like structure, called Profile Bunch Graph (PBG), to change the local matching strategy used in the standard ASM.

We choose N face images randomly as our training set to model the variations of the profiles. In Sec. 4.1, we will solve how to fix on the length of our training set.

After the training set has been chosen, we first marked n landmarks by hand on each training face to get the accurate positions so that all the profiles are reliable to establish the PBG, following are the steps:

1. For each feature point i in face image j, find the direction which passes through the landmark in question, perpendicular to the boundary formed by the landmark and its neighbors.
2. Select n_p pixels, centered at the target landmark, of which the gray values consist of the profile of the landmark, denoted by
$$g_{ij} = \left[g_{ij0} \; g_{ij1} \; \cdots \; g_{ijn_p-1} \right]^{\mathrm{T}} . \tag{4}$$
3. Calculate the derivative profile, and the normalized one is given by:
$$y_{ij} = \frac{dg_{ij}}{\sum_{k=0}^{n_p-2} |dg_{ijk}|} . \tag{5}$$
where,
$$dg_{ij} = \left[g_{ij1} - g_{ij0} \; g_{ij2} - g_{ij1} \; \cdots \; g_{ijn_p-1} - g_{ijn_p-2} \right]^{\mathrm{T}} . \tag{6}$$
4. Collect y_{ij} to build a profile bunch in PBG, denoted by:
$$B_i = (y_{i0} \; y_{i1} \; \cdots \; y_{ij} \; \cdots \; y_{iN}) . \tag{7}$$
where $i = 0, 1, \cdots, n$, and $j = 0, \cdots, N$; and
$$B = (B_0 \; B_1 \; \cdots \; B_i \; \cdots \; B_n) . \tag{8}$$
where B is the PBG got from our training set.

One point to be noticed is that, at step 3) we do not work with the actual gray vector, but the normalized derivative one, because this can give invariance to the offsets and uniform scalings of the gray shape model (Cootes et al [5]).

3.3 Initializing the Bunch-ASM

Since the matching strategy of Bunch-ASM depends on the local profiles, the initialization becomes very important. Better initialization would less lead to incorrect local minimal, tending to avoid local optimization.

The standard ASM uses the mean shape as the initialization. Obviously this need to truncate each face image to keep the same size. Moreover, it can not guarantee to get fairly accurate initial position of each feature point. Many methods have been brought forward to improve the performance of the initialization such as Zhao et al [12] and Wang et al [9]. In this paper, we chose the latter, since the former is very inefficient because of the Garbor transposition. With the positions of the two irises, we can calculate the parameters of the scale, rotation, and translation for the target face in the image.

3.4 The Matching Strategy of the Bunch-ASM

After initializing the Bunch-ASM, we begin to use the information obtained from modeling the gray statistics around each landmark, which has been described in detail in Sec. 3.2, to obtain the desired movement or adjustment of each landmark to better fit the target face image.

To find such adjustments, we search along a line passing through the target landmark and particular to the boundary formed by this landmark and its neighbors, which is called a search profile, Cootes et al [5]. We look for a sub-profile which best matches the corresponding profiles in PBG. The progress is showed as follows:

1. For each feature point in the Bunch-ASM on a target face image, find the search profile, which is similar to what is described in Sec. 3.2 at step 1.
2. Get the n_s pixels centered at the feature point in question, of which the gray values make up of the search profile vector, which is denote by:

$$s_j = [s_{j0}\ s_{j1}\ \cdots\ s_{jn_s-1}]^{\mathrm{T}} . \tag{9}$$

and the derivative searching profile and the normalized one would be (10) and (11):

$$ds_j = [s_{j1} - s_{j0}\ s_{j2} - s_{j1}\ \cdots\ s_{jn_s-1} - s_{jn_s-2}]^{\mathrm{T}} . \tag{10}$$

$$y_{sj} = \frac{ds_j}{\sum_{k=0}^{n_s-2} |ds_{jk}|} . \tag{11}$$

3. Examine y_{sj} for a sub-profile that matches PGB best.

   At step 3, we first calculate the Euclidean distance between each sub-profile and the corresponding profile in FBG, and select the smallest one. Secondly, the smallest one among all the searching profile is picked up as the desired movement of the feature landmark in question. Through this way, we can almost capture all of possible variations of the active shape.

3.5 The Procedure of the Bunch-ASM

Before, we have introduced our training set, establishing Bunch-ASM, initializing our feature point shape and the matching strategy of the Bunch-ASM. Following, we give the working procedure of our Bunch-ASM:

1. Initialize the Bunch-ASM on a novel face image, as is described in Sec. 3.3, we get the start position of each feature point in ASM.
2. From the positions got at the previous step, update the location of each landmark by the matching strategy illustrated in Sec. 3.4.
3. Based on the prior knowledge, we adjust the shape to ensure that the shape is specific to the class of face images.
4. Go to step 2 until convergence, or the iteration has reached the maximum time, or no considerable change is observed.

4 Experiment Results

4.1 The Influence of the Length of the Training Set

The size of our training set would certainly influence the effectiveness of the Bunch-ASM. Table 1 shows the correlations between the length of training set, the average location error and the time cost. Each time we added 30 face images into our training set, except the last time, 20 face images.

Table 1. The influences of the length of the training set

Length	40	70	100	130	160	190	220	240
Aver Time	1.152	1.395	1.811	2.110	2.899	3.680	4.003	3.974
Aver Error	3.230	3.084	3.131	3.112	3.081	3.028	3.116	3.127

Table 1 indicates that with the length of training set becoming longer, the time costs more, while the average location error tends to be smaller. We should give a balance between the time cost and the average location error. In this paper, we choose 70 as the length of our training set, as clarified in Sec. 3.2.

4.2 The Performance of Our Bunch-ASM

Our experiment is based on 362 manually labeled face images, most of which are near frontal. We randomly selected 122 ones as our testing set, and the others for training, including the selection of the length, showed in Sec. 4.1. To evaluate the performance of our algorithm, the average Euclidean distance error is calculated by the following equation:

$$E = \frac{1}{N}\sum_{j=1}^{N}\left(\frac{1}{n}\sum_{i=1}^{n}\sqrt{\left(x_{ij}-x_{ij}^{'}\right)^2+\left(y_{ij}-y_{ij}^{'}\right)^2}\right) . \tag{12}$$

where N is the total number of test images, and n is the number of the landmarks in a face image, (x_{ij}, y_{ij}) is the ith manually labeled landmark location of the jth test image; and $\left(x_{ij}^{'}, y_{ij}^{'}\right)$ is the corresponding i^{th} landmark location we calculated.

We also calculated the overall improvement percentage of our algorithm to the standard ASM by:

$$\text{Im} = \frac{\text{Er}_{\text{ASM}} - \text{Er}_{\text{Bunch-ASM}}}{\text{Er}_{\text{ASM}}} \times 100\% . \tag{13}$$

Table 2 lists our final experimental results on 122 test images and 70 training face images. The average error for ASM with iris-refinement is about 3.452 pixels, while the results of our Bunch-ASM is about 3.084 pixels, with the improvement of about 26.0%.

Table 2. Performance of our method

Methods	Ave Error (pixels)	Improvement
ASM	4.169	–
ASM with iris-refinement	3.452	17.2%
Bunch-ASM	3.084	26.0%

Figure 2 lists some matching results of our algorithm as well as the ASM with iris-refinement. Through the comparison, we can see our algorithm improves the searching accuracy significantly.

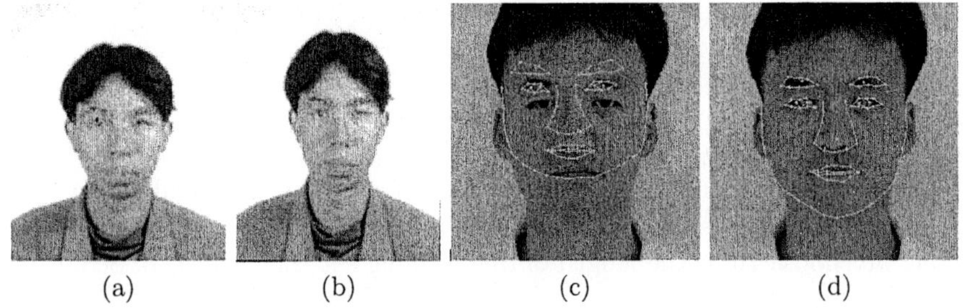

(a) (b) (c) (d)

Fig. 2. The comparison between the ASM with iris-refinement and the Bunch-ASM. And (a), (c) are results of the ASM with iris-refinement; (b), (d) are results of the Bunch-ASM.

5 Conclusions and Further Work

In this research, we proposed a novel method called Bunch-ASM, based on the standard ASM, which not only improves the alignment accuracy greatly but also confines the increase of time consumption. We chose 70 face images at random as our training set, on each of which 103 landmarks are labeled by hand. By clustering the corresponding profiles of each landmark, we built the structure of the Bunch-ASM, called PBG, to which the Euclidean distance from each candidate profile along the searching profile is calculated. The smallest one among all of the candidate profiles is picked up as the updating result at one iterative step. Till convergence, or the iteration has reached the maximum time we set at first, or no considerable change is observed, the iteration ends. Experimental results show that our algorithm performs much better than the standard ASM and the ASM with iris-refinement.

Future work will focus on how to extend the length of the training set without bringing much more time. In this paper we have pointed out that the training set would greatly influence the locating accuracy, more training face images would lead to more accuracy, but would cost more time at the same time. How to settle the contradiction is the emphasis of the future work.

References

1. Zhao, W., Chellappa, R., Rosenfeld, A., Phillips, P.J.: Face Recognition: A Literature Survey. ACM Computing Surveys. **35** Issue 4. (2003) 399–458
2. Blackburn, D.M., Bone, M., Phillips, P.J.: Facial Recognition Vendor Test 2000: evaluation Report. (2001) http:/ /www .frvt.org/frvt2000/
3. Shan, S., Chang, Y., Gao, W., Cao, B.: Curse of Mis-Alignment in Face Recognition: Problem And A Novel Mis-Alignment Learning Solution. Proceeding of The 6th International Conference on Face and Gesture Recognition. (2004) 314–320
4. Kass, M., Witkin, A., Terzopoulos, D.: Active Contour Models. The 1st International Conference on Computer Vision. London (1987) 259–268
5. Cootes, T.F., Taylor, C.J., Cooper, D.H., Graham, J.: Active Shape Models - Their Training and Application. Computer Vision and Image Understanding. **61** No.1. (1995) 38–59
6. Cootes, T.F., Edwards, G.J., Taylor, C.J.: Active Appearance Models. Proc. European Conf. Computer Vision. **2** (1998) 484–498
7. Ginneken, B.V., Frangi, A.F.: A Non-linear Gray level Appearance Model Improves Active Shape Model Segmentation. IEEE Workshop on Mathematical Models in Biomedical Image Analysis. (2001) 205–212
8. Rogers, M., Graham, J.: Robust Active Shape Model Search. Proceedings of the European Conference on Computer Vision. (2002) 517–530
9. Wang, W., Shan, S., Gao, W., Cao, B.: An Improved Active Shape Model For Face Alignment. The 4th International Conference on Multi-modal Interface, IEEE ICMI 2002. Pittsburgh, USA. (2002) 523–528
10. Wiskott, L., Fellous, J.M., Kruger, N., Malsburg, C.V.C.: Face Recogniton by Elastic Bunch Graph Matching. IEEE Trans. On PAMI. **19** No. 7. (1997) 775–779
11. Kirby, M., Sirovich, L.: Application of the Karhunen-Loeve procedure for the haracterization of human faces. IEEE Transactions on Pattern Analysis and Machine Intelligence, **12** No. 1. (1990) 103–108
12. Zhao, S., Gao, W., Shan, S., Yin, B.: Enhance the Alignment Accuracy of Active Shape Models Using Elastic Graph Matching. ICBA'04. (2004) 52–58

Facial Signs of Affect During Tutoring Sessions*

Dirk Heylen[1], Mattijs Ghijsen[2], Anton Nijholt[1], and Rieks op den Akker[1]

[1] University of Twente
[2] University of Amsterdam, The Netherlands

Abstract. An emotionally intelligent tutoring system should be able to taking into account relevant aspects of the mental state of the student when providing feedback. The student's facial expressions, put in context, could provide cues with respect to this state. We discuss the analysis of the facial expression displayed by students interacting with an Intelligent Tutoring System and our attempts to relate expression, situation and mental state building on Scherer's component process model of emotion appraisal.

1 Introduction

INES is an Intelligent Tutoring System that the Human Media Interaction group of the University of Twente is developing as a test-bed for research on multimodal interaction, intelligent agent technology and affective computing ([1] and [2]). In previous work we have investigated strategies for the tutoring agent to give appropriate emotionally intelligent feedback. Ultimately, one would want the system to choose it actions fitting the personality of the students, their reactions to what is happening, their motivation and other aspects of their mental state, in the hope that this will optimize the learning process. In the work described in [3] we discussed how, in the system developed so far, the choice of teaching strategy, the kind of feedback and the form in which this was realized - the kind of dialogue act and stylistic features of the utterance - were co-determined by an hypothesized emotion model of the student. The model changed dynamically on the basis of the level of student activity and the way the student performed the exercise (the number and type of errors). This model and the resulting system was evaluated by having the system generate responses in a number of scenario's and letting people judge the appropriateness of the sessions for different settings of the system.

The design of a tutoring system is a fertile ground for further studies on affective interaction. An obvious issue on the agenda is how we can detect more accurately what the student is actually experiencing during the exercise. The idea that facial expressions may provide cues for this is something that readily springs to mind ([4],[5]), but which is not without its problems. The (marked) facial expressions displayed during interactions might only be few in number

* Part of this work was carried out in the context of the EU Project HUMAINE (IST-2002-507422).

J. Tao, T. Tan, and R.W. Picard (Eds.): ACII 2005, LNCS 3784, pp. 24–31, 2005.

and it is may not be easy to recognize expressions automatically. Moreover, as is well-known, the expressions that are being displayed cannot be taken as simple read outs of the mental state. Associating an expression displayed with an emotion experienced is not a trivial problem (also from a methodological point of view). The remark in [6] that "None of the methods I describe claim to recognize the underlying emotion, but only the expression on the user's face." (p. 175) is telling in this respect. Besides, many facial expressions are determined by other factors than the emotional state: they may be adaptors, have a conversational function, or be expressive of a meta-cognitive state as "thinking face" described in [7], for instance. And, finally, even if we were somewhat confident that the cues we interpret tell us something about the mental state this may not be something useful for optimizing the tutoring process. We therefore started a pilot experiment in which we looked for answers to the following questions: what kinds of facial expressions occur on student's faces during interactions with the INES system and how can we make sense of them. We collected video material from students interacting with the system and explored a method to describe the affective information.

We collected over one hour of video material of students interacting with the INES system. In this paper we will discuss our analysis of the number and kind of facial expressions displayed and the situations in which they occurred. The question we are interest in is what the expressions tell us about the mental state and what events in the context triggered the state/expression. This information can be used by the tutoring system to adapt its strategy. There are various ways one could go about, none completely reliable. One way to proceed to get information about the mental state is to ask the students post-hoc. Another method is to rely on the experimenter's interpretative skills: how do people who view the video interpret the expression in context. For our pilot we relied on this second approach, which is not without its limitations but becomes more reliable when judgements of different people agree. A third method would be to look up the displays in the dictionary of facial expressions and determine their meaning in that way. Of course, the problem is that no dictionaries of this kind exist that can be used for this purpose. Moreover, it is clear that if such a dictionary existed it would list multiple meanings for each expression and map multiple expressions to the same meaning. Nevertheless, emotion theorists, communication researchers and facial expression specialists have made inventories of associations between expression and mental state. These attempts at mapping may be used heuristically or as a first model of what happens. With this in mind we have compiled a kind of facial expression dictionary[1] from the hints in the literature and made an attempt to evaluate this on our data. We have looked at Scherer's component process approach to find a way to come to grips with the relation between facial expressions, the situation they occur in and the mental state of the student ([8] and [9], [10]). The aim is to derive a table associating elements

[1] We are reluctant to use the word dictionary as the term expresses a rather naive view on the relation between facial expression and emotion. On the other hand, for the system to be implemented simplifications will have to made anyway.

of the tutoring situation, the facial expressions that occur in that situation and the mental state one might assume to hold that is consistent with the data and that might be of use for the tutoring system. In the next section we describe how we collected and analyzed the data.

2 INES

The current demo version of INES implements an exercise which teaches students how to give a subcutaneous injection in the arm of a virtual patient. Students can interact with the patient using speech. The objects in the virtual world that are needed to give the injection are manipulated using a haptic device (a Phantom). The tutoring agent provides instructions and feedback through spoken natural language output and haptic feedback through the haptic device. The tutor is also represented by a talking head.

Fig. 1. Camera positions

We used two webcams (as is shown in Figure 1) in the experiment. One webcam was placed on top of the screen of the system where the student is working with the INES system. The other webcam was placed behind the student and captures the actions with the phantom and the screen. All subjects received an explanation of the exercise in advance (as would be the case with an actual nursing student). They carried out the exercise three times in succession.

2.1 The Exercise

An exercise consists of the following steps:

1. The student has to ask (speech) the patient if she wants to place her right arm on the table and roll up the sleeve of the right arm.
2. Next, the student needs to disinfect the region on the upper arm where he or she wants to inject the medicine. This is done by using the haptic device. When the student moves the haptic device a 3D graphical representation of a pair of tweezers holding a ball of sterile cotton will also be moving accordingly.

3. Next, the student has to insert the needle into the skin of the patient. This is again done by using the haptic device and a 3D representation of a syringe. The tip of the needle has to be positioned right under the skin. Because of the force feedback from the device the student can feel the depth of the needle in the skin layer and the force that needs to be used to get the needle at the required depth.
4. The final step is to inject the medicine and withdraw the needle. This again is done by use of the haptic device.

The actual exercise a nurse has to perform, consists of many more steps before and after this sequence ([11]) but the steps shown above are the only ones were used in the experiment [2]. Table 1 shows a transcript of a part of the exercise.

Table 1. Transcript of an exercise

```
Student: Put your right arm on the table.
Patient: I didn't understand what you said, could you repeat the sentence?
Patient: Where do I have to put my arm?
<student raises eyebrows and pulls down mouth corners>
Student: Put your right arm on the table.
Patient: OK
<patient places her arm on the table>
Student: Could you pull up your sleeve?
Patient: Which sleeve should I pull up?
Student: Of your right arm.
Patient: OK
<patient pulls up sleeve>
<student starts disinfecting the arm of the patient>
<student smiles>
<student has finished disinfecting the arm of the patient>
<student smiles>
<student starts injecting the medicine>
<student has completed the task>
<student smiles>
```

3 Expressions

Each time a subject performed the exercise it was recorded in a take. By watching the takes, the marked facial expressions were put in a table, together with the situation in which they occurred. Table 2 summarizes the result of all takes.

A variety of facial expressions occur but on the whole most of the time the students remain largely 'expressionless'. The table shows, for instance, that when the patient asks for clarification ("Which arm should I put on the table") this is accompanied by several movements: eyebrows are raised, a frown shows, and the head is tilted backwards. They can be interpreted as an instance of slight surprise. The student does not expect the patient to say something except for "I did not understand what you said". When the patient pulls up her sleeve similar displays occur: smiles, eyebrow raises, a head nod, and a pulling back of the head. The head nod in this particular instance functions as a kind of acknowledgement. The table shows that seemingly autonomous actions by the patient are greeted with quite a few expressions.

Table 2. The occurrence of facial expressions in different situations

Situation / Facial Expression	smile	brows up	mouth down	frown	nod	tilt	head back
P. does not understand S.							
P. asks for clarification		2		1			1
P. repeatedly does not understand S.	2						
P. does not respond to what S. says	1	1	1				
P. says something unexpected							
S. asks P. to do something		1					
S. gives P. more information	1						
P. pulls up her sleeve	4	2			1		1
P. puts arm on the table	1	2			2	1	
S. disinfects the arm	7	1					
S. finished disinfecting	2						
S. injects the medicine	3						
S. finished injecting the medicine	1	2	1				
OTHER	1	2	1				

A second class of situations that brings forth expressions on the face contains the cases where the student manipulates the haptic device. When disinfecting and injecting a lot of smiles occur and some other expressions.

Most of the time it is not difficult for us, when looking at the video, to imagine what state of mind the student is in when displaying the particular expression. It is almost always obviously what event triggers the occurrence of a marked expression. But in order to use this information in a tutoring system, we wanted to describe the relation between situation, expression and ascribed state more systematically. We looked at the literature for a way to help us explain what is it about the situation and particularly the student's appraisal of it that triggers the facial expression. We chose to explore the use of Scherer's component process analysis as one way to describe the relation between facial expression, type of situation and mental state by stimulus evaluation checks.

4 Interpretation

In [9], Scherer describes a model that explains how an organism evaluates stimuli in a series of appraisal checks. The general idea is that the outcome of these checks result in specific facial expressions. This can be used to relate stimulus (situation), facial expression and appraisal (mental state). Table 3 show the various checks for dimensions such as novelty (suddenness, familiarity, predictability), pleasantness, goal significance (relevance, expectation of outcome, etcetera), coping potential and compatibility standards. These are related to facial expressions, indicated by Action Unit numbers. The table is adapted from [10].

Table 3. Predictions of Facial Expression Changes

Appraisal dimension	Outcome A	Outcome B
Novelty	**High**	**Low**
Suddenness	1 + 2 + 5 + 26/27	–
Familiarity	–	4b + 7
Predictability	–	4b + 7
Intrinsic pleasantness	**High**	**Low**
	5a + 26a	4 + 7/43)/44 + 51/52 + (61/62)

If we look at our data, one can think about each of the types of situation that occur and make educated guesses as to what kinds of appraisals these situations are likely to give rise to. For instance, in our case, one could come up with something as in Table 4 (this is part of the table only).

Table 4. Situations expressed in terms of SECs

	Situation description	Novel	Pleasant	Goal	Coping
(1)	Patient does not understand what the student has said.	-	Low	Obstruct	Low
(2)	Patient asks for clarification.	-	Neutral	Neutral	Low
(3)	Patient repeatedly does not understand what the student has said.	-	Low	Obstruct	Low
(4)	Patient does not respond at all to anything the student says.	-	Low	Obstruct	Low
(5)	Patient says something unexpected.	-	Low	Neutral	Low
(6)	Student asks the patient to do something.	-	Neutral	Conducive	High

It should be noted that we have greatly reduced the number of stimulus evaluation checks for the pilot. If the patient pulls up her sleeve, after the student has asked her as part of the exercise, then this is conducive to the goal of the student but the control the student has is low (control being one aspect of coping potential). Novelty is not scored in this table because it is typically not a property of situation types but rather of actual situations. This table gives us then an idea of the *relation between situation and expected appraisal* (**A**).

From the opposite perspective, one can look at the expressions that occur and look up what appraisal dimensions might have led to these expressions, using associations as in Table 3. Here appraisal dimensions are associated with Facial Action Units. Of course the ambiguity of the expression and the nature of the appraisal process operating in real life make these things much more complicated. The theory was not designed to be used as a dictionary. Let alone, that it is designed to be complete. It is obvious that we are reducing the complexity, hoping to arrive at a reasonable guess about how the student experiences the situation. However, what we get out of this is a crude indication of the *relation between facial expression and appraisal* (**B**).

The data about the actually occurring expressions with the situation when they occur has been tabulated as well. They were derived from the transcripts. This indicates the *relation between facial expression and situation* (**C**). Given **A** and **B**, a system could infer aspects of the mental state of a student when presented with **C**. Either the facial expression will correspond with what can be expected from the theory or the tables will not provide direct information about how to relate the expression and the situation at all. In that case, the system could decide that the student is experiencing something different from what would be expected and can use the association between expression and appraisal (**B**) to make a guess about the most probable mental state or about something deviant that may have happened. All this assumes that the various associations make sense. At the early stages of data collection, however, incompatibilities will lead more likely to adjustments of the 'dictionary' (refining the situation descriptions, changing the analysis in terms of the evaluation checks or changing the associations).

It is also possible to attempt an interpretation of the actually occurring expressions in terms of stimulus evaluation checks, by looking at the expressions and make judgements about the mental state[2]. Such an analysis is presented in Table 5. This table shows how the facial expressions (smile, raise eyebrows, pull down mouth corners and frown) correspond with the characteristics of the situation (expressed as SEC parameters). It shows that smiles often occur in situations that we assume to have a high pleasantness and a conducive goal significance, as one might expect.

Table 5. Results of comparing facial expressions and situations

Facial expression	Novel	Pleasant	Goal	Coping
Smile (Total=22)	3	18	19	14
Raise eyebrows (Total=11)	7	4	2	0
Pull down mouth corners (Total=2)	2	1	1	1
Frown (Total=1)	0	0	0	1

5 Discussion

Looking at the real data one can thus evaluate the predictions of the theory - the adapted dictionary - further. Such investigations can be used as a heuristic procedure to derive more detailed triples (situation, expression, presumed mental state). In case there are mismatches between the conjectured Stimulus Evaluation Checks and the ones that are associated with the facial expressions

[2] One could adopt various methods to attempt this, with more or less reliability ([12]).

one might assume that either the situation specification should be refined or the relations between expression and appraisal might need to be revisited. Clearly, for the simple case we have presented we know that both of these will have to be refined. Our classification of situations, for instance, is too coarse grained. The particular situation with all the contextual features is what gives rise to the actual appraisals. By collecting and analyzing more data in this way one can refine the specification of the associations between expression, appraisal and situation.

Our goal with looking at the facial expressions during tutoring sessions is to get information about aspects of the mental state of the student that may be useful to know for the system in order to adapt its teaching strategy. It remains to be seen whether the facial expressions are a useful cue, whether valid inferences can be made and whether they can lead to useful actions of the system. One of the issues related to this is whether the stimulus evaluation checks provide the information that is appropriate for the system to react to.

References

1. Hospers, M., Kroezen, E., Nijholt, A., op den Akker, R., Heylen, D.: 9. In: An agent-based intelligent tutoring system for nurse education. Volume Applications of intelligent agents in health care. Birkhauser, Basel (2003) 143–159
2. Kole, S.: Tactile, spoken, and visual interaction within an intelligent tutoring system. Master's thesis, Department of Electical Engineering, Mathematics, and Computer Science, University of Twente, Enschede (2004)
3. Heylen, D., Vissers, M., op den Akker, R., Nijholt, A.: Affective feedback in a tutoring system for procedural tasks. In André, E., Dybkjaer, L., Minker, W., Heisterkamp, P., eds.: Affective Dialogue Systems, Heidelberg, Springer (2004) 244–253
4. D'Mello, S.K., Craig, S.D., Gholson, B., Franklin, S., Picard, R., Graesser, A.: Integrating affect sensors in an intelligent tutoring system. In: Affective Interactions, Workshop at IUT (2005)
5. Lisetti, C., Schiano, D.: Facial expression recognition: where human computer interaction, artificial intelligence, and cognitive science intersect. Pragmatics and Cognition **8** (2000) 185–235
6. Picard, R.: Affective Computing. The MIT Press, Cambridge, Massachusetts (2000)
7. Goodwin, M., Goodwin, C.: Gesture and coparticipation in the activity of searching for a word. Semiotica **62** (1986) 51–75
8. Scherer, K.: 14. Approaches to Emotions. In: On the Nature and Function of Emotion: A Component Process Approach. Lawrence Erlbaum Associates, Hillsdale, New Jersey (1984) 293–318
9. Scherer, K.: Toward a dynamic theory of emotion: The component process model of affective states. Copy retrieved [02-26-2004] from: http://www.unige.ch/fapse/emotion/publications/list.html (1987)
10. Wehrle, T., Kaiser, S., Schmidt, S., Scherer, K.: Studying the dynamics of emotional expression using synthesized facial muscle movements. Journal of Personality and Social Psychology **78** (2000) 105–119
11. Hospers, M., Kroezen, L.: I.N.E.S. intelligent nursing education software. Master's thesis, Departement of Computer Science University of Twente (2002)
12. Ekman, P., O'Sullivan, M.: Facial expression: Methods, means, and moues. (In Feldman, R.S., Rimé, B., eds.: Fundamentals of nonverbal behavior) 163–199

Towards Unsupervised Detection of Affective Body Posture Nuances

P. Ravindra De Silva, Andrea Kleinsmith, and Nadia Bianchi-Berthouze

Database Systems Laboratory, University of Aizu, Aizu Wakamatsu 965-8580, Japan
{d8052201, nadia}@u-aizu.ac.jp,
andi@andisplanet.com

Abstract. Recently, researchers have been modeling three to nine discrete emotions for creating affective recognition systems. However, in every day life, humans use a rich and powerful language for defining a large variety of affective states. Thus, one of the challenging issues in affective computing is to give computers the ability to recognize a variety of affective states using unsupervised methods. In order to explore this possibility, we describe affective postures representing 4 emotion categories using low level descriptors. We applied multivariate analysis to recognize and categorize these postures into nuances of these categories. The results obtained show that low-level posture features may be used for this purpose, leaving the naming issue to interactive processes.

1 Introduction

Piller [1] states that computers are entering into a new radical era called affective computing, which is able to identify a large variety of affective states. At the moment, most of the studies have attempted to model three to nine discrete emotions for creating affective gesture recognition systems. However, in everyday life, humans use a richer and more powerful language for defining affective states. Whissell [2]lists 109 words for describing affective states and Plutchik [3] lists 142. Also in daily life people define and express affective states differently in different situations and at different times.

Many emotion recognition systems can recognize mainly basic universal expressions of emotion. However, the human face and body are capable of displaying many more emotional expressions, and little research has been conducted in this direction, mainly due to the limited availability of data on other expressions. Only recently, nuances of emotion have started to be explored in the domain of speech synthesis and facial expression [4][5]. Another interesting work in this direction is described in [6]. They proposed to arrange the six basic emotions as equally distant on the border of a disc according to their similarity. To every point on the disc, a facial expression was associated which was computed by linear interpolation between the closest basic emotions. Their distance from the circle center described their intensity. In the same study, the authors presented a second method to obtain new expressions based on PCA. However, the created

J. Tao, T. Tan, and R.W. Picard (Eds.): ACII 2005, LNCS 3784, pp. 32–39, 2005.

expressions were somewhat awkward, meaning that significant PCA components for representing new affective states were not identified.

While this work focuses on generating new affective states, we aim at recognizing nuances of affective states. We will focus on affective states expressed through body gestures. Although it has previously been argued that body posture is not the primary channel for conveying emotion [7], more recent findings indicate that the body is used for emotional display more than formerly thought [8]. In fact, the role of posture in affect recognition has been accepted and researched within several research areas including psychology. However, amongst computer scientists it is currently a novel approach [9][10]. Most of the research on affective communication has, in fact, focused on face, hand gesture, and voice.

Our main goal is to investigate the possibility of grounding nuances of affective states on a low level description of human postures using an unsupervised method. This is a very important issue in affective human interaction since it would reduce the necessity of continuous feedback. Recently, [11] proposes a recognition system that integrates supervised and unsupervised learning mechanisms to recognize affective postures and lets a common affective lexicon emerge through the interaction of the system with the user. The results show that the system can quite well learn to discriminate between different emotions. However, the authors did not address the problem of nuances.

This paper is organized as follow. In section 2, we report on the way of collecting the set of affective postures and the description method used. In section 3, we describe the model for discriminating between nuances of emotions. In section 4 we discuss the posture features that support such discrimination.

2 Affective Posture Description

In a previous work [12], we used a motion capture system (32 markers) to capture 3D affective gestures from 13 human subjects. The actors were asked to perform an in-place motion to express anger, fear, happiness, and sadness. As there were no constraints placed on the actors, each person was able to freely express the emotion. The capturing sessions were scheduled such that the actors were not allowed to observe each other. In total, 181 gestures were collected. For each gesture, we selected the frame (i.e., a static posture) that the actor evaluated as being the most expressive instant of the gesture. We used a set of 24 low-level posture features (Table 1) to describe each posture. The low-level features of each posture were automatically computed on the basis of the 3D position of the 32 markers describing the selected frame.

In order to assess the affective state conveyed by the postures (and not by the facial expression), we used the 3D coordinates of the selected frames to build faceless avatars. 40 Japanese undergraduate students were asked to assign to each posture an emotion label, chosen from a list of 8 emotions, and an intensity value between 1 and 5. This 8-word list was comprised of pairs of labels indicating two different nuances of the same emotion: anger (*upset*, *angry*), sadness (*sad*, *depressed*), happiness (*happy*, *joyful*) and fear (*fearful*, *surprised*). Table 2 shows

Table 1. The table lists the set of posture features proposed. The Code column indicates the feature codes used in the paper. The following short-cuts are used: L: Left, R: Right, B: Back, F: Front.

Code	Posture Features	Code	Posture Features
V4	$Orientation_{XY}$: B.Head - F.Head axis	V5	$Orientation_{YZ}$: B.Head - F.Head axis
V6	$Distance_z$: R.Hand - R.Shoulder	V7	$Distance_z$: L.Hand - L.Shoulder
V8	$Distance_y$: R.Hand - R.Shoulder	V9	$Distance_y$:L.Hand - L.Shoulder
V10	$Distance_x$:R.Hand - L.Shoulder	V11	$Distance_x$:L.Hand - R.Shoulder
V12	$Distance_x$:R.Hand - R.Elbow	V13	$Distance_x$:L.Hand - L.Elbow
V14	$Distance_x$: R.Elbow - L.Shoulder	V15	$Distance_x$: L.Elbow - R.Shoulder
V16	$Distance_z$: R.Hand - R.Elbow	V17	$Distance_z$:L.Hand - L.Elbow
V18	$Distance_y$: R.Hand - R.Elbow	V19	$Distance_y$:L.Hand - L.Elbow
V20	$Distance_y$: R.Elbow - R.Shoulder	V21	$Distance_y$:L.Elbow - L.Shoulder
V22	$Distance_z$: R.Elbow - R.Shoulder	V23	$Distance_z$:L.Elbow - L.Shoulder
V24	$Orientation_{XY}$: Shoulders axis	V25	$Orientation_{XZ}$: Shoulders axis
V26	$Orientation_{XY}$: Heels axis	V27	$3D - Distance$: R.Heel - L.Heel

Table 2. English and Japanese terms and example of their nuances

English	Japanese	Nuance
Angry	Okotta	*I'm so angry, they stole my car*
Upset	Nayanda	*I'm upset, I cannot solve this problem*
Happy	Tanoshii	*I'm really enjoying my time*
Joy	Yorokobi	*Yahoo, I won the lottery*
Fear	Osore	*I'm afraid he will beat me*
Surprise	Odoroki	*Ahhh! What was that big noise*
Sad	Kanashii	*I'm so sad, I have just received a very bad news*
Depressed	Yuutsuna	*I feel so depressed because I cannot find a job*

the Japanese translation of the 8 labels and an example of their use of such words to understand the nuance meant.

Each static posture P_i was then associated with a triplet (X_i, O_i, I_i, E_i) where $X_i = x_{i1}, ..., x_{i24}$ is the 24 posture features vector (see Table 1), O_i indicates the label most frequently associated by the observers to the posture P_i, I_i is the average intensity level associated to this label, and E_i is the emotion category to which the label belongs.

3 Affective Nuance Discrimination Model

To understand if the proposed set of features could automatically identify nuances within a same emotion, we applied Mixed Discriminant Analysis (MDA) to the numerical description of the collected postures. MDA[13] is a statistical technique used to discriminate between two or more categories or groups. Similar to factor analysis, it computes group discrimination using a set of discriminant functions, i.e., a weighted combination of continuous variables. Using the MDA discriminant functions (i.e., dimensions), it is possible to map the postures onto a multidimensional discriminant space defined by the axes that maximize the separation between groups and minimize the variance within groups. The dimensionality of the space is determined in such a way to reduce the discrimination error. The number of clusters to be identified within each category (i.e. group) is defined by an input parameter. In our experiment, the parameter 2 was chosen

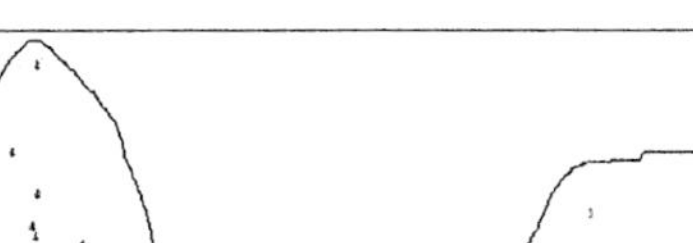
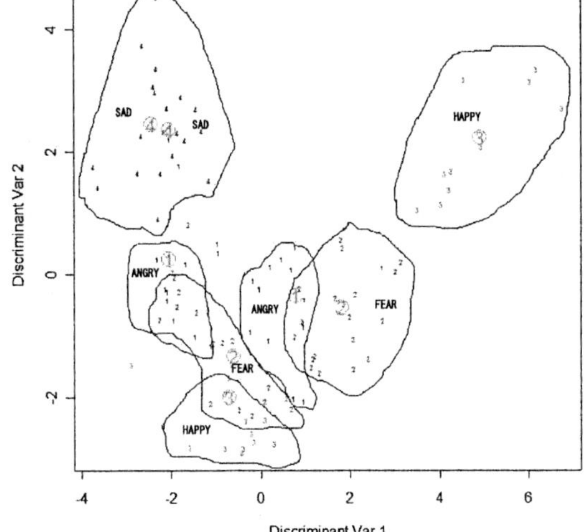

Fig. 1. 2D projections of the set of postures according to the prediction of the MDA model built for the 4 emotion categories

by the unsupervised EM clustering algorithm as the optimal number of clusters for 3 of the categories on the basis of the posture training set.

The MDA model was created using 109 postures as a training set, and 72 postures as a testing set. The division in training set and testing set was dictated by the different periods in which the postures were collected. For each posture P_i, we used the vectors X_i describing its postural features (computed on the original motion capture data), and the emotion category E_i (one of the 4 categories) associated to the postures. The training was repeated 20 times, obtaining on average 84% correct classification on the training set and 56% correct classification on the testing set. Figure 1 shows the 2D-projection of the postures in one of the 20 MDA models built. Since this MDA model produced the highest performance (94%) on the training set, it was used as the best representative for reflecting the way the average observer evaluated the set of 109 affective postures. The first 2 dimensions shown in the Figure cover 80% of the variance. From the plotting of the MDA model, we can see that each emotion is represented by 2 clusters. While the 2 clusters for *sad* are very close to each other, the other clusters are well separated. Each posture is represented by a number indicating the classification of the posture predicted by the model. The number refers to the emotion category E_i according to alphabetical order.

To evaluate the meaning of these clusters in terms of possible nuances of the corresponding emotion categories, for each posture P_i, we plotted the observers' label O_i (the 8 nuance labels) in the 2D model (Figure 2). The labels are represented by a number from 1 to 8 according to their alphabetical order.

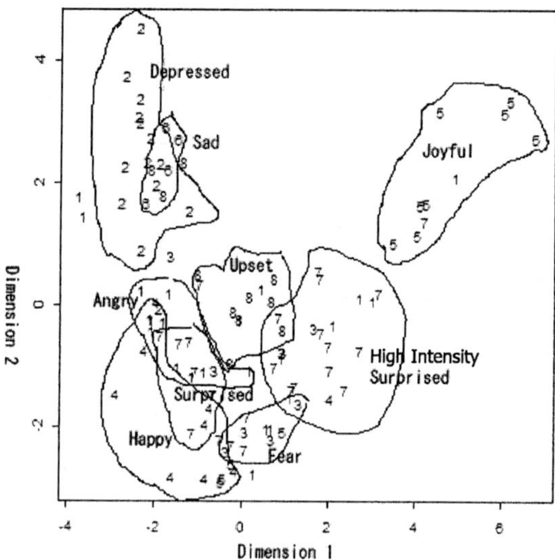

Fig. 2. 2D projection of the 4-category discrimination space using the 8 labels and the intensity values assigned by the observers to the postures

For example the label *angry* is represented by the number 1 while the number 8 represents the label *upset*. We can easily see that the clusters already appear to fit the different nuances of each emotion category in the first 2 dimensions of the model. While naming the clusters would require an interactive process, the unsupervised method was able to detect nuances that well overlap with the one identified by the average observer.

Using an iterative process, the MDA algorithm creates the model based on linear combinations of the most discriminating features. The complexity of the model can be increased by considering non-linear combinations of such features. For our purpose, we considered that the linear combinations were obtaining sufficient accuracy. The third column of Table 3 lists the features used by the MDA model of Figure 1 for discriminating between the 4 categories of affective postures. The number in each cell indicates the ranking of the features in the discrimination process. Lower numbers correspond to higher discriminative power. In order of importance: the vertical extension of the arms (*V6, V16*); the bending and rotation of the head (*V5, V4*); the inclination of the shoulders (*V25*); the lateral opening of the body (*V15*); and finally, the frontal extension of the arms (*V18, V19, V20*).

4 Grounding Nuances on Posture Features

To ground the discrimination of two nuances within each emotion category (e.g. the clusters identified in Figure 1), we applied the MDA algorithm to each category separately. The relevant features for discriminating between each pair of

Table 3. Posture features relevant for discriminating between affective states and between nuances of these affective states

—		MDA single emotion category models								—
Body Features		Emotions	Nuances							Total
Direction	Code	A-F-H-S	H-J	U-A	F-Su	lSu-hSu	F-lSu	F-hSu	FlSu-hSu	Score
Head	V4	4								14
	V5	3		1	1		2			77
Vertical	V6	1		3				14		62
	V7									0
	V16	2						10		20
	V17							4		6
	V22					1				17
	V23							1	1	25
Lateral	V10			2					5	33
	V11							17		2
	V12					3		11		20
	V13		3							18
	V14		1				1	3	2	66
	V15	5		4				15		33
Frontal	V8							9		5
	V9		4							18
	V18	7				2		8	6	48
	V19					4		12		19
	V20	8						7		17
	V21					7		13		16
Shoulder	V24			5				5		22
	V25	6				6		16	4	49
Heels	V26		2		2	5		6		60
	V27							2	3	29
Correct Classification		94%	100%	100%	82%	100%	80%	100%	100%	

nuances within an emotion category were automatically identified by the MDA model built for that category and they are shown in Table 3.

The fifth column of the of Table 3 lists the relevant features for the MDA model built for the nuances Upset and Angry. The main features discriminating between the two nuances are the degree of the bending of the head (V5) and the lateral opening of the arms (V10). In fact, in the *upset* postures, Figure 3(a), the head is slightly bent and the hands are generally close to the center of the body, while in the *angry* postures, Figure 3(b), the avatar is generally looking straight up and the arms are more open. The separation is even stronger in the case of the emotion *happy* (Figure 1). Cluster 4 (label *happy*, Figure 3(c)) and cluster 5 (label *joyful*, Figure 3(d)) lay on the two opposite sides of the space. As shown in the fourth column of the table, the main features discriminating between these two nuances are the lateral opening of the arms (V14, V13) and the distance between the feet (V26).

More interesting is the separation between *surprise* and *fear*. From closer inspection, these two clusters relate to the average intensity values associated with the postures. One cluster contains the low-intensity *surprised* postures, Figure 3(e), and the *fear* postures, Figure 3(f). The other clusters contain the high-intensity *surprised* postures, Figure 3(g). The similarity between *fear* and low surprise could be partially due to the fact that the *fear* postures all have low-intensity, on average. First of all, what mainly discriminates *fear* from *surprised* is the bending of the head (V5) (see column F-Su of the table). In the case of *surprised* the head is bent slightly backward and also is generally turned. In the case of the *fear* nuance, the head is straight or slightly bent forward as in a gesture of protection. The discrimination between these 2 classes reach only 80% as shown in the last row of the table.

We compared also the two intensities of *surprised* (see column lSu-hSu). Their main difference is the vertical position of the elbow with respect to the

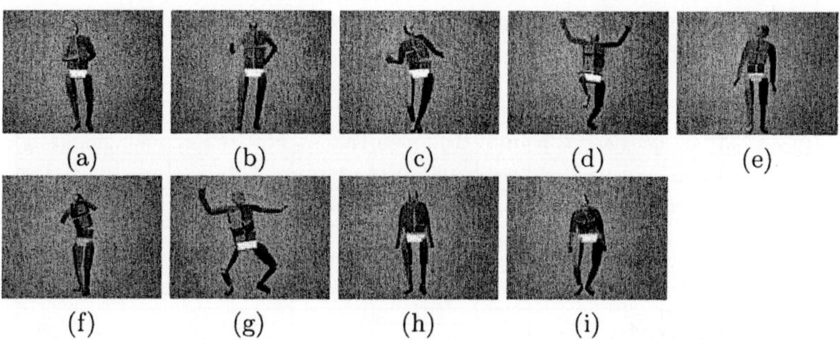

Fig. 3. Examples of 3D affectively expressive avatars for each nuances of emotion. (a) Upset (b) Angry (c) Happy (d) Joyful (e) Low-intensity Surprise (f) Fear (g) High-intensity Surprise (h) Sad (i) Depressed.

shoulder. In the case of low intensity, the arms are stretched down along the body. Instead, in the case of high intensity, the hands are brought up in front of the body (V18, V19) at the shoulders or at the face level as a means of protection. In the latter case, the elbows are also more laterally open than the hands assuring a good protection. Still in the latter case the legs are more open. To discriminate between *fear* and *low surprised* only 2 features are considered relevant (V14 and V5) and the model reaches only 80% of correct classification. This means that these two nuances share similar posture features. This could be due to the fact that the actors have represented a negative type of *surprised* expression (since they were asked to express *fear*) and that the observers have associated low intensity to each posture that they have recognized as expressing *fear*. To distinguish the *fear* nuance from high intensity *surprised*, many features are used, nevertheless it reaches 100% discrimination. Again, in high intensity *surprised* postures, the hands are used to protect the body (V22, V14, V17).

The last column of Table 3 shows the relevance score totalized by each feature. The score is computed in the following way: $score(f_i) = \sum_j w_{ij} * (nf - r_{ij} + 1)$ where: $w_{ij} = (nf - mf_j)/nf$, i = 1,..,24 (i.e. feature index); j = 1,..,7 (i.e. model index); nf = 24 (i.e. total number of features); mf_j = total number of features used by the model j; r_{ij} = ranking of the feature i in the model j; and f_i = feature i. We can see that the most relevant feature is the bending of the head, followed by the lateral opening of the elbow with respect to the shoulder, and by the vertical extension of the arm with respect to the shoulder. A similar score was assigned to the orientation of the heels axis. The general low rank of the frontal features may be due to the fact that the avatars were shown according to their frontal view.

5 Conclusion

In this paper, we used statistical techniques to determine the saliency of a set of posture features in discriminating between nuances of emotions. The proposed low-level features seem to automatically capture affective nuances in postures (in terms of labels used and in terms of the intensity rating of the human) obtaining a very low discrimination error. Using an unsupervised clustering method, the created clusters of postures reflect the nuances of affective states of the average human observers. These results are encouraging to support human-machine affective interaction based on a richer affective language than the one of basic emotions.

Acknowledgments

This study was supported by a grants-in-Aid for Scientific Research from the Japanese Society for the Promotion of Science granted to Nadia Bianchi-Berthouze.

References

1. Piller, C.: A Human Touch for Machines- The radical movement affective computing is turning the filed of artificial intelligence upside down by adding emotion to the equation. Los Angeles Times, Los Angeles (2002)
2. Whissell, C.: The dictionary of affect in language, Emotion: Theory, research and experience, vol.4, The measurement of emotions. Academic press, New York (1995)
3. Plutchik, R.: Emotion:A psychoevolutionary synthesis. Harper and Row (1989)
4. Schröder, M.: Dimensional emotion representation as a basis for speech synthesis with nonextreme emotions. In: Proc. Workshop on Affective Dialogue Systems, Germany (2004) 209–220
5. Tsapatsoulis, N., Raousaiou, A., Kollias, S., Cowie, R.: Emotion recognition and synthesis based on mpeg-4 faps. In MPEG-4 Facial Animation - The standard, implementations, applications (2002) 141–167
6. Ruttkay, Z., Noot, H., Hagen, P.: Emotion disc and emotion squares:tools to explore the facial expression space. Computer Graphics Forum **22** (2003) 49–53
7. Ekman, P.: Emotion in the Human Face. Cambridge University Press (1982)
8. Argyle, M.: Bodily Communication. Methuen & Co. Ltd, London (1988)
9. Coulson, M.: Attributing emotion to static body postures: recognition accuracy, confusions, and viewpoint dependence. Journ. of Nonver. Behav. **28** (2004) 117–139
10. Kleinsmith, A., de Silva, P.R., Bianchi-Berthouze, N.: Recognizing emotion from postures: Cross-cultural differences in user modeling. In: to be published in UM2005 User Modeling: Proceedings of the Tenth International Conference, Springer-Verlag (2005)
11. Bianchi-Berthouze, N., Kleinsmith, A.: A categorical approach to affective gesture recognition. Connection Science special issue on Epigenetic Robotics - Modeling Cognitive Development in Robotic Systems **15** (2003) 259–269
12. De Silva, R., Bianchi-Berthouze, N.: Modeling human affective postures: An information theoretic characterization of posture features. Journal of Computer Animation and Virtual Worlds **15** (2004) 269—276
13. Hastie, T., Tibshirabi, R.: Discriminant analysis by gaussian mixture. Journal of the Royal Statistical Society **B** (1996) 155–176

Face Alignment Under Various Poses and Expressions

Shengjun Xin and Haizhou Ai

Computer Science and Technology Department, Tsinghua University,
Beijing 100084, China
ahz@mail.tsinghua.edu.cn

Abstract. In this paper, we present a face alignment system to deal with various poses and expressions. In addition to global shape model, we use component shape model such as mouth shape model, contour shape model in addition to global shape model to achieve more powerful representation for face components under complex pose and expression variations. Different from 1-D profile texture feature in classical ASM, we use 2-D local texture feature for more accuracy, and in order to achieve high robustness and fast speed it is represented by Haar-wavelet features as in [5]. Extensive experiments are reported to show its effectiveness.

1 Introduction

Face alignment, whose goal is to locate facial feature points, such as eye-brows, eyes, nose, mouth and contour, is very important in face information processing including face recognition, face modeling, face expression recognition and analysis, etc. Since face information is very critical in human to human interaction, it is a key technology to make machine be able to process it in order to realize a natural way of human to machine interaction. In many complex face information processing researches, such as face expression analysis, as a fundamental preprocess to collect and align data, the face alignment algorithm is required workable under various poses and expressions. In this paper, this problem is discussed.

In the literature, Cootes et al. [1] [2] proposed two important methods for face alignment: Active Shape Model (ASM) and Active Appearance Model (AAM). Both methods use the Point Distribution Model (PDM) to constrain a face shape and parameterize the shape by PCA, but their feature models are different. In ASM, the feature model is 1-D profile texture feature around every feature point, which is used to search for the appropriate candidate location of every feature point. However, in AAM, the global appearance model is introduced to conduct the optimization of shape parameters. Generally speaking, ASM outperforms AAM in shape localization accuracy and more robust to illumination but has local minima problem, the AAM is sensitive to illumination and noisy background but can get optimal global texture. In this paper, we focus our work on ASM. In recent years, many new derivative methods have been proposed, such as that of ASM-based, TC-ASM [3], W-ASM [4], and Haar-wavelet ASM [5], that of AAM-based, DAM [6], AWN [7]. However the problem is still an unsolved one for practical applications since their performances are very sensitive to large variations in face pose and especially in face expression although usually they can acquire good results on neutral faces, which may be caused

J. Tao, T. Tan, and R.W. Picard (Eds.): ACII 2005, LNCS 3784, pp. 40 – 47, 2005.

by the global shape model that is not so powerful to represent changes in face components under complex pose and expression variations.

As mentioned above, classical ASM use 1-D profile texture feature perpendicular to the feature point contour as its local texture model. However, this local texture model, which is related to a small area, is not sufficient to distinguish feature point from its neighbors, so ASM often suffer from local minima problem in the local searching stage. To overcome this problem, we follow the approach in [5] to use 2-D local texture feature and represent it by Haar-wavelet features for robustness and high speed.

In this paper, we extend the work [5] to multi-view face with expression variations, and we use component shape model such as mouth shape model, contour shape model in addition to global shape model to achieve more powerful representation for face components under complex pose and expression variations. This approach is developed over a very large data set and the algorithm is implemented in a hierarchical structure as in [8] for efficiency.

This paper is organized as follow: In Section 2, the overview of the system framework and the pose-based face alignment algorithm is given. In Section 3, experiments are reported. Finally, in Section 4, conclusion is given.

2 Overview of the System

The designed system consists of four modules: multi-view face detection (MVFD) [10], facial landmark extraction [11], pose estimation [12], and pose-based alignment, as illustrated in Fig. 1 and Fig. 2 (first two pictures are from FERET[14]). In this paper, pose-based alignment module will be introduced in detail.

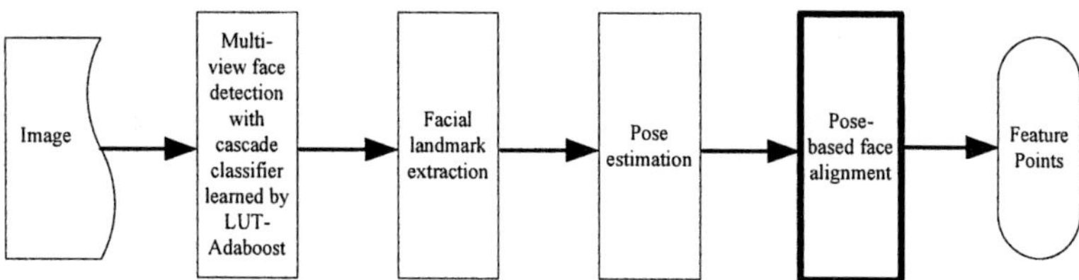

Fig. 1. Framework of the system

2.1 Pose Based Shape Models

Considering face pose changes in off image plane from full profile to frontal (not losing generality, here we consider from right full profile to frontal), five types of global shape of Point Distribution Model (PDM) are defined as shown in Fig. 3, which are 37 points for $[-90^\circ,-75^\circ)$, 50 points for $[-75^\circ,-60^\circ)$, 59 points for $[-60^\circ,-45^\circ)$ and 88 points for $[-45^\circ,-15^\circ)$ and $[-15^\circ,+15^\circ]$. So, over corresponding training sets totally five PDMs are set up as posed based shape models.

In addition to the above global shape models, component shape models for local shape representation are introduced in order to capture accurate shape changes due to large variations in poses and expressions as shown in Fig.4. The reason for this is that global shape model is too strong to represent local shape changes. Taking a face with open mouth as an example (the picture is from AR[13]) shown in Fig.5a, we found that many of mouth feature points truly reach their correct positions in local search stage, but due to their contribution in global level is too little to have significant effects in the final shape they will leave their correct positions under the global shape model constraint shown in Fig.5e. However, if component shape model, that is, mouth shape model is used, their contribution is big enough to change the final shape shown in Fig.5f.

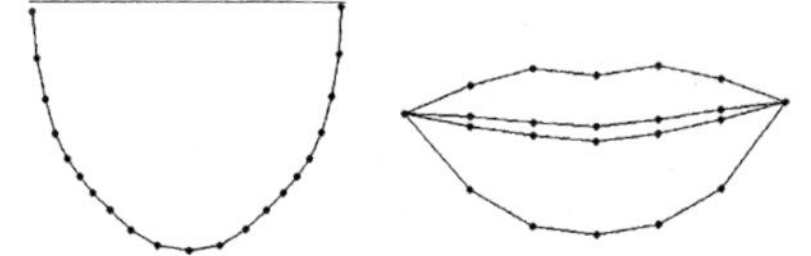

Fig. 2. Component shape model for frontal face (mean contour and mean mouth)

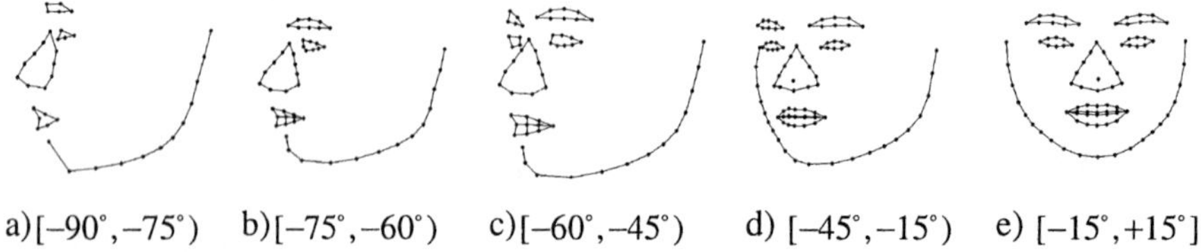

Fig. 3. Pose based shape model (mean shape) from right full profile to frontal

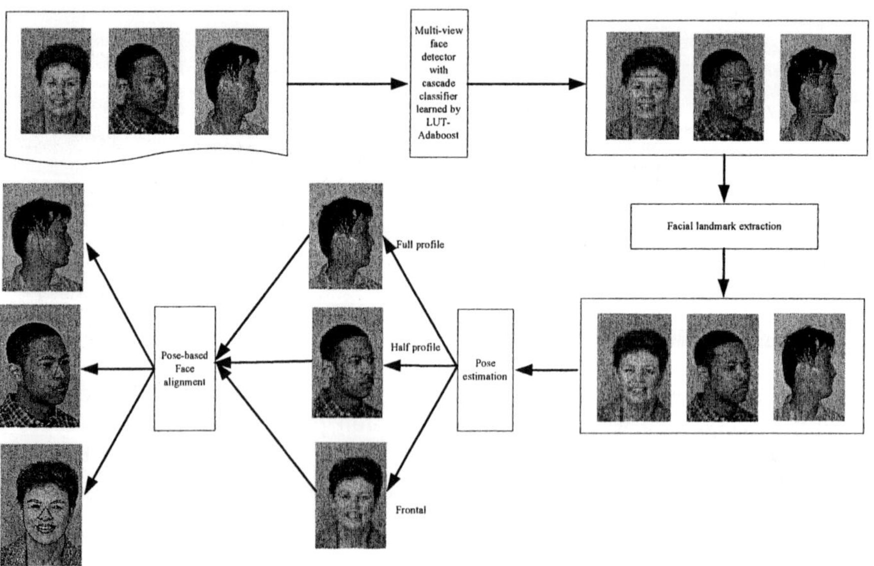

Fig. 4. Pose-based face alignment

In summary, the face alignment consists of two-stage processing, the first stage using global ASM model, the second stage using component ASM model with the initialization from the first stage, see Fig. 5 for an example. In this way, the accuracy is improved significantly.

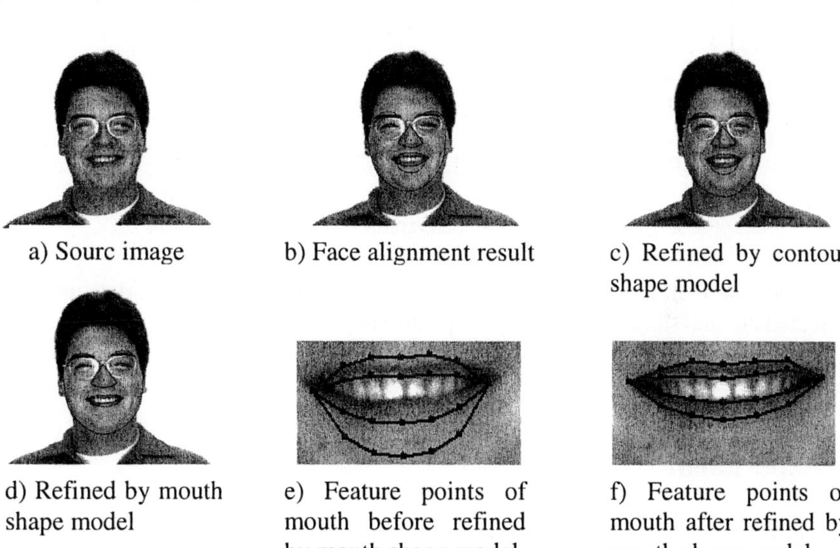

a) Sourc image
b) Face alignment result
c) Refined by contour shape model
d) Refined by mouth shape model
e) Feature points of mouth before refined by mouth shape model
f) Feature points of mouth after refined by mouth shape model

Fig. 5. Face alignment using global & component shape mode

2.2 Local Texture Model

The 2-D local texture feature represented by Haar-wavelet features proposed in [5] as illustrated in Fig. 6 (the picture is from AR[13]) is adopted. For each point, over training set those features are clustered by K-means clustering into several representative templates.

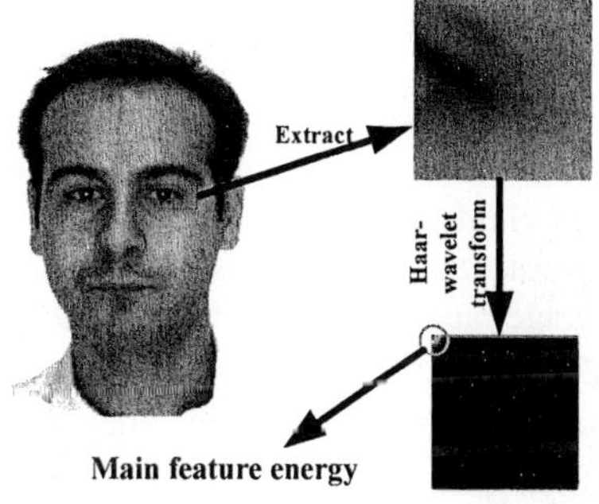

Fig. 6. Haar-wavelet feature extraction

2.3 Alignment

In the hierarchical alignment algorithm shown in Fig. 7, for a given face image, first supposing several facial landmark points are known (for example, by way of manually labeling), a regression method is used to initialize a full shape from those given points to start the ASM algorithm. Second the Haar-wavelet feature of every feature point and its neighbors (a 3×3 area) are computed (described in section 2.2) to select current candidate point based on Euclidean distance between the current

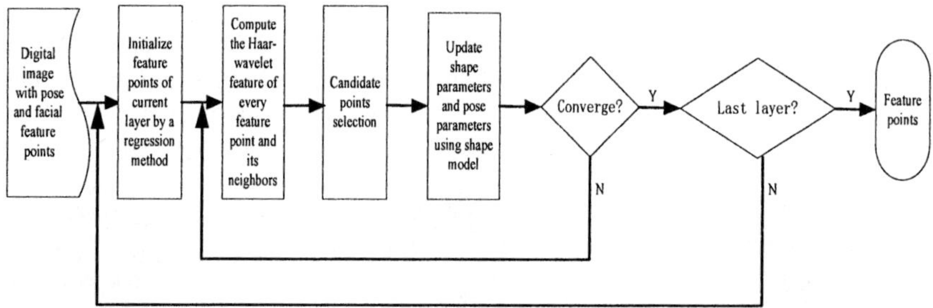

Fig. 7. Flowchart of the hierarchical alignment algorithm

Haar-wavelet feature and the trained templates. Third those candidate points are projected to the shape space to get update shape parameters and pose parameters. Repeat from the second step until the shape converges in current layer. If this layer is the last layer, then stop, otherwise move to the next layer.

3 Experiment

3.1 Training and Testing Data Set

Different from the view ranges presented in [6], that is $[-90^\circ,-55^\circ)$, $[-55^\circ,-15^\circ)$, $[-15^\circ,15^\circ]$, $[15^\circ,55^\circ]$, $[55^\circ,90^\circ]$, we divide the pose of full range multi-view face into the following intervals based on the visibilities of facial feature points and fine mode of shape variations: $[-90^\circ,-75^\circ)$, $[-75^\circ,-60^\circ)$, $[-60^\circ,-45^\circ)$, $[-45^\circ,-15^\circ)$, $[-15^\circ,+15^\circ]$, $(15^\circ,45^\circ]$, $(45^\circ,60^\circ]$, $(60^\circ,75^\circ]$, $(75^\circ,90^\circ]$. The view $[-15^\circ,+15^\circ]$ corresponds to frontal. The experiments are conducted on a very large data set. For frontal view, the data set consists of 2000 images including male and female aging from child to old people, many of which are with exaggerated expressions such as open mouths, closed eyes, or have ambiguous contours especially for old people. The average face size is about 180x180 pixels. We randomly chose 1600 images for training and the rest 400 for test. For the other views, we labeled feature points of 300 images of one side of view, such as $[-90^\circ,-75^\circ)$ with a semi-automatic labeling tool as their Ground Truth Data for training, and used the 300 mirrored images of its symmetric view, such as $(75^\circ,90^\circ]$ for testing.

In the system illustrated in Fig. 1, right now 'Facial landmark extraction' [11] is implemented for frontal faces and 'Pose estimation' [12] can only be used for the views $[-45^\circ,-15^\circ)$, $[-15^\circ,+15^\circ]$, $(15^\circ,45^\circ]$. So for the other part, manually picking several points and selecting the corresponding pose interval are necessary to start the experiments.

3.2 Performance Evaluation

The accuracy is measured with relative pt-pt error, which is the point-to-point distance between the alignment result and the ground truth divided by the distance between two eyes (If the face is not frontal, then we use the distance between the eye corner and mouth corner that can be seen). The feature points were initialized by a linear regression from 4 eye corner points and 2 mouth corner points of the ground truth. After the alignment procedure, the errors were measured.

In Fig. 8a, the distributions of the overall average error are compared with Classical ASM [1], Gabor ASM [4], Haar-wavelet ASM [5]. It shows that the presented method of Haar-wavelet ASM with component model is better than the other three. In Fig. 8b, the average errors of the 88 feature point are compared. The distributions of the overall average errors of the four views except frontal are compared in Fig. 9 and the average error of each feature point of the other four views are showed in Fig. 10. The average execution time per iteration is listed in Table 1.

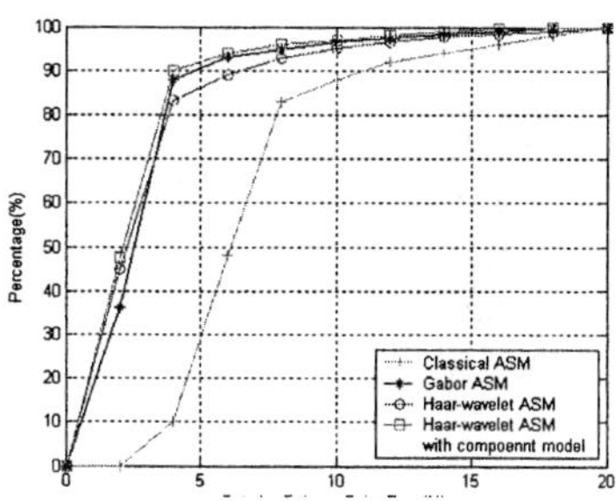

a) Distribution of relative average pt-pt error

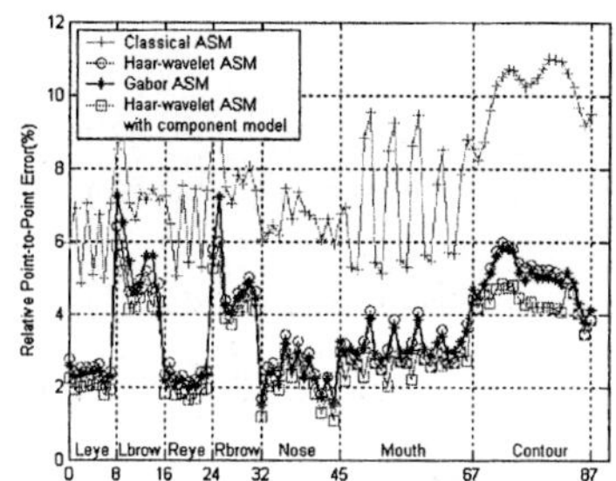

b) Relative average pt-pt error for each feature point

Fig. 8. Comparison of classical ASM, Gabor ASM, Haar-wavelet ASM and Haar-wavelet ASM with component model

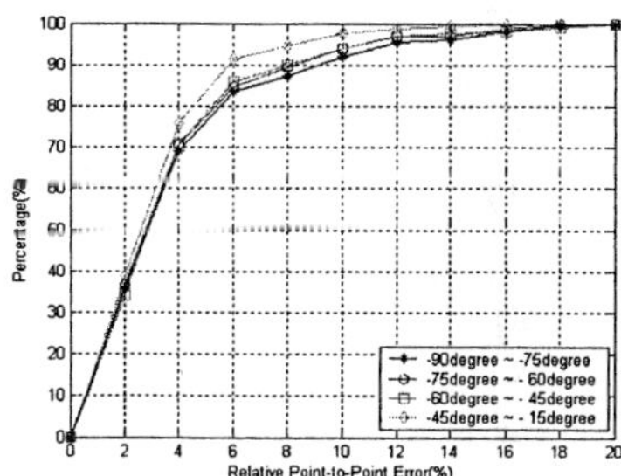

Fig. 9. Distribution of relative average pt-pt error of multi-view

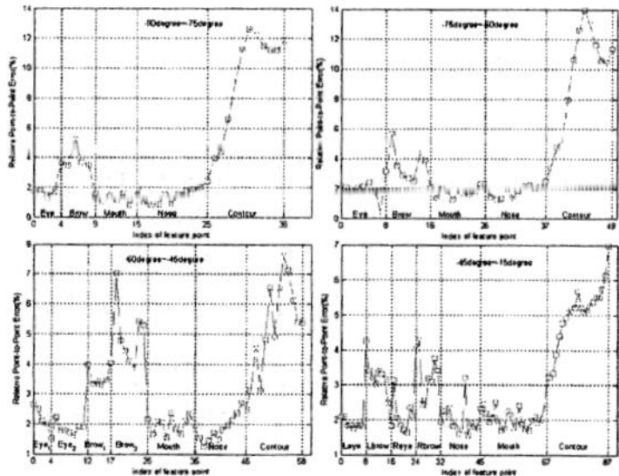

Fig. 10. Relative average pt-pt error for each feature point of multi-view

Some experimental results on images from FERET[14], AR[13], and internet which are independent of the training/testing set with large poses and expression variations are shown in Fig. 11, Fig. 12, Fig. 13.

Table 1. The average execution time per iteration

Algorithm		Execution time (per iteration)
Classical ASM		2ms
Gabor ASM		576ms
Haar-wavelet ASM		30-70ms
Haar-wavelet ASM with component model of this paper	Frontal	53ms
	-45degree ~ -15degree	58ms
	-60degree ~ -45degree	54ms
	-75degree ~ -60degree	45ms
	-90degree ~ -75degree	35ms

Fig. 11. Multi-view face alignment results

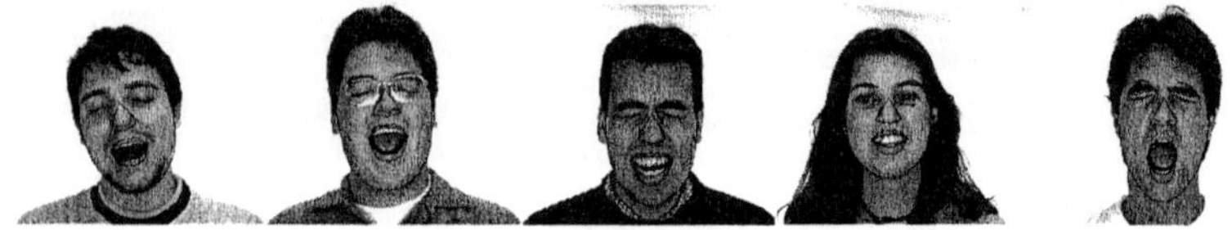

Fig. 12. Some results on face database of AR [13]

Fig. 13. Some results on face database of FERET [14] and Internet pictures

4 Conclusions

In this paper, we extend the work [5] to multi-view face with expression variations using component shape model such as mouth shape model, contour shape model in addition to global shape model. A semi-automatic multi-view face alignment system is presented that combines face detection, facial landmark extraction, pose estimation and pose-based face alignment into a uniform coarse-to-fine hierarchical structure based on Haar-wavelet features. With component shape model, we can deal with faces with large expression variation and ambiguous contours. Extensive experiments show that the implemented system is very fast, yet robust against illumination, expressions and poses variation. It could be very useful in facial expression recognition approaches, for example, to collect shape data.

Acknowledgements

This work is supported by NSF of China grant No.60332010.

References

1. T Cootes, D Cooper, C Taylor, and J Graham, Active shape models – their training and application. Computer Vision and Image Understanding, 61(1):38-59, 1995
2. T Cootes, G Edwareds, and C Taylor, Active appearance models. IEEE Transactions on Pattern Analysis and Machine Intelligence, 23(6):681-685, 2001
3. Shuicheng Yan, Ce Liu, Stan Z. Li, Hongjiang Zhang, Heung-Yeung Shum, Qiansheng Cheng. Texture-Constrained Active Shape Models.
4. Feng Jiao, Stan Li, Heung-Yeung Shum, Dale Schuurmans, Face Alignment Using Statistical Models and Wavelet Feature, Proceedings of IEEE Conference on CVPR, pp. 321-327, 2003.
5. Fei Zuo, Peter H.N. de With, Fast facial feature extraction using a deformable shape model with Haar-wavelet based local texture attributes, Proceedings of IEEE Conference on ICIP, pp. 1425-1428, 2004.
6. S. Z. Li, S. C. Yan, H. J. Zhang, Q. S. Cheng, Multi-View Face Alignment Using Direct Appearance Models, In Proceedings of The 5th International Conference on Automatic Face and Gesture Recognition. Washington.DC, USA, 2002
7. C. Hu, R. Feris, and M. Turk Active Wavelet networks for Face Alignment In British Machine Vision Conference, East Eaglia, Norwich, UK, 2003
8. Ce Liu, Heung-Yeung Shum, and Changshui Zhang, Hierarchical Shape Modeling for Automatic Face Localization, Proceedings of ECCV, pp.687-703, 2002.
9. P. Viola and M. Jones, Rapid object detection using a boosted cascade of simple features, in Proc. CVPR, 2001, pp. 511–518.
10. Bo WU, Haizhou AI, Chang HUANG, Shihong LAO, Fast Rotation Invariant Multi-View Face Detection Based on Real Adaboost, In Proc. the 6th IEEE Conf. on Automatic Face and Gesture Recognition (FG 2004), Seoul, Korea, May 17-19, 2004.
11. Tong WANG, Haizhou AI, Gaofeng HUANG, A Two-Stage Approach to Automatic Face Alignment, in Proceedings of SPIE Vol. 5286, 558-563, 2003.
12. Zhiguang YANG, Haizhou AI, et.al, Multi-View Face Pose Classification by Tree-Structured Classifier, The IEEE Inter. Conf. on Image Processing (ICIP-05), Genoa, Italy, September 11-14, 2005.
13. http://rvl1.ecn.purdue.edu/~aleix/aleix_face_db.html
14. P. J. Phillips, H. Wechsler, J. Huang, and P. Rauss, "The FERET database and evaluation procedure for face recognition algorithms", Image and Vision Computing J, Vol. 16, No. 5, pp 295-306, 1998.

A Voting Method and Its Application in Precise Object Location

Yong Gao[1], Xinshan Zhu[2], Xiangsheng Huang[1], and Yangsheng Wang[1]

[1] CASIA-SAIT HCI Joint Lab,
Center for Biometric Research & Testing,
National Laboratory of Pattern Recognition,
Institute of Automation, Chinese Academy of Sciences
[2] Institute of Computer Science & Technology of Peking University,
Beijing 100080, China
{ygao, xszhu, xshuang, wys}@mail.pattek.com.cn

Abstract. It has been demonstrated that combining the decisions of several classifiers can lead to better recognition results. The combination can be implemented using a variety of schemes, among which voting method is the simplest, but it has been found to be just as effective as more complicated strategies in improving the recognition results. In this paper, we propose a voting method for object location, which can be viewed as generalization of majority vote rule. Using this method, we locate eye centers in face region. The experimental results demonstrate that the locating performance is comparable with other newly proposed eye locating methods. The voting method can be considered as a general fusion scheme for precise location of object.

1 Introduction

It has been observed that sets of patterns misclassified by different classifiers would not necessarily overlap. This suggested that different classifiers potentially offered complementary information about the patterns to be classified, which could be used to improve the performance of classification. Hence there has been a movement toward combining the decisions of several classifiers in order to obtain improved recognition results in the domains, such as OCR, Biometrics etc. The combination can be implemented using a variety of strategies, such as statistical approaches [1], Bayesian [2] and Dempster-Shafer theories of evidence [3]. In all these cases, it was found that using a combination of classifiers has resulted in a remarkable improvement in the recognition results, and this is true regardless of whether the classifiers are independent or make use of orthogonal features.

Among all the classifier combination rules, majority vote is the simplest for implementation. It does not assume prior knowledge of the behavior of the individual classifier (also called *expert*), and it does not require training on large quantities of samples. Yet, many study, such as [4,5] show that the majority vote is just as effective as the other more complicated schemes in improving the recognition rate.

J. Tao, T. Tan, and R.W. Picard (Eds.): ACII 2005, LNCS 3784, pp. 48–55, 2005.

In this paper, we propose a new kind of voting method which is just like the election in real life. Different from the majority vote which is used to improve the recognition performance, the proposed voting method is used to improve location performance. We use this fusion scheme to combine several eye detectors for eye location in face region. The experimental results demonstrate eye location based on the method is encouraging.

The paper is organized into the following sections. In section 2, we propose the voting method for object location. Section 3 describes implementation of the voting method. Section 4 contains the experiments that use the voting method to precisely locate eye centers. Finally, the summary and conclusions are given in Section 5.

2 Voting Method for Object Location

Object location problem, such as eye location in face region, can be converted to a two-class (*object and non-object*) recognition problem by employing a window-scanning strategy like face detection[6]. Let us assume that we have R such classifiers each representing the given pattern by a distinct measurement vector. Denote the measurement vector of the ith classifier by x_i. In the measurement space object and non-object class $\omega_k, (k = 0, 1)$ is modeled by the probability density function $p(x_i|\omega_k)$ and its a priori probability of occurrence is denoted $P(\omega_k)$. We consider the models to be mutually exclusive which means that only one model can be associated with each pattern.

According to the Bayesian theory, given measurements $x_i, i = 1, ..., R$, the pattern Z should be assigned to class ω_j provided the a posteriori probability of that interpretation is maximum, i.e.

$$\begin{gathered} assign \quad Z \rightarrow \omega_j \quad if \\ P(\omega_j|x_1, ..., x_R) = \max_k P(\omega_k|x_1, ..., x_R) \end{gathered} \tag{1}$$

The hardening of the a posteriori probabilities $P(\omega_k|x_i)$ to produce binary valued function $\triangle_{ki}$ as

$$\triangle_{ki} = \begin{cases} 1 & if \quad P(\omega_k|x_i) = \max_{j=1}^{m} P(\omega_j|x_i) \\ 0 & otherwise \end{cases} \tag{2}$$

results in combining decision outcomes rather than combining a posteriori probabilities.Under the assumption of equal priors and that the representations used are conditionally statistically independent, by hardening the probabilities according to (2), we can obtain the majority voting rule [5]

$$assign \qquad Z \rightarrow \omega_j \qquad if \quad \sum_{i=1}^{R} \triangle_{ji} = \max_{k=1}^{m} \sum_{i=1}^{R} \triangle_{ki} \tag{3}$$

Let us return to object location problem. Assume we have knowledge that there is one object in a known region D of input image, the aim of location is to decide, (x_o, y_o), the location of the object. We use $Z(x, y)$ denote the pattern in (x, y). The R object classifiers jointly classify every pattern in the region D into two classes: object ω_1 or non-object ω_0. According to the majority vote rule,

$$assign \quad Z(x,y) \rightarrow \omega_1 \qquad if \ \sum_{i=1}^{R} \triangle_{1i}(x,y) > R/2 \tag{4}$$

Consequently, we have the following corresponding locating rule

$$(x_o, y_o) = (x, y) \quad if \qquad \sum_{i=1}^{R} \triangle_{1i}(x,y) > R/2 \tag{5}$$

Although above derivation is reasonable, the locating rule (5) is not feasible in practice except that all classifiers have very high performance. There are two situations that the locating rule will fail — patterns of more than one position being classified as object and no patterns being classified as object. When the performance of classifiers does not reach certain level or the image region D is clutter the two cases may happen. To cope with this problem, we relax the decision rule of majority vote by

$$assign \quad Z(x,y) \rightarrow \omega_1 \qquad if \ \sum_{i=1}^{R} \triangle_{1i}(x,y) \geq C \tag{6}$$

where C is a dynamic threshold, so that the outcomes of the locating rule has only one location:

$$C = \max_{(x,y)\in D} \sum_{i=1}^{R} \triangle_{1i}(x,y) \tag{7}$$

We have two reasons to support above change on classifying rule. The first is we have prior knowledge that there is only one object in the region D, so it is reasonable to limit the number of pattern assigned to object class to one. The second is there are relatively a large number of possible mistakes, and the probability that all classifiers make mistakes in the same position is very low. As long as performances of the classifiers are not too bad, we have reasons to believe that the pattern of the object, $Z(x_o, y_o)$ will received more votes of object class than patterns of non-objects in region D. Thus we obtain a new locating rule

$$(x_0, y_0) = (x', y') \quad if \qquad \sum_{i=1}^{R} \triangle_{1i}(x', y') = \max_{(x,y)\in D} \sum_{i=1}^{R} \triangle_{1i}(x,y) \tag{8}$$

From the above analysis, we can see that the voting method can be viewed as an generalization of majority voting rule under certain conditions in object location problem. It is a locating rule of multiple object detectors, while majority voting rule is a classification rule of multiple classifiers.

3 Implementation of the Voting Method

It is demanding that individual object detector is capable of precisely locating object center. Usually the point best located is around the actual object center. Directly implementation of above fusion scheme would lead to no consensus. So we convert voting on object center point into voting on object center area and a special image, called response image, is devised for this purpose. The response image has the same size with the region D and every pixel value is set to zero initially. We use it to record vote number. Let N_i be the number of object center candidates detected by object detector i , and (x_{ki}, y_{ki}) be the k-th $(1 \leq k \leq N_i)$ object center candidate among them. We define a round candidate area of object center

$$D_{ki} = \{x, y : (x - x_{ki})^2 + (y - y_{ki})^2 < c^2\} \tag{9}$$

where c is radius of the area, decide its size. The larger the size, the larger the probability that the eye center is located in D_{ki}. Then we add a constant *value* to all pixels in the corresponding area of response image. Suppose M be the number of object detectors, the last response image can be represented as

$$R(x, y) = \sum_{i=1}^{M} \left[\sum_{k=1}^{N_i} I_{((x,y) \in D_{ki})}(x, y) \cdot value \right] \tag{10}$$

where I is indicator function. In response image, gravity center of the area with the maximum response is viewed as object center.

4 Experiment: Eye Location Using Voting Method

Eye location is a crucial step towards automatic face recognition and man-machine interaction such as gaze tracking and expression recognition. In this section, we use voting method as fusion scheme to locate eye center from locating results of several different eye detectors. The block diagram of our eye location experiment is shown in figure 1. After face detection, four eye detectors detect eye candidates in face region respectively. A response image is created and records all locating results. In the response image, eye centers are located using ordinary image processing methods.

4.1 Eye Detectors

All eye detectors used in our system were trained using Gentle AdaBoost [7] combined with cascade structure [6]. To take advantage of different classification capability of different patterns, two kinds of features are used. The first kind of features are the over-complete haar-like features [6]. The second kind of features are Sobel-like features [9] which extract the edge information. They are robust to illumination variation. Both kinds of features can be computed very fast in constant time by means of integral image.

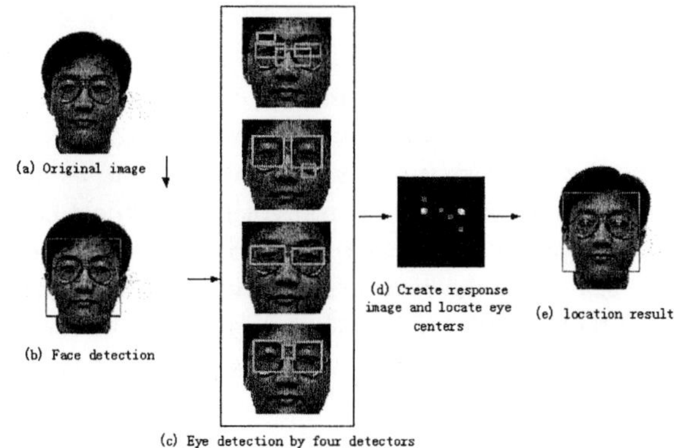

Fig. 1. Diagram of eye location using voting method

Fig. 2. The rectangle and square training examples

At the same time, two kinds of positive eye samples are used. The first kind of eye samples, which only include eye, are rectangle image patches centered on eye center. Some examples of this kind are shown in the left part of Fig.2. The second kind of eye samples, which include eye and a small amount of space below and above eye, are square image patches centered on eye center. Some examples of this kind are shown in the right part of Fig.2. The first kind of eye samples are normalized to 24×12 pixels, and the second kind 16×16 pixels. The negative samples are image patches without eye or image patches randomly displaced a small distance from eye centers and selected using bootstrapping method [10].

From above two kinds of features and two kinds of samples, we obtained four kinds of training combinations: rectangle eye samples with Haar-like feature, rectangle eye samples with Sobel-like feature, square eye samples with Haar-like feature and square eye samples with Sobel-like feature. Consequently, we totally trained four different eye detectors.

4.2 Experiment Results

The training set is drawn from FERET, BioID, Caltech and ORLFace database. Totally 7,000 rectangle eye samples and 7,000 square eye samples are cropped and normalized for training. The test set consists of NLPR face (600 images), open set of CASIA face (1904 images), Yale (165 images) and CDS008 of XM2VTS face [13] (1180 images). Totally 3,849 images are used for evaluation of our algorithm's performance. Among these face databases, Feret, BioID, Caltch, and Yale are open database. NLPR face is built by National Laboratory of Pattern Recognition, Institute of Automation, Chinese Academy of Sciences. The face images in the database are captured in two different time spans and demonstrate significant variations in pose. CASIA face is a subset of multi-modal biometric database built by the Center of Biometrics Research and Testing, Institute of Automation, Chinese Academy of Sciences, and characterized by a large variety of illumination, expression, pose, face size, and complex background.

To evaluate the precision of eye location, a scale independent location criterion [11] is used. Let d_l and d_r be the Euclidean distances between ground truth eye centers and the detected eye centers, d_{lr} be the Euclidean distance between the ground truth eye centers. Then the relative location error is defined as follows:

$$err = \frac{max(d_l, d_r)}{d_{lr}} \tag{11}$$

For comparison, We tested three algorithms on the test set. The first is our fusion-based method. The second is the method in [12], here we call it probability-based method. We implemented it using the training set described above, and 7,000 eye samples and 12,000 eye-pairs samples were used to train the eye classifier and eye-pair classifier respectively. The third is ASM [14].

The distribution of location error is shown in Fig.3. From the figure, we can see our method locates eye centers more precisely than the probability-based method and ASM on the test set. Some eye locating examples of our method are shown in figure 4. We attribute this mainly to our fusion scheme – voting method. The four different eye detectors locate eye positions using different information or knowledge. More information is used than one detector decision. It is well known, compared with global constraint, local constraint is precise but plagued by false positives. Here this disadvantage is overcome by voting method. So we achieved this success. We also observed that ASM is robust, though it is not as precise as the other two algorithms. This is because of its global shape constraint.

On a PIII 900MHz, 256M memory system, speed of the three algorithms was compared. For face region with the size $120 \times 120 pixels$, the average eye location time of our method is $130ms$ while the time of probability-based method and ASM are about $250ms$ and $350ms$ respectively.

5 Summary and Conclusions

We have proposed a kind of voting method for object location, which can be viewed as a relaxation or generalization of majority vote rule in object location problem. A novel way for its implementation has also been presented. Instead of directly seeking gravity center of results of different object detectors, we use a response image to record the results of them, then find gravity center of the area with maximum response as the object center. We use this method to locate eye centers in face region. Experimental results demonstrate that the performance

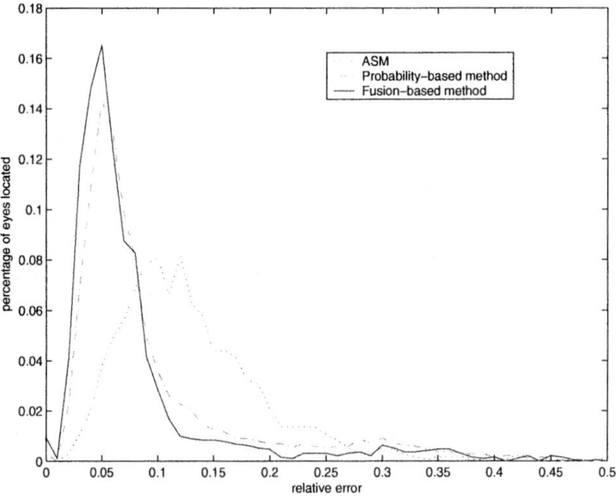

Fig. 3. Distribution of relative error on the test set

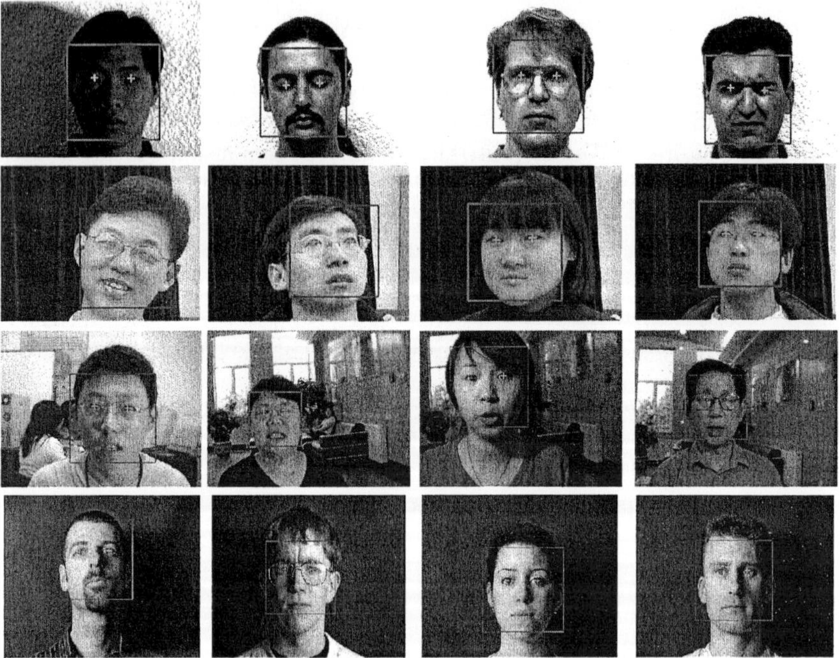

Fig. 4. Example location results

of our method is comparable to other newly proposed algorithms. Therefore the voting method can be regarded as an effective fusion scheme for object location, especially in the case that we know there are one object in a rough region.

References

1. J. Franke and E. Mandler: A comparison of two approaches for combining the votes of cooperating classifiers. in Proc. 11th Int. Conf. Pattern Recognition. The Hague, The Netherlands, vol. 2 (1992) 611–614
2. Y.H. Wang, H.Y. Liu and T.N. Tan: Identity verification base on voice and fingerprint. Sinobiometrics'03 (2002)
3. X.J. Gao, H.X. Yao, W. Gao, and W. Zeng: Fusion of Biometrics Based on D-S Theory. PCM, (2001) 1120–1125
4. D.-S. Lee and S.N. Srihari: Handprinted digit recognition: acomparison of algorithms. in Proc. 3rd Int. Workshop Frontiers Handwriting Recognition. Buffalo, NY, (May 1993) 153–163.
5. J. Kitter, M. Hatef, R. Duin, and J. Matas: On Combining Classifiers. IEEE Trans. Pattern Analysis and Machine Intelligence, vol.20, no.3 (Mar. 1998) 226-239,
6. P. Viola, M. Jones: Rapid object detection using a Boosted cascade of simple features. Proc. Of IEEE conf. On CVPR, (2001) 511-518
7. Y. Freund and R. E. Schapire: Experiments with a new boosting algorithm. In Machine Larning: Proceedings of the Thirteenth International Conference. Morgan Kauman, San Francisco, (1996) 148-156
8. J. Friedman, T. Hastie and R. Tibshirani: Additive logistic regression: a statistical view of boosting. The Annals of Statistics, 38(2) (2000) 337-374
9. X.S. Huang, Stan Z. Li and Y.S. Wang: Evaluation of Face Alignment Solutions Using Statistical Learning. Proc. Of 6th IEEE conf on AFG (2004)
10. H. Schneiderman, T, Kanade: A statistical model for 3D object detection applied to Faces and Cars. Proc. Of IEEE Conf. On CVPR, (2000)
11. O. Jesorsky, K.J. Kirchberg, and R.W. Frischholz: Robust Face Detection Using the Haudorff Distance. In Proc. Third International Conference on Audio- and Video-based Biometric Person Authentication. Halmastad, Sweden (2001)
12. Y. Ma, X.Q. Ding, Z.E. Wang and N. Wang: Robust precise eye location under probabilistic framework. Proc. Of 6th IEEE conf on AFG (2004)
13. The XM2VTS database: http://www.ee.surrey.ac.uk/Research/VSSP/xm2vtsdb/
14. T.F. Cootes, G.J. Taylor, D.H. Cooper, and J. Graham: Active shape models - their training and application. Computer Vision and Image Understanding, vol.61, no. 1 (1995) 38-59

Face Tracking Using Mean-Shift Algorithm: A Fuzzy Approach for Boundary Detection

Farhad Dadgostar[1], Abdolhossein Sarrafzadeh[1], and Scott P. Overmyer[2]

[1] Institute of Information and Mathematical Sciences, Massey University, 102 904 NSMC, Auckland, New Zealand
{F.Dadgostar, H.A.Sarrafzadeh}@massey.ac.nz
[2] Department of Electrical Engineering & Computer Science, South Dakota State University, Brookings, SD 57007, USA
Scott.Overmyer@sdstate.edu

Abstract. Face and hand tracking are important areas of research, related to adaptive human-computer interfaces, and affective computing. In this article we have introduced two new methods for boundary detection of the human face in video sequences: (1) edge density thresholding, and (2) fuzzy edge density. We have analyzed these algorithms based on two main factors: convergence speed and stability against white noise. The results show that "fuzzy edge density" method has an acceptable convergence speed and significant robustness against noise. Based on the results we believe that this method of boundary detection together with the mean-shift and its variants like cam-shift algorithm, can achieve fast and robust tracking of the face in noisy environment, that makes it a good candidate for use with cheap cameras and real-world applications.

1 Introduction

Tracking human body parts in motion is a challenging but essential task in human computer interaction (HCI). It is particularly of interest to those working on the detection of emotional state from non-verbal cues. While facial expression recognition provides a platform from which affect can be evaluated, it has been suggested that facial expression alone is not sufficiently reliable for use as a sole measured indication of emotional state. For example, simply tracking head motion (e.g., nodding and shaking) may provide additional, well understood cues as to emotional states such as approval/disapproval, understanding/disbelief, and agreement/negation [9]. Also, there have been proposals on using postural features in a similar way [1]. In an intelligent tutoring context, a special interest of this research group, the value of such additional cues to emotional state is obvious and significant.

There are several approaches available for hand and face tracking. Some of these approaches require the attachment of devices to the users' body and are considered intrusive. Vision-based methods do not require physical attachments to the users' body, are considered to be less intrusive, and are more likely to be accepted by end users. Vision-based hand and face tracking has shown promising results, and thus considered as one of the popular research subjects in this area. On the other hand some applications like HCI and real-time video processing, require fast image

J. Tao, T. Tan, and R.W. Picard (Eds.): ACII 2005, LNCS 3784, pp. 56–63, 2005.

processing techniques in addition to the challenges posed by real-world problems like camera noise, and lighting conditions.

The mean-shift algorithm in tracking of skin color segments has been shown to be one of the fastest methods for hand and face tracking, because it requires a few integer CPU instructions per pixel [2].

The main idea of the mean-shift algorithm for detecting and tracking the segmented face in HCI, is the classic problem of finding exremum of a function. The algorithm for solving this problem has been addressed in Bradski [2] and Cheng [3]. The main steps in the mean-shift algorithm, are as follows:

1. **Initialize the size and position of the search window**
2. **Find the centre of gravity of the search window**
3. **Calculate the distance vector between the centre of the search window and centre of gravity, and shift the search window equal to the distance vector**
4. **Repeat from step 2 until convergence**

The search window has been called "kernel" in some literature, which we will use throughout this paper. For a kernel in quantized 2D space, the coordinates of the centre of gravity calculate as follows:

$$M_{00} = \sum_y \sum_x M(x, y) \quad M_{01} = \sum_y \sum_x x \cdot M(x, y) \quad M_{10} = \sum_y \sum_x y \cdot M(x, y) \quad x_c = \frac{M_{01}}{M_{00}} \quad y_c = \frac{M_{10}}{M_{00}}$$

M(x, y) is the weight of each point within the kernel, which is 0 or 1 for a binary image, and is 0 to 255 for grey-scale image.

Initializing the kernel and resizing it are still two open questions. The first placement of the kernel leads us to the classic problem of finding the extremum point of a function. For face tracking applications, placing the kernel near a local maxima (e.g. putting it on the hand area instead of the face area) may result in finding a local maximum instead of absolute maximum. Kernel size on the other hand, is a crucial parameter to the performance of the mean-shift algorithm. If the kernel size is chosen too large, it will contain too many background pixels. Choosing a kernel size that is too small is also a problem. Kernels that are too small can "roam" around on the object, and lead to a poor object localization. Changing the size may be necessary due to changes on the shape of the tracking object (e.g. rotation, moving toward or away from the camera).

In this article we introduce strategies for initializing the kernel, and resizing it. In Section 2, we present the research background. Two methods for detecting the boundaries of the kernel are introduced in Section 3. In Section 4, the results of experiments in both a noiseless and a noisy environment are presented and in Section 5 conclusions are drawn.

2 Research Background

Although using the mean-shift algorithm for blob tracking is not new to the computer vision community (first application 1998 [2]), there are few research studies on boundary detection.

Applications of the mean-shift algorithm in image processing were originally introduced by Cheng [3]. Bradski [2] introduced a new variation of the mean-shift algorithm for blob tracking in video sequences, called the "Continuously Adaptive Mean-shift" or CAM-Shift algorithm. His main assumption was that the face silhouette is the only silhouette in the image. He proposed the following equation for calculating the kernel size in each frame:

$$w = 2 \times \sqrt{\frac{M_{00}}{256}} \qquad h = 1.2 \times w$$

Where w and h are width and height of the new kernel and M_{00} is the sum of the weights of pixels in the previous kernel that is in the range 0 to 255. In this paper, we call this method "*kernel density-based*" or for the sake of simplicity, *sqrt(m00)*, because the kernel size is based on square root of the kernel density.

Sherrah and Gong [10] proposed a similar method for tracking discontinuous motion of multiple occluding body parts of an individual from a single 2D view. They used the following width and height for estimating the kernel size for face tracking :

$$w = \sqrt{n_{skin}} \qquad h = 1.2 \times w$$

Where n is the number of none-zero pixels inside the kernel. Comaniciu, et al. [5] suggested repeating the mean-shift algorithm at each iteration using kernel sizes of plus or minus 10 percent of the current size. KaeTraKulPong and Bowden [8] proposed a method to track low-resolution moving objects in the image, using color, shape and motion information. The height and width of the kernel were modeled by a white noise velocity model, based on the assumption that the bounding box does not change extensively. We should note that for some applications, including face tracking in HCI, this assumption is not valid.

Collins [4] indicated that setting the window size based on the CAM-Shift algorithm does not result in a reliable estimation of the object boundaries when weights are negative. Alternatively he proposed a method for resizing the search window based on the weight of the samples and the scale of the mean-shift kernel. The scale space is generated by convolving a filter bank of spatial DOG (Difference Of Gaussian) filters with a sample weight image. The results are then convolved with an Epanichikov kernel in the scale dimension. Although this method produces more reliable results for a wider range of applications, computational expense for calculating convolutions is very high. This makes the approach unfavorable for real-time applications.

3 Initialization and Boundary Detection of the Kernel

For face tracking purposes, our observations show that selecting a large kernel size equal to the input image together with resizing it with a proper algorithm can find the biggest blob, which in this case is the face region (Figure 1). This method has advantages in comparison to other methods, e.g. the random positioning of the kernel, which may or may not find the extremum point.

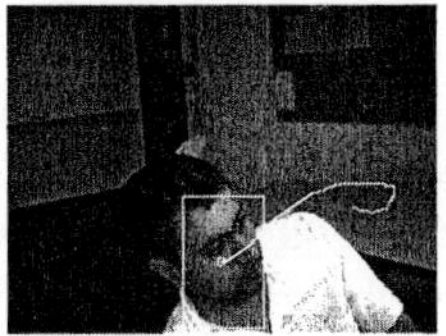

Fig. 1. Face tracking using mean-shift algorithm and boundary density thresholding method

3.1 Skin Detection

The primary process for using the mean-shift tracking algorithm is giving a weight to the pixels of the image. In this research, we have used *hue thresholding* for classifying skin pixels and filtering the image. After applying this filter, skin pixels have a value of 1, and the background pixels have a value of 0 (Figure 2). Filtering the image was done based on the algorithm originally proposed by Dadgostar, Sarrafzadeh, et al. [6, 7]. The tracking algorithm was implemented based on Bradski [2] with a rectangular kernel and a modified kernel resizing procedure.

(a)

(b)

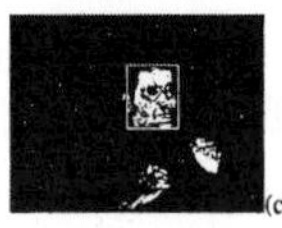
(c)

Fig. 2. Setting the kernel equal to the main image. (a) Original input, (b) Choosing a large kernel size for initialization, (c) Final detected boundaries.

3.2 Boundary Detection Based on Edge Density Thresholding

In this section we propose, a threshold-based approach for calculating the kernel boundaries. It is expected that in normal conditions the kernel size changes together with the weight of inner points. For instance, when the user moves toward the camera, the size of the kernel around his face should be enlarged together with the size of face's silhouette.

Based on this idea, we implemented an algorithm based on edge density of the kernel. Shrinking or enlarging the kernel is done based on measuring of the density of the kernel (counting the number of pixels with the value of 1 on the edges of the kernel by the size of the edge), as follows:

```
ni = calculate the density of the boundary of the kernel
if (ni > UpperThreshold) Then
   enlarge the kernel by 1
elseif (ni < LowerThreshold) Then
   shrink the kernel  by 1
else
   // no resize
endif
```

Our observations show this algorithm is suitable for detecting and tracking the face as the biggest blob in the image, but it also has two disadvantages: (1) In a noisy environment (e.g. camera noise), after reaching the boundary of the image it starts vibrating on the detected blob, and (2) it counts some unnecessary pixels when it is far from the target. Thus, it is not to the optimal solution and there is room for improvement in the convergence speed.

We believe shrinking or enlarging based on the edge density combined with a fuzzy approach can improve the convergence speed and therefore provide faster boundary detection, in either noiseless or noisy environments.

3.3 Fuzzy Boundary Detector

For resizing the kernel, a fuzzy approach based on the following characteristics was developed and tested. The input to the system is the density of the kernel boundaries, and the output is the resize factor. The fuzzy controller for resizing the kernel is defined as follows:

Fuzzifier. The fuzzifier changes the input values to fuzzy values. For input values, we have considered 3 different stages. These stages are based on the thresholds we have empirically determined for the *edge-density-thresholding* method (Section 3.2). The range of values for input parameters is from 0% to 100% and the membership function for the "Edge density thresholding" was defined as illustrated in Figure 3a. Empirical results show that the proposed number of levels is sufficient for face tracking.

Inference Engine. The inference procedure for the proposed fuzzy controller is presented in Table 1. We have considered three fuzzy values for changing the output as indicated in Figure 3c.

Defuzzifier. For evaluating *fuzzy_AND* and *fuzzy_OR*, *min* and *max* operators have been used, and output values calculated based on the centre of gravity method.

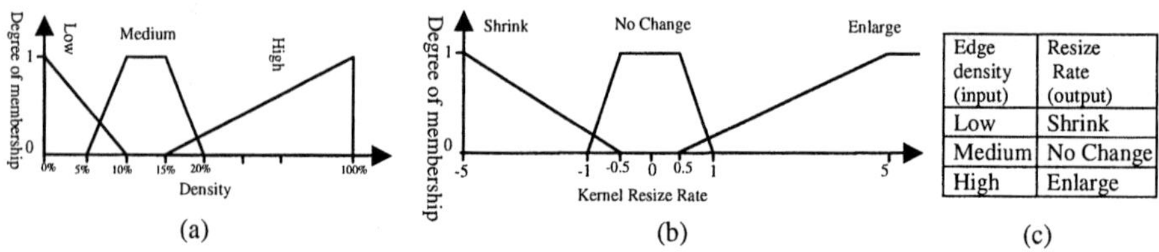

Edge density (input)	Resize Rate (output)
Low	Shrink
Medium	No Change
High	Enlarge

Fig. 3. (a) Fuzzy input, (b) Fuzzy output, (c) Fuzzy controller

4 Experiments and Results

In this section we present the experiments and the results depicting the behavior of the three algorithms presented in this paper: (i) Edge density thresholding, (ii) Edge density fuzzy, and (iii) *sqrt(m00)* in noiseless and noisy environment. The parameters for sqrt(m00) considered for tracking a face-like silhouette were the same as in Bradski [2]. We analyzed (a) the position of the top-left corner, (b) the position of the centre of gravity, and (c) the area of the kernel, that together give an overview of the stability of the kernel.

The experimental platform was a manually segmented face image (Figure 4a) as the input video sequence. The purpose of using a fixed frame instead of a real video sequence was having the ability to control the noise level and not having to deal with other variables including camera noise and change in lighting condition. The noise model was white noise up to a certain percentage in each experiment. The noise might change the value of a skin pixel that causes it to not appear as a skin pixel in the silhouette image (Figure 4c, 4d).

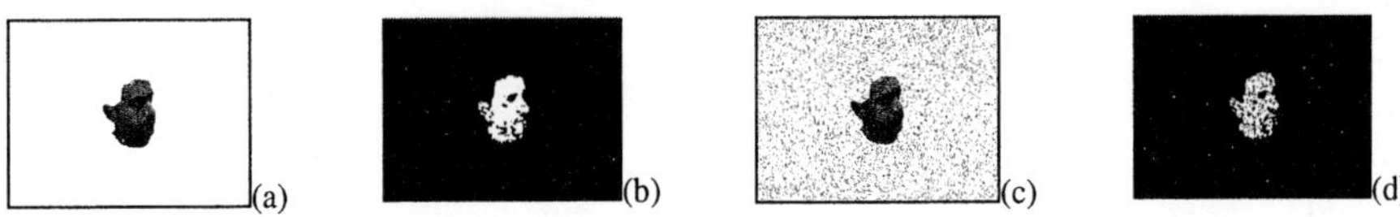

Fig. 4. (a) Input image, (b) Image silhouette filtered by hue thresholding algorithm, (c) Input image with noise, and (d) Noisy silhouette

4.1 Behavior of the Three Algorithms in a Noiseless Environment

The experiment measurements in noiseless environment for kernel's centre of gravity were approximately the same. But, the convergence speeds are different. The fastest convergence speed belongs to *sqtr(m00)*. The fuzzy method was second best and "edge-density thresholding" algorithm was the slowest (Figure 5).

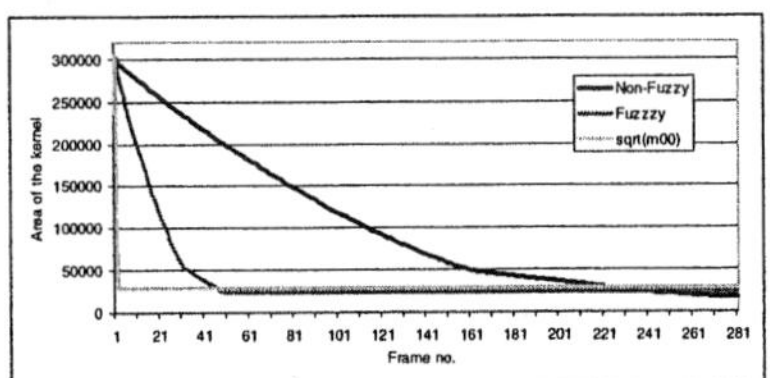

Fig. 5. Convergence speed of the three algorithms: Edge density thresholding (the slowest), Edge density fuzzy, and sqrt(m00) (the fastest)

4.2 Behavior of the Algorithms in Noisy Environment

We applied three noise levels to the input image: 10%, 20% and 25%. The results of our experiments show that the stability of the algorithms decreases with the increase of the noise level. For noise levels in excess of 25%, all three algorithms were unstable because of too few pixels in the region of interest. Consequently none of the algorithms could track the object properly.

By starting to add noise to the image, all three algorithms started to vibrate around the object because of the change in the kernel's inner and edge density. For a noise level up to 10%, all three algorithms could still track the face boundaries with similar stabilities. Adding more noise up to 25% causes more vibration in measurement factors, including "*detected centre of gravity*", "*boundaries*" and "*area*".

4.2.1 Behavior of the Kernel Density-Based Algorithm in Noisy Environment

By increasing the noise, the reliability of the *sqrt(m00)* method decreased until it could no longer properly specify the boundaries of the face. However, there is a logical explanation for this behavior. For specifying the boundaries, this method is dependent on the density of the kernel. Adding noise to the kernel causes a decrease in the density by a power of two, and therefore smaller width and height size for the kernel. By increasing the noise level, this method starts to loose the track more frequently (Figure 6).

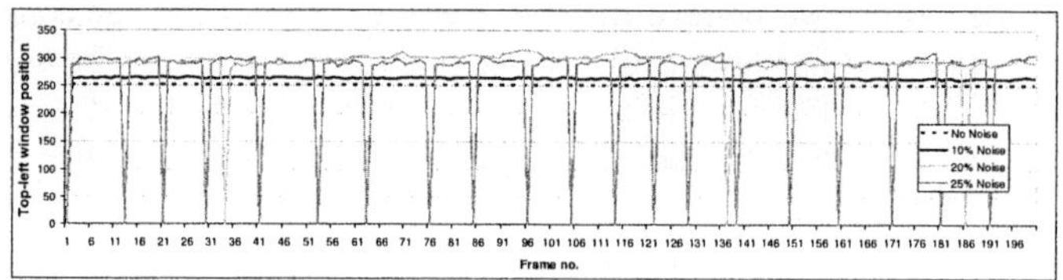

Fig. 6. Sensitivity of the sqrt(m00) to a noise level of 20%

4.2.2 Behavior of the Boundary-Based Algorithms in Noisy Environment

The two boundary-based algorithms proposed in this article, show more robustness against white noise. After locating the approximate position of the object, they deal with boundary density instead of kernel density, which makes them more robust against change of the density inside the kernel. In the highest noise level, the fuzzy-based approach represents significant stability in comparison to the other two algorithms. In Figure 7, the correct boundary is detected by the fuzzy-based approach and is stable over the entire period. The edge density thresholding algorithm has lost the correct track after frame 561. The kernel density-based algorithm was completely unstable, and the "roaming effect" can be seen in Figure 7a.

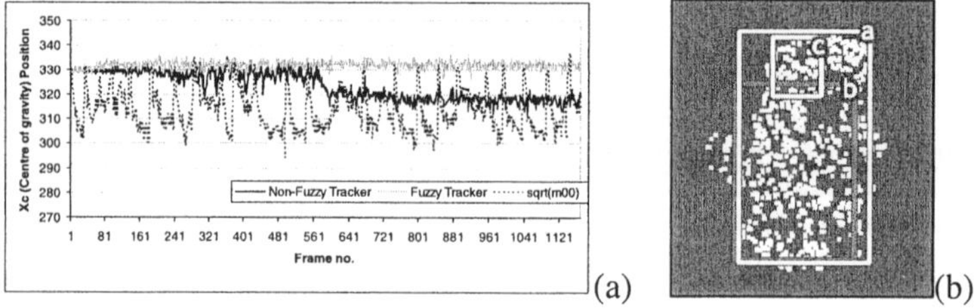

Fig. 7. (a), the next correct determined by Edge density-thresholding (b), and the smallest rectangle is the result of kernel density-based – *sqrt(m00)* – method

5 Conclusion

In this article we have presented strategies for boundary detection for the mean-shift algorithm in face tracking for HCI. We have introduced two new methods for boundary detection and compared them with the method introduced by Bradski [1] as the original application of the mean-shift algorithm for face tracking.

We have analyzed these three algorithms based on two main factors: convergence speed and stability against white noise. The results show that Bradski's approach is faster in convergence speed, but it is more vulnerable to the effects of noise. On the other hand the "fuzzy edge density" approach shows a convergence speed between Bradski's approach and the "edge density" approach with significant robustness against noise.

Based on the results we believe that this method of boundary detection together with the mean-shift and its variants like the cam-shift algorithm can be useful for fast and robust tracking of the face in noisy environment. Moreover, the performance makes it a good candidate for use with inexpensive cameras. Since inexpensive cameras have become commonplace in society among computer and hand-held device users, we believe that this increases the probability that affect-sensitive, adaptive user interfaces will become a reality for the average user.

References

1. Bianchi-berthouze, N. and Kleinsmith, A.A. A categorical approach to affective gesture recognition. *Journal of Neural Computing, Artificial Intelligence & Cognitive Research, 15* (4). 259-269.
2. Bradski, G.R. Computer Vision Face Tracking For Use in a Perceptual User Interface, Microcomputer Research Lab, Santa Clara, CA, Intel Corporation, 1998.
3. Cheng, Y. Mean shift, mode seeking, and clustering. *IEEE Transactions on Pattern Analysis and Machine Intelligence, 17* (8). 790-799.
4. Collins, R.T., Mean-shift Blob Tracking through Scale Space. in *IEEE Conference on Computer Vision and Pattern Recognition*, (2003).
5. Comaniciu, D., Ramesh, V. and Meer, P., Real-Time Tracking of Non-Rigid Objects using Mean Shift. in *IEEE Computer Vision and Pattern Recognition*, (2000), 142-149.
6. Dadgostar, F., Sarrafzadeh, A. and Johnson, M.J., An Adaptive Skin Detector for Video Sequences Based on Optical Flow Motion Features. in *International Conference on Signal and Image Processing (SIP)*, (Hawaii, USA, 2005).
7. Dadgostar, F., Sarrafzadeh, A. and Overmyer, S.P., An Adaptive Real-time Skin Detector for Video Sequences. in *International Conference on Computer Vision*, (Las Vegas, USA, 2005).
8. KaewTraKulPong, P. and Bowden, R., An Adaptive Visual System for Tracking Low Resolution Colour Targets. in *BMVC'01*, (Manchester, UK, 2001), 243-252.
9. Kapoor, A. and Picard, R.W., A real-time head nod and shake detector. in *Proceedings of the Workshop on Perceptive User Interfaces*, (Orlando, Florida, USA, 2001).
10. Sherrah, J. and Gong, S., Tracking Discontinuous Motion Using Bayesian Inference. in *ECCV*, (2000), 150-166.

Modelling Nonrigid Object from Video Sequence Under Perspective Projection*

Guanghui Wang[1,3], Yantao Tian[2], and Guoqiang Sun[1,2]

[1] Department of Control Engineering, Aviation University of Airforce, Changchun 130022, P.R. China
[2] School of Communication Engineering, Jilin University, Changchun 130022, China
[3] National Laboratory of Pattern Recognition, Institute of Automation, Chinese Academy of Sciences 100080, China
ghwang@ee.cuhk.edu.hk, tianyt@mail.jlu.edu.cn

Abstract. The paper is focused on the problem of estimating 3D structure and motion of nonrigid object from a monocular video sequence. Many previous methods on this problem utilize the extension technique of factorization based on rank constraint to the tracking matrix, where the 3D shape of nonrigid object is expressed as weighted combination of a set of shape bases. All these solutions are based on the assumption of affine camera model. This assumption will become invalid and cause large reconstruction errors when the object is close to the camera. The main contribution of this paper is that we extend these methods to the general perspective camera model. The proposed algorithm iteratively updates the shape and motion from weak perspective projection to fully perspective projection by refining the scalars corresponding to the projective depths. Extensive experiments on real sequences validate the effectiveness and improvements of the proposed method.

1 Introduction

The problem of recovering both structure and motion from 2D image sequences is an important and essential task in the field of computer vision. During the last two decades, many approaches have been proposed for different applications. Among which, factorization based methods are widely studied and attracted many attentions in the computer vision society, since this kind of approaches deal with all the data in all images uniformly, thus may achieve good robustness and accuracy.

The factorization method was first proposed by Tomasi and Kanade [1] in early 90's. The main idea of this algorithm is the use of rank constraint to factorize a measurement matrix, which contains all the features tracked across the entire sequence, into the motion and structure at the same time. The algorithm assumes an orthographic projection model. It was then extended to paraperspective and weak perspective projection model by Poelman and Kanada [2].

* The work is partly supported by the National Natural Science Foundation of China.

J. Tao, T. Tan, and R.W. Picard (Eds.): ACII 2005, LNCS 3784, pp. 64–71, 2005.

Christy and Horaud [3] proposed an iterative method to estimate the Euclidean structure under perspective camera model by incrementally performing the reconstruction process with either a weak or a paraperspective projection. The above methods assume the camera is calibrated. In the case of uncalibrated camera, Triggs [4] proposed to achieve the projective reconstruction via similar factorization scheme, where, the projective depth was computed via epipolar geometry. The method was further studied by Heyden and Berthilsson [5] and Mahamud and Hebert [6].

The above methods work only for rigid object or static scenes. While in real world, most objects are nonrigid and the scenes are dynamic, such as human faces carrying different expressions, lip movements, moving vehicles, etc. Many extensions stemming from the factorization algorithm were proposed to relax the rigidity constraint. Costeira and Kanade [7] first discussed how to recover the motion and shape of several independent moving objects via factorization under orthographic projection. The same problem was further discussed by Han and Kanade [8]. Bascle and Blake [9] proposed a method for factoring facial expressions and poses based on a set of preselected basis images.

Breler *et.al.* [10] proposed to describe the 3D shape of nonrigid objects as weighted combination of a set of shape bases, then the shape bases, combination coefficients and camera motion were factorized simultaneously under the rank constraint of the tracking matrix. Torresani *et.al* [11] introduced an iterative algorithm to optimize the recovered shape and motion. Brand [12] generalized the method and proposed nonrigid subspace flow for the searching of correspondences. The above methods use only the orthonormal (rotation) constraints to the Euclidean reconstruction after factorization, this may cause ambiguity to the combination of shape bases. To solve this ambiguity, Xiao *et.al.* [13] introduced the basis constraints that implicitly determine the bases uniquely. They also studied the degenerate cases for nonrigid deformation in [14]. Del Bue and Agapito [15] extended the method to the stereo camera case and introduced a nonlinear optimization step to select the correct shape and motion.

To our best knowledge, previous factorization methods for nonrigid shape and motion are all based on affine camera model. This is a zero-order (weak perspective) or first-order (paraperspective) approximation to the real imaging condition and is only valid when the depth variation of the object is small compared to the distance between the object and the camera [16]. Therefore, large reconstruction errors may be caused when the object is close to the camera. In this paper, we will extend the algorithm in [3] to the nonrigid case and recover 3D structure of nonrigid object under general perspective projection. Experiments demonstrate the improvements to the reconstruction results.

The remaining parts of the paper are organized as follows: In section 2, we first analyze the relationship between perspective and weak perspective projection, then present the nonrigid factorization method under weak perspective assumption, followed by the algorithm and analysis of the proposed method. Some experiment results are given in section 3. Finally, the conclusions of this paper are given in section 4.

2 Nonrigid Factorization with Perspective Camera Model

2.1 Perspective vs. Weak Perspective Projection

Suppose the camera is calibrated and we are working with normalized image coordinates, then the projection between a space point $\mathbf{X}'_i \in \Re^3$ and its image $\mathbf{x}_i \in \Re^2$ can be modelled as:

$$s\tilde{\mathbf{x}}_i = \mathbf{R}'\mathbf{X}'_i + \mathbf{T}' \tag{1}$$

where, $\tilde{\mathbf{x}}_i = [\mathbf{x}_i^T, 1]^T$ is the homogeneous form of $\mathbf{x}_i$, $\mathbf{R}' = [\mathbf{r}_1^T, \mathbf{r}_2^T, \mathbf{r}_3^T]^T$ is the rotation matrix with $\mathbf{r}_i$ the ith row of the matrix, $\mathbf{T}' = [t_x, t_y, t_z]^T$ is the translation vector of the camera, s is a non-zero scalar. Suppose the normalized image coordinates of $\mathbf{x}_i$ is $[u_i, v_i]^T$, expanding equation (1) will give:

$$\begin{cases} u_i = \frac{\mathbf{r}_1\mathbf{X}'_i + t_x}{\mathbf{r}_3\mathbf{X}'_i + t_z} = \frac{\mathbf{r}_1\mathbf{X}'_i/t_z + t_x/t_z}{1 + \mathbf{r}_3\mathbf{X}'_i/t_z} = \frac{\mathbf{r}_1\mathbf{X}'_i/t_z + t_x/t_z}{1 + \varepsilon_i} \\ v_i = \frac{\mathbf{r}_2\mathbf{X}'_i + t_x}{\mathbf{r}_3\mathbf{X}'_i + t_z} = \frac{\mathbf{r}_2\mathbf{X}'_i/t_z + t_x/t_z}{1 + \mathbf{r}_3\mathbf{X}'_i/t_z} = \frac{\mathbf{r}_2\mathbf{X}'_i/t_z + t_x/t_z}{1 + \varepsilon_i} \end{cases} \tag{2}$$

Under weak perspective assumption, the depth variation of the object is small compared with the distance to the camera, i.e. $\varepsilon_i \approx 0$. This is equivalent to a zero-order approximation of perspective projection. Let $\mathbf{X}_i = \mathbf{X}'_i/t_z$, $\mathbf{R} = [\mathbf{r}_1^T, \mathbf{r}_2^T]^T$, $\mathbf{T} = [t_x/t_z, t_y/t_z]^T$, and $\lambda_i = 1 + \varepsilon_i$, then the weak perspective projection can be modelled as:

$$\mathbf{x}_i = \mathbf{R}\mathbf{X}_i + \mathbf{T} \tag{3}$$

From equation (2) we can easily find the relationship between the perspective and weak perspective projection.

$$\mathbf{x}'_i = \lambda_i \mathbf{x}_i \tag{4}$$

Lemma 1. *Under weak perspective projection, the centroid of a set of space points and that of their image points correspond to each other.*

The proof of this Lemma is obvious since the mapping from space point to its image is linear according to equation (3).

2.2 Nonrigid Factorization Under Weak Perspective Projection

Given a sequence of m video frames and n tracked feature points across the sequence. Let $\{\mathbf{x}_i^{(j)} \in \Re^2\}_{i=1,\ldots,n}^{j=1,\ldots,m}$ be the coordinates of these features. The aim is to recover the shape $\mathbf{S}^{(j)} \in \Re^{3\times n}$ (i.e. the corresponding 3D coordinates of the features) and the motion $\mathbf{R}^{(j)} \in \Re^{2\times 3}$ of each frame.

As described in [10], the nonrigid shape can be represented as weighted combination of k shape bases, i.e. $\mathbf{S}^{(j)} = \sum_{l=1}^{k} w_l^{(j)} \mathbf{S}_l$, where, $\mathbf{S}_l \in \Re^{3\times n}$ is one of the shape bases, $w_l^{(j)} \in \Re$ is the deformation weight (a perfect rigid object would correspond to the case of $k = 1$ and $w_l^{(j)} = 1$). Under weak perspective assumption of (3), we have:

$$[\mathbf{x}_1^{(j)}, \mathbf{x}_2^{(j)}, \ldots, \mathbf{x}_n^{(j)}] = \mathbf{R}^{(j)}(\sum_{l=1}^{k} w_l^{(j)} \mathbf{S}_l) + \mathbf{T}^{(j)}, \ j = 1, \ldots, m \tag{5}$$

If we register all image points to the centroid in each frame, then the translation term $\mathbf{T}^{(j)}$ can be eliminated according to Lemma 1. Stacking all equations in (5) frame by frame will give:

$$\begin{bmatrix} \mathbf{x}_1^{(1)} & \cdots & \mathbf{x}_n^{(1)} \\ \vdots & \ddots & \vdots \\ \mathbf{x}_1^{(m)} & \cdots & \mathbf{x}_n^{(m)} \end{bmatrix}_{2m\times n} = \begin{bmatrix} w_1^{(1)}\mathbf{R}^{(1)} & \cdots & w_k^{(1)}\mathbf{R}^{(1)} \\ \vdots & \ddots & \vdots \\ w_1^{(m)}\mathbf{R}^{(m)} & \cdots & w_k^{(m)}\mathbf{R}^{(m)} \end{bmatrix}_{2m\times 3k} \begin{bmatrix} \mathbf{S}_1 \\ \vdots \\ \mathbf{S}_k \end{bmatrix}_{3k\times n} \tag{6}$$

The above equation can be written in short as $\mathbf{W}_{2m\times n} = \mathbf{M}_{2m\times 3k}\mathbf{B}_{3k\times n}$. It is easy to see from the right side of (6) that the rank of the tracking matrix $\mathbf{W}$ is at most $3k$ (usually $2m$ and n are larger than $3k$ respectively). By performing singular value decomposition (SVD) on the tracking matrix and imposing the rank constraint, $\mathbf{W}$ may be factored as $\mathbf{W} = \tilde{\mathbf{M}}\tilde{\mathbf{B}}$ [2]. However, the decomposition is not unique since it is only defined up to a non-singular $3k \times 3k$ linear transformation as $\mathbf{W} = (\tilde{\mathbf{M}}\mathbf{G})(\mathbf{G}^{-1}\tilde{\mathbf{B}})$. If the correct transformation is obtained, the shape bases can be recovered from $\mathbf{B} = \mathbf{G}^{-1}\tilde{\mathbf{B}}$, while the rotation matrix $\mathbf{R}^{(j)}$ and weighting coefficient $w_l^{(j)}$ may be recovered from $\mathbf{M} = \tilde{\mathbf{M}}\mathbf{G}$ by procrustes analysis such as sub-block factorization [10][12] or a further iterative optimization step proposed in [11].

For the computation of $\mathbf{G}$, many researchers [10][11][12] use the rotation constraint to $\mathbf{M} = \tilde{\mathbf{M}}\mathbf{G}$. While, as proved in [13], only the rotation constraint may be insufficient when the object deforms at varying speed. In real applications, it is better to combine the basis constraint [13] together with the rotation constraint to compute the correct transformation matrix.

We can now obtain the solution of the shape $\mathbf{S}^{(j)}$ and the motion $\mathbf{R}^{(j)}$. Nevertheless, a reversal ambiguity still remains which is inherent with any affine camera model [3]. If we denote ($\mathbf{S}^{(j)}$,$\mathbf{R}^{(j)}$) as "positive" solution, then a "negative" solution ($-\mathbf{S}^{(j)}$,$-\mathbf{R}^{(j)}$) is also hold true to the algorithm.

2.3 Recursive Factorization Under Perspective Projection

As given in equation (4), the difference between perspective and weak perspective projection is depicted by the scalar λ_i, which is related to the projection depth of the feature point. We may rewrite the relationship as $\mathbf{x}_i'^{(j)} = \lambda_i^{(j)}\mathbf{x}_i^{(j)}$ for the whole sequence. Let us define a weighted tracking matrix as follows:

$$\mathbf{W}' = \begin{bmatrix} \lambda_1^{(1)}\mathbf{x}_1^{(1)} & \cdots & \lambda_n^{(1)}\mathbf{x}_n^{(1)} \\ \vdots & \ddots & \vdots \\ \lambda_1^{(m)}\mathbf{x}_1^{(m)} & \cdots & \lambda_n^{(m)}\mathbf{x}_n^{(m)} \end{bmatrix}_{2m\times n} \tag{7}$$

If we can recover all the scalars $\{\lambda_i^{(j)} \in \Re\}_{i=1,\ldots,n}^{j=1,\ldots,m}$ that are consistent with (4), the factorization of $\mathbf{W}'$ will give the correct shape and motion under perspective projection of the object. Here we adopt a similar method as [3] (which is for rigid case) to recursively estimate the value of the scalars. The algorithm is summarized as follows:

1. Set $\lambda_i^{(j)} = 1$ for $i = 1, \ldots, n$ and $j = 1, \ldots, m$;
2. Update $\mathbf{W}'$ according to (7);
3. Perform weak perspective factorization of $\mathbf{W}'$ according to section 2.2;
4. Estimate the new value of $\lambda_i^{(j)}$ according to (2);
5. Return to step 2 if $\lambda_i^{(j)}$ does not converge.

The geometrical explanation of the algorithm is very clear as illustrated in Fig. 1. The initial tracking matrix is composed of the images $\mathbf{x}_i$, which is actually formed by perspective projection, the weighted tracking matrix $\mathbf{W}'$ of (7), which may be composed of the points $\mathbf{x}_i' = \lambda_i \mathbf{x}_i$, varies in accordance with the newly updated scalars of step 4. Upon convergence, the image points are modified to $\hat{\mathbf{x}}_i$ such that they fit the weak perspective projection. Thus, the process of the algorithm is to recursively change the image coordinates from the position of perspective projection to that of weak perspective position by adjusting the scalar $\lambda_i^{(j)}$. While the image of the centroid ($\mathbf{x}_c$) remains untouched during the iteration.

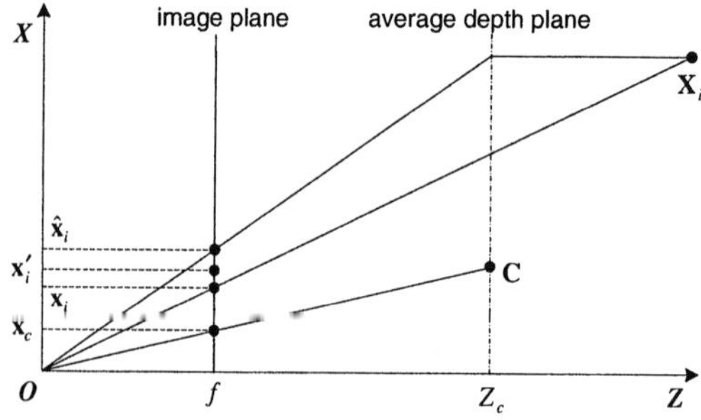

Fig. 1. Cross-sectional view of perspective approximation from weak perspective projection. Where O is the optical center, with $Z = f$ the image plane. $\mathbf{C}$ is the centroid of the object, Z_c is the average depth plane, $\mathbf{X}_i$ is a point on the object, $\mathbf{x}_i$ is the image under perspective projection, $\hat{\mathbf{x}}_i$ is the image under weak perspective projection.

Remark 1. On determining the convergence in step 5, we may arrange all the scalars at the tth iteration into a matrix $\omega(t) = [\lambda_i^{(j)}]_{2m\times 3k}$. Check the scalar variations as the Frobenius norm of the difference with the previous iteration, i.e. $\delta = \|\omega(t) - \omega(t-1)\|_F$. The algorithm will converge ($\delta \to 0$) usually after several iterations.

Remark 2. In step 3 of the algorithm, we do not take the reversal ambiguity as stated in section 2.2 into consideration. However, this ambiguity may be easily solved here. We can reproject the "positive" and the "negative" solutions to each frame and form two new tracking matrices, say $\mathbf{W}^+$ for the "positive" and $\mathbf{W}^-$ for the "negative". Check the Frobenius norms of $\|\mathbf{W}' - \mathbf{W}^+\|_F$ and $\|\mathbf{W}' - \mathbf{W}^-\|_F$. The one with the smaller error would be the correct solution.

Remark 3. One may have noted that the solution obtained by the algorithm is just an approximation to the fully perspective projection. A further step of nonlinear optimization may be needed by minimize the image reprojection error $\left(\min_{\mathbf{R}^{(j)},\mathbf{S}_l,\omega_l^{(j)}} \left\|\mathbf{W} - \hat{\mathbf{W}}\right\|_F\right)$ just as the scheme of bundle adjustment in [16], where $\mathbf{W}$ is the initial tracking matrix, $\hat{\mathbf{W}}$ is the reprojected tracking matrix.

3 Experiments with Real Sequences

We have tested the proposed method on several real video sequences. Here we will only show the results of Franck sequence due to space limitation.

The Franck video and tracking data is downloaded from the European working group on face and gesture recognition (`www-prima.inrialpes.fr/FGnet/`), which contains 5000 frames. While only 65 frames with various facial expressions are used in the experiment. There are 68 automatically tracked feature points using the active appearance model (AAM) method. The camera is assumed to be constant during shooting, we use a simplified camera model with square pixel and the principal point at the image center. The only unknown parameter (focal length) is estimated by the method proposed in [17].

Fig. 2 shows the reconstructed wireframes and VRML models with texture mapping correspond to three frames, which are obtained at the 10th iteration. We may see from the results that the models at different frame, as well as the different facial expressions, are correctly recovered. However, the positions of some reconstructed points may be not very accurate. This is mainly caused by the errors of the tracked features and the camera parameters. We are still working on this problem.

During iteration, we recorded the scalar variations as stated in Remark 1, as well as the reprojection errors $\|\mathbf{W} - \mathbf{W}(t)\|_F$ of the reconstructed shape and motion, where, $\mathbf{W}$ is the initial tracking matrix, $\mathbf{W}(t)$ is the reprojected tracking matrix at the$t$th iteration. The results are shown in Fig. 3.

It can be seen from Fig. 3 that the algorithm converges after 4 or 5 iterations. The reprojection error of the weak perspective based methods corresponds to that at the first iteration as shown in the right of Fig. 3, from which we can see the improvements to the solutions by the proposed algorithm. One may noted that a small residual error still exists even after convergence due to the inherent property of the algorithm. Nevertheless, the results are accurate enough for normal purposes such as visualization and recognition. Better reconstruction results may be expected by the nonlinear optimization of Remark 3.

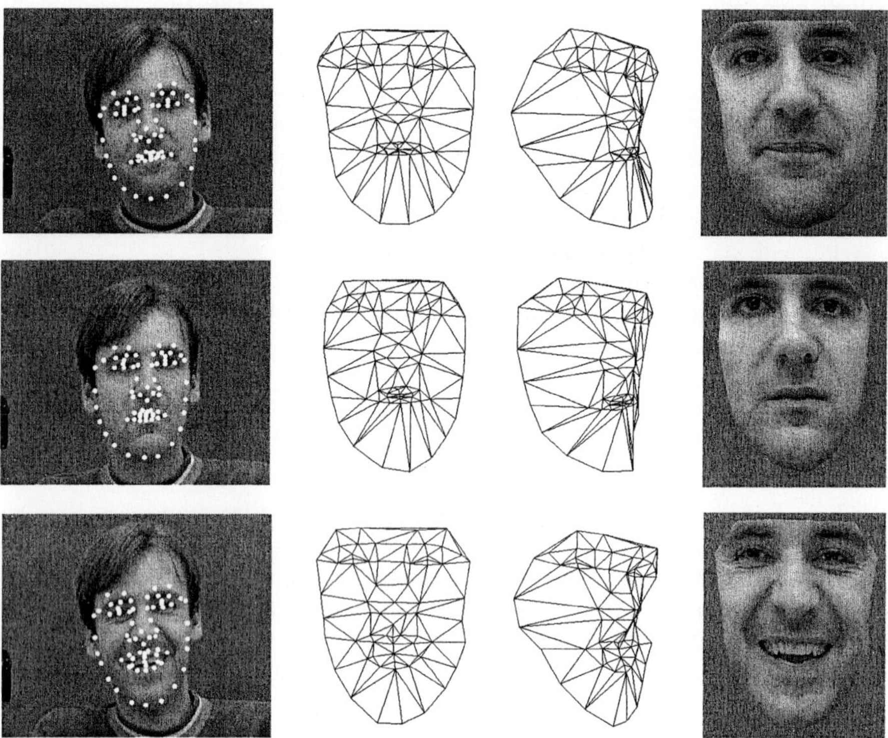

Fig. 2. Reconstruction results of three frames with different facial expressions from the Franck sequence. Left column: three key frames from the sequence overlaid with 68 tracked feature points; Middle two columns: wireframe models corresponding to the left column at different viewpoints; Right column: the corresponding reconstructed VRML models with texture mapping.

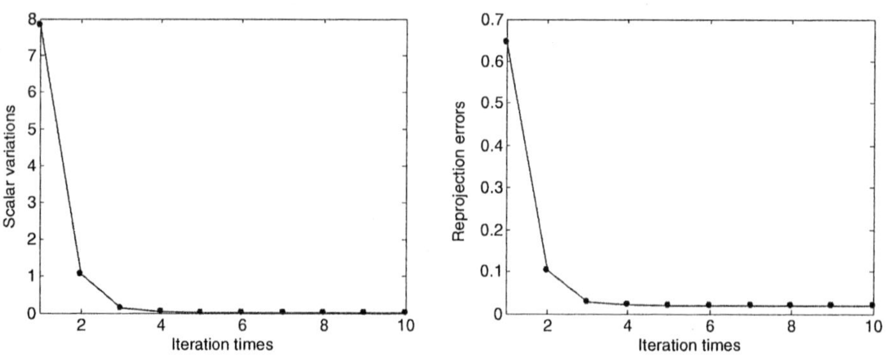

Fig. 3. Left: scalar variations of the algorithm at each iteration; Right: reprojection errors of the reconstructed shape and motion at each iteration

4 Conclusions

In this paper, we have introduced a recursive algorithm to update previous nonrigid factorization methods from weak perspective assumption to the case of perspective projection. We have also given a geometrical explanation of the method. Experiment results with real sequences validate the algorithm and show the improvements compared with weak perspective reconstruction. We are currently working towards an extension of the method to more challenging cases that usually happen in real applications, such as how to deal with large errors in the tracked features or even work with some missing feature points. Another problem is the influence of the calibration results to the final solutions and how to accurately calibrate the cameras.

References

1. C. Tomasi, T. Kanade, Shape and motion from image streams under orthography: A factorization method, IJCV, vol.9(2): 137-154, 1992.
2. C. Poelman, T. Kanade, A paraperspective factorization method for shape and motion recovery, IEEE T-PAMI, vol.19(3): 206-218, 1997.
3. S. Christy, R. Horaud, Euclidean shape and motion from multiple perspective views by affine iterations, IEEE T-PAMI, vol.18(11): 1098-1104, 1996.
4. B.Triggs, Factorization methods for projective structure and motion, In: Proc. CVPR,1996.
5. R. Heyden, Berthilsson, et.al, An iterative factorization method for projective structure and motion from image sequences, Image and Vision Computing, vol.17(13), 1999.
6. S. Mahamud, M. Hebert, Iterative projective reconstruction from multiple views, In: Proc. CVPR, vol.2: 430-437, 2000.
7. J.P. Costeira, T. Kanade, A multibody factorization method for independently moving-objects, IJCV, vol.29(3):159-179, 1998.
8. M. Han, T. Kanade, Reconstruction of a scene with multiple linearly moving objects, In: Proc. CVPR, 2000.
9. B. Bascle and A. Blake, Separability of pose and expression in facial tracing and animation, In: Proc. ICCV, pp.323-328, 1998.
10. C. Bregler, A. Hertzmann, H. Biermann, Recovering non-rigid 3D shape from image streams, In: Proc. CVPR, 2000.
11. L. Torresani, D. Yang, et.al. Tracking and modeling non-rigid objects with rank constraints, In: Proc. CVPR, 2001.
12. M. Brand, Morphable 3D models from video, In: Proc. CVPR, vol.2: 456-463, 2001.
13. J. Xiao, J. Chai, T. Kanade, A closed-form solution to non-rigid shape and motion recovery, In: Proc. ECCV, pp. 573-587, 2004.
14. J. Xiao, T. Kanade, Non-rigid shape and motion recovery: Degenerate deformations, In: Proc. CVPR, pp. 668-675, 2004.
15. A. Del Bue, L. Agapito, Non-rigid 3D shape recovery using stereo factorization. In: Proc. ACCV, 2004.
16. R. Hartley and A, Zisserman, Multiple view geometry in computer vision, Cambridge University Press, 2000.
17. M. Pollefeys, R. Koch and L. Van Gool. Self-calibration and metric reconstruction in spite of varying and unknown internal camera parameters, IJCV, vol.32(1): 7-25, 1999.

Sketch Based Facial Expression Recognition Using Graphics Hardware

Jiajun Bu, Mingli Song, Qi Wu, Chun Chen, and Cheng Jin

Zhejiang University, Hangzhou 310027, P.R. China
{bjj, brooksong, bugtony, chenc, chengjin}@zju.edu.cn

Abstract. In this paper, a novel system is proposed to recognize facial expression based on face sketch, which is produced by programmable graphics hardware-GPU(Graphics Processing Unit). Firstly, an expression subspace is set up from a corpus of images consisting of seven basic expressions. Secondly, by applying a GPU based edge detection algorithm, the real-time facial expression sketch extraction is performed. Subsequently, noise elimination is carried out by tone mapping operation on GPU. Then, an ASM instance is trained to track the facial feature points in the sketched face image more efficiently and precisely than that on a grey level image directly. Finally, by the normalized key feature points, Eigen expression vector is deduced to be the input of MSVM(Multi-SVMs) based expression recognition model, which is introduced to perform the expression classification. Test expression images are categorized by MSVM into one of the seven basic expression subspaces. Experiment on a data set containing 500 pictures clearly shows the efficacy of the algorithm.

1 Introduction

Facial expression is an important way to perform communication between humans. Expression recognition will be a necessary component of future HCI[1], which can make the interaction between human and computer more natural and interesting. This inspired many researchers to analyze facial features and measure their movement so as to categorize different facial expressions. Extensive studies have been performed on the relationship between emotion and facial expressions since 1970s. Ekman[2,3] grouped the facial expressions into six "universality" ones. Those are so called joy, sadness, anger, fear, surprise, and disgust. Some approaches[4] extract the facial features from the image, and these features are used as inputs into a classification system to categorize different facial expressions automatically. The basic idea of these approaches is measuring the motion of the facial features to deduce the AU component, then take a rule based expression recognition. However, tracking the movement of facial features is not so robust since the variation of the background, illumination, texture, etc. Though the temporal information is very useful for studying the motion of the face, static images are important for obtaining configurational information about facial expressions. Since a minute's clip of a video tape take approximately one

J. Tao, T. Tan, and R.W. Picard (Eds.): ACII 2005, LNCS 3784, pp. 72–79, 2005.

hour or more to manually score in terms of features definition. Furthermore, to capture the expression features in a video sequence requires more calculating workload and more expensive equipments, which is an obstacle to apply the method widely in industry. For the static image based expression recognition, actually, the final accuracy depends on the facial feature tracking result. Namely, if the expression features tracking results are promised and robust, the expression recognition accuracy will be higher and consistent, and vice versa. In our case, a GPU enhanced facial tracking method is proposed, then one-to-rest SVM[5] based classification is carried out to determine the certainty of the basic expression it belongs to.

Active Shape Model[6] is a good algorithm to track facial features for its rapidness and lower computing workload. But sometimes it cannot reach convergence or give out a precise location because of the noise and ambiguity in the image. Enhancing the edge or boundary between the components in the image will make the tracking more precise and efficient. But the time cost of this operation is heavy on CPU. GPU has more than one processing pipeline working in parallel. Ian Buck[7] estimated that the nVIDIA GeForce FX 5900 GPU performance peaks at 20GigaFlops. Recent advances in the programmability permit GPU to grow as a powerful vector coprocessor to the CPU. It can implement fast Matrix-Vector operations to improve techniques for executing a set of instructions during the vertex or fragment processing. Considering the parallel nature of implementing custom image processing with filters using pixel shaders to process the image, this new graphics hardware is a suitable candidate for implement them at an extremely high speed. This can be used for sharpen and edge detection filtering for the face expression image to get the corresponding sketch. With the sketched image, ASM based tracking is carried out with fewer iterations while the location is more precise. Then the tracked feature points are normalized to deduce an eigen expression vector. As for the expression classification, in this paper, we treat the neutral face as the seventh expression. With trained MSVM instance, the expression vector are classified into one of the seven basic categories: neutral, joy, anger, surprise, disgust, sadness and fear.

2 System Overview

Fig. 1. shows an overview of our GPU enhanced facial expression recognition system. Our system consists two parts: Sketch based facial feature extraction, and MSVM based expression recognition. In the former section, the GPU based edge detection and sharpen filtering are performed firstly. Then, the very high frequency noise information in the sketched image is filtered out by a tone mapping operation on GPU. The facial feature points are located by an ASM instance in the sketched image, which give a better result with fewer iterations.

Later, in the latter section, the eigen expression vector deduced from the tracked feature points is analyzed by the trained MSVM, which consists of several one-to-rest SVMs. The likelihoods of the classification result are used to determine what basic expression the face is.

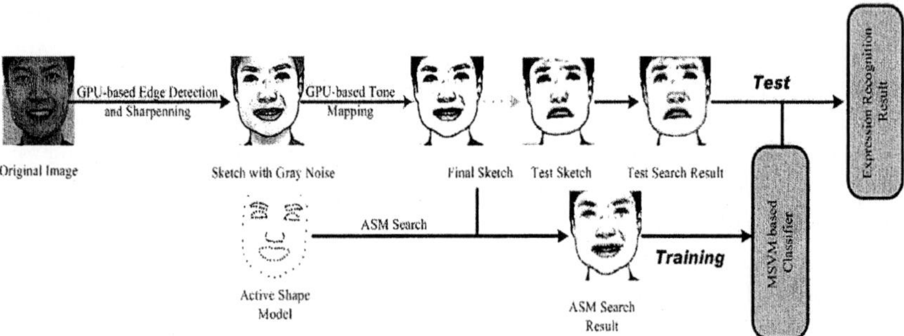

Fig. 1. System Overview

3 Facial Feature Extraction

Given a corpus of facial expression images, we filter them into a sketch set firstly, then with the sharpened edge, ASM can locates the feature points and gives out the face shape more precisely and quickly.

3.1 GPU-Based Sketch Generation

Modern graphics hardware technology gives GPU a powerful capability to carry out Matrix-Vector operations. Therefore a series of filtering operation on image can be performed at a extremely high speed. Edge detection, sharpening and luminance filtering are typical operations in image processing. It is suitable for GPU to implement such operations to obtain a high quality sketch at a high speed.

To obtain the corresponding sketch for an expression face image, a filter kernel based operator is employed to detect and sharpen the edge of the contour of face component. We adopt the a general equation mentioned in [8] to carry out such operation, which is

$$P = \frac{s^2}{4}(a+c+g+i) + (\frac{s-s^2}{2}(a+d+f+h) + (1-s)^2 e) \qquad (1)$$

Here s is the sample window's edge from the center texel, and a,b,c,d,e,f,g,h,i are the texels in the sample window. In the edge detection stage, firstly, the color of each pixel is converted to luminance value and the square diagonal differences are computed. Secondly, sum up the differences. Thirdly, the result is inverted to display edges black on white. Finally, we multiply the edge image with a large number to make the values visible to obtain the final result.

However, the result obtained from the method mentioned above still contains many noises make the tracking process slow and unreliable. So in our approach, a further step is taken to eliminate these high frequency noise by changing the tonal range, which can also be run extremely fast on GPU. For the world luminance L, it can be defined with the equation below [9].

a	b	c
d	e	f
g	h	i

Fig. 2. Sample Window

$$TM(L) = LDMAX \frac{C(L) - C(L_{min})}{C(L_{max}) - C(L_{min})} \tag{2}$$

In our case, the mid-tone and the highlight are 0.25 and 175 respectively to compute L_{max} and L_{min}. As shown in Fig. 3, we can see the luminance filtered sketch is cleaner than the initial one while keeping the detail of the face.

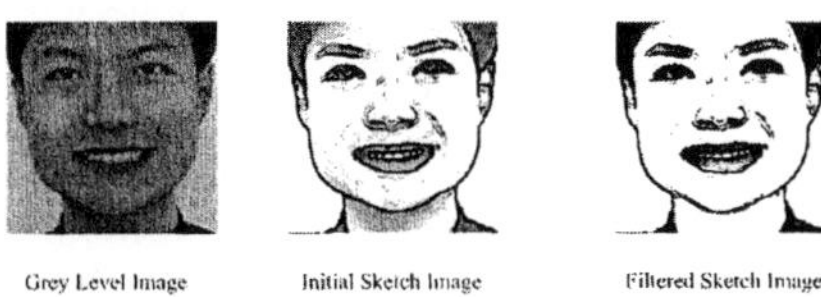

Fig. 3. GPU-Based Sketch Extraction and Noise Elimination

3.2 Facial Feature Tracking

ASM and AAM are both good models to track objects in image. Because ASM only use data around the model points, and do not take advantage of all the grey-level information available across an object, in general, ASM is believed being faster and achieving more accurate feature point location than the AAM.

In our system, 128 feature points are defined to describe the face configuration (Fig. 4). For tracking the facial feature points mentioned above, we apply ASM to track the facial feature points. The image database for the training of the shape model is obtained using the method of Covell and Bregler [10]. And the images in the training database are all in sketch form. The images from the data set are labelled manually. Then, ASM is trained by using these labelled sketches. Finally, the facial eigen expression vector is deduced from the location of these tracked feature points using the trained model.

For an ASM searching issue, if we expect the model boundary to correspond to an edge, "we can simply locate the strongest edge (including orientation if known) along the profile. The position of this gives the new suggested location for the model point" [?]. So it takes much less time to converge on a sketched image. Table 1 shows the average convergence time for ASM searching the feature points on grey level and sketched expression image respectively. Furthermore, since the

Fig. 4. Face Configuration by 128 Feature Points

edge of the components in the face is enhanced, which makes the derivative of the sampled profile in ASM more sensitive, the feature points locating becomes more precise. The sketch based ASM searching is shown in Fig. 5.

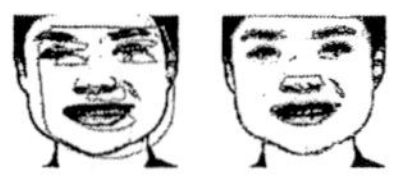

Fig. 5. Sketch based ASM Tracking

For a set of 128 tracked feature points $f_1, \cdots, f_{128}$ on the face define the face configuration, it's not necessary for us to form them into the the expression vector. PCA is performed to lower the dimension of the tracking result. Finally we get a 19 dimension vector $\overrightarrow{f}$, where $\overrightarrow{f} = [f_1^x, f_1^y, \cdots, f_{19}^x, f_{19}^y]$. We first normalize $\overrightarrow{f}$ and convert it into a standard expression vector $\overrightarrow{f_s} = [f_1^x/S^x, f_1^y/S^y, \cdots, f_{19}^x/S^x, f_{19}^y/S^y]$, $S^x = \sum_{i=1}^{19} f_i^x$, $S^y = \sum_{i=1}^{19} f_i^y$.

Table 1. Average Convergence Time on Grey Level and Sketched Image

	Grey Level	Sketch
GPU Time	0	0.001s
Searching Time	2.531s	1.323s
Total	2.531s	1.324s

4 Facial Expression Recognition

As an important human behavior for conveying psychological information, expression has been studied for some ten's of years in different modal: visual, speech, audio-visual, etc [11,12,13]. Seven expressions are recognized in our system: neutral, joy, anger, surprise, disgust, sadness and fear.

4.1 Expression Recognition Model

SVM(Support Vector Machine) can be trained quickly, and the training data are separated from the recognition process after we obtain the classifier. In our approach, SVM using RBF(Radial Basis Function) kernels below is adopted to be the component of the classifier.

$$R_i(P) = exp[-\frac{\|P - C_i\|^2}{\sigma_i^2}] \tag{3}$$

Seven one-to-rest SVMs are formed into a MSVM system being trained to distinguish one type from the six others. For a tracked eigen expression vector $\overrightarrow{f_s}$ and the trained classifiers $S_i(\overrightarrow{f_s})(i = 1, \cdots, 7)$,

$$\begin{cases} \overrightarrow{f_s} \;\; is \;\; accepted \; : \; if \;\; S_i(f) > 0 \\ \overrightarrow{f_s} \;\; is \;\; rejected \; : \; if \;\; S_i(f) < 0 \end{cases} \tag{4}$$

4.2 Training Data

In order to build a system which is flexible enough to cover the most typical variation of face, we have collected more than 840 sketched pictures from 40 people with different basic expressions as a data set (Fig. 6).

Fig. 6. Samples From Training Set

5 Experiment and Evaluation

We select 252 sketched and grey facial expression images in the data set to perform the test with MSVM classifiers. Table 2 and Table 3 shows their performance respectively. It is noticeable that the overall performance of the sketch based approach is better than the grey based.

Another benefit of MSVM is it can give out the confidence of recognition, which can be treated as combination of several basic ones. For example, as shown in Fig. 7, the expression on the left can be treated as a combination of the following two basic joy and neutral ones, which makes the recognition interesting.

Table 2. Sketch Based Expression Recognition Results. (Confusion matrix of the expression recognition. Columns represent the expression elected in first choice for samples belonging to the expression of each row.)

	Anger	Disgust	Fear	Neutral	Sadness	Joy	Surprise	Ratio
Anger	30	4	0	0	2	0	0	83.33%
Disgust	0	30	0	0	6	0	0	83.33%
Fear	0	0	36	0	0	0	0	100%
Neutral	0	0	0	30	4	2	0	83.33%
Sadness	0	0	0	0	36	0	0	100%
Joy	0	0	0	0	0	36	0	100%
Surprise	0	0	0	0	0	0	36	100%
Total	30	34	36	30	48	38	36	92.86%

Table 3. Gray Based Expression Recognition Results

	Anger	Disgust	Fear	Neutral	Sadness	Joy	Surprise	Ratio
Anger	32	2	0	0	2	0	0	88.89%
Disgust	6	28	0	0	2	0	0	77.78%
Fear	4	0	31	0	0	0	1	86.11%
Neutral	0	0	0	30	6	0	0	83.33%
Sadness	0	0	0	2	34	0	0	94.44%
Joy	0	0	0	2	0	34	0	94.44%
Surprise	5	0	0	0	0	2	29	80.56%
Total	47	30	31	34	44	36	30	88.01%

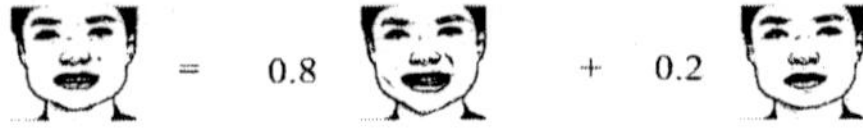

Fig. 7. Basic Expression Combination

6 Conclusion and Future Work

In this paper, a GPU enhanced facial expression recognition system is proposed. The grey level face image is filtered by GPU to be a sketch at extremely high speed. Then an ASM instance is trained to track the facial feature points in the sketched image with much less convergence time. The feature points is much easier to be located because of the sharpened edge. The normalized feature points construct a 19 dimensional eigen expression vector. In the final, the eigen expression vector is classified into one of seven basic expressions by an trained MSVM model with RBF kernel. Also, the recognition result can be considered as the combination of different basic expressions at different levels. Experiment result shows that our approach can make the recognition process more quick and precise.

In future work, more effort will be paid on facial expression intensity recognition by employing the face wrinkle to carry out the subtle expression recognition. In addition, the research on driving the sketched facial expression animation will be performed by applying NPR (Non Photo Realistic) rendering and parameterization technique.

Acknowledgements

The work is supported by National Natural Science Foundation of China (60203013), 863 Program (2004AA1Z2390) and Key Technologies R&D Program of Zhejiang Province (2004C11052 & 2005C23047).

References

1. Maja Pantic and Leon J.M. Rothkrantz: Towards an affect-sensitive multimodal human-computer interaction. Proceedings of the IEEE, **91(9)** (2003) 1370–1390
2. P. Ekman, W.V. Friesen: Facial Action Coding System: Investigator's Guide. Consulting Psychologists Press, (1978)
3. P.Ekman: Strong Evidence for Universals in Facial Expressions: A Reply to Russel's Mistaken Critique. Psychological Bulletin, **115(2)** (1994) 268–287
4. Ira Cohen, Nicu Sebe, Fabio G. Cozman, Marcelo C. Cirelo, Thomas S. Huang: Learning Bayesian Network Classifiers for Facial Expression Recognition with both Labeled and Unlabeled data. In Proceedings of IEEE CVPR03 (2003) 585–601
5. N. Cristianini and J. Shawe-Taylor: An Introduction To Support Vector Machines. Cambridge University Press (2000)
6. T. Ahmad, C.J.Taylor, A.Lanitis, T.F.Cootes: Tracking and Recognising Hand Gestures using Statistical Shape Models. Image and Vision Computing, **15(5)** (1997) 345–352
7. M. Macedonia: The gpu enters computing's mainstream. IEEE Computer (2003)
8. Bryan Dudash: Filter Blit Example. nVidia SDK White Paper (2004)
9. Michael Ashikhmin: A Tone Mapping Algorithm for High Contrast Images. Eurographics Workshop on Rendering (2002) 1–11
10. M. Covell, C. Bregler: Eigen-Points. Proceedings of IEEE ICIP'96 (1996)
11. Albino Nogueiras, Asuncin Moreno, Antonio Bonafonte, José B. Mariño: Speech Emotion Recognition Using Hidden Markov Models. Proceedings of EUROSPEECH01 (2001)
12. Ira Cohen, Nicu Sebe, Fabio G. Cozman, Marcelo C. Cirelo, Thomas S. Huang: Learning Bayesian Network Classifiers for Facial Expression Recognition with both Labeled and Unlabeled data. Proceedings of IEEE CVPR03 (2003) 595-601
13. Mingli Song, Jiajun Bu, Chun Chen, Nan Li: Audio-Visual based Emotion Recognition-A New Approach. Proceedings of IEEE CVPR04 (2004) 1020–1025

Case-Based Facial Action Units Recognition Using Interactive Genetic Algorithm*

Shangfei Wang and Jia Xue

University of Science and Technology of China, Hefei, Anhui 230027, P.R. China
sfwang@ustc.edu.cn

Abstract. This paper proposes a case-based automatic facial AU recognition approach using IGA, which embeds human's ability to compare into target system. To obtain AU codes of a new facial image, IGA is applied to retrieve a match instance based on users' evaluation, from the case base. Then the solution suggested by the matching case is used as the AU codes to the new facial image. The effectiveness of our approach is evaluated by 16 standard facial images collected under controlled imaging conditions and 10 un-standard images collected under spontaneous conditions using the Cohn _ Kanade Facial Expression Database as case base. To standard images, a recognition rate of 77.5% is achieved on single AUs, and a similarity rate of 82.8% is obtained on AU combinations. To un-standard images, a recognition rate of 82.8% is achieved on single AUs, and a similarity rate of 93.1% is obtained on AU combinations.

1 Introduction

The Facial Action Coding system (FACS) developed by Ekman and Friesen is the leading standard for measuring facial expressions both in the behavioral sciences [1] and computer science. It decomposes facial expressions into 44 unique Action Units (AUs), which roughly correspond to independent muscle movements in the face, as well as several categories of head and eye positions and movements.

Presently, FACS coding is mainly performed manually by human experts. It is slow, and requires extensive training. Automatic FACS coding could have revolutionary effects on the development of computer systems that understand facial expressions. However, achieving AU recognition by a computer remains difficult.

Few approaches have been reported for automatic recognition of AUs in images of faces. (Please refer to [2], [3], [4], [5], [6], and [7]) The main methodology of previous work consisted of firstly extracting the parameters describing the facial features, and then recognizing AUs using machine learning techniques. In order to make the problem of facial feature detection more tractable, most of the previous work relied on data-sets of posed expressions, collected under controlled imaging conditions, e.g., with subjects deliberately facing the camera, with no facial hair or glasses, with constant illumination. This is one of

* This paper is supported by NSFC project (NO. 60401004).

J. Tao, T. Tan, and R.W. Picard (Eds.): ACII 2005, LNCS 3784, pp. 80–87, 2005.

the major impediments that hinder the extension of these systems to realistic applications.

In contrast to these previous approaches, the research reported here addressed the problem of automatic AU recognition using Interactive Genetic Algorithm (IGA) directly without the stage of facial feature detection, which is sensitive to imaging conditions. Images with coded AUs, which are the training data in previous researches, are regarded as case base here. The AU codes of these case images are the solutions. To obtain AU codes of a new facial image, IGA is applied to retrieve a most similar instance to the new image from the case base, based on users' evaluation. Then the solution suggested by the matching case is used as the AU codes to the new facial images. The approach is easy and has the latent capacity to detect AU codes from facial images and image sequences insensitive to pose and occlusions. The effectiveness of our approach is evaluated through 16 standard images and 10 un-standard images using Cohn _ Kanade Facial Expression Database [8] as case base.

The basic idea and the details of our approach are explained in Section 2. The experimental results are presented in Section 3. Section 4 gives the conclusion.

2 Case-Based Facial Action Detection Using IGA

IGA is a GA in which human's subjective evaluation is regarded as the fitness function [9]. It combines human sensory, perception and cognition ability with GA's search ability. Over the past 10 years, IGA has been widely used in the fields of computer graphics [10], signal processing [11], multimedia retrieval [12] and many others. This paper extends IGA application to a new field, Facial Action Units Detection from facial images.

2.1 Basic Idea

Previous research on AUs detection follows a two stage approach, first, some approaches such as facial motion analysis, holistic spatial analysis and local spatial analysis, are applied to extract features. Secondly, machine learning techniques, such as NN, are used to obtain the mapping function between features and AUs. This approach has obtained some good results, however, feature extraction requires some controlled imaging conditions, which limits the real application of this research. Our approach presented here is to recognize facial actions without feature extracting stage by using IGA.

Although inexperienced subjects without any training can not detect AU from facial images, they can easily recognize facial behavior such as open mouse, frown, and stare, from images. These facial behavior are anatomically related to contraction of facial muscles, which correspond to the definition of various AUs. Furthermore, subjects have excellent capacity to grasp the similarities and differences between two images in view of facial behavior, even if they are not from the same person, or include some occlusion(e.g., glasses, facial hair). The basic idea here is to use human's ability to compare with GA to realize AU detection. GA searches in the facial case base and displays the retrieval results to human, human gives fitness to these results according to their similarities to the new facial image. This retrieval process repeats until the most similar case image is found. Then, the AU codes of this image are used as those of the new image.

2.2 Facial Action Recognition

Fig. 1 gives the overview of our proposed approach.

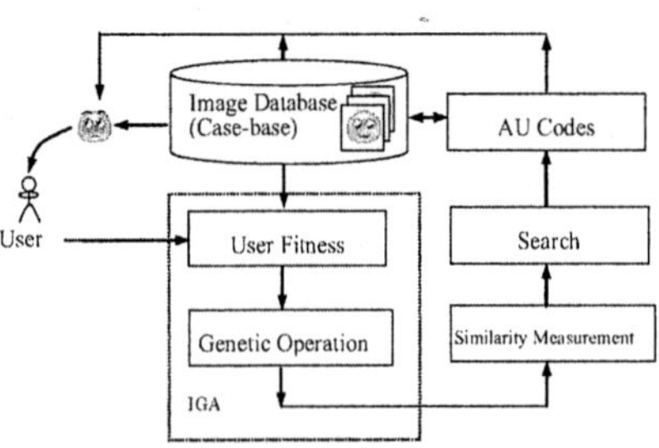

Fig. 1. Framework of IGA-based facial action detection

Here, the case base consists of facial images with known AU codes, which are usually regarded as training data set in other researches. The AU codes of these case images are the solutions. When new facial image with unknown AU codes comes, the system displays the initial population, consisting of N randomly selected case images from the case base. Users evaluate the similarity between each displayed case image and the new image in the view of facial behavior, then give the fitness to case images on a 7-point similarity scale. Based on users' evaluation, the system creates the next generation case images through genetic operations and displays them. The procedure is repeated until the user obtains the case image that is most similar to the target image. After that, the solution suggested by the matching case is used as the AU codes of the new facial image.

Chromosome Representation
AU codes of case images are translated into 92-bit binary string ($J = 92$) as the chromosome representation shown in Table 1, which includes the most frequently used AUs and their position information, such as, left, right, top and below. Intensity of AUs is not considered in the present state of our coding.

Table 1. Chromosome representation

AU1	AU2	L	R	AU4	L	R	...

Genetic Operation
Roulette wheel selection stage, multi-point crossover method, and random mutation are used to generate N candidates of next generation.

Similarity Measurement
After N candidates are obtained, to find N case images of next generation, the similarity between the images in case base and candidates is calculated by using Hamming distance as showed in Eq.1. N case images with the minimal distance values are provided as the individuals of next generation. Then the user gives fitness values to these N case images. The process of interactive genetic algorithm is repeated until the users find the most similar case image.

$$dist(j,i) = sum_{k=1}^{J}(FI_j(k) \bigoplus FC_i(k)) \tag{1}$$

where, $FI_j(k)$ is the kth bit AU codes of case image j and $FC_i(k)$ indicates the kth bit chromosome of candidate i.

3 Experiments

3.1 Experimental Condition

Five adult volunteers from our university attended the experiment. They range in age from 22 to 29 years. Three of them are male, and the others are female. None of them are expert AU coders. Only one of them participated in the design of the system, so she has some basic knowledge of AUs. Others don't have any knowledge of either facial expression measurement or our system. The parameters of IGA of the experiments are given in Table 2. Fig. 2 gives the interface of our system.

Table 2. Parameters of IGA

Parameters	Population size (N)	Bit length (J)	Crossover rate	Mutate rate
Values	12	92	0.8	0.01

3.2 Experimental Results of Standard Test Images

The final frames in 481 image sequences, from Cohn_Kanade AU-Coded Facial Expression Database, with AU codes are divided into two sets, one set of 465 images as the case base, and the other set of 16 images as test data, which called standard test images, since they were collected under controlled imaging conditions. A subject compared the test image and other 12 images displayed by the system, and gave fitness to the 12 images separately according to their similarity to the test image. Each subject did the tests of 16 test images. Thus, totally 80 ($16 * 5$) experimental results were obtained. The statistical results of these 80 experiments are given in Table 3 and Table 4.

Fig. 2. Interface of IGA-based facial action detection

Table 3. Experiment results to single AU

AU No.	1	2	4	5	6	7	9
Recognition Rate	84.0%	95.0%	70.0%	90.0%	55.0%	46.7%	80.0%
AU No.	12	15	17	25	26	27	
Recognition Rate	100.0%	90.0%	100%	80.0%	66.7%	50.0%	

Recognition rate to each AU is listed in Table 3. The average recognition rate is about 77.5%. From Table 3, it also can be seen that some AUs, such as AU2, AU12 and AU17, which are defined as outer brow raiser, lip corner puller, and chin raiser separately, are easier to detect from static images than other AUs, such as, AU6, AU7 and AU27, which correspond to cheek raiser, lid tightened and mouth stretch. These AUs with lower recognition rate may be obvious in image sequences rather than in a static image. Also, the recognition rate may be affected by the human's attention span.

Table 4 lists similarity rate and the average interaction number for each test image. Here, we define that the similarity rate is the ratio of the number of AUs in both real codes of test images and case images to the number of AUs in test images. From Table 4, we can see that the mean of interaction is 2.8, and the average similarity is 82.8%. The result signifies that usually after three interactions, a most similar case image can be found. It costs about 2 minutes. The similarity rate between the test image and matching case is more than 80.0%.

3.3 Experimental Results of Un-standard Images

We downloaded 10 face images collected under spontaneous conditions from a number of websites as un-standard test images. 481 images with AU codes, from Cohn_Kanade AU-Coded Facial Expression Database, are used as the case base. The experimental process is similar to that described in Section 3.2. The time of processing one test image for one subject is about 2.5 minutes. It is a little longer than that, 2 minutes in Section 3.2, since there exits some interference

Table 4. Experiment results to AU combinations

Image No.	AU Combination	Average No. of Interactions	Similarity Rate
1	1+2+5+27	3.40	75.0%
2	4+17	3.40	70.0%
3	1+2+27	2.80	86.7%
4	1+4+15+17	3.00	75.0%
5	6+12+25	2.40	100.0%
6	4+7+9+17	2.60	80.0%
7	1+2+26	2.60	80.0%
8	15+17	2.00	90.0%
9	1+2+5+26	2.40	75.0%
10	12+25	2.60	70.0%
11	4+6+7+9+17	3.00	68.0%
12	6+12	3.20	80.0%
13	25	2.80	100.0%
14	26	2.80	100.0%
15	6+7+12+25	2.40	75.0%
16	12	2.60	100.0%

signals, such as glasses, facial hair, complex background, inconstant illumination, in the images, and subjects need spend some time to get rid of such interference. However, the time difference that subjects used between standard image test and un-standard image test is negligible.

Table 5 and Table 6 give the statistical results of the 50(10 ∗ 5) person-time experiments.

Table 5. Experiment results to single AU

AU No.	4	6	7	9	12	17	25
Recognition. Rate	100.0%	85.7%	60.0%	40.0%	97.1%	100.0%	97.1%

Recognition rate for each AU is listed in Table 5. The average recognition rate is about 82.8%. From Table 5, it can be seen that the recognition rate of AU9 is rather low. However, this has not occured in section 3.2. AU9 appeared in the 6th test image, in which, there are two faces, an adult face and a boy-face. The boy-face is the object of our experiments. However, the boy-face is too small to display clearly, which could be is the reason why the AU9 could not be detected effectively.

To avoid copyright issues, the 10 test images are not displayed in this paper. The first column of Table 6 describes the interference in the images. From Table 6, we can see that the mean of interaction is 2.53, and the average similarity is 93.1%. This means that, usually after three interactions, the most similar case image can be found, and the similarity rate between the test image and matching case is more than 90.0%.

Table 6. Experiment results to AU combinations

Image No. & Description	AU Combination	Average Number of Interactions	Similarity Rate
1, with glasses	6+12+25	2.40	100.0%
2, with glasses, complex background	6+12+25	2.60	100.0%
3, with glasses, profile face	6+12+25	2.60	100.7%
4, with complex background, profile face	6+12+25	2.40	100.0%
5, with facial hair, complex background	25	2.60	100.0%
6, with complex background	4+6+7+9+17	2.60	68.0%
7, with beard, hat	12	2.40	100.0%
8, with hat	6+12	2.20	70.0%
9, with glasses, complex background	6+12+25	2.40	93.3%
10,with hat	25	2.80	100.0%

4 Conclusion

A robust way to detect facial actions from facial images and image sequences, insensitive to pose, and occlusion, remains the key research challenge in the domain of automatic facial expression analysis. This paper has proposed a case-based approach that recognizes AUs using interactive genetic algorithm. This approach is quite novel in the research of facial action recognition. Also, it is a new application field of IGA. The experimental results on 16 standard facial images and 10 un-standard images using Cohn _ Kanade Facial Expression Database as case base are reported. To standard images, a recognition rate of 77.5% is achieved on single AUs, and a similarity rate of 82.8% is obtained on AU combinations. To un-standard images, a recognition rate of 82.8% is achieved on single AUs, and a similarity rate of 93.1% is obtained on AU combinations.

Although the proposed approach is easy and effective, it is still a preliminary work. There are several possible directions for future investigation.

Firstly, only AUs detection from static images is presented in this paper. The next step is to extend the approach to image sequences, and also to add the intensity of AU to chromosome coding. Secondly, comparison experiments between our approach and others on the same data should be done in the near future. Thirdly, the multiplicity of facial images in the case base is important in our approach. If a match case can not be found, the performance of recognition will be reduced. Interactive and dynamic case revision will be addressed for further research.

Acknowledgments. The authors would like to thank Dr. Jeffrey Cohn and his colleges for supplying Cohn-Kanade database and permission to use some images as illustration of the paper. http://vasc.ri.cmu.edu/idb/html/face/facial_expression/index.html.

References

1. Ekman, P., Froesem, W.: Facial action coding system: a technique for the measurement of facial movement. Palo Alto, CA: Consulting Psychologists Press (1978)
2. Bartlett, M.S., Hager, J.C., Ekman, P., Sejnowski T.J.: Measuring facial expression by computer image analysis. Psychopshysiology **36** (1999) 253–263
3. Donato, G., Bartlett, M.S., Hager, J.C., Ekman, P., Sejnowski, T.J.: Classifying facial actions. IEEE trans. on Analysis and Machine Intelligence **21** (1999) 974–989
4. Cohn, J.F., Zlochower, A.J., Lien, J. Kanade, T.: Automated face analysis by feature point tracking has high concurrent validity with manual FACS coding. Psychophysiology **36** (1999) 35–43
5. Tian, Y.L., Kanade, T., Cohn, J. F.: Recognizing action units for facial expression analysis. IEEE Trans. on Pattern Analysis and Machine Intelligence, **23(2)** (2001) 97–115
6. Kapoor, A.: Automatic facial action analysis. Master thesis MIT (2002)
7. Pantic, M., Rothkrantz, L.J.M.: Facial action recognition for facial expression analysis from static face images. IEEE Transactions on Systems, Man, and Cybernetics - Part B **34(3)** (2004) 1449–1461
8. Kanade, T., Cohn, J.F., Tian, Y.L.: Comprehensive database for facial expression analysis. Preceedings of the Fourth IEEE International Conference on Automatic Facial and Gesture Recognition (2000)
9. Takagi, H.: Interactive evolutionary computation: fusion of the capacities of EC optimization and human evaluation. Proceedings of the IEEE , **89(9)** (2001) 1275–1296
10. Smith, J. R.: Designing biomorphs with an interactive genetic algorithm. Proceedings of the Fourth International Conference on Genetic Algorithms: (1991) 535–538
11. Lutton, E., Jacques, P. G., Vehel, L, : An interactive EA for multifractal bayesian denoising. EvoWorkshops 2005 274–283
12. Wang, Sh. F.: Interactive Kansei-oriented image retrieval. AMT01 Lecture Notes in Computer Science 2252 (2001) 377–388

Facial Expression Recognition Using HLAC Features and WPCA

Fang Liu, Zhi-liang Wang, Li Wang, and Xiu-yan Meng

School of Information Engineering,
University of Science & Technology Beijing, China
Liufangustb@sohu.com

Abstract. This paper proposes a new facial expression recognition method which combines Higher Order Local Autocorrelation (HLAC) features with Weighted PCA. HLAC features are computed at each pixel in the human face image. Then these features are integrated with a weight map to obtain a feature vector. We select the weight by combining statistic method with psychology theory. The experiments on the "CMU-PITTSBURGH AU-Coded Face Expression Image Database" show that our Weighted PCA method can improve the recognition rate significantly without increasing the computation, when compared with PCA.

1 Introduction

Facial expression is a visible manifestation of the affective state, cognitive activity, intention, personality, and psychopathology of a person; it not only expresses our emotions, but also provides important communicative cues during social interaction. Reported by psychologists, facial expression constitutes 55 percent of the effect of a communicated message while language and voice constitute 7 percent and 38 percent respectively[1]. So it is obvious that analysis and automatic recognition of facial expression can improve human-computer interaction or even social interaction.

FER provided by us is the shortened form of computer automatic recognition of human facial expression, in detail it means using computer to extract facial features automatically and classify them to six basic expressions [2]. As a principle component of artificial psychology and affective computing, facial expression recognition will have widely application domains such as HCI, tele-teaching, tele-medical treatments, Car surveillance, PC-GAME, affective robots etc[3].

2 Common Steps and Content of FER

Automatic systems for facial expression recognition usually take the form of a sequential configuration of processing blocks, which adheres to a classical pattern recognition model (see Figure 1). The main blocks are: image acquisition, pre-processing, feature extraction, classification, and post-processing.

J. Tao, T. Tan, and R.W. Picard (Eds.): ACII 2005, LNCS 3784, pp. 88 – 94, 2005.

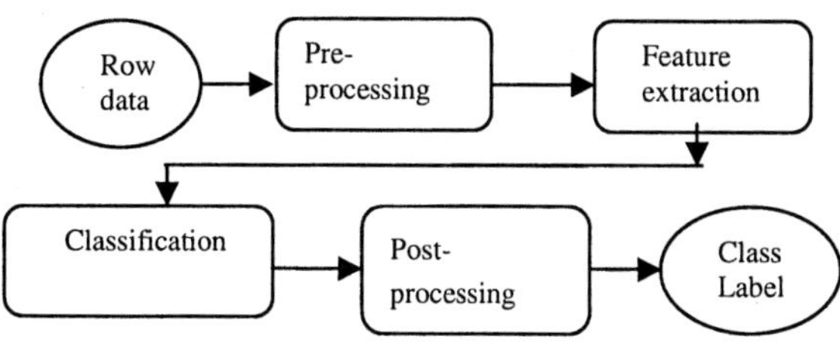

Fig. 1. Flowchart of facial expression recognition system

The main steps embedded in the components of an automatic expression recognition system are feature extraction and classification. Feature extraction converts pixel data into a higher-level representation –shape, motion, color, texture, and spatial configuration of the face or its components. Geometric, kinetic, and statistical, or spectral-transform-based features are often used as alternative representation of the facial expression. Then a wide range of classifiers, covering parametric as well as non-parametric techniques, has been applied to automatic expression recognition problem. For example, LDA classifier, ANN classifier[4], SVM classifier, HMM classifier, Bayesian network classifiers [5]etc.

3 Higher-Order Local Auto-correlations Features

Higher-order Local Auto-Correlation (HLAC) features developed by Otsu are widely used in many computer vision applications, such as character recognition and face recognition [6]. It is a derivative of a higher-order autocorrelation function, which is defined by the following equation:

$$x(a_1,...,a_N) = \int I(r)I(r+a_1)...I(r+a_N)dr = \int h(r)dr \tag{1}$$

where $I(r)$ represents an image, r is a reference point in the image, $h(r)$ represents a local feature defined at a pixel r, $(a_1,...,a_N)$ is a set of displacements, N is the order of the autocorrelation function, and x is a primary statistical feature of the image. We can define an infinite number of higher-order autocorrelation functions by changing the set of displacements $(a_1,...,a_N)$ and N above .We must reduce the number of functions to a reasonably small number to produce higher-order autocorrelation functions that are useful in practical applications.

Limiting the order of autocorrelation function N to the second (N=0,1,2), restricting the displacements a_i within one pixel, and taking into account the equivalence of duplications by translation, the number of displacement patterns reduces to 35. Fig. 2 shows 3 types of local displacement patterns (each type is called a *mask*).Using all the masks, we can compute 35 types of primary statistical features of an image. These features are called HLAC features. Fig. 3 shows the original gray image, the binary image computed by threshold method, and (c) shows the processed image, It is obtained by adding the three matrixes which is computed by moving the three mask (showed in figure 2)on the given binary image.

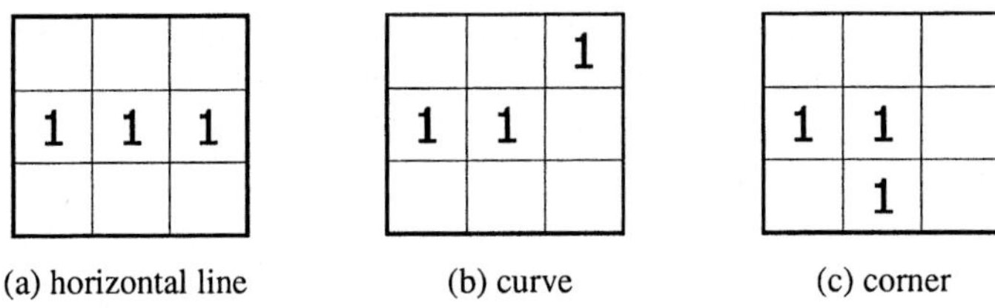

(a) horizontal line (b) curve (c) corner

Fig. 2. Type of local displacement patterns for HLAC functions

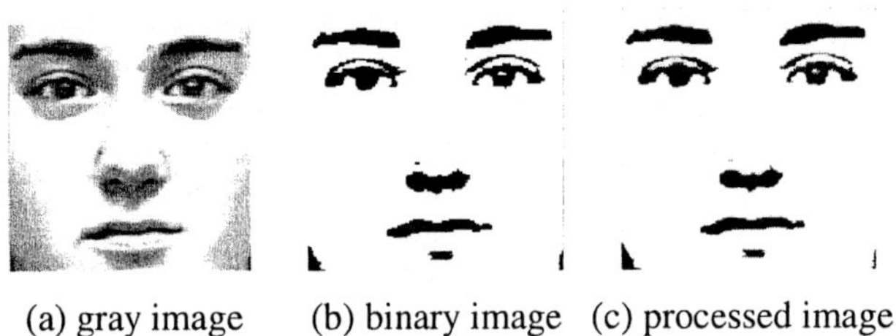

(a) gray image (b) binary image (c) processed image

Fig. 3. Type of face image

4 Weighted PCA

Science every area (e.g. area around the eyes) may contain important features for classification of expressions while other areas (e.g. area around the forehead) may not, here we use the *Weighted PCA* approach to find the optimal weight map vector [7].

Let the training set of feature images be $h_1, h_2, ..., h_k$ .The average feature image of the set is defied by $\bar{h} = 1/k \sum_i h_i$, the covariance matrix of our sample set H =[$h_1, h_2, ..., h_k$] is $S = \sum_i (h_i - \bar{h})(h_i - \bar{h})^T$, and $U = [u_1, u_2, ..., u_q]$ is the eigenvectors corresponding to the largest eigenvalue of the scatter matrix. Then the feature image can transformed into its eigenface components by a simple operation:. $y = U^T (x - \bar{h})$

Principal Component Analysis (PCA) seeks a projection that best represents the data in a least-squares sense[8]. It use the variance criterion J to optimize the matrix U , as follows:

$$J_1(U) = \sum_{k=1}^{p} \| (\bar{h} + Uy_k) - h_k \|^2 = \sum_{k=1}^{p} ((\bar{h} + Uy_k) - h_k)^T ((\bar{h} + Uy_k) - h_k) \tag{2}$$

Where h_k represents training samples, y_k represents their projections.

In facial expression recognition, it is natural to think that some areas (e.g. area around the eyes) may contain important features for classification of expressions while other areas (e.g. area around the forehead) may not. Concurrent with this idea, we propose a new feature projection method using weighted coefficient in principal component analysis to distinguish the different areas' contributions to facial expression recognition. Then we construct sample - x_m 's weighted reconstruction error function:

$$J_2(U^{'},x_m)\sum_j w_j((x_{0j}+Uy_{kj})-x_{mj})^2 = \sum_{k=1}^{p}((x_0+Uy_k)-x_m)^T W((x_0+Uy_k)-x_m) \quad (3)$$

Where the weighted coefficient diagonal matrix W = Diagonal[$w_1, w_2, w_3, ..., w_n$], $w_1, w_2, w_3, ..., w_n$ =n ; Then the aim is to find matrix $U^{'}$, which can minimize the variance criterion $J_2(U)$.

$$J_2(U^{'})=\sum_m J_2(U^{'},x_m)=\sum_m (x_m-x_0)^T (U^{'}U^{'T}-I)W(U^{'}U^{'T}-I)(x_m-x_0) \quad (4)$$

In this way, the basis of weighted PCA is the row vectors of matrix $U^{'}$.

Of course we can obtain the matrix $U^{'}$ by optimization method. But in fact, especially in real-time recognition, there is an approximate method, Given the weighted coefficient diagonal matrix W , the covariance matrix defined as follows:

$$S=\sum_{k=1}^{p}(x_k-x_0)W(x_k-x_0)^T \quad (5)$$

Then, we could use the eigenvectors of matrix S in place of $U^{'}$. But How to decided W?

Presently, most computer facial analysis and recognition methods are based on Ekman's Face Action Coding System (FACS)[9], which is proposed in 1978, and widely admitted in psychology domain. It is the most comprehensive method of coding facial displays.FACS action units are the smallest visibly discriminable changes in facial display, and combinations of FACS action units can be used to describe emotion expressions and global distinctions between positive and negative expression.

In this paper, for analysis and recognition facial expressions, we use FACS interpretation and FACS'AU to model six basic type of facial expressions- Anger, Disgust, Fear, Happiness, Sadness and Surprise. In other words, that is to make each facial expressions corresponds to AU weighted combinations. (see table 1)

According to table, we selected different weighted in the area around the eyes, brows and lip, y the rule of letting them corresponding to the AU contribution. For example, In "Fear" expression, we decided that the area's weighted of eyes, mouth and others are 0.6, 0.3, 0.1 respectively.

Table 1. FACS prototypes for modeled expressions

Expression	Created prototype	Detail description
Anger	AU4+5+7+15+24	Brow Lowerer + Upper Lid Raiser + Lid Tightener + Lip Corner Depressor + Lip Pressor
Disgust	AU9+10+17	Nose Wrinkler+ Upper Lip Raiser+ Chin Raiser
Fear	AU1+2+4+5+7+20+25	Inner Brow Raiser + Outer Brow Raiser + Brow Lowerer + Upper Lid Raiser + Lid Tightener + Lip Stretcher + Lips Part
Happiness	AU6+12+25	Cheek Raiser + Lip Corner Puller + Lips Part
Sadness	AU1+4+7+15+17	Inner Brow Raiser + Brow Lowerer + Lid Tightener + Lip Corner Depressor + Chin Raiser
Surprise	AU1+2+5+25+26	Inner Brow Raiser + Outer Brow Raiser + Upper Lid Raiser +Lips Part +Jaw Drop

5 Tests and Results

We evaluated the performance of our facial expression recognition method on the CMU-Pittsburgh AU-Coded Face Expression Image Database, Which contains a recording of the facial behavior of 210 adults who are 18 to 50 years old; 69% female and 31% male; and 81% Caucasian, 13% African, and 6% other groups. In this database, Image in this database sequences from neutral to target display were digitized into 640 by 480 or 490 pixel arrays with 8-bit precision for grayscale values.

In our experiment, we choice 560 images from the CMU database randomly. Those images are classified into 7 basic expressions- nature, anger, disgust, fear, joy, sadness, and surprise. 70% of the 80 images of each facial expression are used for training, while others are used for testing. In PCA method, we use the pictures of human faces, while in WPCA method, we should extract the local areas in one's face by integral projection method as Figure 4. Figure 5 shows the first three acquired Eigeneyes and Eigenmouths.

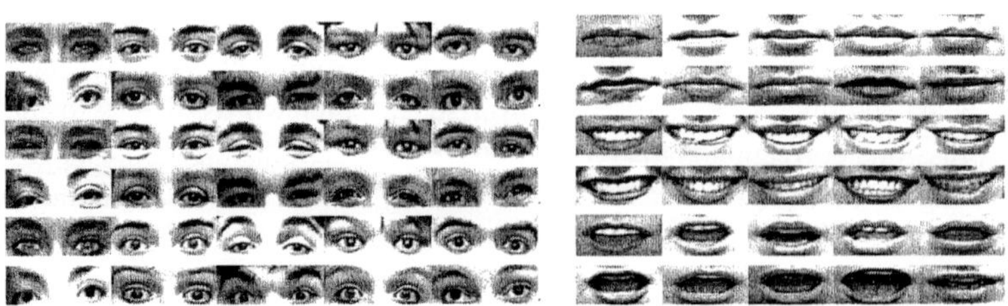

Fig. 4. Expressions areas of our Sample images

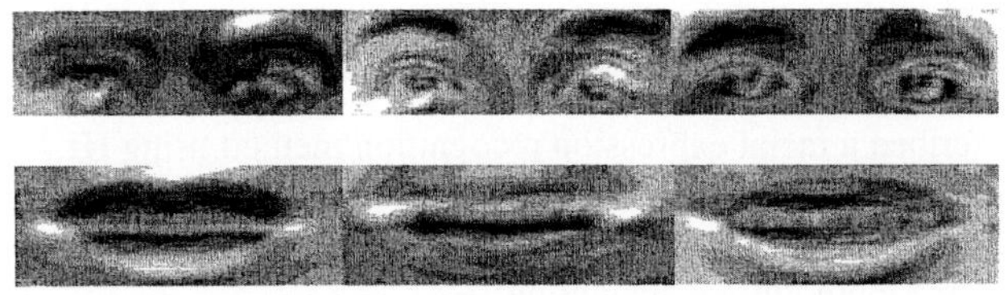

Fig. 5. The Eigeneyes(Up) / Eigenmouth(Down) in our experiment

Our experiment used the PCA, WPCA and HLAC+WPCA method to train and test the system. The recognition rate was obtained by averaging the recognition rates of all 7 types of facial expressions. The recognition rate of our method using the HLAC+WPCA was 83.9%, while PCA method was 71.3% and WPCA method was 78.9%.(as table 2 shows)Our hybrid method outperformed the others, and by using WPCA, we compute the eigenface and eigenmouth in place of the whole face ,so it can reduce our computation.

Table 2. Recognition rates of different method

Method	Rate(%)
PCA	71.3
WPCA	78.9
HLAC+WPCA	83.9

In table 3, we show our HLAC+WPCA method's recognition rates of different facial expressions, respectively. The first row presents the recognition results, while the left row means the real facial expressions. It is easy to know from the table that "joy" and "surprise" gained better recognition rates, because their facial action are obvious.

Table 3. Recognition rates for 7 basic facial expression(%)

Results / Facts	nature	anger	disgust	fear	joy	Sad	surprise
nature	68.5	7.2	12.7	0	0	11.6	0
anger	6.1	81.9	2.2	0	0	9.8	0
disgust	11.1	5.5	79.6	0	0	3.8	0
fear	0	0	3.8	89.5	0	0	6.7
joy	7.8	0	0	0	91.2	0	0
Sad	0	0	4.8	13.1	0	82.1	0
surprise	0	0	0	5.5	0	0	94.5

6 Concluding Remarks

This paper described a facial expression recognition method using HLAC features and Weighted PCA. Our method is a hybrid of two approaches: geometric based approaches[10] and statistic based approaches. We generalized and combined these approaches from a more unified standpoint.

We quantified and visualized relative importance (weights) of facial areas for classification of expressions. Besides, we proposed a new idea to confirm the weight coefficient, which is combined statistic method with psychology theory. Furthermore, the proposed method can be used with other types of local features and with more complicated but powerful classification methods (e.g. neural networks, support vector machines, kernel-based Fisher discriminant analysis, etc).

Given that facial expression and emotion are dynamic process, for future work, we will add subtle and blended facial expressions recognition to our research and pay more attention to extract kinetic features and transitory changings, such as facial wrinkles, etc. And to implement human-Computer Interaction tasks related to real-time facial expressions, we will also investigate the algorithm's efficiency and delays.

Acknowledgments

The paper supported by the key lab named Advanced Information Science and Network Technology of Beijing (No. TDXX0503) and the key foundation of USTB.

References

1. A. Mehrabian. Communication without words. *Psychology Today*, 2(4):53–56, 1968.
2. Yang Guoliang, Wang Zhiliang1, Ren Jingxia. Facial expression recognition based on adaboost algorithm, Computer Applications. Vol 25.No 4,Apr 2005.
3. C. L. Lisetti and D. J. Schiano. Automatic Facial Expression Interpretation: Where Human-Computer Interaction, Arti cial Intelligence and Cognitive Science Intersect. Pragmatics and Cognition (Special Issue on Facial Information Processing: A Multidisciplinary Perspective), 8(1):185-235, 2000.
4. Neil Alldrin, Andrew Smith, Doug Turnbull. Classifying Facial Expression with Radial Basis Function Networks, using Gradient Descent and K-means. CSE253, 2003
5. Ira Cohen, Nicu Sebe, Fabio G. Cozman. Learning Bayesian network classifiers for facial expression recognition using both labeled and unlabeled data. CVPR '03- Volume I.-p. 595
6. T. Kurita, N. Otsu, and T. Sato, "A Face Recognition Method Using Higher Order Local Autocorrelation and Multivariate Analysis," *in Proc. IAPR Int. Conf. on Pattern Recognition*, pp. 213–216, 1992.
7. Qiao Yu, Huang Xiyue, Chai Yi. Face recognition based on Weighted PCA. Journal of Chongqing University. Vol 27, No 3, Mar 2004.
8. M.Turk and A. Pentland, "Eigen Faces for Recognition," *Journal of Cognitive Neuroscience*, vol. 3, pp. 71–86, 1991.
9. P. Ekman et al1, Facial Action Coding System" ,Consulting Psychologists Press ,1978.
10. Philipp Michel, Rana El Kaliouby, "Real time Facial Expression Recognition in Video using Support Vector Machines", ICMI'3, November 5-7 ,2003

Motion Normalization

Yan Gao, Lizhuang Ma, Zhihua Chen, and Xiaomao Wu

Department of Computer Science and Engineering,
Shanghai Jiao Tong University, Shanghai 200030, China
{gaoyan, Zhihua, wuxiaomao}@sjtu.edu.cn
ma-lz@cs.sjtu.edu.cn

Abstract. This paper presents a very simple but efficient algorithm to normalize all motion data in database with same skeleton length. The input motion stream is processed sequentially while the computation for a single frame at each step requires only the results from the previous step over a neighborhood of nearby backward frames. In contrast to previous motion retargeting approaches, we simplify the constraint condition of retargeting problem, which leads to the simpler solutions. Moreover, we improve Shin et al.'s algorithm [10], which is adopted by a widely used Kovar's footskate cleanup algorithm [6] through adding one case missed by it.

1 Introduction

Nowadays, motion capture is an increasingly popular approach for synthesizing human motion. Various editing techniques for adapting existing motion data to new situations [1, 2] have been developed in the past few years. As commercial motion capture systems are widely applied, large numbers of motion capture data become public available [e.g., 3]. As a result, how to efficiently organize and retrieve these motion data becomes an important problem.

Usually, the difference between skeletons in motion data will affect the results of motion retrieval or motion graph [4]. So it is desirable if each skeletal segment for all motions in motion database shares a common length. Similar to the image normalization, we call such process motion normalization.

Motion retargeting [5] adapts an animated motion from one character to another while maintains its constraints unchanged. This seems to be the same as our work. However, the goal of motion retargeting is different from ours. As an editing means, motion retargeting has to consider how to interact with surrounding environment as well as maintain the motion details. In contrast, the relative positions of motion data in database are important than their global positions. Such property simplifies the complicacy of motion retargeting, which makes possible the simpler solution.

In this paper, we present a motion normalization method to adapt each skeletal segment for motion data in database with common length automatically. Our method first adjusts root positions in an online manner. Footskates are then cleaned up using kovar's post-process algorithm [6]. Though Kovar's algorithm is widely used, we find

J. Tao, T. Tan, and R.W. Picard (Eds.): ACII 2005, LNCS 3784, pp. 95 – 101, 2005.

that one step in his algorithm don't consider all possible cases, which may introduce visual artifacts.

2 Related Works

A number of researchers have developed techniques for mapping a motion from one performer to the target performer. Hodgins et al. [7] present an algorithm that adjusts the parameters of control system for adapting existing simulated behaviors to new characters. However, such approach risks losing qualities of the original motion. Pollard [8] describes a fast technique for modifying human motion sequences in a way that preserves physical properties of the motion. However, some physical parameters needed for his algorithm are not available for most motion data.

Glercher[4] uses spacetime constraints method for motion retargeting. Such approach considers duration of motion simultaneously in a computation, at the cost of increasing complication along with the motion's length. Lee and Shin [9] propose a hierarchical motion editing approach for adapting existing motion to have the desired features. However, for motion normalization purpose, their approach is reduced to solve one large optimization problem. Shin et al.'s importance based approach [10] determines what aspects of the performance must be kept in the resulting motion through the importance of each end-effector position. In contrast, our method considers that joint angles are always more important than end-effector's positions. Other methods such as Choi and Ko's *inverse rate control* based method [11] and Seyoon et al.'s [12] per-frame Kalman filter algorithm are also not suitable for our purpose. The most difference between our approaches with the others is that none of these approaches explicitly consider the root placement problem because all previous methods are proposed as motion editing means.

3 Motion Normalization Method

Our algorithm includes three steps: constraints detection, skeleton adaptation and footskate cleanup.

3.1 Constraints Detection

Our algorithm needs to consider only two kinds of constraints:

1. A point on the character is in the same place at two different times. Note this position is unspecified so that can be adjusted.
2. A point on the character must beyond the floor. This prevents the toes penetration.

It is trivial to identify constraints of the second type. We only discuss how to identify the first type here. We use *Velocity and bounding box criteria* [13] to identify footplants semi-automatically. We find such simple algorithm works quite well for our purpose so that user seldom need edit the results by hand as Kovar[6] mentioned.

3.2 Skeleton Adaptation

We select one skeleton from the input motions as a reference skeleton, which is closest to the average bone lengths. Our goal is to adjust the other skeletons to the reference one. The naive skeleton adaptation will destroy the constraints in the original motion so that footskate occurs. Kovar's footskate cleanup algorithm [6] can be used to remove such artifacts. However, the errors of foot sliding will accumulate, which lead to unnatural resulting motions. To get a more desirable result, we must place the root positions reasonably before call his algorithm.

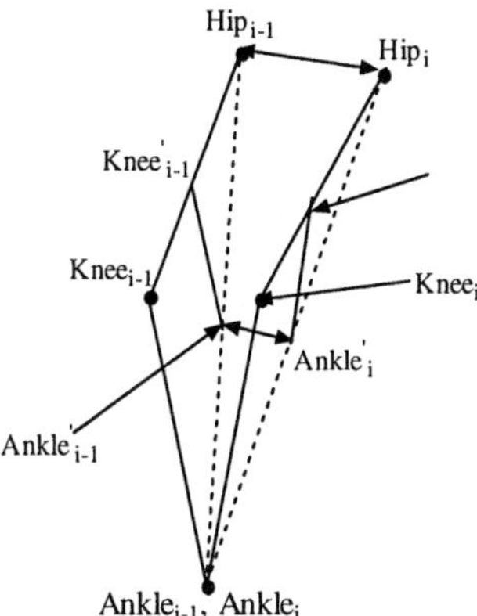

Fig. 1. The relation between root's displacement and ankle's offset. Suppose subscript represents frame. Knee' and Ankle' are knee and ankle in the reference skeleton that is λ of the size of the input skeleton. It's easy to prove that $A'_{i-1}A'_i=H_{i-1}H_i*\lambda$.

From figure 1, we can see that if the reference skeleton is λ of the size of the input, the ratio of root velocities between the result motion and original motion is just λ. However, if we scale root's velocity by λ simply, the foot sliding errors will also accumulate because different bones in different persons are hardly scaled at the same proportion. We use an algorithm to remove such errors as follows.

1. For each frame, place root position in an incremental way. Define R_i is the target root position while source_R_i is the source root position for frame i. Then R_i is

$$R_i = R_{i-1} + (source\_R_i - source\_R_{i-1}) * \lambda \tag{1}$$

   Translate root position to R_i and update all joint positions.
2. For each constrained frame, determine the feet positions. If one foot is constrained and not initially constrained, the position F_i is at the same constraint position of frame i-1; else F_i is just the current foot position.
3. For each constrained frame, compute the constrained positions for the ankles.
4. For each constrained frame, translate the root to compensate the ankles offset between current positions and constrained positions. If only one foot is constrained, the final root displacement is such offset for the constrained ankle;

else the average offset for both ankles is used as the final root displacement. Translate the root with such displacement.

5. For each frame, translate the root position so that its y value equal to that of the source motion.

Now the root positions in the resulting motion have been placed more rationally than naïve skeleton adaptation. However, while we don't introduce discontinuities when constraints are held over multiple frames, discontinuities may occur when a constraint become active or inactive. We use a blend function as [6]

$$\alpha(t) = 2t^3 - 3t^2 + 1 \tag{2}$$

to blend off such discontinuities. The algorithm proceeds as follows. For each frame F_i, we look backward L frames to check whether or not the current constraint state changes. Here we use the terms *miss* and *hit* in [6]. If the constraint states in all frames that we encountered remain unchanged, we have a *miss*; otherwise we have a *hit*. Say that the first *hit* frame is F_{i-k1} for the left foot and F_{i-k2} for the right. The offset for the left ankle between it current position and it constraint position is δ_{Li} while such offset for the right one is δ_{Ri}.

1. Constraints exist for both feet at frame F_i. If we have a *hit*, the root adjustment for frame F_i we seek is

$$\delta_i = \begin{cases} (\alpha(\frac{k_1}{L+1}) * \delta_{Li} + \alpha(\frac{k_2}{L+1}) * \delta_{Ri})/2, & 0 < k_1 \le L, 0 < k_2 \le L \\ \alpha(\frac{k_1}{L+1})\delta_{Li}, & 0 < k_1 \le L \\ \alpha(\frac{k_2}{L+1})\delta_{Ri}, & 0 < k_2 \le L \\ (\delta_{Li} + \delta_{Ri})/2, & \text{otherwise} \end{cases} \tag{3}$$

2. Constraints exist for either foot at frame F_i. If we have a hit that we assume in the left foot, the root adjustment for frame F_i we seek is

$$\delta_i = \begin{cases} \alpha(\frac{k_1}{L+1}) * \delta_{Li}, & 0 < k_1 \le L \\ \delta_{Li}, & \text{otherwise} \end{cases} \tag{4}$$

3. Constraints exist for neither foot at frame F_i. If we have a hit at frame F_{i-k} and the root adjustment applied to F_{i-k} is δ_{i-k}, the root adjustment for frame F_i we seek is

$$\delta_i = \begin{cases} \alpha(\frac{k}{L+1}) * \delta_{i-k}, & 0 < k \le L \\ 0, & \text{otherwise} \end{cases} \tag{5}$$

3.3 FootSkate Cleanup

We use Kovar's approach [6] as our footskate cleanup algorithm. His approach is divided into five phases:

1. Determine a position for each plant constraint.
2. Determine ankle's position and orientation.
3. Calculate root's position.
4. Meet the target ankle configuration.
5. Final processing.

The process in step 3 was first proposed by [10]. However, we find that this step in his algorithm omits one possible case so that may introduce visual artifact. The process is shown as figure 2.

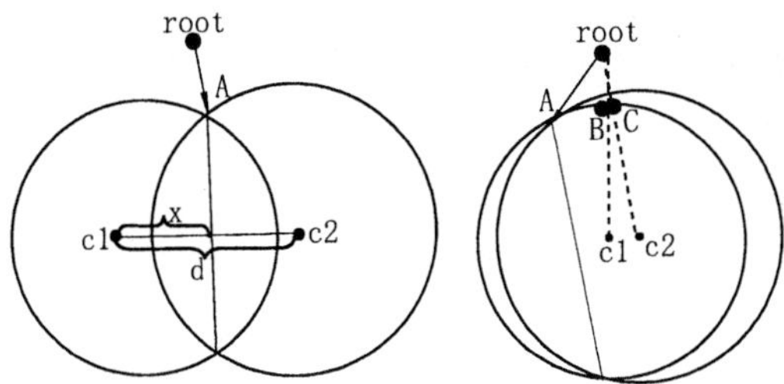

Fig. 2. The left figure is Shin's solution. However, for the right figure, the root will place to A, which will cause root swings. We give our solution is either B or C, which is determined by its distance between root.

In Figure 2, the sphere C_1 is centered about P_A-O_H, where P_A is the target left ankle position and O_H is the hip offset. The radius of C_1, C_2 is the length of the left and right lower limb, respectively. Suppose the distance between C_1 and C_2 is d. Because the radius of C_1 and C_2 are far more than d, the right case may occur. Root will be placed outside the region [C_1, C_2] so that root swings occur. We can judge this situation through the distance x, e.g. formula (28) in [10]. If x is less than 0, we compute the intersection B between root- C_1 and sphere C_1 as well as the intersection C between root- C_2 and sphere C_1. The nearer one of B and C to root is the solution. If x is larger than d, we compute the solution in a similar way using C_2 instead.

4 Results

We implemented our normalization algorithm and tested it on a database containing 137605 frames of motion capture data, which are composed of 31 different skeletons. The motions in our database include various types such as walking, running, boxing, jumping etc. The experiments were run on a 1.8GHz Pentium 4 with 384M of main memory. In our experiments L was 6 frames. To verify our algorithm's capability, we halve all joints' lengths for each skeleton in our database and compare the resulting motions with the original ones. The sample motions are shown in figure 3.

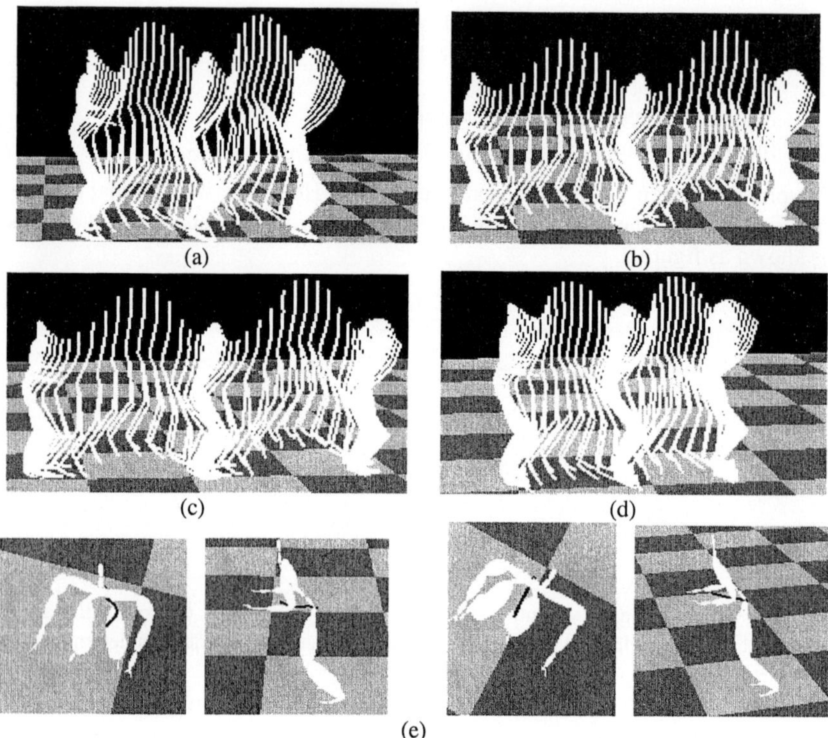

Fig. 3. (a) the original motion. (b) the resulting motion that halves the original skeleton lengths without footskates cleanup process. (c) the motion in (b) after footskate cleanup. (d) the result using our algorithm. (e) Shin's root placement algorithm may cause root swings (the black line in the left two figures), the right two figures show the result using our algorithm.

5 Discussions

In this paper, we present a simple and efficient algorithm to normalize all motion data in database with same skeleton length. The resulting motions of our algorithm are quite similar to the input ones so that have little influence on motion retrieval. We also find that one case is missed in Shin et al.'s algorithm [10], which may cause root swings. Though we only discuss the motion adaptation problem between different skeletons here, our framework can be used in more general cases. For example, the framework of root placement + footskate cleanup in this paper can be also used to replace an original motion into another terrain. In the future we plan to analyze the new terrain's influence on the placement of the root positions for a natural result. In consequence, a new path transformation algorithm will be developed.

Acknowledgements

The motion data used in this project was obtained from mocap.cs.cmu.edu. This work is supported by Microsoft Research Asia (Project-2004-Image-01).

References

1. Bruderlin, A., Williams, L.: Motion signal process. In: *proc. ACM SIGGRAPH 95*, ACM Press /ACM SIGGRAPH. Computer Graphics Proc. Annual Conf. Series (1995) 97-104.
2. Witkin, A., Popvic, Z.: Motion warping. In: *proc. ACM SIGGRAPH 95*, ACM Press/ ACM SIGGRAPH. Computer Graphics Proc. Annual Conf. Series (1995) 105-108
3. CMU. Carnegie-Mellon Mocap Database. (2003) http://mocap.cs.cmu.edu.
4. Kovar, L., Gleicher, M., Pighin, F.: Motion graphs. In: *Proceedings of ACM SIGGRAPH 2002*, Annual Conference Series, (2002).
5. Gleicher, M. Retargeting motion to new characters. In: *Proceedings of ACM SIGGRAPH 98*, Annual Conference Series, ACM SIGGRAPH (1998) 33–42.
6. Kovar, L., Schreiner, J., Gleicher, M.: Footskate cleanup for motion capture editing. In: *Proceedings of ACM SIGGRAPH Symposium on Computer Animation 2002*. ACM SIGGRAPH (2002).
7. Hodgins, J.K., Pollard, N.S.: Adapting simulated behaviors for new characters. In: *Proceedings of SIGGRAPH 1997* (1997) vol. 31, 153–162.
8. Pollard, N.S.: Simple Machines for Scaling Human Motion, In: *Eurographics Workshop on Animation and Simulation*, Milan, Italy, ISBN 3-211-83392-7 (1999)
9. Lee, J., Shin, S.Y.: A hierarchical approach to interactive motion editing for human-like figures. In: *Proceedings of ACM SIGGRAPH 99*, Annual Conference Series, ACM SIGGRAPH (1999) 39–48.
10. Shin, H.J., Lee, J., Gleicher, M., Shin, S.Y.: Computer puppetry: an importance-based approach. In: *ACM Transactions on Graphics 20*, 2 (2001), 67–94.
11. Kwang-Jin Choi, Hyeong-Seok Ko: On-line motion retargetting.In: *Pacific Graphics 99*, Held in Seoul, Korea (1999).
12. Tak Seyoon, Hyeong-Seok Ko: A Physically-Based Motion Retargeting Filter, ACM Transactions on Graphics (2005) Vol. 21, Issue 3, 98-117.
13. Bodik, P.: Automatic footplant detection inside flmoview. Student Summer Project Report Web Page. http://www.cs.wisc.edu/graphics/Gallery/PeterBodik/

Fusing Face and Body Display for Bi-modal Emotion Recognition: Single Frame Analysis and Multi-frame Post Integration

Hatice Gunes and Massimo Piccardi

Faculty of Information Technology, University of Technology, Sydney (UTS), PO Box 123, Broadway, NSW 2007, Australia
{haticeg, massimo}@it.uts.edu.au

Abstract. This paper presents an approach to automatic visual emotion recognition from two modalities: expressive face and body gesture. Face and body movements are captured simultaneously using two separate cameras. For each face and body image sequence single "expressive" frames are selected manually for analysis and recognition of emotions. Firstly, individual classifiers are trained from individual modalities for mono-modal emotion recognition. Secondly, we fuse facial expression and affective body gesture information at the feature and at the decision-level. In the experiments performed, the emotion classification using the two modalities achieved a better recognition accuracy outperforming the classification using the individual facial modality. We further extend the affect analysis into a whole image sequence by a multi-frame post integration approach over the single frame recognition results. In our experiments, the post integration based on the fusion of face and body has shown to be more accurate than the post integration based on the facial modality only.

1 Introduction

The case for affective computing is supported by the observation that humans display a rich set of emotional cues while communicating with other humans. In such human-human communications, a subject playing the role of the source-end uses a variety of cues such as gestures, tone of the voice, facial expressions that will be interpreted by the subject at the receiver-end. Such a rich set of emotional cues will be wasted in human-computer interaction until computers as the receiver-end will be capable of recognizing them to a human-like extent.

Significant research results have been reported in recognition of emotional cues from facial expressions (e.g. [2]). The level of acknowledgement for emotion recognition via body movements and gestures is lower since it has only recently started attracting the attention of computer science and HCI communities [13]. However, the interest is growing with works similar to those presented in [1], [4] and [14]. So far, most of the work in affective computing has focused on only a single channel of information (e.g. facial expression). However, reliable assessment typically requires the concurrent use of multiple modalities (i.e. speech, facial expression, gesture, and gaze) occurring together [13]. Multimodal interfaces operate in a more efficient way, modalities usually complement each other and help improve the accuracy and robustness of affective and perceptual interfaces.

J. Tao, T. Tan, and R.W. Picard (Eds.): ACII 2005, LNCS 3784, pp. 102 – 111, 2005.

Relatively few papers have focused on implementing emotion recognition systems using affective multimodal data [17]. There exist several works in the literature (e.g. [7, 9]) that combined facial video and audio information either at a feature-level [7] or at a decision-level [9]. More recently, Kapoor et al. [14] combined sensory information from the face video (manually extracted features), the posture sensor (a chair sensor) and the game being played in a probabilistic framework to detect children's affective states. However, they do not focus on gestures of the hands and other bodily parts. Balomenos et al. [1] combined facial expressions and hand gestures for recognition of six prototypical emotions by using facial points from MPEG-4 compatible animation and defining certain hand movements under each emotion category. They fused the results from the two subsystems at a decision level using pre-defined weights.

Similarly, the aim of our research is to combine face and upper-body gestures in a bi-modal manner to recognize emotions automatically. Compared to the work in [1], we use a higher number of hand gestures and postures combined with the displacement of the other bodily parts (e.g. shoulders). Moreover, we compare the experimental results from feature-level and decision-level fusion of the face and body modalities to determine which fusion approach is more suitable for our work. Our motivation for multimodality is based on the fact that all of the aforementioned studies have improved the performance of their emotion recognition systems by the use of multimodal information [1, 7, 9, 14].

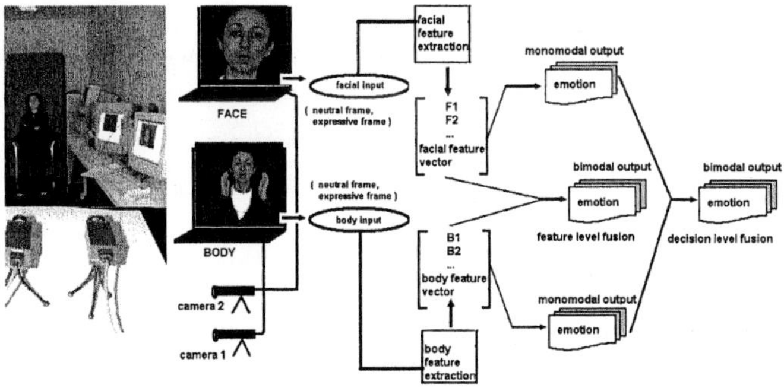

Fig. 1. Our system framework for mono-modal and bi-modal emotion recognition.

2 Methodology

Initially, we present the two modalities, namely facial expressions and expressive body gestures, as described in the following sections. Our task is to analyze expressive cues within HCI which mostly take place as dialogues from a sitting position; hence, we focus on the expressiveness of the upper part of the body in our work. Since we were not able to find a publicly available database with bi-modal expressive face and body gesture we created our own bi-modal database (FABO) by capturing face and body simultaneously from 23 people using two cameras as shown in Fig.1. Our database consists of recordings of the participants performing required face and body expressions. Moreover, after the recordings we conducted a survey asking the participants to evaluate their own performance. Based on their statement we considered a number of recorded sequences as outliers and did not include them in this work.

Table 1. List of the facial emotions recognized by our system and the changes that occur on the face when they are displayed (based on [6])

anxiety ▪ lip bite ▪ stretching of the mouth ▪ eyes turn up/down/left/right ▪ lip wipe	**fear** ▪ brows raised and drawn together ▪ forehead wrinkles drawn to the center ▪ upper eyelid is raised and lower eyelid is drawn up ▪ mouth is open ▪ lips are slightly tense or stretched and drawn back
anger ▪ brows lowered and drawn together ▪ lines appear between brows ▪ lower lid is tensed and may or may not be raised ▪ upper lid is tense and may or may not be lowered due to brows' action ▪ lips are either pressed firmly together with corners straight or down or open	**happiness** ▪ corners of lips are drawn back and up ▪ mouth may or may not be parted with teeth exposed or not ▪ cheeks are raised ▪ lower eyelid shows wrinkles below it, and may be raised but not tense ▪ wrinkles around the outer corners of the eyes
disgust ▪ upper lip is raised ▪ lower lip is raised and pushed up to upper lip or it is lowered ▪ nose is wrinkled ▪ cheeks are raised ▪ brows are lowered ▪ tongue out	**uncertainty** ▪ lid drop ▪ inner brow raised ▪ outer brow raised ▪ chin raised ▪ jaw sideways ▪ corners of the lips are drawn downwards

Table 2. List of the body emotions recognized by our system and the changes that occur in the upper-body when they are displayed (based on [4, 8, 11])

anxiety ▪ hands close to the table surface ▪ fingers moving ▪ fingers tapping on the table	**anger** ▪ body extended ▪ hands on the waist ▪ hands made into fists and kept low, close to the table surface	**disgust** ▪ body backing ▪ left/right hand touching the neck
fear ▪ body contracted ▪ body backing ▪ hands high up, trying to cover bodily parts	**happiness** ▪ body extended ▪ hands kept high ▪ hands made into fists and kept high	**uncertainty** ▪ shoulder shrug ▪ palms up

2.1 Modality 1: Facial Expression

The leading study of Ekman and Frisen [10] formed the basis of visual automatic facial expression recognition. Their studies suggested that anger, disgust, fear, happiness, sadness and surprise are the six basic prototypical facial expressions recognized universally. Brave and Nass also provide details of the facial cues for displayed emotions in [6]. We base our facial feature extraction module on distinguishing these cues from the neutral face and from each other. Table 1 provides the list of the facial emotion categories (anger, disgust, fear, happiness, uncertainty and anxiety) recognized by our system based on the visual changes occurring on the face.

2.2 Modality 2: Expressive Body Gesture

Human recognition of emotions from body movements and postures is still an unresolved area of research in psychology and non-verbal communication. There are numerous works suggesting various opinions on this area.

In his paper [8], Coulson presented experimental results on attribution of 6 emotions (anger, disgust, fear, happiness, sadness and surprise) to static body postures by using computer-generated figures. He found out that in general, anger, happiness, and sadness are being attributed to certain postures, with some identified by 90%. For instance, arms open and raised above shoulder level constituted the posture receiving the highest concordance for the emotion "happiness". From his experiments he concluded that human recognition of emotion from posture is comparable to recognition from the voice, and some postures are recognized as well as facial expressions. Burgoon et al. clearly discuss the issue of emotion recognition from bodily cues and provide useful references in a recent publication in the context of national security [4]. They claim that emotional states are conveyed by a set of cues: "The natural expression, we may suppose, is a total made up of a certain facial expression, certain gestures, and a bodily posture" [4]. They focus on the identification of emotional states such as positivity, anger and tension in video from body and kinesics cues. In their paper, Boone and Cunningham [3] suggest that propositional expressive gestures are described as specific movements of certain bodily parts or postures corresponding to stereotypical emotions (e.g. bowed head and dropped shoulders showing sadness). Non-propositional expressive gestures are, instead, not coded as specific movements but form the quality of movements (e.g. direct/flexible).

In this paper we focus on the propositional gestures only as they can be easily extracted from individual frames. Table 2 is based on the cues described by Burgoon et al. [4], Coulson [8], Givens [11]; and provides the list of the body gestures and the correlation between the gestures and the emotion categories currently recognized by our system.

3 Feature Extraction

In our experiments we select a whole frame sequence where an expression is formed in order to perform feature extraction and tracking. For feature extraction we processed all available sequences and we classify only apex frames where an expression is fully formed. For each apex frame, we use a manually selected neutral frame and a set of previous frames for feature extraction and tracking. We assume that initially the person is in frontal view, the upper body, hands and face are visible and not occluding each other.

We apply a segmentation process based on a background subtraction method in each frame in order to obtain the silhouette of the upper body. We then apply thresholding, noise cleaning, morphological filtering and connected component labeling [18]. We generate a set of features for the detected foreground object, including its centroid, area, bounding box and expansion/contraction ratio as reference for body movement. We extract the face and the hands automatically from individual frames of the face and body independently, by exploiting skin color information. The hand position consists of the position of the centroid and in-plane rotation. We employ the Camshift algorithm [5] for tracking the hands and predicting their locations in the subsequent frames (see Fig. 2). Orientation feature helps to discriminate between different poses of the hand together with the edge density information. For the face, we detect the key features in the neutral frame and define the bounding boxes for each facial feature (forehead, eyes, eyebrows, nose, lips and chin). Once the face and its features are detected, for tracking the face and obtaining its orientation for the next sequence we use again the Camshift algorithm. We also calculate the optical flow by comparing the displacement from the neutral face to the expressive face using the Lucas-Kanade algorithm [16]. Further details of our approach are explained in [12].

Fig. 2. Camshift tracking for face and two hands

4 Single Frame Analysis

In this experiment, we processed 58 sequences in total, 29 for face and 29 for body from 4 subjects. We processed about 1750 frames for the face and 1750 for the body overall. However, we used only the "expressive" or "apex" frames for training and testing and we omitted the frames with intermediate movements. We used nearly half of these for training and the other half for testing purposes. For training we used the following sequences (one version for face and one for body): fear (1 sequence), happiness (3 sequences), anger (5 sequences), anxiety (2 sequences), uncertainty (2 sequences), and disgust (2 sequences). Similarly, the following sequences were used for testing: fear (1 sequence), happiness (3 sequences), anger (4 sequences), anxiety (2 sequences), uncertainty (2 sequences), and disgust (2 sequences). After obtaining the feature vector for face and body separately, we performed emotion recognition using Weka, a tool for automatic classification [19].

4.1 Mono-modal Emotion Recognition

Before the automatic recognition procedure all frames were initially labeled by two human experts. The ground truth in this work was established based on participants' own evaluation of their performance and the authors as human experts labeling all the frames. Further validation from a large pool of human experts will be done as future work. We created a separate class for each emotion, for face and body separately. The face feature vector consists of 148 attributes and the body vector consists of 140 attributes. We then fed these feature vectors into separate classifiers for mono-modal emotion recognition.

Table 3. Mono-modal emotion recognition results for 4 subjects using BayesNet

Modality	Training	Testing	Attributes	Number of classes	Correctly classified
Face	414	386	148	6	82.9 %
Body	424	386	140	6	100 %

For the face, we used 414 frames for training and 386 for testing. For the body, we used 424 frames for training and 386 for testing. BayesNet [19] provided the best classification results both for face and body emotion recognition (results are presented in Table 3).

4.2 Bi-modal Emotion Recognition

In general, modality fusion is to integrate all incoming single modalities into a combined single representation [20]. Typically, fusion is either done at a feature-level or deferred to the decision-level [20]. To make the fusion issue tractable the individual modalities are usually assumed independent of each other. In this work, to fuse the affective facial and body information we implemented both approaches: feature-level and decision-level fusion.

Feature-Level Fusion. Feature-level fusion is performed by using the extracted features from each modality and concatenating these features into one large vector. The resulting vector is input to a single classifier which uses the combined information to assign the testing samples into appropriate classes. We fuse face and body features of the corresponding expressive frames from the corresponding videos obtained from face and body cameras. We experimented various classifiers on a dataset that consists of 412 training and 386 testing instances. For the feature set with 288 attributes, BayesNet provided the best classification accuracy again (100% in this test). For the emotions considered, we observe that using the two modalities achieves better recognition accuracy in general, outperforming the classification using the face modality alone. To correctly interpret these results, it is important to recall that our experiments test unseen instances from the same subjects used for the training phase. Accuracy might be significantly lower for totally unseen subjects.

Decision-Level Fusion. Decision-level (late) integration is the most common way of integrating asynchronous but temporally correlated modalities [20]. Each modality is first pre-classified independently and the final classification is based on the fusion of the outputs from the different modalities. Designing optimal strategies for decision-level fusion is still an open research issue. Various approaches have been proposed: sum rule, product rule, using weights, max/min/median rule, majority vote etc. [15]. We used the first three techniques mentioned above for our system: sum, product and weight criteria. We describe the general approach of late integration of the individual classifier outputs as follows: $X = (x_f, x_b)$ represents the overall feature vector consisting of the face feature vector, x_f, and the body feature vector, x_b. X must be assigned to one of M possible classes, $(\omega_1, \ldots \omega_k, \ldots \omega_M)$ having maximum posterior probability $p(\omega_k|X)$. An early integration approach would compute such a probability explicitly. In late integration, instead, two separate classifiers provide the posterior probabilities $p(\omega_k|x_f)$ and $p(\omega_k|x_b)$ for face and body, respectively, to be combined into a single posterior probability $p(\omega_k|X)$ with one of the fusion methods described in the following. Moreover, in the infrequent case in which the combined $p(\omega_k|X)$ "fires" the same value for two or more classes, we resort to the classification provided by the face classifier since this is the major mode in our bi-modal approach. If the same happens for $p(\omega_k|x_f)$, we arbitrarily retain the first class in appearance order. The description of the three criteria we used (sum, product and weight) is given in Table 4.

Table 4. Description of the three late-fusion criteria used: sum, product and weight

assign $X \rightarrow \omega_k$	Sum rule	$k = \arg\max_{k=1..M} \left(\left(p(\omega_k \mid x_f) + p(\omega_k \mid x_b)\right)\right)$
	Product rule	$k = \arg\max_{k=1..M} \left(p(\omega_k \mid x_f)\, p(\omega_k \mid x_b)\right)$
	Weight criterion	$k = \arg\max_{k=1..M} \left(\lambda_f\, p(\omega_k \mid x_f) + \lambda_b\, p(\omega_k \mid x_b)\right)$

In our case, the face modality has the lead and the body modality needs to be integrated. Thus, when using the weight criteria we assigned arbitrary weights as follows: $\lambda_f = 0.7$ for the face modality and $\lambda_b = 0.3$ for the body modality. The late fusion results for sum, product and weight criteria are all presented in Table 5.

Table 5. Bi-modal emotion recognition results for 4 subjects using BayesNet

	Recognition rates on the testing set (%)		
Emotion	Sum Rule	Product Rule	Weight criterion ($\lambda_\phi = 0.70$, $\lambda_\beta = 0.30$)
Overall	91	88	83
Anger	80	76	75
Disgust	100	100	97
Fear	94	83	77
Happiness	100	100	98
Uncertainty	78	76	63
Anxiety	98	93	83

5 Multi-frame Post Integration

In order to provide a generalized affect analysis for a whole video we apply a multi-frame post integration approach on the single frame recognition results. The post integration combines single frame recognition results first by calculating the total number of recognized frames for each emotion category and then choosing the emotion with the maximum value as the "assigned emotion" or final decision for a whole video. We further analyze how the mono-modal and bi-modal multi-frame post integration approaches can differently prove useful for affect analysis of a whole video with two experiments:

Experiment 1. We used video #2 as an illustrative test case. The test results for "video #2" are shown in Table 6.

Experiment 2. We applied the multi-frame post integration analysis to all the testing videos. The test results are shown in Table 7.

The results obtained from both tables are analyzed in Section 6.

Table 6. Results of single frame recognition and multi-frame post integration for video #2

		face video	body video	early fusion	late fusion		
frame index #	actual emotion	single frame recognition result	single frame recognition result		sum	product	weights
59	uncertainty	disgust	uncertainty	uncertainty	disgust	disgust	disgust
60	uncertainty	anxiety	uncertainty	uncertainty	uncertainty	uncertainty	anxiety
61	uncertainty	anger	uncertainty	uncertainty	uncertainty	uncertainty	uncertainty
62	uncertainty	happy	uncertainty	uncertainty	happy	disgust	happy
63	uncertainty	happy	uncertainty	uncertainty	happy	disgust	happy
65	uncertainty	happy	uncertainty	uncertainty	happy	disgust	happy
66	uncertainty	happy	uncertainty	uncertainty	happy	disgust	happy
67	uncertainty	happy	uncertainty	uncertainty	uncertainty	uncertainty	happy
68	uncertainty	happy	uncertainty	uncertainty	uncertainty	uncertainty	happy
69	uncertainty	uncertainty	uncertainty	uncertainty	uncertainty	uncertainty	uncertainty
70	uncertainty	happy	uncertainty	uncertainty	uncertainty	uncertainty	happy
71	uncertainty	happy	uncertainty	uncertainty	happy	disgust	happy
72	uncertainty	happy	uncertainty	uncertainty	happy	disgust	happy
73	uncertainty	happy	uncertainty	uncertainty	happy	disgust	happy
74	uncertainty	happy	uncertainty	uncertainty	happy	disgust	happy
75	uncertainty	happy	uncertainty	uncertainty	happy	disgust	happy
76	uncertainty	uncertainty	uncertainty	uncertainty	uncertainty	uncertainty	uncertainty
77	uncertainty	happy	uncertainty	uncertainty	uncertainty	disgust	happy
78	uncertainty	happy	uncertainty	uncertainty	uncertainty	uncertainty	happy
79	uncertainty	happy	uncertainty	uncertainty	uncertainty	uncertainty	happy
post integration		disgust 1 happiness 15 fear 0 anger 1 uncertainty 2 anxiety 1	disgust 0 happiness 0 fear 0 anger 0 uncertainty 20 anxiety 0	disgust 0 happiness 0 fear 0 anger 0 uncertainty 20 anxiety 0	disgust 1 happiness 9 fear 0 anger 0 uncertainty 10 anxiety 0	disgust 11 happiness 0 fear 0 anger 0 uncertainty 9 anxiety 0	disgust 1 happiness 15 fear 0 anger 0 uncertainty 3 anxiety 1
final decision		**happiness**	**uncertainty**	**uncertainty**	**uncertainty**	**disgust**	**happiness**

Table 7. Results of multi-frame post integration for all testing videos

	emotion recognized							
actual emotion	**face only**		**early fusion**		**late fusion**			
		# of frames		**# of frames**	**sum**	**# of frames**	**product**	**# of frames**
anger 26 frames	**disgust** happiness others	**22** 4 0	**anger** others	**26** 0	**disgust** anger others	**21** 5 0	**disgust** anger others	**25** 1 0
uncertainty 20 frames	**happiness** uncertainty others	**15** 2 3	**uncertainty** others	**20** 0	**uncertainty** happiness others	**10** 9 1	**disgust** uncertainty others	**11** 9 0
anxiety 41 frames	**anxiety** disgust others	**26** 13 2	**anxiety** others	**41** 0	**anxiety** disgust others	**37** 3 1	**anxiety** disgust others	**35** 6 0
disgust 15 frames	**disgust** anger others	**14** 1 0	**disgust** others	**15** 0	**disgust** others	**15** 0	**disgust** others	**15** 0
disgust 27 frames	**disgust** others	**27** 0	**disgust** others	**27** 0	**disgust** others	**27** 0	**disgust** others	**27** 0
fear 18 frames	**fear** anger others	**14** 3 1	**fear** others	**18** 0	**fear** happiness others	**17** 1 0	**fear** disgust others	**15** 3 0
happiness 31 frames	**happiness** others	**31** 0	**happiness** others	**31** 0	**happiness** others	**31** 0	**happiness** others	**31** 0
happiness 25 frames	**happiness** others	**24** 1	**happiness** others	**25** 0	**happiness** others	**25** 0	**happiness** others	**25** 0
happiness 28 frames	**happiness** others	**28** 0	**happiness** others	**28** 0	**happiness** others	**28** 0	**happiness** others	**28** 0
anger 35 frames	**anger** others	**35** 0	**anger** others	**35** 0	**anger** others	**35** 0	**anger** others	**35** 0
uncertainty 26 frames	**uncertainty** others	**26** 0	**uncertainty** others	**26** 0	**uncertainty** others	**26** 0	**uncertainty** others	**26** 0
anger 46 frames	**anger** others	**46** 0	**anger** others	**46** 0	**anger** others	**46** 0	**anger** others	**46** 0
anxiety 48 frames	**anxiety** uncertainty others	**47** 1 0	**anxiety** others	**48** 0	**anxiety** others	**48** 0	**anxiety** others	**48** 0

6 Analysis and Conclusions

This paper presented an approach to automatic visual analysis of expressive face and upper body gesture and associated emotions suitable for use in a vision-based affective multimodal framework.

Initially, we focused on facial expressions and body gestures separately and analyzed the individual frames, namely neutral and expressive frames. We presented experimental results from four subjects. Firstly, individual classifiers were trained separately with face and body features for mono-modal classification into labeled emotion categories. We fused affective face and body modalities for classification into combined emotion categories (a) at the feature-level ("early" fusion), in which the data from both modalities are combined before classification and (b) at the decision-level ("late" fusion). Our experimental results show that: (a) the emotion classification using the two modalities achieved a better recognition accuracy in general, outperforming the classification using the face modality only; (b) by comparing the experimental results, early fusion seems to achieve a better recognition accuracy compared to late fusion; (c) Table 5 shows that the sum rule proved the best way to fuse the two modalities.

We further extended affect analysis into a whole video sequence by a multi-frame post integration approach over the single frame recognition results in order to output a decision for the whole video sequence with two experiments. Table 6 shows that: (a) single frame recognition accuracy from the face is not high; (b) the mono-modal multi-frame post integration from the face results in 10% accuracy for affect analysis of the whole video and wrongly labels it as "happiness"; (c) the bi-modal multi-frame post integration based on early fusion results in 100% accuracy for affect analysis of the whole video and correctly labels it as "uncertainty"; (d) the bi-modal multi-frame post integration based on late fusion with sum criterion results in 50% accuracy for affect analysis of the whole video; if the maximum is chosen (10 out of 20), then this criteria correctly labels the video as "uncertainty". Similarly, Table 7 shows that: (a) both mono-modal and bi-modal multi-frame post integration approaches prove to be useful for affect analysis of a whole video; (b) mono-modal post integration most often provides accurate results when maximum is chosen (11 out of 13 videos); (c) the bi-modal post integration based on early fusion provides 100% accuracy for affect analysis of all testing videos by correctly labeling 13 out of 13 videos; (d) the bi-modal post integration based on late fusion provides 92% accuracy by correctly labeling 12 out of 13 videos; (e) the bi-modal multi-frame post integration based on early fusion provides more accurate results than late fusion; (f) the bi-modal post integration based on late fusion with sum criterion provides better results than the other late fusion criteria.

From our experiments we can conclude that using expressive body information adds substantial accuracy to the emotion recognition based solely on the face. Furthermore, the use of body cues helps disambiguate the recognition of emotions for those cases where emotions appear very similar in terms of facial features alone. A logical explanation for that is that body gestures can be more reliably recognized than small-scale facial actions by means of image analysis techniques in many real cases.

References

1. Balomenos, T., et al.: Emotion Analysis in Man-Machine Interaction Systems, Springer MLMI 2004 Lecture Notes, 3361 (2004), 318-328.
2. Bartlett, M.S., et al.: Machine learning methods for fully automatic recognition of face expressions and face actions, Proc. of IEEE SMC (2004) 592-597.
3. Boone, R. T. & Cunningham, J. G.: Children's decoding of emotion in expressive body movement: The development of cue attunement, Developmental Psyc. 34 (1998)1007-1016.
4. Burgoon, J. K., et al.: Augmenting Human Identification of Emotional States in Video, Proc. of Int. Conference on Intelligent Data Analysis (2005) (in press).
5. Bradski, G. R.: Computer vision face tracking for use in a perceptual user interface, Intel Techn. J. 2nd Quarter (1998).
6. Brave, S. & Nass, C.: Emotion in HCI. In J. Jacko & A. Sears (Eds.), The HCI Handbook, Hillsdale, NJ: Lawrence Erlbaum Associates (2002).
7. Chen, L.S. & Huang, T.S.: Emotional expressions in audiovisual human computer interaction, Proc. of IEEE ICME, 1 (2000) 423-426.
8. Coulson, M.: Attributing Emotion to Static Body Postures: Recognition Accuracy, Confusions, and Viewpoint Dependence, J. of Nonverbal Behavior, 28 (2) (2004).
9. De Silva, L. C. & Ng, P. C.: Bi-modal emotion recognition, Proc. FG (2000) 332–335.
10. Ekman, P. & Friesen, W. V.: Unmasking the face: a guide to recognizing emotions from facial clues, Imprint Englewood Cliffs, N.J.: Prentice-Hall (1975).
11. Givens, D. B. , The Nonverbal Dictionary of Gestures, Signs & Body Language Cues, Washington, Center for Nonverbal Studies Press, (2005).
12. Gunes, H. & Piccardi, M.: Fusing Face and Body Gesture for Machine Recognition of Emotions, Proc. IEEE RO-MAN 2005, Nashville, USA, (2005) (in press).
13. Hudlicka, E.: To feel or not to feel: The role of affect in human-computer interaction, Int. J. Hum.-Comput. Stud., 59 (1-2) (2003) 1-32.
14. Kapoor, A., et al.: Probabilistic Combination of Multiple Modalities to Detect Interest, Proc. IEEE ICPR (2004).
15. Kuncheva, L. I.: A Theoretical Study on Six Classifier Fusion Strategies, IEEE Trans. on PAMI, 24(2) (2002).
16. Lucas, B.D. & Kanade, T.: An iterative image registration technique with an application to stereo vision, Proc. of 7th Int. Jnt. Conf. on Artificial Intelligence (1981) 674–680.
17. Pantic, M. & Rothkrantz, L.J.M.: Towards an affect-sensitive multimodal human-computer interaction, Proc. of the IEEE, 91(9) (2003) 1370-1390.
18. Shapiro, L.G. & Rosenfeld, A.: Computer Vision and Image Processing, Boston, Academic Press (1992).
19. Witten, H. & Frank, E.: Data Mining: Practical machine learning tools with Java implementations, Morgan Kaufmann, San Francisco (2000).
20. Wu, L., Oviatt, S. L. & Cohen, P. R. Multimodal Integration-A Statistical View, IEEE Trans. on Multimedia, 1(4) (1999)334-341.

A Composite Method to Extract Eye Contour

Ke Sun and Hong Wang

State Key Laboratory of Intelligent Technology and Systems,
Department of Computer Science and Technology, Tsinghua University,
Beijing 100084, P.R. China
sunk@mails.tsinghua.edu.cn, wanghong@tsinghua.edu.cn

Abstract. An eye contour extraction method which combines a simplied version of Active Shape Model(ASM) with a gradient method is proposed. Considering the large amount of calculations required by ASM, it is only used to extract eyelids. As iris is considered to have some more regular shape, the detection of iris is done by the simple but fast gradient method, which is improved by introducing gradient value to the weight matrix. Our detection method has been implemented in the C programming language and experimental results shows good accuracy and efficiency.

1 Introduction

Eyes reveals a lot of human affection. Extracting information from eyes would be the basic step in the study of Affective Computing. In a geometrical point of view, we should get the contour of eyes first. Then the extraction results could be taken for further processing or analysis, such as iris recognition, gaze detection, eye animation and eye motion tracking.

Deformable templates is a well-known method for detecting eye features [7] [8]. It describes an arbitrary shape as a parameterized template, and requests for altering the parameters to minimize an energy function, which is defined linking the edges, peaks and valleys in the image. It works well after the energy function is determined, which ultimately depends on the weight of each energy term. However, determing the weights is time consuming [8]. And this method, which would ultimately use some search technique, is not efficient enough, sometimes tends to reach some local minima and mistake them for the real contours.

Active Shape Model (ASM) is a powerful tool in facial feature extraction and medical image analysis [1] [4]. It uses Point Distribution Model(PDM) and iterates to interpret the image. During iteration, a search is performed on each model point to find a new position which best matches the texture of the landmark, then the parameters describing the position and shape of the object are updated to get the model points closer to the new positions. This method has a very flexible shape model and the model can only deform in ways found in the training set. But ASM, being an iterative method, relies on the initial pose and shape of the object to be detected and requires a large amount of calculations.

There are also methods based on luminance edges or valleys in the luminance map [6]. Unlike deformable templates or ASM, which need search or iterate,

J. Tao, T. Tan, and R.W. Picard (Eds.): ACII 2005, LNCS 3784, pp. 112–118, 2005.

these methods are sometimes more efficient. But they often make some assumption about the eyelid shape, polynomial curve for example, which is not always the case.

In order to accomplish the eye contour detection task more efficiently, we propose a composite method, which combines a simplified version of the traditional ASM with a gradient method based on the face localization method proposed by G. Kukharev etc [2]. Our detection algorithm requires the approximate positions of the eye corner points as input, which can give a good estimation of the initial shape in the ASM iteration. Section 2 describes the detection method. In section 3 and 4, experimental results and summary are presented.

2 Eye Contour Extraction

Our detection method is accomplished in two steps. First of all we use the simplified ASM to extract the eyelid contour. Then the possible range of iris position is known, and it will guide the iris localization method, which uses the gradient method in [2].

2.1 Detect Eyelids

The eyelid detection step follows the basic idea of the traditional ASM given by [1], but simplifies the alignment step in the training stage and jumps over the pose adjusting step in the detection stage. Thus it gets more efficient.

First a training set with labeled landmarks is needed. From the classification of landmarks given by [4], the eyelids contour can only contain two obviously mathematical landmarks, that is, the eye corners. All the others is pseudo-landmarks, and we should make them span equally along the eyelids. Figure 1 demonstrates two such eye images used in our experiments.

Some facial feature extraction systems using ASM mark the whole face with hundreds of landmarks. Thus the relationship among the positions of unconnected parts of face is learned (Eye would not be under nose in the detection result, for example), so that they perform better globally. But each part cannot deform independently, unless a large amount of principal components are used in the ASM iteration, which is not an efficient choice. We propose to use the global ASM with fewer landmarks to extract the position and approximate contour of each part, then use our method and some other homologous methods (local ASM) to extract the accurate contour locally.

The alignment of training shapes is performed by translating, rotating and zooming the original landmarks of each image so as to map the two corner points

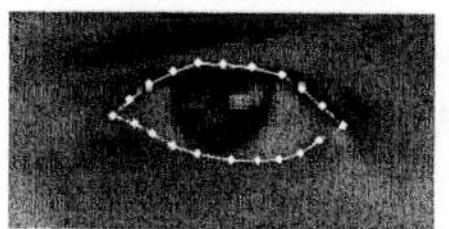
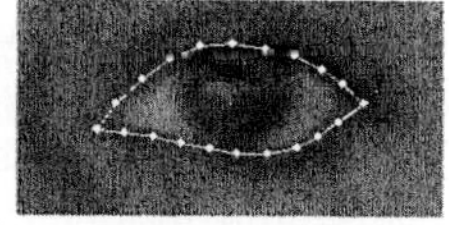

Fig. 1. Eyes with landmarks

to some standard position, $(-100, 0)$ and $(100, 0)$ for example. After that, each training sample could be represented as a vector of $2n$ dimensions, where n is the number of landmarks:

$$x_i = (x_{0i}, y_{0i}, x_{1i}, y_{1i}, \ldots, x_{(n-1)i}, y_{(n-1)i})$$

Following [1], we could calculate the mean shape $\overline{x}$ and the matrix $P = (p_1\ p_2\ \ldots\ p_t)$ where p_i is the i'th principal component, after performing Principal Component Analysis (PCA) on the training set. And we could model the statistics of the grey level appearance around each model point by extracting a profile g_{ij} of length n_p pixels, along the bisector direction and centered at this point. Then the mean normalized derivative profile $\overline{g_i}$ and the $n_p \times n_p$ covariance matrix S_{gi} of each model point is calculated.

Given a new eye image and the rough position of eye corners, we could estimate the initial model points by translating, rotating and zooming the mean shape $\overline{x}$ so as to map the eye corners from standard position (e.g. $(-100, 0)$ and $(100, 0)$) to the given position. Then we iterate to fit the model points to the eye image. The iteration is performed in two steps:

1. Look along bisectors through each model point to find the best local match
2. Update the shape parameters to best fit the model points to the new positions

Here we have omitted the pose adjusting step in the traditional ASM because of the known eye corner positions. They are unchanged during the iteration, while the only thing we need to update is the shape parameters. We use the cost function given in [1] to determine the best local match for each model point:

$$f(d) = (h(d) - \overline{g})^T S_g^{-1} (h(d) - \overline{g}) \tag{1}$$

Then we transform the current and the new shape to our standard position, that is, map the two corners to $(-100, 0)$ and $(100, 0)$. Thus we could obtain two 2n-dimension column vectors, namely x_0 and x_0', corresponding to the two shapes respectively. Then we update the current shape using equation 2.

$$x_1 = x_0 + PP^T \cdot (x_0' - x_0) \tag{2}$$

Then x_1 is transformed back from standard position to the known eye position. Thus one iteration is finished, step 1 pulls each model point from current position to some new position where the gray level appearance around there best match the statistic results we have learned, while step 2 ensures the stableness of the shape during iteration.

There is another simplification, which is risky but efficient. The traditional ASM assumes the valid shapes are drawn from a normal distribution, that is, they lie in some hyper sphere in the 2n-dimension space. Therefore when updating the shape model, we should ensure the updated shape also lie in the hyper sphere. However, equation 2 doesn't ensure this, as we only use the first two principal components in our eye shape model (but they are enough to represent most eyelid contours), and the projection operation in equation 2 will not drive the shape too far from the current shape instance in this case.

2.2 Locate Iris

If the open height of eye is below a certain value, we would assume the eye is closed so there's no need to detect iris. Otherwise, we use the gradient method proposed in [2] to estimate the rough iris location. After that, the center position and radius of iris are adjusted using some search technique.

Having detected the eyelids, the possible range of iris location is known. The original eye image is smoothed with a 3×3 median filter to get rid of noise. Then we apply sobel operator to each point, thus we could obtain the gradient value g_x and the unit vector v_x along the gradient direction of each point x:

$$g_x = \sqrt{d_h^2(x) + d_v^2(x)} \tag{3}$$

$$v_x = \left(\frac{d_h(x)}{g_x}, \frac{d_v(x)}{g_x}\right) \tag{4}$$

where $d_h(x)$ and $d_v(x)$ are the horizontal and vertical luminance derivative values of point x, respectively.

Having known the eye corner positions, the rough iris radius in pixels is known because of the physiological scale. Following [2], the "matrix of hits", namely M, which has the same size as the eye image and has all entries initialized 0, is filled to determine the iris center. For each point x, if g_x is above a certain value and x lies in the eyelid rectangle, a supposed iris center is calculated:

$$c_x = x + R \cdot v_x \tag{5}$$

where R is the supposed iris radius. If c_x is in the rectangle where iris center possibly exists(could be obtained after the eyelid detection step), then we add the 3×3 matrix

$g_x/3$	$g_x/2$	$g_x/3$
$g_x/2$	g_x	$g_x/2$
$g_x/3$	$g_x/2$	$g_x/3$

to M with the "g_x" term added to the point in M who has the same coordinates as c_x. Intuitively speaking, each point will vote another point as well as its neighbors, then add weights to them. Here we have abandoned the constant weight matrix proposed in [2] to fill the "matrix of hits", while gradient value (the "g_x" term) has been introduced in our weight matrix, therefore, points with larger gradient value will generate larger weight matrix so as to speak louder in the vote. This simple modification has largely improved the accuracy in our experiments.

Experimental results have shown that the "matrix of hits" always has one or several peaks, and in high probability the peak with highest value appears at the iris center. The typical hits matrix is shown in Figure 2. Accordingly we search matrix M for the point c with maximum value, then c would be the rough position of iris center.

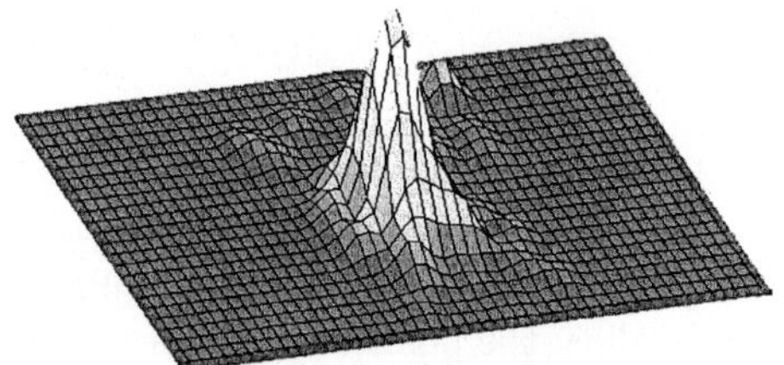

Fig. 2. Matrix of hits

To locate the iris accurately, we disturb the center position (x_0, y_0) and radius r of iris with a small value, then search the triple (x_0, y_0, r) which maximizes the cost function proposed in [5]:

$$f(x_0, y_0, r) = G_\sigma(r) * \frac{\partial}{\partial r} \int_{\theta \in \Theta} \frac{I(x_0 + r\cos\theta,\ y_0 + r\sin\theta)}{2\pi r} d\theta \qquad (6)$$

And it would be the final detection result.

3 Experimental Results

We have used an eye data set cropped from the *BioID face database* [3] to test our algorithm. Each eye has a resolution of 100×50 and is marked with 20 landmarks. A training set is constructed with 70 such eyes. The PCA result has shown that the first two principal components is flexible enough to represent most eye shapes. Figure 3 shows the effect of these principal components.

We use our composite method to detect the contour of each eye unless the eye image is so blurred that even human can hardly recognize the contour. Our

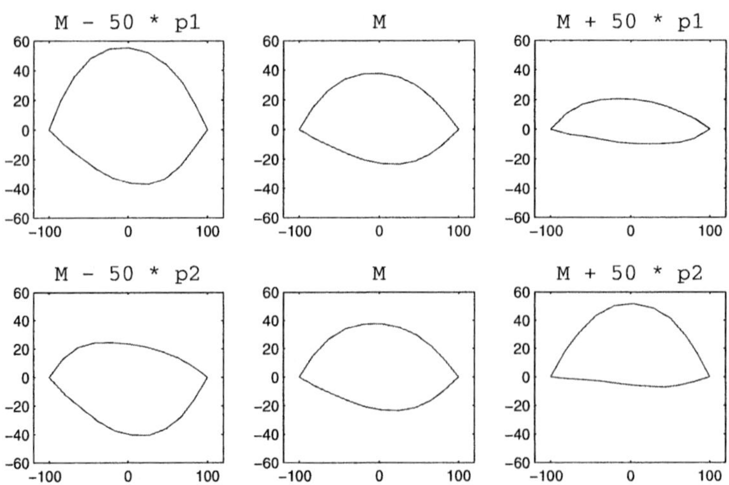

Fig. 3. The effect of the first two principal components

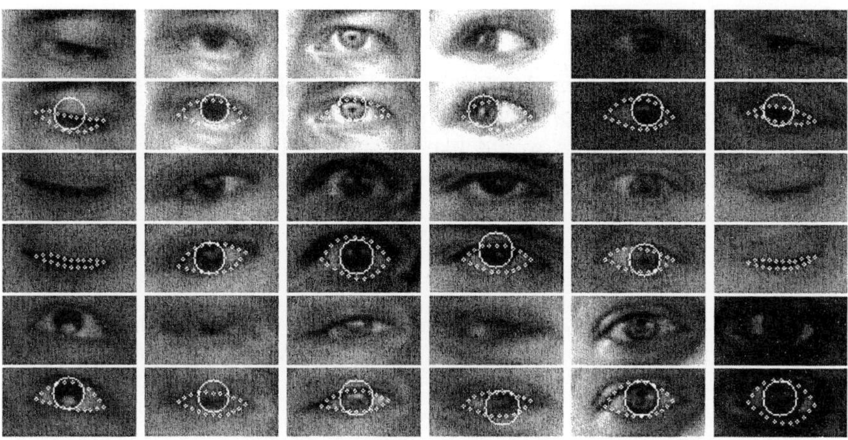

Fig. 4. Typical detection results

Fig. 5. Bad results

method could achieve a speed of 26fps, and the accuracy is about 93% on a subset of our database which contains 1000 eye images. Figure 4 has shown some typical detection results and their corresponding eye images. Note that the method is robust of eyes under different luminance conditions as well as different gaze directions. However, there are also bad results, as figure 5 has shown. They are all representative in the wrongly detected contours. The first one is caused by highlight in iris. While the second and third are caused by the wrongly direction of model points movement during ASM iteration.

4 Conclusion

We have presented an eye contour extraction method combining ASM and a gradient method. The simplification of traditional ASM has made the iteration more efficient, and ASM is only used to detect eyelids. The iris circle is extracted by the face detection method proposed in [2], which has been improved by relating gradient value to the weight matrix. The algorithm described here is implemented and proved to be efficient and accurate.

In studies to follow, we will work on introducing the relationship between eyelids and iris position to the detection system. It would report error when the relationship gets wrong, and some error correcting technique would be designed and implemented. We will also study on tracing the eye contour using our composite method, which requires realtime processing.

Acknowledgements

This work is a part of Research on Affective Computing Theory and Approach, which is a key program project of National Natural Science Foundation of China(NSFC). The authors would like to thank Mr. Wenchao Cai's valuable discussion and help.

References

1. T.F.Cootes, A.Hill, C.J.Taylor and J.Haslam: The Use of Active Shape Models for Locating Structures in Medical Images. Image and Vision Computing. **12** (1994) 355-366.
2. G.Kukharev, P.Masicz, P.Masicz: A Fast and Accurate Faces Localization using Gradient Method. WSCG SHORT Communication papers proceedings WSCG'2004, Feb. 2-6, 2004, Plzen, Czech Republic. (2004) 149-156.
3. O.Jesorsky, K.Kirchberg, R.Frischholz: Robust Face Detection using the Hausdorff Distance. Third International Conference on Audio and Video based Biometric Person Authentication. (2001) 90-95.
4. M.B.Stegmann, D.D.Gomez: A Brief Introduction to Statistical Shape Analysis. Lecture Notes of Image Analysis & Computer Graphics. (2002) 15.
5. J.G.Daugman: High Confidence Visual Recognition of Persons by a Test of Statistical Independence. IEEE Transactions on Pattern Analysis and Machine Intelligence.**15** (1993) 1148-1161.
6. V.Vezhnevets, A.Degtiareva: Robust and Accurate Eye Contour Extraction. Proc. Graphicon-2003, Moscow, Russia. (2003) 81-84.
7. A.L.Yuille, P.W.Hallinan and D.S.Cohen: Feature Extraction from Faces using Deformable Templates. International Journal of Computer Vision. **8** (1992) 99-111.
8. Yuwen Wu, Hong Liu and Hongbin Zha: A New Method of Detecting Human Eyelids Based on Deformable Templates. IEEE International Conference on Systems, Man and Cybernetics. (2004).

Simulated Annealing Based Hand Tracking in a Discrete Space*

Wei Liang, Yunde Jia, Yang Liu, and Cheng Ge

Department of Computer Science and Engineering,
Beijing Institute of Technology, Beijing 100081, PR China
{liangwei, yjiar, liuy, gecheng}@bit.edu.cn

Abstract. Hand tracking is a challenging problem due to the complexity of searching in a 20+ degrees of freedom (DOF) space for an optimal estimation of hand configuration. This paper represents the feasible hand configurations as a discrete space, which avoids learning to find parameters as general configuration space representations do. Then, we propose an extended simulated annealing method with particle filter to search for optimal hand configuration in this discrete space, in which simplex search running in multi-processor is designed to predict the hand motion instead of initializing the simulated annealing randomly, and particle filter is employed to represent the state of the tracker at each layer for searching in high dimensional configuration space. The experimental results show that the proposed method makes the hand tracking more efficient and robust.

1 Introduction

Gesture is one of the most common and natural communication means among human beings. Rather than the traditional mice and keyboards, hand gesture is a more natural and convenient way for human-computer interaction. Cyber-glove was firstly used to capture hand motion in real time, but it is not natural and friendly. In recent years, many researchers in computer vision have been trying to seek more effective methods to solve this problem. However, highly articulated human hand motion always presents complex rotation, translation and self-occlusion, which make hand tracking difficult especially in unconstrained environment.

Different visual methods have been proposed to track hand motion. The appearance-based approach [9,10] is one choice. This kind of methods estimates hand configurations from image features directly. Once the mapping is learned, they can quickly get the configurations. But it is difficult to determine the structure of the mapping function and the optimal set of training data for the learning process. Another strategy for tracking hand motion is model-based approach [4,6]. This kind of methods compares real hand image features with several hand model projections, and estimate current hand configuration by searching for the best match. Although with a well

* This work is supported by the National Natural Science Foundation (No.60473049) of China.

J. Tao, T. Tan, and R.W. Picard (Eds.): ACII 2005, LNCS 3784, pp. 119–126, 2005.

initialization, these methods can produce an accurate estimate, they still have to search in a high dimensional space. Fortunately, Lee and Kunii [2] showed that the dimensionalities of hand configuration can be decreased significantly by hand motion constraints. To take advantage of the hand motion constraints, a suitable representation of feasible hand motion configuration space and an efficient searching algorithm associated with this representation are necessary. Some works [4,8] represent the manifold using linear assumption. But it is still a difficult problem in constructing an accurate manifold approximation.

In this paper, we represent feasible hand configurations as a discrete space which avoids learning to find parameters and eliminates the error rising from incorrect approximate. KD-tree is utilized to arrange the discrete data for fast nearest neighbor retrieval and it is modified easily when new data are embedded. To search in this discrete space, we propose an extended simulated annealing method with particle filter, in which the state of tracker is represented by particle filter at each layer to search in high dimensional configuration space, and simplex search on the KD-tree is employed to predict the hand motion at each step instead of initialization randomly.

2 A Discrete Hand Configuration Space

Human hand is a highly articulated object composed of 27 skeletons, which is divided into three parts: wrist bones (wrist, 8 pieces), metacarpal bones (palm, 5 pieces), and phalanx bones (fingers, 14 pieces). Each finger could be treated as a kinematical chain. Generally, hand motion includes global motion (palm motion) and local motion (fingers motion). Although the global and local hand motion could be estimated separately, the finger motion still involves 20 DOFs.

In this section, we utilize a discrete space to represent feasible local hand configurations from a set of data which are collected manually from various hand motions and KD-tree is employed to arrange data of this discrete space. The entire feasible hand motion configuration space ξ is represented by a set of nodes θ_i , $i=1,\cdots,N$ on the KD-tree, where $\theta_i \in R^{20}$ .To store N hand configurations at the leaves of a tree, about $\log_2(N)$ levels are required, and about $\log_2(N)$ comparisons are required to arrive at the first leaf which contains the first nearest neighbor candidate. The true nearest neighbor may actually reside in a neighboring leaf or further.

This discrete representation is a good choice for three reasons. Firstly, the discrete representation avoids learning to find parameters and eliminates the error rising from incorrect learning. Secondly, the space is easy to be modified when new data are embedded due to the way of data arrangement. And finally, the KD-tree supports fast nearest neighbor retrieval.

3 Multi-directional Simplex Search

In the discrete space, although we could write objective function for each configuration, it is difficult to get a formal description for all configurations and the gradient of objective function. Simplex search is a good choice to deal with this problem. There are some simplex search methods, such as the original method proposed by Spendley et al. [1], the variation version presented by Nelder and Mead [3], and so on.

In this section, Multi-Directional simplex search is performed on the KD-tree to get a prediction for time *t* from the configuration at time *t-1*. Multi-Directional search is a greater overall sampling of the objective function than other simplex search methods and it is designed to run on the multi-processor by calling multiple functions simultaneously, so it's more efficient. Different from the other simplex search methods, during the reflection step, rather than reflecting the 'worst' vertex with greatest function value through the centroid of the other vertices, Multi-Directional search reflects all the vertices through the 'best' vertex. The 'best' and the 'worst' are decided by the objective function. We give the formal description of Multi-Directional simplex search with vertices $< v_0^0, v_1^0, \cdots, v_n^0 >$ in details in Fig.1.

$\alpha \in (0,1)$
min $\leftarrow \arg_i \min\{f(v_i^0), i = 0, \cdots n\}$
swap v_{min}^0 and v_0^0
for $k = 0, 1, \cdots$
  Check the terminate criterion
  for $i = 0, 1, \cdots, n$ /*reflection step
    $v_i^{k+1} \leftarrow 2v_0^k - v_i^k$
    Calculate $f(v_i^{k+1})$
  if $(\min\{f(v_i^{k+1}), i = 1, \cdots, n\} < f(v_0^k))$ then
    for $i = 1, \cdots, n$ /*expansion step
      $v_{e_i}^k \leftarrow (1-\mu)v_0^k + \mu v_i^{k+1}$
      Calculate $f(v_{e_i}^k)$ for $i = 1, \cdots n$
    if $(\min\{f(v_{e_i}^k), i = 1, \cdots, n\} < \min\{f(v_i^{k+1}), i = 1, \cdots, n\})$
      $v_i^{k+1} \leftarrow v_{e_i}^k$ for $i = 1, \cdots, n$
  else
    for $i = 1, \cdots, n$ /*contraction step
      $v_i^{k+1} \leftarrow (1+\alpha)v_0^k - \alpha v_i^{k+1}$
      Calculate $f(v_i^{k+1})$ for $i = 1, \cdots n$
  endif
  min $\leftarrow \arg_i \min\{f(v_i^{k+1}), i = 1, \cdots n\}$
  if $(f(v_{min}^{k+1}) < f(v_0^k))$ swap v_{min}^{k+1} and v_0^k

Fig. 1. Multi-Directional simplex search

These searches are free of any interdependencies, so they can be performed in parallel. $f(\cdot)$ is the objective function. The terminate condition is written as Eq.(1).

$$[\frac{1}{n+1}\sum_{i=0}^{n}[f(v_i)-\mu]^2]^{\frac{1}{2}} < \varepsilon . \tag{1}$$

where $\mu \in (1, +\infty)$, $\mu = \frac{1}{n}\sum_{i=1}^{n} f(v_i)$, and ε is a small tolerance constant.

Given the hand motion configuration θ_{t-1} estimated at time *t-1*, the Multi-Directional search begins with generating an initial simplex S_{t-1}^{0} around θ_{t-1}, with vertices $< v_0^0, v_1^0, \cdots, v_n^0 >$. The vertices are generated from the importance function as described in [6]. After k^{th} iteration, the predicted configuration θ_t at time t is the centroid of the converged simplex:

$$\theta_t = \frac{1}{n+1} \sum_{v_j \in S_t^k} v_j \,. \tag{2}$$

Although human hand is highly constrained, the basic Multi-Directional search does not embed the motion constraints into the search process. It might lead to getting a best matching configuration during the search process which makes the objective function converge towards minimum, while the real hand joints can never reach that configuration. So we restrict the simplex search on the KD-tree instead of performing the unconstrained search in continuous domain. At k^{th} iteration, after computing configuration θ_t in Eq.(2), we have a new configuration θ_t by finding a nearest θ_i on the KD-tree by Eq.(3).

$$\theta_t = \arg\min_{\theta_i \in \xi} \left\| \theta_t - \theta_i \right\| . \tag{3}$$

4 Simulated Annealing (SA) Searching in the Discrete Space

Simulated annealing has become a popular search technique for solving optimization problems. In this section, we employ this method together with Multi-Directional simplex to search in the discrete space.

4.1 SA Particle Filter

The Markov chain based simulated annealing method was developed as a way of handling multiple modes in an optimization context [7]. Given a series of distribution, p_0 to p_M, varying slightly, samples are drawn from it. The distribution p_M is designed so that the Markov chain used to sample from it allows movement between all regions of the search space. The usual method is set as $p_m(x) \propto p_0(x)^{\beta_m}$, for $1 = \beta_0 > \beta_1 > \cdots > \beta_M$. The simulated annealing begins with some initial state, from which a Markov chain designed to converge to p_M is first simulated. Then a Markov chain designed to converge to p_{m-1} is simulated next, starting from the final state of the previous simulation. This process is continued in this way, using the final state of the simulation for p_m as the initial state for the simulation for p_{m-1}, until the chain designed to converge to p_0 is finally simulated.

In this section, the state of mth layer of an annealing is represented by a set of N weighted particles $\{s_m^{(n)}, \pi_m^{(n)}\}_{n=1}^{N}$, where $\pi_m^{(n)} \propto \omega_m(z, s_m^{(n)})$. At $m-1^{th}$ layer, the set of samples at m^{th} layer are resampled to get $\{s_{m-1}^{(n)}\}_{n=1}^{N}$. The process is repeated until arriving at 0th layer with $\{s_0^{(n)}, \pi_0^{(n)}\}_{n=1}^{N}$.

1. From the 'old' sample-set $\{s_{t-1,0}^{(n)},\pi_{t-1,0}^{(n)}\}_{n=1}^{N}$ at time-step *t-1*, predict a 'new' sample-set $\{s_{t,M}^{(n)},\pi_{t,M}^{(n)}\}_{n=1}^{N}$ at time *t*, where N is the number of the samples.

   1.1 Resample.

   Get $\{\tilde{s}_{t-1,0}^{(n)}\}_{n=1}^{N}$ from $\{s_{t-1,0}^{(n)},\pi_{t-1,0}^{(n)}\}_{n=1}^{N}$ according to the weights $\pi_{t-1,0}^{(n)}$ and for each sample in $\{\tilde{s}_{t-1,0}^{(n)}\}_{n=1}^{N}$,

   $\tilde{s}_{t,0}^{(n)}=\tilde{s}_{t-1,0}^{(n)}+B_0$

   where B_0 is a muti-variate Gaussian random with variance p_0 and mean 0.

   1.2 Predict.

   Construct initial simplex $S^{(n)_0}$ around each sample in $\{\tilde{s}_{t,0}^{(n)}\}_{n=1}^{N}$. Perform simplex search on the KD-tree as described in Section 3 to get new samples $\{s_{t,M}^{(n)}\}_{n=1}^{N}$, where $s_{t,M}^{(n)}$ is the result of searching on simplex $S^{(n)_0}$.

2. Simulated annealing particle filter

   Let $m=M$

   2.1 Weight.

   Each sample is assigned a weight:

   $\pi_{t,m}^{(n)}\propto\omega_m(z_t,s_{t,m}^{(n)})$,

   where $\omega_m(z_t,s_{t,m}^{(n)})$ is achieved by $\omega_m(z_t,s_{t,m}^{(n)})=\omega(z_t,s_{t,m}^{(n)})^{\beta_m}$ for $1=\beta_0>\beta_1>\cdots>\beta_M$. $\pi_{t,m}^{(n)}$ is normalized so that $\sum_N\pi_{t,m}^{(n)}=1$. In this paper, $\omega(\cdot)$ is written as the weighting function and z_t is the observations at time *t*. The samples are then written as $\{s_{t,m}^{(n)},\pi_{t,m}^{(n)}\}_{n=1}^{N}$.

   2.2 Resample.

   The N particles are from $\{s_{t,m}^{(n)},\pi_{t,m}^{(n)}\}_{n=1}^{N}$ according to their weights. The nth sample at $m-1^{th}$ layer are produced as:

   $s_{t,m-1}^{(n)}=s_{t,m}^{(n)}+B_m$

   where B_m is a muti-variate Gaussian random with variance p_m and mean 0.

   2.3 $m=m-1$

   2.4 Repeat 2.1-2.3.

   Terminate until arriving at $\{s_{t,0}^{(n)},\pi_{t,0}^{(n)}\}_{n=1}^{N}$, the hand configurations at time t is written as:

   $\theta_t=\sum_{n=1}^{N}s_{t,0}^{(n)}\pi_{t,0}^{(n)}$

Fig. 2. Simulated annealing in the discrete space

4.2 Prediction with Multi-directional Simplex Search

Most of the typical tracking methods are based on Bayesian system. The object state at time t is denoted by x_t, and its history is $X_t=\{x_1,\cdots,x_t\}$. Similarly the set of image features at time t is z_t with history $Z_t=\{z_1,\cdots,z_t\}$. All these methods estimate x_t at time t through Bayesian formulation:

$$p(x_t \mid Z_t) \propto p(z_t \mid x_t) p(x_t \mid Z_{t-1}) . \tag{4}$$

where $p(x_t \mid Z_{t-1}) = \int_{x_{t-1}} p(x_t \mid x_{t-1}) p(x_{t-1} \mid Z_{t-1}) dx_{t-1}$.

We assume that it is a Markov process, in which the state at time t only depends on the state at time t-1. Given the hand configuration at time t-1, we suppose that the prediction is performed by Multi-Directional simplex search in the discrete space as described in Section.2. The simulated annealing method is then extended as shown in Fig. 2.

5 Experiment Results

We employ edges and foreground silhouette to construct the observation model. The detail description could be referred to [4]. And the objective function in the Multi-Directional simplex search is defined as the negative of the observation density.

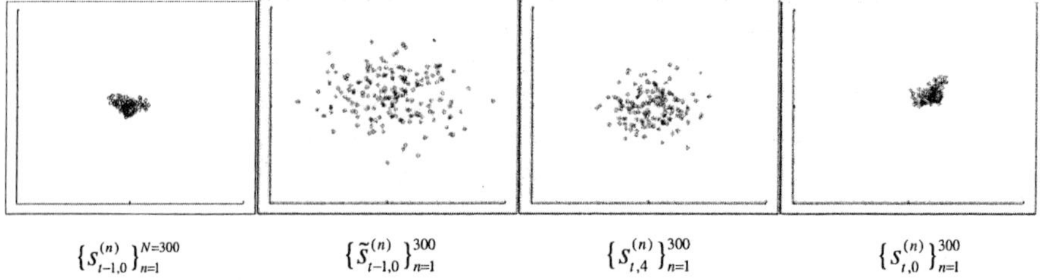

Fig. 3. The process of the sequential simulated annealing. $\{s_{t-1,0}^{(n)}\}_{n=1}^{N=300}$ is resampled to get $\{\tilde{s}_{t-1,0}^{(n)}\}_{n=1}^{300}$, and then searching in the discrete space to get $\{s_{t,4}^{(n)}\}_{n=1}^{300}$. After 5 layers annealed, $\{s_{t,0}^{(n)}\}_{n=1}^{300}$ is gotten. The layers 3 to 1 are omitted for brevity.

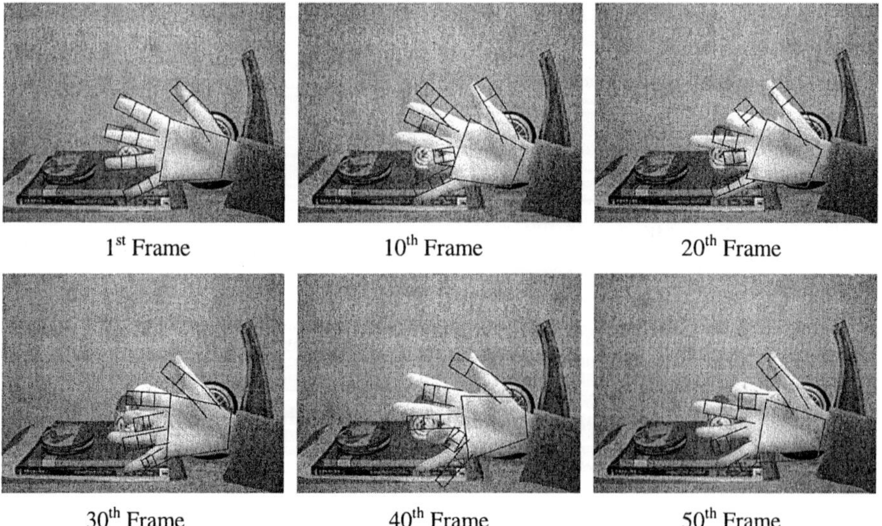

Fig. 4. Hand motion configurations from Condensation with 300 samples

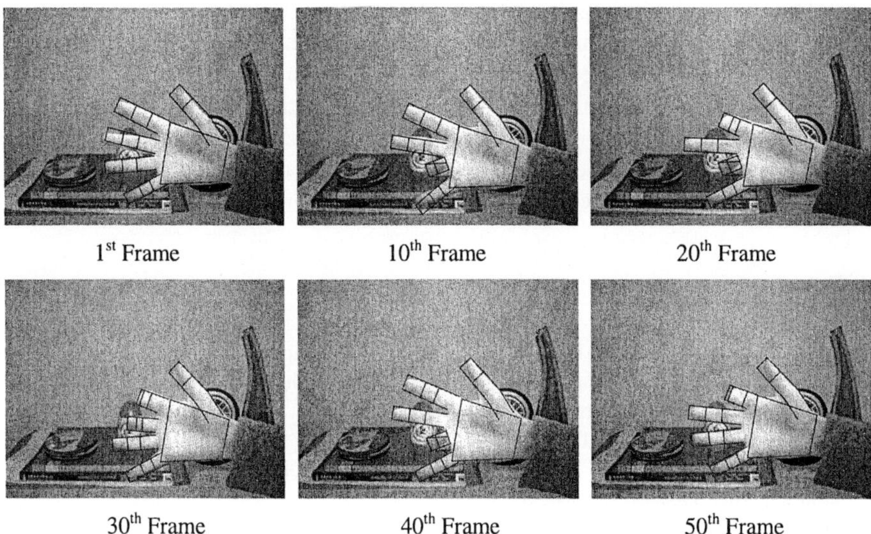

Fig. 5. Hand motion configurations from sequential simulated annealing method with 300 samples and 5 layers

We take a group of image sequence with little global motion by calibrated camera. All the experiment is performed in a cluttered background. Fig.3 gives the process of simulated annealing when hand is tracked as shown in Fig.5. Only two angles are shown, one for Distal Interphalangeal (DIP) of middle and one for DIP of index. Five layers are taken. The hand configurations described by a set of samples $\{s_{t-1,0}^{(n)}, \pi_{t-1,0}^{(n)}\}_{n=1}^{N}$ at time *t-1* is used to form $\{s_{t,4}^{(n)}, \pi_{t,4}^{(n)}\}_{n=1}^{N}$ by the method of Multi-Directional simplex search on KD-tree. The particles are then annealed over 5 layers to produce $\{s_{t,0}^{(n)}, \pi_{t,0}^{(n)}\}_{n=1}^{N}$ which is clustered around the maximum of the weighting function. We also implemented standard simulated annealing method to track the same sequential images. With the same number of samples, the standard simulated method got the equivalent tracking results after more than 10 layers annealing.

A comparison of our method and CONDENSATION[5] method can be seen in Fig.4 and Fig.5. Both methods take 300 samples to track hand. The CONDENSATION lost the hand quickly. Even with 3000 samples, the tracking results are negative. Obviously, the method of the simulated annealing based hand tracking in discrete space is more robust than CONDENSATION and the standard simulated annealing method. In fact, the simulated annealing method with single layer could be considered as the same with CONDENSATION.

6 Conclusion

In this paper, we utilize a discrete space to represent the feasible hand motion configurations and KD-tree is employed to organize the data set. The advantage of this representation is that it avoids learning to find parameters and eliminates the error rising from incorrect learning. It supports fast nearest neighbor retrieval and it is easy to be modified when new data are embedded. And then, the method of SA particle filter in this discrete space is proposed to track the hand motion in which the Multi-Directional simplex search is employed to predict the hand configurations. Although the simulated annealing search is not influenced by the initialization at each step, it is time-consuming. Our method makes the search process more efficient and robust by beginning the search near the global optimal configurations at each step.

References

1. W. Spendley, G. R. Hext, F. R. Himsworth.: Sequential application of simplex designs in optimization and evolutionary operation. Technometrics, 4(4), November, (1962), 441-461
2. J.Lee, T.L.Kunii, Model-based analysis of hand posture. IEEE Computer Graphics and applications, September, (1995), 77-86
3. J.A. Nelder and R. Mead: A simplex method for function minimization. The Computer Journal, 7(4): January, (1965), 308-313
4. John Y.Lin, Ying Wu, Thomas S. Huang: 3D Model-Based Hand Tracking Using Stochastic Direct Search Method. Proceedings of the Sixth IEEE International Conference on Autumatic Face and Gesture Recogniton FGR, (2004), 693-698
5. Isard, M., Blake, A.:CONDENSATION - conditional density propagation for visual tracking. IJCV, vol. 29, no. 1 (1998) 5-28
6. Y.Wu and T. S. Huang. Capturing articulated human hand motion: A divide-and-conquer approach. In Proc. of IEEE Int'l Conf. Computer Vision, (1999), 606–611
7. J. Deutscher, A.Blake and Ian Reid: Articulated Body Motion Capture by Annealed Particle Filtering. CVPR, (2000), 126-133
8. J. Ho, M.-H. Yang, J. Lim, K.-C. Lee, and D. Kriegman: Clustering appearancs of objects under varying illumination conditions. In Proc. of IEEE Conf. on Computer Vision and Pattern Recognition, volume I, (2003), 11–18
9. Ying Wu, Ting Yu, Gang Hua: Tracking Appearances with Occlusions. Proceedings of the 2003 IEEE Computer Society Conference on Computer Vision and Pattern Recognition. (2003), 789-795
10. S. Z. Li, X G. Lv, and H. J Zhang: View-based clustering of object appearances based on independent subspace analysis. In Proc. IEEE Int'l Conf. on Computer Vision, Vancouver, Canada, July, (2001), 295-300

Modulation of Attention by Faces Expressing Emotion: Evidence from Visual Marking

Fang Hao[1,2], Hang Zhang[1,2], and Xiaolan Fu[1,*]

[1] State Key Laboratory of Brain and Cognitive Science,
Institute of Psychology, Chinese Academy of Sciences,
Beijing 100101, China
{haof, zhangh, fuxl}@psych.ac.cn
[2] Graduate School of the Chinese Academy of Sciences, Beijing 100049, China

Abstract. Recent findings demonstrated that negative emotional faces (sad, anger or fear) tend to attract attention more than positive faces do. This study used the paradigm of visual marking to test the perspective that mentioned and explored whether the preview benefit still existed when using schematic faces as materials. The results found that preview benefit was significant in the search of affective materials. In a gap condition, it was faster to search negative faces than to search positive faces. However, this advantage did not appear in half-element condition when negative faces as distractors, which indicated that the view that negative faces capture attention more efficiently is not always like this.

1 Introduction

There has been a long history that researchers make study on attention by the paradigm of visual search [15] [19]. In recent years, researchers turned their interest to emotion and facial expression by this classical paradigm and applied their research results into facial expression aspect [2]. They testified that different kinds of emotion would play a distinct role in the search of facial expression.

The majority of the experiments that used the paradigm of visual search indicated that negative faces capture attention more efficiently than positive faces do [3][6]. Hansen et al. (1988) showed that RTs (reaction times) in negative target-positive distractors condition were faster than positive target-negative distractors condition, which also reflected the asymmetry search of different valences of facial expression [8]. White (1995) received the similar conclusion instead of using schematic facial expression as materials [18]. Ohman et al (2001) found it was faster to search angry faces or fear-relevant stimuli than to search positive faces [11].

The paradigm of visual search is especially well suited for examining whether facial expression can be perceived outside the focus of attention and can guide focal attention. If a face expressing either positive or negative emotion is embedded among different numbers of distractors and the time taken to locate the target face is measured, the relative contribution of unattended positive and negative facial expressions in guiding focal attention can be assessed by comparing the performance of the search [14].

* Corresponding author.

J. Tao, T. Tan, and R.W. Picard (Eds.): ACII 2005, LNCS 3784, pp. 127–134, 2005.

Many experiments made schematic faces as materials to study emotion. Although the schematic faces were impoverished as compared with photographs of real human faces, they appeared to be potent affective facial stimuli. Schematic faces appeared to communicate emotional meaning effectively [1] and showed disruptions in perception when inverted similar to those found with photographed faces [5]. Furthermore, it has recently been shown that schematic faces elicit event-related potentials that are similar to those elicited by photographs of faces [4]. Therefore, given that schematic faces contain fewer feature confounds than photographs and appear to be effective affective face stimuli, it may actually be preferable to use schematic faces in studies in which the perception of facial expression is studied.

Visual marking, which is postulated recently, has more reasonably explained the phenomena of prioritizing selection that occur in temporal asynchrony between two groups of items in visual search [17]. In this present experiment, we altered some aspects of the standard paradigm and applied it into visual search of the emotional faces. In visual marking, participants search for the presence or absence of a target item among some distractor elements. There are three conditions. In a half-element condition, the target differs from the distractors by the possession of a unique feature. In an all-element condition, the other distrcators which had different features were also presented besides the distractors in half-element condition. In a gap condition, some items (old items) are presented for 1000ms, and then the other items (new items) are displayed. If the target appears, it will only be presented in the new items [7] [12]. Researchers found that the search performance in the gap condition is as efficient as the half-element condition in which old items are not displayed and more efficient than the all-element condition in which two groups of items are presented synchronously. This performance benefit has been called 'preview benefit' [17].

Detecting negative faces quickly and responding to them as efficiently as possible has an evolutionary benefit that is argued to have formed the basis for selection [10]. In addition, visual system can anticipate the appearance of new visual information. It would be adaptive to be able to selectively prioritize (or deprioritize) relevant objects, even if those faces have yet to emerge.

The present study sought to test whether it was faster to search a negative face than to search a positive face in the paradigm of visual marking [13]. We also especially wanted to know whether the negative faces captured more attention than the positive faces when the negative faces were used to be target and distractors respectively. On the other hand, the experimental materials were often letters in the study of visual marking. It was important to use schematic faces that express emotion as materials either because they accessed more to the reality or because they attributed to the research of shape change in visual marking [16]. Therefore, we also tested whether the preview benefit still exist when using affective materials.

2 Method

2.1 Participants

Eleven undergraduates (5 men and 6 women) were paid to serve as participants. All had self-reported normal or corrected-to-normal vision.

2.2 Stimuli and Apparatus

All stimulus generation and response recording were conducted by Matlab 7.0 program. Stimuli were randomly plotted in the cell of a 10×10 virtual matrix. The overall matrix dimensions were 20cm wide×20cm high. The visual search items consisted of schematic faces of positive emotion (happy faces, see Fig. 1. the left one), neutral emotion(neutral faces, see Fig. 1. the middle one) and negative emotion (sad faces, see Fig. 1. the right one) presented on a black background. The individual stimuli faces were 18mm wide×18mm high. In the all-element and gap conditions, the display size was 6, 8 or 10 items. An equal number of old items and new items were always present in the display. The target was present on 50% of the trials.

Fig. 1. The Example of the stimulus displays used in Experiment

2.3 Design and Procedure

Each trial started with a white fixation cross in the center of the screen for 1000ms. Following this, the search display was presented and remained until the participants responded to either the presence or absence of the face that searched. After the participants responded or did not respond after 3000ms, the display disappeared and a new trial began.

There were three main conditions: half-element, all-element and gap conditions. Every condition had six search types. The six search types of half-element condition were as following: search a happy face from neutral faces or negative faces, search a negative face from happy faces or neutral faces, and search a neutral face from happy faces or negative faces. The search types of all-element condition were the same as the half-element condition except that another kind of faces were also presented in the display, such as searching a happy face from negative faces and neutral faces, and so on; thus the display size was double that of the half-element condition. For the gap condition, following the fixation cross, some faces were first displayed for 1000ms, after which the other kinds of faces were added to the display. For example, some happy faces appeared for 1000ms, and then a negative face and some neutral faces were displayed.

All participants completed 18 blocks of trials lasting approximately 90min, with block order counterbalanced across the participants. Each block had 60 trials, with an equal number of present and absent trials within a block was presented in random order. Before each block of trials, the participants received a short practice block. If the participants had a low correct percent, they would have to engage the practice again until they passed.

3 Results

Before the data analyse, error trials were first identified and then removed. Outliers, identified as RTs of less than 250msec, and outside ± 3 SD, were removed from the data, resulting in a loss of 1.18% of the trials.

In the data analyse, at first, we analyzed whether the preview benefit existed when we searched the schematic faces and then analyzed the difference of the three kinds of schematic faces in search in detail.

3.1 Preview Benefit

Half-element condition, all-element condition and gap condition. The RTs for correct trials for each of the three conditions were entered into a three-way within-subject analysis of variance (ANOVA) with condition (half-element, all-element or gap condition), target (present or absent) and display size (6, 8, 10) as the main variables. For the half-element condition, the display size was matched to those in the all-element condition.

All of three main effects were significant: Condition, $F(2, 9) = 393.92$, $p < 0.001$; Target, $F(1, 10) = 398.62$, $p < 0.001$; and Display size, $F(2, 9) = 193.11$, $p < 0.001$. Present trials were faster than absent trials, RTs increased as the display size increased, and RTs were fastest in the half-element condition and slowest in the all-element condition (see Fig. 1.).

The two separate two-way within-subject ANOVAs showed the comparison of the gap condition and each of the two other conditions. RTs in the gap condition and half-element condition had no significant difference, $F(1, 10) = 1.437$, $p = 0.258$, which showed the performance in the gap condition was as efficient as the half-element condition. RTs were faster in the gap condition than in the all-element condition, $F(1, 10) = 593.63$, $p < 0.001$, which showed the performance in the gap condition was more efficient than the all-element condition.

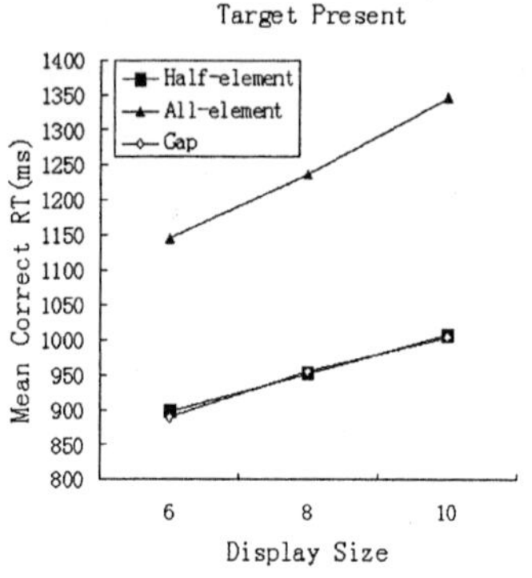

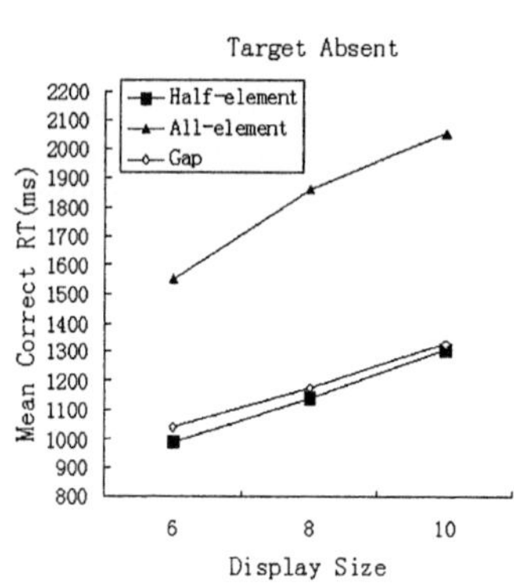

Fig. 2. Mean correct reaction times (RTs) as a function of condition and display size for present trials (the left) and absent trials (the right)

3.2 The Difference Among Happy Faces, Sad Faces and Neutral Faces in Visual Marking

Search a happy face, a sad face and a neutral face respectively. All of the three main effects were significant: Face type, $F(2, 9) = 128.64$, $p < 0.001$; Target, $F(1, 10) = 381.90$, $p < 0.001$; and Display Size, $F(2, 9) = 182.46$, $p < 0.001$. RTs were fastest in the search of a neutral face and slowest in the search of a happy face, present trials were faster than absent trials, and RTs increased as the display size increased. There was also a significant Face Type×Display Size interaction, $F(4, 7) = 9.51$, $p < 0.01$, and Target×Display Size interaction, $F(2, 9) = 459.26$, $p < 0.001$. No other interactions were significant.

Search a happy face in sad faces versus search a sad face in happy faces. The difference of the two kinds of search was significant: RTs in the search of a sad face in happy faces were faster than in the search of a happy face in sad faces, $F(1, 10) = 8.69$, $p < 0.05$. The results showed the search was asymmetry.

Search a happy face in neutral faces versus search a sad face in neutral faces. The difference of the two kinds of search was significant: RTs in the search of a sad face in some neutral faces were faster than in the search of a happy face, $F(1, 10) = 6.09$, $p < 0.05$.

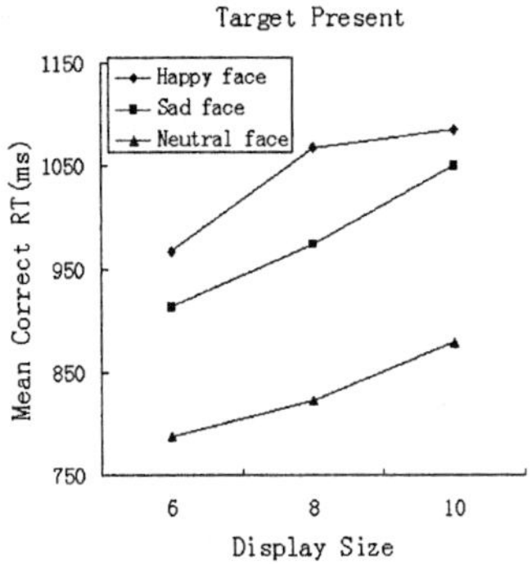

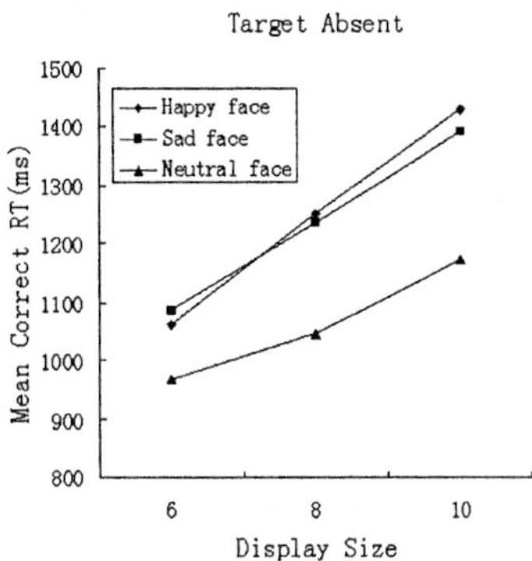

Fig. 3. Mean correct reaction times (RTs) as a function of three kinds of faces in gap condition and display size for present trials (the left) and absent trials (the right)

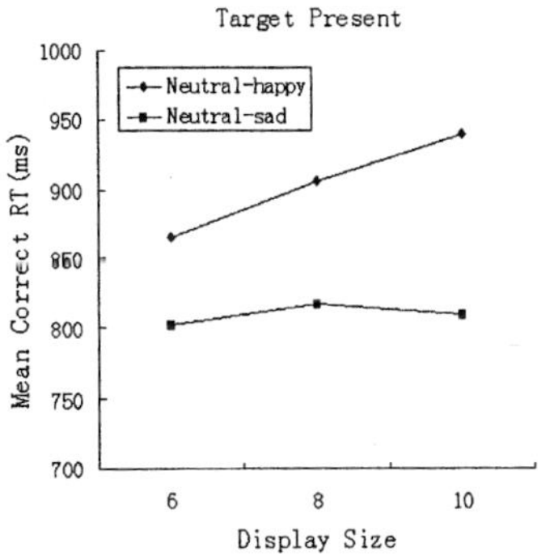

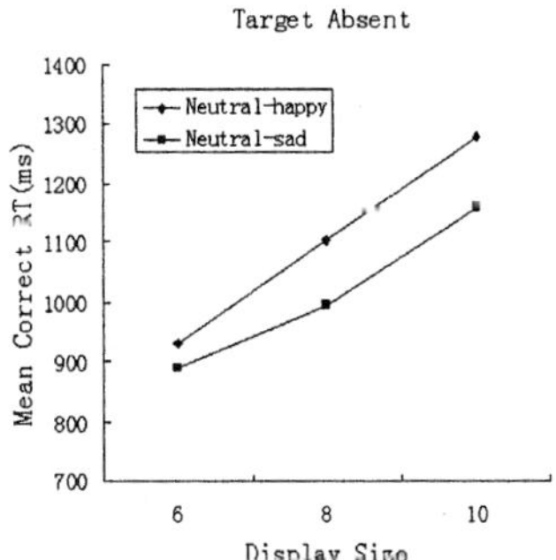

Fig. 4. Mean correct reaction times (RTs) as a function of three kinds of faces in half-element condition and display size for present trials (the left) and absent trials (the right)

3.3 The Analyses of the Sad Face as the Target or Distractors Separately

At first, we concerned the condition that a sad face was used to be the target. When the target was presented in gap condition (see Fig. 3.), the difference of the search of the three kinds of face was significant, $F(2, 9) = 135.59$, $p < 0.001$. In addition, RTs were faster in the search of a sad face than in the search of a happy face, $F(1, 10) = 22.31$, $p = 0.001$.

On the other hand, we concerned the condition that sad faces were used to be distractors so that we analyzed the difference between searching a neutral face in sad faces and in happy faces respectively. So we analyzed the half-element conditions (see Fig. 4.). Searching a neutral face in sad faces was faster than searching a neutral face in happy faces, $F(1, 10) = 6.82$, $p < 0.05$.

4 Discussion

The present experiment showed that the performance in gap condition was as efficient as the half-element condition and more efficient than all-element condition, which proved that the preview benefit still existed when using affective materials. When a sad face was used as the target, it was faster to search a sad face than to search a happy face. However, when sad faces were used to be distractors, they did not slow the RTs of searching a neutral face.

The results showed that it was faster when searching a sad face than searching a happy face in gap condition. However, in half-element condition, when sad faces and happy faces were both to be used as distractors, it was faster when searching a neutral face in sad faces than in happy faces. Mack and Rock (1998) found the participants detect the presence of a positive face more easily than detect a negative face. By this view, it seemed suspectable to draw a conclusion that negative faces capture attention more effectively than positive faces. One possible explanation is that the results are different in different search condition and different tasks [4].

The results showed that it was usually faster to search a neutral face than to search a happy face or a sad face. This difference might be induced by the local feature of the mouth in the faces (see Fig. 1.). However, Eastwood et al. (2001) approved that the differential guidance of focal attention was due to holistic face perception instead of part differences [4].

In gap condition, the preview benefit still existed when using the emotional faces as experimental materials and distractors could be effectively and efficiently ignored when they preceded by a preview display. In the all-element condition, the additional set of faces distractors affected search to the extent that it became slower than in the half-element condition, in which only two kinds of faces were present. In gap condition, search performance was as efficient as the half-element condition, indicating that the previously presented faces had no influence on search efficiency. We could confidently conclude that the present combination of stimuli and compound search task provides a solid basis for the occurrence of the preview benefit [9]. In addition, the results of this experiment provided more materials to the research of visual marking which has few kinds of figures as materials in the past and attributed to the influence of the shape change of stimulus on the preview benefit [16].

In summary, the present findings extended previous studies of the deployment of attention to emotionally expressive faces, while also contributing to our understanding of visual marking and attention. Future studies need to explore more specifically the constriction of attention by negative faces and positive faces.

Acknowledgement

This research was supported in part by grants from 973 Program of Chinese Ministry of Science and Technology (2002CB312103), from the National Natural Science Foundation of China (60433030 and 30270466), and from the Chinese Academy of Sciences (0302037).

References

1. Aronoff, J., Barclay, A. M., Stevenson, L. A.: The recognition of threatening facial stimuli. Journal of Personality & Social Psychology. 54 (1988) 647-655
2. Dolan, R. J.: Emotion, cognition and behavior. Science. 298 (2002) 1191-1194
3. Eastwood, J. D., Smilek, D., Merikle, P. M.: Negative facial expression captures attention and disrupts performance. Perception & Psychophysics. 65 (2003) 352-358
4. Eastwood, J., Smilek, D., Merikle, P. M.: Differential attentional guidance by unattended faces expressing positive and negative emotion. Perception & Pshchophysics. 63 (2001) 1004-1013
5. Farah, M. J., Wilson, K. D., Drain, M., Tanaka, J. N.: What is "special" about face perception? Psychological Review. 105 (1998) 482-498
6. Fenske, M. J., Eastwood, J. D.: Modulation of focused attention by faces expressing emotion: evidence from flanker tasks. Emotion. 3 (2003) 327-343
7. Gibson, B., S., Jiang, Y.: Visual marking and the perception of salience in visual search. Perception & Psychophysics. 63 (2001) 59-73
8. Hansen, C. N., Hansen, R. D.: Finding the face in the crowd: an anger superiority effect. Journal of Personality & Social Psychology. 54 (1988) 917-924
9. Kunar M A, Humphreys G W, Smith K J, etc. When a re-appearance is old news: visual marking survives occlusion. Journal of Experimental Psychology: Human Perception and Performance. 29 (2003) 185-198
10. Lipp, O. V., Derakshan, N., Waters, A. M., Logies, S.: Snakes and cats in the flower bed: fast detection is not specific to pictures of fear-relevant animals. Emotion. 4 (2004) 233-250
11. Ohman, A., Lundqvist, D., Esteves, F.: The face in the crowd revisited: A threat advantage with schematic stimuli. Journal of Personality & Social Psychology. 80 (2001) 381–396
12. Olivers, C. N. L., & Humphreys, G. W.: Visual marking inhibits singleton capture. Cognitive Psychology. 47 (2003): 1-42
13. Olivers, C. N. L., & Humphreys, G. W.: When visual marking meets the attentional blink: more evidence for top-down, limited-capacity inhibition. Journal of Experimental Psychology: Human Perception and Performance. 28 (2002) 22-42
14. Smilek, D., Eastwood, J. D., Merikle, P.: Does unattended information facilitate change detection? Journal of Experimental Psychology: Human Perception & Performance. 26 (2000) 480-487

15. Treisman, A., Souther, J.: Search asymmetry: a diagnostic for preattentive processing of separable features. Journal of Experimental Psychology: General. 114 (1985) 285-310
16. Watson D G, Humphreys G W. Visual marking and visual change. Journal of Experimental Psychology: Human Perception and Performance. 28 (2002) 379-395
17. Watson, D. G., Humphreys, G. W.: Visual marking: prioritizing selection for new objects by top-down attentional inhibition of old objects. Psychological Review. 104 (1997) 90-122
18. White, M.: Preattentive analysis of facial expressions of emotion, Cognition & Emotion. 9 (1995) 439-460
19. Wolfe, J.: Asymmetries in visual search: an introduction. Perception & Psychophysics. 63 (2001) 381-389

An Intelligent Algorithm for Enhancing Contrast for Image Based on Discrete Stationary Wavelet Transform and In-complete Beta Transform

Changjiang Zhang, Xiaodong Wang, and Haoran Zhang

College of Information Science and Engineering, Zhejiang Normal University, Postcode 321004, Jinhua, China
{zcj74922, wxd, hylt}@zjnu.cn

Abstract. Having implemented discrete stationary wavelet transform (DSWT) to an image, combining generalized cross validation (GCV), noise is reduced directly in the high frequency sub-bands which are at the better resolution levels and local contrast is enhanced by combining de-noising method with in-complete Beta transform (IBT) in the high frequency sub-bands which are at the worse resolution levels. In order to enhance the global contrast for the image, the low frequency sub-band image is also enhanced employing IBT and simulated annealing algorithm (SA). IBT is used to obtain non-linear gray transform curve. Transform parameters are determined by SA so as to obtain optimal non-linear gray transform parameters. In order to avoid the expensive time for traditional contrast enhancement algorithms, a new criterion is proposed with gray level histogram. Contrast type for original image is determined employing the new criterion. Gray transform parameters space is given respectively according to different contrast types, which shrinks gray transform parameters space greatly. Finally, the quality of enhanced image is evaluated by a total cost criterion. Experimental results show that the new algorithm can improve greatly the global and local contrast for an image while reducing efficiently gauss white noise (GWN) in the image. The new algorithm is more excellent in performance than histogram equalization (HE), un-sharpened mask algorithm (USM), WYQ algorithm and GWP algorithm.

1 Introduction

Traditional image enhancement algorithms are as following: point operators, space operators, transform operators and pseu-color contrast enhancement[1]. Recently, some new algorithms for image enhancement have been proposed. Such as Ramar and Shang-ming Zhou gave two kinds of algorithms for contrast enhancement based on fuzzy operators respectively[2-3]. However, the algorithm, which was proposed by Shang-ming Zhou, cannot be sure to be convergent. Performance of the algorithm is affected greatly by mathematic model[4]. Lots of improved histogram equalization algorithms were proposed to enhance contrast for kinds of images[5-9]. The visual quality cannot be improved greatly with above algorithms. Tubbs gave a simple gray transform algorithm to enhance contrast for images[10]. However, the computation burden of the

J. Tao, T. Tan, and R.W. Picard (Eds.): ACII 2005, LNCS 3784, pp. 135 – 143, 2005.

algorithm was large. Based on Tubbs algorithm, Zhou Ji-liu gave a new kind of genetic algorithm to optimize non-linear transform parameters[11]. Although the algorithm can enhance contrast for image well, the computation burden is larger. Existing many enhancement algorithms' intelligence and adaptability are worse and much artificial interference is required.

To solve above problems, a new algorithm employing incomplete Beta transform (IBT), DSWT and SA is proposed. To improve optimization speed and intelligence of algorithm, a new criterion is proposed based on gray level histogram. Contrast type for original image is determined employing the new criterion. Contrast for original images are classified into seven types: particular dark (PD), medium dark (MD), medium dark slightly (MDS), medium bright slightly (MBS), medium bright (MB), particular bright (PB) and good gray level distribution (GGLD). The new algorithm is still a kind of gray transform method. IBT operator transforms original image to a new space. A certain criterion function is used to optimize non-linear transform parameters. SA, which was given by William, is used to determine the optimal non-linear transform parameters. Having made DSWT to the original image, the global contrast is enhanced directly employing IBT in the low frequency sub-band image. The local contrast is enhanced employing de-nosing algorithm combining IBT, which was proposed by Tubbs in 1997[10]. We expand the IBT to SWT domain so as to extrude the detail in the original image. Noise is reduced directly at the better resolution levels by the de-noising algorithm. The de-noising asymptotic thresholds can be obtained employing GCV without the accurate statistic information of the noise. Local enhancement is enhanced combining de-noising algorithm with IBT. In order to evaluate the quality of the enhanced image, a new total cost criterion is proposed. Experimental results show that the new algorithm can enhance efficiently the global and local contrast for the image while the gauss white noise in the image can be reduced well. The total performance of the new algorithm is more excellent than the HE, USM, GWP algorithm and WYQ algorithm[11-12].

2 Transform Parameters Optimization with IBT and SA

Tubbs employed unitary incomplete Beta function to approximate above three non-linear functions[10]. The incomplete Beta function can be written as following:

$$F(u) = B^{-1}(\alpha,\beta) \times \int_0^u t^{\alpha-1}(1-t)^{\beta-1}dt, \quad 0 < \alpha, \beta < 10 \tag{1}$$

Let x shows gray level of original image, g indicates unitary gray level. We have:

$$g = \frac{x - \min(x)}{\max(x) - \min(x)} \tag{2}$$

Where $\min(x)$ and $\max(x)$ shows the minimum gray level and the maximum one in original image respectively. g is mapped to g':

$$g' = IB(a, b, g) \tag{3}$$

Let x' shows gray level of enhanced image, we have:

$$x' = [\max(x) - \min(x)]\, g' + \min(x) \tag{4}$$

Objective function in Ref. [1] is employed to evaluate the quality of enhanced image. The function can be written as following:

$$f = \frac{1}{MN}\sum_{i=1}^{M}\sum_{j=1}^{N} g'^2(i,j) - \left[\frac{1}{MN}\sum_{i=1}^{M}\sum_{j=1}^{N} g'(i,j)\right]^2 \tag{5}$$

Where M, N show width and height of original image. $g'(i,j)$ Shows gray level at (i,j) in enhanced image. More f is, more well proportioned the distribution of image gray level is.

Contrast classification criterion can be described in Fig.1:

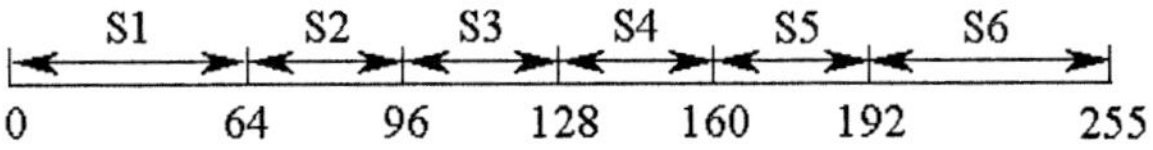

S1	S2	S3	S4	S5	S6
0–64	64–96	96–128	128–160	160–192	192–255

Fig. 1. Image classification sketch map based on gray level histogram

Given that original image has 255 gray levels, the whole gray level space is divided into six sub-spaces: S1, S2, S3 , S4 , S5 , S5。 Where Si (i=1, 2, ···, 6) is the number of all pixels which distribute in the ith sub-space. Let,

$$S = \max_{i=1}^{6} S_i, \quad S_1 = \sum_{k=2}^{6} \mathbf{Sk}, \quad S_2 = \sum_{k=2}^{5} \mathbf{Sk}, \quad S_3 = \sum_{k=1}^{5} \mathbf{Sk},$$

$$S_4 = S1 + S6, \quad S_5 = S2 + S3, \quad S_6 = S4 + S5,$$

Following classification criterion can be obtained:

$if\ S = S1\ \&\ S1 > S_1$

Image is PB;

$elseif\ S_2 > S_4\ \&\ S_5 > S_6\ \&\ S_5 > S1\ \&\ S_5 > S6\ \&\ S2 > S3$

Image is MD;

$elseif\ S_2 > S_4\ \&\ S_5 > S_6\ \&\ S_5 > S1\ \&\ S_5 > S6\ \&\ S2 < S3$

Image is MDS;

$elseif\ S_2 > S_4\ \&\ S_5 < S_6\ \&\ S1 < S_6\ \&\ S6 < S_6\ \&\ S4 > S5$

Image is MBS;

$elseif\ S_2 > S_4\ \&\ S_5 < S_6\ \&\ S1 < S_6\ \&\ S6 < S_6\ \&\ S4 < S5$

Image is MB;

$elseif\ S = S6\ \&\ S6 > S_3$

Image is PB;
else
Image is GGLD;
end

Where symbol $\&$ represents logic "and" operator.

We will employ the SA, which was given by William L. Goffe, to optimize transform parameters[5]. The range of α and β can be determined by Tab.1.

Table 1. Range of α and β

Parameter	PD	MD	MDS	MBS	MB	PB
α	[0 , 2]	[0 , 2]	[0 , 2]	[1 , 3]	[1 , 4]	[7 , 9]
β	[7 , 9]	[1 , 4]	[1 , 3]	[0 , 2]	[0 , 2]	[0 , 2]

Let $\mathbf{x} = (\alpha, \beta)$, $F(\mathbf{x})$ is function to be minimized, corresponding to (4). Where $a_i < \alpha, \beta < b_i$ $(i = 1,2)$, a_i and b_i $(i = 1,2)$ can be determined by Tab.1.

Having made lots of experiments and tests, a satisfactory result will be obtained to all contrast types of images when parameters above are determined as follows: $N_S = 20, N_T = 100, c_i = 2, \quad i = 1,2, T_0 = 5, r_T = 0.95$. Detail steps on SA can be found in Ref. [13].

3 Global Contrast Enhancement Based on SWT and IBT

SWT has been independently discovered several times, for different purpose and under different names[14]. The transform matrix exists a left inverse and its computation complexity is $O(N \log N)$.

Based on discrete stationary wavelet transform, IBT is employed to enhance the global and local contrast for image. The low frequency sub-band image is enhanced employing IBT. According to section 2, proper non-linear gray transform parameter α and β are selected to enhance the global contrast for the image.

4 Local Contrast Enhancement Based on SWT and IBT

I. M. Johnstone has proved that wavelet transform of the correlated noise is still stationary at all scales of every resolution level[15]. We consider discrete image model as follows:

$$\mathbf{g} = \mathbf{f} + \boldsymbol{\varepsilon} \tag{6}$$

Where, $\mathbf{g}=\{g[i,j]\}_{i,j}$ shows observation signal, $\mathrm{f}=\{f[i,j]\}_{i,j}$ indicates un-corrupted original image, $\boldsymbol{\varepsilon}=\{\varepsilon[i,j]\}_{i,j}$, $i=1,\cdots,M; j=1,\ldots,N$ is stationary signal. DSWT is implemented to equation (7):

$$\mathbf{X}=\mathbf{S}\mathbf{f} \tag{7}$$

$$\mathbf{V}=\mathbf{S}\boldsymbol{\varepsilon} \tag{8}$$

$$\mathbf{Y}=\mathbf{S}\mathbf{g} \tag{9}$$

$$\mathbf{Y}=\mathbf{X}+\mathbf{V} \tag{10}$$

Where $\mathbf{S}$ shows two-dimension stationary wavelet transform operator. "Soft-threshold" function is employed to reduce the noise in the image:

$$\mathbf{Y}_{\boldsymbol{\delta}}=\mathbf{T}_{\boldsymbol{\delta}}\circ\mathbf{Y} \tag{11}$$

$$\mathbf{X}_{\boldsymbol{\delta}}=\mathbf{T}_{\boldsymbol{\delta}}\circ\mathbf{X} \tag{12}$$

The total operator can be expressed as:

$$\mathbf{Z}_{\boldsymbol{\delta}}=\mathbf{S}^{-1}\circ\mathbf{T}_{\boldsymbol{\delta}}\circ\mathbf{S} \tag{13}$$

Where $\mathbf{T}_{\boldsymbol{\delta}}$ is correlated to threshold δ and input signal $\mathbf{g}$. If the statistic properties of the noise are employed to approximate the optimal threshold δ, standard variance σ will be used[15]. This will be almost impossible in practice according to above discussion. Generalized cross validation principle is employed to solve the problem[16].

Let the original signal $f[i,j]$ can be expressed employing the linear combination of its neighbor elements. Consider $\tilde{g}[i,j]$ is a linear combination of $g[k,l]$, thus special noise can be reduced. $g[i,j]$, which is the $[i,j]$ element of $\mathbf{g}$, is replaced by $\tilde{g}[i,j]$:

$$\tilde{\mathbf{g}}=\mathbf{Z}\cdot(g[1,1],\ldots,\tilde{g}[i,j],\ldots,g[M,N])^{T} \tag{14}$$

The same processing is repeated to all the components and proper thresholds can be obtained employing following equation:

$$OCV(\delta)=\frac{1}{MN}\sum_{i=1}^{M}\sum_{j=1}^{N}(g[i,j]-\tilde{g}_{\delta}[i,j])^{2} \tag{15}$$

The forms of $\tilde{g}[i, j]$ are many kinds, here let $\tilde{g}_\delta[i, j] = \tilde{g}[i, j]$, we have:

$$g[i, j] - \tilde{g}_\delta[i, j] = \frac{g[i, j] - g_\delta[i, j]}{1 - \tilde{z}[i, j]} \tag{16}$$

Where, $\tilde{z}[i, j] = \dfrac{g_\delta[i, j] - \tilde{g}_\delta[i, j]}{g[i, j] - \tilde{g}_\delta[i, j]} \approx z'[m, n] = \dfrac{\partial g_\delta[i, j]}{\partial g[k, l]}$

However, in equation (16), $z'[m, m]$ is either zero or 1. Thus "generalized cross validation" formula in the wavelet domain will be given as follows:

$$SGCV(\delta) = \frac{\frac{1}{MN} \cdot \left\| \mathbf{Y} - \mathbf{Y}_\delta \right\|^2}{\left[\frac{trace(\mathbf{I} - \mathbf{Z}'_\delta)}{MN} \right]^2} \tag{17}$$

Let $\delta^* = \arg\min MSE(\delta)$, $\tilde{\delta} = \arg\min GCV(\delta)$, M. Jansen has proved that $\tilde{\delta}$ is an asymptotic optimal solution[17].

5 Evaluation Criterion for Enhanced Image

The quality for enhanced image is evaluated employing following function[1]:

$$C_{contrast} = \frac{1}{MN} \sum_{x=1}^{M} \sum_{y=1}^{N} f'^2(x, y) - \left| \frac{1}{MN} \sum_{x=1}^{M} \sum_{y=1}^{N} f'(x, y) \right|^2 \tag{18}$$

Where $f'(x, y)$ is enhanced image. More the value of equation (18) is, better the contrast of the image is. Combining the ratio of signal-to-noise, a total evaluation criterion is propose as follows:

$$C_{total} = \frac{C_{contrast} * C_{snr}}{\beta} \tag{19}$$

More the value of equation (19) is, better the total visual quality is.

6 Experimental Results

Fig.2 shows gray transform curve, where $\alpha = 2.1924$, $\beta = 1.9542$. The transform curve is employed to enhance the global and the local contrast of Fig.3. Fig.4 (a) is a Lena image, which is corrupted by GWN ($\sigma = 8.8316$). In order to extrude excellent performance of the new algorithm, two traditional contrast enhancement algorithms are compared with the new algorithm. They are HE and USM respectively. Fig.4 (b)-Fig.4 (f) show enhanced images by HE, USM, the new algorithm, GWP and WYQ algorithm respectively.

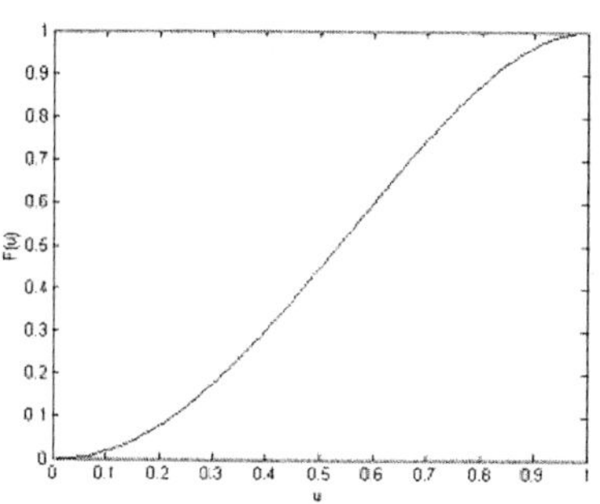

Fig. 2. Gray levels transform curve

Fig. 3. Lena image

($\alpha = 2.1924$, $\beta = 1.9542$) ($\alpha = 1.9819$, $\beta = 3.3340$)

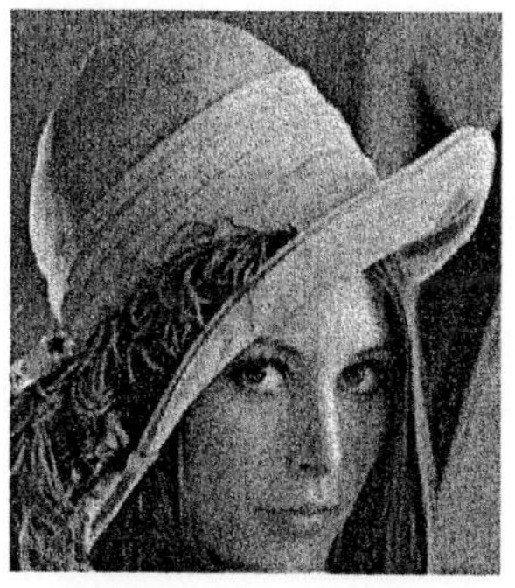

(a) Lena image corrupted by AGWN

(b) Enhanced image by HE

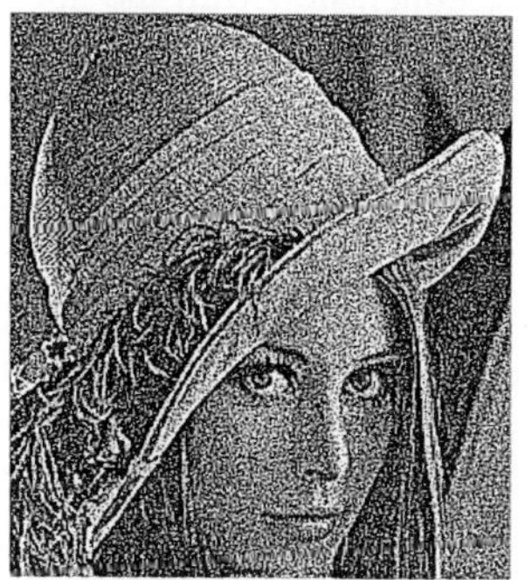

(c) Enhanced image by USM

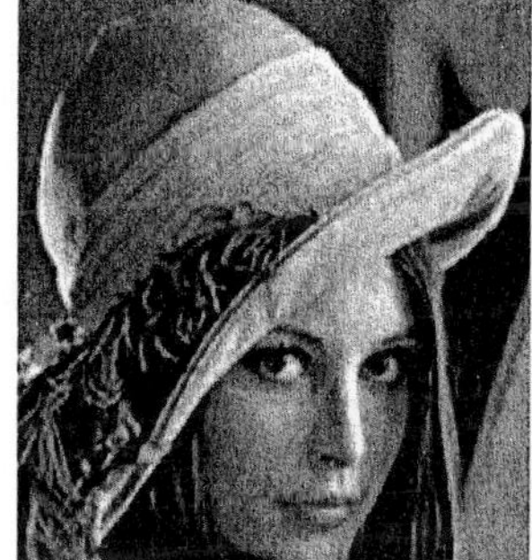

(d) Enhanced image by the new algorithm

Fig. 4. Enhanced images by five algorithms

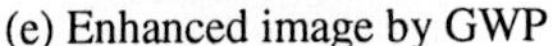

(e) Enhanced image by GWP (f) Enhanced image by the WYQ

Fig. 4. (*Continued*)

According to section 3, the contrast type of Fig.4 (a) is "MBS". From the experimental results above, the noise in the image is enhanced greatly when USM and HIS enhance the image, which is obvious in Fig.4 (b)-(c). Noise reduction is also considered in Ref.[11] and Ref.[12]. The total contrast is better employing GWP algorithm, however, it is not efficient to reduce the noise in the image. From Fig.4 (e), it is obvious that the noise in the image is enhanced greatly and the background clutter is also enlarged. This is very obvious in Fig.4 (e). Although WYQ algorithm can reduce the noise in the image well, the whole brightness of the image is too high so that some detail in the image lost. Lots of burr is produced in Fig.4 (f), such as the hat of Lena. Compared with the above four algorithms, the new algorithm can reduce efficiently GWN in the image while enhance the contrast for the image well. It is obvious that the new algorithm is more excellent in the total performance than USM, HIS, GWP and WYQ.

In order to explain further the efficiency of the new algorithm, equation (19) is used to evaluate the quality of enhanced images. The total cost of enhanced images by HIS, USH, SWT, GWP and WYQ in Fig.5 are 27.0131, -95.5358, 38.5407, 8.7313 and –2.9249 respectively. This can draw the same conclusion with the above analysis to enhanced images.

7 Conclusion

Employing GCV, the asymptotic optimal de-noising threshold can be obtained when the accurate statistic properties are not prior-known. The global contrast of the image is enhanced directly combining IBT and SA. The local contrast of the image is enhanced combining de-nosing algorithm and IBT. Experimental results show that the new algorithm can enhance adaptively the global and local contrast for image effectively while keeping detail information in the original image well. The total performance of the new algorithm is more excellent than HE, USM, GWP and WYQ algorithm. The total computation complexity of the new algorithm is O (MN) log (MN), where M and N are the width and height of the original image.

References

1. Azriel Rosenfield, Avinash C K.: Digital Picture Processing. New York: Academic Press, (1982)
2. Ramar K, Arumugam S, Sivanandam S N.: Enhancement of noisy and blurred images: A fuzzy operator approach. Advances in Modeling and Analysis, **42** (1992) 49-60
3. Shang-Ming Zhou, Qiang Gan: A new fuzzy relaxation algorithm for image contrast enhancement. Proceedings of the 3rd International Symposium on Image and Signal Processing and Analysis, **1** (2003) 11-16
4. Ming Tang, SongDe Ma, Jing Xiao: Model-based adaptive enhancement of far infrared image sequences. Pattern Recognition, **30** (2000) 827-835
5. Stark, J.A.: Adaptive image contrast enhancement using generalizations of histogram equalization. IEEE Transactions on Image Processing, **9** (2000) 889-896
6. Joung-Youn Kim, Lee-Sup Kim: An advanced contrast enhancement using partially overlapped sub-block histogram equalization. IEEE Transactions on Circuits and Systems for Video Technology, **11** (2001) 475-484
7. Seungjoon Yang, Jae Hwan Oh, Yungjun Park: Contrast enhancement using histogram equalization with bin underflow and overflow. International Conference on Image Processing, 2003. Proceedings, **1** (2003) 881-884
8. Soong-Der Chen, Ramli, A.R.: Contrast enhancement using recursive mean-separate histogram equalization for scalable brightness preservation. IEEE Transactions on Consumer Electronics, **49** (2003) 1301-1309
9. Soong-Der Chen, Ramli, A.R.: Minimum mean brightness error bi-histogram equalization in contrast enhancement. IEEE Transactions on Consumer Electronics, **48** (2003) 1201-1207
10. Tubbs J D.: A note on parametric image enhancement. Pattern Recognition, **30** (1997) 616-621
11. GONG Wu-Peng, WANG Yong-Zhong: Contrast enhancement of infrared image via wavelet transforms. Chinese Journal of National University of Defense Technology, **22** (2000) 117-119
12. WU Ying-Qian, SHI Peng-Fei: Approach on image contrast enhancement based on wavelet transform. Chinese J. Infrared and Laser Engineering, **32** (2003) 4-7
13. William L. Goffe, Gary D. Ferrier, John Rogers: Global optimization of statistical functions with simulated annealing. Journal of Econometrics, **60** (1994) 65-99
14. M.Lang,H.Guo,J.E. odegend, C.S. Burrus, R.O.Wells, Jr.: Nonlinear processing of a shift-invariant DWT for noise reduction. In SPIE Conference on wavelet applications, **2491** (1995) 76-82
15. I.M.Johnstone, B.W.Silverman: Wavelet threshold estimators for data with correlated noise. Journal of the Royal Statistical Society, Series B, **59** (1997) 319-351
16. P. Hall and I. Koch: On the feasibility of cross-validation in image analysis. SIAM J.Appl. Math, **52** (1992) 292-313
17. Maarten Jansen, Geert Uytterhoeven, Adhemar Bultheel: Image de-nosing by integer wavelet transforms and generalized cross validation. Technical Report TW264, Department of Computer Science, Katholieke Universiteit, Leuven, Belguim, August 1997

Automatic Facial Expression Recognition Using Linear and Nonlinear Holistic Spatial Analysis

Rui Ma and Jiaxin Wang

State Key Laboratory of Intelligent Technology and Systems,
Department of Computer Science, Tsinghua University, Beijing, 100084, P.R. China
mr02@mails.tsinghua.edu.cn

Abstract. This paper is engaged in the holistic spatial analysis on facial expression images. We present a systematic comparison of machine learning methods applied to the problem of automatic facial expression recognition, including supervised and unsupervised subspace analysis, SVM classifier and their nonlinear versions. Image-based holistic spatial analysis is more adaptive to recognition task in that it automatically learns the inner structure of training samples and extracts the most pertinent features for classification. Nonlinear analysis methods which could extract higher order dependencies among input patterns are supposed to promote the performance of classification. Surprisingly, the linear classifiers outperformed their nonlinear versions in our experiments. We proposed a new feature selection method named the Weighted Saliency Maps(WSM). Compared to other feature selection schemes such as Adaboost and PCA, WSM has the advantage of being simple, fast and flexible.

1 Introduction and Motivation

1.1 Background of Facial Expression Analysis

Recent intelligent systems have devoted a great deal of efforts to the effective affective communication between human beings and mechanical entities in the virtual environment. The conveying and understanding of affective information via facial expression, voice, pose and gesture features largely in person-to-person communication. The purpose of affective communication is to incorporate such natural ways of communication in the person-to-machine interaction, and ultimately enlarging to the scope of natural machine-to-machine communication.

One of the bases in affective communication is the automatic recognition of human emotional expressions. Human face can significantly reflect the emotional state of a person, and thus maybe one of the most natural means in human-machine interaction. Although the authentic emotions are affected by a variety of factors and might not be exactly revealed by the exterior visible facial clues, the explicit facial expression is evidently the most direct indicator of a person's inner feelings. Human facial expression recognition is indispensable to a robust intelligent system as speech and gestures.

Automatic facial expression recognition has been explored by researchers in a few decades and various methods were proposed in the relevant literature. Generally, facial expression recognition falls into two major categories: recognizing facial expression type and detecting visible facial actions. The former approach assigned each

J. Tao, T. Tan, and R.W. Picard (Eds.): ACII 2005, LNCS 3784, pp. 144 – 151, 2005.

face image to be one of the seven primary emotions postulated by Ekman and Friesen in 1971 or other trained expression types. These basic emotions which are ubiquitous across all human cultures comprise anger, disgust, fear, joy, neutral, sadness and surprise. In the latter case, it is more emphasized on the visible LOCAL facial features demonstrated in an image. Recognition methods fallen in this scenario attempt to detect and recognize the appearance of one single facial action unit or a combination of several facial action units descirbed in a FACS system, not necessarily assigning the face image as a specific type of expression.

The pioneering work of facial expression analysis by Mase and Pentland employed optical flow to estimate the activity of 12 facial muscles. Other methods have been proposed to focus on the analysis of facial motions. However, these motion-based approaches ignored other important aspects of facial expression than the motion clues[1]. Via a set of measurable facial features, one of the earliest works to identify facial expressions concentrated on using a flexible face model and classification was made on these predefined features. Feature location and displacement were analyzed by optical flow or active appearance model. Facial actions or expressions were determined with neural networks or nonlinear embedding[11]. These approaches drastically reduced the dimensionality of input features, but might lose vital information in the process. As an alternative to feature-based methods, the holistic analysis takes into account all the information contained in an image and focuses on discovering the intrinsic structural information via a set of sample images. Unsupervised holistic analyses such as principal component analysis(PCA) and independent component analysis(ICA) have been used to reveal the statistical dependencies among input features and to find the adaptive subspaces for classification[4,5]. Lyons applied the supervised Fisher linear discriminant analysis(FDA) to learn an adequate linear subspace from class-specified training samples and the samples projected to this subspace can be best separated[9].

1.2 Motivation and Proposed Approach

However, both PCA and FDA address the linear projection. Representation of PCA and FDA projection encodes pattern information based on second order dependencies. In fact, the underlying features most useful for facial expression classification may lie within the higher order statistical dependencies among input features. Bartlett demonstrated that the ICA is superior to PCA in human face recognition in that ICA learns the higher-order dependencies in the input besides the correlations[1]. However, ICA seems to be time-consuming and whether the facial expression is composed of a set of independent components is not clear yet. People still try to seek out other solutions for this task. Our method is motivated by this concern and the nonlinear holistic spatial analysis based on kernel methods would be investigated on the task of automatic facial expression recognition.

Kernel trick is one of the vital reasons that make Support Vector Machine successful in solving nonlinear separable problems. Scholkopf combined kernel method with classical PCA and the extended Kernel PCA showed its good ability in extracting nonlinear features for efficient classification[10]. Likewise, Kernel FDA was also investigated and employed to many applications in computer vision. Existing works demonstrated the ability of Kernel FDA in seeking out the nonlinear discriminant features among the input patterns. In this paper, both the kernel based analyses will be applied to facial expression recognition.

Another important aspect is about feature selection. Dailey et al. pointed out that local PCA carried out on random windows on face image can obtain better results in facial expression classification than performing PCA on a whole image[4]. While Bartlett indicated that the holistic PCA and local PCA has the same effect, what contributes to this difference is the selection of random windows[1]. Lyons worked out a saliency map on human face that could facilitate facial expression recognition[9]. This map was actually a set of feature points such as eye corners sorted by their discriminating powers. Littlewort employed Adaboost to select features which were then fed into the SVM classifiers for recognition[8]. These measures not only improve the classification accuracy but also speed up the recognition step which makes the real-time facial expression recognition possible. The idea of feature selection will also be incorporated in our system. We proposed a novel feature selection method named Weighted Saliency Maps, see section 3.1.

2 Nonlinear Holistic Spatial Analysis

The proposed approaches in this paper address nonlinear holistic spatial analysis on face images in extracting higher order statistical dependencies of training samples. Two kernel-based methods are examined: Kernel PCA and Kernel FDA.

2.1 Kernel Principal Component Analysis

The idea of Kernel Principal Component Analysis is to find a feature space through kernel method, and then apply PCA in this space to seek the orthonormal components that denote the maximal variances of input features.

Given a set of centered samples(zero mean, unit variance) $\{x_1, x_2, \ldots\ldots, x_N\}$, $x_k \in R^n$, classical PCA finds a set of orthonormal vectors by solving the eigenvalue problem: $\lambda v = Cv$, where C is the covariance matrix of input $x_k, k = 1 \ldots N$, eigenvalues $\lambda \geq 0$, and eigenvectors $v \in R^n \setminus \{0\}$.

In Kernel PCA, each vector of x is projected from the input space to a higher feature space F. $y = \phi(x)$, and $y \in F$. The dimensionality of F can be arbitrarily large. Applying PCA in F is equivalent to the eigenvalue problem: $\lambda v^{\phi} = C^{\phi} v^{\phi}$, where C^{ϕ} is the covariance matrix. It is often infeasible to compute C^{ϕ} and work out the v^{ϕ} in the high dimensional space F. Actually, kernel trick informs us that if we could represent any algorithm as the inner product of samples, we might easily construct the nonlinear version of it.

In fact, all solutions of v^{ϕ} with $\lambda \neq 0$ must lie in the span of $\phi(x_1), \phi(x_2), \ldots\ldots \phi(x_N)$, that is $v^{\phi} = \sum_{i=1}^{N} \alpha_i \phi(x_i)$, where coefficients $\alpha_i \in R, i = 1, \ldots, N$. Consider the following equation

$$\lambda(\phi(x_k) \cdot v^{\phi}) = (\phi(x_k) \cdot C^{\phi} v^{\phi}),\ \forall k = 1, \ldots, N$$

If we define a $N \times N$ matrix K by $K_{ij} = (\phi(x_i) \cdot \phi(x_j)) = k(x_i, x_j)$, combining the above equations, we could get the eigenvalue problem of Kernel PCA:

$$N\lambda K\alpha = K^2\alpha \equiv N\lambda\alpha = K\alpha$$

Eigenvector $\alpha = [\alpha_1, \alpha_2, ..., \alpha_N]^T$. Then normalize the each eigenvectors by their corresponding eigenvalues with $1 = \lambda(\alpha \cdot \alpha)$.

2.2 Kernel Fisher Discriminant Analysis

Similarly, Kernel Fisher Discriminant Analysis first maps the input patterns to a higher dimensional feature space by a nonlinear mapping, and then applies Fisher Linear Discriminant Analysis to obtain a reduced space for better classifying the patterns. Given a set of centered samples(zero mean, unit variance) $\{x_1, x_2, ..., x_N\}$ labeled as c classes, $x_k \in R^n$, and N_i samples are within class x_i, $N = \sum_{i=1}^{c} N_i$. In KFDA, the optimal projection w^ϕ is the solution of following equation:

$$w^\phi = \arg\max_{w^\phi} J(w^\phi) = \arg\max_{w^\phi} \frac{(w^\phi)^T S_B^\phi w^\phi}{(w^\phi)^T S_W^\phi w^\phi}.$$

S_B^ϕ and S_W^ϕ is the within-class and between-class scatter matrix respectively.

$$S_B^\phi = \sum_{i=1}^{c} N_i(\mu_i^\phi - \mu^\phi)(\mu_i^\phi - \mu^\phi)^T,$$

$$S_W^\phi = \sum_{i=1}^{c} \sum_{x_k \in X_i} (\phi(x_k) - \mu_i^\phi)(\phi(x_k) - \mu_i^\phi)^T,$$

where $\mu^\phi = \frac{1}{N}\sum_{k=1}^{N}\phi(x_k)$, $\mu_i^\phi = \frac{1}{N_i}\sum_{k=1}^{N_i}\phi(x_k)$, $i = 1, ..., c$.

Likewise, all solutions of w^ϕ must lie in the span of $\phi(x_1), \phi(x_2), ...\phi(x_N)$, that is, there exists $\alpha = [\alpha_1, \alpha_2, ..., \alpha_N]^T$, such that $w^\phi = \sum_{i=1}^{N} \alpha_i \phi(x_i) = \Phi\alpha$,

where $\Phi = [\phi(x_1), ..., \phi(x_N)]$. Project $\phi(x_k)$ on w^ϕ, we get

$$(w^\phi)^T \phi(x_k) = \alpha^T \Phi^T \phi(x_k) = \alpha^T \begin{bmatrix} (\phi(x_1) \cdot \phi(x_k)) \\ \vdots \\ (\phi(x_N) \cdot \phi(x_k)) \end{bmatrix} = \alpha^T \begin{bmatrix} k(x_1, x_k) \\ \vdots \\ k(x_N, x_k) \end{bmatrix} = \alpha^T \xi_k.$$

Denote $K_B = \sum_{i=1}^{c} N_i(m_i - m)(m_i - m)^T$, $K_W = \sum_{i=1}^{c} \sum_{\xi_k \in F_i} (\xi_k - m_i)(\xi_k - m_i)^T$, $m_i - \sum_{k=1}^{N_i} \xi_k$,

then, $(w^\phi)^T S_B^\phi w^\phi = \alpha^T K_B \alpha$ and $(w^\phi)^T S_W^\phi w^\phi = \alpha^T K_W \alpha$. Kernel FDA is then equivalent to solving $\alpha = \arg\max_\alpha J(\alpha) = \arg\max_\alpha \frac{\alpha^T K_B \alpha}{\alpha^T K_W \alpha}$.

3 Facial Expression Classification

The Japanese JAFFE expression database is employed in our experiments for the evaluation of our methods. It comprises 213 gray-level images of ten Japanese female subjects, each one expressing seven basic types of expressions. Several factors add difficulty to classification: the images have some variation in lighting, and some faces have slight in-plane and out-of-plane rotation. The original 256*256 pixels images were preprocessed to get the 70*50 pixels down-sampled aligned face images, with most of the background eliminated. The database was then enlarged to 426 images with the mirrored pictures.

3.1 Features and Feature Selection

The features been used in the literature include the pixel intensity values of original images, diff.-images[5] and Gabor filtered images. 2D Gabor representation is obtained by filtering the images with a set of Gabor wavelets of different orientations and frequencies[4, 8, 9]. Since human face expressions differ with subtle changes in local areas, we would investigate how to capture these pertinent features to facilitate the classification. Thus the aim of feature selection is to reduce the dimensionality of input patterns to make the computation feasible, meanwhile, to retain the most salient features that would reflect the expressional changes. In [4, 5] features are selected on the fixed grid called Gabor Jet. Littlewort et al. used Adaboost to iteratively select features. We here propose a new method named Weighted Saliency Maps(WSM) to select the appropriate features for facial expression recognition. The idea partly comes from selecting ICs in[1]. We compute the ratio of between-class variance and within-class variance of each feature across all the training samples. Denote an arbitrary feature as $[f_1, f_2, ..., f_N]$, N is the number of training samples, then the ratio is:

$$\sigma_k = \frac{Var_B}{Var_W}, \quad k = 1, ..., n$$

where between-class variance $Var_B = \sum_{i=1}^{c} \left(\frac{1}{N_i} \sum_{j=1}^{N_i} f_j - \frac{1}{N} \sum_{k=1}^{N} f_k \right)$,

within-class variance $Var_W = \sum_{i=1}^{c} \sum_{j=1}^{N_i} \left(f_j - \frac{1}{N_i} \sum_{k=1}^{N_i} f_k \right)^2$,

n is the number of features. All the features are computed with above equations and sorted according to the obtained ratios(weights) in descending order. The first 500 features sensitive to each of the seven basic facial expressions are shown in Fig.1. They are marked in the image as grayscale points. The darkness of each pixel is proportional to its weight.

Fig. 1. Weighted Saliency Maps for seven basic expressions

Compared to the fixed feature points in Gabor Jet, feature selection methods based on learning are more promising to produce a better feature set. Adaboost iteratively selects a set of features based on their recognition errors respectively. PCA finds a subspace by solving an eigen problem. Input patterns project onto this space and transform to new features. In comparison with PCA, Adaboost and WSM only investigate the classification ability of each feature solely, while PCA takes into account the whole distribution of training samples. Nonetheless, Adaboost and WSM utilize the class label of each sample in learning the discriminant power of each feature, which to some extent would yield better result than PCA. Adaboost is an iterative process which may be not very fast to re-select pertinent features in a real-time application. WSM is much faster than PCA and Adaboost, and it has the flexibility of employing different criteria to promote the performance. In our experiment, WSM could remarkably reduce the dimensionality of input feature space and speed up the training process, with a little promotion of performance with certain classifiers.

3.2 Experiments

We compared the performance of machine learning methods applied to the problem of automatic facial expression recognition, including supervised subspace analysis such as FDA and MDA, unsupervised subspace analysis such as PCA and ICA, SVM classifier and their nonlinear versions. We choose the polynomial kernel in KPCA, KFDA and RBF kernel in SVM. In the reduced space, recognition was performed based on the Nearest Neighbor Classifier except in SVM approach. Generalization performance was tested using the leave-one-subject-out cross-validation. Since FDA and SVM make binary decisions, the one-against-the-rest scheme was adopted. In other words, in each round of training, we computed seven projection matrices in subspace-based approach, and seven SVM classifiers in SVM-based approach.

We first compare the performance of FDA, KFDA, linear SVM and SVM with RBF kernels under different feature selection schemes(Fig.2). There are 3500 possible features in the grayscale images. We can see that with PCA feature selection or no feature selection, the performances for each of the four methods are the same. With WSM feature selection, the performances promote a little in linear SVM but drop in FDA.

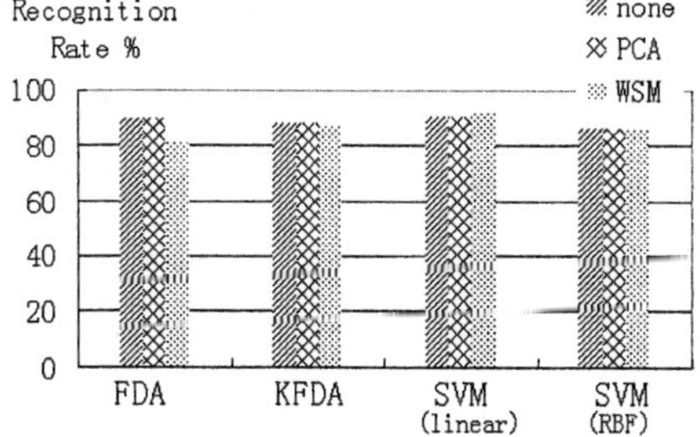

Recognition Rate (%)	Feature selection		
	None	PCA	WSM
FDA	89.5	89.5	80.5
KFDA	87.7	87.7	07.0
SVM (linear)	90.7	90.7	91.4
SVM (RBF)	85.7	85.7	85.7

Fig. 2. Leave-one-out generalization performance of FDA, KFDA, linear SVM and SVM with RBF kernels(70*50 pixels images). They are compared with no feature selection, with feature selection by PCA, and with feature selection by WSM.

We then compare the leave-one-out generalization performance of PCA, FDA, MDA, ICA, SVM, KPCA, and KFDA on facial expression recognition(Fig. 3). The

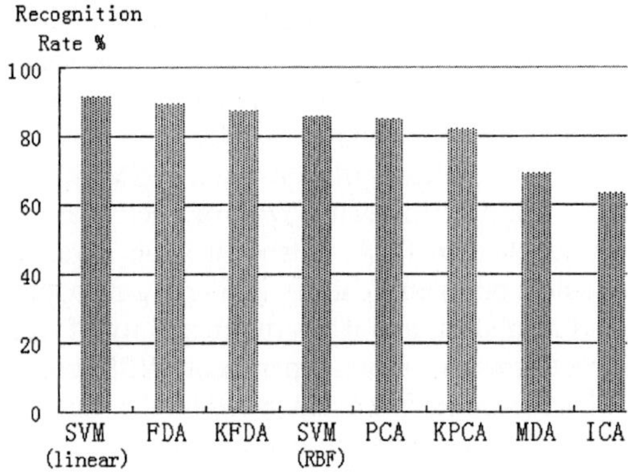

Method	Recognition Rate (%)
SVM (linear)	91.4
FDA	89.5
KFDA	87.7
SVM (RBF)	85.7
PCA	85.0
KPCA	81.9
MDA	69.0
ICA	63.0

Fig. 3. Leave-one-out generalization performance of linear SVM, FDA, KFDA, SVM with RBF kernels, PCA, KPCA, MDA and ICA (70*50 pixels images)

best performance was gained with linear SVM and 1900 WSM features. We obtained the following conclusions from the experiments:

1) Supervised vs. unsupervised learning. Supervised learning methods showed a better performance than unsupervised ones, such as SVM and FDA outperformed PCA and ICA, and so did their nonlinear versions. The class labels of training samples were utilized in supervised learning, thus facilitated the classification.
2) *Nonlinear vs. linear methods.* The linear methods outperformed their kernel-based nonlinear versions in our experiments, as illustrated in linear SVM vs. SVM with RBF kernels, PCA vs. KPCA, and FDA vs. KFDA with polynomial kernels.
3) *Binary decision vs. multiple decision.* The multiple decision classifiers MDA and ICA yielded the recognition rate of 69.0% and 63.0%, respectively. Overall, the binary decision classifiers outperformed multiple decision classifiers.

4 Conclusions

We generally make the comprehensive comparison and discussion on facial expression classification by using the holistic spatial analysis methods, including supervised and unsupervised subspace analysis, SVM and their nonlinear versions. Compared with model-based and feature-based approach to facial expression recognition, image-based holistic spatial analysis is more adaptive to different recognition task. Features relevant to expression classification or the most discriminant subspaces are learned directly from training images.

We proposed a novel feature selection method named Weighted Saliency Maps(WSM). Compared with other feature selection schemes, as Adaboost randomly select features by testing their exclusive performance on a weak classifier iteratively and PCA tries to solve an eigenvalue problem to produce an orthonormal set for projection, WSM has the advantage of being simple, fast and flexible. The features are extracted with supervised learning, which makes them different and superior to those predefined features in feature-based approach.

References

1. M.S.Bartlett: Face Image Analysis by Unsupervised Learning. Boston: Kluwer Academic Publishers. 2001
2. M.S.Bartlett, J.R.Movellan and T.J.Sejnowski: Face Recognition by Independent Component Analysis. IEEE Transaction on Neural Networks. **13**(2002):1450-1460
3. P.N.Belhumeur, J.P.Hespanha and D.J.Kriegman: Eigenfaces vs. Fisherfaces: Recognition Using Class Specific Linear Projection. IEEE Transaction on Pattern Analysis and Machine Intelligence. **19**(1997):711-720
4. M.N.Dailey and G.W.Cottrell. PCA = Gabor for Expression Recognition. UCSD Computer Science and Engineering Technical Report CS-629, October 26 1999
5. G.Donato, M.S.Bartlett et al.: Classifying Facial Actions. IEEE Transaction on Pattern Analysis and Machine Intelligence. **21**(1999):974-989
6. R.O.Duda, P.E.Hart and D.G.Stork: Pattern Classification. Second Edition. New York: Wiley, 2000
7. B.Fasel and J.Luettin: Automatic Facial Expression Analysis: A Survey. Pattern Recognition. **36**(2003):259-275
8. G.Littlewort, M.S.Bartlett,I.Fasel,J.Susskind and J.Movellan: Dynamics of Facial Expression Extracted Automatically from Video. In IEEE Conference on Computer Vision and Pattern Recognition. Workshop on Face Processing in Video. 2004.
9. M.J.Lyons, J.Budynek and S.Akamatsu: Automatic Classification of Single Facial Images. IEEE Transaction on Pattern Analysis and Machine Intelligence. **21**(1999):1357-1362
10. B. Scholkopf, A.Smola, and K.R.Muller: Nonlinear Component Analysis as A Kernel Eigenvalue Problem. Neural Computation, **10**(1998):1299-1319
11. Ya Chang, Chang Hu, and Matthew Turk. Probabilistic Expression Analysis on Manifolds. Proc. IEEE Conference on Computer Vision and Pattern Recognition. **2**(2004):520-527

A Novel Regularized Fisher Discriminant Method for Face Recognition Based on Subspace and Rank Lifting Scheme

Wen-Sheng Chen[1], Pong Chi Yuen[2], Jian Huang[2], Jianhuang Lai[3], and Jianliang Tang[1]

[1] Department of Mathematics, Shenzhen University, P.R. China 518060
[2] Key Laboratory of Mathematics Mechanization, CAS, Beijing, P.R. China 100080
{chenws, jtang}@szu.edu.cn
[3] Department of Computer Science, Hong Kong Baptist University, Hong Kong
{pcyuen, jhuang}@comp.hkbu.edu.hk
[4] Department of Mathematics, Sun Yat-Sen University, P.R. China 510275
stsljh@zsu.edu.cn

Abstract. The null space $N(S_t)$ of total scatter matrix S_t contains no useful information for pattern classification. So, discarding the null space $N(S_t)$ results in dimensionality reduction without loss discriminant power. Combining this subspace technique with proposed rank lifting scheme, a new regularized Fisher discriminant (SL-RFD) method is developed to deal with the small sample size (S3) problem in face recognition. Two public available databases, namely FERET and CMU PIE databases, are exploited to evaluate the proposed algorithm. Comparing with existing LDA-based methods in solving the S3 problem, the proposed SL-RFD method gives the best performance.

Keywords: Face recognition, linear discriminant analysis, small sample size problem, Regularized method, Null space.

1 Introduction

In appearance-based approaches, linear discriminant analysis (LDA) is a popular statistic method, which was developed in 1997 [1]. After that, a large number of LDA-based algorithms/systems have been proposed. LDA is theoretically sound and a number of LDA-based face recognition algorithms/systems have been developed in the last decade [1]-[11]. However, the major drawback of LDA is the so-called Small Sample Size (S3) problem. This problem always occurs when the total number of training samples is smaller than the dimensionality of feature vector. Under this situation, the within-class scatter matrix S_w becomes singular and direct applying LDA approach is impossible. To overcome S3 problem, some algorithms, such as Fisherface method [1], subspace methods (Direct LDA [2], Huang et al's method [7]) and regularized discriminant analysis (RDA) method [8] etc, are developed to solve S3 problem. Fisherface and Direct LDA are implemented in the sub-feature-space, not in the full feature space. So it maybe

J. Tao, T. Tan, and R.W. Picard (Eds.): ACII 2005, LNCS 3784, pp. 152–159, 2005.

lost some useful discriminant information in subspace for PR. For existing RDA method [8], it proposed 3-parameter method to solve S3 problem. Although this method is executed in the full sample space, it's complexity and difficult to determine three optimal parameters.

Huang et al proposed a improved null space method. It was shown in [7] that the null space of the total scatter matrix S_t is the intersection of the null spaces of within-class scatter matrix S_w and between-class scatter matrix S_b, i.e., $N(S_t) = N(S_w) \cap N(S_b)$. Moreover, this intersection set $N(S_t)$, the null space of S_t, contains no useful information for pattern classification. So, they first discard the null space $N(S_t)$ for dimensionality reduction without loss useful discriminant information. This dimensionality reduction technique will be exploited in this paper.

In many situations, it is known that $\text{rank}(S_w) = N - C$, where N is the total number of training data, C is the number of classes. To deal with S3 problem, we first show a rank lifting theorem by linear algebraic theory. According to this theorem, a single parameter t is introduced to lift the rank of matrix Φ_w and to obtain a d by N full rank matrix $\tilde{\Phi}_w$. Also, the rank of within-class scatter matrix $S_w(= \Phi_w \Phi_w^T)$ is lifted from $N - C$ to N. Namely, we can obtain a semi-regularized within-class scatter matrix $\tilde{S}_w(= \tilde{\Phi}_w \tilde{\Phi}_w^T)$, the rank of which is N. Subsequently, the null space of S_t is discarded for dimensionality reduction and the semi-regularized within-class scatter matrix $\tilde{S}_w$ is mapped to a full rank matrix S'_w in sub-feature space $\overline{N(S_t)}$, where $\overline{N(S_t)}$ is the complement space of $N(S_t)$. After above two procedures, the traditional LDA method can be performed in subspace $\overline{N(S_t)}$ directly and will not loss any discriminant power.

Two public available databases, namely FERET and CMU PIE face databases are used to evaluate the proposed method for face recognition. Comparing with the existing LDA-based methods, the results are encouraging.

The rest of this paper is organized as follows. Our proposed SL-RFD method is given in Section 2. The experimental results and computational complexity are reported in Section 3. Finally, Section 4 draws the conclusions.

2 Proposed SL-RFD Method

In this section, we proposes and develops a novel regularized Fisher discriminant method for face recognition based on subspace and rank lifting scheme. Details are discussed as follows.

2.1 Some Definitions

Assume d be the dimensionality of original sample feature space and C be the number of sample classes, the total original sample $X = \{X_1, X_2, \cdots, X_C\}$, the jth class X_j contains N_j samples, i.e., $X_j = \{x_1^{(j)}, x_2^{(j)}, \cdots, x_{N_j}^{(j)}\}, j = 1, 2, \cdots, C$. Let N be the total number of original training samples, $\bar{x}_j = \frac{1}{N_j} \sum_{x \in X_j} x$ be the mean of the sample class X_j and $\bar{x} = \frac{1}{N} \sum_{j=1}^{C} \sum_{x \in X_j} x$ be the global mean of the total original sample X. The within-class scatter matrix S_w, between-class scatter matrix S_b and total scatter matrix S_t are defined respectively as:

$$S_w = \frac{1}{N}\sum_{j=1}^{C}\sum_{x\in X_j}(x-\bar{x}_j)(x-\bar{x}_j)^T = \Phi_w\Phi_w^T, \tag{1}$$

$$S_b = \frac{1}{N}\sum_{j=1}^{C}N_j(\bar{x}_j-\bar{x})(\bar{x}_j-\bar{x})^T = \Phi_b\Phi_b^T, \tag{2}$$

$$S_t = \frac{1}{N}\sum_{j=1}^{C}\sum_{x\in X_j}(x-\bar{x})(x-\bar{x})^T = \Phi_t\Phi_t^T, \tag{3}$$

where Φ_w, $\Phi_t \in R^{d\times N}$ and $\Phi_b \in R^{d\times C}$.

The goal of Fisher linear discriminant analysis is to find an optimal projection $W^* : R^d \to R^m$, $d > m$, such that

$$W^* = \arg\max_W \mathrm{tr}(W^T S_b W)\mathrm{tr}(W^T S_w W)^{-1} \tag{4}$$

where $\mathrm{tr}(A)$ denotes the trace of matrix A. The problem (4) is equivalent to solve the eigenvalue problem: $S_w^{-1}S_bW = W\Lambda$, where Λ is a $d\times d$ diagonal eigenvalue matrix.

2.2 Regularization Strategy

The proposed regularized technique includes the following two stages.

Rank Lifting Scheme. In this subsection, we shall need the following rank lifting theorem (The proof is ommited).

Theorem 1. *If vector set* $\bigcup_{i=1}^{k}\{\alpha_j^{(i)}|j = 1,2,\cdots,n_i\}$ *is a linearly independent set and* $m_i = \frac{1}{n_i}\sum_{j=1}^{n_i}\alpha_j^{(i)}$, $i = 1,2,\cdots,k$, *then for any constant* $t\,(t \neq 1)$, *the following vector set*

$$\bigcup_{i=1}^{k}\{\alpha_1^{(i)}-m_i,\ \alpha_2^{(i)}-m_i,\cdots,\alpha_{n_i-1}^{(i)}-m_i,\ \alpha_{n_i}^{(i)}-t\cdot m_i\}$$

is a linearly independent set as well.

Define matrix $\tilde{\Phi}_w$ as follows

$$\tilde{\Phi}_w = \frac{1}{\sqrt{N}}[x_1^{(1)}-\bar{x}_1|\cdots|x_{N_1}^{(1)}-\bar{x}_1+t\cdot\bar{x}_1|,\cdots,|x_1^{(C)}-\bar{x}_C|\cdots|x_{N_C}^{(C)}-\bar{x}_C+t\cdot\bar{x}_C], \tag{5}$$

where $t \neq 0$. By rank lifting theorem 1, we know that matrix $\tilde{\Phi}_w$ is a full rank matrix, i.e., $\mathrm{rank}(\tilde{\Phi}_w) = N$. The rank of semi-regularized within-class scatter matrix $\tilde{S}_w(=\tilde{\Phi}_w\tilde{\Phi}_w^T)$ is lifted from $N-C$ to N. If $\tilde{S}_w$ is nonsingular, the classical LDA method can be applied directly. Otherwise, we shall apply dimensionality reduction technique proposed in [7] to $\tilde{S}_w$ and get the final nonsingular within-class scatter matrix S_w'.

In addition, it derived from (5) that

$$\tilde{S}_w = S_w + \frac{t}{N} S_1 + \frac{t^2}{N} S_2 \tag{6}$$

where $S_1 = M\alpha^T + \alpha M^T - 2MM^T$, $S_2 = MM^T \in R^{d\times d}$, $\alpha = [x_{N_1}^{(1)}, x_{N_2}^{(2)}, \cdots, x_{N_C}^{(C)}]$, $M = [\bar{x}_1, \bar{x}_2, \cdots, \bar{x}_C] \in R^{d\times C}$.

It is easy to see from equation (6) that $\tilde{S}_w$ approaches to S_w, as parameter t tends to 0.

Discard the Null Space of S_t. From the statistical point of view, the null space of S_b can not provide any useful information for pattern classification. It showed in paper [7] that $N(S_t) = N(S_w) \bigcap N(S_b)$. Therefore, discarding the null space of S_t will not loss useful discriminant information. In many situations, rank$(S_w) = N - C$. By rank lifting technique, S_w can be lifted to $\tilde{S}_w$ with rank$(\tilde{S}_w) = N$. Perform eigenvalue decomposition: $S_t \overset{\text{evd}}{=} U_t D_t U_t^T$, where $U_t = [u_1, \cdots, u_d] \in R^{d\times d}$ is an orthonormal matrix, the diagonal matrix $D_t = \text{diag}\{\lambda_1, \cdots, \lambda_\tau, 0, \cdots, 0\} \in R^{d\times d}$ with $\lambda_1 \geq \cdots \geq \lambda_\tau > 0$, where $\tau \leq N-1$. Denote $U_\tau = [u_1, \cdots, u_\tau] \in R^{d\times\tau}$, then in $\overline{N(S_t)}$, the complement subspace of $N(S_t)$, the lifted within-class scatter, between-class scatter and total scatter matrices $\tilde{S}_w, S_b, S_t$ can be projected into $\overline{N(S_t)}$ as follows:

$$S'_w = U_1^T \tilde{S}_w U_1, S'_b = U_1^T S_b U_1, S'_t = U_1^T S_t U_1, \tag{7}$$

where $S'_w, S'_b, S'_t \in R^{\tau\times\tau}$ and S'_w usually is a full rank matrix, i.e., rank$(S'_w) = \tau$.

2.3 The Proposed SL-RFD Algorithm

Based on above sections, our SL-RFD algorithm is designed as follows.

Step 1: Perform eignvalue decomposition on $N\times N$ matrix $\Phi_t^T\Phi_t \overset{\text{evd}}{=} V_t\Lambda_t V_t^T$, where $V_t = [v_1, \cdots, v_N] \in R^{N\times N}$ is an orthonormal matrix, the diagonal matrix $\Lambda_t = \text{diag}\{\lambda_1, \cdots, \lambda_\tau, 0, \cdots, 0\} \in R^{N\times N}$ with $\lambda_1 > \cdots > \lambda_\tau > 0$. Calculate $u_i = \Phi_t v_i / \|\Phi_t v_i\| \in R^{d\times 1}$ $(i = 1, \cdots, \tau)$ and construct a $d\times\tau$ matrix $U_\tau = [u_1, \cdots, u_\tau]$, where $\tau \leq N-1$.

Step 2: Set regularized parameter t=0.01 and let

$$\begin{aligned}\tilde{\Phi}_w &= \frac{1}{\sqrt{N}}[x_1^{(1)} - x_1|\cdots|x_{N_1}^{(1)} - x_1 + t\cdot x_1|, \cdots, |x_1^{(C)} - x_C|\cdots|x_{N_C}^{(C)} - x_C + t\cdot x_C] \\ &= \Phi_w + \frac{t}{\sqrt{N}}[\underbrace{0, \cdots, 0}_{N_1-1}, m_1|\underbrace{0, \cdots, 0}_{N_2-1}, m_2|, \cdots, |\underbrace{0, \cdots, 0}_{N_C-1}, m_C].\end{aligned}$$

and calculate $\tilde{S}_w = \tilde{\Phi}_w\tilde{\Phi}_w^T$.

Step 3: Caculate $S'_w = U_\tau^T\tilde{S}_w U_\tau$ and $S'_b = U_\tau^T S_b U_\tau$. Perform SVD: $S'_w \overset{\text{svd}}{=} U_w\Lambda_w U_w^T$. Let $Y = \Lambda_w^{-1/2}U_w^T$ and $\tilde{S}_b = YS'_bY^T$

Step 4: Perform SVD: $\tilde{S}_b \overset{\text{svd}}{=} V_b\Lambda_b V_b^T$. Denote $V_b = [v_1, \cdots, v_{C-1}, v_C, \cdots, v_\tau] \in R^{\tau\times\tau}$ and let $V_{C-1} = [v_1, v_2, \cdots, v_{C-1}] \in R^{\tau\times(C-1)}$.

Step 5: The optimal projection matrix: $W_{SLRFD} = U_\tau U_w\Lambda_w^{-1/2}V_{C-1}$

---

3 Experimental Results

In this section, FERET and CMU PIE databases are selected to evaluate the performance of our proposed SL-RFD algorithm. In all experiments, the value of regularized parameter is given as $t = 0.01$.

In FERET database, we select 120 people, 4 images for each individual. Face image variations in FERET database include pose, illumination, facial expression and aging. The original images with resolution 112x92 are reduced to wavelet feature face with resolution 30x25 after two-level D4 wavelet decomposition. Images from two individuals are shown in figure 1.

Fig. 1. Images of two persons from FERET database

In CMU PIE face database, there are totally 68 people. There are 13 pose variations ranged from full right profile image to full left profile image and 43 different lighting conditions, 21 flashes with ambient light on or off. In our experiment, for each people, we select 56 images including 13 poses with neutral expression and 43 different lighting conditions in frontal view. The original images with resolution 112x92 are reduced to wavelet feature face with resolution 57x47 after one-level D4 wavelet decomposition. Several images of one people are shown in figure 2.

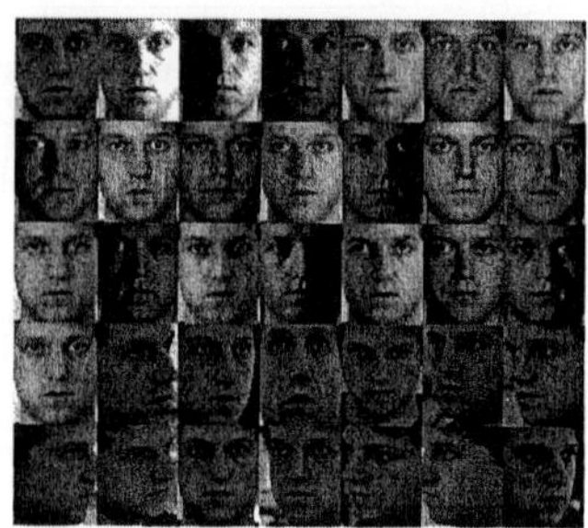

Fig. 2. Images of one person from CMU PIE database

3.1 Results on FERET Database

The section reports the results of the proposed SL-RFD method on FERET database. We randomly select 2 images from each people for training ($2\times120=240$ images for training), while the rest of images of each individual are selected for testing ($2\times120=240$ images for testing). The experiments are repeated 10 times and the average accuracies of rank 1 to rank 5 are recorded in table 1 and shown in the Figure 3(a). The recognition accuracy of our method increases from 80.00% with rank 1 to 89.38% with rank 5. Comparing with other LDA-based methods,

Table 1. Performance comparison on FERET Database

	Rank 1	Rank 2	Rank 3	Rank 4	Rank 5
DLDA [2]	75.17%	80.08%	82.75%	84.17 %	85.33%
Fisherface [1]	76.79%	81.67%	83.79%	84.83%	86.50%
Huang et al [7]	77.46%	81.79%	83.96%	85.33%	86.38%
Our Method	80.00%	85.08%	87.13%	88.29%	89.38%

namely, Fisherface [1], direct LDA (DLDA) [2] and Huang et al methods [7], the recognition accuracies of Fisherface, direct LDA and Huang et al methods increase from 76.79%, 75.17% and 77.46% with rank 1 to 86.50%, 85.33% and 86.38% with rank 5 respectively.

3.2 Results on CMU PIE Face Database

The section reports the results of the proposed SL-RFD method on CMU PIE database. We randomly select 14 images from each people for training (14x68=952 images for training), while the rest of images of each individual are selected for testing (42x68= 2856 images for testing). The experiments are repeated 10 times and the average accuracies of rank 1 to rank 3 are recorded and shown in table 2 and plotted in Figure 3(b). The recognition accuracy of our method increases from 76.38% with rank 1 to 79.67% with rank 3. Comparing with other LDA-based methods, namely, Fisherface [1], direct LDA (DLDA) [2] and Huang et al methods [7], the recognition accuracies of Fisherface, direct LDA and Huang et al methods increase from 75.71%, 75.54% and 75.67% with

Table 2. Performance comparison on CMU PIE face database

	Rank 1	Rank 2	Rank 3
DLDA [2]	75.54%	77.58%	78.74%
Fisherface [1]	75.71%	78.08%	79.20%
Huang et al [7]	75.63%	78.30%	79.44%
Our Method	76.38%	78.52%	79.67%

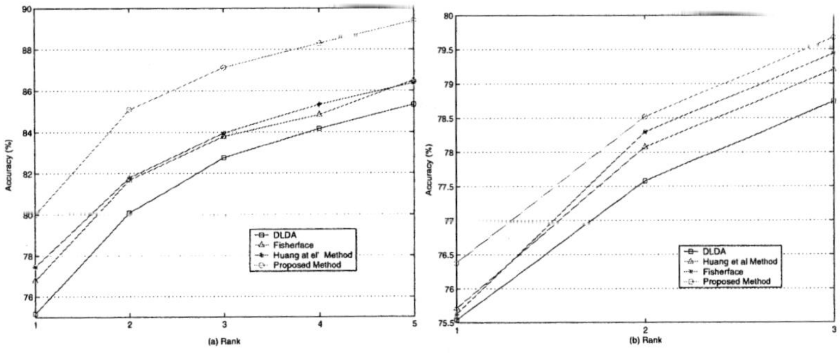

Fig. 3. Performance on (a) FERET datebase and (b) CMU PIE database

rank 1 to 79.20%, 78.74% and 79.44% with rank 3 respectively. The results show our proposed method gives the best performance.

3.3 Computational Complexity

The major difference on complexity of different methods is on the training process to solve eigensystems. The computational cost of Fisherface includes solving one N by N eigensystem, $O(N^3)$, and two $(N-C) \times (N-C)$ eigensystem, $O((N-C)^3)$. In Direct LDA, the computational cost involves solving one C by C eigensystem, $O(C^3)$ and one $m \times m\,(m \leq C-1)$ eigensystem, $O(m^3)$. In Huang's method, the computational cost consists of three parts. The first part is to solve one N by N eigensystem, $O(N^3)$. The rest parts are to solve one $(N-1)$ by $(N-1)$ eigensystem, $O((N-1)^3)$ and one $(C-1) \times (C-1)$ eigensystem, $O((C-1)^3)$. The computational cost of our proposed method consists of three parts, which involves solving one N by N eigensystem, $O(N^3)$ and two $\tau \times \tau$ $(\tau \leq N-1)$ eigensystem, $O(\tau^3)$.

4 Conclusions

A new subspace and rank lifting scheme-based regularized Fisher discriminant algorithm has been developed and reported in this paper for solving the small sample size problem (S3) in face recognition. The proposed regularized strategy includes two stages: • **Rank Lifting Step** semi-regularization $(S_w \rightarrow \tilde{S}_w)$; • **Discard Null Space Step** perform dimensionality reduction and leads to final regularization $(\tilde{S}_w \rightarrow S'_w)$. It is also shown that the semi-regularized within-class scatter matrix $\tilde{S}_w$ will approach to original within-class scatter matrix S_w as parameter t tends to zero. The proposed method has been evaluated with two public available databases, namely FERET and CMU PIE databases. A comprehensive comparison with the existing LDA-based methods, namely Fisherface, Direct LDA and Huang et al methods, is also performed. Comparing with these three methods, the proposed method gives the best performance for both databases.

Acknowledgement

This project was supported by SZU R/D Fund (200548). The authors would like to thank for the US Army Research Laboratory for contribution of the FERET database and CMU for the CMU PIE database.

References

1. Belhumeur, P. N., Hespanha, J.P., Kriegman, D.J.: Eigenfaces vs. Fisherfaces: recognition using class specific linear projection. IEEE Trans. Pattern Anal. Mach. Intell. **19**, No. 7 (1997) 711–720

2. Yu, H. and Yang, J.: A direct LDA algorithm for high-dimensional data — with application to face recognition. Pattern Recognition **34** (2001) 2067–2070
3. Chen, L., Liao, H., Ko, M., Lin, J. and Yu, G.: A new LDA-based face recognition system, which can solve the small sample size problem Pattern Recognition **33**, No. 10, (2000) 1713–1726
4. Jin, Z., Yang, J.Y., Hu, Z. S. and Lou, Z.: Face recognition based on the uncorrelated discriminant transform. Pattern Recognition **34** (2001)1405–1416
5. Martinez, A. M. andKak, A. C.: PCA versus LDA. IEEE Trans. Pattern Anal. Mach. Intell. **23** (2001) 228–233
6. Zhao, W., Chellappa, R. and Phillips, P. J.: Subspace linear discriminant analysis for face recognition. Technical Report CAR-TR-914, CS-TR-4009, University of Maryland at College Park, USA (1999)
7. Huang, R., Liu, Q., Lu, H. and Ma, S. D.: Solving small sample size problem in LDA. Proceeding of International Conference in Pattern Recognition (ICPR 2002) **3**(2002)
8. Dai, D. Q. and Yuen, P. C.: Regularized discriminant analysis and its application on face recognition. Pattern Recognition, **36** (2003) 845–847
9. Lu, J., Plataniotis, K. N. and Venetsanopoulos, A. N.: Face Recognition Using LDA Based Algorithms. IEEE Transactions on Neural Networks, **14**, No.1 (2003) 195–200
10. Duin, R.P.W. and Loog, M.: Linear dimensionality reduction via a heteroscedastic extension of LDA: the Chernoff criterion. IEEE Transactions on Pattern Analysis and Machine Intelligence, **26**, No. 6 (2004) 732 - 739
11. Ye J. P. and Li O.: A Two-Stage Linear Discriminant Analysis via QR-Decomposition. IEEE Transactions on Pattern Analysis and Machine Intelligence, **27**, No. 6 (2005) 929 - 941.

Hand Motion Recognition for the Vision-Based Taiwanese Sign Language Interpretation

Chia-Shiuan Cheng, Pi-Fuei Hsieh, and Chung-Hsien Wu

Department of Computer Science and Information Engineering,
National Cheng Kung University, Taiwan

Abstract. In this paper we present a system to recognize the hand motion of Taiwanese Sign Language (TSL) using the Hidden Markov Models (HMMs) through a vision-based interface. Our hand motion recognition system consists of four phases: construction of color model, hand tracking, trajectory representation, and recognition. Our hand tracking can accurately track the hand positions. Since our system is recognized to hand motions that are variant with rotation, translation, symmetric, and scaling in Cartesian coordinate system, we have chosen invariant features which convert our coordinate system from Cartesian coordinate system to Polar coordinate system. There are nine hand motion patterns defined for TSL. Experimental results show that our proposed method successfully chooses invariant features to recognition with accuracy about 90%.

1 Introduction

Hand motion recognition has many applications in human computer interaction (HCI) such as hand gesture recognition and sign language recognition. However, sign language recognition have many important applications in virtual reality (VR), where gesturing would certainly provide a nature and efficient way for human computer interaction. Formally, a phoneme is defined to be the smallest contrastive unit in a language; that is, a unit that distinguishes one word from another. Phonemes are especially interesting for recognition purpose, because their number is limited in any language, as opposed to an unlimited number of words that can be built from the phonemes. The TSL linguistics assures that a sign gesture can be decomposed into sign words that are composed of a finite set of phonemes. For example, Stokoe's transcription system [1] assumes that signs in ASL can be broken into three phonemes which consist of the location of the sign (tabula or tab), the hand shape (designator or dez), and the movement (signation or sig). In this paper, we present a hand motion system for TSL recognition.

Campbell and et al [2] compared recognition performance on ten different feature vectors derived from a single set of 18 T'ai Chi gestures. They used ten different feature vectors to test in a gesture recognition which utilizes 3D data gathered in real-time from stereo video cameras. Montero and Sucar [3] tested the gesture recognition rate using HMMs with different: (i) number of discrete symbol, (ii) number of hidden states, (iii) combinations of feature. Their results showed a high variation on the recognition rate depending on these parameters, from 50% to more than 95%. Therefore,

J. Tao, T. Tan, and R.W. Picard (Eds.): ACII 2005, LNCS 3784, pp. 160–167, 2005.

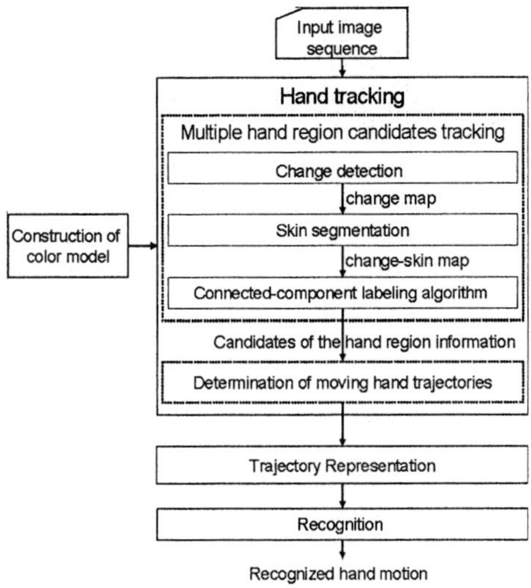

Fig. 1. The flow diagram of the hand motion system for TSL recognition

we can see that the success of a gesture recognition system depends on an adequate set of feature vectors representing the patterns.

The diagram of the hand motion system for TSL recognition is shown in Fig. 1.

2 Hand Tracking

The objective of the hand tracking phase is to extract the hand position in a 2D space from a video sequence. There are two stages: (i) multiple hand region candidates tracking and (ii) determination of moving hand trajectories. In the multiple hand region candidates tracking stage, we propose an effective method to record the candidates of the hand region information. In order to track the positions of moving hands more accurately, we develop a method for tracking multiple hand regions. By this means, the effect of noise caused by improper lighting conditions can be eliminated. Also, those incautious movements can be detected and removed from the list of candidates. When a signer performs one-hand sign language, he might incautiously move the other hand or his head. Because of these conditions, we probably track the wrong hand regions. Using multiple hand region candidates tracking can solve these problems because the final trajectory is determined by the following stage that can remove noise. In the determination of moving hand trajectories stage, we analyze the candidates of hand region information to extract the moving hand trajectory.

2.1 Multiple Hand Region Candidates Tracking

We present a hand tracking method that applies the color and motion cues to a sign language video sequence. The multiple hand region candidates tracking stage consists of three stages: change detection, skin segmentation and connected-component labeling algorithm.

In the change detection stage, we first convert color space from RGB color space to YIQ color space, since the I-component in YIQ color space is sensitive to skin color [4]. We derive the temporal information by segmenting a video sequence into moving (i.e. foreground) and stationary (i.e. background) regions. We use image difference for our change detection since change detection by image differencing is a very simple procedure. It just differences two images of original or transformed, and then gives a threshold to label change or un-change. After change detection, we generate a change map that labels change or un-change for skin segmentation. In the change map, we remove the most of background information and noise, so it can reduce the number of processing pixels for skin segmentation. The change detection methods generally cost less computation time than the motion estimation and optical-flow methods. The change detection methods would therefore promote real-time segmentation [5].

In the skin-color segmentation stage, image pixels are classified as skin or background using the Bayes linear classifier. However, skin segmentation is feasible because the human skin has a color distribution that differs significantly, although not entirely, from those of the background objects. We classify the image pixels that respond to changed pixels in the change map to generate the change-skin map and record the number of change-skin pixels for the determination of moving hand trajectories.

In order to record the candidates of the hand region information, we perform the connected-component labeling algorithm to the change-skin map. We record centroid and the number of pixels of the top three connected-components, because everyone has three obviously skin connected-component such as two hands and head.

2.2 Determination of Moving Hand Trajectories

In determination of moving hand trajectories stage, we determine the final moving hand trajectories from the candidates of the hand region information. There are two thresholds that set up in advance. One is the threshold of the size of one hand that one hand at least contains pixel number in a frame. The other is the threshold of frame number of two hands that two moving hands appear in a sign language video. We first determine that the trajectory is one- or two-hand trajectory by counting the frame number of two hands which region size of second conned-component of every frame exceeds the threshold of pixel number of one hand. If frame number of two hands exceeds the threshold of frame number of two hands, we determine that two moving hand trajectories in the sign language video or one moving hand trajectory.
The following is the procedure for determination of final moving one-hand trajectory:

1. Find the frame which contains the maximum change-skin pixels in the change-skin map and set it as seed frame.
2. The maximal connected-component is the most possible moving hand region in the seed frame and records its centroid of moving hand in this frame.
3. Calculate the centroid of forward and backward the seed frame by minimize the displacement of hand between two consecutive frames.

The procedure for determination of final moving two-hand trajectory is similar to the procedure for determination of final moving one-hand trajectory.

3 Trajectory Representation

After hand tracking, we get the trajectory that is represented as a set of point-tokens in a spatio-temporal space, as describe in, (1).

$$G = \{(x_1, y_1), (x_2, y_2), \dots, (x_T, y_T)\}\,, \tag{1}$$

where T is the trajectory length.

The original trajectory G in the Cartesian system is dependent on the variance of translation, rotation, symmetry and scaling of a trajectory. Yoon et al [6] show that all of the features are based on only three basic characteristics of a hand motion trajectory: (i) distance to the origin (ρ) (ii) angle (θ) (iii) velocity (v). However, in our system, we suppose that our trajectories are performed smoothed, so the v feature does not assist to our hand motion recognition system and we do not use it in our system. We transfer coordinate system from the Cartesian coordinate system to the polar coordinate system. Under the polar coordinate system, the feature sets are robust to and independent of size and angle variations [3].

We first choose the center of trajectory as the new origin in order to deal with the variance of translation of a trajectory, as described in (2).

$$(C_x, C_y) = \left(\frac{1}{T}\sum_{t=1}^{T} x_t, \frac{1}{T}\sum_{t=1}^{T} y_t\right), \tag{2}$$

where (C_x, C_y) is the center of a trajectory.

In order to deal with the variance of rotation, we calculate the rotation angle, Θ which is the angle obtained between first point of the trajectory and the center of the trajectory.

$$\Theta = \tan^{-1}\left(\frac{y_1 - C_y}{x_1 - C_x}\right), \tag{3}$$

where (x_1, y_1) is the position of the trajectory.

We translate the origin and rotate all trajectories with the angle Θ as follow:

$$\begin{bmatrix} \overline{x}_t \\ \overline{y}_t \end{bmatrix} = \begin{bmatrix} \cos\Theta & -\sin\Theta \\ \sin\Theta & \cos\Theta \end{bmatrix} \begin{bmatrix} x_t - C_x \\ y_t - C_y \end{bmatrix}. \tag{4}$$

We can deal with the variance of translation and rotation under the above transformation, but there is symmetry situation in our experiment. We just only rotate the trajectory to normalize the preceding points of the trajectory to be located at the first quadrant.

After the above coordinate transformation, these features, ρ and θ are used for the HMMs recognition. ρ_t is the distance between the center of the hand motion trajectory and the t-th point of the hand trajectory:

$$\rho_t = \left(\sqrt{(x_t - C_x)^2 + (y_t - C_y)^2}\right). \tag{5}$$

$r_{\max}$ is the maximum distance from the center point to every point in the hand motion trajectory.

$$\rho_{\max} = \max_{t=1}^{T}(\rho_t)\,. \tag{6}$$

We normalize the ρ_t to deal with the variance of scaling as follows:

$$\overline{\rho}_t = \rho_t / \rho_{\max}, \tag{7}$$

where $\overline{\rho}_t$ is a normalized value between 0~1.

θ_t is the angle obtained between the center of the hand motion trajectory and the t-th point of the hand trajectory:

$$\theta_t = \tan^{-1}\left(\frac{y_t - C_y}{x_t - C_x}\right). \tag{8}$$

4 Hidden Markov Models

HMMs have become the preferred technique for visual recognition of human gestures. If the hands move faster or more slowly during a test gesture, the Viterbi algorithm will compensate for this; effectively performing dynamic time warping. HMMs are rich in mathematical structures and it serves as the theoretical basis for wide range of application. The effectiveness of this model class lies in its ability to deal with non-stationary that often in the observation sequence and model spatio-temporal information in a natural way. When HMMs apply properly, they will work very well in practice for several important applications. They have been applied to speech recognition [7], behavior models, and more recently gesture recognition [8].

5 Experiment

The goal of our experiment is to (i) confirm our hand tracking that can accurately track the moving hand regions (ii) confirm our feature selection and feature representation invariant to the hand motion of TSL (iii) find the lowest image resolution that we can accept.

5.1 Data Sets

In the experiments, the subject, who performed sign language, was sitting before any stationary background with normal lighting condition. We have tested 19 different words selected from TSL. Each word may contain one or two hand trajectories. Each word of TSL was performed 3 times by 6 different subjects. Each subject smoothly performed sign language in natural situation. The sign language video sequences were

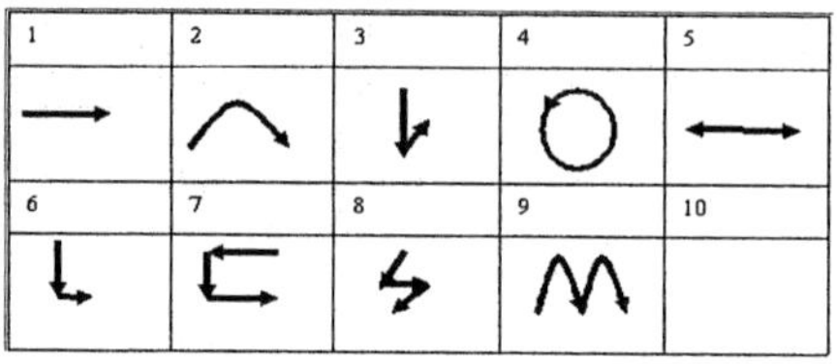

1	2	3	4	5
6	7	8	9	10

Fig. 2. Nine hand motion patterns of TSL

acquired using a digital video camera that has 24-bit RGB colors and a 352 x 240 resolution with 30 frames per seconds (FPS). There are nine hand motion patterns of TSL as shown in Fig. 2.

5.2 Results

Fig. 3(a) shows the result of multiple hand region candidates tracking. After multiple hand region candidates tracking, we record the information of hand region candidates such as region size, region position, and so on. We input the information to extract the final hand motion of TSL. Fig. 3(b) showed the result of trajectory determination. We can see that if we used the max hand region candidate, we may track the other hand. Using our hand tracking method can accurately track the hand motion of TSL.

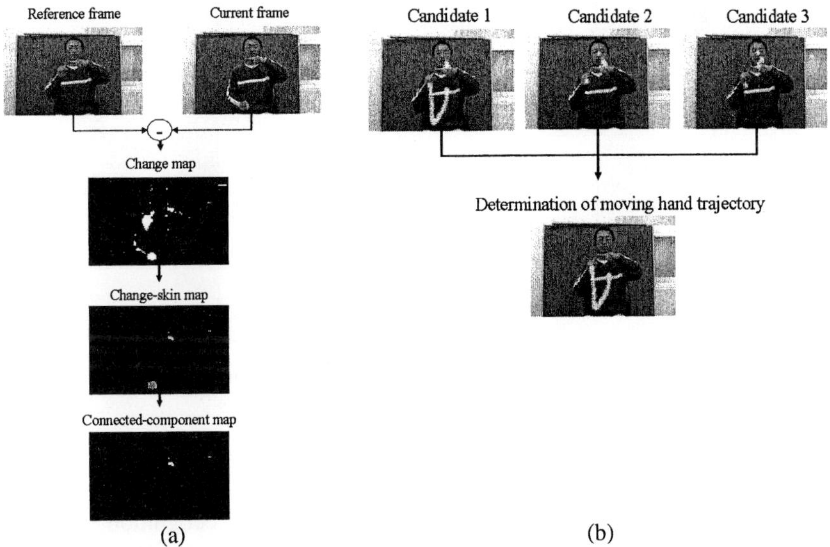

Fig. 3. (a) Result of multiple hand region candidates tracking (b) Result of determination of moving hand trajectories

5.2.1 Preprocessing

In order to choose features that are invariant to scale, we normalize the feature data. Before the HMMs recognition, we tried to use three kinds of preprocessing methods to these hand motion data, (i) Reduce redundant observation number (Rm), (ii) Calculate more accurate center of trajectory (Cc), (iii) Apply mean filter to remove noise (Sm), and these three kinds method can be combined to use. To reduce observation number, we remove the points of trajectory which appear the same position in previous time instance. Since the hand motion of TSL position data often change sharply due to hand trembling, unintentional movements or unstable image processing, they are smoothed as the mean value of a specified point and two neighbor points. In the calculating more accurate center of trajectory method, we first applied Reduce redundant observation number to our hand motion data, and then calculate the center of new hand motion data. Since segmenting the meaningful part from sign language video sequences task was not perfect, there would be many redundant points in original trajectory data. The best recognition accuracy was about 92% which combined the three kind of preprocessing methods.

5.2.2 Effect of Image Resolution on Recognition Accuracy

In order to speed up our system, we experimented to show how the image resolution affected the system performance. Fig. 4 showed the relation between accuracy and image resolution. We can conclude that decreasing image resolution down to 140 x 96 does not affect the system performance, but our hand motion of TSL recognition must combine hand shape information to recognize TSL. However, the hand shape of TSL recognition need higher image resolution.

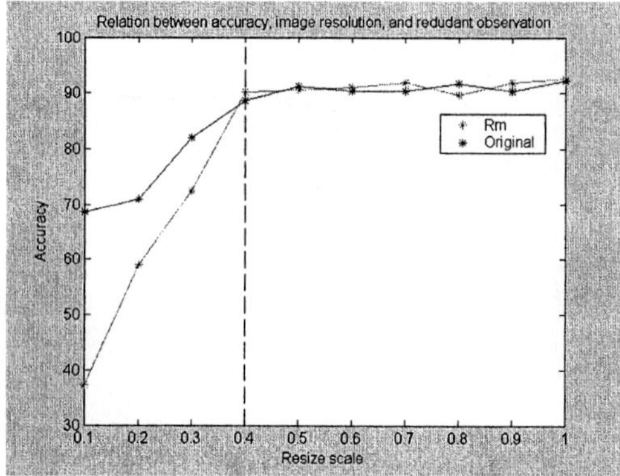

Fig. 4. The relation between accuracy and decrease image resolution scale

6 Conclusion

In this study we have developed a vision-based hand motion recognition system for TSL. Our hand tracking method can extract moving hand trajectories from a video sequence more accurately than other methods. This method can remove the affect caused by the lighting conditions and the signer's incautious movements of his body. Our hand motions of TSL are varied with rotation, translation, symmetry, and scaling in the Cartesian coordinate system. By converting our coordinate system from the Cartesian coordinate system to the Polar coordinate system and choosing invariant features to deal with those variations. We use the three preprocessing methods to improve our system such that the recognition accuracy can reach about 92%. It shows that by using invariant features and HMMs, our recognition is an effective tool for hand motion recognition. In order to speed up the system for real-time processing, we analyze the relation between the accuracy and the image resolution. If we do not combine the hand shape information for the TSL recognition, we can conclude that decreasing image resolution down to 140 x 96 does not affect the system performance. We can also apply our system to the applications such as the object manipulation in VR, and the remote control of robots, as well as graphic primitive and alphanumeric editing.

Acknowledgment

The authors would like to thank the National Science Council, Taiwan, for financially supporting this research work under Contract No. NSC93-2213-E-006-072. The authors would also like to thank Miss Gong-Ru Lin for her assistance in TSL experiments.

References

1. W. C. Stokoe, *Sign Language Structure: An outline of the Visual Communication System of the American Deaf*, Buffalo, N.Y.: Univ. of Buffalo, 1960.
2. L. W. Campbell, D. A. Becker, A. Azarbayejani, A. F. Bobick, and A. Pentland, "Invariant Features for 3-D Gesture Recognition," *Proc. IEEE Int'l Conf. FG*, pp. 157-162, Zurich 1996.
3. J. A. Montero V. and L. E. Sucar S., "Feature Selection for Visual Gesture Recognition Using Hidden Markov Models," *Proc. IEEE Int'l Conf. Computer Science*, pp. 196-203, Mexican, 2004.
4. H. K. Lee and J. H. Kim, "An HMM-based Threshold Model Approach for Gesture Recognition," *IEEE Trans. Pattern Anal. Machine Intell.,* vol. 21, no. 10, pp. 961-973, 1999.
5. N. Habili, C. C. Lim, and A. Moini, "Segmentation of the Face and Hands in Sign Language Video Sequences Using Color and Motion Cues," *IEEE Trans. Circuits Syst. Video Techn.*, vol. 14, no. 8, Oct. 2004.
6. H.S. Yoon, J. Soh, B.W. Ming, and H. S. Yang, "Recognition of Alphabetical Hand Gestures Using Hidden Markov Model," *IEICE Trans. Fund. Electr.*, vol. 87, pp. 1358-1366, Jul. 1999.
7. L. R. Rabiner, "A Tutorial on Hidden Markov Models and Selected Applications in Speech Recognition," *IEEE Trans ASSP*, vol. 77, no. 2, pp. 257-286, 1989.
8. M. H. Yang, N. Ahuja, and M. Tabb, "Extraction of 2D Motion Trajectories and Its Application to Hand Gesture Recognition," *IEEE Trans. Pattern Anal. Machine Intell.,* vol. 24, no. 8 pp. 1061-1074, Aug. 2002.

Static Gesture Quantization and DCT Based Sign Language Generation

Chenxi Zhang[1], Feng Jiang[1], Hongxun Yao[1], Guilin Yao[1], and Wen Gao[1,2]

[1] School of Computer Science and Technology, 15 00 01,
Harbin Institute of Technology, P.R.C
{cxzhang, fjiang, yhx, glyao}@vilab.hit.edu.cn
[2] Institute of Computing Technology, CAS, 10 00 85,
Beijing, P.R.C
wgao@ict.ac.cn

Abstract. To collect data for sign language recognition is not a trivial task. The lack of training data has become a bottleneck in the research of singer independence and large vocabulary recognition. A novel sign language generation algorithm is introduced in this paper. The difference between signers is analyzed briefly and a criterion is introduced to distinguish the same gesture words of different signers. Basing on that criterion we propose a sign word generation method combining the static gesture quantization and Discrete Cosine Transform (DCT), which can generate the new signers' sign words according to the existed signers' sign words. The experimental result shows that not only the data generated are distinct with the training data, they are also demonstrated effective.

1 Introduction

The purpose of Sign Language Recognition (SLR) is to provide an effective and accurate mechanism to translate sign words to texts or common language, to make it more convenient to communicate between the deaf and the normal by computers. Many researchers have documented methods for recognizing sign language from instrumented gloves at high accuracy while these systems suffer from notable limitations: signer-dependent and small vocabulary [1-5].

The main methods of Chinese Sign Language Recognition are based on HMM. Later ANN/HMM [6], DGMM/HMM [7] SOFM/HMM [8], DTW/HMM [9] recognition systems were presented. These systems implemented the signer-independent SLR with a large vocabulary. Although the systems are signer independent, there are only 7 signers' gesture words during the training the testing process which restricts the signer-independent SLR's effectiveness. In SLR, one of the problems is to collect enough data. Data collection for both training and testing is a laborious but necessary step. All of the statistical methods used in SLR suffer from this problem. However, sign language data cannot be gotten as easily as speech data. We must invite the special persons to pantomime. If Datagloves are used to collect the data, the difficulty will increase enormously. Data gloves are extremely expensive, so there are maybe only one or two pairs in a research institution. Signers have to pantomime one by one. Besides, the sensors on the data gloves are brittle. The lack of data makes the

J. Tao, T. Tan, and R.W. Picard (Eds.): ACII 2005, LNCS 3784, pp. 168 – 178, 2005.

research, especially the large vocabulary signer-independent recognition, very formidable. Due to the very large Chinese sign vocabulary, one more signer to sample the training data, much more time and money it would cost. Therefore, generating new signers' sign words from the existed signers' sign words is an imperative job.

In order to achieve effective generation performance, the critical problem is Signal Analysis. This paper first analyzes the sign word signals of different signers, and presents a sign word generation approach that comes from static gesture quantization and DCT method. We also propose a criterion to measure the common and distinct features of the same sign word from different signers. The experiment demonstrates that the generated sign word data not only differ from the existed training data, they are also demonstrated correct after recognizing by our recognition system.

The remainder of this paper is organized as following. In section 2, sign word data and the features that different signers perform are analyzed; Section 3 describes the sign word generation approach basing on static gesture quantization and DCT in detail. Experimental result is presented in the last section.

2 Sign Language Data Analysis

Data gloves are adopted in this paper as the input equipment. American Virtual Technologies Company's CyberGlove with 18 sensors and three Polhemus FASTRAK 3-D position trackers are utilized as input devices. The 51-dimension vectors got from two CyberGloves and position trackers in every moment, function as the final input data.

Fig. 1. The three part of the word of "aunt"

Communicative gestures can be decomposed into three motion phase: preparation, stroke, and retraction. Psycholinguistic studies show that stroke may be distinguished from the other gesture phases, since stroke contains the most information. Generally speaking, stroke is composed of three parts: the beginning gesture, the terminative gesture, and the transition movement from the beginning to the terminative gesture in Chinese sign language. The variation process of the word 'aunt' can be obviously saw from figure 1, the first sub-figure is the sign word's beginning static gesture, the third sub-figure is the sign word's terminative static gesture, the middle stage is the partition period from the beginning gesture to the terminative gesture.

Different signers have their own rhythms which include time length, range, and data change when they are performing sign words. This paper considers these three characteristics as the criterion to measure the differences of the sign words of different signers.

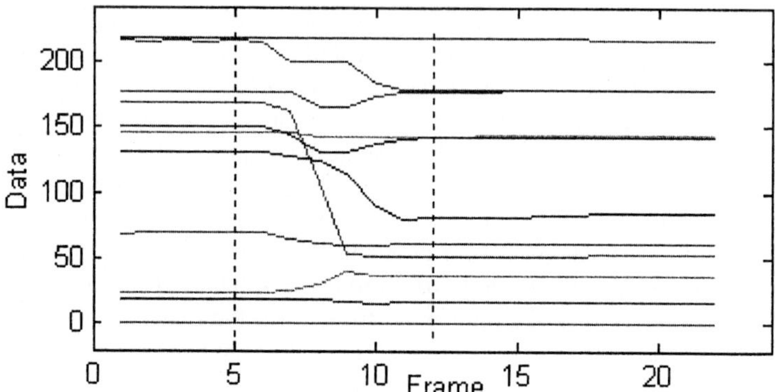

Fig. 2. Partial original data of the sign word 'aunt' obtained from the sensors. The lines represent the values changing with the time of the sensors. The two vertical lines divide all the curves into three parts. In the first part, the curves change gently, which means the signers are in the beginning static period; all the curves in the third part that change little indicate that the signers are in the terminative static gesture period; the curves between them are in the middle variation period.

2.1 Time Length Analysis

Time length is the length of time that the signers perform. It reflects the speed of individual signer. The time length we define here is just the middle part in figure 2. We omit the beginning and the terminative time because the errors that data collection procedure brings are very big. In the ideal situation, the beginning and the terminative static gesture are both one frame. Thus in order to find the middle period and compute the time length in the middle stage of each sign word, we must dissect the word first. To compute time length is to find the critical points, namely the X-coordinates of the two vertical lines. The steps are composed of forward and backward searching. Forward Searching is to find backward from the first frame in every dimension. If the subtract of current frame and the average of the following two frames is smaller than 1, stops searching and record the current X-coordinate. Or continue searching. The Backward Searching is similar to the Forward, which searches every dimension from the back to the beginning. In this paper K and K' represent the forward and backward searching result.

$$\text{AverageTime} = \frac{\sum_{i=1}^{N} K'^{(i)} - K^{(i)} + 1}{N}, \quad N = 4942$$

AverageTime is the average time length of the sign word an individual signer performs in average. Here the time is measured by the frame number of the data collection. $K'^{(i)} - K^{(i)'} + 1$ denotes the varying frame number in the middle stage of i th sign word. Compute the AverageTime as below.

Table 1. The comparison of the average time of one sign word 5 signers perform in average. The 4942 sign words performed by 5 signers independently are used as training sample.

Names of the signers	pfz	lwr	ljh	mwh	ygy
AverageTime (frame)	18.59	19.18	19.68	20.25	21.61

We can see from table 1 that the average performing speed of different signers are different. Thus time length can be used to measure the differences among different signers.

2.2 Range Analysis

The same sign word's curves' changing trend is the same, whereas every sensor's value range is different. For instance, the value of a certain sensor of the data glove can reflect the bending extent of the thumb. Apparently, every signer has different bending extent. Therefore we could find all the value ranges of the 51-dimension data and their average value to measure the range feature of every signer. This difference measuring function $Distance(i, j)$ of each signer is presented later. The algorithm is as following:

Definition 1: The form of a word is $O = \{A_1, A_2, \cdots, A_i, \cdots, A_N\}$, where N represents the number of the dimension (in this paper $N = 51$), A_i is the 51-dimension vector: $A_i = < a_1, a_2, a_3, \cdots, a_{51} >^T$, $A_i(j) = a_j$ denotes that the value of time j for the ith sensor is a_j, $O_k(A_i)$ denotes the kth word of the i th sensor.

Definition 2: Matrix $D = \{min, max, mean\}$, min, max and $mean$ are all 51-dimension vectors. $min(i)$, $max(i)$, $mean(i)$ respectively denote the minimum, the maximum and the average of the i th sensor.

1. Compute $min(i)$ and $max(i)$. $frame(k)$ is the frame number of the k th gesture word. N is the overall number of the training words 4942. $i = 1, 2, \cdots 51$

$$min(i) = \min\{O_k(A_i(j)) \mid j = 1, 2, \cdots frame(k); k = 1, 2, \cdots, N\}$$

$$max(i) = \max\{O_k(A_i(j)) \mid j - 1, 2, \cdots frame(k); k = 1, 2, \cdots, N\}$$

2. Compute $mean(i)$.

$$M = \sum_{k=0}^{N} frame(k), \quad mean(i) = \frac{1}{M} \sum_{k=1}^{N} \sum_{j=1}^{frame(k)} O_k(A_i(j)).$$

where $i = 1, 2, \cdots 51$.

Construct a feature Matrix for each signer. $Matrix_{3\times51} = \{min, max, mean\}$. Now define the formula $Distance(1, 2)$ that measures the two signer's $Matrix1 = \{min1, max1, mean1\}$ and $Matrix2 = \{min2, max2, mean2\}$ (1, 2 refers to two person):

$$Distance(1,2) = \alpha_1 \|min1 - min2\| + \alpha_2 \|max1 - max2\| + \alpha_3 \|mea1 - mean2\|$$

where $\alpha_1, \alpha_2, \alpha_3$ are weights.

Table 2. *Distance* comparison of 5 signers. Consider the 4942 sign words that five different signers perform as the training sample.

Name \ Name	pfz	lwr	ljh	mwh	ygy
pfz	63.04	255.27	332.60	346.59	365.13
lwr	—	91.19	372.29	362.57	428.13
ljh	—	—	54.01	339.31	341.15
mwh	—	—	—	64.54	360.69
ygy	—	—	—	—	57.04

We can see from Table 2 that the values on the diagonal are the result of the same signer who performs twice, '—' means the value is the same with the value that is symmetrical to the diagonal and are thus omitted. It is clearly shown the *Distance* of the same signer is smaller than 100, and the *Distance* of different signers is at least 255. It is arrived that the *Distance* of the same signer is much smaller than the *Distance* of different signers. By this token, *Distance* can be used to measure the range feature of different signers.

2.3 Data Variation Analysis

Data variation this paper analyzes is the varying period in the middle stage shown in Figure1 and Figure 2. The curves are almost the same as for the value of the same sign word of a certain dimension. Just as shown in Figure 3.

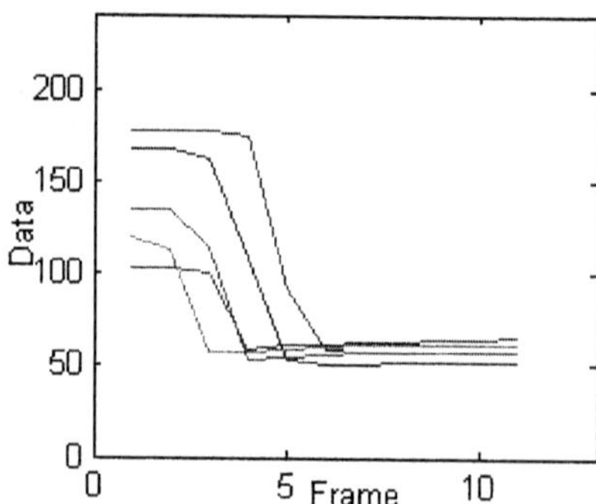

Fig. 3. Value variation curves of 'aunt' that is performed by 5 signers of the same dimension

We can clearly see that the curves' changing trends are the same: changing descendingly. Their initial values and terminative values are distinctive. The initial and terminative values are determinative and the middle data variation is aid to them. We are going to use this variation to aid the change of the initial and terminative values when generating sign words in the following Section.

3 Generating Sign Language

According to the above analysis, now we are proposing a sign language generation method basing on the static gesture quantization and DCT methods. The principle is to generate the beginning static gesture and the terminative static gesture for every sign word respectively, later modulate the data variation curve in the middle process without changing their curves to make them satisfy both the beginning and the terminative static gestures.

3.1 The Generation of Static Gesture

We have found every sensor's value range of each signer: the minimum $min(i)$ and the maximum $max(i)$ from Section 2.1. Now quantize $min(i)$ and $max(i)$ in every dimension, and get the value in the quantization table for every sign word's beginning and terminative static gesture. We choose five signers' data.

1. Compute the quantization range of every dimension, RANGE is the quantization step length.

$$List_i(\mathrm{j})=\mathrm{j}\times(max(\mathrm{i})-min(\mathrm{i}))/\mathrm{RANGE}+min(\mathrm{i})$$

   where $j = 1, 2, \cdots \mathrm{RANGE}$, $i = 1, 2, \cdots, 51$
2. Get the quantization value of the beginning and the terminative static gesture of every sign word: $O_k(frontG_i)$ and $O_k(backG_i)$ denote the beginning and the terminative static gesture quantization value of the i th dimension, the k th sign word. $O_k(frontG_i)$, $O_k(backG_i)$ have the following relationship:

$$List_i(\mathrm{j}) < List_i(O_k(frontG_i)) \le List_i(\mathrm{j}+1)$$

$$List_i(\mathrm{j}) < List_i(O_k(backG_i)) \le List_i(\mathrm{j}+1)$$

   where $k - 1, 2, \cdots, 4942$.
3. The beginning and the terminative static gesture for each sign word are $O_k{}^j(frontG_i)$, $O_k{}^j(backG_i)$ ($k = 1, 2, \cdots, 5$. denotes 5 persons) Find the repeated values from the five $O_k{}^j(frontG_i)$ and give it to $O_k(generateFG_i)$. If the five numbers differ from each other, let $O_k(generateFG_i)$ is the median of the five numbers. Generate $O_k(generateBG_i)$ in the same way. $O_k(generateFG_i)$, $O_k(generateBG_i)$ denote the beginning and the terminative quantization value of the k th sign word respectively.

4. Generate the original values with reference to $O_k(generateFG_i)$ and $O_k(generateBG_i)$. $O_k(gestureF(i))$, $O_k(gestureB(i))$ denote the generation of the i th dimension value of the k th sign word's beginning and terminative static gesture, where $max^{'}(i)$ and $min^{'}(i)$ are the given maximum and minimum value.

   $$O_k(gestureB(i)) = (max^{'}(i) - min^{'}(i)) \times (O_k(generateBG_i) + rand()) / \text{RANGE} + min^{'}(i)$$

   $$O_k(gestureF(i)) = (max^{'}(i) - min^{'}(i)) \times (O_k(generateFG_i) + rand()) / \text{RANGE} + min^{'}(i)$$

   where $i = 1, 2, \cdots, 4942$, $rand() \in [0,1]$. The algorithm stops here.

We choose the repeated value when computing $O_k(generateFG_i)$ in the third step, because when making statistics for the 4942 sign words, the probability of the number repeating of these 5 numbers is 64% (RANGE is chosen 50). The repeatability fully exhibits the common features when different signers are performing the same sign word. In the fourth step, $max^{'}(i)$ and $min^{'}(i)$ can be decided by ourselves, and this work is the very crucial point when generating data. $max^{'}(i)$ and $min^{'}(i)$ can reflect the range value of the newly generated virtual signer's data.

3.2 Generation of Data Variation Curve

We generated the static gesture in the above section, now we are going to generate the varying data in the middle stage. From Figure 3 in Section 2, it is seen that the trend of the same sensor's value variation curves are the same when different signers are performing the same sign word, so the main purpose of this section is to find this sameness. The steps of this algorithm are as follows:

1. Dissect each sign word using the dissecting algorithm discussed in Section 2.1, find the stage of the middle variation.
2. Process Discrete Cosine Transformation for every dimension data. Find the DCT variation range of five signers' training data. $O_k(DCT\text{coefficient}_i(j))$ denotes the j th cosine coefficient of the i th dimension data, the k th sign word in the middle variation stage. Find its maximum value $O_k(DCTmax_i(j))$ and the minimum value $O_k(DCTmin_i(j))$ for every j. To simplify the algorithm, it is supposed the middle varying frames of each sign word's five data are the same. $j = 1, 2, \cdots, frame$
3. Generate new cosine coefficients. $O_k(DCTgenerate_i(j))$ denotes the generated j th cosine coefficient of the i th dimension data, the k th sign word in the middle variation stage.

   $$O_k(DCTgenerate_i(j)) = (O_k(DCTmax_i(j)) - O_k(DCTmin_i(j)) \times rand() + O_k(DCTmin_i(j)$$

Do inverse discrete cosine transform (IDCT) to $O_k(DCTgenerate_i(j))$ to get the final result.

Because the changing trend of the same dimension's sensor is the same, randomly select the coefficients in $[O_k(DCTmax_i(j)), O_k(DCTmin_i(j))]$ will not change the curve's changing trend. We have generated all the three parts of a sign word till now, but these three parts may not be continuous as is shown in Figure 4.

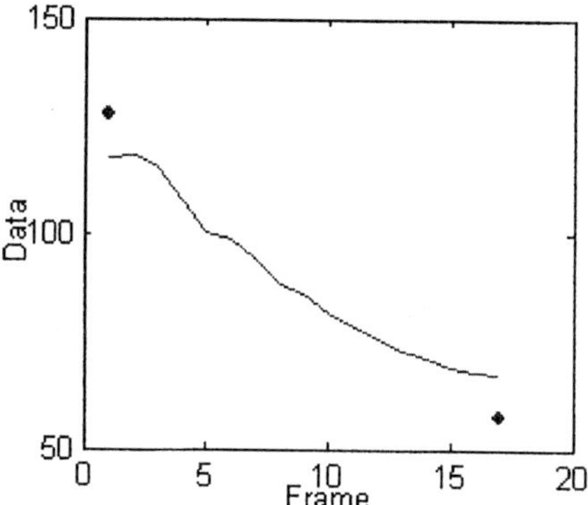

Fig. 4. Discontinuity of IDCT transformed curves and the static gesture

IDCT transformed curves and the static gesture values are discontinuous, how to solve this problem? Considering the characteristics of DCT coefficient, let's make some modifications to DCT coefficient in order to meet the needs of continuity of the curves and the discrete points without changing the shape of the figure. The algorithm is described below:

1. Shift the curve to make the curve's two ends located in the middle or outside of the two discrete points, also make the distances from the curve's two ends to the two discrete points the same(as shown in Figure 4). This step just indicates changing the direct current sub-value of the DCT coefficient $O_k(DCTgenerate_i(0))$.
2. If the ends of the curve locate in the middle part of the two discrete points, change the value of $O_k(DCTgenerate_i(1))$. δ is the speed factor.

$$O_k(DCTgenerate_i(1)) = O_k(DCTgenerate_i(1)) + \delta .$$

3. If the ends of the curve locate outside of the two discrete points, change the value of $O_k(DCTgenerate_i(1))$.

$$O_k(DCTgenerate_i(1)) = O_k(DCTgenerate_i(1)) - \delta$$

4. When the distances from the ends of the curve to the two discrete points are the same, finish this algorithm; Or else, repeat Step 2 or Step 3.

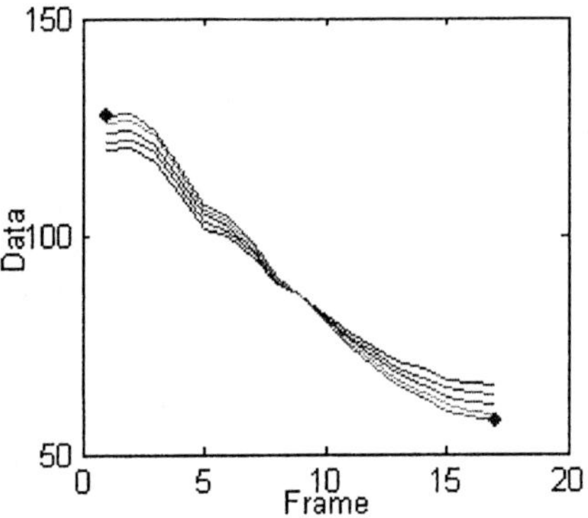

Fig. 5. The curve after modulating is continuous with the static gesture points

From Figure 5 we can clearly understand the process shifting the curve closer and closer to the discrete points, which did not change the shape. According to compressible characteristic of DCT, the higher the DCT's frequency, the closer to 0 the coefficient is, thus we are able to change the frame number by increasing or reducing the high frequency coefficient without changing the shape.

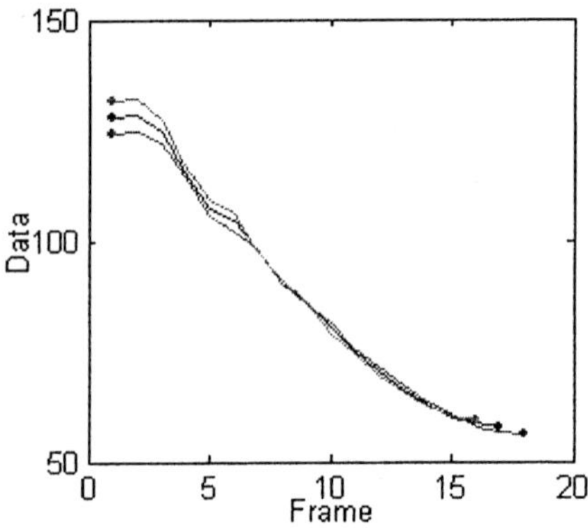

Fig. 6. Change the number of the high frequency coefficients in order to change the length of the curve. This is the picture after doing DCT transformation for one dimension's middle transitional stage, increasing a 0 to the high frequency coefficient, reducing the last high frequency and doing inverse transformation. We can see that even though the frame number changed, the shape did not change.

4 Experimental Result

In this paper, the sign words performed by 5 signers are considered as training data. Sign words are the 4942 words chosen from 《Chinese Sign Language Dictionary》. We generate three different signers' 4942 sign words by using the method described in Section 3, and measure the newly generated sign words by using the criterion given in Section 2.

Table 3. Comparison of the AverageTime and Recognition accuracy of the newly generated 3 signers' data

New data	A	B	C
AverageTime (frame)	19.54	20.42	21.29
Recognition accuracy in %	80.19	80.43	80.01

We can know from Table 3 the AverageTime of the newly generated 3 signers' data are different, because we changed the frame number in the middle transitional stage by changing DCT high frequency coefficient. We tested the newly generated sign word data by using the DGMM Recognizer in reference 7. The experiment shows the newly generated three signers' data all have the recognition accuracy above 80%, thus the method to generate sign word data presented in this paper is correct.

Table 4. Comparison of *Distance* of the newly generated 3 signers' data and the training data

Training data \ New data	A	B	C
pfz	377.86	363.80	325.53
lwr	407.23	396.51	276.81
ljh	339.45	426.75	378.17
mwh	298.14	342.69	297.98
ygy	317.61	387.55	416.44

Table 4 indicates all the *Distance* of the newly generated data and the training data are far above 255 which fully demonstrates the newly generated data can be distinguished from the training data. We can also see that the maximum number in Table 4 is 426.75 that is between signer ljh and the generated signer B. That means the feature difference between the generated signer B and signer ljh is the biggest.

We have generated another 3 person's data, which deviate the original signers' rhythm feature in the training data on the premise of accuracy, and successfully arrived at the purpose of generating sign language.

5 Conclusion

This paper analyzes the features of the rhythm of the same sign word performed by different signers, presents the formula for measuring the characteristics of time length, range and data variation of different signers. The sign language generation method basing on static gesture quantization and DCT which can generate new signer's sign word data according to the sign word data performed by the existed signers is then given. This method is demonstrated by the experimental result that the new data are accurate and differ from the training data.

References

1. Charayaphan C, Marble A. Image processing system for interpreting motion in American Sign Language. Journal of Biomedical Engineering, 1992, 14 (15): 419-425
2. S. S. Fels and G. Hinton, "Glove Talk: A neural network interface between a DataGlove and a speech synthesizaer", IEEE Transactions on Neural Networks, 1993, Vol. 4, pp.2-8.
3. M. W. Kadous, "Machine recognition of Auslan signs using PowerGlove: Towards large-lexicon recognition of sign language", proceeding of workshop on the Integration of Gesture in Language and Speech, Wilmington, DE, 1996, pp.165-174.
4. R.H. Liang, M. Ouhyoung, "A Real-time Continuous Gesture Recognition System for Sign Language", In Proceeding of the Third International Conference on Automatic Face and Gesture Recognition, Nara, Japan,1998, pp. 558-565.
5. C. Vogler, D. Metaxas, "Toward Scalability in ASL Recognition: Breaking Down Signs into Phonemes", In Proceedings of Gesture Workshop, Gif-sur-Yvette, France,1999, pp. 400-404.
6. Wu Jiangqin and Gao Wen. Sign Language Recognition Method on ANN/HMM. Computer science and application.No.9, pp 1-5.1999.
7. Wu Jiang-Qin,Gao Wen.A Hierarchical DGMM Recognizer for Chinese Sign Language Recognition. Journal of Software. Vol.11.No.11, pp 552-551.2000
8. Gaolin Fang, Wen Gao, Jiyong Ma, "Signer-Independent Sign Language Recognition Based on SOFM/HMM", IEEE ICCV Workshop on Recognition, Analysis and Tracking of Faces and Gestures in Real-time Systems (RATFG-RTS 2001), Vancouver, Canada, 2001: 90-95
9. Feng Jiang, Hongxun Yao, Guilin Yao. "Multilayer Architecture in Sign Language Recognition", Proceedings of the 5th International Conference on Multimodal Interfaces, 2004:102-104.

A Canonical Face Based Virtual Face Modeling

Seongah Chin

Division of Multimedia, Sungkyul University, Anyang-City, Korea
solideo@sungkyul.edu

Abstract. The research presented here is to create 3D virtual face based on the canonical face model derived from a clustering method on facial feature points. The algorithm efficiently transforms feature points of the canonical face model into those of the new face model for input images without creating new face manually. By comparative experiments, we have shown both facial models generated by manually and automatically. In conclusion, both facial models are quite identical visually whereas efficiency is totally different.

1 Introduction

In recent years, modeling virtual human face has attracted more and more attention from both research and industrial community. By advances in algorithms and new development in the supporting hardware, one can reside in a virtual environment moving, talking and interacting with other virtual characters or even real humans positioned at local or remote sites.

The face is a relatively small part of a virtual human, but it plays an essential role in communication [1],[2],[5]. Hence, it is very important to model human facial anatomy exactly, including its movements with respect to structural and functional aspects [3], [4].

Several issues are involved in modeling a virtual human face model such as acquisition of human face data, realistic high-resolution texture and functional information for animation of the human face [11].

There are various approaches to the reconstruction of a face using sculptor, laser scanner, stereoscopic camera, and face cloning, etc.[7],[10],[12]. These systems have tradeoffs in cost, accuracy, speed and expertise knowledge. Most of them concern precision and accuracy, which result in the intensive needs for high cost, expertise knowledge and a special environment setting in using them. Thus, those systems have limitations when compared practically to a commercial product such as mobile devices for the input of data for 3D face reconstruction and animation.

Recent developments in facial animation include physically-based approximation to facial tissue and the reconstruction of muscle contractions from several photos. Comparatively, face cloning technique, which reproduces a virtual model of a real person in virtual world, is much cheaper and easier to use when utilizing photos. This method is considered in this work for animation and face recognition. Developing a facial clone model requires a framework for describing geometric shapes and animation capabilities. Attributes such as surface color and textures must be taken into account. Prerequisite for cloning a face are analysis of several aspects necessary for its reconstruction such as shape and movements due to both emotion and speech. This

J. Tao, T. Tan, and R.W. Picard (Eds.): ACII 2005, LNCS 3784, pp. 179 – 186, 2005.

requires techniques from various fields. Shape includes geometrical form as well as other visual characteristics such as color and texture. Input for shape reconstruction may be drawn from photographs. The synthesis of facial motion involves deforming its geometry over time according to physical or ad hoc rules for generating movements conveying facial expressions.

In this paper, the methodology of acquisition of an animatable and canonical young Korean male face model with a realistic appearance is addressed. Our goal is to develop a technique that enables an easy cloning of real Korean male person on the canonical Korean male face model having the ability to be applicable into various areas properly and produced at a low cost.

2 3D Canonical Face Modeling

First of all 42 facial feature points on the sample image should be defined with respect to 3D feature vertices on the reference model. 42 feature points for one half of the face are based on 9 muscles for one half of the face related to animation parameters defined by Parke [13] and FACS(Facial Action Coding System) [14] as shown in Figure 1. Figure 1 shows frontal (left) and side (right) view of 42 feature points corresponding to 3D feature vertices. Accordingly facial feature points determining facial patterns should be defined in terms of usability and distinction between models.

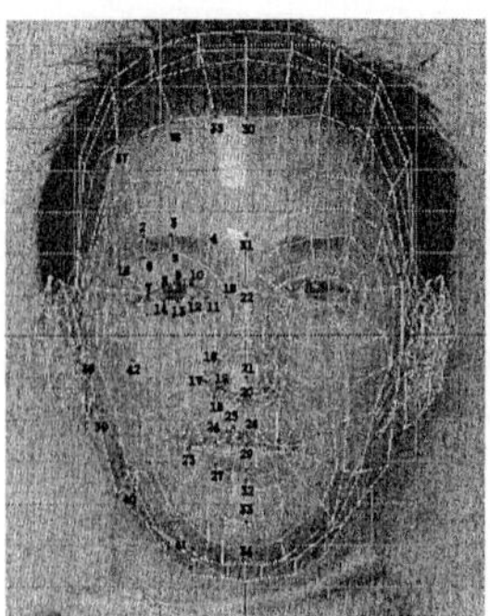

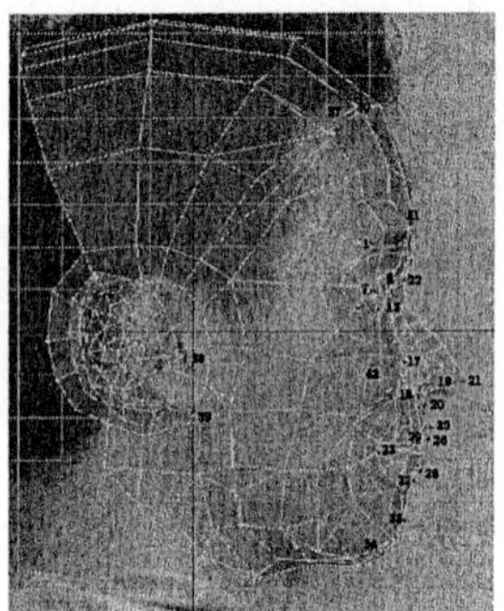

Fig. 1. 42 feature vertices on the 3D ref. model corresponding to feature points for a sample picture(frontal and side views)

In the sequel facial features can be utilized in facial expressions or facial recognition. Intentionally our facial feature points note both key aspects carrying reusability such as muscle motion directions for facial animation, eye, nose, mouth and shape of the face for facial recognition.

Then it is required to collect sample images from young Korean men and align the feature vertices on a reference 3D mesh model to the corresponding feature points of the sample images. We locate the sample images behind the 3D reference mesh model

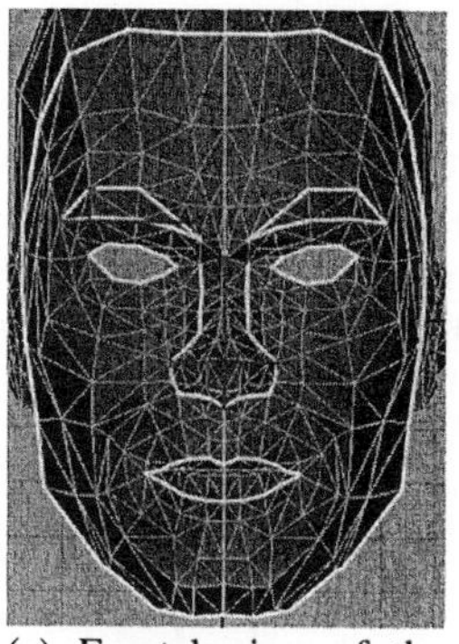
(a) Frontal view of the ref. mesh model

(b) Side view of the ref. mesh model

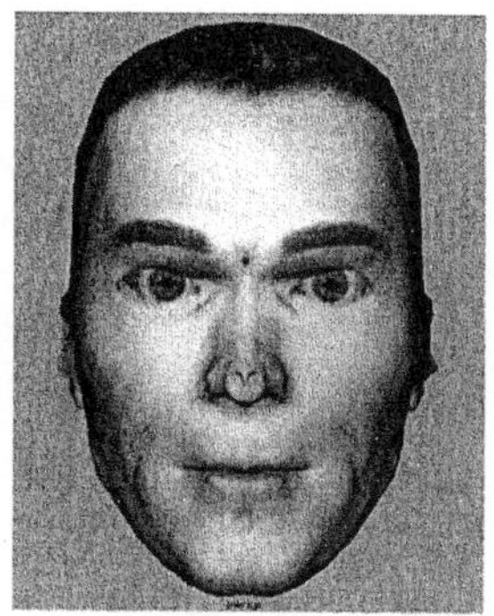
(c) Ref. model after texture mapping

Fig. 2. Reference model applied into creating Korean Canonical face model

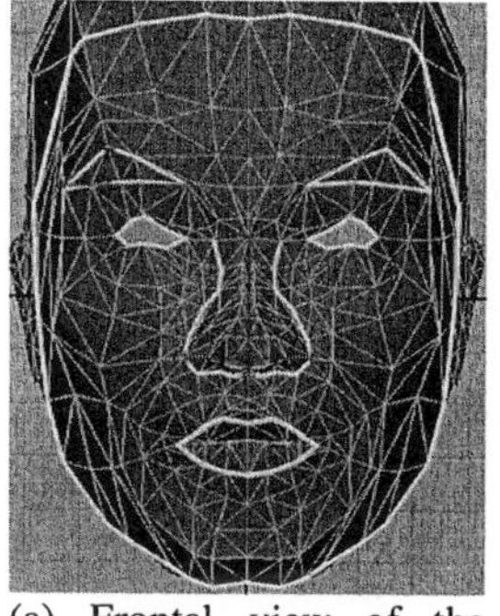
(a) Frontal view of the clustering mesh model

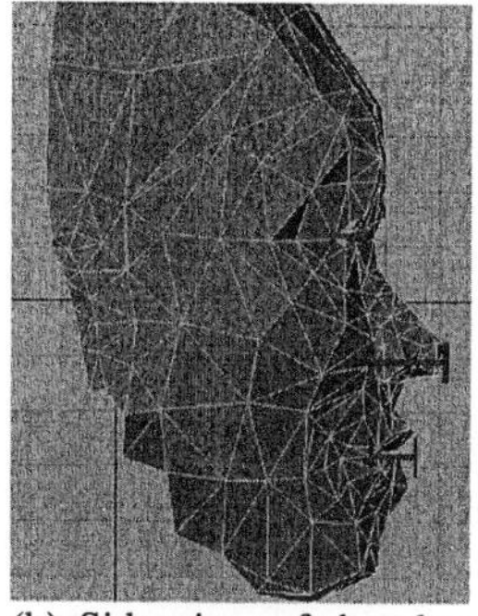
(b) Side view of the clustering mesh model

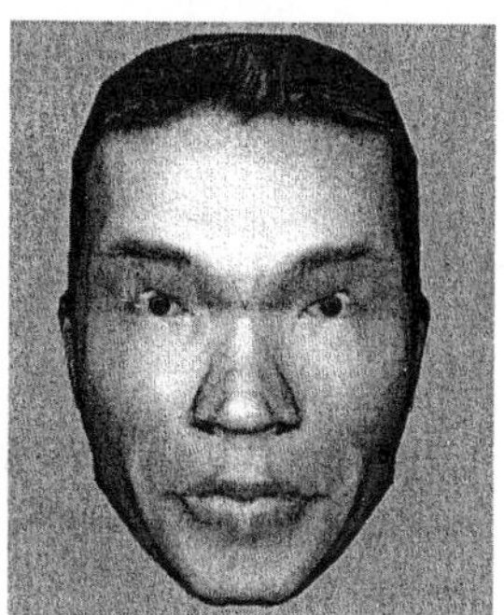
(c) Clustering model after texture mapping

Fig. 3. Canonical face model generated by FCM

in Fig. 2 so that it is possible to align feature vertices to feature points in a sample image by moving feature vertices as shown in Figure 3. At last Fuzzy c-mean algorithm has been applied to compute clustering center vertices standing for feature vertices of young Korean men. Standard Korean faces are usually characterized by the relatively round facial contours, and wide nostril and lips. Chins look prominent outward a little bit, which makes the forehead look shortened inwardly. These kinds of features are considered to be faithfully reflected in the FCM model, which is determined as a canonical Korean face model.

3 Defining Φ for Face Reconstruction

After setting up the canonical model as a reference 3D model, some distance-related functions should be employed to calculate displacement of non-feature points related to detected feature points from photos for cloning. Let p_i' be a point in an input image corresponding to vertex p_i in the canoniccal model. And let q_i be a vertex for a new face model. Now we derive transfer filter Φ_s computing vertices of a new face mesh model for an input image by converting vertex p_i of the canonical model into vertex q_i for a new face mesh model. Let q_i and q_i be a vertex in a new face model. We define vector l_s' consisting of p_i' and p_j' in an input image. The following equations are creating new vertices for input images.

$$q_i = \Phi_s'^i p_i$$

$$= \begin{bmatrix} 1\;0\;0 & \frac{1}{2}(\|l_s^x\|\Delta w - \|l_s^x\|') \\ 0\;1\;0 & \frac{1}{2}(\|l_s^y\|\Delta h - \|l_s^y\|') \\ 0\;0\;1 & \frac{1}{2}(\|l_s^z\|\Delta d - \|l_s^z\|') \\ 0\;0\;0 & 1 \end{bmatrix} \begin{bmatrix} x_i \\ y_i \\ z_i \\ 1 \end{bmatrix} = \begin{bmatrix} x_i + \frac{1}{2}(\|l_s^x\|\Delta w - \|l_s^x\|') \\ y_i + \frac{1}{2}(\|l_s^y\|\Delta h - \|l_s^y\|') \\ z_i + \frac{1}{2}(\|l_s^z\|\Delta d - \|l_s^z\|') \\ 1 \end{bmatrix} \tag{1}$$

Where $\Delta w = \frac{W'}{W}$, $\Delta h = \frac{H'}{H}$, *and* $\Delta d = \frac{D'}{D}$ if W′>W, H′>H and D′>D

$$q_j = \Phi_s'^j p_j$$

$$= \begin{bmatrix} 1\;0\;0 & -\frac{1}{2}(\|l_s^x\|\Delta w - \|l_s^x\|') \\ 0\;1\;0 & -\frac{1}{2}(\|l_s^y\|\Delta h - \|l_s^y\|') \\ 0\;0\;1 & -\frac{1}{2}(\|l_s^z\|\Delta d - \|l_s^z\|') \\ 0\;0\;0 & 1 \end{bmatrix} \begin{bmatrix} x_j \\ y_j \\ z_j \\ 1 \end{bmatrix} = \begin{bmatrix} x_j - \frac{1}{2}(\|l_s^x\|\Delta w - \|l_s^x\|') \\ y_j - \frac{1}{2}(\|l_s^y\|\Delta h - \|l_s^y\|') \\ z_j - \frac{1}{2}(\|l_s^z\|\Delta d - \|l_s^z\|') \\ 1 \end{bmatrix} \tag{2}$$

And where $\|l_s^x|$ is norm of the vector obtained by the projection of p_i and p_j onto xz plane followed by x axis. Similarly $\|l_s^y|$ is calculated by the projection of p_i and p_j onto xy plane followed by y axis and $\|l_s^z|$ is acquired by the projection of p_i and p_j onto yz plane followed by z axis. Finally we can obtain Φ(P) expressing vertices in the new face for an input image where P is a set of vertices on the canonical model.

There is quite enough number of such vectors defined in order to keep acuteness of the new face model. In addition, let us define vector l_s calculated by p_i and p_j on the canonical model corresponding to l_s' in an input image as shown in Figure 4 in (a) illustrating dotted circle l_s' in the input image and l_s is on the canonical model in (c).

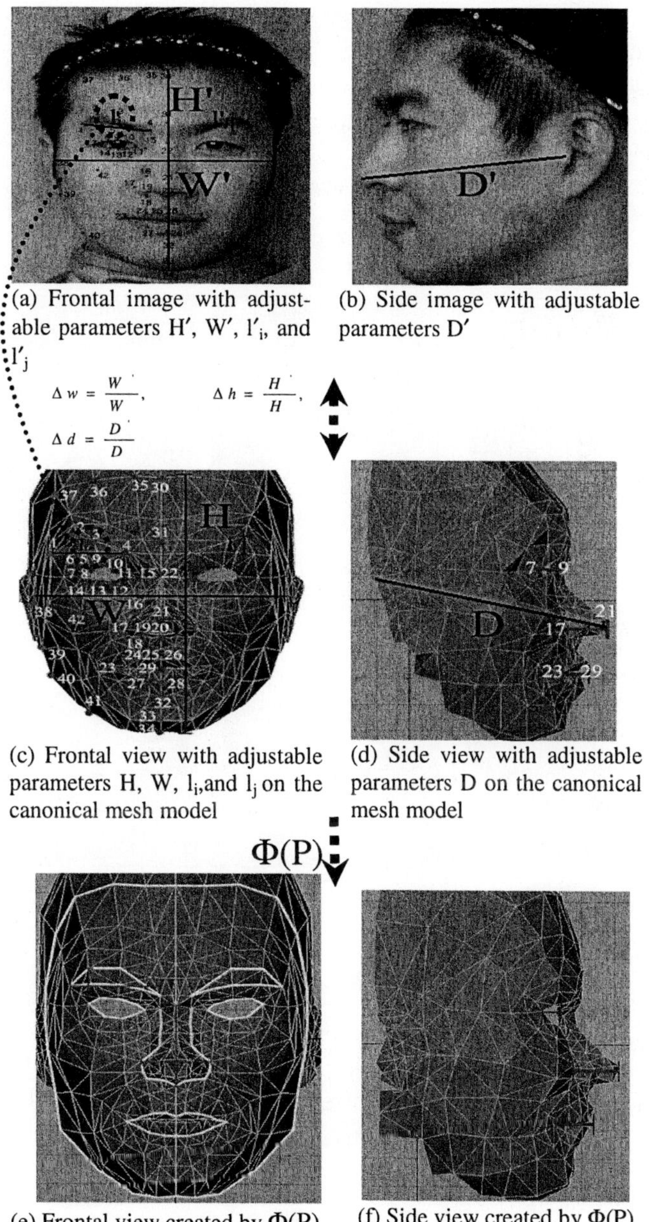

(a) Frontal image with adjustable parameters H′, W′, l'_i, and l'_j

(b) Side image with adjustable parameters D′

(c) Frontal view with adjustable parameters H, W, l_i,and l_j on the canonical mesh model

(d) Side view with adjustable parameters D on the canonical mesh model

(e) Frontal view created by Φ(P)

(f) Side view created by Φ(P)

Fig. 4. Face model generated by Φ(P) where P is a set of feature vertices on the canonical face model and Φ(P) is a set of feature vertices on the face mesh model suitable for the input image

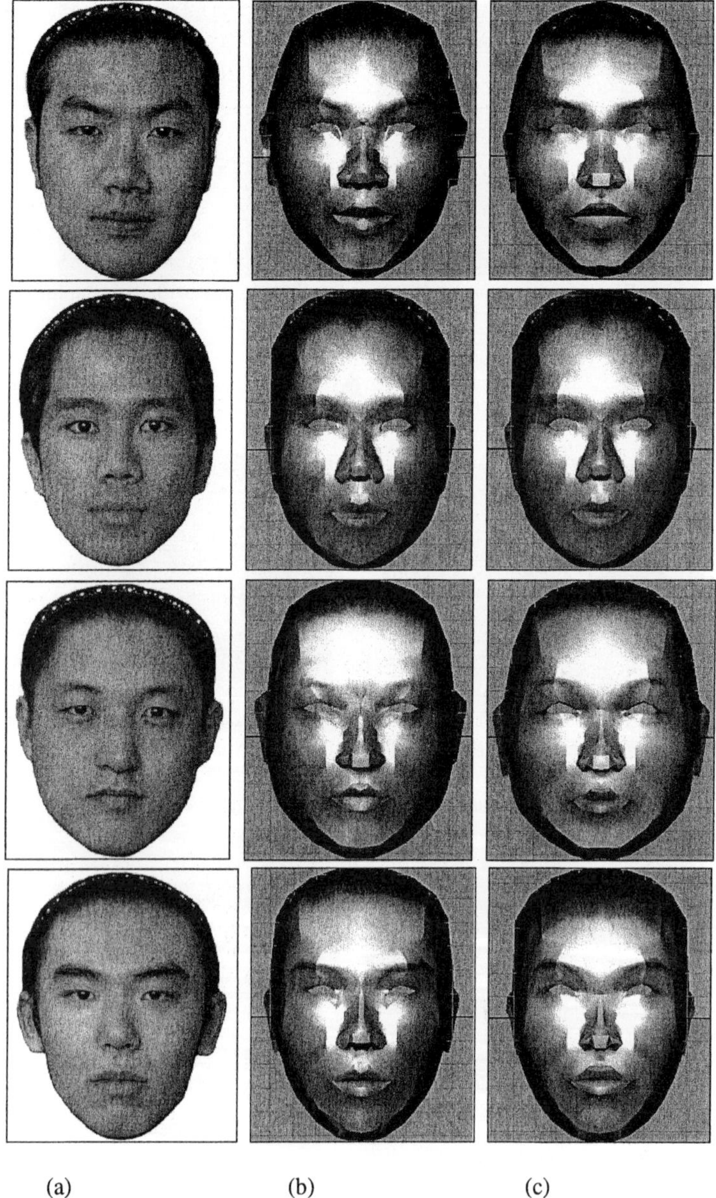

Fig. 5. The original photos in front view in (a), the 3D models created by manually in (b) and the 3D models obtained by the proposed method in (c)

4 Results and Discussion

The process of modification of canonical model fitting feature points detected from two orthogonal photos are as follows :

First, 42 feature vertices on the canonical model which are corresponding to feature points detected from two views of a person are defined. Then the global transformations such as transformation and scaling are applied to bring detected feature points to canonical model's 3D space. To construct the 3D structure of feature points, two eyes extremities in canonical model and a specific person are compared for scaling. And the center of rightmost, leftmost, up most, down most, front most, backmost points of the head are checked for translation. After this preliminary process, the transformation using faceline features are applied on the points of the canonical head using the formula (1) and (2). After computing the displacement of feature vertices, the displacement of non-feature vertices are calibrated by taking the relative distances between them into accounts manually. Figure 5 shows the result of experiments for the purpose of comparison the fully manually constructed model with the numerically developed method using canonical Korean face model. Finally we have found 3D faces created by the proposed method is as same as manually generated ones providing very simplicity and time efficiency.

In this paper, the process for developing a canonical Korean male face model using photos is introduced. This generic model is constructed for the photo-realistic animatable virtual human cloning. Two photos from front and side views are used to extract 3D face feature vertices. The collected 3D feature vertices are numerically computed for setting up canonical 3D facial positions. The computation of displacement for cloning is done by simple faceline linear transformation. Several photo pairs of real persons are tested for the plausibility of this method. The result shows that the suggested method is very simple, efficient and robust for reconstruction of 3D face model for animation and recognition. We plan to integrate this face cloning method with facial expression generation and recognition methods.

Acknowledgments

This work has been partially supported by University Industrial Technology Force (UNITEF). The author would like to thank to Ms. H. Park, Ms. J. Seo and lots of students for providing sample data and help.

References

1. Albert Mehrabian : Communication without words, Communication : Concepts and Process(editor : Joseph A. DeVito), Prentice-Hall, (1971) 106-114
2. Albert Mehrabian and James A. Russell : An Approach to Environmental Psychology, MIT Press, 1974
3. P. Ekman, & W. V. Friesen : Facial Action Coding System(FACS), Consulting Psychologist Press, Palo Alto. (1978)
4. P. Ekman, ,& W. V. Friesen : Emotion in the Human Face System, Cambridge University Press, San Francisco, CA, 2nd Edition (1982).
5. F.Hara and H.Kobayashi : Use of Face Robot for Human-Computer Communication, IEEE Conference on SMC, (1995) 1515-1520
6. F. I. Parke, Keith Waters : Computer Facial Animation, A K Peters Wellesley, (1996)
7. L. Moccozet and N. M.-Thalmann, Dirichlet free-form deformations and their application to hand simulation, Proc. Computer Animation, (1997)

8. Milan Sonka, et. al, : Image Processing, Analysis, and Machine Vision, PWS Publishing, (1999)
9. N. M. Thalmann, D. Thalmann : The direction of Synthetic Actors in the film Rendez-vous a Montreal, IEEE Computer Graphics and Applications, 7(12): (1987) 9-19
10. P. Fua and Y.G. Leclerc : Taking Advantage of Image-Based and Geometry-Based Constraints to Recover 3-D Surfaces, Computer Vision and Image Understanding, 64(1): (1996) 111-127
11. W.S. Lee, Jin Gu, N.M. Thalman : Generating Animatable 3D Virtual Humans from Photographs, Eurographics 2000, Paris
12. Y. Lee,., et. al, : Realistic Modeling for Facial Animation, Computer Graphics, (1996) 55-62
13. F. I., Parke, K. Waters: Computer Facial Animation. A K Peters. (1996)
14. P. Ekman, W.V Friesen : Manual for the Facial Action Coding System. Consulting Psychologist Press, Palo Alto. (1978)
15. P. Ekman, & W. V. Friesen : Emotion in the Human Face System, Cambridge University Press, San Francisco, CA, 2nd Edition (1982)
16. S.Chin, & S. Kim, : Deriving Facial Patterns for Specifying Korean Young Men's 3D Virtual Face from muscle based features, LNCS3309, (2004) 251-257
17. K.C. Lee, et. al, : Acquiring Linear Subspaces for Face Recognition under Variable Lighting, IEEE Transactions on PAMI, Vol. 27, No.5, (2005) 684-698
18. Y. Zhang, Qiang. Ji : Active and Dynamic Information Fusion for Facial Expression Understanding from Image Sequences, IEEE Transactions on PAMI, Vol. 27, No.5, (2005) 699-714
19. Y. Tian, T. Kanade, & J. Cohn : Recognizing Action Units for Facial Expression Analysis, IEEE Transactions on PAMI, Vol. 23, No.2, (2001) 97-114
20. M. Pantic, L. Rothkrantz, J.M. : Automatic Analysis of Facial Expressions : The State of the Art, IEEE Transactions on PAMI, Vol.22., No.12, (2000) 1424-1445
21. S. Kshirsagar, S. Garchery, G. Sannier & N. M. Thalmann, Synthetic Faces : Analysis and Applications, International Journal of Image Systems & Technoloogy, Vol. 13, (2003) 65-73
22. Y. Zhang, E.C. Prakash, E. Sung : Constructing a realistic face model of an individual for expression animation, International Journal of Information Technology, Vol.8. (2002)
23. B. Guenter, C. Grimm, D. Wood, H. Malvar, F. Pighin, : Making Faces. Proc. ACM SIGGRAPH98 Conf. (1998)

Facial Phoneme Extraction for Taiwanese Sign Language Recognition

Shi-Hou Lin, Pi-Fuei Hsieh, and Chung-Hsien Wu

Department of Computer Science and Information Engineering
National Cheng Kung University, Taiwan

Abstract. We have developed a system that recognizes the facial expressions in Taiwanese Sign Language (TSL) using a phoneme-based strategy. A facial expression is decomposed into three facial phonemes of eyebrow, eye, and mouth. A fast method is proposed for locating facial phonemes. The shapes of the phonemes were then matched by the deformable template method, giving feature points representing the corresponding phonemes. The trajectories of the feature points were tracked along the video image sequence and combined to recognize the type of facial expression. The tracking techniques and the feature points have been tailored for facial features in TSL. For example, the template matching methods have been simplified for tracking eyebrows and eyes. The mouth was tracked using the optical flow method, taking lips as homogeneous patches. The experiment has been conducted on 70 image sequences covering seven facial expressions. The average recognition rate is 83.3%.

1 Introduction

A number of work on facial expression recognition is focused on a small set of prototypic expressions of emotions [1] such as joy, surprise, anger, sadness, fear, and disgust. These expressions typically involve simultaneous changes in multiple regions of the face. In everyday life, however, such prototypic expressions occur relatively infrequently. Most emotions and paralinguistic communication, as seen in sign languages, are conveyed by changes in only one or two more local regions on the face. Action units (AUs) [2] have been defined for analytical descriptions of facial expressions. Facial expression recognition becomes a task to recognize AUs and their combinations. In [3], the various shapes of facial features, such as eyes, eyebrow, mouth and cheeks, are described for 16 AUs by multistate templates. The parameters of these multistate templates are used to recognize the AUs and their combinations by a Neural Network based classifier. However, the templates are required to be initialized manually in a video sequence. In [4], three upper face AUs and six lower face AUs are recognized using dense-flow, feature point tracking, and edge extraction. A separate hidden Markov model (HMM) was used for each AU and each combination of AUs. However, it is intractable to model more than 7000 AU combinations separately.

It is found that almost any facial expression in sign languages can be decomposed and described as a unique combination of primitive features of eyebrow, eye, and mouth. Therefore, the analysis platform can be lowered to the level of primitive features, making the recognition task scalable. Since sign languages are generally parallel to ordinary languages in phonologic analysis, the primitive features for facial

J. Tao, T. Tan, and R.W. Picard (Eds.): ACII 2005, LNCS 3784, pp. 187 – 194, 2005.

expressions are referred to as facial phonemes in this study. To enjoy the advantage of scalability gained by the divide-and-conquer strategy, we divide the recognition system of facial expressions into three modules, each for one phoneme. It inherits the property of the AUs. In addition, an analysis at the phoneme level is also beneficial for paralinguistic communication, where facial phonemes are to be combined with other hand gestures to express a whole sign word perfectly.

In this paper, we present an automatic system to recognize facial expressions in Taiwanese Sign Language (TSL). This system consists of three stages, as shown in Fig. 1. Assume that a sequence of image frames is acquired by a digital video camera as an input to our system. First, eyebrows, eyes, and mouth are located automatically. The deformable template method is used to match the shapes of facial phonemes in the first image frame, and the feature points are extracted from these shapes. In the next stage, these feature points are tracking in the following image sequence. Finally, based on the trajectories resulting from the stage of feature point tracking, features of phonemes are combined to decide the type of facial expression.

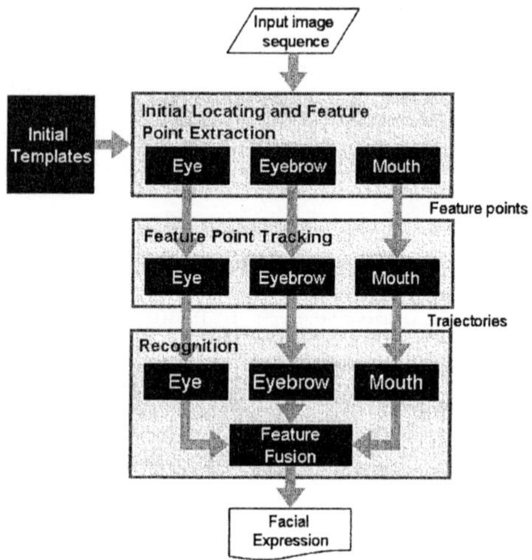

Fig. 1. Flow chart of the facial expression recognition system

2 Initial Locating and Feature Point Extraction

We propose a process to locate facial phonemes and extract feature points automatically. The process has seven steps:

1. Convert the first image frame from the RGB domain to the YIQ domain. From the new finding that the mouth is characterized by higher Q-values than skin and the background, we can obtain the rough location of the mouth.
2. Use the deformable template method [5] to obtain the exact shape and location of the mouth. Here the energy functions used in template matching have been modified.
3. Detect the human face and filter out the background using a threshold in domain.

4. Conjecture the rough location of the eyes based on the exact location and shape of the mouth. Locate the pupils in the conjectured area of the eyes by minimizing an energy function of pupils.
5. Find the center of the eyes from the neighboring pixels of the pupils. Match the exact shapes of the eyes with the template by minimizing an energy function [6] of eyes.
6. Locate the eyebrows from the neighboring pixels of the centers of the eyes by anthropometry. Match the exact shapes of eyebrows with the eyebrow template by minimizing an energy function [7] of eyebrows.
7. Generate 19 feature points (P_1-P_{19} as shown in Fig. 3) from the shapes of the facial phonemes obtained in the above steps, including six feature points from eyebrows, eight feature points from eyes, and five feature points from the mouth.

3 Feature Point Tracking

For each of the three phonemes, we track the corresponding feature points and record their trajectories for the subsequent stage. Due to distinct characteristics of phonemes, we specialized the tracking techniques for different phonemes. For example, eyebrows are tracked as rigid objects using a simplified template matching method whereas the lips of the mouth are tracked as homogeneous patches using the optical flow method.

3.1 Eyebrow Tracking

We utilize the property of lower intensity to design the energy function for tracking the eyebrow position because eyebrows respond with lower intensity values than the skin in the forehead. By regarding an eyebrow as a rigid object, the size and the shape remain unchanged. A deformable template method can thus be simplified with the eyebrow position as the only parameter. The eyebrow position is obtained from minimizing the energy function [7] in the $t+1$ frame from the neighboring position of the eyebrow in t frame, as shown in Fig. 2(a).

3.2 Eye Tracking

We use a simplified eye's deformable template [6] with two fixed points to track the eye's shape. The inner corner and the outside corner of an eye are assumed two fixed points in an image sequence. The template matching process yields the height of the upper eyelid in the $t+1$ frame, as shown in Fig. 2(b).

3.3 Mouth Tracking

First, we use the optical flow method [8] [9] to track lips To comply with the constraint of the optical flow method, we select points $P_u^{(t)}$ and $F_l^{(t)}$ as the feature points to be tracked, where $P_u^{(t)} = (P_{16}^{(t)} + P_{19}^{(t)})/2$ and $P_l^{(t)} = (P_{18}^{(t)} + P_{19}^{(t)})/2$ are shown in Fig. 2(c).

When the two points $P_u^{(t+1)}$ and $F_l^{(t+1)}$ have been tracked, we calculate the center point of the mouth ($P_m^{(t+1)}$) by averaging the two points $P_u^{(t+1)}$ and $F_l^{(t+1)}$ in the $t+1$ frame. Next, we project the rough area (A) that contains the mouth onto the x-axis in the edge field to estimate the width (b_m) of the mouth. Assume that the center point of the mouth ($P_m^{(t+1)}$) and two corners of the mouth $P_{15}^{(t+1)}$ and $F_{17}^{(t+1)}$ have the same y-coordinate, we obtain the positions of the two corners $P_{15}^{(t+1)}$ and $F_{17}^{(t+1)}$ in the $t+1$ frame from b_m and $P_m^{(t+1)}$.

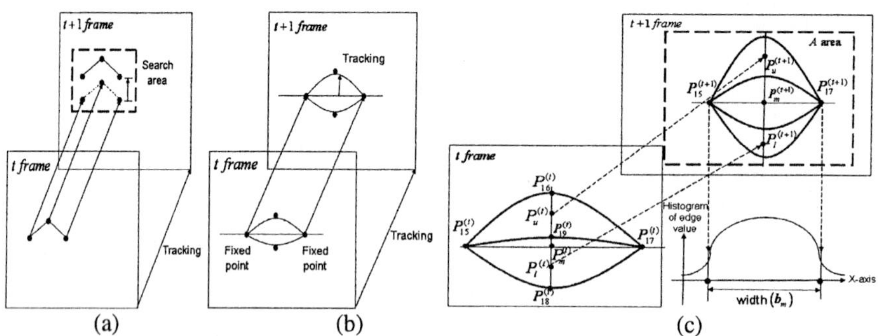

Fig. 2. (a) Eyebrow tracking by a simplified template matching method. (b) Eye tracking by a simplified template matching method. (c) Mouth tracking by the optical flow method and a projection method.

4 Recognition

Assume that the expression in the first frame of a video sequence is neutral. We have defined several distances based on the feature points. The distances used are illustrated in Fig. 3 and described in Table 1. The normalized differences of these distances between in first frame and last frame are chosen as features for recognition of the eyebrows, eyes, and mouth. That is, features for recognition are generated by

$$f_i = \left(d_i^{(T)} - d_i^{(1)}\right) / d_i^{(1)}, \tag{1}$$

where d_i are distances defined in Table 1.

In addition, we have found a feature useful for recognition of the mouth. We record the all pixels' intensity values on the line formed of the two feature points on the upper and lower lips. The intensity value can be used as a feature to recognize the opening and the closing of the mouth.

For recognition of Taiwanese Sign Language, we define three eyebrow positions (neutral/normal, raised, and furrowed), three eye shapes (neutral, wide-open, and closed), and five mouth shapes (neutral, whistle-shaped, Ah-shaped, Smile, and Oh-shaped).

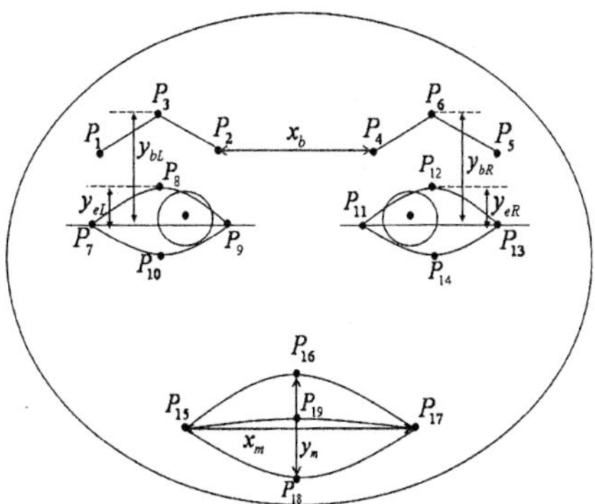

Fig. 3. Feature points and the related distances

Table 1. Description of the distances used for generating the features of recognition

Phoneme	Distance, $d_i^{(t)}$	Description
Eyebrow	$d_1 = y_{bL}$	● Distance from the center point of the left eye to the feature points in the middle of the left eyebrows
	$d_2 = y_{bR}$	● Distance from the center point of the right eye to the feature points in the middle of the right eyebrows
	$d_3 = x_b$	● Distance between the left and the right eyebrows
Eye	$d_4 = y_{eL}$	● Distance from the center point of the left eye to the upper left eyelid
	$d_5 = y_{eR}$	● Distance from the center point of the right eye to the upper right eyelid
Mouth	$d_6 = y_m$	● The length of the mouth
	$d_7 = x_m$	● The width of the mouth

5 Experiments and Results

Experiments were conducted in two levels: facial phonemes and facial expressions (sign words). In the phoneme level, we focus on the recognition of the facial phonemes. In the sign-word level, we focus on the recognition of the sign words that are combinations of the facial phonemes.

5.1 Result of Feature Point Extraction

A video sequence that contains a facial expression of a person is an input to our system. The resolution of each image frame is 352x240 pixels. Fig. 4 shows the results of detected facial features in the first frames of two image sequences.

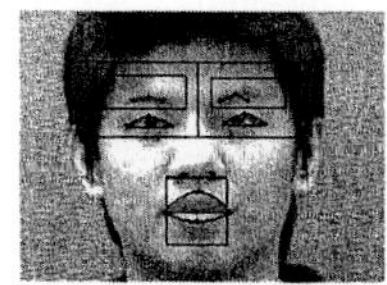 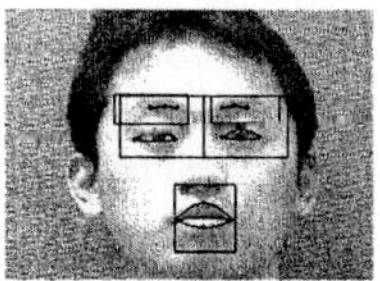

Fig. 4. The detection results of facial phonemes

5.2 Recognition of Facial Phonemes

In this level for phoneme recognition, we devise three experiments to evaluate the performance of our system. The image sequences used include five distinct people. There are 11 expressions for each one and five samples for each expression. There are 165 training samples and 110 testing samples for each phoneme. The results of the phonemes tracked and the recognition are shown in Fig. 5 and Table 2, respectively.

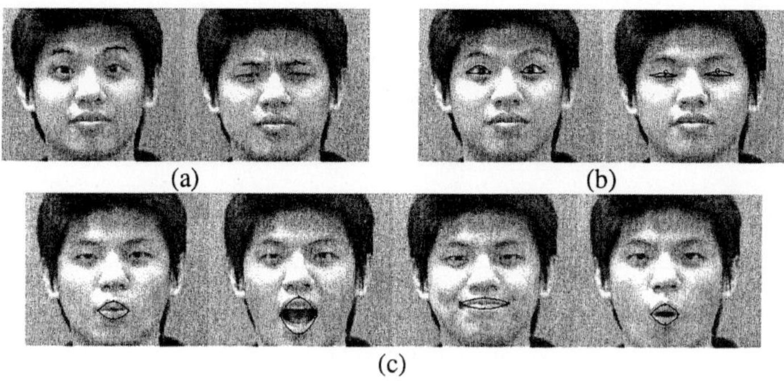

Fig. 5. Various phoneme tracking

Table 2. Recognition results of phonemes

	Eyebrow		Eye		Mouth	
Class no.	Class	Acc.	Class	Acc.	Class	Acc.
1	Neutral	94.0	Neutral	92.5	Neutral	92.3
2	Raised	92.3	Wide-open	76.9	Whistle-shaped	60.0
3	Furrowed	94.7	Closed	79.3	Ah-shaped	78.9
4	-	-	-	-	Smile	82.3
5	-	-	-	-	Oh-shaped	60.5
Total accuracy (%)		93.5		83.3		82.4

5.3 Recognition of Facial Expressions

We chose seven facial expressions that could be used alone to represent sign words sufficiently. The phonemic compositions of the facial expressions are listed in Table 3. Here, this experiment is devised to evaluate the performance of the recognition of the facial expressions in our system. The video sequences of the tested

Table 3. Sign words that are conveyed by facial expressions

Sign word	Eyebrow	Eye	Mouth
Have	Neutral	Neutral	Whistle-shaped
Wooden	Neutral	Neutral	Oh-shaped
Shock	Raised	Wide-open	Ah-shaped
Ha	Neutral	Neutral	Ah-shaped
Sour	Furrowed	Closed	Smile
Look	Raised	Wide-open	Neutral
Happy	Neutral	Neutral	Smile

facial expressions were the inputs to the system. The image sequences were acquired from five people. Each facial expression was repeated by every signer for five times, giving a total of 175 samples. There were 105 samples used for training and 70 samples for testing. The percentage of the correctly classified samples by the Maximum Likelihood classifier is 83.8%.

6 Discussion

In the experiments for recognition of facial phonemes, individual recognition accuracy of the eyebrows, eyes, and mouth are 90.7%, 80.2%, and 86.0%, respectively. Some errors of the recognition occur in the extraction of the facial phonemes. The others occur in the tracking process. In the tracking process, the main problem is head motion. Head motion is serious problem if we use the distances as features for recognition. For the eyebrows, we track directly the positions of the eyebrows and use the relative distances between the eyebrows and eyelids as the features. For the mouth, we track the feature points of the upper and lower lips and calculate the new center of the mouth from the two points to update the position of the mouth. The two phonemes of the eyebrows and mouth do not have such hand motion problem. For eyes, however, we regard inner and outer corners as fixed points. It is serious problem if the head motion occurred. Therefore, we adjust the tracking method of the eyes. We permit these fixed points can shift toward up and down to match the correct position of the eyes' inner and outer corners. It can overcome light head motion and increase the accuracy of the recognition. The result improved is shown in Fig. 6. There is still a failure if the head motion occurred with a large distance.

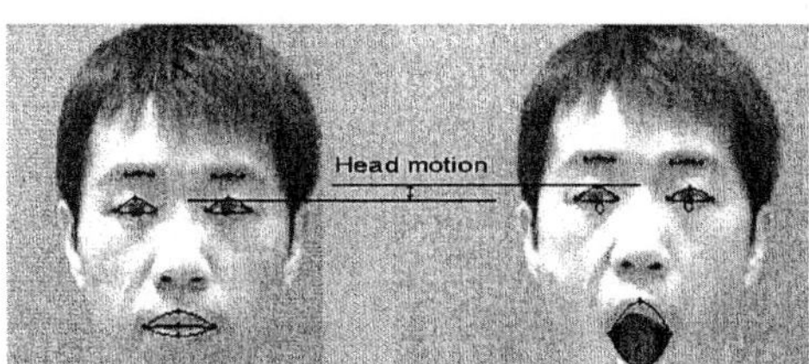

Fig. 6. The result improved of the head motion

There is still a problem for the recognition of the mouth. If we use the length and width of the mouth as the features for the recognition of the mouth, the shapes of the Whistle-shaped and Oh-shaped mouth classes are too similar to separate the two classes for recognition in the xy-coordinates, though there is a difference in z-coordinate.

7 Conclusions

A facial expression recognition system is designed and developed on the basis of phonemes for Taiwanese Sign Language. This system includes several tracking techniques especially suitable for the facial features in TSL. Our experimental results have demonstrated the feasibility of the system for the recognition of facial expressions in Taiwanese Sign Language. In the future, we will investigate the problems of the serious head motion and similar shapes of the mouth.

Acknowledgment

The authors would like to thank the National Science Council, Taiwan, for financially supporting this research work under Contract No. NSC93-2213-E-006-072. The authors would also like to thank Miss Gong-Ru Lin for her assistance in TSL experiments.

References

1. P. Ekman, "Facial expression and emotion," *American Psychologist,* Vol. 48, no. 4, pp. 384-392, Apr. 1993.
2. P. Ekman, W. V. Friesen, "Facial action coding system investigator's guide," *Consulting Psychologist Press,* Palo Alto, CA, 1978.
3. Y. Tian, T. Kanade, and J. F. Cohn, "Recognizing action units for facial expression analysis," *IEEE Trans. Pattern Anal. Machine Intell.*, Vol. 23, no. 2, pp. 97-115, 2001.
4. J. Lien, T. Kanade, J. Cohn, and C. C. Li, "Detection, tracking and classification of action units in facial expression," *Journal of Robotics and Autonomous Systems*, Vol. 31, no. 3, pp. 131-146, May 2000.
5. L. Yin and A. Basu, "Generating realistic facial expressions with wrinkles for model-based coding," *Computer Vision and Image Understanding*, Vol. 84, no. 2, pp. 201-240, Nov. 2001.
6. A. Yuille, D. Cohen and P. Hallinan, "Feature extraction from faces using deformable templates," *Proc. IEEE Conf. CVPR*, pp. 104-109, Jun. 1989.
7. F. Hara, K. Tanaka, H. Kobayashi, and A.Tange, "Automatic feature extraction of facial organs and contour," *Proc. IEEE Int'l Workshop on Robot and Human Communication*, Vol. 29 Sept.-1, pp. 386-391, Oct. 1997.
8. B. Horn and B. Schunck, "Determining optical flow,' *Artif. Intell.*, Vol. 17 ,pp. 185-203, Aug. 1981.
9. L. Yin, A. Basu, and M.T. Yourst, "Active tracking and cloning of facial expressions using spatio-temporal information,' *Proc. ICTAI 2002.*

What Expression Could Be Found More Quickly? It Depends on Facial Identities

Hang Zhang[1,2], Yuming Xuan[1], and Xiaolan Fu[1,*]

[1] State Key Laboratory of Brain and Cognitive Science, Institute of Psychology, Chinese Academy of Sciences, Beijing 100101, China
{zhangh, xuanym, fuxl}@psych.ac.cn
[2] Graduate School of the Chinese Academy of Sciences, Beijing 100049, China

Abstract. Visual search task was used to explore the role of facial identity in the processing of facial expression. Participants were asked to search for a happy or sad face in a crowd of emotional face pictures. Expression search was more quickly and accurate when all the faces in a display belonged to one identity than two identities. This suggested the interference of identity variance on expression recognition. At the same time the search speed for a certain expression also depended on the number of facial identities. When faces in a display belonged to one identity, a sad face among happy faces could be found more quickly than a happy face among sad faces; otherwise, when faces in a display belonged to two identities, a happy face could be found more quickly than a sad face.

1 Introduction

Recognizing facial expressions is a fundamental and important ability people possess to understand emotions of other people and to communicate with others efficiently. It is also becoming a crucial element for the new generation of human-computer interfaces, such as vision-based or camera-based interfaces, which require the computer to identify the user's emotional status and change its behavior accordingly to provide better support [11]. Understanding the mechanism of human's recognition of facial expressions could be useful and helpful to make computers achieve matchable or acceptable performance.

Human faces contain a series of semantic information besides expression, such as identity, gender, age and race, and a natural question is whether the extraction and coding of certain kinds of information, especially, expression and identity, are independent of each other. The answer relies on two aspects. The first one is the physical separability of facial information. A principle component analysis of the pixel intensities of facial expression pictures revealed that different information is responsible for expression coding and identity coding [3]. For example, eye width and jaw drop were important expression components, while face width was an important identity component. Another study suggested that high-frequency components of a face might be important for the recognition of facial expression [14]. But these are not doubtless

* Corresponding author.

J. Tao, T. Tan, and R.W. Picard (Eds.): ACII 2005, LNCS 3784, pp. 195–201, 2005.

evidences for the separation of expression and identity information, but only imply that people may have different biases towards the two processes. The other aspect is whether there are independent systems in the brain respectively for the processing of expression and identity. "Fusiform face area" (FFA), i.e., the middle lateral fusiform gyrus, a region responding more to faces than to other object categories, which contributed to distinguishing new faces from old ones [13], might be the area for identity processing. In contrast, expression processing was thought to relate with the superior temporal sulcus and the amygdala [8]. But it was shown that the FFA was also sensitive to variations in expression even for identity processing or passive viewing of faces [7]. Therefore, whether expression recognition and identity recognition are parallel or interactive is still a question in debate.

Most behavioral evidences for the interaction between the processing of expression and identity came from studies using Garner's task [1][6]. Participants were asked to do speeded classification according either to identity or to expression. When the classification task was on one dimension, the other dimension was correlated, constant, or orthogonal. The reaction time difference between these three conditions for expression classification reflected the interference of identity variance on the processing of expression. Is this effect robust enough to be replicated with other paradigms? The present study aimed to use visual search paradigm to explore whether and how facial identity would affect the processing of facial expression.

The basic logic of our study is as follows: If searching for an expression among faces of more than one identity is more difficult than searching among faces of a single identity, it implies that automatic identity activation could exert an effect on expression processing.

In a visual search task, participants may be required to search for a target with a predefined property or a property distinct from other items on a certain dimension. Search is usually more efficient in the former condition than in the latter condition, because a predetermined target allows people to expect what it looks like and have more top-down guidance accordingly [16]. In our study the effect of target certainty on search was also examined to evaluate to what extent expression search is modulated by top-down information.

In previous studies about facial expression perception, a famous but debatable finding was the search asymmetry between different expressions. Negative expressions were observed to be found more promptly than positive expressions in some studies, but this result failed to be replicated in other studies [10][12]. But items to be searched in these experiments were mainly schematic faces or faces of one identity at a time. In the present study, identity of faces was manipulated to investigate its possible effects on negative-face advantage in visual search.

2 Method

2.1 Participants

Eleven paid undergraduate students took part in our experiment. Among them, eight were males, three were females, and all had normal or corrected-to-normal vision.

2.2 Stimuli and Apparatus

Stimuli were black-and-white pictures of two female faces (A & B, Fig. 1) with happy or sad expressions. Seven independent raters categorized expressions of about 20 digital photographs into happiness, anger, fear, sadness, disgust, surprise or neutral expression. The four stimuli pictures selected from the photographs had happy or sad expressions agreed by at least half of the raters, and had no irrelevant salient features, and were polished with Photoshop 7.0 to diminish their differences in image attributes.

  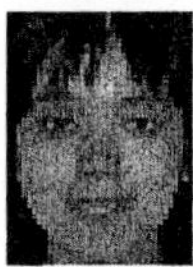 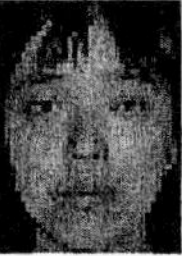

Fig. 1. Pictures of faces used in the experiment

Stimuli were presented on black background in the center of a 17 inch monitor. Matlab PsychToolbox [2] was used to control the experiment and record responses. Participants were seated about 65 cm from the monitor.

Stimuli were composed of several faces, each of which extended 1.9 deg in width and 2.6 deg in height. They scattered randomly in an imaginary four-by-three grid covering 9.5 × 9.5 deg in the center of the screen. Each unit of the grid was 2.4 × 3.2 deg and an individual face could appear anywhere in its display unit on a random basis.

2.3 Procedure

Each trial started with a centered "+" fixation point for 1 s, and after it disappeared, four, six or eight happy or sad faces was displayed until a response was made or for a maximum duration of 3 s. The interval between trials varied from 1 s to 1.8 s.

There were three kinds of tasks. In Searching-for-Happy-Faces (SHF) blocks, participants were told that the displays were a happy face among a crowd of sad faces, or all sad faces, and they had to decide the presence of happy face. In Searching-for-Sad-Faces (SSF) blocks, participants were told that the displays were a sad face among a crowd of happy faces, or all happy faces, and they had to decide the presence of sad face. In Searching-for-Different-Faces (SDF) blocks, participants were told that there might be a happy face among a crowd of sad faces, or all sad faces, or a sad face among a crowd of happy faces, or all happy faces, and they had to decide if there was a face of different expression than others. The numbers of target-present trials and target-absent trials were equal. Half of the participants were instructed to press the "z" key with left index finger for "yes" response and "/" with right index finger for "no" response, and the other half were told the reverse. They were asked to respond as promptly and accurately as possible. Accuracy and reaction time were recorded for experimental trials.

2.4 Design

In each task, faces could belong to female A only, or female B only, or half faces were A and the other were B. Multiplied with three kinds of tasks, there were nine conditions altogether. The displays in each condition had the same possibility to consist of four, six, or eight items.

Each of blocks of SHF or SSF with A's or B's faces had 6 practice and 60 experimental trials. Blocks of SHF or SSF with A and B's faces, and blocks of SDF with A's or B's faces had 12 practice and 120 experimental trials each. The condition of SDF in A and B's faces was split into two blocks, both had 12 practice and 120 experimental trials. Participants were tested through all the ten blocks in one of four counterbalance orders.

There were five independent variables: target state (present vs. absent), number of items (four, six, or eight), target certainty (one certain expression vs. one of the two expressions), target expression (happy vs. sad), and number of identities (one identity vs. two identities).

3 Results

All the participants completed the experiment and the lowest accuracy was 0.89. Accuracy and reaction time for correct responses were analyzed respectively.

3.1 Reaction Time

A repeated-measures ANOVA of reaction time was conducted on the five independent variables. The main effects of target state, number of items, target certainty, and number of identities were significant. As expected, responses were faster for target-present conditions (1476 ms) than for target-absent conditions (1794 ms), $F(1, 10) = 227.3$, $p < 0.001$. There were significant differences among four-item conditions (1434 ms), six-item conditions (1674 ms), and eight-item conditions (1828 ms), $F(2, 9) = 99.3$, $p < 0.001$. Effects of target certainty and number of identities on searching performance were shown in table 1. Searching was faster when target was a certain expression (1517 ms) than when target was an uncertain distinct expression (1770 ms), $F(1, 10) = 62.8$, $p < 0.001$. Expression search was done more quickly in one person's face crowds (1519 ms) than in two persons' face crowds (1769 ms), $F(2, 9) = 99.3$, $p < 0.001$, suggesting that the irrelevant dimension, facial identity, could influence expression processing.

Table 1. Mean reaction time (ms) and percentage correct (%) under two conditions of number of identities (one vs. two) by two conditions of target certainty (certain vs. uncertain)

	Reaction Time		**Percentage Correct**	
	Number of Identities		Number of Identities	
Target Certainty	One	Two	One	Two
Certain	1401	1637	95.45	91.86
Uncertain	1640	1908	93.11	87.50

The interaction between target state and number of items was significant, $F(2, 9) = 54.6$, $p < 0.001$,which indicated search slope difference under target-present and target-absent conditions. In the four conditions shown in table 1, target-present slopes ranged from 55 to 63 ms/item, target-absent slopes from 123 to 152 ms/item, and slope ratios (target-absent to target-present) from 2.25 to 2.48, suggesting patterns of typical serial and self-terminating search [15].

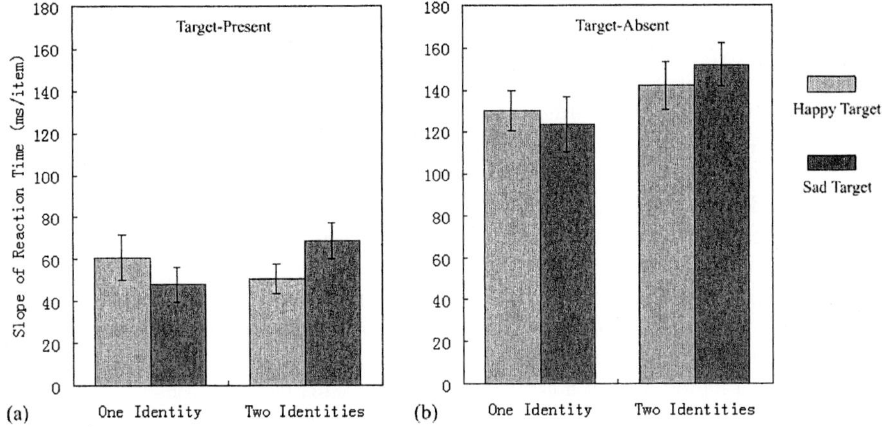

Fig. 2. Slopes of reaction time for target-present conditions (a) and target-absent conditions (b)

An interesting result was the three-way interaction of number of items by target expression by number of identities, $F(2, 9) = 8.52$, $p = 0.008$. Since "no" response might involve some special strategy unlike "yes" response, separate analyses were made on slopes under target-present and target-absent conditions. Main results were shown in Fig. 2. When there was a target face in the display, the interaction between number of identities and target expression was significant, $F(1, 10) = 8.99$, $p = 0.013$. A sad face among happy faces would be more quickly found than a happy face among sad faces if all faces in a display belonged to one person; but if two persons' faces were involved simultaneously in a search, a happy face would be found more quickly. When target was absent, there was no statistically significant interaction, but the trend was similar.

3.2 Percentage Correct

A repeated-measures ANOVA of percentage correct was conducted on the five independent variables. The main effects of target state, number of items, target certainty, and number of identities were significant, and the directions of difference was consistent with those of reaction time data, i.e., the conditions under which participants had faster responses were also the conditions under which more accurate responses were made, thus excluding the possibility of speed-accuracy tradeoff. Main results of percentage correct were given in table 1. There was also no interaction between target certainty and number of identities.

4 Discussion

Consistent with earlier studies [10][12], expression search in our experiment is serial and self-terminating, which means participants indeed searched for expressions and so the accompanying effects can't be simply attributed to some salient feature irrelevant to facial expression. As expected, the reaction time and accuracy data show that search is faster and more accurate when the identity of faces keeps constant than when it varies, indicating that identity information can't be fully neglected in the coding of facial expression. The present result from visual search adds positive evidences to the hypothesis that the processing of expression may be interfered with the processing of identity.

Target certainty also has effects on the efficiency of expression search. Knowing the target is a happy or sad face facilitates the search, compared with the conditions in which target expression is uncertain and may vary from trial to trial. The number of identities and target certainty has no interaction, implying the effects of identities on expression recognition are more likely mediated by a bottom-up mechanism but not top-down expectations.

The new finding of the present study is that what expressions could be easily found depends on the number of identities involved in the searching. When all the faces are of a single identity, searching for a sad face in a crowd of happy faces is faster than searching for a happy face in a crowd of sad faces. This result is consistent with previous studies demonstrating faces with negative expressions capture more attention [4][5]. But this is only one side of the coin. When two identities are involved, the happy face among sad faces is more promptly found than the sad face among happy faces. There was evidence that the expression of happiness is more consistent between different people than the expression of sadness is [9]. Supposed this is the case in our study, in a display involved two identities, happy faces should be more easily identified because of their higher similarity. When the effect of high similarity of happiness expression outweighs the capturing-attention effect of negative expressions, a reverse result appears.

5 Conclusion

In this study visual search task was used to investigate the possible influence of facial identity on facial expression. Switching from faces of one person to faces of another person has cost on the processing of expression. And the number of identities for expression search affects which expression, happiness or sadness, could be searched faster.

Acknowledgements

This research was supported in part by grants from 973 Program of Chinese Ministry of Science and Technology (2002CB312103), from the National Natural Science Foundation of China (60433030 and 30270466), and from the Chinese Academy of Sciences (0302037).

References

1. Baudouin, J.-Y., Martin, F., Tiberghien, G., Verlut, I., Franck, N.: Selective Attention to Facial Emotion and Identity in Schizophrenia. Neuropsychologia. 40 (2002) 503-511
2. Brainard, D.H.: The Psychophysics Toolbox. Spat. Vis. 10 (1997) 433–436
3. Calder, A.J., Burton, A.M., Miller, P., Young, A.W., Akamatsu, S.: A Principal Component Analysis of Facial Expressions. Vision Res. 41 (2001) 1179-1208
4. Eastwood, J.D., Smilek, D., Merikle, P.: Negative Facial Expression Captures Attention and Disrupts Performance. Perception & Psychophysics. 65 (2003) 352-358
5. Fenske, M.J., Eastwood, J.D.: Modulation of Focused Attention by Faces Expressing Emotion: Evidence From Flanker Tasks. Emotion. 3 (2003) 327-343
6. Ganel, T., Goshen-Gottstein, Y.: Effects of Familiarity on the Perceptual Integrality of the Identity and Expression of Faces: The Parallel-Route Hypothesis Revisited. Journal of Experimental Psychology: Human Perception and Performance. 30 (2004) 583-597
7. Ganel, T., Valyear, K.F., Goshen-Gottstein, Y., Goodale, M.A.: The Involvement of the "Fusiform Face Area" in Processing Facial Expression. Neuropsychologia. In Press
8. Haxby, J.V., Hoffman, E.A, Gobbini, M.I.: The Distributed Human Neural System for Face Perception. Trends Cogn. Sci. 4 (2000) 223-233
9. Kohler, C.G., Turner, T., Stolar, N.M., Bilker, W.B., Brensinger, C.M., Gur, R.E., et al.: Differences in Facial Expressions of Four Universal Emotions. Psychiatry Research. 128 (2004) 235-244
10. Nothdurft, H.C.: Faces and Facial Expressions Do Not Pop Out. Perception. 22 (1993) 1287-1298
11. Porta, M.: Vision-Based User Interfaces: Methods and Applications. Int. J. Human-Computer Studies. 57 (2002) 27-73
12. Purcell, D.G., Stewart, A.L., Skov, R. B.: It Takes a Confounded Face to Pop Out of a Crowd. Perception. 25 (1996) 1091-1108
13. Rossion, B., Schiltz, C., Crommelinck, M.: The Functionally Defined Right Occipital and Fusiform "Face Areas" Discriminate Novel from Visually Familiar Faces. NeuroImage. 19 (2003) 877-883
14. Tsurusawa, R., Goto, Y., Mitsudome, A., Tobimatsu, S.: An Important Role for High-spatial Frequencies in Recognition of Facial Expressions. Int. Congress Series. 1278 (2005) 53-56.
15. Wolfe, J.M.: What Can 1 Million Trials Tell Us About Visual Search? Psychol. Sci. 9 (1998) 33-39
16. Wolfe, J.M., Butcher, S.J., Lee, C., Hyle, M.: Changing Your Mind: On the Contributions of Top-Down and Bottom-Up Guidance in Visual Search for Feature Singletons. Journal of Experimental Psychology: Human Perception and Performance. 29 (2003) 483-502

Using an Avatar to Develop a System for the Predication of Human Body Pose from Moments

Song Hu and Bernard F. Buxton

Department of Computer Science, University College London,
Gower Street, London WC1E 6BT, UK
{s.hu, b.buxton}@cs.ucl.ac.uk

Abstract. Tracking people using movie sequences is not straightforward because of the human body's articulation and the complexity of a person's movements. In this paper we show how a person's 3D pose can be reconstructed by using corresponding silhouettes of video sequences from a monocular view. Currently, a virtual avatar is used to train the model for inferring the pose and a different avatar is used to produce novel examples not in the training set in order to evaluate the approach. The approach was subsequently tested using the silhouettes of walking people.

1 Introduction

In recent years, computer vision researchers have been interested in tracking people in video sequences since such a capability may enable a wide variety of applications in surveillance, entertainment, sports, computer games and even robotics. However, the task is not easy because of the human body's articulation and the complexity of a person's movements. Some work has been carried out to track a pedestrian's shape, for example in 2D [1]. However, instead of only tracking a person's 2D shape from the video frames, we aim to track a person's pose in 3D, which describes the movement more precisely than the 2D shapes do.

Bowden *et al* and Grauman *et al* have attempted to achieve 2D to 3D mapping by combining 2D and 3D data in single or mixture models [2,5] similar to local linear embeddings. In their approaches, 2D landmarks are labelled on the person's silhouette contour in each frame to represent the shape of the moving person through an image sequence (400 points are used in Bowden's work and 200 points are used in Grauman's work). This approach requires an accurate and reliable method to label each landmark at the same place of the silhouette contour otherwise the model cannot represent the changes of the moving person's shape reliably. The landmarks should also be located on important parts of the object, so that, for example, each anatomically important part (such as the hands and face) will be labelled with at least one landmark point to ensure that objects are modelled fully. Using more landmark points or even using the whole contour can reduce the possibility of missing important parts of the object and can also lower the requirements on landmark labelling accuracy. However, using

J. Tao, T. Tan, and R.W. Picard (Eds.): ACII 2005, LNCS 3784, pp. 202–209, 2005.

many landmark points is not ideal since it raises the dimension of the 2D data dramatically and does not provide, from contour data, a concomitant increase in the information available.

Thus, we have developed an approach based on global features of the silhouette contour such as its moments which, though they might be expected to be quite sensitive to noise and to details of the silhouette shape give us the benefit of a compact description and avoid the difficulties of building an accurate and reliable landmark labelling system. To achieve the goal of tracking 3D pose, we analyse the correlation between the silhouette's moments and the corresponding 3D pose of the body. To capture this correlation, we build a combined 2D and 3D statistical model, which can later be used to infer a moving person's 3D pose from a single video frame. In principle, the 3D pose may be inferred from 2D data by calculation of the posterior distribution from the combined 2D and 3D joint distribution. In practice, this is only straightforward when the distributions are Gaussian and the posterior may be obtained analytically. However, we also adjust the inferred 3D pose in order to optimise the reconstruction in case the distributions are significantly non-Gaussian or the moments unduly sensitive to noise and details of the silhouette shape, either of which could mean that the algebraic prediction is not accurate.

Training the model in order to capture the correlation between the 2D image and 3D pose requires access to both 2D image and 3D pose data. Such data could be provided by means of a specialised motion tracking system [4]. However, in the context of ordinary laboratory work and simple movements such as walking, it is more convenient to use data from an avatar to train the system. Use of an avatar gives full control over both its movement and of the virtual camera environment with the result that it is straightforward to obtain 2D image and corresponding 3D pose data. Our aim is thus to show: (i) that an avatar can be used to train such a system in this manner, (ii) that a few low-order normalised central moments may be used to capture sufficient information from the silhouette shape for a first prediction of the 3D pose from the trained model, (iii) that the pose predicted in this manner may be refined and corrected by using the avatar model to match directly to the shape of the silhouette, thereby (iv) overcoming to a large extent both the potential sensitivity of the moment features and the limitations of the assumed Gaussian model. The accuracy of the pose reconstruction is evaluated from simulation experiments and that of the matching from both simulated and real data. We begin, however, in the next section, with a description of the data representation used.

2 Data Representation and Gaussian Model

We represent a person's 3D pose by the rotation of key joints, such as the root joint, which determines the balance and the orientation of the person, the knees, hips, elbows, shoulders *etc* as in Biovision's BVH format [11]. This approach, unlike others that represent 3D pose as a set of 3D joint locations (e.g. [5]), gives the potential of easily applying the estimated 3D pose to other objects, which have different physique from the one being tracked. If we suppose there are L key joints, then the column vector

$$s = [x_1, y_1, z_1, \cdots, x_i, y_i, z_i, \cdots, x_L, y_L, z_L]^T , \tag{1}$$

in which x_i, y_i, z_i stand for the rotations of the ith joint around the X, Y, Z axes, will represent a person's 3D pose. To parameterise the silhouette, instead of using landmarks as in [2,5], we use normalised central moments η_{pq} [7] which are invariant to image rotation and approximately invariant to changes in viewing distance. This is an attractive option as the moments are easily computable in real-time on an ordinary, up to date, desktop workstation from the bounding contour of the silhouette, S_t, obtained, for example by thresholding of the image [6]. Moreover, the moments are not dependent on the presence of particular landmark points which may sometimes be obscured and, by focusing first on the low-order (e.g. 2nd, 3rd, 4th and 5^{th}order) moments, can be introduced in a way that progressively introduces more detail of an object's shape. However, care must be taken in order to combat the known sensitivity of moments, even of comparatively low order, to noise and to details of the silhouette shape. This is one reason why, as described in section 3, after using the low-order moments to infer the 3D pose, we use the silhouette itself to correct and refine the pose estimates.

By definition, the zero order normalised moment is one and the first order central moments vanish. We therefore use moments of order $2 \leq p+q \leq l$ to represent the shape of the silhouette in the image by means of the $(l+4)(l-1)/2$ dimension column vector

$$m = [\eta_{20}, \eta_{11}, \eta_{02}, \cdots, \eta_{(l-1)}, \eta_{0l}]^T . \tag{2}$$

The vectors s and m are not in the same space and not of similar scale. Thus, principal component analysis (PCA) [8] is applied to both data sets:

$$s = \bar{s} + P_s b_s , \qquad m = \bar{m} + P_m b_m , \tag{3}$$

where b_s, $\bar{s}$ and P_s are respectively the weight parameters, mean vector and matrix of principal components of the 3D pose data set, and b_m, $\bar{m}$ and P_m are the weight parameters, mean vector and matrix of principal components of the silhouette moments data set. The matrices P_s and P_m are respectively chosen to contain the first t_s and t_m eigenvectors in each space, so as to explain a fraction f of the variation. Typically, $f = 90, 95, 98$ or 99%. Given the weights b_s and b_m for each training example, we can balance them by as suggested by Cootes [3] and use the scaled weights $b_s^{'}$ and $b_m^{'}$ after whitening to represent the 3D pose and the corresponding silhouette. Training data obtained from animation of the avatar implicitly enables us to construct the joint distribution $p(s, m)$. In practice, this is characterised by the means $\bar{s}$ and $\bar{m}$ and the covariance, which is calculated in the combined space of the vectors $b_s^{'}$ and $b_m^{'}$.

If we assume the joint distribution of the whitened weights $b_s^{'}$ and $b_m^{'}$ is Gaussian, then the conditional density $p(b_s^{'} \mid b_m^{'})$, which defines the distribution of the b'_s given b'_m is also Gaussian. Moreover, the mean $\bar{b}'_{s|m}$ and covariance $C_{s|m}$ of the conditional density are given by:

$$\bar{b}'_{s|m} = C_{s,m} C_m^{-1} b'_m \,, \qquad C_{s|m} = C_s - C_{s,m} C_m^{-1} C_{m,s} \,, \tag{4}$$

where C_m^{-1} is the inverse covariance matrix of the b'_m and $C_{s,m}$ is the $t_s \times t_m$ cross-covariance matrix. It is important to note that, according to 4, the conditional mean $\bar{b}'_{s|m}$ is a function of the b'_m. This means that, given a new example of whitened PCA weights b'_m, the most likely corresponding 3D pose weights b'_s can be estimated as the mean of the conditional density $p(b'_s \mid b'_m)$.

3 Adjusting the 3D Pose

The system described in the preceding section uses the Gaussian approach to predict the 3D pose from image data. As we shall see from the results to be presented in section 4, such a system performs quite well, but owing to the assumption of Gaussian statistics, and the sensitivity of the moments to noise and details of the silhouette shape, is not always accurate. In this section, the pose estimates are refined and more accurate results obtained by using a search algorithm to adjust the initial pose estimates obtained from the Gaussian assumption to fit better to the observed image silhouette. Owing to the fact that the pose PCA parameter space b'_s usually has fewer dimensions than the original space of the joint angles, the search is carried out in the space b'_s. Furthermore, in PCA, the eigenvectors of the matrix P_s are sorted with respect to the magnitudes of their variances, so successive weights contribute less to the manipulation of pose in equation 3. This encourages us to treat each pose PCA weight separately during the search process and starting with the most important weights will enable us to correct the largest errors first. Adjustment of the next weight then corrects for the next largest contribution to the remaining error and so on.

A one-dimensional golden section search [9] was carried out in this way to adjust the PCA pose weights. For each b'_s obtained from the conditional mean $\bar{b}'_{s|m}$ as described in section 2, a pose is generated using equation 3 and applied to a virtual avatar that is similar to the moving person or target. The avatar's silhouette S_a is then obtained by projection onto a virtual plane. The accuracy of the match between S_a, regarded as a binary image with value one inside the silhouette and zero elsewhere, and the given target silhouette S_t, similarly encoded, was defined as:

$$D_S = \frac{2 \times (S_a \cup S_t - S_a \cap S_t)}{S_a \cup S_t + S_a \cap S_t} \,. \tag{5}$$

The search algorithm is iterative, so when we finish the golden section search on the last of the pose PCA weights, we return to the first and continue the pose adjustment until the system converges (i.e. the change in D_S is small enough). However, because at each point of the search the avatar has to be regenerated, the computation cost rises with the number of iterations.

4 Experiments and Evaluation

Our approach was tested on a walking movement. An avatar was used to train the model as described in sections 2. Another avatar, which had a different physique was used to evaluate the system's performance. We also tested our method using the silhouettes of walking persons from the *Southampton Human ID at a Distance* database [10].

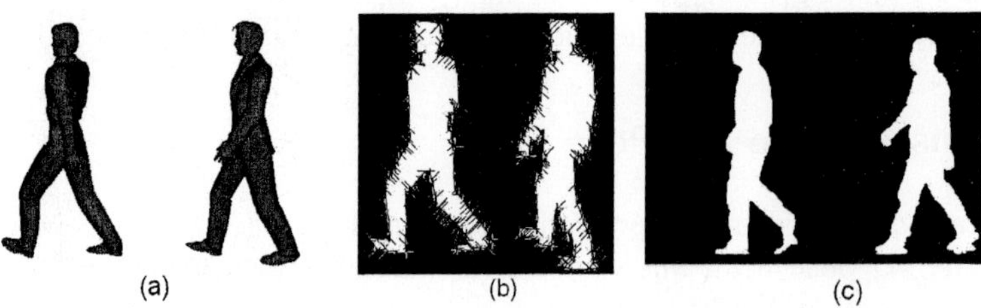

Fig. 1. (a) Examples of avatars used for training and evaluation. (b) Examples of avatar silhouettes with added random noise at a level of 12 pixels. (c) Examples silhouettes from the *Southampton Human ID at a Distance* database.

During the training process, we placed the virtual camera in front of the training avatar and made the avatar walk from right to left which was the same as for the real silhouette examples from the image database as shown in figure 1. Walking sequences were collected from different orientations at 60, 70, 80, 90, 100, 110 and 120 degrees from the front view (clockwise). The moments of the avatar's silhouettes, together with their corresponding 3D pose information, were collected as the training data set and were used to calculate the inverse of the covariance matrix C_m^{-1} and the covariance $C_{s,m}$ described in section 2. These matrices were then used in equation 4 for initial estimation of gait pose when given a new example silhouette. Adjustments to the 3D pose were then made as described in the section 3 to fine-tune the reconstructed pose by searching for a better match between the silhouette of the reconstructed avatar and the given new silhouette.

Because the data from the walking people lacks 3D pose information, evaluation of the accuracy of the 3D pose reconstruction was carried out using a virtual avatar. In order to test the robustness of our method, we used a different avatar from that used in training. The test avatar was constructed to perform movements similar to those of the avatar in the training set, while the orientation was set at different directions from those used in the training process (at $65, 75, 85, 95, 105$ and 115 degrees, respectively).

Noise was also introduced on the test silhouettes in order to evaluate the method's performance in a noisy situation. Figure 1 shows some examples of noisy silhouettes. The noise was added randomly to the avatar's silhouette contour along the normal of each contour pixel. A noise level of 12 pixels, as indicated in figure 1 means we randomly generated a number between -12 and 12. If the random number obtained was positive, we added this number of noise pixels outside the silhouette contour along the direction of the contour's normal, while if the random number was negative, we similarly added noise pixels inside the silhouette.

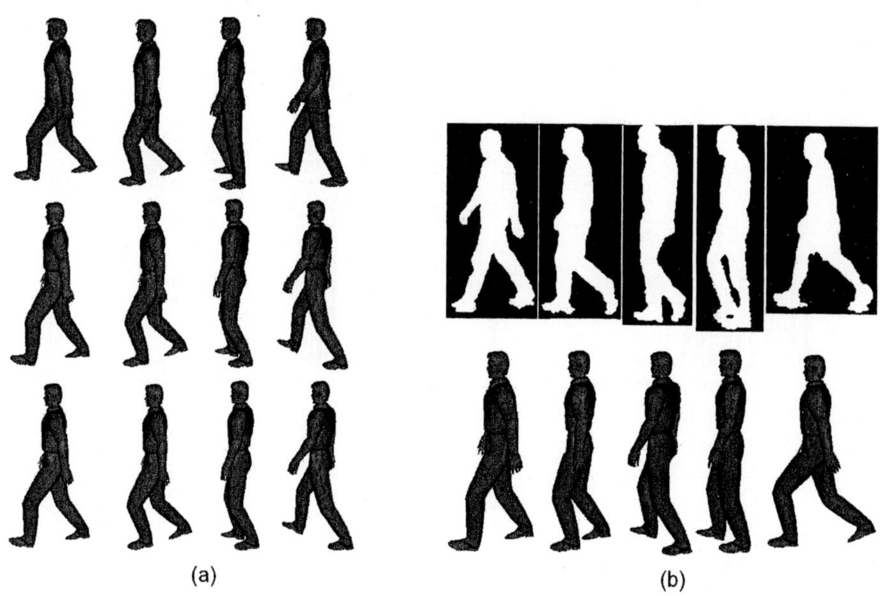

Fig. 2. (a) The first row at the top shows the ground truth test examples, the second row shows the reconstructed poses in a noise free situation, while the third row shows the reconstructed poses in a noisy situation. (b) Real silhouettes (first row) and corresponding reconstructed avatar poses (second row).

Figure 2 shows some examples of ground truth test poses and the reconstructions obtained as described in sections 2 and 3 in both noise free and noisy situations. There is little perceptible difference between the ground truth 3D poses and the reconstructions and it can be seen that adding noise on the test silhouette contour does not affect the reconstruction performance too adversely.

For each test example, the mean absolute difference (MAD) over 26 key joints between the angles of these key joints in the reconstructed pose and their ground truth values were used to assess the pose reconstruction performance. To do so, we represented the estimated and ground truth orientations of each key joint i as orthogonal matrices $q_r(i)$ and $q_t(i)$ respectively and, by solving $q_t(i) = q_r(i) \cdot q_e(i)$ we obtained the matrix $q_e(i)$ that would rotate $q_r(i)$ into $q_t(i)$. The angular difference $\theta(i)$ between the estimated and ground truth rotations for each key joint i may then be obtained from the fact that $tr(q_e(i)) = 1 + 2\cos(\theta(i))$.

As shown in figure 3, for both noisy and noise free situation, an accuracy of about 3 degrees mean absolute angular difference is achieved, which corresponds approximately to 2cm if we assume the average distance between key joints is

40 cm. It can also be seen that, although the 3D pose adjustment introduced extra errors for a few examples, the average performance is improved after the fine-tuning of the iterative search.

Our approach was also tested on real walking people's silhouettes provided by the *Southampton Human ID at a Distance* database. For testing on the real data, the virtual camera was set approximately the same as the real camera so that the real silhouette and the virtual avatar's silhouette were of the same scale. Some examples of the test on real silhouettes are shown in figure 2.

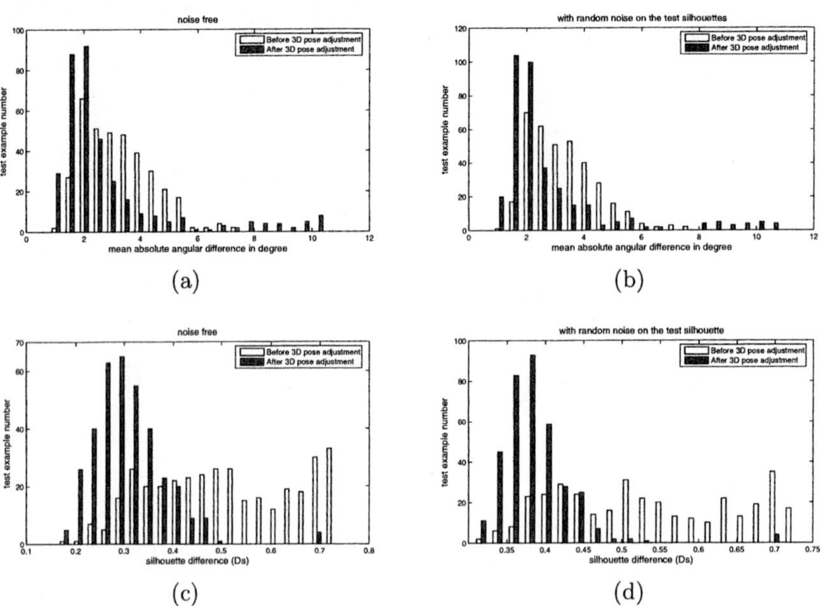

Fig. 3. (a) and (b) are the histograms of the angular MAD for noise free and noisy experiments respectively. Prior to the 3D pose adjustment the MAD is 3.23 degrees for noise free experiments and 3.28 for noisy ones, whilst after the 3D adjustment they are reduced to 2.87 degrees and 2.82 degrees respectively. (c) and (d) are the histograms of D_s for noise free and noisy experiments respectively. The mean of D_s is 0.5 in the noise free experiment and 0.53 in the noisy experiment prior to 3D pose adjustment, reduced to 0.31 and 0.39 respectively after 3D pose adjustment.

5 Conclusion and Future Work

As discussed in previous sections, by using the system described in section 2 we can estimate an avatar's 3D pose by using information from the avatar's silhouette. The accuracy of the pose predicted from the conditional mean was acceptable (i.e to within a few degrees when a test avatar was used) and we were able to improve it by adjusting the initial estimated 3D pose to fit the silhouette. This reduces the average reconstruction errors and, as inspection of the sequence of reconstructed poses shows, the jitter. At present, there is no representation of temporal coherence in our model. However we intend to introduce temporal constraints in the future, for example, by use of a Kalman filter to eliminate the jitter and to make the model more accurate and specific.

Acknowledgment

The authors would like to thank the ISIS research group at the University of Southampton for providing access to the Automatic Gait Recognition for Human ID at a Distance database.

References

1. A. M. Baumberg and D. C. Hogg. An efficient method for contour tracking using active shape models. Technical Report 94.11, April 1994.
2. R. Bowden, T.A. Mitchell, and M. Sarhadi. Reconstructing 3d pose and motion from a single camera view. In John N. Carter and Mark S. Nixon, editors, *In Proceedings of the British Machine Vision Conference*, volume 2, pages 904–913, University of Southampton, September 1998.
3. T. F. Cootes and C. J. Taylor. Statistical models of appearance for computer vision. Technical report, University of Manchester, Manchester M13 9PT, U.K., March 2004.
4. Ascension Technology Corporation. Real-time motion capture. [Online] Available at http://www.ascension-tech.com/products/motionstar.pdf, 2000. (accessed 03 March, 2005).
5. Kristen Grauman, Gregory Shakhnarovich, and Trevor Darrell. Inferring 3d structure with a statistical image-based shape model. In *ICCV '03: Proceedings of the Ninth IEEE International Conference on Computer Vision*, pages 641–648, Washington, DC, USA, 2003. IEEE Computer Society.
6. S. Hu and B. F. Buxton. A real-time tracking system developed for an interactive stage performance. In *WEC'05*, Istanbul, Turkey, April 2005.
7. Anil K. Jain. *Fundamentals of digital image processing.* Number 0-13-336165-9. Prentice-Hall, Inc., Upper Saddle River, NJ, USA, 1989. page 377-380.
8. I.T. Jolliffe. *Principal Component Analysis.* Springer-Verlag, New York, 1988.
9. William H. Press, Saul A. Teukolsky, William T. Vetterling, and Brian P. Flannery. *Numerical Recipes in C: The Art of Scientific Computing, 2nd edition.* Cambridge University Press, New York, NY, USA, 1992. page 397-402.
10. ISIS research group. Southampton human id at a distance database. [Online] Available at http://www.gait.ecs.soton.ac.uk/database/index.ph3, February 2004. (accessed 03 March, 2005).
11. J. Thingvold. Biovision bvh format. [Online] Available at http://www.cs.wisc.edu/graphics/Courses/cs-838-1999/Jeff/BVH.html, (accessed 03 March, 2005), 1999.

Real-Time Facial Expression Recognition System Based on HMM and Feature Point Localization

Yumei Fan, Ning Cheng, Zhiliang Wang, Jiwei Liu, and Changsheng Zhu

University of Science and Technology, Beijing 100083
kinchengning.student@sina.com,
kinchengning@263.net

Abstract. It is difficult for computer to recognize facial expression in real-time. Until now, no good method is put forward to solve this problem in and abroad. In this paper, we present an effective automated system that we developed to recognize facial gestures in real-time. According to psychologists' facial expression classification, we define four basic facial expressions and localize key facial feature points exactly then extract facial components' contours. We analyze and record facial components' movements using information in sequential frames to recognize facial gestures. Since different facial expressions can have some same movements, it is necessary to use a good facial expression model to describe the relation between expression states and observed states of facial components' movements for achieving a good recognition results. HMM is such a good method which can meet our requirement. We present a facial expression model based on HMM and get good real-time recognition results.

1 Introduction

Facial expression recognition is to extract and analyze human facial expression information, then classify and comprehend this information according to human cognition and thinking mode knowledge and make computer to think and reason, further to analyze and understand human emotions such as: happiness, surprise, anger, and sadness, etc. Facial expression is caused by the change of facial muscles and glands and is the most important manner which expresses emotions and also is the representation of human psychology states [3]. In the book of 《The Expression of the Emotions in Man and Animals》 which published in 1872, according to his research to facial expressions and lives of animals and primitives, Darwin points out that expression has the function of conveying information and signals, so it has important meaning for animal lives and it has been developed in the process of adaptation to circumstance. Psychologist points out that: Emotion expression=7%language + 38%voice + 55%facial expression. So we can find that facial expression has close relation with emotion expression. Automatic computer facial expression recognition as one important aspect of harmonious human computer interaction and at the same

J. Tao, T. Tan, and R.W. Picard (Eds.): ACII 2005, LNCS 3784, pp. 210–217, 2005.

time also as one important research content of affective computing attracts more and more attentions. In recent decades, computer facial expression recognition has developed to a new hot research fields.

Automatic computer facial expression recognition is a very complex problem. ① Facial expressions are diversity and easy to change. People in different country may have different expressions and even the people in same country may also have different expressions because of expression diversity, different personality and customs. How to make a uniform expression classification is a problem which psychologists and biologists have researched for many years and it has still no uniform standard until now. ② Real-time facial expression recognition requires computer to have good pattern recognition ability, but because computer has no knowledge and experience itself, so it needs a good recognition algorithm for computer. Furthermore, because the quality of computer images is affected by conditions of circumstance and illumination, etc, automatic computer recognition is more difficult, many recognition algorithms which already exist are based on still images, and for real-time facial expression recognition, it has no very effective algorithm until now.

The purpose of this paper is to design an effective real-time facial expression recognition system. We first extract facial features exactly, then analyze the facial components' movement, at last put forward a facial expression model based on HMM and get good real-time recognition results. In Fig.1, we show the system structure flow chart.

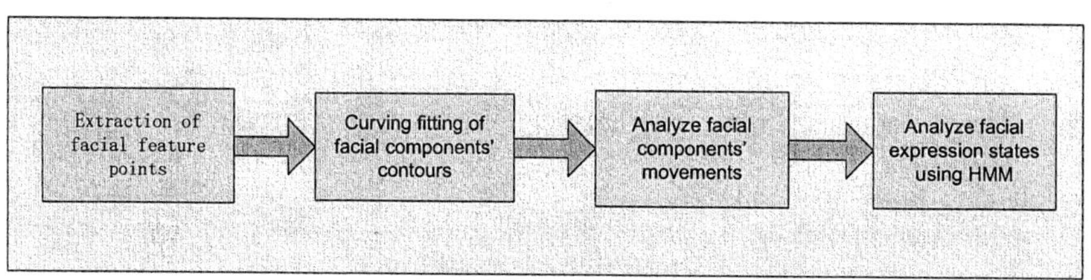

Fig. 1. System structure flow chart

2 Facial Expression Classification

How to classify facial expression is an unsolved problem and it still has no uniform standard until now. However, there are still many classifications which proposed by psychologists and biologists. Ekman[2] gives a classification based on psychology and anatomy knowledge and his classification is broadly used now. According to Ekman's classification and for the reason of feasibility, we just define four basic facial expressions: surprise, happiness, anger and sadness to recognize. In Table 1, we show the four classification and corresponding facial components' movements.

Table 1. Facial expression classification and corresponding facial components' movements

	Eyebrows	Eyes	Mouth
Surprise	Pulled upward	Eye opening widened	Open but not stretched
Happiness	Pulled downward	Eye opening narrowed	①lip corners pulled upward and backward ②mouth widened
Anger	Wrinkled, pulled downward	Upper eyelids is pulled downward and lower eyelids is pulled upward	①mouth may have two states : shut , lip corners stretched or pulled downward ; open, likely to shout②nostrils may widen
Sadness	Inner corners wrinkled, pulled upward	Inner corners' upper eyelid is pulled upward	Mouth corner is pulled downward

3 Facial Features Localization

3.1 Feature Point Localization

There are many methods for feature point localization, but some of these methods rely on hand or special hardware such as infrared illumination, electrodes to place on face, high resolution camera, etc. These methods can't meet the requirement of real-time or can't suit for general people. We want to design an inexpensive system suit for general people, so we can't use any special hardware and have to use low-resolution camera. At last, we decide to use an inexpensive USB camera and to realize our system on low-resolution images.

In our facial feature localization algorithm, eye localization is foundation of the others because eye is an important and stable character in human face. Based on eye localization, we localized mouth, eyebrows and nostrils.

3.1.1 Eye Feature Points Localization

Face detection is the first step for eye localization. We detect face using skin-color model[5], then transfer color face images to gray images and get the binary images by using appropriate threshold to process gray images. In binary images, we find eyes using followed rules:

1. The left eye block and the right eye block have similar areas.
2. The ratio of left eye width W_1 to the distance of two eye centers D is in a limited range. The same to right eye width W_2.
3. The gravity centers of two eyes have similar height.
4. The ratio of W_1 to W_2 is in a limited range.

Proved by experiments, using these rules, you can find a pair of regions which meet requirements and this region pair is just formed by eyes.

After eye localization, next we need to do is to localize the eye corners using local search method. We find the most left point, the most right point, the highest point and the lowest point in eye region as the left corner, right corner, upper eyelid highest point and lower eyelid lowest point and use the integral projection method to localize pupil center.

3.1.2 Other Feature Points Localization

Using similar method, we can find eyebrows in above eye region and localize the eyebrow corners. Using lip-color model, we can find mouth and localize four feature points as: left corner, right corner, upper lip's highest point and lower lip's lowest point. Based on some rules, we can find a pair of small areas near to face midline in the region between eye and mouth. Proved by experiments, this area pair is just formed by nostrils.

3.2 Extraction of Facial Feature Shapes

3.2.1 Eye Curve Fitting

We use a circle and four parabola segments to fit eye.

Upper eyelid curve fitting: Using upper eyelid highest point as parabola vertex and dividing point, we draw parabola segments on each side of it. The corresponding parabola equation is as follow:

$$y = -k_i (x - x_1)^2 + y_1, i = 1,2 \tag{1}$$

Point of (x_1, y_1) is upper eyelid highest point. k_1 is quadratic coefficient of left parabola segment and k_2 is quadratic coefficient of right parabola segment. $k_i > 0$.

Lower eyelid curve fitting: Using lower eyelid lowest point as parabola vertex and dividing point, we draw parabola segments on each side of it. The corresponding parabola equation is as follow:

$$y = k_i (x - x_2)^2 + y_2, i = 3,4 \tag{2}$$

Point of (x_2, y_2) is lower eyelid lowest point. k_3 is quadratic coefficient of left parabola segment and k_4 is quadratic coefficient of right parabola segment. $k_i > 0$.

The equation of pupil circle is as follow:

$$y = \pm\sqrt{r^2 - (x - x_c)^2} + y_c . \tag{3}$$

(x_c, y_c) is circle center coordinate. r is circle radius.

3.2.2 Eyebrow Curve Fitting

Eyebrow curve fitting is similar to eye curve fitting, we don't say more about it here.

3.2.3 Mouth Outer Contour Curve Fitting

Since mouth has a long contour curve, if just use four parabola segments to fit it, we can't get good result, so mouth curve fitting needs more feature points to get better result. According to the positions of two mouth corners, we divide the mouth width into 20 equal segments. It has totally 21 points. On each point, using a vertical line to intersect with the contour of lip, we get 42 intersection points. Affected by binary image quality, some of these points may leave the right position of real mouth contour too far, so we have to discard these points and replace them with the linear interpolation of neighboring points. According to mathematic knowledge, when there are too many points, it is hard to construct a curve to go through all these points. One method to solve this problem is to choose a low degree function and make it to be the closest curve to these points in some meanings. We use least square method to construct this approximation curve. The approximation function is $y = f(x)$. Let $f(x)$ to be m degree multinomial:

$$f(x) = \sum_{j=0}^{m} \alpha_j x^j \tag{4}$$

Approximation effect is measured by square sum of departures. To solve the followed extremal function, we get coefficients α_j:

$$\varphi(\alpha_j) = \sum_{i=1}^{n} [f(x_i) - y_i]^2 = \sum_{i=1}^{n} [\sum_{j=0}^{m} \alpha_j x^j - y_i]^2 \tag{5}$$

To put α_j into the function $f(x)$, we get the approximation function we need. Using this approximation function, we can get a good curve fitting of mouth.

3.2.4 Nostril Curve Fitting

The nostril corresponding circle equation is

$$y = \pm\sqrt{r^2 - (x - x_i)^2} + y_i, i = 1,2 \tag{6}$$

(x_1, y_1) is left nostril circle center coordinate and (x_2, y_2) is right nostril circle center coordinate.

4 Facial Expression Modeling

We extract facial components' contours above, so our next work is to analyze the facial expression states. Our method is to use facial components' movement information to determine expression states. Because even different people have similar facial movements information for same facial expression, this method usually has a good recognition result. We choose the second method to analyze facial expression states. In order to get good recognition results, it is necessary to model facial expressions. To each facial component, some different expressions may have some similar movements, so we need to use an appropriate method which can describe the relation between expression states and observed facial components' movements well to construct our model. HMM is such a good method which can meet our requirement, so we do our modeling using HMM. We construct one model for each facial component's movements, so we totally have three models corresponding to eye, eyebrow and mouth. First, we analyze and record the movement information for each component. Second, according to HMM, we get the optimal expression states sequence. Third, we compute the ratio of each expression state in the sequence. Last, we weight and synthesize the statistic data then use the highest ratio corresponding expression state as the recognition result, e.g. mouth may have the higher weight than eye and eyebrow because its movement is more accurate and obvious. HMM can be described using parameters as follow:

1. Element N: it is the states number in the model. Let state space as $S = \{S_1, S_2, \cdots, S_N\}$, each state is corresponding to one facial expression.
2. Element M: it is the possible observed states number in each expression state. The observed states are marked as $V = \{V_1, V_2, \cdots, V_M\}$ and each observed state is corresponding to one movement state.
3. States transferring probability distribution $A = \{a_{ij}\}$: in which $a_{ij} = P[q_{t+1} = S_j \mid q_t = S_i], 1 \le i, j \le N$, it is the transferring probability among each states. This distribution is predefined.
4. The observed states probability distribution in state j: $B = \{b_j(k)\}$, in which $b_j(k)$ =[at the time t, V is observed| $q_t = S_j$],1≤j≤N, 1≤k≤M, it is the probability distribution of movement states in one facial expression state.
5. Initial state distribution $\pi = \{\pi_j\}$, in which $\pi_j = P[q_1 = S_j], 1 \le j \le N$. It is also predefined.

Using forward-backward algorithm to get the optimistic state, define:
Forward variable:

$$\alpha_t(i) = P(O_1 O_2 \cdots O_t, q_t = S_i \mid \lambda) \tag{7}$$

1. Initial condition:

$$\alpha_1(i) = \pi_i b_i(O_1), 1 \le i \le N \tag{8}$$

2. Induction:

$$\alpha_{t+1}(j) = [\sum_{i=1}^{N} \alpha_t(i) a_{ij}] b_j(O_{t+1}), 1 \le t \le T-1, 1 \le j \le N \tag{9}$$

3. Result:

$$P(O \mid \lambda) = \sum_{i=1}^{N} \alpha_T(i) \tag{10}$$

Backward variable:

$$\beta_t(i) = P(O_{t+1}O_{t+2}\cdots O_T \mid q_t = S_i, \lambda) \tag{11}$$

1. Initial condition:

$$\beta_T(i) = 1, 1 \le i \le N \tag{12}$$

2. Induction:

$$\beta_t(i) = \sum_{j=1}^{N} a_{ij} b_j(O_{t+1}) \beta_{t+1}(j), t = T-1, T-2, \ldots, 1, 1 \le i \le N \tag{13}$$

Define variable $\gamma_t(i)$:

$$\gamma_t(i) = \frac{\alpha_t(i)\beta_t(i)}{P(O \mid \lambda)} = \frac{\alpha_t(i)\beta_t(i)}{\sum_{i=1}^{N} \alpha_t(i)\beta_t(i)}, \sum_{i=1}^{N} \gamma_t(i) = 1 \tag{14}$$

The solution - expression state q_t is:

$$q_t = \arg\max_{1 \le i \le N} [\gamma_t(i)], 1 \le t \le T \tag{15}$$

Based on state sequence q_t, we can get the recognition result using the method mentioned above. We show some recognition results in Fig. 2. We use red curve to fit eye, eyebrow, mouth contours and use green circle to fit pupils.

Fig. 2. Real-time recognition results of four facial expressions as: surprise, happiness, sadness and anger

5 Experiment Result

We use four facial expressions mentioned above to do experiments and ask twenty different persons to do each of the four expressions in real time. Real-time recognition rate achieves 75%. Our system ran at a rate of 15frames/second on a PC with a Pentium Ⅳ 1.70GHz CPU without any special hardware. Our next work is to improve our system both from detection technology and expression model to develop a better system. We believe that along with the development of pattern recognition, affective computing, psychology, etc, real-time facial expression recognition will get more achievements and serve people's lives well in near future.

References

1. Zhiliang Wang, Lun Xie, Artificial Psychology—an Attainable Scientific Research on the Human Brain[J]. IPMM'99(KEYNOTE PAPER), Honolulu, USA, July 10-15, 1999(ISTP)
2. Ekman P, Friesen W V, Facial Action Coding System. California: Consulting Psychologists Press, 1978
3. Liu jinmin, Psychology[M]. Beijing：Press of Chinese three gorge, Page109, 1999
4. Maja Pantic, Member, IEEE, and Leon J. M. Rothkrantz, Facial Action Recognition for Facial Expression, Analysis From Static Face Images, IEEE TRANSACTIONS ON SYSTEMS, MAN, AND CYBERNETICS—PART B: CYBERNETICS, VOL. 34, NO. 3, JUNE 2004
5. Quan Huynh-Thu, MitsuhikoMeguro, Masahide Kaneko, Skin-Color Extraction in Images with Complex Background and Varying Illumination, Proceedings of the Sixth IEEE Workshop on Applications of Computer Vision (WACV'02), 2002

Appendix: Support Foundation

Foundational project: Supported by the key Lab named Advanced Information Science and Network Technology of Beijing (No.TDXX0503) and the key foundation of USTB of Beijing.

Discriminative Features Extraction in Minor Component Subspace

Wenming Zheng[1], Cairong Zou[2], and Li Zhao[2]

[1] Research Center for Learning Science, Southeast University, Nanjing, Jiangsu 210096, China
[2] Engineering Research Center of Information Processing and Application, Southeast University, Nanjing, Jiangsu 210096, China
{wenming_zheng, cairong, zhaoli}@seu.edu.cn

Abstract. In this paper, we propose a new method of extracting the discriminative features for classification from a given training dataset. The proposed method combines the advantages of both the null space method and the maximum margin criterion (MMC) method, whilst overcomes their drawbacks. The better performance of the proposed method is confirmed by face recognition experiments.

1 Introduction

Discriminative features extraction for classification is a very important issue in pattern recognition. One of the most popular techniques of extracting the discriminative features from a given training dataset is the Fisher's linear discriminant analysis (LDA). It finds the optimal discriminant vectors that maximize the Fishers' criterion: $J_F(\omega) = \frac{\omega^T \mathbf{S}_B \omega}{\omega^T \mathbf{S}_W \omega}$, where the between-class scatter matrix $\mathbf{S}_B$ and the within-class scatter matrix $\mathbf{S}_W$ are respectively defined as

$$\mathbf{S}_B = \sum_{i=1}^{c} N_i (\mathbf{u}_i - \mathbf{u})(\mathbf{u}_i - \mathbf{u})^T \tag{1}$$

$$\mathbf{S}_W = \sum_{i=1}^{c} \sum_{j=1}^{N_i} (\mathbf{x}_i^j - \mathbf{u}_i)(\mathbf{x}_i^j - \mathbf{u}_i)^T \tag{2}$$

where $\mathbf{x}^T$ represents the transpose of the vector $\mathbf{x}$, $\mathbf{x}_i^j$ is the j th sample in the i th class, $\mathbf{u}_i$ is the mean of the i th class samples and $\mathbf{u}$ is the mean of all samples:

$$\mathbf{u}_i = \frac{1}{N_i} \sum_{j=1}^{N_i} \mathbf{x}_i^j, \quad \mathbf{u} = \frac{1}{N} \sum_{i=1}^{c} \sum_{j=1}^{N_i} \mathbf{x}_i^j \tag{3}$$

The classical approach of solving the LDA problem is to solve the following generalized eigenequation:

J. Tao, T. Tan, and R.W. Picard (Eds.): ACII 2005, LNCS 3784, pp. 218–223, 2005.

$$\mathbf{S}_B\boldsymbol{\omega} = \lambda\mathbf{S}_W\boldsymbol{\omega} \tag{4}$$

However, when the dimensionality of the input space is larger than the number of the training samples, the within-class scatter matrix will be singular, which is referred to as the so-called "small sample size" problem [2]. To overcome this problem, Belhumeur et al. [1] proposed the well-known Fisherfaces method. This method uses the principal component analysis (PCA) firstly to reduce the dimensionality of the training samples such that the within-class scatter matrix becomes nonsingular, and then performs the traditional LDA method. Recently, Chen et al. [2] proved that the most optimal discriminant vectors of LDA lie in the null space of $\mathbf{S}_W$ as for the case of the "small sample size" problem, thereafter proposed the Null Space method, which aims to find the most discriminant vectors of LDA in the subspace $\mathbf{S}_W(0)$, where $\mathbf{S}_W(0)$ denotes the null space of $\mathbf{S}_W$. A major drawback of this method is that it discards the within-class scatter information, which will probably result in the over-fitting problem because of the difficulty of ensuring any test samples belonging to the same class be exactly projected into the same projection point.

More recently, Li et al. [4] proposed another discriminant method based on a new criterion $J_M(\boldsymbol{\omega}) = \boldsymbol{\omega}^T(\mathbf{S}_B - \mathbf{S}_W)\boldsymbol{\omega}$, called maximum margin criterion (MMC), to overcome the "small sample size" problem. However, one could not guarantee that the within-class variance is small enough just according to the maximum margin criterion. Motivated by the null space method and the MMC method, we proposed a new method for extracting discriminative features in this paper, which combines the advantages of both methods.

2 The Proposed Method

From the theory of discriminant analysis, we know that it is better for a discriminant vector that makes the between-class scatter distance as large as possible, whilst the with-class scatter distance as small as possible. However, it is also notable that if the within-class scatter distance is too small (e.g., the case of the null space method), it will very probably produce the over-fitting problem. Motivated by the null space method and the MMC method, we propose a new method in this section to solve the "small sample size" problem of LDA. We will firstly project the training samples onto the minor component subspace, which is spanned by the eigenvectors corresponding to the smallest eigenvalues (including the zero eigenvalue) of $\mathbf{S}_W$, and then perform the MMC problem in the projection space.

Suppose that $\lambda_1 \geq \lambda_2 \geq \cdots \geq \lambda_n \geq 0$ are the complete eigenvalues of the matrix $\mathbf{S}_W$ and $\varphi_1, \varphi_2, \cdots, \varphi_n$ are the associated eigenvectors. Suppose that the first M largest eigenvalues of $\mathbf{S}_W$ satisfy $\sum_{i=1}^{M}\lambda_i >> \sum_{j=M+1}^{n}\lambda_i$. Let $\mathbf{\Omega}$ be the subspace spanned by $\varphi_1, \varphi_2, \cdots, \varphi_M$, $\mathbf{\Omega}^\perp$ be the orthogonal complement of $\mathbf{\Omega}$. For any training sample x_i^j, we decompose $\mathbf{x}_i^j$ as the following forms:

$$\mathbf{x}_i^j = \mathbf{y}_i^j + \mathbf{z}_i^j \tag{5}$$

where $\mathbf{y}_i^j \in \mathbf{\Omega}$ and $\mathbf{z}_i^j \in \mathbf{\Omega}^{\perp}$.

Let $\mathbf{P} = [\varphi_1 \quad \varphi_2 \quad \cdots \quad \varphi_M]$. Then we have $\mathbf{y}_i^j = \mathbf{P}\mathbf{P}^T\mathbf{x}_i^j$ and $\mathbf{z}_i^j = \mathbf{x}_i^j - \mathbf{y}_i^j = \mathbf{x}_i^j - \mathbf{P}\mathbf{P}^T\mathbf{x}_i^j$. Thus our goal turns to find the optimal discriminant vectors trained on the decomposed samples $\{\mathbf{z}_i^j\}$. Let $\tilde{\mathbf{S}}_B$ and $\tilde{\mathbf{S}}_W$ denote the between-class scatter matrix and the within-class scatter matrix of the training samples $\{\mathbf{z}_i^j\}$, respectively. Then we have

$$\tilde{\mathbf{S}}_B = \sum_{i=1}^{c} N_i(\tilde{\mathbf{u}}_i - \tilde{\mathbf{u}})(\tilde{\mathbf{u}}_i - \tilde{\mathbf{u}})^T \tag{6}$$

$$\tilde{\mathbf{S}}_W = \sum_{i=1}^{c}\sum_{j=1}^{N_i}(\mathbf{z}_i^j - \tilde{\mathbf{u}}_i)(\mathbf{z}_i^j - \tilde{\mathbf{u}}_i)^T \tag{7}$$

where $\tilde{\mathbf{u}}_i = \frac{1}{N_i}\sum_{j=1}^{N_i}\mathbf{z}_i^j$, $\tilde{\mathbf{u}} = \frac{1}{N}\sum_{i=1}^{c}\sum_{j=1}^{N_i}\mathbf{z}_i^j$.

In the next step, we adopt the MMC method to solve the optimal discriminant vectors, which is equivalent to solving the eigenvectors of the following eigenequation corresponding to the m ($\geq c-1$) largest eigenvalues:

$$(\tilde{\mathbf{S}}_B - \tilde{\mathbf{S}}_W)\boldsymbol{\varphi} = \lambda\boldsymbol{\varphi} \tag{8}$$

Let $\boldsymbol{\varphi}_1, \boldsymbol{\varphi}_2, \cdots, \boldsymbol{\varphi}_m$ be the eigenevectors corresponding to the m largest eigenvalues of the eigenequation (8), and let $\mathbf{Q} = [\boldsymbol{\varphi}_1 \quad \boldsymbol{\varphi}_2 \quad \cdots \quad \boldsymbol{\varphi}_m]$. Then the final projection matrix can be expressed as:

$$\mathbf{W} = \mathbf{Q} - \mathbf{P}\mathbf{P}^T\mathbf{Q} \tag{9}$$

For a test sample $\mathbf{x}$, the discriminative features can be obtained using the following expression:

$$\mathbf{f} = \mathbf{W}^T\mathbf{x} = (\mathbf{Q} - \mathbf{P}\mathbf{P}^T\mathbf{Q})^T\mathbf{x} \tag{10}$$

3 Experiments

We will use the Yale face database [1] and the AR face database [3], respectively, to test the performance of the proposed method. The Yale face database contains 15 subjects, each of which contains 11 face images with variations in both facial expression and lighting condition. Figure 1 shows the 11 images of one subject in Yale face database. Note that the normal facial expression image and the without glasses image (or with glasses if subject normally wears glasses) in subjects numbered 2, 3, 6, 7, 8, 12 and 14 are copies of each other. We remove the normal facial expression image (numbered 6) from every subject. The original face images are sized 243×320 pixels

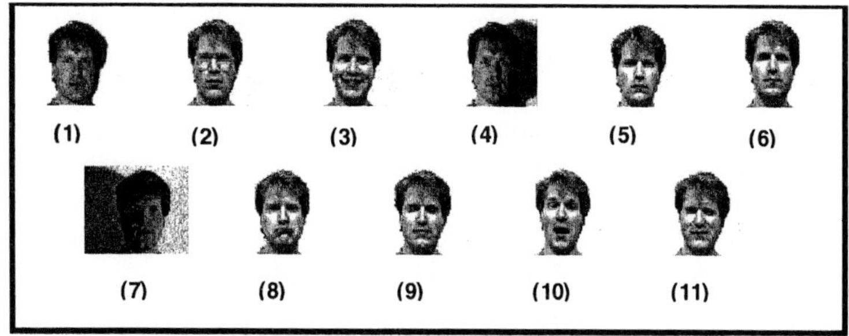

Fig. 1. The 11 face images of one subject from the Yale face database

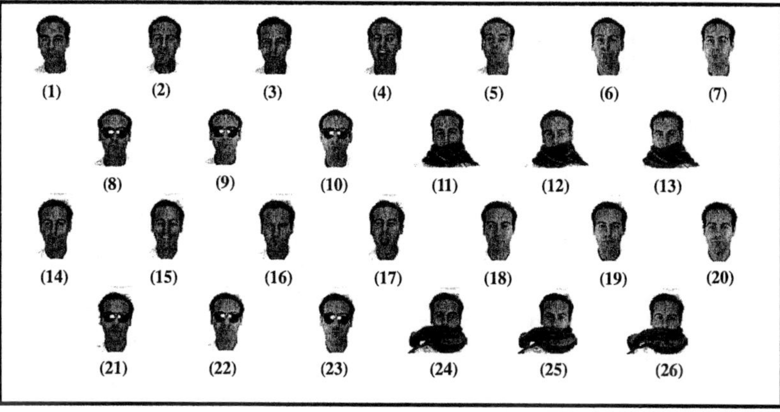

Fig. 2. The 26 images of one subject in the AR face database

with a 256-level gray scale. To reduce the computation complexity, we centered and cropped each image into a size of 190×170 pixels, and then downsample the cropped image into size of 57×51 using the bicubic interpolation method.

The AR face database consists of over 3000 facial images of 126 subjects. Each subject contains 26 facial images recorded in two different sessions separated by two weeks, where each session consists of 13 images. The original image size is 768×576 pixels, and each pixel is represented by 24 bits of RGB color values. Figure 2 shows the 26 images for one subject, where the images numbered from 1 to 13 are taken in the first session, and those numbered from 14 to 26 are taken in the second session. Among the 126 subjects, we randomly select 70 subjects (50 males and 20 females) for this experiment. Similar to [6], only the nonoccluded images, i.e., the images numbered 1-7 and 14-20, are used for the experiment. Before the experiment, all images are centered and cropped to the size of 468×476 pixels, and then downsampled into the size of 46×47 pixels.

We adopt the "leave-one-out" strategy and the two fold cross-validation strategy [7] to perform the experiments on Yale and AR face databases, respectively. For the comparison purpose, we also conduct the same experiments using the Eigenfaces method [5], the Fisherfaces method, the MMC method, and the null space method, respectively. The nearest neighbor (NN) classifier is used over the experiments. Table 1 and Table 2 show the experimental results of the average recognition rates on the two face databases. From Table 1 and Table 2, we can see that the proposed method achieves the best recognition rate among the various systems.

Table 1. Comparison of Recognition Rate on Yale Face Database

Methods	Reduced Space	Recognition Rate (%)
Eigenfaces	40	72.00
Fisherfaces	14	94.67
MMC	14	86.67
Null space method	14	95.33
Our method	14	96.67

Table 2. Comparison of Test Error Rate on AR Face Database

Methods	Reduced Space	Recognition Rate (%)
Eigenfaces	70	96.84
Fisherfaces	69	97.15
MMC	69	97.86
Null space method	69	98.07
Our method	69	98.47

4 Conclusion

In this paper, we have proposed a novel discriminant analysis and applied to the face recognition task. The proposed method combines the advantages of the MMC method and null space method, whilst overcomes the drawbacks of the two methods. The experimental results of face recognition on Yale face database and AR face database confirm that the proposed method can achieve better recognition performance than the MMC method and the null space method.

Acknowledgment

This work was supported in part by the Jiangsu Natural Science Foundations under Grants BK2005407.

References

1. Belhumeur P.N., Hespanha J.P., Kriegman D.J.: Eigenfaces vs. Fisherfaces: recognition using class specific linear projection, IEEE Transactions on Pattern Analysis and Machine Intelligence, 19 (7) (2004) 711-720.
2. Chen L.-F., Liao H.-Y. M., Ko M.-T., Lin J.-C., & Yu G.-J., A new LDA-based face recognition system which can solve the small sample size problem, Pattern Recognition, 33 (2000) 1713-1726.
3. Martinez A.M. and Benavente R., The AR Face Database, CVC Technical Report #24, 1998.
4. Li H., Jiang T., Zhang K.: Efficient and robust feature extraction by maximum margin criterion, Proceedings of Advances in Neural Information Processing Systems 16 (2004) 97-104, Cambridge, MA, MIT Press.
5. Turk M.A. and Pentland A.P.: Face recognition using eigenfaces, in Proc. Int. Conference on Pattern Recognition (1991) 586-591.
6. Cevikalp H., Neamtu M., Wilkes M., & Barkana A.: Discriminiative common vectors for face recognition", IEEE Transactions on Pattern Analysis and Machine Intelligence, 27 (2005) 4-13.
7. Fukunaga, K.: Introduction to statistical pattern recognition, (1990) Orlando, FL: Academic Press.

Vision-Based Recognition of Hand Shapes in Taiwanese Sign Language

Jung-Ning Huang, Pi-Fuei Hsieh, and Chung-Hsien Wu

Department of Computer Science and Information Engineering,
National Cheng Kung University, Tainan

Abstract. The pixel-based shape representation has been sensitive to rotation. In this paper, we propose a pixel-based descriptor that is invariant with rotation and scale for the hand shape recognition in Taiwanese Sign Language (TSL). Based on the property that a hand shape is characteristic of a unique pointing direction, angle normalization is used to meet the rotation-invariant requirement. With angle normalization, the traces of class covariance matrices have been reduced almost all over the classes of hand shapes, implying a less overlap between classes. It is confirmed by the experiments that show an increase in recognition accuracy.

1 Introduction

A sign language that is the preference language of the hearing-impaired usually seems to be a foreign language to most of the hearing-normal people who live in the same area. A sign language interpretation system is developed in hope that this tool helps for better communication between the hearing-impaired and others. Sign languages are not a universal language. Each has its special lexicon, though the techniques for recognition signs may be transferable between different sign languages. In this study, we adopt a vision-based approach to recognition of the hand shapes in Taiwanese Sign Language (TSL), which is the most popular sign language in Taiwan. The techniques for vision-based hand shape recognition are related to those used in vision-based object recognition [1,2]. There are several problems to be faced with. For example, when an input image is acquired under an over-lighting condition, a serious image noise problem occurs. The lighting inconsistency problem always causes difficulty in detecting skin correctly. Modeling of a hand shape in an image is another issue. Although the Fourier descriptor on the contour of a hand shape gives a representation that is invariant with rotation and scale [3,4,5], it does not work for discriminating between similar hand contours. Noting that similar hand contours differ in the texture inside the hand shape, we turn to the pixel-based representation that contains discriminant information about the hand texture. In a pixel-based representation, a hand shape is modeled in the first place with an ordered set of all pixel values in the image containing a hand shape. The scaling problem in the pixel-based representation can be easily overcome by normalizing images to a standard size. The rotation problem is taken care of in this study by rotating images to the principal pointing direction. For the rotation problem, one can choose to define several classes of pixel-based descriptions for a hand shape corresponding to various

J. Tao, T. Tan, and R.W. Picard (Eds.): ACII 2005, LNCS 3784, pp. 224–231, 2005.

rotation angles. For example, one can define a class every 45 degrees, giving eight classes for a shape. It usually turns out to be a large number of classes in processing, and more importantly, the large variation in a class often leads to misclassification.

The functional block diagram for hand shape recognition is given in Fig. 1(a). The image segment that contains a hand shape is first separated from the input image. Subsequently, the hand shape is described with a pixel-based representation and recognized by a classification process.

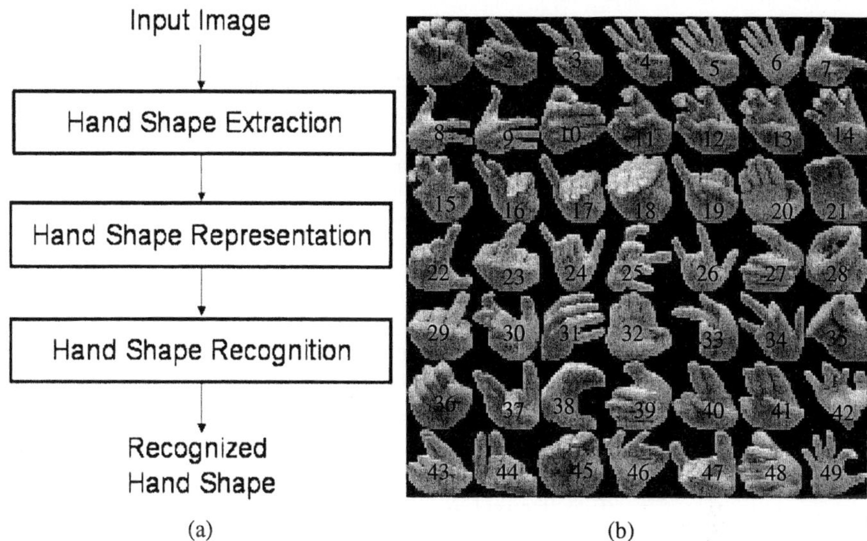

Fig. 1. (a) Functional block of vision-based hand shape recognition. (b) 49 hand shapes in TSL.

2 Hand Shape Extraction

Out of the 51 basic hand shapes in TSL, we took the 49 static hand shapes that are performed by hands, as shown in Fig. 1(b). The remaining shapes, worm and arm, are not within the scope of this study because 'worm' is not static and 'arm' is not performed by a hand. The process of hand shape extraction consists of the following stages, namely skin detection, morphological operation, connected component, and attention image generation.

2.1 Skin Detection

In the first step of hand shape extraction, skin is detected based on the color feature of the skin. Any parts other than skin, such as clothes, hair, and wall, are all included into the background. Accurate detection results can be obtained only if the contrast between the skin and the background is significant. Notice that the background is sometimes in a similar color to the skin, and this may pose problems. When the color distribution of the skin is not entirely different from the background, skin detection can hardly be done accurately by RGB image processing [6]. There are some limitations to be taken into account for a skin-color detection algorithm. It is important to choose an appropriate color space for skin-color detection. Choices of color spaces include the YCbCr [6,7], HSV [8,9], RGB [10], and YIQ [11], where Y(luminance), I(hue), and Q(saturation) are defined by the National Television Systems Committee (NTSC). We choose the YIQ color space in this study since it is discriminative in modeling the human skin-color, especially in Y-domain. The conversion from the RGB domain to the YIQ domain is given by

$$\begin{bmatrix} Y \\ I \\ Q \end{bmatrix} = \begin{bmatrix} 0.229 & 0.587 & 0.114 \\ 0.596 & -0.275 & -0.321 \\ 0.212 & -0.523 & 0.311 \end{bmatrix} \begin{bmatrix} R \\ G \\ B \end{bmatrix} \tag{1}$$

We perform skin detection by segmenting an input image into skin and background classes in the YI subspace, where the skin can be discriminated from the background.

2.2 Skin Model

Let $\mathbf{v} = [\mathrm{Y\ I}]^T$ be the feature vector of a pixel. The luminance Y and the hue I of the YIQ color space span a feature space for skin detection. Assume that the skin-color distribution in the feature space can be modeled as a normal distribution with mean vector $\boldsymbol{\mu}_s$ and covariance matrix Σ_s. The values of μ_s and Σ_s are estimated from the training pixels of the skin class. The Mahalanobis distance [12] from $\mathbf{v}$ to $\boldsymbol{\mu}_s$ is given by

$$d^2 = (v - \mu_s)^T \Sigma_s^{-1} (v - \mu_s) \tag{2}$$

The Mahalanobis distance is used to determine if a pixel with feature $\mathbf{v}$ is within a confidence region of the skin. Note that the background might be better modeled with multiple normal distributions, depending on the complexity of the background.

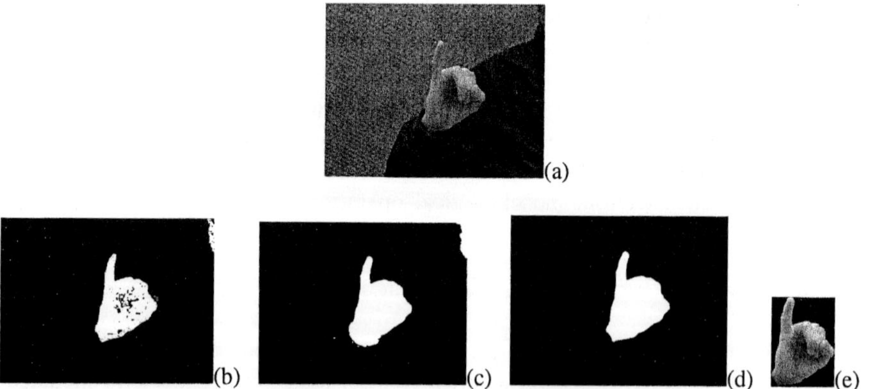

Fig. 2. (a) Original image. (b) The binary image resulting from skin detection. (c) The result of a morphological operation. (d) The maximum connected component. (e) Attention image.

2.3 Hand Shape Modification

The skin detection based on skin features usually produces a hand shape in fragments. Subsequent cosmetic processing is required to yield a reliable hand shape for recognition. An example of hand shape extraction is illustrated in Fig. 2. The image processing techniques used include a morphological operation for edge smoothing and connected component for shape integrating. The morphological operation used is the dilation operation [13]. To obtain the integrity of a hand shape, we apply the maximum component method to the fragmented image based on the Hoshen-Kopelman algorithm [14].

3 Hand Shape Representation

Let an attention image be the smallest rectangular image that is compacted by a hand shape along the x- and y- axes. Attention images are obtained directly from the images resulting from hand shape detection. In the representation process, an attention image is to be transformed into a feature vector representing the hand shape. A representative feature vector carries discriminant information for hand shape recognition. In this representation process, an attention image is rotated by using the proposed angle normalization method and subsequently resized to a square image of standard size.

3.1 Normalization

3.1.1 Angle Normalization for Rotation Invariance

There are some factors that cause variation in samples of the same hand shape. For example, a certain number of people are unable to gesture the special shapes correctly. More frequently, a hand shape is presented in an image with various orientations. When samples in various angles are included into a class, it is inevitable to produce a large covariance for the class. A larger covariance matrix often increases the overlap with other classes, leading to confusion of recognition. It has been presented that the contour-based representation achieves higher accuracy in object recognition than pixel-based representation [3,4]. The key advantage of the contour-based representation over the pixel-based representation is the property of rotation invariance. In view of this, we propose angle normalization for reducing the variation in samples of the same class.

From the observation of hand shapes, we have found the property that there exists a unique principal direction for each hand shape in a 2-D plane. The principal direction is almost parallel with the direction of finger pointing. By normalizing the angles of the principal axis on attention images, the clustering of samples in each class can be improved. We utilize the PCA to find the principal axis. First, collect the coordinates of the skin pixels from an attention image and compute the covariance matrix of the coordinates. The eigenvector that corresponds to the largest eigenvalue of the covariance matrix gives the principal direction of the hand shape in the attention image. The angle between the principal direction and the x-axis is the measure to be normalized. An example is depicted in Fig. 3. An attention image is

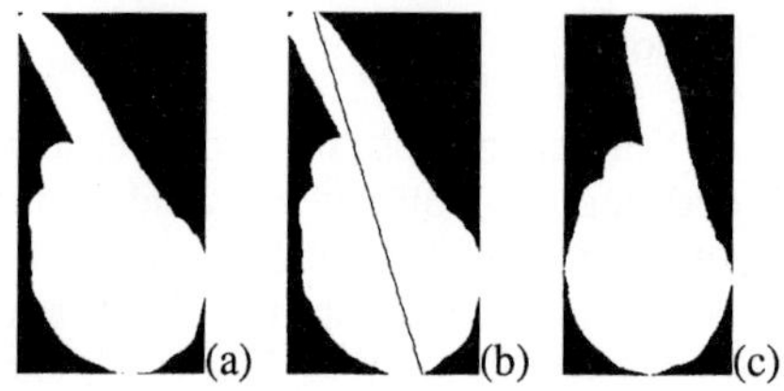

Fig. 3. (a) An attention image of n rows and m columns. (b) The principal direction of the hand shape. (c) The image resulting from angle normalization.

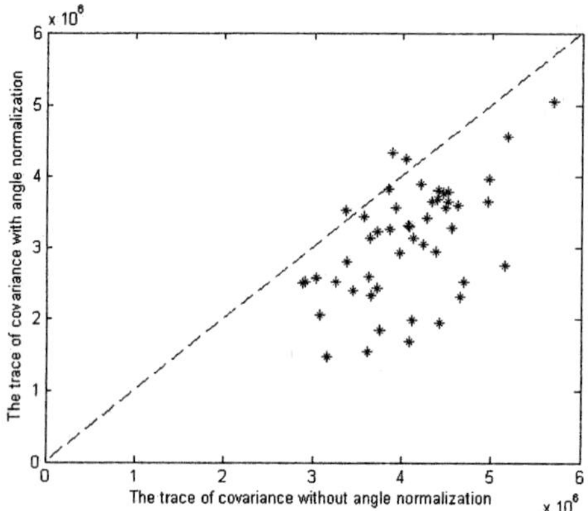

Fig. 4. The effect of angle normalization on the variation within a class. In terms of the trace of class covariance, the variation within a class has been reduced by angle normalization.

shown in Fig. 3(a). The principal direction found by PCA is demonstrated by a line in Fig. 3(b). The angle between the principal direction and the x-axis is 106°. To normalize the angle to 90° so that the principal direction is parallel with the y-axis, the image is rotated clockwise by an angle of 16°, giving a result in Fig. 3(c).

The effect of angle normalization on the variation within a class is investigated in an experiment with the samples collected from all 49 classes of hand shapes in TSL. Consider the variation of the samples within a class in terms of the trace of the class covariance matrix. A large trace implies a large variation in samples. The relationship between the original and the new traces after angle normalization can be figured out in a plot of the new traces versus the original traces, as shown in Fig. 4. Each point represents a class with x- and y- coordinates for the original and the new traces, respectively. The fact that almost all the points are located below the line $y=x$ suggests that the new traces are likely to be less than the original traces. This indicates that the variation within a class has been reduced by angle normalization.

3.1.2 Size Normalization for Scale Invariance

In order to model the hand shape to be invariant with scales, a simple yet effective approach is to normalize each attention image to be in a standard size. For example, a standard size of 40 by 40 is chosen in our experiment and yields a 1600-dimensional data sample for recognition processing.

4 Hand Shape Recognition

The pixel-based representation of a standard-size image are still of large dimensionality (e.g., 1600), compared to the number of samples available for a class. To mitigate the singularity problem of class covariance matrix, the principal component analysis (PCA) [12] is used to reduce the dimensionality of data (e.g., 60) for efficient and effective processing. The maximum likelihood classification method is used for recognition of 49 hand shapes in TSL.

5 Experiments

To evaluate the performance of the proposed hand-shape recognition, a collection of static images was obtained from nine individuals who repeat each of 49 hand shapes for three times. There were 27 samples acquired for each class of hand shape and a total of 1323 samples collected in the database. In the experiment, K samples were randomly selected out of the 27 samples from each of 49 classes as a training set, and the remaining were left as a test set. The experiments were repeated for 20 times by changing the training set through a random selection.

The recognition result is listed in Table I. In the cases of test sizes K=1 and K=2, the recognition accuracy achieved near 90%. In these cases, the test samples and the training samples were likely to be drawn from the same individuals. This makes the recognition accuracy tend to be optimistic. The hold-out recognition accuracy of K=13 is lower than 80% partly because an insufficient number of training images was used and partly because the samples from a single individual were all excluded in training.

As mentioned before, similar hand shapes may cause misclassification. By analysis on the confusion matrix and also by visual inspection, we have found that the classes (1, 18, 36, 45), (17, 19), (27, 39), (2, 29), (35, 48), and (46, 49) are groups of similar hand shapes because they were often misclassified with each other. In considering the feasibility of a recognition system, it is reasonable to combine the groups of similar classes. Our combination was applied to the recognition result rather than to the samples before the training process. If the combination was performed prior to the training process, it may cause inaccurate estimation of the data distribution, leading to a serious overlap with other classes. Fig. 5 illustrates an example of the two combination methods. The average results of combining the similar classes give a recognition accuracy higher than 90% for test sizes K=1 and K=2, as shown in Table I.

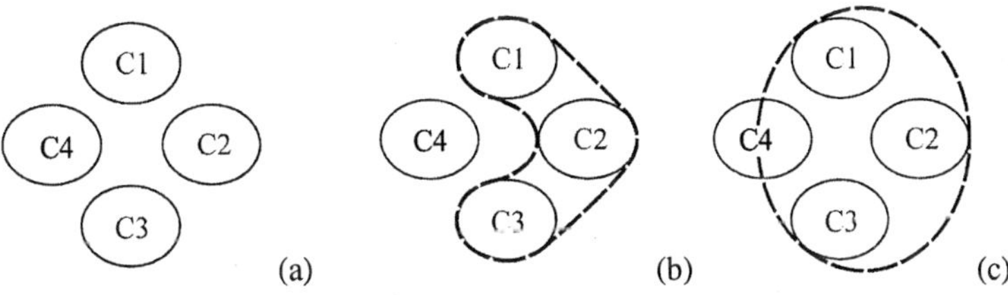

Fig. 5. (a) The distribution of the three classes. (b) Combine the results of classification. (c) Combine the samples of classes into one class.

Table I. Recognition accuracy of hand shapes in various cases

Cases	Test Accuracy, % K=1	K=2	K=13	Training Acc., %
49 classes (contour-based image model)	71.02	70.35	84.48	100
49 classes (without angle normalization)	72.35	72.24	62.78	100
49 classes (with angle normalization)	**89.08**	**87.14**	**78.07**	100
41 classes (with class combination)	92.65	90.87	82.11	100

(K: Number of test samples)

6 Conclusion

We propose a rotation-invariant pixel-based representation for hand shapes. The major advantage of this representation is that it overcomes the rotation-sensitive problem of the conventional pixel-based representation. The experimental results have shown that the proposed method has outperformed the conventional one in recognition of the hand shapes of Taiwanese sign language.

Acknowledgment

The authors would like to thank the National Science Council, Taiwan, for financially supporting this research work under Contract No. NSC93-2213-E-006-072. The authors would also like to thank Miss Gong-Ru Lin for her assistance in TSL experiments.

References

1. Y. Cui and J. Weng, "A learning-based prediction-and-verification segmentation scheme for hand sign image sequence," *IEEE Trans. Pattern Anal. Machine Intell.*, vol. 21, no. 8, Aug. 1999.
2. N. H. Habili, and C.C. Lim, and A. Moini, "Segmentation of the face and hands in sign language video sequences using color and motion cues," *IEEE Trans.Circuit Syst. Video Technol.*, vol.14, no. 8, Aug. 2004.
3. J. Cai and Z.Q. Liu, "Hidden markov models with spectral feature for 2D shape recognition," *IEEE Trans. Pattern Anal. Machine Intell.*, vol. 23, no. 12, Dec. 2001.
4. H. Kauppinen, T. Seppanen and M. Pietikaainen, "An experimental comparison of autoregressive and fourier-based descriptors in 2D shape classification," *IEEE Trans. Pattern Anal. Machine Intell.*, vol. 17, no. 2, Feb. 1995.
5. K. Arbter, W. E. Snyder, H. Burkhardt and G. Hirzinger, "Application of affine-invariant Fourier descriptors to recognition of 3-D objects," *IEEE Trans. Pattern Anal. Machine Intell.*, vol. 12, no.7, July 1990.
6. D. Chai and K. N. Ngan, "Face segmentation using skin-color map in videophone applications," *IEEE Trans. Circuits Syst. Video Technol.*, vol. 9, pp. 551–564, June 1999.
7. H. Wang and S.-F. Chang, "A highly efficient system for automatic face region detection in MPEG video," *IEEE Trans. Circuits Syst. Video Technol.*, vol. 7, pp. 615–628, Aug. 1997.
8. K. Sobottka and I. Pitas, "A novel method for automatic face segmentation, facial feature extraction and tracking," *Signal Process. Image Commun.*, vol. 12, pp. 263-281, June 1998.

9. X. Zhu, J. Yang, and A. Waibel, "Segmenting hands of arbitrary color," in *Proc. IEEE 4th Int. Conf. FG*, Grenoble, France, pp. 446-453, Mar. 2000.
10. M. J. Jones and J. M. Rehg, "Statistical color models with application to skin detection," in *Proc. CVPR*, Ft. Collins, Colorado, pp. 274-280, June 1999.
11. J. R. Parker, *Algorithms for Image Processing and Computer Vision*, in Chapter 5, Addison-Wesley Pub. Comp., New York, 1996.
12. K. Fukunaga, *Introduction to Statistical Pattern Recognition*, New York: Academic Press, 1990.
13. R. C. Gonzalez and R. E. Woods, *Digital Image Processing*, Addison-Wesley, 2002.
14. R. M. Haralick and L. G. Shapiro, *Computer and Robot Vision*, Volume I, Addison-Wesley, pp. 28-48, 1992.

An Information Acquiring Channel —— Lip Movement

Xiaopeng Hong, Hongxun Yao, Qinghui Liu, and Rong Chen

Department of Computer Science and Engineering,
Harbin Institute of Technology, Harbin 150001, China
{xphong, yhx, qhliu, rchen}@vilab.hit.edu.cn

Abstract. This paper is to prove that lip-movement is an available channel for information acquiring. The reasoning is given by describing two kinds of valid applications, which are constructed on lip movement information only. One is lip-reading, the other is lip-movement utterance recognition. The accuracy of the former system with speaker-dependent could achieve 68%, and of the latter achieves over 99.5% for test-independent (TI) and nearly 100% for test-dependent (TD) in experiments till now. From this conclusion, it could be easily got that lip-reading channel is an effective one and can be applied independently.

1 Introduction

The role of labial channel appears out in computer vision field gradually. Speech recognition using both audio and video information has been demonstrated to have a better performance than using audio channel alone [1-3, 7-9]. Some famous automatic speech systems has existed, such as the audio-visual speech recognition (AVSR) systems, Intel Co. [7] and the system introduced by Neti [8]. Also, acoustic and labial speaker recognition and identification also have been shown to work [5, 6].

Although most of the systems using the labial channel which have existed now are integrated with acoustic information, applications using information from lip movement alone are still expected. At least two such applications: lip-reading and utterance recognition, are possible (Fig.1). Lip-reading is to recognition what the people say while utterance recognition to determine who makes the lip movement (we call him/her lip actor in this paper). Take utterance recognition for example. Face recognition research has shown some promising results [9]. As we all know, the mouth or lip area occupies a large part of the human face so that most of the facial information can be gained from this area. Meanwhile, lip movement offers dynamic information which can make the recognition result more stable and robust. Because of these, an utterance recognition system using lip movement information alone is available.

This paper describes two systems which we developed: a lip-reading system and a lip movement utterance recognition system to show the validity of the sole labial channel, which can be seen from the experimental results. Thus the rest of this paper describes the implement of the two kinds of system, and model the lip movement utterance using both static and dynamic information. Experimental results and conclusion are arranged in the end.

J. Tao, T. Tan, and R.W. Picard (Eds.): ACII 2005, LNCS 3784, pp. 232 – 238, 2005.

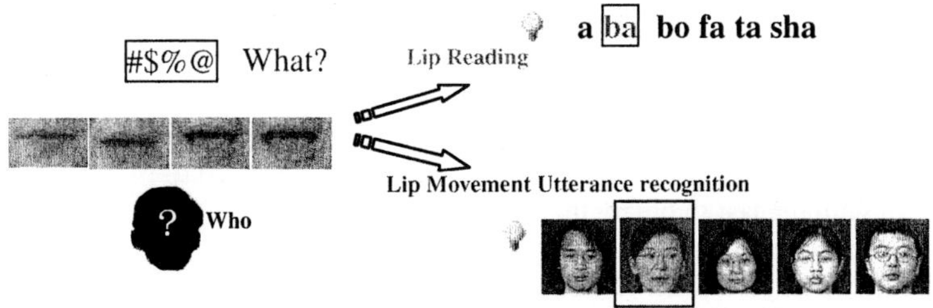

Fig. 1. Two applications using labial information alone

2 Overview of the Two Systems Using Labial Information

Because of the valid appearance of the lip-reading system and the lip movement utterance recognition system which we constructed, it is proved that information acquiring channel from the sole channel of lip movement is effective enough. This section gives an overview of them. Key problems are also discussed. The experimental results shown in section 2.5 give us encouraging conclusion, although some key problems still need to be studied further.

No matter which application, lip-reading or utterance recognition, it is for, there are several key problems a system using the labial channel should face: 1. how can we find the mouth and lip area? 2. What features describe lip movement best and what is the key information to differ one lip actor to another? 3. How to model the visual features we get from step 2? Thus the two systems have many similarities in solving the corresponding problem. Because of this, we can use a general flowchart to describe the solution to these problems in the two different applications, as seen in Fig. 2. Thus the rest of this section lies in the following: lip tracking, feature extracting, modeling, data collection and experimental results.

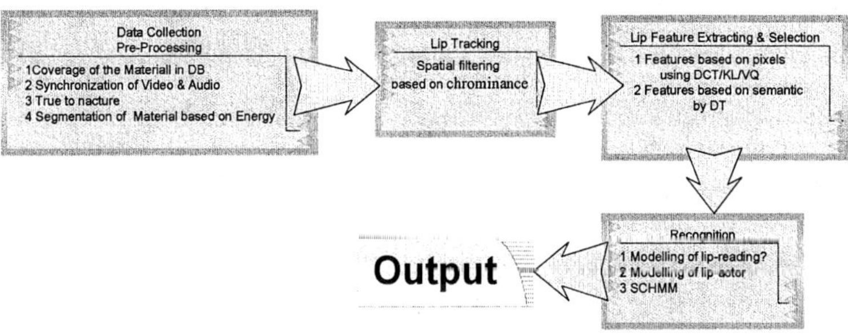

Fig. 2. Flowchart of the system suing labial information alone

2.1 Lip Detection and Tracking

We use spatial filter based on chrominance enhancement that follows [2] to locate the lip. Coordinate transformation from RGB space to YIQ space is used to improve contrast between chrominance of lip and face area.

1 Detect the position of face and eyes approximately.
2 Determine the region of interest (ROI) that contains lip
2 Coordinate transform the pixels of ROI.
4 Learn the maximum Q value of the data from face region and the minimum Q value of the data form lip region as thresholds. The front is used to filter the skin pixel around lip with the last to binary the ROI.
5 Use some operator of edgy detection to get the corner of the lip.
6 Use a lip contour model to characterize the shape information of lip.

Fig. 3. Lip Tracking Algorithm

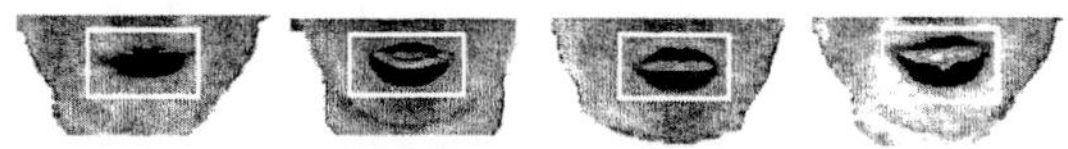

Fig. 4. Results of Lip Tracking

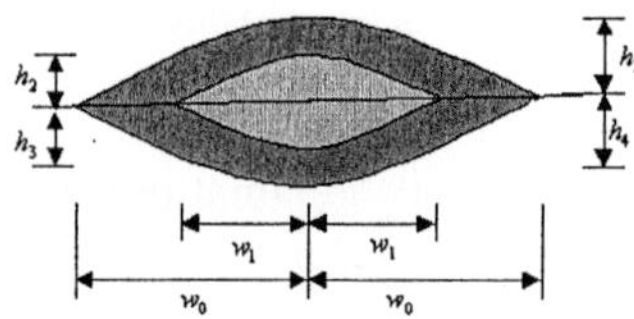

Fig. 5. Lip contour model

The whole procedure of tracking can be described in the following Fig.3. We can see some examples in Fig.4. :

The contour model used in the 6th step of the algorithm is four parabola curves shown in Fig.5. Here w0, w1, h1, h2, h3, h4 are parameters of the lip contour model. The equations to describe the lip contour can be seen in [2].

2.2 The Visual Feature Extracting

In this sub section, we need to find what features should be extracted from the effective region that have the best contribution to two applications. According to [3], all the methods to extract features from mouth area can be classified into 2 categories: bottom-up and top-down. The front method estimates feature vectors directly from lip image data while the last uses some templates and models to characterize the lip. Both pixel based and model based features are examined in our works. We use the lip contour model [2] in Fig.4 to acquire the shape information and also gain the intensity information from the lip region by the image transformation [2].

In the bottom-up method, the detected lip region is scaled to size of 32*16. The data from zoomed region is then transformed to YIQ space. We use the feature vectors forming by the transformed coefficients for classification. The transformations investigated in our work include the Discrete Cosine Transformation (DCT) and the Karhunen-Loeve Transformation (KLT).

While in the top-down approach, the parameters used in Fig.5 are combined and examined. As a conclusion, $(w_0, w_1, h_2 + h_3, h_1 + h_4)^T$ is used to lip-reading [2]. The contribution towards speaker recognition of these parameters is still being experimented.

One thing to be noted here is the truth that DCT can only reflect the frequency of the overall image. While we believe that the local frequency information may characterize movements of the lip better. To handle this problem, we divide the whole 256*256 image into 8 blocks (Fig. 6), each transformed respectively. All the experiment results tested are shown in Table 1.

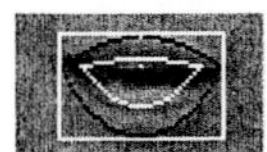
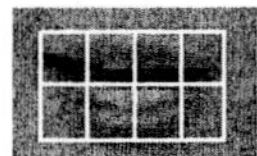

Fig. 6. Division of image for DCT

2.3 The Lip-Reading and Lip Movement Utterance Models

In this sub section, we discuss the modelling problems in lip-reading and lip movement utterance recognition respectively.

For languages like English, most of the experiments on lip-reading have been done on words. Unlike English, the unit of Chinese is syllable but not word. Totally, there are 400 syllables in Chinese, many of which are similar. Because of this, modelling every category of similar syllables seems to be a good choice for lip-reading. At this point in time, we have modeled the most common syllables [4]. It can be easily expanded to all syllable categories in Chinese.

Left to right Semi-continuous Hidden Markov Model (SCHMM) is used. For every tester in lip-reading experiment, 200*2 sentences are used to train the HMM models of the corresponding syllables, the rest 200*1 examples to test. All the HMM models for lip-reading are in six states, eight mixtures topology [2], while the HMM models for lip movement utterance recognition are in six states, ten mixtures.

Modelling for lip movement utterance recognition always follows this way: using the dynamic information from the image sequences and modelling the sentences for each lip actor. In this manner, the static information is always ignored. Because static information and the characteristic of the lip movement are both used to tell one lip actor to anther most of the time when we have the only choice to focus on the mouth area, a merger of static and dynamic information is necessary. Thus, we use a novel method to model the lip actor using both the static and dynamic information.

Against the method that only uses the dynamic information or the method that regards the two kinds of information as two separated channels, we combine the two kinds of information in a single channel. We consider it in a Text-Dependent (TD) way, while in Text-Independent (TI) way, it is similar, of course.

Let a sentence observation sequence $O = O_1O_2...O_i...O_T$ and O_i , $1 \le i \le T$, denote the corresponding feature vector of the ith observation. Let $S_1, S_2, ..., S_N$ mean the static models of the N lip actors. S_j comes in following: take several natural images of the jth speaker, acquire the feature vectors of them and get the mean vector, which is S_j. Then we get N difference vector sequences: $D_1, D_2, ..., D_N$. Here $D_j = d_1d_2...d_i...d_T$, $d_i = O_i - S_j$, $1 \le j \le T$. D_j is then tested against the jth HMM model H_j. The lip actor, supposed the kth, who owns the highest probability is selected. Here $k = \arg\max_j(P(D_j/H_j))$. The N HMM models are trained by the N difference vector sequences, not by the direct feature vector sequences that we have observed, obviously.

The method above exploits both the static and the dynamic information from the mouth area in a single channel. It only needs N extra mean vectors against any additional HMM models. It's natural and easy to realize.

In TD way, we train a HMM model for every phase; in TI way, all the 20*4 phases are trained to form a single HMM model.

The results of the corresponding experiments are shown in Table 1.

2.4 Data Collection and Pre-processing

For our research, two bi-modal databases are designed according to linguistics and built onto high quality digital image sequences. The database for lip-reading is called HIT Bimodal Chinese Audio-Video Database (HIT Bi-CAVDB)[2], which includes 10 people (5 males and 5 females), each person 200 sentences (each 3 times). All the sentences are designed according to linguistics. The other database for lip movement utterance recognition is called HIT Lip-Movement Utterance Recognition Database (HIT LUDB), still being expanded, which includes 28 people (15 males 13 females), each person 20 phases (each 5 times). All the images are captured in 25Hz, and stored in 24bits, 256*256 BMP files while the audio materials are 11025Hz, 8 bits PCM stored.

As introduced above, our research on lip-reading is based on Chinese syllables. Thus, material segmentation based on energy is done.

2.5 System Performances

All the lip-reading tests are done on the HIT Bi-CAVDB while the lip movement utterance recognition experiments are done on the HIT LUDB. Table 1 shows correct recognition rate of characters in lip-reading tests. Table 2 shows the result of lip actor recognition tests on all the last phase of the 5 in LUDB (420 phases in total).

The results shown in Table 2 are promising. It is revealed that (1) Utterance recognition from a lip movement channel is effective. (2) The accuracy of lip-reading can be improved, compared to [2] [3]. Thus the applications using a single labial channel are available.

Table 1. Result of speech recognition in Speaker Dependent

Feature extracted method(s)	Parameters from lip contours	ASM+PCA[3]	DCT	KL
Dimensions	4 $(w_0, w_1, h_2 + h_3, h_1 + h_4)^T$	-	6×8	48
Contribution to lip-reading	25.6%	26.9%	67.2%	66.8%

Table 2. Result of lip actor recognition (by the top 24 DCT coefficients)

	TD	TI
Correct rate	100%	99.5%

3 Conclusion

This paper has paid attention to the validity of the labial channel. Two applications: the lip-reading system and the system with lip movement utterance for identification, using information acquiring from lip movement alone, have been discussed. The two systems have achieves encouraging results in the experiment by far. A novel method to model the lip movement utterance has also been presented, regarding both the static and dynamic labial information as a single channel. Applications using information from lip movement alone are demonstrated effective.

Considering the HIT LUDB's still being built, further experiments are necessary to evaluate the performance of the method for a larger number of subjects. The accuracy of lip-reading still needs to be improved further, and it is possible to improve because there are contours and structure features not to be used in both systems. So, in both of them, we shall test further to investigate the benefit of different combination of features in the future.

References

1. E.D.Petajan. Automatic Lipreading to Enhance Speech Recognition. Ph.D. thesis of University of Illinois at Urbana_Champain. 1984: 1~261
2. Hongxun Yao. Research and implementation on some key problems of lip-reading recognition technology. Ph.D. thesis of Department of Computer Science and Technology, Harbin Institute of Technology, China , 2003
3. Matthews, I., Cootes, T. F., Bangham, J. A., Cox, J. A., and Harvey, R.:Extraction of visual features for lipreading. IEEE Transactions on Pattern Analysis and Machine Intelligence, vol. 24, no. 2, pp. 198-213, Feb.2002.

4. Xiaopeng Hong, Hongxun Yao, Minghui Xu. BioModel Database and Its Material Segmentation for Lip-Reading Recognition on Sentence (in Chinese). Chinese Journal Computer Engineering and Application, 2005, 41(3):174-177,190
5. J. Luettin. Visual Speech and Speaker Recognition. Ph.D. thesis of Department of Computer Science University of Sheffield, UK, 1997: 1~14
6. Ara V. Nefian, Lu Hong Liang, Tieyan Fu, and Xiao Xing Liu. A Bayesian Approach to Audio-Visual Speaker Identification. J. Kittler and M.S. Nixon (Eds.): AVBPA 03, pp. 761–769, 2003.
7. Ara V Nefian, Lu Hong Liang, Xiao Xing Liu, Xiaobo Pi and Kevin Murphy, "Dynamic Bayesian networks for audio-visual speech recognition", EURASIP, Journal of Applied Signal Processing, vol. 2002, no 11, p. 1274-1288, 2002.
8. C. Neti, G. Potamianos, J. Luettin, I. Matthews, D. Vergyri, J. Sison, A. Mashari, and J. Zhou. Audio visual speech recognition. In Final Workshop 2000 Report, 2000.
9. Shiguang Shan. Study on Some Key Issuses in Face Recognition. Ph.D. thesis of Institute of Computing Technology, Chinese Academy of Sciences, China, 2003.

Content-Based Affective Image Classification and Retrieval Using Support Vector Machines

Qingfeng Wu, Changle Zhou, and Chaonan Wang

Institute of Artificial Intelligence, Computer Science Department,
Xiamen University, 361005 Fujian, P.R. China
jlwu@xmu.edu.cn

Abstract. In this paper a new method to classify and retrieve affective images is proposed. First users express the affective semantics of the images with adjective words; process the data got by Semantic Differential method to obtain main factors of affection and establish affective space; extract low-level visual features of image to construct visual feature space; calculate the correlation between affective space and visual feature space with SVMs. The prototype system that embodies trained SVMs has been implemented. The system can classify the images automatically and support the affective image retrieval. The experimental results prove the effectiveness of this method.

1 Introduction

The goal of affective computing is to establish harmonious human-machine environment by enabling computer to observe, understand and synthesize emotions of human [1]. The research on the process of emotional information is inevitable in order to realize the "harmonious human-machine interaction". Visual emotional information is the main information which human get from the world, and it accounts for 80% of all.

On the other hand, with the rapid growing amount of images, the management and access of huge image library is becoming a headachy experience for users. Under such background, content-based image retrieval attracts attention widely and becomes a hot research area. The early research of this area is focused on the extraction of low-level visual features, such as color, texture and shape [2]. With the rapid development of affective computing, one of the important research subjects of content-based image retrieval is enabling retrieval system to simulate feelings of human to process and understand affective images. The study in this paper follows this idea.

Research on affective computing has been done in many countries such as US, Japan and so on [1, 3, 4]. Their research is mainly focused on facial expression recognition [5], affective speech recognition [6] and so on. The research of affective semantics of images is still on the stage of exploration. Different images arouse different emotions. Based on the careful research of the rule about the psychological effect and emotions aroused by visual features of images, some proper methods should be used to describe and extract these features quantificationally. Based on the research of art image visual psychology, Carlo Colombo *et al.* [7] established a set of rules to map

J. Tao, T. Tan, and R.W. Picard (Eds.): ACII 2005, LNCS 3784, pp. 239 – 247, 2005.

the visual contents of images to image semantics. Low-level visual features including color and line were selected to represent the image contents. The affections expressed by art images are first explained, and then users could retrieve images by visual features of images. The problem of the above method lies in the simplicity of features selected to express the visual contents of images, and the effects of human feeling and psychology are not considered well when low-level visual features are extracted. It is a key step in affective computing to map the relation between visual features and human affections. Yoshida *et al.* [8] realized it with linear mapping in ART museum. Considering the complexity of the relation between image features and affection, linear mapping obviously cannot fully display their relation.

In this paper a new method to classify and retrieve affective images is proposed. Some adjective words are collected first which are usually used by people when observing images, such as the word of lovely and beautiful etc. Users are invited to evaluate the images in the training set, and through factor analysis main factors are recognized. In addition affective space of image is constructed according to the thought of "dimensions". Visual features of images are extracted and visual feature space of image is also constructed. We calculate the mapping between affective space and visual feature space by SVMs. The trained SVMs are embodied in the prototype system, which can classify and retrieve affective images.

The rest part of the paper is organized as follows. Creation of affective space is introduced in Section 2. In Section 3 visual features of image which are suitable for the affective retrieval are described. The classification and retrieval of affective images using Kernel SVMs are introduced in Section 4. In Section 5, experimental results and analysis are presented. In section 6, conclusions and further work are given.

2 Creation of Affective Space

Obviously for better accomplishing the task of recognition and retrieval of affective image, human emotion should be categorized reasonably and clearly first. But it is relatively difficult. Emotion research involves many fields such as psychology, physiology, philosophy and so on, and there is no unified theory about categorization and description of emotion by far [9, 10].

In the field of facial expression recognition, different kinds of emotions can be described by defining the value of n dimensions of emotion [9, 11]. Adopting the idea of dimensions, this paper illustrates that an affective space can be constructed by proper method and every kind of emotion can be mapped to a vector in this space.

The creation of affective space includes the following main steps [12]:

1. First for specific image database, N adjective word pairs such as "beautiful-ugly", "natural-artificial" and so on, are selected to express the emotions of observers when they are viewing an image.
2. Collect data by Semantic Differential method and form the emotion database. That is, users examine the sample images and put a score for each adjective word pairs given previously against an image. The value of the score is -2, -1, 0, 1or 2.

3. Preprocess the emotion database. z_{mnk} is the value of image m evaluated by user k for the nth adjective word pairs. With formula 1 the average values can be got and with formula 2 they are standardized, and the emotion matrix X can be obtained.

$$y_{mn} = \frac{1}{K}\sum_{k=1}^{K} z_{mnk} , \tag{1}$$

$$x_{mn} = \frac{y_{mn} - \overline{y_n}}{s_n} , \tag{2}$$

where, $\overline{y_n} = \frac{1}{M}\sum_{m=1}^{M} y_{mn}$, $s_n^2 = \sum_{m=1}^{M} (y_{mn} - \overline{y_n})^2$.

4. Create affective space. Apply factor analysis to matrix X . And factor analysis can be formulated in 3.

$$X = FA^T + e , \tag{3}$$

where, F is the factor variable; A is the factor loading matrix.

In this paper, F and A are calculated by Principal Component Analysis (PCA). Using the PCA, the original space of adjective word pairs with N dimensions is reduced to orthogonal affective space with L ($L < N$) dimensions. The values of vector $a_{1 \le n \le N}$ in matrix A correspond to the coordinate of nth adjective word pairs in affective space with L dimensions.

3 Extraction of Image Visual Features

Different shape, color, texture and so on of objects will arouse different psychological reaction of people under the perceptual effect. Through visual observation of people, the appearance of any object will drive the exposure of emotions, such as the psychological activity of love, excitement, calmness and disgust [1, 9, 13]. So the well-selected visual features of image should not only have strong ability to represent the visual contents of images but also the ability to express observers' affection.

3.1 Color Feature of Image

Color is one of the main perceptual features for people to recognize image and also the most extensively used visual content for image retrieval. At the same time people realize that color has the power to arouse emotions [13].

Before extracting color feature, color space must be determined first. In this paper, HSV (hue, saturation and value) space is adopted because it is considered to be more preferable to RGB space for affective image retrieval. RGB coordinates are translated to HSV coordinates by formula 4. Moreover the color in HSV space is quantized to 256 bins.

$$
\begin{aligned}
&Max = \max(R,G,B) \\
&Min = \min(R,G,B) \\
&V = 0.299R + 0.587G + 0.114B \\
&S = \begin{cases} 0 & , \text{if } Max = 0 \\ (Max - Min) / Max, & else \end{cases} \\
&H = \begin{cases} 0 & , \text{if } Max = Min \\ 60(G-B)/(Max-Min) & , \text{if } Max = R \text{ and } G > B \\ 360 + 60(G-B)/(Max-Min), & \text{if } Max = R \text{ and } G < B \\ 60(2+(B-R)/(Max-Min)), & \text{if } Max = G \\ 60(4+(R-G)/(Max-Min)), & else \end{cases}
\end{aligned}
\tag{4}
$$

By far the widely-used color describers include color histogram, color moment, color correlogram, etc. Because color correlogram was proposed to characterize not only the color distributions of pixels, but also the spatial correlation of pairs of colors, it is adopted in this paper. Please refer to ref. [14] for the detailed formula.

3.2 Texture Feature of Image

Texture is an inherent property of the object surface. Different material leads to the different structure of surface, and gives viewers different feelings. Smooth can arouse the delicate feeling, whereas coarseness arouses the aged feeling, and they all produce different visual psychological effect.

The widely-used methods to represent texture include co-occurrence matrices, Markov random field, Tamura feature and so on. The Tamura features, including coarseness, contrast, directionality, linelikeness, regularity and roughness, are designed in accordance with psychological studies on the human perception of texture. The first three components of Tamura features are adopted in this paper. The computations of these three features are given in ref. [15].

3.3 Shape Feature of Image

Shape is one of the features which describe the object essential. Shape of objects in images can stimulate the emergence of human sensibility knowledge. For example, lines with different directions can express different emotions. Horizontal lines always associate with stillness and width, and communicate calmness and relaxation; vertical lines are clear and direct, and communicate dignity and eternality; slant lines are unstable and communicate notable dynamism.

Classical shape representation uses a set of moments which are invariant to translation, rotation, and scale. This paper adopts moment invariants as shape describer. Please refer to ref. [16] for the detailed formula.

4 SVMs Applied in Affective Image Classification and Retrieval

Considering affective space and visual feature space of image belong to different domains, SVMs is used to learn the mapping correlation between these two spaces.

4.1 Support Vector Machines

It is known that SVMs [17, 18] can give an optimal separating hyperplane with a maximal margin if the data is linearly separable. In linearly non-separable but nonlinearly separable case, the data will be mapped into a high-dimensional space where the two classes of data are more readily separable. Such mapping is formed by a kernel representation of data.

Consider the problem of separating a set of training examples which belong to two classes, $(x_i, y_i)_{1\le i\le N}$, where each example $x_i \in R^d$, d being the dimension of the input space, belong to a class labeled by $y_i \in \{-1,+1\}$. Once a kernel $K(x_i, x_j)$ satisfying Mercer's condition has been chosen, an optimal separating hyperplane will be constructed in the mapping space. The optimization problem can be achieved by maximizing the objective function with Lagrange multiplies,

$$L(a) = \sum_{i=1}^{N} a_i - \frac{1}{2}\sum_{i,j=1}^{N} a_i a_j y_i y_j K(x_i, x_j) , \tag{5}$$

where a_i is Lagrange multiplies and then the decision function will be:

$$f(x) = \mathrm{sgn}\left(\sum_{i-1}^{N} a_i y_i K(x_i, x) + b\right) . \tag{6}$$

Possible choices of kernel functions include: polynomial, Gaussian radial basis function and Multi-Layer perception function. In this paper, we use Gaussian radial basis function kernel, which is defined in formula 7, since it was empirically observed to perform better than other two.

$$K(x, y) = \exp\left(-\rho\|x-y\|^2\right) . \tag{7}$$

In this case, the number of centers, or number of support vectors, the centers themselves, or the support vectors, the weights (a_i) and the threshold (b) are all produced automatically by the SVMs training and give excellent results.

SVMs are designed for binary classification. To discriminate several classes simultaneously, we must construct a multi-class classifier. Here we use the one-against-others SVM-based classifiers.

In the one-against-others SVM-based classifiers, n hyperplanes are constructed, where n is the number of classes. Each hyperplane separates one class from the other classes. Namely, we will get n decision functions $(f_k)_{1\le k\le n}$. The class of a new point x is given by

$$C(x) = \arg\max_k \{f_k(x)\} . \tag{8}$$

4.2 Classification and Retrieval of Affective Image

In this paper SVMs is used to learn the mapping correlation between affective space and visual feature space of image. The visual features of sample images are provided to SVMs as input, and the output is the coordinates of different emotions in affective space. After being trained, parameters of SVMs present the correlation between affective space and visual feature space of image. Trained SVMs can be used to estimate and classify images automatically.

Our implemented prototype system allows users to retrieve images from the image database of affective scenery by scoring adjective word pairs. The retrieval procedures are described as follow:

1. User puts a score as weight for each impression word pairs provided by system, and then a vector Q is obtained.
2. Apply the relation of mapping A to Q, namely $Q \cdot A$. Calculate the coordinates of adjective word pairs in affective space.
3. Retrieval system that embodies trained SVMs will decide the candidate images and send them to users.

5 Experiments and Results

1420 color scenery images are collected. The retrieval system extracts the low-level visual features of images automatically. These low-level visual features are stored in the database. By excluding the ambiguous images, we choose respectively 150 images as the training set and testing set from image database. To avoid giving heavy load to users, we elaborately select only 9 adjective word pairs listed in Table 1.

5.1 Affective Space Experiment

The twelve users examine the sample images of training set and put a score for each adjective word pairs mentioned above to each image. Then, the emotion database is got. Preprocess data in the emotion database by formula 1 and formula 2. Apply factor analysis to matrix X . Eigen values of matrix X are 4.380, 2.403 and 1.023, and their accumulating contribution is 85.447%. So three main factors are drawn and original factor loading matrix for these three main factors are calculated by PCA. The structure of loading matrix is adjusted for simplification and maximal variance orthogonal rotation matrix is figured out in Table 1.

Shown in Table 1, the adjective word pairs $Pair_1$, $Pair_2$, $Pair_3$ and $Pair_4$ have large weights for the first main factor, and it reflects the human feeling of "evaluation". The adjective word pairs $Pair_5$ and $Pair_6$ have large weights for the second main factor and it conveys the feeling of "naturalness". The adjective word pairs $Pair_7$, $Pair_8$ and $Pair_9$ have large weights for the third main factor and it is the reflection of "complexity".

Through the process described above, the original space of adjective word pairs with N ($N = 9$) dimensions is transformed into orthogonal affective space with

$L(L < N)$ dimensions and each vector in affective space stands for the semantic description of some kind of emotion.

5.2 Experiment of Selection of Visual Feature

The selection of visual features has direct influence on learning effect. We also made experiments on the selection of visual features, and the result is shown in Table 2.

Based on the experimental result, the following conclusions can be drawn: 1) Accuracy rate of color feature is higher than that of texture and shape, and this means color of an image may give viewers more impression. In other words, different visual features of image have the influence of different degree on human affections; 2) Combination of visual features gets a higher accuracy rate than exclusive visual feature. That is to say, we should not use exclusive visual feature to represent image because exclusive feature doesn't have strong ability to convey users' affections.

5.3 Experiment of Affective Image Retrieval

Figure 1 shows an example of retrieval of affective image. It shows the best 14 candidates for the adjectives: "beautiful", "dynamic" and "natural" whose weights are 2, 1 and 1 respectively.

Table 1. Maximal Variance Orthogonal Rotation Matrix

$Pair_n$	Adj. Word Pair	1	2	3
1	Beautiful-Ugly	0.951	0.189	-0.237
2	Dynamic-Static	0.936	0.281	-0.185
3	Cheerful-Gloomy	0.932	-0.231	-2.72E-02
4	Active-Passive	0.661	-0.592	-0.308
5	Natural-Artificial	0.115	0.975	8.851E-02
6	Tense-Relaxed	0.106	-0.956	0.104
7	Simple-Complex	2.76E-01	-0.666	0.760
8	Bright-Dark	-2.06E-02	-0.576	0.539
9	Hot-Cold	-0.348	7.612E-02	0.849

Table 2. Comparison of Retrieval Rate with Different Visual Features

Combination of visual features	Number of correct retrieval sample	Number of error retrieval sample	Accuracy rate (%)
Color	67	13	84.0
Texture	64	16	79.6
Shape	65	15	81.3
Color+Shape	71	9	88.4
Color+Texture	66	14	82.5
Color+Texture+Shape	75	5	93.3

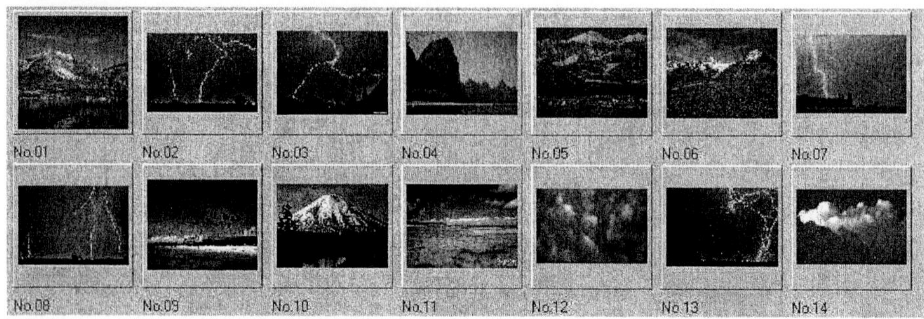

Fig. 1. Result of Affective Image Retrieval

6 Conclusions

In this paper, we present the procedure to create the affective space and the low-level visual feature space of image. And calculate the correlation between these two spaces using SVMs. Prototype system that embodies trained SVMs can classify affective images and support affective retrieval. Experimental results prove the effectiveness of our method.

In our future work, we will focus on: 1) building up the mechanism to evaluate the validity of adjective word pairs selected for expressing the affections of human; 2) analyzing and extracting visual features which can better represent users' affection.

Acknowledgment

This work was supported by National Science Foundation of P.R. China (60275023).

References

1. Changle Z.: An introduction to Mental Computation. Tsinghua University Press, Beijing (2003)
2. Amold W. M., Semeulders, *et al.*: Content-Based Image Retrieval at the End of Early Years. IEEE Trans on Pattern Analysis and Machine Intelligence. 22(12), (2000) 1349–1380
3. Picard R. W: Affective Computing. MIT Press, Cambridge (1997)
4. Nagamachi M.: Emotion Engineering. Kaibundo Publishing. Tokyo, Japan (1997)
5. Essa I A, Pentlang A.: Coding, Analysis, Interpretation and Recognition of Facial Expressions. IEEE Tran. on Pattern Analysis and Machine Intelligence. 19(7), (1997) 757–763
6. Roy D, Pentland A.: Automatic Spoken Affect Analysis and Classification. In: Proceedings of the Second International Conference on Automatic Face and Gesture Recognition, Killington, VT, (1996) 363–367
7. C Colombo, A Del Bimbo, P Pala: Semantics in Visual Information Retrieval. IEEE Multimedia. 6(3), (1999) 38–53
8. Yoshida K, Kato T, Yanaru T.: Image Retrieval System Using Impression Words. In: Proceedings of IEEE International Conference on Systems, Man, and Cybernetics, Vol. 3, San Diego, CA, (1998) 2780– 2784

9. Weining W., Yinglin Y.: A Survey of Image Emotional Semantic Research. Journal of Circuits and Systems. 8(5), (2003) 101–109
10. Ortony A, Clore G L, Collins A.: The Cognitive Structure of Emotions. Cambridge University Press. Cambridge, UK (1988)
11. Lang P J. The Emotion Probe: Studies of Motivation and Attention. American Psychologist. 50(5), (1995) 372–385
12. Teruhisa Hochin, Keiichi Yamada, Tatsuo Tsrji: Multimedia Data Access Based on the Sensitivity Factors. In: Proceedings of International Database Engineering and Applications Symposium, Yokohama, Japan, (2000) 319–326
13. Jonhannes Itten: The Art of Color. Shanghai People's Art Press, Shanghai (1992)
14. Huang J., Kumar S. R., Mitra M., Zabih R. : Image Indexing Using Color Correlograms. In: Proceedings of IEEE Computer Society Conference on Computer Vision and Pattern Recognition, Puerto Rico, (1997) 762–768
15. Tamura H, Mori S, Yamaki T: Texture Features Corresponding to Visual Perceptions. IEEE Trans. On System, Man and Cybernetics. 8(6), (1978) 460–473
16. Ming-Kei Hu: Visual Pattern Recognition by Moment Invariants. IEEE Trans. on Information Theory. 8(2), (1962) 179–187
17. Vapnik V N: The Nature of Statistical Learning Theory. New York: Springer-Verlag (2000)
18. Nello Cristianini, John Shawe-Taylor: An Introduction to Support Vector Machines and Other Kernel-based Learning Methods. Publishing House of Electronics Industry. Beijing (2004)

A Novel Real Time System for Facial Expression Recognition

Xiaoyi Feng[1], Matti Pietikäinen[2], Abdenour Hadid[2], and Hongmei Xie[1]

[1] College of Electronics and Information, Northwestern Polytechnic University, 710072 Xi'an, China
{fengxiao, xiehm}@nwpu.edu.cn
[2] Machine Vision Group, Infotech Oulu and Dept. of Electrical and Information Engineering, P. O. Box 4500 Fin-90014 University of Oulu, Finland
{hadid, mkp}@ee.oulu.fi

Abstract. In this paper, a fully automatic, real-time system is proposed to recognize seven basic facial expressions (angry, disgust, fear, happiness, neutral, sadness and surprise), which is insensitive to illumination changes. First, face is located and normalized based on an illumination insensitive skin model and face segmentation; then, the basic Local Binary Patterns (LBP) technique, which is invariant to monotonic grey level changes, is used for facial feature extraction; finally, a coarse-to-fine scheme is used for expression classification. Theoretical analysis and experimental results show that the proposed system performs well in variable illumination and some degree of head rotation.

1 Introduction

Fully automatic and real time facial expression recognition plays an important role in human-computer interaction, telecommunication and psychological research etc, while it is still a challenging problem due to the influence of illumination and head movement etc. During the past years, few works have addressed this issue [1-8].

In this paper, we propose a fully automatic and real time system for facial expression recognition. In the face detection step, face areas are detected by using a skin color model and eyes are located by face segmentation. In the feature extraction step, LBP operator is used to efficiently describe facial expressions. In the classification step, a coarse-to-fine scheme is proposed. The proposed system is insensitive to illumination changes due to the insensitiveness of the skin detection and eyes location methods to illuminations and the invariance of the LBP operator to monotonic grey level changes. Besides of this, the system is able to deal with head movement to some degree because its features are holistic.

The rest of the paper is organized as follows. The structure of the system is introduced in section 2 and the face preprocessing procedure is described in section 3. In section 4, we present our facial feature representation method. In section 5, we introduce the classification method. System evaluation is described in section 6. Finally in section 7 we conclude this paper.

J. Tao, T. Tan, and R.W. Picard (Eds.): ACII 2005, LNCS 3784, pp. 248–256, 2005.

2 Structure of the System

Fig. 1 illustrates implementation of the system. A commercial digital camcorder is connected to a computer for image acquisition and one example of images caught from the video stream is shown in Fig.2.

The preprocessing procedure includes three steps: face detection, eyes location and face normalization. First, skin color locus in [9] is used to detect face candidates. Then, a color-ratio image is used for face segmentation and a geometrical face model is adopted for eyes location. Finally, face area is normalized and cropped.

In the feature detection stage, the preprocessed face area is divided into several small blocks and the LBP histograms is calculated and combined into a feature vector.

Finally, a coarse-to-fine scheme is employed for expression classification.

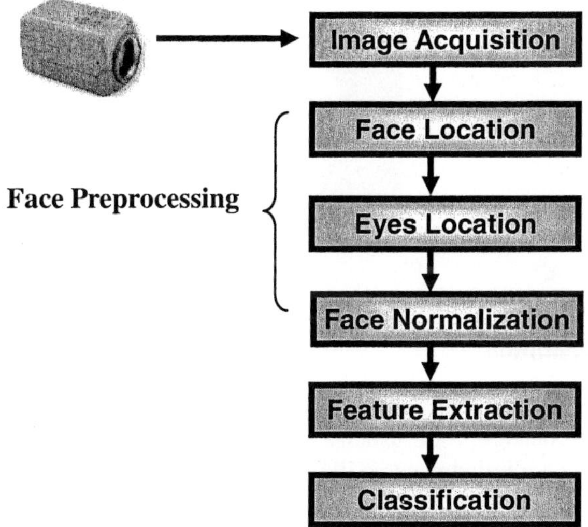

Fig. 1. Implementation of the system

Fig. 2. Acquired Image

3 Face Preprocessing

3.1 Face Detection with a Skin Locus

Martinkauppi et al. found that the Normalized Color Coordinates (NCC) combined with the skin locus most appropriate for skin detection under varying illumination. Three steps are included in creating a skin locus: I. Collecting the image material for different camera calibration and prevailing conditions. II. Selecting skin area for further processing manually or automatically. III. Converting the selected skin RGBs into a chromatically space and modeling them using a polynomial [9].

To detect face-like area, the image presented in RGB color space is converted to the NCC space *r, g* and *b*. if *r* and *b* of a pixel fall into the area of the skin locus, the pixel belongs to skin. The result of skin detection is shown in Fig.3. Considering real application, we select the largest skin component and regard it as face area (see the part inside the green box in Fig.3).

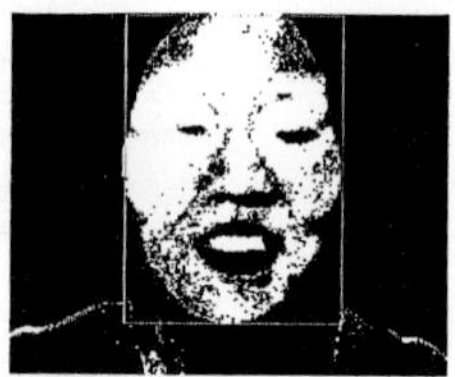

Fig. 3. Face detection result

3.2 Face Segmentation

Based on the knowledge that facial features are darker than their surroundings, morphological valley detectors are usually used for eyes detection, while these feature detection methods are failed in some illumination conditions (See Fig.4).

Here we propose a novel method for facial feature detection based on color information that is insensitive to illuminations. Based on the observation that eyes and eyebrows contain less and lips contain more red elements than skin, face region is converted to grey level image named color-ratio image as follows:

$$f(x,y) = \min(255, {b \times 255}/{r}) \tag{1}$$

Here $f(x,y)$ is grey value of a pixel in position (x,y) in the color-ratio image and r and b are two chromaticities in NCC space. The color-ratio image corresponding to the image in Fig. 2 is shown in Fig. 5(a).

The upper part and the lower part of the color-ratio image are then segmented respectively, according to the rules of minimizing intra-class variance and the results are shown in Fig. 5(b) and Fig. 5 (c).

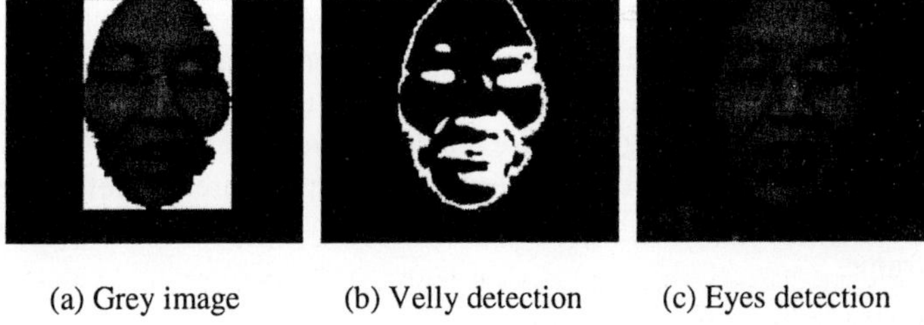

(a) Grey image (b) Velly detection (c) Eyes detection

Fig. 4. Velly-based eyes detection

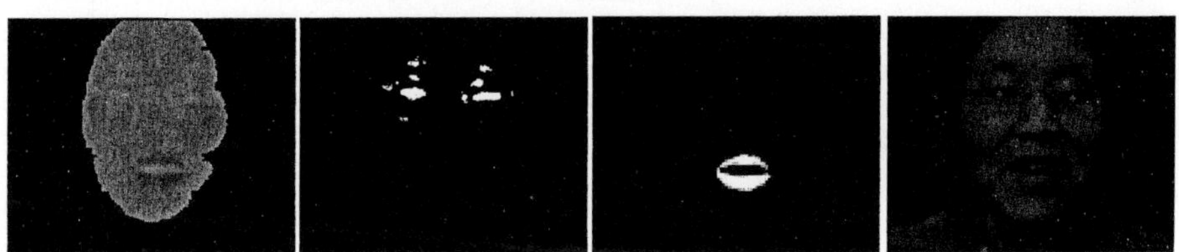

(a)Color-ratio image (b)Upper face segmentation (c)Lower face segmentation (d)Eyes detection

Fig. 5. Color-based eyes detection

3.3 Eyes Location and Tracking

After the possible facial features are detected, a similar method as proposed in [10] is applied to evaluate feature constellations, using a geometrical face model including eyes, eyebrows and mouth. Based on experiments we have modified the face model to make the tracking procedure accurate and fast.

We first select facial features locating at the upper half of face area as eyes candidates and evaluate each eye candidate pair as follows:

$$E_{eyepair} = 0.5\exp(-10(\frac{D_{eyes} - 0.4B_{width}}{D})^2) + 0.25\left|\theta_{eyeleft} + \theta_{eyeright} - 2\times\theta\right| \quad (2)$$

Here B_{width} is the width of face bounding. Let $D = 0.8B_{width}$. D_{eyes} is real distance a eye candidate pair. $\theta, \theta_{eyeleft}, \theta_{eyeright}$ indicate directions of base line (line passing through center of a eye candidate pair), left eye candidate and right eye candidate, respectively.

For each eye candidate pair, other facial features are searched for and evaluated.

$$E_{feature} = \exp(-10(\frac{d_{feature} - D_{feature}}{D})^2) \quad (3)$$

Where $features = \{mouth, eyebrows\}$, $d_{feature}$ and $D_{feature}$ are real distance and reference distance from features to base line.

The total evaluation value is a weighted sum of the values for each facial features. The weights for each pair of eyes, mouth, and eyebrows are 0.4, 0.3, 0.1 and 0.05, respectively. The constellation with the largest evaluation value is assumed to real facial features. Fig.4 (c) and Fig.5 (d) are results of eyes detection.

It should be pointed out that during eyes tracking procedure, the reference distances are replaced by corresponding real distances, which can be obtained from the just processed frame.

3.4 Face Normalization

Face normalization is based on the position of two eyes and the distance between them. After face normalization, eyes position and distance between two eyes are the same. Fig. 6 shows one face normalization result. The size of each normalized image is 150×128.

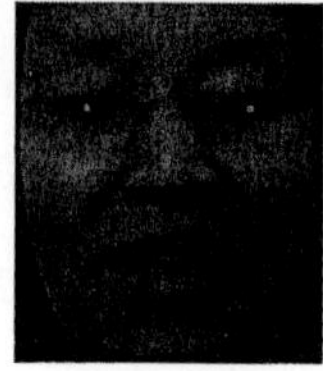

Fig. 6. Normalized face

4 Face Feature Extraction

Fig.7 is an illustration of the basic LBP operator [11]. The original 3×3 neighbourhood at the left is thresholded by the value of the centre pixel, and a binary pattern code is produced. The LBP code of the centre pixel in the neighbourhood is obtained by converting the binary code into a decimal code. It is obviously that LBP is invariant to grey level changes.

The LBP operator has been applied to many problems with excellent performance [12][13]. In our work, face images are seen as a composition of micro-patterns, which can be well described by LBP:

18	10	17
21	15	4
25	22	13

Threshold ⟹

1	0	1
1		0
1	1	0

Local binary pattern

Fig. 7. The basic LBP operator

Binary code: 11100101 LBP code: 229

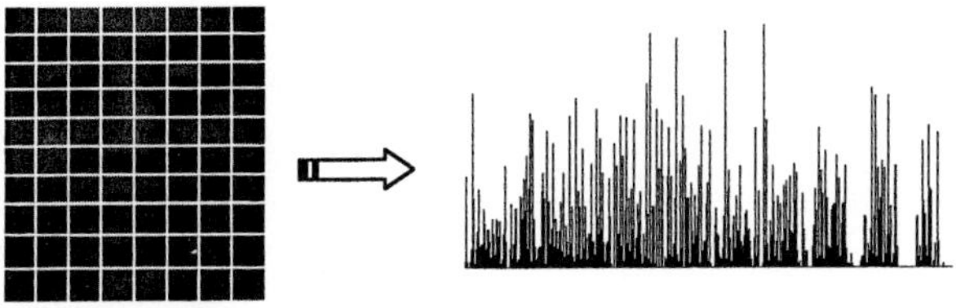

(a) Image blocks (b) LBP histogram

Fig. 8. An example of a facial image divided into 10×8 blocks

1. **Divide the face image into small regions**. After experimenting with different block sizes, we choose to divide the image into 80 (10×8) non-overlapping blocks (see Fig.8 (a)).
2. **Calculate the LBP histogram from each region.**
3. **Concatenate the LBP feature histograms into a single feature vector.** LBP histogram of each region is combined together to form a single feature vector representing the whole image (See Fig.8 (b)).

The reasons for our feature extraction are: First, LBP is capable of presenting facial appearances and so it can be used for representing facial expressions; Second, LBP is invariant to grey level changes.

5 Expression Classification

A coarse-to-fine classification scheme is used here. In the coarse classification step, the combination of the chi square statistic and the nearest neighbor classifier is used to reduce a seven-class classification problem to a two-class one. In the fine classification step, the weighted chi square statistic [12] and the nearest neighbor classifier to further discriminate the two expressions.

5.1 Coarse Classification

Consider a training set X containing n d -dimensional feature vectors is divided into seven subsets and each subset corresponds to one expression.

Let $X_c = \{x_i^c | 0 \le i < n_c\}$ denotes the cth subset with n_c $(c = 1,2,...7)$ vectors and x_i is the ith feature vector. So

$$X = \bigcup_{c=1}^{7} X_c \qquad n = \sum_{c=1}^{7} n_c \tag{4}$$

The model vector (denoted as m^c) of the cth expression class is the cluster center of the cth subset:

$$m^c = \frac{1}{n_c} \sum_{i=0}^{n_c - 1} x_i^c \tag{5}$$

A chi square (χ^2) statistic is used as dissimilarity measure between a testing sample and models. Suppose s is the test vector and s_j is its jth element, we have

$$\chi^2(s, m^c) = \sum_{j=0}^{d-1} \frac{(s_j - m_j^c)^2}{s_j + m_j^c} \tag{6}$$

Instead of classifying the test sample into one expression class, here we choose two expression candidates $cc = \{c1, c2\}$, $c1$ and $c2$ subject to

$$\begin{aligned} \chi^2(s, m^{c1}) &= \min_{1 \le c \le 7} \chi^2(s, m^c) \\ \chi^2(s, m^{c2}) &= \min_{1 \le c \le 7,\, c \ne c1} \chi^2(s, m^c) \end{aligned} \tag{7}$$

5.2 Fine Classification

The weighted chi square (χ_w^2) statistic [12] is defined as follows

$$\begin{aligned} \chi_w^2(s, m^c) &= \sum_{j=0}^{d-1} w_j \frac{(s_j - m_j^c)^2}{s_j + m_j^c} \\ \chi_w^2(s, m^c) &= \min_{1 \le cc \le 2} \chi_w^2(s, m^{cc}) \end{aligned} \tag{8}$$

Fig. 9 shows the classification result for original image in Fig. 2.

Fig. 9. Classification result

6 Evaluation

The recognition performance of our system is tested as follows.

(1) **Person-dependent recognition:** In the training stage, ten individuals are asked to pose seven basic expressions, which are input into the system for training. In the recognition stage, these individuals posed expressions again and the system recognized them. Each individual labels his expressions in the original image sequences. Results of the system are compared to the labels and then we have the recognition rate. The average recognition accuracy is 92%. Some results are shown in Fig.10.

(2) **Person-independent recognition:** Five individuals' expressions are used for training and five other persons' expressions are used for testing. The average recognition rate is 76%.

7 Conclusions

Real time, fully automatic facial expressions recognition is one of the challenging tasks in face analysis. This paper presents a novel real time system for it. The face pre-processing is implemented based on the skin detection and face segmentation, which can assure correct eyes detection under large illumination variation and some degree of head movement. The Local Binary Pattern operator is used here to describe face efficiently. The features detection procedure is insensitive to grey level changes. The holistic features also make the proposed system insensitive to some degree of head rotation. At last, a coarse-to-fine classification scheme is used for expression classification. Experimental results demonstrate that our system performs well in illumination changes and some degree of head movement.

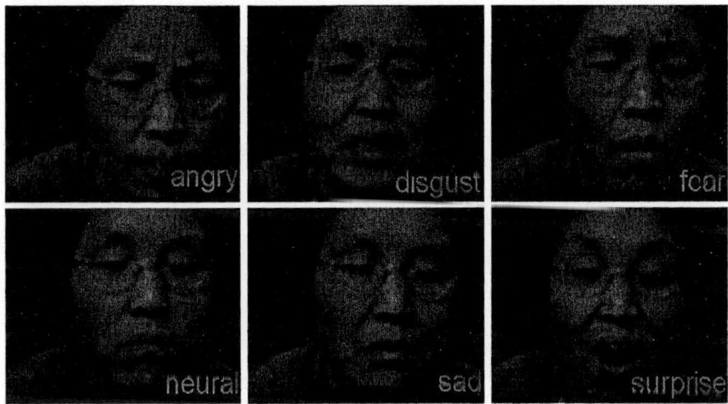

Fig. 10. Examples of correct recognition

References

1. M. Pantic, Leon J.M. Rothkrantz: Automatic analysis of facial expressions: the state of the art, IEEE Transactions on Pattern Analysis and Machine Intelligence, Vol. 22 (2000) 1424-1445
2. B. Fasel and J. Luettin: Automatic facial expression analysis: A survey, Pattern Recognition, Vol. 36 (2003) 259-275
3. Li.Stan Z & K.Anil, Handbook of face recognition, Springer-Verlag, 2004.9
4. P. Michel and R. E. Kaliouby: Real time facial expression recognition in video using support vector machines, Proceedings of the 5th International Conference on Multimodal Interfaces, (2003) 258-264
5. I. Kotsia and I. Pitas: Real time facial expression recognition from image sequences using support vector machines, Proceedings of Visual Communication and Image Processing, (2005), in press
6. H. Park and J. Park: Analysis and recognition of facial expression based on point-wise motion energy, Proceedings of Image Analysis and Recognition (2004) 700-708
7. X. Zhou, X. Huang, B. Xu and Y. Wang: Real time facial expression recognition based on boosted embedded hidden Markov model, Proceedings of the Third International Conference on Image and Graphics (2004), 290-293
8. K. Anderson and P. w. Mcowan: Real-time emotion recognition using biologically inspired models, Proceedings of 4th International Conference on Audio- and Video-Based Biometric Person Authentication (2003) 119-127
9. B. Martinkauppi, Face color under varying illumination-analysis and applications, Dr.tech Dissertation, University of Oulu, Finland, 2002
10. J.Hannuksela: Facial feature based head tracking and pose estimation, Department of Electrical and Information Engineering, University of Oulu, Finland, 2003
11. T. Ojala, M. Pietikäinen, T. Mäenpää: Multiresolution grey-scale and rotation invariant texture classification with Local Binary Patterns, IEEE Transactions on Pattern Analysis and Machine Intelligence, Vol. 24(2002) 971-987
12. T. Ahonen, A. Hadid and M. Pietikäinen, Face recognition with local binary patterns. The 8th European Conference on Computer Vision (2004), 469-481
13. T. Ojala, M. Pietikäinen and T. Mäenpää. Multiresolution grey-scale and rotation invariant texture classification with Local Binary Patterns. IEEE Transactions on Pattern Analysis and Machine Intelligence Vol.24 (2002): 971-987

Fist Tracking Using Bayesian Network

Peng Lu, Yufeng Chen, Mandun Zhang, and Yangsheng Wang

Institute of Automation, Chinese Academy of Sciences,
Beijing 100080, China
{plu, wys}@mail.pattek.com.cn

Abstract. This paper presents a Bayesian network based multi-cue fusion method for robust and real-time fist tracking. Firstly, a new strategy, which employs the latest work in face recognition, is used to create accurate color model of the fist automatically. Secondly, color cue and motion cue are used to generate the possible position of the fist. Then, the posterior probability of each possible position is evaluated by Bayesian network, which fuses color cue and appearance cue. Finally, the fist position is approximated by the hypothesis that maximizes a posterior. Experimental results show that our algorithm is real-time and robust.

1 Introduction

With the ever increasing role of computers in society, HCI has become an increasingly important part of our daily lives. One long-term goal in HCI has been to migrate the "natural" means that humans employ to communicate with each other into HCI. In this paper we mainly investigate the fist tracking algorithm, which can be used as a natural racing car game control interface.

Tracking objects efficiently and robustly in complex environment is a challenging issue in computer vision. Many researches have been done on this area. Currently, particle filter [1] [2] and mean shift[3] [4]are two successful approaches taken in the pursuit of robust tracking. Particle filters, to apply a recursive Bayesian filter based on propagation of sample set over time, maintain multiple hypotheses at the same time and use a stochastic motion model to predict the position of the object. Maintaining multiple hypotheses allows the tracker to handle clutters in the background, and recover from failure or temporary distraction. However, there are high computational demands in the approach, and this is the bottleneck to apply particle filtering in real time systems. On the other hand, mean shift explores the local energy landscape, using only a single hypothesis. This approach is computational effective, but it is susceptible to converge to local maximum.

In this paper, we propose a novel fist tracking algorithm. First, some hypotheses about the fist's position are generated based on the motion cue and color cue. In this way, the number of the hypotheses is very limited. Then all the hypotheses are evaluated by the Bayesian network, which fuses appearance cue and color cue. Based on Bayesian network the tracking results are more robust.

J. Tao, T. Tan, and R.W. Picard (Eds.): ACII 2005, LNCS 3784, pp. 257–262, 2005.

In the remainder of this paper, section 2 introduces how to generate hypothesis. Section 3 describes the evaluating of the hypothesis by Bayesian network. Some experiments are shown in section 4.

2 Hypothesis Generation

Skin is arguably the most widely used primitive in human image processing research, with applications ranging from face detection and person tracking to pornography filtering. Color is the most obvious feature of the fist. It indicates the possible position of the fist. In order to use color cue of the fist ,a probability distribution image of the desired color must be created firstly. Many algorithms employ a manual process to extract color information in their initialization stage, such as CAMSHIFT. By this way an accurate skin color model can be obtained. But semi-automation is the main shortcoming of these algorithms. For achieving automation, the most popular method is to learn the skin color distribution from a large number of training samples. However, due to the different illumination and different camera lens, this color distribution is not always exact in real condition.

In this paper, we proposed a novel scheme to acquire the color distribution of the fist. Generally speaking, the skin color of hand and face, which belong to the same person, are the same or similar. For face detection, there are many successful algorithms. So we gain the skin distribution from the face of the player instead of the fist. In our scheme, three steps are needed for creating color model. The first stage is face detection. In this stage, our Haar-Sobel-like boosting [5] algorithm is used. Haar and sobel features are used as feature space, and GentleBoost is used to select simple classifiers. Haar features are used to train the first fifteen stages. And then sobel features are used to train the rest fourteen stages. The second stage is face alignment. At this stage, active shape model (ASM) [6] is used. The last stage is creating color model. The hues derived from the pixels of the face region are sampled and binned into an 1D histogram, which is used as the color model of the fist. Through this histogram, the input image from the camera can be convert to a probability image of the fist.

In order to deal with the skin-colored objects in the background, motion cue is used for our algorithm. We differentiate the current frame with the previous frame to generate the difference image using the motion analysis method in [7]. The method is to compute the absolute value of the differences in the neighborhood surrounding each pixel. When the accumulated difference is above a predetermined threshold, the pixel is assigned to the moving region.

Since we are interested in the motion of skin-colored regions, the logical AND operator is applied between the color probability distribution image and the difference image. And as a result the probability distribution image is obtained.

Suppose human hand is represented by a rectangle window, the possible position of the fist is gained as follows:

1. We sample the image from 320x240 to 160x120.
2. A subwindow x, y, w, h, where x and y are the left-top coordinate, w and h are the size of the rectangle, moves on the probability distribution image. And the sum of the pixels in subwindow is calculated. In our experiment, the w is 28 and the h is 35.
3. If the sum is below a certain threshold, it returns to step 2. And if the sum is above the threshold, the CAMSHIFT [8] is applied to getting the local maximum and the local color region size. And the center point of CAMSHIFT region is saved.
4. The pixels in CAMSHIFT region are set to zero. And it goes to step 2.

Based on these saved points, multiple hypotheses of the position and size of the fist are generated. For each saved point (x, y), four rectangle regions are taken out as four hypotheses. These regions have the same center (x, y), but differ in size. So the total number of the hypotheses is $Num \times 4$, where Num is the number of saved point.

3 Inference in the Bayesian Network

For robust tracking, we must eliminate the effect of other skin-color objects, which are also in motion, such as face. So besides skin-color feature more features should be taken into consideration. Fist appearance is the most significative feature and it can be used for differentiating fist from other objects. In our algorithm, two main features, color feature and appearance feature, are employed.

Bayesian network [10] is useful when we are trying to fuse more cue for tracking fist. Thus the posterior probability of fist region given observations of the other variables can be computed as follows:

$$P(X_k|C, A, X_{k-1}, X_{k-2}) \tag{1}$$

where C denotes color cue, A denotes appearance cue, X_{k-1} and X_{k-2} are the previous object state, X_k is the current object state.

The Bayesian network is shown in Fig.1.

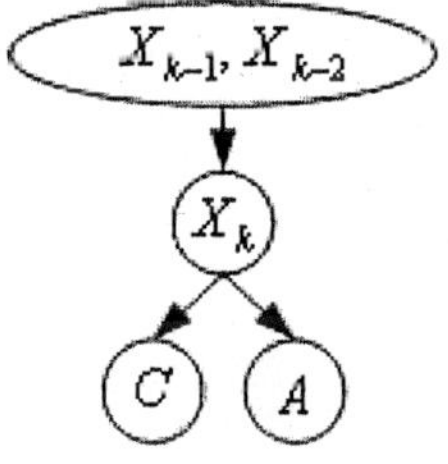

Fig. 1. The Bayesian network

By using conditional independence relationships we can get

$$\begin{aligned} &P(X_k|C, A, X_{k-1}, X_{k-2}) \\ &\propto P(X_k, C, A, X_{k-1}, X_{k-2}) \\ &\propto P(C|X_k)P(A|X_k)P(X_k|X_{k-1}, X_{k-2}) \end{aligned} \tag{2}$$

Prior Model. The prior model $P(X_{k-1}, X_{k-2})$ is derived from the dynamics of object motion, which is modelled as a simple second order autoregressive process(ARP).

$$X_k - X_{k-1} = X_{k-1} - X_{k-2} + W_k \tag{3}$$

where W_k is a zero-mean Gaussian stochastic component.

The parameters of ARP model are learned from a set of pre-labeled training sequences.

Computation of the Color Marginal Likelihood. We define the color likelihood as follows:

$$P(C|X) = \frac{1}{n_c} \sum_{i,j} P_c(i, j) \tag{4}$$

where n_c is the scale of the likelihood, and $P_c(i, j)$ is the pixel in color cue image.

Computation of the Appearance Marginal Likelihood. Based on assumption of a Gaussian distribution, the probability of input pattern A, which belongs to fist class X can be modelled by a multidimensional Gaussian probability density function:

$$P(A|X) = \frac{exp[-\frac{1}{2}(A-\mu)^T \Sigma^{-1}(A-\mu)]}{(2\pi)^{N/2}|\Sigma|^{1/2}} \tag{5}$$

where μ is the mean vector of class X, Σ is the covariance matrix of class X.

By using PCA to reduce the dimension of X, the $P(A|X)$ is approximately estimated by equation (6), more detail about equation (6) can be found in [9].

$$\hat{P}(A|X) = exp\left[-\frac{1}{2}\sum_{i=1}^{M}\frac{y_i^2}{\lambda_i}\right] exp\left[-\frac{\epsilon^2(x)}{2\rho}\right] \tag{6}$$

where $\hat{P}(A|X)$ is the estimation value of $P(A|X)$, $\epsilon^2(x)$ is the residual error, λ_i is eigenvalue of Σ, M is the dimensional of principal subspace, N is the dimension of total subspace.

In our experiment, the appearance parameters μ and Σ are learned from more than 5000 labelled images, which are collected from one hundred persons with three kinds of illumination. Some samples are shown in the Fig.2.

Fig. 2. Some samples used for training

4 Experimental Result

In order to compare with the mean shift algorithm, two experiments are done. In the first experiment, the color-motion based mean shift algorithm is used. When player's fist and face overlap, the tracker loses the fist. Some key frames of this experiment are shown in Fig.3. And it has no chance to recover. This is because the mean shift is a local optimal algorithm. In the second experiment, the proposed algorithm is applied. Based on multi-hypotheses it overcomes the local optimal. And using more cues, our algorithm becomes more robust. Some key frames of this experiment are shown in Fig.4.

All the experiments are done on a P4 1.7G machine with 512M memory. The normal recognition speed of our algorithm is about 29 fps.

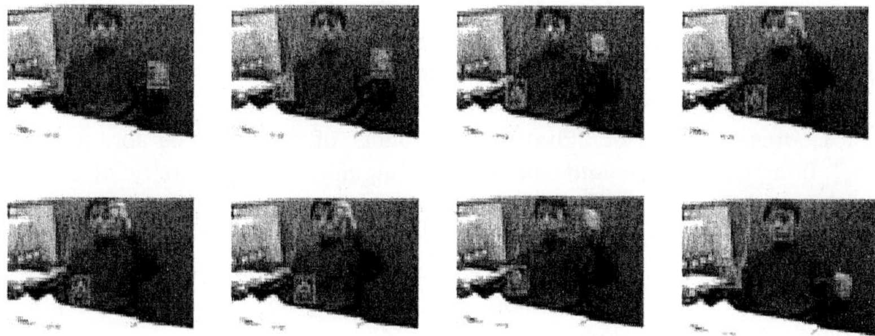

Fig. 3. Tracking failure by color and motion based Mean Shift algorithm

Fig. 4. Tracking by Bayesian network

5 Summarize

In this paper,a Bayesian network based fist tracking algorithm is introduced. Comparing with particle filter, the proposed algorithm, which uses more information to generate hypotheses, reduces significantly the number of hypotheses needed for robust tracking. And at the same time it overcomes the shortcoming of local optimal of the mean shift algorithm.

References

1. S. Maskell and N.Gordon, "A Tutorial on Particle Filters for On-line Nonlinear/Non-Gaussian Baysian Tracking", in Proc. IEE Workshop "Target Tracking: Algorithms and Applications", Oct. 2001
2. C.F. Shan, Y.C Wei, T.N. Tan, "Real Time Hand Tracking by Combining Particle Filtering and Mean Shift", The 6th International Conference on Automatic Face and Gesture Recognition (FG2004).
3. D. Comaniciu and V. Ramesh, "Mean Shift and Optimal Prediction for Efficient Object Tracking", ICIP, Vancouver, Canada, 2000, pp. 70-73.
4. D. Comaniciu, P. Meer, Mean Shift Analysis and Applications, Proc. Seventh Int'l Conf. Computer Vision, pp. 1197-1203, Sept. 1999.
5. P.Lu, X.S.Huang, Y.S.Wang,"A New Framework for Handfree Navigation in 3D Game," Proceedings of the International Conference on CGIV04.
6. T.F. Cootes, C.J.Taylor "Statistical Models of Appearance for computer vision," Imaging Science and Biomedical Engineering, University of Manchester, Manchester M13 9PT, U.K. March 8, 2004.
7. H. P. Graf, E. Cosatto, D. Gibbon, M. Kocheisen, and E. Petajan, "Multi-Modal System for Locating Heads and Faces", AFG, Killington, Vt, 1996, pp. 88-93.
8. G. R. Bradski, "Computer Vision Face Tracking For Use in a Perceptual User Interface", Intel Technology Journal Q2, 1998.
9. B. Moghaddam and A. Pentland, "Probabilistic visual learning for object representation", IEEE Transactions on Pattern Analysis and Machine Intelligence, 19(7):696-710, July 1997.
10. D. Heckerman, "A Tutorial on Learning With Bayesian Networks", Microsoft Research Technical Report,MSR-TR-95-06

Grounding Affective Dimensions into Posture Features

Andrea Kleinsmith, P. Ravindra De Silva, and Nadia Bianchi-Berthouze

Database Systems Laboratory, University of Aizu, Aizu Wakamatsu 965-8580, Japan
andi@andisplanet.com
{d8052201, nadia}@u-aizu.ac.jp

Abstract. Many areas of today's society are seeing an increased importance in the creation of systems capable of interacting with users on an affective level through a variety of modalities. Our focus has been on affective posture recognition. However, a deeper understanding of the relationship between emotions in terms of postural expressions is required. The goal of this study was to identify affective dimensions that human observers use when discriminating between postures, and to investigate the possibility of grounding this affective space into a set of posture features. Using multidimensional scaling, arousal, valence, and action tendency were identified as the main factors in the evaluation process. Our results showed that, indeed, low-level posture features could effectively discriminate between the affective dimensions.

1 Introduction

Due to the ever-increasing importance of computers in many areas of today's society, i.e., eLearning, tele home-health care, entertainment, and everyday tasks, their ability to interact well with humans is essential. We believe that a key technology to achieving this is the ability to recognize affect and emotion from whole body postures. We base this belief on the increasingly accepted scientific argument that emotion is comprised of both mental and physical events, and that emotion expression occurs through various combinations of verbal and nonverbal channels [13].

Recently, researchers have attempted to propose models for categorizing affective nonverbal expressions into discrete emotion categories. Refer to [3][1][13][5] to name a few. While these results are important, we believe that it is necessary to go beyond discrete categories, and to allow for a more refined description of the affective dimensions of affective expressions. We believe this to be important as, in general, it is difficult to precisely label one emotion expression with a single emotion label. To handle this, Cowie et al [4] have developed a system called FEELTRACE, which allows a person to view and/or listen to a recording and to track emotion variation over time on a 2 dimensional space representing activation (from active to passive) and evaluation (from positive to negative). The circular 2D space is represented on a computer screen and observers move a cursor within the space to rate their impression of the degree

J. Tao, T. Tan, and R.W. Picard (Eds.): ACII 2005, LNCS 3784, pp. 263–270, 2005.

(as a combination of emotion terms) of the emotional state of the person they are listening to/watching. But now the question becomes, how can a computer be made to assign a position to an emotion expression in an affective space?

There has been considerable research on mapping facial expressions [16][14][2] and voice [17] to affective dimensions. In fact, Breazeal [2] has mapped a series of facial expression photos onto Russell's [16] arousal-valence dimensions. We have been unable to find similar research using posture. Typically, postures are more ambiguous than facial expressions and emotional states are often complex, signifying a combination of emotion labels.

Our motivation is to offer a basic framework on which to ground affective posture recognition models that exploit the same affective dimensions used by human observers. In order to reach this goal, we aim at identifying these dimensions and the postural descriptors on which they are grounded. To this purpose, we use a general and task-independent affective posture description framework based on low-level body features (i.e. joint relations) proposed in [1][18].

This paper is organized as follows: Section 2 describes our analysis to determine the main affective dimensions used by humans (observers) in the posture affective recognition process. In Section 3 we propose an affective posture recognition model grounded on the low level posture features. We end with our conclusions in Section 4.

2 Affective Space

The first goal of our study was to identify the affective dimensions that human observers use when discriminating between postures. Towards this purpose we carried out a psychological experiment using 109 affectively expressive avatars to collect data on the evaluation of affective postures by human observers.

Prospective subjects (called observers hereafter) were asked to choose an emotion label from a predefined list of 8 labels (*angry, depressed, fear, happy, joyful, sad, surprised*, and *upset*), and to rate the intensity of the emotion on a scale from 1 (least intense) to 5 (most intense). These emotions were chosen on the basis that they are included in the set of universal emotions defined by Ekman and Friesen [6], and various structural models also have been proposed to describe these emotions in terms of affective dimensions [15][16]. 40 Japanese observers participated. Please refer to [8][18] for more details on the collection of the data.

Given that postures are multidimensional stimuli, we applied multidimensional scaling (MDS) [10] to represent their affective perception into a reduced multidimensional space. MDS is a mathematical technique that is able to uncover the hidden structure of data, and represent it in a reduced multidimensional space reflecting distances between data. Our data here are the emotion labels whose distances are measured according to their relation with the postures. As a distance between a pair of labels we use the averaged normalized difference between the agreements obtained on each of the two labels for each of the postures. By applying MDS to the 8x8 non-diagonal dissimilarity matrix, we obtained a 3 dimensional affective space (with a Kruskal-stress = 0.13895). Figure 1(a,b,c) shows the 2D projections in the affective space.

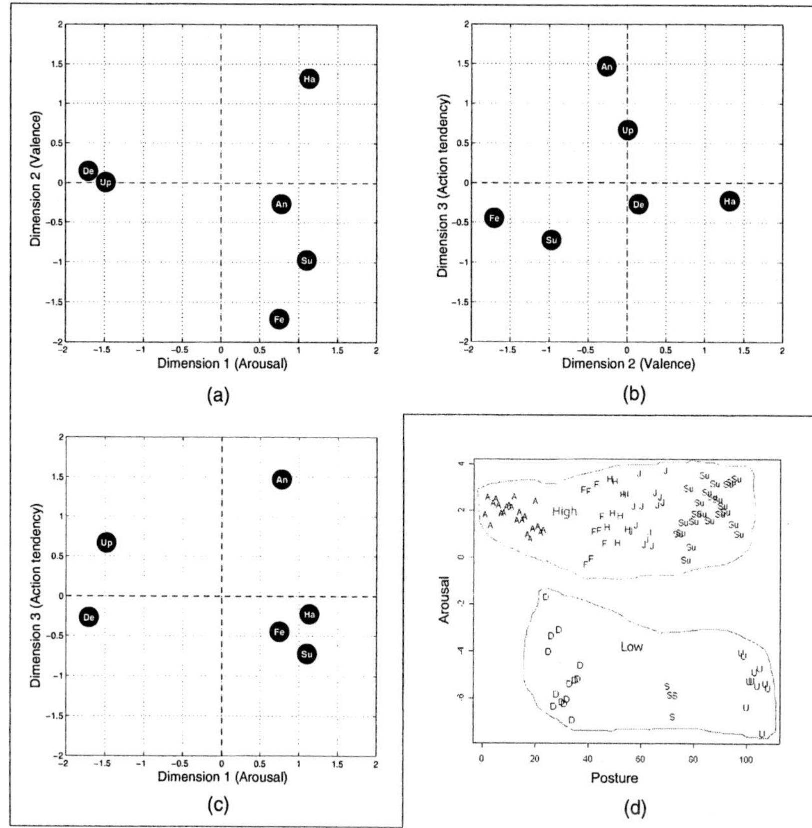

Fig. 1. (a,b,c) shows the 3D model of the affective space created with MDS. The space represents the distances between labels according to the evaluation judgment of the observers. According to the "layout" of the labels, dimension 1 shown in (a,c) appears to correspond with the affective dimension of arousal, dimension 2 shown in (a,b) relates to the valence of the emotion posture, and dimension 3 shown in (b,c) correpsonds to the action tendency of each posture. (d,e,f) shows the 3 models created using MDA to discriminate posture according to levels of the 3 affective dimensions. Each symbol in each model represents a posture. The black dots represent the centroid of each affective level. The "layout" of the centroids along one dimension of each model reflect one affective dimension: (d) arousal, (e) valence, and (f) action tendency.

Observing the distribution of the labels along the 3 dimensions of the space, we can derive the meaning associated to these dimensions. Dimension 1 (refer to Fig. 1(a,c)) separates the categories *sad, depressed and upset* from the others (*angry, fear, happy, joy*, and *surprised*). Note that in the space, sad and depressed overlap, as well as joyful and happy. According to the Watson and Tellegen two-factor structure of affect [12], these two sets of emotions identify two opposite levels of arousal (low in the first case and high in the second case). Thus, arousal appears to be the first dimension used to evaluate the affective state conveyed by postures.

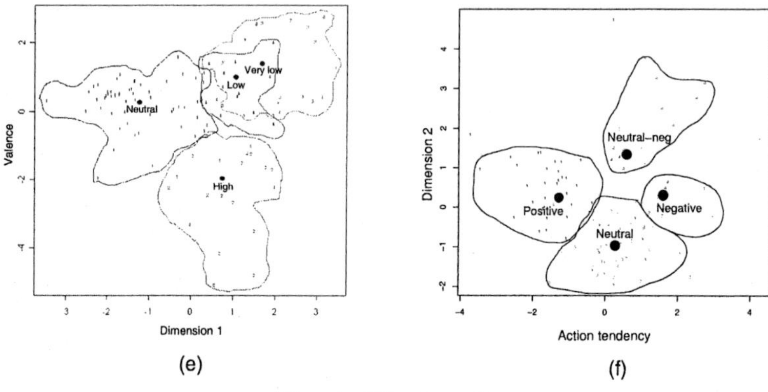

Fig. 1. (*Continued*)

The second dimension (refer to Fig. 1(a,b)) proposed by the MDS could be associated to the valence dimension used to describe emotional states. In fact, according to the same structure of affect, it separates the negative emotions (*fear/surprise*) from the positive emotions (*happy/joyful*), figuring the other 4 emotion labels (carrying a lower level of negativity in the sense of survival and pleasantness) at the center of the axis. We consider *surprised* as a negative state since it was used as a nuance for the category *fear* in the experiment [18][8].

The third dimension (refer to Fig. 1(b,c)) of this space represents action tendency. The circumplex created by the layout of the 8 emotion labels on the plane defined by dimension 1 (arousal) and dimension 3 (action tendency) approximates the emotion wheel of Plutchik [15]. On this plane, the third dimension separates the emotions *fear/surprise* from *anger*. The latter affective state represents a desire and readiness to react, while the former represent more a sense of *protection*. The emotion labels in the center of the axis carry a more neutral/acceptance value with respect to this dimension.

3 Grounding the Affective Space into Posture Features

To understand the relation between emotion dimensions and postural expressions we describe the postures according to the 24 features introduced in [18] and listed in Table 1. We chose these features because they are context-independent. Furthermore, they were used to discriminate between the same set of emotions and resulted in a correct classification of 90%. Specifically, direction and volume of the body were described by projecting each marker on the 3 orthogonal planes and measuring the lateral, frontal, and vertical extension of the body, body torsion, and the inclination of the head and shoulders. For more details see [1]. Each static posture P_i was then associated with a pair (X_i, O_i) where $X_i = x_{i1}, ..., x_{i24}$ is the vector of 24 posture features (Table 1) and O_i indicates the label most frequently associated by the observers to the posture P_i.

In order to ground the dimensions of the affective space (arousal, valence, and action tendency) onto the 24 postural features, three more labels were as-

Table 1. The table lists the set of posture features proposed. The Code column indicates the feature codes used in the paper. The following short-cuts are used: L: Left, R: Right, B: Back, F: Front.

Code	posture features	Code	posture features
V4	$Orientation_{XY}$: B.Head - F.Head axis	V5	$Orientation_{YZ}$: B.Head - F.Head axis
V6	$Distance_z$: R.Hand - R.Shoulder	V7	$Distance_z$: L.Hand - L.Shoulder
V8	$Distance_y$: R.Hand - R.Shoulder	V9	$Distance_y$:L.Hand - L.Shoulder
V10	$Distance_x$:R.Hand - L.Shoulder	V11	$Distance_x$:L.Hand - R.Shoulder
V12	$Distance_x$:R.Hand - R.Elbow	V13	$Distance_x$:L.Hand - L.Elbow
V14	$Distance_x$: R.Elbow - L.Shoulder	V15	$Distance_x$: L.Elbow - R.Shoulder
V16	$Distance_z$: R.Hand - R.Elbow	V17	$Distance_z$:L.Hand - L.Elbow
V18	$Distance_y$: R.Hand - R.Elbow	V19	$Distance_y$:L.Hand - L.Elbow
V20	$Distance_y$: R.Elbow - R.Shoulder	V21	$Distance_y$:L.Elbow - L.Shoulder
V22	$Distance_z$: R.Elbow - R.Shoulder	V23	$Distance_z$:L.Elbow - L.Shoulder
V24	$Orientation_{XY}$: Shoulders axis	V25	$Orientation_{XZ}$: Shoulders axis
V26	$Orientation_{XY}$: Heels axis	V27	$3D - Distance$: R.Heel - L.Heel

Table 2. Important features for discriminating between emotions

Emotions	Head		Vertical					Lateral						Frontal	Heels	Error	N. dims
Model	V4	V5	V6	V7	V16	V23	V25	V10	V11	V12	V13	V14	V15	V20	V27		
Arousal	2	1	7				9	3	6	10		4	8	5		1%	1
Valence		2	3		1	6			4		5	8			7	20%	3
Action tendency		4	7	5	3	2					6		1			25%	3

signed to each posture P_i: i) a label indicating the arousal level (low, high); ii) a label indicating the valence degree (very low, low, middle, and high); and 3) a label indicating the direction of the action tendency (positive, neutral, neutral-negative, and negative). The labels were decided according to the most frequent observer label O_i of the posture P_i, and the clustering of the labels along the 3 dimensions in the affective space (Fig. 1(a,b,c)).

We then applied mixture discriminant analysis (MDA) [11][7] which is a statistical technique used to discriminate between two or more categories or groups. Using the MDA dimensions, it is possible to map the postures onto a multidimensional discriminant space defined by the axes that maximize the separation between groups and minimize the variance within groups. The dimensionality of the space is determined in such a way as to reduce the discrimination error.

We applied the MDA method for each of the 3 affective dimensions. Using an iterative process, the MDA algorithm creates a model based on linear combinations of the most discriminating features. The 3 models obtained are shown in Figure 1(d,e,f), respectively, and the last two columns of Table 2 give the percentage of classification error for each model and the number of dimensions identified by the MDA algorithm. Each symbol in each of the 3 models represents a single posture. The black dots in Figure 1(e,f) show the centroid for each affective level. Also, Figure 1(e,f) show only the two main dimensions of the 3D models. These two dimensions respectively cover 90% and 82% of the variance. In Figure 1(d), we can see that by using 2 labels to signify levels of arousal, only one dimension is necessary to completely discriminate the affective postures into two sets. Figure 1(e) shows the model for discriminating postures according to 4 levels of valence with an error of 20%. We can observe also that the layout of the centroids along the second dimension (vertical axis) reflect the valence dimension. Similarly, the model in Figure 1(f) discriminates the affective postures according to 4 levels of action tendency with an error of 25%. In this case, the layout of the centroids along the first dimension (horizontal axis) reflects the action tendency dimension.

The remainder of Table 2 reports the set of features that were used by the discrimination functions of each model. The number in each entry represents the rank of importance of the features. Lower numbers correspond to higher discriminative power. For conciseness, we report in this Table only the features selected by at least one of the 3 models.

The first line of the Table corresponds to the model in Figure 1(d). In the input to the model, the postures were labeled according to level of arousal of the affective space (see Fig. 1(a)), i.e. postures labeled by the observers as *sad, depressed,* and *upset* were labeled as *low arousal*, the others were labeled as *high arousal.* We can see from the Figure that the two classes are well separated. The most important features for this model were the bending and the torsion of the head *V5* and *V4*, the lateral distance of the arm and the elbow from the body *V10* and *V14*. In the case of *low arousal*, refer to Figure 2(a) for examples, the head was mostly bent and not turned. The hands were close to the side of the body with the elbow seldom slightly bent. The vertical feature *V6* also plays an important role in the discrimination. The *low arousal* postures, differently from the others (Fig. 2(b)), generally have the arm stretched down along the body.

The second line of the Table corresponds to the model in Figure 1(e). In the input to the model, the postures were labeled according to the valence level of the affective space (see Fig. 1(b)), i.e. postures labeled by the observers as *surprised/fear* were labeled as *(very) low valence*, the ones labeled as *happy/joyful* were labeled as *high valence*, the others were labeled as *neutral valence.* We can see from the Figure that the four classes reflect the distribution of the four classes in the affective space. The most important features for this model were the vertical extension of the arms *V16* and *V6*, the bending of the head *V5*, and the lateral distance of the hand from the body. In the case of *low valence* (Fig. 2(c)), the head is slightly bent forward and the hands are raised in front of the face (i.e. the body is very closed according to the lateral dimension). In the *high valence* postures (Fig. 2(d)), the head is upright or bent backward and generally the arms are raised higher, and are more distant from the body.

The third line of the Table corresponds to the model in Figure 1(f). In the input to the model, the postures were labeled according to the action tendency level of the affective space (see Fig. 1(c)), i.e. postures labeled by the observers as *surprised/fear* were labeled as *negative, neutral-negative action tendency*, the ones labeled as *angry* were labeled as *positive action tendency*, the others were labeled as *neutral action tendency.* We can see from the Figure that again the four classes reflect the distribution of the four classes in the affective space. The

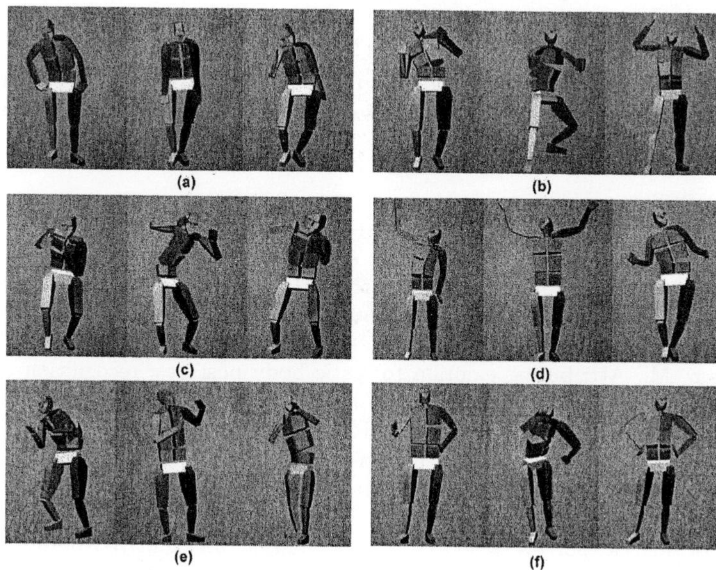

Fig. 2. Examples of affective postures representing (a) low arousal (b) high arousal (c) low valence (d) high valence (e) negative action tendency and (f) positive action tendency

most important features for this model were the lateral distance of the elbow from the body *V15* and the vertical extension of the arms *V23* and *V16*. In the case of *negative action tendency* (Fig. 2(e)), the hands are raised in front of the face, and the body remains fairly closed along the lateral dimension. In the case of *positive action tendency* (Fig. 2(f)), generally the elbows are bent and away from the side of the body, and the arms are raised to about hip level.

4 Conclusions

In this paper, we determined a set of affective dimensions for affective postures following Plutchik's [15] emotion wheel and Watson and Tellegen's two factor structure of affect [12]. We then used statistical techniques to ground these dimensions into a set of low-level, context-independent posture features for discriminating between postures along the 3 dimensions, arousal, valence, and action tendency. The features proposed seem to reflect the criteria human observers exploit when evaluating affective postures. However, by adding motion features, such as direction and speed of movement (proposed in [9]), we may be able to increase discrimination for the action tendency dimension. As discussed by [3], the addition of motion features seem to be necessary for discriminating fear postures specifically. The set of features described in this paper prove to be a valid framework to build recognition models at different levels of granularity. Using these features, each posture could be assigned to a position in an affective space instead of to a discrete emotion label only.

Acknowledgment

This study was supported by a grants-in-Aid for Scientific Research from the Japanese Society for the Promotion of Science granted to N. Bianchi-Berthouze.

References

1. Bianchi-Berthouze, N. and Kleinsmith, A., A categorical approach to affective gesture recognition, Connection Science, **15**, (2003), 259-269.
2. Breazeal, C., Emotion and sociable humanoid robots, International Journal of Human-Computer Studies, **59**, (2003), 119–155.
3. Coulson, M., Attributing emotion to static body postures: recognition accuracy, confusions, and viewpoint dependence, Jour. of Nonv. Behav., **28**, (2004), 117-139.
4. Cowie, R., Douglas-Cowie, E., Savvidou, S., McMahon, E., Sawey, M., and Schroder, M., 'FEELTRACE': An instrument for recording perceived emotion in real time, Proc. ISCA Workshop on Speech and Emotion, (2000), 19–24.
5. Dailey, M.N., Cottrell, G.W., Padgett, C., and Adolphs, R., EMPATH: A neural network that categorizes facial expressions, Journal of Cognitive Neuroscience, **14**, (2002), 1158–1173.
6. Ekman, P. and Friesen W., Unmasking the Face: A Guide to Recognizing Emotions from Facial Expressions, Prentice Hall, 1975.
7. Hastie, T. and Tibshirabi, R., Discriminant analysis by Gaussian mixture, Journal of the Royal Statistical Society, **B:58**, (1996), 155–176
8. Kleinsmith, A., De Silva, P.R., Bianchi-Berthouze, N., Building User Models Based on Cross-Cultural Differences in Recognizing Emotion from Affective Postures, Int'l Conf. on User Modeling, to appear, Edinburgh, July, (2005), 50–59.
9. Kleinsmith, A., Fushimi, T., and Bianchi-Berthouze, N., An incremental and interactive affective posture recognition system, Proc. Workshop on Adapting the Interaction Style to Affective Factors, to appear, Edinburgh, July, (2005).
10. Kruskal, J.B. and Wish, M., Multidimensional Scaling, Series: Quantitative Applications in the Social Sciences, Sage University paper,1978.
11. Lachenbruch, P.A., Discriminant Analysis, NY, Hafner, (1975).
12. Larsen, J.T., McGraw, A.P., and Cacioppo, J.T., Can People Feel Happy and Sad at the Same Time?, Journ. of Pers. and Social Psych., **81**, (2001), 684–696.
13. Picard, R., Toward Agents that Recognize Emotion, Actes Proc. IMAGINA, (1998), 153-165.
14. Plutchik, R., Emotions: A general psychoevolutionary theory., Approaches to Emotion, Scherer, K., Ekman, P. (Eds.), Lawrence Erlbaum Associates, NJ, (1984).
15. Plutchik, R., The Nature of Emotions, American Scientist, **89**, (2001), 344–350.
16. Russell, J., Reading emotions from and into faces: resurrecting a dimensional-contextual perspective, The Psychology of Facial Expression, Russell, J., Fernandez-Dols, J. (Eds.), Cambridge University Press, Cambridge, UK, (1997).
17. Schroder, M., Dimensional emotion representation as a basis for speech synthesis with non-extreme emotions, Proc. Workshop on Affective Dialogue Systems, Germany, (2004), 209–220.
18. de Silva, P.R. and Bianchi-Berthouze, N., Modeling human affective postures: An information theoretic characterization of posture features. Journal of Computer Animation and Virtual Worlds, **15**, (2004), 269—276.

Face and Facial Expression Recognition with an Embedded System for Human-Robot Interaction

Yang-Bok Lee, Seung-Bin Moon, and Yong-Guk Kim

School of Computer Engineering, Sejong University, Seoul, Korea
ykim@sejong.ac.kr

Abstract. In this paper, we present an embedded system in which face recognition and facial expression recognition for Human-Robot Interaction are implemented. To detect face with a fast and reliable way, AdaBoost algorithm is used. Then, Principal Component Analysis is applied for recognizing the face. Gabor wavelets are combined with Enhanced Fisher Model for facial expression recognition. Performance of the facial expression recognition reaches to 93%. The embedded system runs on 150MHz and the processing speed is 0.6 frames / second. Experimental result demonstrates that face detection, recognition and facial expression can be implemented with an embedded system for the Human-Robot Interaction.

1 Introduction

There are six prototypical (or basic) facial expressions, i.e. surprise, fear, sadness, anger, disgust and happiness according to the previous researches [3, 5], which are known to be universal across human ethnicities and cultures. Such studies provide a convenient framework, by which we test and compare different facial expression recognition systems. Accurate measurement of facial actions has many potential applications such as intelligent human-robot interaction (HRI), entertainment devices, psychiatry [5] and neurology.

To represent facial expression images effectively, several methods have been proposed such as PCA (Principal Component Analysis), ICA (Independent Component Analysis), Gabor representation, Optic flow, and geometrical tracking method [4, 9]. Among them, the Gabor representation has been favored among many researchers because of its better performance and biological implication [1, 7].

The Enhanced Fisher discrimination Model (EFM) is very effective in a face recognition task [8]. Moreover, when it is combined with the Gabor representation, the face recognition performance is improved greatly. Given that there is evidence that Gabor representation is effective for the facial expression image, we thought that Gabor representation with the EFM could be used effectively in the facial expression task as well.

This paper is organized as follow. Section 2 describes face detection, and section 3 Gabor Wavelets for facial expression recognition. We compare PCA and EFM in section 4. Section 5 shows on implementation of the embedded system. Section 6 is performance evaluation and finally we conclude in section 7.

J. Tao, T. Tan, and R.W. Picard (Eds.): ACII 2005, LNCS 3784, pp. 271 – 278, 2005.

2 Face Detection Using Adaboost Method

Recently, Viola and Jones have proposed a multi-stage classification procedure based upon Adaboost method that reduces the processing time substantially while achieving almost the same accuracy as compared to a much slower and more complex single stage classifier [11]. This paper extends their rapid object detection framework. Their basic and over-complete set of Haar-like features is extended by an efficient set of 45° rotated features, which add additional domain-knowledge to the learning framework and which is otherwise hard to learn. These novel features can be computed rapidly at all scales in constant time. And, it is shown that Gentle Adaboost outperforms (with respect to detection accuracy) Discrete and Real Adaboost for object detection tasks, while having a lower computational complexity, i.e., requiring a lower number of features for the same performance. Also, the usage of small decision trees instead of stumps as weak classifiers further improves the detection performance at a comparable detection speed. Fig. 1 shows the block diagram how to detect using Adaboost and PCA by which we can verify a face among many candidate faces. Below that, the procedure of the AdaBoost algorithm adopted in our system is given in detail.

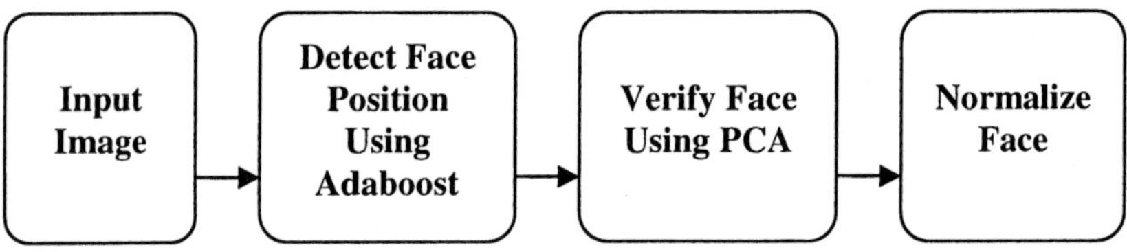

Fig. 1. A Face Detection System using Adaboost

< AdaBoost Training Algorithm >

- Given N examples $(x_1,y_1),\ldots,(x_n,y_n)$ with $x \in \Re^k, y_i \in \{-1,+1\}$
- Start with weight $w_i = 1/n$, $i = 1,\ldots, n$.
- Repeat for $t=1,\ldots, T$.
  - (a) Fit the classifier $f_t(x) \in \{-1,+1\}$ using weight w_i on the training data $(x_1,y_1),\ldots,(x_n,y_n)$.
  - (b) Compute error $e_j = \sum_{i=1}^{n} w_i \left| f_j(x_i) - y_i \right|$, $\alpha_t = \log\left((1-\varepsilon_t)/\varepsilon_t\right)$.
  - (c) Set $w_i \leftarrow w_i \cdot \exp\left(\alpha_t \left| F_t - y_i \right|\right)$, $i = 1,\ldots,n$ and re-normalize weight $w_i \leftarrow w_i \Big/ \sum_{j=1}^{n} w_j$.
- Output the classifier:

$$F_{\text{strong}}(\mathbf{x}) = \begin{cases} 1 & \text{if } \sum_{t=1}^{T} \alpha F_t(\mathbf{x}) > \lambda_i \\ -1 & \text{otherwise} \end{cases}$$

3 Gabor Wavelets Representation for the Facial Expression Images

Since Daugman [1] proposes a way where Gabor wavelets are applied to the 2D image, it becomes a standard method for representing faces, fingerprints or facial expressions. As Gabor wavelets consists of orientation component as well as spatial frequency components, they have an advantage in representing any object in an image, compared to the conventional edge detectors, which tends to focus on orientation of the object. In our study, we used five frequencies (from 0 to 4) and eight orientations at each image point within the grid (22 x 22), that drawn over the cropped facial image. Fig.2 shows the steps from face detection to Gabor wavelet application via normalization step.

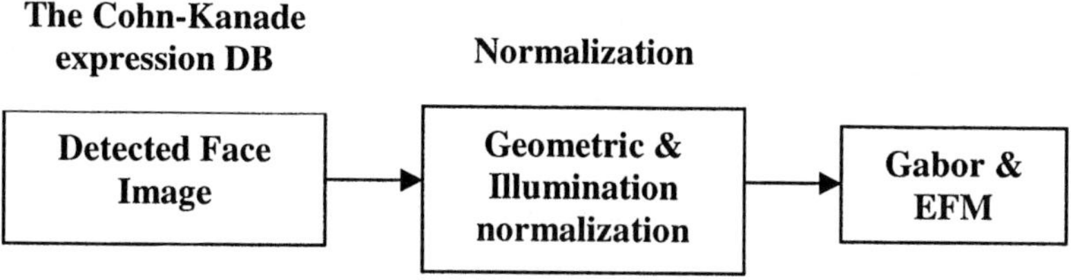

Fig. 2. A Facial Expression Recognition System using Gabor & EFM

4 PCA and EFM Classifiers

4.1 PCA

PCA generates a set of orthonormal basis vectors, known as principal components (PCs) that maximize the scatter of all the projected samples [10]. Let $X \in R^N$ be a random vector representing an image, where N is the dimensionality of the corresponding image space. The covariance matrix of X is defined as follows:

$$\sum X = E\{[X - E(X)][X - E(X)]^t\} \tag{1}$$

where $E()$ is the expectation operator; t denotes the transpose operation $\sum X \in R^{N \times N}$. The PCA of a random vector factorizes the covariance matrix into the following form:

$$\sum X = \Phi \Lambda \Phi^t \tag{2}$$

where $\Phi = [\phi_1 \phi_2 ... \phi_N] \in R^{N \times N}$ is the orthonormal eigenvector matrix; $\Lambda = diag\{\lambda_1, \lambda_2, ..., \lambda_N\} \in R^{N \times N}$ is the diagonal eigenvalue matrix with diagonal elements in decreasing order $(\lambda_1, \lambda_2, ..., \lambda_N)$. Then the first leading eigenvectors define matrix P

$$P = [\phi_1, \phi_2, ..., \phi_m] \tag{3}$$

An application of PCA is the dimensionality reduction

$$Y = P^t X \tag{4}$$

The lower dimensional vector $Y \in R^m$ captures the most expressive features of the original data X as shown at the top row of Fig. 3. For the present embedded system, we have used 30 lower components of PCA and EFM, respectively.

4.2 EFM Classifier

We have adopted an EFM classifier [8] that determines the discriminative features for the reduced image space. The EFM is introduced to improve on the generalization ability of the standard Fisher Linear Discriminant (FLD) based methods. The EFM applies first Principle component analysis (PCA) for dimensionality reduction before proceeding with FLD type of analysis. Then, it discriminate the reduced PCA subspaces.

Let Y be a random vector representing the lower dimensional feature. Let $w_1, w_2, ..., w_L$ and $N_1, N_2, ..., N_L$ denote the classes and the number of images within each class, respectively. Let $M_1, M_2, ..., M_L$ and M be the mean of the classes and the grand mean. The within-and between-class covariance matrices Σ_w and Σ_b are defined as follows:

$$\Sigma w = \sum_{i=1}^{L} P(w_i) E\{(Y - M_i)(Y - M_i)^t \mid w_i\} \tag{5}$$

$$\Sigma b = \sum_{i=1}^{L} P(w_i)(M_i - M)(M_i - M)^t \tag{6}$$

EFM first diagonalizes the within-class covariance matrix Σw

$$\Sigma w \Xi = \Xi \Gamma \text{ and } \Xi^t \Xi = I \tag{7}$$

$$\Gamma^{-1/2} \Xi^t \Sigma w \Xi \Gamma^{-1/2} = I \tag{8}$$

where Ξ, Γ are the eigenvector and the diagonal eigenvalue matrices of Σw. The EFM proceeds then to compute the between-class covariance matrix as follows:

$$\Gamma^{-1/2} \Xi^t \Sigma b \Xi \Gamma^{-1/2} = K_b \tag{9}$$

Diagonalize the new between-class covariance matrix K_b

$$K_b \Theta = \Theta \Delta \text{ and } \Theta^t \Theta = I \tag{10}$$

where Θ, Δ are the eigenvector and the diagonal eigenvalue matrices of K_b. The overall transformation matrix of the EFM is now defined as follows:

$$T = \Xi \Gamma^{-1/2} \Theta \tag{11}$$

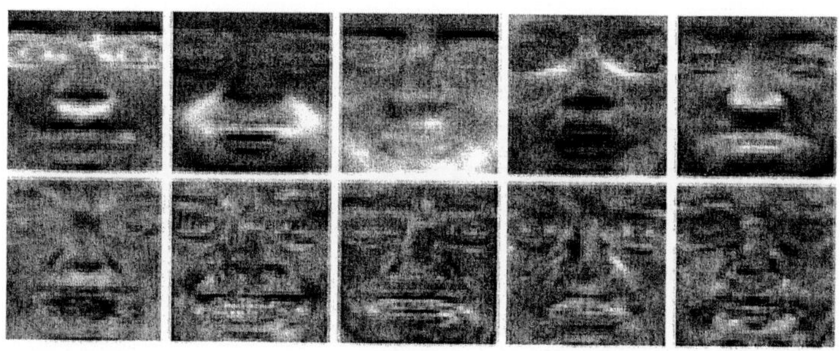

Fig. 3. Visual representation of the lower components (or base vectors) of PCA (top row) and EFM (bottom row) of the face, respectively

5 Implementation of Embedded System

5.1 Vision Processing Module Framework

We implemented the face recognition and facial expression algorithm as robot interface and loaded the embedded system as shown in Fig 4. The hardware components of the embedded system as follow.

5.2 Vision Processing Module Hardware Specification

- TMS320C6711 150MHz
- 32MB SDRAM
- 16MB Flash memory
- 2CH 0.3M Pixels (640 x 480) Mono CMOS Camera
- RS-232 1 Port (38400bps)

5.3 Memory Map

Flash Map TOTAL = 01000000h, 80h Blocks

90000000 h	Boot Loader	00020000 h (01h blks)
90020000 h	FPGA ISP	00020000 h (01h blks)
90040000 h	Serial Loader Program	00020000 h (01h blks)
90060000 h	Serial Loader Status -Header (4) -Length (4) -CRC (4)	00020000 h (01h blks)

90080000 h	User Program	00100000 h (08h blks)
90180000 h	User Data	00E80000 h (74h blks)

Memory Map TOTAL = 02000000h

80000000 h	VECTOR	00001000 h
80001000 h	APPL	01EBF000 h
81EC0000 h	LOADER	00040000 h
81F00000 h	LDBUFF	00100000 h

5.4 System Implementation

All algorithms are implemented with C/C++, and loaded within the flash memory. The training data (or model) are generated in PC, and then uploaded them into the flash memory. And these data are use to detect face and to recognize face identification and facial expression.

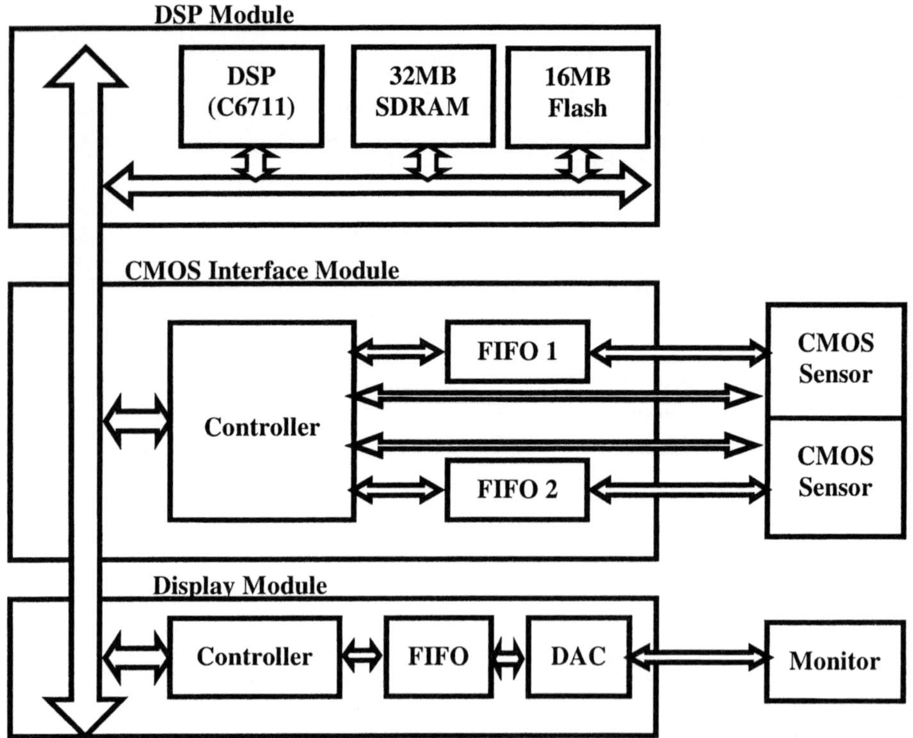

Fig. 4. Block Diagram of Embedded Hardware system

6 Performance Evaluation

Our method has been tested on 500 images using the Cohn-Kanade Database [6]. In this experiment, we sampled the half of the image database for the training purpose and the test was performed by using the remaining half of the images. We repeated these tests for 20 times and averaged the results. The test was carried out for face detection, face identification and facial expression recognition, respectively.

For the face detection task where Adaboost algorithm is used, the detection rate was 95%. For the face recognition where the PCA is used, the recognition rate was 92%. Finally, the rate of the facial expression recognition was 93% when the Gabor wavelets are combined with EFM method. The processing speed of the embedded system was about 0.6 frames per second.

7 Discussion and Conclusions

The study presents an embedded system for HRI. It implements the Adaboost for face detection, the PCA for face identification, and the EFM for the facial expression recognition task, respectively. It turns out that the Adaboost algorithm was faster than the SVM or Neural Network case. And the EFM performance was higher than the PCA case. In particular, when the EFM was combined with the Gabor representation, it is even better than the EFM alone. Our results suggest that it can be successfully applied to the facial expression case. It is known that human capability to classify human facial emotions is about 90% correction [2]. The best result with the EFM was 93%, which is even higher than human's capability. The present system was installed within a service robot, which identifies his user and recognize the emotional states.

Acknowledgement

This research was performed for the Intelligent Robotics Development Program, one of the 21st Century Frontier R&D Programs funded by the Ministry of Commerce, Industry and Energy of Korea.

References

1. J. Daugman, Uncertainty relationship for resolution in space, spatial frequency, and orientation optimized by two-dimensional visual cortical filters. Journal of the Optical Society of America A, 2: 1160-1169, 1985.
2. M. Dailey, G. Cottrell, and C. Padgett, EMPATH: A neural network that categorizes facial expressions, Journal of Cognitive Neuroscience, 13, 513-532, 2002.
3. C. Darwin, *The expression of emotions in man and animals.* John Murray, London, 1872.
4. G. Donato, M. Bartlett, J. Hager, P. Ekman and T. Sejnowski, Classifying facial actions, IEEE PAMI, 21, 10, 974-989, 1999.
5. P. Ekman and W. Friesen, Unmasking the Face. A guide to recognizing emotions from facial clues. Palo Alto. Consulting Psychologists Press, 1975

6. T. Kanade, J. Cohn, and Y. Tian, Comprehensive database for facial expression analysis, Proc. Int'l Conf Face and Gesture Recognition, 46-53, 2000.
7. M. Lades, J. Vorbruggen, J. Buhmann, L. Lange, C. von der Malsburg, R. Wurz, and W. Konen, Distortion invariant object recognition in the dynamic link architecture, IEEE Computers, 42, 300-311, 1993.
8. C. Liu and H. Wechsler, Gabor feature based classification using the enhanced Fisher linear discriminant model for face recognition, IEEE Image Processing, 11, 4, 467-476, 2002.
9. M. Pantic and L.J.M. Rothkrantz, Towards an Affect-Sensitive Multimodal Human-Computer Interaction, Proc. of IEEE, vol. 91, 1370-1390.
10. M. Turk and A. Pentland, Face recognition using eigenfaces, Proc IEEE Conf in Comp Vision and Pattern Recognition, 586-591, 1991.
11. P. Viola and M. J. Jones. Rapid Object Detection using a Boosted Cascade of Simple Features. IEEE CVPR, 2001.
12. Z. Zhang, M. Lyons, M. Schuster, and S. Akamatsu, Comparison between geometry-based and Gabor-based expression recognition using multi-layer perceptron, Proc. Int'l Conf Face and Gest

Combining Acoustic Features for Improved Emotion Recognition in Mandarin Speech

Tsang-Long Pao, Yu-Te Chen, Jun-Heng Yeh, and Wen-Yuan Liao

Department of Computer Science and Engineering, Tatung University
tlpao@ttu.edu.tw
d8906005@ms2.ttu.edu.tw

Abstract. Combining different feature streams to obtain a more accurate experimental result is a well-known technique. The basic argument is that if the recognition errors of systems using the individual streams occur at different points, there is at least a chance that a combined system will be able to correct some of these errors by reference to the other streams. In the emotional speech recognition system, there are many ways in which this general principle can be applied. In this paper, we proposed using feature selection and feature combination to improve the speaker-dependent emotion recognition in Mandarin speech. Five basic emotions are investigated including anger, boredom, happiness, neutral and sadness. Combining multiple feature streams is clearly highly beneficial in our system. The best accuracy recognizing five different emotions can be achieved 99.44% by using MFCC, LPCC, RastaPLP, LFPC feature streams and the nearest class mean classifier.

1 Introduction

Speech signals are air vibration produced by air exhaled from the lungs modulated and shaped by the vibrations of the glottal cords and the vocal tract as it is pushed out through the lips and nose and are the most natural form of communication for humans and many animal species. Speech sounds have a rich temporal-spectral variation. In contrast, animals can only produce a relatively small repertoire of basic sound units.

Just as written language is a sequence of elementary alphabet, speech is a sequence of elementary acoustic symbols. Speech signals convey more than spoken words. The additional information conveyed in speech includes gender information, age, accent, speaker's identity, health, prosody and emotion [1].

Recently acoustic investigation of emotions expressed in speech has gained increased attention partly due to the potential value of emotion recognition for spoken dialogue management [2-4]. For instance, complain or anger due to unsatisfied services about user's requests could be dealt with smoothly by transferring the user to human operator. However, in order to reach such a level of performance we need to extract a reliable acoustic feature set that is largely immune to inter- and intra-speaker variability in emotion expression. The aim of this paper is to use feature combination (FC) to concatenate different features to improve emotion recognition in Mandarin speech.

J. Tao, T. Tan, and R.W. Picard (Eds.): ACII 2005, LNCS 3784, pp. 279 – 285, 2005.

This paper is organized as follows. In Section 2, the extracted acoustic features used in the system are described. In Section 3, we will describe feature selection and combination in more detail. Experimental results are reported in Section 4. Finally, conclusions are given in Section 5.

2 Extracted Acoustic Features

The speech signal contains different kind of information. From the automatic emotion recognition task point of view, it is useful to think about speech signal as a sequence of features that characterize both the emotions as well as the speech. How to extract sufficient information for good discrimination in a form and size which is amenable for effective modeling is a crucial problem.

All studies in the field point to the pitch as the main vocal cue for emotion recognition. The other acoustic variables contributing to vocal emotion signaling are: vocal energy, frequency spectral feature, formants and temporal features [5]. Another approach to feature extraction is to enrich the set of features by considering some derivative features such as MFCCs (Mel-Frequency Cepstral Coefficients) parameters of signal or features of the smoothed pitch contour and its derivatives. It is well known that the MFCCs are among the best acoustic features used in automatic speech recognition. The MFCCs are robust, contain much information about the vocal tract configuration regardless the source of excitation, and can be used to represent all classes of speech sounds. In [6], the authors proposed using MFCC coefficients and Vector Quantification to perform speaker-dependent emotion recognition. From the experimental results, the correct rate of energy or pitch is about 36% in comparison with performance of MFCC 76% and the influence of these features when combined with MFCC is unclear.

Instead of extracting pitch and energy features, in this paper, we estimated the following: formants (F1, F2 and F3), Linear Predictive Coefficients (LPC), Linear Prediction Cepstral Coefficients (LPCC), Mel-Frequency Cepstral Coefficients (MFCC), first derivative of MFCC (dMFCC), second derivative of MFCC (ddMFCC), Log Frequency Power Coefficients (LFPC), Perceptual Linear Prediction (PLP) and RelAtive SpecTrAl PLP (Rasta-PLP). Formants are used in a wide range of applications such as parameter extraction for a TTS system, as acoustic features for speech recognition, as analysis component for a formant based vocoder and for speaker identification, adaptation and normalization. There are at least three methods defined to estimate formant positions: LPC root, LPC peak-picking of the LPC envelope and LPC peak-picking of the cepstrally smoothed spectrum. In this paper, we adopted the second method.

For the past years, LPC has been considered one of the most powerful techniques for speech analysis. In fact, this technique is the basis of other more recent and sophisticated algorithms that are used for estimating speech parameters, e.g., pitch, formants, spectra, vocal tract and low bit representations of speech. The LPC coefficients can be calculated by either autocorrelation method or covariance method [1] and the order of linear prediction used is 16. After 16 LPC coefficients are obtained, the LPCC parameters are derived using the following equation:

$$c_k = a_k + (1/k)\sum_{i=1}^{k-1} i c_i a_{k-i} \quad 1 \le k \le p \tag{1}$$

where a_k are the LPC coefficients and p is the LPC analysis order.

Mel Frequency Cepstral Coefficients (MFCCs) are currently one of the most frequently used feature representations in automatic speech recognition system as they convey information of short time energy migration in frequency domain and yield satisfactory recognition results for a number of tasks and applications. The MFCCs are extracted from the speech signal that is framed and then windowed, usually with a Hamming window. A set of 20 Mel-spaced filter banks is then utilized to get the mel-spectrum. The natural logarithm is then taken to transform into the cepstral domain and the Discrete Cosine Transform is finally computed to get the MFCCs. Spectral transitions play an important role in human speech perception. Including the first and second order derivatives of MFCC features are adopted in this paper.

LFPC can be regarded as a model that follows the varying auditory resolving power of the human ear for various frequencies. In [7], it is found that the short time LFPC gives better performance for recognition of speech emotion compared with LPCC and MFCC. A possible reason is that LFPCs are more suitable for the preservation of fundamental frequency information in the lower order filters. The computation of short time LFPC can be found in [7]. The bandwidth and the center frequency of the first filter for a set of 20 bandpass filters are set at 54 Hz and 127 Hz respectively.

A combination of DFT and LP techniques is perceptual linear prediction (PLP). The analysis steps for PLP are critical band warping and averaging, equal loudness pre-emphasis, transformation according to the intensity loudness power law and all-pole modeling. All-pole model parameters are converted to cepstral coefficients which are liftered to approximately whiten the features. For a model of order p we use p=20 cepstral coefficients.

The word RASTA stands for RelAtive SpecTrAl technique [8]. This technique is an improvement of the traditional PLP method and consists in a special filtering of the different frequency channels of a PLP analyzer. The previous filtering is done to make speech analysis less sensitive to the slowly changing or steady-state factors in speech. The RASTA method replaces the conventional critical-band short-term spectrum in PLP and introduces a less sensitive spectral estimation.

3 Feature Selection and Combination

Despite the successful deployment of speech recognition applications, there are circumstances that present severe challenges to current recognizers – for instance, background noise, reverberation, fast or slow speech, unusual accents etc. In the huge body of published research there are many reports of success in mitigating individual problems, but fewer techniques that are of help in multiple different conditions. What is needed is a way to combine the strengths of several different approaches into a single system.

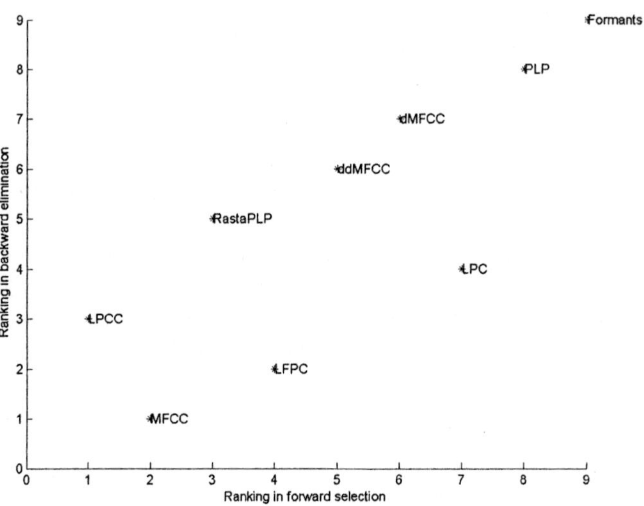

Fig. 1. Features ranking

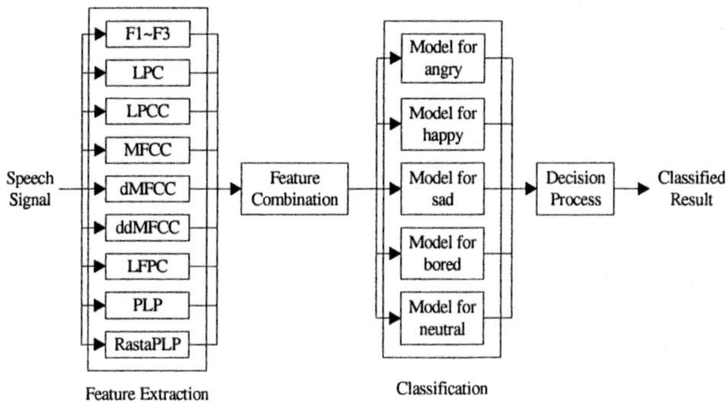

Fig. 2. The block diagram of the proposed system

Feature combination is a well-known technique [9]. During the feature extraction of speech recognition system, we typically find that each feature type has particular circumstances in which it excels, and this has motivated our investigations for combining separate feature streams into a single emotional speech recognition system. For feature combination, all possible feature streams would be concatenated. Due to the highly redundant information in the concatenated feature vector, a forward feature selection (FFS) or backward feature selection (BFS) should be carried out to extract only the most representative features, thereby orthogonalizing the feature vector and reducing its dimensionality. Figure 1 is a two-dimensional plot of 9 features ranked with nearest class mean classifier by forward selection and backward elimination. Features near origin are considered to be more important. The resulting feature vector is then processed as for a regular full-band recognizer. The block diagram of Mandarin emotional speech recognition system with feature combination is shown in Fig. 2.

4 Experimental Results

In order to carry out the experimentations, we have constructed an acted speech corpus recorded from two Chinese, one male and one female, in 8-bit PCM with a sampling frequency of 8k Hz. To provide reference data for automatic classification experiments, we performed human listening tests with two other listeners. Only those data that had complete agreement between them were chosen for the experiments reported in this paper. From the evaluation result, angry is the most difficult category to discriminate in our database, which had the lowest accuracy rate. Finally, we obtained 637 utterances with 95 angry, 115 bored, 113 happy, 150 neutral, and 164 sad utterances.

The Mandarin emotion recognition system was implemented using "MATLAB" software run under a desktop PC platform. The correct recognition rate was evaluated using leave-one-out (LOO) cross-validation which is a method to estimate the predictive accuracy of the classifier.

The task of the classifier component proper of a full system is to use the feature vector provided by the feature extractor to assign the object to a category. To recognize emotions in speech we tried the following approaches: minimum distance classifier with Euclidean distance, minimum distance classifier with Manhattan distance and nearest class mean classifier.

Table 1. Experimental results (%) with each feature stream

	Minimum distance (Euclidean)	Minimum distance (Manhattan)	Nearest class mean
F1~F3	32.81	32.52	36.44
LPC	63.67	60.90	59.18
LPCC	78.71	78.00	82.05
MFCC	71.44	73.50	92.62
dMFCC	65.70	65.03	46.13
ddMFCC	52.37	49.92	29.56
LFPC	62.75	64.96	80.64
PLP	67.00	68.58	77.24
RASTAPLP	56.65	60.13	78.43

Table 2. The best accuracy and the combined feature streams in different classifiers

Classifier	Minimum distance (Euclidean)	Minimum distance (Manhattan)	Nearest class mean
Best accuracy	79.98	81.03	99.44
Combined features	LPCC, MFCC, LPC, LFPC, RASTA-PLP	LPCC, MFCC, LPC, LFPC, RASTA-PLP	MFCC, LPCC, RASTA-PLP, LFPC

The nearest class mean classification is a simple classification method that assigns an unknown sample to a class according to the distance between the sample and each class's mean. The class mean, or centroid, is calculated as follows:

$$m_i = \frac{1}{n}\sum_{j=1}^{n_i} x_{i,j} \tag{2}$$

where $x_{i,j}$ is the jth sample from class i. An unknown sample with feature vector x is classified as class i if it is closer to the mean vector of class i than to any other class's mean vector. Rather than calculate the distance between the unknown sample and the mean of every classes, the minimum-distance classification estimates the Euclidean and Manhattan distance between the unknown sample and each training sample.

The experimental results of individual feature stream are described in Table 1 and the best accuracy of feature combination based on different classification method is given in Table 2.

5 Conclusions

We express our emotions in three main ways: the words that we use, facial expression and intonation of the voice. Whereas research about automated recognition of emotions in facial expressions is now very rich, research dealing with the speech modality, both for automated production and recognition by machines, has only been active for very few years and is almost for English.

Some of the state-of-the-art ASR systems employ multi-stream processing in which several data streams are processed in parallel before their information is recombined at a later point. Combination of the different streams can be carried out either before or after acoustic modeling, i.e. on the feature level or on the decision level.

In this paper, the feature selection and the feature combination were used to perform an exhaustive search for the optimal selection of the best feature vector combination. For each feature combination the classifier performance was tested by means of the leave-one-out method. Five basic emotions of anger, boredom, happiness, neutral and sadness are investigated. The experimental results show that the MFCC and LPCC play the role of primary features and the best feature combination in our proposed system are MFCC, LPCC, RastaPLP and LFPC. The highest accuracy of 99.44% is achieved with nearest class mean classifier. Contrary to [7], LPCC and MFCC achieve better performance for recognition of speech emotion compared with short time LFPC.

In the future, it is necessary to collect more and more acted or spontaneous speech sentences to test the robustness of the best feature combination. Furthermore, it might be useful to measure the confidence of the decision after performing classification. Based on confidence threshold, classification result might be classified as reliable or not. Unreliable tests can be for example further processed by human. Besides, trying to combine the information of different features and diverse classifiers in emotion recognition system is still a challenge for our future work.

Acknowledgement

The authors would like to thank the National Science Council (NSC) for financial supporting this research under NSC project NO: NSC 93-2213-E-036-023.

References

1. Rabiner L.R. and Juang B.H. Fundamentals of Speech Recognition. Prentice-Hall, Englewood Cliffs, NJ, 1993.
2. Lee, C. M., and Narayanan, S., "Towards detecting emotion in spoken dialogs," IEEE Trans. on Speech & Audio Processing, in press.
3. Cowie, R., Douglas-Cowie, E., Tsapatsoulis, N., Votsis, G., Kollias, S., Fellenz, ans Taylor, J., "Emotion Recognition in Human-Computer Interactions", IEEE Sig. Proc. Mag., vol. 18, pp.32-80, Jan 2001.
4. Litman, D., ad Forbes, K. "Recognizing Emotions from Student Speech in Tutoring Dialogues," In proceedings of the ASRU'03, 2003.
5. Banse, R. and Scherer, K.R. "Acoustic profiles in vocal emotion expression," Journal of Personality and Social Psychology, pp.614-636, 1996.
6. Xuan Hung Le; Quenot, G.; Castelli, E.; "Recognizing emotions for the audio-visual document indexing", Proceedings of Computers and Communications, ISCC, 2004, pp. 580-584.
7. Tin Lay Nwe, Foo Say Wei, Liyanage C De Silva, "Speech Emotion Recognition using Hidden Markov models," Speech Communication, 2003.
8. H. Hermansky and N. Morgan, ``RASTA Processing of Speech'', IEEE Transactions on Speech and Audio Processing, Vol. 2 No. 4, October 1994.
9. Ellis, DPW (2000a). "Stream combination before and/or after the acoustic model." Proc. of the Int. Conf. on Acoustics, Speech, and Signal Processing (ICASSP 2000).

Intonation Modelling and Adaptation for Emotional Prosody Generation

Zeynep Inanoglu and Steve Young

Cambridge University Engineering Department,
Machine Intelligence Laboratory, Cambridge, UK
zi201@cam.ac.uk, sjy@eng.cam.ac.uk

Abstract. This paper proposes an HMM-based approach to generating emotional intonation patterns. A set of models were built to represent syllable-length intonation units. In a classification framework, the models were able to detect a sequence of intonation units from raw fundamental frequency values. Using the models in a generative framework, we were able to synthesize smooth and natural sounding pitch contours. As a case study for emotional intonation generation, Maximum Likelihood Linear Regression (MLLR) adaptation was used to transform the neutral model parameters with a small amount of happy and sad speech data. Perceptual tests showed that listeners could identify the speech with the sad intonation 80% of the time. On the other hand, listeners formed a bimodal distribution in their ability to detect the system generated happy intontation and on average listeners were able to detect happy intonation only 46% of the time.

1 Introduction

Emotional speech synthesis requires the appropriate manipulation of a wide range of parameters related to voice quality and prosody. In this paper, we focus on the generation of pitch contours which constitute the building blocks of human intonation. Such prosodic generation schemes can plug into a variety of speech synthesis or voice conversion frameworks. We argue that a robust model-based approach can provide an adaptive framework which allows new emotional intonations to be generated with little training data using model adaptation algorithms.

The popularity of concatenative synthesis and unit-selection schemes have made the prospect of emotional speech synthesis more viable, given the improvement in quality over formant-based approaches. One approach that has been explored is to record neutral as well as emotional speech databases and select the units with the appropriate emotional qualities [1][2][3]. However this gives only limited capability for generating new emotions, since each new emotion requires an extensive data collection effort. At the other end of the spectrum, exploring dimensional approaches has proved valuable, particularly for generating non-extreme emotions and emotion build-up over time [4]. Due to lack of a

J. Tao, T. Tan, and R.W. Picard (Eds.): ACII 2005, LNCS 3784, pp. 286–293, 2005.

comprehensive theory of emotion, however, it is unclear how all emotions can be represented within this dimensional space.

We propose an HMM-based representation of intonation, where each HMM represents a syllable-length intonational unit. Previous work on intonation modelling based on HMM has been carried out by [6][5][7]. We revisit this approach with the purpose of automatic contour synthesis and adaptation. Our motivation is twofold: to create a set of unified models that can be used to both recognize and synthesize natural sounding intonation patterns and to generate emotional intonation by adapting model parameters with a small amount of emotional speech data. Our results show that syllable-based HMMs can generate very natural sounding intonation contours. Adaptatation to a very small amount of sad speech data also resulted in considerably sadder prosody, as confirmed by preference tests. Adaptation to happy data was not as effective, suggesting that intonation may not be the only key element in producing happy sounding speech.

Section 2 describes the models in detail. Section 3 presents the performance of our models in a recognition framework, where two levels of context-sensitivity are explored. Section 4 reviews the HTS(HMM-based speech synthesis) system which has been adapted to generate continuous pitch contours from HMMs and illustrates the contours that result from our models. Section 5 describes the MLLR adaptation method and demonstrates the results of adaptation to happy and sad speech data. Section 6 summarizes conclusions and future work.

2 Intonation Models

A set of seven basic units, which constitute the parts of an intonational phrase, were chosen (Table 1). Each syllable is assumed to belong to one of the seven units of intonation. This label set is based on the work done on the Tilt intonation model [7]. An accent is represented by **a** and any intonation movement that is not an accent is either a falling or rising boundary tone (**fb**,**rb**) or an unstressed segment of speech(**c**). For the cases when an accent and a boundary tone coincide, the combination units (**arb**, **afb**) are used. Silence is also included as a marker for intonational boundaries.

The basic models were trained on a female speaker from the Boston Radio Corpus [12]. This is a corpus of news stories read by a professional news reader. About 48 minutes of the female speaker's speech was labelled with the intonation units. Out of the thirty-four news clips, five were set aside for testing. To achieve speaker independence, raw fundamental frequency values were normalized by speaker mean and two orders of dynamic coefficients were computed (delta and

Table 1. List of Intonation Units

a	accent	**c**	unstressed
rb	rising boundary	**fb**	falling boundary
arb	accent + rising boundary	**afb**	accent + falling boundary
sil	silence		

delta delta). The models have three states, each with a single Gaussian distribution. Training was carried out using HTK (Hidden Markov Model Tool Kit)[11]. A number of iterations of embedded Baum-Welch algorithm were performed. Context-sensitive models were also explored using incremental levels of context around each intonation unit. A **tri-unit** model set was built by replicating models based on their left and right neighbours and performing further iterations of embedded training. The use of tri-unit models is analogous to the use triphones in speech recognition. In order to overcome the problems of data sparsity and unseen contexts, decision-tree based parameter tying was used, where states of the models are clustered based on a log-likelihood criterion[10]. A **full-context** model set was also built incorporating sixteen contextual factors. The goal here was to capture more long distance intonation dependencies and take advantage of more detailed information such as the relative location of the vowel in the syllable. An intonational phrase (IP) is defined as the sequence of labels between two silences. Based on this definition, the contextual factors incorporated in the full-context models are as follows:

- identity of the unit to the left
- identity of the unit to the right
- relative position of current syllable in current IP
- the total number of each of **a/c/rb/fb/arb/afb**s in current IP
- the number each of **a/arb/afb/rb/fb**s before current syllable in current IP
- relative position of the vowel in current syllable
- total number of phones in current syllable

Decisions on how much context to incorporate in the models can depend on the framework within which one wishes to use the system. In a speech synthesis framework, for instance, access to phonetic information is straightforward and further context can be incorporated. In a voice conversion framework, it may be preferable to work with intonation units only.

3 Recognition Accuracy of Intonation Models

Evaluating the models in a recognition framework is important for two reasons: to understand how effective our models are as a means to capture and analyze intonation patterns and to ensure that they reliably represent the individual intonation units since failing to do so would also degrade the quality of synthesis. Recognition is performed using the Viterbi algorithm in HTK. Given consecutive raw f0 values extracted from an utterance of any length, the Viterbi algorithm finds the sequence of intonation units that maximizes the likelihood of the observations. In addition to the label sequence, the syllable boundaries are also determined by this process. The test data consisted of five news stories each lasting for about two minutes, with an average syllable count of 200. Table 2 shows the percent accuracy and percent correct rates for models of varying contextual complexity. The difference between percent correct and percent accuracy is that the latter also takes into consideration insertion errors (i.e. errors where a

Table 2. Recognition results of varying mixture components in the no context case as well as single mixture component with tri-unit and full context. Ten mixtures was the optimal rate for the no-context case.

Model Set	Number of Mixtures	%Correct	%Accuracy
Basic	N=1	53.26	44.52
	N=2	53.36	45.48
	N=4	54.65	46.31
	N=10	59.58	50.40
Tri-Unit	N=1	61.50	49.75
Full Context	N=1	64.02	55.88

redundant intonation unit was inserted between two correctly recognized units) and is therefore a more informative evaluation metric.

To illustrate the power of context we have also included the best results that can be achieved by increasing the number of Gaussian mixture components when context is ignored. Incorporating full context significantly improves the performance even when compared with the best performance achieved by the optimal configuration of mixtures components(N=10).

4 Intonation Synthesis from HMM

We have adapted the HMM-based speech synthesis(HTS)[9] system to generate continuous pitch values. HTS is a stand-alone speech synthesizer, which can generate speech waveforms from a set of context-sensitive phone HMMs. We have applied its cepstral parameter generation framework[8] to produce interpolated pitch values from our continuous density intonation HMMs. The key idea behind the parameter generation algorithm is the fact that in addition to f0 values, dynamic features (delta f0 and delta delta f0) are also used to optimize the likelihood of the generated parameter sequence. Without the incorporation of these dynamic features, the generated sequence would consist of the state mean vectors regardless of immediate context.

The input to our system is an intonation label sequence with corresponding syllable boundaries as well as a speaker mean value. The intonation models are then concatenated according to the label sequence to form a larger HMM network that represents the entire contour. The parameter generation algorithm is then applied to generate an interpolated f0 contour. Since training includes a mean normalization for the speaker, the input mean value is added to the generated f0 values. Currently the system also assumes that syllable boundaries are given since our focus is on intonation generation and a precise syllable-based duration model will require a separate investigation of its own. We have generated contours from both tri-unit and full-context model sets. Figure 1 illustrates the interpolated contours generated by our system given two different sequences of intonation units for an utterance with six syllables. The introduction of accents and boundary tones in the contour is clearly observable in these plots. Figure 2 is a comparison of a sample contour generated by the tri-unit and full context models for the same label sequence. We were able to observe that, compared with the tri-unit model, the full context model may shift accents slightly to the right or to the left, based on the location of the vowel in the syllable. The full context model was also found to frequently vary the amplitude of a pitch accent based on the number of preceding accents. For instance, in an utterance with many accents, some of the later ones may not be as pronounced as the earlier ones. A number of these contextual modifications are observable in Figure 2.

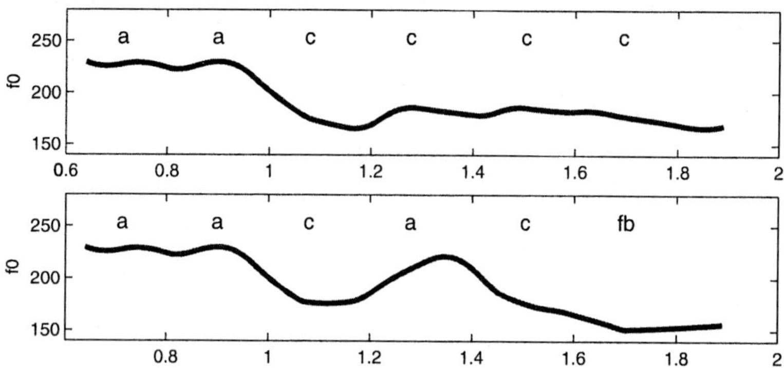

Fig. 1. Contours generated from two different label sequences using tri-unit model set with mean f0=200Hz

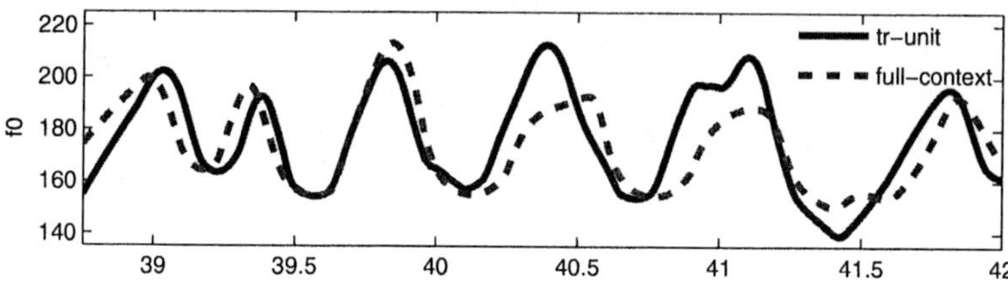

Fig. 2. Contours generated by tri-unit and full context models for the same label sequence, mean f0=180Hz

The perceptual evaluation framework was based on transplanting the contours onto naturally spoken utterances. In order to focus on the effects of the generated contours, real utterances were modified using the PSOLA algorithm [14] to replace their existing f0 contours with those generated by the intonation models. We were able to transplant our contours onto a wide range of recordings from different speakers and still obtain very natural sounding results. A brief perceptual test was conducted to quantify the naturalness of generated contours. Listeners were asked to rate eight utterances on a scale of 1 to 5 for their naturalness, 1 corresponding to least natural and 5 to very natural. Four of the utterances were presented with their original, unmodified pitch contours and the other four had the synthetic contours generated by our tri-unit models. The utterances were presented in random order. The objective of the test was to ensure that the utterances with synthetic contours had ratings that overlapped sufficiently with those of the original recordings. The mean rating was 4 out of 5 for the unmodified utterances and 3.55 for the modified utterances. A t-test ($p<0.05$) on the two samples confirmed that the samples are not statistically distinguishable.

5 MLLR Adaptation of Intonation Models with Happy and Sad Speech

MLLR is an adapatation technique frequently used in speech recognition to adapt phone models to different regional dialects[13]. The algorithm estimates a set of linear transformations for the mean and variance parameters of the Gaussian distributions for each state. Using HTK, MLLR can be applied flexibly depending on the amount of training data available. A regression tree is used to cluster the Gaussian parameters based on a similarity criteria and different transformations can be applied to different nodes of the tree based on the data available.

Thirty nine and ninety short segments of speech were acquired for sad and happy emotions, respectively. The data came from the Emotional Prosody Speech Corpus[15], which contains neutral and emotional utterances of four syllable phrases, mainly dates and numbers. Since these are extremely short utterances with limited long-distance context, tri-unit models were used for adaptation. Figure 3 illustrates sad, happy and neutral contours all generated by their respective model sets for a given label sequence. Detailed analysis of the emotion-specific changes in intonation is beyond the scope of this paper. However, it was observed that both happy and sad contours generally had a higher mean pitch, while the pitch range for happy contours was frequently wider than both sad and neutral contours, particularly in the case of accents and accents with rising boundaries. Sad contours manifested very unpronounced intonation units, particularly accents.

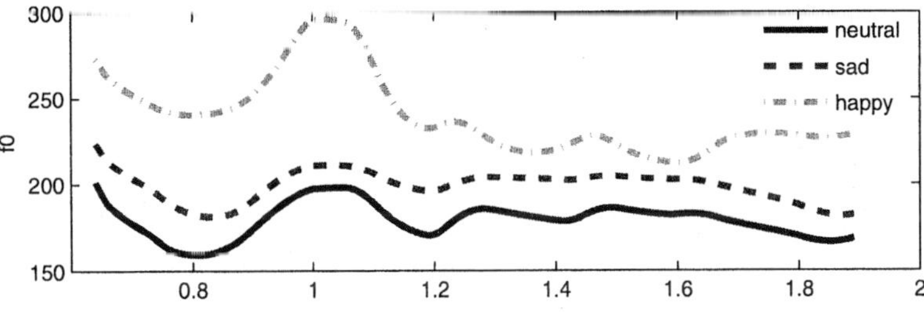

Fig. 3. Synthesized sad, happy and neutral contours by tri-unit models for the label sequence: **c arb c c c c.** mean f0=200Hz

A two-part, perceptual preference test was conducted to compare the two types of generated contours: neutral and emotional. In part one, listeners were asked to listen to twenty pairs of short utterances and decide which utterance out of each pair sounds happier. In part two, the same procedure was repeated for sad speech. In order to evaluate the relative performance of emotional models over neutral ones, a forced choice was required between a generated neutral contour and a generated emotional contour. The utterances were taken from five different speakers: 3 female and 2 male. The presented contours covered all of the seven basic intonation units. Fourteen listeners took the test and a total of 280 choices were made in each part. The speech with sad contours were identified as sounding sadder 80% of the time. This was statistically significant (Chi-Square, $p<0.01$). On the other hand, only 46% of listener's choices associated the happy contours with happier sounding speech. While we would have hoped that our models performed better for the happy case, our results seem to confirm previous attempts in emotion synthesis[3][2].

When analyzed on a per listener basis, the distribution of preferences in part one (happy) suggest strong bimodality: eight of the fourteen listeners had a mean identification rate of 5 out of 20, while the remaining six had a mean identification rate of 15. Figure 4 illustrates the distribution of speakers in both parts. Clearly the intonational correlates of happiness are not universally sufficient on their own to express the full texture of the emotion. On the other hand, there may also be differences in imagined context for the two groups of listeners who seem to disagree on the effectiveness of our models.

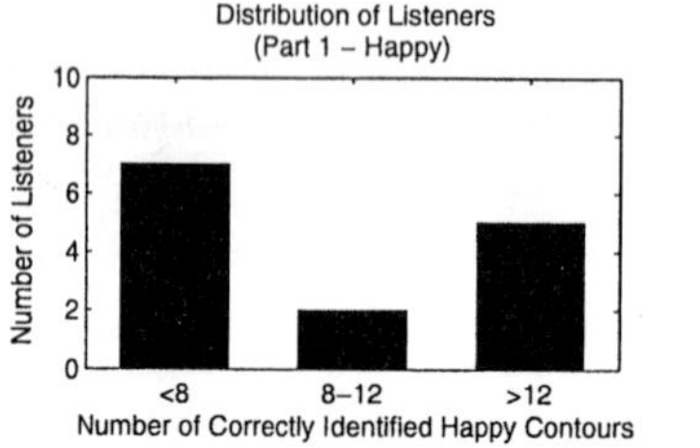

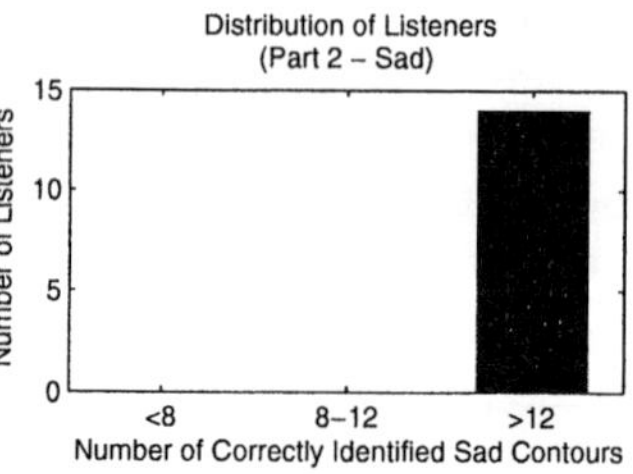

Fig. 4. Distribution of listener agreements with system

An interesting observation was made on the possible dependence of system performance on the actual label sequence. In part one, the utterance where thirteen out of fourteen listeners agreed with the contours produced by happy models, consisted of six consecutive accents. The same label sequence was also the least successful in part two, meaning that listeners consistently preferred neutral contours over sad ones for sadder sounding speech. These facts suggest that the frequency and organization of certain constituents such as accents may be directly correlated with the proper expression of the two emotions at hand, contributing to the generative power of our models. More rigourous analysis of correlations between intonation unit sequences and emotions will be part of future work.

6 Conclusions and Future Work

A novel approach to synthesizing pitch contours based on syllable-based intonation models has been proposed. The effectiveness of these models was assessed both in a classification framework through recognition accuracy figures as well as in a generative framework through perceptual tests. Model adaptation to sad data proved successful while adaptation to happy data resulted in a division between groups of listeners. One of our immediate objectives is to analyze the dependence of emotions on the actual intonation unit sequence. Incorporation of an emotion-specific pattern of basic units may actually improve the perception of difficult emotions such as happiness. Since the poor performance of the happy synthesis may also be a consequence of the limited context in the specific adaptation data, richer data sources will be evaluated. Further work on emotion recognition using adapted intonation models will also be pursued in order to explore advantages of recognition/synthesis duality.

References

1. Akemi, I., Campbell, N., Higuchi, F., Yasamura, M.: A Corpus-based Speech Synthesis System with Emotion. Proc. of Speech Communication **40** (2003) 161–187
2. Montero, JM., Arriola, J., Colas, J., Enriquez, E., Pardo, J.M.: Analysis and Modelling of Emotional Speech in Spanish. Proc. of ICPhS **2** (1999) 957–960
3. Bulut, M., Narayanan, S., Syrdal, A.: Expressive Speech Synthesis Using a Concatenative Synthesizer. Proc. of ICSLP (2002)
4. Schroder, M.: Dimensional Emotion Representation as a Basis for Speech Synthesis with non-extreme emotions. Workshop on Affective Dialogue Sys. (2004) 209–220
5. Jensen, U., Moore, R.K., Dalsgaard, P., Lindberg B.: Modelling Intonation Contours at the Phrase Level using Continuous Density Hidden Markov Models Computer Speech and Language **8** (1994) 247–260
6. Ljolje, A., Fallside, F.: Recognition of Isolated Prosodic Patterns using Hidden Markov Models Speech and Language **2** (1987) 27–33
7. Taylor, P.: Anaysis and Synthesis of Intonation using the Tilt Model. Journal of the Acoustical Society of America **107(3)** (2000) 1697–1714
8. Tokuda, K., Yoshimura, T., Masuko, T., Kobayashi, T., Kitamura, T.: Speech Parameter Generation Algorithms for HMM-Based Speech Synthesis Proc. of ICASSP Processing **3** (2000) 1315–1318
9. Tokuda, K., Zen, H., Black, A.: An HMM-Based Speech Synthesis System Applied To English. IEEE Speech Synthesis Workshop (2002)
10. Odell, J.J.: The Use of Context in Large Vocabulary Speech Recognition. PhD Dissertation, Cambridge University (1995)
11. http://htk.eng.cam.ac.uk
12. Ostendorf, M., Price, P.J., Shattuck-Hufnagel, S.: The Boston University Radio Corpus. Technical Report ECS-95-001 (1995)
13. Gales, M., Woodland, P.: Mean and Variance Adaptation within the MLLR Framework. Computer Speech and Language **10** (1996)
14. Moulines, E., Charpentier, F.: Pitch Synchronous Waveform Processing Techniques for Text-to-speech Synthesis Using Diphones. Speech Communication **9** (1990) 453–467.
15. http://www.ldc.upenn.edu/Catalog/LDC2002S28.html

Application of Psychological Characteristics to D-Script Model for Emotional Speech Processing

Artemy Kotov

Department of Theoretical Linguistics,
Russian State University for Humanities, Moscow, Russia
kotov@harpia.ru
http://www.harpia.ru/d-scripts-en.html

Abstract. D-scripts model is originally developed for description of affective (emotional) mass media texts and with extension also applies to emotional speech synthesis. In this model we distinguish units for "rational" inference (r-scripts) and units for "emotional" processing of meaning (d-scripts). Basing on a psycholinguistics study we demonstrate relations between classes of emotional utterances in d-script model and psychological characteristics of informants. The study proposes a theoretical framework for an affective agent simulating given psychological characteristics in it's emotional speech behaviour.

1 Introduction

The concept of d-scripts was initially developed for the purposes of linguistic expertise and was aimed at finding emotional texts and speech insults in mass media [10]. The proposed model included two types of units (scripts) for the interpretation of incoming text: *d-scripts* (dominant scripts) for emotional processing and *r-scripts* (rational scripts) for "rational", neutral processing. It is supposed that "emotional" or "affective" texts activate d-scripts during text comprehension and tend to leave r-scripts inactive. This concept of speech analysis was further developed with orientation on CogAff architecture discussed in particular in [5, 6, 7]. CogAff (Cognition and Affect project) proposes a model for autonomous agent, experiencing and expressing emotions in interaction with the environment, so the d-scripts extension (where d-scripts correspond to "alarm system" in CogAff) offered a possibility of describe not only behavioural, but also emotional speech interaction, including speech synthesis.

CogAff architecture suggests that actual output of an agent may be controlled and affected by a hierarchy of controlling states, in particular by *personality, attitudes, preferences, moods* etc. [1]. In our study we wanted to find specific links between psychological characteristics and particular speech replies in emotional situations, defined by Rosenzweig Picture frustration test (PFT). As the d-script model provides detailed analysis of the emotional utterances, each actual reply can be associated with a specific class in d-script model, which in tern may be correlated with psychological

J. Tao, T. Tan, and R.W. Picard (Eds.): ACII 2005, LNCS 3784, pp. 294 – 302, 2005.

characteristics of a respondent, measured in parallel psychological tests. For the discovered correlations this allows to define possible classes of utterances and construct specific replies for a given set of psychological characteristics, which we want to simulate at the interface.

2 Structure and Functioning of a D-Script

The list of d-scripts for negative processing contains 13 units, responding for 'danger', 'limitation', 'inadequacy' and other affective meanings[1]. A particular d-script SUBJV, shown here as an example, is responsible for 'subjective actions' and is revealed in sentences (1) *You think only about yourself* - for conflict communication, and (2) *The government is concerned only about it's salary* - for influence or complaint communication [3]. Initial activation of the d-script by the listener may force utterances like (1) while an attempt to force the listener to activate the d-script may result utterances like (2). Starting model of this script fixes a situation of 'subjectivity', represented as a semantic graph (in a simple case – as a predicative structure) or in a form similar to a dictionary definition. Starting model includes slots AGGR – for person or entity, whose actions seem to be subjective, and VICT – for person, who is affected. Starting model of SUBJV is defined in the following way:

SUBJV(AGGR, VICT, M^S, P_{AGGR}, M^G): AGGR doesn't consider relevant factors of the situation and is effecting or is going to effect [all the possible] actions P_{AGGR} upon discovering of the stimulus M^S or to achieve a goal M^G; AGGR and VICT are linked with a relation $R_{AGGR-VICT}$.

Some nodes of the representation are also appended by semantic markers, responsible for emotional processing – *critical elements*. The value of the critical elements allows to distinguish emotional text and a neutral text containing the same semantic graph. The analysis of mass media and conflict texts gives us a notion on the list of critical elements for each d-script. Above all, the following critical elements are relevant to SUBJV: **<number of AGGR>$^+$** (*Everybody thinks only about himself!*), **<timeframe/quantity of P_{AGGR}>$^+$** (*He always talks about football!*), **<intensity of P_{AGGR}>$^+$** (*Why do you start shouting, when I mention the washing machine?*), **<importance of M_2>$^-$** (*Luzhkov shall bite to death everybody in order to be the first to congratulate Eltsin with his birthday!*). Definition of each d-script includes from 6 to 20 critical elements, discovered from actual text analysis and collected from linguistic studies of emotional texts [8, 9]. Critical elements may apply during text synthesis in emotional state and further may be extracted from text and contribute to emotional processing during text comprehension. In linguistic analysis meaning shifts in critical elements serve as criteria to identify emotional texts.

The sensitivity of a d-script may vary, depending on the control states: in nervous condition the of d-scripts are pre-activated and may respond to texts having very little shifts in critical elements or no shifts at all (neutral texts). In reply, the system may respond with a more emotional utterance, supporting a dialogue as:

---

[1] For the list of negative d-scripts see: http://www.harpia.ru/d-scripts-en.html

(3) – *The government is working on the budget.*
– *They all always shout only about their budget/such trifles!*

Activation of a d-script may result text synthesis not only from the starting model (description of "a terrible situation") but also from target models of aggression or flight (*I shall kill you! / I have to go away!*). Out purpose is to test the dependency between such control states as personal characteristics and the preferency of d/r-scripts in a psychological survey study.

3 Application of D-Script Model to the Results of Rosenzweig PFT

In standard Rosenzweig PFT a participant is asked to reply to a speaker in situation of frustration, represented by a picture (the test is projective). Sample situations include:

a. [a woman tells a person, who broke a vase:] *You broke the favourite vase of my mother!* ('vase' situation) and
b. [a driver tells a pedestrian:] *I'm sorry to spoil your suite, although I tried to avoid the puddle!* ('driver' situation).

In a task of incoming text processing a d-script must detect a predicative structure, so application of the model to the processing of a situation (as in PFT) needs some extensions as no predicative structure is given a priori. In this case activation of d/r-scripts is based on a segmentation of the situation with further extraction of a typical predicative structure from each of the segments. The analysis of the set of utterances received in the experiment shows that the following segmentation of a situation appears sufficient to describe most of the actual utterances.

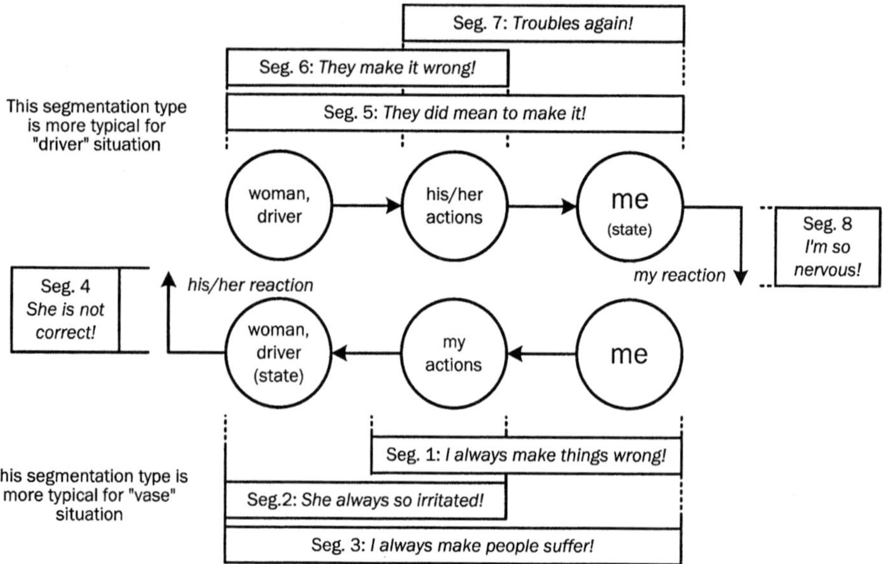

Fig. 1. Segmentation and extraction of a predicative structure from Rosenzweig situations

The scheme represents speaker ('me') making some actions or experiencing some state when being affected by some other actions. The actions of the speaker may affect the addressee – this interaction may be segmented in three different ways, depending on which components of the situation speaker takes into account: 'I make some actions' (Seg. 1), 'some actions (possibly not mine) affect the addressee' (Seg. 2) and a combination of the two – 'I make some actions affecting the addressee' (Seg. 3). Further, the speaker may construct a representation for the addressee who has some true of false understanding of what has happened (Seg. 4), and the four segments should be symmetrically doubled to represent possible actions of the addressee in relation to the speaker ('myself') and speaker's understanding (Seg. 5-8). Each of these segments has a clear predicative structure, which can be processed in the model. During processing each segment may activate r-scripts with 'rational' speech output or d-scripts with 'emotional' reply – the latter is shown on the scheme for each segment.

In fact, most of the studied PFT situations may be represented by any of the selected segments, but there are still some preferences. 'Vase' situation is concentrated on the speaker's actions in respect to the addressee ('I broke his/her vase'), so the possible segmentation would be Seg.1-4 with the most complete – Seg. 3. On the other side 'driver' situation represents addressee's actions and is segmented by Seg. 5-8. Speaker may violate this tendency and treat 'vase' situation, for example, as Seg. 5 (*Is it a long time that the vase stands here?* – resulted by 'someone contrived it'), and 'driver' situation as Seg. 1 (*I have to be more attentive!* – resulted by 'I'm inadequate'). Each of the segments (represented as a predicative structure) arrives to the input of d/r-script set and activates one or several scripts with further speech output. A sample scheme for a segment processing is shown on Fig. 2.

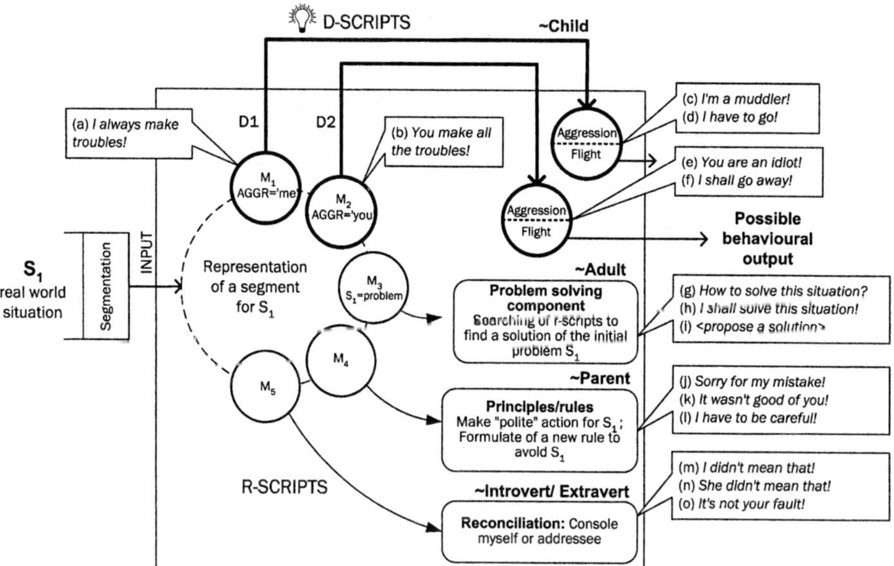

Fig. 2. Processing of a single component through d/r-scripts and possible outputs

D-script processing may differ depending on the actant of AGGR valency – it can be the speaker himself – D1 (*I always make troubles!*) or the addressee – D2 (*You make all the troubles!*). In all cases the speaker also occupies VICT valency, as he is suffering from the situation (other types of emotional communication like "communication of victims" and "speech persuasion", not observed here, may assign VICT valency to other participants). The selection between D1 and D2 is defined by the preferred segment: Seg. 1, 3, 8 activate a d-script in D1 scheme, and Seg. 2, 4, 5, 6 – activate D2 (we assume, that preference of reaction D1 or D2 influences extraction of a particular segment from the situation). The positions D1 and D2 may be occupied by different d-scripts from the 13 d-scripts list, e. g. we may treat other's actions (D2) ad inadequate, subjective, dangerous, etc. Each of the d-scripts may result speech output from it's starting models (M_1, M_2) with corresponding utterances falling in classes (a) and (b), and from it's final models of aggression or flight: classes (c-f).

The other way to process a segment is to activate an r-script. Since there was no given list of r-scripts or criteria for their selection (like critical elements for d-scripts), r-scripts were extracted from actual utterances basing on the similarity of their supposed initial models and semantics of speech output. Finally, selected r-scripts were categorized in three blocks: problem solving, principles/rules and reconciliation (minor speech output classes are here omitted). In problem solving block a speaker treats an initial segment as a problem and proposes a solution (i), offers to propose a solution (h) or requests a solution from the addressee (g). In principles/rules block a speaker follows etiquette (j), appeals to addressee to make him follow a rule (k) or formulates a new rule for himself or addressee (l). In reconciliation block speaker pays attention to his own emotional state or emotional state of the addressee (here emotional state is described as an activation of a d-script by speaker and/or addressee); here speaker has to detect a particular d-script (emotional state) and minimize it's activation by changing a representation of the initial situation. Speaker can represent his actions as less harmful for the addressee (m), justify addressee's actions for himself (n) or falsify the addressee's harmful actions (o).

The analysis in Fig. 2 has to be multiplied on the number of segments, selected in a particular situation with further combination and deletion of non-existing classes. For 'vase' situation with consideration of Seg. 1-5 this gives 28 general classes with the possibly of further classification (e.g. for emotional/reconciliation we may analyse, which exactly d-script is activated or is supposed to be activated etc.).

The segmentation allows to mark-up the utterances, received in the actual experimental study and to form a database. The proposed analysis offers more detailed classification than the standard PFT key (only 9 classes) and for many classes defines linguistic rules to construct utterances for this class in a speech interface. This allows not only to step from particular utterances to psychological characteristics (as in standard psychological interpretation of test results) but also to construct a set of possible utterances once a particular class is selected for output synthesis.

The next important task is to find out which class of utterances in d/r-script model is selected in a given situation for particular psychological characteristics. The question can be solved theoretically: we can assume, that aggressive participants may prefer D2 reaction while diffident participants – D1 reaction. We may suppose that a tendency to transfer control to a specific component of the model (as on Fig. 2) may correspond to different ego-states like "wish/fear-oriented" behaviour (d-scripts), "rational" behaviour (problem solving) or "rule-oriented" behaviour (principles/rules). On Fig. 2 we have proposed a shallow mark-up of the components, following E. Berne concept of ego-states: Child, Adult and Parent [2]. Further, reconciliation may be speaker-oriented (speaker calms himself) or addressee-oriented (speaker trys to calm the addressee). This may follow introvert / extravert psychological distinction. The other approach is to test the correspondence between psychological characteristics and preferred utterance experimentally.

4 Experimental Study

The experimental study was carried out on several groups of respondents and included several PFT pictures (from 2 to 5) and supplementary tests, different for each group. We used an extended study of PFT, where the participants were asked several questions, in particular: *What would you say in this situation?* (WWYS) *What would you think?* (WWYT) and *What would you do, if you were not limited?* (WWYD). The following groups took part in the survey:

Adults – 100 respondents (2 PFT situations, no supplementary tests); University entrants – 110 respondents (5 PFT situations, Leary test, Lichko test); Practicing therapeutics and surgeons – 50 respondents (2 PFT situations, emotional degression test). The participants were native russian speakers, all the protocols were in Russian. The results of the survey were organized in a database, giving access to all actual utterances of a particular d/r-script class. The database can be used to adjust the representation of utterances in each specific class to meet actual speech practice. Further the database includes a set of psychological characteristics for participants.

Shallow results. The results for WWYS question for 'vase' situation remain quite stable and don't change for the three groups, staying at the following levels: (j) *Sorry! Excuse me!* – 43-46%, (h) *I shall compensate it!* – 26-30%, (m) *I didn't mean that!* – 14-21%. These three classes of results cover the majority of replies in WWYS (89-96%). This gives us a shallow understanding that a computer agent can be pre-programmed to produce a limited number of "etiquette" utterances and doesn't require any extensional reactions. The results however are motivated by the purpose of PFT – to verify the socialization of participants. Stability in replies do confirm the socialization, however, for an emotional agent we further require an adequate performance in WWYT and WWYD tasks, which can be usual for everyday communication and in addition may produce communicative stimulus, allowing the agent to initiate communication.

Answer filtering. For adults group the replics in WWYS and WWYT groups significantly differed. Some answers ((j) *Sorry*) are dedicated to the addressee – participants 'say' them, but don't 'think' this way, other classes ((a) *I'm a muddler!*) are selected in WWYT task and are suppressed in WWYS. We interpret the results as an activity of utterance filter, which rises the activation of "etiquette" classes (the answers are produced, even if there is a doubtful opportunity to prefer them), and lowers activation of some emotional classes, not allowed by politeness.

Answer filtering suggests to us a mechanism of class substitution: where an emotional utterance like (b) *You accuse me of what I haven't done!* is suppressed by the filter, it can exploit another more competent class like (m) *I didn't mean that!*

giving to this utterance a distinctive emotional prosody (as in *Don't you see, that I didn't mean that?!*).

Correlations in Lichko test. Studies of personal psychological accentuations, measured in Lichko test, and classes of utterances, marked by d/r-scripts (University entrants, 5 PFT situations) give a list of correlations (relevant at p<0,05), in particular:

(i) psychasthenic level correlates with d-script answers: participants with psychasthenic accentuation prefer answers, defined by starting or target models of d-scripts – classes (a-f);
(ii) sensitivity – flight (d, f): sensitive participants tend to report flight plans, either because they are upset about their own actions (class (d)) or because they are affected by the actions of addressee (class (f)); further, if the addressee is responsible for the situation (e. g. he has spoiled out suit) sensitive participants don't justify his actions and don't propose answers (o) *It's not your fault!*
(iii) schizoid participants (as sensitive) don't justify the addressee in case of his fault;
(iv) level of sincerity correlates with d-script answers: sincere participants propose more "emotional" answers described by d-scripts, the answers may fall both in D1 (accuse myself) or D2 group (accuse the addressee);
(v) dissimulation correlates with extrovert d-script answers: insincere participants tend to propose emotional utterances, accusing the addressee – (b, e).

Correlations in Leary test. The results of Leary test give a list of correlations with the classes of produced utterances (relevant at p<0,05). Most of them seem trivial, but can be treated as a valuable dependency between "high-level" control states like emotional characteristics and "low-level" linguistic definitions of a particular utterance class, in particular: (vi) egoistic level negatively correlates with the sum of points for utterances, aimed at the addressee; (vii) aggressive level correlates with D2 (extroversive) d-script utterances (b, e, f).

Other results are less trivial and are worthy of notice, in particular: (viii) friendliness correlates with the sum of points for emotional utterances – on one side, and with the sum of D1 utterances plus sum r-script utterances, aimed at the speaker (like to consulate myself, formulate a rule for own actions etc.).

Correspondence between the number of emotional replies (assigned to d-scripts) and sincerity – on one side (Lichko test) and friendliness – on the other side (Leary test) may suggest a reverse dependency: to look friendly a computer agent might simulate emotions and report emotional utterances when interacting with a human in emotional situation. As expected, this behaviour must be refined by accurate application of critical elements to distinguish the case of sincerity from psychasthenic behaviour. As expected, "friendly" emotional interaction may contain both ironic aggression (Ironically: *Do you understand, what you've said?*) and sincere utterances (*Sometimes I make people suffer!*). These classes and their distinction from corresponding aggressive and self-accusation texts constitute one the most interesting areas for further studies.

5 Conclusion and Future Work

In the present report we have represented an application of a d-script model to mark-up of experimental data set and consecutive findings on the correlations between psychological characteristics of participants and classes of utterances, as defined by the theoretical linguistic model. As expected the correlations may allow creating a computer agent interacting with a human in a natural domestic or office environment and simulating certain mood or character in emotional speech interaction. As we propose, an important feature of the agent is to simulate and report it's internal emotional states thus setting up a friendly mood in communication.

Future work on the project is dedicated to the extension of psychological studies and extension of linguistic characteristics, assigned to each class of utterances. We intend: (a) to extend the created corpora of emotional utterances in Rosenzweig test for different age and professional groups of participants, linked with psychological characteristics – this allows to refine the structure for each class of utterances, as proposed by the d-script theory, and to produce accurate output in text synthesis tasks. (b) As the intonation serves as a distinctive feature for most of the classes – it is important to include it in the description; studies are based on the project "Intonation of a Russian dialogue" (Moscow State University). (c) PFT test considers situations where the dialogue is initiated by an event, in other cases it is important to detect and keep certain dialogue mood and sometimes to support a dialogue atmosphere, proposed by a speaker; as d-script model offers quite accurate means for definition of dialogue mood, the development of the corresponding classification is one of the future priorities. (d) Interjections offer a typical start for an emotional utterance but are actually omitted by participants of PFT; cooperating with project of Multimedia dictionary of interjections (RSUH) we work to equip the classes of emotional utterances in d-scripts model by typical interjections, to be produced during text synthesis.

References

1. Allen R. S. Concern Processing in Autonomous Agents. Ph. D. thesis. School of Computer Science, University of Birmingham (2001)
2. Berne, E. Games People Play: The Psychology of Human Relationships. Ballantine Books (1996)
3. Kotov, A. A. D-scripts model for speech influence and emotional dialogue simulation. In Proceedings of the 7th Annual Colloquium for the UK Special Interest Group for Computational Linguistics. University of Birmingham (2004) 134-140
4. Kotov, A. D-script model for synthesis and analysis of emotional speech : Proceedings of "Speech and Computer" SPECOM'2004, St.-Petersburg (2004) 579-585
5. Sloman, A. Beyond Shallow Models of Emotion. In Cognitive Processing, Vol. 1 (2001)
6. Sloman, A. Varieties of Affect and the CogAff Architecture Schema : C. Johnson (ed.), Proceedings Symposium on Emotion, Cognition and Affective Computing AISB'01 Convention, York, March (2001) 39-48
7. Sloman, A., Chrisley, R. Virtual Machines and Consciousness. In Journal of Consciousness Studies. Vol. 10, No. 4-5, April/May (2003) 133-172
8. Апресян В. Ю. Имплицитная агрессия в языке = Apresian U. Implicit aggression in speech. In Компьютерная лингвистика и интеллектуальные технологии: Тр. Междунар. конференции Диалог 2003. – М.: Наука (2003) 32-35

9. Гловинская М. Я. Гипербола как проявление и оправдание речевой агрессии = Glovinskaya M. Hyperbole as an expression and justification of speech aggression. In Сокровенные смыслы. Сборник статей в честь Н. Д. Арутюновой (2004) 69-76
10. Теория и практика лингвистического анализа текстов СМИ в судебных экспертизах и информационных спорах = Theory and practice of linguistic analysis of mass media texts in juridical expertises and information disputes. In Сборник материалов научно-практического семинара. Москва 7-8 декабря 2002 г. Часть 2. – М.: Галерия (2003)

A Hybrid GMM and Codebook Mapping Method for Spectral Conversion

Yongguo Kang[1], Zhiwei Shuang[2], Jianhua Tao[1], Wei Zhang[2], and Bo Xu[1]

[1] Institute of Automation, Chinese Academy of Science
[2] China Research Lab, IBM
{ygkang, jhtao}@nlpr.ia.ac.cn, {shuangzw, zhangwei}@cn.ibm.com, xubo@hitic.ia.ac.cn

Abstract. This paper proposes a new mapping method combining GMM and codebook mapping methods to transform spectral envelope for voice conversion system. After analyzing overly smoothing problem of GMM mapping method in detail, we propose to convert the basic spectral envelope by GMM method and convert envelope-subtracted spectral details by GMM and phone-tied codebook mapping method. Objective evaluations based on performance indices show that the performance of proposed mapping method averagely improves 27.2017% than GMM mapping method, and listening tests prove that the proposed method can effectively reduce over smoothing problem of GMM method while it can avoid the discontinuity problem of codebook mapping method.

1 Introduction

Starting from speech signal uttered by a speaker, voice conversion aims at transforming the characteristics of the speech signal in such a way that a human naturally perceives the target speaker's own characteristics in the transformed speech[1]. An important task in voice conversion system is to map speech features which represent the speaker individuality between source and target speech. The underlying meaning of mapping is to find the relation between two sets of multi-dimension vectors.

There are a lot of mapping methods such as codebook mapping[2] [3], Linear Multivariate Regression (LMR)[8], , Neural Networks[9][10], Gaussian Mixture Model (GMM)[4][5] and Hidden Markov Model (HMM)[11]. Among these mapping methods, codebook mapping and GMM methods are two representative and popular mapping algorithms. Motivated by the fact that the disadvantages of two methods respectively are overly smoothing and discontinuity, a method combining GMM and codebook mapping is proposed. This method tries to grasp the basic spectral envelope using GMM and retain converted spectrum details using offset codebook mapping method. By this means, the problems of smoothing and discontinuity can be counteracted.

This paper is organized as follows. Section 2 describes the conventional GMM mapping methods and then investigates the reason of GMM's overly smoothing problem. Section 3 describes the proposed hybrid method combining GMM and

J. Tao, T. Tan, and R.W. Picard (Eds.): ACII 2005, LNCS 3784, pp. 303–310, 2005.

codebook mapping to convert source spectrum. Evaluation and discussions are given in section 4 while the conclusions are drawn in section 5.

2 Analysis of GMM Mapping Algorithms

2.1 Gaussian Mixture Model

The GMM assumes the probability distribution of the observed parameters takes the following form:

$$p(x) = \sum_{i=1}^{m} \alpha_i N(x; \mu_i, \Sigma_i), \sum_{i=1}^{m} \alpha_i = 1, \alpha_i \geq 0 \tag{1}$$

where $N(x; \mu_i, \Sigma_i)$ denotes the m-dimensional normal distribution with mean vector μ and covariance matrix Σ, α_i is normalized positive scalar weight. The parameters (α, μ, Σ) can be estimated with the expectation-maximization algorithm.

The parameter of the conversion function is determined by the joint density of source and target features [5]. The combination of source and target vectors $z = [x^T y^T]^T$ is used to estimate GMM parameters (α, μ, Σ). The conversion function can be yielded using regression:

$$F(x) = \sum_{q=1}^{Q} p_q(x)[\mu_q^Y + \Sigma_q^{YX}(\Sigma_q^{XX})^{-1}(x - \mu_q^X)] \tag{2}$$

where $p_q(x)$ is the conditional probability of a GMM class q given x:

$$p_q(x) = \frac{\alpha_q N(x; \mu_q^X, \Sigma_q^X)}{\sum_{p=1}^{Q} \alpha_p N(x; \mu_p^X, \Sigma_p^X)} \tag{3}$$

$$\Sigma_q = \begin{bmatrix} \Sigma_q^{XX} & \Sigma_q^{YX} \\ \\ \Sigma_q^{XY} & \Sigma_q^{YY} \end{bmatrix}; \mu_q = \begin{bmatrix} \mu_q^X \\ \\ \mu_q^Y \end{bmatrix}$$

and Q is the number of GMM components. The performance of GMM method has been proved that it can be as good as or better than other conversion function implementations. However, the conventional GMM based conversion tends to generate overly smoothed spectrum [13][7].

2.2 Analysis of Overly Smoothing Problem

In the conventional GMM method, the transforming function includes two parts: the mean item and correlation item, as shown in Equation (4):

$$F(x) = \underbrace{\sum_{q=1}^{Q} p_q(x)\mu_q^Y}_{mean} + \underbrace{\sum_{q=1}^{Q} p_q(x) \underbrace{\Sigma_q^{YX}(\Sigma_q^{XX})^{-1}}_{covariance} \underbrace{(x - \mu_q^X)}_{offset}}_{correlation} \tag{4}$$

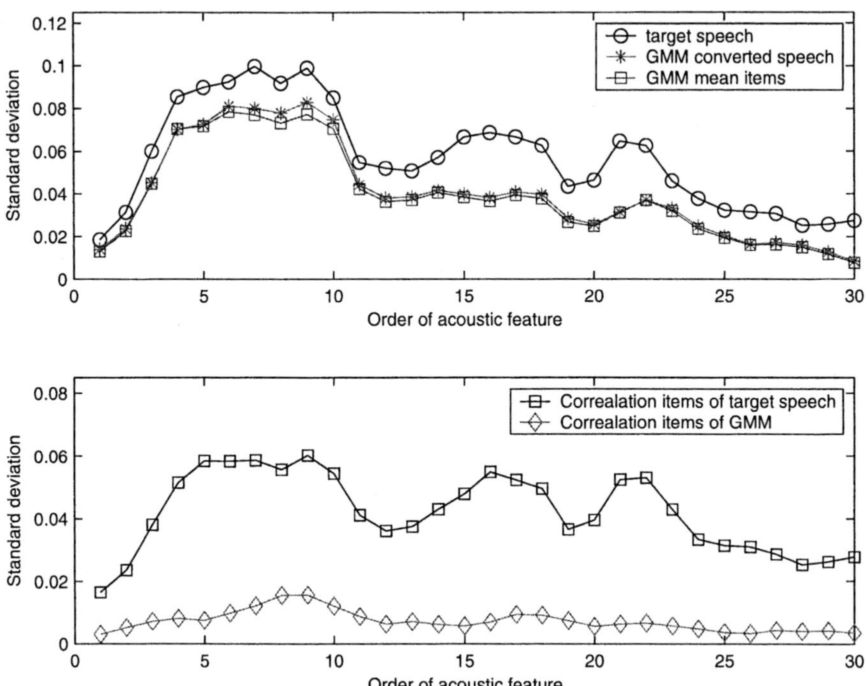

Fig. 1. The top are standard deviations of acoustic feature from target speech, GMM converted speech and hybrid method converted speech; The bottom are those from correlated items of target speech, GMM converted speech and hybrid method converted speech

It can be concluded that the mean item grasps the basic shape of converted feature while the correlation item try to convert spectral details using the offset vector $((x - \mu_q^X))$. Toda [6] has pointed that the covariance matrices between a source feature and a target feature is critical to convert speech features continuously In GMM mapping method. However, the correlation is difficult to accurately estimate in particular using full covariance matrices. Chen [7] has point out the most items in the correlation matrix is nearly zero, thus the converted features are in fact close to the first item.

In this study, standard deviation is employed to describe the smoothing level of acoustic feature. Figure 1 shows the standard deviations calculated from the following acoustic features: 1) target speech; 2) GMM converted features 3) GMM mean items; 4) correlation items of target speech, i.e. acoustic features from target speech subtracted GMM mean features; 5) GMM correlation items. It can be observed that standard deviations of GMM converted features are less than those of target speech, and the smaller standard deviations can indicate the overly smoothing problem. However, it is worth noting that the standard deviations of GMM correlation items are distinctly less than those of correlation items from target speech. Thus it can explain that in GMM methods, the basic envelope of ideally converted features is remained but the spectral details are lost.

3 A Hybrid Mapping Method

Based on the analysis of previous section, the overly smmothing problem to be solved is how to reuse the offset vector $(x - \mu_q^X)$ and rebuild the missed spectral details. We will apply this phoneme-tied codebook mapping method to convert the offset vector in order to recover the spectral details. The procedures combining GMM and Mapping codebooks are described as:

- *Training procedure:*
  1. GMM training is first carried out.
  2. Generating offset codebook entries. For each joint vectors $z = [x^T y^T]^T$, the offset code words are defined as:

$$x^{\mathrm{offset}} = \sum_{q=1}^{Q} p_q(x)(x - \mu_q^X) \tag{5}$$

$$y^{\mathrm{offset}} = \sum_{q=1}^{Q} p_q(x)(y - \mu_q^Y) \tag{6}$$

- *Converting procedure:*
  1. Converting input source vector x only using corresponding target mean vectors:

$$\hat{y}^{\mathrm{mean}} = \sum_{q=1}^{Q} p_q(x)\mu_q^Y \tag{7}$$

$$\hat{y}^{\mathrm{corr}} = \sum_{q=1}^{Q} p_q(x)\Sigma_q^{YX}(\Sigma_q^{XX})^{-1}(x - \mu_q^X) \tag{8}$$

  2. Converting offset vector using codebook mapping method with phoneme-tied weighting :

$$\hat{y}^{\mathrm{offset}} = F^{\mathrm{offset}}(x^{\mathrm{offset}}) \tag{9}$$

  where F^{offset} is the transforming function obtained by codebook mapping method, and x^{offset} is defined by equation (5);
  3. The final converted feature is:

$$\hat{y} = \hat{y}^{\mathrm{mean}} + (1 - \lambda)\hat{y}^{\mathrm{corr}} + \lambda\hat{y}^{\mathrm{offset}} \tag{10}$$

The smooth converted spectrum is added spectral details using mapping offset codebook, and the new converted spectrum is shown in Fig.2. From Fig.2, it can be observed that the converted spectrum is much closer to the target spectrum than the smooth spectrum and the over smoothing problem is avoided.

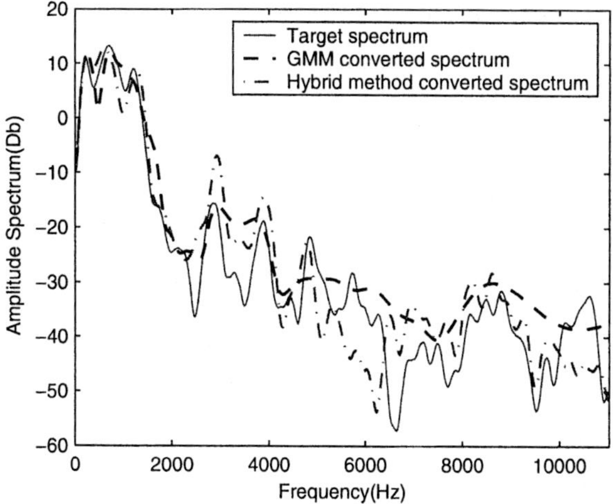

Fig. 2. The target spectrum, converted spectrum by GMM method and converted spectrum using hybrid mapping method

4 Experiment and Evaluation

4.1 Experiment

The corpus used for the experiments was recorded by two female speakers reading the same text. We use 22050 Hz's sampling rate and 16 bits per sample to store the speech data. The corpus has been segmented (manually supervised) into phonemes. There are 180 sentences which consist of 28037 vectors to train the transforming function and 12 sentences which consist of 2097 vectors to test voice conversion system.

Because STRAIGHT (Speech Transformation and Representation using Adaptive Interpolation of weighted spectral envelope) algorithm can reproduce high quality speech from its coefficients and modify duration, F0 and spectral coefficients separately in large scale with little degradation to the quality, it is employed to analyze and synthesize speech signal. In this experiment we utilize the all-pole model to fit spectral envelope obtained by STRAIGHT, and employ linear spectral pair (LSP) parameter resulted from all-pole model as the mapping feature.

The pitch contour is converted using a linear transformation. The converted pitch $\hat{f}_t$ is obtained using:

$$\hat{f}_t = \mu_t + \frac{\sigma_t}{\sigma_s}(f_s - \mu_s) \tag{11}$$

where (μ_s, σ_s) and (μ_t, σ_t) are the mean and variance of source and target pitch contours respectively.

4.2 Objective Evaluation

The objective evaluation of mapping algorithms is based on spectral distance rather than acoustic feature distance. The spectral distance is measured using Kullback-Leibler (KL) distance:

$$D_{kl}(X,Y) = \int X(\omega)\log(\frac{X(\omega)}{Y(\omega)})d\omega \tag{12}$$

where $X(\omega)$ and $Y(\omega)$ are two spectral envelopes to be measured. Because the KL distance has the important property that it emphasizes differences in spectral regions with high energy more than differences in spectral regions with low energy, spectral peaks are emphasized more than valleys between the peaks and low frequencies are emphasized more than high frequencies [14].

To compare the performance of voice conversion system, the performance indices[5] is used in objective evaluation on converted spectral envelope, which is defined as:

$$P_{sd} = 1 - \frac{D_{sd(t(n),\hat{t}(n))}}{D_{sd(t(n),s(n))}} \tag{13}$$

Where $D_{sd(t(n),\hat{t}(n))}$ is the spectral distance between target speech and converted speech while $D_{sd(t(n),s(n))}$ is the spectral distance between target and source speech. It is noted that the objective evaluation is performed on spectral envelope rather than spectral feature.

As shown in equation (10), the λ value adjusts the proportion between GMM method and codebook mapping method in final converted offset vector. The proposed method is traditional GMM method when $\lambda = 0$, while the offset vector is entirely converted by codebook mapping method when $\lambda = 1$.

The results with various λ using different training method are shown in Fig.3. From these figures, it is noted that the performance initially improves with the

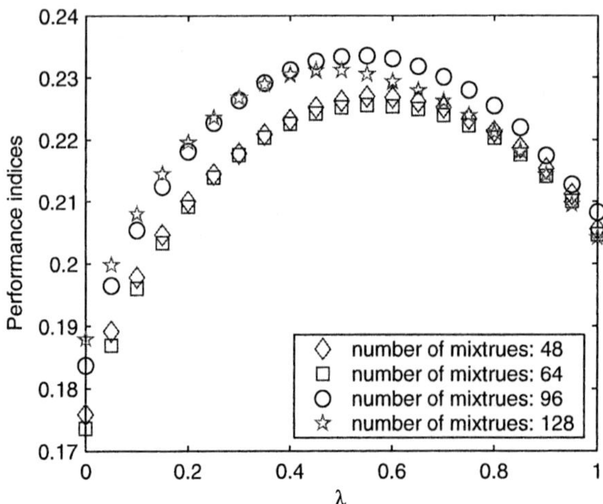

Fig. 3. Spectral distance with different λ using training method1

increase of λ, but then degrades after an optimal λ value, which is about 0.5. As well-known facts, the converted offset vector by GMM is overly smoothing while the results from codebook mapping method have so much spectral details that the converted spectrum is discontinuous. This evaluation indicates that the smoothing problem and the discontinuous problem can be properly counteracted with an optimal λ . The hybrid method with the optimal λ averagely improves 27.2017% than GMM mapping method.

5 Conclusion

In this paper, we propose a new voice conversion method combining the Gaussian Mixture Model (GMM) and codebook mapping method with phoneme-tied weighting. When transforming spectral features, the basic spectral envelopes are converted by GMM method and the envelope-subtracted spectral details are transformed by phone-tied codebook mapping method and GMM method. Evaluations are performed on speech quality and speaker individuality. All experiments shows that the converted speech using the proposed method both reduce the over smoothing problem of GMM method and avoid the discontinuity problem in spectrum of codebook mapping method.

Acknowledgements

This work is fulfilled as an intern in China Research Lab of IBM. I especially thank Liqin Shen for her giving the opportunity to study in CRL, and I am very grateful for studying together with IBM colleagues: Xijun Ma, Yi Liu, Qin Shi, Haiping Li, Yong Qin and Weibin Zhu.

References

1. Moulines. E and Sagisaka.Y, .Voice conversion: State of the art and perspectives,. Speech Communication, vol. 16, no. 2, pp. 125-126, Feb 1995.
2. L. M. Arslan and D. Talkin, .Voice Conversion by Codebook Mapping of Line Spectral Frequencies and Excitation Spectrum, in Proc: of the Eurospeech'97, Rhodes, Greece, 1997.
3. Zhi-Wei Shuang, Zi-Xiang Wang, Zhen-Hua Ling, and Ren-Hua Wang, .A novel voice conversion system based on codebook mapping with phoneme-tied weighting,. In Proc. ICSLP, Jeju, Oct. 2004.
4. Y. Stylianou and et al, .Continuous probabilistic transform for voice conversion,. IEEE Transactions on Speech and Audio Processing, vol. 6, no. 2, pp. 131.142, March 1998.
5. Alexander Blouke Kain, High Resolution Voice Transformation, Ph.D. thesis, Oregon Health and Science University, October 2001.
6. T. Toda, H. Saruwatari, and K. Shikano, .Voice conversion algorithm based on gaussian mixture model with dynamic frequency warping of straight spectrum,. In Proc. Of ICASSP, 2001, pp. 841.944.

7. Yining Chen, Min Chu, and et al, .Voice conversion with smoothed gmm and map adaptation,. in Proc. Eurospeech, Geneva, Switzerland, Sept. 2003, pp. 2413-2416.
8. H Valbret, et al. Voice transformation using PSOLA technique [J]. Speech Communication. 1992, 11(2-3): 175-187.
9. M Narendranath, et al. Transformation of formants for voice conversion using artificial neural networks [J]. Speech Communi- cation. 1995, 16(2): 207-216.
10. T Watanabe, et al. Transformation of Spectral Envelope for Voice Conversion Based on Radial Basis Function Networks . Proc. ICSLP'2002 [C]. Denver, USA. Sept. 2002: 285-288.
11. E K Kim, et al. Hidden Markov Model Based Voice Conversion Using Dynamic Characteristics of Speaker [A]. Proc. Eurospeech [C]. Rhodes, Greece, 1997: 2519-2522.
12. M. Abe, S. Nakamura, K. Shikano, and H. Kuwabara. Voice conversion through vector quantization. J. Acoust. Soc. Jpn. (E), Vol. 11, No. 2, pp.7176, 1990.
13. T. Toda, Alan W Black, Keiichi Tokuda. Spectral conversion based on maximum likelihood estimation considering global variance of converted parameter, In Proc. Of ICASSP, 2005.
14. Esther Klabbers, Raymond Veldhuis. Reducing Audible Spectral Discontinuities, IEEE TRANSACTIONS ON SPEECH AND AUDIO PROCESSING, VOL. 9, NO. 1, pp 39-51, JANUARY 2001.

Speech Emotional Recognition Using Global and Time Sequence Structure Features with MMD

Li Zhao[1,2], Yujia Cao[1,2], Zhiping Wang[2], and Cairong Zou[2]

[1] Research Center of Learning Science, Southeast University, Nanjing, 210096, China
[2] Department of Radio Engineering, Southeast University, Nanjing, 210096, China
zhaoli@seu.edu.cn

Abstract. In this paper, combined features of global and time-sequence were used as the characteristic parameters for speech emotional recognition. A new method based on formula of MMD (Modified Mahalanobis Distance) was proposed to decrease the estimated errors and simplify the calculation. Four emotions including happiness, anger, surprise and sadness are considered in the paper. 1000 recognizing sentences collected from 10 speakers were used to demonstrate the effectiveness of the new method. The average emotion recognition rate reached at 95%. Comparison with method of MQDF [1] (Modified quadratic discriminant function), Data analysis also displayed that the MMD is better than MQDF.

1 Introduction

Speech emotion recognition is one of the important parts in emotion processing. The research of the speech emotion can be applied in great many fields, such as Virtual Reality and military affairs. Emotions can be recognized by speech prosody when all word meanings are filtered out [3, 4, 5, and 6]. In addition, many methods are being developed. The multivariable regression and principle component analysis methods have already achieved an average recognition rate above 87.1% [10], while neural net cannot achieve a satisfied result due to the problem of constringency [9]. The global characteristics, which make the whole sentence as a unit, have once been utilized in our research, and the result was good [7]. However, the structure features of time-sequence, which reflects the dynamic characteristics of the emotional change, also have great influences on the recognition of speech emotion. But now, little research focuses on the time sequence, key words and phrases [8]. In this paper, a new emotion recognition method MMD (modified Mahalanobis Distance) based on the combined features of global and time-sequence such as the time, amplitude, pitch and formant construction were presented. And the MQDF [1] method was introduced to compare with MMD. The speech signals, which represent the emotion of happiness, anger, surprise and sadness, have been compared with the neutral speech to find the different emotion

J. Tao, T. Tan, and R.W. Picard (Eds.): ACII 2005, LNCS 3784, pp. 311–318, 2005.

features' distribution. The result showed that the new method has recognition rate of 95% among 1000 recognizing sentences collected from 10 speakers. The data analysis also showed that MMD is better than MQDF.

2 Data Collection

Two aspects were taken into account during selecting speech materials in this paper. Firstly, the sentences don't have any emotional tendency; secondly, the sentences can involve all kinds of emotions for analysis and comparison. In addition, the length of the sentence, the construction of consonants, auxiliary words structure and sexual difference were also been taken into consideration. Here, 60 sentences were selected as the speech materials [11]. Neutral, happiness, anger, surprise, and sadness were involved. 10 (males) healthy students (age 20 to 35) were selected in the experiments. The speech signals sampled at a rate of 12KHZ with 16-bit. 3000 sentences (10 speakers×5 emotions×60 sentences) were collected. The data's validity was tested before the experiments, all materials were played randomly, and five listeners (none of the speakers) decided the type of emotions involved in each sentence by their perception subjectively. After repeated comparison and tested by Mcnemar analytical rule [12], the materials, which were ambiguous in emotion, were discarded and they were recorded again until the materials met the need. Among 3000 sentences, 2000 sentences were used for training and 1000 ones were used for test.

3 The Analysis and Extraction of Emotional Characteristics

The global features used in this paper include the ratio of duration, changing rate of F_0 (pitch), and F_1 (the first formant), the difference of average amplitude power, mean pitch, maximum pitch, average frequency of the first formant, dynamic range of F_1 and amplitude power between the speech. And the time-sequence features were extracted from the part of pitch in the whole sentence. In MMD the pitch was divided into M parts according to the time and then selected the mean, maximum value and dynamic range of pitch, amplitude power and the frequency of F_1 in each part as the characteristics of time series. While in MQDF, the division is not needed.

3.1 Time

Two parameters were analyzed in time construction: duration of emotional sentence T and the average rate of speaking (syllable/s). T included the parts of silence because these parts contribute to the emotion. An analytic result is shown in figure (1).

3.2 Amplitude

The amplitude of signals closely relates with all kinds of emotional information [8]. Here, the average amplitude energy (A) and the dynamic range (A_{range}) were analyzed. The result is shown in figure (2).

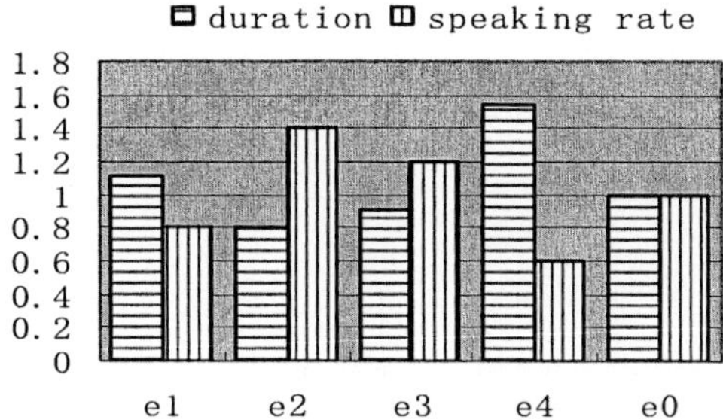

Each word in figure (1) means:

e1 happiness

e2 anger

e3 surprise

e4 sadness

e0 neutral speech

Fig. 1. Time construction

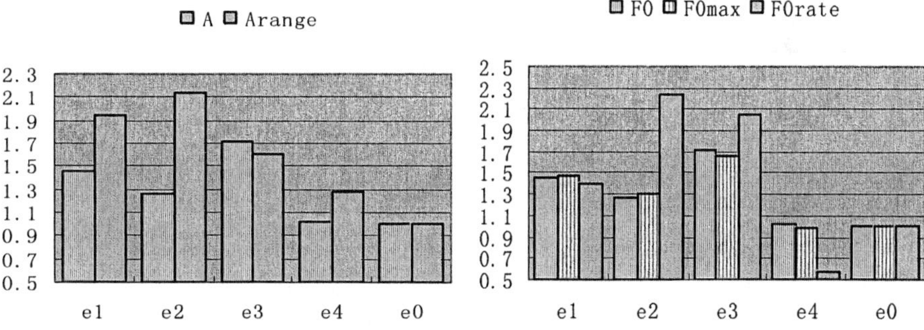

Fig. 2. Amplitude construction

Fig. 3. Pitch construction

3.3 Pitch

The pitch is also an important feature that reflects emotional information [8]. The analyzing characteristics include the average pitch, maximum pitch and the changing rate (F_0, F_{0max}, F_{0rate}) of different emotional speech signals. Here F_{0rate} referred to the mean absolute value of the difference of pitch in each speech signal's frame. Analytic result is shown in figure (3). In addition, because the envelope curve of surprising speech signals is inclined to rise at the end of the sentence, we can distinguish surprise from other emotions.

3.4 Formant

The formant is an important parameter reflecting the features of track, so we researched the parameters of average, dynamic range and changing rate (F_1, F_{1range}, F_{1rate}) of the first formant in our paper. The analytic result is presented in figure (4).

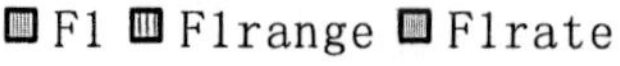

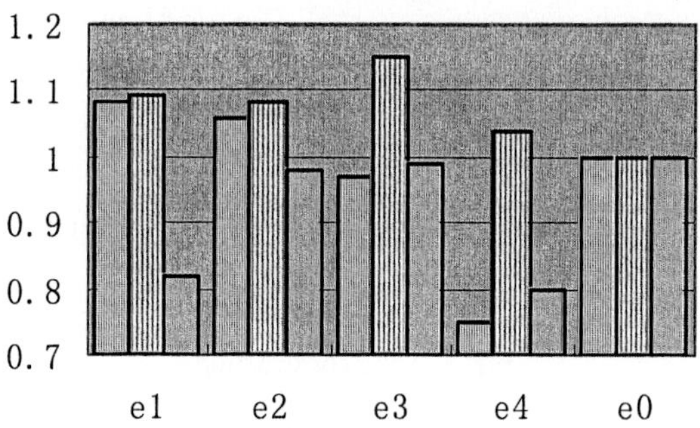

Fig. 4. Formant construction

3.5 Conclusion

According to the above discussion, we got Tab 1 as follow:

Table 1. The variability of the parameters in emotional speech

	T	F_0	$F_{0\ max}$	$F_{0\ rate}$	A	A_{range}	F_1	$F_{1\ range}$	$F_{1\ rate}$
Happiness	+	+	+	+	+	++	+	+	_
Anger	_	+	+	++	+	++	+	+	_
Surprise	_	++	++	++	++	++	_	+	_
Sadness	++	-	-	__	-	+	__	+	__

(+: increase, ++: increase more, _: decrease, _ _: decrease more, -: no change)

4 Method of Recognition

In this part, MMD is presented in detail firstly, and then MQDF [1] is introduced simply to compare with MMD.

4.1 MMD

The original formula of Mahalanobis Distance is shown in formula (1).

$$d^2(X) = (X - \mu)^t \Sigma^{-1} (X - \mu) \tag{1}$$

Where $X(x_1, x_2, \cdots, x_p)$ is a P-dimension original characteristic vector, μ is mean vector of training samples, Σ is the covariance matrix of the training samples. It is known that the necessary multiplication times of calculating Σ are $p^2 + p$. So the complexity of calculation, EMS memory capacity and the estimation errors of Σ will increase with the increasing of the dimensions of X. Then the recognition percent will decrease. To avoid the above problems, we modified the formula (1). Suppose λ_k is the i th eigenvalue of Σ, ϕ_k is the eigenvector corresponding to λ_k, then we have

$$\Sigma = \sum_{i=1}^{p} \lambda_i \cdot \vec{\phi}_i \cdot \vec{\phi}_i^{\,t} \tag{2}$$

Based on formula (1) and (2), formula (3) could be got.

$$d^2(X) = \sum_{k=1}^{P} \frac{1}{\lambda_k + b} (X - \mu, \phi_k)^2 \tag{3}$$

In order to reduce the effect of the estimated error of eigenvalues on recognizing rate, the offset b was introduced and its value was chosen based on the experimental result. However, because of the application of combined features, the dimension of features space was very big. Moreover, the training data were small relatively, so formula (3) can't simplify calculation to the full extent and raise the recognizing rate. We modified the formula (3) supposing that the covariance matrix of normal Mahalanobis Distance could be segmented as the following form (shown in formula (4)).

$$\Sigma = \begin{bmatrix} \Sigma_1 \cdots\cdots\cdots\cdots 0 \\ \Sigma_2 \cdot\cdot \\ \cdot \\ 0 \cdots\cdots\cdots\cdots \Sigma_M \end{bmatrix} \tag{4}$$

Where $\Sigma_1, \Sigma_2 ... \Sigma_M$ is the phalanx of $k \times k$ ($K \times M = P$) . Then the normal *M*ahalanobis *Di*stance had the following form (shown in formula (5)).

$$d^2(X) = (X-\mu)^t \Sigma^{-1} (X-\mu) = \sum_{i=1}^{M} (X_i - \mu_i)^t \Sigma_i^{-1} (X_i - \mu_i) = \sum_{i=1}^{M} \sum_{k=1}^{K} \frac{1}{\lambda_{ik} + b} (X_i - \mu_i, \phi_{ik})^2 \tag{5}$$

Where X_i and μ_i are k-dimension vectors and composed by the data from $K_{i-1}+1$ to K_i of vector X and μ respectively. λ_{ik} is the kth eigenvalue of Σ_i, ϕ_{ik} is the eigenvector corresponding to the λ_{ik}. Obviously, the multiplication of formula (5) ($O(K^2 M) = O(PK)$) is the $1/M$ times to that of formula (1). Moreover, because the P -dimension vector is segmented to M k-dimension vectors, the ratio of dimension and learning data increase M times for the same amount of learning data when we calculate the covariance matrix of $k \times k$, and the reliability of calculating covariance matrix is more high.

4.2 MQDF

The discriminant criterion based on QDF (quadratic discriminant function) is given as follows:

$$P(\vec{X} \mid k) = \tfrac{1}{2}\ln|\Sigma_k| + \tfrac{1}{2}\left[(\vec{X} - \vec{\mu}_k)^t \Sigma_k^{-1} (\vec{X} - \vec{\mu}_k)\right] - \ln p(k) \tag{6}$$

Introduced (2) into (6), we got the modified criterion which is defined as formula (7)

$$P(\vec{X} \mid k) = \sum_{i=1}^{p} 1/\lambda_{ik} \left[\vec{\phi}_{ik}{}^t (\vec{X} - \vec{\mu}_k)\right]^2 + \ln \prod_{i=1}^{p} \lambda_{ik} - 2\ln p(k) \tag{7}$$

Because the estimative errors of eigenvalues and eigenvectors for high-order Σ were higher than them of low-order Σ, a constant $N_0\sigma^2/(N+N_0)$ was used to replace each eigenvalue in $(\lambda_{m+1}, \lambda_{m+2}, \cdots, \lambda_p)$ which exceeds the threshold of m. Where N represents the total numbers of learning samples, N_0 is a constant, σ^2 is a value which has relation with the eigenvalues. If $N_0/(N+N_0) = \alpha$ $(0 < \alpha < 1)$, $\alpha\sigma^2 = V^2$, introduced the formula (8) into (7),

$$\sum_{i=1}^{p} \left[\vec{\phi}_{ik} (\vec{X} - \vec{\mu}_k)^t\right]^2 = \| \vec{X} - \vec{\mu}_k \|^2 \tag{8}$$

We got the final calculation formula (9) of MQDF

$$P(\vec{X} \mid k) = \frac{1}{V^2}\left[\| \vec{X} - \vec{\mu}_k \|^2 - \sum_{i=1}^{m} \frac{V^2 - \lambda_{ik}}{\lambda_{ik}} \left(\vec{\phi}_{ik}{}^t (\vec{X} - \vec{\mu}_k)\right)^2\right] + \ln\left(V^{2(p-m)} \prod_{i=1}^{m} \lambda_{ik}\right) - 2\ln P(k) \tag{9}$$

5 Results

1000 sentences have been used to the experiment. Let b as 1.3, let M as 4, 6, 8, 10 respectively, and the difference of results was compared. The result is listed in Tab 2.

From Tab 2, it can be see that the recognition result is not always being improved with the raising of *M*. Because of the increase of *M* in each fixed length sentence, the

Table 2. Recognition Result (%)

Emotion \ *M*	4	6	8	10
Happiness	89	90	94	91
Anger	91	92	95	92
Surprise	87	88	92	90
Sadness	98	100	100	98
Average	91	93	95	93

amount of data in each part will decrease. Consequently, the analyzing precision will decrease and all these will have influence on the recognition results. So the choice of *M* should be appropriate.

The following list the compared results performed by four methods. In method 1, the global characteristics and MD (Mahalanobis Distance (shown in formula 1)) were used. In method 2, the combined features of global and time-sequence and MD (*M* is 8) were applied. While in method 3, besides the combined features, the MMD presented in this paper was involved to recognize the emotional speech (*M* is 8). And in method 4, the combined features and MQDF were used. The compared results were shown in Tab 3:

Table 3. Recognition Rates [%]

Emotion	Method 1	Method 2	Method 3	Method 4
Happiness	84	82	94	92
Anger	85	83	95	94
Surprise	83	79	92	87
Sadness	95	92	100	100
Average	87	84	95	93

From the Tab 3, it could be seen that the method 3 is excelled to the method 1, 2 and 4. Moreover, the recognizing rate of sadness is higher than any other methods, while the recognizing rate of surprise is lowest among four emotions. And the table also shows that the difference of combined features between the sadness and other emotions (happiness, anger, surprise) is bigger expect for surprise.

6 Conclusion

To find out the distributing rules of different emotional signals, the emotional recognizing method based on the MMD is presented in this paper. The speech signals comprise of four emotions: happiness, anger, surprise and sadness. And MQDF is introduced to compare with MMD. The simulation with 1000 emotional speech sentences was done by MATLAB. We got the result which is closed to the usual behaviors of human. But there is still some work need to do to improve the recognition rate. The more efficient parameters and other modified method will be investigated further.

Acknowledgments

The paper has got the financial support of Education Revitalization Program Oriented to the 21st Century under the Chinese Ministry of Education.

References

[1] *Lili Cai, Chunhui Jiang, Zhiping Wang, Li Zhao, Cairong Zou*, "A Method Combining The Global And Time Series Structure Features For Emotion Recognition In Speech", IEEE Int. Conf. Neural Networks & Signal Processing, 2003.

[2] *Akemi Iida, Nick Campbell, Soichiro Iga, Fumito Higuchi, Michiaki Yasumura*, "Acoustic Nature and perceptual testing of corpora of emotional speech."

[3] *Banse, R. & Scherer, K. R.*, "Acoustic profiles in vocal emotion expression," Journal of Personality and Social Psychology, 70(3), 1996.

[4] *Mozziconacci. S.*, "Speech Variability and Emotion: Production and Perception." Eindhoven, Netherlands, Technische Universiteit Eindhoven, 1998.

[5] *Scherer, K. R.*, "Speech and Emotional States." In Darby, J. K. (Ed.) Speech Evaluation in Psychiatry. New York, Grune and Stratton, 1981.

[6] *Soskin W. F. & Kauffman, P. E.*, "Judgements of Emotions in Word-free Voice Samples." Journal of Communication, 1961.

[7] *Zhao Li, Qian Xiangmin, Zou Cairong, Wu Zhenyang,* "A Study on Emotional Recognition in Speech Signal," Journal of Software, Vol.12, No.7 2001.7.

[8] *Cowie.R.* "Emotion Recognition in Human-Computer Interaction," IEEE Signal Processing Magazine, 18(1): 32-80, 2001.

[9] *S.Muraka,* "Emotional Constituents in Text and Emotional Components in Speech,"[Ph. D. Theis] Kyoto, Kyoto Institute of Technology, Japan, 1998.

[10] *M.Shigenaga,* "Features of Emotionally Uttered Speech Revealed by Discriminant Analysis (VI)," The preprint of the acoustical society of Japan, 2-p-18 1999.9.

[11] *Zhao Li, Qian Xiangmin, Zou cairong, Wu Zhenyang,* "A Study on Emotional Feature Analysis and Recognition in Speech Signal," Journal of China Institute of Communications, Vol.21, No.1, pp18-25 2000.

[12] *Zhao Li, Qian Xiangmin, Zou cairong, Wu Zhenyang,* "A Study on Emotional Feature Extract in Speech signal," Data Collection and Process, Vol.15, No.1, pp120-123 (2000).

Emotional Metaphors for Emotion Recognition in Chinese Text

Xiaoxi Huang[1], Yun Yang[2], and Changle Zhou[1,2]

[1] College of Computer Science, Zhejiang University, 310027, P.R. China
itshere@zju.edu.cn
[2] Institute of Artificial Intelligence, Xiamen University, 361005, P.R. China
onenaomi@163.com, dozero@xmu.edu.cn

Abstract. The affections of a person can be expressed by non-verbal methods such as facial expressions, gestures, postures and expressions from eyes. While implicit language like emotional metaphor is also an important way to express one's affections. Different kinds of emotional metaphors in Chinese and their characteristics are proposed, including happiness, sadness, anger, fear and surprise. Experiment result shows the characteristics of Chinese emotional metaphors are reasonable. The importance of emotional metaphors in emotion recognition is also discussed.

1 Introduction

The latest scientific findings have indicated that emotions lead an important role in human intelligence, such as decision-making, inter-communication and more. As Marvin Minsky said in his "the society of mind"[1], "The question is not whether intelligent machines can have any emotions, but whether machines can be intelligent without any emotions", if we want computers to be vividly intelligent and to interact with us more naturally and socially, we should let the computers have the abilities to recognize, understand, and even to express emotions[2].

To date, much of the work studying affective computing has concentrated on facial expressions, gestures, postures, and properties of speech. Although much emotional expression is conveyed in physiological features or speech's acoustic realizations, it is equally important to trace into how it is conveyed in the linguistic content[3]. In written language, the interpretation of emotional states is more complex. It can be referred to directly, for instance, "I am angry", but usually it is not explicit and the reader or hearer must infer it. The cues for inferring it can come from grammatical structures, vocabulary forms and verbal inflections, etc. Metaphor is useful for abstract concepts, and the function of a metaphor is to express, clarify or explain some concept through a better understood, and generally concrete, concept. For example, in metaphor "Time is money", the concept "time" is an abstract concept, while "money" is a concrete concept. Since emotions are abstract concepts, it is natural that metaphor is an effective method for expressing emotion. In fact, one of the major functions of metaphor is to express emotion[4, 5]. Through metaphor, an emotion can be related to some other concept, which tends to make it more concrete.

J. Tao, T. Tan, and R.W. Picard (Eds.): ACII 2005, LNCS 3784, pp. 319 – 325, 2005.

In this paper, the different emotional metaphors and the characteristics of Chinese emotional metaphor are discussed. We think that emotional metaphor plays an important role in emotion recognition for text. Taking emotional metaphor into account will make up the insufficiency of merely focusing on emotion keywords.

The rest of the paper is organized as follows: Section 2 describes some backgrounds about metaphors and emotional metaphor. Section 3 discusses the different kinds of emotional metaphor according to the source domain. And then, the characteristics of five primary emotions of happiness, sadness, anger, fear and surprise are proposed in section 4. Related works are introduced in section 5. At last, the conclusions and future work are given in section 6.

2 Metaphors and Emotional Metaphor

The study for metaphor can trace back to the era of Aristotle. Since then, the traditional view to metaphor is that metaphorical language is decorative and secondary, while literal language is the primary. However, along with the development of metaphor research, researchers have realized that metaphor is prevalent in natural language, and is the center of language and human thinking[6]. Lakoff and Johnson proposed that metaphor is a means of understanding one domain of experience, called the source domain, in terms of the conceptual structure of another domain, called the target domain. Their study indicates that the cognitive system of human itself is a metaphorical system. Metaphor is not merely decoration of language, but also an important method of human thinking and cognition[6].

Many linguists have researched about emotional metaphor in English. The results indicate that the emotions of human are generally expressed through metaphors about body perceptions in a way[6-8]. Some researchers have compared the emotional metaphors between Chinese and English[7, 8]. Yu Ning[8] discussed the metaphorical expressions about Chinese emotional concept "愤怒"(anger) and "喜悦"(happy). He demonstrates that the metaphorical schemas of emotions in Chinese is the same to those in English, which are "ANGER IS HEAT" and "HAPPY IS UP". There are two derived conceptual metaphor for this schema, namely, "anger is fire" and "anger is a hot fluid/gas in a container". Here, based on the research result on emotional metaphors from linguists, through analyzing different kind of emotional metaphors, we divide emotional metaphors into following kinds in section 3.

3 Kinds of Emotional Metaphor

In this section, we will discuss 3 types of emotional metaphors, namely, orientational metaphors, body metaphors and nature metaphors. The main standard is the source domain of emotional metaphors.

3.1 Orientational Metaphors

In Lakoff's conceptual metaphor theory, emotions are generally understood in terms of orientational metaphors, such as "HAPPY IS UP", "SAD IS DOWN". From these root metaphors, we can derive many emotional metaphors as follows.

(1) 他 今天 情绪 看起来 很高/低落.
He seems in high/low spirits today.
(2) 老师 高度 评价 了 他的 成果.
The teacher remarked highly of his achievements.
(3) 战士们 士气 高昂/低落.
The soldiers were elated/downcast.
(4) 别 看低 他 的 本领.
Don't look down upon him.

Example (1)-(3) uses the orientational concept "high" ("low") to express one's emotion about happiness (sadness). In (4), the orientational concept "down" is used to express the agent's scorn emotion.

3.2 Body Metaphors

Emotions are generally expressed through the physiological state of human body[6, 9]. Researchers have investigated different languages such as Chinese and English, and have found that many emotional metaphors are in forms of mapping the physiological changes into the emotion domain[6, 7, 10]. In section 1, we have introduced that most of existing emotion recognition methods are through facial expressions, gestures, postures and physiological features. When it comes to written language, it is also a good approach to recognize emotions through the words which describing the physiological features of the agent. In body metaphors, the states of eyebrows, facial colors, hairs and hearts are usually used to express different emotions.

3.2.1 Eyes and Brows

In Chinese, there are many methods to express emotions through eyes and brows. We can find these phenomena from many Chinese idioms. For instance, "眉飞色舞"(brows flying and eyes dancing), "喜上眉梢"(joys on the brows), "舒眉展眼"(be all smiles) and "眉开眼笑"(brows expanding and eyes smiling) all express the happy feelings; both "愁眉苦脸" and "眉头紧锁" mean sadness; "横眉" and "皱眉" mean anger and worry respectively.

3.2.2 Facial Colors

Facial color is an effective source feature reflecting agent's emotion. In written language, using facial colors to describe emotion is ubiquitous. For examples, "脸色苍白"(pale or white) in Chinese is generally used to express "fear" or "fright"; "红晕"(flush) is used for "shame" or "embarrassment"; "急红了脸"(red with anger) and "面红耳赤"(be flushed) mean "anger". Sometimes, red is also used to express "happy", such as "红光满面"(in ruddy health).

3.2.3 Heart

Heart also plays an important role in expressing human emotion, especially in written text, when characterizing people's mental activities. We may use "心碎"(heart broken) and "心如刀割"(to feel as if a knife were piercing one's heart) to express the extremity of sadness or depression, heartbroken,"心花怒放"(a flower blossoms in the heart) and

"心旷神怡"(relaxed and happy, cool) are generally used to convey the happiness, While "心惊肉跳" and "心惊胆战" are used to express fear, which means that the heart is shaking with fear.

3.2.4 Behaviors

Ordinarily, emotions can also be expressed through behaviors. If someone is dancing and skipping with joy, then he may be happy. If someone is grinding one's teeth, he may be angry. "hair stands on end" means fear, and that "weeping" means sadness.

(5) 孩子们 拿到 礼物 后, 都 欢蹦乱跳 起来.

The children were dancing and skipping with joy, after they got their presents.

(6) 听了 这个 故事, 大家 都 觉得 毛骨悚然.

When having heard the story, we all felt hair stands on end.

(7) 得知 这个 消息 后, 她 低下了头 默默 流泪.

When heard of the message, she crouched and wept.

(8) 遇到 不人道 的 事情, 大家 都 咬牙切齿.

We all gnash for inhumanity.

3.3 Nature Metaphors

The nature is the closest thing human can feel directly. In traditional culture of China, "red" is one of the symbols for happy events such as weddings, festivals etc., and "black" is used to express sadness such as bereavements. In English, "blue" represents sadness, but "gray" is used in Chinese for sadness, such as (9).

(9) 今天的心情就像这天空一样, 是灰色的.

The feeling is gray, like the color of today's sky.

Goatly[4] has pointed out that most of the language for emotion or emotional states come from the words for weather or weather changes.

(10) 她脸上带着灿烂的笑容.

There are sunny smiles on her face.

(11) 刚才还是晴空万里, 现在就变为乌云密布, 女人的心真难琢磨.

Sun shining a moment ago has turned heavily cloudy, it's so hard to tell women's mood.

(12) 老板突然来了一个晴天霹雳, 大家都沉默了.

Suddenly, the boss got thunderstorm and we all kept silent.

(13) 她对我大发雷霆.

She blew up at me.

In (10), the term "sunny" which comes from weather domain is used as a modifier for smile, to express the happiness of the subject. In (11) to (13), "乌云密布"(cloudy), "晴天霹雳"(a lightning bolt) and "雷霆"(thunder) all represent anger.

In Lakoff's conceptual metaphor theory, "ANGER IS FIRE" is a famous conceptual metaphor. In Chinese, anger is usually described as gas[8]. For examples,

(14) 他在发脾气

He is losing control of himself.

(15) 别惹他发火

Don't make him get angry.

4 Characteristics of Chinese Emotional Metaphor

In this section, we summarize the characteristics of Chinese emotional metaphor, based on section 3. We only consider the five primary emotions of happiness, sadness, anger, fear and surprise. The result is in table 1. The left column represents emotions, and the top row represents source domains of emotional metaphors. The cell contents are the features of source domains used to describe emotions.

Table 1. Characteristics of Chinese emotional metaphor for 5 primary emotions

Emotion	Orien-tation	Body				Nature	
		Eyebrow	Facial color	Heart	Behavior	Color	Weather
Happy	Up High	Open Free	Flush, Red	Open	Dancing Singing Flying Jumping Smiling	Red	Sunny Spring Warm
Sad	Down Low	Tighten Lour	Cyan White	Broken Pain	Crouch, Weeping	Black White Gray	Rainy Cloudy Autumn Dark
Angry	Up	Frown, Glare	Red		Gnash Fist Stomp Long-face	Red	Fire Storm Thunder Summer
Fear		Close	Pale White	Shake Tighten	Shiver Breathe-hurry	White	Thunder Light Cold
Surprise		Stare			Gapemout-hed		

To verify the characteristics summarized above, we collect 100 Chinese emotional metaphors from a large corpus. According to the characteristics in table 1, the distribution of emotions in this collection is 25% for happiness, 25% for sadness, 25% for anger, 15% for fear, and 10% for surprise. 30 subjects who are undergraduate students from Xiamen University are given the forms. Every form consists of a sentence of Chinese emotional metaphors; the subjects should select one and only one of the primary emotions or other for the sentence. 24 out of the 30 subjects returned them. Then we calculate the values of a sentence as a particular emotion with the following formula:

$$v(i,k) = \frac{num(i,k)}{S} \tag{1}$$

Where, $v(i,k)$ means the value of sentence i as emotion k (that is happiness, sadness, anger, fear or surprise), $num(i,k)$ is the total number of subjects that vote sentence i to emotion k. S is the number of subjects, here S=24. Obviously, v is range from 0 to 1.

According to the characteristics described in table 1, if sentence i expresses emotion k is denoted as $u(i,k)=1$, otherwise, $u(i,k)=0$. The correlation r_k between v and u for emotion k is decided by the Pearson's correlation as follow.

$$r_k = \frac{\sum_i v(i,k)u(i,k) - \frac{\sum_i v(i,k)\sum_i u(i,k)}{N}}{\sqrt{(\sum_i v(i,k)v(i,k) - \frac{(\sum_i v(i,k))^2}{N})(\sum_i u(i,k)u(i,k) - \frac{(\sum_i u(i,k))^2}{N})}} \tag{2}$$

Where, N is the number of emotional metaphor in the collection, here N=100. The resulting correlations are showed in table 2.

Table 2. The correlation values for emotions between decided by subjects and that by characteristics in table 1

Emotion	happiness	sadness	anger	fear	surprise
Correlation value	0.984007	0.869635	0.939065	0.951250	0.833278

The correlation values show that the characteristics in table 1 are reasonable for Chinese emotional metaphor.

5 Related Work

According to phrasal conventions of Chinese and the conclusions from linguists, Xu & Tao[11] proposed an emotion system of Chinese, including love, disgust, happiness, anger, sadness, fear and desire. Based on semantic annotation on adjective and verb dictionary, they further categorized the emotion system into mental experience based emotions and expressive force based emotions. The dictionary-based method of Xu & Tao gives a good reference for emotion classification, but they haven't thought of the importance and prevalence of metaphors. We think that emotion is context sensitive, and metaphor is related greatly with cultures and background knowledge. Thus, the dictionary-based method combined with metaphorical knowledge may give a more effective support for emotion classification and recognition.

6 Conclusions and Future Work

Emotion recognition from text is an important part of affective computing. In this paper, the prevalence of metaphors and emotional metaphors are discussed, and different kinds of emotional metaphors in Chinese and their characteristics are proposed. Experiment shows that the characteristics described in this paper are reasonable for Chinese emotional metaphor.

Metaphor is pervasive in natural language, and emotional metaphor is an effective method to express emotions. To construct efficient and lifelike affective computing system, especially Text To Speech (TTS) system, it is important to process emotional metaphor. In the future work, we will propose a computational model for metaphorical mechanism. And the further relation between characteristics of emotional metaphors and the emotional keywords also need to be further investigated.

Acknowledgements

This work is supported partly by the National Natural Science Foundation of China (no. 60373080).

References

1. Minsky, M.: The society of mind. New York: Simon and Schuster(1985)
2. Picard, R.: Affective Computing. Cambridge: MIT Press(1997)
3. Ying, Y., Zhou, F. and Zhou. C.L.: A Research on Emotion Tagging of Chinese Understanding by Designing an Experiment System. Journal of Chinese Information Processing(2002). 16(2): p. 27-33
4. Goatly, A.: The Language of Metaphors. London: Routledge(1997)
5. MacCormac, E.R.: A Cognitive Theory of Metaphor. London: MIT Press(1990)
6. Lakoff, G. and M. Johnson: Metaphors We Live By. Chicago: The University of Chicago Press(1980)
7. Zhou, H.: Similarities between English and Chinese emotion metaphors. Journal of Sichuan International Studies University(2001). 17(3): p. 90-92
8. Yu, N.: The Contemporary Theory of Metaphor: A Perspective from Chinese. Amsterdam: John Benjamins Publishing Company(1998)
9. Peng, D.L., General Psychology. 2001, Beijing: Beijing Normal University Press.
10. Chen, W.C., A cognitive view to emotional expression for metaphorical concept. Journal of Nanhua University(Social Science Edition)(2002). 3(3): p. 84-87
11. Xu, X. and Tao, J.H: Study on emotion classification in Chinese emotion system. in The 1st Chinese Conference on Affective Computing and Intelligent Interaction(ACII'03). Beijing(2003)

Voice Conversion Based on Weighted Least Squares Estimation Criterion and Residual Prediction from Pitch Contour

Jian Zhang, Jun Sun, and Beiqian Dai

Electronic Science and Technology Department, University of Science and Technology of China 230026, Hefei, Anhui, China
{jianzhang, sunjun}@ust.edu

Abstract. This paper describes an enhanced system for more efficient voice conversion. A weighted LMSE (Least Mean Squared Error) criterion is adopted, instead of conventional LMSE, for the spectral conversion function training. In addition, a short-term pitch contour mapping algorithm together with a new residual codebook formed from pitch contour is presented. Informal listening tests prove that convincing voice conversion is achieved while maintaining high speech quality. Evaluations by objective tests also show that the proposed system reduces speaker individual discrimination compared with the baseline system in LPC based analysis/synthesis framework.

1 Instruction

Voice conversion methods attempt to modify the characteristics of speech by a given source speaker, so that it sounds as if it was uttered by some designated target speaker. The applications include the production of additional voices from a single-speaker database, the "personalization" of a text-to-speech (TTS) synthesis system to speak with any desired voice after an adaptation process, and the preprocessing of affective voice modification [1,2].

In general, a voice conversion system includes two parts: the training procedure and the converting procedure. In the training stage, the source and target speakers pronounce speech data with the same text contents and then conversion rules are summarized. In the converting stage, arbitrary speeches from the source can then be converted to sound like the target by using the derived conversion rules. Various approaches have been proposed for achieving high quality conversion, most of which focused on the spectral properties of the vocal tract and the excitation at the vocal folds [3,4,5]. The GMM based mapping algorithm [5,6] is a typical spectral conversion method, which manages to realize relatively accurate spectral conversion. But during the training stage, just like other methods, the parameters of the conversion function are derived by minimizing the mean squared error. However this least squares optimization treats all the aligned training data equivalently regardless of their difference in original source-to-target spectral distance. As a result, spectral distance of many

J. Tao, T. Tan, and R.W. Picard (Eds.): ACII 2005, LNCS 3784, pp. 326–333, 2005.

frames after conversion becomes even larger than original distance. Lots of experimental results indicate that the excitation plays an important role in speaker individuality. Kain predicted spectral residual from the LP envelope in the pitch synchronous sinusoidal model [7]. However less attempt has been done with the excitation in LPC based model, early conversion system based on LPC model used just the excitation of the source speaker, which greatly degraded the quality of converted speech.

In this paper, we proposed a revised least squares estimation criterion weighted by the original spectral distance on a frame by frame basis between the two speakers. Effect of different dimensions of the feature vector also has been taken into account in operation. Here we use Kain's residual prediction ideas for reference, but the target's residual codebook created by our novel method are stored in waveform and predicted from the converted short-term pitch contour. This paper is organized as follows. In Sect. 2, the weighted LMSE criterion is described. In Sect. 3, the short-term pitch contour mapping algorithm as well as residual prediction method is presented. In Sect. 4, experimental conditions and baseline system are outlined, and then test results are given before presenting overall conclusions in Sect. 5.

2 Spectral Conversion Based on Weighted LMSE Criterion

Our voice conversion system uses the source-filter model for speech signal representation and modification. Let $\boldsymbol{X} = [\boldsymbol{x}_1 \boldsymbol{x}_2 \ldots \boldsymbol{x}_N]$ and $\boldsymbol{Y} = [\boldsymbol{y}_1 \boldsymbol{y}_2 \ldots \boldsymbol{y}_N]$ after time-aligned be the spectral vectors of source and target speaker extracted from every frame in the training data, each spectral vector with p dimensional elements. The GMM based locally linear transformation [6] is chosen for spectral conversion such that the converted spectral vector is given by

$$F(\boldsymbol{x}) = \left(\sum_{m=1}^{M} h_m(\boldsymbol{x}) \boldsymbol{W}_m \right) \bar{\boldsymbol{x}} \ . \tag{1}$$

where $\bar{\boldsymbol{x}} = [\boldsymbol{x}', 1]'$ is the extended vector of $\boldsymbol{x}$ arbitrarily chosen from the train set $\boldsymbol{X}$ ($'$ denotes transposition), and h_m is the interpolation weight of transform matrix $\boldsymbol{W}_m$ which is equal to the posterior probability that $\boldsymbol{x}$ belongs to the mth Gaussian component of GMM trained on the source data.

The parameters of the conversion (transform matrices) are deduced by minimizing some error measure. Generally the problem is solved by least squares optimization on the training data so as to minimize the total square conversion error.

$$\varepsilon_{\text{LS}} = \sum_{t=1}^{N} [\boldsymbol{y}_t - F(\boldsymbol{x}_t)]' \, [\boldsymbol{y}_t - F(\boldsymbol{x}_t)] \ . \tag{2}$$

Obviously this LS optimization is not suitable for lack of considering the difference of original spectral distance from each frame of source speaker to its aligned frame of target speaker, denoted by d_t. To every frame couple $(\boldsymbol{x}_t, \boldsymbol{y}_t)$, the same spectral error left after conversion has different effects. So it is the *relative* conversion error not the *absolute* conversion error that we should minimize. On the other hand, each dimension of spectral vectors has its distinct distribution and contributes differently to speaker individuality. So in the computation of conversion error, influence of each dimension should be considered separately. Here we derive the unknown parameters by minimizing the weighted mean squared error, which is given by

$$\varepsilon_{\mathrm{WLS}} = \sum_{t=1}^{N} \left[\boldsymbol{y}_t - F(\boldsymbol{x}_t)\right]' \boldsymbol{P}_t{}' \boldsymbol{P}_t \left[\boldsymbol{y}_t - F(\boldsymbol{x}_t)\right] \ . \tag{3}$$

where $\boldsymbol{P}_t$ is a diagonal matrix, which acts as a weighted matrix. In our experiment we used a simple form of $\boldsymbol{P}_t$ just like: $1/d_t \cdot \mathrm{diag}\left\{1/\sigma_1, 1/\sigma_2, \ldots, 1/\sigma_p\right\}$, and σ_i is the deviation of the ith dimension of target's spectral vectors computed on training data.

Due to the linear nature of the conversion function given by (1), the weighted least squares optimization of its parameters is equivalent to the solution of the following overdetermined linear matrix equation [8]

$$\widetilde{\boldsymbol{Y}} = \left[\boldsymbol{P}_1 F(\boldsymbol{x}_1) \quad \boldsymbol{P}_2 F(\boldsymbol{x}_2) \quad \ldots \quad \boldsymbol{P}_N F(\boldsymbol{x}_N)\right] \ . \tag{4}$$

where $\widetilde{\boldsymbol{Y}}$ is a $p \times N$ matrix that contains the weighted target spectral vectors ordered as

$$\widetilde{\boldsymbol{Y}} = \left[\boldsymbol{P}_1 \boldsymbol{y}_1 \quad \boldsymbol{P}_2 \boldsymbol{y}_2 \quad \ldots \quad \boldsymbol{P}_N \boldsymbol{y}_N\right] \ . \tag{5}$$

for the convenience of discussion, we rewrite the above symbols and define

$$\begin{aligned} \boldsymbol{\Lambda}(\boldsymbol{x}_t) &= \frac{1}{d_t} \left[h_1(\boldsymbol{x}_t)\bar{\boldsymbol{x}}_t' \quad \ldots \quad h_M(\boldsymbol{x}_t)\bar{\boldsymbol{x}}_t'\right]'_{((p+1)\times M)\times 1} \\ \bar{\boldsymbol{W}} &= \left[\boldsymbol{W}_1 \quad \boldsymbol{W}_2 \quad \ldots \quad \boldsymbol{W}_M\right]_{p\times((p+1)\times M)} \\ \boldsymbol{A} &= \mathrm{diag}\left\{1/\sigma_1,\ 1/\sigma_2,\ \ldots,\ 1/\sigma_p\right\} \end{aligned} \ . \tag{6}$$

after such assumption, (4) can be written in the following concise form

$$\widetilde{\boldsymbol{Y}} = \boldsymbol{A}\bar{\boldsymbol{W}}\left[\boldsymbol{\Lambda}(\boldsymbol{x}_1) \quad \boldsymbol{\Lambda}(\boldsymbol{x}_2) \quad \ldots \quad \boldsymbol{\Lambda}(\boldsymbol{x}_N)\right] = \boldsymbol{A}\bar{\boldsymbol{W}}\boldsymbol{\Lambda}(\boldsymbol{X}) \ . \tag{7}$$

then the weighted least squares problem can be solved by solving the normal equation

$$\widetilde{\boldsymbol{Y}}\boldsymbol{\Lambda}'(\boldsymbol{X}) = \boldsymbol{A}\bar{\boldsymbol{W}}\boldsymbol{\Lambda}(\boldsymbol{X})\boldsymbol{\Lambda}'(\boldsymbol{X}) \ . \tag{8}$$

using matrix inversion, the unknown transform matrices $\bar{\boldsymbol{W}}$ can be obtained

$$\bar{\boldsymbol{W}} = \boldsymbol{A}^{-1}\widetilde{\boldsymbol{Y}}\boldsymbol{\Lambda}'(\boldsymbol{X})\left(\boldsymbol{\Lambda}(\boldsymbol{X})\boldsymbol{\Lambda}'(\boldsymbol{X})\right)^{-1} \ . \tag{9}$$

3 Residual Prediction Scheme

As we predict the LPC residual from the pitch contour, the preliminary step is to realize the conversion of pitch contour. Previous pitch conversion methods focused most on its static characteristic and considered rarely its evolution transformation [9]. Here we combine pitches of consecutive frames and associated Δpitches into a multi-dimension vector. Suppose that $\boldsymbol{P}^s = [\boldsymbol{p}_1^s \ldots \boldsymbol{p}_n^s]$ and $\boldsymbol{P}^t = [\boldsymbol{p}_1^t \ldots \boldsymbol{p}_n^t]$ are the combined pitch vectors sequences of source speaker and target speaker after time-aligned. Each combined pitch vector has the form like: $\boldsymbol{p}_i^{s,t} = [p_{i1} \ldots p_{iL}, \Delta p_{i1} \ldots \Delta p_{iL}]$, which is combined with pitches and Δpitches extracted from L consecutive frames. By using conventional GMM based methods to $\boldsymbol{P}^s$ and $\boldsymbol{P}^t$, we get the pitch contour mapping function. Then a c-mixture GMM, which is also the size of residual codebook, is trained on $\boldsymbol{P}^t$, and the ith residual codeword $rc_i\,(i = 1, 2, \ldots, c)$ of target speaker is chosen as follows

$$\begin{array}{ll} \text{if} & j = \arg \max\limits_{k=1,2,\ldots,n} \{p(i/\boldsymbol{p}_k^t)\} \\ \text{then } rc_i = r_j & \end{array} \quad . \tag{10}$$

where $p(i/\boldsymbol{p}_k^t)$ is the posterior probability of target speaker's combined pitch vector $\boldsymbol{p}_k^t$ belonging to the ith Gaussian component of GMM, r_k is the residual obtained by inversely filtering the speech waveform from frames associated with $\boldsymbol{p}_k^t$.

The block diagram in Fig. 1 illustrates how the target residual codebook is generated. After the residual and pitch contour are extracted, the pitches and Δpitches from L consecutive frames are bound to form a combined pitch vector by "frames binding", and the associated residual from these frames is labeled together with it. At last the residual codebook is generated after the training of GMM and comparison of the posterior probabilities of all the combined vectors, described in detail as above.

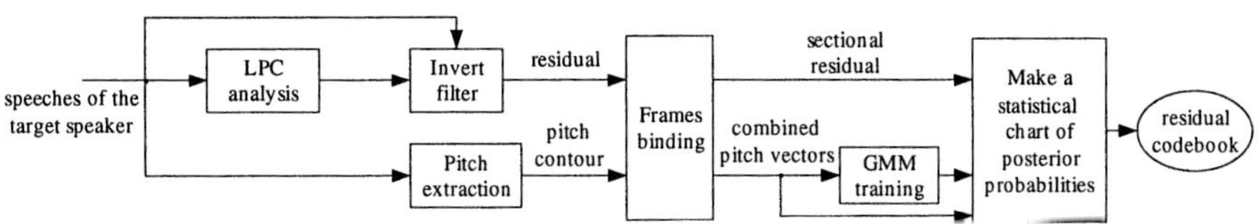

Fig. 1. Construction of target residual codebook in the training stage

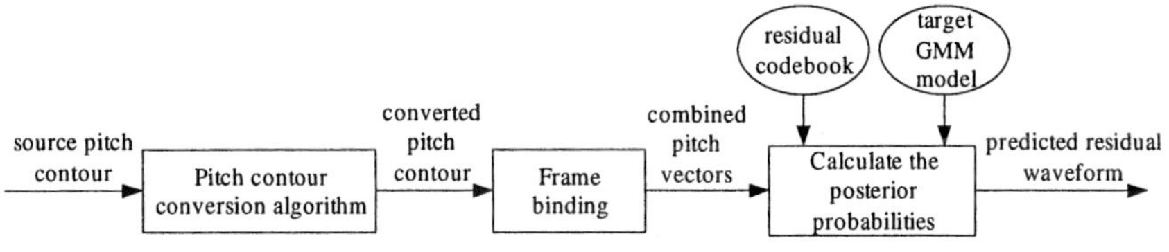

Fig. 2. Residual prediction in the converting stage

In the converting stage, as shown in Fig. 2, the posterior probabilities of a combined pitch vector after conversion are calculated and the residual codeword of the class which posterior probability is maximum, is picked as the predicted residual. Finally the residual waveform is passed through the converted LPC filter to synthesize the converted speech. As for the unvoiced part, the associated residual of source speech is directly coped to the converted speech.

4 Experimental Performance

In order to investigate the effectiveness of our proposed algorithm in LPC based analysis/synthesis framework, we compared it with the baseline system. The conventional GMM based conversion was chosen as the baseline system, which adopted LMSE criterion in spectral envelope training and outputted the converted speech by using source speaker's residual. Finally the PSOLA technique was used for the pitch modification of synthesis speeches.

4.1 Experimental Conditions

We performed four group male-to-male voice conversion using MSRA mandarin database consisting of 100 male speakers [10]. We selected 16 sentences as a training set from the total 22 sentences based on a binary split vector quantization so that the diphone coverage for all sentences was maximized. Then the remaining 6 sentences were chosen as a test set.

Before extracting feature parameters, the speech data were downsampled to 8kHz and all silence parts were removed. The LPC based analysis/synthesis framework was adopted for parameters extraction and converted speech synthesis. Bark-scaled, 12 order linear spectral frequencies (LSFs) were used to represent the spectral envelope. In our experiment, the optimal numbers of mixtures for spectral envelope conversion and short-term pitch contour conversion were 8 and 12 respectively. And the size of residual codebook was set to 32.

4.2 Objective Evaluations

Spectral Conversion. The Itakura distance [11] is used as an objective measure of the spectral distortion

$$d_{\mathrm{I}}\left(1/\left|A_p\right|^2, 1/\left|A\right|^2\right) = \log\left\{\int_{-\pi}^{\pi} \frac{|A|^2}{|A_p|^2}\frac{d\omega}{2\pi}\right\} = \log\frac{\boldsymbol{a}'\boldsymbol{R}_p\,\boldsymbol{a}}{\sigma_p^2} \ . \tag{11}$$

where A is an inverse filter whose coefficients are determined by $\boldsymbol{a}$, p represents the subscript of the referring pattern and $\boldsymbol{R}$ is the autocorrelation matrix.

A distortion ratio is then used to compare the converted-to-target distortion with the source-to-target distortion, which is defined as

$$D = \sum_{i=1}^{T} \frac{d_{\mathrm{I}}(t_i, c_i)}{d_{\mathrm{I}}(t_i, s_i)} \Big/ T \ . \tag{12}$$

Table 1. Spectral conversion distortion compared weighted LMSE with LMSE criterion

	s1/t1	s1/t2	s2/t1	s2/t2
weighted-LMSE	0.585	0.637	0.589	0.654
LMSE	0.637	0.698	0.683	0.726

Table 2. Pitch conversion error when the number of bound frames (L) varies from 1, 3, 5 to 7 (unit: Hz)

L	s1/t1	s1/t2	s2/t1	s2/t2
1	16.26	17.79	19.03	19.08
3	14.18	16.37	17.79	17.95
5	14.15	16.25	17.45	17.78
7	14.84	16.85	17.93	18.05

where s_i, t_i and c_i are the source, target and converted power spectrum of the ith frame calculated from respective LPC coefficients. T is the total number of test spectral vectors.

The results shown in Table 1 demonstrate that the converted spectral envelope sequence having more similar characteristics to the target is estimated by applying weighted LMSE training criterion.

Pitch Conversion. The mean pitch error from the converted speeches to the target speeches in the test set is used to evaluate the pitch conversion quality.

Table 2 indicates that binding pitches and associated Δpitches of consecutive 5 frames together to form a vector for converting the pitch contour is an optimal scheme. A conversion sample of pitch contour is also demonstrated in Fig. 3. As can be seen, the converted pitch contour tallies well with that of the target, which illuminates the validity of this new pitch conversion algorithm.

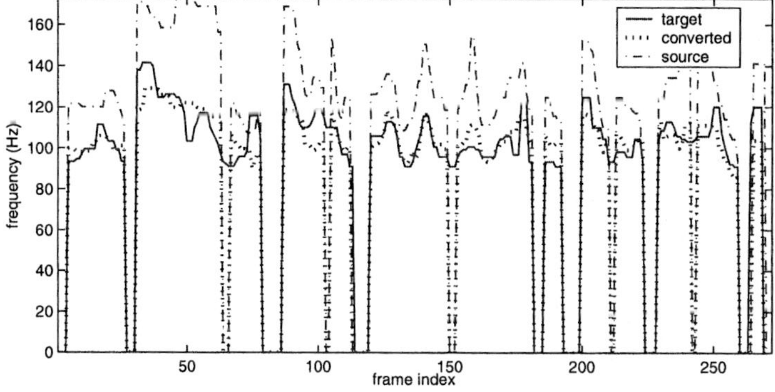

Fig. 3. An example of pitch contour conversion for a test sentence

Table 3. Results from the ABX test

Baseline System	Enhanced System
61.0%	87.5%

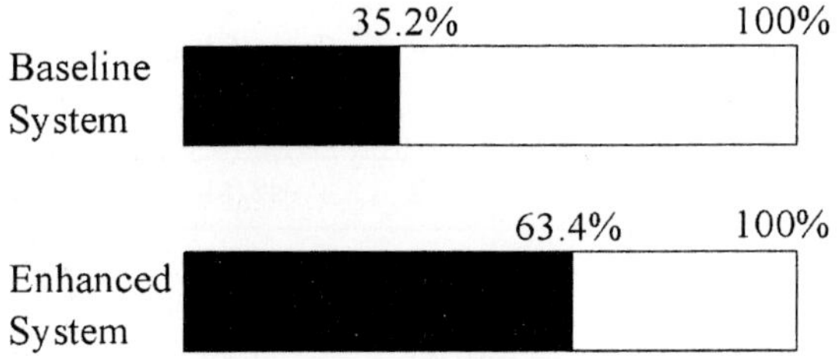

Fig. 4. Results from the preference test

4.3 Subjective Evaluations

Subjective listening tests were also carried out to assess the perceptual performance of the enhanced system against the baseline system. Specifically, two kinds of listening tests were performed: the standard ABX test and a preference test. The evaluation has been carried out using five continuously uttered sentences of about 5 seconds duration each. Ten listeners participated in each of these experiments.

In the ABX test, the converted speech was presented as X, and A and B were either the source speech or the target speech. Listeners were asked to judge whether X sounded closer to A or B in terms of speaker identity. Twenty triads covering all possible speaker conversion combination were presented to the listeners. Table 3 gives the percentage of the converted utterances that were chosen as closer to the target for each case. The results clearly reveal that the enhanced system integrating all the improved techniques outperforms the baseline system in speaker identity transformation. To assess converted speech quality between the baseline system and the enhanced system, a preference test was designed where pairs of utterances generated by the baseline system and the enhanced system respectively were presented to the listeners, and then listeners were asked to judge which one has the better speech quality. Results of this preference test shown in Fig. 4 indicate most listeners were in favor of the converted speech generated by the enhanced system.

5 Conclusions

This paper has described an enhanced voice system for higher quality voice conversion. The improvement includes a new weighted LMSE training criterion and short-term pitch contour conversion algorithm together with the residual prediction from pitch contour. The weighted LMSE criterion emphasizes on the accurate conversion of some dimensions of the feature vector that contribute greatly to speaker identity, and manifests the conversion difficulty degrees of different source-to-target frames. By joining pitches and its dynamic elements from several frames together, we introduce a short-term pitch contour conversion algorithm and a residual waveform prediction scheme based on GMM.

Experimental results show that the weighted LMSE criterion decreases the spectral distortion obviously compared with LMSE criterion. It is also found that the new pitch contour algorithm can realize the conversion of short-term pitch evolution and the residual prediction from short-term pitch contour can succeed in capturing target speaker's excitation characteristics to some extent. Informal listening tests confirm that the proposed methods can improve speaker individuality of converted speeches while maintaining high speech quality in vivid contrast with the baseline system.

References

1. E. Moulines, et. al.: Voice conversion: state of the art and perspectives. Elsevier, **16(2)** (1995) 125-126
2. Kuwabara H., Sagisaka Y.: Acoustic characteristics of speaker individuality: control and conversion. Speech communication, **16(2)** (1995) 165–173
3. M. Abe, et. al.: Voice conversion through vector quantization. Proceedings of ICASSP (1988) 655–658
4. Y. Stylianou, O. Cappe and E. Moulines: Continuous probabilistic transform for voice conversion. IEEE trans. in Speech & Audio processing, **6** (1998) 131–142
5. A. Kain and M. Macon: Spectral voice conversion for text-to-speech synthesis. Proceedings of ICASSP, **1** (1998) 285–288
6. Ye Hui and Young Steve: Perceptually weighted linear transformation for voice conversion. Eurospeech (2003) 2409-2412
7. A. Kain and M. Macon: Design and evaluation of a voice conversion algorithm based on spectral envelope mapping and residual prediction. proceedings of ICASSP (2001) 813–816
8. Charles L. Lawson and Richard J. Hanson: *Solving Least Squares Problem*, Englewood Cliffs, N. J. Prentice-Hall International, Inc.
9. A. Kain and Y. Stylianou: Stochastic modeling of spectral adjustment for high quality pitch modification. proceedings of ICASSP (2000) 949–952
10. Eric Chang, Y. Shi, J.Zhou, and C. Huang: Speech lab in a box: a mandarin speech toolbox to jumpstart speech related research. Eurospeech (2001) 2799-2802
11. L. Rabiner and Biing-Hwang Juang: *Fundamentals of Speech Recognition*, Chap. 4. Prentico Hall, Inc.

Modifying Spectral Envelope to Synthetically Adjust Voice Quality and Articulation Parameters for Emotional Speech Synthesis

Yanqiu Shao, Zhuoran Wang, Jiqing Han, and Ting Liu

School of Computer Science and Technology,
Harbin Institute of Technology, Harbin, China
{Yqshao, jqhan}@hit.edu.cn
{zrwang, tliu}@ir.hit.edu.cn

Abstract. Both of the prosody and spectral features are important for emotional speech synthesis. Besides prosody effects, voice quality and articulation parameters are the factors that should be considered to modify in emotional speech synthetic systems. Generally, rules and filters are designed to process these parameters respectively. This paper proves that by modifying spectral envelope, the voice quality and articulation could be adjusted as a whole. Thus, it will not need to modify each of the parameter separately depending on rules. Accordingly, it will make the synthetic system more flexible by designing an automatic spectral envelope model based on some machine learning methods. The perception test in this paper also shows that when prosody and spectral features are all modified, the best emotional synthetic speech will be obtained.

1 Introduction

Speech is the most convenient way for human to communicate with each other. Besides the linguistic information, a great deal of non-linguistic information such as emotion and attitude are included in speech. Unfortunately, this useful non-linguistic or para-linguistic information in speech is largely missing from modern speech synthesis system. The direct result is that the synthesized speech is lack of variability and it is still readily identifiable as being machine-generated.

The development of emotional speech synthesis has closely related to different synthetic methods. By using DECtalk, a formant synthesis system, Janet Cahn's Affect Editor generated six kinds of emotions including anger, fear, gladness, sadness, disgust and surprise[1]. In Cahn's system, 17 associated prosodic and voice quality parameters have been selected to express emotion. Formant synthesis system is also used in Iain Murray's HAMLET system[2]. It is easy for formant synthesis system to adjust those parameters that can affect the result, but the speech generated by formant synthetic system sounds unnatural and robot-like. In recent decade, concatenative synthesis has been putting into use.

In concatenative synthesis, diphone recordings are concatenated to generate the synthetic speech, and the result is more natural than that of formant synthesis. However, only F0 and duration can be adjusted in this kind of system, while the

J. Tao, T. Tan, and R.W. Picard (Eds.): ACII 2005, LNCS 3784, pp. 334–341, 2005.

control of voice quality is not quite convenient. Rank and Pirker tried to synthesize Austria emotional speech including anger, sadness, fear and disgust by concatenative system[3]. In their system, the synthesized speech which is generated by prosody model and concatenation, is put into a filter which can add bandlimited noise to the speech to modify the voice quality, and then some kinds of emotional speech can be output. However, the experiment results are not very good. Maybe it is because those emotions all belong to negative emotions, and are too similar to distinguish.

The most natural synthetic speech is generated by those systems which apply unit selection technology. Iida and Campbell developed an emotional speech synthesis system based on CHATR to help those disabilities to express three kinds of emotions, i.e. sadness, anger and joy[4].Perceptual experiments show that the synthetic emotional speech were identifiable, nevertheless, it is very hard to build so many large emotional speech database. Moreover, in this kind of synthesis, if appropriate units are found in the database, the result can be very good, otherwise, it will be very bad.

Whatever the synthetic method is used, it is still very important for an emotional speech synthesis system to make a model on those features that can play a great role in emotional perception. However, the process of human's emotional perception is very complex. Only part of features could be extracted to describe emotion such as prosody feature F0 and duration, voice quality like breathy, creaky and harsh, or articulation precision such as nasality and vowel quality. But in concatenative synthesis, except for prosody features, it is hard to extract voice quality and articulation features. It is still a question that whether F0 and duration is enough to express emotion, and different study has different answer. Nagasaki reported that synthesized emotions can be recognized reasonably well while prosody features are modified[5], whereas Gobl[6] emphasized the importance of voice quality and articulation. In Gobl's experiment, six parameters are selected to enhance the expression of emotion, breathy, whispery, lax-creaky, modal, and harsh. The results show that after adding the voice quality, the tendency of the emotion is much obvious than that of the speech only being modified pitch. Moriyama and Ozawa[7] pointed out that good results could be obtained by modifying prosody features to synthesize surprise, sadness and anger, but, it is not enough to distinguish happy and fear only depending on prosody features. So, maybe it is effective on some kinds of emotions only by modifying their prosody features, and some emotions need to be changed the spectrum.

As mentioned above, many related features and synthetic methods that can effect the emotion have been studied. But up to now, the majority of these methods are based on some rules or pre-designed filters to modify voice quality and articulation features separately. In this paper, we tried to prove that those voice quality and articulation features could get integrated adjustment by modifying the spectrum envelope, and then it will be possible to avoid changing each parameter respectively. The significance is that if the proper spectral envelope, which can be represented as LPC or LSF parameters, could be generated automatically by some machine learning methods, a flexible emotion synthesis system will be able to realize.

2 Emotional Speech Corpus

Before recording emotional speech data, the number of emotional types must be decided. Now, there are two main ways of emotion representation, i.e. discrete and dimensional description.Discrete representation contains basic emotion and extended emotion. The arousal and evaluation are often used to represent dimension. The number of basic emotions considered in the literature ranges from 2 to 9. Considering about the arousal and evaluation in emotion space, we selected three basic emotions in our research. They are sadness, anger and happiness. Anger and happiness are related to high arousal, and sadness belongs to low arousal. Sadness and anger are negative emotion and happiness is positive.

In order to avoid the semantic influence on emotion, 310 neutral sentences without special emotion tendency are selected. The average length of every sentence is about 7.5 Chinese characters. These sentences are uttered respectively by a well-trained female speaker with standard articulation. Each sentence was read in four different styles, i.e. neutral, sad, angry and happy. Before the speaker read the formal sentences with emotion, she would read some other corresponding emotional passages to incite her attitude. For example, when she began to read the happy sentences, she would read some happy news or some jokes at first. Then she would keep cheerful spirits to read those formal sentences. Then ten students, who did not have any experience on speech synthesis, took part in the forced-choice perception test of the emotional speech corpus. 100 sentences are selected randomly from the corpus and listened to by the students. The recognition rate of happiness, anger and sadness are 100%,100% and 98% respectively. It can be seen that the majority of the emotional recordings can express the proper emotion.

3 Experiments

In order to prove the supposition of that the modification of spectrum envelope could synthetically change the voice quality and articulation, and to prove that whether the combined prosody and spectrum changing could obtain the best synthetic result, three groups experiments were done. (1) Only prosodic parameters are modified. (2) Only spectrum is modified. (3) Both prosodic and spectral parameters are modified. 20 sentences are selected and each sentence has four corresponding emotional speech including neutral emotion. Moreover, each utterance was extracted its pitch contour and every syllable boundary was labeled manually by “praat”.

3.1 To Synthesize Emotional Speech by Modifying Prosody Features

In this experiment, neutral utterance was looked as the original speech, and the prosody parameters of the other three emotional speech were used to modify the original speech signal. Then, the emotional synthetic speech was got. Concretely, every syllable of the neutral utterance was segmented, and the corresponding pitch contour, duration and energy of the syllable from emotional utterance were calculated. Then depending on these values, PSOLA technology was applied to modify the

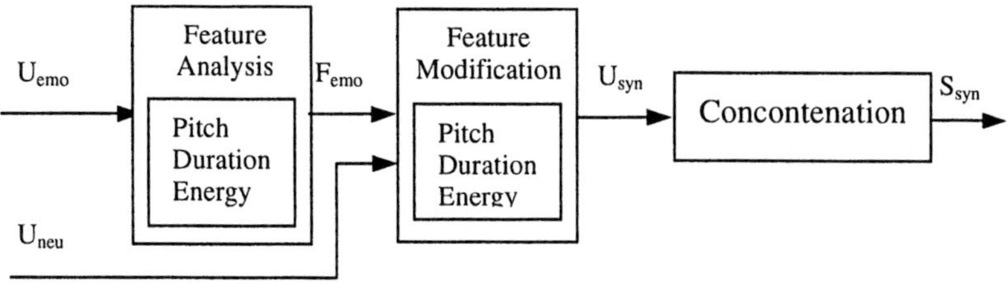

Fig. 1. Modifying prosody features to synthesize emotional speech (U: Unit, F: Feature, S: Speech, emo: emotional, neu: neutral, syn: synthetic)

corresponding neutral syllable parameters. At last, every modifiable syllable was concontenated to output. The flow chart is given by Fig. 1.

Because the pitch contour, duration and energy are all got from the real emotional speech, the prosody parameters could be looked as an ideal value from an ideal prosody model. Thus, the effect of prosody model in a speech synthetic system needs not to be considered. The focus could be concentrated on whether the perception parameters are good or not.

However, from the auditory perception, it can't be felt that the sentences have very obviously emotional tendency. The synthetic sentences sound just like those ones with a little expression on the intonation. For example, the pitch value of happiness and anger becomes higher and the pitch of sadness becomes lower. It shows that only depending on modifying prosody features to generate emotional effect is not enough.

3.2 To Synthesize Emotional Speech by Modifying Spectral Envelope

The articulation parameters include nasality, vowel quality, tension of vocal tract muscles and so on. They are all related to the state of the vocal tract. So, these parameters have close relations with the shape of spectral envelope, formant position and bandwidth[8]. On the other hand, the voice quality parameters, like "breathy" and "creaky" are all related to the laryngeal state, but some of them can be expressed through the spectrum. For example, "breathy" can increase the inter-harmonic noise among the high frequency harmonious wave, and the quantity of air flow through the glottis can effect the first harmonics and the first formant bandwidth; When "creaky" occurs, the pulse of glottis is very narrow and the spectrum will become smooth [9]. It can be seen that the spectral envelope has loaded a lot of information of articulation and voice quality. So, this paper proposed to modify the spectral envelope to accomplish the purpose of adjusting the articulation and voice quality as a whole.

In frequency domain, the speech signal spectrum can be looked as a product of residue spectrum and vocal tract spectrum. If the LPC parameters are calculated, the vocal tract spectral envelope and residue spectrum will be got. In this experiment, neutral utterance was still looked as the original speech. Both of the original speech and the emotional speech are analyzed by LPC. Because of the short-time stationarity of speech signal, 16-order LPC coefficients are gained for every 20ms-long analysis frame. Then the spectrum of each frame of original and emotional speech was

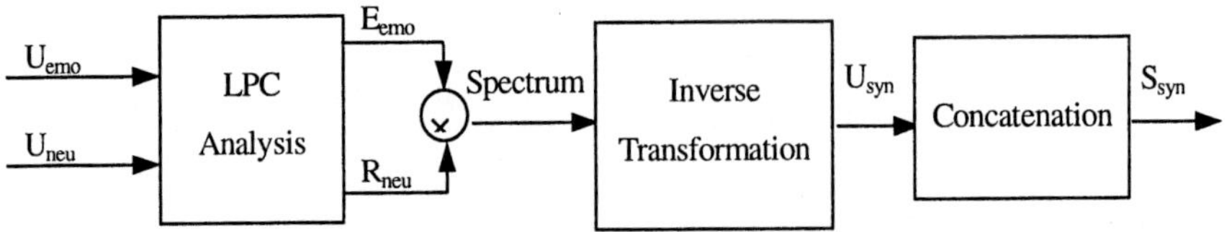

Fig. 2. Modifying spectrum to synthesize emotional speech (E: Envelope, R: Residue)

resolved into vocal spectral envelope and residue spectrum. The vocal envelope of the original speech was replaced by emotional envelope. Then combined with original residue, new synthetic emotional spectrum was generated. At last, the wave was obtained by inverse transformation. This process is showed in Fig. 2.

From the auditory perception, it could be felt obviously that the voice quality was modified. Happiness and anger could be felt, but sadness was not very obviously. Because the prosody parameters were not changed, the intonation did not sound very obviously. After all, only modifying the spectral envelope is not enough to fully express the emotion, especially when pitch is largely modified.

3.3 To Synthesize Emotional Speech by Modifying Envelope and Prosody Feature

In this experiment, both of the spectral envelope and prosody feature are modified to synthesize emotional speech. Firstly, depending on the emotional prosody features, the original neutral speech is modified according to the way introduced in section 3.1, and then the method in 3.2 is used to modify the spectral envelope. Fig. 3 shows the pitch contour of the original recording speech and the synthetic speech which is modified on the basis of neutral speech according to the angry speech prosody parameters. From the figure, it can be seen that these two pitch contours are relatively similar, so, the intonation of synthetic emotional speech is natural on the whole.

Fig. 4 is the comparison of the spectrum and envelop of a Chinese syllable “再” from an angry sentence. As can be seen that after being modified the envelope, the

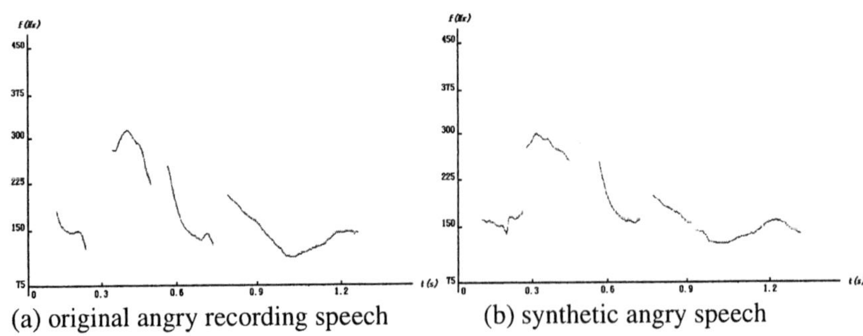

Fig. 3. Two pitch contours of Chinese sentence “我不想再玩了！” (“I don’t want to play anymore!”)

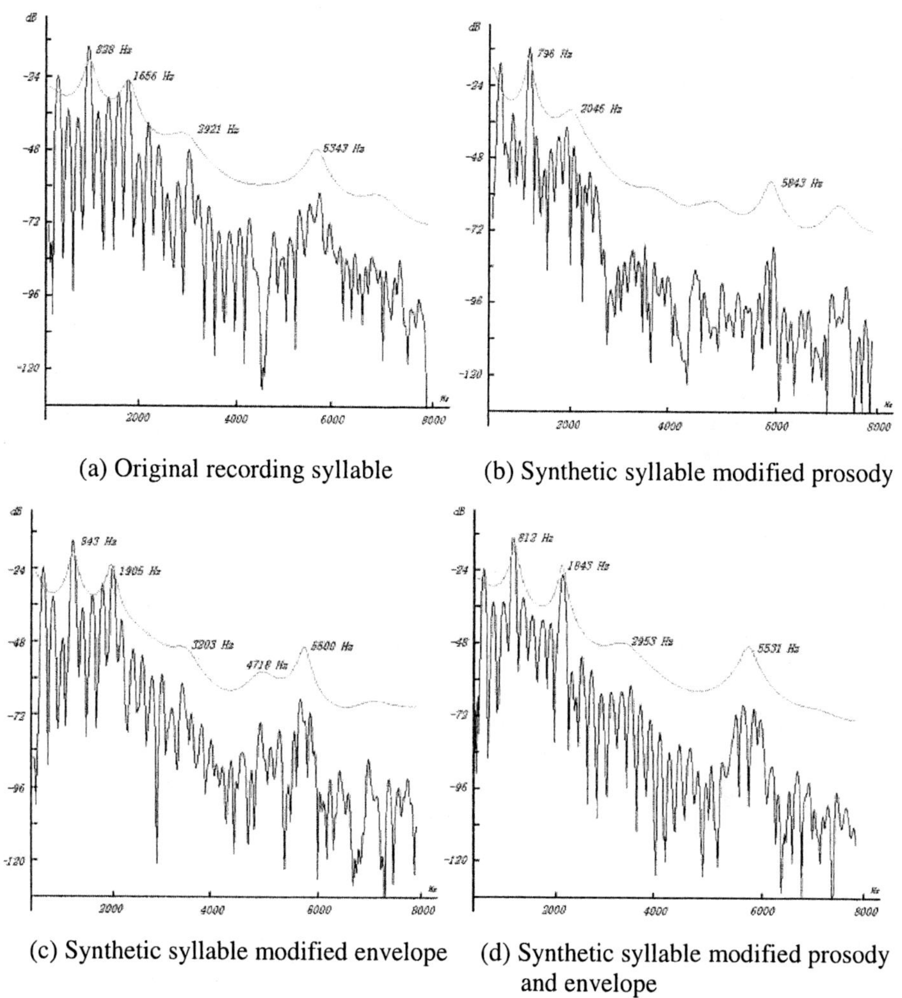

(a) Original recording syllable

(b) Synthetic syllable modified prosody

(c) Synthetic syllable modified envelope

(d) Synthetic syllable modified prosody and envelope

Fig. 4. The spectrum and envelop of an Chinese syllable "再" from an angry sentence

formant position and bandwidth, and the envelope shape of the synthetic speech are all similar to those of original recording speech. So, it proved that by modifying the envelope, the voice quality and articulation could be synthetically adjusted. From the auditory perception, it can also be felt that the synthetic speech is more natural when the prosody feature and spectrum envelope are modified together.

4 Evaluation

In order to evaluate the effect of different methods, two perception tests are given in this paper, i.e. emotion recognition test and comparison test based on support rate.

4.1 Emotion Recognition Test

Based on the above methods, twenty sentences were selected to generate three different emotional utterances. Thus, three groups, which are corresponding to three different methods, were obtained. Each group has 60 utterances related to three different emotions. Then the utterances in each group are mixed confusedly. Ten students who did not have any experience on speech synthesis were invited to do a forced-choice of each sentence only depending on the auditory perception of the synthetic speech. The results are given bellow. From table1, it can be known that compared with the method of modifying spectral envelope, prosody modification is much better. It can also be seen that when the prosody and spectrum are all modified, the best result could be obtained.

Table 1. The recognition results of emotional synthetic speech based on different methods

Subjective response to different modification of parameters		Emotional synthetic speech		
		Happy	Angry	Sad
Prosody	Happy	63%	29.5%	11.5%
	Angry	20.5%	65.5%	4.5%
	Sad	16.5%	5%	84%
Envelope	Happy	61%	25.5%	17%
	Angry	19.5%	44%	10%
	Sad	19.5%	30.5%	73%
Prosody & Envelope	Happy	79.5%	7.5%	5.5%
	Angry	14%	88%	3.5%
	Sad	6.5%	4.5%	91%

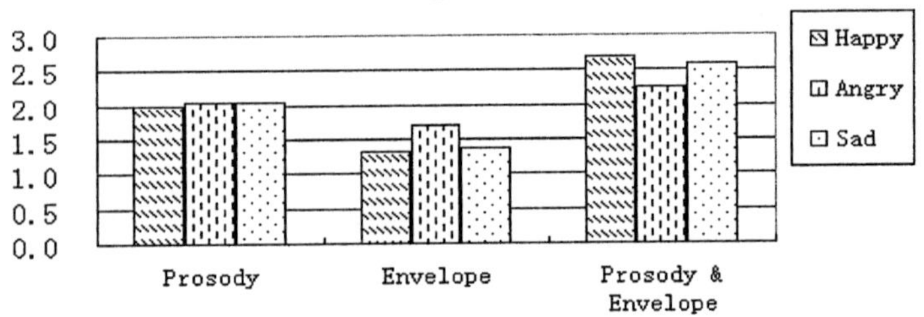

Fig. 5. The results of support rate of different methods

4.2 Comparison Test Based on Support Rate

Because the recognition test is a forced-choice test, it amounts rather to a discrimination task than an identification task. In order to compare the quality of these three methods, a support rate test is given. Ten students took part in this experiment. Each sentence generated by different methods was compared by every student, and each student gave a score of the sentence. The best one got a score of 3, the worst one got 1 and another got 2. Equation (1) is the average support rate, where n is the number of the sentences, N is the number of subjects and mark is the score. Fig. 5 gives the results of support rate test. This test proved further that by modifying prosody and spectrum together could get the best result.

$$S = \sum_{N}\sum_{n} mark_n \Big/ (N \times n) \tag{1}$$

5 Conclusion

In this paper, three methods are applied to synthesize emotional speech depending on neutral speech, i.e. the method of modifying prosody parameters, spectral envelope and both of the prosody and spectrum. The recognition test and the comparison test based on support rate have further proved that when prosody and spectrum are all modified, the best result would be obtained. Compared with spectral feature, prosody feature has a tenuous advantage. In fact, both of these two kinds of features are important for synthesizing emotional speech. Theoretically, the changing of spectral envelope always accompanies the changing of voice quality and articulation, so, it does not need to modify each parameter of voice quality and articulation, and it does not need to design rules or filters to synthesize emotional speech. A better way is to automatically generate the spectral envelope model by some machine learning method. For different emotion and application, it just needs different training data to build the spectral envelope and it does not need to re-design the model. If so, it will make the emotional speech synthesis more flexible. How to build the spectral envelope model is our next research work. Some technology in the field of voice transformation will be considered to apply to the emotional speech synthesis field.

References

1. Cahn, J.E.: Generating expression in synthesized speech. Master's thesis, Massachusetts Institute of Technology, (1989)
2. Murray,I.R., Arnott,J.L.: Implementation and testing of a system for producing emotion-by-rule in synthetic speech. Speech Communication, Vol. 16. (1995) 369-390
3. Rank,E., Pirker, H.: Generating emotional speech with a concatenative synthesizer. In:Proceedings, ICSLP '98, Vol.3. Sydney, Australia (1998) 671–674
4. Iida A, Campbell N, Iga S, Higuchi F, Yasumura M,:A Speech synthesis system with emotion for assisting communication, In: Proceedings of ISCA Workshop (ITRW) on Speech and Emotion. Newcastle, Northern Ireland (2000) 167-172
5. Nagasaki Y, Komatsu T: Can people perceive different emotions from a non-emotional voice by modifying its F0 and duration? In: Proceedings of Speech Prosody 2004. Nara, Japan (2004)
6. Gobl C., Bennett E., N'i Chasaide A.: Expressive synthesis: How crucial is voice quality? . In: Proceedings of IEEE Workshop on Speech Synthesis, Santa, Monica (2002)
7. Moriyama T., Ozawa S.: Emotion recognition and synthesis system on speech. IEEE ICMCS 99, (1999)
8. Hawkins S., Stevens K.: Acoustic and perceptual correlates of the non-nasal nasal distinction for vowels. Journal of the Acoustical Society of America (1985) 77, 1560-1575
9. Klatt D., Klatt L.: Analysis, synthesis, and perception of voice quality variations among female and male talkers. Journal of the Acoustical Society of America (1990) 87, 820-857

Study on Emotional Speech Features in Korean with Its Application to Voice Conversion

Sang-Jin Kim[1], Kwang-Ki Kim[1], Hyun Bae Han[2], and Minsoo Hahn[1]

[1] Speech and Audio Info. Lab., Information and Communications Univ., Korea
{sangjin, kkkim, mshahn}@icu.ac.kr
[2] International Network Planning & Management Team, Network Group, KT, Korea
sunshine@kt.co.kr

Abstract. Recent researches in speech synthesis are mainly focused on naturalness, and the emotional speech synthesis becomes one of the highlighted research topics. Although quite a many studies on emotional speech in English or Japanese have been addressed, the studies in Korean can seldom be found. This paper presents an analysis of emotional speech in Korean. Emotional speech features related to human speech prosody, such as F0, the duration, and the amplitude with their variations, are exploited. Their attribution to three different types of typical human speech is tried to be quantified and modeled. By utilizing the analysis results, emotional voice conversion from the neutral speech to the emotional one is also performed and tested.

1 Introduction

Recently, in many countries, due to the progress in speech synthesis technology and the availability of very large speech databases, it is not hard to find some acceptable quality speech synthesizers in the sense of intelligibility. And researchers concern has smoothly started to move onto the improvement of naturalness. One of the presently popular issues is emotional speech synthesis, and various attempts to add emotional information to synthetic speech have been made over the decade. It is clear that prosodic features, such as the pitch, the duration, and the energy, are closely correlated with emotions in human speech. Hence, many researchers have analyzed emotional speech and tried to find the cues for emotional speech, but basically, most of the cues are found to be same as the features mentioned above. The literatures, however, are mostly about English and Japanese[1][2][3][4][5][6][7]. Not only are the letters and grammar different among the languages, the way of speaking, like intonation and rhythm, is also different. And it is inevitable to exploit the emotional cues for each language separately but it is not easy to find the studies about Korean emotional speech. Firstly, this paper analyzes Korean emotional speech with some well-acknowledged emotional features. Then emotional information is introduced onto neutral synthetic speech by utilizing the features in order to realize emotional voice conversion. With this converted speech, the role of each feature can be more easily confirmed. Added emotion types are joy, sadness, and anger. This

J. Tao, T. Tan, and R.W. Picard (Eds.): ACII 2005, LNCS 3784, pp. 342–349, 2005.

paper consists as follows: In Section 2, emotional speech materials for our experiments are described. In Section 3, Korean emotional speech data are analyzed with prosodic features while the emotional voice conversion experiment is given in Section 4. Section 5 is for our experimental results showing the behavior of the parameters in Korean emotional speech. Finally, Section 6 concludes our discussions including the future works.

2 Emotional Speech Material

The speech data were recorded in a noise-free room on a digital audio tape(DAT). Four male speakers were employed to pronounce emotional speech. Each speaker uttered five rather short, i.e., less than 1.5 second duration, sentences five times without emotion and with three different types of emotion; joy, sadness, and anger. Hence, the total number of our speech data becomes 400. All the utterances successfully convoyed the emotions. The sentences were carefully designed to convoy the emotions into the sentences rather easily by the speakers. Finally, the speech samples are sampled at 16 kHz with 16 bit resolution.

3 Emotional Speech Analysis

Emotional speech features exploited in this paper are the pitch, the energy, and the duration with their contours. For more detailed analysis, each sentence speech is divided into three parts; the beginning, the middle, and the end parts. Then feature values are evaluated for these three different parts of the sentence separately.

3.1 Pitch

Table 1 shows the behavior of the pitch information along with the emotional types. The ratios are evaluated between the emotional speech and the neutral, i.e., emotionless speech. When the emotional information is added to the neutral speech, the pitch tends to become higher. Fig. 1 shows a typical example of the pitch ratio change for different types of emotions while Table 1 summarizes the pitch ratio statistics according to the emotional type and the analyzed part. From Table 1 and Fig. 1, we can see that the pitch for angry emotion is shorter than that for the other emotions while the pitch for joyful emotion is shorter than that for sad emotion. Another thing we can find is that the pitch is getting shorter slightly in the end part of the sentence than in the beginning part for angry and sad emotions. In case of joyful emotion, the pitch remains rather unchanged throughout a sentence. Our discussion on the pitch can generally be summarized as follows.

$$\text{Pitch} : \text{Anger} < \text{Joy} < \text{Sadness} < \text{Neutral}$$

3.2 Energy

Table 2 is for the behavior of the energy information according to the different emotions. The values in the table are also the energy ratios between each

Table 1. Pitch ratio(msec/msec) of each emotional speech to neutral speech

Sentence	Ratio To Neutral	Begin Part	Middle Part	End Part
1	Anger	0.80	0.70	0.67
	Joy	0.86	0.81	0.83
	Sadness	0.99	0.94	0.90
2	Anger	0.76	0.67	0.64
	Joy	0.83	0.82	0.83
	Sadness	0.95	0.93	0.92
3	Anger	0.81	0.75	0.65
	Joy	0.88	0.86	0.82
	Sadness	0.96	0.94	0.89
4	Anger	0.70	0.69	0.66
	Joy	0.75	0.77	0.76
	Sadness	0.95	0.90	0.89
5	Anger	0.81	0.75	0.66
	Joy	0.89	0.80	0.76
	Sadness	0.95	0.95	0.88

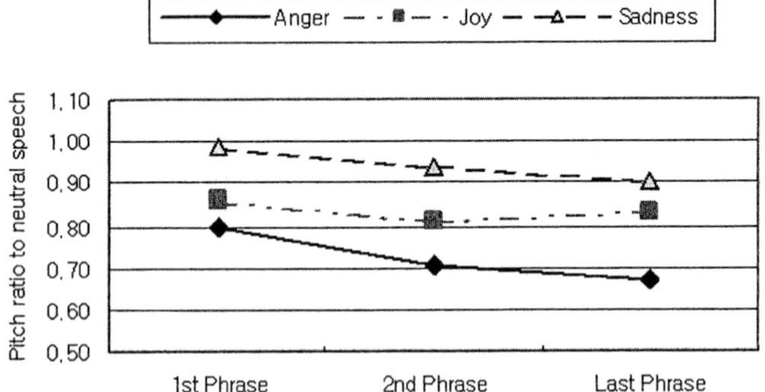

Fig. 1. Example of the pitch ratio variation

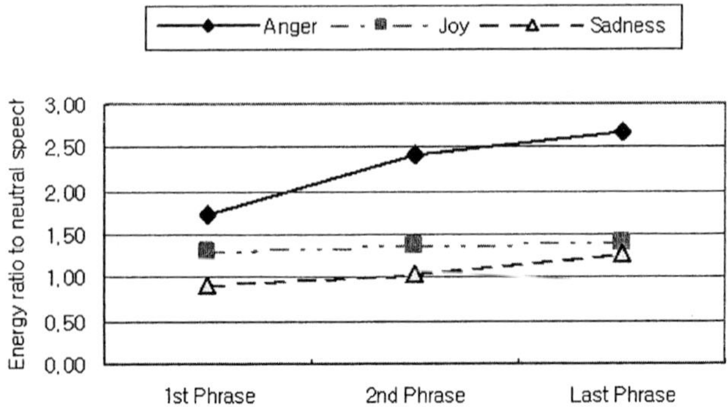

Fig. 2. Example of the pitch energy variation

Table 2. Energy ratio(dB/dB) of each emotional speech to neutral speech

Sentence	Ratio To Neutral	Begin Part	Middle Part	End Part
1	Anger	1.67	2.30	2.53
	Joy	1.16	1.52	1.35
	Sadness	0.77	0.88	1.05
2	Anger	1.71	2.40	2.67
	Joy	1.31	1.36	1.42
	Sadness	0.90	1.04	1.28
3	Anger	1.58	2.21	2.41
	Joy	1.21	1.50	1.43
	Sadness	0.90	0.97	1.15
4	Anger	2.04	2.36	2.15
	Joy	1.55	1.67	1.61
	Sadness	0.90	0.92	1.08
5	Anger	1.74	1.65	2.65
	Joy	1.18	1.23	1.58
	Sadness	1.02	0.96	1.13

emotional and emotionless speech. Fig. 2 shows a typical example of the typical energy change in a sentence. Table 2 and Fig. 2 show that the energy of the emotional speech is mostly larger than that of the neutral speech. As expected, in case of angry emotion speech, the energy is much larger than that of the other emotional ones, especially in the end part. Our observations on the energy feature changes are as follows.

$$\text{Energy} : \text{Neutral} <= \text{Sadness} < \text{Joy} < \text{Anger}$$

3.3 Duration

The behavior of the duration information for different emotions is shown in Table 3 and a typical example for the duration ratio change is introduced in Fig. 3. Both the table and the figure show that the durations of joyful and angry emotional speech are much smaller than that of the neutral speech, and are getting longer gradually in the end part of the sentence. In case of the sad speech sentences, the duration varies relatively small except in the end part of the sentence. The duration of the sad speech is slightly shorter than that of the neutral speech in the sentence, but becomes longer in the end part of the sentence. All the aboves can be represented as follows,

$$\text{Duration: Anger, Joy} < \text{Neutral} <= \text{Sadness}$$

3.4 Feature Analysis

Table 4 shows the overall ratios of the emotional features for different emotions of the total speech database. The variation of each feature according to the phone and the phrase positions of the sentences is not considered. In case of the

Table 3. Duration ratio(msec/msec) of each emotional speech to neutral speech

Sentence	Ratio To Neutral	Begin Part	Middle Part	End Part
1	Anger	0.68	0.75	0.98
	Joy	0.72	0.82	1.16
	Sadness	0.94	0.94	1.37
2	Anger	0.65	0.80	0.97
	Joy	0.69	0.86	0.96
	Sadness	0.94	1.05	1.20
3	Anger	0.74	0.78	0.93
	Joy	0.95	0.81	0.95
	Sadness	0.98	0.94	1.19
4	Anger	0.77	0.82	1.00
	Joy	0.76	0.85	1.09
	Sadness	1.27	1.04	1.27
5	Anger	0.80	0.75	1.01
	Joy	0.83	0.77	1.12
	Sadness	1.01	0.90	1.31

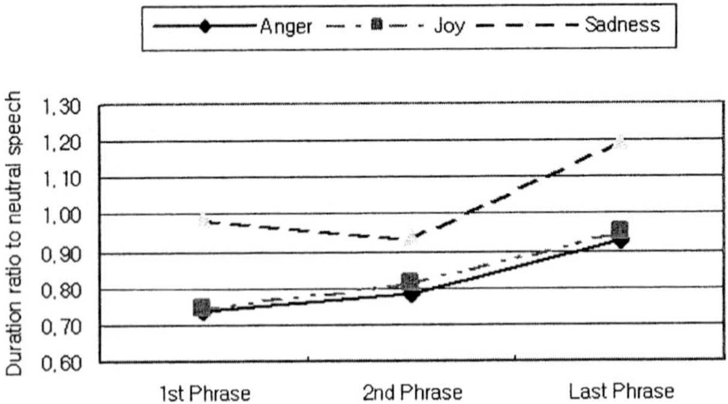

Fig. 3. Example of the duration ratio variation

Table 4. Overall feature ratio of emotional speech to neutral speech

Feature	Joy	Anger	Sadness
Pitch	0.82	0.72	0.93
Energy	1.41	2.14	0.95
Duration	0.88	0.83	1.09

joyful speech, the features decrease except energy. The anger speech has much larger energy but shorter pitch and duration. The sad speech has slight changes in the features, which makes it difficult to convey sad emotion in the neutral speech.

4 Emotional Voice Conversion System

In order to verify the relationship between each emotion and the feature parameters including their variations more closely, a voice conversion system is utilized. The simple block diagram for the system is described in Fig. 4. The conversion

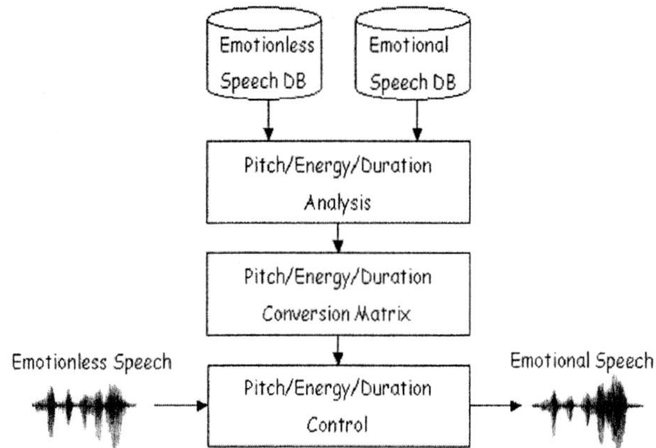

Fig. 4. Block diagram of emotional speech conversion

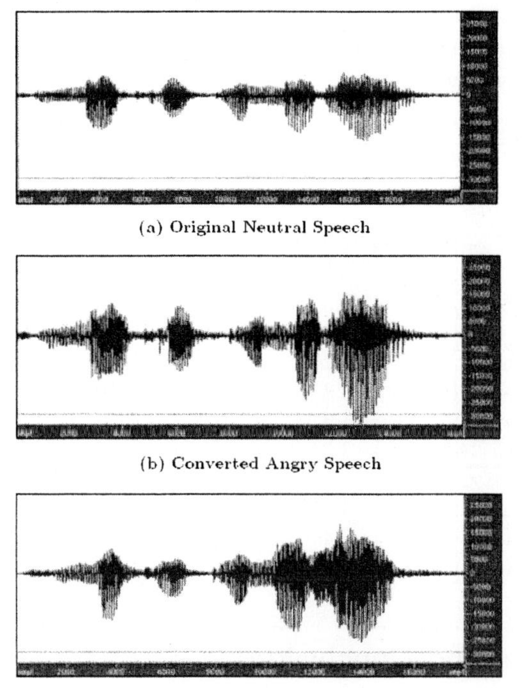

Fig. 5. Original, target and converted speech waveforms

table between the emotionless source speech and the target emotional speech is constructed by utilizing our analysis results of the whole emotional speech data. The conversion is carried out based on the phone unit. The pitch and phones are previously labeled manually as is the case for the synthesis speech data preparation. Each parameter is manipulated not only individually but also simultaneously to find which parameter affects most. The original neutral speech, the conversion target speech, and the converted speech waveforms are presented in Fig. 5.

5 Experimental Results

Table 5 shows the MOS test results of the conversion. Ten people participated in the test. Vote values mean how many people selected in the table, and score values mean the closeness to each emotions varying from 1 to 5. Firstly, each feature parameter is controlled, then, all three of them were modified simultaneously. Separate control of the feature parameter shows that the angry emotion is relatively easier to be added to the neutral speech than the other emotions. The major parameter to control the angry emotion is the duration. When all the parameters were modified, 9 people out of 10 selected the intended emotion successfully. In case of the joyful emotion, no specific parameter contributes in the target emotion generation. When all three parameters were controlled, 6 people voted on the joyful emotion correctly. From the table we can see that the energy is important in sad emotion control. When all the parameters were manipulated the score for the sad emotion became a little higher.

Table 5. MOS test results of emotional voice conversion

Cnvtd. \ Rcgnzd.		Neutral		Anger		Joy		Sadness	
		vote	score	vote	score	vote	score	vote	score
Anger	Duration	5	3.2	5	3.0	-	-	-	-
	Energy	6	3.5	3	2.0	1	1.0	-	-
	Pitch	3	1.3	3	1.3	-	-	4	2.0
	All	1	1.0	9	2.7	-	-	-	-
Joy	Duration	3	2.7	7	2.7	-	-	-	-
	Energy	7	3.8	3	1.3	-	-	-	-
	Pitch	3	1.3	2	2.5	-	-	5	1.6
	All	1	3.0	3	2.0	6	1.7	-	-
Sadness	Duration	9	3.4	-	-	-	-	1	2.0
	Energy	5	4.2	-	-	-	-	5	2.2
	Pitch	7	2.4	2	2.0	-	-	1	1.0
	All	4	2.5	1	2.0	-	-	5	2.4

6 Discussion and Conclusion

In this paper, we tried to verify the relationship between well-known emotional features and the emotional speech in Korean. The emotional speech data were rather short sentences usually containing 3 phrases. The pitch, the energy, and the duration of the emotional speech data are analyzed the beginning, the middle, and the end part of the sentence separately. When a sentence was uttered with emotions, the pitch values of the speech became smaller than that of the emotionless speech. On the contrary, the energy values became larger. The variation of the features fails to show any consistent trend for each type of emotion. The duration and the energy were the major affecting features for the angry and the sad emotions, respectively. In case of the joyful emotion, no feature becomes dominant. When all the parameters were modified, the intended joyful emotion was recognized fairly well. For the angry emotion, we got relatively good conversion results. However, for more successful emotional color conversion, we have to admit that much more intense studies are needed with larger databases. And not only the prosodic features but the acoustics ones have to be analyzed further at the same time to mimic the changed acoustic property in emotional speech more faithfully.

References

1. Vine, D.S.B., Sahandi R.: Synthesis of Emotional Speech using RP-PSOLA. IEE Colloquium on the State of the Art in Speech Synthesis. (2000)
2. Murray, I., Arnott, J.: Implementation and Testing of a System for Producing Emotion-by-Rule in Synthetic Speech. Speech Communication. (1995) 369–390
3. Jun, S., Shigeo, M.: Emotion Modeling in Speech Production using Emotion Space. IEEE International Workshop on Robot and Human Communication. (1996) 472–477
4. Tsuyoshi, M., Shinji, O.: Emotional Recognition and Synthesis System on Speech. Proceedings of IEEE International Conference on Multimedia Computing and Systems. (1999) 840–844
5. Erhard, R., Hannes, P.: Generating Emotional Speech with a Concaternative Synthesizer. Proceedings of ICSLP-98. (1998) 671–675
6. Galanis, D., Darsinos, V., Kokkinakis, G.: Investigating Emotional Speech Parameters for Speech Synthesis. Proceedings of ICECS-96. (1996) 1227–1230
7. Kazuhito, K., Hirotaka, S., Hiroaki, S.: Prosodic Parameters in Emotional Speech. Proceedings of ICSLP-98. (1998) 679–682

Annotation of Emotions and Feelings in Texts

Yvette Yannick Mathieu

Laboratoire de Linguistique formelle – CNRS,
Université Paris 7- CP 7031 – 2, place Jussieu,
75005 Paris cedex 05 – France
ymathieu@linguist.jussieu.fr

Abstract. In this paper, a semantic lexicon in the field of feelings and emotions is presented. This lexicon is described with an ontology. Then, we describe a system to annotate emotions in a text and, finally, we show how these annotations allow a textual navigation.

1 Introduction

A semantic lexicon in the field of feelings, emotions and psychological states is presented here. This lexicon is described with an ontology, and a knowledge base. Our goal is to use this ontology for automatically annotating emotions in texts, in order to navigate through linguistic units with specific criteria.

2 Description of the Lexicon

We studied 950 French words for emotions and psychological states. Among them, 600 are verbs, like *aimer* (to love), *effrayer* (to frighten), and 350 are nouns, like *amour* (love), *colère* (anger), etc. We propose a semantic classification, in which verbs and nouns are split into 38 semantic classes, according to their meanings (cf. Table 1). Each class is labeled by the affect described, such as Peur (fear) class which contains nouns and verbs related to a sensation of fear (fear, to frighten, to fear, etc.).

Table 1. Semantic classes of French psychological words

Amertume	Amour	Amusement	Apaisement	Consternation
Déception	Dédain	Dégoût	Déprime	Dérangement
Désapprobation	Désir sexuel	Embarras	Émerveillement	Émotion
Ennui	Étonnement	Fascination	Haine	Indifférence
Indignation	Inhibition	Insensibilité	Intérêt	Irritation
Jubilation	Obsession	Offense	Orgueil	Passion
Peur	Pitié	Satisfaction	Tracas	Souffrance
Soulagement	Stimulation	Tristesse		

J. Tao, T. Tan, and R.W. Picard (Eds.): ACII 2005, LNCS 3784, pp. 350–357, 2005.

There are three clusters of words:

a -) Negative words which mean the experience or the causation of a rather unpleasant feeling, such as fear or disappointment. They are divided into 22 classes, like Peur (fear), Tristesse (sadness), etc.

b -) Positive words which mean the experience or the causation of a rather pleasant feeling, such as interest or love. They are divided into 14 classes like Intérêt (interest), Passion (passion), etc.

c -) Neutral Words which mean the experience or the causation of a feeling that is neither pleasant nor unpleasant. They belong to two classes: Étonnement (astonishment) and Indifference.

3 Relationships Between Semantic Classes

Semantic classes are linked by meaning, intensity and antonymy relationships, represented with simple graphs.

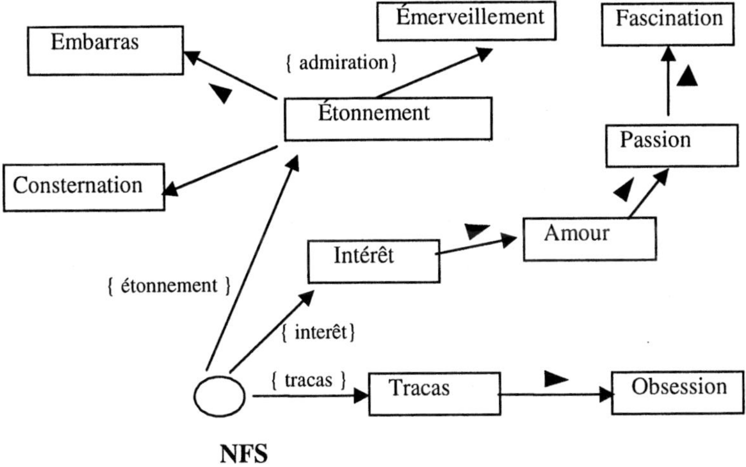

Fig. 1. Meaning and Intensity relationship between semantic classes

Meaning and Intensity graphs are connected graphs, oriented according to intensity of experienced feeling. A graph contains antonymy links between classes. These graphs are shown partially on Fig. 1 and Fig. 2.

There is a "no feeling state" represented by a white circle noted NFS. Labeled arcs join this state to semantic classes. For example, the arc labeled "intérêt" (interest) joins the no feeling state to the Intérêt class. These arcs can be labeled by intensity degree represented by the symbol ▸ or by more specific features like "admiration".

For example, an interest increase on Intérêt class words (interest, attraction, etc.), is described by Amour (love) class words. A stronger emotion of love is reflected by Passion (passion) class words (passion, excitement, etc.), and a stronger emotion of passion is reflected by Fascination class (fascination, to bewitch, etc.).

The antonymy between classes is represented with an arc and the symbol ↔. For example, the Irritation class is antonymous with the Apaisement (calm) class, meaning that each verb or noun in the first class is antonymous with at least one verb or noun respectively in the second class and vice versa.

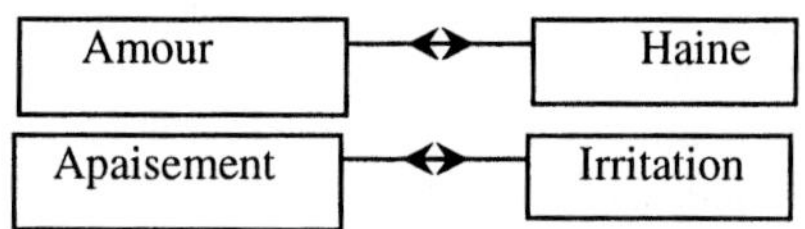

Fig. 2. Subset of Antonymy relationships between semantic classes

4 Semantic Properties of Verbs

We describe here a subset of properties, for a full description see [1], [2], [3].

4.1 Simple Properties

French verbs of feelings, and psychological states occur in two kinds of structures, as illustrated in (1) and (2), respectively:

(1) *Paul irrite Mary*
Paul irritates Mary

(2) *Mary hait Paul*
Mary hates Paul

These structures differ by the syntactic position of the person (*Mary*), called the "experiencer", who has the feeling or the emotion. In (1), the experiencer is the complement, and the subject (*Paul*) is the cause of her feeling (*irritation*). In (2), the experiencer is the subject and the complement *Paul* is the object of her feeling (*hate*). About 500 verbs belong to the first category and 100 to the second one.

This property is called [Experiencer], its value is "subject" for verbs like *aimer*, and "complement" for verbs like *irriter*.

The property "the subject is agentive or non agentive" indicates that *Luc effraye Marie* (Luc frightens Marie) has two possible meanings: that Luc frightens Marie because he wants it, or he frightens her unintentionally, by his behavior or his appearance, or something else. This property is called [Agentivity].

Some verbs have a psychological meaning only, like *aimer*, while others, such as *irriter*, have two meanings: one which is "basic" (3), and one psychological by metaphor (4):

(3) *Le soleil irrite Mary* (sa peau)
The sun irritates Mary (her skin)

(4) *Paul irrite Mary* (par son comportement)
Paul irritates Mary (by his behavior)

This property is called [Metaphor].

Intensity relationships link verbs and nouns inside each class. Thus, *exaspérer* (to exasperate) and *irriter* are in the same class, but *exaspérer* is stronger than *irriter*. These internal intensity relationships between words are described by the property [Intensifier] with the value "neutral" for *irriter*, and the value "high" for *exaspérer*.

A subset of these properties for Irritation class is shown in Table 2 . Each row is a verb (*agacer, énerver,* etc.), and each column is a property .

A plus sign indicates that a verb accepts the property.

Table 2. Simple properties of verbs

	Agentivity	*Experiencer*	*Intensifier*	*Metaphor*
agacer	+	complement	neutral	-
courroucer	+	complement	*high*	-
crisper	+	complement	neutral	+
énerver	+	complement	neutral	+
exaspérer	+	complement	*high*	-
horripiler	-	complement	*high*	-
irriter	+	complement	neutral	+
stresser	+	complement	neutral	-
trépigner	+	subject	*high*	+

4.2 Complex Properties

Whereas simple properties are attribute-value pairs, others are more complex such as arguments selection and arguments structure. For example, when the experiencer is complement, it is always a person, like Mary in sentence (1) *Paul irrite Mary*, or some metonymical expressions referring to a person. There are three main categories of expressions, according to how distant the metonymy is from the person ; it can be (1) a body part (or "soul part") like *coeur* (heart), (2) a feeling or quality name like *colère* (anger), *vanité* (vanity), etc., or (3) a noun such as *espoirs* (hopes) or convictions.

Some verbs select nouns of the first category only, like *briser* (to break) in *Mary a brisé le coeur de Luc* (Mary broke Luc's heart), Some verbs select nouns of the second category also, like *apaiser* ou *calmer* in *La chanson a apaisé/ calmé la colère de Mary* (The song calmed down Mary's anger), while others accept all nouns denoting psychological states, such as *satisfaire* (to satisfy) in *Les paroles de Mary ont satisfait les espoirs/ la curiosité de Luc* (Marie's words satisfied Luc's hopes / curiosity). Moreover, 110 verbs like *irriter* or *déconcerter* (to disconcert) accept non strictly human complement, although with difficulty.

5 Ontology of Emotions and Feelings

In order to make this semantic lexicon usable by people and software agents, it had to be described with an electronic and standard format. For this reason, we built an ontology and a knowledge base in this domain of emotion and feeling.

We consider an ontology as a formal explicit description of concepts, with a set of properties for each concept describing various features of the concept, and relationships between individual members of the class and other items [4].

We built our ontology using Protégé-2000, a framed-based system where concepts are described by classes, and properties by attributes of each class [5]. An ontology with a set of individual instances of classes constitutes a Knowledge base. The classes are linked by a inheritance relation. All subclasses of a class inherit attributes and relationships of that class. A subset of this ontology is given in Fig. 3.

```
MOTS DE SENTIMENTS (Feeling Words)
    MOTS DE POLARITÉ NÉGATIVE (negative polarity words)
        Irritation
            Noms d'irritation
            Verbes d'irritation
        Peur
            Noms de peur
            Verbes de peur
        Tristesse
            Noms de tristesse
            Verbes de tristesse
        etc.
    MOTS DE POLARITÉ POSITIVE (positive polarity words)
        Amour
            Noms d'amour
            Verbes d'amour
        Fascination
            Noms de fascination
            Verbes de fascination
        etc.
    MOTS NEUTRES (neutral words)
        Étonnement
            Noms d'étonnement
            Verbes d'étonnement
```

Fig. 3. Ontology of Emotions and feelings

To the root MOTS DE SENTIMENTS is associated a set of attributes [category, word, metaphor, antonymous class] inherited by each subclass.

MOTS DE POLARITÉ NÉGATIVE are words of unpleasant feeling such as Irritation, Peur, etc., which are divided into nouns and verbs. To each of these class is associated a set of specific attributes. For example, the class Irritation contains the property [higher class] inherited by its subclass "Verbes d'irritation", which contains the properties [experiencer, higher verb, agentivity].

Verbs of irritation (*agacer, énerver, irriter, exaspérer,* etc.) are the instances of this class "Verbes d'irritation". They inherit all the attributes and relationships of the hierarchy.

6 Annotation in Texts

Our goal is to use this ontology for annotating emotion in texts, in order to propose a navigation through a text, with specific criteria. The example given here has been implemented in *NaviTexte* [6],[7], a workstation dedicated to textual visualization and navigation.

NaviTexte applies to a text model based on typed units (TU), marked using XML format. Each unit has one type and an unlimited number of attributes. Navigation is carried out by operations which links two typed units, a source and a target. Furthermore, *NaviTexte* allows us to specify several conditions and a span of text.

Each operation must specify a type of moving by using one of these pre-definite instructions: {*First, Last, Forward(i), Backward(i)*}. *First, Last,* indicates that the search of the target is absolute: the TU displayed will be the first or the last TU, in the specified span, which checked the conditions. *Forward(i), Backward(i),* indicates that the search is carried out relatively to the source (before or after) and indexed by the integer *i*. For example, {*Forward(3)*} is interpreted as the search of the third TU located after the source, provided that its attributes match the conditions. It must be emphasized that all this navigation knowledge (the set of navigation operations), which are declared in specific cartridges, are independent of the annotated text.

For navigating through the text, we have chosen one type of textual units, which specifies navigation operations and makes it possible to establish feeling links between them. Thus, the navigation allows us to track different types of feeling and to identify their linguistic realization in a given language.

The text we consider here is extracted from *Madame Bovary* by Gustave Flaubert [8]. The navigation through this novel allows a reader to follow, for example, the evolution of Emma's feelings to her husband Charles, or to her lovers (Léon, then Rodolphe). An example of dynamic interface proposed by *NaviTexte* is shown in Fig. 4. In this part of text, we focus on the irritation Emma feels to Charles. Given a textual unit, a verb of irritation, here "exaspérée", the system proposes an oriented navigation towards verbs of the same emotion with the same intensity level: <Continuer vers même intensité> (Going to the same Intensity), or with a lower or higher intensity level: <Continuer vers diminution d'intensité> (Going to lower Intensity), <Continuer vers augmentation d'intensité> (Going to higher Intensity).

To realize this example, we first define two attributes: {Semantic Class, Intensity}, and a set of navigation operations which apply to these attributes. A subset is given below:

{<Continuer vers même intensité (Going to same intensity), Semantic Class Irritation ILN (Intensity Level = Neutral), NEXT Semantic Class Irritation ILN>.

<Continuer vers diminution d'intensité (Going to a lower intensity), Semantic Class Irritation ILH (Intensity Level = High), NEXT Semantic Class Irritation ILN>.

Then, to each verb inside the text, we associate the value of the semantic class it belongs to, and its intensity level. The definition of attributes, navigation operations and text annotations are written in XML format. An example of annotations is shown in Fig. 5.

Given the verb source ("exaspérée") and the navigation operation <Continuer vers diminution d'intensité>, *NaviTexte* find out automatically which first target satisfies the condition: a verb with the same meaning (same semantic class) with a lower intensity, and it proposes “irritée”.

In order to be usable by *NaviTexte*, we had to rewrite the ontology knowledge into a specific format. Our goal is to allow the system to use this ontology for automatically annotating emotions in texts, and automatically navigate through the text with specific conditions. For instance, by consulting the ontology, the system will know that the verbs *exaspérer* and *irriter* are in the same semantic class, and that *exaspérer* is stronger than *irriter*. And given the operation <Continuer vers diminution d’intensité > (Going to a lower intensity), the system will use the ontology to find out between which classes this operation applies.

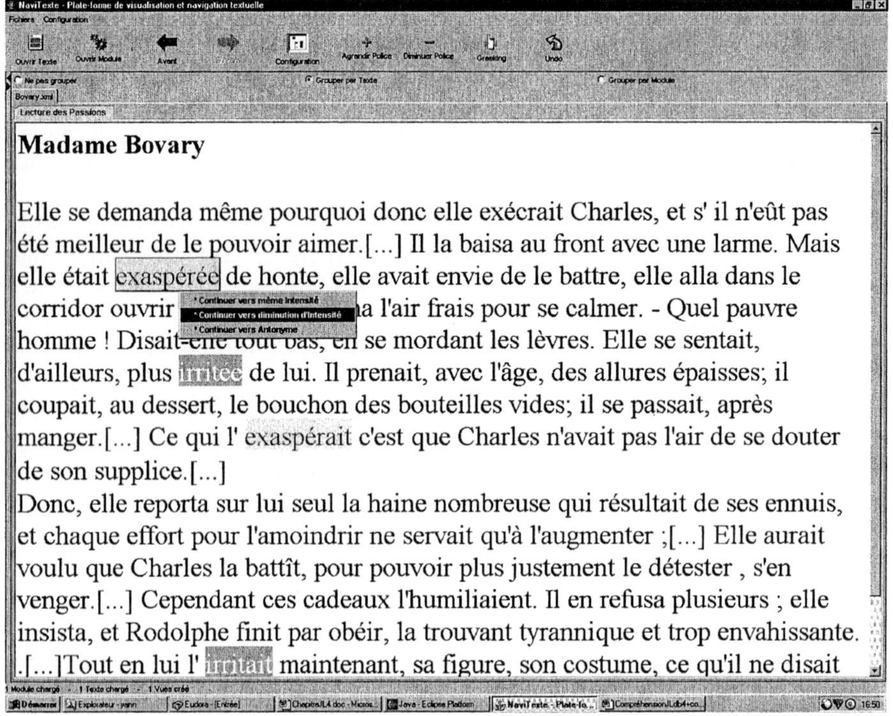

Fig. 4. Example of dynamic interface

[...]-<UT Type="segment" Nro="15"> <Chaine>Il la baisa au front avec une larme. Mais elle était </Chaine></UT>
-<UT Type="verbe" Nro="2">
<Attribut Nom=" Semantic Class ">Class Irriter ILH</Attribut>
<Attribut Nom="Intensity">2</Attribut>
<Chaine>exaspérée</Chaine> </UT>

Fig. 5. Annotations of the unit “exaspérée”

7 Conclusion

We have presented a semantic lexicon in the field of feelings and emotions, as well as its representation into an ontology. Then, we described a system to annotate emotions in texts semi-automatically and, finally, we have shown how these annotations make a textual navigation possible. Our goal is to offer a system which uses an ontology to annotate and navigate through a text automatically.

Acknowledgments

We thank Jean-Luc Minel for offering valuable suggestions and stimulating discussions during the course of this work.

References

1. Mathieu, Y. Y. Les verbes de sentiments. De l'analyse linguistique au traitement automatique, CNRS Editions, Paris (2000)
2. Mathieu, Y. Y. Linguistic Knowledge and Automatic Semantic Representation of Emotions and Feelings. », *International Conference on Information Technology*, ITCC 2004, IEEE Computer Society (2004) 314–318
3. Mathieu, Y. Y. A Computational Semantic Lexicon of French Verbs of Emotion. In Shanahan, G., Qu, Y., Wiebe, J. (eds.): Computing Attitude and Affect in Text. Springer, Dordrecht, The Netherlands (2005 , to be appear)
4. Uschold, M ;,Gruninger, M. Ontologies: Principles, Methods and Applications. Knowledge Engineering Review 11(2) (1996)
5. Protégé. The Protégé Project. http://protege.stanford.edu, (2000)
6. Couto J., Minel J.-L. Outils dynamiques de fouilles textuelles, actes de RIAO, Avignon (2004) 420-430
7. Couto J., Lundquist l., Minel J.-L. Using *NaviTexte* to teach French as a second language, *Proceedings of Recent Research Developments in Learning Technologies,* Carceres, Spain (2005)
8. Flaubert, G. Madame Bovary, Gallimard, Paris (2001)

IG-Based Feature Extraction and Compensation for Emotion Recognition from Speech

Ze-Jing Chuang and Chung-Hsien Wu

Department of Computer Science and Information Engineering,
National Cheng Kung University, Tainan
{chwu, bala}@csie.ncku.edu.tw

Abstract. This paper presents an approach to emotion recognition from speech signals. In this approach, the intonation groups (IGs) of the input speech signals are firstly extracted. The speech features in each selected intonation group are then extracted. With the assumption of linear mapping between feature spaces in different emotional states, a feature compensation approach is proposed to characterize the feature space with better discriminability among emotional states. The compensation vector with respect to each emotional state is estimated using the Minimum Classification Error (MCE) algorithm. The IG-based feature vectors compensated by the compensation vectors are used to train the Gaussian Mixture Models (GMMs) for each emotional state. The emotional state with the GMM having the maximal likelihood ratio is determined as the final output. The experimental result shows that IG-based feature extraction and compensation can obtain encouraging performance for emotion recognition.

1 Introduction

Human-machine interface technology has been investigated for several decades. Recent research made more emphasis on the recognition of nonverbal information, especially on the topic of emotion reaction. Scientists have found that emotional skills can be an important component of intelligence, especially for human-human communication. Although human-computer interaction is different from human-human communication, some theories have shown that human-computer interaction is essentially following the basics of human-human interaction [1]. In this paper, an emotion recognition approach from speech signals is proposed. This method consists of the definition and extraction of intonation groups (IGs), IG-based feature extraction, and feature compensation.

In the past years, many researchers have paid their attention to emotion recognition via speech signals. Several important recognition models have been applied to the emotion recognition task, such as Neural Network (NN)[2], Hidden Markov Model (HMM)[3], and Support Vector Machine (SVM)[4][5]. Besides the generally used prosodic and acoustic features, some special features are also applied for this task, such as TEO-based features [6]. Although lots of features and recognition models have been tested in these works, large overlaps between the feature spaces for different emotional states is rarely considered. Besides, the pre-trained emotion recognition model is highly speaker-dependent.

J. Tao, T. Tan, and R.W. Picard (Eds.): ACII 2005, LNCS 3784, pp. 358–365, 2005.

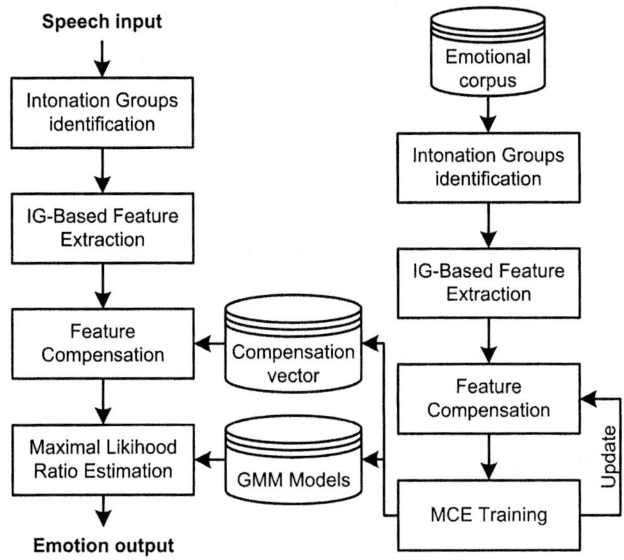

Fig. 1. Block diagram of the proposed emotion recognition approach

To solve the above questions, this paper proposes an approach to emotion recognition based on feature compensation. The block diagram of the approach is shown in Fig.1. In order to identify the most significant segment, the intonation groups (IGs) of the input speech signals are firstly extracted. Following the feature extraction process [7], the prosodic feature sets are estimated for the IG segments. Then all the feature vectors compensated by compensation vectors are modeled by a Gaussian Mixture Model (GMM). Finally, the minimum classification error (MCE) training method [8] iteratively estimates all the model parameters.

The rest of the paper is organized as follows. Sec.2 describes the definition of Intonation Group and the extraction of the prosodic features. Then the feature compensation technique and MCE training is provided in Sec.3. Finally, experimental results and conclusion are drawn in Sec.4 and Sec.5, respectively.

2 Feature Extraction

2.1 Intonation Group Extraction

The intonation group, also known as breath-groups, tone-groups, or intonation phrases, is usually defined as the segment of an utterance between two pauses.

As shown in Fig. 2. The intonation group is identified by analyzing the smoothed pitch contour (the gray-thick line in Fig. 2). Three types of smoothed pitch contour patterns are defined as the intonation group:

- **Type 1**: a complete pitch segment that starts from the point of a pitch rise to the point of the next pitch rise,

- **Type 2**: a monotonically decreasing pitch segment,
- **Type 3**: a monotonically increasing pitch segment.

For all identified IG segments, only those IGs that match the following criterion are selected for feature extraction:

- the complete IGs with the largest pitch range or duration,
- the monotonically decreasing or increasing IGs with the largest pitch range or duration,
- the monotonically decreasing or increasing IGs at the start or end of a sentence.

In the example of Fig. 2, only three IGs are selected for feature extraction.

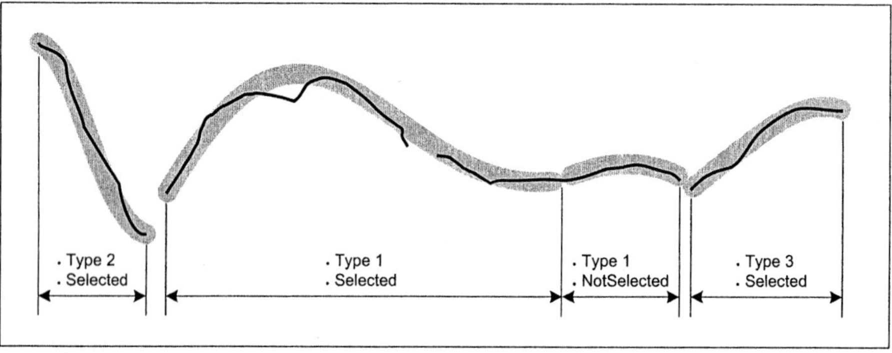

Fig. 2. An illustration of the definition and extraction of Intonation Groups. Four IGs are extracted from the smoothed pitch contour (the gray-thick line), but only three IGs (the first, second, and forth IGs) are selected for feature extraction.

2.2 IG-Based Feature Extraction

Emotional state can be characterized by many speech features, such as pitch, energy, or duration [9]. In this paper, we use the following 64 prosodic features as the input features for emotion recognition:

- Speaking rate and relative duration (2 values),
- Pause number and relative pause duration (2 values),
- Average, standard deviation, maximum, and minimum of pitch, energy, zero-crossing-rate, and F1 (formant one) values (16 values),
- Average and standard deviation of jitter (for pitch) and shimmer (for energy) (4 values),
- Relative positions where the maximal and minimal pitch, energy, zero-crossing-rate, and F1 value occur (8 values),
- Fourth-order Legendre parameters of pitch, energy, zero-crossing-rate, and F1 contours of the whole sentence and the "rapidest part" (32 values), which is the segment between the positions with the maximum and minimum values.

Jitter is a variation of individual cycle lengths in pitch-period measurement, and shimmer is the same measurement for energy [10].

3 Compensation Vector Estimation Using MCE

The goal of feature compensation is to move the feature space of an emotional state to a feature space more discriminative to other emotional states. Given a sequence of the training data $\mathbf{X}^e = \{x_n^e\}_{n=1}^N$, where x_n^e indicates the n-th feature vector that belongs to emotional state E_e. The feature vector extracted for each intonation group contains the prosodic features mentioned above. With the assumption of linear mapping between feature spaces in different emotional states, the vector compensation function is defined as:

$$\tilde{x}_n^{e\to f} = x_n^e + p\left(E_e \middle| x_n^e\right) r_{e\to f}, \tag{1}$$

where $r_{e\to f}$ is a compensation vector of emotional state E_e with respect to the reference emotional state E_f. The conditional probability of the emotional state E_e given the input feature vector x_n^e is estimated as:

$$p\left(E_e \middle| x_n^e\right) = \frac{p\left(x_n^e \middle| E_e\right) p\left(E_e\right)}{\sum_i p\left(x_n^e \middle| E_i\right) p\left(E_i\right)}. \tag{2}$$

Minimum classification error (MCE) training based on the generalized probabilistic descent (GPD) method is applied in our study. We assume that the probability of a mapped feature vector $\tilde{x}_n^{e\to f}$ given an emotional state E_c follows the distribution of a mixture of Gaussian density function:

$$g_c\left(\tilde{x}_n^{e\to f}\right) \equiv p\left(\tilde{x}_n^{e\to f} \middle| E_c\right) = \sum_m w_m^c \cdot N\left(\tilde{x}_n^{e\to f}; \mu_m^c, \delta_m^c\right), \tag{3}$$

where $N\left(\cdot\,; \mu_m^c, \delta_m^c\right)$ denotes the normal distribution with mean μ_m^c and diagonal covariance matrix δ_m^c, and w_m^c is the mixture weight. To estimate the mapping coefficients and GMM parameters jointly by MCE training, the misclassification measure is defined as:

$$D_e \equiv D(\mathbf{X}_e) = -g_e(\mathbf{X}_e) + \frac{1}{\eta}\log\left[\frac{1}{\mathrm{C}-1}\sum_{c\neq e}\exp(\eta\, g_c(\mathbf{X}_e))\right], \tag{4}$$

where $\mathbf{X}_e$ denotes a set of data compensated from the emotional state E_e, $\mathbf{X}_e = \left\{\tilde{x}_n^{e\to f}\right\}_{f\neq e}$, $\mathbf{C}$ is the number of emotional state, and η is a penalty factor. The function $g_c\left(\mathbf{X}_e\right)$ is the average likelihood estimated by the GMM of the emotional state E_c given $\mathbf{X}_e$. Based on the GPD iterative theory, the parameters will approximate the global optimization using the iterative equation:

$$\Theta_{t+1} = \Theta_t - \varepsilon \cdot \nabla l. \tag{5}$$

The loss function is defined as a sigmoid function of misclassification measure. And the gradient of loss function ∇l is the partial differential to the updated parameter. Using chain rule, the gradient of loss function can be divided into three components. The first component can be derived to a closed form $a \cdot l_e \cdot (1 - l_e)$, and the second component is assumed as:

$$\frac{\partial D_e}{\partial g_c} = \begin{cases} -1 & ,e = c \\ 1 & ,e \neq c \end{cases}. \tag{6}$$

Since there are four different parameters needed to be updated, the last component of the gradient with respect to each parameter is obtained as:

$$\frac{\partial g_e}{\partial r_{e \to f}} = \frac{-1}{\mathbf{N}(\mathbf{C}-1)} \sum_n \sum_m \frac{w_m^e \left(\tilde{x}_n^{e \to f} - \mu_m^e \right) p\left(E_e \middle| x_n^e \right)}{\left(\delta_n^e \right)^2} N\left(x_n^e ; \mu_m^e, \delta_n^e \right), \tag{7}$$

$$\frac{\partial g_e}{\partial w_m^e} = \frac{1}{\mathbf{N}(\mathbf{C}-1)} \sum_n \sum_r N\left(\tilde{x}_n^{e \to f} ; \mu_m^e, \delta_m^e \right), \tag{8}$$

$$\frac{\partial g_e}{\partial \mu_m^e} = \frac{1}{\mathbf{N}(\mathbf{C}-1)} \sum_n \sum_r \left[w_m^e \left(\tilde{x}_n^{e \to f} - \mu_m^e \right) \left(\delta_m^e \right)^{-2} N\left(\tilde{x}_n^{e \to f} ; \mu_m^e, \delta_m^e \right) \right], \tag{9}$$

$$\frac{\partial g_e}{\partial \delta_m^e} = \frac{1}{\mathbf{N}(\mathbf{C}-1)} \sum_n \sum_e \left[w_m^e \left(\left(\tilde{x}_n^{e \to f} - \mu_m^e \right)^2 - \left(v_m^e \right)^2 \right) \left(v_m^e \right)^{-3} N\left(\tilde{x}_n^{e \to f} ; \mu_m^e, \delta_m^e \right) \right]. \tag{10}$$

Given an input feature vector y, the recognized emotional state E_e^* is determined according to the following equation:

$$E_e^* = \arg\max_e \left[\sum_{i \neq e} g_e \left(y + p\left(E_e \middle| y \right) r_{e \to i} \right) \Big/ \sum_{j \neq e} g_j \left(y + p\left(E_j \middle| y \right) r_{j \to e} \right) \right], \tag{11}$$

4 Experimental Results

In this experiment four kinds of emotional states: Neutral, Happy, Angry, and Sad was adopted. The emotional speech corpus was collected in 8KHz and 16bits. 40 sentences for each emotional state were recorded by 8 volunteers.

Besides the proposed prosodic features, we also evaluated the recognition rate for Mel-Frequency Cepstrum Coefficient (MFCC) features, which is generally used in speech recognition task. To investigate the performance of the proposed method, we tested both the proposed method and a baseline system, which is a GMM emotion recognition system without any preprocessing before feature extraction.

4.1 Mixture Number Determination

The number of mixtures in the GMM is firstly determined for each emotional state. Assuming that the number of mixtures is greater than 3, the average likelihood of all training data given the GMM with different mixture number is calculated. Figure 3 shows the plot of GMM likelihoods using both prosodic and MFCC features.

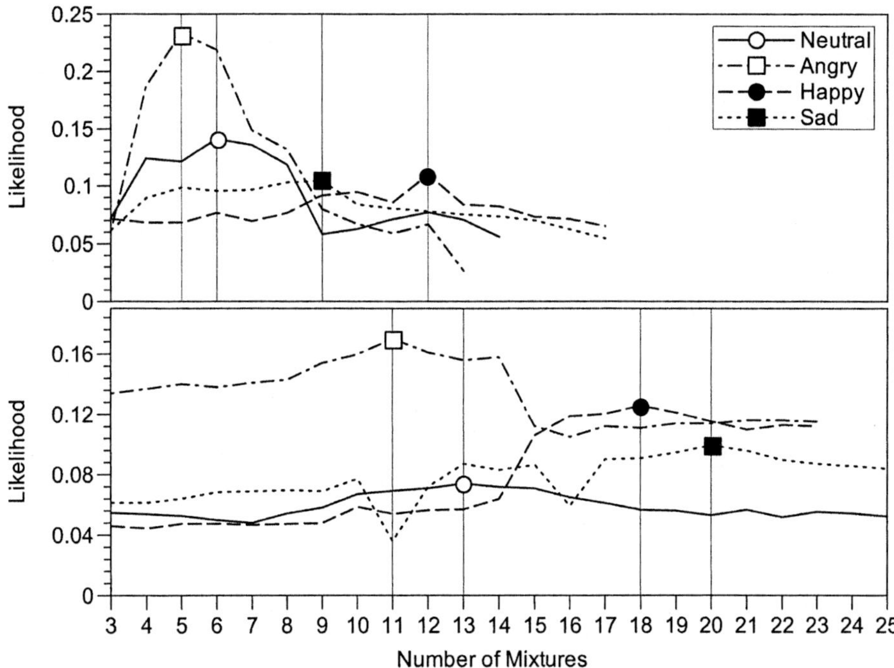

Fig. 3. The likelihood contours of GMMs with increasing mixture number. The upper part is the plot using prosodic features, and the lower part is the plot using MFCC features.

Accordingly, the numbers of mixtures using prosodic features is set to 6, 5, 12, and 9 for neutral, angry, happy, and sad emotion, respectively. To evaluate MFCC features, the number of mixtures was also evaluated using the same method. The contours of the likelihood using MFCC features is shown in Fig. 4, and the mixture numbers for neutral, angry, happy, and sad emotions are set to 13, 11, 18, and 20, respectively.

4.2 Experiments on Emotion Recognition

Table 1 shows the results for emotion recognition, including the proposed approach and the baseline system.

Although MFCC feature outperforms prosodic features in the inside test, prosodic features achieved better performance in both outside-open and outside-closed tests. The reason of this result is that the MFCC features contain much information from speech content and speaker. To model the emotional state using MFCC features become to model the speech content and speaker. Therefore, a GMM can perfectly model the distribution of MFCC features, but cannot well characterize the unseen features in outside test. In the proposed approach, MFCC features remain its higher recognition rate in inside test, and the prosodic features obtain the best overall performance. From the above experiments, an increase in recognition rate for the approaches with IG-based feature extraction is about 5% to 10% compared to that without IG-based feature extraction. Furthermore, an improvement of 10% in recognition rate for the approach with feature compensation is obtained compared to that without feature compensation.

Table 1. The emotion recognition result. The abbreviation **FC** indicates the method using **F**eature **C**ompensation. The abbreviation **In, OO**, and **OC** indicate the results from **In**side, **O**utside-**O**pen, and **O**utside-**C**losed tests, respectively.

Approach	Prosodic	MFCC	Prosodic+IG	MFCC+IG
Without FC (In)	74.33%	99.96%	76.32%	99.24%
Without FC (OO)	49.78%	35.15%	51.07%	35.01%
Without FC (OC)	55.95%	37.22%	59.90%	42.13%
With FC (In)	80.72%	95.12%	83.94%	91.32%
With FC (OO)	55.19%	41.27%	60.13%	49.10%
With FC (OC)	61.03%	41.03%	67.52%	52.86%

5 Conclusion

In this paper, an approach to emotion recognition from speech signals is proposed. In order to obtain crucial features, the IG-based feature extraction method is used. After feature extraction, the feature vector compensation approach and MCE training method are applied to increase the discriminability among emotional states. The experiments show that it is useful to integrate IG-based feature extraction and feature compensation to emotion recognition. The result of emotion recognition using the proposed approaches is 83.94% for inside test and 60.13% for outside-open test. We also demonstrate that the prosodic feature is more suitable for emotion recognition than the acoustic MFCC features in speaker-independent task.

The future work of this research is to improve the recognition accuracy for outside data. Though the feature compensation is useful for emotion recognition, the compensation vector is still speaker-dependent. An adaptation method will be useful to adapt compensation vectors for emotional speech with different speaking styles.

References

1. Reeves, B., Nass, C.: The Media Equation: How People Treat Computers, Televi-sion, and New Media Like Real People and Places. University of Chicago Press (1996)
2. Bhatti, M.W., Wang, Y., Guan, L.: A neural network approach for human emotion recogni-tion in speech. IEEE International Symposium on Circuits and Systems, Vancouver, Canada (2004) 181-184
3. Inanoglu, Z., Caneel, R.: Emotive alert□HMM-based emotion detection in voicemail messages. IEEE Intelligent User Interfaces '05, San Diego, California, USA (2005) 251-253
4. Kwon, O.W., Chan, K., Hao, J., Lee, T.W.: Emotion Recognition by Speech Signals. 8th European Conference on Speech Communication and Technology, Geneva, Switzerland (2003) 125-128
5. Chuang, Z.J., Wu, C.H.: Multi-Modal Emotion Recognition from Speech and Text. International Journal of Computational Linguistics and Chinese Language Processing, Vol. 9, No. 2 , August 2004 1-18

6. Rahurkar, M.A., Hansen, J. H.L.: Frequency Distribution Based Weighted Sub-Band Approach for Classification of Emotional/Stressful Content in Speech. 8th European Conference on Speech Communication and Technology, Geneva, Switzerland (2003) 721-724
7. Deng, L., Droppo, J., Acero,A.: Recursive estimation of nonstationary noise using iterative stochastic approximation for robust speech recognition. IEEE Transactions on Speech and Audio, Vol. 11 Issue 6 , (2003) 568-580
8. Wu, J. Huo, Q.: An environment compensated minimum classification error training approach and its evaluation on aurora2 database. 7th International Conference on Spoken Language, Denver, Colorado, USA (2002) 453-456
9. Ververidis, D., Kotropoulos, C., Pitas, I.: Automatic emotional speech classification. IEEE International Conference on Acoustics, Speech, and Signal Processing, Montreal, Montreal, Canada (2005) 593-596
10. Levity, M., Huberz, R., Batlinery, A., Noeth, E.: Use of prosodic speech characteristics for automated detection of alcohol intoxication. Prosody in Speech Recognition and Understanding, Molly Pitcher Inn, Red Bank, NJ, USA (2001)

Toward a Rule-Based Synthesis of Emotional Speech on Linguistic Descriptions of Perception

Chun-Fang Huang and Masato Akagi

School of Information Science, Japan Advanced Institute of Science and Technology, 1-1 Asahidai, Nomi-shi, Ishikawa, Japan
{chuang, akagi}@jaist.ac.jp

Abstract. This paper reports rules for morphing a voice to make it be perceived as containing various primitive features, for example, to make it sound more "bright" or "dark". In a previous work we proposed a three-layered model, which contains emotional speech, primitive features, and acoustic features, for the perception of emotional speech. By experiments and acoustic analysis, we built the relationships between the three layers and reported that such relationships are significant. Then, a bottom-up method was adopted in order to verify the relationships. That is, we morphed (resynthesized) a speech voice by composing acoustic features in the bottommost layer to produce a voice in which listeners could perceive a single or multiple primitive features, which could be further perceived as different categories of emotion. The intermediate results show that the relationships of the model built in previous work are valid.

1 Introduction

Traditionally, human-computer interaction is a sequence of instruction-reaction steps. The computer does what humans tell it to do. This interaction model requires self-adapting of human working habits to meet the responsive style of the computer. This model may be adequate for a computing environment such as a computer terminal. But in the current ever-changing environment and burgeoning information era, a new computer interaction model is required. In order to create such a new interaction model, we could follow one of two paths. One would be to create a computing environment that is designed by considering how human minds work, and making it as easy as possible [1]. The other is to create a computing environment that instead of asking humans to behave in a self-adapting way, programs the computer to respond differently to coordinate with the human's emotional state [2]. With regard to the second situation, in order to create a computer-adapting environment, we must give computers the ability to sense human emotional states. There are many ways that humans express their emotional states intentionally or spontaneously, such as through facial expression [3] or voice [4]. Due to the maturity of voice recognition technology, one of the most effective ways to help computers adapt themselves might be by voice.

Generally, research on expression in speech falls into two categories. One is the perception of emotional states in speech; the other is the production of emotional

J. Tao, T. Tan, and R.W. Picard (Eds.): ACII 2005, LNCS 3784, pp. 366–373, 2005.

speech. There are many different synthesis techniques for producing emotional speech. Formant synthesis [5][6][7][8] provides a non-pre-recorded-voice approach and uses a set of rules to control different acoustic parameters. The resulting synthesis voice is less natural but has richer degree of control over varying parameters [10]. Conversely, concatenative synthesis concatenates pre-recorded speech segments (mostly triphones and diphones) to form the speech voice. The resulting synthesis voice, when compared to formant synthesis, is more natural but there is less control over varying parameters [10][11][12][13]. Another technique is morphing. It also uses pre-recorded speech of completed sentences and can be used to manipulate recordings [14][15].

For emotional speech, Figure 1 shows a conceptual diagram of the perceptual model proposed by Huang and Akagi [16]. Unlike most other studies that deal with the direct relationship between emotional speech and acoustic features [5][6][7], this model consists of three layers, emotional speech, primitive features, and acoustic features, where the emotional speech includes five categories, *Neutral* (N), *Joy* (J), *Cold Anger* (CA), *Sadness* (S), and *Hot Anger* (HA). The primitive features are considered as a set of adjectives often used to describe speech, such as bright or dark. The acoustic features are a set of the acoustic features of speech signals. The concept is based on the assumption that humans perceive emotion from speech according to a combination of different primitive features that they give to the utterance they hear. The concept is inspired from an observation that when listening to the voice of a speaker, our first sense is something like "it sounds very bright and slightly fast", which we then interpret as "the speaker is happy". From the observation, we conclude (1) the emotion we perceive in speech may depend on what we have sensed, such like "bright", from the voice; (2) humans describe their perception of phenomenon with vague linguistic forms, not precise values, and this human vagueness should be considered; and (3) although human nature is vague, a precise analytical/mathematic approach to deal with that vagueness is needed.

A two-phase approach was taken to build the model. The first phase builds the model by a top-down method and the second phase verifies the model by a bottom-up

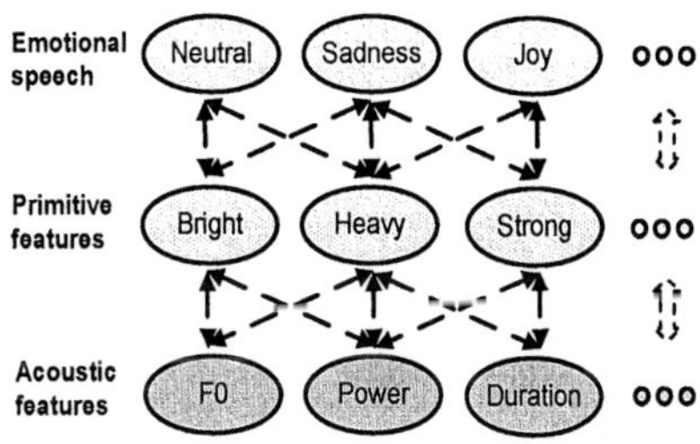

Fig. 1. Conceptual diagram of the perceptual model

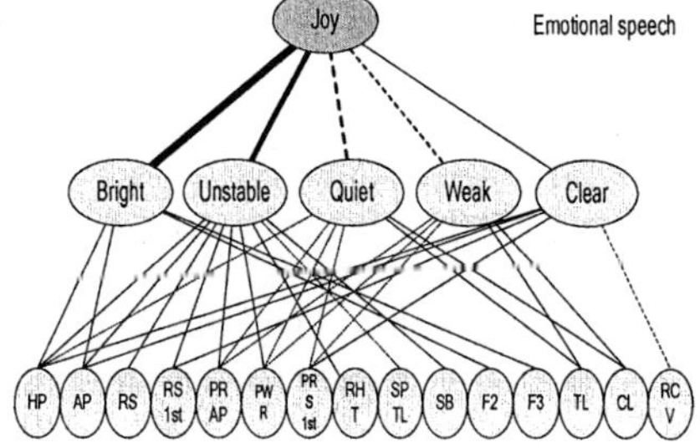

Fig. 2. Resultant perceptual model of emotion Joy. The solid lines indicate the relation is a positive correlation, and the dotted ones indicate a negative correlation. The thicker the line is, the higher the correlation.

method, where the top-down method is analysis and the bottom-up method is synthesis. In our previous work, the first phase was accomplished. We built the perceptual model that includes two relationships. The first relationship, between categories of emotion and primitive features, was built by conducting three experiments and applying fuzzy inference systems. The second relationship, between primitive features and acoustic features, was built by analyzing acoustic features in speech signals. Combining the two relationships, we showed an efficient model for perception of emotional speech. Fig 2 shows one of the resultant perceptual models of the emotion "Joy".

The purpose of our current research is to verify the model, which is the second phase of model building. Our approach is to morph (resynthesize) a speech voice by composing the acoustic features of the bottommost layer to produce speech with the perception of single or multiple primitive features, which can further be perceived as different categories of emotion. To this end, the verification phase was divided into two stages. In the first stage, rules for morphing speech to make it be perceived as various primitive features were established. In the second stage, the rules of primitive feature perception were combined to produce rules for morphing speech to make it be perceived as different emotions. This paper describes how the rules in the first stage were established according to the results of experiments and acoustic analysis and an experiment that was conducted to evaluate the rule performance of relations between acoustic features and primitive features. The second stage is an item of future work.

The remainder of this paper is organized as follows. Section 2 describes the working flow of the current research and the principles of rule establishment. Section 3 gives the results for the rules of primitive features. Section 4 describes our conclusion and future work.

2 Rules of Primitive Features

In this section, the principles of rule establishment and the working flow of current research are described.

2.1 Principles

There are three mandating principles and one optional principle of rule establishment.

1. *Rules are monotonous.* This means any newly added rule will not weaken the perception of an existing rule
2. *Rules are general.* This means rules are applied to general perception, not any specific personality consideration.
3. *Rules are dynamic.* This means a newly added rule changes the configuration of existing rules but still be monotonous.

One optional principle is *the pursuit of naturalness*. The fact that it is optional does not imply naturalness is unimportant or undesirable to achieve. It is only because the focal point of our research is finding the effectiveness of synthesizing on the basis of primitive features. If we try to pursue naturalness along with the other principles, the focus of the research will be lost.

2.2 Working Flow of the Second Phase

Figure 3 shows the working flow of our current research. For each stage of the verification phase, there are two steps, production and evaluation.

With regard to the first stage to create morphed voice for primitive feature perception, two types of rules for primitive features, atomic rules and compound rules (see Fig. 4), are developed that are designed for resynthsizing the speech voice so that it will be perceived as having different kinds of primitive features. It is an iterative process that includes:

1. Develop atomic rules for resynthesizing speech so that it might be perceived as one or more primitive features. More details about how the rules are developed based on the results of the acoustic analysis and experiments in our previous work will be introduced in the next section.
2. Implement rules using STRAIGHT [14].
3. Conduct perception experiments to verify the rules.
4. Refine rules according to the results of experiments.

Compound rules are for resynthesizing speech to make it be perceived as multiple types of primitive features. The process is identical to that for atomic rules. Compound rules are more complex than atomic rules. Currently only atomic rules have been developed.

In the evaluation step, we evaluate the effectiveness of our rules for primitive features. In this step, atomic rules and compound rules are used to resynthesize the speech voices, to make them be perceived as different types of primitive features and categories of emotional speech, and to conduct perception experiments to verify them. This method is also designed to verify the relationships built by the top-down method. In the following session, the establishment of atomic rules and the results are described.

An atomic rule is defined for each primitive feature. It defines the configurations of acoustic features that participate in it. A *configuration* consists of three types of parameters, the multi-regression correlation coefficient between the primitive feature and all acoustic features, a percentage variation, and ranges of values (maximum and minimum).

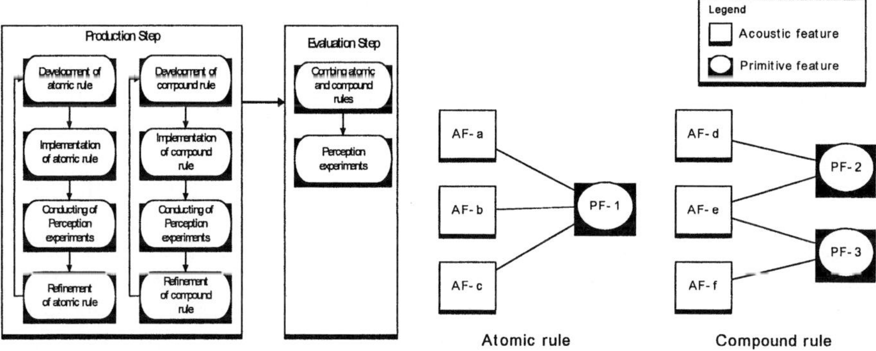

Fig. 3. Working flow of current research

Fig. 4. Atomic rules and compound rules

3 Methodology

In this section, the method of rule establishment and the intermediate experimental results are described.

3.1 Establishment of Rules

There are three steps for creating rules.

Step 1: Analysis of Acoustic Feature
As was reported in our previous work [16], we measured acoustic features on the basis of two aspects – accentual phrase and overall utterance – because most people do not speak continuously. For example, in Japanese the sentence /a ta ra shi i ku ru ma o ka i ma shi ta/[1] was always spoken with pauses in such a way / a ta ra shi i ku ru ma o ka i ma shi ta/, forming 3 accentual phases. Nine acoustic features are measured from the F0 contour, eight from the power envelope, five from the power spectrum, and six from the duration. The acoustic features are the following.

F0 Contour: for the accentual phrase aspect, the features are mean value of rising slope (RS), mean value of rising duration, mean value of falling slope, mean value of falling duration, and mean value of pitch range, where *pitch range* is the band width of the range bounded by the lowest and highest F0 of each phase. For overall utterance aspect, they are average F0 (AP), pitch range, highest F0 (HP), and rising slope of the first accent phrase (RS1st).

Power Envelope: for the accentual phrase aspect, the features are mean value of rising slope (RS), mean value of rising duration, mean value of falling slope, mean value of falling duration, and mean value of power range (PRAP). For overall utterance aspect, they are power range (PWR), rising slope of the first accent phrase (RS1st), and the ratio between the average power in high frequency portion (over 3 kHz) and the average power (RHT).

Spectral: the features are first formant (F1), second formant (F2), third formant (F3), spectral tilt (ST), and spectral balance (SB).

Time Duration: pause length, phoneme length, total length (TL), consonant length (CL), vowel length, ratio between consonant length and vowel length (RCV)

Step 2: Selection of Participant Acoustic Feature
This step was to find out that what acoustic features are most related to each primitive feature. First, values of correlation coefficients between acoustic features and those primitive features that have at least one correlation coefficient over 0.6 were considered significant and were chosen. There were a total of 16 acoustic features, which were briefly described above.

Next, multi-regression analysis was applied; because not all of the 16 acoustic features are related to every primitive feature, it was also necessary to reveal which acoustic features are more related to each primitive feature. The criterion is the absolute value of any acoustic feature that is higher than the average of absolute values of all the acoustic features. The selected acoustic features that were used to establish rules are listed in the third column of Table 1.

[1] In English translation, it means “we bough a new car”.

Table 1. Results of the perception experiment and rules of primitive features

Primitive Feature	Accuracy Rate	Rules of Percentage Variation (%)
Bright	63%	AP:6.8971, PWR:8.961, PRAP:7.4674, F3:4.2405
Dark	100%	AP: -8.6915, RS1st: -74.618, PRAP:-15.541
High	100%	AP: 6.6863, HP: 8.0809, PWR: 9.327, RRAP: 9.3739, F3: 3.6476, RCV: -6.9915
Low	88%	AP: -9.9074, HP: -8.9125, PWR: -13.191, RRAP: -12.786, TL: 3.2754, RCV: -14.604
Strong	75%	AP: 6.2975, HP: 8.2056, RS: 45.65, PWR: 14.6, RRAP: 16.33, F2: -1.4528, H1A3: -51.204, RCV: 0.60943
Weak	75%	AP: -8.064, HP: -8.7019, PWR: -14.609, RRAP: -16.788, TL: 14.715, CL: 24.708, RCV: -11.72
Calm	75%	AP: -5.5793, RS:-27.871, PWR:-9.484, PRAP:-11.567, F2:-0.0916, TL:6.207
Unstable	50%	AP:6.4277, RS:43.568, PWR:12.953, PRAP:26.326, F2:-1.0208, H1A3:-55.649, RCV:2.095
Well-modulated	63%	AP:6.9762, HP:8.3081, RS:30.157, PWR:11.681, PRAP:20.318, F2:-0.052032, RCV:2.3622
Mono-tonous	75%	AP:2.3465, HP:2.502, RS:0.00046194, RCV:2.8654
Heavy	75%	AP:-9.4597, PWR:10.384, RS1st_A:2.556, PRAP:12.759, H1A3:15.605, RCV:-15.241
Clear	63%	AP:6.3306, RS:33.116, RHT:10.321, RS1st_A:2.2046, PRAP:5.326, RCV:-5.6828
Noisy	100%	AP:6.2975, HP:8.2056, RS:31.105, RS1st:20, PWR:25.486 , PRAP:24.698, F2:-1.4528, H1A3:-51.204
Quiet	63%	HP:-4, RS:-21.978, RS1st:-35.131, PWR:-14.609, F2:0.15395, F3:-1.4341, TL:10.715
Sharp	63%	AP:6.2975, HP:8.2056, RS:16, RS1st:11.003, PWR:13, PRAP:10, F2:-1.4528
Fast	75%	HP:-1.9229, RS:11.953, RS1st:-33.776, PRAP:-5.1078, F2: 1.5146, TL:-10.2257, CL:11.767
Slow	63%	AP:1.4565,F1:-1.7676, TL:12.4309, CL:-4.907, RCV:0.69847

Step 3: Calculation of Percentage Variation

This step calculated the percentage variation of acoustic features against a primitive feature. For each primitive feature, 10 utterances with higher perceptual values of primitive features were selected, where perceptual values were rated by perceptual experiments in a previous work. In order to reduce bias in the data, utterances that have the highest differentiated values with the mean of 10 utterances were excluded. Based on the remaining 9 utterances, the percentage variation was calculated by subtracting values of acoustic features from the corresponding values of acoustic features of neutral utterances and then dividing the results by the values of the acoustic features of neutral utterances.

$$\frac{v\_AF - v\_N\_AF}{v\_N\_AF}$$

where v_AF is the value of acoustic features of a primitive feature within selected utterances and v_N_AF is the value of acoustic features of a primitive feature within its corresponding neutral utterance.

Based on the acoustic features selected in step 2 and the percentage variation calculated in step 3, rules of primitives feature were established; they are listed in the third column of Table 1.

3.2 Experiments

The resultant rules were then implemented by STRAIGHT and a perceptual experiment was also conducted. There were 17 voices morphed from one natural utterance, one for each of 17 primitive features. Eight subjects were asked to compare the morphed voices with a neutral voice and choose which voice could be most associated with each primitive feature. The accuracy rates are shown in the second column of Table 1. The result shows that it is possible to make rules for primitive features with our method, and also that the model built in the first phase was successful, because the establishment of rules is based on the results of experiments and acoustic analysis.

4 Conclusion and Future Work

For emotional speech, a three-layered model, consisting of emotional speech, primitive features, and acoustic features, was proposed in the previous work. A two-phase approach was taken to build the model. In the first phase, the model was built by a top-down method. In this paper, we report the work of the second phase, which was to verify the model by a bottom-up method. A set of rules for primitive features was built from acoustic features and implemented by morphing. They were used to verify the relationships of the model that was built in the first phase. A total of 16 acoustic features have been identified and measured for each primitive feature. For each acoustic feature of a primitive feature, two types of parameters were calculated, percentage variations and ranges of value of acoustic features. The significance of this research is that the rules are designed in terms of primitive features instead of emotions. They can be used to verify the proposed model. The results of the perception experiments also show that the relationships built in the first phase are appropriate.

With regard to future work, we will first implement the rules in the morphing engine. Then we will conduct perception experiments to verify the reliability of the rules and refine the rules by experimental results.

Acknowledgement

This research is conducted as a program for the "21st Century COE Program" funded by the Ministry of Education, Culture, Sports, Science and Technology. We sincerely thank Fujitsu Laboratory for permission to use their voice database.

References

[1] Raskin, J.: Humane Interface: New Directions for Designing Interactive Systems. Addison-Wesley, Boston (2000).
[2] Picard, R. W.: Affective Computing. MIT, (2000).
[3] Massaro, D.W.: Perceiving Talking Faces. MIT, (1998).
[4] Tatham, M. & Morton, K.: Expression in Speech. Oxford University, (2004)
[5] Cahn, J. E.: Generating Expression in Synthesized Speech, Masters Thesis, MIT, (1989). http://www.media.mit.edu/~cahn/masters-thesis.html
[6] Murray, I. R., & Arnott, J. L.: Toward the simulation of emotion in synthetic speech: a review of the literature on human vocal emotion, JASA, 93, p. 1097-1108.
[7] Murray, I. R., & Arnott, J. L.: Implementation and testing of a system for producing emotion-by-rule in synthetic speech, Speech Communication, 16, p. 369-390 (year?).
[8] Montero, J. M., Gutiérrez-Arriola, J., Palazuelos, S.,Enríquez, E., Aguilera, S., & Pardo, J. M.: Emotional speech synthesis: from speech database to TTS, ICSLP 98, Vol. 3, p. 923-926.
[9] Schröder, M.: Emotional speech synthesis: a review. Proc. Eurospeech 2001
[10] Vroomen, J., Collier, R., & Mozziconacci, S. J. L.: Duration and intonation in emotional speech, Eurospeech 93, Vol. 1, p. 577-580.
[11] Heuft, B., Portele, T., & Rauth, M.: Emotions in time domain synthesis, ICSLP 96.
[12] Edgington, M.: Investigating the limitations of concatenative synthesis, Eurospeech 97. (1997)
[13] Iida, A., Campbell, N., Higuchi, F. & Yasumura, M., A corpus-based speech synthesis system with emotion, Speech Communication, 40, p.161-187. (2003)
[14] Kawahara, H., Masuda-Katsusa, I. & de Cheveign'e, A.: Restructuring speech representations using a pitch adaptive time-frequency smoothing and an instantaneous-frequency-based F0 extraction: possible role of a repetitive structure in sounds, Speech Communication, 27, p. 187-207, (1999).
[15] Matsui, H. & Kawahara, H.: Investigation of emotionally morphed speech perception and its structure using a high quality speech manipulation system, Proc. Eurospeech'03, p.2110-16, (2003)
[16] Huang, C-F. & Akagi, M.: A multi-layer fuzzy logical model for emotional speech perception. Proc. EuroSpeech'2005 (accepted)

Emotional Speech Synthesis Based on Improved Codebook Mapping Voice Conversion

Yu-Ping Wang, Zhen-Hua Ling, and Ren-Hua Wang

iFlytek Speech Laboratory,
University of Science and Technology of China, Hefei
{ypwang2, zhling}@ustc.edu, rhw@ustc.edn.cn

Abstract. This paper presents a spectral transformation method for emotional speech synthesis based on voice conversion framework. Three emotions are studied, including anger, happiness and sadness. For the sake of high naturalness, superior speech quality and emotion expressiveness, our original STASC system is modified by introducing a new feature selection strategy and hierarchical codebook mapping procedure. Our result shows that the LSF coefficients at low frequency carry more emotion-relative information, and therefore only these coefficients are converted. Listening tests prove that the proposed method can achieve a satisfactory balance between emotional expression and speech quality of converted speech signals.

1 Introduction

In recent years, with the development of TTS(Text-To-Speech) systems, the speech quality and naturalness of the synthesizer have reached a high level, so more requests lead us to new areas of research such as emotional speech synthesis.

Analysis of acoustic features of emotional speech and its synthesis rules have been studied[1], especially from the viewpoint of prosody. But spectrum of the emotional speech is still a problem. Corpus-based approach is realized by waveform unit selection from a large size emotional speech corpus[2][3], this method can achieve high speech quality, but problems still remain with database designing, recording and labeling.

Therefore, in order to generate spectrum of emotional speech automatically, voice conversion system is adopted here to transform the spectrum of neutral voice to emotional one. Generally, there are two methods for spectrum conversion: codebook mapping and GMM based method. Codebook mapping [4] is adopted here because each codebook represents one segment of training data, which can preserve the information in the training data well, whereas in GMM methods, overall optimized conversion function for a group of data may lose information of some training data and cause smoothing effects of speaker's or emotion's characteristics.

In this paper, emotional spectrum is converted from that of neutral, to achieve high accuracy in spectrum conversion, base on the analysis, only the LSF coefficients at low frequency are converted and DAL is introduced in to modify the converted LSF and also a hierarchical codebook mapping procedure is used to improve the speech quality of conversion output.

J. Tao, T. Tan, and R.W. Picard (Eds.): ACII 2005, LNCS 3784, pp. 374 – 381, 2005.

Three emotions are synthesized from reading style speech by the presented method: *anger, happiness* and *sadness*. Comparing the results of the original voice conversion system and the improved one, speech quality has been improved and meanwhile the identification rate of emotion type still remains stable.

This paper is arranged as follows: section 2 will introduce the baseline voice conversion system, the experiment data and the details of proposed improving methods. The following section will describe experimental results. After discussion, we conclude this paper.

2 Method

2.1 Basic Idea

Codebook mapping voice conversion is used to convert emotional speech from neutral speech, according to the results of the analysis of conversion parameters, only the LSF coefficients at low frequency are converted because they are proved to carry more emotion-relative information and DAL (Distance of Adjoin dimension LSF coefficients) is introduced in to modify converted LSF and also a hierarchical codebook mapping procedure is used to improve the speech quality of conversion output.

2.2 Baseline Voice Conversion System

The baseline system is based on codebook mapping for spectral conversion[5]. In order to reduce smoothing effects, the system uses a phoneme-tied weighting strategy which takes into account the phoneme types and state types of code words in addition to the objective distance between spectral coefficients. The new strategy can reduce the smoothing effects while maintaining high speech quality. And for prosodic conversion, decision tree is adopted here.

STAIGHT is adopted here for speech analysis and all-pole model is used to present the spectrum of analysis output. 40 poles are used to make a precise model of the spectrum of speech data with 16kHz sampling rate. Then these poles are transferred to LSF coefficients, which are the spectral parameters used in the conversion procedure.

2.3 Speech Database

Target emotions are anger, happiness and sadness, the selection is based on the concept that they are primary emotions and they can be expressed continuously in speech. Our experiments show that texts with emotions are helpful for emotional expression. As emotion text collection is difficult, texts with or without emotions are obtained first, then by adding, deleting or changing a few key words to obtain emotional texts.

For each emotion, 100 emotional sentences are collected. One female speaker reads the texts in target emotion style and neutral style respectively. For each emotional voice and neutral one, 10 sentences are selected randomly from the recorded database for listening test. Ten listeners are asked identify which emotion each sentence

Table 1. Result of identification test for the emotional speech database(%)

Emotion Type	Neutral	Anger	Happiness	Sadness	Fear
Neutral	**92.5**	0.75	1.5	2.75	2.5
Anger	3.75	**89.75**	3.75	0.5	2.25
Happiness	8.0	6.0	**83.75**	0.75	1.5
Sadness	6.5	0.25	0.5	**82.75**	10.0

belongs to with 5 choices: neutral, anger, happiness, sadness and fear. Table1 shows the result of identification test.

For each emotion type, only the first 50 emotional and the corresponding neutral sentences are used for training in the voice conversion system.

2.4 Improvement on Feature Selection

2.4.1 Significant Analysis of LSF Coefficients at Different Order

In order to analyze the significance of LSF coefficients in presenting the spectral differences between neutral and emotional speech, an analysis is conducted here. Accurate alignments are first made between emotional and corresponding neutral utterances, and then 10000 frames of LSF coefficients on vowels are analyzed by Paired-Samples T-Test. Figure1 shows the LSF significance of different order in

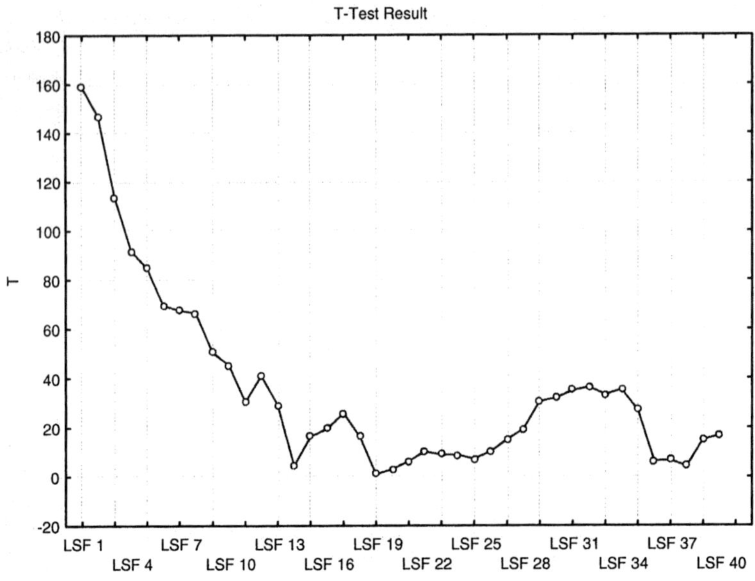

Fig. 1. T-Test result of significant analysis

distinguishing neutral and happy speech. The results for angry and sad speech are similar and not listed here.

The following conclusions can be drawn from Figure 1:

1. There explicitly exists spectral component that can strongly distinguish neutral and emotional speech, and it must be adjusted as emotion changes.
2. The spectral component that can strongly distinguish neutral and emotional speech is mainly presented in the low orders of LSF coefficients, the high orders of LSF coefficients are not so significant in distinguish them;

As high orders of LSF coefficients are not so significant in distinguishing neutral and emotional speech, which means, high order LSF coefficients of neutral and emotional are close to each other, so when LSF coefficients are converted from neutral to emotional, only the low orders are converted and leave the high orders unchanged, this can avoid smooth effect in high frequency and achieve more natural and clear speech. So, in this experiment, only the lowest 10 orders are converted and the other 30 left unchanged.

2.4.2 LSF Modification Based on DAL Conversion

Though the quality of output speech has been improved by only converting the LSF of lowest 10 orders, it is still not good enough as neutral voice. One of the problems is the synthesized speech is not clear enough, because the smooth effects make speech formant unclear, so in order to improve the synthesized speech, the formants should be made clear. As we all know, DAL (in formula 1) has a strong correlation with speech formants,

$$DAL[i] = LSF[i+1] - LSF[i] \tag{1}$$

So, DAL is added into the parameter space to join training and conversion.. After all the coefficients have been generated and assume $DAL[i]$ and $LSF[i]$ are the generated DAL and LSF coefficients, DAL is used to modify the LSF data as formula 2:

$$LSF[i] = LSF[i-1] + DAL[i-1] + \frac{DAL[i-1]^2}{DAL[i-1]^2 + DAL[i]^2}[(LSF[i+1] - LSF[i-1]) - (DAL[i] + DAL[i-1])] \tag{2}$$

After modification, new LSF coefficients are generated. They are then converted into spectrum and used to synthesize emotional speech with prosody information.

2.5 Hierarchical Codebook Mapping

The precision of predicted spectrum affects speech quality of the synthesized speech, so if the precision can be improved, high quality speech can be achieved, as our synthesis system is based on codebook mapping, smooth effect is inevitable. Some attempts [6][7] have been made to reduce the smooth effect. Here a hierarchical codebook mapping method is proposed to improve the precision of spectral conversion.

Assuming $LSF_n[i]$ and $LSF_p[i]$ the natural LSF parameters and the predicted LSF parameters, $Res[i] = LSF_n[i] - LSF_p[i]$ will also be converted and used to modify $LSF_p[i]$ to achieve more reasonable LSF coefficients.

Here, a hierarchical codebook mapping method is introduced to predict $Res[i]$. The conversion residual of LSF coefficients in the training set are combined with the neutral LSF to constructed a residual codebook, which is used to predict $Res[i]$ in the general codebook mapping way during conversion procedure. The final LSF will be modified in the following way:

$$LSF[i] = LSF_p[i] + Res[i] \tag{3}$$

The flowcharts of constructing residual codebook and conversion process of hierarchical codebook mapping method are shown in Fig. 2 and 3.

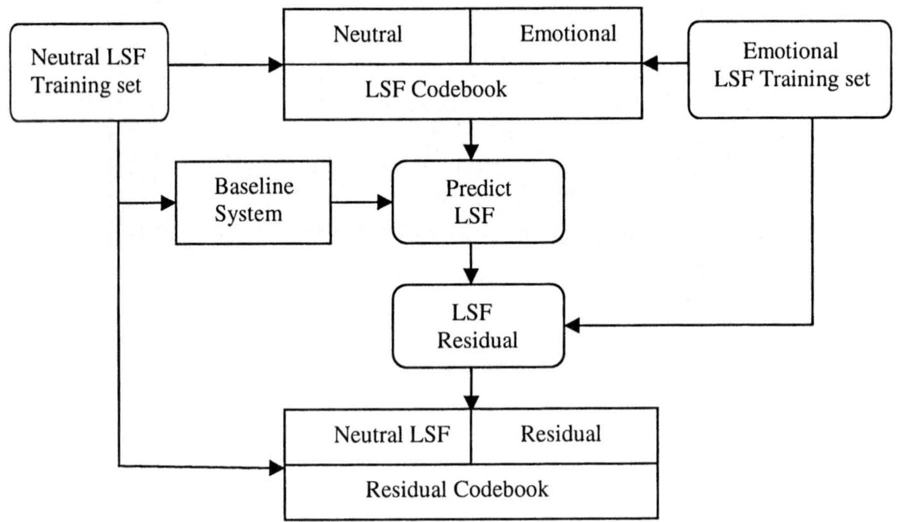

Fig. 2. The flowchart of constructing residual codebook

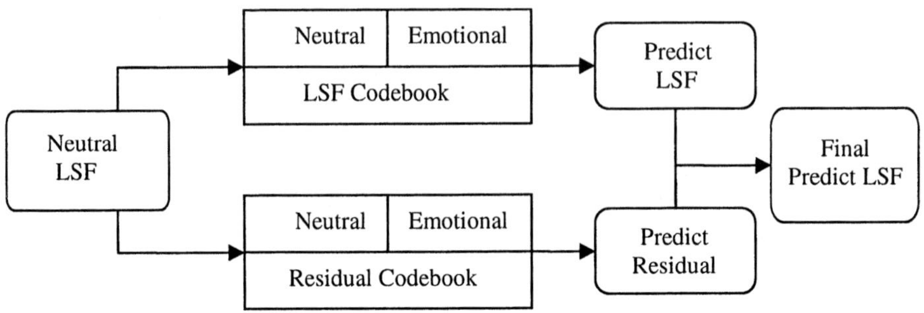

Fig. 3. The conversion process of hierarchical codebook mapping method

3 Experiments

3.1 Spectrum Comparison

In order to test the effect of the improvements, four conversion systems are used separately to convert emotional spectrum from that of neutral, the comparison of converted sad spectrum between the four systems and natural is shown in Figure 4.

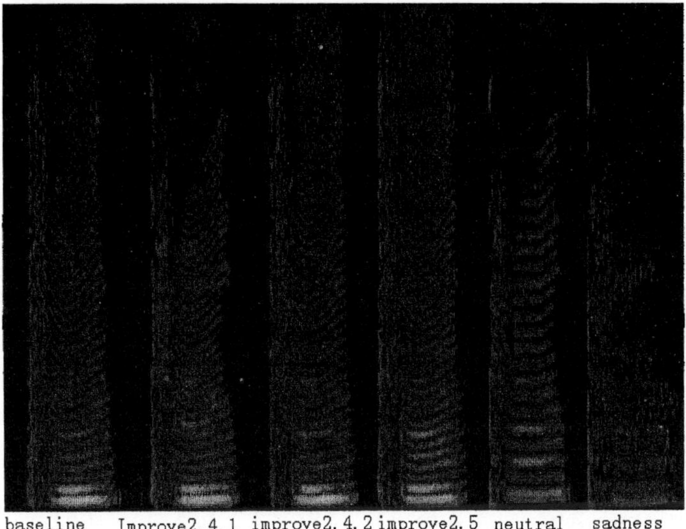

Fig. 4. Comparison of converted spectrum

From left to right, the spectrum are the generation of baseline system, improved system by 2.4.1, improved system by 2.4.2, improved system by 2.5, neutral spectrum and sadness spectrum separately.

As shown in Figure 4, when LSF difference coefficients are added or only convert low orders of LSF or use spectrum residual to modify LSF, the formants of synthesized speech become clearer, listening tests also shows speech quality becomes better.

3.2 Listening Tests

To evaluate effect of conversion and improvement, listening tests is conducted here. 10 listeners are asked to listen to the synthetic speech to, on one hand, identify the emotion type of synthetic speech(carried out as a force-choiced test, four choices: anger, happiness, sadness and neutral), on the other hand, give a Mean Opinion Score(MOS) to the quality of each utterance.

For each emotion type, only the first 50 emotional and the corresponding neutral sentences are used for training in the voice conversion system. Six systems described below are used for the listening tests:

A. **Converted prosody with neutral spectrum** Prosody is converted by decision tree with no spectrum conversion.
B. **Baseline System** Both spectrum and prosody are converted
C. **Baseline System with improvement2.4.1** Only the lowest 10 orders of LSF parameters are converted
D. **Baseline System with improvement2.4.2** DAL modification
E. **Baseline System with improvement2.5** Spectrum residual modification
F. **Baseline System with all three improvements**

20 sentences of each emotion are selected and synthesized by each system. Table 2 and Table 3 show the results of the listening tests:

Table 2. Identification rate of the emotion type for different conversion system(%)

Emotion	A	B	C	D	E	F
Anger	**56.0**	**76.0**	**76.0**	**78.0**	**76.0**	**78.0**
Happiness	**76.0**	**84.0**	**82.0**	**82.0**	**84.0**	**82.0**
Sadness	**28.0**	**60.0**	**62.0**	**62.0**	**62.0**	**60.0**

Table 3. The MOS socre for different conversoin system

Emotion	A	B	C	D	E	F
Anger	**4.03**	**3.03**	**3.32**	**3.14**	**3.10**	**3.34**
Happiness	**3.88**	**3.18**	**3.36**	**3.22**	**3.20**	**3.40**
Sadness	**2.62**	**2.26**	**2.97**	**2.75**	**2.83**	**3.10**

We can conclude from Table 2 and Table 3 that prosodic features mainly contribute to emotion in speech especially for *anger* and *happiness*, and also the converted spectrum reinforce the emotional expression, as for *sadness*. Because the spectrum of neutral speech is so different from that of sad speech and spectrum is also important in emotional expression, so when neutral spectrum with sadness prosody are combined to synthesis sadness speech, both identification rate and MOS are low, but after spectrum is converted and the improvements, the identification rate and MOS are acceptable.

4 Discussion

As our listening test shows, prosodic features are important in emotional expression especially for *anger* and *happiness*, when neutral spectrum with emotional prosody are combined to synthesis emotional speech, the identification rate of emotions in the synthetic speech is acceptable, and after spectrum is converted, the identification rate is much higher, that's to say, prosodic features mainly contribute to emotion in speech and spectrum reinforce the emotional expression, as for sadness, spectrum in emotional expression is comparatively more important. So when use the converted spectrum rather than the original spectrum, the identification rate increases a lot. To achieve high accuracy in spectrum conversion, only the LSF coefficients at low frequency are converted and DAL is introduced in to modify the converted LSF and also a hierarchical codebook mapping procedure is used to improve the speech quality of conversion output.

5 Conclusion

In this paper, we describe our emotional speech synthesis system based on codebook mapping, prosodic parameters are predicted by decision tree and meanwhile spectrum is converted from neutral to emotional, as smooth effect deteriorate speech quality, some improvements are applied to improve speech quality of the synthesized speech, listening tests shows the proposed methods can effectively improve the speech quality of the synthesizer and meanwhile the identification rate of the perception test remains high. However, there are still a lot of problems stay unresolved, for example, the accuracy of the converted prosodic features is still low, and so is the spectrum. More work should be done in these areas in the near future to generate high quality emotional speech.

References

1. I. R. Murry, et al : Towards the Simulation of Emotion in Synthetic Speech : A Review of the Literature of Human Vocal Emotion, *J. of ASA, 93, No.2, pp.1097-1108(1993)*
2. A. Iida, et al.:A Speech Synthesis System with Emotion for Assisting Communication, *Proc. ICSA Workshop on Speech And Emotion, pp.167-177(2000)*
3. Iida, A., Campbell, N.: A corpus-based speech synthesis system with emotion, *Speech Communication 40 (2003)*
4. M. Abe, S. Nakamura, K. Shikano and H. Kuwabara.: Voice Conversion through vector quantization, *Proceedings of ICASSP 1988, pp.655-658*
5. Shuang, Z.W, Z.X.Wang, Z.H.Ling, and R.H.Wang, A Novel Voice Conversion System based on Codebook Mapping with Phonome-tied Weighting, *ISCSLP 2004, pp. 1197-1200*
6. Noriyasu Maeda, Banno Hideki, Shoji Kajita, Speaker conversion through NoN-Linear frequency warping of STRAIGHT spectrum, Proc. Of EUROSPEECH 1999, pp.827-830
7. Toda, T., Saruwatari, H., voice conversion algorithm based on Gaussian Mixture Model with dynamic frequency warping of STRAIGHT spectrum, *Proc. Of ICASSP, 2001, pp.841-944*

Improving Speaker Recognition by Training on Emotion-Added Models

Tian Wu, Yingchun Yang, and Zhaohui Wu

College of Computer Science and Technology,
Zhejiang University, Hangzhou 310027, P.R. China
{wutian, yyc, wzh}@zju.edu.cn

Abstract. In speaker recognition applications, the changes of emotional states are main causes of errors. The ongoing work described in this contribution attempts to enhance the performance of automatic speaker recognition (ASR) systems on emotional speech. Two procedures that only need a small quantity of affective training data are applied to ASR task, which is very practical in real-world situations. The method includes classifying the emotional states by acoustical features and generating emotion-added model based on the emotion grouping. Experimental works are performed on Emotional Prosody Speech (EPS) corpus and show significant improvement in EERs and IRs compared with baseline and comparative experiments.

1 Introduction

Current speaker verification and identification systems are limited by the effect on speech of transient state changes to speakers, such as cognitive and physiological stress, emotional state and speaker attitude. The variability of intra-speaker in these situations can cause unacceptably high error rates [1]. In order to improve the performance of automatic speaker recognition (ASR) systems, vocal tract is considered. Its information has been popular adopted because the envelop shape could provide speaker dependent characters [2].

K.R.Scherer [3] has presented a method called "structured training" to enhance the performance of automatic speaker verification systems[4]. However, this approach requires a large amount of training data with emotional information to enhance the performance. As is well known, it is difficult to obtain enough data with emotional information in the real-world applications. Therefore, a method that can improve the ASR system on affective speech with limited emotional speech data is needful. To arrive at this goal, research is focused on two parts:

1. 14 emotional states are divided into 3 groups according to the acoustical features. The decision-making depends on the research that explores the acoustical correlations of emotional speech. Mean pitch, pitch range, pitch variance, pitch skewness and pitch expansion types are investigated as the criteria.

2. The second step is called "emotion-added training". The modified speaker model is built by adding very few information of emotional states. By this means

J. Tao, T. Tan, and R.W. Picard (Eds.): ACII 2005, LNCS 3784, pp. 382–389, 2005.

the speaker model is integrated with intra-speaker variability caused by different psychological states of the speaker. Test is also performed in emotion groups respectively.

Experiments are performed on emotional speech database and achieve good performance in the ASR task.

The remainder of this paper is organized as follows: the speech database is introduced in section 2. The description of acoustical features, the statistical analysis and interpretation of the parameters are given in section 3. Then, the strategies and the results are described in section 4 and 5. Section 6 presents the conclusions.

2 Speech Database

Collecting large scale affective speech corpus is a very tough task. By far, the Emotional Prosody Speech (EPS) corpus is the only one related to emotional speech provided by Linguistic Data Consortium (LDC), which supplies the top-ranking and authoritative speech database. The corpus is recorded by 8 speakers, including 3 men and 5 women who are actors and actresses. It is divided into two parts, Distance Continuum and Emotion Continuum. The first section of the recording expresses a dimension of dominance and a dimension of distance. In the second section of the recording, the speakers are asked to read lines in 14 specific emotional states. These states are: neutral (unemotional), anxiety, boredom, cold anger, contempt, despair, disgust, elation, hot anger, interest, panic, pride, sadness and shame. The categories of emotions are chosen based on Banse & Scherer's selection criteria [5]. They were drawn from over 3,800 descriptions of emotional experiences as well as the situations that elicited these responses [7]. Each speaker read 10 to 40 sentences of different types portraying the states above. For each person, the database contains 5-minute emotional speech and 0.5-to-1-minute neutral speech. The signal is sampled at 22050Hz and is quantized to 16 bits.

3 Acoustical Features

From earlier studies [3] [5] [8], many parameters like fundamental frequency (F0), voice quality, or articulation precision have been used in emotional speech synthesis. Pitch is investigated because it relies greatly on broad classes of sounds and indicates emotion characters [9].

3.1 Description of the Parameters

The following describes the acoustical features that are used in the perception experiments.

- mean pitch: Mean pitch indicates the average level of speaker's voice frequency, which varies greatly under different emotional states. The mean pitch of an utterance can be calculated as:

$$\overline{f} = \frac{\sum_{i=1}^{N} f_i}{N} \tag{1}$$

Where f_i is the pitch value of frame i, and N is the number of pitch values in the utterance.

- pitch range: The pitch range of an utterance is the interval between the smallest and largest values:

$$f_r = f_{max} - f_{min} \tag{2}$$

f_{max} is the maximal value in a set of pitch of an utterance and f_{min} is the minimum.

- pitch variance: Pitch variance is a measure of how spread out the distribution is. To reduce the complexity of calculation, the standard deviation is used.

$$f_v = (\frac{1}{N-1}(\sum_{i=1}^{N}(f_i - \overline{f})^2))^{\frac{1}{2}} \tag{3}$$

- pitch skewness: Skewness is a measure of symmetry, or more precisely, the lack of symmetry. A distribution of pitch is symmetric if it looks the same to the left and right of the center point. Pitch skewness is calculated as

$$f_s = (\frac{1}{N}(\sum_{i=1}^{N}(f_i - \overline{f})^3))^{\frac{1}{3}} \tag{4}$$

- range expansion: Fig. 1 depicts the various theoretically possible ways that range can be expanded [5]. They are NR (Normal Range), RU (Expansion from the bottom of the range up), RD (Expansion from the top of the range down), and RB (Expansion radiating from the middle of the range outward in both directions).

3.2 Statistical Analysis and Interpretation of the Results

F.Burkhardt and W.F.Sendlmeier [6] give a presentation of systematic variation of acoustical features which are used for reference in this paper. An experiment was set up comprising five features (mean pitch, pitch range, pitch variance, pitch skewness and pitch expansion), which vary in the following way:

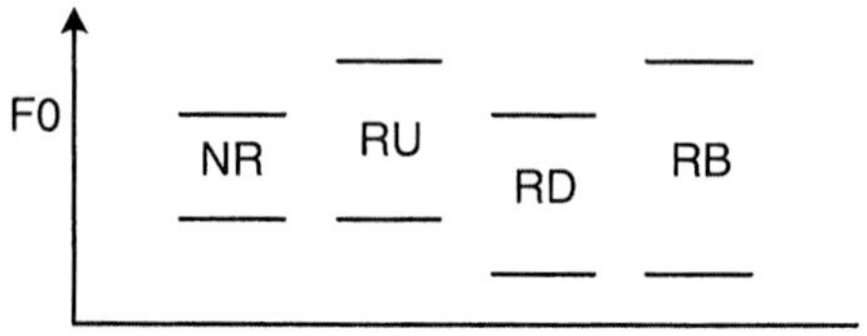

Fig. 1. Theoretically possible ways in which pitch range can be expanded [7]

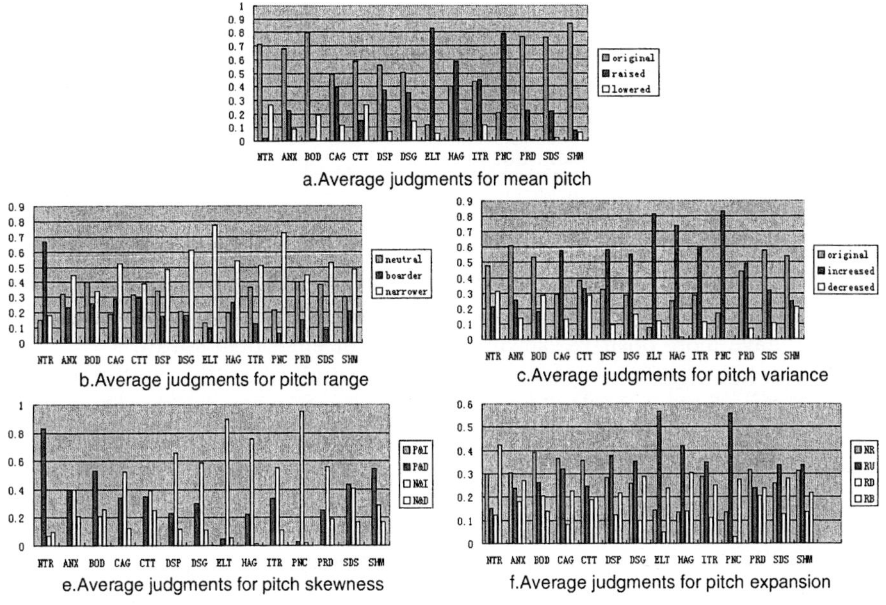

Fig. 2. Average judgments for mean pitch. The emotional states are: NTR (neutral), ANX (anxiety), BOD (boredom), CAG (cold anger), CTT (contempt), DSP (Despair), DSG (disgust), ELT (elation), HAG (hot anger), ITR (interesting), PNC (panic), PRD (pride), SDS (sadness), SHM (shame).

- mean pitch (3 levels): original, 30% raised and 20% lowered. Mean pitch from unemotional speech is chosen to be the original standard.
- pitch range (3 levels): original, 20% narrower and 20% broader. It is aware that a 20% larger range does not necessarily result in a 20% increase in variance.
- pitch variance (3 levels): original, 50% increased and 10% decreased. Pitch has wider range of distribution only when the pitch variance is increased.
- pitch skewness (4 types): P&I (Skewness is positive and increased), P&D (Skewness is positive and decreased), N&I (Skewness is negative and increased in absolute value), N&D (Skewness is negative and decreased in absolute value).
- range expansion (4 types): normal range, expansion from the bottom of the range up, expansion from the top of the range down, expansion radiation from the middle of the range outward both directions.

A statistical analysis is executed on EPS corpus in terms of criteria above (see Fig. 2). Pitch is determined by SHR (Subharmonic-To-Harmonic Ratio) method provided by Sun [11]. We try to detect he commonness among emotion states. The interpretation is as following:

Table 1. The classification of emotion stats

grouops	details
Group0	anxiety, boredom, neutral, shame
Group1	cold anger, contempt, interest, pride, sadness
Group2	elation, hot anger, panic, despair, disgust

- neutral, anxiety, boredom and shame: They were almost in original mean pitch. Equal distribution in three levels of variance is a typical character. They have more positive skewness than other emotional states.
- elation, hot anger and panic: Utterances are judged as this kind of emotion when they had a raised mean pitch, a broad range, increased variance. The majority of the data are smaller than the mean, so the absolute value of skewness is quite large. Most of their pitch can be expanded into upper range.
- despair and disgust: The five parameters of this kind of emotions distributed equally on the levels. By comparison, 50%-60% of their pitch fall in original mean pitch, increased variance. Besides, 55%-65% of the skewness are negative and decreased.
- cold anger, contempt, interest, pride and sadness: More than 50% of them have original mean pitch. Comparatively, skewness distribute equally over positive&decreased and negative&increased.

According to the results, 14-emotional states are divided into 3 groups (see Table 1). In each group, the changes of mean pitch, pitch range, pitch variance, pitch skewness and pitch expansion are similar .

4 Strategies

4.1 Emotion-Added Model

The 14 emotional states are divided into 3 groups (Table 1) according to the statistical analysis. In this case, 4-to-5-second emotional speech materials are used for adding emotion information to the neutral model $\lambda_{s,u}$. Therefore, for each speaker, three models, $\lambda_{s,e0}$, $\lambda_{s,e1}$, $\lambda_{s,e2}$ are generated for recognition (Figure 3). These models could be called "emotion-added model".

Global Test. Test data are not separated. It is tested on each model in the set $\{\lambda_{s,e0},\lambda_{s,e1},\lambda_{s,e2}\}$.

Local Test. Training materials and test data are both classified to three groups according to the criterion guided by the pitch. For an utterance in the EPS corpus, it is tested by one certain group of the emotion-added models. Test data are also divided into three groups according to Table 1. Then, each sentence has corresponding models to match.

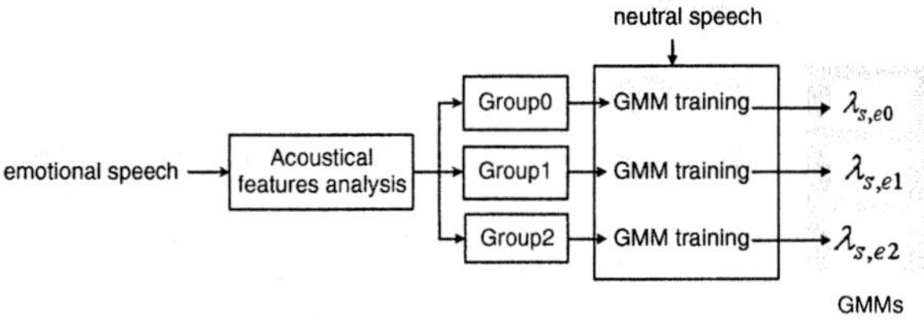

Fig. 3. Block diagram of the proposed emotion-added model training method

4.2 Comparative Strategy

Baseline. The baseline strategy uses unemotional utterances for training. Hence, one model $\lambda_{s,u}$,for each speaker is generated without any emotion information. It is more like a traditional ASR system.

Random Grouping. Emotional states are classified randomly (see Table 2). Three new models for each speaker are $\lambda_{s,e3}$, $\lambda_{s,e4}$, $\lambda_{s,e5}$, which are used for comparing the recognition rate with the experiment using emotion-added model. In this part, the data are tested locally.

Table 2. The random grouping of emotion stats

groups	details
Group3	cold anger, disgust, interest, panic, sadness
Group4	anxiety, contempt, hot anger, pride, shame
Group5	elation, boredom, despair, elation, neutral

5 Experiments and Results

Four groups of experiments were performed respectively in accordance with the strategies in section 4. The speech signal was segmented into 32 ms with 16 ms overlapped frames, reemphasized and Hamming windowed. 32 MFCC (Mel Frequency Cepstrum Coefficients) is used to describe the speakers' characters. Pitch is extracted by SHR (Subharmonic-To-Harmonic Ratio) [11]. 32 GMMs (Gaussian Mixture Model) are used with a Universal Background Model (UBM) [12].

EER (Equal Error Rate) and IR (Identification Rate) are chosen as the criteria of performance.

Tables 3, 4, 5, 6 report both EER and IR, which are the verification and identification results respectively, observed with the four techniques: 1) global test, 2) local test, 3) baseline (training without any emotion information), 4) random grouping.

Compared to the baseline, the other three experiments achieve lower EERs and higher IRs. Hence, a conclusion can be drawn: Using the emotion-added model, both the EER and IR of the system are improved.

Table 3. The results of global test

Group Name	EER(with UBM)(%)	IR(%)
Group0	19.55	68.01
Group1	18.76	76.29
Group2	16.33	84.99
Average	18.21	76.43

Table 4. The results of local test

Group Name	EER(with UBM)(%)	IR(%)
Group0	8.54	92.54
Group1	10.72	90.68
Group2	13.39	88.35
Average	10.88	90.52

Table 5. The results of baseline

EER(with UBM)(%)	IR(%)
19.61	67.91

Table 6. The results of random grouping

Group Name	EER(with UBM)(%)	IR(%)
Group3	22.56	60.81
Group4	17.29	72.42
Group5	18.33	72.15
Average	19.39	68.46

The result of global test is listed in table 3 while local test in table 4. It is displayed that the latter achieves higher performance. The greatest decrease in EER is 11.01% (Group0) and the least is 2.94% (Group2) compared with global test. When a speaker identification is held, the greatest increase in IR is 24.53% (Group0) and the least is 3.36% (Group2). The results indicate that for each group local test yields a improvement in performance.

Random grouping experiment is carried out to demonstrate the validity of the grouping rule. For local test, the average of EER is 8.51% lower than random grouping while the average of IR is 22.06% higher. It is observed that local test yields much better recognition performance.

As is known in the results of experiments, our approach gain better performance in ASR system with only a tiny amount of emotional training data, while Scherer's techniques need a lot [1] [3] [4].

6 Conclusions

We present a method for improving ASR system under emotional situation, including two steps: 1)classifying emotional states by statistical analysis for mean pitch, pitch range, pitch variance, pitch skewness and range expansion, 2)adding emotion information to speaker model. Using the emotion-added model, the performance of ASR system is significantly improved. For real life applications of ASR, this method can be very practical.

Acknowledgment

This work is supported by National Natural Science Foundation of P.R.China (No.60273059), Zhejiang Provincial Natural Science Foundation(No.M603229) and National Doctoral Subject Foundation of P.R.China (20020335025).

References

1. Scherer, K.R., Johnstone, T., Klasmeyer, G., Banziger, T.: Can Automatic Speaker Verification be Improved by Training the Algorithms on Emotional Speech? Proceedings of the 6th International Conference on Spoken Language Processing Beijing, China. (2000)
2. Atal, B.S.: Automatic recognition of speakers from their voices, Proc. IEEE. 64(1976) 460-475
3. Scherer, K.R., Johnstone, T., Banziger, T.: Verification of emotionally stressed speakers: The problem of individual differences. Proc. of SPECOM98, 1998
4. Klasmeyer, G., Johnstone, T., Banziger, T., Sappok, C., Scherer, K.R.: Emotional Voice Variability in Speaker Verification, ISCA Workshop on Speech and Emotion, 2000
5. Banse, R., Scherer, K.R.: Acoustic profiles in vocal emotion expression. J Pers Soc Psychol. 1996 Mar; 70(3):614-36
6. Burkhardt, F., Sendlmeier, W.F.: Verification of Acoustical Correlates of Emotional Speech using Formant-Synthesis. ISCA Workshop on Speech and Emotion, 2000
7. LDC: The Linguistic Data Consortium: web pages at www.ldc.upenn.edu
8. Schroder, M.: Emotional Speech Synthesis: A Review. EUROSPEECH'01 Volume1, 2001.
9. Schuller, B., Rigoll, G., Lang, M.: Speech Emotion Recognition Combining Acoustic Features and Linguistic Information in a Hybrid Support Vector Machine-belief Network Architecture. ICASSP 2004
10. Patterson, D.: A Linguistic Approach to Pitch Range Modelling. thesis for the degree of Doctor of Philosophy to the University of Edinburgh, 2000
11. Sun, S.: Pitch Determination and Voice Quality Analysis Using Subharmonic-To-Harmonic Ratio. IEEE International Conference on Acoustics, Speech, and Signal Processing, May 13-17, 2002
12. Reynolds, D.A., Quatieri, T.F., Dunn, R.B.: Speaker Verification Using Adapted Gaussian Mixture Models. Digital Signal Processing 10, 19-41(2000)

An Approach to Affective-Tone Modeling for Mandarin

Zhuangluan Su and Zengfu Wang

Department of Automation,
University of Science and Technology of China, Hefei 230027, China
zfwang@ustc.edu.cn

Abstract. Mandarin is a typical tone language in which a syllable possesses several tone types. While these tone types have rather clear manifestations in the fundamental frequency contour (F_0 contour) in isolated syllables, they vary considerably in affective speech due to the influences of the speaker's mood. In the paper the Fujisaki model based on the measured F_0 contour is modified to adapt for affective Mandarin, and a novel approach is proposed to extract the parameters of the model automatically without any manual labels information such as boundary labels, tone types and syllable timing, etc. The preliminary statistic result shows the model is feasible for the affective speech study.

1 Introduction

The contour of the speech fundamental frequency (henceforth F_0 contour) plays an important role in expressing the prosody of an utterance including the affective information. Mandarin is a tonal language including four basic tone types and a so-called 'light' tone. The F_0 contour is composed of three elements [1]: 1. a syllable's tone, 2. the variety of tone in continuous utterance, and 3. the movement caused by mood, so-called intonation of the sentence. Since tone and intonation may occur together, tone shape and range are affected by mood.

Fujisaki Model is originally designed for Japanese [2]. The fundamental idea is that F_0 contour generally consists of slowly-varying components corresponding to phrases and clauses and rapidly-varying components corresponding to word accents or syllable tones. Fujisaki Model has been modified to develop adaptive models to several other languages [3,4,6]. Some researchers have addressed the problem of automatic extraction of the model parameters for Mandarin. In their researches, the major problem is how to deal with both positive and negative components. They generally use labels information such as boundary labels [5], tone types [7], syllable timing [8], etc. to deal with polarity problem. Furthermore, the linguistic meaning is required, so in their methods the preprocessing step for an observed F_0 contour is firstly applied to remove the tone shape changes caused by mood etc. The types of these tones are then regarded to be normal in later processing steps. However, the above methods for removing affective influences from the observed F_0 contour cannot be directly applied to emotion related research work.

J. Tao, T. Tan, and R.W. Picard (Eds.): ACII 2005, LNCS 3784, pp. 390–396, 2005.

This paper presents how to modify the Fujisaki Model to obtain a novel affective-tone model for Mandarin and how to extract the corresponding parameters without any labels information.

2 The Affective-Tone Model for Mandarin

The Fujisaki Model for Mandarin [9] is a command-response model that describes F_0 contours in the logarithmic scale as the sum of phrase components, tone components and a baseline level. The model diagram is shown in Fig. 1. In the model, the F_0 contour is expressed by the following equations. The symbols in the equations were indicated in [3].

$$log_e F_0(t) = log_e F_b + \sum_{i=1}^{I} Ap_i Gp(t-T_{oi}) + \sum_{j=1}^{J} Aa_j\{Ga(t-T_{1j}) - Ga(t-T_{2j})\} \quad (1)$$

$$Gp(t) = \begin{cases} \alpha^2 t\exp(-\alpha t) & t \geq 0 \\ 0 & t < 0 \end{cases} \quad (2)$$

$$Ga(t) = \begin{cases} min[1-(1+\beta t)\exp(-\beta t), \gamma] & t \geq 0 \\ 0 & t < 0 \end{cases} \quad (3)$$

During the model expresses the micro-movement caused by mood with high fitting accuracy, T_{2j} may be requested to be much closed to T_{1j}. In (3), $Ga(t)$ is not continuous at the time of t_x, if $Ga(t_x) = \gamma$ for the first time. As shown in Fig. 2, this discontinuity will result in an unexpected distortion in the fitting processing. As a result, an unexpected accent command will be extracted because of the distortion.

In order to solve the above problem, (3) is needed to be modified. This paper gives a modification of (3) below. As shown in (4), $Ga(t)$ is continuous after modification, and the unexpected distortion emerged in the original model will also not appear. The modification improves the model's ability of expressing affective speech based on F_0 contour.

$$Ga(t) = \begin{cases} 1-(1+\beta t)\exp(-\beta t) & t \geq 0 \\ 0 & t < 0 \end{cases} \quad (4)$$

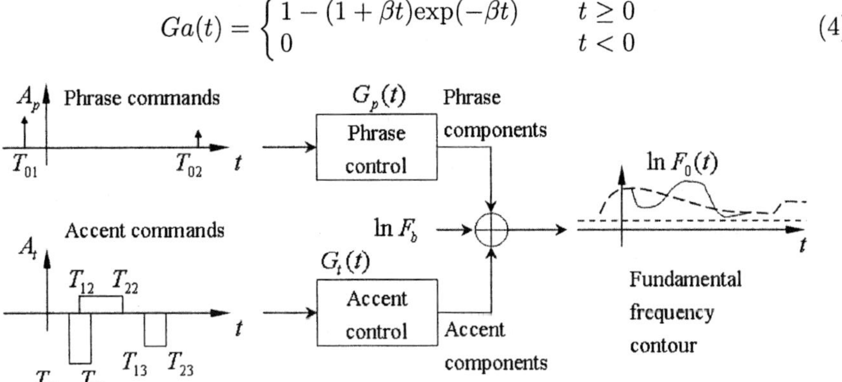

Fig. 1. The Fujisaki Model for Mandarin

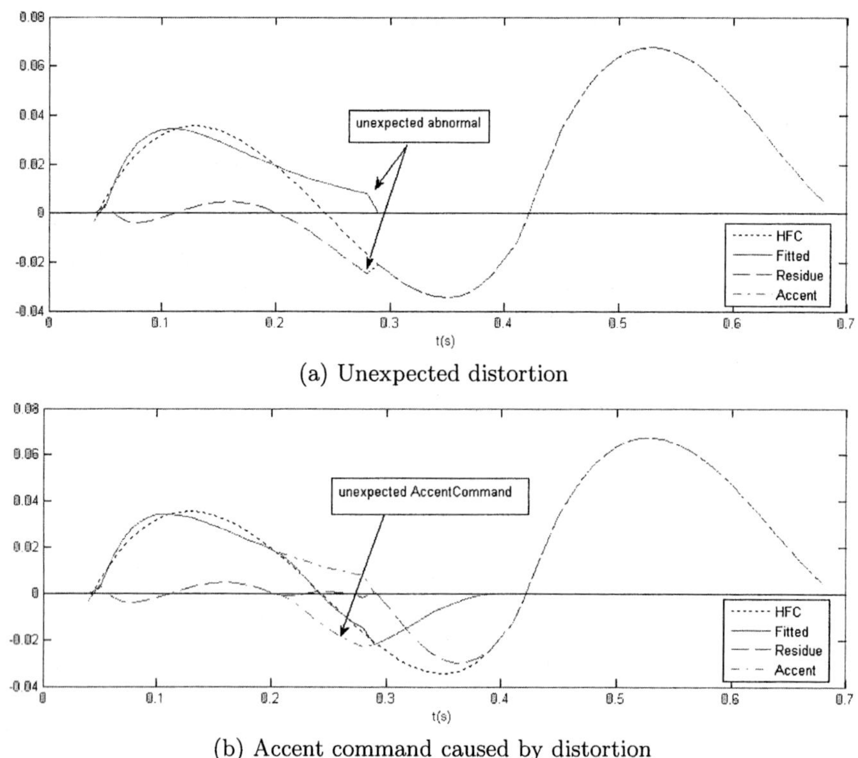

(a) Unexpected distortion

(b) Accent command caused by distortion

Fig. 2. 'HFC' is the target for fitting, 'Fitted' is the fitting result, 'Residue' is the fitting residue, and all 'Accent' parts form 'Fitted'

3 Estimation of Parameters

To estimate the parameters of the affective-tone model for Mandarin from the observed F_0 contour, approximation is one successive method. In [4], a multi-stage approach was proposed to derive the first-order estimation. In this paper, we use the same framework, but modify the details for each stage to satisfy the needs for affective speech. The procedure consists of the following stages:

3.1 Obtaining a Continuous and Smooth F_0 Contour

After cubic Hermite interpolating for unvoiced segments and smoothing by tow serial filters with different length, a mainly measured F_0 contour is obtained. Then tow serial piecewise three-order polynomial fittings are applied to smooth the contour. The F_0 contour obtained in such way is continuous and smooth everywhere.

3.2 High-Pass Filtering and Component Separation

As mentioned above, the model produces a particular F_0 contour in the logarithmic domain by superimposing three components. In order to separate the tone component from the phrase component and F_b, the logeF_0 contour is passed through a high-pass filter with a cut-off frequency at 0.5Hz. The output of the high-pass filter (henceforth called 'high frequency contour' or HFC) is then subtracted from the smooth F_0 contour to yield a 'low frequency contour' (LFC) which contains the sum of phrase component and F_b, where F_b is initially set to the overall minimum of the LFC for simplicity. The filter is optimized by maximizing the matching degree between the manual label and the phrase command onset time.

3.3 Extraction of Tone Commands from HFC

The tone command consists of several accent commands. It is known from (4) that each accent command is essentially a semi-infinite function of time starting from the onset of the command. So any accent command will not influence the accent commands located on the left side. Accordingly, a process of extracting an accent command is repeated from left to right in turn to extract all accent commands from the tone component of F_0 contour.

In the repeated process, the HFC is searched for the first segment whose first-order derivative has same polarity and whose amplitude at the right end is larger than a given threshold. Obviously, such a segment is corresponding to the rising part of a positive accent command or the falling part of a negative accent command. The amplitude at the right end of the segment is assigned to the amplitude of the corresponding accent command where the right end is adopted as the offset time. The onset time is set back to $1/\beta$ before the point whose first-order derivative is maximal in the segment, and the parameter β is set to 20/s as first-order approximation. Finally, all the parameters are optimized by successive approximation with the least mean squared error. The resultant accent command is subtracted from the HFC and the residue is set to the HFC for the next repeated process.

We can extract all the accent commands until no one can be detected from the current HFC with a pre-defined threshold in the repeated process. Figure 2 illustrates the first and the second repeated process.

3.4 Extraction of Phrase Commands from LFC

It is known from (2) that the phrase command has the similar response characteristic with the accent command. In the same way, a left-to-right procedure is applied to obtain parameters of phrase command from the LFC.

In each repeated process, the LFC is searched for first and second local minima with a minimum distance threshold of 1.2s between consecutive phrase commands. And the segment between the local minima is corresponding to a phrase command and the first minimum point is assigned to onset time. Then the maximum of the segment is adopted as magnitude of the corresponding phrase command. And α is set to 2.0/s as first-order approximation.

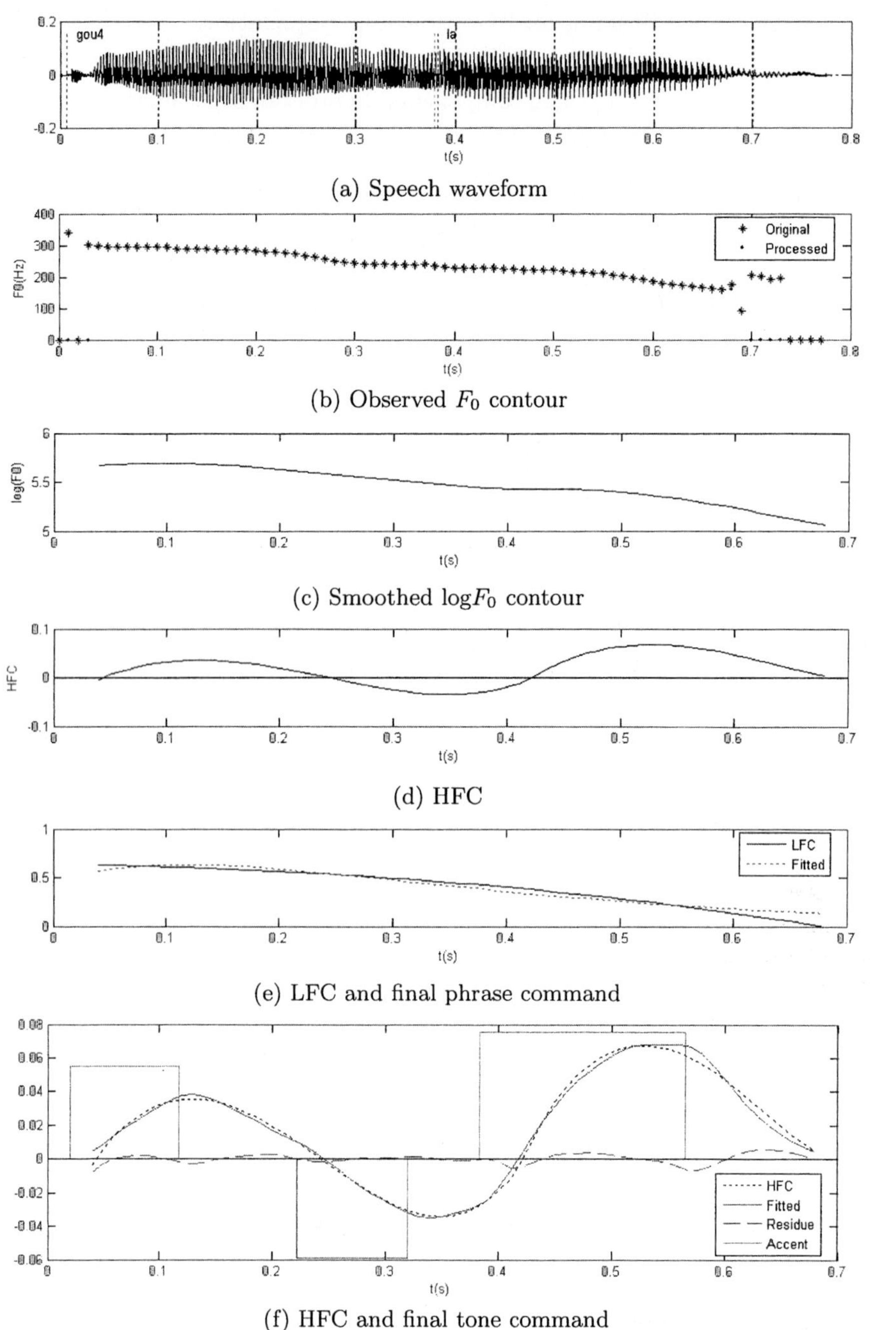

(a) Speech waveform

(b) Observed F_0 contour

(c) Smoothed $\log F_0$ contour

(d) HFC

(e) LFC and final phrase command

(f) HFC and final tone command

Fig. 3. Illustration of extraction for the model

4 Statistics for Emotion Based on Parameters of Fujisaki

4.1 Speech Material

Seven sentences with different contents were used as the speech materials in this paper. Each sentence is read respectively with 7 different moods including angry, disappointment, fear, joy, normal, sad and wonder. So the speech material for the present study was totally 49 affective Mandarin sentences uttered by a native female speaker. The speech signal was digitized at 22.05 kHz with 16-bit precision, and F_0 was extracted at 100Hz by a modified autocorrelation algorithm.

4.2 Preliminary Results

Figure 3 shows the process of the extraction of model parameters. While Mandarin tone types have rather clear manifestations in the F_0 contour in isolated syllables, they vary considerably in connected affective speech due to the influences of such factors as tones of adjacent syllables, syntactic and affective information of the whole utterance. So the fitting error is defined as criterion for the proposed method. In the entire corpus of 224 syllables, all the phrase commands can be extracted well and the tone commands can be approximated with maximal 1% error.

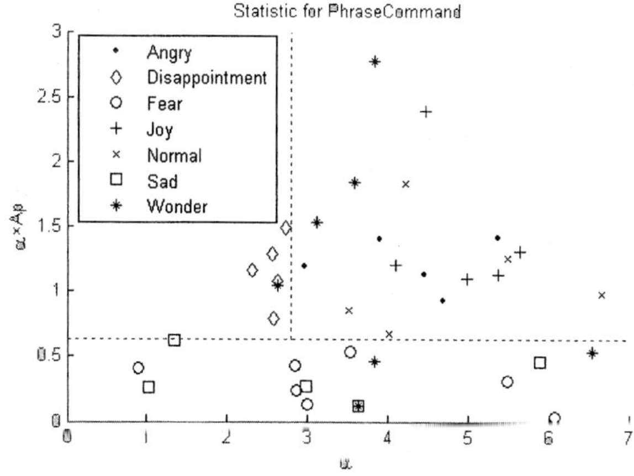

Fig. 4. Parameters of phrase command differ among several moods

It can be deduced that the magnitude of LFC is in proportion to phrase parameter's product, $\alpha \star A_p$, and the change rate of LFC is in proportion to α. The LFC is generally regarded as intonation of the sentence. Figure 4 illustrates the phrase parameters with 7 different moods. The statistical results of the parameters show that the modified model is feasible. It can be used for the affective speech study.

5 Conclusions

In this paper, the Fujisaki model is adapted to affective Mandarin. The modification introduced in this paper avoids the distortion during the parameters' extraction and improves the expressive ability of the model. A novel approach is introduced to extract the model parameters of Mandarin employing a cubically smoothed contour as the intermediate approximation target. The method reserves the pitch movement caused by mood and does not need any manual labels information. The statistical results of the parameters show that the modified model is feasible for the affective speech study.

Future work will focus on a closer analysis of the relationship between model parameters and affective information.

Acknowledgements

This work is partly supported by Open Foundation of National Laboratory of Pattern Recognition, China. We would like to thank Dr. Tieniu Tan and Dr. Jianhua Tao for their helps.

References

1. Zhao YuanRen: Problems of Language, Commercial Press of China (1980)
2. Fujisaki H., and Hirose K.: Analysis of voice fundamental frequency contours for declarative sentences of Japanese. Journal of the Acoustical Society of Japan (E), Vol. 5, No. 4, (1984) 233-241
3. Narusawa S., Minematsu N., Hirose K. and Fujisaki H.: Automatic extraction of model parameters from fundamental frequency contours of English utterances, Denver, ICSLP-2002, (2002) 1725-1728
4. Mixdorff, H.: A novel approach to the fully automatic extraction of Fujisaki model parameters, Istanbul, ICASSP-2000, Vol. 1, (2000) 1281-1284
5. Mixdorff, H., Fujisaki, H., Chen, GaoPeng, Hu, Yu: Towards the automatic extraction of fujisaki model parameters for Mandarin, In EUROSPEECH-2003, (2003) 873-876
6. Seresangtakul, Pusadee, Takara, Tomio: Study on pitch contour of Thai polysyllabic tone sequences using a generative model, Nara, SP-2004, (2004) 483-486
7. Chen GaoPeng, Hu Yu, Wu YiJian, Wang RenHua: A concatenative-tone model with its parameters' extraction, Nara, SP-2004, (2004) 455-458
8. Gu Wentao, Hirose, K., Fujisaki, H.: A method for automatic tone command parameter extraction for the model of F0 contour generation for Mandarin, Nara, SP-2004, (2004) 435-438
9. Fujisaki, H., Hallê, P., Lei, H.: Application of F0 contour command-response model to Chinese tones. Reports of Autumn Meeting, Acoustical Society of Japan (1987) 197-198

An Emotion Space Model for Recognition of Emotions in Spoken Chinese

Xuecheng Jin and Zengfu Wang

Department of Automation, University of Science and Technology of China, Hefei, Anhui, 230027, China
zfwang@ustc.edu.cn

Abstract. This paper presents a conception of emotion space modeling using psychological research for reference. Based on this conception, this paper studies the distribution of the seven emotions in spoken Chinese, including joy, anger, surprise, fear, disgust, sadness and neutral, in the two dimensional space of valence and arousal, and analyses the relationship between the dimensional ratings and the prosodic characteristics in terms of F0 maximum, minimum, range and mean. The findings show that the conception of emotion modeling is helpful to describe and distinguish emotions.

1 Introduction

The recognition of emotion in human speech has gained increasing attention in recent years as the need for machines to understand human well in human-machine communication has grown [1]. A great deal of methods of emotion recognition in speech have been proposed by many scholars [2,3,4,5,6,7,8]. Most of them focus on classifying inputted emotional speech into some emotional state. How to define the states of emotions? Various opinions have been proposed [9], but there is no an accepted answer about the problem up to now. In fact, sometimes it is difficult to exactly classify some emotional speech into a specific emotion state. If the emotions can be modeled according to an 'emotional' space which is similar to the HSI representation of color and can be described in some mathematical way, then the problem of recognition of emotion in speech can be easily solved.

This paper presents a conception of constructing an emotion space model based on the results from psychological research and reports a perceptual experiment. In the experiment, we have studied how the seven emotions of spoken Chinese including joy, anger, surprise, fear, disgust, sadness and neutral distribute in the emotion space we constructed. Furthermore, we have studied the relationship between the prosodic characteristics and the mean ratings in the two dimensional space of valence and arousal by using the pitch information extracted from inputted emotional speech.

J. Tao, T. Tan, and R.W. Picard (Eds.): ACII 2005, LNCS 3784, pp. 397–402, 2005.

2 Emotion Space Model

According to Osgood, Suci and Tannenbaum's theory [10] and subsequent psychological research [11,12], the emotion computing can be conceptualized as three major dimensions of connotative meaning: valence, arousal and power. The valence dimension refers to how positive or negative the emotion is. The arousal dimension refers to how excited or apathetic the emotion is. And the power dimension refers to the degree of power or sense of control over the emotion. Regarding the three dimensions as axes, and using Plutchik emotion model and the constitution of HSI model of color for reference, a reasonable space of emotion can be modeled as Figure 1.

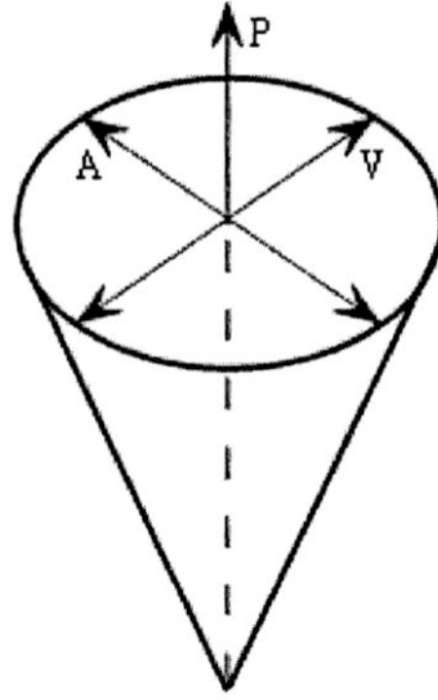

Fig. 1. Three dimensions of emotion space (V-valence, A-arousal, P-power)

3 Experimental Results and Discussion

3.1 Corpus of Emotional Data

To collect speech material, 10 Chinese sentences that are fitting to reflect the basic emotion were chosen for each of six basic emotions, including joy, anger, surprise, sadness, fear and disgust. And four professional actors were recruited. Each actor was asked to speak each sentence for twice, respectively in manner of neutral and corresponding emotion. In this way, 240 emotional utterances were obtained, each with a corresponding one in neutral.

To eliminate the utterances whose emotion are not obvious, listening tests were used: eight test subjects who were university students of adult education were recruited to listen to the data. The test subjects were requested to hear the speech samples in random order. In the forced choice test, the emotional labels were the same as those actually expressed by the speakers. The utterances corresponding to mistaken emotion given by more than two test subjects were eliminated. After the listening tests, 214 utterances that can reflect the corresponding basic emotion properly were left.

3.2 Distribution of Emotions in Valence-Arousal Space

In this paper, just the distributions of the seven emotions in valence-arousal space were studied. Each of the two dimensions was represented by 7 gradations, e.g. on the dimension of valence -3 for very negative, -2 for negative, -1 for slightly negative, 0 for neither negative nor positive, 1 for slightly positive, 2 for positive, 3 for very positive.

Then 20 normally-hearing listeners were asked to listen to the 214 emotional utterances that were selected in the first listening test, and to rate each utterance on 7 gradations on the two dimensions of valence and arousal. While listening,

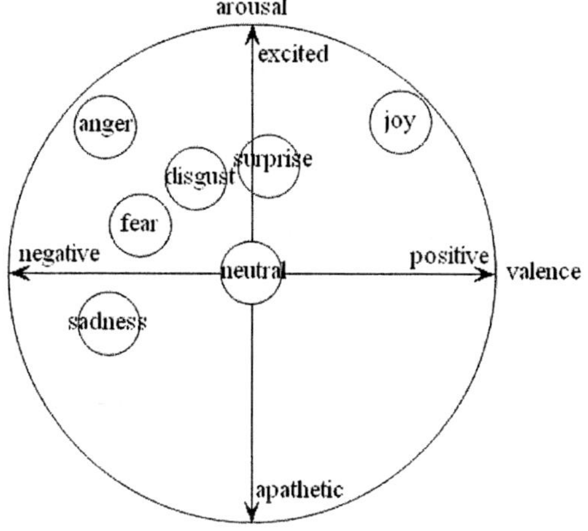

Fig. 2. Distribution of the seven emotions in valence-arousal space

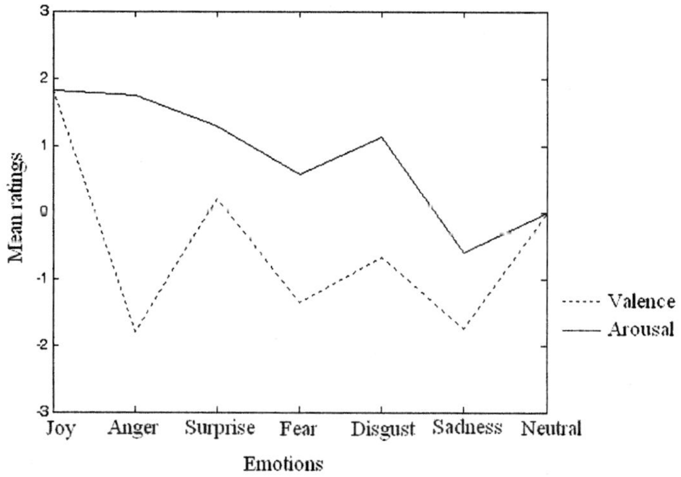

Fig. 3. Mean dimensional ratings of the seven emotions

the listeners could contrast the emotional utterances with their corresponding neutral ones, whose ratings were about the origin (0, 0). Figure 2 shows the statistical distribution result of each emotion in valence-arousal space, and Figure 3 shows the mean rating on each dimension for each emotion.

Joy and anger show nearly exactly the same highest rating on the dimension of arousal, followed by surprise, disgust, fear, neutral, then sadness. On the dimension of valence, the highest rated emotion was joy too, followed by surprise, neutral, disgust, fear, sadness then anger. Figure 3 shows that the variety of the ratings on the arousal dimension is smaller than that on the valence dimension.

In this experiment, the distributions of joy, anger, sadness, disgust and neutral on the dimension of valence mostly match the research of Osgood [10]. Disgust has positive ratings on the dimension of arousal in this experiment, whereas Osgood research had 'boredom' at the very negative end. The reason of this result might be the disgust emotion in this research can be explained to be hot antipathy whereas the boredom in Osgood research could be understood to be apathetic annoyance.

3.3 Prosodic Characteristics-Fundamental Frequency

Previous research has shown some statistics of the pitch (fundamental frequency F0) to be the main vocal cue for emotion recognition [13], also other prosodic characteristics, e.g. energy and speaking rate.

In this paper, pitch was extracted with a cepstrum-based method [14], to study the relationship between the prosodic characteristics and the mean ratings on the two dimensions of valence and arousal. The mean of the statistical measurements of the pitch for each emotion are shown in Figure 4.

In Figure 4, sadness has the lowest F0 mean and maximum and the smallest differences between maximum and minimum. Joy and anger have significantly higher F0 mean than other emotions except for surprise. These results match the

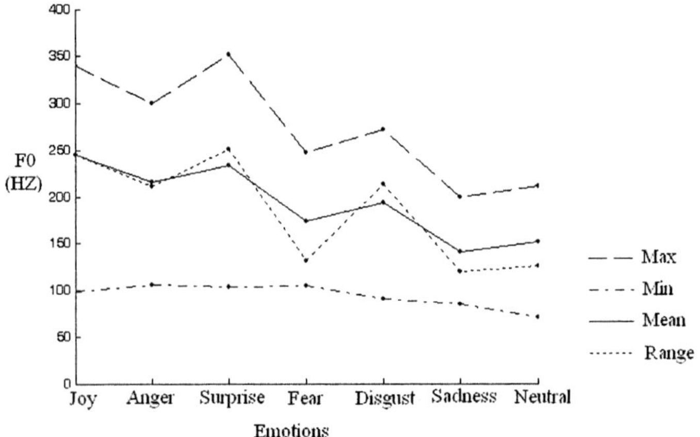

Fig. 4. The mean of the statistical measurements of F0 of the seven emotions

research of Paeschke [13] well (Paeschke didn't study surprise). But significant difference to the research of Paeschke is that the mean and maximum of F0 of fear are lower than those of disgust, whereas in Paeschke research fear had higher mean and maximum than boredom. The reason is similar to that discussed previously.

3.4 Correlations Between Dimensional Ratings and Pitch

To study the relationship between the dimensional ratings and pitch, the correlation coefficients between the mean ratings and the maximum, minimum, range and mean of F0 were calculated, and shown in Table 1.

Table 1. Correlation coefficients between dimensional ratings and the pitch measurements

Correlation coefficients	F0 min	F0 max	F0 range	F0 mean
Valance	-0.0643	0.4783	0.4654	0.4933
Arousal	0.5938	0.7674	0.7591	0.8069

From Table 1, one can see that the dimension of valence correlates positively with F0 mean, max, range, and correlates insignificantly negatively with F0 min. The dimension of arousal correlates positively and significantly with F0 mean, max, range and min. This result is similar to Pereira's findings for male in [15], in which author expressed his research on the three dimensions of five emotional meaning: cold anger, hot anger, happiness, sadness and neutral.

4 Conclusion and Prospect

The experimental results show that all of the emotions are significantly different from each other in at least one dimension, which suggests the dimension information is helpful to distinguish emotions and the conception of emotion space modeling is reasonable to describe emotions.

The result of listening tests shows that the emotions with a similar level of arousal are easy to be confused for each other. At the same time, the analysis of correlations between dimensional ratings and pith indicates that the emotions with a similar level of arousal share prosodic characteristics in terms of F0 maximum, range and mean, which suggests that F0 is reasonable to be used as the feature to distinguish the emotions that have significantly different ratings on the dimension of arousal.

In the subsequent research, we will study the distribution of the emotional meaning on the dimension of power, and analysis the relationship between the dimensional ratings and other acoustic characteristics besides F0, in order to select more efficient features to distinguish emotions in spoken Chinese. Furthermore we hope to describe the emotion space model with a reasonable mathematic method and hope to find a new approach for recognition of emotion in speech.

Acknowledgements

This work is partly supported by Open Foundation of National Laboratory of Pattern Recognition, China. We would like to thank Dr. Tieniu Tan and Dr. Jianhua Tao for their helps.

References

1. Cowie R. , Douglas-Cowie E. ,Tsapatsoulis N. , Votsis G. , Kollias S. , Fellenz W. and Taylor J.G. : Emotion Recognition in Human-Computer Interaction. IEEE Signal Proc. Mag., 18(1), (2001) 32-80
2. Dellaert F. , Polzin T. , Waible A. :Recognizing Emotion In Speech, Proceedings of the ICSLP, Philadelphia, PA, (1996) 1970-1973
3. Nicholson J., Takahashi K., Nakstsu R.:Emotion Recognition in Speech Using Neural Networks, Neural Information Processing, 1999. Proceedings. ICONIP '99. 6th International Conference, 2(11), (1999) 495 - 501
4. Nogueiras A. , Moreno A. , Bonafonte A., and Mariño J. : Speech Emotion Recognition Using Hidden Markov Models, Eurospeech 2001, Poster Proceedings,Scandinavia, (2001) 2679-2682
5. Yu F. , Chang E. , Xu Y.-Q. and Shum H.-Y. :Emotion detection from speech to enrich multimedia content, Proceedings of the Second IEEE Pacific-Rim Conference on Multimedia, Peking, (2001) 550-557
6. Schuller B. , Rigoll G., and Lang M. : Hidden Markov Model-based Speech Emotion Recognition, Proceedings of IEEE-ICASSP, (2003) 401-405
7. Yacoub S. , Simske S. ,Lin X. , Burns J.: Recognition of Emotions in Interactive Voice Response Systems, Eurospeech, HPL-2003-136, (2003)
8. Pao Tsang-Long, Chen Yu-Te , Yeh Jun-Heng , Lu Jhih-Jheng : Detecting Emotions in Mandarin Speech Proceeding ROCLING XVISep. (2004)
9. Kleinginna P. R. and Kleinginna A.M. : A Categorized List of Emotion Definitions with Suggestions for a Consensual Definition, Motivation and Emotion, (1981) 345-379
10. Osgood C.E. , Suci J.G. and Tannenbaum P.H. : The Measurement of Meaning, University of Illinois Press, (1957) 31-75
11. Davitz, Joel R. : Auditory correlates of vocal expression of emotional feeling, In The communication of emotional meaning, ed, (1964) 101-112
12. Mehrabian A. and Russel J.: An Approach to Environmental Psychology, Cambridge MA: MIT Press, (1974) 192-203
13. Pasechke A. and Sendlmeier W.F. : Prosodic Characteristics of Emotional speech: Measurements of Fundamental Frequency Movements, In SpeechEmotion-2000, (2000) 75-80
14. Ahmadi S. , and Spanias A. S. : Cepstrum-based pitch detection using a new statistical V/UV classification algorithm, IEEE Transaction on Speech and Audio Processing, Vol. 7, NO. 3, (1999) 333-338
15. Pereira C. : Dimensions of Emotional Menming in Speech, Proceedings of the ISCA-Workshop on Speech and Emotion, (2000)

Emotion-State Conversion for Speaker Recognition

Dongdong Li, Yingchun Yang, Zhaohi Wu, and Tian Wu

Department of Computer Science and Technology,
Zhejiang University, Hangzhou, P.R. China, 310027
{lidd, yyc, wzh, wutian}@cs.zju.edu.cn

Abstract. The performance of speaker recognition system is easily disturbed by the changes of the internal states of human. The ongoing work proposes an approach of speech emotion-state conversion to improve the performance of speaker identification system over various affective speech. The features of neutral speech are modified according to statistical prosodic parameters of emotion utterances. Speaker models are generated based on the converted speech. The experiments conducted on an emotion corpus with 14 emotion states shows promising results with an improved performance by 7.2%.

1 Introduction

Biometrics system based on voice is a friendly approach to authenticate a person because speech communications is the most effective way in human-to-human and human-machine interaction. Affective factors can cause an unacceptably high error rate, which limits the commercial viability of such systems. In [1,2],an approach called structured training is proposed, in which speaker models built on a variety of utterances elicited under different affective states rather than the standard neutral samples lead to an improvement in the performance of speaker verification systems. However, additional affective speech is required during the enrollment.

In order to endow the speaker recognition system with the ability to deal with different types of emotional arousal without special requirement in enrollment, a novel text-independent emotion-state conversion approach is presented based on the elicitation of emotional speech synthesis [3]. The residual signal [4] which carries the specific speaker information is modified to change the duration, pitch and the amplitude of the speech according to the corresponding prosodic parameters [5] in affective speech. The preliminary converted speech is generated by Linear Predictive Coding (LPC) synthesis with the transformed feature. The prosodic information representing the affective states is complemented to the neutral in the process of speech conversion leading to considerably improvement of system performance.

This paper is organized as follows. The emotional corpus is introduced in section 2, followed by the description of system architecture in section3. In section 4, the implement of proposed system is discussed in detail. The experimental protocol and comparison is presented in section5. Finally, we give a conclusion in Section 6.

J. Tao, T. Tan, and R.W. Picard (Eds.): ACII 2005, LNCS 3784, pp. 403 – 410, 2005.

2 Database

The data we used for the experiments are the Emotional Prosody Speech and Transcripts corpus from the Linguistic Data Consortium (LDC) [6]. The main objective of the corpus is to support research in emotional prosody. The corpus contains two recording sessions including audio recordings as well as corresponding transcripts of 8 actors taken at eight month intervals. In the first section, the actors were asked to express a dimension of dominance and a dimension of distance. While, the second section consists of a series of semantically neutral utterances (dates and numbers) spanning fourteen distinct emotional categories [7]. The fourteen specific emotional states are: hot anger, cold anger, panic, anxiety, despair, sadness, elation, happiness, interest, boredom, shame, pride, disgust, contempt. The utterances were recorded at a sampling rate of 22.05 KHz on 2 channels and directly saved into WAVES+ data files.

3 Framework Overview

Figure 1 shows the block diagram for the speaker recognition system with affective speech based on a proposed text-independent emotion-state conversion. The system in this work relies on 3 modules:

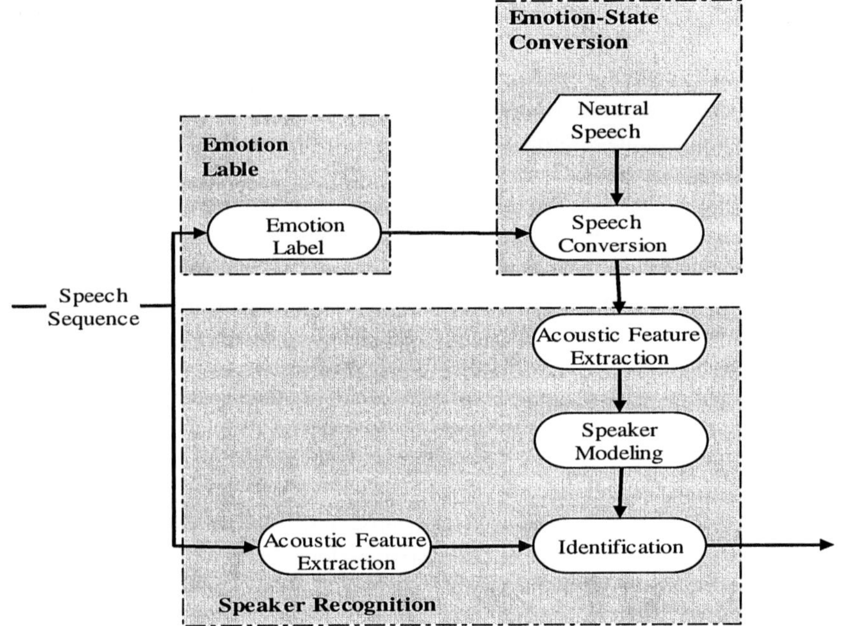

Fig. 1. The architecture of speaker recognition based on emotion-state conversion

- The *emotion label* which provides the affective information to the next module to decide the converted state. In this work, the state of the affective speech is assumed to be classified before feature extraction. The problem could also be achieved by emotion recognition which has been addressed by different researcher and with different methods [8], to implement the automatic speaker recognition.
- The *emotion-state conversion* which analyses the emotional speech, modifies the prosodic information of neutral speech and generates the converted speech. The prosodic information refers to duration of the speech, average pitch, pitch range, average amplitude and amplitude range. Linear Predictive Coding (LPC) analysis is applied to extraction the LPC coefficients representing the phoneme character and residual signal with pitch information. These two features are modified according to prosodic information and synthesized to a converted speech.
- The *speaker recognition* which extracts the feature from the converted speech, generates speaker models, matches the test utterances with the models and makes the final decision. This task is based on the use of Mel Frequency Cepstral Coefficients (MFCC) as the parameters, and the Gaussians Mixtures Models (GMM) for the classification.

The proposed approach focuses on the second module (the emotion-state conversion). The details of this process are explained in the next chapter.

4 Emotion-State Conversion

The implement of emotion-state conversion comprises two main stages: the analysis of prosodic parameters in affective speech and the modification of features in neutral speech.

4.1 Prosodic Parameters

Phonetic research reveals that prosodic information could predict the changes in the speech signal with emotional states [5].

The prosodic parameters we analyzed are duration of the speech, average pitch (AP), pitch range (PR), average amplitude (AA) and amplitude range (AR). Duration is counted from the number of voiced frames by LPC analysis. The change of Duration can be calculated as:

$$D = f_e / f_n \tag{1}$$

Where f_e and f_n are the frame number of emotional speech and neutral ones, respectively.

Pitch is determined by Subharmonic-TO-Harmonic Ratio (SHR) method provided by Sun [9].The change of average pitch can be calculated as:

$$AP = \frac{\sum_{i=1}^{K} E_i}{K} - \frac{\sum_{i=1}^{L} N_i}{L} \tag{2}$$

Where E_i and N_i is the pitch value of frame i of emotion and neutral speech respectively, and K is the number of pitch values in the emotion utterances. L is the number of pitch values in the neutral utterances.

The change of pitch range can be calculated as:

$$PR = (E_{\max} - E_{\min})/(N_{\max} - N_{\min}) \quad (3)$$

Where $E_{\max}$ and $E_{\min}$ are the maximal and minimal value in a set of pitch of emotion utterance. $N_{\max}$ and $N_{\min}$ are the maximal and minimal value in a set of pitch of emotion utterance.

Amplitude is referred to the short time mean amplitude. The change of Amplitude can be calculated the same as the formula as Equation (2) and (3) with replacing corresponding features.

Table 1 shows the values of parameters changes for each emotion.

Table 1. The changes of parameters for each emotion

emotion	Prosodic Parameter changes				
	Duration (%)	AP (Hz)	PR (%)	AA	AR (%)
hot anger	0.992406	125.84718	2.115069	0.006468	3.965434
cold anger	1.087478	41.438710	1.333915	0.003122	2.403157
panic	1.082492	92.857509	1.403321	0.001422	2.858753
anxiety	1.064805	30.073901	1.086914	-0.000011	1.012111
despair	1.036088	41.231239	1.189985	-0.000006	1.200300
sadness	1.139990	22.912141	1.125422	-0.000001	1.332440
elation	1.004447	44.420044	1.340661	0.000012	1.614118
neutral	1.034974	24.515332	1.170365	-0.000032	1.277464
interest	0.990863	20.741113	1.186989	-0.000035	0.948060
boredom	0.996848	4.594516	1.099803	0.000046	0.955415
shame	1.016246	10.479784	1.093688	-0.000035	0.967273
pride	1.038735	24.683332	1.251838	-0.000028	1.812363
contempt	1.028349	20.764525	1.268763	-0.000029	1.494658
disgust	1.145482	19.374581	1.247953	-0.000007	1.524762

4.2 Speech Conversion

The theory of linear predictive coding (LPC), as applied to speech, has been well understood for many years. The residual signal by LPC analysis carries significant speaker specific information [10] and shows the correlation with a subjective evaluation of voice properties. The whole residue is often summarized in one number representing F0 used as prosodic features to characterize the source contribution.

In this stage, two features, LPC coefficients and residual signal are extracted from neutral training speech sample on a frame by frame basis. The results of LPC analysis are a new representation of the signal.

$$s(n) = \sum_{i=1}^{p} a_i s(n-i) + Gu(n) \quad (4)$$

where $s(n)$ is the original speech signal. a_i and $u(n)$ are the outputs of the LPC analysis with a_i representing the LPC coefficients. The $u(n)$ term represents the normalized excitation source, or the residual. The G factor is a gain term.

The converted speech is derived by modifying the LPC coefficients and residual signal of neutral utterances according to prosodic information. Prosodic parameters which have the emotional feature of speeches are analyzed by the same mentioned in chapter 4.1.

The frames are reconstructed for the duration modification. Excessive frames are cut to reduce its duration; and appropriate frames are repeated to expand its duration. Residual signal is changed directly by average pitch and pitch range:

$$u_{ci} = (u_n + AP_i) * PR_i \tag{5}$$

Amplitude is changed by average amplitude and amplitude range after LPC synthesis, and can be calculated as:

$$a_{ci} = (a_n + AA_i) * AR_i \tag{6}$$

Where x_{ci} and y_n is the modified feature of i th affective state of converted speech and the original neutral one respectively, x, y could be the residual signal u and amplitude a . Z_i represents the prosodic parameters of emotion i, Z could be average pitch (AP), pitch range (PR), average amplitude (AA) and amplitude range (AR).

Fig 2 shows the process of emotion-state conversion.

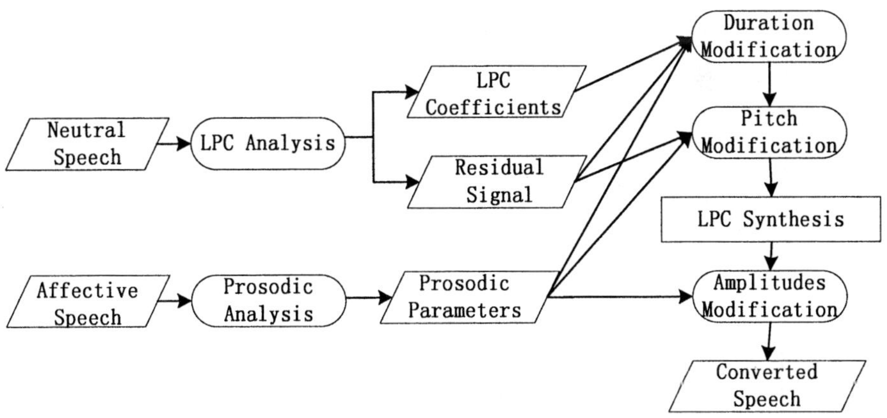

Fig. 2. The flow chart of emotion-state conversion

5 Experiments and Discussion

5.1 Experiment Protocol

The protocol is defined to evaluate the performance of speaker authentication on even more varied speech. The Emotional Prosody Speech and Transcripts corpus was divided into three set: training set, evaluation set, and test set. The training set is used to build client models, and consists of the neutral utterances in a general conversation from the first sessions. The evaluation set is selected to produce the affective parameter representing the difference between the neutral and affective speech of the same content. The test set is selected to simulate real authentication tests using the remainder emotion recordings. For this description, each subject appears only in one set which is an important requirement to ensure the realistic evaluation of the system.

5.2 Strategies

Three experiments are designed in this work to evaluate the performance of the proposed approach:

- *Baseline*: In a first set of experiments, we conducted a baseline strategy. The approach to recognize the speaker identity is based on the use of the MFCC as the parameters and the Gaussians Mixtures Models (GMM) for the classification task. This strategy is used to provide the initial results for speaker recognition with affective speech.
- *Unmodified LPC*: In another series of experiments, a module that estimates the system performance with LPC analysis and synthesis is included. The recordings are divided to LPC coefficients and its residual signal by LPC analysis, and then synthesized using the unmodified features extracted before. The following processes are the same as mentioned in the baseline strategy.
- *Speech-State Conversion*: Compared with the Unmodified LPC strategy, the proposed approach modifies the LPCC and residual signal of training data before LPC synthesis. Converted speech is generated for acoustic feature extraction.

In each strategy, the 16 MFCC coefficients and their delta coefficients are used. A pre-emphasis filter whose constant α value is 0.94 is generally used before spectral analysis, followed by a sliding Hamming window with a length of 32 ms and a shift of 16 ms. In LPC analysis, speech is cut in overlapping frames of 30ms duration stepped each 20ms. After pre-emphasis with $u = 0.9378$, each frame is fed to LPC with p=14 as analysis order.

Table 2. The results of the speaker identificaation with three stragies

Approaches	Baseline (%)	Unmodified LPC (%)	Speech-State Conversion (%)
IR	62.81	62.34	70.22

5.3 Results and Discussion

Table 2 reports the identification rate (IR) of the whole speaker authentication system observed with the three techniques: 1) Baseline (feature extracted directly from original speech by MFCC), 2) Unmodified LPC (feature extracted from the speech synthesized by LPC with the unmodified features), 3) Speech-State Conversion (feature extracted from the converted speech). The details of IR for the fourteen kinds of affective speech tested independently are shown in the Fig. 3.

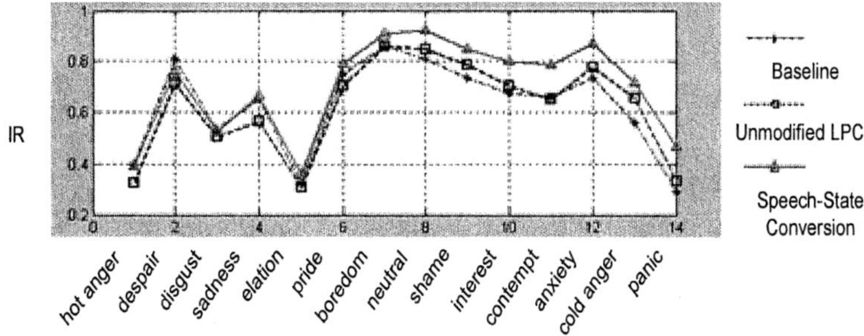

Fig. 3. The identification rate of the three strategies on fourteen affective states

The result shows that the baseline system yields the lowest IR of 62.81%. The neutral state of speech gives the highest one of 81.25% among all the affective states. This technique demonstrates that the performance of speaker recognition system drops sharply on emotional speech and the consistence speech state of the training and test utterances is important.

The fluctuation but steadiness of the performance between the baseline strategy and the unmodified LPC strategy shows the feasibility of speech by the preliminary process of LPC analysis followed by the LPC synthesis. The specific speaker information is maintained in the wave files synthesized by LPC.

With the task of speaker identification, the profit in performance increases by 7.4% for all emotional testing utterances, along with 17.73% in the best case for affective state of panic using proposed approach compared with the baseline technique. However, there are three sorts of emotion indicating a loss in performance, 0.71% for hot anger, 4.62% for despair and 1.11% for disgust. The main reason lies on the debased quality of these three states, which results from the process of LPC analysis and synthesis. In the unmodified LPC strategy, the performance decreases by 3.33%, 8.61%, and 1.25% for hot anger, despair and disgust respectively compared with the baseline experiment. The proposed approach enhances the overall identification rate by 7.8% compared with the case of unmodified LPC, and each kind of affective speech gains the profit.

6 Conclusion

This paper has presented a robust speaker modeling technique capable of operating on speech corrupted with the multi-affective states. An approach of emotion state conversion was proposed to modify the prosodic parameter of neutral speech in text-independent speaker recognition system. The converted speech incorporated with corresponding affective information is derived by changing the duration, pitch, and amplitude of the neutral speech. The large improvement of performance demonstrates the promisingness of the proposed work.

Further experiments on conversion of the affective states to neutral states will focus on reversibleness with respect to states transform.

Acknowledgement

This work is supported by National Natural Science Foundation of P.R.China(60273059), Zhejiang Provincial Natural Science Foundation (M603229) and National Doctoral Subject Foundation (20020335025).

References

1. Scherer, K. R., Johnstone, T., Klasmeyer, G.: Can automatic speaker verification be improved by training the algorithms on emotional speech? Proceedings of the 6th International Conference on Spoken Language Processing Beijing, China. (2000),
2. Scherer, K. R., Johnstone, T., and Bänziger, T.: Automatic verification of emotionally stressed speakers: The problem of individual differences. Proc. of SPECOM98, (1998)
3. Sato J. and Morishima. S.: Emotion modeling in speech production using emotion space. in Proc. IEEE Int. Workshop on Robot and Human Communication. (1996)
4. Thévenaz, P., Hügli. H.: Usefulness of the LPC-Residue in Text-Independent Speaker Verification. Speech Communication, vol. 17, (1995) 145-157
5. Galanis, D., Darsinos, V., Kokkinakis, G.: Investigating Emotional Speech Parameter for Speech Synthesis. ICECS96 (1966) 1227-1230
6. LDC: The Linguistic Data Consortium: web pages at www.ldc.upenn.edu
7. Banse, R., Scherer, K. R.: Acoustic profiles in vocal emotion expression. Journal of Personality and Social Psychology, 70 (1996) 614-636
8. Frank, D., Thomas, P. and Alex W.: Recognizing Emotion in Speech. ICSLP'96 (1996) 1970-1973
9. Sun, s.: Pitch Determination and Voice Quality Analysis Using Subharmonic-TO-Harmonic Ratio. IEEE International Conference on Acoustics, Speech, and Signal processing (2002)
10. Feustel, T. C. Velius, G. A. Logan R. J.: Human and Machine Performance on Speaker Identity Verification. *Speech-Tech'89*, (1989) 169-170.

Affect Editing in Speech

Tal Sobol Shikler and Peter Robinson

Computer Laboratory, University of Cambridge, Cambridge, UK

Abstract. In this paper we present an affect editor for speech. The affect editor is a tool that encompasses various editing techniques for expressions in speech. It can be used for both natural and synthesized speech. We present a technique that uses a natural expression in one utterance by a particular speaker to other utterances by the same speaker or by other speakers. Natural new expressions are created without affecting the voice quality.

1 Introduction

Editing affect in speech has many desirable applications. Editing tools have become standard in computer graphics and vision, but speech technologies still lack simple transformations to manipulate expression of natural and synthesized speech. Such editing tools are relevant for the movies and games industries, for feedback and therapeutic applications, and more.

There is a substantial body of work in affective speech synthesis, see for example, the review by Schröder [6]. Morphing of affect in speech, meaning regenerating a signal by interpolation of auditory features between two samples, was presented by Kawahara and Matsui [3]. This work explored transitions between two utterances with different expressions in the time-frequency domain. Further results on morphing speech for voice changes in singing were presented by Pfitzinger [5], who also reviews other morphing related work and techniques.

However most of the studies explored just a few extreme expressions, and not nuances or subtle expressions. The methods that use prosody characteristics consider global definition, and only few integrated the linguistic prosody categorizations like f_0 contours [1, 4]. The morphing examples are of very short utterances (one short word each), and few extreme acted expressions. None of these techniques leads to editing tools for general use.

In this paper we suggest an editing tool for affect in speech. We describe its architecture and a possible implementation which is based on known processing techniques. We also suggest a set of transformations of f_0 contours, energy, duration and spectral content, for the manipulation of affect in speech signals. This set includes operations like selective extension, shrinking, and actions like 'cut and paste'. In particular, we demonstrate how a natural expression in one utterance by a particular speaker can be transformed to other utterances, by the same speaker or by other speakers. The basic set of editing operators can be extended gradually to encompass a larger variety of transformations and effects. In the following sections we outline the method, show examples of subtle

J. Tao, T. Tan, and R.W. Picard (Eds.): ACII 2005, LNCS 3784, pp. 411–418, 2005.

expression editing of one speaker, demonstrate simple manipulations, and apply a transformation of an expression using another speaker's speech. We present here initial results. The techniques and their implementation still require refining and further validation with users and listeners.

2 Affect Editor

The affect editor, shown schematically in Figure 1, takes an input speech signal X, and allows the user to modify its conveyed expression, in order to produce an output signal $\tilde{X}$, with a new expression. The expression can be of an emotion, mental state or attitude. The modification can be a nuance, or might be a radical change. The operators that affect the modifications are set by the user.

The editing operators are derived in advance by analysis of an affective speech corpus. They can include a corpus of pattern samples for concatenation, or target samples for morphing. A complete system may allow the user to choose either a desired target expression that will be automatically translated into operators and contours, or choose the operators and manipulations manually. The editing tool should offer a variety of editing operators, such as changing the intonation, speech rate, the energy in different frequency bands and time frames, or add special effects.

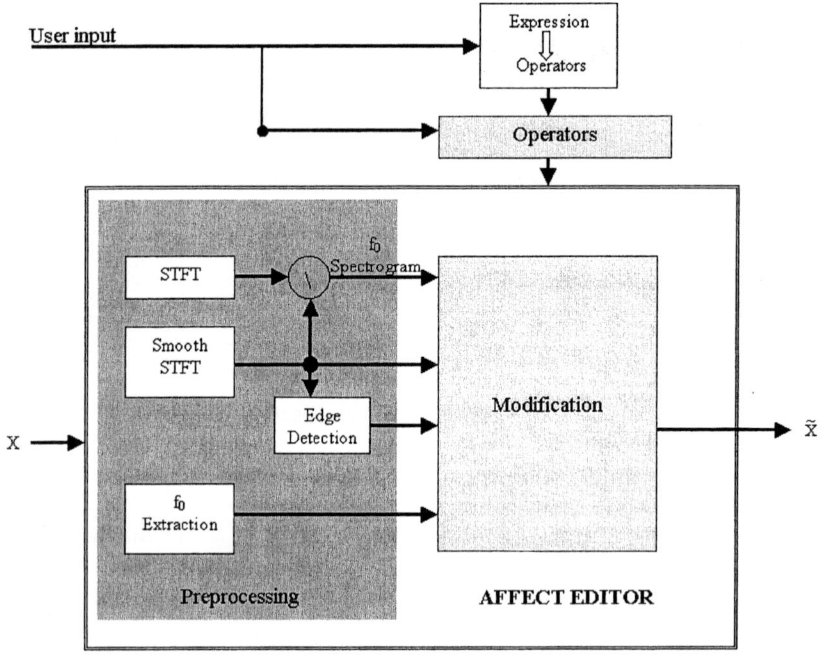

Fig. 1. A schematic description of an affect editing system

Extensions of this system rely heavily on an expressive inference system that should supply reliable operators and transformations between expressions and the related operators. Other extensions may include a graphical user interface that allows navigation among expressions and gradual transformations in time.

3 Implementation

The editor requires a preprocessing stage before editing an utterance. Post-processing is also necessary for reproducing a new speech signal. The input signal is preprocessed in a way that allows processing of different features separately. The method we use for preprocessing and reconstruction was described by Slaney [7], who used it for speech morphing. It is also close to Kawahara's method for morphing of affect. It is based on analysis in the time-frequency domain. The time-frequency domain is used because it allows for local changes of limited durations, and of specific frequency bands. From human computer interaction point of view, it allows visualization of the changeable features, and gives the user graphical feedback for most operations. We also use a separate f_0 extraction algorithm, so a contour can be seen and edited. These features make it a helpful tool for the psycho-acoustic research of features' importance.

The pre-processing stages include:

1. Short Time Fourier Transform, to create a spectrogram.
2. Calculating the smooth spectrogram using Mel-Frequency Cepstral Coefficients (MFCC). The coefficients are computed by resampling a conventional magnitude spectrogram to match critical bands as measured by auditory perception experiments. After computing logarithms of the filter-bank outputs, a low-dimensional cosine transform is computed. The MFCC representation is inverted to generate a smooth spectrogram for the sound which does not include pitch.
3. Divide the spectrogram by the smooth spectrogram, to create a spectrogram of f_0.
4. Extracting f_0. This stage simplifies the editing of f_0 contour.
5. Edge detection on the spectrogram, in order to find significant patterns and changes, and to define time and frequency pointers for changes. Edge detection can also be done manually by the user.

The pre-processing stage prepares the data for editing by the user. The affect editing tool allows editing of f_0 contour, spectral content, duration, or energy. Different implementation technique can be used for each editing operation, for example:

1. Changing the intonation can be done both by mathematical operations, or by using concatenation. Another method for changing intonation is to borrow f_0 contours from different utterances of the same speaker and other speakers. The user may change the whole f_0 contour, or only parts of it.

2. Change the energy in different frequency ranges and time frames. The signal is divided into frequency bands that relate to the frequency response of the human ear. A smooth spectrogram which represents these bands is generated in the preprocessing stage. Changes can then be made in specific frequency bands and time frames, or over the whole signal.
3. Change the speech rate. Extend and shrink the duration of speech parts by increasing and decreasing the overlap between frames in the inverse short-time Fourier transform. This method is good for the voiced parts of the speech, where f_0 exists, and for silence. The unvoiced parts, where there is speech but no f_0 contour, can be extended by interpolation.

These changes can be done on parts of the signal or on all of it. As will be shown below, operations on the pitch spectrogram and on the smooth/spectral spectrogram are almost orthogonal in the following sense. If one modifies only one of the spectrograms and then calculates the other from the reconstructed signal it will have minimal or no variations compared to the one calculated from the original signal. The editing tool has built-in operators and recorded speech samples. The recorded sample are for borrowing expression parts, and for simplifying imitation of expressions.

After editing, the system has to reconstruct the speech signal. Post-processing includes:

1. Regeneration of the new full spectrogram by multiplying the modified pitch spectrogram with the modified smooth spectrogram.
2. Spectrogram inversion, as suggested by Griffin and Lim [2]. Spectrogram inversion is the most complicated and time-consuming stage of the post-processing. It is complicated because spectrograms are based on absolute values, and do not give any clue regarding the phase of the signal. The aim is to minimize the processing time in order to improve the usability, and to give direct feedback to the user.

4 Examples

In this section we show some of the editing operations, with a graphical presentation of the results. We wanted to check if an affect editor is feasible with the current technology. The goal was to check if we could get new speech signals, that sound natural and convey new or modified expressions, and to experiment with some of the operators. We examine basic forms of the main desired operations, including changing f_0 contour, changes of energy, spectral content, and speech rate. For our experiment we used utterances from the Doors database, which consists of recordings of 15 people speaking Hebrew. Each speaker was recorded uttering repeatedly the same two sentences during a computer game, with approximately a hundred iterations each. The game elicited natural expressions and subtle expressions. It also allows tracking of dynamic changes among consecutive utterances.

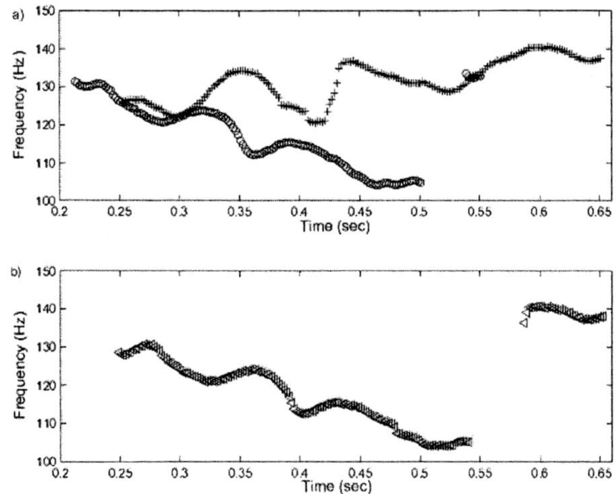

Fig. 2. Fundamental frequency (f_0) curves of 'sgor de-let'. a) original curves. The upper curve of 'uncertainty', the lower curve of 'determination' b) the curve of the edited signal, with combined pitch curve, and the energy and spectral content of 'uncertainty'.

Figure 2 presents features of the utterances 'sgor de-let' which means in Hebrew 'close door', uttered by a male speaker. Figure 2a represents the fundamental frequency curves of two original utterances. The higher curve shows the expression of uncertainty, and the lower curve shows determination. The uncertainty curve is long, high, and has a mildly ascending slope, while the determination curve is shorter and has a descending slope.

Figure 2b represents the curve of the edited utterance of uncertainty, with the combined f_0 curve generated from the two original curves, after reconstruction of the new edited signal. The first part of the original uncertainty curve, between 0.25sec and 0.55sec, was replaced by the contour from the determination curve. The location of the transformed part and its replacement were decided by using the extracted f_0 curves. The related parts from the f_0 spectrograms were replaced. A spectrogram of the new signal was generated by multiplying the new f_0 spectrogram by the original smoothed energy spectrogram. The combined spectrogram was then inverted. The energy and spectral content remained as in the original curve.

This manipulation yields a new natural speech signal, with a new expression, which is the intended result. We have intentionally chosen an extreme combination in order to check the validity of the editing concept, so the new expression is not necessarily identifiable. An end-user should be able to treat this procedure as the 'cut and paste', or 'insert from file' commands that are used by other types of editors. The user can use pre-recorded files, or to record the required expression to be used.

Figure 3 presents another set of operations on the utterance 'ptach de-let zo', which means 'open door this' (open this door) in Hebrew. First we manipulated local features of the fundamental frequency, as presented in Figure 3. We took an

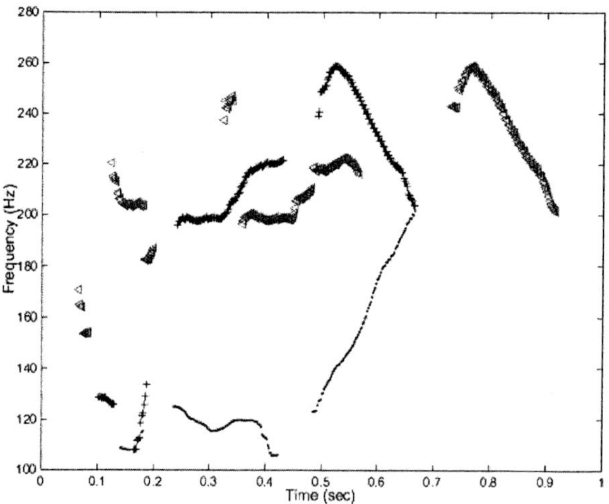

Fig. 3. f_0 contours of 'ptach delet zo' uttered by a female speaker (triangles), and a male speaker (dots), and the pitch of the edited male utterance (crosses)

utterance by a male speaker, and replaces part of its f_0 contour with a contour of an utterance by a female speaker, with a different expression, using the same technique as in the previous example. The pitch of the reconstructed signal is shown in crosses. As can be seen, both the curve shape and its duration were changed. The duration was extended by inverting the original spectrogram with smaller overlap between frames. The sampling rate of the recorded signals was 32KHz, the short-time Fourier transform, and the f_0 extraction algorithm used frames of 50ms with original overlap of 48ms, which allow precision, calculation of low f_0, and flexibility of duration manipulations. After changing the intonation, we took the edited signal and changed its energy, by multiplying it by a Gaussian, so that the center of the utterance was multiplied by 1.2, and the sides, the beginning and the end of the utterance, were multiplied by 0.8. The new signal sounds natural, with the voice of the male speaker. The new expression is a combination of the two original expressions.

The goal here was to examine editing operators and get natural results. We employed a variety of manipulations, such as replacing parts of intonation contours with different contours by the same speaker and by another speaker, changing the speech rate, and changing energy by multiplying the whole utterance by a time dependent function. The results were new utterances, with new natural expressions, in the voice of the original speaker. These results were confirmed by initial evaluation with Hebrew speakers. The speaker was always recognized, and the voice sounded natural. On several occasions the new expression was perceived as unnatural for the specific person, or the speech rate too fast. It happened in utterances in which we had intentionally chosen slopes and f_0 ranges which are extreme for the edited voice. In some utterances the listeners heard an echo. It occurred when the edges chosen for the manipulations were not precise.

Using pre-recorded intonation contours and borrowing contours from other speakers enable a wide range of manipulations of new speakers' voices, and may add expressions that are not part of a speaker's repertoire. A relatively small reference database of basic intonation curves can be used for different speakers. Time-related manipulations, such as extending the shrinking durations, and applying time dependent functions, extend the editing scope even farther. The system allows flexibility and a large variety of manipulations and transformations and yields natural speech.

Gathering these techniques and more, under one editing tool, and defining them as editing operators create a powerful tool for affect editing. However, for a full system, which is suitable for general use the algorithms should be refined, especially synchronization between the borrowed contours and the edited signal. Special consideration should be taken for the differences between voiced, where there is f_0, and unvoiced speech. Usability aspects should also be addressed, including processing time.

5 Summary

In this paper we have suggested the application of affect editing for non-verbal aspects of speech. Such an editor has many useful applications. We have demonstrated some of the capabilities of such a tool for editing expressions of emotion, mental state and attitudes, including nuances of expressions and subtle expressions.

We examined the concept using several operations,including borrowing f_0 contours from other speech signals uttered by the same speaker and by other speakers, changing speech rate, and changing energy in different time frames and frequency bands. We managed to reconstruct natural speech signals of the same speaker, with new expressions. These experiments demonstrate the capabilities of such an editing tool, although the details of the implementation should be refined. Future work should extend the scope of the operators and take into account usability issues including real-time processing.

Further extensions should include input from affects inference systems and labeled reference data for concatenation, automatic translation mechanism from expressions to operators, and a user interface that allows navigation among expressions.

References

1. Burkhardt F., Sendlmeier W. F.: Verification of Acoustical Correlates of Emotional Speech using Formant-Synthesis, ISCA Workshop on Speech & Emotion, Northern Ireland 2000, p. 151-156.
2. Griffin D. W., Lim J. S.: Signal Estimationm from Modified Short-Time Fourier Transform IEEE Trans. ASSP. **22** 1984 236-247.
3. Kawahara H., Matsui H.: Auditory Morphing Based on an Elastic Perceptual Distance Metric, in an Interference-Free Time-Frequency Representation, ICASSP'2003, pp.256-259, 2003.

4. Mozziconacci S. J. L., Hermes, D. J.: Role of intonation patterns in conveying emotion in speech, ICPhS 1999, p. 2001-2004.
5. Piftzinge H. R.: Unsupervised Speech Morphing between Utterances of any Speakers, Proceedings of the 10th Australian International Conference on Speech Science & Technology Macquarie University, Sydney, December, 2004. 545-550.
6. Schröder M.: Emotional speech synthesis: A review. In Proceedings of Eurospeech 2001, pages 561-564, Aalborg.
7. Slaney M., Covell M., Lassiter B.: Automatic Audio Morphing (ICASSP96), Atlanta, 1996, 1001-1004.

Pronunciation Learning and Foreign Accent Reduction by an Audiovisual Feedback System

Oliver Jokisch[1], Uwe Koloska[2], Diane Hirschfeld[2], and Rüdiger Hoffmann[1]

[1] Dresden University of Technology, Laboratory of Acoustics and Speech Communication, 01062 Dresden, Germany
{oliver.jokisch, ruediger.hoffmann}@ias.et.tu-dresden.de
[2] voice INTER connect GmbH, Research and Development, 01067 Dresden, Germany
{koloska, hirschfeld}@voiceinterconnect.de

Abstract. Global integration and migration force people to learn additional languages. With respect to major languages, the acquisition is already initiated at primary school but according to their missing daily practice, many speakers keep a strong accent for longterm which may cause integration problems in new social or working environments. The possibility of later pronunciation improvements is limited since an experienced teacher and single education are required. Computer-assisted teaching methods have been established during the last decade.

Common methods do either not include a distinct user feedback (vocabulary trainer playing a reference pattern) or widely rely on fully automatic methods (speech recognition regarding the target language) causing evaluation mistakes, in particular, across the border of language groups.

The authors compiled an audiovisual database and set up an automatic system for the accent reduction (called AZAR) by using recordings of 11 native Russian speakers learning German and 10 native German reference speakers. The system feedback is given within a multi modal scenario.

1 Introduction

Teaching local Russian migrants in improving their German skills, in particular, their pronunciation, the authors were dissatisfied with existing computer-assisted tools. Common systems do either not include a distinct user feedback or they widely rely on fully automatic methods (speech recognition on the target language, e. g. using standard HMM) causing evaluation mistakes and, partly, marking wrong phenomena or pronunciation positions. In particular, students with strong Eastern-Slavic accent require further assistance for their homework. Supported by companies for further education and by a speech technology provider, the authors established a network of teachers, phoneticians and technicians aiming at an *Automat for Accent Reduction* (German acronym: AZAR). The AZAR project is focusing on two issues:

– Stronger consideration of phonetic aspects, mainly the language group dependency during the analysis of the accented source speech,

J. Tao, T. Tan, and R.W. Picard (Eds.): ACII 2005, LNCS 3784, pp. 419–425, 2005.

- The parallel usage of synchronized multi-modal information (in particular the lip movement).

In this paper, the authors summarize the multi-modal processing. The results can be used to improve the decisions of the underlying speech recognition technology and to adapt the acoustic feedback of reference speech (generated by a text-to-speech synthesizer). In a first version, AZAR enabled the interactive training of second language pronunciation for adolescent and adult learners (native speakers from the Slavic area). The current state includes a visual feedback mode. Further versions will include new language groups (pairs of source and target accent). The AZAR system includes an extensive curriculum for the production and perception training of difficult segmental contrasts.

2 Concept of Interactive Pronunciation Training

2.1 State-of-the-Art Technology

Most prevalent speech training aids are computer-based audiovisual language courses. Advanced PC-based learning systems (like *Pronunciation Power*, *American Sounds*, *Phonics Tutor*, *Eyespeak*) include (verify [1]):

- Speech analyzing windows or frames,
- Internet-based features like email answering, online help and chat sessions with human tutors,
- Animated views of the articulatory mechanics, video clips showing jaw, lip and tongue movement and waveform patterns of sound samples.

Users are able to record sound files and to acoustically compare a graphical representation of their sound utterances with the instructor's one. A few systems, such as *Fonix iSpeak 3.0* and *Pro-Nunciation*, include synthesized speech or TTS solutions [2]. During the last decade, speech recognition technology was implemented into innovative interactive systems like ISTRA and PRONTO [3] and in the European research project *Interactive Spoken Language Education* [4].

2.2 Language Group Dependency

One specific contribution of the AZAR project was to identify a set of phones which occur in the speech of Russian students as allophonic variants of German phonemes (during the second language learning). In accented utterances of Russian students, the authors identified a set of 48 phones. The phonetic investigation focuses on the typical segmental (phoneme) errors of students caused by interference with their native language phonology and phonetics.

Figure 1 shows the interference of Russian and German vowels but the Slavic-Germanic language group transition causes many other phonological or phonetic interference effects. The authors expect similar interferences between other language groups and also within one language group.

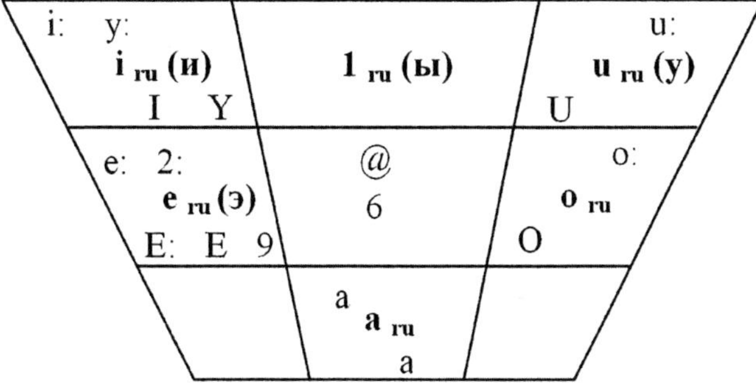

Fig. 1. Merged vowel trapezes of Russian and standard German (phoneme symbols according to [5])

2.3 Audiovisual Feedback on Pronunciation Quality

Common tools for the detection of the pronunciation errors of users rely on ASR systems and in some cases on other special detectors. The AZAR project combines the objective features of an ASR system with the expert knowledge of a human expert. The system cannot detect all errors which the human teacher could find

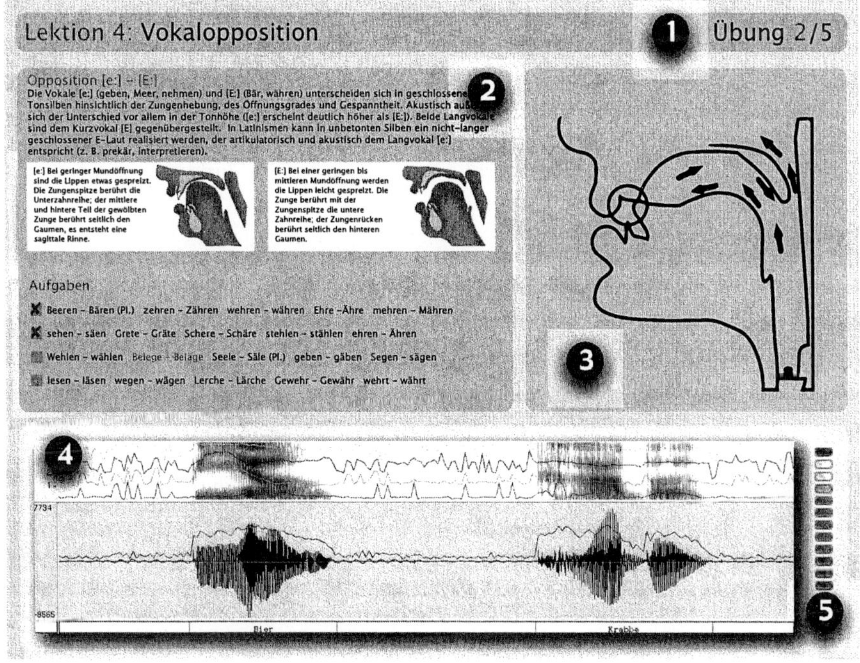

Fig. 2. First prototype of the AZAR user interface

(and in contrast to other approaches) does not try to so. Nevertheless, it is able to reliably detect errors which the human expert has identified for a given corpus of test utterances.

Figure 2 shows the prototype of the user interface including the main system features which need to be complemented.

❶ The navigational bar which shows the position inside the curriculum and which enables module navigation.
❷ The place where the instructions and exercises are presented.
❸ Several visual feedback functions (reference video, animated pictures of the vocal tract, etc.) are presented here.
❹ Analytical feedback providing a waveform, formant graphs, energy plots, etc.
❺ Direct feedback with regard to signal quality and speech volume.

All parts of the display are easily customizable by the learners to fit their individual needs. It is impossible to see all implemented modules at once to reduce the complexity of the interactive system.

2.4 Authoring System

Beside the audiovisual support tools as important part of the program features, the project focuses on the expert knowledge to define a clear curriculum and to parametrize the analysis of test sentences and word pairs. This expert knowledge-base is language-specific for each pair of (source accent and target) languages. The authors are creating an authoring system for the language expert to easily transfer his knowledge into the system without being an expert of speech analysis technology. Currently, this authoring system is a compariably simple XML-driven textual interface to the knowledge database which will be extended to provide more comfort and control possibilities for the language expert.

3 Audiovisual Speech Database

The database includes reading speech of German (studio recordings, large membrane microphone and EGG signal, 44.1kHz, 16bit) of 11 adult speakers (6 male, 5 female), born and raised in the Eastern-Slavic area (mainly Russia and Ukraine). Each speaker read 140 constructed sentences or phrases which provoke typical pronunciation errors. The speakers are subdivided into three education levels: Beginner, Intermediate and Advanced. A second database contains the regarding reference speech of 10 native speakers (5 male and 5 female) of German. For analyzing the interference with the source accent, the authors created a third database including 330 Russian phrases and items. The automatic phoneme labeling is considering the SAMPA convention for German and Russian [5]. If existing, the authors always assumed German target allophones. If necessary, typical phoneme substitutions (Russian accent) were annotated with Russian SAMPA. The very few intermediate allophones (neither Russian nor German) are marked with an enhanced transcription set based on SAMPA. All automatic segmentations and annotations were manually checked.

Synchronously to the audio recordings, the speaker's faces were captured by a high-quality web camera. Thus, the resulting database consists of combined audio and video tracks enabling development and evaluation of the algorithms.

4 System Performance

4.1 Audio Based Feedback

Using the audiovisual database described before, tools for audiovisual feedback were trained and tested. Special interest was laid on the tools suitability to detect deviations from standard articulation in the target language.

For the auditive feedback, a German phoneme recognizer was trained and adapted to the specific German speech data (recorded in the reference database). This German recognizer was considered as a baseline system for the adaptation done by the Russian speech expert. German phonemes, which have Russian contrast phonemes, were split (reproduced) and adapted using the Russian speech database. The alignment to generate the spoken transcription for the educational speech material was carried out by a mixed German and Russian phoneme recognizer, considering a lexicon with several alternatives for each word.

The best-scored phone sequence wins over the alternative sequences. The dynamic matching between canonical and aligned phone sequence provides a warping function of temporal information and information about the best-matching areas of the speech signal. By considering articulatory features to compare phone symbols from the canonical and the automatically aligned form, the distance between the phone symbols can be expressed quantitatively. The system marks the potential area of wrong pronunciation in the utterance and suggests suitable exercises to reduce the speaker-specific pronunciation errors.

4.2 Video Based Feedback

For the visual feedback, a video based feature extraction was developed by support of the INTEL openCV library. The video recordings are analyzed in order to find the face and looking for regular structures. After identifying the eyes and the nose, the mouth region is detected. In order to refine the mouth region and to find the current mouth width and height, a black and white picture is

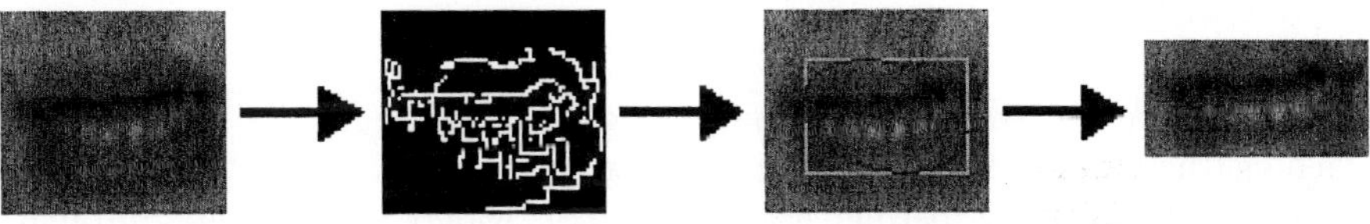

Fig. 3. Lip recognition process

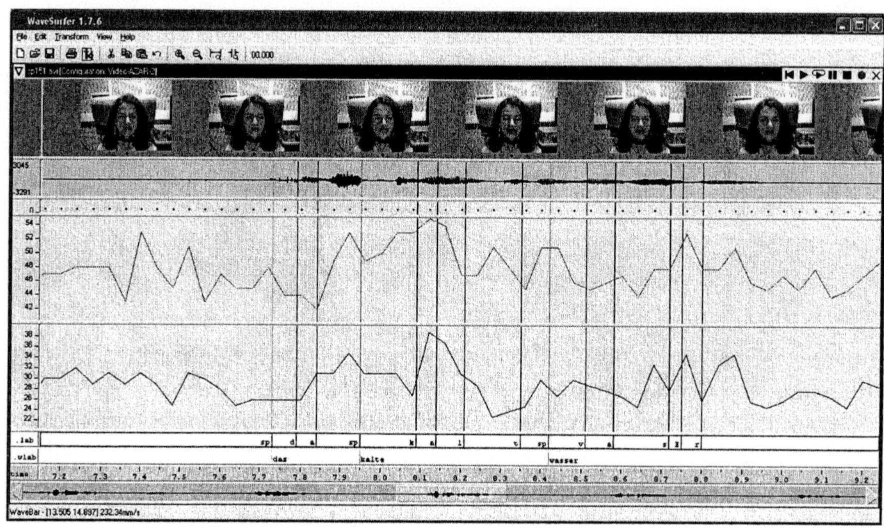

Fig. 4. Synchronized audiovisual processing of the signals; lip width and lip height

generated to detect the lip edges. Finally, an ellipse is assigned to the lips in order to compensate a possible tilt of the lips (see figure 3).

The features width and height are extracted from the video and can be used to separate voice and pause phases in a robust manner. Figure 4 shows video snapshots and speech signal, including the tracks of the features lip width over lip height (units in pixels) for the utterance *"das kalte Wasser"* (*the cold water*). In a later version of AZAR, the information will be used to judge pronunciation differences concerning the lip-tooth contact, lip opening and rounding as well as the position of the tongue in front consonants.

Theoretically, it would be also possible to derive motivation and involvement from the eyes end eyebrows to give some suggestions for repetitions or new lectures but there is no robust feature extraction for this purpose currently available.

Region of interest (ROI) detection and feature extraction are robustly working for about 72 % of the persons examined within the own experiments. Some male persons with beard or strong hair growth cause difficulties, because the lip edge detector often fails in these cases.

5 Conclusions

Interactive spoken language teaching methods (in particular for pronunciation teaching) have been established during the last decade. Common approaches do either not include a distinct user feedback or widely rely on fully automatic acoustic methods (speech recognition for foreign speakers) causing potential evaluation mistakes.

The automatic system for the accent reduction AZAR includes an audio-visual database of 11 native Russian speakers (source accent) and 10 native German reference speakers (for the target language) uttering 140 different phrases and sentences.

The synchronized processing of audio and video information in an education context is basically possible. For this purpose, the complexity of the user interface needs to be restricted and the system requires an intelligent navigation concept. To ensure the overall robustness, the training material should consist of selected utterances which contain typical pronunciation mistakes. This curriculum can be analogously compiled by native language experts for new languages using a special authoring tool. For general acceptance, both audio and visual algorithms (like phoneme recognition or region of interest recognition) require further improvements.

References

1. J. Finley et al., Pronunciation Power. Educational Software Review, Learning Village homepage. [Online] http://www.learningvillage.com/html/guide.html
2. J. Burston (Ed.), The CALICO Software Review. Computer Assisted Language Instruction Consortium homepage. [Online] http://calico.org/CALICO_Review/
3. J. Dalby and D. Kewly-Port, Explicit Pronunciation Training Using Automatic Speech Technology. CALICO Journal, vol. 16, no. 3, 425-445, 1999.
4. Interactive Spoken Language Education (ISLE), project homepage of Hamburg University. [Online] http://nats-www.informatik.uni-hamburg.de/~isle/
5. J. C. Wells, SAMPA - computer readable phonetic alphabet. project homepage [Online] Available: http://www.phon.ucl.ac.uk/home/sampa/home.htm

Prosodic Reading Style Simulation for Text-to-Speech Synthesis

Oliver Jokisch, Hans Kruschke, and Rüdiger Hoffmann

Dresden University of Technology, Laboratory of Acoustics and Speech Communication, Dresden, Germany
{oliver.jokisch, hans.kruschke, ruediger.hoffmann}@ias.et.tu-dresden.de

Abstract. The simulation of different reading styles (mainly by adapting prosodic parameters) can improve the naturalness of synthetic speech and supports a more intelligent human machine interaction. The article exemplarily investigates the reading styles News and Tale. For comparison, all examined texts contained the same genre-neutral paragraphs which have been read without a specific style instruction: Normal but also faster, slower, rather monotone or more emotional which led to corresponding artificial styles.

The measured original intonation and durations style patterns control a diphone synthesizer (mapped contours). Additionally, the patterns are used to train a neural network (NN) model.

Within two separate listening tests, different stimuli presented as original signal/style, respectively, with mapped or NN generated prosodic contours have been evaluated. The results show that both, original utterances and artificial styles are basically perceived in their intended reading styles. Some reciprocal confusions indicate the similarities between different styles like News and Fast, Tale and Slow as well as Tale and Expressive. The confusions are more likely for synthetic speech. To produce e. g. the complex style Tale, different features of the prosodic variations Slow and Expressive are combined. The training method for the synthetic styles requires a further improvement.

1 Motivation

State of the art text-to-speech (TTS) systems usually provide a good intelligibility and a satisfying segmental naturalness (corpus synthesis). To improve the naturalness and also the flexibility of the human machine interface, the authors intend to simulate different speaking styles on synthetic speech.

The authors define a speaking style as manner of the speech under certain conditions and for a certain purpose which is characterized by distinctive features of ekto-semantic (not immediately information-coding) language attributes. Repeating language features under similar conditions leads to style patterns respectively style associations, which alternate according to historical, cultural or social origins. Speaking styles support the communication task and carry information but require overlapping style associations among communicating subjects.

J. Tao, T. Tan, and R.W. Picard (Eds.): ACII 2005, LNCS 3784, pp. 426 – 432, 2005.

2 Prosodic Style Simulation Approach

Considering the ekto-semantic language attributes, speaking styles are characterized by following aspects of the speech production:

(a) Laryngeal excitation and corresponding voice quality features,
(b) Segmental features and
(c) Prosodic features.

There are only few studies about the relevance of these feature levels on the overall perception of certain styles. In [5], the authors examine the influence of different prosodic parameters on the discrimination between spontaneous and read speech. Other studies propose a dependency of the relevant feature level on the chosen speaking styles [1].

Considering the application in a speech synthesizer, the speaking style simulation should mainly consider the style features which are distinguishable from the synthetic speech output of the baseline system. This study was carried out using the Dresden Speech Synthesizer (DRESS) and its derived low-resource version MicroDRESS with an overall memory consumption of less than 1 megabyte [2]. These synthesizers are basing on diphone concatenation and use an algorithm comparable to TD-PSOLA. Excitation and segmental features are widely predefined by these technical constraints.

Consequently, from scientific and technical viewpoints, the authors decided for the simulation of speaking styles by adapting prosodic parameters. Considering the acoustic database of the synthesizer (usually extracted from read carrier words or phrases), the experiments were focused on speaking styles which are produced while reading texts aloud. Consecutively, the authors use the term *reading style*.

2.1 Selection of Reading Styles and Speech Database

The reading style implicates a communication purpose as already mentioned. Different text genres can cause variations in conditions and purpose. A professional female speaker adequately produced the according speaking styles in a professional sound studio at Dresden University. The authors examined the genres *News* basing on texts from the German radio station *Deutschlandfunk* and *Tale* using two German fairy tales of the *Grimm* brothers.

Additionally, all texts were embedded into genre-neutral contents, at which each paragraph contained four or five sentences. Consecutively, these texts are named as *genre-neutral paragraphs*. The prosodic manipulation in speech synthesis usually includes the levels/parameters intonation (mainly f_0 contour), segmental durations and speech intensity (amplitude). The amplitude is neglected here. In the current study, the speaker was instructed to consciously vary these parameters on the genre-neural paragraphs.

In the following, the authors compare the resulting additional reading styles *Normal, Fast, Slow, Monotone* and *Expressive* with the "real" reading styles News and Tale.

3 Perceptual Experiment on Original Speech Recordings

The reading style assignment of the recorded speech database was evaluated in a forced-choice listening test. The stimuli contained five genre-neutral paragraphs which were presented in random order (as mixure of text and styles). 19 listeners participated in the test.

The relative style assignment (in %) is shown in the confusion matrix in figure 1. The highest scores are located within the diagonal and clearly differ from random probability. The styles are perceived as intended. There are some reciprocal confusions between Normal and News, Fast and News, Expressive and Tale, respectively, Normal and Tale.

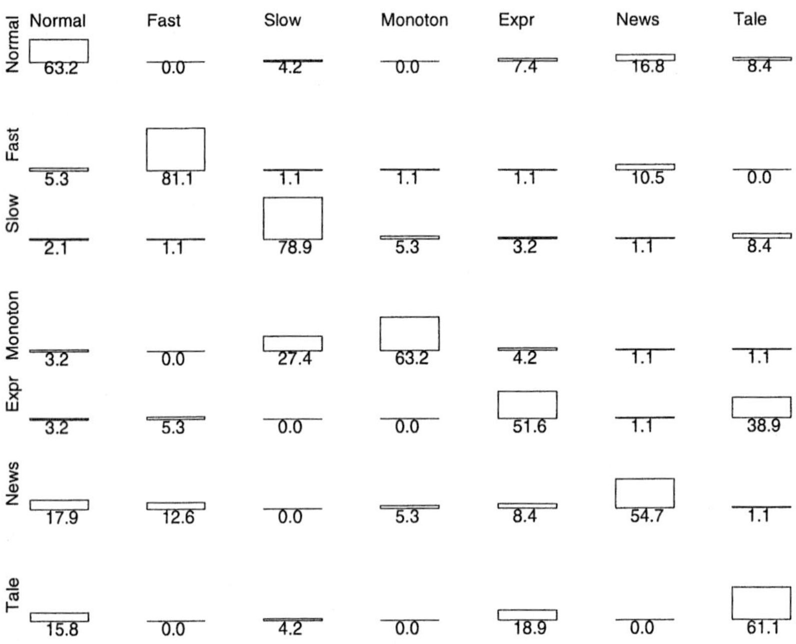

Fig. 1. Relative reading style assignment of (in %) on original speech. Rows indicate the intended style. Columns show the perceived style.

4 Reading Style Simulation on Synthetic Speech Using Original Prosody Contours

The assumption of this article implies that style simulation on synthetic speech with style-adapted prosody is possible - at least with a certain degree of recognition. To confirm this assumption for the investigated styles, the parameters f_0 and duration were extracted from the recorded utterances of the five genreneutral paragraphs.

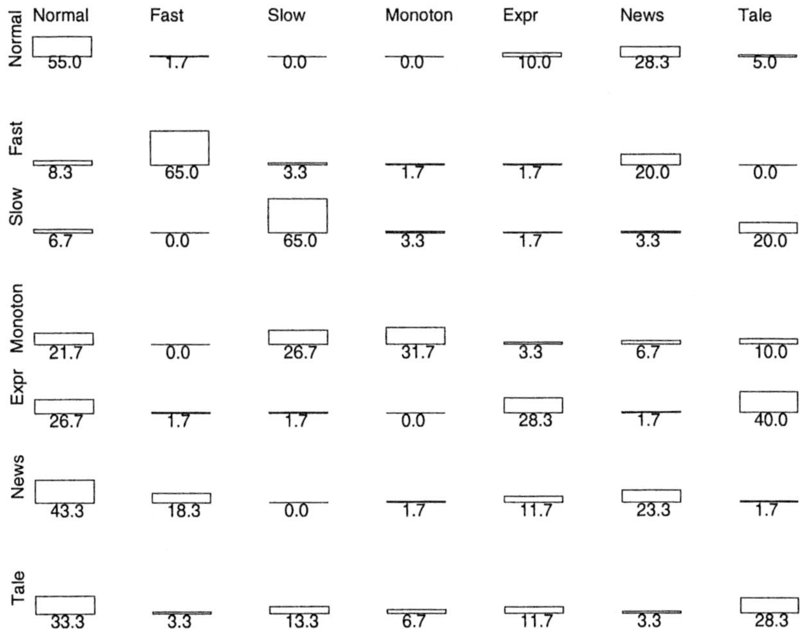

Fig. 2. Relative reading style assignment of listeners (in %) on synthetic speech (with mapped prosody). Rows indicate the intended style. Columns show the perceived style.

For duration analysis the utterances were automatically labeled using a dynamic time warping (DTW) aligner, matching TTS generated phonemes to original speech. All labels were manually corrected. The f_0 contour was coded with the well known Fujisaki model. For this purpose, smoothing of extracted f_0 contour was done with a method described in [4] and afterwards, the model parameters were extracted using the algorithm in [6]. The model-generated f_0 values were applied to control the mentioned synthesizer DRESS. Table 1 shows an overview about the prosodic analysis.

The test setup with mapped (original) prosody separates prosodic features from segmental properties of reading styles. It also represents the case that prosodic parameters can be adequately generated by the TTS system itself. Analogously, the style assignment was evaluated in a forced-choice listening test as already described in section 3 and 12 listeners participated. Additionally, this test included synthetic speech with NN generated prosody (section 5).

The assignment results for mapped prosody are given in figure 2. Not all reading styles were perceived as intended before. There was a tendency to assign them as Normal. The reciprocal confusions were stronger compared to the test on original speech recordings. The reciprocal confusions between Tale and Slow increased and were stronger than the confusions between Tale and Expressive. Monotone was often confused with Slow and Normal but not in the reciprocal direction.

Table 1. Overview about the prosodic analysis of genre-neutral paragraphs

Style	f_0 mean	f_0 range	Tempo (phones/s)	Pause no.	Mean pause duration(ms)
Normal	214	150 - 340	19.3	57	657
Fast	210	160 - 330	22.8	34	505
Slow	208	150 - 300	15.2	79	747
Monotone	196	150 - 265	16.8	51	803
Expressive	235	165 - 390	19.6	64	527
News	223	165 - 325	20.2	67	498
Tale	221	160 - 350	18.7	64	770

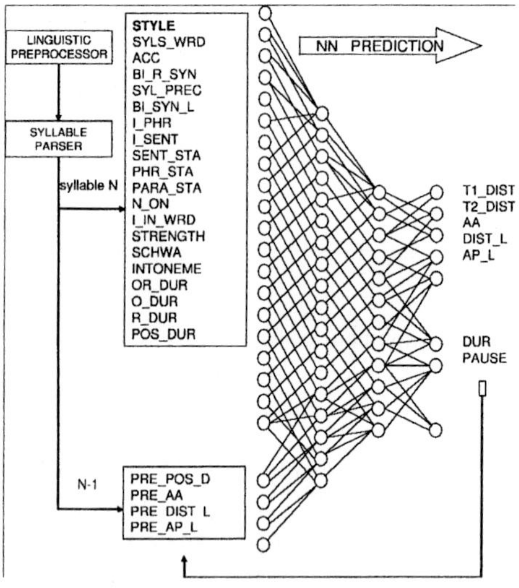

Fig. 3. MFN based model predicting reading style-specific prosody

5 Adapting Reading Styles by Neural Network Training

Usually, prosodic parameters in a TTS system are generated by rule based or data driven algorithms. A data driven algorithm can be adapted to a new language, to new speakers or to several speaking styles.

The authors trained a multi-layer feed-forward neural network (MFN) with 24 input and 8 output neurons. The underlying integrated prosody model approach is described in [7]. The multilingual use of this model was tested, too [3]. The algorithm works on a syllabic level and predicts Fujisaki parameters for generating the f_0 contour, syllable and pause durations, respectively, syllable intensity.

For this study, the input vector is slightly modified by a style-coding component (compare figure 3). To reduce potential error sources, only the manually corrected phone labels are used. At first, the Fujisaki model parameters are extracted as described in section 4. The training data set contains both, News and Tale styles and a single input neuron identifies the current reading style. Afterwards, the NN predicted prosody (of an independent test set) is applied to the synthesizer.

The authors performed the synthesis evaluation together with the evaluation of stimuli of the mapped (original) prosody described in section 4, but the results are given separately in table 2. The styles News and Tale were not recognized as the intended styles. According to the mapped prosody stimuli, News and Tale were mostly confused with Normal. The style News was additionally confused with Fast as expected but also with Expressive and Slow. The Tale style shows numerous confusions with Slow and Expressive as observed among the mapped stimuli.

Table 2. Relative reading style assignment of listeners (in %) on synthetic speech (NN predicted prosody). Rows indicate the intended style. Columns show the perceived style.

	Perceived						
Intended	Normal	Fast	Slow	Monotone	Express.	News	Tale
News	28.3	28.3	13.3	5.0	18.3	3.3	3.3
Tale	36.7	3.3	28.3	3.3	10.0	8.3	10.0

6 Conclusions

The authors are aiming at a simulation of different reading styles by modifying prosodic parameters (*style-adapted prosody*) for a standard TTS system. The genre-specific reading styles *News* and *Tale* are investigated in conjunction with five variations of *normal* reading including the base style *Normal.*

Both, original recordings and synthetic speech with either mapped original prosody or NN predicted prosody were evaluated in perceptive experiments. Most of the listeners could perceive the intended reading styles of original speech. Nevertheless, also concerning the original speech, some reciprocal confusions can be observed such as between News and Fast, Tale and Expressive or Tale and Slow. By testing styles on synthetic speech, the number of confusions increases.

Compared to unmarked reading without any instruction, the News reading style is faster. Similarly, the Tale style is slower and more expressive. Controlling these parameters, the synthesizer can be adapted towards the intended reading style. Testing a stepwise scaled style configuration on synthetic speech can enhance the understanding of reading strategies and human style production.

The challenge of the experiments in this study is caused by the selection of the styles Normal, Fast, Slow, Monotone and Expressive since they do not directly correlate with a real-life scenario. The listeners have no distinguished reference pattern in their mind when evaluating these styles. This issue becomes more critical for distorted synthetic speech, in particular, if NN predicted prosodic contours are used, which are a second source of distortion. The authors will focus on clear separable reading styles like News and Tale and will avoid the usage of style categories like "Normal".

Furthermore, the used automatic algorithm for the Fujisaki parameter extraction and the neuronal network training concerning the automatic style-specific prosody generation require further improvements.

Acknowledgement. The authors would like to thank Ursula Hirschfeld, Kati Hannken-Illjes and Peter Müller from University of Halle for their support during the recording of the speech database. Hongwei Ding, Dresden University of Technology, assisted the speech data preparation and Hansjörg Mixdorff, Berlin University of Applied Sciences, provided tools for extracting Fujisaki parameters.

References

1. M. Bulut, S. S. Narayanan, and A. K. Syrdal. Expressive speech synthesis using a concatenative synthesizer. In Proc. International Conference on Spoken Language Processing, ICSLP, pages 1265–1268, Denver, USA, 2002.
2. R. Hoffmann, O. Jokisch, D. Hirschfeld, G. Strecha, H. Kruschke, and U. Kordon. A multilingual TTS system with less than 1 mbyte footprint for embedded applications. In Proc. IEEE International Conference on Acoustics, Speech and Signal Processing, ICASSP, pages 532–535, Hong Kong, 2003.
3. O. Jokisch, H. Ding, and H. Kruschke. Towards a multilingual prosody model for Text-to-Speech. In Proc. IEEE International Conference on Acoustics, Speech and Signal Processing, ICASSP, pages 421–424, Orlando, USA, 2002.
4. H. Kruschke. Advances in the parameter extraction of a command-response intonation model. In Proc. IEEE International Symposium on Intelligent Signal Processing and Communication Systems, ISPACS, Nashville, USA, 2001.
5. G. P. M. Laan and D. R. van Bergem. The contribution of pitch contour, phonem durations and spectral features to the character of spontaneous and read aloud speech. In Proc. Eurospeech, pages 569–572, Berlin, 1993.
6. H. Mixdorff. A novel approach to the fully automatic extraction of fujisaki model parameters. In Proc. IEEE International Conference on Acoustics, Speech and Signal Processing, pages 1281–1284, Istanbul, Turkey, 2000.
7. H. Mixdorff and O. Jokisch. Building an integrated prosodic model of German. In Proc. Eurospeech, pages 947–950, Aalborg, Denmark, 2001.

F0 Contour of Prosodic Word in Happy Speech of Mandarin*

Haibo Wang, Aijun Li, and Qiang Fang

Phonetics Lab, Institute of Linguistics, Chinese Academy of Social Sciences

Abstract. This paper focuses on analyzing the F0 contour of happy speech. We designed some declarative sentences and recorded them in happy and neutral expressive states. All of our speakers were asked to express these sentences in the same imaginary scene. It is known that emotion can be expressed through modifying acoustic features of speech in various ways, such as pitch, intensity, voice quality and so on. In this study, we compared the difference of F0 contour between happy and neutral speech through which we found that: (1) F0 contour plays an important role when happiness is expressed. (2) The F0 contour of happy speech displays a kind of declination pattern, but the degree of declination is less than that of neutral speech. (3) Contrasting to neutral speech, the pitch register of happy speech is higher, and the slope of F0 contour of the final syllable of each prosodic word is bigger, especially for the syllable at the end of the sentence.

1 Introduction

Speech can convey not only literal meanings, but also mood and emotion. Many researchers have found that F0 contour is an important acoustic parameter when emotions are expressed. "Happiness, fear, shyness and to some extend sadness show similarities. F0 is even and quite high, in relation to the other emotion; surprise, anger, and dominance have a strongly varying F0." [6]. "In Chinese, the prosody of F0 of anger and joy is high and has big fluctuation; that of fear is high and has small fluctuation. That of sadness is low and has small fluctuation." [7]. "Some of the detailed results suggest that aspects of contour shape (such as the height of selected accents and the final F0 movement) may well differentially affect emotion inferences." "It is argued that pitch contours have to be considered as configurations that acquire emotional meaning only through interaction with a linguistic and paralinguistic context." [8].

In this study, we take Prof. Wu Zongji's intonation theory as the framework. He claims that tonal variation unit is the basic unit of intonation. Within this unit, the pattern of the F0 contour can be controlled by phonetic and syntactic rules. Then, the intonation can be generated by adjusting the range and register of the units within the sentence. Several kinds

* This paper is revised from one part of an MA thesis (Wang Haibo 2004), funded by NSF, Project No. 60275015.

J. Tao, T. Tan, and R.W. Picard (Eds.): ACII 2005, LNCS 3784, pp. 433 – 440, 2005.

of factors affect the F0 contour, such as linguistic factors of "stress", "rhythm", "sentence function", and paralinguistic factors of "emotion" and so on. [1][2][3]

We hypothesize that the difference in pitch contour is mostly due to different expressiveness when analyzing the parallel speech of the happy and neutral with the same script. By this way, F0 contour patterns of prosodic words were analyzed and modeled.

2 Corpus Design and Annotation

We designed a prompt file with 100 sentences taking some factors into account, such as sentence length (SL), prosodic word length (PWL), syntax, semantic focus (SF), affective key words (KW), neutral tone syllable (NT), etc. In the designed prompts, each prosodic word contains 2 syllables, and each sentence contains 4 prosodic words, which are denoted "the 1st, 2nd, 3rd, 4th prosodic word" respectively. The details are shown in Table 1.

Table 1. Factors considered in the prompt design

Factors	KW	SL	PWL	Syntax	SF	NT
Values	None	8 syllables	2 syllables	statement	None	None
Sample	bei3jing1 ren2min2 guang3bo1 dian4tai2 (People's Broadcast Station of Beijing)					

Two young actors and two young actresses were recruited to express the designed prompts in neutral and happy states of emotion in a sound proof room. Both vocal and EGG signals were recorded (22 kHz, 16bits) to yield 800 utterances in total (100 sentences * 4 speakers * 2 states).

During recording, subjects were asked to imagine that they were in the same happy state, and express the designed sentences alternately, as if they were having a dialog. In this way, speakers could stimulate each other to have a similar expressive style. If the sentence was not good enough, the speakers were asked to repeat[1].

Table 2. Details of annotation

Information	Annotation Options
Segments	Time aligned boundaries of initials and finals with tones
Emotions	Happy or neutral
Locations	The first, second, third, and fourth prosodic words
Breaks	Intonation breaks , prosodic word breaks
Stresses	Sentence stresses

Here, only intonation phrase break and prosodic word break are annotated in breaks tier, and sentence stress is annotated in stress tier. The detail of annotation information is shown in Table 2.

[1] All these sentences are part of the emotional corpus, CASS-EMC.

3 Speech Data Analysis

Prosodic words are taken as the basic units for analysis. The F0 data are extracted by Praat and amended by hand. The highest and lowest point within the prosodic word and the duration of the prosodic word are also extracted. Then frequency values in hertz domain are transformed to semitone values according to formula (1). All the following analysis is done in the domain of semitone. The pitch range of a prosodic word is defined as the difference between the highest and lowest values of F0 within the prosodic word.

$$F_{ST} = 12 \times [\ln(F_x / F_r)] / \ln 2 \tag{1}$$

Where, F_X is the original F0. F_{ST} is the transformed F0. F_r is the reference value, 50Hz for male and 100 Hz for female.

Here, we analyzed the difference between happy speech and neutral speech in the aspects of the highest and lowest point of F0 within the prosodic word, the pitch range and register of prosodic word, the slope of F0 contour of each syllable in the prosodic word, and the declination of the utterance. We have two male and two female speakers. There are four kinds of instances for the location of prosodic words in sentences: 1st, 2nd, 3rd, and 4th. And the distribution of stress also includes 4 kinds of instances: (1) The prosodic word carries sentence stress in both happy and neutral speech; (2) The prosodic word do not carry sentence stress in both happy and neutral speech; (3) The prosodic word carries sentence stress only in happy speech; (4) The prosodic word carries sentence stress only in neutral speech.

3.1 T-Test for the Highest and Lowest Points of F0

At first, we thought that speakers, the location of prosodic words in the sentence and the distribution of stress may affect F0 contour. After covariance analysis, we found that both speakers and location of prosodic words had prominent effects at the highest and lowest points, pitch range and duration whereas the distribution of stress only had prominent effects on duration. Based on the results, we took speakers, the location of prosodic words and the distribution of stress as partition options.

Then one-sample t-test was applied to investigate the difference between happy speech and neutral speech in the aspect of F0 value. Detailed to say, we get the differences of pitch value between happy and neutral prosodic words which have the same script, then compared the differences value with the test value "0". If $p <= 0.01$, it means the difference is very prominent, if $0.01 < p <= 0.05$, it means the difference is prominent, if $p > 0.05$, it means the different isn't prominent. (95% confidence interval, 2-tailers, test value=0).

Through which we found that: contrasting to neutral speech, both the highest and lowest points of F0 contour in prosodic words of happy speech are higher than those of the neutral speech (Confined to paper space, we can't list all t-test results, just list the mean results of t-test for all speakers and all stress distribution, as shown in Table 3).

Table 3. The mean results of t-test for all speakers and all stress distribution

Location In sentence	The highest point Within prosodic word		The lowest point within prosodic word		The pitch range of prosodic word		Duration of prosodic word	
	Random	p	Random	p	Random	p	Random	p
1st	24	0.000	24	0.000	24	0.067	24	0.072
2nd	24	0.000	24	0.000	24	0.261	24	0.104
3rd	24	0.001	24	0.002	24	0.080	24	0.076
4th	24	0.002	24	0.016	24	0.035	24	0.235

3.2 Analysis of the Highest-Lowest Points

Here, the data of the highest points and lowest points within the prosodic words are analyzed. There are still four speakers and four location instances. F, the mean of the lowest or highest points of pitch, is given by formula (2).

$$F = \sum_{i=1}^{N} F_i / N \tag{2}$$

Where, F_i is the actual value of the highest or the lowest points within the prosodic words. N is the number of prosodic words in each category classified by the distribution of stress and position.

As shown in Fig. 1-Fig. 4, The patterns of four speakers are similar. There are 4 groups of high-low points in every figure, they are the 1st, 2nd, 3rd, and 4th prosodic word respectively. And each group also has 4 instances which are "non-sentence stress in neutral speech", "non-sentence stress in happy speech", "sentence stress in neutral speech", "sentence stress in happy speech".

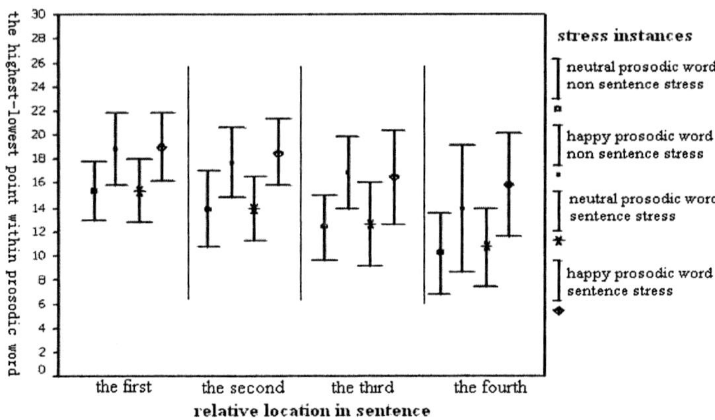

Fig. 1. F0 patterns (average highest and lowest values) of prosodic words according to the stress and position for speaker 1

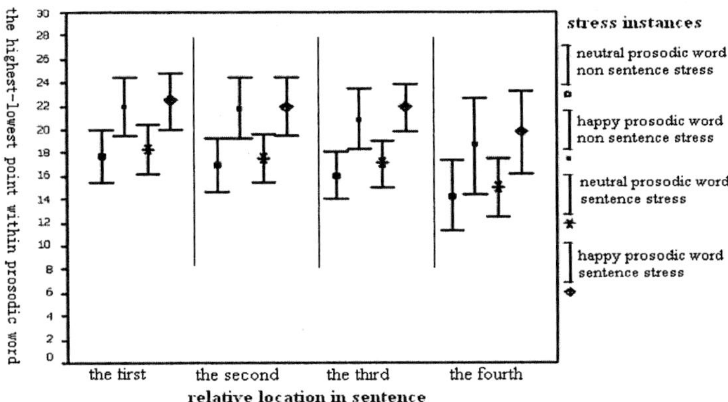

Fig. 2. F0 patterns (average highest and lowest values) of prosodic words according to the stress and position for speaker 2

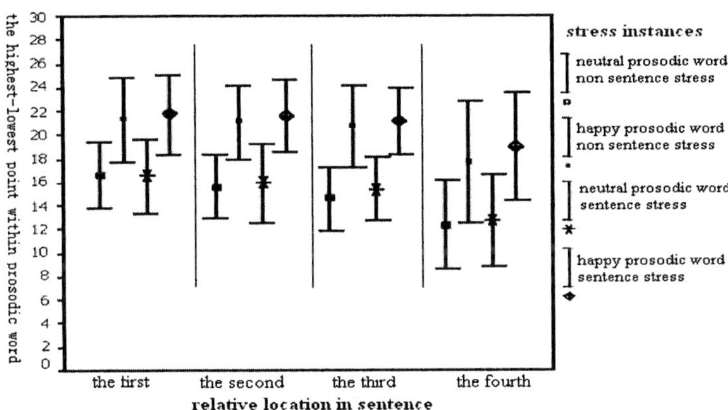

Fig. 3. F0 patterns (average highest and lowest values) of prosodic words according to the stress and position for speaker 3

It's consistent that the register of happy speech is higher than that of neutral speech, and F0 contours have declination in both happy and neutral speech.

Furthermore, the mean value of difference, F, is given by formula (3).

$$F = \sum_{i=1}^{N} (F_{i\_happy} - F_{i\_neutral}) / N \quad (3)$$

Here, "F_{i_happy} - $F_{i\_neutral}$" is the difference between happy and neutral highest F0 value. N is the number of prosodic words in each category.

As shown in Fig. 5, for all the four speakers, the distribution of the difference of the highest points between happy speech and neutral speech become larger and larger from sentence initial to end. It means the declination degree of happy speech is less than that of neutral speech, although both of them have declination.

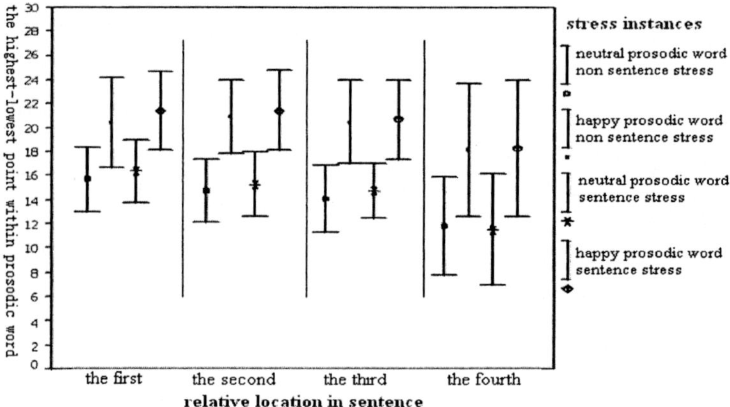

Fig. 4. F0 patterns (average highest and lowest values) of prosodic words according to the stress and position for speaker 4

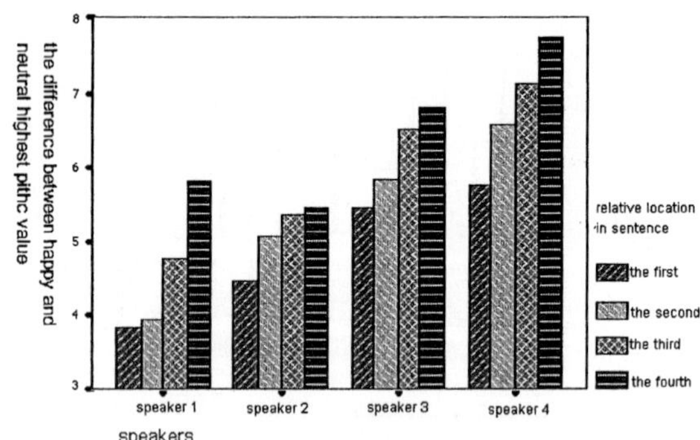

Fig. 5. The distribution of the difference of the highest points between happy speech and neutral speech

3.3 The Frame of F0 Contour of a Prosodic Word

In this part, we will investigate the change of the frame of F0 contour through the tonal variation unit of tone3 and tone1 combination, because tone3 and tone1 have the reliable low and high tonal features respectively. In this way, we can get the general frame of F0 contour within a prosodic word. Before analysis, the duration of each syllable is normalized to a 10-point span at the same distance.

In order to remove influence of sentence stress, we select 454 prosodic words which carry no sentence stresses in either happy or neutral speech. We get the F0 contour of "tone3 + tone1" by averaging the corresponding values in each category which is classified by speaker and location of prosodic words. As shown in fig6-fig9, four speakers have similar patterns of F0 contour. The register of happy speech is

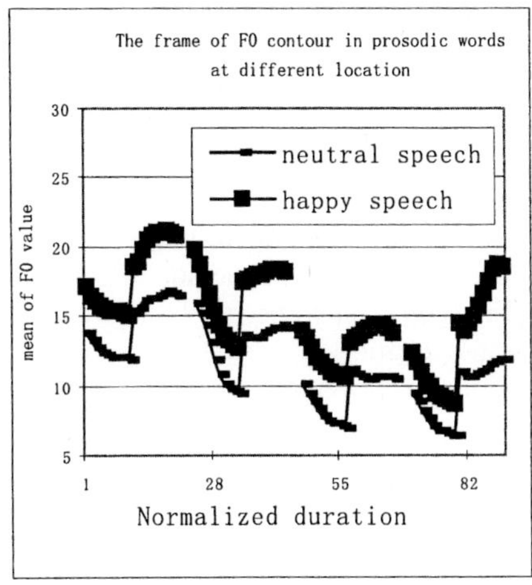

Fig. 6. Speak 1, F0 contour of "tone 3 and tone 1" prosodic word

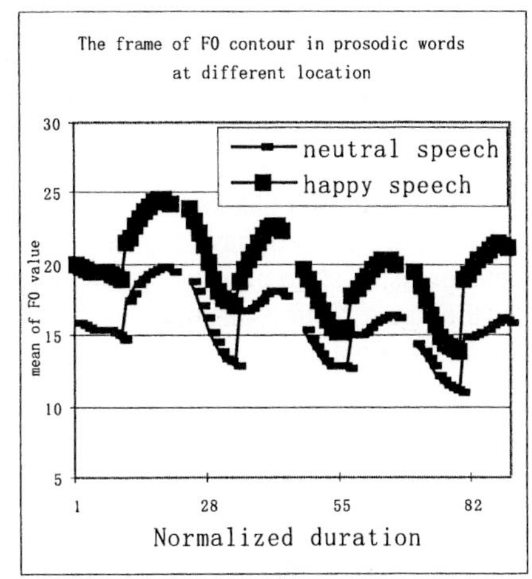

Fig. 7. Speak 2, F0 contour of "tone 3 and tone 1" prosodic word

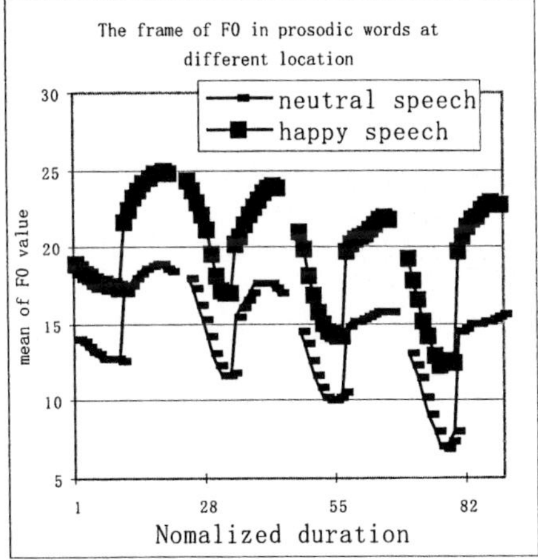

Fig. 8. Speak 3, F0 contour of "tone 3 and tone 1" prosodic word

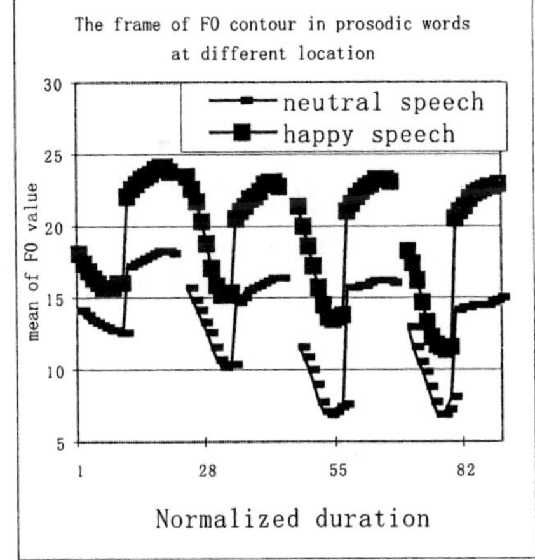

Fig. 9. Speak 4, F0 contour of "tone 3 and tone 1" prosodic word

higher than that of neutral speech, and the slope of F0 contour of the final syllable of the prosodic word is larger in happy speech than in neutral speech, which is similar to the former findings [4], especially when the word is at the end of a sentence. The frame of stressed prosodic word hasn't been taken into account for insufficient data.

4 Discussion

F0 contour plays an important role in expressing happiness. Speech will sound happy if we adjust the F0 contour of neutral speech by elevating the register, decreasing the declination degree of the sentence, and increasing slope of F0 contour of the final syllable in the prosodic word, especially for the final syllable of sentences.

Here, emotional stress of happy speech is not discussed. It doesn't mean that stress has no effects on expressing emotion. It's found that stress had great influence on expressing friendly attitude [5]. Both happy emotion and friendly attitude are positive. Thus, stress should have some effects on expressing happiness.

The four speakers have similar expressive style in our experiment. It doesn't mean the expressive style of all people will be the same. And we can't conclude that we will get the same results throughout different corpus with happy speech. Otherwise, the speech of human beings would be dull rather than colorful.

Here we will give our thanks to PhD. Ziyu Xiong for providing the Praat scripts.

References

[1] Wu, Zongji.: Basic contour patterns of intonation of Standard Chinese Essays for Anniversary of Professor Wang Li. Commercial Press. (1990)

[2] Wu, Zongji.: Further experiments on spatial distribution of phrasal contours under different range registers in Chinese intonation Proceedings of International Symposium on Prosody. Yokohama, Japan. (1994)

[3] Wu, Zongji.: New method of Standard Chinese intonation processing based on the relation between tone and melody Collected Essays dedicated to 45 Anniversary of Institute of Linguistics, CASS. (1997)

[4] A. Paeschke, M. Kienast, W.F. Sendlmeier.: F0-CONTOURS IN EMOTIONAL SPEECH. The 14th International Congress of Phonetic Sciences, San Francisco. (1999).

[5] Wang, Haibo: The acoustic analysis of affective speech in Mandarin. Unpublished MS. Dissertation. (2004).

[6] Åsa Abelin, Jens Allwood.: Cross linguistic interpretation of emotional prosodic. ISCA work group on emotion 2000. (2000)

[7] Yuan, Jiahong, Liqin Shen, Fangxin Chen.: The acoustic realization of anger, fear, joy and sadness in Chinese. ICSLP 2002. (2002).

[8] Tanja Bänziger et al.: Is there an emotion signature in intonational patterns? And can it be used in synthesis? Eurospeech 2003. (2003).

A Novel Source Analysis Method by Matching Spectral Characters of LF Model with STRAIGHT Spectrum

Zhen-Hua Ling, Yu Hu, and Ren-Hua Wang

iFlytek Speech Laboratory,
University of Science and Technology of China, Hefei
zhling@ustc.edu, yuhu@iflytek.com, rhw@ustc.edu.cn

Abstract. This paper presents a voice source analysis method by studying the spectral characters of LF model and their representation in output speech signal. The estimation of source features is defined as the set of LF parameter whose spectrum has the most similar characters in frequency domain, including glottal formant and spectral tilt, with the corresponding characters held by the STRAIGHT spectrum of speech signal for analysis. Besides, the concept of analyzable frame is introduced to ensure the feasibility and improve the reliability of proposed method. Evaluation with synthetic speech proves this method is able to estimate the LF parameters with satisfactory precision. Furthermore, the experiment with emotional speech shows the effectiveness of proposed method in describing voice quality variety among speech with different emotions.

1 Introduction

In emotional speech analysis and synthesis, voice quality, which is determined by the characters of glottal waveform during voice production, has been proved to be an important acoustic feature in expressing and distinguish different kinds of emotions [1,2]. Although many methods have been presented by previous researchers to analysis glottal waveform from speech signal and estimate related parameters, it is still far from finding a reliable and robust solution. Most of these methods are based on inverse filtering in time domain by applying a filter to the speech signal with a transfer function which is the inverse of the vocal tract transfer function and then fitting the residual signals to glottal source models, such as LF model[3]. In these methods, vocal tract estimation is essential for reasonable inverse filter construction and it is realized by LPC analysis of speech signal in most cases[4,5]. In order to canceling the glottal effect on articulation filter during the estimation of vocal tract transfer function, it is important to select appropriate temporal positions for LPC analysis, such as the Glottal Closure Instant (GCI). However, to detect GCI in continuous speech is quite difficult a task. Furthermore, for some kinds of glottal source signal, such as breathy voice, the closed quotient within a pitch period is so short that there are no clear GCI events.

Here we try to study this problem from another point of view — the frequency representation of source signal. If the voice source is assumed to be the output of an

J. Tao, T. Tan, and R.W. Picard (Eds.): ACII 2005, LNCS 3784, pp. 441 – 448, 2005.

LF model, its spectral characters can be measured, including glottal formant and spectral tilt. After vocal tract filtering, the temporal structure of glottal waveform is always destroyed, while these frequency characters are more likely to be preserved by the spectrum of output speech. So it provides us the possibility to realize glottal parameter estimation by studying these spectral characters of voice source presented in speech spectrum.

STRAIGHT (Speech Transformation and Representation using Adaptive Interpolation of weiGHTed spectrum)[6], as a vocoder type speech analysis-synthesis algorithm is adopted here for speech spectrum analysis, which is implemented by pitch adaptive spectral smoothing in both time and frequency domains. In the outputs of STRAIGHT analysis, the excitation consists of only pitch information. So the smoothed spectral envelop is the integration of both spectral presentation of glottal waveform and vocal tract transfer function according to general speech production hypothesis. In previous works, we used Mixtures of Gaussians (MOG) to model the source related spectral component within STRAIGHT spectrum of speech signals[7]. However, only the character of glottal formant was taken into account and it failed to give a quantitative estimation of source parameters. In this paper, an improved method is proposed. After STRAIGHT analysis frame by frame, the continuous speech signals are divided into analyzable frames and unanalyzable frames at first. For each analyzable frame, the voice source parameters can be estimated by selecting an LF parameter set whose spectrum matches the frequency characters of source signal presented by speech spectrum most appropriately.

In the following parts of this paper, a detailed introduction to proposed method is given in section 2. Section 3 presents the result of evaluation with synthetic speech and experiment with emotional speech. Section 4 is conclusion.

2 Method

2.1 Framework

The flowchart of presented method is shown as Fig. 1, which includes 3 main steps:

1. Analysis of acoustic features. The pitch, spectrum and amplitude of aperiodic component are analyzed from input speech signal by STRAIGHT at 5ms frame shift. At the same time, the formant frequencies are estimated by Praat. The frequency of the first formant and the amplitude of aperiodic component are used for analyzable frame decision in the following step.
2. Selection of analyzable frames. According to the output of acoustic analysis, analyzable frames are selected from continuous speech signals, which can support more reliable source analysis. The details will be discussed in Section 2.3.
3. Estimation of LF parameter. Here, the optimization algorithm is realized in a discrete way. For each analyzable frame, the spectrums of 717 candidates of LF parameter set are calculated according to current pitch value. These candidate spectrums are used to match the source-related spectral characters of speech spectrum one by one. The parameter set with minimum matching error is selected as the estimation result of source parameter for this frame. The calculation of matching error will be discussed in Section 2.5.

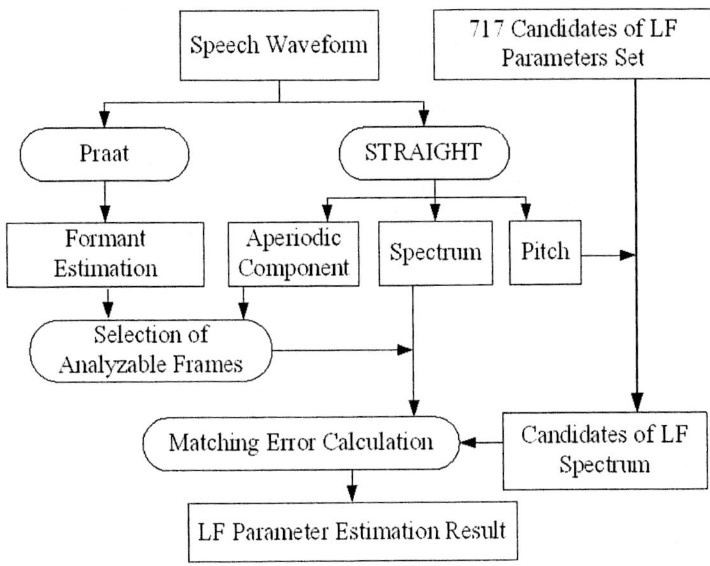

Fig. 1. Flowchart of proposed source parameter estimation method

2.2 The Frequency Representation of LF Model

The spectral characteristics of voice source are studied based on LF model[3], which describes the shape of differential glottal waveform using the following four parameters — *EE, RA, RG, RK*, together with pitch period T_0. The open quotient of source signal is related to both *RG* and *RK*: $OQ = (1+RK)/(2RG)$. As mentioned in[8], the spectrum of LF model has two main characteristics:

1. Glottal formant (F_g). Assuming an abrupt closure of glottal waveform (when $RA=0$), the spectrum of differential glottal waveform has a (+6, -6)dB/oct asymptotic behavior. So there exists a maximum at frequency F_g, called glottal formant. The position of the glottal formant can be calculated as:

$$F_g = 1/(2\pi \cdot OQ \cdot T_0) \cdot f(RK) \tag{1}$$

where *f(RK)* means a function of *RK*.

From Eq 1 we can see that the position of glottal formant is dependent on both T0 and source parameters — OQ and RK. After vocal tract filtering, the glottal formant can also be presented by STRAIGHT spectrum of output speech signal. When the first formant of vocal tract is high, such as vowel /a/, glottal formant can be observed as an isolated peak with frequency position lower than the first formant; while for the vowels whose first formant is not high enough, such as /i/ or /u/, the glottal formant would be merged with the first formant and can not be observed directly.

Fig. 2 shows the spectrogram of a Chinese syllable /jia/ pronounced by a female speaker and corresponding STRAIGHT spectrums at 50, 60 and 70ms respectively.

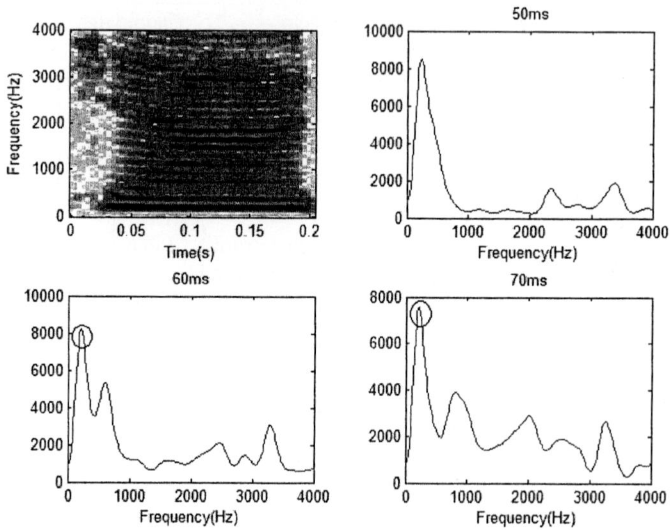

Fig. 2. An example for the representation of glottal formant in STRAIGHT spectrum of continuous speech signals (the circles indicate glottal formant positions at 60 and 70 ms)

From this figure, the separation of glottal formant from the first vocal tract formant at the transition part from /i/ to /a/ can be observed clearly with the rising of first formant.

2. Spectral tilt. When the vocal fold is closed smoothly with positive *RA*, an additional -6 or -12dB/oct spectral tilt will be added to the spectrum of glottal flow above a specific cut-off frequency. In the STRAIGHT spectrum, the spectral tilt is presented by the decline of spectral amplitude along frequency axis.

2.3 Definition of Analyzable Frame

As discussed above, some spectral characters, such as glottal formant, can not be observed directly in every frame of speech spectrum. Therefore in order to ensure the feasibility and reliability of measuring such characters for continuous speech, the concept of analyzable frame is defined here to choose frames satisfying following conditions for source analysis:

1. The frame is located within a voiced segment;
2. The amplitude of aperiodic component is lower than -12 dB;
3. There existed a distinct spectral peak whose frequency is at least 400 Hz lower and amplitude is at least 2/3 greater than the first formant in STRAIGHT spectrum.

2.4 Candidate Generation of LF Parameter Set

The four features *TP RK RA* and *EE* are used to construct LF parameter set, where *TP* can be derived from *RG* mentioned in Section 2.2 as $TP = 2/RG$. At the same time, the open quotient can be calculated as $OQ = TP(1+RK)$.

In our method, only the three temporal parameters *TP RK* and *RA* are estimated. In order to simplify the procedure of optimization, some candidates of LF parameter set are generated for finding the optimal one. In these candidates, the distributions of parameters are listed as follows:

- *TP*: 0.20~0.80, 0.05 interval
- *RK*: 0.05~0.45, 0.05 interval
- *RA*: 0.02~0.16, 0.02 interval

Besides, in order to make sure that the LF waveform can descend to zero at the end of each pitch period, *OQ+RA* is restricted to be no greater than 0.92.

Finally, 717 candidates of LF parameter set are generated, which are used to calculate candidate LF spectrums with the pitch value of current frame for analysis.

2.5 Calculation of Spectral Matching Error

For each analyzable frame, the matching error d_i, $i=1...717$ between STRAIGHT spectrum of speech signal $S(\omega)$ and each candidate LF spectrum $G_i(\omega)$ is calculated according to the spectral characters of source signal, including glottal formant and spectral tilt. d_i is composed of following four parts:

1. d_gf_i, to measure the distance of glottal formant position between $S(\omega)$ and $G_i(\omega)$. It is set to infinite if the difference is greater than 10%. Then $S(\omega)$ and $G_i(\omega)$ are normalized according to the amplitude at the glottal formant of speech spectrum.
2. d_tilt_i, to measure the distance where $G_i(\omega)$ is greater than $S(\omega)$ as Eq. 2.

$$d\_tilt_i^2 = \frac{1}{f_S/2 - GF_S} \int_{GF_S}^{f_S/2} \left[\frac{1}{2}(G_i(\omega) - S(\omega) + \left| G_i(\omega) - S(\omega) \right|) \right]^2 d\omega \quad (2)$$

where f_s and GF_s means the sampling rate and glottal formant of speech spectrum.

3. d_all_i, to measure the overall distance between $G_i(\omega)$ and $S(\omega)$ as Eq. 3.

$$d\_all_i^2 = \frac{2}{f_s} \int_0^{f_s/2} \left| G_i(\omega) - S(\omega) \right|^2 d\omega \quad (3)$$

4. d_lpc_i, which is calculated as the error of fitting $S(\omega)/G_i(\omega)$ to an all pole model, where $S(\omega)/G_i(\omega)$ presents the estimated transfer function of vocal tract according to parameter set *i*.

The final matching error d_i is the weighted sum of d_gf_i d_tilt_i d_all_i and d_lpc_i. Here d_tilt_i is used to measure the similarity of candidate LF spectrum and speech spectrum in spectral tilt because the function of vocal tract is commonly considered as amplifying specific frequency ranges of source signal. d_all_i is for a comprehensive consideration for measuring the differences of glottal formant and spectral tilt. d_lpc_i is based on the assumption that a reliable estimation of vocal tract transfer function is able to be present by an all pole filter. The final estimation result is defined as the LF parameter set which has the minimum matching error. Fig. 3 shows the estimated LF spectrum from one STRAIGHT spectrum compared with other two LF spectrum candidates which has greater matching error.

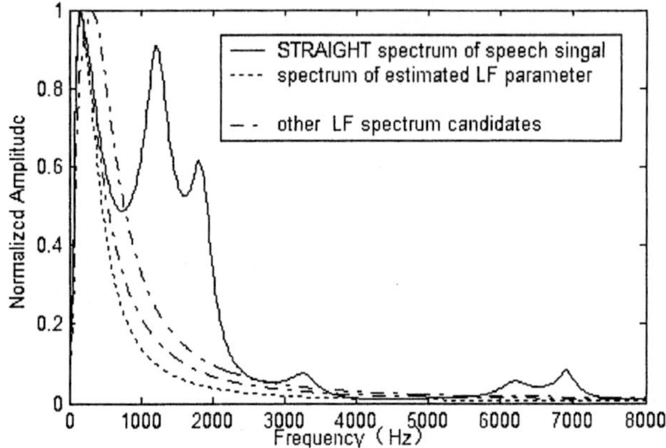

Fig. 3. A comparison between estimated LF spectrum and other LF spectrum candidates

3 Experiment

3.1 Evaluation with Synthetic Speech

In order to evaluate the performance of proposed method, experiment with synthetic speech signals is implemented. The synthetic speech signals are produced by LPC filtering. The glottal waveforms are generated from random LF parameter sets. The distribution ranges for pitch, *TP*, *RK* and *RA* are 100~300Hz, 0.2~0.8, 0.05~0.45 and 0.02~0.16. The LPC order is 16 for 16kHz sampled speech and the shape of this filter is derived from vocal tract transfer function of a vowel /a/.

Table 1. The difference and correlation between estimated and original LF parameters

	Ave. Rel. Diff (%)	*Ave. Abs. Diff.*	*Correlation*
TP	11.13	0.0585	0.7491
OQ	8.69	0.0568	0.8044
log RA	10.15	0.2493	0.8346

100 synthetic speech signals whose spectrums meet the conditions of analyzable frame are used for evaluation. The difference and correlation between estimated source parameters (*es*) and original ones (*or*) are shown in Table 1. Here *OQ* is evaluated instead of *RK* and *RA* is logarithmized. The average relative difference and average absolute difference are calculated as follows, here *N* is 100:

$$Ave.Rela.Diff = \frac{1}{N}\sum_{i=1}^{N}\frac{|es_i - or_i|}{or_i}; \quad Ave.Abs.Diff = \frac{1}{N}\sum_{i=1}^{N}|es_i - or_i| \tag{4}$$

Comparing the results in Table.1 with other source parameter estimation methods, such as the SIM method introduced in[9], where the average relative difference and correlation for these three parameters are 15.9%, 19.0%, 13.0% and 0.76, 0.69, 0.76

respectively, the method proposed here can give the estimation of LF parameters for synthetic speech signal with satisfactory precision.

3.2 Experiment with Emotional Speech

The LF parameter estimation experiment with emotional speech is carried out here to test the ability of proposed method for discriminating the voice quality characters of different emotional speech. Our emotional speech database used for analysis is recorded by an actress and consists of three emotions: happiness, sadness and anger with corresponding neutral utterances. 5 sentences are selected for each emotion and each sentence is analyzed by proposed source estimation method. For the estimation results of all analyzable frames of each emotion, the mean value, median value and standard deviation of *TP RK OQ* and *RA* are calculated and shown in Table 2.

Table 2. The analysis results of source parameter for emotional speech

		TP	RK	OQ	RA
Neutral	Mean	0.5246	***0.3566***	***0.7089***	***0.1131***
	Median	0.5000	0.3500	0.7250	0.1200
	Std. Dev.	0.0675	0.0920	0.0807	0.0312
Happiness	Mean	0.5138	***0.4131***	***0.7268***	0.1070
	Median	0.5500	0.4500	0.7700	0.1100
	Std. Dev.	0.0590	0.0578	0.0946	0.0387
Sadness	Mean	0.5038	0.3759	0.6936	0.1095
	Median	0.5000	0.4000	0.7250	0.1200
	Std. Dev.	0.0737	0.0650	0.1072	0.0383
Anger	Mean	0.5300	***0.4200***	***0.7518***	***0.0900***
	Median	0.5250	0.4500	0.7250	0.0800
	Std. Dev.	0.0340	0.0677	0.0488	0.0397

The following conclusions can be derived from Table 2:

1. For angry and happy voice, the *RK* and *OQ* are greater than netural voice. That means the voice quality of these two emotions vary towards breathy voice, the open quotient of glottal waveform is longer and the shape is more symmetrical. This is consistent with common views[1].
2. For angry voice, *RA* is smaller than netural speech. That means the high freqnecy component of source spectrum is richer and explains why angry voice always sounds sonorous and blaring.
3. There exist no obvious differences between the source parameters of neutral and sad voice. However, the source spectrum is determined by both LF paramters and pitch value. Because the pitch of sad voice is much lower than neutral one, their difference in source spectrum is still distinct.

4 Conclusion

In this paper, an LF parameter estimation method for voice source analysis is proposed. The spectral characters of source signal represented by STRAIGHT spectrum of speech signal are studied and used to measure the difference between candidate LF parameters and actual ones. In order to ensure the feasibility and reliability of spectral matching procedure, the speech signals are divided into analyzable frames and unanalyzable frames. Evaluation with synthetic speech demonstrates the proposed method can give satisfactory precision for LF parameter estimation; analysis experiment with emotional speech proves the proposed method is effective in discriminate the voice quality character among different emotional speech. However, there still exist some limitations with this method. The most evident one is how to get reliable estimation for unanalyzable frames after introducing the concept of analyzable frame. To improve the robustness of proposed method will be the goal of our future research.

References

1. Murray, I. and J.L. Arnott, Towards the Simulation of Emotion in Synthetic Speech: A review of the Literature on Human Vocal Emotion. Journal of the Acoustic Society of America, 1993: p. 1097-1108.
2. Gobl, C., The voice source in speech communication - production and perception experiments involving inverse filtering and synthesis. 2003, Department of Speech, Music and Hearing, KTH, Stockholm.
3. Fant, G., J. Liljencrants, and Q. Lin, A four-parameter model of glottal flow. STL-QPSR, Speech, Music and Hearing, Royal Institute of Technology, Stockholm, 1985. **4**: p. 1-13.
4. Hedelin, P. High quality glottal LPC-vocoder. in Proceedings of IEEE International Conference on Acoustics, Speech, and Signal Processing. 1986.
5. Alku, P., Glottal wave analysis with pitch synchronous iterative adaptive inverse filtering. Speech Communication, 1992. **11**: p. 109-118.
6. Kawahara, H., I. Masuda-Katsuse, and A. Cheveigné, Restructuring speech representations using a pitch adaptive time frequency smoothing and a instantaneous frequency based F0 extraction: Possible role of a repetitive structure in sound. Speech Communication, 1999. **27**: p. 187-207.
7. Ling, Z., et al. Modeling Glottal Effect on the Spectral Envelop of STRAIGHT using Mixture of Gaussians. in International Symposium on Chinese Spoken Language Processing. 2004.
8. d'Alessandro, C. and B. Doval. Voice quality modification for emotional speech synthesis. in Eurospeech. 2003.
9. Fröhlich, M., D. Michaelis, and H.W. Strube, SIM — simultaneous inverse filtering and matching of a glottal flow model for acoustic speech signals. Journal of the Acoustical Society of America, 2001. **110**: p. 479-488.

Features Importance Analysis for Emotional Speech Classification

Jianhua Tao and Yongguo Kang

National Laboratory of Pattern Recognition (NLPR), Institute of Automation,
Chinese Academy of Sciences, P.O.X. 2728, Beijing 100080
{jhtao, ygkang}@nlpr.ia.ac.cn

Abstract. The paper analyzes the prosody features, which includes the intonation, speaking rate, intensity, based on classified emotional speech. As an important feature of voice quality, voice source are also deduced for analysis. With the analysis results above, the paper creates both a CART model and a weight decay neural network model to find acoustic importance towards the emotional speech classification and to disclose whether there is an underlying consistency between acoustic features and speech emotion. The result shows the proposed method can obtain the importance of each acoustic feature through its weight for emotional speech classification and further improve the emotional speech classification.

1 Introduction

More and more efforts have been made for the research of emotional speech recently. It is a widely known fact that the emotional speech differs with respect to the acoustic features [2]. Some prosody features, such as pitch variables (F0 level, range, contour, and jitter), speaking rate are analyzed [2]. Parameters describing laryngeal processes on voice quality were also taken into account [3]. The method of using acoustic prosodic cues to classify emotions or speaking style has been adopted by many researchers. Huber used 50 neutral and 50 angry utterances and multi-layer perceptions for classification. Results reached around 90% of accuracy in the simplified tasks of distinguishing emotional from non-emotional utterances. Dellaert *et al.* [8] compared three classifiers: the maximum likelihood Bayes classification, kernel regression, and k-nearest neighbor (K-NN) method with particular interest in sadness, anger, happiness, and fear. They used features from the pitch contour. An accuracy of 60%~65% was achieved. Valery A. Petrushin[9] performed an experimental study on vocal emotions and the development of a computer agent for emotion recognition. Noam Amir[10] used a corpus that had been studied extensively through subjective listening tests. Best results obtained using distance measures based classifiers. Lee *et al.*[11] used linear discriminant classification with Gaussian class-conditional probability distribution and K-NN method to classify utterances into two basic emotion states, negative and non-negative. Tato *et al.* [12] discussed techniques that exploit emotional dimension other than prosody. Their experiments showed how "quality features" were used in addition to "prosody features." Yu *et al.* [13] used SVMs for emotion detection. An average accuracy of 73% was reported.

J. Tao, T. Tan, and R.W. Picard (Eds.): ACII 2005, LNCS 3784, pp. 449 – 457, 2005.

In the paper, to know how the acoustic features affect the final perception results, we did some more analysis about feature importance for emotional speech classification. We have built both a CART model and a weight decay neural network to learn the relationships between the acoustics and the perceptual characteristics. Based on this, the importance of acoustic features was analyzed.

The whole paper is broken down into several major parts. Section 2 introduces the corpus which supports all of the later work in the paper. Furthermore, the paper makes some analysis on acoustic features (F0 mean, F0 top, F0 bottom, speaking rate, voice source, etc.) according to the different emotion states. In section 3, the paper creates a CART to do the emotion classification based on above acoustic parameters. The acoustic importance is analyzed according to the training results. In section 4, the paper describes a weight decay neural network which is used for automatic analysis of feature importance. Finally, the feature importance analysis results from two models are compared and discussed in section 5. Some other factors which might influence the perception will also be discussed here.

2 Corpora and Statistic Results of Acoustic Features

The corpora used for analysis contains 1,2000 sentences (8 hours), which are performed by 2 actors and 2 actresses with 5 emotions, neutral, fear, sad, angry, happy. They are segmentally and prosodically annotated with break index, F0 contours, syllable boundaries, transcription, etc. All of the results are manually checked. From previous research [2], we know F0, speaking rates, intensity and voice quality form the important features for emotion classification. To know the behavior of each parameter in different emotion states, we made more experiment on the parameters' distributions. The results are shown in Fig.1 and Fig.2. In both Fig.1 and Fig.2, the X-coordinate means the different type of emotion states, from neutral to happy. Y-coordinate denotes the mean value (dots) and standard deviation (vertical lines) of each parameter within the single emotion state.

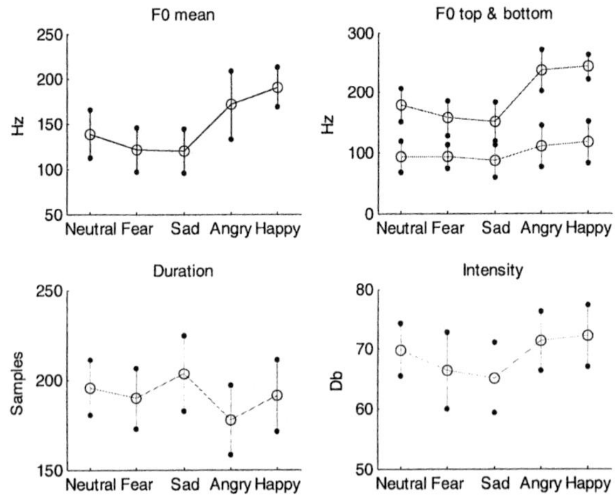

Fig. 1. Relationship between normalized F0s (top), syllable duration (bottom left), intensity (bottom right) and emotion states

Fig.1 shows the distribution of prosody features. In the figure, it shows that "happy" and "angry" make a very high F0, while "sad" generates lower value than neutral state. F0 parameters of "fear" make quite similar behaviors as "sad". "sad" utterances are normally slower than those of other emotions, while "angry" is the fast. "Angry" and "happy" have relatively higher power than other emotions, while "fear" and "sad" are the lowest. All of the results confirm the previous research results [6].

From Fig.1, we also can find the overlap of F0 mean and F0 top in different emotions is less than that of F0 bottom. That means F0 mean and F0 top seem to be the better "resolving power" for perception than F0 bottom. It gives us a brief impression on which is might be more important in distinguishing the emotional speech.

Normally, we think voice quality is a kind of timbre for speech, and is determined by laryngeal characteristics. There are some kinds of phonation modes, such as breathy, whisper, falsetto, creaky, normal, and so on, which correspond to certain laryngeal characteristics respectively. However, there would be some subtypes within one category. In normal mode, one end of the continuum of subtypes approaching breathy voice, where the laryngeal muscles controlling vocal fold adduction are relatively relaxed. At the other end, tension in the musculature begins to limit the vibration of the folds and voice verges on laryngealized or creaky voice [6, 7].

Usual acoustic measurements of breathiness could be classified into two main categories of source parameters and spectral parameters according to the estimate procedure [6]. A general source model is a four-parameter liljencrants-fant(LF) model [5], whose parameters are Ee (the excitation strength), Ra (the measure of the return phase), Rk (the measure of the symmetry/asymmetry of the glottal pulse), and Rg (the measure of the opening branch of the glottal pulse). The familiar parameter, open quotient (Oq), is defined as (1+Rk)/2Rg. The statistic results of the voice source parameters are shown in Fig.2.

From Fig.2, we can see that the mean values of "sad" utterances' glottal sources are distinctly less than those of other emotional utterances'. The low Ee of "sad" utterances indicates its overall weak source signal as well as whispery voice. Consistent with Johnstone's experiments [7], extremely low Ra values indicate a sharp instantaneous closure of the glottis. In this regard, "sad" utterances, which are likely to reflect the relatively high degree of laryngeal tension, are similar to tense voice [10]. Thus "sad" utterances have the trend of exhibiting whispery and tense voice qualities. However, compared to higher Sq of tense voice, the mean value of Sq of "sad" utterances is lower too. The wildly suggested association of "angry" emotion with tense voice is not supported in this study. Although the mean values are employed in the current research, it can be indicated that the relation between emotion and voice quality is not one to one and an emotional speech can exhibit several characteristics of different voice qualities. In other words, concluded by Gobl [3], a given quality tends to be associated with a cluster of affective attributes.

Corresponding with their range, it can also be observed from the figures that standard deviations of Sq are the largest and standard deviations of Ra are the smallest among the six glottal parameters. Comparing the five emotional states, "angry" utterances have the largest standard deviation for Ee and Sq, while "sad" utterances have the largest standard deviation for other four parameters. The standard deviation represents the distribution of parameters, so it can be indicated that the variation of spectral intensity is the largest in "angry" utterances while the variation of voice quality is largest in "sad" utterances.

As mentioned above, Ee is the absolute value of the negative peak of the differentiated glottal flow and is correlated with the overall intensity of the signal. Generally speaking, "angry" utterances sound louder than those of other emotions and should have larger Ee too. So, larger Ee is not critical for producing "angry" utterances, in particular "angry" female utterances.

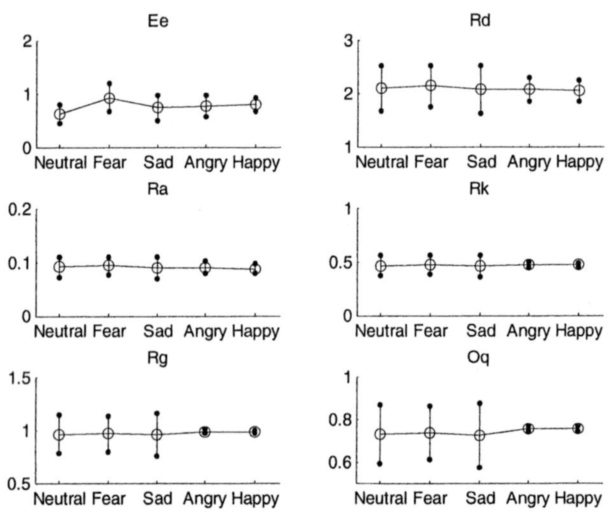

Fig. 2. Voice source properties among different emotions

Previous work has confirmed the following features to be useful for emotional speech classification: utterance duration, f0-range, f0-variation, f0-maximum, f0-minimum, f0-mean, power-level, power-mean and voice source parameters. To simulate the stress information, we add some more parameters, position of f0 peak in the utterance, position of f0-minimum in the utterance, position of duration peak in the utterance, position of the duration minimum in the utterance. After we got the general idea of the influence between the emotional speech and the groups of acoustic features, we still wish to know more subtle acoustic influence of each acoustic parameter on emotions. In next two sections, classification and regression tree (CART) and weight decay neural network methods are employed to analyze the importance of every acoustic feature.

3 Acoustic Importance Analysis with CART Model

This section, we built a CART model to learn the relationships between the acoustics and the emotion states in order to predict the most likely response for each speech token for a reclassification. We used simple first-order statistics derived from the acoustics as the independent variables. The tree correctly predicted 69% of categories using 26 leaf nodes. After training, we used a function that passed the same acoustic data to each of the classification trees, and allowed each to output a probability indicating the likelihood of a sub-parameter of expressiveness vector. These likelihoods were ranked and an ordered list of relevant categories was produced for each speech token.

To know how the acoustic features affect the final stimuli perception, we made further analysis. As we know, variable importance, for a particular predictor, is the sum across all nodes in the tree of the improvement scores that the predictor has when it acts as a primary or surrogate (but not competitor) splitter. Specifically, for node i, if the predictor appears as the primary splitter, then it has a contribution toward the importance as:

importance_contribution_node_i = improvement

If, instead, the predictor appears as the n'th surrogate instead of the primary predictor, the expression is:

*importance_contribution_node_i = (p ^ n) * improvement*

in which p is the "surrogate improvement weight": a user controlled parameter which is equal to 1.0 by default and can be set anywhere between 0 and 1. Linear combination splits do not contribute in any way to variable improvement.

If, in the absence of linear combinations, the improvement weight is greater than 0, and the variable has importance = 0.0, it does not appear in the tree as a primary or surrogate splitter, although it may appear as a competitor.

With this method, we got the factors related to each input acoustic parameters after the training in Table 1.

Table 1. Ranking score of input acoustic parameters

Parameters	Ranking Score
F0 mean	100.00
F0-maximum	98.79
F0-range	98.64
Ee	57.63
Duration mean	48.34
Duration Range	38.78
Position of F0 minimum	36.36
Power	34.86
Rd	33.52
F0 minimum	33.46
Ra	30.31
Position of F0 maximum	29.86
Rk	27.12
Rg	23.40
Power range	15.07
Position of maximum duration	14.02
Oq	13.18
Position of minimum duration	1.56

The parameters, whose ranking score are zero, are not listed in the table. It is easy to find that the F0 mean assumes the most important role in emotion perception. Ee is the most important parameter related to voice quality for the model. Position of F0 minimum is, then, the most important word stress feature for emotion perception.

4 Acoustic Importance Analysis with Weight Decay Neural Network

The weight decay concept is well known in neural network theory as a type of regularization [1]. Regularization is typically used to reduce the complexity of a NN by adding a penalty term $P(w)$ to the error function $F(w)$:

$$\overline{F}(w) = F(w) + \lambda \cdot P(w) \tag{1}$$

where w denotes a vector containing all weights in the NN and λ controls the influence of the penalty term. In the scope of this work $P(w) = \sum_i w_i^2$, which is known as standard weight decay (i=1, …, number of weights). λ is then typically referred to as decay rate.

During training, weights will be adopted on the basis of this function (using gradient descent):

$$w^{i+1} = w^i - \eta \nabla \overline{F}(w) \tag{2}$$

The parameter η is generally referred to as learning rate and controls the step size used to adapt the weights. In our case η and λ are kept constant in all steps i.

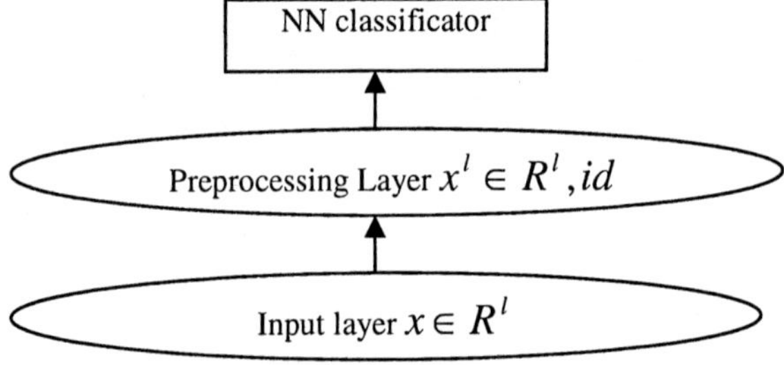

Fig. 3. NN with preprocessing layer

To find out which of the input parameters are important to the NN for a specific task, a preprocessing layer is inserted between the input and the network. The input signals $x \in R^l$ are propagated to this preprocessing layer via a diagonal matrix $w_{diag} = diag(w_1,\dots,w_l)$ to give the output signals $x^l \in R^l$ of the preprocessing layer. Figure 3 shows the resulting network architecture. The weight decay concept is applied only to weights of the diagonal matrix. Thus, w_{set} contains all elements of

$w_{set} = w_l = \{w_1,...,w_l)$. For the neurons of the preprocessing layer, the identity function is chosen as activation function.

At the beginning of the training process all elements of the diagonal matrix are initialized with 1. Thus, the input signals are transferred to the hidden layer without modification. In each training epoch i eq. (3) is applied to obtain the new values for epoch (i+1) for the weights in the diagonal matrix. It is important to carefully choose the decay rate λ. λ should generally be as small as possible. This way the influence of the learning rate η on weight adaptation (eq.(3)) is stronger than the influence of the decay rate λ. Therefore, non-linear relations hidden in the data can be captured. On the other hand λ should be large enough, so that it effects the weights in the diagonal matrix. After several training epochs and application of eq.(3) to the weights in w_l, the following behavior is observed: For some elements of w_l the influence of the learning rate η is stronger than the influence of the decay rate λ. For other elements of w_l, however, the influence of the decay rate λ is stronger than the influence of the learning rate η. By choosing λ / η right, some weights can be pushed towards zero, while others range higher. Those weights close to zero, or below a certain threshold, are considered to be of less importance to the training success of the auto-associator classificatory network. All weights of the auto-associator classificatory network are trained without the penalty term $P(w)$ of (1) at the same time as the weights in w_l.

The table 2 shows the value w_l, Some relatively high values can clearly be identified.

Again, the parameters whose ranking score is zero are not listed in the table. Similar to the results deduced from CART model, F0 mean also plays the most important role in emotion perception. Ee is the most important parameter related to voice quality. Unlike the previous results, position of F0 maximum seems to be the most important word stress feature with NN model.

Table 2. w_l of input parameters

Parameters	w_l
mean F0	0.51
maximum F0	0.42
Ee	0.38
mean Duration	0.36
position of maximum F0	0.35
Intensity	0.35
Rd	0.32
minimum F0	0.28
Ra	0.25
Rk	0.25
Rg	0.24
Oq	0.21

5 Discussion

In the sections above, two methods including CART and neural network are used to explore the importance of each acoustic feature. Although the results of two methods are not entirely identical, the underlying relationship between acoustic features and emotional states is disclosed to a certain extent. Observed from these results, The F0 features such as f0 mean are most important features, while duration, intensity and voice source features are useful features for emotional speech classification in turn.

The above analyses are just based on the one person's speech. As we know, there are different properties of acoustic features among the speakers, even though there is no difference in emotion expression. To show how the speech differs from the different persons we make some more statistic results of parameter Rg among five people. It is shown in Fig.3.

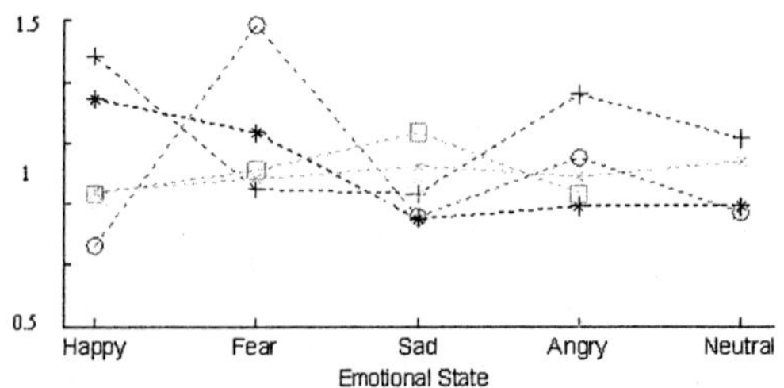

Fig. 3. Rg distribution among five different people

We see Rg is quite unstable among the persons. It may be helpful for speaker identification system, but may be not suitable for creating a speaker independent emotion classification system. Similar analysis of other parameters will be done in our future work. The importance order of the acoustic parameters might be changed, while using the speech from several persons.

6 Conclusion

In this paper we make some analysis on the acoustic parameters, especially the voice source parameters, in different emotional speech. Based on that, classification tree and the weight decay concept known from neural network theory have been applied in the emotion speech classification. By applying above two methods, the importance of acoustic parameters could be evaluated. The results will be much helpful for the later research on the emotion classification and emotional speech synthesis.

References

[1] Nick Campbell, "Perception of Affect in Speech - towards an Automatic Processing of Paralinguistic Information in Spoken Conversation", ICSLP2004, Jeju, Oct, 2004.

[2] Jianhua Tao, "Emotion control of chinese speech synthesis in natural environment," in EUROSPEECH- 2003, pp. 2349–2352.

[3] C. Gobl and A. N´ı Chasaide, "The role of voice quality in communicating emotion, mood and attitude," Speech Communication, vol. 40, pp. 189–212, 2003.
[4] Scherer K.R., "Vocal affect expression: A review and a model for future research," Psychological Bulletin, vol. 99, pp. 143–165, 1986.
[5] G. Fant, Liljencrants J., and Q. Lin, "A four- arameter model of glottal flow," STL-QPSR 4, Speech, Music and Hearing, Royal Institute of Technology, Stockholm, pp. 1–13, 1985.
[6] Yildirim, Serdar Bulut, Murtaza Lee, Chul Min Kazemzadeh, Abe Deng, Zhigang Lee, Sungbok Narayanan, Shrikanth Busso, Carlos (2004): "An acoustic study of emotions expressed in speech", In INTERSPEECH-2004, 2193-2196.
[7] T. Johnstone and K. R. Scherer, "The effects of emotions on voice quality," in Proceedings of the XIVth International Congress of Phonetic Sciences, 1999.
[8] Dellaert, F., Polzin, t., and Waibel, A., Recognizing Emotion in Speech", In Proc. Of ICSLP 1996, Philadelphia, PA, pp. 1970-1973, 1996.
[9] Petrushin, V. A., "Emotion Recognition in Speech Signal: Experimental Study, Development and Application." ICSLP 2000, Beijing.
[10] Amir, N., "Classifying emotions in speech: a comparison of methods". Holon Academic Institute of technology, EUROSPEECH 2001, Escandinavia.
[11] Lee, C.M.; Narayanan, S.; Pieraccini, R., Recognition of Negative Emotion in the Human Speech Signals, Workshop on Auto. Speech Recognition and Understanding, Dec 2001.
[12] Tato, R., Santos, R., Kompe, R., Pardo, J.M., Emotional Space Improves Emotion Recognition, in Proc. Of ICSLP-2002, Denver, Colorado, September 2002.
[13] Yu, F., Chang, E., Xu, Y.Q., and Shum, H.Y., Emotion Detection From Speech To Enrich Multimedia Content, in the second IEEE Pacific-Rim Conference on Multimedia, October 24-26, 2001, Beijing, China.

Toward Making Humans Empathize with Artificial Agents by Means of Subtle Expressions

Takanori Komatsu

Future University-Hakodate, 116-2 Kamedanakano, Hakodate 041-8655, Japan
komatsu@fun.ac.jp

Abstract. Can we assign attitudes to a computer based on its represented subtle expressions, such as beep sounds and simple animations? If so, which kinds of beep sounds or simple animations are perceived as specific attitudes, such as "disagreement", "hesitation" or "agreement"? To examine this issue, I carried out two experiments to observe and clarify how participants perceive or assign an attitude to a computer according to beep sounds of different durations and F0 contour's slopes (Experiment 1) or simple animations of different durations and objects' velocities (Experiment 2). The results of these two experiments revealed that 1) subtle expressions with increasing intonations (Experiment 1) or velocities (Experiment 2) were perceived by participants as "disagreement", 2) flat intonations and velocities with longer duration were interpreted as "hesitation", and 3) decreasing intonations and velocities with shorter duration were taken as "agreement."

1 Introduction

Recently, various interactive agents have been applied to intelligent user interfaces in our ordinary life, such as those for home information appliances and network communication terminals. Obviously, we humans have to create a smooth means of communicating with these agents to obtain the maximum benefits of their abilities and capacities. To create such interactive agents, many studies have developed humanoid robots (e.g., Ishiguro et al., 2001) that can exist in the same physical space with users and life-like (or character) agents (e.g., Prendinger et al., 2004) that appear on computer screens. Both kinds of agents have human-like shapes or faces to express certain gestures or facial expressions so that users will perceive them as having attitudes and emphasize with them. This is believed to facilitate communication between these agents and humans.

In contrast, some researchers have reported that humans perceive the attitudes of others from their expressed information even if this information is simpler than that derived from gestures or facial expressions (for example, Suzuki et al., 2004). Nagasaki & Komatsu (2004) examined whether humans' perception of the attitudes of others are affected by simple prosodic components of speech sounds: F0 contour's slopes and durations. Concretely, participants were asked

J. Tao, T. Tan, and R.W. Picard (Eds.): ACII 2005, LNCS 3784, pp. 458–465, 2005.

to hear various Japanese interjection "eh" [1] pronounced without any specific attitudes but with different durations and F0 contour's slopes, and then asked to answer the question of which kind of attitudes of information sender they felt. As a result, this study showed that different durations and F0 contour's slopes of semantically neutral speech sounds can cause participants to perceive different attitudes. Therefore, if even subtle expressions presented by an agent without a human-like shape or face meet certain requirements, one may expect that these expressions would also cause users to perceive different attitudes and to assign specific attitudes to this agent. Moreover, this perception might induce the users' empathy toward the agent and eventually trigger smooth communication between them.

As a preliminary study to achieve such a relationship between users and agents, I have focused on a normal laptop computer as the agent without a human-like shape or face, and on beep sounds (sound stimuli) and simple animations (visual stimuli) as subtle expressions presented to humans. Specifically, in the first experiment, I conducted an experiment in which various beep sounds were presented to participants from a laptop computer to observe and analyze how participants assign the specific attitudes to the computer based on the presented beep sounds (Experiment 1). In the second experiment, I conducted an experiment in which various simple animations were presented (Experiment 2).

2 Experiment 1: Beep Sounds as Sound Stimuli

2.1 Purpose and Settings

In this experiment, as sound subtle expressions, I prepared 44 different types of beep sounds with four different durations and 11 different F0 contours. Specifically, the four durations were 189, 418, 639, and 819 ms. The 11 F0 contours were set so that the transition range of F0 values between the onset and end-point in the sound stimuli were 0, $\pm 25, \pm 50, \pm 75, \pm 100$, or $\pm$ 125, and these were linearly downward or upward (Figure 1 (a)). All these 44 stimuli have the same F0 average 131 Hz.

2.2 Procedure

Participants were 23 Japanese (17 men and 6 women; 20 - 42 years old). Hearing tests established that no participants had any hearing problems. An experimenter explained that beep sounds would be presented to participants, and asked them to assume that these stimuli were answering speeches in a telephone conversation. At first, as an experimental trial, one randomly selected sound stimulus among the 44 sounds was presented to participants. They were then asked to answer a question like *"Did you feel that [***] was this computer's attitude based on this beep sound?"*; [***] was the randomly selected attitude among the following three: **1) Disagreement**, e.g., surprising, doubting,

[1] In Japanese, this interjection can be used in situations of agreement, hesitation, or disagreement to show one's thought.

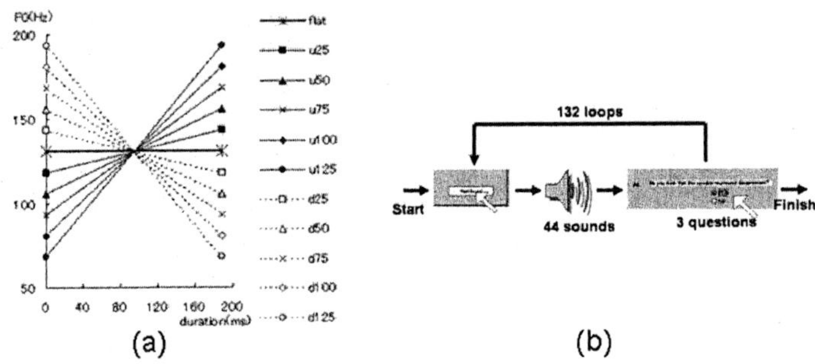

Fig. 1. (a) Eleven different F0 contours (duration; 189 ms). For example, "u25" indicates that F0 transition range was 25 Hz with upward slope (increasing intonation). (b) Specific Procedure used in this experiment 1.

2) Hesitation, e.g., being lost for words, and **3) Agreement**, e.g., acceptance. These three attitudes were reorganized to be complementary to each other. In addition, it can be said that these attitudes might correspond to valence evaluations such as "good/bad"; "disagreement" corresponds to the negative valence value ("bad"), "agreement" to the positive value ("good"), and "hesitation" to a neutral.

Specifically, each participant experienced 132 trials (44 different sounds x 3 attitudes, see Figure 1 (b)). The presenting orders of stimulus-question pairs were counterbalanced among participants, and it is assumed that all participants have contingent tendencies of judgment of each trial.

2.3 Results

The results were divided into three attitudes, and each attitude was statistically analyzed to observe how the following three sound properties affected the interpretation of a particular computer's attitudes; 1) rising tone or falling tone, 2) duration of stimulus, and 3) transition range of F0 contour's slope (in rising tone and falling tone). Figure 2 (a) shows which sounds were interpreted as the computer's attitude of "disagreement," Figure 2 (b) presents the sounds identified as "hesitation," and Figure 2 (c) those accepted as "agreement." In these figures, the horizontal axis lists the types of F0 contours and the labels on this axis, such as "u25" or "d100," are the same ones used to distinguish the contours in Figure 1 (a). The vertical axis shows the **interpretation rates (IR)** that give the proportion of participants answering "yes" in the corresponding trials. There are four lines indicating the duration of sound stimuli.

Case1 : Disagreement. In the results, no significant differences were found among different durations ($F(3,66)=.70$, n.s.) and different F0 transition ranges in falling tones ($F(4,88)= 1.68$, n.s.). On the other hand, rising tones showed a significant higher IR than falling tones (rising tone: 89.1%, falling tone: 15.4%, $F(1,22)=219.7$, $p<.01$), and wider F0 transition ranges in a rising tone showed higher IR (u25: 73.9% < u125: 95.6%, $F(4,88)= 9.81$, $p<.01$). To sum up, **when**

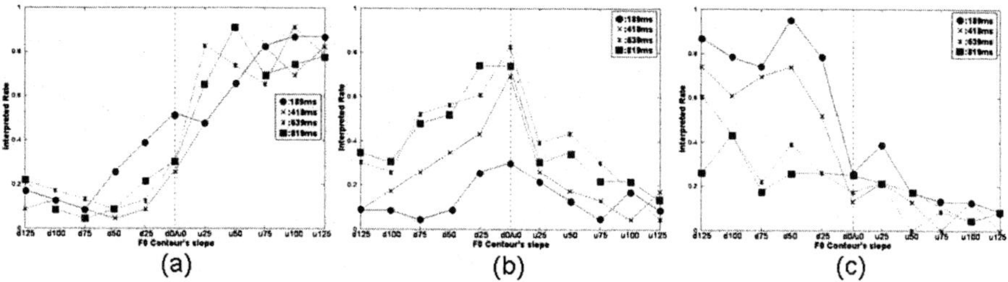

Fig. 2. Relationship between F0 contours and rate of "disagreement (a)", "hesitation (b)" and "agreement (c)" interpretation for each duration

the sounds with upward slopes (increasing intonation) regardless of their duration were presented from the computer, this computer's attitude was interpreted as "disagreement."

Case 2: Hesitation. The sounds with longer duration showed the higher IR (189 ms: 14.6% < 819 ms: 44.7%, F(3,66)=18.1, p<.01), and falling tones showed the higher rate than the rising tones (rising tone: 22.8%, falling tone: 37.0%, F(1,22)=11.64, p<.01). Moreover, narrower F0 transition range in both rising and falling tones showed the significant higher IR (d25: 57.6% > d125: 20.6%, F(4,88)=11.23, p<.01, u25: 36.9% > u125: 12.0%, F(4,88)= 8.89, p<.01). In summary, **when the slower downward slopes (decreasing intonation) with longer duration were presented, the computer's attitude was interpreted as "hesitation."**

Case 3: Agreement. The sounds with the shorter duration showed the higher IR (189 ms: 53.4% > 819 ms: 29.3%, F(3,66)=19.42, p<.01) and falling tones showed the significantly higher rate than rising tones (rising tone: 12.4%, falling tone: 62.4%, F(1,22)= 67.5, p<.01). And wider F0 transition range in falling tone showed rather higher rates than narrower ones (d25: 53.3% < d125: 70.7%, F(4,88)= 3.12, p<.05), and in rising tones, narrower transition range showed higher rates than wider ones (u25: 23.9% > u125: 9.8%, F(4,88)= 5.48, p<.01). To sum up, **when the downward slopes with shorter duration were presented, the computer's attitude was interpreted as "agreement."**

Thus, it can be said that beep sounds with different durations and F0 contour's slopes caused users to perceive the different attitudes and were assigned specific attitudes to this computer.

3 Experiment 2: Simple Animations as Visual Stimuli

3.1 Purpose and Settings

In this experiment, as visual subtle expressions, I utilized the simple animations that a white rectangle is moving from left to right on a black background (Figure 3 (c)). I then prepared 36 different animations with four different durations and nine different rectangle's velocity slopes. Specifically, the four du-

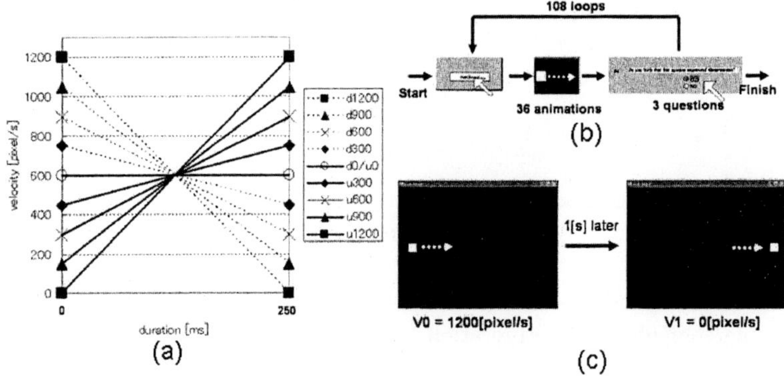

Fig. 3. (a) Nine different velocity slopes (duration; 250 ms). For example, "u1200" indicates that velocity transition range was 1200 pixel/s with increasing velocity. (b) Animation of "d1200" velocity slope and 1000 ms duration. (c) Specific Procedure used in this experiment 2.

rations were 250, 500, 750, and 1000 ms. The nine velocity slopes were designed like the F0 contours in Experiment 1 that were set so that the transition range of velocity between onset and endpoint in visual stimuli were 0, ±300, ±600, ±900, or ± 1200 [pixel/s], and these were also linearly downward or upward (Figure 3 (a)). Each animation window was 640 x 480 pixels and its physical size on the 11-inch computer display used in this experiment was about 13 x 10 cm.

3.2 Procedure

Participants were 21 Japanese (16 men and 5 women; 18 - 25 years old). An experimenter explained that simple animations would be presented to participants, and asked them to assume that these visual stimuli were a part of the trajectory of a sign language speaker's[2]

The experimental procedure was followings; One randomly selected animation among the 36 animations was presented to participants. Afterward, they were asked to answer a question like *"Did you feel that [***] was this computer's attitude based on this animation?"*; [***] was the randomly selected attitudes among disagreement, hesitation and agreement. Each participants experienced 108 trials (36 animations x 3 attitudes, see Figure 3 (b)).

3.3 Results

Similar with Experiment 1, each of three attitudes was statistically analyzed to observe how the following three properties affected the interpretation of a

[2] Actually there are no Japanese signs corresponding to rectangle's motion in these animations, but Japanese sign language speakers usually changes the actions' velocity to express the intensities of its sign. However, all participants did have any specific knowledge about the above issues.

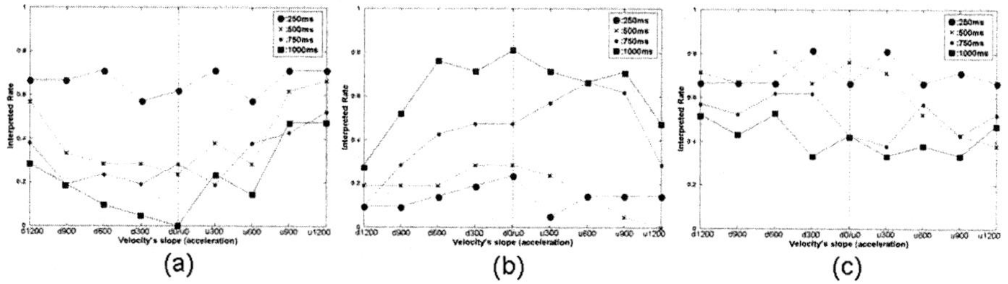

Fig. 4. Relationship between velocity slopes and rate of "disagreement (a)", "hesitation (b)" and "agreement (c)" interpretation for each duration

particular computer's attitudes; 1) increasing or decreasing velocity, 2) duration of stimulus, and 3) transition range of velocity slope (in increasing and decreasing velocity). Figure 4 (a) shows which animations were interpreted as the computer's attitude of "disagreement." Figure 4 (b) presents the sounds identified as "hesitation" and Figure 4 (c) those accepted as "agreement."

Case 1: Disagreement. The animations with shorter duration showed the higher IR (250 ms: 66.1% < 1000 ms: 22.2%, $F(3,60)=13.22$, $p<.01$), and increasing velocity showed the higher IR (increasing velocity: 47.6%, decreasing velocity: 35.4%, $F(1,20)=11.36$, $p<.01$). Moreover, wider velocity range in increasing velocity showed the higher IR (u300: 47.6% < u1200: 60.7%, $F(3,60)=3.63$, $p<.05$). No significant differences were found among different velocity transition range in decreasing velocity ($F(3,60)=2.40$, n.s.). To sum up, **when the animations with faster increasing velocity were presented from a computer, this computer's attitude was interpreted as "disagreement."**

Case 2: Hesitation. The animation with longer duration showed the higher IR (250 ms: 13.7% < 1000 ms: 62.4%, $F(3,60)=18.17$, $p<.01$). Although no significant differences were found between increasing and decreasing velocity (increasing: 35.1%, decreasing: 30.9%, $F(1,20)=.95$, n.s.), smaller velocity transition in both increasing and decreasing velocity showed the significant higher IR (u300: 35.7% > u1200: 22.6%, $F(3,60)=4.69$, $p<.01$, d300: 33.3% > d1200: 13.1%, $F(3,60)=8.19$, $p<.01$). In summary, **when the narrower velocity transitions with longer duration were presented, the computer's attitude was interpreted as "hesitation."**

Case 3: Agreement. The animation with shorter duration showed the higher IR (250 ms: 71.9% > 1000 ms: 47.8%, $F(3,60)=6.29$, p.<.01), and ones with decreasing velocity showed the rather higher IR (increasing: 52.6%, decreasing: 61.6%, $F(1,20)=3.28$, $p<.075$). However, no significant differences were found among different among velocity transitions in both increasing and decreasing velocity (decreasing, $F(3,60)=.69$, n.s.; increasing, $F(3,60)=1.32$, n.s.). To sum up, **when the decreasing velocity transition with shorter duration were presented, the computer's attitude was interpreted as "agreement."**

Thus, it can be said that animation with different durations and rectangle's velocities caused users to perceive the different attitudes and were assigned specific attitudes to this computer. Moreover, this result is quite similar with ones observed in Experiment 1.

4 Discussion and Conclusions

From the results of Experiment 1 and 2, it can be said that these two results showed similar tendencies (Table 1). For example, this table showed that the sounds with decreasing intonation with shorter duration and the animations with decreasing velocity with shorter duration were interpreted as the computer's attitudes as "Agreement"; thus both kinds of presented information (beep sounds and simple animations) are continuously decreasing their values (F0 and rectangle's velocity). At a glance, it seems that these two values are different kinds of information, however, it can be said that their dimensions are quite similar; F0 [Hz=1/s] and velocity [pixel/s]. Therefore, to assign specific attitude to a computer for users regardless of the kinds of utilizing information, it can be said that it required changing its values (more specifically, the acceleration value) of the presented information as follows: *1) When the presented information is increasing its value (positive acceleration), this information sender's attitude was interpreted as "disagreement," 2) When the presented information is not changing its value, without velocity changes (zero acceleration), this information sender's attitude was "hesitation," and 3) When the presented information is decreasing its value (negative acceleration) were observed, this was "agreement."*

At this point, the reason why changing its value of presented information cause to perceive the different attitudes for information receivers was still unclear and controversial (for example, one possibility is "whether the expressed information violate the natural energy flow such as preservation of energy might be the one of the candidate hypothesis to resolve this reason"). It can be said that the most reasonable hypothesis for explaining the above phenomena is caused by linguistic aspects (especially "Japanese" in this study, e.g., "Japanese sentences with increasing intonation are normally interrogative,"). Therefore, it strongly

Table 1. Results of Experiment 1 and 2

Computer's Attitude		Experiment 1 (sound)	Experiment 2 (visual)
Disagreement	Transition	Increasing Intonation	Increasing Velocity
	Duration	-	Shorter
Hesitation	Transition	No change	No change
	Duration	Longer	Longer
Agreement	Transition	Decreasing	Decreasing
	Duration	Shorter	Shorter

requires conducting consecutive experiments to recruit the non-Japanese participants and analyzing these results to consider the effects of participants mother tongue on interpreting attitudes of an information sender.

In any case, the results of the two experiments insured that the different subtle expressions can be interpreted as different attitude of a information sender, so that there are enough possibilities to apply these to an actual application. Same statement was argued by Lin & Picard (2003) as their "subtle expressivity" study. For example, it can be expected that implementing this result into an actual computer would create effective interactions between users and interfaces. For example, when the computer responds to a certain action of users by presenting "beep sounds with increasing intonation," users would intuitively assign the particular attitude (in this case "disagreement") to the computer from this beep sound: "Umm... this computer seems to have some doubts about my last command..." Thus, this result would contribute to achieving an interface that enables users to assign or interpret particular attitudes to a computer intuitively and effectively.

References

1. Ishiguro, H., Ono, T., Imai, M., Maeda, T., Kanda, T., & Nakatsu, R. (2001). Robovie: an interactive humanoid robot. *International Journal of Industrial Robot, 28(6)*, 498–503.
2. Liu, K., & Picard., W. R. (2003). Subtle Expressivity in a Robotic Computer. In *Proceedings of the CHI2003 Workshop on Subtle Expressivity for Characters and Robot.*
3. Nagasaki, Y., & Komatsu, T. (2004). Can People Perceive Different Emotions from a Non-emotional Voice by Modifying its F0 and Duration? In *Proceedings of the 2nd International Conference on Speech Prosody (SP2004)*, (pp. 667–670).
4. Prendinger, H. DeCampus, S., & Ishizuka, M. (2004). MPML: A Markup Language for Controlling the Behavior of Life-like Characters. *Journal of Visual Languages and Computing, 15(2)*, 183–203.
5. Suzuki, N., Kakehi, K., Takeuchi, Y., & Okada, M. (2004). Social effects of the speed of hummed sounds on human-computer interaction. *International Journal of Human-Computer Studies, 60*, 455–468.

Evaluating Affective Feedback of the 3D Agent Max in a Competitive Cards Game*

Christian Becker[1], Helmut Prendinger[2], Mitsuru Ishizuka[3], and Ipke Wachsmuth[1]

[1] Faculty of Technology, University of Bielefeld, 33594 Bielefeld, Germany
[2] National Institute of Informatics, 2-1-2 Hitotsubashi, Chiyoda-ku, Tokyo 101-8430, Japan
[3] Graduate School of Information Science and Technology, University of Tokyo, 7-3-1 Hongo, Bunkyo-ku, Tokyo 113-8656, Japan

Abstract. Within the field of Embodied Conversational Agents (ECAs), the simulation of emotions has been suggested as a means to enhance the believability of ECAs and also to effectively contribute to the goal of more intuitive human–computer interfaces. Although various emotion models have been proposed, results demonstrating the appropriateness of displaying particular emotions within ECA applications are scarce or even inconsistent. Worse, questionnaire methods often seem insufficient to evaluate the impact of emotions expressed by ECAs on users. Therefore we propose to analyze non-conscious physiological feedback (bio-signals) of users within a clearly arranged dynamic interaction scenario where various emotional reactions are likely to be evoked. In addition to its diagnostic purpose, physiological user information is also analyzed online to trigger empathic reactions of the ECA during game play, thus increasing the level of social engagement. To evaluate the appropriateness of different types of affective and empathic feedback, we implemented a cards game called *Skip-Bo*, where the user plays against an expressive 3D humanoid agent called *Max*, which was designed at the University of Bielefeld [6] and is based on the emotion simulation system of [2]. Work performed at the University of Tokyo and NII provided a real-time system for empathic (agent) feedback that allows one to derive user emotions from skin conductance and electromyography [13]. The findings of our study indicate that within a competitive gaming scenario, the absence of negative agent emotions is conceived as stress-inducing and irritating, and that the integration of empathic feedback supports the acceptance of Max as a co-equal humanoid opponent.

1 Introduction and Motivation

Embodied Conversational Agents are computer-generated, humanoid characters that are able to conduct a natural face-to-face dialogue with human users [12], whereby the types of communication channels range from purely textual input

* This paper builds on the joint project outline described in [3].

J. Tao, T. Tan, and R.W. Picard (Eds.): ACII 2005, LNCS 3784, pp. 466–473, 2005.

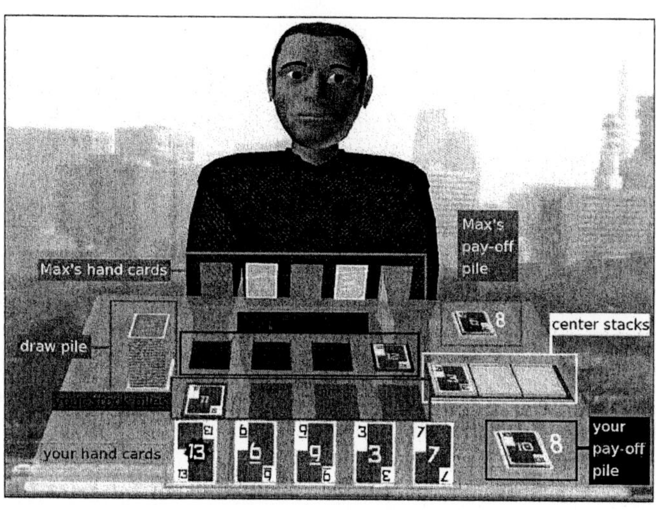

Fig. 1. The card game *Skip-Bo* as an interaction scenario for an Empathic Max

to multi–modal speech–gesture interfaces. In scenarios where autonomous ECAs are designed to assist human users [6,7] it is questionable if the implementation of negative emotions is useful or not even contra-productive. In the context of affective gaming, however, our expectation was that the simulation and expression of negative emotions would increase the believability and naturalness of the synthetic opponent dramatically as most games are designed to evoke various kinds of emotions (positive and negative) to intensify the game experience.

Moreover, research in affective computing is offering promising results on interpreting human physiological information as emotions [11]. In accord with the two-dimensional (arousal, valence) model of [8], we claim that all emotions can be characterized in terms of judged valence (positive or negative) and arousal. Since skin conductance increases with a person's level of overall arousal and stress, and electromyography correlates with negatively valenced emotions, named emotions can be identified in the arousal–valence space. A real-time system based on [8] is described in [13]. In our work, the behavior of the ECA is modulated by both its own and the human interlocutor's emotional state. Consequently, the agent may be experienced as a more sensible and sociable interaction partner.

As our ECA, we use a 3D agent called *Max* that has been developed by the Artificial Intelligence Group at the University of Bielefeld [6] (see Fig. 1). Max has basic abilities for multi-modal interaction such as synchronized auditory speech, and facial and bodily gestures, and is controlled by a cognitively motivated architecture that enables him to conduct deliberative as well as reactive behavior. Max uses a concurrent emotion simulation system based on dimensional emotion theories [2]. The gaming scenario described in this paper provides the deliberative module with a clearly defined goal (to win the game), and it may thus derive a power relationship between the human player and itself in any given (game) state. This information enables the agent to distinguish between the emotion categories "fear" (low dominance) and "anger" (high dominance), and adapt the behavior of Max accordingly.

The rest of the paper is organized as follows. Section 2 describes the setup of our empirical study and in Section 3, we present our results based on questionnaires and the analysis of the physiological data recorded during game play. Section 4 concludes the paper.

2 Empirical Study

As an affective gaming scenario, the classical cards game *Skip-Bo* has been implemented as a face-to-face interaction scenario between a human player and the Max agent (see Fig. 1). In the game, players have the conflictive goal of getting rid of the eight cards on the pay-off piles to the right side of the table by playing them to the shared white center stacks. As on these center stacks the order of cards from one to twelve is relevant, the hand and stock cards must be used strategically by the players to achieve this overall goal, and win the game.

The 'physical' objects necessary to play the game were modelled as 3D objects and enriched by semantic information, so that intuitive point-and-click interaction by the human player as well as natural gestural interaction by Max (e.g. moving cards on the table) were easily realized [9].

Max displays different types of facial emotions within the pleasure-arousal-dominance space that reflect his current emotional state [2]. Speech was not seen as important in the cards game setting and has therefore not been implemented. However, when in a negative affective state, Max utters a variety of grunts and moans. Moreover, he continuously simulates and modulates breathing and eye-blinking, giving the user the impression of interacting with a life-like agent.

Visual and auditory feedback was also given whenever the human player was selecting or moving cards. Moreover, the Max agent gave visual feedback to the user by dynamically looking at the objects (cards) selected by himself or the user for a short period of time, and then looking straight ahead again in the direction of the user. Max also performs a simple type of turn–taking by nodding whenever he starts or completes his move. These behaviors are intended to increase the user's perception of interacting with an agent that is aware of its environment and the actual state of the game.

2.1 Design

In order to assess the effect of simulated emotions and empathic feedback in the context of human–computer interaction we designed the following four conditions within the proposed gaming scenario (see [4] for a similar set of conditions):

1. *Non-Emotional* condition: Max does not display emotional behavior.
2. *Self-Centered Emotional* condition: Max appraises his own game play only, and displays e.g. (facial) happiness when he is able to move cards.
3. *Negative Empathic* condition: Max shows self-centered emotional behavior and responds to those user actions that thwart his own goal of winning the

game. Consequently, he will e.g. display distress when the user performs a good move or is detected to be positively aroused. This condition implements a form of 'negative' empathy.
4. *Positive Empathic* condition: Here, Max is also self-centered emotional, but user actions are appraised 'positively' so that he is "happy for" the user's game progress. If the user can be assumed to be distressed, Max will display "sorriness" for the user. This condition implements 'positive' empathy.

Note that Max follows a competitive playing strategy in all conditions.

2.2 Subjects

The study included 14 male and 18 female subjects. All but one subject were Japanese, and two of them had never played a card game before. The age of the subjects ranged from 22 to 55 years and the average age was 30 years. Subjects were given a monetary reward of 500 Yen for participation. They were told in advance that they would get an extra reward if they won against Max. Subjects were randomly assigned to the four conditions (eight in each condition).

2.3 Procedure

Subjects received written instructions of the card game (in Japanese) with a screenshot of the starting condition before they entered the room with the experimental setup. Subjects entered the room individually and were seated in front of a 50 inch plasma display with attached loudspeakers on both sides (see Fig. 2). They were briefed about the experiment, in particular that they would play a competitive game. Then, subjects could play a short introductory game against a non-emotional Max, which allowed them to get used to the mouse based point-and-click interface, and also provided subjects the possibility to ask clarifying questions about the game. Every subject won this first game easily.

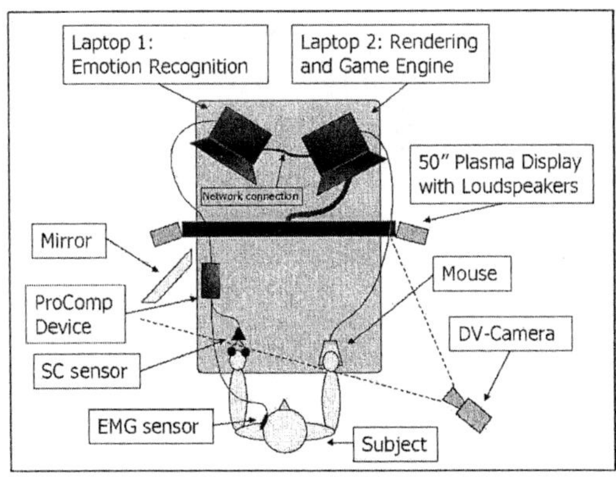

Fig. 2. Experimental setup

Next, the biometrical sensors of the ProComp Infinity encoder [15] were attached to the subject and the subject was assured that these sensors were not harmful. Upon consent, a skin conductance (SC) sensor was attached to the index finger and the small finger of the non-dominant hand. The electromyography (EMG) sensor was attached to the subject's left (mirror-oriented) cheek to measure the activity of the masseter muscle. Then a relaxation phase of three minutes started, with Max leaving the display and the subject being advised not to speak. This phase was necessary to obtain a baseline for the normalization of the bio-signals, since values may greatly vary depending on subject.

From now on, the experimenter remained visually separated from the subject (behind the screen) only to supervise the experiment. After the baseline was set, Max re-entered to the screen and the subject was asked to start the game. After the game was completed, the subjects were asked to fill in a questionnaire in English presented on the screen, together with a Japanese translation on hard-copy. The questionnaire contained 25 questions that were related to the participant's subjective experience while playing the game.

The whole interaction was recorded with a digital video camera positioned to the right behind the subject. In order to capture both the interaction on the screen as well as the human player's facial expression, a mirror was set up to acquire in indirect image of the human players face. Each game lasted for about ten minutes. A protocol of the development of the game, the acquired physiological data, and the video data were recorded for later analysis.

3 Results

Both questionnaires and biometrical data were evaluated to estimate the impact of different forms of emotional agent behavior (or their absence) on human users. Our findings will be presented in the following sections.

3.1 Questionnaire Results

The questionnaire contained twenty-five questions, which can be grouped into the following categories: (i) *Overall Appraisal*: Seven questions about the experimental condition, including questions about whether subjects liked playing the game or how they felt during game play; (ii) *Affective Qualities of Max*: Twelve questions related to the emotionality, personality, and empathic capability of Max; (iii) *Life-Likeness of Max*: Six questions about user judgements of the human-likeness of Max' behavior and outward appearance.

Questions were rated on a 7 point Likert scale. Due to space limitations, only selected questions will be discussed. (The full set of questions and results can be obtained from the authors.) With respect to the first group of questions (Overall Appraisal), all but two subjects liked to play the game and everyone wanted to play it again. A nearly significant effect of the two empathic conditions in comparison with the Non-Emotional and Self-Centered Emotional conditions could be found. Subjects in the empathic conditions tended to feel less lonely ($t(30) = 1.66$; $p = 0.053$).[1]

The second group of questions (Affective Qualities of Max) – while not providing results of statistical significance – showed that subjects had a tendency to perceive Max as hiding his 'true feelings' in the Non-Emotional and Self-Centered Emotional conditions and showing his true feelings in both empathic

[1] The level of statistical significance is set to 0.05.

conditions ($t(30) = -1.49$; $p = 0.073$). Also, Max was experienced as more caring about the human players' feelings when playing a positive empathic manner then when playing in a negative empathic manner ($t(14) = -1.6$; $p = 0.068$).

Concerning the third group of questions (Life-Likeness of Max), the agent was more perceived as "a human being" when playing in an empathic way, opposed to playing in a non-emotional or self-centered emotional way ($t(30) = -3.42$; $p = 0.001$). Moreover, Max' outward appearance was judged as more attractive when reacting empathically as compared to the Non-Emotional and Self-Centered Emotional conditions ($t(30) = -2.2$; $p = 0.018$).

3.2 Results of Biometrical Data Analysis

In order to analyze the recorded physiological data (skin conductance and electromyography), we focused on game situations where emotional reactions in the human player as well as Max were likely to occur. Specifically, we assumed emotional reactions whenever either of the players was able to play at least two pay-off pile cards in a row, which are moves towards winning the game, and found eighty-seven such situations.

Determining the exact duration of emotions is a notoriously hard problem [10]. We chose to analyze periods of ten seconds, consisting of five seconds before the last card was played, and the succeeding five seconds. For those periods and each of the four experimental conditions, the arithmetic means (averages) were calculated for both normalized skin conductance and normalized electromyography values (see Fig. 3). For each data set (each subject and each signal type), normalization was performed by first subtracting the average baseline value from the current signal value and dividing the resulting value by the range of values applicable to each subject (maximum minus minimum).

Regarding skin conductance, we found a significant difference between the Negative Empathic condition and the Positive Empathic condition ($t(48) = -3.48; p = 0.0006$), as well as between the Non-Emotional condition and the Negative Empathic condition ($t(44) = 1.81$; $p = 0.04$). Moreover, the Self-Centered Emotional and Positive Empathic conditions were statistically significantly different ($t(38) = -3.1$; $p = 0.002$).

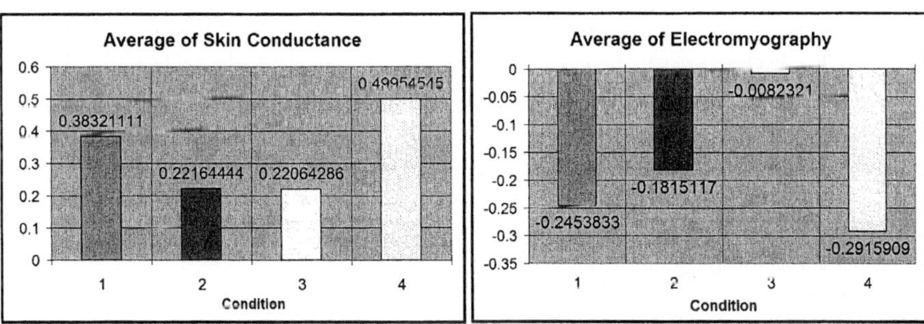

Fig. 3. The average values of normalized skin conductance and electromyography data within dedicated segments of the interaction. Explanation: 1 (Non-Emotional), 2 (Self-Centered Emotional), 3 (Negative Empathic), 4 (Positive Empathic).

As high skin conductance is an indicator of stress [5], the human player was seemingly most stressed in the Positive Empathic condition where Max was mostly "happy for" for the human player's success and giving positive empathic feedback by smiling back whatever the emotional or game state of the user was. Although counter-intuitive at first sight, it is important to note that in the setting of a competitive game, positive empathic behavior is quite unnatural and may thus induce user stress. The relatively high stress level in the Non-Emotional condition further supports our argumentation that inappropriate behavior (relative to an interaction task) leads to higher stress levels. These results are consistent with the corresponding questionnaire item, asking whether Max' behavior is seen as irritating. Here, Max was perceived as most irritating in Non-Emotional condition, followed by the Positive Empathic condition.

Regarding EMG, only the Negative Empathic condition differs significantly from all other conditions, whereby all p-values are smaller than 0.012. (Observe that in Fig. 3 all values are below zero, meaning that the baseline period was not experienced relaxing in terms of muscle tension.) High values of electromyography are primarily an indicator of negative valence [1]. The highest value was achieved in the Negative Empathic condition, where Max was designed to evoke negative emotions in the human player by showing negative empathic feedback, e.g. a sarcastic smile to the user's (assumed) frustration. Notably, the lowest EMG values can be observed in the Positive Empathic condition where Max performed a "calm down" gesture whenever the human player was assumed to be frustrated or angry. The same tendency can be found in the questionnaire as the subjects were judging Max as most caring in the Positive Empathic condition and the least caring in the Negative Empathic condition.

4 Conclusion

To our knowledge, this is the first study that systematically investigates the impact of different types of emotional behavior on human physiology. Emotions were displayed by the highly sophisticated 3D agent Max that was integrated into a realistic game setting. While previous similar studies only considered positive emphatic response [13,14], the current experiment also analyzes the utility of displaying negative emotions. Our chief finding is that – within a competitive game scenario – the absence of negative empathy is conceived as stressful (derived from SC) and irritating, as it might also be experienced when playing against a human player. A complementary result is that negatively emphatic behavior induces negatively valenced emotions (derived from EMG) in the user. While emotion simulation systems such as [2] or emotion recognition systems such as [13] cannot be validated directly, the use of physiological information seems to be a promising approach to evaluate their effects on human users.

Acknowledgements

We would like to express our cordial thanks to Arturo Nakasone for fruitful discussion and for implementing the emotion recognition module, and Avinash

Lavania for helping with the bio-signal analysis. Christian Becker is supported by a JSPS Pre-Doctoral Fellowship. This research was supported by the Research Grant (FY1999–FY2003) for the Future Program of the Japan Society for the Promotion of Science (JSPS), by a JSPS Encouragement of Young Scientists Grant (FY2005–FY2007), and an NII Joint Research Grant (FY2005).

References

1. J. L. Andreassi. Psychophysiology. Human Behavior & Physiological Response. Lawrence Erlbaum Associates, Mahwah, NJ, 4th edition, 2000.
2. C. Becker, S. Kopp, and I. Wachsmuth. Simulating the emotion dynamics of a multimodal conversational agent. In Proceedings of the Tutorial and Research Workshop on Affective Dialogue Systems (ADS-04), LNAI 3068, pages 154-165, Berlin Hei- delberg, 2004. Springer.
3. C. Becker, H. Prendinger, M. Ishizuka, and I. Wachsmuth. Empathy for Max (Preliminary project report). In The 2005 International Conference on Active Media Technology (AMT-05), pages 541-545. IEEE, 2005.
4. S. Brave, C. Nass, and K. Hutchinson. Computers that care: Investigating the effects of orientation of emotion exhibited by an embodied computer agent. International Journal of Human-Computer Studies, 62(2):161-178, 2005.
5. J. Healey and R. Picard. Detecting stress during real-world driving tasks. IEEE Transactions on Intelligent Transportation Systems, 2005.
6. S. Kopp, B. Jung, N. Lessmann, and I. Wachsmuth. Max - a multimodal assistant in virtual reality construction. *KI Zeitschift (German Magazine of Artificial Intelligence), Special Issue on Embodied Conversational Agents*, 2003.
7. S. Kopp, P. Tepper, and J. Cassell. Towards integrated microplanning of language and iconic gesture for multimodal output. In Proceedings of the International Conference on Multimodal Interfaces (ICMI-04), 2004.
8. P. J. Lang. The emotion probe: Studies of motivation and attention. American Psychologist, 50(5):372-385, 1995.
9. M. E. Latoschik, P. Biermann, and I. Wachsmuth. Knowledge in the loop: Semantics representation for multimodal simulative environments. In Proceedings of the 5th International Symposium on Smart Graphics, 2005.
10. R. W. Levenson. Autonomic specificity and emotion. In R. J. Davidson, K. R. Scherer, and H. H. Goldsmith, editors, Handbook of Affective Sciences, pages 212-224. Oxford University Press, Oxford, 2003.
11. R. W. Picard. Affective Computing. The MIT Press, Cambridge, MA, 1997
12. H. Prendinger and M. Ishizuka, editors. Life-Like Characters. Tools, Affective Functions, and Applications. Cognitive Technologies. Springer Verlag, Berlin Heidelberg, 2004.
13. H. Prendinger and M. Ishizuka. The Empathic Companion: A character-based interface that addresses users' affective states. International Journal of Applied Artificial Intelligence, 19(3):267-285, 2005.
14. H. Prendinger, J. Mori, and M. Ishizuka. Using human physiology to evaluate subtle expressivity of a virtual quizmaster in a mathematical game. International Journal of Human-Computer Studies, 62(2):231-245, 2005.
15. Thought Technology Ltd., 2002. URL: `http://www.thoughttechnology.com`.

Lexical Resources and Semantic Similarity for Affective Evaluative Expressions Generation

Alessandro Valitutti, Carlo Strapparava, and Oliviero Stock

ITC-irst, Istituto per la Ricerca Scientifica e Tecnologica,
I-38050 Povo Trento, Italy
{alvalitu, strappa, stock}@itc.it

Abstract. This paper presents resources and functionalities for the selection of affective evaluative terms. An affective hierarchy as an extension of the WordNet-Affect lexical database was developed in the first place. The second phase was the development of a semantic similarity function, acquired automatically in an unsupervised way from a large corpus of texts that allows us to put into relation concepts and emotional categories. The integration of the two components is a key element for several applications.

1 Introduction

Affective states have a direction. Generally we feel an emotion toward something or someone. The verbal communication of emotions allows us to express and evoke not only the affective states, but also their evaluative characteristic. An affective utterance may communicate an affective evaluation towards some object, expressing the attitudes of the sender or inducing them in the recipient.

If we want to realize a system that automatically generates evaluative expressions related to some target, we have to provide a suitable knowledge of affective concepts and lexicon. On the other hand, we have to provide it with the ability to associate an input concept to the most appropriate affective category. An important issue to consider is that the system, to be effective, should deal with the full lexicon, without any restriction.

The main contributions of this work consist on (i) the development of an affective lexical resource based on an extension of WordNet, and on (ii) a selection function (named *affective weight*) based on a semantic similarity mechanism acquired automatically in an unsupervised way from a large corpus of texts (100 millions of words). Applied to a set of concepts that are semantically similar, this function selects subsets characterized by some given affective constraints (e.g. referring to a particular emotional category or valence).

As we will see, we are able to focus selectively on positive, negative or neutral types of emotions. For example, given "difficulty" as input term, the system suggests as related emotions: IDENTIFICATION, NEGATIVE-CONCERN, AMBIGUOUS-EXPECTATION, APATHY. Moreover, given an input word (e.g. "university") and the indication of an emotional valence (e.g. positive), the system suggests a set of related words through some positive emotional category (e.g. "professor"

J. Tao, T. Tan, and R.W. Picard (Eds.): ACII 2005, LNCS 3784, pp. 474–481, 2005.

"scholarship" "achievement" found through the emotions ENTHUSIASM, SYMPATHY, DEVOTION, ENCOURAGEMENT.

These fine-grained kinds of affective lexicon selection can open up new possibilities in many applications that exploit verbal communication of emotions.

2 Resources and Tools

This section gives some details about the main resources and tools to deal with affective terms selection: the affective lexicon (an extension of WordNet-Affect) and the affective semantic similarity based on the Latent Semantic Analysis.

2.1 Affective Lexical Resources

The first attempts to build a lexical structure for affective terms concerned studying which terms are really representing emotions, and what classification criteria to consider. In particular, lexical semantic approaches are grounded on the belief that "it is possible to infer emotion properties from the emotion words" [1,2]. In our approach to the affective lexicon, the center of interest is not to study the nature of emotions, but how the affective meanings are expressed in natural language. In fact to generate affective sentences, it it necessary to have an affective lexicon organized into categories representing the affective states that people generally refer to in the linguistic use.

We enriched and restructured WordNet-Affect, an extension of WordNet lexical database [3] that we developed in a previous work [4].

WordNet-Affect. For the development of WordNet-Affect, we considered as a starting point WordNet Domains [5], a multilingual extension of WordNet, developed at ITC-irst. In WordNet Domains each synset has been annotated with at least one *domain label* (e.g. Sport, Politics, Medicine), selected from a set of about two hundred labels hierarchically organized. A domain may include synsets of different syntactic categories: for instance the domain Medicine groups together senses from Nouns, such as `doctor#1` (i.e. the first sense of the word doctor) and `hospital#1`, and from Verbs such as `operate#7`.

For WordNet-Affect, our goal was to have an additional hierarchy of "affective domain labels", independent from the domain hierarchy, with which the synsets representing affective concepts are annotated. Starting from WordNet we selected a subset of synsets suitable to represent affective concepts. Similarly to our method for domain labels, we assigned to a number of WordNet synsets one or more affective labels (*a-labels*) that contribute to precise the affective meaning. For example, the affective concepts representing emotional states are individuated by synsets marked with the a-label EMOTION, according to [6]. Other a-labels are present for concepts representing moods, situations eliciting emotions, or emotional responses (see Table 1 for a complete list of a-labels). WordNet-Affect is freely available for research purpose at `http://wndomains.itc.it`. See [4] for a complete description of the resource.

Table 1. A-Labels in WordNet-Affect and some corresponding synsets

A-Labels	Examples
EMOTION	noun `anger#1`, verb `fear#1`
MOOD	noun `animosisy#1`, adjective `amiable#1`
TRAIT	noun `aggressiveness#1`, adjective `competitive#1`
COGNITIVE STATE	noun `confusion#2`, adjective `dazed#2`
PHYSICAL STATE	noun `illness#1`, adjective `all_in#1`
EDONIC SIGNAL	noun `hurt#3`, noun `suffering#4`
EMOTION-ELICITING SITUATION	noun `awkwardness#3`, adjective `out_of_danger#1`
EMOTIONAL RESPONSE	noun `cold_sweat#1`, verb `tremble#2`
BEHAVIOUR	noun `offense#1`, adjective `inhibited#1`
ATTITUDE	noun `intolerance#1`, noun `defensive#1`
SENSATION	noun `coldness#1`, verb `feel#3`

Table 2. Number of elements of the emotional hierarchy

	# Synsets	*# Words*	*# Senses*
Nouns	280	539	564
Adjectives	342	601	951
Verbs	142	294	430
Adverbs	154	203	270
Total	918	1637	2215

Emotional Hierarchy. Recently, we provided WordNet-Affect with a set of additional a-labels, hierarchically organized, in order to specialize synsets with a-label EMOTION.

Starting from the set of synset tagged with a-label EMOTION, we considered only hyponyms of the noun synset `feeling#1`. For each of these, we defined a new a-label corresponding to the first synonym of the considered synset and representing an emotional category. Thus we obtained a hierarchy modeled on the WordNet *isa* relation. Each new label was put at the end of a sequence of a-labels, representing the position of the considered category in the hierarchy, and named *affective path* or *a-path*. Table 5 shows some synsets with the corresponding synonym-list and the a-path.

Stative/Causative Tagging. An important aspect of the affective lexicon, concerning mainly adjectival interpretation is the stative/causative dimension [7]. An emotional adjective is said *causative* if it refers to some emotion that is caused by the entity represented by the modified noun (e.g. 'amusing movie'). In a similar way, an emotional adjective is said *stative* if it refers to the emotion owned or felt by the subject denoted by the modified noun (e.g. 'cheerful/happy boy').

We are interested to the stative/causative distinction because it is connected to the subjective/objective quality of the affective evaluative utterances. As claimed by [8], the rhetorical effect of an evaluative predicate is different whether the evaluation is expressed as subjective or objective. Actually, stative terms are

Table 3. Two emotional categories with some related stative and causative terms

emotional category	*stative terms*	*causative terms*
DISGUST	disgusted	disgusting disgust disgustingly
ENCOURAGEMENT	encouraged bucked_up	encouraging encourage encouragingly

Table 4. Stative and causative tagging

	# Stative Synsets	*# Causative Synsets*
Adjectives	237	105
Verbs	68	74
Adverbs	112	42
Total	417	221

generally used in subjective utterances, in which there is an explicit expression of the emotional state of the subject. Causative terms, instead, are normally included in objective utterances and presented as an objective, observer-free property of the target, with a considerably stronger rhetorical effect. Following the approach of [9] and [7] on emotional adjectives, we marked with the STATIVE or the CAUSATIVE label all the synsets of the emotional hierarchy with Part of Speech *adjective*. Therefore, assumed an analogue distinction for verbs and adverbs, we extended this tagging to the *verb* and *adverb* synsets. See Table 3 for some examples.

Valence Tagging. As explained above, the hierarchical structure of new a-labels was modeled on the WordNet hyperonym relation. In a second stage, we introduced some modifications, in order to distinguish synsets according to emotional valence. For example, the synset `fear#1` includes hyperonym `horror#1` (with negative valence), but also `frisson#1` (with positive valence).

We defined four addictional a-labels: POSITIVE, NEGATIVE, AMBIGUOUS, NEUTRAL. The first one corresponds to "positive emotions", defined as emotional states characterized by the presence of positive edonic signals (or pleasure). It includes synsets such as `joy#1` or `enthusiasm#1`. Similarly the NEGATIVE a-label identifies "negative emotions" characterized by negative edonic signals (or pain), for example `anger#1` or `sadness#1`. Synsets representing affective states whose valence depends on semantic context (e.g. `surprise#1`) were marked with the tag AMBIGUOUS. Finally, synsets referring to mental states that are generally considered affective but are not characterized by valence, were marked with the tag NEUTRAL.

Table 5. Concepts and affective categories

Synset	*A-Path*
joy, joyousness, joyfulness	EMOTION → POSITIVE → GENERAL-JOY → JOY
scare, panic_attack	EMOTION → NEGATIVE → NEGATIVE-FEAR → SCARE
surprise	EMOTION → AMBIGUOUS → SURPRISE
indifference	EMOTION → NEUTRAL → NEUTRAL-UNCONCERN → INDIFFERENCE

Having classified synsets according to valence, it was necessary to add a further number of a-labels, in order to distinguish hyponyms of the same synset but different valence. For example, we defined a-label NEGATIVE-FEAR, including `fear#1`, and POSITIVE-FEAR, including `frisson#1`.

2.2 Affective Semantic Similarity

A crucial issue is to have a mechanism for evaluating the similarity among generic terms and affective lexical concepts. To this aim we estimated term similarity from a large scale corpus, exploiting the assumption that semantic domains are sets of very closely related terms. In particular we implemented a variation of Latent Semantic Analysis (LSA) in order to obtain a vector representation for words, texts and synsets.

In LSA [10], term co-occurrences in the documents of the corpus are captured by means of a dimensionality reduction operated by a Singular Value Decomposition (SVD) on the term-by-document matrix. For the experiments reported in this paper, we run the SVD operation on the British National Corpus[1].

The resulting LSA vectors can be exploited to estimate both term and document similarity. Regarding document similarity, Latent Semantic Indexing (LSI) is a technique that allows us to represent a document by means of a LSA vector. In particular, we used a variation of the *pseudo-document* methodology described in [12]. This variation takes into account also a *tf-idf* weighting schema (see [13] for more details). Each document can be represented in the LSA space by summing up the normalized LSA vectors of all the terms contained in it. Also a synset in WORDNET (and then an emotional category) can be represent in the LSA space, perfoming the pseudo-document technique on all the words contained in the synset. Thus it is possible to have an affective synset representation in the LSA space. In this way, we can compute a similarity measure among terms and affective synsets. For example, the term "sex" shows high similarity with respect to the positive emotional category AMOROUSNESS, with the negative category MISOGYNY, and with the ambiguous valence tagged category AMBIGUOUS_EXPECTATION. The noun "gift" is highly related to the emotional categories: LOVE (with positive valence), COMPASSION (with negative valence), SURPRISE (with ambiguous valence), and INDIFFERENCE (with neutral valence).

3 Algorithm and Examples

WORDNET-AFFECT emotional hierarchy and the affective similarity are the basis for the automated and selective generation of affective evaluative lexicon. In this section, we describe the algorithm developed to realize that generation.

The first step of the procedure consists of the insertion and the internal representation of the input-target. This is represented as a WORDNET synset, and it is individuated through a word (the *input-term*), the part of speech (noun, adjective, verb, or adverb), and the sense number. Using the pseudo-document

[1] The British National Corpus is a very large (over 100 million words) corpus of modern English, both spoken and written [11].

representation technique described in section 2.2, this synonym set is represented as a vector (named *input-vector*) in the LSA vectorial space.

In a second step the algorithm uses LSA in order to generate a list of terms that are semantically similar to the input-term. We limit the length of this list to 400 terms. In a similar way, a set of *emotional vectors* is created from the corresponding set of emotional categories.

Thus, the vectorial representation in the Latent Semantic Space allows us to represent in a *uniform* way emotional categories, terms, concepts and possibly full documents. An appropriate metric (e.g. cosine, dot product, ...) allows us to have a semantic similarity measure among all these objects.

Thus we defined the *affective weight* as the similarity value between an emotional vector and an input term vector.

The affective weight function can be used in order to select the emotional categories that can best express or evoke valenced emotional states with respect to input term. Moreover, it allows us to individuate a set of terms that are semantically similar to the input term and that share with it the same affective constraints (e.g. emotional categories with the same value of valence).

For example, given the noun *university* as input-term, it is possible to ask the system for related terms that have a positive affective valence, possibly focussing only to some specific emotional categories (e.g. SYMPATHY). On the other hand given two terms, it is possible to check whether they are semantically related, and with respect to which emotional category. Table 6 shows a portion of affective lexicon related to "university" with some emotional categories grouped by valence.

Table 6. Some terms related to "university" through some emotional categories

Related Emotional Term	*Positive Emotional Category*	*Emotional Weight*
university	enthusiasm	0.36
professor	sympathy	0.56
scholarship	devotion	0.72
achievement	encouragement	0.76
	Negative Emotional Category	
university	downheartedness	0.33
professor	antipathy	0.46
study	isolation	0.49
scholarship	melancholy	0.53
	Ambiguous Emotional Category	
university	ambiguous-hope	0.25
career	earnestness	0.59
rector	reverence	0.57
scholar	reverence	0.67
	Neutral Emotional Category	
university	withdrawal	0.12
faculty	apathy	0.13
admission	withdrawal	0.31
academic	distance	0.35

4 Possible Applications

Computer Assisted Creativity. WordNet-Affect and the affective-weight function can be useful for computer assisted creativity. The automated generation of evaluative expressions with a bias on some valence orientation are a key component for automatic personalized advertisement, computational humor [14] and persuasive communication.

Verbal Expressivity of Embodied Conversational Agents. Emotions expression by synthetic characters is considered now a key element for their believability. Intelligent dynamic words selection is crucial for realizing appropriate and expressive conversations.

Sentiment Analysis. The emotional weight function can be employed in text analysis as a sentiment analysis technique [15] (e.g. text categorization according to affective relevance, opinion exploration for market analysis, etc.)

5 Conclusions

In this paper, we presented some resources and functionalities for the selection of affective evaluative terms. We developed an affective hierarchy as an extension of the WordNet-Affect lexical database. This includes an indication of valence and stative/causative tagging of the synsets. In addition, we implemented a functionality based on a semantic similarity mechanism automatically acquired in an unsupervised way from a large corpus, providing relations among concepts and emotional categories. Exploiting this mechanism, it selects for a set of LSA-similar terms those elements found through a particular emotional category or valence. This way of organizing and using the affective lexicon is useful for the generation of explicit evaluative expressions. In fact, careful selection of affective words plays a crucial role in communication. For example, stative affective words are preferred in evaluative utterances. Causative affective words, instead, are preferred for example in persuasive communication.

Exploitation of these techniques will be at the basis of various possible applications such as automatic advertisement, improvements of expressiveness of embodied conversational agents, sentiment analysis.

References

1. Ortony, A., Clore, G.L.: Disentangling the affective lexicon. In: Proceedings of the Third Annual Conference of the Cognitive Science Society, Berkeley (1981)
2. Fiehler, R.: How to do emotions with words. In Fussell, S., ed.: The Verbal Communication of Emotion. Lawrence Erlbaum (2002) 79–106
3. Fellbaum, C.: WordNet. An Electronic Lexical Database. The MIT Press (1998)
4. Strapparava, C., Valitutti, A.: WordNet-Affect: an affective extension of WordNet. In: Proceedings of LREC 2004, Lisbon (2004) 1083 – 1086
5. Magnini, B., Cavaglià, G.: Integrating subject field codes into wordnet. In: Proceedings of LREC-2000, the Second International Conference on Language Resources and Evaluation, Athens, Greece (2000) 1413–1418

6. Ortony, A., Clore, G.L., Foss, M.A.: The psychological foundations of the affective lexicon. Journal of Personality and Social Psychology **53** (1987) 751–766.
7. Goy, A.: Lexical semantics of emotional adjectives. In Feist, S., Fix, S., Hay, J., Moore, J., eds.: : Proceedings of Student Conference in Linguistics. MIT Working Papers in Linguistics 37. MIT Press (2000)
8. Jackendoff, R.: Language, Culture, Consciousness: Essays on Mental Structure. Chapter 7: Experiencer Predicates and Theory of Mind. in press (2005)
9. Bouillon, P.: Mental states adjectives: the perspective of generative lexicon. In: Proceedings of COLING-96, Copenhagen (1996)
10. Deerwester, S., Dumais, S.T., Furnas, G.W., Landauer, T., Harshman, R.: Indexing by latent semantic analysis. Journal of the American Society for Information Science **41** (1990) 391–407
11. BNC-Consortium: British national corpus `www.hcu.ox.ac.uk/bnc`. (2000)
12. Berry, M.: Large-scale sparse singular value computations. International Journal of Supercomputer Applications **6** (1992) 13–49
13. Gliozzo, A., Strapparava, C.: Domain kernels for text categorizations. In: Proceedings of 9th Conference on Computational Natural Language Learning (CONLL05), Ann Arbor (2005)
14. Stock, O., Strapparava, C.: Getting serious about the development of computational humour. In: Proceedings of the 8th International Joint Conference on Artificial Intelligence (IJCAI-03), Acapulco, Mexico (2003)
15. Turney, P., Littman, M.: Measuring praise and criticism: Inference of semantic orientation from association. ACM Transactions on Information Systems (TOIS) **21** (2003) 315–346

Because Attitudes Are Social Affects, They Can Be False Friends…

Takaaki Shochi, Véronique Aubergé, and Albert Rilliard

Institut de la Communication Parlée, UMR CNRS 5009, Grenoble, France
{Takaaki.Shochi, Veronique.Auberge, Albert.Rilliard}@icp.inpg.fr
http://www.icp.inpg.fr

Abstract. The attitudes of the speaker during a verbal interaction are affects built by language and culture. Since they are a sophisticated material for expressing complex affects, using a channel of control that is surely not confused with emotions, they are the larger part of the affects expressed during an interaction, as it could be shown on large databases by Campbell [3]. strong Twelve representative attitudes of Japanese are given to be listened both by Japanese native speaker and French native speaker naive in Japanese. They include "*doubt-incredulity*", "*evidence*", "*exclamation of surprise*", "*authority*", "*irritation*", "*admiration*", "*declaration*", "*interrogation*", and four socially referenced degrees of politeness: "*simple politeness*", "*sincerity-politeness*", "*kyoshuku*" and "*arrogance-impoliteness*" (Sadanobu [11]). Two perception experiments using a closed forced choice were carried out, each attitude *being* introduced by a definition and some examples of real situations. The 15 native Japanese subjects discriminate all the attitudes over chance, with some little confusion inside the politeness class. French subjects do not process the concept of degree of politeness: they do not identify the typical Japanese politeness degrees. The prosody of "*kyoshuku*", highest degree of politeness in Japanese, is misunderstood by French on contrary meaning as "impoliteness", "authority" and "irritation".

1 Introduction

The affects in speech are expressed following different cognitive processing levels, from involuntary controlled expressions to the intentionally control of attitudes and the meta-linguistic control of expressivity. Attitudes are sometimes assimilated with emotions since both use to be expressed the direct acoustic channel. But emotion expressions are carried by voice in parallel to speech (often called extra-linguistic controlled, we prefer para-linguistic control), only constrained but not controlled but the language building. The attitudes expressions are part of the language interaction building (not para but intra lingustic building), even if some concepts (like authority, doubt) and prosodic implementations can be supposed as quite universal, but not innate. Since they are a sophisticated material for expressing complex affects, they are the larger part of the affects expressed during an interaction, as it could be shown on large databases by Campbell [3].

Attitudes expressed by the speaking agent, human or machine, are essential communicative values because they carry the speaker's intentions and points of view

J. Tao, T. Tan, and R.W. Picard (Eds.): ACII 2005, LNCS 3784, pp. 482–489, 2005.

(surprise, confirmation, politeness etc.), that are not deduced from the phonetic/syntactic string. Because attitudes are constructed socially for and by the language, they can exist or not from one language to the other, and prosodic realization of one specific attitude in a specific language may not be recognized or may be ambiguous in the learner's language.

A human who would not use this attitudinal dimension (that is would generate only declaration and question modalities) would be interpreted as having special intentions and even could be considered as a pathological speaker. Not to give to an expressive clone such kind of prosodic dimensions is to substrate one essential information channel to the human-machine interaction, moreover that can be very specific to one language, and from which must be evaluated (and predicted and minimized by the clone) the misunderstanding from a non-native listener. The perceptive measurements are essential in order to give to the expressive clone this dimension of expression, both at the dialog conception level (knowing with panel of attitudes can/must be controlled by the clone) and at the speech synthesis level.

We built a Japanese corpus according to the method previously developed for French and English (Aubergé et al.[1], Morlec et al. [9] and Diaferia [4]). In these studies have been perceptually evaluated, and acoustically modeled by global prosodic contours, 6 French attitudes and 11 English attitudes for native listeners.

In addition to these two European languages, Japanese was also a target of research to reveal cultural specificities or cross cultural common attitudes and prosodic implementations of these attitudes.

After verifying that native listeners recognize their language attitudes, it has been perceptually measured how do non-native speakers recognize cross-language attitudes. Concerning attitudes concepts shared by the native and non-native language, they may be performed prosodically different or similar. Listeners from each language can recognize or confuse such attitudes in one other language. Therefore, the objective of the first step of cross cultural research treating two target languages (e.g. French and Japanese) is to reveal the two following points: can specific attitudes connected to Japanese culture be perceived only by Japanese listeners or by both Japanese and French listeners? Another aim is to check if common attitudes in Japanese and French are perceived differently or recognized like similar attitudes.

2 Selection of 12 Japanese Attitudes

We have selected a representative group of 12 attitudes for Japanese: *"doubt-incredulity"* [DO], *"evidence"*[EV], *"exclamation of surprise"*[EX], *"authority"*[AU], *"irritation"*[IR], *"arrogance-impoliteness"*[AR], *"sincerity-politeness"*[SIN], *"admiration"*[AD], *"kyoshuku"*[KYO], *"simple-politeness"*[PO], *"declaration"*[DC] and *"interrogation"*[QS]. In this set of attitudes, there is four cultural specific attitudes linked to Japanese politeness strategy; *"simple politeness"*, *"arrogance-impoliteness"*, *"sincerity-politeness"* and *"kyoshuku"*. The attitude of *"sincerity-politeness"* appears when speaker is inferior facing to his interlocutor who is superior in Japanese society. The speaker expresses by this prosodic attitude that his intention is serious and sincere. And attitude of *"kyoshuku"* is also a typical Japanese cultural attitude. It appears when the speaker wants to express this contradictory opinion on a situation in which his social states is inferior to his interlocutor, or when the speaker is willing to get a favour from his superior. In this context, the speaker has to show an attitude which is "*a mixture of suffering ashamedness and embarrassment, comes from the speaker's consciousness of the fact that his/her utterance of request imposes a burden to the hearer*" (Sadanobu [11] p. 34).

3 The Corpus

First step is the recording of a very controlled corpus, constructed according to theoretical principles. The construction of opposed minimal pairs allows observing the effect of the targeted factor only. On the basis of such controlled corpora, an acoustic analysis leads to a statistical model of prosodic variations, which can be used in order to synthesize the captured prosodic variations by analysis-resynthesis methods.

In order to validate this work, a compared analysis of the competences of natural prosody contained in the corpus vs. the performances of the synthetic prosody extracted by analysis will be realized in order to define a description of the observed prosody.

The corpus is based on seven sentences ranging from one to eight moras. The syntactic structure of the sentences used in the corpus is either a single word, or a simple verbal object structure. For the eight-moras utterances, the position of lexical accent may be on the first, second, and third mora or absent. In order to express some attitudes like "doubt" or "surprise", the vowel [u] may be inserted at phrase final position, and lexical accent will be realized at the seventh mora too. The sentences were constructed in order to have no particular connotations in any region of Japan. Each sentence is produced with all the attitudinal functions.

One male Japanese native language teacher produced recorded all the attitudes for this corpus. We already mentioned that the attitudes are socially constructed for each language. Therefore foreign language learners have to learn prosodic attitudes corresponding to the target language and culture, and languages teachers are able to elicit different types of attitudes for didactic/pragmatic reasons.

The complete corpus contains 84 stimuli, i.e. seven utterances produced with twelve different attitudes. All stimuli are used for the perception test.

Table 1. Corpus of Japanese attitudes: 7 utterances of different length with different position of the lexical accent, which is marked with a star, each produced with the 12 different attitudes

Number of mora	Utterance	Translation
1	Me	The eye
2	**Na***ra	Nara
5 (3+2)	**Na***rade neru	He sleeps in Nara
8 (4+4)	**Na***goyade nomimas	He drinks in Nagoya
8 (4+4)	Na**ra***shide nomimas	He drinks in Nara Town
8 (4+4)	Matsu**ri***de nomimas	He drinks at the party
8 (4+4)	Naniwade nomimas	He drinks at Naniwa

4 Perception Experiments

In this study, Japanese native listeners perceptively validate the prosodic attitudes of Japanese on the one hand, and French listeners also test these Japanese attitudes, which belong to a distant culture comparing to the French one.

4.1 Listeners

30 listeners participated in this experiment: 15 Japanese listeners (11 females and 4 males) who speak the Tokyo dialect, and 15 French listeners (10 females and 5 males) who have never heard the Japanese language. The mean age is 29.5 for Japanese listeners, and 25.4 for French listeners. Listeners don't report to suffer of any listening disorder.

4.2 Experimental Protocol

Subject listens to each stimulus one time only. For each stimulus, they were asked to answer the perceived attitude amongst the twelve possible attitudes. The presentation order of the stimuli was randomized in a different order for each subject.

Two types of perceptual test's interface (e.g. the French and the Japanese versions) were used, on which short instructions are presented. The choice of the twelve attitudes, with their definitions is indicated.

5 Results

5.1 Validation with Japanese Listeners

According to a chi-square test, all attitudes were above the chance level. Then, we tested a possible effect of the stimuli length for the distributions of selected attitudes. The results show a significant difference of the length between two and five-moras sentences and also between the five and eight-moras one. But, there is no effect of the lexical accent.

In order to determine which attitude listeners recognized over chance, a criterion was used: the mean identification rate must be over twice the theoretical chance level.

According to this criterion, seven attitudes (i.e. "*arrogance-impoliteness*", "*declaration*", "*doubt-incredulity*", "*simple-politeness*", "*exclamation of surprise*", "*irritation*" and "*interrogation*") have been recognized without any particular confusion.

"*Authority*" was confused with "*evidence*". One possible explanation is that, concerning the self-confidence of speaker, these two attitudes are, in fact, similar: when imposing authority, the speaker is certainly sure of himself.

"*Evidence*" was confused with "*arrogance-impoliteness*". "*Evidence*" shows that speaker is confident of himself, and this expression of certainty can sometimes be perceived like disrespect to interlocutor.

Curiously, two typical Japanese attitudes like "*sincerity-politeness*" and "*kyoshuku*" were confused with each other. These two attitudes express essentially the humility of a speaker facing a superior person in the social hierarchy. It is important to note that "*sincerity-politeness*" was also confused with "*simple-politeness*", whereas this confusion with "*simple-politeness*" was absent for "*kyoshuku*".

Concerning the attitude of "*admiration*", we observed confusion with "*simple-politeness*". These two attitudes are interconnected each other in the Japanese society. This evidence can be explained by the lexical polysemy of items like "*sonkee*" [admiration / politeness], and "*keifuku*" [admiration / politeness]

Table 2. Confusion matrix in percentages for 15 Japanese listeners: [solid box] well recognized, [hatched] recognized well with confusion, [shaded]: significant recognition, but confused with other attitudes, [dotted box]: significant confusion (over 16.6%).

Japanese	Percentage – Presented attitudes											
Recognized attitudes	AD	AR	AU	DC	DO	EV	EX	IR	KYO	PO	QS	SIN
AD	21.9%	0.0%	0.0%	0.0%	1.9%	0.0%	1.0%	0.0%	1.9%	4.8%	0.0%	3.8%
AR	1.9%	72.4%	5.7%	10.5%	5.7%	21.0%	0.0%	2.9%	1.9%	0.0%	1.0%	0.0%
AU	0.0%	9.5%	51.4%	2.9%	1.0%	9.5%	1.0%	11.4%	15.2%	0.0%	1.9%	1.0%
DC	4.8%	5.7%	10.5%	65.7%	0.0%	12.4%	0.0%	0.0%	2.9%	8.6%	1.9%	9.5%
DO	0.0%	0.0%	0.0%	0.0%	56.2%	0.0%	14.3%	0.0%	0.0%	1.0%	3.8%	0.0%
EV	8.6%	5.7%	17.1%	7.6%	0.0%	45.7%	5.7%	0.0%	10.5%	1.9%	1.0%	3.8%
EX	9.5%	0.0%	0.0%	0.0%	14.3%	4.8%	59.0%	0.0%	1.0%	1.9%	1.0%	1.9%
IR	1.0%	5.7%	4.8%	1.0%	13.3%	2.9%	4.8%	85.7%	12.4%	0.0%	1.0%	1.0%
KYO	11.4%	0.0%	0.0%	0.0%	0.0%	0.0%	0.0%	0.0%	24.8%	9.5%	1.0%	27.6%
PO	26.7%	1.0%	4.8%	11.4%	0.0%	1.0%	0.0%	0.0%	2.9%	64.8%	8.6%	17.1%
QS	0.0%	0.0%	0.0%	0.0%	7.6%	2.9%	14.3%	0.0%	0.0%	1.0%	77.1%	1.9%
SIN	14.3%	0.0%	5.7%	1.0%	0.0%	0.0%	0.0%	0.0%	26.7%	6.7%	1.9%	32.4%

5.2 Behavior of French Listeners

The distribution of all attitudes was above of chance. A significant effect of the length was identified between the one and two-moras sentences. It was not possible to identify any significant effect of the lexical accent for French subjects.

By using the same criterion that for the Japanese listeners, the following results were extracted:

Figure 1. shows that "*authority*", "*irritation*" and "*admiration*" have been perceived with no significant confusion according to our criteria. But, attitude of "*arrogance-impoliteness*" showed week identification score by French listeners. This attitude was confused with "*declaration*" and "*authority*".

French listeners did not recognized two particular attitudes of politeness connected in Japanese society like "*sincerity-politeness*" and "*kyoshuku*".

Moreover, "*Sincerity-politeness*" was confused with "*simple-politeness*" and "*kyoshuku*" which are others expressions of politeness.

On the contrary, attitude of "*kyoshuku*" was recognized like "*irritation*", "*arrogance-impoliteness*" and "*authority*". This result was expected, since these attitudes do not exist at all in the French society, nor such voice quality does not match any politeness expression in French.

French listeners confused also "*interrogation*" with "*declaration*". This result shows a possibility for French people to perceive Japanese Yes-No question like simple declaration.

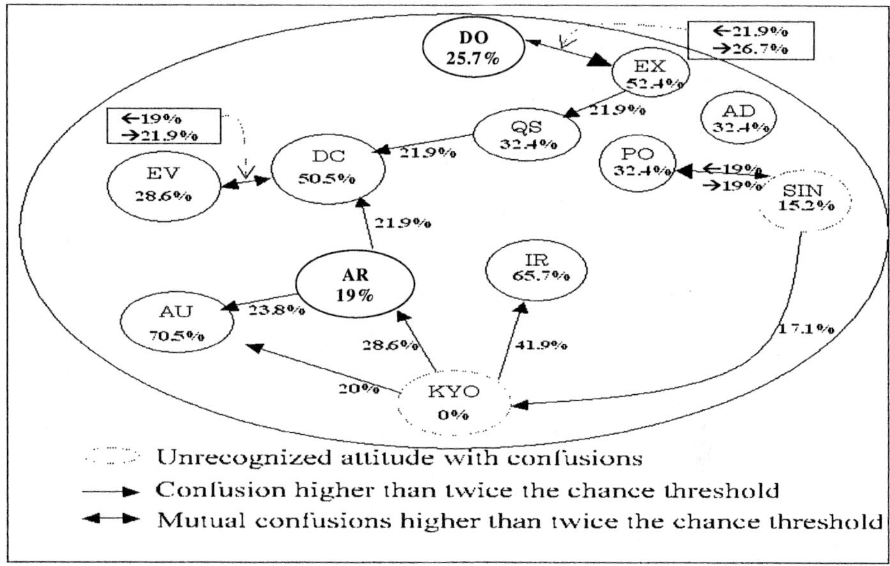

Fig. 1. Confusion graph: percentages inside the frame indicate the confusion rate in percentages. Other percentages written under the labels of each attitude represent the identification rates of attitude in percentages.

They show significant reciprocal confusions between "*declaration*" and "*evidence*", between "*doubt-incredulity*" and "*exclamation of surprise*", and between "*simple-politeness*" and "*sincerity-politeness*".

6 Conclusion

After two perception tests carried out on this Japanese corpus, it can concluded that at first, the distribution of attitudes is above chance for all attitudes, both for Japanese and French listeners. The Japanese listeners validate prosodic expressions and attitudes concepts. A length effect can be observed between one and two-moras sentences for French listeners, and between two and five-moras, and also five and eight-moras sentences for Japanese listeners. The effect of lexical accent was not observed for both groups of listeners. The Japanese subjects showed confusions of three politeness levels inside the politeness class. "*Sincerity-politeness*" and "*kyoshuku*" are confused each other. "*Sincerity-politeness*" is also confused over chance with "*simple politeness*" which is well identified. The "*evidence*" attitude is confused over chance with "*arrogance-impoliteness*" (and "*authority*" with "*evidence*") for Japanese listeners. On the contrary, the concept of degree of politeness is not processed by French subjects: they recognize the "simple-politeness" (as well as "admiration", "authority and "irritation"), but they do not identify the typical Japanese politeness degrees "*kyoshuku"* and "sincerity-politeness". "Sincerity-politeness" is confused with "simple politeness" and "*kyoshuku",* then "simple politeness" is confused with "sincerity-politeness". This weak recognition might come from the absence of this concept in French society on one hand, and this particular voice quality which express this Japanese politeness manifest a completely different signification (or intention) for French native speakers on the other hand. It is to be noted that *"kyoshuku"* is misunderstood with "arrogance-impoliteness", and also with "authority" and "irritation". This is typically a "false friend". After this result, an acoustic analysis of the corpus should reveal the prosodic characteristics of each attitude. It is important to test confusions due to cross-cultural differences with the stimuli composed of French sentences and superposed Japanese prosodic attitudes.

To reveal common attitudes and cultural specific attitudes, it is very interesting to carry out perception tests between Japanese and English, and also between Japanese and Chinese or Korean, which are cultures closer from the Japanese one. Moreover, it is also important to implement a perception test for these two groups of listeners using a gating paradigm to envisage if listeners can predict attitudinal values early in the utterance, in the same way that the results shown by Aubergé et al. [1].

Acknowledgment

This work was held as a part of the Crest-JST "Expressive Speech Processing" Project, directed by Nick Campbell, ATR, Japan. We especially thank T. Sadanobu, from Kobe University, for his help in studying Japanese attitudes.

References

1. Aubergé, V., Grépillat, T., Rilliard, A.: Can we perceive attitudes before the end of sentences ? The gating paradigm for prosodic contours. In 5th European Conference On Speech Communication And Technology, Vol.2, Greece (1997) 871-874
2. Ayuzawa, T.: Nihongo no gimonbun no inritsuteki tokucyou. In Nihongo no inritsu ni mirareru bogo no kansyou(2), Grand-in-aid for Scientific research on Priority areas (D1), research report 1992 (1992) 1-20
3. Campbell, N.: Modelling Affect in Speech Communication, Beiing (2003).
4. Diaferia, M.L.: Les Attitudes de l'Anglais : Premiers Indices Prosodiques. Mémoire de DEA en Science Cognitives, Institut National Polytechnique de Grenoble France (2002)
5. Erickson, D., Ohashi, S., Makita, S., Kajimoto, N., Mokhtari, P.: Perception of naturally-spoken expressive speech by American English and Japanese listeners. In CREST International Workshop on Expressive Speech Processing (2003) 31-36
6. Ito, M.: The Contribution of Voice Quality to Politeness in Japanese. In VOQUAL'03, Geneva (2003) 157-162
7. Ko, M.: Teinei hyougen ni mirareru nihongo onsei no inritsuteki tokucyou. In the Phonetic Society of Japan 1993 Annual Convention (1993) 35-40
8. Matsumoto, E., Sadanobu, T.: Nihongo no inritsu niokeru rikimi to, nihongo gakushuusha no rikaido. In: Departement of Japanese Studies, The Chinese University of Hong Kong and Society of Japanese Language Education (eds.): Quality Japanese Studies and Japanese Language Education in Kanji-Using Areas in the New Century, Hong Kong Himawari Publishing Co. (2001) 455-461

9. Morlec, Y., G. Bailly, and V. Aubergé *Generating prosodic attitudes in French: data, model and evaluation.* Speech Communication, (2001) 33(4): p. 357--371.
10. Ofuka, E., McKeown, J.D., Waterman, M.G. , Roach, P.J.: Prosodic cue for rated politeness in Japanese speech. In Speech Communication, 32 (2000) 199-217
11. Sadanobu, T.: A natural history of Japanese pressed voice. In Journal of the Phonetic Society of Japan, Vol.8. No.1 (2004) 29-44
12. Van Bezooijen, R.: Sociocultural aspects of pitch differences between Japanese and Dutch women. In Language and Speech 38, 3 (1995) 253-266

Emotion Semantics Image Retrieval: An Brief Overview

Shangfei Wang and Xufa Wang

University of Science and Technology of China, Hefei, Anhui, 230027, P.R. China
sfwang@ustc.edu.cn

Abstract. Emotion is the most abstract semantic structure of images. This paper overviews recent research on emotion semantics image retrieval. First, the paper introduces the general frame of emotion semantics image retrieval and points out the four main research issues: to exact sensitive features from images, to define users' emotion information, to build emotion user model and to individualize the user model. Then several algorithms to solve these four issues are analyzed in detail. After that, some future research topics, including construction of an emotion database, evaluation of the user model and computation of the user model, are discussed, and some resolved strategies are presented elementarily.

1 Introduction

Current computer vision techniques allow for the automatic extraction of low-level features from images, such as color, texture, shape and spatial location of image elements, but it is difficult to extract high level features automatically, such as names of objects, scenes, behaviors and emotions. This is the semantic gap [1] [2]. Bridging the semantic gap between the simple visual features and the abundant semantic request of users is the biggest chanllenge in the research of image retrieval. The semantic structure of images contains spatial relationship, object, event, behavior and emotion. Among those, emotion semantics is the most abstract and highest, which is usually described in adjective form. It closely relates to cognitive models, culture backgrounds and aesthetic standards of users. Because of the enrichment of information in images and the variety of human's subjective factors, there are many difficulties in emotion semantics image retrieval research.

This paper gives a survey on recent research trends on emotion semantics image retrieval. A general framework of emotion semantics image retrieval is presented first, and four main research issues are pointed out. After that, some algorithms to solve these four issues are analyzed in detail. Finally, three critical problems, including management of emotion database, evaluation of user model and interest drift of user, faced in emotion image retrieval are explained, and some resolved strategies are presented elementarily.

J. Tao, T. Tan, and R.W. Picard (Eds.): ACII 2005, LNCS 3784, pp. 490–497, 2005.

2 General Framework of Emotion Semantics Image Retrieval

Emotion semantics image retrieval has started to attract attention in the recent years. Several prototype systems also have been developed, such as ART MUSEUM [3], K-DIME [4],emotional information acquiring system [5]. Fig. 1 gives the general frame of emotion semantics image retrieval [6]. First, users put forward emotional retrieval demand, for example, to retrieve *beautiful* images. Then, acquisition subsystem obtains candidate images based on emotion user model and displays them to users. After that, users give their feedback to the system through the interactive user interface. The system records them and uses an appropriate learning mechanism to adjust user's emotion model dynamically in order to realize individual emotion semantics image retrieval. From Fig. 1, it can be seen that emotion semantics image retrieval involves four aspects:

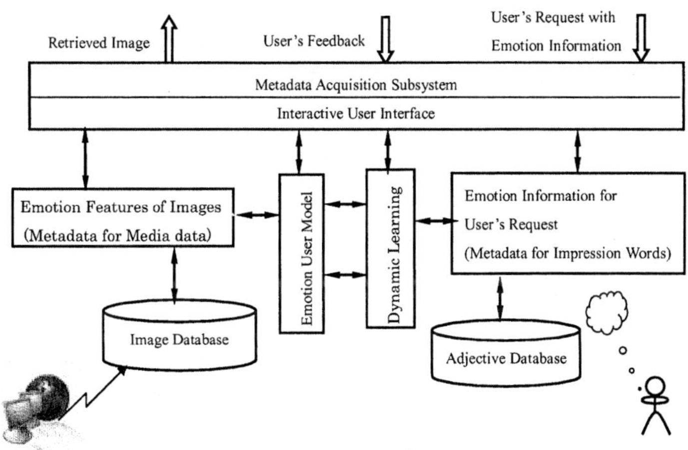

Fig. 1. General framework of emotion semantics image retrieval

- Extracting emotion features from images (metadata definition for media data). This refers to the extraction of sensitive features which can evoke users' emotional response easily;
- Defining emotion information for users' requests (metadata definition for impression words). This requires the analysise of adjectives or impression words that are often used by users to express their feelings;
- Building emotion user models, which requires the calculation of the semantic correlations of emotion features of images and users' emotion demands;
- Individualizing emotion user models, which means adapting emotion user model according to individual variation and improving accuracy of the retrieval results by dynamic learning mechanism.

3 Main Issues

3.1 Extracting Emotion Features from Images

Emotion features are the features that can stimulate users' emotional change easily. Current computer vision techniques allow for the automatic extraction of various low-level features from images. So, the key problem here is how to choose sensitive features so that the retrieval result can be close to human's psychological impression of images.

Now, there are two methods of extracting image's emotion features. One is domain-based, which extracts relevant features based on special knowledge of application field, especially in art images. For example, Arnheim discussed the relationships between artistic form and perceptive processes [7]. Itten [8] formulated a theory about the use of color or color combination in art and about the semantics it induces. He also pointed out the Itten sphere model. Line slope also contributes to the semantics of an image. An oblique slope communicates dynamism and action, while a flat slope, such as a horizon, communicate calmness and relaxation. These research results can be a guide when we choose features for images [5] [9].

The other method of extracting emotion features is to analyze which kinds of features have significant impact on users through psychology experiments. Mao analyzed the emotion characteristics of different images by semantic difference (SD) method[10]. She proved that the fractal dimensions (FDs) of images are related to the images' affective properties, and more FD makes people feel more messy. The FD of a monotonous image is the least, which is 2.37, the FD of messy images is the largest, at 2.91, and the FD of harmonious images is the medial, at 2.68. Shoji Tanaka [11] concluded that the contribution of color, spatial frequency, and size to attractiveness follows the order of color > size > spatial frequency, and the contribution of each features heterogeneity to attractiveness follows the order of color heterogeneity > size heterogeneity > shape heterogeneity > texture heterogeneity. Though experiment, Yuichi Kobayashi [12] also pointed out that psychological responses depended on the discrimination of material of a texture at first, and second.

3.2 Defining Emotion Information for Users' Requests

Usually, adjectives are used to express people's feelings and emotions, such as happy, beautiful etc. Defining users' emotion information means processing adjectives and constructing a psychological space in computers.

Now, there exist two approaches to construct a psychological space: implicit one and explicit one. Cho and Hagiwara used the first approach [13] [14], which uses users' subjective evaluation to define users' emotion and expression. By using the first approach, new adjectives can be added to system directly. However the deficiency here is redundancy since there is no analysis of adjectives.

The second approach is to retrieve databases by explicitly constructing the psychological space. One of these approaches is semantic differential(SD) method

[15]. The flow of the SD method [16] to construct the space is as follows: (1)collecting adjective pairs that express the impression of medias, (2)recording subjects' rating data to the given image on the scale for each adjective pair based on their impression, and (3) analyzing the ratings from (2) by factor analysis. After that, an orthogonal psychological space is constructed. Another method is to use impression word dictionary. Hideyuki Kobayashi has built such a dictionary including more than 800 adjectives [17]. Concept structure of the dictionary is the same as that of the WorldNet. Through semantic network, the dictionary gives not only the relationships between adjectives (synonymy, antonym, concept of high level and low level), but also gives value of adjectives in the form of fuzzy function. The advantage of the second approach is that it can build an orthogonal psychological space, and can measure the similarity of adjectives in the space. But new adjectives can not be easily added to the existing psychological space.

3.3 Building Emotion User Model

The emotion user model in an image retrieval system is a kind of semantic relationship between images' sensitive features and users' emotion demands.

There exist two kinds of methods to build the mapping between images and visual impression: one is linear method such as regression, multi-variable analysis, quantification theory and relevance calculation. For example, Sato put forward an linear calculating formula of adjective and CIELAB color space [18]. Yoshida mapped graphical feature (GF) space and users' subjective feature (SB) space to a unified feature (UF) space through multi-factor analysis, and then realized image's emotional retrieval through correlation computing in UF space [19]. The other method is nonlinear such as neural networks (NN), fuzzy theory (FT), interactive genetic algorithm (IGA) and rough sets etc. Hagiwara used NN to build the mapping function between image features and impression words [20]; Yukuo and Kouji applied fuzzy sets to construct a relative emotion model [21]. Sung-Bae Cho used IGA to realize emotion image retrieval [13]. The authors [5] used support vector machine (SVM) to build the common user model.

3.4 Individualizing Emotion User Models

Systems might not always select accurate and appropriate data items from database, because the judgment of accuracy for the retrieval results is strongly dependent on individual variation. So it is necessary to build an individual emotion user model in order to adapt retrieval results according to individual variation by using a proper learning mechanism. Just like people understanding each other through communication, this learning mechanism should also be interactive, dynamic and adaptive.

Three main approaches have been adopted to perform these tasks: content-based, collaborative and hybrid [22]. The first is based on the tenet that each user exhibits a particular behavior under a given set of circumstances, and that this behavior is repeated under similar circumstances. The second is based on the tenet that people within a particular group tend to behave similarly under a given set of circumstances. The third is based on the tenet that human emotion consists of both common emotion and individual emotion. Common Emotion is an *average* emotion or *objective* emotion, which means that a certain number of people might agree to some extent, while individual emotion reflects the difference between one another.

Thus, in the content-based approach, the retrieval candidate of a user is predicted from his/her past retrieval behavior. The advantage of this approach is that it can tailor a system's retrieval result according to the specific requirements of a particular user. However, this approach requires each user to provide relatively large amounts of data to enable the construction of an individual emotion user model. In the collaborative approach, the retrieval candidate of a user is predicted from the retrieval behavior of other like-minded people. It reduces the data collection burden for individual users. However, the emotion user model in these systems is not an individual but only an *average* user model, since the approach makes predictions about the behavior of a single user from observations of many users. It does not support the tailoring of a system according to the requirements of a particular user. The third approach involves hybrid adaptive processes, in which the initial stage is based on common emotion user model, and the individual emotion user model is realized step by step though interaction and feedback. This approach can alleviate the burden of data collection and online learning, since the initial retrieval candidate of a user is predicted from the retrieval behavior of other like-minded people. Furthermore, it can satisfy individual demand through interaction and learning from the user's feedback. So we think it is the most potential approach.

4 Thoughts for the Future

When users are looking for images, mostly it is the semantic structure conveyed by these media which should be key for selection. The goal of emotion semantics image retrieval is to acquire satisfying images according to the subjectivity of different individuals by using proper user models. However, users' subjectivity is very complex because it is affected by their goals and by their past experience, which vary over time. Similar information can be judged differently even by the same person according to the experience recalled by his/her brain. Furthermore, the information in an observed image is also very versatile. Human's visual system uses selection and attention mechanisms to filter the information from the observed object to the brain. So the mapping between still images and dynamic users' impression that arises in users is highly complex and difficult to explicit. Although many efforts have been performed to build individual emotion user model, it is still remains as the core research topic of emotion semantics image retrieval in the future. Relating to emotion user model, this section will discuss three future research topics: construction of emotion information database, evaluation of user model and computation of user model.

4.1 Construction of Emotion Information Database

In order to analyze users' feedback information and adjust individual user model, we need to construct an emotion information database to record users' profile (i.e. users' ID, gender, interest), feedback information(i.e. relevant or not relevant) and classified images by users(i.e. image ID, emotion features, relevant adjective). However, few research has been comprehensively done on this topic until now. Traditional database system do not deal well with such complex structures that are needed to represent users' subjectivity. The needs of emotion information database system are summarized by Yoshida as data independency, integrity consistency, non-redundancy, security, privacy, data sharing, soncurrent access, adaptability, and data migration etc [23].

How to build and index emotion database integrating traditional database is worthy of further research.

4.2 Evaluation of User Model

To date, there is no standard to evaluate user models in emotion semantic image retrieval. In theory, recall rate and precision rate, which are borrowed from the field of information retrieval, can be used. Recall rate is a measure of the number of satisfying retrieved images with respect to the number of all satisfying images in the database, and precision rate is a measure of the number of satisfying retrieved images with respect to the number of all retrieved images. The rates are higher, the models are more effective. But in fact, the judgment of the satisfying images is strongly dependent on individual variation. It means the judgment is subjective. So, the key issue here is how to define a objective evaluation to measure users' subjective visual impression. Empirical evaluation and statistic test borrowed from psychology might be a good solution [24].

4.3 Computation of Emotion User Model

Adaption of Emotion User Model. How to handle the variability intrinsic to subjective aspects of users' personality is a very complex issue. Presently, the main idea of adjusting user model is to learn from users' feedback during the interaction. However, most learning methods have their limits, such as the limit of local minimum. Thus, they can only solve this issue partly. New learning mechanism inspired from human's visual and emotional information process might be useful. It is a potential trend to build multi-level hybrid emotion user model using some research results of cognition science and visual psychology, such as visual selection and attention models.

Classification of Users. It need to assign a user to a certain group, when collaborative and hybrid approaches are applied to individualize emotion user models. The most often used method today is to assign users based on the similarity of their profiles. This is easy, but rough. A person' past retrieval behavior also can be a guide to classify him/her. So combining past retrieval behavior with profiles may improve the performance of individual emotion user model.

Interest Drift. An implicit working assumption of many user models is that of the *persistence of interest*, whereby users maintain their behavior or interests over time [22]. However, it has been reported many times that users change their interests during the retrieval process. Considering the interest drift for user model, we think there are three approaches. The first is simply to place less weight on older data of the user. The second is to retraining the user model periodically. The last is to use a dual model that classifies instance by first consulting a model trained on recent data. If this fails, then a model trained over a longer time period is used.

Computation of Impression words. In addition, according to computer description of impression word, computing with words [25] based on fuzzy logic might be a research orientation which is worthy of notice.

In Summary, emotion semantics image retrieval is still an open question for discussion, which is closely relevant to human's visual and emotional information processing. It is necessary in the future to cooperate with many research fields, such as cognition, psychology, artificial intelligence, pattern recognition, image processing and information retrieval, in order to realize individual emotion image retrieval through diversified approaches.

Acknowledgment. This paper is supported by NSFC project (NO. 60401004).

References

1. Amold, W.M. Semeulders Et Al.: Content-Based image retrieval at the end of early years. IEEE Trans. On Pattern Analysis And Machine Intelligence. **22(12)** (2000) 1349–1380
2. Zhao, R., William, I. Grosky: Bridging the semanitic gap in image retrieval. Distributed multimedia databases: techniques & applications. Idea Group Publishing Hershey PA USA (2002) 14 – 36
3. Ozaki, K., Abe, S., Yano, Y.: Semantic retrieval on art museum database system. IEEE International Conference on Systems Man and Cybernetics **3** (1996) 2108–2112
4. Bianchi-Berthouze, N., Kato, T.: K-DIME: An adaptive system to retrieval images from the WEB using subjective criteria. IEEE International Conference on System Man and Cybernetic'99, Tokyo Japan **6** (1999) 358–362
5. Wang, S.F.: Research on Emotion Information Processing and Its Application in Image Retrieval. Doctoral Dissertation, University of Science and Technology of China, May, (2002)
6. Uemura, S., Arisawa, H., Arikawa, M., Kiyoki, Y.: Digital media information base. IEICE Transaction on Information and System **E82-D(1)**(1999) 22–33
7. Arnheim, R.: Art and visual perception: A psychology of the creative eye. Palo Alto Calif.: Regents of the University of California(1954)
8. Itten, J.: Art of Color. Ravensburg Germany: Otto Maier Verlag(1961)
9. Corridoni, M., Bimbo, A. Del, Pala, P.: Retrieval of Paintings using Effects Induced by Color Features. 1998 International Workshop on Content-Based Access of Image and Video Databases (CAIVD '98)
10. Mao, X., Chen, B., Muta, I.: Affective property of image and fractal dimension. Chaos Solitions and Fractals **13**(2003) 905–910
11. Tanaka, S., Iwadate, Y., Inokuchi, S.: An attractiveness evaluation models based on the physical features of image regions. IEEE 15th International Conference on Pattern Recognition. Barcelona, Spain, (2000) 793–796

12. Kobayashi, Y., Kato, P.: Multi-contrast based texture model for understanding human subjectivity. 15th International Conference on Pattern Recognition, Barcelona, Spain, **3** (2000) 917–922
13. Sung-Bae, Cho.: Emotional image and musical information retrieval with interactive genetic algorithm. Proceedings of the IEEE **92(4)** (2004) 702 - 711
14. Hayashi, T., Hagiwara, M.: An image retrieval system to estimate impression words from images using a neural network. IEEE International Conference on Systems Man and Cybernetics 'Computational Cybernetics and Simulation'. Orlando FL USA **1**(1997) 150–155
15. Shibata, T., Kato, T.: "Kansei" image retrieval system for street landscape: discrimination and graphical parameters based on correlation of two images. IEEE International Conference on System Man and Cybernetic'99 Tokyo Japan (1999) 247–252
16. Charles, E. Osgood, George J. Suci, Percy H. Tannenbaum: The measurement of meaning. Urbana: University of Illinois Press (1957)
17. Kobayashi, H., Ota, S.: The semantic network of KANSEI words. 2000 IEEE International Conference on Systems Man and Cybernetics Nashville TN USA **1**(2000) 690–694
18. Sato, T., Kajiwara, K., Xin, J., Hansuebsai, A., Nobbs, J.: Numerical expression of colour emotion and its application.
19. Yoshida, K., Kato, T., Yanaru, T.: Image retrieval system using impression words. 1998 IEEE International Conference on Systems, Man, and Cybernetics **3** (1998) 2780–2784
20. Hayashi, T., Hagiwara, M.: Image query by impression words-the IQI system. IEEE Transactions on Consumer Electronics **44(2)** (1998) 347–352
21. Miura, K., Ozawa, J., Imanaka, T.: Information retrieval system based on a relative KANSEI model. Methodologies for the conception, Design and Application of Soft Computing, Proceedings of IIZUKA'98 239–242
22. Zukerman, I., Albrecht, D.W.: Predictive statistical models for user modeling. User Model and User-Adapted Interaction **11** (2001) 5–18
23. Yoshida, K., Kato, T.: Database system for Kansei-oriented communication. Industrial Electronics Society . IECON 2000. 26th Annual Conference of the IEEE Nagoya Japan **3** (2000) 1604 –1607
24. Chin, David, N.: Empirical Evaluation of user models and user-adapted systems. User Model and User-Adapted Interaction. **11** (2001) 181–194
25. Lotfi, A. Zadeh: Applied Soft computing-foreword. Applied soft computing (2001) 1–2

Affective Modeling in Behavioral Simulations: Experience and Implementations

Robert A. Duisberg

University of Washington, Seattle WA 98195, USA

Abstract. Recent studies have convincingly demonstrated the critical role of affect in human cognitive development and expression, supporting the case for incorporating affective representation into behavioral simulations for artificial intelligence. Music provides a powerful and concise mechanism for evoking and indeed representing emotions, and thus studying the ways in which music represents affect can provide insights into computer representations. That music can be understood as a multidimensional structure leads to the consideration of systemic grammars for this representation. A systemic grammar of emotions is presented which has proven effective as the basis for a concrete – and marketable – implementation of behavioral simulations for virtual characters, by allowing the system to parse interactions between characters into representations of emotional states, and using the attributes of those determined states as determinants of subsequent behavior.

Le coeur a ses raisons, que la raison ne connait point.
– Blaise Pascal

1 Background and Motivation

Early successes of classical artificial intelligence (AI), in such endeavors as logic, algebra, and chess, generated much enthusiasm, since these activities had been the province of intelligent, well-educated humans. Over the years, as limitations of classical AI become apparent, we have gained an appreciation of the critical role of other less "rational" factors at play in the development and exercise of cognition or intelligence. While excelling at formal tasks, AI engines have faltered in common-place activities that depend on understanding of world and such things as intentions, goals and desires. Even a pioneer of classical AI, Marvin Minsky, acknowledges that "only the surface of reason is rational."[11]

To know the world at all requires that we interpret experience. This process of interpretation occurs at all levels, from the basic processing of raw sensory input into elementary percepts, up to high-level conceptualization. The epistemological frameworks of Polanyi and Kuhn take these notions further, asserting that the application of such perceptual categories or higher concepts is essentially "tacit"[12] in that the criteria by which we choose to apply them are not rational or verbalized, but are instead aesthetic in nature and a matter of a

J. Tao, T. Tan, and R.W. Picard (Eds.): ACII 2005, LNCS 3784, pp. 498–504, 2005.

passionate personal commitment to our interpretation. This aspect of personal emotional commitment as a foundation of epistemology is central to Polanyi's notion of "personal knowledge." In this view a scientist applies a conceptual paradigm to data by virtue of an aesthetic judgement expressed as an emotional commitment to a belief that the paradigm is appropriate, to the extent that it is not possible to interpret knowledge "in the absence of at least some implicit body of intertwined theoretical and methodological belief that permits selection, evaluation, and criticism" [7].

Even at the most basic level of perception, an infant's innate need (and thus desire) for connection to its mother becomes love that drives its learning to recognize her language-specific phonemes and intonations. These patterns become hard-wired into the infant's developing neurology to the degree that in later life, the adult is unable to even distinguish salient phonemes from other languages.[9]. Given studies of the the terrible neurological and cognitive damage to mammalian offspring which suffer emotional (or "limbic") deprivation[6], one might fairly assert that love, as the efflorescence of basic physical needs, underlies and prefigures cognition itself.

Thus we are impelled toward the judgement that any theory or application of artificial intelligence will be seriously deficient if it does not adequately account for the ways in which emotions motivate and shape learning and cognition at every level. For while symbolic calculus is something we humans learn in higher schooling and which computers can do reasonably well (albeit without insight), what computer has ever been programmed to recognize and long for the sound of its mother's voice, and has engaged in expensive and complex tasks of learning in order to earn her love? For something of this sort would certainly be needed to pass a Turing test or even to take seriously the implication of "user friendliness" in an interface.

This paper presents some approaches and implementations, the intent of which have been to address this lacuna by explicitly modeling affective states and parsing interactions for their emotional content as inputs to such a model.

1.1 Insights from Music

If we accept the premise that emotion is the precursor to intelligence and cognition, then we may be motivated to seek ways by which to represent affective states and ways to "reason" by means of them.

As "the language of emotions," music can undeniably depict and evoke emotions with remarkable precision. The process of creating sound design and composing music for theatre is convincing in this regard, for in that context it is readily apparent that particular music may be quite right or entirely wrong emotionally for a given dramatic sequence. So we ask how this precision of emotional evocation can possibly take place, and understanding this process might help us design computer models. It is also remarkable to note that the representation of emotion in music can be in fact an entirely numerical artifact – for example, if the music is stored as a MIDI file. We are thus faced with the irrefutable experiential evidence and experience that emotions can be and often are accurately represented by numerical constructs. It is useful to understand how this can happen, and how it is done.

In the parlance of aesthetics[4], *expressive* symbols such as segments of music are effective insofar as they in some sense possess attributes of the referent they express. This is in contrast to the function of a *denotative* symbol, such as the word "table," which can in no way be said to possess legs or a surface upon which to place things. However, when we say that a piece of music "is sad," we are actually saying that it possesses the attributes of sadness, albeit by virtue of a metaphorical transference. That is, sad music *literally* possesses musical attributes which may described as "dark" (in terms of timbre or harmonic color), "slow" (in terms or tempo or rhythm), "downward" moving (in terms of the direction of melodic gesture), and so on which correspond directly to actual attributes of sadness similarly experienced in the emotional realm. That there is some specificity and precision in such representations can be confirmed by imagining how a passage involving presto pizzicato and glockenspiel would simply be a very incorrect representation of anything like sadness. Thus we can see that music manages to represent and express emotions through a mapping of affective attributes of the emotion onto numerous sonorous dimensions available to the composer.

1.2 The Affective Dynamics of Interactions

Following the direction indicated by these considerations, we are led toward a design for representing an emotional state as a multidimensional object, where the dimensions in the structure may be analogous to the kinds of attributes mapped into musical representations of emotional states. This kind of multidimensional representation lends itself well to be expressed, analyzed and recognized in the terms of a systemic-functional grammar[5], and indeed Winograd has employed just such a systemic approach to the analysis of standard musical harmony[15].

A systemic grammar presumes that a linguistic structure is the outcome of simultaneous decisions made in multiple dimensions. This is in contrast to transformational or generative grammars, more commonly used in computer science applications such as compiler technologies, in which a linear sequence of incremental decisions yields a single tree structure mapping the derivation of a well formed statement. In a simple example, the declension of an English pronoun results from simultaneous choices in four systems: person (1st, 2nd or 3rd), number (singular or plural), gender (applicable only in 3rd person, singular), and case (nominative, dative, genitive). Winograd's systemic grammar for harmony presents a more complex and less familiar example in which the type and function of a particular chord is determined from its constituent notes by simultaneously evaluating the choices in a number of systems, including ones identifying root, completeness, inversion, type, diatonic level, alteration, etc.

An analogous and particularly compelling multidimensional model of emotions was developed by the psychologist Joseph de Rivera. He proposes a "matrix of emotions" (see figure) describing the emotions as positions in what is effectively a four dimensional space, in which "any particular emotion is the outcome

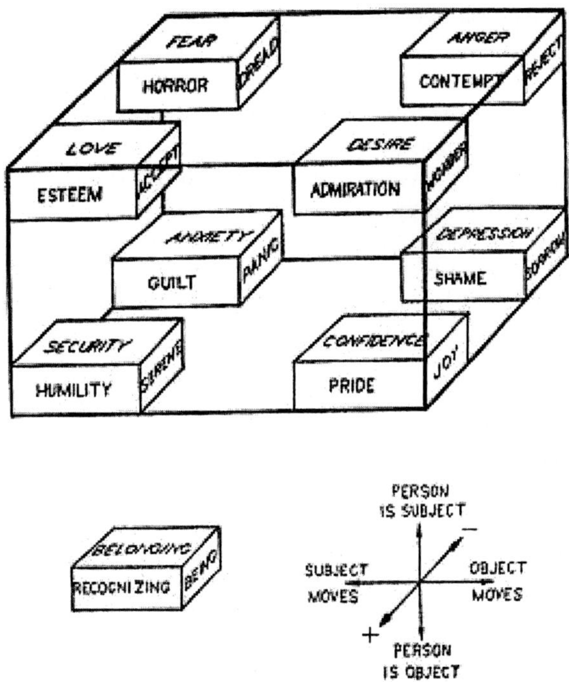

Fig. 1. The Matrix of Emotions (De Rivera, 1977)

of a pattern of 'choices' that organize our relationship with the other."[1] The four dimensions or systems in which choices are manifest are:

- the direction of motion, increasing or decreasing the distance between subject and object
- who does the moving, the subject or the object
- whether the person experiencing the emotion is the subject or the object of the motion
- the psychological aspect associated with the emotion (being, belonging, or recognition).

This structure has the advantage, for our purposes, of representing emotions as arising from interpersonal *motions*, or changes in a relationship often observable as changes in physical position and posture. The advantage is that these positional and attitudinal changes are external and measurable, and when when interpreted with this matrix, we have an elegant operational basis for parsing interactions into emotional states. For example, if I wish to move toward another because of what I recognize in her, this parses out as "esteem," whereas if were to reject her along similar lines, she may well understand that as an expression of "contempt."

The value of an agent's being able to parse an interpersonal interaction for its affective content is in allowing it to predict future actions in an effective way, shifting the agent's behavior and "worldview." Or a system may use this matrix to computationally parse a human operator's behaviors, then with its new "understanding" of the human's emotions, shift its own response and user-model toward a more "user-friendly" pattern that especially suits this particular human. These kinds of computations associated with machine learning are typically computationally expensive, so the affective framework may function as a gate or a trigger to these kinds of activities.

2 Implementation

In the nineteen-nineties, at WizBang! Software Productions Inc., we implemented a series of virtual reality simulations, whose design was strongly influenced by these considerations. A major goal was to populate a virtual environment with believable AI characters, interspersed with avatars controlled by real people. The ability to parse qualities of interactions among AI and human controlled characters was crucial to an AI character's ability to be appropriately adaptive in subsequent encounters. For example, if a human controlled character had been particularly aggressive in one engagement, then subsequently the AI character may behave in a shy or defensive manner on another encounter. The design was motivated by the kinds of user interface considerations considered by Brenda Laurel in her *Computers as Theatre*[8], with the intent of providing a user experience akin to that found in interactive theatre productions or "theatre sports."

2.1 The Structure of the AdLib Language and Run-Time System

The system we developed in house for these purposes (and which we subsequently licensed to Microsoft for use in a number of their products[10]) is known as AdLib (A Declarative Language for Interactive Behaviors). The AdLib system has three parts:

1. A declarative language for describing characters' behaviors and interactions
2. An authoring environment for the language
3. A run-time system that operates over the state diagrams constructed from the declarative specifications in the language, to generate executable sequences of actions.

The descriptions of characters' behaviors and motivations are called `Plans`, effectively AdLib "programs," and have been responsible for controlling with considerable clarity and ease, virtually every dynamic aspect of a three dimensional virtual scene, including sound, camera work, context-sensitive input, in addition to animation and AI. The AdLib plan language is a declarative, object-oriented language with an extensible vocabulary for specifying high-level descriptions of behaviors and interactions. A `Plan` consists of a collection of `Behavior` declarations and declarations of sets of `Interactors` associated with each `Behavior`.

The high concept here is that a behavior is a set of activities executed "unthinkingly" on each frame of a simulation (e.g. when we are walking or riding a bike, having made the decision to do so, we do not reconsider our goals with every step or pedal stroke). In any behavior there are any number of interactions, arrival points or events to which we can expect to be responsive (e.g. if we meet a friend on our walk, or a dog runs out to chase us on our bike), and in considering how to respond at that point (i.e. when an `Interactor` object is activated), we may invoke any computational model we wish in order to explore the options, consider revising our goals, etc. It is at this juncture, within the active `Interactor` object, that the influences of an affective model can be invoked to influence the choice and parameterization of subsequent behaviors (e.g. we really like our friend and decide to walk together, or have a fear of dogs and so veer quickly down a side street to get away).

The results of this design were at least two-fold. First we were able to maintain excellent run-time performance while performing credible AI, since generally the "reasoning" was restricted to being occasional (much less than on every frame) and local (the currently active `Behavior` providing context for the decisions being made within an `Interactor`). We were also able to experiment with characters' responsiveness, since the resources available for decision making within an `Interactor` can be most anything at all that a developer might implement, from random choices, to discrete conditional branches, to small local neural networks, to full implementations of affective matrices. Finally, coming full circle, we were also able to use elements of affective modeling to provide hints as to what sort of musical accompaniment to provide in some virtual scenes.

3 Future Work

AdLib was originally implemented in C++, but is being reimplemented with extensions based upon lessons learned and a conviction in the applicability of its methodology to other fields where there is a need for autonomous intelligent agents in simulations. The principal extensions in the new version will address issues of the complexity and number of agents in a simulation. The complexity of models will be supported by adopting a hierarchical design, in which an AdLib object possessing `Plans` and `Behaviors` may in turn contain other such objects with their own `Plans`. The extension of AdLib to handle very large numbers of agents will also be supported through distributed techniques and array processing packages. The motivation for these extensions is to be able to use AdLib's mechanism in the context of large scale econometric simulations[14], which while aspiring to "behavioral microsimulation," typically resort in their implementation to statistical techniques. An exception in this field is the problem of commuter traffic modeling, which is essential for urban planners. These models are generally implemented using cellular automata, and are extremely expensive to run. In these simulations would benefit from the ability to model populations of commuters with diverse characteristics, needs and behaviors, and even varying propensities for impatience or road rage, which might motivate them to seek alternative routes. The new implementation will be in Python and will be made available as an open source package. A progress report on the new implementation will be given at the presentation of this paper in October 2005.

References

1. de Rivera, Joseph: A structural theory of the emotions. Psychological Issues Monograph **40** New York:International Universities Press (1977) 71
2. Duisberg, Robert A.: On the Role of Affect in Artificial Intelligence and Music. Perspectives of New Music **23:1** (1984) 6-35
3. Duisberg, Robert A.: Animation using temporal constraints: an overview of the Animus system. Human-Computer Interaction **3:3** (1987) 275-307
4. Goodman, Nelson: Languages of Art. Hackett Publishing:Indianapolis (1976)
5. Halliday, M.A.K., Hasan, R.: Language, context, and text: aspects of language in a social-semiotic perspective. Oxford: Oxford University Press (1985)
6. Kraemer, G.W.: A psychobiological theory of attachment. Behavioral and Brain Sciences **15** (1992) 493-541
7. Kuhn, Thomas S.: The Structure of Scientific Revolutions Chicago: University of Chicago Press (1962) 16-17
8. Laurel, Brenda: Computers as Theatre Boston: Addison-Wesley (1993)
9. Lewis, Thomas, Amini, Fari, Lannon, Richard: A General Theory of Love. Vintage, Random House:New York (1990)
10. Microsoft Corp. Press Release:
Microsoft pitches a perfect game with "Baseball 2001".
`http://www.microsoft.com/presspass/press/2000/Feb00/Baseball2001pr.asp`
Redmond, WA (Feb. 16, 2000)
11. Minsky, M.: Music, mind, and meaning. Computer Music Journal **5:3** (1981) 28
12. Polanyi, Michael: Personal Knowledge: Towards a Post Critical Philosophy. London: Routledge (1958, 1998)
13. Rosen, Stuart, Duisberg, Robert: The making of hyperblade. Game Developer Magazine **Aug/Sep** (1996) 22-25
14. Waddell, Paul: UrbanSim: modeling urban development for land use, transportation and environmental planning. Journal of the American Planning Association **68:3** (2002) 297-314
15. Winograd, Terry: Linguistics and the computer analysis of tonal harmony Journal of Music Theory. **12:1**(1968). pages 22- 49. Reprinted in M.A.K. Halliday and J.R. Martin (eds.). Readings in Systemic Linguistics. London: Batsford Academic (1981) 257-270

An Ontology for Description of Emotional Cues

Zeljko Obrenovic[1], Nestor Garay[2], Juan Miguel López[2], Inmaculada Fajardo[2], and Idoia Cearreta[2]

[1] Laboratory for Multimodal Communications, School of Business Administration, University of Belgrade
obren@fon.bg.ac.yu
[2] Laboratory of Human-Computer Interaction for Special Needs, Computer Science Faculty; University of the Basque Country
{nestor, juanmi, acbfabri}@si.ehu.es, icearreta001@ikasle.ehu.es

Abstract. There is a great variety of theoretical models of emotions and implementation technologies which can be used in the design of affective computers. Consequently, designers and researchers usually made practical choices of models and develop ad-hoc solutions that sometimes lack flexibility. In this paper we introduce a generic approach to modeling emotional cues. The main component of our approach is the ontology of emotional cues. The concepts in the ontology are grouped into three global modules representing three layers of emotions' detection or production: the emotion module, the emotional cue module, and the media module. The emotion module defines emotions as represented with emotional cues. The emotional cue module describes external emotional representations in terms of media properties. The media module describes basic media properties important for emotional cues. Proposed ontology enables flexible description of emotional cues at different levels of abstraction. This approach could serve as a guide for the flexible design of affective devices independently of the starting model and the final way of implementation.

1 Introduction

Design of computing systems that detect and produce emotional cues is not a mean task, as there are many practical problems that have to be solved. Currently, there is a great variety of theoretical models of emotions that can frame the design of affective computers, and there are different technologies that can be used for their implementation. For that reason, designers and researchers often made practical choices of models, and develop solutions in order to recognize a fixed set of emotional states, with limited flexibility. In addition, although there are many common properties, emotional cues are not universal: they are differently expressed in different cultures and languages, while many emotional properties are individual. There is rarely a one-size-fits-all solution for the growing variety of computer users and interactions [1]. Therefore, emotionally-aware applications have to be designed flexible if they want to serve a wider class of users.

Having in mind the presented problems, this paper proposes a generic approach to defining emotional cues that could serve as a guide for flexible design of affective devices with independence of the starting model and the final way of implementation [2]. The essence of this solution is the ontology of emotional cues, which introduces

J. Tao, T. Tan, and R.W. Picard (Eds.): ACII 2005, LNCS 3784, pp. 505–512, 2005.

concepts that can enable flexible description of emotional cues at different levels of abstraction. The concepts in the ontology are grouped into three modules, representing three layers of emotions' detection or production: the emotion module, the emotional cue module, and the media module.

In next section, a brief revision of the theoretical models of emotions is presented, in order to illustrate different points of view among researchers, and it presents a theoretical background for this research. After that, the basic idea of this approach is presented. Then, the ontology of emotional cues is introduced. Next, it is discussed how the proposed ontology can lead toward creation of new types of flexible emotionally aware applications. In the end, a short discussion and conclusions are given.

2 Models of Emotions

There are many possible ways how parameters of emotions can be registered, interpreted or implemented by computers. Models of emotions proposed by cognitive psychologist could be a useful starting point. Generally speaking, models of emotions can be classified in two main groups:

- Dimensional emotional models, and
- Categorical emotional models.

One of the most relevant dimensional models of emotions is the Bio-Informational Model of Peter Lang [3], who defined emotions according to three dimensions: arousal, valence and control.

Instead of using dimensions for defining emotions, other authors have proposed defining discrete categories of emotions, such as fear, happiness, or sadness [4, 5]. For practical reasons, categorical models of emotions have been more frequently used in affective computing. For example, Picard has implemented several algorithms that recognize eight categories of emotions based on facial expressions [6]. Pierre-Yves has developed such algorithms for production and recognition of five emotions based on speech parameters [7].

Lang also proposed analyzing of emotions according to three systems involved in the expressions of emotions [3]:

- *Subjective or verbal information*: reports about perceived emotions described by users,
- *Behavioral or conductal*: facial and postural expressions and speech paralinguistic parameters,
- *Psychophysiological answers*: such as heart rate, galvanic skin response –GSR–, and electroencephalographic response.

The subjective, behavioral and physiological correlates of emotions should be taken into account when possible. The correlations among the three systems could help computers to interpret ambiguous emotions. For instance, a person with apraxia could have problems in the articulation of facial gestures, but subjective information written down with assistive technology, could be used by a computer to interpret her/his emotional state. At the same time, if a voice synthesizer can express emotions not only by means of the word's meanings but also by means of the tone, speed or intensity of the speech, it could provide more emotional cues to its interlocutor (computer or human being). In that sense, more specific models or classifications which describe the components of each system of expression can be found in the literature and selected according to the particular case, for example, dictionary of emotional speech [8], acoustic correlates of speech [5], or facial expressions [4].

We think that a generic ontology, as the one that we present here, could be useful for the description of emotional cues according to the different systems of emotional expression (subjective, conductal or physiological) and to the different theoretical models (dimensional or categorical).

3 An Ontology for Description of Emotional Cues

The basic motivation of our solution is to allow flexible definitions of emotional cues at different levels of abstraction. Therefore, our first step was to develop a conceptual ontology that would allow such logical division of concepts. An ontology is usually defined as an explicit specification of an abstract, simplified view of a world we want to represent. It specifies both the concepts inherent in this view as well as their inter-relationships [9]. In our case, an ontology can give us a common and standardized language for sharing and reusing knowledge about emotions.

As one of our main aims is to produce tools that can be used for affective mediation and that can be easily personalized to each user. Personalization is necessary for more efficient interaction, and for fine tuning and better acceptation of the system. Each person reflects emotions in a personal way, so there is a need to properly adjust parameters to each one of them.

The essence of proposed solution is the Emotional Cues Ontology, which introduces concepts and mechanisms used in the affective computing domain. This ontology can be viewed as a metamodel that formally describes important affective computing concepts, and introduces concepts used to create models of concrete emotions. Consequently, in our work we have focused on two main topics:

- *The design of the Ontology of Emotional Cues*, in which we have synthesized the knowledge and common concepts from different domains relevant to affective computing into a single uniform view;
- *Applying the Ontology of Emotional Cues*, to the modeling of emotional cues, and the design of affective applications.

4 The Ontology of Emotional Cues

The concepts in the ontology are grouped into three global modules representing three layers of emotions' detection or production (Figure 1a): the emotion module, the emotional cue module, and the media module. The emotion module defines emotions as represented with emotional cues. The emotional cue module describes external emotional representations in terms of media properties. The media module describes basic media properties important for emotional cues.

Figure 1b shows simplified structure of the emotion module. This module introduces the concept of emotions, and its relation to emotional cues: emotional cues are modeled as external representations of emotions. Every emotion can have one or more emotional cues, represented in different media. Which of the emotional cues will be

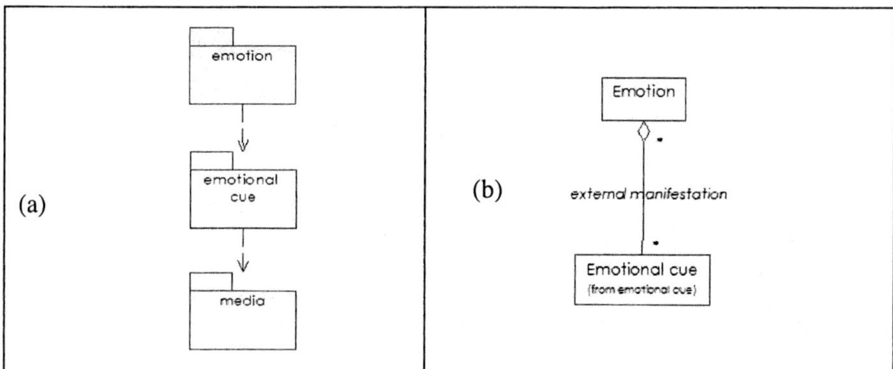

Fig. 1. Structure of the ontology of emotional cues (a), and the model of emotions and emotional cues (b)

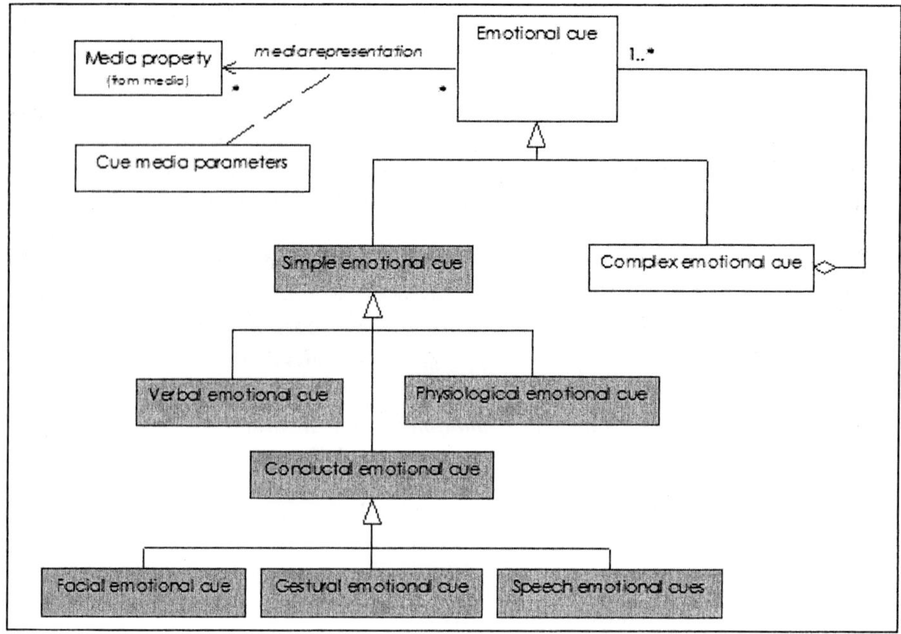

Fig. 2. The model of emotional cues

included when a concrete emotion is modeled depends on the purpose of the model and on the available communication channels. For example, if you are developing a system that recognizes emotions in a telephone speech, then facial and physiological emotional cues are irrelevant as they cannot be detected [10].

Figure 2 shows a simplified structure of the emotional cues module. The basic concept is an emotional cue, classified as a simple or complex emotional cue. Emotional

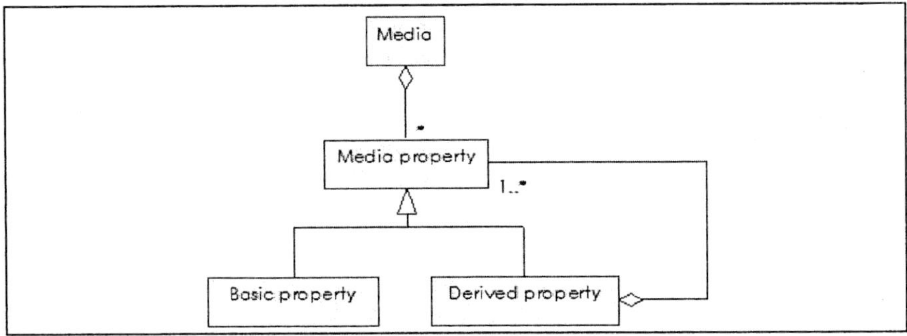

Fig. 3. The model of media

cues can be connected with media properties from which they are derived. This relation among emotional cues and media properties can be parameterized, enabling different settings for different emotional cues. This parameterization is important as different emotions are often based on analysis of the same media properties, but with different intensity.

Simple emotional cues are basic signals, usually derived directly from the media properties. We have identified three types of simple emotional cues [3]: verbal emotional cues, such as the used vocabulary, conductal emotional cues, such as smiling, and physiological emotional cues, such as GSR. Difference between speech and verbal emotional cues is that speech emotional cues are related to speech parameters (tone, intonation, etc.), while verbal emotional cues are related to the content. Complex emotional cues integrate two or more emotional cues. For instance, speaking loudly telling insults suggests that the person is angry. We enable parameterization of this integration, so that it is possible, for example, to say what level of response is necessary to form the complex emotional cue.

In similar way we describe the media module (Figure 3). Media is described with various media properties. A media property can be simple, such as intensity of sound, or derived, such as variations in the intensity of sound. These media properties are used for description of emotional cues which they form.

5 Discussion: Applying the Ontology in Developing Generic Tools for Recognition and Generation of Emotional Cues

The main expected benefit of our solution, is to establish a formal description of emotional cues in an easily understandable way, using concepts defined in the ontology. Moreover, proposed ontology enables more abstract description of emotional cues in various ways. It is possible to define emotions as composed of complex emotional cues, which are composed of other simple emotional cues, which are based on some media properties. Recognition of emotions, therefore, can be viewed as a bottom-up process. Firstly, we detect simple media properties, and then derive complex media properties. By analyzing complex media properties, we get simple emotional cues, and by combining these cues, we get complex emotional cues, which represent some emotion. On the other hand, production of emotions can be viewed as a reverse, top-down process.

In order to illustrate how complex emotional cues can be described using defined concepts, Table 1 presents description of Joy and Desire in speech according to a categorical approach to emotions [5]. According to [11], Joy is represented with different simple emotional cues in speech. It is characterized with the increase of the average tone from 10% to 15%, increase in tone variability for 120%, fast inflection of tone, stable intensity, and decrease in duration of silences for 20%. Each of this simple emotional cues has some representation in media, e.g. in sound. For example, change of average tone is calculated by comparing average tone in time. Average tone is a complex speech media property, based on analysis of speech tone.

Desire is characterized with the decrease of intensity stability (around 20 dB), the decrease of average tone (around 10%), the tone variability decreases between 5% and 10%, the tone inflection is slow, the discourse fragmentation is smaller and there are exhalations at the end of phonetic groups [11]. These cause that the total time change increases.

Table 1. Describing some of the properties of Joy and Desire in speech, using terms defined in the proposed ontology

Complex emotional cues ⟸	**Simple emotional cues**	⟸ **Complex media properties**	⟸ **Simple media properties**
Joy in speech	Change of average tone (10% to 50%)	Average tone	Tone
	Change of tone variability (120%)	Tone variability	
	Speed inflection of tone (fast)	Inflection of tone	
	Change in duration of silences (-20%)	Silence duration	Speech intensity
	Change of intensity stability (stable)	Intensity change	
Desire in speech	Change of average tone (-10%)	Average tone	Tone
	Change of tone variability (-5% to -10%)	Tone variability	
	Speed inflection of tone (slow)	Inflection of tone	
	Change of intensity stability (<20dB)	Intensity change	Speech intensity

Other categories of emotions, such as Fear, or Surprise, can be described in a similar way. Moreover, emotions can also be described according to a dimensional approach of emotions.

Proposed ontology defines a generic approach for modeling emotional cues. These models of emotional cues can be used for various purposes. For example, they can serve as a description or metadata about some emotions, or as a part of user profile. Furthermore, most modeling tools allow transformation of models using formats such as Extensible Markup Language (XML) so afterwards they can be used by other tools (Figure 4).

Based on the ideas from proposed ontology, we are working on applications which produce or recognize emotional cues that do not have "built in" complete knowledge about recognition of emotional cues. In order to be more flexible they can be param

```
<emotional-cue name="joy in speech">
- <composed-of>
  - <emotional-cue name="Change of average tone">
      <range lower="10%" upper="50%" />
      <derived-from media="speech" property="average tone" />
    </emotional-cue>
  - <emotional-cue name="Change of tone variability">
      <range lower="120%" upper="" />
      <derived-from media="speech" property="tone variability" />
    </emotional-cue>
  </composed-of>
</emotional-cue>
```

Fig. 4. A simplified fragment of one possible XML encoding of emotional cues

eterized for particular emotional cues, using models of emotional cues. Generic applications can be created so that they have built-in media layer, combining it with the simple emotional cue layer and the complex emotional cue layer, parameterized with our models.

In the HCI field, different models and approaches have been defined in order to better capture relevant concepts from user interaction, some of them based on software engineering paradigms. For example, Unified Modeling Language (UML) [12] is a modeling language consisting of a collection of semiformal graphical notations, including case diagrams, activity diagrams, class diagrams, interaction diagrams, and state diagrams. These notations can be used to support different development methodologies [13, 14]. Nunes [15] proposed a UML profile for interactive system development that leveraged on HCI domain knowledge under the common notation and semantics of the UML. At the moment, we are working on integration of proposed ideas into software developing environments, and we have developed several profiles in order to allow descriptions of emotional cues using UML. Besides the possibility to use existing modeling tools, standardization provides a significant driving force for further progress because it codifies best practices, enables and encourages reuse, and facilitates interworking between complementary tools [16].

6 Conclusions and Future Work

In this paper, we have presented an ontology that can be used to describe emotional cues. This ontology is mainly devoted to the use of affective mediation, but it can also be used within other areas of the affective computing. The formalization can be used by developers to construct tools for a generic description of emotions that can be personalized to each user, language and culture.

We are currently expressing emotional cues and have some descriptions made based on UML. We are working on tools that could be parameterized with XML descriptions of the models. The results that are achieved are going to be tested in order to establish whether this work will be usable for other people and which level of usability is achieved, in order to maximize this level.

So far, we have described models for the transmission of emotions via speech and using the categorical model [2]. We also plan to study emotions according to categorical and dimensional models of emotions [3, 4, 5] in our future work.

Acknowledgements

The involved work has received financial support from the Department of Economy of the local government "Gipuzkoako Foru Aldundia".

References

1. Picard R.: Perceptual user interfaces: affective perception, Communications of the ACM, Vol. 43, No. 3 (March 2000) 50-51
2. Obrenovic Z., Garay N., López J.M., Fajardo I.: A Generic Framework for Description of Emotional Cues. Internal Technical Report EHU-KAT-IK-08-05 (2005)
3. Lang P. J.: A bio-informational theory of emotional imagery. Psychophysiology, 16, (1979) 495-512
4. Ekman P.: Expression and nature of emotion. In K. Scherer and P. Ekman (Eds.): Approaches to emotion. Hillsdale, Nueva Jersey: Erlbaum, (1984)
5. Scherer K. R.: Vocal affect expression: A review and a model for future research. Psychological Bulletin, vol. 99 (1986) 143-165
6. Picard R. W.: Towards Agents that Recognize Emotion, Acts Proceedings IMAGINA (Monaco), (1998) 153-165
7. Pierre-Yves, O.: The production and recognition of emotions in speech: features and algorithms. International Journal of Human-Computer Studies, Volume 59 , Issue 1-2 (July 2003) 157 - 183
8. Bradley M.M., Lang P.J. and Cuthbert N.B.: Affective Norms for English Words (ANEW). NIMH Center for the Study of Emotion and Attention, University of Florida, (1997)
9. Obrenovic Z., Starcevic D., Devedzic V.: Using Ontologies in Design of Multimodal User Interfaces. In M. Rauterberg, M. Menozzi, and J. Wesson (Eds.): Human-Computer Interaction - INTERACT '03, IOS Press & IFIP, (2003), 535-542
10. Garay N., Abascal J., Gardeazabal L.: Adaptive Emotional Interface for a Telephone Communication Aid. 6th European Conference for the Advancement of Assistive Technology. AAATE 2001. Ljubljana, Slovenia, 2001. In C. Marincek, et al. (eds.) Assistive Technology - Added Value to the Quality of Life. IOS Press, (2001) 175-179
11. Iriondo I., Guaus R., Rodríguez A., Lázaro P., Montoya N., Blanco J. Mª, Bernadas D., J. Oliver M., Tena D., Longhi L.: Validation of an Acoustical Modelling of Emotional Expression in Spanish Using Speech Synthesis Techniques. Proceedings of the ISCA Workshop on Speech and Emotion. http://www.qub.ac.uk/en/isca/index.htm (2000)
12. UML™ Resource page. http://www.uml.org (2005)
13. Fowler M, Scott K.: UML distilled: Applying the standard object modeling language. Addison-Wesley (1997)
14. Quatrani T.: Visual modeling with Rational Rose and UML. Addison-Wesley (1998)
15. Nunes N., Falcao J.: Towards a UML profile for user interface development: The Wisdom approach. Proceedings UML'2000, LNCS Springer-Verlag (2000) 50-58
16. Obrenovic Z., Starcevic D.: Modeling Multimodal Human-Computer Interaction, IEEE Computer, Vol. 37, No. 9, (2004) 65-72.

The Reliability and Validity of the Chinese Version of Abbreviated PAD Emotion Scales

Xiaoming Li[1,2], Haotian Zhou[1,2], Shengzun Song[1,2], Tian Ran[1,2], and Xiaolan Fu[1,*]

[1] State Key Laboratory of Brain and Cognitive Science, Institute of Psychology, Chinese Academy of Sciences, Beijing 100101, China
lixm@psych.ac.cn, zhou-ht@mails.tsinghua.edu.cn, songshenzun@163.com, rant@psych.ac.cn, fuxl@psych.ac.cn
[2] Graduate School, Chinese Academy of Sciences, Beijing 100039, China

Abstract. The study aimed at testing the reliability and validity of the Chinese version of Abbreviated PAD Emotion Scales using a Chinese sample. 297 Chinese undergraduate students were tested with the Chinese version of Abbreviated PAD Emotion Scales; 98 of them were retested with the same scales after seven days in order to assess the test-retest reliability; and 102 of them were tested with SCL-90 at the same time which was intended as criteria for validity to assess the criterion validity. The results showed that the Chinese version of Abbreviated PAD Emotion Scales displayed satisfying reliability and validity on P (pleasure-displeasure), only moderate reliability and validity on D (dominance-submissiveness), but quite low reliability and validity on A (arousal-nonarousal).

1 Introduction

Nowadays affective computing has become the hotspot in computer science, and effective methods for annotating emotion have been regarded as of particular importance to the success of affective computing. Various methods have been used to annotate emotion, such as categorical annotation scheme [1] or 2 dimensional annotation scheme [2]. The problem with most of these tools in a view of affective computing was that they did not meet the requirement of psychological measurement for reliability and validity. The development of a more precise emotion annotation tool put forward based on many demonstration researches in psychology should be emphasized for the sake of affective computing.

The PAD Emotion Scales was build upon the PAD Emotional State Model [3] . It was an elaborate tool for measuring emotions developed by Dr Mehrabian of UCLA and had been used in many practical researches [4, 5, 6, 7]. There are three nearly independent dimensions that are used to describe and measure emotional states in the PAD emotional-state Model: pleasure-displeasure (P), arousal-nonarousal (A), and dominance-submissiveness (D). "pleasure-displeasure" distinguishes the positive-negative quality of emotional states, "arousal-nonarousal" refers to a combination of physical activity and mental alertness, and "dominance-submissiveness" is defined in terms of control versus lack of control [3]. Specific emotional states can be visualized as points in a three-dimension PAD emotion space. When the PAD scale scores are

* Corresponding author.

J. Tao, T. Tan, and R.W. Picard (Eds.): ACII 2005, LNCS 3784, pp. 513 – 518, 2005.

standardized, each emotion can be described using corresponding values on the pleasure-displeasure, arousal-nonarousal, and dominance-submissiveness coordinates. For example, "anger" can be represented with (-.51, .59, .25) (scores on each PAD scale ranging from -1 to +1), which indicates that it is a highly unpleasant, highly aroused, and moderately dominant emotional state.

Although The full-length (34-item) PAD Emotion Scales was strongly recommended for most experimental applications [3], it was realized that researchers sometimes need to require participants rating a large number of stimuli and completing such a lengthy questionnaire for many times, and it could be an extremely irritating experience to the participant which might jeopardize the credibility of data obtained. Therefore, a 12-item abbreviated version had been prepared with each dimension consisting of four items.

Each item of the PAD Emotion Scales consists of a word pair that is separated by nine spaces. The two words on each line refer to feelings and highlight a special contrast between the two feelings. For items measuring P, the two words in each item differ only on P (but the same or similar on A and D), and the principle is the same with items for A and D. Participants are required to indicate which end of the scale is heavier or stronger (and by how much) as an accurate description of your feelings by placing a check-mark in one of the nine spaces. Check-marks in the left-most to the right-most spaces are transformed to scores that range from -4 to +4, and the check-mark in the middle space is coded as zero.

Half of the items on each dimension are inverted (worded negatively) to minimize response bias and to render the scale more opaque (i.e., less obvious) to respondents. In addition, the PAD Emotion Scales provides a set of equations for computing from the PAD scores the values of some specific emotion, such as exuberant, bored, anxious, fearful and so on, which can be weighed against each other to determine the dominant emotion under a given circumstances. The PAD Emotion Scales is a versatile psychological measuring instrument in accordance with the dimensional and categorical approach to emotion classification and is capable of adapting to a variety of applications including emotion annotation.

The primary goal of the present study was to test the reliability and validity of the Chinese version of Abbreviated PAD Emotion Scales in a Chinese sample.

2 Methods

2.1 Participants

297 (male 132; female 165) undergraduate students in Beijing and Hebei were tested with the Chinese version of Abbreviated PAD Emotion Scales. 98 of them (male 53; female 45) were retested with the same scales after seven days in order to assess the test-retest reliability. To assess the criterion validity, 102 of them (male 57; female 45) were tested with SCL-90 at the same time which was intended as criteria for validity test.

2.2 Testing Tools

(1) The Chinese version of Abbreviated PAD Emotion Scales. Firstly, a prototype of the Chinese version of Abbreviated PAD Emotion Scales was obtained by translating

the original English version through the collaboration of one psychology professional and three graduate students of psychology major. Then this prototype was back-translated into English by an expert in English to be compared with the original English version. The final version used in this study was formed through appropriate subsequent modification; (2) SCL –90. SCL –90 was intended as criteria for validity test which has eleven statistic indexes including Somatization, Obsessive-Compulsive, Interpersonal sensitivity, Depression, Anxiety, Hostility, Photic anxiety, Paranoid ideation, Psychoticism, Others, and GSI (General Symptomatic Index).

3 Results

3.1 Reliability Analysis

Cronbach's α was computed to gauge the inter-item consistencies for P, A, and D. Correlation analysis was used to analyzing the test-retest reliabilities for P, A, and D. The detailed results were displayed in Table 1.

Table 1. The Inter-item Consistencies and Test-retest Reliabilities for P, A, and D

Dimension	the Inter-item Consistency (Cronbach's α)	Test-retest Reliability
P (pleasure-displeasure)	.692	.427**
A (arousal-nonarousal)	.235	.380**
D (dominance-submissiveness)	.467	.565**

Note: **means $P < 0.01$

Table 2. Exploratory Factor Analysis for 12 items

Item	Factor		
	1 (P)	2 (D)	3 (A)
10	***.758***	.192	.100
1	***.747***	.207	.130
7	***.698***	.213	.004
4	***.545***	-.019	-.214
6	.002	***.726***	.066
2	.146	***.628***	-.071
3	.212	***.621***	-.143
12	.187	***.554***	.110
5	.035	-.136	***.713***
11	-.094	.039	***.634***
9	-.284	.387	***.502***
8	.244	-.012	***.400***

3.2 Validity Analysis

3.2.1 Construct-Related Validity

The construct-related validity was assessed using exploratory factor analysis by Varimax – rotated method, and the detailed results were displayed in Table 2. The three factors accounted for 22.47%, 12.90%, and 10.58% of the total variance respectively. All 4 items of P had their highest loadings on factor 1(P); three items of D and one item of A (item2) had their highest loadings on factor 2(D); and three items of A and one item of D (item9) had their highest loadings on factor3 (A).

3.2.2 Criterion-Related Validity

SCL—90 served as criteria for criterion-related validity test in the present study, and correlation analysis was used to test the criterion-related validity. The detailed results were displayed in Table 3.

Table 3. Coefficients of Correlation between P, A, D and SCL-90

	P	**A**	**D**
Somatization	-.343**	-.093	-.298**
Obsessive-Compulsive	-.312**	-.162	-.250*
Interpersonal sensitivity	-.380**	-.177	-.348**
Depression	-.448**	-.205*	-.354**
Anxiety	-.416**	-.093	-.245*
Hostility	-.419**	-.165	-.172
Photic anxiety	-.363**	-.181	-.276**
Paranoid ideation	-.461**	-.271**	-.203*
Psychoticism	-.282**	-.188	-.277**
Others	-.398**	-.055	-.303**
GSI	-.484**	-.203*	-.359**

Note: *means *P*< 0.05 level; **means *P*< 0.01 level

4 Discussion

For the inter-item consistency, the Cronbach's α for P and D met the conventional requirement for the inter-item consistency of common psychological measurement tools, whereas the Cronbach's α for A was not good enough. The results differed drastically from those of Mehrabian's study in which Alpha internal consistency coefficients for P, A, and D were 0.95, 0.83, and 0.78 respectively [3]. As for the test-retest reliability, the coefficients of correlation of P, A, and D between the two sessions with a time interval of seven days were all significant at .01level. Considering the fact that emotion is more variable than personality and intelligence, the test-retest reliabilities for P, A, and D were acceptable.

The results of exploratory factor analysis for the construct-related validity illustrated that one item of A (item2: Wide-awaken----Sleepy) were factored into factor2 (D), and one item of D (item9: Humble ----Superior) were factored into factor3 (A) which were contrary to expectation. As mentioned above, for any item of a particular dimension, two kinds of emotions described by the two words are of similar values on the other two dimensions. Since the PAD scores for Sleepy is (.20,-.70,-.44), the value of D for Wide-awaken should also be negative (submissive). In the same way, the terms "Humble" and "Superior" should be similar in A. The unexpected outcomes may be caused by the distortion in meanings resulted from the translation. The corresponding Chinese translation ("qingxingde") for Wide-awaken might have been considered to be more dominant than its counterpart for Sleepy("kunjuande") by Chinese participants. Similarly, the Chinese terms for "Humble" ("qianbeide") and "Superior" ("gaoaode") might also have been rated differently on A with "Superior" judged to be more aroused.

SCL-90 is a 90-item self-report symptom inventory designed primarily to reflect the psychological symptom patterns of psychiatric and clinical patients. All of the eleven indexes of SCL-90 represent relatively negative emotions. The results of the correlation analysis between P and SCL-90 showed that P had significantly negative correlations with all the eleven statistic indexes of SCL-90, meaning that the criterion-related validity for P was good. D was found to be significantly negatively correlated with all the indexes of SCL-90 but Hostility. Therefore, D was moderately valid in terms of criterion-related validity. However, A had poor criterion-related validity indicated by the absence of statistically significant correlation between A and SCL-90.

5 Conclusion

In conclusion, the Chinese version of Abbreviated PAD Emotion Scales had satisfying reliability and validity on P, only moderate reliability and validity on D, but quite low reliability and validity on A. The disparity between the present study and the study of Mehrabian might be caused by the difference in testing methods selected. According to Mehrabian, the most desirable way to check the PAD Emotion Scales was to administer the questionnaire under as many circumstances as possible. A systematic list of 80 such circumstances had been provided in [5] and [7]. These descriptions constituted a balanced representation of a large variety of everyday settings, and included 10 replications of eight categories of PAD combinations (+P +A +D, +P +A–D, +P –A +D, +P –A –D, –P +A +D, –P +A –D, –P –A +D, –P –A –D). Further work needs to be done before any credible conclusion can be drawn about the applicability of the Chinese version of Abbreviated PAD Emotion Scales.

Acknowledgement

We thank Professor Mehrabian for authorizing us to use the PAD Emotion Scales in the construction of our multi-modal emotional database and offering invaluable comment on this study.

This research was supported in part by grants from 973 Program of Chinese Ministry of Science and Technology (2002CB312103), from the National Natural Science Foundation of China (60433030 and 30270466), and from the Chinese Academy of Sciences (0302037).

References

1. Craggs, R., Wood, M.M.: A 2 dimensional annotation scheme for emotion in dialogue. In: Proceedings of AAAI Spring Symposium on Exploring Attitude and Affect in Text: Theories and Applications, Stanford University (2004)
2. Craggs, R., Wood, M.M.: A categorical annotation scheme for emotion in the linguistic content of dialogue. In: Elisabeth André, Laila Dybkjaer, Wolfgang Minker and Paul Heisterkamp (eds.): Affective Dialogue System, Vol. 3068. Springer. (2004) 89-100
3. Mehrabian, A.: Framework for a comprehensive description and measurement of emotional states. Genetic, Social, and General Psychology Monographs. 121 (1995) 339-361
4. Mehrabian, A.: Comparison of the PAD and PANAS as models for describing emotions and for differentiating anxiety from depression. Journal of Psychopathology and Behavioral Assessment. 19 (1997) 331-357
5. Mehrabian, A.: Correlations of the PAD emotion scales with self-reported satisfaction in marriage and work. Genetic, Social, and General Psychology Monographs. 124 (1998) 311-334
6. Mehrabian, A., Blum, J.S.: Physical appearance, attractiveness, and the mediating role of emotions. Current Psychology: Developmental, Learning, Personality, Social. 16 (1997) 20-42
7. Mehrabian, A., Wihardja, C., Ljunggren, E.: Emotional correlates of preferences for situation-activity combinations in everyday life. Genetic, Social, and General Psychology Monographs. 123 (1997) 461-477

Representing Real-Life Emotions in Audiovisual Data with Non Basic Emotional Patterns and Context Features

Laurence Devillers, Sarkis Abrilian, and Jean-Claude Martin

LIMSI-CNRS, BP133, 91403 Orsay Cedex, France
{devil, abrilian, martin}limsi.fr

Abstract. The modeling of realistic emotional behavior is needed for various applications in multimodal human-machine interaction such as emotion detection in a surveillance system or the design of natural Embodied Conversational Agents. Yet, building such models requires appropriate definition of various levels for representing: the emotional context, the emotion itself and observed multimodal behaviors. This paper presents the multi-level emotion and context coding scheme that has been defined following the annotation of fifty one videos of TV interviews. Results of annotation analysis show the complexity and the richness of the real-life data: around 50% of the clips feature mixed emotions with multi-modal conflictual cues. A typology of mixed emotional patterns is proposed showing that cause-effect conflict and masked acted emotions are perceptually difficult to annotate regarding the valence dimension.

1 Introduction

The modeling of emotional behavior is needed for various applications in audio-visual signal processing or multimodal human-machine interaction, such as emotion detection in a surveillance system or the design of animated interactive characters also called Embodied Conversational Agents (ECAs). Yet, building such models requires representing multiple levels involved in emotional processes: the emotional context, the emotion itself and associated multimodal behaviors. Furthermore, modeling emotional behavior for realistic applications implies the challenge of exploring real-life data instead of basic and acted emotions. Real-life multimodal corpora are indeed very few despite the general agreement that it is necessary to collect databases that highlight naturalistic expressions of emotions [1]. Yet, the existing multimodal emotional behavior studies are based mostly on acted basic emotions. In Human Computer Interaction, researchers are studying the usefulness of expressivity and movement quality for the design of expressive ECAs [2].

Three types of emotion annotation are generally used in research on emotion: appraisal dimensions, abstract dimensions and most commonly verbal categories. These verbal categories include both "primary" labels (anger, fear, joy, sadness, etc. [3]) and "secondary" labels for social emotions (e.g. love, submission). Plutchik [4] also combined primary emotions to produce other labels for "intermediate" emotions. For example, love is a combination of joy and acceptance, whereas submission is a combination of acceptance and fear. Yet, the number of labels required for annotating

J. Tao, T. Tan, and R.W. Picard (Eds.): ACII 2005, LNCS 3784, pp. 519 – 526, 2005.

real-life emotions might be very high when compared to basic emotions. Actually, most of the emotion modeling studies has used a minimal set of labels to be tractable [5]. Instead of using this limited number of categories, some researchers define emotions using continuous abstract dimensions: Activation-Evaluation [1], Activation-Evaluation-Control [6]. This scheme needs to be refined by adding new abstract dimensions in order to distinguish some emotions such as fear and anger which both can be active, negative and uncontrolled. Finally, the appraisal model is useful for describing the perception / production of emotion. The major advance in this theory is the detailed specification of appraisal dimensions that are assumed to be used in evaluating emotion-antecedent events (pleasantness, novelty, etc) [7]. Some authors combine verbal labels and appraisal dimensions [8].

We have developed the EmoTV corpus [9], which features 51 videos samples of TV interviews with emotional behavior. Its highly emotional content during monologues is also quite relevant to our research since we do not want to focus on the analysis of communicative functions. Real-life emotions are more complex to annotate than the basic acted emotions. Our multi-level scheme allows describing emotion, context and high-level multimodal behavior. The main difficult point of this representation is to find the useful levels of description in term of granularity and temporality. A new representation of emotion with a soft emotion vector which allows the annotation of blended emotions has been proposed [9, 10]. We included both verbal categories and abstract dimensions in order to study their redundancy and complementarity's. Some appraisal descriptors derived from the appraisal model [7] such as time-of-event have been also added in the context part of the scheme.

A part of the corpus has been annotated (by three annotators) with the multi-level annotation scheme including emotion, context and high level multimodal description documented in an annotation guide. In this paper, we present some annotations results showing the complexity of our data. 50% of the clips feature mixed emotions and propose a typology of mixed emotion patterns. Correlations between different annotations of our multi-level coding scheme are also proposed as validation procedures of annotations. A low-level multimodal cues annotation scheme has been also defined [11, 12]. Our long-term goal is to investigate the relations between multi-modal cues, emotions and context, and to use the annotated corpus to pilot ECAs [13].

Section 2 introduces the corpus used for a first manual annotation phase done with two expert annotators [9] using the Anvil tool [14]. Section 3 details the annotation scheme: emotion, context and high-level multimodal annotations. Section 4 illustrates some correlation between these levels and shows the complexity of the data.

2 Corpus

Studying emotion raises several questions concerning ethics, naturalism of the emotion, contextual dependencies, etc. Recording actors aimed at providing controlled answers to these questions. How to collect more real-life corpus? It is necessary to find a context where the video-taped person forgets the presence of the camera and does not act. TV interviews during news are generally more natural than talk show or reality TV. Furthermore, the required size of such a corpus and the granularity of annotations depend on the research goals. For detection purposes, statistical approaches are greedy for large data sets. For realistic generation purposes, a fine-grained annotation of a smaller corpus might be more relevant. Other constraints concern the context of interaction such as the type of interaction (monologue or interaction with 2 or more people), the characters' position (in front of the camera, etc). EmoTV video clips have been selected with the following constraints: Interviews during news (2 people, only one visible), no spoken feedback from the journalist who interviews, people are recorded in the same position in front of the camera with their upper body visible. Our corpus is well balanced between positive and negative emotions. It is also rich in blended emotions such as conflictual valences, i.e. positive relief blended with sadness. Clips also show rich emotional behaviors expressed by gestures, facial expressions and speech (prosody and verbal content). The EmoTV corpus is in French and consists of 48 subjects, the total duration of the corpus is 12mn (average length of 14s per clip) and the lexicon size is 800 words (total number of words: 2500).

3 Multi-level Emotion Annotations Scheme

In a first manual annotation phase, two expert annotators created emotional segments where they felt it was appropriate for all the videos [9]. Annotations were done both at the global level of the video and for these individual emotional segments. The contextual descriptors were defined at the global level. We evaluated the quality of these annotations at each level using inter-coder agreement measures, and correlation between different cues that are logically dependent, such as the valence dimension and the classes of negative or positive labels. The attributes which are deterministic were checked automatically; for the other attributes a manual verification was made.

In this first annotation phase, the annotators could select only one label per segment. Inter-coder agreement measures were very low (e.g. kappa value 0.37) [9]. This was not due to bad labelling but rather to the fact that we use real-life exploratory data with a lot of blended emotions and conflictual multimodal cues, by example, cry to bring relief. Based on the careful study of these disagreement cases, we have defined a typology of non-basic emotional patterns, and enabled the annotation of each segment with two emotional labels. A temporal evolution of the emotions' intensity is useful for dynamic character animation so a coarse temporal annotation of emotion intensity inside each segment has been added to the annotation scheme.

To summarize, the specificities of our multi-level coding scheme are to enable annotation of: 1) both emotion labels and abstract dimensions and a coarse temporal description of intensity variation in each segment, 2) non-basic emotional patterns, 3) the emotional context including some appraisal-based dimensions and 4) a global description of perceived signs of emotion in the different modalities.

3.1 Emotion Representation

A combination of two theories for representing emotions is used in our scheme: dimensions and labels. Both verbal categories and abstract dimensions are included in order to study their redundancy and complementarity. The redundancy allows verifying the reliability of the annotations by correlation between dimensions and labels.

For example, valence should be correlated with emotion class. We present some correlation measures for validating our annotations in section 4.

In order to find an appropriate list of emotional labels, different strategies can be used [15]. The two expert annotators labeled the emotion they perceived in each emotional segment, each time selecting one label of their choice (free choice). This resulted in 176 fine-grain labels (after a normalization phase) which were classified into the following set of 14 broader categories: anger, despair, disgust, doubt, exaltation, fear, irritation, joy, neutral, pain, sadness, serenity, surprise and worry. We have kept several levels of granularity. The coarse-grained level is composed of the 6 well-known Ekman classes [3] plus the "neutral" and "other" classes.

Our coding scheme features two classical abstract dimensions [16]: activation (passive, normal, active) and valence (negative, neutral, positive). Intensity (low, normal, high) and control dimensions (controlled, normal, uncontrolled) were added since they provide relevant information for the study of real-life emotion. Furthermore, for each segment we added coarse temporal descriptors for intensity variation (rising, decreasing, etc) and the type of emotional pattern: basic or non-basic.

3.2 Emotion Mixtures

The real-life emotions we observed led us to propose an annotation scheme with two emotional labels for each segment and to propose the following typology of non-basic emotional patterns:

- blended emotions: two emotions are merged, and occur at the same time,
- masked acted emotion: the videotaped person is masking her real emotion, like a joy mask (by smiling) with a real disappointment behind,
- sequence: two emotions, one occurring shortly after the other, in a single emotional segment,
- cause-effect conflict: for example positive/negative conflict (e.g. to cry for joy and relief),
- ambiguity between two emotions in a same broad class (e.g. anger and irritation).

3.3 Contextual and Appraisal Emotion-Causes Information

Emotions found in real-life data are highly dependent on the context. The EmoTV is rich in different topics (politic, law, sport, etc). Five sets of attributes represent the context in our scheme for EmoTV. The first set is named the "emotional context" and includes some appraisal dimensions describing the reason that cause the emotions: degree-of-implication (low, normal, high), cause-event (free-text), person-event relation (society subject, true story by himself or by kin) and time of event (near, recent, present, future). The other sets are the "interview context": theme, place, the videotaped person: age, gender, race, the overall communicative goal of the video-taped person, which combines consequence-event and communicative function: what-for (to claim, to share a feeling, etc.), to-whom (kin, colleagues, public, etc.); and the "recording context": camera (static, dynamic), character (static, dynamic), acoustic quality, video quality.

3.4 Multimodal High Level Annotation

Annotation of perceived signs of emotions is done with high level descriptors at the level of the video (free text description for each modality: speech, eyes, mouth, head, brows, gestures, torso and shoulders), and for each emotional segment of the video (boolean value for each modality). The goal of the EmoTV corpus is to provide knowledge on the coordination between modalities during non-acted emotionally rich behaviors. A fine-grained multimodal cues annotation scheme has also been defined [12].

4 Annotations Analysis

The low kappa measures obtained in our first emotion annotation phase do not appear to be due to bad labelling but are rather to the complexity of real-life data. A large part of EmoTV consists of blended emotions and contradictory multimodal cues, by example cry to bring relief despite sadness.

A subset of EmoTV (11 clips, 48 segments) has been annotated by three expert labelers using the annotation scheme described above. An average time of 15mn is necessary to annotate each clip.

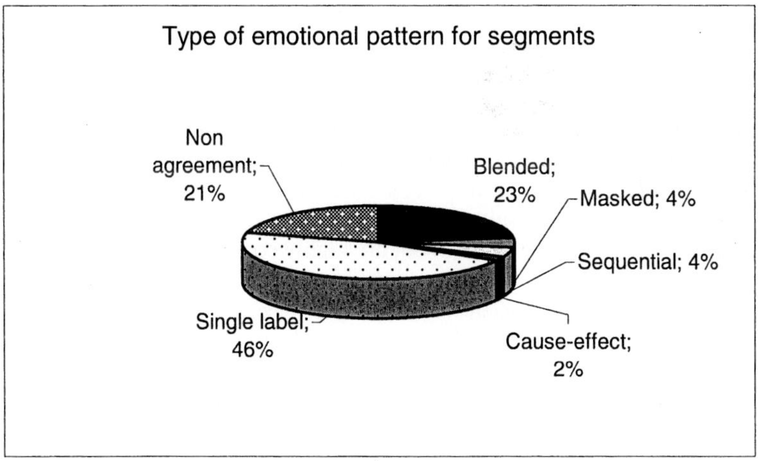

Fig. 1. Repartition of type of emotional pattern for the 48 segments after majority voting

Figure 1 summarizes the types of global pattern reported. It uses majority voting, i.e. a description is accepted if at least 2 of the 3 raters use it. On that criterion, the proportion of segments with no agreed label is 21%. The key point is that segments rated as showing a specific non-basic pattern (33%) were nearly as common as segments showing a pure emotion (46%). In such a situation, it is not surprising that asking raters to assign a single label leads to inter-coder disagreement.

The new annotation scheme with two labels per segment (Major and Minor) is used to describe a 'soft' coding as a way of representing everyday emotion mixes. A soft emotion vector is computed considering a combination of Major and Minor emotions rated by 2 (or more) coders (weights 2 for Major, 1 for minor). On 48 segments, 90% of the soft vectors (obtained with 3 raters) get a "winner" label, which gives better reliability scores than using one single label (77% of agreement for Major only).

The reliability of the dimensions annotation is also measured at the two levels (global and segmental). The Cronbach's alpha coefficient has been computed for continuous dimensions. Results show a high level of reliability (Table 1) for Intensity and Valence and more generally a higher reliability for the global clip than for each segment. The self-control seems to be difficult to evaluate on local segments. Globally speaking, in this experiment, activation (active/passive) is the less reliable dimension. Intensity seems to be more reliable than activity in our corpus. The reason might be the context of interviews of our corpus (the action is to talk).

Table 1. Cronbach's Alpha for each annotated dimension

Dimension	Alpha on global clip	Alpha on 48 segments
Intensity	0.896	0.750
Valence	0.739	0.761
Self-control	0.826	0.464
Activation	0.455	0.448

The negative communicative goals (to criticize, to complain, etc) annotated in the global emotional context (called what-for in our scheme) are highly correlated to the negative valence annotations obtained after majority voting. But when the type of emotional patterns is annotated as "cause-effect conflict" or "masked acted", there is no agreement between the raters for the valence and furthermore the communicative goal annotated does not explain the valence of the sequence (for example to explain, to share a story, etc). This result is reinforced by the fact that the valence dimension and the labels annotated for each segment are highly correlated except for the cases of

Table 2. Frequency with which different cue types were reported relevant to emotion judgments (a cue is accepted if at least 2 of the 3 raters use it). The percentage of each cue is given for Negative segments and Neutral/Positive segments in the two last columns. The proportion of segments (on the 48 segments) annotated with negative labels (winner of the soft vector) is 65%.

Multimodal Cues	#segments (total of 48 segments)	% cues All segments	% cues NEG Segments	% cues NEU/P0S Segments
Speech	44	92%	96%	82%
Eyes	40	83%	84%	82%
Mouth	31	65%	64%	65%
Head	29	60%	61%	59%
Brows	16	33%	29%	41%
Gestures	10	21%	29%	6%
Torso	4	8%	13%	0%
Shoulders	3	6%	10%	0%

those mixed emotions. The correlation between valence and verbal labels is a way to validate our annotations but also to point out the complexity of some segments.

Raters have been also asked to identify the cues that they considered to be important in reaching their rating. Table 2 summarizes the results. The main point is that both audio and facial cues were involved in the great majority of segments. There were in fact no cases where only one modality was judged relevant. The average number of multimodal cues by segment is between 3 and 4 cues (i.e. 177/48). The "uncontrolled" annotations appear mainly for anger and irritation. Furthermore, in the sub-set of the corpus studied, the presence of gestures, torso and shoulders movements appear in the segments labelled with negative verbal labels (see Table 2).

An analysis of the correlations between intensity and control obtained after majority voting and the number of multimodal cues in a segment has been carried out. 74% of the segments with a number of multimodal cues superior to the average have been annotated with a high level of intensity. When the control is high, the trend is that the number of multimodal annotations decreases.

Such analyses allow validating our annotation scheme and studying the correlation between high-level multimodal cues and emotion representations.

5 Conclusion and Future Directions

As a conclusion of these experiments, in real-life emotional behaviors, different channels are usually active, and they are as likely to conflict as to add. We identified some types of mixed emotions such as cause-conflict and masked emotional patterns which are very difficult to judge and annotate even for valence dimension.

The high and intermediate level of representation we propose will be completed with low-level information coming partially from automatic analysis of signal (for speech) and annotations for the other modalities (e.g. speed, frequency for gestures). We intend to validate our coding scheme by using the annotations of the EmoTV corpus as one source of knowledge for the specification of multimodal emotional behavior in ECA. This will enable various controlled experiments and perceptual tests with the ECA and the original videos.

Acknowledgements

This work was partly funded by the FP6 IST HUMAINE Network of Excellence (http://emotion-research.net).

References

1. Douglas-Cowie, E., Campbell, N., Cowie, R., Roach, R.: Emotional speech, Towards a new generation of databases. Speech Communication (2003).
2. Maya, V., Lamolle, M., Pelachaud, C.: Influences on Embodied Conversational Agent's Expressivity: Toward an Individualization of the ECAs. AISB (2004) convention. Symposium on Language, Speech and Gesture for Expressive Characters.

3. Ekman, P.: Basic emotions. In: T. Dalgleish, M. J. Power, (eds.): Handbook of Cognition & Emotion. John Wiley. New York (1999) 301–320.
4. Plutchik, R.: The psychology and Biology of Emotion. New York: Harper Collins College (1994).
5. Batliner, A., Fisher, K., Huber, R., Spilker, J., Noth, E.: Desperately seeking emotions or: Actors, wizards, and human beings. SpeechEmotion (2000).
6. Schröder M.: Dimensional Emotion Representation as a Basis for Speech Synthesis with Non-extreme Emotions. Affective Dialogue Systems (2004) 209-220.
7. Scherer, K. R.: Appraisal theories. In: T. Dalgleish, M. Power (eds.): Handbook of cognition and emotion. Wiley. Chichester, UK (1999) 637-639.
8. Gratch, J., Marsella, S.: Domain-independent Framework for Modeling Emotion. Journal of Cognitive Systems Research, Volume5, Issue 4 (2004) 269-306.
9. Abrilian, S., Devillers, L., Buisine S., Martin, J.-C.: EmoTV1: Annotation of Real-life Emotions for the Specification of Multimodal Affective Interfaces. HCI International (2005a), Las Vegas, USA.
10. Devillers, L. Vidrascu, L. Lamel, L.: Challenges in real-life emotion annotation and machine learning based detection. Journal of Neural Networks, Elsevier, to appear (2005).
11. Abrilian, A., Martin, J.-C., Devillers, L.: A Corpus-Based Approach for the Modeling of Multimodal Emotional Behaviors for the Specification of Embodied Agents. HCI International (2005b), Las Vegas, USA.
12. Martin, J.-C., Abrilian, S., Devillers, L.: Annotating Multimodal Behaviors Occuring during Non Basic Emotions. ACII (2005).
13. Lamolle, M. Mancini, M., Pelachaud, C., Abrilian, S., Martin, J.-C., Devillers, L.: Contextual Factors and Adaptative Multimodal Human-Computer Interaction:Multi-Level Specification of Emotion and Expressivity in ECAs. Context (2005).
14. Kipp, M.: Anvil - A Generic Annotation Tool for Multimodal Dialogue. Eurospeech (2001).
15. Cowie, R.: Emotion recognition in human-computer interaction. IEEE Signal processing Magazine (2001).
16. Cowie, R., Douglas-Cowie, E., Savvidou, S., McMahon, E., Sawey, M., Schröder, M.: FEELTRACE: An Instrument for Recording Perceived Emotion in Real Time. ISCA Workshop on Speech & Emotion. Northern Ireland (2000) 19-24.

The Relative Weights of the Different Prosodic Dimensions in Expressive Speech: A Resynthesis Study

Nicolas Audibert, Véronique Aubergé, and Albert Rilliard

Institut de la Communication Parlée,
Université Stendhal/INPG/CNRS, Grenoble, France
{audibert, auberge, rilliard}@icp.inpg.fr
http://www.icp.inpg.fr/Emotion

Abstract. The emotional prosody is multi-dimensional. A debated question is to understand if some parameters are more specialized to convey some emotion dimensions. Selected stimuli, expressing anxiety, disappointment, disgust, disquiet, joy, resignation, satisfaction and sadness, were extracted from the acted part of a French corpus supposed to include only variations of direct emotional expressions. These stimuli were used as a basis for the synthesis of artefactual stimuli integrating the emotional contour of each prosodic parameter separately, which were evaluated on a perceptual experiment. Results indicate that (1) no parameter alone is able to carry the whole emotion information, (2) F0 contours (not only the global F0 value) reveal to bring more information on positive expressions, (3) voice quality and duration convey more information on negative expressions, and (4) the intensity contours do not bring any significant information when used alone.

1 Introduction

The multi-dimensionality of prosody is a complex problem relatively to its emotional function. A large debate remains open on the question of the specificity of some emotional cues [17]: is F0 relative to positive or/and active dimension; is the voice quality relative to some specific aspects, such as the breathy quality relative to the degree of care [10]? Another important point of this discussion is that if one can suppose that some prosodic dimensions are related to some emotional dimensions, the question of their characterization still has to be addressed: by global values of the parameters supposed to be relevant (for instance, is F0 "higher" for positive emotions?), or by a global contour, from which quantitative values could possibly be extracted as sufficient cues [4]? The aim of this paper is to address the question of the relative weight of each parameter, taking as hypotheses that (1) the whole morphology of a contour is required to describe an emotional dimension (even when a global value is sufficient), and (2) one parameter cannot be in a one-to-one relation with an emotional dimension, even when it has a predominant weight.

In order to evaluate the weight of each prosodic parameter in the vocal morphology of emotions, and thus in the perception of their expressions, we have to evaluate how stimuli carrying these expressions are perceived when parameters are tuned separately. Since the variation of these parameters results from a global control of the

J. Tao, T. Tan, and R.W. Picard (Eds.): ACII 2005, LNCS 3784, pp. 527 – 534, 2005.

vocal tract rather than separate controls, it doesn't seem possible to naturally collect such stimuli, even if those expressions were produced by specifically trained actors.

We adopt a resynthesis-based approach to evaluate such phenomena, i.e. we perform an acoustic analysis of reference stimuli, prior to the synthesis of new stimuli using the values of extracted parameters as an input. Those parameters may be voluntarily altered, and either the whole set or only part of them may be used, according to the aim of the experiment. Eventually, generated stimuli can be perceptually evaluated to assess tested hypotheses.

Such a method was already used in experiments focusing on affective expressions in speech. For instance, Gobl et al. [13] evaluated the role played by voice quality in emotional expressions using stimuli resynthesized from a reference glottal flow waveform, and modified to express different voice qualities. In another experiment [8], prosodic parameters (limited to F0 variations and duration) analyzed from emotional expressions in English of anger, happiness and sadness as well as neutral expressions were applied to diphones recorded with the same set of emotional expressions in a concatenative synthesizer. Stimuli with prosodic parameters matched to diphones set, as well as mismatched stimuli, were generated this way. Looking at identification scores obtained by mismatched expressions, authors concluded that anger expressions were mainly carried by diphones, sadness by prosodic parameters, when no clear pattern could be observed from expressions of happiness. Eventually, in other studies such as [1] or [6], stimuli were synthesized from multiparametric measurements in order to evaluate the relevance of extracted parameters for the perception of emotional expressions.

2 A Corpus of Authentic Emotional Speech

The choice of a corpus of authentic expressive speech recorded in lab was made for several reasons. First, evidence from neurophysiology showed that acted emotion do not follow the same neural mechanism as non-acted one [11], as they are not due to physiological changes. Moreover, as shown by Aubergé and Cathiard [3], acted amusement for instance can be discriminated from non-acted one, with a strong interjudge effect. This implies that one cannot make sure that acted productions are identical to non acted emotional expressions, as the ability of an actor to reproduce exactly spontaneous emotional expressions cannot be evaluated in an objective way.

On the other hand, acoustic analyses require a high-quality recording that can only be performed in lab condition [9], which implies to develop protocols for the induction of emotional states. In addition, the choice of such a method enables the control of phonetic and linguistic contents by the use of a command language that constraints the subjects' vocal expression. Eventually, it allows the collection on the same utterances of various emotional states.

In order to set up experiments based on the Wizard of Oz paradigm (which consists in imitating the behavior of a complex person-machine interface) and enabling to collect corpora of authentic emotional speech, a dedicated platform, E-Wiz, was developed at ICP in Java language, with a client/server architecture [5]. This platform makes possible to design and set up various emotional induction scenarios, with the common frame of imitating a voice recognition-based software.

One of the developed scenarios, Sound Teacher, is presented as a software based on the neuropsychological findings of perception-action theory, and enabling the subject to improve his cognitive abilities for the phonetic learning of languages. The subjects are chosen to be strongly motivated by this task. The Sound Teacher scenario aims at inducing first positive then negative emotional states to the subjects by manipulating their performances. In this scenario the subject is convinced to communicate exclusively with a machine, through a very poor and strict word command language, in order to avoid the use of attitudinal expressiveness, thus restricting the subject's production to direct expressions of emotions.

Each recording session lasted around 50 minutes, for the 17 subjects recorded up to now. For each session, the speech data consist in the command words [paʒ sɥivɑ̃t] (*'next page'*) repeated 50 to 60 times, and in five monosyllabic (to avoid timing and long-term prosodic effects) color names shared in the phonological space ([ʀuʒ], [ʒon], [sabl], [vɛʀ], [bʀik]), repeated 11 to 50 times. Acoustic, video, biophysiological and articulatory signals were recorded synchronously.

7 out of 17 subjects were professional actors, for which an extra protocol was designed: immediately after having been trapped by Sound Teacher, those subjects were asked to reproduce the expressions of the emotional states they had been encountering during the experiment, using actor's methods. This task was performed both on the utterances used in the spontaneous part and on 10 semantically neutral sentences. In addition of that, actors were asked to express the 'big six' [11] emotions (happiness, anger, surprise, fear, disgust, sadness) on the same stimuli (command words as well as longer sentences).

The first emotional labeling was done by the subject himself after the experiment: he was given a VHS video tape, as well as a pre-filled grid, with the task of describing the different emotional states he had been feeling along the experiment. The collected emotions expressed by 17 subjects are close to what was expected: concentration, satisfaction, joy, relief, stress, anger, discouragement, boredom, anguish. An interesting observation is that highly coherent groups of reaction appear within subjects, surely linked to their psychological profile.

3 Generation of Synthesized Stimuli

3.1 Choice of Reference Data

We selected 10 monosyllabic reference stimuli, extracted from the acted part of the E-Wiz / Sound Teacher corpus [5] and composing a subset of the 72 acted stimuli produced by a male actor and previously evaluated by 26 subjects on a perception study [15], which showed that emotions expressed by monosyllabic stimuli were as well recognized as those expressed by longer sentences. Those 10 stimuli were used as a basis to generate the 42 synthetic stimuli evaluated in this study. They express the following emotional states: anxiety, disappointment, disgust, disquiet, happiness, resignation, satisfaction and sadness on the French monosyllabic words [ruʒ] and [sabl]. Moreover, neutral expressions of those two words were selected as a reference for the comparison of multiparametric contours. The relevance of a neutral expression for the selected speaker is validated by the presence in his spontaneous production of expressions labeled as 'nothing' by the speaker himself [4].

3.2 Stimuli Design

Parameter contours were analyzed and used in resynthesis using the Praat software [7] following a semi-automatic procedure driven by a specific script. The process was to stylize F0 and intensity contours extracted from a source stimulus, to apply one or both of them to a target stimulus with respect for duration events, and eventually to generate a new wave file combining properties of both source and target stimuli using the TD-PSOLA-based synthesis function of Praat. Contours stylization (to ensure no salient point was missed) as well as their transplantation to the target stimulus were user-monitored tasks.

For each original stimulus carrying an emotional expression, 5 distinct synthetic stimuli were generated: (i) A control stimulus labeled *full resynthesis* built by applying the stylized F0 and intensity contours of the source stimulus to itself, as a way to evaluate possible resynthesis artifacts. (ii) A stimulus labeled *F0 only*, built by applying the F0 contour of the source stimulus to the neutral expression stimulus with the same phonetic material. (iii) A stimulus labeled *intensity only*, built by applying the intensity contour of the source stimulus to the corresponding neutral expression stimulus. (iv) A stimulus labeled *F0 and intensity*, obtained by applying both F0 and intensity source stimulus contours to the neutral expression stimulus. (v) A stimulus labeled *voice quality and duration* stimulus. This last condition was designed by applying the F0 and intensity of the corresponding neutral expression stimulus to the source stimulus. As a result, only voice quality and timing phenomena of the source stimulus remain, when its emotion-specific pitch and intensity are neutralized.

In addition to these 40 stimuli generated from the 8 selected emotional expressions, a stimulus in *full synthesis* condition was generated from each neutral expression original stimulus.

A drawback of the method used for the generation of stimuli in the *voice quality and duration* condition is that it does not enable us to study voice quality and duration phenomena separately, since we cannot process directly at least one of them. However, as we assume that direct emotional expression belong to a time domain different from the one of other affective expressions [2], we decided not to rely on a linguistic – and potentially not relevant to direct affective expressions – time model to analyze duration events. Moreover, as we don't have a method to perform contour tracking on a voice quality parameter [16], we are not yet able to process voice quality in a reliable way.

4 Perceptual Evaluation

The 42 generated stimuli were rated by 40 judges (all native French speakers, 6 male, 34 female, mean age: 23.3 years) at the lab in a soundproof room, each stimulus being presented three times to each judge. Stimuli were presented in a random order, controlled to prevent the same stimulus from being presented twice consecutively. A graphical interface was developed with the Revolution software to present the stimuli and record subject's responses.

Subjects were asked to choose one category between the 8 emotional labels proposed (anxiety, disappointment, disgust, disquiet, happiness, resignation, satisfaction and sadness) or to select the neutral label when the presented stimulus was perceived as expressing no emotion. In addition of that, they were asked to rate the perceived emotional intensity on a 1-10 scale by moving the cursor of the chosen label.

5 Results

Results of the perceptual evaluation were processed separately for each resynthesis condition. In a first time, we did examine only identification scores compiled into confusion matrices for each resynthesis condition, regardless of the emotional intensities indicated by subjects.

Chi-square tests indicate that observed responses distributions are significantly different from chance (p=.001) for the *full resynthesis* and *voice quality and duration* conditions. Though observed patterns for other conditions also seem to differ from chance, low scores attributed to some categories (especially to disgust) resulted in expected numbers too small to allow us to perform chi-square validation.

Due to the number of confusions observed, we cannot easily draw other conclusions straight from raw confusion matrices. However, we can already notice some tendencies: for instance the expression of *satisfaction* (recognized with a score of 24.2% in control condition) obtains almost as high scores in *F0 only* (21.7%) and *F0 and intensity* (22.5%) conditions. Moreover, the expression of anxiety (identified at 57.5% in control condition) also obtains a high identification score in *voice quality and duration* condition.

Taking major confusions into account, a category clustering is proposed to make main tendencies appear more clearly: the expressions of happiness and satisfaction are grouped into a category labeled joy*;* anxiety and disquiet labels are grouped into a *fear* category; sadness, disappointment and resignation are grouped into a *sadness* category; *disgust* and *neutral* remain separate categories. In the following, joy, fear and sadness stand for these clustered categories.

New confusion matrices were computed to take those clusters into account, scores being balanced with the number of original labels clustered. Chi-square tests for clustered matrices data indicate that distributions of responses significantly differ from chance distribution for all resynthesis conditions (p=.001 for all conditions except *intensity only* condition: p=.01).

Figure 1 shows a set of diagrams presenting clustered results for each resynthesis condition, as well as a comparison of identification scores across conditions. Clustered categories positions in diagrams are function of their identification score and attractiveness. For a given label, attractiveness was defined as the sum of responses wrongly attributed to other labels, balanced with the theoretical maximum score. Moreover, arrows between labels indicate confusions over chance level, thickness being proportional to the confusion value.

In *full resynthesis* condition, many subjects confused neutral expressions with sadness. The first observation is that no category obtains identification scores as high in manipulated condition than in control condition, which enables us to conclude that no parameter contour carries the whole affective information alone.

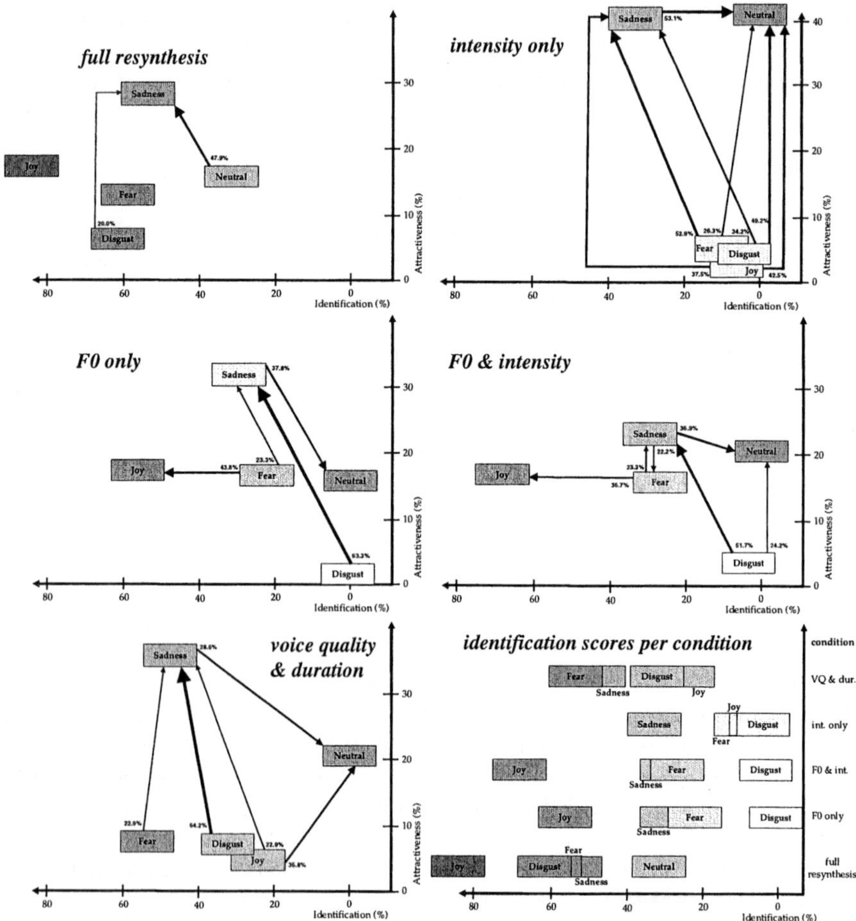

Fig. 1. Visualization of identification and confusion scores after categories clustering, for each resynthesis condition. Figure on bottom-right compares identification scores across conditions.

In *intensity only* condition, most expressions were very poorly recognized, with scores under 10%, except expressions of sadness, identified at 35.6%. However, this difference may be explained by the fact that subjects rating *intensity only* stimuli as sadness were the same as those confusing neutral expressions with sadness in control condition. We therefore conclude that intensity contours alone do not carry enough information to make generated stimuli perceptually different from neutral expressions.

In *F0 only* and *F0 & intensity* condition, joy was well recognized (respectively at 56.3% and 67.5% vs. 85.4% in *full resynthesis* condition), when fear and sadness were identified with a score only slightly over chance, and disgust was systematically confused.

In a second time, emotional intensities indicated by subjects were normalized with the number of times the corresponding category was selected for each resynthesis condition, to obtain mean intensities for each element of the confusion matrices. If we look at these values for clustered categories, we observe that, though attributed intensities are not significantly correlated to identification scores, similar patterns may be observed. Indeed, highest values are observed in the control condition (overall mean: 4.3) than in other conditions, especially for the expressions of disgust and joy, and lower values are observed in the *intensity only* condition (overall mean: 3.1). Expressions of joy obtained the highest scores in *F0 only* and *F0 and intensity* conditions, when expressions of disgust, sadness and fear were attributed highest values in *voice quality and duration*. The only remarkable difference when compared with identification scores is that the expression of disgust obtains the highest mean intensity both in control condition (7.4) and *voice quality and duration* condition (5.8), in spite of identification scores not better than those of other expressions. This last observation is coherent with the observed inter-judge effect found in [15] for the perception of disgust in audio-only condition: only a part of subjects are able to perceive expressions of disgust, but these subjects perceive it with a good accuracy.

6 Conclusion

This work was conducted on stimuli supposed to include prosodic variations limited to involuntary emotions, the others affects changes (attitudes and expressivity) being frozen in such mono-syllabic mono-words. The stimuli synthesized with separate parameters variation for a limited panel of emotional expressions (first expressed in authentic tasks and labeled by the subjects themselves before being re-played) are artifacts. However the listeners were able to identify some salient parts of the global morphology of this chimera prosody in a Gestalt-like processing. These results inform us on the weight of the parameters on which it is necessary to be vigilant when modeling prosody for the synthesis of expressions, the interest to synthesize the less relevant parameters in order to generate a non chimera form, and point out the contours as a relevant feature for characterizing expressions over a global value of the parameter. The voice quality dimension was not directly processed in this study, but an adequate voice quality synthesis tool is being studied with France Telecom R&D division, and will make possible to test hypotheses on that prosodic dimension in future studies.

Acknowledgment

This work was supported by the Japanese CREST Expressive Speech Processing project, by the French Pegasus program, and by France Telecom R&D. Special thanks to Nick Campbell for our constructive discussions.

References

1. Abadjieva, E., Murray, I. R., Arnott, J. L.: Applying analysis of human emotional speech to enhance synthetic speech. Eurospeech'93, Berlin, Germany (1993) 909-912
2. Aubergé, V. A Gestalt Morphology of Prosody Directed by Functions: The Example of a Step by Step Model Developed at ICP, 1st Speech Prosody, Aix-en-Provence, France (2002) 151-154

3. Aubergé, V., Cathiard, M.: Can we hear the prosody of smile ? Special issue Emotional Speech, Speech Communication Review 40 (2003) 87-97
4. Aubergé, V., Audibert, N., Rilliard, A.: Acoustic Morphology of Expressive Speech: What about Contours? 2nd Speech Prosody, Nara, Japan (2004) 201-204
5. Aubergé, V., Audibert, N., Rilliard, A.: E-Wiz: A Trapper Protocol for Hunting the Expressive Speech Corpora in Lab. 4th International Conference on Language Resources and Evaluation, Lisbon, Portugal (2004) 179-182
6. Bänziger, T. : Communication vocale des émotions. Perception de l'expression vocale et attributions émotionnelles. PhD thesis, University of Geneva (2004).
7. Boersma, P., Weenink, D.: Praat: doing phonetics by computer. http://www.fon.hum.uva.nl/ praat
8. Bulut, M., Narayanan, S. S., Syrdal, A. K.: Expressive speech synthesis using a concatenative synthesiser: 7th ICSLP, Denver, Colorado, USA (2002).
9. Campbell, N.: Databases of Emotional Speech. ISCA Workshop on Speech and Emotions, Newcastle, Northern Ireland (2000) 34-38.
10. Campbell, N., Mokhtari, P.: Voice Quality: the 4th Prosodic Dimension. 15th International Congress of Phonetic Sciences, Barcelona Spain (2003) 2417-2420
11. Cornelius, R. R.: The science of emotion. Research and tradition in the psychology of emotion. Upper Saddle River (NJ): Prentice-Hall (1996).
12. Damasio, A. R.: Descartes' error. Emotion, reason, and the human brain. A. Grosset/ Putnam Books (1994)
13. Gobl, C., Ní Chasaide, A.: Testing affective correlates of voice quality through analysis and resynthesis. ISCA Workshop on Speech and Emotions, Newcastle, Northern Ireland (2000) 178-183
14. Juslin, P. N., Laukka, P.: Communication of emotions in vocal expression and music performance: Different channels, same code? Psychological Bulletin (2003) 129(5), 770-814
15. Rilliard, A., Aubergé, V. and Audibert, N.: Evaluating an Authentic Audio-Visual Expressive Speech Corpus. 4th International Conference on Language Resources and Evaluation, Lisbon, Portugal (2004) 175-178
16. Rossato, S., Audibert, N., Aubergé, V.: Emotional Voice Measurement: A Comparison of Articulatory-EGG and Acoustic-Amplitude Parameters. Speech Prosody 2004, Nara, Japan (2004) 749-752
17. Scherer K. R., Johnston T., Klasmeyer G.: Vocal Expression of Emotion. In R.J. Davidson, K.R. Scherer, H.H. Goldsmith (Eds). Handbook of Affective Sciences (2003) 433-456

An XML-Based Implementation of Multimodal Affective Annotation

Fan Xia[1], Hong Wang[1], Xiaolan Fu[2], and Jiaying Zhao[2]

[1] State Key Laboratory of Intelligent Technology and Systems, Department of Computer Science and Technology, Tsinghua University, Beijing 100084, P.R. China

[2] State Key Laboratory of Brain and Cognitive Science, Institute of Psychology, Chinese Academy of Sciences, Beijing 100101, P.R. China

Abstract. In simple cases, affective computing is a computational device recognizing and acting upon the emotions of its user or having (or simulating having) emotions of its own in complex cases. Multimodal technology is currently one of the hottest focuses in affective computing research. However, the lack of a large-scale multimodal database limits the research to some respective and scattered fields, such as affective recognition by video or by audio. This paper describes the development and implementation of an XML-based multimodal affective annotation system which is called MAAS (Multimodal Affective Annotation System). MAAS contains a hierarchical affective annotation model based on the 3-dimensional affect space derived from Mehrabian's PAD temperament scale. The final annotation file is formed in XML format in order to interchange the resources with other research groups conveniently.

1 Introduction

In psychology, affect is an emotion or subjectively experienced feeling, or the involvement of such processes in a psychological system or theory, different from mood which is more sustained [11]. Affective computing is an area of computer science research aimed to simulate emotional processes or make use of human emotion in human-computer interaction. In simple cases, affective computing is a computational device recognizing and acting upon the emotions of its user or having (or simulating having) emotions of its own in complex cases.

Multimodal technology is a key issue of emotion recognizing and understanding in affective computing research. The development of multimodal database has attracted the attention of some researchers in the past few years. This is motivated by the fact that the lack of a large-scale multimodal database limits the research of affective computing. Our work is a sub-project of the RACTA (Research on Affective Computing Theory and Approach), a key research project of NSFC (National Nature Science Foundation of China), with the purpose of establishing a large-scale affect database. In this paper, we present an approach to annotate human emotions precisely and conveniently, as well as its implementations.

J. Tao, T. Tan, and R.W. Picard (Eds.): ACII 2005, LNCS 3784, pp. 535–541, 2005.

In achieving our goal, a series of experiments have been designed. Participants were stimulated in order to induce some real affect. A few problems arised such as how to evaluate the stimulation materials and how to annotate the various affect precisely and conveniently. In the following sections, we will present an annotation system named MAAS with a useful toolkit to solve these problems.

2 Approaches of Affective Evaluation

There is no exact definition of affect in psychology. Nonetheless, various psychologists have attempted to provide temporary definitions, among which Leverson's theory is the most acceptable - affect is "a transient psychological-physiological behavior, which represents the model that the organism adopted to adapt the variety environment" [1].

Adopting a universal evaluation standard will be greatly helpful to allow the easy interchange of annotation files and the sharing of annotation model among different research groups. There are two different theoretical approaches to the study of affect: categorical and dimensional.

The categorical approach considers that there are several basic types of affect; each type has its special experiential characters, physiological arousal pattern and performance pattern. The different combinations of the basic affect form the entire human affect [2]. According to this approach, commonly proposed members include happiness, surprise, fear, sadness, anger, disgust, contempt, shame, and guilt [12].

Another one is the dimensional approach. This theory shows that the human affect consists of several dimensions. The dimensional theorists consider affect as gradual and smooth transformation. In this approach, similarity and differ-

The following sample ratings illustrate definitions of various emotion terms when scores on each PAD scale range from -1 to +1:

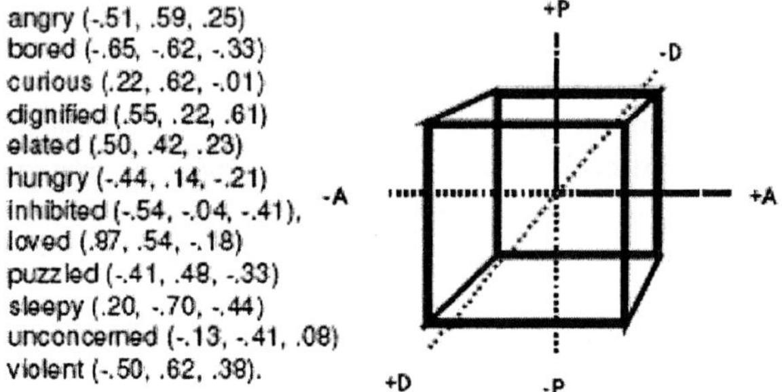

The emotional state "angry" is a highly unpleasant, highly aroused, and moderately dominant emotional state. The "bored" state implies a highly unpleasant, highly unaroused, and moderately submissive state.

From: Albert Mehrabian's (1980) PAD Scales.

Fig. 1. 3-dimensional affect space [5] [10]

ence between two types of affect is expressed as the distance in the dimensional space. The most acceptable dimensional pattern is a two-dimension space can be described as below: (a) valence or in other word hedonic tone, this dimension is based on negative-positive affect's separation-activation; (b) arousal or activation, this dimension indicates the activated power intensity associated with the affect status. However, this approach doesn't hold good in all cases. For example, it fails to specify the difference between fear and anger [6].

In MAAS, Mehrabian's PAD temperament scale is used [5] [6] [7].The PAD scale determines emotions using a three-dimensional emotion space representing pleasure-displeasure, arousal-nonarousal and dominance-submissiveness. Pleasure-displeasure represents the positive or negative quality of the emotion; arousal-nonarousal refers to a combination of physical activity and mental alertness; and dominance-submissiveness is defined in terms of levels of control [5]. According to Mehrabian, every possible human emotion can be represented as definite points in the three dimensions. The following emotions exist as points in that space: angry, bored, curious, dignified, elated, hungry, inhibited, loved, puzzled, sleepy, unconcerned, and violent [5], as shown in Figure 1. Violent, for instance, represents a displeased, highly aroused, and highly dominant emotional state.

Furthermore, the work of Yuxia Huang and her colleagues based on IAPS (International Affective Picture System) [3] shows that basic affect has a corresponding position in the dimensional affective space. For example, the affect of happiness always has a corresponding position on the aroused and positive dimensions, and the affect of sadness on the nonaroused and negative dimensions. Through the research they also discover that the dimensional affective space has no absolute relation with the basic affect, which means that there is no precise transformation between basic affect and the position in dimensional affect space.

Further analysis shows the correspondence between the two approaches [3]. In some cases, they are similar in some ways. Like the categorical approach, the dimensional approach also includes the existence of basic affect. Moreover, the multidimensional and dynamical nature of affect should be considered while describing the complicated human affect.

3 MAAS: An XML-Based Affective Annotation System

3.1 Issues in the Design of a Multimodal Affective Annotation System

An effective annotation approach needs to be able to represent the entire human affect. The representation should be precise and convenient for researchers. MAAS assumes that human affect consists of three parts: subjective experience, performance or in another word expression and physiological arousal. The system should be useful when annotating a person's affect in a particular scene, describing his or her performance and tracking the physiological data.

The implementation of multimodal annotation is another important issue that needs to be considered. Due to the complexity and multi-causality of affect, any single subject like video is not enough for affect recognition. Thus we must integrate the multimodal data: physiological, audio-visual in the annotation process in MAAS.

3.2 The Hierarchical Annotation Model

Considering the convenience of annotation process and the representation of various human affect, MAAS employs a hierarchical structure to describe both affect information and other data sources. There are mainly two top layers in MAAS's hierarchical structure: the affect annotation layer and the data layer.

First in affect annotation MAAS assumes that there are ten basic categories of affect: exuberant, bored, dependent, disdainful, relaxed, anxious, docile, hostile, fearful and disgusted. Each affect in these categories has a value in the form of (P, A, D) in the three dimensional affective space. For example, anger is labeled with a value (-.51,.59,.25) and curious with a value (.22,.62,-.01). During the annotation process, MAAS divides the annotation into two parts: the person's self-evaluation and an objective-evaluation by others. Self-evaluation and objective-evaluation are respectively corresponded to the features of subjective experience and performance of affect. In the following steps, some scattered elements can be added to the annotation, such as the mode which represents how the person performs his or her affect, by expression or gesture; the scene which represents the description of the experiment environment and the person's background, etc..

In the data layer there are now three sub-layers: video, audio and physiology. The data recorded during the experiments will be stored into the data layer in required format. The notable key is that data layer represents not only the physiological arousal but also multimodal factors related to the affect.

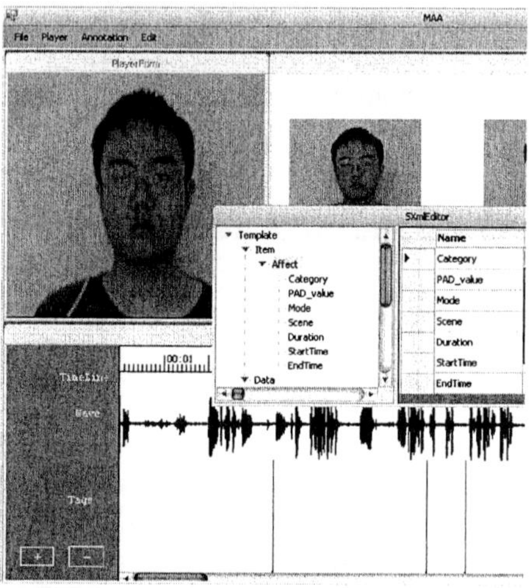

Fig. 2. MAAS-toolkit's main window

3.3 MAA: An XML-Based Affective Annotation Tool

A demo picture of MAAS's toolkit is given in Figure 2. It shows how to use the MAAS's toolkit to annotate a person's affect. The main window contains a video-window, a wave-window and a thumbnail-window. Before the annotation process, the video and the audio source should be specified respectively. In the center of Figure 2, there is a simple XML-based annotation content editor, which appears when a segment is specified as Figure 3 shows. The MAAS toolkit will automatically track the data to the annotation content editor and save it to the result files.

When the large-scale affective resource database is established, the most imperative problem is how to extract a particular piece of data from a vast database rapidly and efficiently. MAAS's toolkit provides an extract wizard for researchers. This tool in MAAS can extract the data with features specified by user from a great capacity of annotation files and sort the result in several ways, as Figure 4 shows. For example, users can extract only the relaxed affect in a series of experiment order by experiment time.

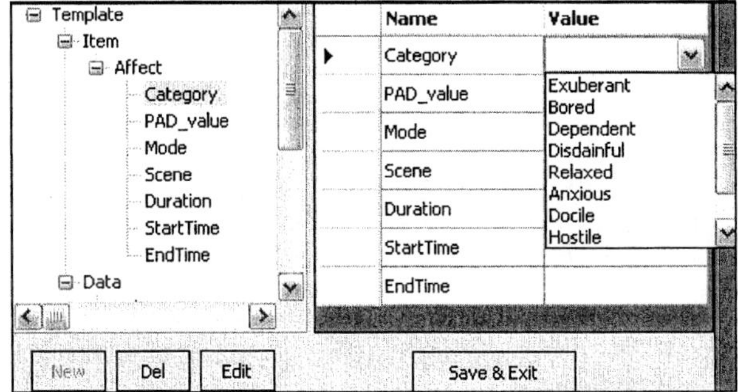

Fig. 3. Annotation content editor

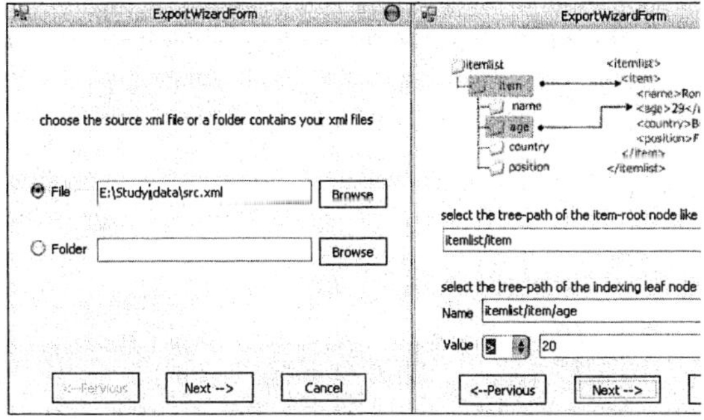

Fig. 4. Extract specified item from annotation file(s)

Here is a simple example of the annotation file:

```
<?xml version="1.0" encoding="utf-8"?>
<affect>
    <Category>Relaxed</Category>
    <PAD_value>(.22, .51, -.10)</PAD_value>
    <mode>expression</mode>
    <scene>in the dormitory</scene>
    <Duration unit=ms>1226</Duration>
    <Other />
</affect>

<data>
    <video> </video>
    <audio> </audio>
    <physiology>   </physiology>
</data>
```

4 Conclusion

A multimodal affective annotation system named MAAS is described in this paper. MAAS and its toolkit are convenient for researchers to annotate common affect and track the data collected in the experiment. It takes the most popular and standard XML format to store the annotation results, which is easy for users to read and to modify. The hierarchical annotation structure which MAAS adopts is flexible enough to expand to be compliant with other particular research.

Acknowledgements

This work is a part of the Research on Affective Computing Theory and Approach, which is a key research project of National Natural Science Foundation of China (NSFC). We would like to thank Prof.Lianhong Cai and other members of the Project Group for their valuable discussion and help.

References

1. R.W.Leverson: The Nature of Emotions [M]. New York, OxfordUniversity Press. (1994) 123-126
2. P.Ekman: An argument for basic emotions [J]. Cognition and Emotion. **6** (1992) 169-200
3. Huang, Y., Luo, J.: Experimental Research based on IAPS in China. Psychology and Sanitation Journal of China. **18** (2004) 631-634
4. J.Broekens, D.DeGroot: Scalable and Flexible Appraisal Models for Virtual Agents. CGAIDE. (2004).

5. A.Mehrabian: Basic Dimensions for a General Psychological Theory. Cambridge, OGH Publishers. (1980).
6. Li, X., Zhou, H., Song, S., Ran, T.,Fu, X.: The reliability and validity of the Chinese version of abbreviated PAD emotion scales. In: Proceedings of the First International Conference on Affective Computing and Intelligent Interaction. (2005)
7. Zhao, J., Fu, X.: An Evaluation-based Hybrid Annotation Scheme for Emotion Using Multimodal Data in Task-oriented Conditions. Submitted to ACM CHI 2006
8. R.W.Picard: Affective Computing. MIT Press, London, England. (1997)
9. E.C.Chang, L.J.Sanna: Optimism, Pessimism, and Positive and Negative Affectivity in Middle-Aged Adults: A Test of a Cognitive-Affective Model of Psychological Adjustment. Psychology and Aging. **16** (2001) 524-531
10. G.A.Hollinger, Z.A.Pezzementi, B.Mitchell, A.Flurie, B.A.Maxwell: Design of a Social Mobile Robot Using Emotion-Based Decision Mechanisms. http://www.engin.swarthmore.edu/ ghollin1/e28/lab5/SocialRobot.pdf
11. http://www.wikipedia.org/wiki/affect
12. M.Pagel: The Evolution of Human Emotions. The Oxford Encyclopedia of Evolution. **1** (2002) 296-299

CHAD: A Chinese Affective Database

Mingyu You, Chun Chen, and Jiajun Bu

College of Computer Science, ZheJiang University, China
{roseyoumy, chenc, bjj}@zju.edu.cn

Abstract. Affective database plays an important role in the process of affective computing which has been an attractive field of AI research. Based on analyzing current databases, a Chinese affective database (CHAD) is designed and established for seven emotion states: neutral, happy, sad, fear, angry, surprise and disgust. Instead of choosing the personal suggestion method, audiovisual materials are collected in four ways including three types of laboratory recording and movies. Broadcast programmes are also included as source of vocal corpus. By comparison of the five sources two points are gained. First, although broadcast programmes get the best performance in listening experiment, there are still problems as copyright, lacking visual information and can not represent the characteristics of speech in daily life. Second, laboratory recording using sentences with appropriately emotional content is an outstanding source of materials which has a comparable performance with broadcasts.

1 Introduction

The interest in emotion expression and recognition by human and animals has attracted more and more attentions. Charles Darwin published the first monograph devoted to this topic in the 19th century [1]. After this milestone work, psychologists began to gradually accumulate knowledge in the field. A new wave of interest attracts not only psychologists but also artificial intelligence researchers. Equipping computers with the ability of perception and expression would lead to a revolution to the human-computer interface nowadays. Affective tutors are more suitable to children. Lifelike software agents help us to be really supported by interactive robots in many science fictions. A new attractive field of AI research as affective computing has been identified [2].

AI experts made contributions to emotion recognition [3] and emotional speech synthesis [4], which depend on adequate training and testing materials. In spite of intensive research in corpus linguistics in the past decades, few speech databases have included emotional information [5]. Unfortunately, there are some limitations which are still under development as below.

Modality. Most of existing emotional databases deal with one modality at a time(i.e. audio or visual). There are databases only focusing on speech corpus in Danish(DES, 1997), Dutch(ELRA corpus S0020, called GRONINGEN) and English(joint project of University Reading and Leeds [6]). On the other hand, databases provided by Yale [7] and Emanuela [8] are just collections of face

J. Tao, T. Tan, and R.W. Picard (Eds.): ACII 2005, LNCS 3784, pp. 542–549, 2005.

pictures. Audiovisual corpus offering multi-modality input stream is necessary to make the computer work like a person and achieve a great increase in emotion recognition accuracy.

Emotion States. Few studies agreed on the same emotional classification because of thousands of emotion definitions in literature and variant concepts of emotional information in different cultures. Chul Min Lee simply classified the human emotions into non-negative and negative [13]. McGilloway et al. [14] set up their researches on four basic emotion states: fear, anger, happiness and sadness. Different from the small emotion sets, Linnankoski [15]requested the speakers to simulate ten emotional connotations: naming, sad, pleading, admiring, content, commanding, astonished, scornful, angry and frightened.

Genuine Emotion. Some of the current databases collected radio or television programmes with relatively strong emotions as main source of materials [9]. The corpora seem to provide obviously emotional materials. However, the problem is that the researcher may have no way to ascertain the intended emotion and how strongly the emotion is expressed. Furthermore, if such authentic materials are accessed, copyright problem is unavoidable. In order to resolve these issues, most of the researchers turned to have a number of speakers simulate emotions in laboratory environments. Professional actors/actresses were preferred to be the speakers because of their better skills in expressing intended emotions [10] that could usually be correctly identified by listeners afterwards. The question here is whether they faithfully represent the characteristics of speech used by ordinary people when naturally experience similar emotions. Instead, some speech corpus chose non-professional speakers to produce more spontaneous data. In order to overcome the problems of acted speech and make the person nature in front of camera lens, omnifarious methods were tried. Noam Amir et al. requested the subjects to recall an emotional event and experience the same feelings that they had felt at the original event [11]. The recordings are maybe satisfactorily emotional but the materials must have relationship with personal information more or less. Ethical validity involved should not be ignored. Geneva's group utilized interactive computer games to elicit emotions [12]. Subjects were videotaped while playing the experimental games. The approach does seem capable of eliciting genuine emotions, it remains to be seen how closely it relates to the way emotion expressed in social contexts and the database gained contains only facial images without speech. How to collect audiovisual materials with genuine emotion is still a difficult problem.

Language. There are emotional speech databases in Danish(DES, 1997), Dutch(ELRA corpus S0020, called GRONINGEN), Russian [16] and English [6] available. Different Chinese linguistic corpora exist but few of them include emotional information. Zhao li [17] has mentioned a Chinese speech corpus produced by five persons. But it lacks visual information and can not be reached publicly.

Considering the importance of emotional database and the lack of Chinese corpus available, CHAD - a Chinese affective database is set up. Audiovisual materials offering multi-modality input stream are collected for high emotion recognition accuracy. The seven emotion states: neutral, happy, sad, fear, angry, surprise and disgust used in our database are the most popular emotion states and also employed in MPEG-4. Instead of choosing the best way only based on researchers' guess, five methods are included to collect spontaneous emotional materials. Listening experiments are performed to evaluate the authenticity and make comparison among different ways. Associated descriptions for data files are also contained in CHAD.

The remainder of the paper is organized as follows. First, data collection methods including laboratory recording, movie and broadcast programme extraction are described in section 2. Then speech corpus evaluation and comparison are focused in section 3. Section 4 presents associated descriptions for data files in our database - CHAD. Conclusion and acknowledgement are given in section 5 and 6 respectively.

2 Creating Database – CHAD

In order to sample genuine emotional states, various methods were tried by artificial intelligence researchers. Discussions about different collection ways frequently appears in papers, but most of them were only based on the authors' personal suggestions. We present five different collection methods in our database and make a detailed comparison among them based on real data obtained from listening experiments. We explore two main sources. First, we make our own laboratory recordings. Second, following the approach pioneered by others, we collect extracts from selected movies and broadcast programmes.

2.1 Laboratory Recording

The prime attractions of making our own recordings are the prospect of controlling materials and avoiding the copyright problem. We design three different methods for materials recording.

In the first way, we select fifteen semantically neutral sentences, which include all the Chinese Initials and Finals, to be the carriers for different emotions. Every sentence will be read with all of the six emotions plus the neutral one. Ten from fifteen sentences are to be selected by the speaker that he or she thinks can be naturally expressed. The following types of sentences are covered: simple declarative sentence, "yes/no" question, alternative question, special question, question-request(structurally an interrogation with negation), exclamatory sentence and imperative sentence. One of the sentences with Chinese phoneme sequence is given below along with English translation in brackets. For this sentence, the frame stories for different emotion categories are described shortly in the following. Angry: "**He** knows it" is uttered by a speaker who warns others off cheating **him**; Happy: it is uttered by a girl who wants **him** know that she love **him**; Surprise: it is uttered by a person who can not believe that **he** knows it; Fear: it is uttered by **his** good friend who "steals" **his** girlfriend; Sad: it is uttered by a friend who wants to keep the news that **his** father died yesterday secret to **him**; Disgust: it is uttered by a person who doesn't want to talk about **him**. He or him with bold font refer to the same person.

ta zhi dao zhe jian shi le
他 知 道 这 件 事 了。(He knows it.)

In the second way, for each of all six emotion states(excluding neutral) fifteen sentences are designed to convey it. Different from the first way, here we use a set of sentences with appropriately emotional content instead of a same carrier for different emotions. Ten of the fifteen sentences in every emotion are chosen by speakers. Every sentence should be expressed in neutral and the required emotions, which will benefit the emotion recognition study.

In the third way, twelve emotionally biased passages are proposed, two for each non-neutral emotion. Different from the two ways listed before, passages can be used to stimulate the feeling of a particular emotion. The last sentence in a passage is the result materials we need, all other sentences contribute to artless expression.

Forty-two Chinese native speakers have taken part in the laboratory recording: eighteen of them are female and twenty-four are male. All of the speakers are students from ZheJiang University in Hangzhou. Nine speakers have been in Hangzhou since their birth or early childhood. Thirty-three speakers have been in Hangzhou for at least three years before the time of recording, but come from other regions. Age of these speakers ranges from nineteen to thirty-two. Non-professional speakers are employed in our recording in order to avoid exaggerated performance and capture the characteristics of speech used by ordinary people.

Speakers were requested to simulate each of the specific emotional contents in front of the camera three times. The most spontaneous one of them was selected into our database. The speech samples were recorded in an anechoic room with Sony DCR-HC20E DAT recorder and Boli-009 microphone. The obtained recordings are converted into audio part with monophonic Windows PCM format at 48kHZ sampling frequency and 16 bits resolution and visual part with resolution 320*240 pixels. Recording data(include audio and visual) for one sentence is stored in a .WAV file with average size of 1.5M and each file for the passages in the third recording type has approximate 16M. So we get 6*10*2*1.5M*42=7.4G data from the first type recording, 10*7*1.5M*42=4.3G data from the second and 6*2*16M*42=7.9G data from the third, 19.6G in total.

2.2 Movie and Broadcast

Regarding more vividly emotional expression, we also collect materials from movies and broadcast programmes. Our group members have watched movies of different theme in several months and picked sentences with required emotions. For all the seven emotion states we study, 1.7G materials are gotten from movies.

Broadcast programmes especially those dramas and conversations are also good source for emotional materials. Vocal performances with different emotions are splendid in broadcast theaters. People recall their emotional events in the conversation with president from which affective expression can be extracted. Altogether, 850M data are collected from broadcast programmes.

3 Data Evaluation

Considering lack of Chinese emotional speech corpus publicly available, our evaluation experiments are focused on audio part of the database. Two main steps are designed for data evaluation: people performance in laboratory recording and emotion portray comparison of different materials sources.

3.1 People Performance

We design experiments to find answers to the following questions:

a. How well can people portray emotions in speech without training ?
b. Which one of the three laboratory recordings is most suitable for speakers to simulate emotions?

The utterances from our database - CHAD are played in random order and listeners are requested to classify every utterance according to the emotional information conveyed in audio part. One hundred and twenty subjects are involved in the evaluation stage, and none of whom has participated in the recording stage earlier in order to avoid unreasonably high recognition accuracy. Table 1 shows the emotion detection confusion matrix for all the three types of laboratory recordings. The rows and the columns represent true and evaluated categories respectively. For example, fourth line tells us that 4.49% of utterances that are portrayed as happy were evaluated as neutral (unemotional), 90.11% as true happy, 0.45% as angry, 3.15% as surprise and none of them is evaluated as sad, fear, and disgust.

From the data displayed, emotional materials obtained from the second type laboratory recording are easiest to be recognized. Compared with the first type, sentences with appropriately emotional contents are easier to be expressed by people without special training. A same carrier for different emotions in the first type sometimes confuses the speakers. They find it difficult to switch between emotions in one sentence. Passages in the third type are used to stimulate emotional expression, but the effect are worse than anticipated. Passages contain several sentences, speakers maybe pay more attention to correctly reading than simulating the emotions. Emotions may be conveyed in all sentences a passage, but only the last sentence is selected to be the materials for listening experiments, which will lead to a lower accuracy.

3.2 Comparison of Different Sources

Emotional information is contained in materials from all sources, but it costs different efforts to decode required emotion.

Table 1. People Performance Matrix for three types laboratory recordings. No1. refers to the first method, No2. refers to the second and No3. refers to the third.

Category		Neutral	Happy	Sad	Fear	Angry	Surprise	Disgust	Not Sure
Neutral	No1.	**86.47**	0	8.08	0	0.40	1.62	0	3.43
	No2.	**84.30**	0.31	3.58	0.31	1.61	0.63	5.19	4.07
	No3.	**82.35**	0	7.65	0	2.35	0	2.94	4.71
Happy	No1.	6.51	**69.03**	0	2.33	0.23	12.33	0.93	8.84
	No2.	4.49	**90.11**	0	0	0.45	3.15	0	1.80
	No3.	0	**73.54**	5.88	0	2.94	0	8.82	8.82
Sad	No1.	12.91	0	**82.92**	0	1.25	0	0	2.92
	No2.	6.39	0	**87.78**	0	0.83	0	3.06	1.94
	No3.	14.44	0	**72.23**	2.22	0	0	2.22	8.89
Fear	No1.	1.48	0	0.74	**77.04**	0	14.07	0	6.67
	No2.	0.69	3.79	0.34	**84.50**	0.34	3.79	0	6.55
	No3.	2.24	0	6.72	**63.43**	0	8.21	5.97	13.43
Angry	No1.	12.22	1.85	2.59	4.44	**42.23**	17.04	10.74	8.89
	No2.	0	0	0.68	0	**79.55**	0	18.86	0.91
	No3.	1.75	0	0	0.88	**80.71**	1.75	12.28	2.63
Surprise	No1.	1.89	2.53	0	4.21	2.53	**82.95**	0	5.89
	No2.	0.22	0	0	0.22	2.25	**87.87**	6.07	3.37
	No3.	3.33	2.22	0	4.44	1.11	**73.34**	0	15.56
Disgust	No1.	20	0	2.56	2.56	12.31	15.90	**35.39**	11.28
	No2.	0.18	0	0.45	0	10.15	1.14	**85.45**	1.82
	No3.	8.18	0.91	6.36	2.73	20.91	1.82	**55.45**	3.64

Table 2. Mean emotion recognition accuracy for materials from different sources

Category	No1. Lab Recording	No2. Lab Recording	No3. Lab Recording	Movies	Broadcast
Neutral	86.47	84.30	82.35	46.0	100
Happy	69.03	90.11	73.54	57.5	80.0
Sad	82.92	87.78	72.23	75.71	96.67
Fear	77.04	84.50	63.43	62.5	100
Angry	42.23	79.55	80.71	66.25	92.14
Surprise	82.95	87.87	73.34	55.0	78.0
Disgust	35.39	85.45	55.45	50.5	66.67
Average	**68.0**	**85.65**	**71.58**	**59.07**	**87.64**

Table 2 shows the mean emotion recognition accuracy for materials from different sources. Ignoring the consideration of copyright, broadcast programmes seem to be the best source for emotional audio materials(with average accuracy 87.64%). But it lacks visual information. From movie source, it's difficult to extract required emotional monolog because most of the play are composed of conversations. And emotions in movie are usually conveyed by actor's gesture instead of voice. Sentences extracted from movies include not only voice but also music and other background sound. All these facts are murderers to high recognition accuracy. Performance of materials from the second type laboratory recording is comparable to the broadcast programmes. Besides, data collected from laboratory recording contain not only speech corpus but also visual information which can also represent the characteristics of speech used by ordinary people when they naturally experience similar emotions.

4 Associated Description

The database has the following structures. The top folder, whose name is CHAD, contains seven folders - Neutral, Happy, Sad, Fear, Angry, Surprise and Disgust. There are five sub-folders, such as No1Recording, No2Recording, No3Recording, Movies and Broadcast in each folder. Each of the five sub-folders includes a folder for every sentence materials with a certain emotion, appointed source. The folder includes a video file containing both audio and visual data recorded, an audio file with only vocal data, a speaker information file, a Chinese phoneme sequence file and a prosody feature statistics file. The speaker information file contains demographic information about speakers, such as speaker ID, gender, age, major, region of birth or living and comments on speaker's performance. The Chinese phoneme sequence file contains labels on word level and phoneme level. Prosody feature statistics file has information like: length of the utterance, percentage of pauses in the utterance, average speaking rate, fundamental frequency (F0)(mean, median, standard deviation, minimum, maximum and range), energy intensity (mean, median, standard deviation, minimum, maximum and range) and First three formants(F1, F2, F3) (mean, median, standard deviation, minimum, maximum and range).

5 Conclusion

A Chinese affective database (CHAD) is designed and established in the paper. This database includes audiovisual materials from three kinds of laboratory recording, and audio materials from broadcast programmes. Seven emotion states are employed: neutral, happy, sad, fear, angry, surprise and disgust. Detailed comparison of materials from different data collection methods is carried out in the first time. Broadcast programmes seem to make excellent performance in data evaluations, but there are problems as copyright, lacking visual information and can not represent the characteristics of speech used by ordinary people. Solving all the problems,laboratory recording using sentence script with appropriately emotional content for different emotion state is an outstanding data collection source, which has a comparable recognition accuracy with broadcasts. Data evaluation in the paper is only based on audio part, experiments testing both of the audio part and visual part of our database should be designed. Emotions can be precisely divided into several intensity levels such as light happy, middle happy and complete happy. Besides, more methods should be tried to collect materials with spontaneous emotions.

Acknowledgement

The work is supported by National Natural Science Foundation of China (60203013), 863 Program (2004AA1Z2390) and Key Technologies R&D Program of Zhejiang Province (2004C11052 & 2005C23047).

References

1. Darwin, Ch.: The expression of the emotions in man and animals. Chicago: University of Chicago Press, (1965) (Original work published in 1872).
2. Picard, R.: Affective computing. The MIT Press. (1997)
3. Dellaert, F., Polzin, Th., and Waibel, A.: Recognizing emotions in speech. ICSLP (1996)
4. Murray, I.R. and Arnott, J.L.: Toward the simulation of emotion in synthetic speech: A review of the literature on human vocal emotions. Journal Acoustical society of America **2** (1993) 1097-1108.
5. Cowie, R. et al.: Emotion recognition in Human-Computer Interaction. IEEE Signal Processing Magazine **18** (2001) 32-80.
6. Roach, P., Stibbard, R., Osborne, J., Arnfield, S. and Setter, J.: Transcriptions of prosodic and paralinguistic features of emotional speech. J.Int.Phonetic Assoc. **2** 83-94.
7. http://cvc.yale.edu/projects/yalefaces/yalefaces.htm
8. Emanuela, M.C., Piero, C., Carlo, D., Graziano, T. and Federica, C.: Modifications of phonetic labial targets in emotive speech: effects of the co-production of speech and emotions. Speech Communication **44** (2004) 173C185
9. Douglas-Cowie, E., Cowie, R. and Schroder, M.: A new emotion database Considerations, sources and scope. ISCA Workshop on Speech and Emotion: A conceptual framework for research (2000)
10. Albino, N., Asuncion, M., Antonio, B., and Jose, B.: Marino Speech Emotion Recognition Using Hidden Markov Models. Eurospeech (2001)
11. Noam A., Samuel R. and Nathaniel L..: Analysis of an emotional speech corpus in Hebrew based on objective criteria. ISCA Workshop on Speech and Emotion: A conceptual framework for research (2000)
12. http://www.unige.ch/fapse/emotion/
13. Chul Min L., Shrikanth, S. N. and Roberto, P.: COMBINING ACOUSTIC AND LANGUAGE INFORMATION FOR EMOTION RECOGNITION. ICSLP (2002)
14. McGilloway, S. al.: APPROACHING AUTOMATIC RECOGNITION OF EMOTION FROM VOICE: A ROUGH BENCHMARK. ISCA Workshop on Speech and Emotion: A conceptual framework for research (2000)
15. Ilkka, L., Lea, L., Minna, V., Maija-Liisa, L. and Synnove, C.: Conveyance of emotional connotations by a single word in English. Speech Communication **45** (2005) 27C39
16. Veronika, M. and Valery A. P.: RUSLANA: a Database of Russian Emotional Utterances. ICSLP (2002) 2041-2044.
17. Li, ZH. , Xiangmin, Q., Cairong, ZH. and Zhenyang W.: A Study on Emotion Recognition in Speech. Journal of Software **12** (2001)

Annotating Multimodal Behaviors Occurring During Non Basic Emotions

Jean-Claude Martin, Sarris Abrilian, and Laurence Devillers

LIMSI-CNRS, BP 133, 91403 Orsay Cedex, France
{martin, abrilian, devil}@limsi.fr

Abstract. The design of affective interfaces such as credible expressive characters in story-telling applications requires the understanding and the modeling of relations between realistic emotions and behaviors in different modalities such as facial expressions, speech, hand gestures and body movements. Yet, research on emotional multimodal behaviors has focused on individual modalities during acted basic emotions. In this paper we describe the coding scheme that we have designed for annotating multimodal behaviors observed during mixed and non acted emotions. We explain how we used it for the annotation of videos from a corpus of emotionally rich TV interviews. We illustrate how the annotations can be used to compute expressive profiles of videos and relations between non basic emotions and multimodal behaviors.

1 Introduction

The design of affective interfaces such as credible expressive characters in story-telling applications requires the understanding and the modeling of relations between realistic emotions and behaviors in different modalities such as facial expressions, speech, body movements and hand gestures. Until now, most experimental studies of multimodal behaviors related to emotions have considered only basic and acted emotions and their relation with mono-modal behaviors such as facial expressions [8] or body movements [18]. Recent tools [11] facilitate the annotation and the collection of multimodal corpora but raise several issues regarding the study of emotions: How should we annotate multimodal behaviors occurring during emotions? What are the relevant behavioral dimensions to annotate? What are the differences between basic acted emotions and non acted emotions regarding the multimodal behaviors?

EmoTV is an audiovisual corpus featuring 51 video clips of emotionally rich monologues from TV interviews (with various topics as politics, law, sports…) that we have collected for studying non acted emotions. We have designed a coding scheme for annotating the context and several dimensions of emotions (categories, intensity, valence …), both at the level of the whole video clip and at the level of the different emotional segments that each clip contain (see [1] for a description of how these segments were defined). The main conclusions of a first annotation phase of the 51 clips were that emotional segments can not be labeled with a single emotion label but rather with a combination of two labels (blend, masked, cause-effect conflict, ambiguous) [6]. Furthermore classical schemes used for detailed annotation of

J. Tao, T. Tan, and R.W. Picard (Eds.): ACII 2005, LNCS 3784, pp. 550 – 557, 2005.

communicative multimodal behaviors revealed to be partly inappropriate for non acted emotions [2]. Such parts of the coding scheme were either removed or modified in order to improve the annotation process.

In this paper we describe this new coding scheme that we have designed for annotating multimodal behaviors during real life mixed emotions. This scheme focuses on the annotation of emotion specific behaviors in speech, head and torso movements, facial expressions, gaze, and hand gestures. We do not aim at collecting detailed data on each individual modality or statistically representative models of the relations between emotions and multimodal behaviors. Instead, our goals are to use the annotations produced with this scheme to identify the required levels of representation for realistic emotional behavior and to explore the coordination between modalities during non acted behaviors observed in individual videos. Section 2 provides a short survey of some studies on multimodal emotional behavior. Section 3 details the coding scheme that we have defined. In section 4, we illustrate the measures that can be done from our annotations such as the computation of expressivity profiles.

2 Studying Multimodal Emotional Behaviors

The experiment described in [16] consisted of asking younger and older adults to evaluate the following parameters from actors' body movements: age, gender and race; hand position; gait; variations in movement form, tempo, and direction; and movement quality. The actors were silent and their faces were electronically blurred in order to isolate the body cues to emotion. In a first part, they identified emotions depicted in brief videotaped displays of young adult actors portraying emotional situations. In a second part, they rated the videotaped displays using characteristics of movement quality (form, tempo, force, and direction) rated on a 7-point scale and verbal descriptors (smooth / jerky, stiff / loose, soft / hard, slow / fast, expanded / contracted, and no action / a lot of action). The ratings of both age groups revealed to be in high agreement and provided reliable information about particular body cues to emotion. The errors made by older adults were linked to exaggerated or ambiguous body cues.

In [18], twelve drama students were asked to code body movement and posture performed by actors. The emotions were acted and mostly basic. Only categories with more than 75% inter-coder agreement between 2 coders were kept: position of upper body, position of shoulders, position of head, position of arms, position of hands, movement quality (movement activity, spatial expansion, movement dynamics, energy, and power) ; body movements (jerky and active), body posture.

The experiment in [4] investigated the accuracy of children to identify emotional meaning in expressive body movement performances. 103 subjects participated in two tasks of nonverbal decoding skill. For this experiment, the subjects were asked to identify, on a TV screen, the emotions expressed by two dancers (i.e. which one of them was feeling happy, sad, angry, or afraid). The following specific cues were used by the adult subjects to discriminate the emotions: Anger (changes in tempo; directional changes in face and torso); Happiness (frequency of arms up, duration of arms away from torso); Fear (muscle tension); Sadness (duration of time leaning forward).

In [5], the authors studied the effects of three variables on the inference of emotions from body movements: sex of the mover, sex of the perceiver, and expressiveness of the movement. 42 adults participated in the experiment, analyzing video-recordings consisting of performances of 96 different movements, each performed by students of expressive dance. The subjects used seven dichotomous dimensions for describing movements: trunk movement (stretching, bowing), arm movement (opening, closing), vertical direction (upward, downward), sagittal direction (forward, backward), force (strong-light), velocity (fast-slow), directness (moving straight towards the end-position versus following a lingering, s-shaped pathway).

Three dimensions of movement are defined in Laban's theory of the Art of Movement [17]: up-down, left-right, and forward-backward. Some body movements and gestures are interpreted (e.g. the wish to communicate is expressed in outward-reached movements and the wish to remain private is expressed in inward movements). This suggests that form and motion are related to emotions.

In the field of Embodied Conversational Agents, [10] proposed a set of expressivity attributes for facial expressions (intensity, temporal course), for gaze (length of mutual gaze), for gesture (strength, tempo, dynamism, amplitude) and global parameters (overall activation, spatial extent, fluidity, power, repetitivity).

Several studies also involve TV material. The Belfast naturalistic database contains similar emotional interviews annotated with continuous dimensions [7]. Other studies deal with multimodal annotation, although not specific to emotion [14]. A coding scheme was designed for the annotation of 3 videos of interviews taken from television broadcasting [3]. It includes annotation of facial displays, gestures, and speech. The coding scheme involves the annotation of both the form of the expression and of its semantic-pragmatic function (e.g. give feedback / elicit feedback / turn managing / information structuring) as well as the relation between modalities: repetition, addition, substitution, contradiction.

As revealed by this short survey, most studies of multimodal behavior during emotions are based on basic and acted emotions and do not always make use of recent tools and advances in multimodal corpora management.

3 A Scheme for Annotating Multimodal Emotional Behavior

We have grounded our coding scheme on requirements collected from both the parameters described as perceptually relevant for the study of emotional behavior (See previous Sect.), and the features of the emotionally rich TV interviews that we have selected. The following measures are thus required for the study of emotional behaviors: the expressivity of movements, the number of annotations in each modality, their temporal features (duration, alternation, repetition, and structural descriptions of gestures), the directions of movements and the functional description of relevant gestures. We have selected some non verbal descriptors from the existing studies listed above. We have defined the coding scheme at an abstract level and then implemented it as a XML file for use with the Anvil tool [11]. This section describes how each modality is annotated in order to enable subsequent computation of the relevant parameters of emotional behavior listed above. Each track is annotated one after the other (e.g. the annotator starts by annotating the 1st track for the whole video and then proceeds to the next track). The duration and order of annotations is available in the annotations.

For the speech transcription, we annotate verbal and nonverbal sounds[1], as hesitations, breaths, etc... Most annotated tags are: "laugh", "cries", "b" (breath), and "pff". We do the word by word transcription using Praat[2].

In the videos only the upper body of people is visible. Torso, head and gestures tracks contain both a description of pose and movement. Pose and movement annotations thus alternate. The direction of movement, its type (e.g. twist vs. bend) and the angles can be computed from the annotations in the pose track. Examples of instructions for annotating torso movements are provided in Table 1. Movement quality is annotated for torso, head, shoulders, and hand gestures. The attributes of movement quality that are listed in the studies reported in the previous section and that we selected as relevant for our corpus are: the number of repetitions, the fluidity (smooth, normal, jerky), the strength (soft, normal, hard), the speed (slow, normal, fast), and the spatial expansion (contracted, normal, expanded). The annotation of fluidity is relevant for individual gestures as several of them are repetitive. The 1st annotation phase revealed that a set of three possible values for each expressive parameter was more appropriate than a larger set of possible values.

Table 1. Annotating torso side and bend movements: example of annotation guide instructions

Torso side movement	Illustrative example	Torso bend movement	Illustrative example
Side right (+20°)		Bend front (+20°)	
Front (0°)		Front (0°)	
Side left (-20°)		Bend back (-20°)	

The head pose track contains pose attributes adapted from the FACS coding scheme [9]: front, turned left / right, tilt left / right, upward / downward, forward / backward. Head primary movement observed between the start and the end pose is

[1] http://www.ldc.upenn.edu/

[2] http://www.fon.hum.uva.nl/praat/

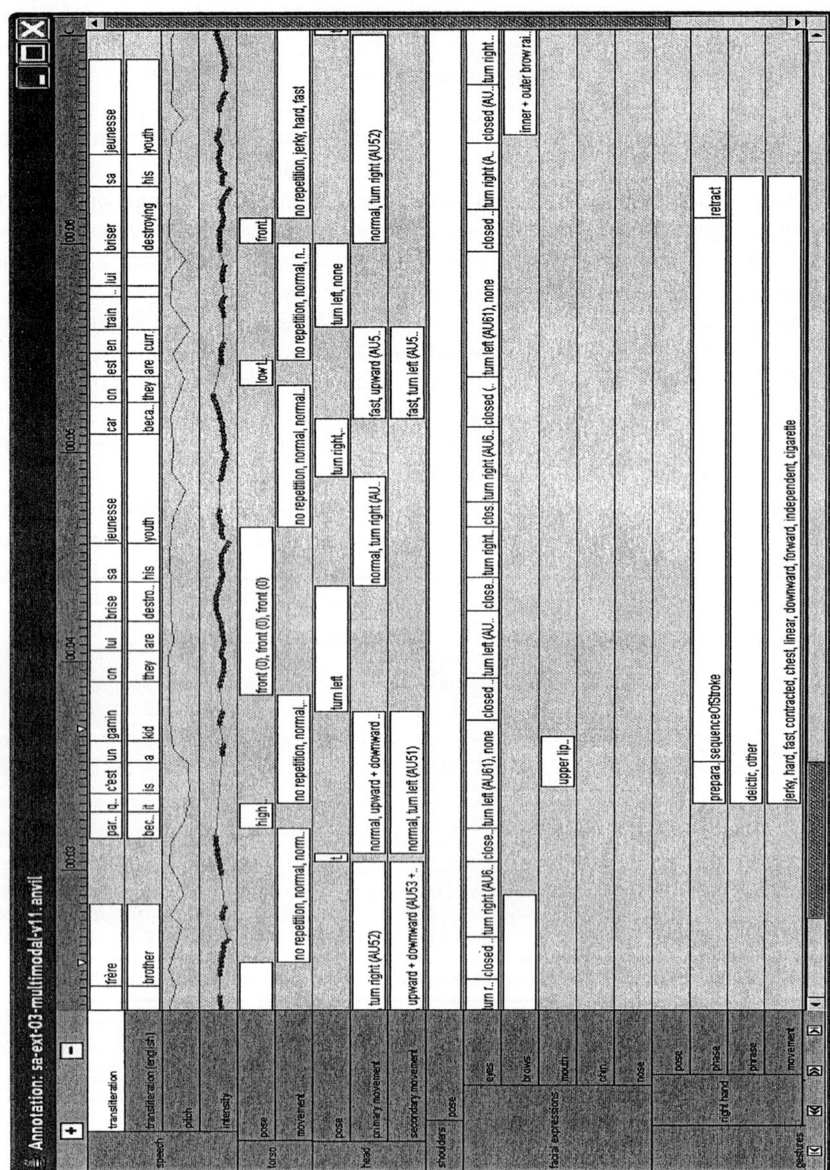

Fig. 1. From top: *(1)* speech tracks, *(2)* alternation of pose and movement for torso, *(3)* head behaviors annotated with one pose and two movement tracks, *(4)* facial expressions (including frequent closed eyes in this example), *(5)* hand gestures including annotation phase, phrase and movement expressivity (jerky, hard, fast, ...)

annotated with the same set of values as the pose attribute. A secondary movement enables the combination of several simultaneous head movements which are observed in EmoTV (e.g. head nod while turning the head). Facial expressions are coded using combinations of Action Units (the low level we used for the 1st annotation phase was based on FAPS and was inappropriate for manual annotation of emotional videos).

As for gesture annotation, we have kept the classical attributes [12, 15] but focused on repetitive and manipulator gestures which occur frequently in EmoTV, as we observed during the 1st annotation phase. Our coding scheme enables the annotation of the structural description ("phases") of gestures as their temporal patterns might be related to emotion: preparation (bringing arm and hand into stroke position), stroke (the most energetic part of the gesture), sequence of strokes (a number of successive strokes), hold (a phase of stillness just before or just after the stroke), and retract (movement back to rest position). We have selected the following set of gesture functions ("phrases") as they revealed to be observed in our corpus: manipulator (contact with body or object, movement which serve functions of drive reduction or other non-communicative functions, like scratching oneself), beat (synchronized with the emphasis of the speech), deictic (arm or hand is used to point at an existing or imaginary object), illustrator (represents attributes, actions, relationships about objects and characters), emblem (movement with a precise, culturally defined meaning). Currently, the hand shape is not annotated since it is not considered as a main feature of emotional behavior in our survey of experimental studies nor in our videos. Direction of movement for shoulders is also annotated as some of them are observed. An example of the annotation of multimodal behaviors is provided in Figure 1.

4 Computing Measures from Annotations

With this new coding scheme, 455 multimodal annotations of behaviors in the different modalities were done by one coder on the 19 emotional segments on 4 videos selected for their multimodally rich content (e.g. expressive gesture) for a total duration of 77 seconds. These annotations have been validated and corrected by a second coder. The average required annotation time was evaluated to 200 seconds to annotate 1 second of such video featuring rich multimodal behaviors. This annotation time might decrease during future annotations as the coders will learn how to use the scheme more efficiently. We developed a software for parsing the files resulting of annotation and for computing measures. It enables to compare the "expressivity profile" of different videos which feature blended emotions (Table 2), similarly to the work done by [10] on expressive embodied agents. For example videos #3 and #36 are quite similar regarding their emotion labels, average intensity and valence (although their durations are quite different).

Modalities involving movements in these videos are also similar (head, then torso, and then hand gestures). The relations between the extreme values of expressive parameters are also compatible in the two videos: fast movements are more often perceived than slow movements; hard movement more often than soft; jerky more often than smooth; contracted more often than expanded. Video #30 with a similar average intensity (4) has a quite different expressive profile with a positive valence but also more head movements and no hand gestures. Even more movements are evaluated as being fast, but compared with videos #3 and #36, movements in this video are more perceived as soft and smooth. The goal of such measures is to explore the dimensions of emotional behavior in order to study how multimodal signs of emotion are combined during non acted emotion.

Table 2. Expressivity profiles of three videos involving blended emotions

Video#	**#3**	**#36**	**#30**
Duration	37s	7s	10s
Emotion labels	Anger (66%), despair (25%), sadness (12%)	Anger (55%), despair (44%)	Exaltation (50%), Joy (25%), Pride (25%)
Average intensity (1: min – 5: max)	5	4.6	4
Average valence (1: negative, 5: positive)	1	1.6	4.3
% head movement	56	60	72
% torso movement	28	20	27
% hand movement	16	20	0
% fast vs. slow	47 vs. 3	33 vs. 13	83 vs. 0
% hard vs. soft	17 vs. 17	20 vs. 0	0 vs. 27
% jerky vs. smooth	19 vs. 8	6 vs. 0	5 vs. 50
% expanded vs. contracted	0 vs. 38	13 vs. 20	0 vs. 33

5 Conclusion and Future Directions

In this paper we have described our work for the study of multimodal behaviors occurring during non acted emotions. We explained the different features of the coding scheme we have defined and illustrated some measures that can be done from the annotations. Currently, the protocol used for validation of annotations is to have a second coder validate the annotations done by a first coder followed by brainstorming discussions. Other validation protocoles are currently under consideration. We are currently investigating the use of such annotations in a copy-synthesis approach for the specification of expressive embodied agents which can be useful for perceptual validation [13]. Future directions include the annotation of other videos of EmoTV with the coding scheme described in this paper, the validation of the annotations by the automatic computation of inter-coder agreements from the annotations by several coders, and the computation of other relations between 1) the multimodal annotations, and 2) the annotation of emotions (labels, intensity and valence), and the global annotations such as the modalities in which activity was perceived as relevant to emotion [6].

References

1. Abrilian, S., Devillers, L., Buisine, S., Martin, J.-C.: EmoTV1: Annotation of Real-life Emotions for the Specification of Multimodal Affective Interfaces. HCI International (2005a) Las Vegas, USA
2. Abrilian, S., Martin, J.-C., Devillers, L.: A Corpus-Based Approach for the Modeling of Multimodal Emotional Behaviors for the Specification of Embodied Agents. HCI International (2005b) Las Vegas, USA

3. Allwood, J., Cerrato, L., Dybkær, L., Paggio, P.: The MUMIN multimodal coding scheme. Workshop on Multimodal Corpora and Annotation , (2004) Stockholm
4. Boone, R. T., Cunningham, J. G.: Children's decoding of emotion in expressive body movement: The development of cue attunement. Developmental Psychology 34 5 (1998)
5. DeMeijer, M.: The attribution of agression and grief to body movements : the effect of sex-stereotypes. European Journal of Social Psychology 21 (1991)
6. Devillers, L., Abrilian, S., Martin, J.-C.: Representing real life emotions in audiovisual data with non basic emotional patterns and context features. First International Conference on Affective Computing & Intelligent Interaction (ACII'2005) (2005) Beijing, China
7. Douglas-Cowie, E., Campbell, N., Cowie, R., Roach, P.: Emotional speech; Towards a new generation of databases. Speech Communication 40 (2003)
8. Ekman, P.: Emotions revealed. Weidenfeld & Nicolson (2003)
9. Ekman, P. W., F.: Facial Action Coding System (FACS). (1978)
10. Hartmann, B., Mancini, M., Pelachaud, C.: Formational Parameters and Adaptive Prototype Instantiation for MPEG-4 Compliant Gesture Synthesis. Computer Animation (2002)
11. Kipp, M.: Anvil - A Generic Annotation Tool for Multimodal Dialogue. Eurospeech (2001)
12. Kipp, M.: Gesture Generation by Imitation. From Human Behavior to Computer Character Animation. Boca Raton, Dissertation.com Florida (2004)
13. Lamolle, M., Mancini, M., Pelachaud, C., Abrilian, S., Martin, J.-C., Devillers, L.: Contextual Factors and Adaptative Multimodal Human-Computer Interaction: Multi-Level Specification of Emotion and Expressivity in Embodied Conversational Agents. 4th International and Interdisciplinary Conference on Modeling and Using Context (Context) (2005) Paris
14. Magno Caldognetto, E., Poggi, I., Cosi, P., Cavicchio, F., Merola, G.: Multimodal Score: an Anvil Based Annotation Scheme for Multimodal Audio-Video Analysis. Workshop "Multimodal Corpora: Models Of Human Behaviour For The Specification And Evaluation Of Multimodal Input And Output Interfaces" In Association with the 4th International Conference On Language Resources And Evaluation (LREC) (2004) Lisbon, Portugal
15. McNeill, D.: Hand and mind - what gestures reveal about thoughts. University of Chicago Press (1992)
16. Montepare, J., Koff, E., Zaitchik, D., Albert, M.: The use of body movements and gestures as cues to emotions in younger and older adults. Journal of Nonverbal Behavior 23 2 (1999)
17. Newlove, J.: Laban for actors and dancers. Routledge New York (1993)
18. Wallbott, H. G.: Bodily expression of emotion. European Journal of Social Psychology 28 (1998)

The Properties of DaFEx, a Database of Kinetic Facial Expressions

Alberto Battocchi, Fabio Pianesi, and Dina Goren-Bar

ITC-irst, via Sommarive, 18, 38050 Povo (Trento), Italy
{battocchi, pianesi}@itc.it
dinag@bgu.ac.il

Abstract. In this paper we present an evaluation study for DaFEx (Database of Facial Expressions), a database created with the purpose of providing a benchmark for the evaluation of the facial expressivity of Embodied Conversational Agents (ECAs). DaFEx consists of 1008 short videos containing emotional facial expressions of the 6 Ekman's emotions plus the neutral expression. The facial expressions were recorded by 8 professional actors (male and female) in two acting conditions ("utterance" and "non utterance") and at 3 intensity levels (high, medium, low). The properties of DaFEx were studied by having 80 subjects classify the emotion expressed in the videos. We tested the effect of the intensity level, of the articulatory movements due to speech, and of the actors' and subjects' gender, on classification accuracy. We also studied the way error distribute across confusion classes. The results are summarized in this work.

1 Introduction

During the last years quite a few efforts have been made to develop interfaces for human-computer communication based on Embodied Conversational Agents (ECAs), virtual characters capable of communicating with users through natural language but also through other non verbal channels such as gestures posture, gaze direction and facial expressions [4]. Parallel to that, interest has raised on methodologies and protocols for evaluating ECAs. Most of the studies conducted so far have addressed the end-to-end evaluation of systems exploiting ECAs, and focusing on dimensions such as the effectiveness and quality of the resulting interaction, the ECA's believability, trust and engagement it promotes; see [12], and [13] for a review of relevant studies and an attempt at providing a general framework.

Other works — e.g., [2], [5], [6], [11] — have addressed the *quality* of facial displays, and those 'low levels' dimensions that arguably determine it: lip-speech synchronisation, facial gestures signalling emotions, or emphasis, punctuation and other discourse-level regulatory characteristics. However, despite the current interest in the topic, and the many efforts towards endowing ECAs with the capabilities of expressing emotional states, neither accepted benchmarks nor agreed methodologies are available to assess those dimensions. Arguably, though, they would provide important information for testing and development purposes, and for comparatively evaluating different platforms.

J. Tao, T. Tan, and R.W. Picard (Eds.): ACII 2005, LNCS 3784, pp. 558 – 565, 2005.

In almost all the studies quoted above, ECAS were evaluated by comparing their expressions to those produced by humans. However, with the exception of [11], authors used their own reference data base, usually consisting of expressions produced by few humans, collected for the purpose of the study under less than ideally controlled conditions, and often being of a less than ideal quality level. Moreover, the statistical properties of those reference corpora are almost always unknown: the comparative study was often the first and sole occasion in which issues such as the recognisability of the various expressions of the corpus was addressed. Still, it is clear that in order to make the comparative approach to the assessment of expressive properties of ECAs widely available, to attain a reasonable level of reliability, and facilitate cross-study comparisons, a reference corpus of facial expressions is necessary, whose expressive properties are well known, and whose technical quality is as controlled as possible. Such a corpus should control a number of important dimensions that either are constitutive of facial expressivity — e.g., intensity — or that are expected to affect recognisability — e.g., the gender of the acting human and of the subject's, the presence/absence of co-occurring articulatory movements due to speech, etc. Finally, the material in the corpus should be of a high video and audio quality.

In this paper we present DaFEx, a corpus of acted emotional expressions that was created with the precise purpose of providing a reference benchmark for the evaluation of the facial expressivity of ECAs. This work is structured as follows: in Section 2 we describe DaFEx, and the methodology we followed to build it. Section 3 presents the results of a recognition study we conducted on the material contained in the DaFEx data base. Finally, in section 4 we draw conclusions and discuss future research work.

2 The Database

DaFEx consists of 1008 short video clips, lasting between 4 and 27 sec., each showing a facial expression corresponding to one of the 6 Ekman's emotions [8], [9] – happiness, surprise, fear, sadness, anger and disgust – plus the neutral expression. The expressions were acted by 8 italian professional actors (4 male and 4 female), who recorded each emotion at 3 intensity levels (low, medium and high), and in 2 recording conditions ("Utterance" and "No utterance"). In the "Utterance" condition, the actor produced the emotional expression while uttering a phonetically rich and visemically balanced sentence *("In quella piccola stanza vuota c'era però soltanto una sveglia*:" In that little empty room there was only an alarm clock). In the "No-utterance" condition emotions were acted without uttering any sentence. The entire set of emotions was recorded by every actor more than once: four times in the "Utterance" condition and twice in the "No-utterance" condition. Examples of the video clips are available at http://tcc.itc.it/research/i3p/ dafex/

Before starting the recording sessions, actors were given appropriate guidelines. They were explained the purposes of the work, and the importance of collecting expressions looking as "natural" as possible. Following [3] and [15], actors were given 6 short emotionally coloured stories; their purpose was to provide actors with identical scenarios for them to act the emotions in, this way facilitating their task, while making the recording conditions as uniform as possible. To reduce the actors' movements in front of the camera, they acted emotions while seating on a chair, which was placed in the same positions for all of them. Before starting the recordings, actors could freely exercise on the emotions they would later produce, checking, if they wished, the results to calibrate the different expressions. Emotions were recorded by every actor in a random order. For every emotion the recording order of the three intensity levels was fixed (low, medium, and then high).

3 A Study of DaFEx

We studied DaFEx by addressing the way the considered dimensions affected: a) the recognition accuracy, and b) the way errors distribute. We followed the methodology of classical judgment studies (e.g. [5], [6] and [7]), in which emotional colored material, e.g., pictures, is evaluated though judgments expressed by human subjects. In our case, participants were asked to watch DAFEx's videos and classify each of them. For the data analysis, we exploited loglinear methods [1], [5], [6].

Participants were 40 women and 40 men (average age: 25.6), all students at the universities of Trento and Padua. They were divided into 8 groups, consisting of 5 women and 5 men each. Each group evaluated the entire set of 126 videos (7 emotions × 3 intensity levels × 6 blocks; each block consisted of the 4 video clips for the 'utterance' condition and the 2 video clips of the 'no-utterance one) recorded by one actor. Subjects watched and evaluated videos in individual sessions, providing their judgments on a paper sheet containing multiple choice forms, one set for each video, and consisting of the 6 Ekman's emotions plus the neutral expressions.

Before starting their sessions, participants underwent a training phase, consisting in the evaluation of 7 videos, different from those they would classify later on.

Videos were presented in a random order on the screen (10.8 × 8.7 cm.) of a laptop computer through Microsoft PowerPoint presentations. Since the focus of the study was on the emotional information conveyed by the face alone, the audio signal was not presented. At the end of each video, participants had 10 seconds to classify the video. Every individual session lasted about 50 minutes, including instructions and training.

3.1 Results – Recognition Rates

Overall recognition rates were quite high, as shown in Table 1. We ran a loglinear (model selection, saturated model) analysis with factors: emotion recognition (2 levels: recognized vs. not recognized), presented emotion (7 levels, corresponding to the six Ekman's emotions plus the neutral expression), acting condition (2 levels: "Utterance" vs. "No-utterance"), intensity level (3 levels: low, medium and high). Here we focus on the results of the tests of partial associations [1]. Then appropriate, post-hoc comparisons were performed through χ^2 tests, with Bonferroni correction for multiple comparisons. In all cases, and unless otherwise explicitly stated, the threshold for the significant results reported below is $p<.05$.

Table 1. Recognition rates

	Anger	Disgust	Fear	Happ.	Surp.	Sadness	Neutral
Utter.	90.6%	79.1%	53%	78.3%	66.1%	77.7%	80.1%
No-utt.	75.6%	72.3%	69,2%	80%	78.1%	74.6%	87.9%

Effects of the Intensity. The intensity level has a main effect on the recognition of emotions. Recognition rates were 83.2% for high intensity, 76.6% for medium intensity, 67% for low intensity. Comparisons showed that, as expected, the stronger contrast is between the high and the low levels.

Intensity significantly interacts with the presented emotion, see Fig. 1, affecting the recognition of all the emotions except happiness (and, obviously, neutral); again, the effect is mainly due to the high vs. low level contrast.

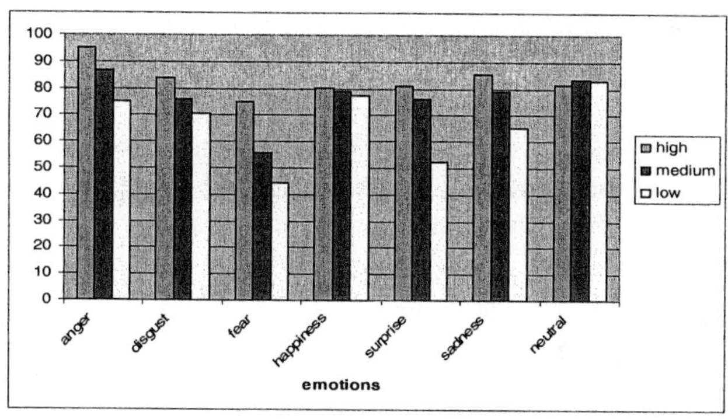

Fig. 1. The effect of intensity on recognition rates

Effects of Emotion Categories. Emotion categories have a significant main effect on decoding accuracy. The recognition rates for the six emotions were compared to those obtained for the neutral expression, taken as the reference category. Multiple tests showed that disgust, fear, surprise and sadness were all recognized worse than the neutral expression. Happiness and anger did not differ from the neutral expression.

Effects of Articulatory Movements. Generally, emotions are slightly better recognized in the "No-utterance" condition (76.8%) than in the "Utterance" one (75.0%). Intensity and condition had a significant, albeit small, interaction. A series of χ^2 tests showed that the effect is due to the differences at high intensity level, where the "No-utterance" condition has a slightly higher recognition rate than the "Utterance" one, see Fig. 2. Recognition rates did not differ significantly between the two conditions at the medium and at the low intensity levels. In conclusion, there is a selective, though small, advantage of "No-utterance" at the high intensity level.

Condition and presented emotion interacted in a significant way, with a selective effect on anger, fear, surprise, and, interestingly, neutral. The recognition rates are higher in 'Utterance' for anger, but lower for fear, surprise and neutral, see Fig. 3.

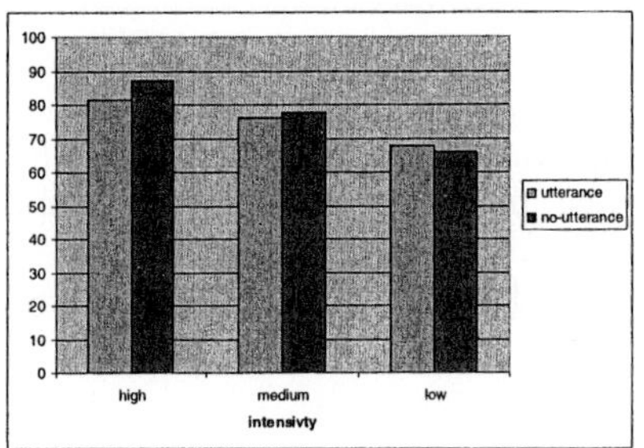

Fig. 2. Recognition rates for intensity*condition

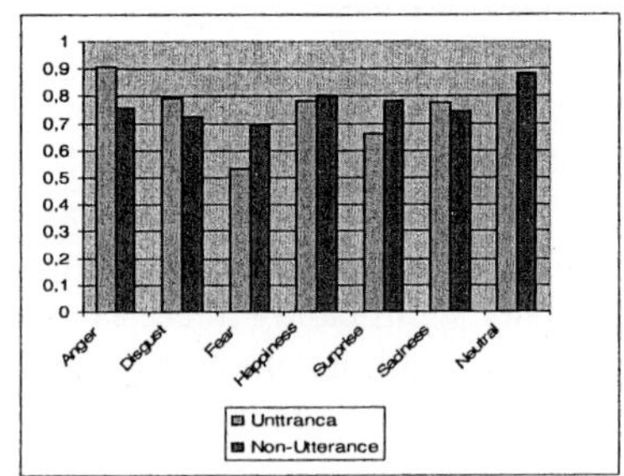

Fig. 3. Effect of the articulatory condition on accuracy

Hence, the articulatory movements due to the speech have a very selective effect on the recognition of emotions: their presence improves the recognition of anger and disgust, and depresses that of fear, surprise and the neutral expression.

Sex-Related Effects. A separate loglinear analysis (factors: recognition, presented emotion, sex of actor (2 levels) and sex of subjects) did not reveal any significant main effects due to subjects' sex, nor any significant interaction with the presented emotion. The sex of the actors produced a small effect, corresponding to a small advantage of actresses (76.7%) over actors (74.5%). The sex of the subjects and that of the actors interacted in a significant way, with male subjects recognizing emotions better when they are expressed by actresses (78.8%) than when expressed by actors (73.2%).

3.2 Error Classes, Error Distributions and Typical Errors

Following [5] and [6], we analyzed errors by means of the information theoretic approach outlined in [14]. We start from indices d_s and d_r: the former measures the effective (geometric) average number of confusion classes per stimulus. When d_s increases, so does the number of possible confusion categories for a given stimulus category, hence its ambiguity. d_r, in turn, informs about the (geometric) average number of stimulus categories a response category collects confusion from. A high value of d_r for a given response class, corresponds to a high number of stimulus categories it can collect errors from (equivocation). Both quantities are normalized for error rates. Table 2 reports the results.

Table 2. Values of d_s and d_r

	Global	Sex		Condition		Intensity		
		Males	Fem.	Utter.	No-Utt	High	Med	Low
Err. rate	0.24	0.26	0.23	0.25	0.23	0.17	0.23	0.33
d_s	3.66	3.53	3.49	3.47	3.42	3.09	3.27	3.45
d_r	3.18	3.66	3.70	3.67	3.60	3.20	3.47	3.88

Both the average ambiguity and the average equivocation are pretty stable across the various conditions, the only exception being the slight increase in both quantities with decreasing intensity levels. Table 3 reports an evaluation of the contribution of each stimulus class to the overall ambiguity. As can be seen, fear is the expression that stably contributes more to the overall ambiguity, in all conditions. Surprise follows, in particular with male actors, in the 'utterance' condition, and at low intensity levels.

Table 3. Contribution of stimulus classes to overall ambiguity

	Global	Sex		Condition		Intensity		
		Males	Fem.	Utter	No-utt	High	Med.	Low
Anger	0.39	1.07	-0.55	-0.75	2.40	-1.62	0.30	1.09
Disgust	1.68	1.73	1.58	1.22	2.49	1.55	1.76	1.46
Fear	**4.22**	**3.76**	**4.69**	**4.62**	**2.95**	**3.63**	**4.43**	**3.85**
Happin.	1.12	0.67	1.45	1.17	0.97	1.52	0.91	0.85
Neutral	0.74	0.74	0.66	1.05	-0.09	2.41	0.50	0.15
Sadness	1.88	1.42	2.28	1.68	2.21	1.37	1.76	1.84
Surprise	**3.03**	**3.34**	2.52	**3.58**	1.48	2.53	2.31	**3.26**

Direct comparisons across the levels of our factors can be pursued by means of two other indices, δ_s and δ_r, computed on pooled confusion matrices, [14]. For matrices M_1 and M_2 pooled into $M=M_1+M_2$, δ_s and δ_r yield the effective fraction of errors in M that fall outside the error categories shared by M_1 and M_2. These indices are corrected for the overall differences in the distribution of stimuli, δ_s, and responses, δ_r, and quantify the extent to which the error distributions of two confusion matrices agree. The lower their values, the higher the error distributions of the pooled matrices overlap. The results are in Table 4.

The similarity of the error distributions across actor sex, condition and (overall) intensity is very high. An interesting results, especially if compared with previous ones obtained with less controlled data bases of emotional expressions, e.g., [5], [6]. The only clear differences emerge on pair-wise comparisons between intensity levels, where the fraction of non-shared errors increases with decreasing intensity levels along both the stimulus and the response dimension. In conclusion, the ambiguity and equivocation values of the emotional expressions of our data base are very stable across the levels of our independent variables. The only (marginal) exception is intensity where, expectedly, both quantities are inversely proportional to the levels. Moreover, the various levels of the independent variables give rise to very similar error distributions, again with the exception of 'intensity' where errors tend to distribute in a less uniform way with decreasing intensities.

Table 4. Non-shared fractions of errors across factors' levels

	Act. sex	Condition	Intensity	Intensity - comparison		
				high-med	med-low	high-low
δ_r	0.05	0.09	0.06	0.04	0.05	0.09
δ_s	0.06	0.11	0.09	0.05	0.09	0.16

Finally, we computed typical error classes from the adjusted (Pearson's standardized) residuals of a series of loglinear analyses (one for each independent variable) under the hypothesis of a uniform distribution of errors. In this paper, a typical error class is a stimulus-class/response-class pair whose residual is greater than 3. The results are summarized in Table 5. As can be seen there is a good symmetry between typical errors, which is complete between disgust and anger, surprise and fear, neutral and sadness, and partial between sadness and fear.

Table 5. Typical error classes. M=males, F=females, U.=utterance, No-u.=no-utterance, H.=high, Me.=medium, L.=low.

	An.	Dis.	Fear	Ha.	Neut.	Sad.	Sur.
An.		**all**				M. No-u. Me.	
Fear	F. U. H.					**M. U.** No-u. **Me.** L.	**all**
Hap.					F L		all
Neut.	all					**all**	
Sad.			**M. U.** H. **Me.**		**M. F. U. No-u. L.**		
Sur.			**M. U. Me No-u. H..**		M. F. U. No-u. L.		

4 Conclusions

DaFEx has a set of desirable properties for a benchmark devoted to the evaluation of the expressivity of ECAs: it consists of high quality videos, with expressions varying in a controlled way according to the sex of the actors, the intensity level and the presence/absence of concomitant speech. Moreover, the results of the recognition study, briefly discussed in this paper, are a valuable source of information about the factors affecting the recognition rates, and the way errors distribute.

As to the future, many aspects deserve further considerations. We are currently pursuing: a) the cross-cultural validation of DaFEx, to make it usable in cross-cultural contexts; b) an investigation of the credibility of the expressions contained in DaFEx; c) a study addressing the subjective assessment of the intensity of facial expressions.

Acknowledgments

This work was carried on within the PF-STAR (http://pfstar.itc.it) and the HUMAINE (http://emotion-research.net/) projects, and partially supported by grants IST-2001-37599 and and IST 2004 507422 from the EU.

References

1. Agresti, A. 2002 *Categorical Data Analysis.* John Wiley & Sons. Hoboken, NJ.
2. Ahlberg, J., Pandzic, I. S., You, L. 2002, Evaluationg MPEG-4 Facial Animation Players. In I. S. Pandzic, R. Forchhimer (editors), *MPEG-4 Facial Animation: the standard, implementation and applications*, Wiley & Sons, Chichester, UK, 287-291.
3. Banse, R., Scherer, K.R. 1996. Acoustic profiles in vocal emotion expression. *Journal of Personality and Social Psychology*, 70(3), 614-636.
4. Cassell, J., Sullivan, J., Prevost, S., Churchill, E. (Eds.): 2000, *Embodied Conversational Agents*. Cambridge, MA: MIT Press.
5. Costantini, E., Pianesi, F., Cosi, P., 2004, Evaluation of Synthetic Faces: Human Recognition of Emotional Facial Displays. In E. Andre', L. Dybkiaer, W. Minker, P. Heisterkamp (eds.), *Affective Dialogue Systems*, pp. 276-287. Springer Verlag, Berlin.
6. Costantini, E., Pianesi, F., Prete, M. 2005. Recognising Emotions in Human and Synthetic Faces: the Role of the Upper and Lower Parts of the Face. In *Proceedings of IUI 2005, International Conference on Intelligent User Interfaces*. San Diego, CA.
7. Ekman, P.; Friesen, W.V. 1971. Constants across cultures in the face and emotion. *Journal of Personality and Social Psychology*, 17, 124-129.
8. Ekman, P., Friesen, W.V., Ellsworth, P. 1972, *Emotion in the Human Face*. Pergamon Press. Elmsdorf, NY.
9. Ekman, P., Friesen W. 1978, *Manual for the Facial Action Coding System.* Consulting Psych. Press. Palo Alto, CA.
10. Izard, C.E. 1977. *Human Emotions*. Plenum Press, New York.
11. Kätsyri, J., Klucharev, V., Frydrych, M., Sams M. 2003. 'Identification of Synthetic and Natural Emotional Facial Expressions'. In *Proceedings of AVSP'2003*, 239-244, St. Jorioz, France.
12. Ruttkay, Z., Doorman, C., Noot, H. 2002. 'Evaluating ECAs - What and How?'. In *Proceedings of the AAMAS02 Workshop on Embodied conversational agents - let's specify and evaluate them!*, Bologna, Italy.
13. Ruttkay, Z., Doorman, C., Noot, H. 2004 'Embodied Conversational Agents on a Common Ground. A Framework for Design and Evaluation'. In Ruttkai, Z. and C. Pelachaud (eds.) *From Brows till Trust*.. Kluwer, Dordrecht.
14. van Son, R.. J. .J. .H.. 1994. 'A Method to Quantify the Error Distribution in Confusion Matrices'. In Proceedings 18, 41-63. Institute of Phonetic Sciences, University of Amsterdam.
15. Wallbott, H.G. 1998. Bodily expression of emotion. *European Journal of Social Psychology*, 28, 879-896.

A Multimodal Database as a Background for Emotional Synthesis, Recognition and Training in E-Learning Systems

Luigi Anolli[1], Fabrizia Mantovani[1,2], Marcello Mortillaro[1], Antonietta Vescovo[1], Alessia Agliati[1], Linda Confalonieri[1], Olivia Realdon[1], Valentino Zurloni[1], and Alessandro Sacchi[1]

[1] CESCOM - Centre for Research in Communication Science, University of Milan – Bicocca, Milan, Italy
{luigi.anolli, fabrizia.mantovani, marcello.mortillaro, antonietta.vescovo, alessia.agliati, linda.confalonieri, olivia.realdon, valentino.zurloni, alessandro.sacchi}@unimib.it
[2] ATN-P LAB – Applied Technology for Neuro-Psychology Lab, Istituto Auxologico Italiano, Milan, Italy

Abstract. This paper presents a multimodal database developed within the EU-funded project MYSELF. The project aims at developing an e-learning platform endowed with affective computing capabilities for the training of relational skills through interactive simulations. The database includes data coming from 34 participants and concerning physiological parameters, vocal nonverbal features, facial expression and posture. Ten different emotions were considered (anger, joy, sadness, fear, contempt, shame, guilt, pride, frustration and boredom), ranging from primary to self-conscious emotions of particular relevance in learning process and interpersonal relationships. Preliminary results and analyses are presented, together with directions for future work..

1 Introduction

Designing an automatic system able to express emotions and to detect the emotional state of a user is one of the main aims of the research field defined as affective computing [1]. The acknowledgment of the user's affective state can improve the effectiveness of a number of computer applications in a variety of fields. In particular, e-learning could be deeply empowered in its effectiveness since emotions are recognized to have a deep influence on the learning process. The Learning Companion project, at MIT, was one of the first experiences trying to address this issue in distance learning and computer-assisted training for children. A number of projects are currently being conducted in order to design e-learning platforms endowed with affective computing capabilities. One of these projects, funded by the European Commission and started in September 2004, is called MYSELF "Multimodal elearning System based on Simulations, Role-Playing, Automatic Coaching and Voice Recognition interaction for Affective Profiling" (www.myself-proj.it) and involves 14 partners (among Universities, research labs, educational and IT companies and SMEs) from 6

J. Tao, T. Tan, and R.W. Picard (Eds.): ACII 2005, LNCS 3784, pp. 566 – 573, 2005.

different EU countries. The target focus of Myself platform will be on training social and relational skills in different professional settings (banking, commerce, health-care, etc.) through interactive simulations. As far as affective computing features are concerned, three main issues are at the moment under investigation: the implementation of a virtual tutor provided with emotional expressive synthesis abilities; a multimodal emotional detection module able to get information on user's state along the learning path; the development of 3D interactive simulations and targeted exercises to improve emotional management, with specific focus on expression and recognition of emotions.

This paper presents preliminary work carried out by the Centre for Research in Communication Science (CESCOM) focusing on building a multimodal emotional database as a background for the development of MySelf platform and simulations.

Much work has been now carried out in the affective computing domain to perform the detection and inference of emotional state detection from physiological correlates [1-3], facial expressions [4,5], vocal-non-verbal features (such as F0, intensity, etc.) [6,7], verbal speech content, questionnaires or self-report measures and the detection of behavioural events (e.g. mouse-clicking) [8]. Since the integration of multiple sources of information could enhance power to achieve a reliable emotional recognition, building multimodal databases to test recognition algorithms is recognized a very important issue for affective computing research. While this need is clearly perceived within research community very few large multimodal databases are available, in particular including also physiological measures. From a review of the state of the art about emotional databases [9] emerged that among more than 40 emotional databases only 10-12 include more than one measure at the same time. Most of the databases deal only with speech or facial expression (in some cases also gestures) and even when considering few more complete multimodal databases available they mostly combine audio and visual (facial behavior) information; very few [10,11] added physiological features. Furthermore, acquiring ecologically valid emotional data with is very complex. Many of the databases available, in fact, ask subjects to act or pose emotions, in order to extract vocal and facial features. In the last years, this lack of naturalism has been severely criticized, and researchers try to induce emotions (rather than asking subjects to simulate them) or to collect data occuring in everyday life [12-14]. Finally, there is growing awareness that it is important to include a broader range of emotions than the six-seven basic ones. The number of databases that include emotions exceeding traditional primary emotions is constantly increasing [11, 13, 15, 16]. Due to the specific objective of Myself project, the range of emotions of interest include also secondary and self-conscious emotions like pride, shame, frustration, boredom, that do play a key role both in learning process and in interpersonal relationships; their investigation is therefore very relevant when trying to design interactive training simulations dealing with relational skills.

Starting from these premises, the present work focuses on *building a multimodal database* taking into account different sources of data (physiological measures, facial expression and posture, vocal non verbal features) for 10 different emotions (anger, joy, sadness, fear, contempt, shame, guilt, pride, frustration and boredom). We intend to systematically investigate the difference between emotions in the considered modalities and to verify the existence of systematic correlation between the different measures. Furthermore, we are interested in investigating whether these measures are modulated by specific personality characteristics and/or emotional management styles, assessed through dedicated self-report measures. This work, as discussed more into depth in section 4, might hold relevant implications for MySelf project, providing useful guidelines for emotional synthesis, recognition and training.

2 Methodology

2.1 Participants and Experimental Design

Participants were 34 students (16 male and 18 female) of the University of Milan-Bicocca (M = 22.62; SD = 1.30).

A 10 (emotion) x 2 (sex) mixed factor design (with repeated measures for emotion) was performed. Emotions considered were: anger, joy, sadness, fear, contempt, shame, guilt, pride, frustration and boredom.

Measures considered were: *physiological measures* (Heart Rate, HR; Skin conductance, SC; Respiration Rate, RR; Respiration Amplitude, RA, Finger Blood Amplitude, BA; Electromyography of the extensor muscle of the forearm, EMG); *nonverbal behavior related to facial expression and posture*: in particular, facial expression was coded using FACS (Facial Action Coding System[17]); *vocal acoustic parameters* referring to time (total duration, partial duration, duration of pauses, speech rate and articulation rate), fundamental frequency (F0) (mean, standard deviation, range, minimum and maximum) and intensity (mean, standard deviation, range, minimum and maximum). Besides these measures we administered a battery of paper-and-pencil tests (*Big Five Questionnaire and Emotion Regulation Questionnaire*) to assess some personality and emotional management style characteristics of the participants, as potential variables modulating the emotional expression at different levels.

2.2 Contextualized Acting for Eliciting Emotions

As general framework, we attempted to induce emotions in the laboratory rather than to merely simulate it using actors according to the suggestions by Bachorowski [18]. To this aim, in a preliminary phase we prepared and validated ten prototypical texts eliciting the ten different emotions. The texts, consisting of 200 to 250 words, were characterized by a clear and univocal emotional episode and in each text an identical standard utterance was included on which to carry out subsequently acoustic comparisons. Each text included a first part describing the situation, and a second part where the protagonist speaks in first person. Such a method was previously adopted in the study of vocal correlates of emotions [16, 19, 20]. Procedure was modified in order to acquire other kind of data: participants were asked to read aloud texts written, trying to identify themselves with the main character of every narration (contextualised acting, similarly to Velten procedure, [21], but adding a contextual dimension through narration). To achieve a higher naturalism degree, naïve readers were chosen, and no direct mention of emotional terms was provided by researchers to the participants.

2.3 Procedure

Participants were introduced in a laboratory setting (individually), they were shortly briefed about the sensors and gave their consent to being video and audio recorded.

First of all, a baseline (3 minutes) for physiological parameters was measured for all participants. Then, the eliciting texts were presented on a single PC screenshot, in randomized order. Participants were asked to read each text first time silently and imagining the situations described, then reading them aloud in a natural and spontaneous way trying to identify themselves with the protagonist. At the end participants were administered the two questionnaires (Big Five and ERQ). The overall recording session took about 30 minutes.

2.4 Materials and Instruments

Physiological data were collected through Procomp Thought Technology, able to detect real-time measure of physiological indices. One desktop PC (NEC, Powermate) was connected to the Procomp, and had the Biograph Infinity software for feature extraction installed. *Video data* were acquired using a webcam (Logitech Quickcam) placed on the top of the screen in front of the participant. Video files were analyzed through Theme software, a tool to code and analyse behavioural events, as well as to detect regularities within behavior, that are graphically translated in time patterns. Time patterns (T-patterns) are repeated sequences of behavioural units occurring in the same order and with approximately the same time distance during an observation period; according to recent studies [22], the use of this tool might provide very interesting insights in the dynamic and hierarchical features of nonverbal behavior organization. *Voice* was acquired through a unidirectional dynamic microphone (Shure, SM 48); vocal features were then extracted and analyzed through Computerized Speech Lab (CSL 4500 by Kay Elemetrics). A laptop PC (ASUS M3000N), ran the PowerPoint text slideshow that participants read.

3 Results

Due to space constraints and to the early stage of analysis, here are presented some preliminary data. Next steps for analysis will include: investigating the correlations between measures taken from different modalities; training and testing computational algorithms for automatic clustering and recognition; identifying individual profiles according to personality and emotional management characteristics.

Physiological Data. We considered the mean value detected during the standard utterance period. Repeated-measure parametric and non parametric tests were performed on all the measures (according to the normality of their distributions). A significant main effect for emotion was acknowledged in ANOVA statistics for mean values of BA ($F_{9, 288} = 3.44$; $p< .01$), RR ($F_{9, 288} = 8.981$; $p< .01$), RA ($F_{9, 288} = 2.753$; $p< .01$). For EMG Friedman's non-parametric test showed a significant main effect for emotion ($Chi^2 = 27.915$; $p< .05$). A number of post hoc analyses showed significance patterns allowing to defining preliminary groupings of variables (Due to their number it is not possible to report all of them here). Results are generally consistent with previous studies: for example, emotions like joy, anger, fear are clearly differentiated from sadness, registering a higher level in skin conductance and EMG and a lower in finger blood amplitude, while other measures like heart rate fails to discriminate. For what concerns self-conscious emotions and emotions connected to learning, Pride and Shame showed similar means for every measure with the exception of RR, while Frustration and Guilt differed in respiration measures (RA and RR) and SC. From a whole consideration of these data subsequent analysis will be directed to the identification of possible physiological patterns for each emotion.

Table 1. Mean and sd of the physiological indices for the 10 emotions considered

	HR		BA		*RR*		RA		*SC*		EMG	
	Mean	SD	Mean	SD	Mean	SD	Mean	SD	Mean	SD	Mean	SD
Anger	91,03	20,3	4,99	4,5	14,32	2,7	3,19	2,1	11,38	4,1	12,03	11,8
Boredom	91,69	17,6	4,53	3,7	14,55	3,2	3,23	2,1	11,35	4,7	7,60	8,1
Contempt	92,43	17,0	4,75	3,8	10,55	3,1	4,06	2,1	11,86	4,7	11,43	12,0
Fear	91,27	20,6	5,13	3,8	12,83	2,9	3,48	1,9	11,56	4,9	10,63	11,6
Frustration	87,35	19,7	6,00	4,8	10,19	2,9	4,14	2,6	11,38	4,9	8,65	10,5
Guilt	87,52	18,5	5,92	4,4	13,47	3,8	2,79	1,7	11,00	4,3	9,61	9,0
Joy	89,22	19,2	4,40	3,5	11,42	3,2	3,59	1,4	11,66	4,9	11,71	11,1
Pride	90,96	16,8	5,44	5,3	12,32	2,8	3,10	1,7	11,26	4,5	11,84	9,1
Sadness	89,74	20,2	5,85	4,9	11,36	3,4	3,65	1,9	11,22	4,4	9,31	11,0
Shame	91,75	18,2	5,06	4,2	13,89	2,6	3,39	2,3	11,32	4,3	11,05	10,5

Vocal Features. A significant main effect of emotion was found in ANOVA statistics for every index considered with the exception of Pause: Speech Rate ($F_{9, 270} = 5.132$; $p< .01$), Articulation Rate ($F_{9, 270} = 12.017$; $p< .01$), Total Duration ($F_{9, 270} = 3.907$; $p< .01$), Partial Duration ($F_{9, 270} = 10.796$; $p< .01$), Intensity mean ($F_{9, 270} = 32.138$; $p< .01$), Intensity SD ($F_{9, 270} = 4.423$; p< .01), F0 mean ($F_{9, 270} = 9.222$; $p< .01$), F0 SD ($F_{9, 27} = 3.628$; $p< .01$). Also for vocal correlates a high number of post hoc analysis resulted significant and allowed a preliminary grouping of emotions according to their vocal nonverbal features profiles. In general, our results are consistent with scientific literature for the primary emotions included in our study. For example emotions like anger, joy and fear showed a significant higher Intensity mean and F0 mean than sadness. For secondary emotions, it emerged that Boredom and Frustration were quite similar (except for Intensity SD), as resulted for Pride and Shame, (except for F0 mean).

Non Verbal Behaviour (Facial Expression and Posture). Video sequences were analyzed and coded frame by frame using Theme Coder and then coded were entered in Theme Software, that generates both the frequency of every behavioural unit observed and Time patterns. A multivariate ANOVA with repeated measures showed a significant main effect of emotion ($F_{33, 2340} = 2.289$; $p< .01$). At univariate tests a significant effect emerged for several nonverbal behaviour units: AU1, inner brow raising ($F_{9, 288} = 2.709$; $p< .05$); AU2, outer brow raising ($F_{9, 288} = 3.469$; $p< .01$); AU4, eyebrow lowering ($F_{9, 288} = 3.514$; $p< .01$); AU6, cheek raising ($F_{9, 288} = 8.393$; $p< .01$), AU7 ($F_{9, 288} = 4.459$; $p< .05$); AU9, nose wrinkling ($F_{9, 288} = 3.098$; $p< .05$); AU10, upper lip raising ($F_{9, 288} = 3.115$; $p< .05$); AU12, lip corners raising ($F_{9, 288} = 22.081$; $p< .00$); AU26, jaw drop ($F_{9,288} = 3.832$; $p < .05$); AU33, cheek blowing ($F_{9,288} = 31.703$; $p < .00$); AU37, lips wiping ($F_{9,288} = 2.646$; $p < .05$); hand on table ($F_{9,288} = 4.203$; $p < .05$); trunk on chair ($F_{9,288} = 3.539$; $p < .05$). Some nonverbal units mean frequencies were significant to identify a typical expressive nonverbal pattern for different emotions. In particular AU1 and AU2 were significantly more manifested in pride, AU4 and "hand on chair" in fear; AU6 and AU12 in happiness; AU33 in boredom and "trunk on chair" in guilt. By way of example, figure 1 represents a T-pattern detected during an emotional sequence, specifically during boredom: a sequence (recurring twice) of cheek blowing (AU33), eyebrow lowering (AU4) and head left inclination (AU55), that seems well represent the typical boredom-related facial expression.

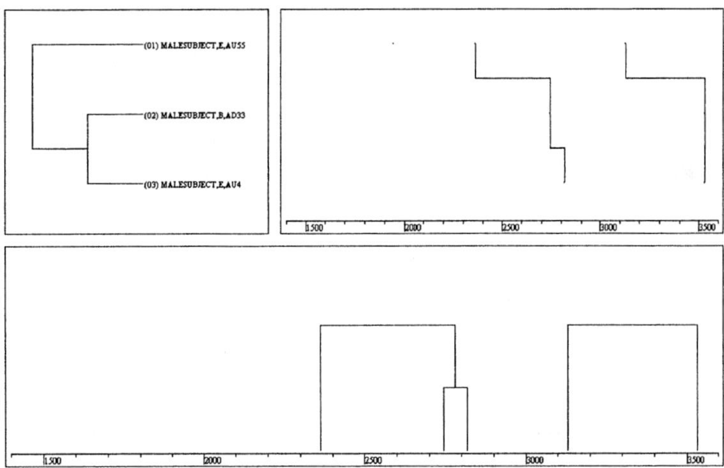

Fig. 1. T-pattern detected in a male subject during boredom sequence. (Legend: Male subject, ends, AU55; male subject, begins, AD33; male subject, ends, AU4).

4 Discussion and Conclusions

In this paper we presented a multimodal emotional database which included vocal non verbal features, physiological signals, facial expression and posture for ten different emotions (anger, joy, sadness, fear, contempt, shame, guilt, pride, frustration and boredom).

Preliminary data presented in this paper supported the hypotheses of the existence of significant differences among emotions in the different modalities investigated; results for the single modalities seem to be, in general, quite consistent with scientific literature. Also, the investigation of complex, self-conscious emotions seemed to show specific multimodal profiles.

This work might have relevant implications for the ongoing MySelf project, at different levels.

First of all, for *emotional expression synthesis:* identifying prototypical nonverbal configurations for the different emotions might provide a useful basis to animate the 3D virtual tutor and the virtual characters of the interactive simulations. Of particular interest are data on facial expression and postural behavior: the use of Theme software allowed to investigate non only differences among emotions in terms of relative frequencies of single action units, but also in terms of emergence of higher order, temporal patterns characteristics of different emotions. We will try to use these prototypical configurations for 3D character animation (virtual tutor and simulation characters) and assess their effectiveness in terms of recognizability and representativeness. Issues related to temporal synchrony across the different modalities are also worth deeper investigation, especially for their inputs to animating virtual characters.

Second, the work might provide useful indications for the implementation of the *user's emotion recognition system:* work for training and testing multimodal recognition algorithms (in line with works like [3, 5, 23]) will be performed in the near future. These analyses should support efforts in the investigation of criteria for feature and algorithm selection, in order to identify the best combination of features and algorithm according to different clustering problems. Furthermore, within the project we will focus on how to integrate in the recognition modules information coming also from verbal speech content, self-report measures and specific events detectable by the e-learning system (such as failing/passing a test, etc.) in order to enhance consistency and reliability.

Third, material gathered within this study could be extremely useful for the implementation of *training exercises* specifically aimed at improving emotional expression and recognition skills.

Future work within the project will be also aiming at building a second database, more context-dependent (given the importance of restricting use domain in order to increase reliability). This work, which will start after the release of the beta version of the platform, will be hopefully able to enhance ecological validity of data gathered and allow a useful comparison with data coming from the first database presented in this paper.

Acknowledgments

The present work is part of the European Commission 6FP research project MYSELF (SME-2003-1-508258). Web site: www.myself-proj.it . The authors would also like to thank Dr. MariaChiara Gritti, Sara Manieri and Simona Raspelli for their active collaboration in this study.

References

1. Picard, R. W.: Affective computing. The MIT Press, Cambridge MA (1997)
2. Prendinger, H., Dohi, H., Wang, H., Mayer, S., Ishizuka, M.:. Empathic embodied interfaces: Addressing users' affective state Tutorial and Research. Workshop on Affective Dialogue Systems (ADS-04). Springer LNAI 3068, Kloster Irsee, Germany: (2004) 53-64
3. Scheirer, J., Fernandez, R., Klein, J., Picard, R. W.: Frustrating the user on purpose: A step toward building an affective computer. Interacting with computers 14 (2002) 93-118
4. Chen, L.S., Huang, T.S., Miyasato, T., Nakatsu, R.: Multimodal human emotion/ expression recognition. In: Proceedings of International Conference on Automatic Face and Gesture Recognition, Nara, Japan, IEEE Computer Society (1998)

5. Kapoor, A., Picard, R.W., Ivanov, Y.: Probabilistic combination of multiple modalities to detect interest. In: Proceedings of International Conference on Pattern Recognition, Cambridge, England (2004)
6. Oudeyer, P-Y.: The production and recognition of emotions in speech: features and algorithms. International Journal of Human Computer Interaction 59 (2003) 157--183
7. Batliner, A., Fischer, K., Huber, R., Spilker, J., Nöth, E.: How to find trouble in communication. Speech Communication, 40 (2003) 117-143
8. Pantic, M., Rothkrantz, L.J.M.: Toward an Affect Sensitive Multimodal Human-Computer Interaction. In: Proceedings of the IEEE Vol. 91, 9 (2003) 1370-1390
9. Douglas-Cowie, E. et al.: Deliverable D5c-Preliminary plans for exemplars: Databases. Project Deliverable of Humaine Network of Excellence (Available online at: http://emotion-research.net/deliverables/) (2004)
10. Amir, N., Ron, S., Laor, N.: Analysis of an emotional speech corpus in Hebrew based on objective criteria. In: Proceedings of ISCA ITRW on speech and emotion, Newcastle, Belfast, Textflow (2000) 29-33
11. McMahon, E., Cowie, R., Kasderidis, S., Taylor, J., Kollias, S.: What chance that a DC could recognise hazardous mental states from sensor outputs? In: Tales of the disappearing computer, Santorini (2003)
12. Campbell, W. N.: Recording Techniques for capturing natural everyday speech. In: Proceedings of LREC, Las Palmas (2002)
13. Douglas-Cowie, E., Campbell, N., Cowie, R., Roach, P.: Emotional speech: towards a new generation of databases. Speech Communication, 40 (2003) 33-60
14. Devillers, L., Vasilescu, I., Vidrascu, L.: . Anger versus Fear detection in recorded conversations. Speech Prosody (2004)
15. Cowie R., Cornelius R.: Describing the emotional states that are expressed in speech. Speech Communication, 40 (2003) 5-32.
16. Banse, R., & Scherer, K. R. (1996). Acoustic profiles in vocal emotion expression. Journal of personality and social psychology, 70 (3), 614-636.
17. Ekman, P., Friesen, W. V.: The Facial Action Coding System: A technique for measurement of facial movement. Palo Alto, CA: Consulting Psychologists Press (1978)
18. Bachorowski, J. A.: Vocal expression and perception of emotion. Current Directions in Psychological Science,. 8 (1999) 53-57
19. Douglas-Cowie, E., Cowie, R., Schroeder, M. (2000). A new emotion database: considerations, sources and scope. Proceedings of ISCA ITRW on speech and emotion, Newcastle, Belfast, Textflow (2000) 39-44
20. Iriondo, I., Guaus, R., Rodriguez, A., Lazaro, P., Montoya, N., Blanco, J., Beradas, D., Oliver, J., Tena, D., Longhi, L.: Validation of an acoustical modelling of emotional expression in Spanish using speech synthesis techniques. In: Proceedings of ISCA ITRW on speech and emotion, Newcastle, 5-7 September 2000, Belfast, Textflow (2000) 161-166
21. Velten, E.: A laboratory task for induction of mood states. Behaviour research and therapy, 6 (1968) 473-482
22. Anolli, L., Duncan, S.Jr., Magnusson, M., Riva, G.: The hidden structure of interaction: From neurons to culture patterns. Amsterdam. IOS Press (2005)
23. D'Mello, S. K., Craig, S. D., Gholson, B., Franklin, S., Picard, R. W., Graesser, A. C.: Integrating affect sensors in an intelligent tutoring system. In: Affective Interactions: The Computer in the Affective Loop, Workshop at 2005 International conference on Intelligent User Interfaces. New York: AMC Press (2005) 7-13

Construction of Virtual Assistant Based on Basic Emotions Theory

Zhiliang Wang, Ning Cheng, Yumei Fan, Jiwei Liu, and Changsheng Zhu

University of Science and Technology, Beijing 100083
kinchengning.student@sina.com
kinchengning@263.net

Abstract. The purpose of this paper is to construct a virtual assistant. Basic emotions theory points out that compound emotion consists of eight prototype basic emotions and "drives" which reflects people's will. According to this theory, we construct a psychology model. By adjusting parameters in it, we can simulate different human psychologies. Based on this model, combining real-time facial expression and voice recognition and synthesizing technology, we construct a virtual assistant. Proved by experiment, our system obeys human emotion rules.

1 Introduction

Artificial psychology is the machine realization of human psychology actives using research methods in information science. The purpose of artificial psychology is to meet users' requirements for life quality and it has many applying fields. For example, harmonious human-computer interaction needs the comfortable interface which can change automatically according to user's feelings. The virtual assistants of automatic commodity selecting may have the ability of automatically supplying commodities which consumers are interesting in. Computer games require virtual roles to have emotion for attracting users, etc. Currently, active research is being conducted on a user-friendly human-machine interface, such as Virtual characters found in the Oz Project [6] and the Virtual Theatre [7], as well as the humanoid robot WR-4 [8], all includes emotion as a fundamental component. Although some progress has been made in creating agents that display believable emotions, there are still many problems need to resolve. Two important problems in them are how to construct model for emotion [9], and affection model how to be applied in agent for improve agent's performance [10]. So our current goal is to try to resolve these problems and to construct a virtual assistant which have emotions and can interact with users. In Fig.1, we show our system structure chart.

Perceptual input layer gets and processes the sensor information which is associated with the emotion parameters in basic emotion equations by voice and facial expression recognition. Basic emotion layer computes the basic emotion intensity according to emotion equation. Motivation layer describes "drives" of virtual assistant which represents its will. Compound emotion layer computes compound emotion using output of basic emotion layer and motivation layer. Behavior layer responds to the user by voice and facial expression synthesizing. Calm layer denotes the calm state of psychology.

J. Tao, T. Tan, and R.W. Picard (Eds.): ACII 2005, LNCS 3784, pp. 574–581, 2005.

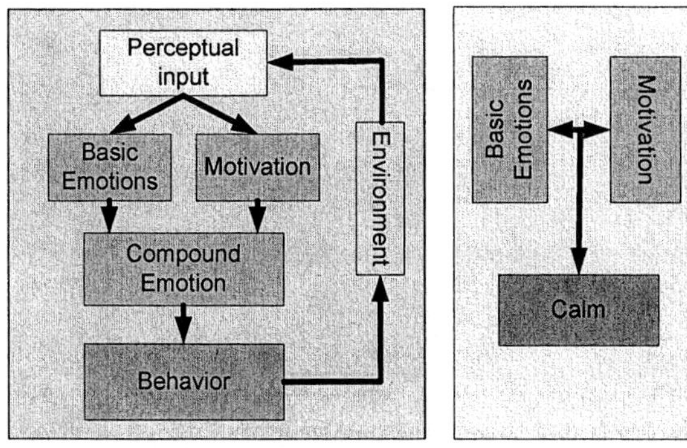

Fig. 1. System structure chart

2 Emotion Model

Psychology model is the core of the system, so we introduce it in detail.

2.1 Emotion Theory

Our emotion theory foundation is basic emotion theory. It points out that emotion has prototypes, i.e. for human, there are many basic emotion types each of which has unique characters, biologic waken mode and display mode. The different combination of these basic emotions form all the human emotions[1]. From the view of individual development, the generation of basic emotions is the result of organism natural mature but not natural study. Plutchik uses one single word to describe each of the eight basic emotions and makes a table as follow[3]:

Table 1. Basic emotions classification and their intensities

Intensity / type	None	Little	middle	strong	Very strong
Happiness	1	2	3	4	5
Acceptance	1	2	3	4	5
Surprise	1	2	3	4	5
Fear	1	2	3	4	5
Sadness	1	2	3	4	5
Disgust	1	2	3	4	5
Interesting	1	2	3	4	5
Anger	1	2	3	4	5

In his book, Frend usually uses the concept of “drives” to represent an inside incentive which is used to affect individual behaviors by adjusting activity contents and types[3]. Emotion has many compound modes. Basic emotions combined with “drives” form the affective experiences such as: content, urgent, eager, etc[3].

2.2 Mathematic Model

Our mathematic model has two parallel parts: motivation driving part and emotion calming down part.

2.2.1 Motivation Driving Part

According to psychology theory mentioned above, we analyze the relations among basic emotions, "drives" and environment information now.

1) Basic Emotion Layer

First, look at basic emotions. We think that people's psychology is a self organization procedure. Self organized natural things have these characters: each part of them exists both relying on other parts and for other parts and these parts interact with each other to integrate as a whole[4]. Think about one basic emotion. Intensity is the most obvious property of emotion and used as order parameter. Let $P(t)$ to be intensity. $P(t)$ changes according to outer stimulations and outer stimulation A is in direct proportion to current emotion intensity, so we induce item $AP(t)$. Because emotion goes to calm over time, we induce another item $-BP^2(t)$. At last, we get the equation:

$$\frac{\mathrm{dP(t)}}{\mathrm{dt}} = AP(t) - BP^2(t) \tag{1}$$

In which, $A \geq 0$, $B > 0$. Initial value is P_0 . When $t \to +\infty$, the solution $P(t) \to \frac{A}{B}$. It means that emotion intensity goes to stable value at last. A is the outer stimulation parameter and B is a predefined value which reflects emotion states. Eight basic emotions correspond to eight such equations:

$$\frac{\mathrm{dP_m(t)}}{\mathrm{dt}} = A_m P_m(t) - B_m P_m^2(t), m = 1,2,\cdots 8 \tag{2}$$

2) Driver Layer

People's motivation ("drives") reflects their will and behavior mode, so it has important position in our model. How to describe motivation precisely is the next problem we need to discuss. Use a vector to denote "drives": $\delta(\delta_1,\delta_2,\delta_3,\delta_4,\delta_5,\delta_6,\delta_7,\delta_8)$. "drives" reflects people's will, so it relates to people's attitudes about outer stimulations. Generally speaking, if outer stimulation is big at one component, "drives" is also big at this component but not in direct proportion to it. Let:

$$\tilde{A} = \frac{A}{\|A\|} = (\tilde{A}_1, \tilde{A}_2, \tilde{A}_3, \tilde{A}_4, \tilde{A}_5, \tilde{A}_6, \tilde{A}_7, \tilde{A}_8),$$

In which, $\|A\| = \sum_{m=1}^{8} A_m$. δ_i *is the component of "drives" vector. When* $0 \le a_i \le a$ *, let* $\delta_i = 0$ *,when* $a < a_i \le 1$ *,let* $\delta_i = 1 - e^{-(A_i - a)^2}$.

3) Compound Emotion Layer

When we get the expression of "drives", we think about the relation between "drives" and compound emotion. When emotion rising, the drive also rise, so emotion strengthens the "drives". However, emotion and "drives" both have decay tendency. According to these, we describe their relation as:

$$\begin{cases} \frac{du}{dt} = -\alpha u + s \\ \frac{ds}{dt} = -\beta s + u^2 \end{cases} \tag{3}$$

In which, s is one basic emotion intensity in compound emotion and u is corresponding component's intensity of "drives". α is the decay coefficient of "drives", so α >0. β is the decay coefficient of emotion, so β>0. $s(t)$ can be expressed as:

$$s(t) = (\frac{1}{\beta} + \frac{2}{\beta^2}\alpha + \frac{4}{\beta^3}\alpha^2)u^2(t) \tag{4}$$

Considered the impact of basic emotions to compound emotion, compound emotion is decided as follow:

$$P(t) = (\frac{1}{\beta} + \frac{2}{\beta^2}\alpha + \frac{4}{\beta^3}\alpha^2)u^2(t) \times p(t) \tag{5}$$

In which, $P(t)$ is a component of compound emotion vector, $u(t)$ is the corresponding component of "drives" vector, $p(t)$ is corresponding basic emotion. α, β are constants which relate to personality and sensitivity and are used to control emotion's fluctuation range. The vector of compound emotion consists of eight components $P_i(t)$.

2.2.2 Emotion Calming Down Parts

After rising states, emotion will go to calm automatically over time, i.e. basic emotion goes to calm under the impact of "drives". In this section, we describe this process. We give a method to describe the relation between "drives" and basic emotions. Generally speaking, people's attitude for one thing is in direct proportion to emotion, but the drive to do thing will also decay over time, so we think that "drives" has self-decay tendency and also has the rising tendency under the impact of basic emotion. Basic emotion is decaying under the impact of "drives" and the decay rate is associated with itself. The bigger its intensity is, the faster it decays. Now, we give the mathematic expressions as follow:

$$\begin{cases} \dfrac{dX}{dt} = k_1X - k_2XY = G_X(X,Y,k_1,k_2) \\ \dfrac{dY}{dt} = k_2XY - k_3Y = G_Y(X,Y,k_2,k_3) \end{cases} \tag{6}$$

In which, X is intensity of one basic emotion and $\frac{dX}{dt}$ is intensity's change rate. Y is intensity of corresponding component of "drives" and $\frac{dY}{dt}$ is this component's change rate. k_1 is basic emotion's rise rate. k_2 is basic emotion's decay rate and is also the rise rate of corresponding component of "drives". k_3 is decay rate of corresponding component of "drives".

We solve this equation set and get the static solution as follow:

$$X_0 = \frac{k_3}{k_2} \quad Y_0 = \frac{k_1}{k_2} \tag{7}$$

Because emotion always has some little disturbance, we analyze the static solution for its stability. Let:

$$X = X_0 + x \quad Y = Y_0 + y \tag{8}$$

In which, $|x| << X_0, |y| << Y_0$.

The result is as follow:

$$\begin{bmatrix} x \\ y \end{bmatrix} = \begin{bmatrix} x_0 \\ y_0 \end{bmatrix} \exp[\pm i\omega t] \tag{9}$$

In which, $\omega = \sqrt{k_1k_3}$. Expression (9) indicates that if emotion is at some initial state of $\begin{bmatrix} X_0 + x_0 \\ Y_0 + y_0 \end{bmatrix}$ which depart static state of $\begin{bmatrix} X_0 \\ Y_0 \end{bmatrix}$, when t=0, over time, emotion neither to go away infinitely, nor to go to the static state infinitely, but fluctuate around the static state of $\begin{bmatrix} X_0 \\ Y_0 \end{bmatrix}$. The fluctuant frequency is $\omega = \sqrt{k_1k_3}$. This result describes the phenomenon that emotion fluctuates around a static state when it is calm.

3 Construction of Virtual Assistant

Based on this psychology model, combining real-time facial expression and voice recognition and synthesizing technology, we construct a virtual assistant.

3.1 Psychology Model Realization

We program to realize our psychology model and show it in Fig. 2. The upper two curve graphs describe the changing process of basic emotion and compound emotion in motivation driving part and the third curve graph describes the emotion calming down process.

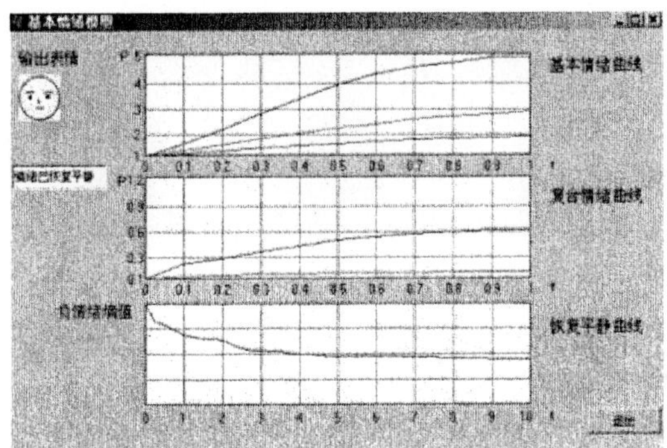

Fig. 2. Realization of psychology model

3.2 Behaviors Database

We construct a rule controlled behaviors database in which we define many usual behaviors and speech such as: can I help you, ok, thank you, etc. For each behavior and speech, we define the applying range rank, so virtual assistant's behavior directly associates with emotion.

3.3 Real Time Expression Recognition and Synthesizing

Real time expression recognition result is used as system input. It is based on exactly character point location. First, we localize the key points of eye, eyebrow and mouth exactly and extract their contours by curve fitting. Second, we analyze and record facial components' movement information, then use our HMM expression model to get recognition result. In Fig. 3, we show a row of recognition results.

Fig. 3. Real-time recognition results of four facial expressions as: surprise, happiness, sadness and anger

We synthesize virtual facial expression to output. We use character polygons to render 3D face. In the polygon mesh, we define the feature points of eyes, nostril, eyebrows, mouth, etc. These feature points are used to describe the shape and position of facial feature. We adopt two methods for face modeling: one is linear flexible model used to generate face, another is muscle model used for animation and expression transformation. In Fig. 4, we show some of our output facial expressions.

Fig. 4. Face expressions as: joy, surprise, sorrow, and calm

3.4 Real Time Voice Recognition and Synthesizing

We use the ASR sdk software to realize voice recognition as system input. We constructed simple word and speech database, store data such as: good, bad, I need you help, etc, to lead virtual assistant's behaviors. We established corresponding relations between these data and emotion parameters, so voice input can directly impact virtual assistant's emotions.

We use Interphonic (Text To Speech) software to realize voice synthesizing to output. We also established database to store word and speech such as: good morning, nice to meet you, can I help you, etc, as the response of the virtual assistant to users. Of course, there are corresponding relations between data and emotion parameters, so virtual assistant can choose word according to his emotion states.

4 Conclusions

Based on psychology model, we use many technologies to construct a virtual assistant who can first recognize user's expressions and voice in real time, then judge by psychology model and last give the response. Proved by experiments, our system obeys human emotion rules. Of course, we also met some problems such as: expression recognition is not exact enough sometimes and the speech's emotion rank is difficult to decide, etc. Our next work is to continue our research and solve the problem we met. We believe that we will design better system and our system will serve people in near future.

References

1. Ekman, P. An argument for basic emotions, Cognition and Emotion[J], 1992b,6,
2. Zhiliang Wang, Lun Xie, Artificial Psychology—an Attainable Scientific Research on the Human Brain[J]. IPMM'99(KEYNOTE PAPER), honolulu, USA, July 10-15,1999(ISTP)
3. Meng zhaolan, Human emotion[M], Shanghai press, 1989

4. Wu tong, Self-organization methods research[M], Tsinghua press, 2001
5. Weimin Xue, Zhehua Wei, Zhiliang Wang, The Research of Artificial Psychology Model[J], IEEE TENCON'02., Vol. I, p691-693, Beijing, China. October 30_31, 2002.
6. J.Bates, The role of emotion in believable agents. Communications Of The ACM,37(7):122-125. 1994.
7. B.Hayes-Roth, and R..van Gent, Story-making with improvisational puppets. in Proc. 1st Int. Conf. On Autonomous Agents, (Marina del Rey, CA, 1997), 1-7.
8. H. Miwa, T.Okuchi, K. Itoh, H. Takanobu, A.Takanishi: A new mental model for humanoid robots for human friendly communication - introduction of learning system, mood vector and second order equations of emotion, Proceedings of The 2003 IEEE International Conference on Robotics and Automation, pp.3588-3593, 2003
9. C.Calhoun, R.Solomon. What is an emotion[M] . London : Oxford University Press, 1984.
10. Camurri, A. Coglio. An architecture for emotional agents[J] . IEEE Multimedia , 5 (4) : 24 – 33,1998.

Appendix: Support Foundation

Foundational project: Supported by the key Lab named Advanced Information Science and Network Technology of Beijing (No.TDXX0503) and the key foundation of UST of Beijing.

Generalization of a Vision-Based Computational Model of Mind-Reading

Rana el Kaliouby and Peter Robinson

Computer Laboratory, University of Cambridge,
15 JJ Thomson Avenue, Cambridge UK CB3 0FD

Abstract. This paper describes a vision-based computational model of mind-reading that infers complex mental states from head and facial expressions in real-time. The generalization ability of the system is evaluated on videos that were posed by lay people in a relatively uncontrolled recording environment for six mental states—agreeing, concentrating, disagreeing, interested, thinking and unsure. The results show that the system's accuracy is comparable to that of humans on the same corpus.

1 Introduction

Existing human-computer interfaces are oblivious to the user's mental states and intentions, and as a result often respond inappropriately, e.g., by deciding to do irrelevant, computationally intensive tasks while a user is frantically working on a deadline. With the increasing complexity of human-computer interaction and the ubiquity of mobile and wearable devices, a new interaction paradigm is needed. In this paradigm, systems need to have socio-emotional intelligence to gather information autonomously about the user's state and to respond adaptively to it. "Theory of mind" or **mind-reading** [1]—the ability to attribute mental states to others by observing their behaviour—is a key component of socio-emotional intelligence in humans, and is equally important for natural user interfaces.

We have developed a computational model of mind-reading that infers mental states from head gestures and facial expressions in a video stream in real-time. The principal contribution of our system is the inference of complex mental states, states of mind that are not part of the set of basic emotions. These encompass affective states such as *interested*, and cognitive states that reveal mental processes such as *thinking* [3]. The automated inference of complex mental states has received almost no attention compared with the automated recognition of basic emotions. By supporting a wider range of mental states beyond the basic emotions, our system has widened the scope of human-computer interaction scenarios in which automated facial analysis systems can be integrated.

In this paper, we test the generalization ability of the computational model of mind-reading on videos that were posed by lay people in a relatively uncontrolled environment, having trained the system on carefully-composed videos from the Mind-Reading DVD [2][1]. We emphasize that training and testing are

[1] Video examples that demonstrate how our system generalizes can be found at `http://www.cl.cam.ac.uk/~re227/demo/`

J. Tao, T. Tan, and R.W. Picard (Eds.): ACII 2005, LNCS 3784, pp. 582–589, 2005.

carried out using different corpora, as opposed to using sampling methods on the same corpus (e.g., cross-validation) since sampling often introduces a bias in the results because of the similarity of recording conditions and actors on a single corpus. Evaluating the generalization ability of supervised systems is important: ultimately we need train the system on some (limited) data-set then deploy it in different scenarios with many users without having to re-train or calibrate it.

2 Related Work

Over the past decade, significant progress has been made with automated facial expression analysis (FEA) (a survey can be found in Pantic and Rothkrantz [15] and in Fasel and Leuttin [6]). The majority of systems are either concerned with the recognition of basic emotions (happy, sad, angry, disgusted, surprised and afraid) or with the automated coding of facial actions. There are two recent exceptions. Gu and Ji [7] present a facial event classifier for driver vigilance (inattention, yawning and state of falling asleep). Kapoor *et al.* [11] devise a multi-modal probabilistic framework for the recognition of interest and boredom. Only a few FEA systems have been evaluated with regards to how well they generalize across different corpora. This is mainly because the collection, filtering and labelling of videos is a labour intensive and time-consuming task. Littlewort *et al.* [12] test their system in recognizing the basic emotions when trained on the Cohn-Kanade database [10] and tested on the Pictures of Facial Affect [4] and vice versa. Even though both corpora contain similar stimuli—prototypic facial representations of the basic emotions and no rigid head motion—an average of 60% was reported compared with 95% when the system was trained and tested on the same corpus. In Michel and el Kaliouby [13], the system's accuracy dropped from 87.5% when trained and tested on the Cohn-Kanade database, to 60.7% when tested with users who were oblivious of the prototypic faces of basic emotions. A similar divergence of results is reported in Tian *et al.* [17] and Pardas *et al.* [16], emphasizing the importance of generalization in FEA systems.

3 Computational Model of Mind-Reading

A person's mental state is not directly available to an observer; instead it is inferred from nonverbal cues such as facial expressions. We present a novel approach to mental state representation based on the theory of mind-reading. Our approach combines vision-based perceptual processing with top-down reasoning to map low-level observable behaviour into high-level mental states.

3.1 Representation of Mental States

As shown in Fig. 1, we use Dynamic Bayesian Networks (DBNs) [14] to model the unfolding of mental states over time $P(\mathbf{X}[t])$, where $\mathbf{X}$ is a vector of events corresponding to different mental states. A DBN is a graph that represents the

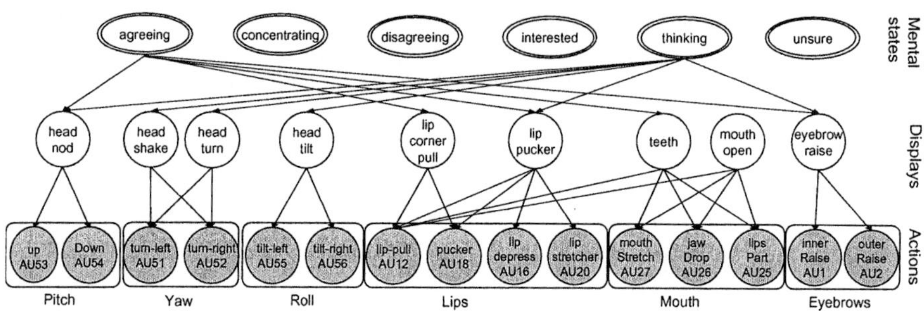

Fig. 1. Multi-level computational model of mind-reading. For clarity, the displays for only two mental states are shown.

causal probability and conditional independence relations among events that evolve over time. The hidden state of each DBN represents an event with two possible outcomes: true whenever the user is experiencing a specific mental state, and false otherwise. The observations or evidence nodes represent the recognized head and facial displays $\mathbf{Y}$. The double circle around a mental state node encodes the temporal dependency between that node in consecutive slices of the network, $X_i[t-1]$ and $X_i[t]$. Having a model for each class means that the hidden state of more than one DBN can be true, so that co-occurring mental states can be represented by the system. The DBN parameters and structure are learnt from exemplar videos using maximum likelihood estimation and feature selection [9].

3.2 Observational Evidence: Head and Facial Displays

The observational evidence consists of the head and facial displays that were recognized up to the current time $P(\mathbf{Y}[t])$ such as a head nod or smile. Each display is represented as a Hidden Markov Model (HMM) of a sequence of head/facial actions, recognized non-intrusively, in real time (Fig. 2). The supported actions and displays are shown in Fig. 1. For instance, a nod is an alternating sequence of head-up and head-down actions. The actions are based on the Facial Action Coding System [5]. Head actions are described by the magnitude and direction of 3 Euler angles, while facial actions are extracted using motion, shape and colour analysis of the lips, mouth and eyebrows. Details of head/facial action recognition and HMM topologies can be found in el Kaliouby [8].

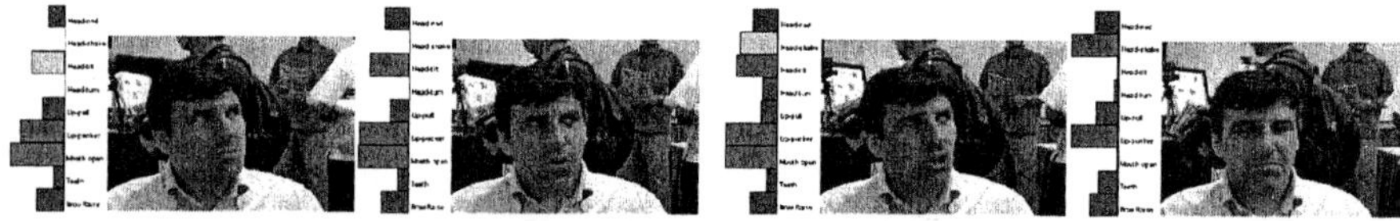

Fig. 2. Real time display recognition (frames sampled every 0.7s). The bars represent the output probabilities of the HMM classifiers (top to bottom): head nod, shake, tilt, turn, lip corner pull, lip pucker, mouth open, teeth and eye-brow raise.

3.3 Inference Framework

Inference involves recursively updating the belief state of hidden states based upon the knowledge captured in the DBNs and available evidence—the head and facial displays that are recognized throughout a video, their dynamics (duration, relationship to each other, and when in the video they occur) and previous mental state inferences. We implement the inference framework as a sliding window of evidence (Algorithm 1). At any instant t, the observation vector that is input to the inference engine is a vector of the w most-recent displays $\mathbf{Y}[t-w:t]$, and the corresponding most-recent mental state inferences $P(\mathbf{X}[t-w:t-1])$. The output is a probability that the observation vector was generated by each of the DBNs. The inference engine uses the unrolled-junction-tree algorithm [14].

Algorithm 1. Mental state inference

Objective: $P(X_i[t])$, the belief state of $1 \leq i \leq x$ mental states over time $1 \leq t \leq T$
Given: x DBNs with y observations nodes; evidence length w and sliding factor dw

```
Instantiate inference engine
for all t in w time slices do
   Get current observations Y[t]
for all t in T time slices do
   Enter evidence so far: Y[t − w : t] and P(X[t − w : t − 1])
   Calculate marginal probabilities P(X[t])
   Advance window t = t + dw
   Get current observations Y[t]
```

---

4 Experimental Evaluation

In el Kaliouby and Robinson [9], we trained and tested our system on videos from the Mind-Reading DVD (MR) [2], a guide to emotions developed for Autism Spectrum Disorders. An upper bound of 88.9% and an average accuracy of 77.4% was achieved for *agreeing*, *concentrating*, *disagreeing*, *interested*, *thinking* and *unsure*. To test if our system generalizes beyond the controlled videos in MR, we collected videos at the IEEE International Conference on Computer Vision and Pattern Recognition (CVPR 2004). Fig. 3 (left) shows frames of both corpora.

4.1 The CVPR 2004 Corpus

We asked 16 conference attendees to act six mental states: *agreeing*, *concentrating*, *disagreeing*, *interested*, *thinking* and *unsure*. The volunteers were *not* given any instructions on *how* to act the mental states, which resulted in considerable within-class variation between the 16 videos of each emotion. They were asked to name the mental state they would act immediately before they started; this was later used to label the videos. Unlike prevalent facial expression databases [10], we placed no restrictions on the head or body movements of volunteers. All 16 volunteers were aged between 16 and 60 and worked in computer-science

Table 1. Characteristics of CVPR corpus "actors". Gender: Male • Female ○; Ethnicity: White • Asian ○; Glasses • Facial hair ○; Looking down • Talking ○.

Subject ID	A	B	C	D	E	F	G	H	I	J	K	L	M	N	O	P
Gender	•	•	○	•	•	•	•	•	○	•	○	•	•	•	•	•
Ethnicity	•	•	•	•	•	○	•	•	•	•	•	•	•	•	•	○
Glasses/Facial hair	○				•	•					• ○					
Frontal	•	•	•	•	•	•	•		•	•	•	•	•	•	•	•
Looking down/Talking		○	○	•				○	•	○						

or engineering; most were males of a white ethnic origin[2]. Their characteristics are summarized in Table 1. The videos were captured at 30 fps at a resolution of 320x240 and were labelled using the audio accompanying the footage. The background of the videos is dynamic: people were moving in and out of the neighbouring demonstration booth. We just relied on the lighting in the conference room at the time. The face-size varies within and between videos as the volunteers moved toward/away from the camera. By contrast, the actors in MR had a frontal pose at a constant distance from the camera, none wore glasses or had facial hair and the videos all had a uniform white background and the lighting was professionally set up. Eight videos (15s) were discarded: three lasted less than two seconds which is when the first DBN invocation occurs, and the system failed to locate the face in five videos. We used the remaining 88 videos (313s).

4.2 Human Baseline

Having been posed by people who are not professional actors, the CVPR videos are likely to include incorrect or bad examples of a mental state, and are weakly labelled. To establish a baseline with which to compare the results of the system, we tested how a panel of people would classify the videos. A forced-choice procedure was adopted, with six choices on each question: *agreeing*, *concentrating*, *disagreeing*, *interested*, *thinking*, *unsure*. Chance responding is 16.7%. Participants were shown a video on a projection screen, and then asked to circle only one mental state word that best matched what the person in the video was feeling. The panel consisted of 18 participants (50.0% male, 50.0% female), mostly software developers between the ages of 19 and 28[3]. The test generated 88 trials per participant for a total of 1584 responses. The distribution of results is shown in Fig. 3 (right). The percentage of correct answers range from 31.8% to 63.6% (mean=53.03%, SD=0.068). The agreement-score of a video—the percentage of panel participants who assigned the same label to a video—varied between 0-100%. Only 11% of the videos achieved an agreement-score of 85% or more on the truth label of the video; these were deemed as good examples of mental states. The confusion matrix of responses is shown in Fig. 5 (left). The classification rate is highest for *disagreeing* (77.5%) and lowest for *thinking* (40.1%). For a false positive rate of 9.4%, the recognition accuracy of the panel was 54.5%.

[2] Ethnicity defined as in the latest UK census, The Focus on Ethnicity and Identity.
[3] The panel did not know any of the "actors" on the CVPR corpus.

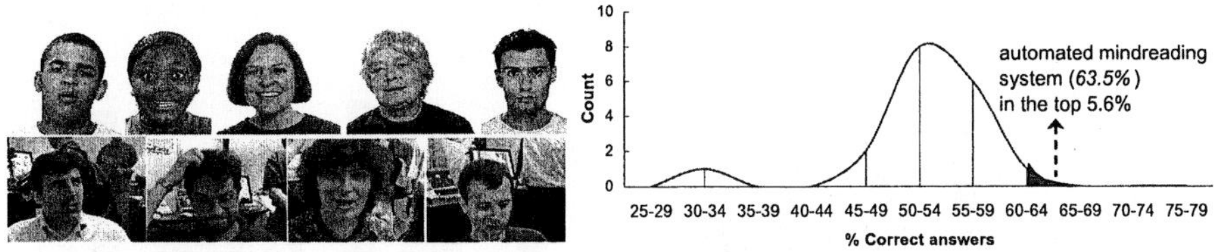

Fig. 3. (top-left) Mind Reading DVD; (bottom-left) CVPR corpus; (right) Distribution of human responses. The accuracy of our system is also shown.

4.3 Results of Computational Model of Mind-Reading

We trained the system on MR videos and tested it on the 88 videos of the CVPR corpus. A classification is correct if the mental state scoring the minimum error (i.e. largest area under the curve) matches the ground-truth label of the video. Fig. 4 shows an example of a 4.3-second long video labelled as *thinking* (77.8% agreement-score). A (false) head shake, a head tilt, a head turn and a lip-pull were recognized. Since *thinking* spans the largest area and this matches the ground-truth label of the video, this is a correct classification. The results are summarized in Fig. 5 (right). The classification rate is highest for *disagreeing* (85.7%) and lowest for *thinking* (26.7%)—all higher than chance responding (16.7%). For a mean false positive rate of 7.3%, the overall accuracy of the system is 63.5%. Compared with the results of humans classifying the exact set

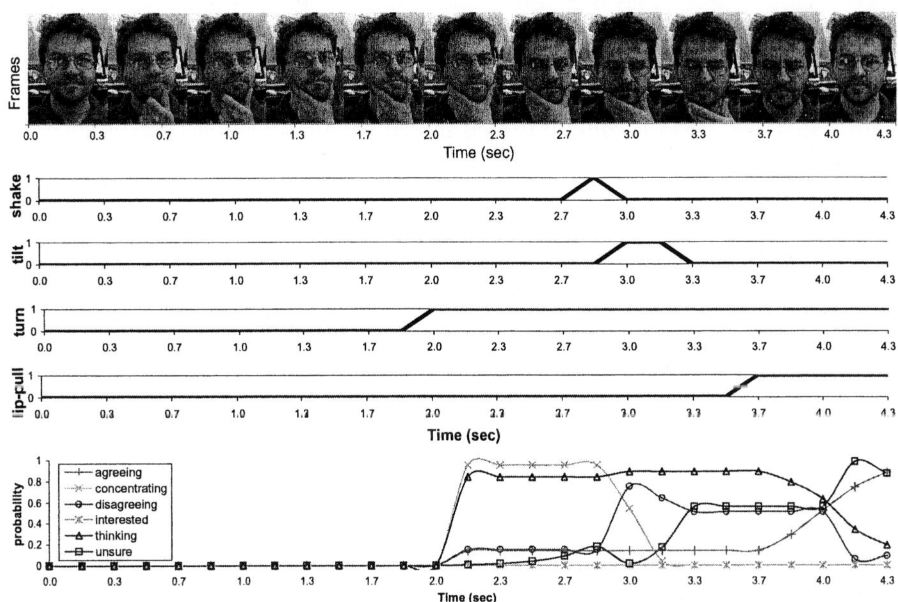

Fig. 4. Mental state inference: (top) frames from a video labelled as *thinking* (CVPR Corpus); (middle) head and facial displays; (bottom) mental state inferences

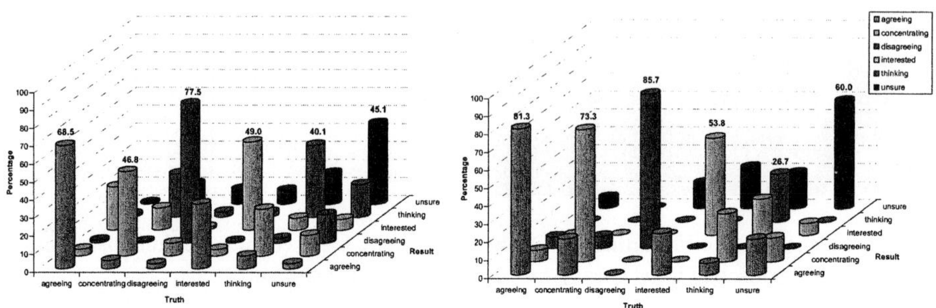

Fig. 5. Confusion matrix of results shown as a 3D bar chart: (left) human recognition results of the CVPR corpus; (right) the system's recognition the CVPR corpus

of videos, the automated mind-reading system scores among the top 5.6% of humans, and 10.2% better than the mean accuracy reported in the sample of 18 people. The result is superimposed on the distribution of human responses shown in Fig. 3 (right). The principal reason why both human recognition (54.5%) and the system's accuracy (63.5%) is generally low is the untrained acting and weak labelling of the CVPR corpus videos. In addition, the recording conditions of the CVPR corpus were much less controlled than that of MR, resulting in challenges in processing these videos automatically (e.g., speech and changes in lighting conditions). The system's recognition accuracy increases to 80% for the 11% of videos with agreement-score of 85% or more, a result similar to that obtained from evaluating the system on MR.

5 Conclusion and Future Directions

This paper described a computational model of mind-reading that infers complex mental states from facial expressions and head gestures in real-time video. The system generalizes well (compared with human recognition) to new examples of mental state enactments, which are posed (and labelled) by lay people in an uncontrolled setup. Albeit posed, the videos were challenging from a machine vision perspective: 1) they contained natural rigid head motion; 2) had overlapping facial expressions and 3) the "actors" expressed the same mental state through different facial expressions, intensities and durations. By recognizing mental states beyond the basic emotions, we widen the scope of applications in which facial analysis systems can be integrated. Moving forward, we will test our system on natural expressions of mental states.

Acknowledgements

Special thanks are due to everyone who took part in our experiments, especially those who volunteered with acting at CVPR 2004. This research was generously funded by the Computer Laboratory's Wiseman Fund, the Overseas Research Student Award, the Cambridge Overseas Trust and Newnham College.

References

1. S. Baron-Cohen. *Mindblindness: An Essay on Autism and Theory of Mind.* Cambridge, MA: MIT Press, 1995.
2. S. Baron-Cohen, O. Golan, S. Wheelwright, and J. J. Hill. *Mind Reading: The Interactive Guide to Emotions.* London: Jessica Kingsley Publishers, 2004.
3. S. Baron-Cohen, S. Wheelwright, J. Hill, Y. Raste, and I. Plumb. The Reading the Mind in the Eyes Test Revised Version: A Study with Normal Adults, and Adults with Asperger Syndrome or High-functioning Autism. *Journal of Child Psychology and Psychiatry*, 42(2):241–251, 2001.
4. P. Ekman and W. V. Friesen. *Pictures of Facial Affect.* Consulting Psychologists, 1976.
5. P. Ekman and W. V. Friesen. *Facial Action Coding System: A Technique for the Measurement of Facial Movement.* Consulting Psychologists, 1978.
6. B. Fasel and J. Luettin. Automatic Facial Expression Analysis: A Survey. *Pattern Recognition*, 36:259–275, 2003.
7. H. Gu and Q. Ji. Facial Event Classification with Task Oriented Dynamic Bayesian Network. In *Proceedings of the IEEE Conference on Computer Vision and Pattern Recognition (CVPR)*, volume 2, pages 870–875, 2004.
8. R. el Kaliouby. *Mind-Reading Machines: Automated Inference of Complex Mental States.* Phd thesis, University of Cambridge, Computer Laboratory, (2005).
9. R. el Kaliouby and P. Robinson. *Real-Time Vision for Human Computer Interaction*, chapter Real-Time Inference of Complex Mental States from Facial Expressions and Head Gestures, pages 181–200. Springer-Verlag, 2005.
10. T. Kanade, J. Cohn, and Y.-L. Tian. Comprehensive Database for Facial Expression Analysis. In *Proceedings of International Conference on Automatic Face and Gesture Recognition*, pages 46–53, 2000.
11. A. Kapoor, R. W. Picard, and Y. Ivanov. Probabilistic Combination of Multiple Modalities to Detect Interest. In *Proceedings of the International Conference on Pattern Recognition (ICPR)*, volume 3, pages 969–972, 2004.
12. G. Littlewort, M. S. Bartlett, I. Fasel, J. Susskind, and J. R. Movellan. Dynamics of Facial Expression Extracted Automatically from Video. In *Face Processing in Video Workshop at the CVPR2004*, 2004.
13. P. Michel and R. el Kaliouby. Real Time Facial Expression Recognition in Video using Support Vector Machines. In *Proceedings of the IEEE International Conference on Multimodal Interfaces (ICMI)*, pages 258–264, 2003.
14. K. P. Murphy. *Dynamic Bayesian Networks: Representation, Inference and Learning.* Phd thesis, UC Berkeley, Computer Science Division, 2002.
15. M. Pantic and L. J. Rothkrantz. Automatic Analysis of Facial Expressions: The State of the Art. *IEEE Trans. on Pattern Analysis and Machine Intelligence (PAMI)*, 22:1424–1445, 2000.
16. M. Pardàs, A. Bonafonte, and J. L. Landabaso. Emotion Recognition based on MPEG4 Facial Animation Parameters. In *Proceedings of Internatoinal Conference on Acoustics, Speech and Signal Procssing*, volume 4, pages 3624–3627, 2002.
17. Y.-L. Tian, L. Brown, A. Hampapur, S. Pankanti, A. W. Senior, and R. M. Bolle. Real World Real-time Automatic Recognition of Facial Expressions. *IEEE workshop on Performance Evaluation of Tracking and Surveillance*, 2003.

Physiological Sensing and Feature Extraction for Emotion Recognition by Exploiting Acupuncture Spots*

Ahyoung Choi and Woontack Woo

GIST U-VR Lab.,
Gwangju 500-712, S.Korea
+82-(0)62-970-2279
{achoi, wwoo}@gist.ac.kr
http://uvr.gist.ac.kr

Abstract. Previous emotion recognition systems have mainly focused on pattern classification, rather than utilizing sensing technologies or feature extraction methods. This paper introduces a method of physiological sensing and feature extraction for emotion recognition that is based on an oriental medicine approach. The specific points for affective sensing were experimentally determine, in which it was found that skin conductance measurements of the forearm region correlate well with acupuncture spots. Features are then extracted by the same way to interpret pulsation signals in diagnosis. We found that the proposed sensing and feature extraction method benefits the recognition of emotion with a neural network classifier.

1 Introduction

In order to realize a smart environment, an intelligent computer should be aware of user's context and situational information to offer personalized services. Over the last decade, many researchers have carried out studies on context awareness such as location, emotion, intention, etc. Among them, implicit contexts such as emotion and intention are essential for obtaining a user's feedback as whether the user is satisfied with the automatically triggered services or not.

One possible approach of emotion recognition is to analyze physiological signal. Picard et al. proposed a physiological feature extraction method that handles the daily variations of the features, and includes a linear classification method which projects numerous features into lower dimensions 1. Daniel Chen et al. measured the mental burden using an ECG (Electrocardiogram) signal and an EEG (Electroencephalogram) signal when the user was stressed and interfered with a certain strong stimuli 2. They categorized user's mental status with a decision table based on scientific background and evidence in combination with the two electronic signals.

However, in previous work 12, the features obtained from physiological signals were largely overlapped among other classes. Each class is a set of features further classified into emotion categories. The reason for the overlapped distribution among the distinct emotional classes might have occurred from physiological sensing

* This work is supported by Seondo project of MIC in Korea.

J. Tao, T. Tan, and R.W. Picard (Eds.): ACII 2005, LNCS 3784, pp. 590 – 597, 2005.

condition such as sensing position, sensing posture or sensing intervals. In case of sensing position, electrodes for sensing skin conductance and PPG (Photoplesysmogrphy) sensor for monitoring the heart activity are placed on the second or third fingertip in previous work. Furthermore, the features were not verified for whether they were appropriate for emotion recognition or not.

In this paper, we propose a physiological sensing method for analyzing emotional status based on a traditional oriental medicine approach. Oriental medical science, especially the Yin and Yang and Five element theory, supports a clear mechanism between an individual's internal status and the external changes of his or her body. The meridian, or acupuncture theory represents the responsible reflection of inside or outside of a body against the stimuli 5. Based on this theory, we determine the forearm acupuncture spots which could be used for affective sensing by conducting an experiment for in which skin conductance measurements correlate well with expected skin conductance of the acupuncture spots. Our experiment was also designed to locate appropriate sensing positions for recognizing the changes in physiological signals by instigating a user with a sound stimulus. In feature extraction step, we deployed a diagnosis method of measuring pulsation and skin conductivity, which support multiple analyses in terms of depth, shape, strength or quality.

We established that the proposed sensing and feature extraction methods benefit the recognition of emotion with a neural network classifier. In addition, the proposed method reduces the number of physiological sensors and features as compared to multimodal technologies which use computer vision technologies and speech recognition technologies. This method supports multiple analyses through the proposed sensing method, as referenced by the detailed description of pulsation and skin humidity.

This paper is organized as follows. The proposed sensing and feature extraction method are described in section 2 and section 3, respectively. In section 4, we analyze and evaluate the experimental results. Finally we give the conclusion in section 5.

2 Physiological Sensing on Acupuncture Spots

2.1 Sensing Condition on Acupuncture Spots

Most physiological signals depend on an environmental factor since they usually are measured in a low frequency and are low in voltage and current. In addition, a human body is highly nonlinear and complex due to the fact that the signals of organs and tissues are combined together in the human body. To compensate for this, we apply a method for measurement, which has gage repeatability and reproducibility (Gage R&R) used for checking the consistency of measurements. In order to estimate Gage R&R measurement, we define both the evaluation factor and measurement factor. A measurement value is an index of meaningful factor from the sensing device. It is defined as the difference of conductivity between an acupuncture spot and a non-acupuncture spot.

$$M = \frac{\sum_{n=0}^{10}(C(n)_{acupoint} - C(n)_{nonacupoint})}{N} \tag{1}$$

where, $C(n)_i$ is the skin conductivity of nth trial when i^{th} event is occurred. And N is the total number of tested data. An evaluation factor defined as a resolution is represented by repeatability and reproducibility for criticizing the output characteristic of the measurement system. The repeatability is determined to be the variance of measurement errors when we measure a physiological signal with the same device and the same experimenter.

We analyzed the process of physiological sensing as shown in Fig. 1. Process analysis objectively illustrates all feasible input variables which have a major influence on the output results in terms of measurement factor.

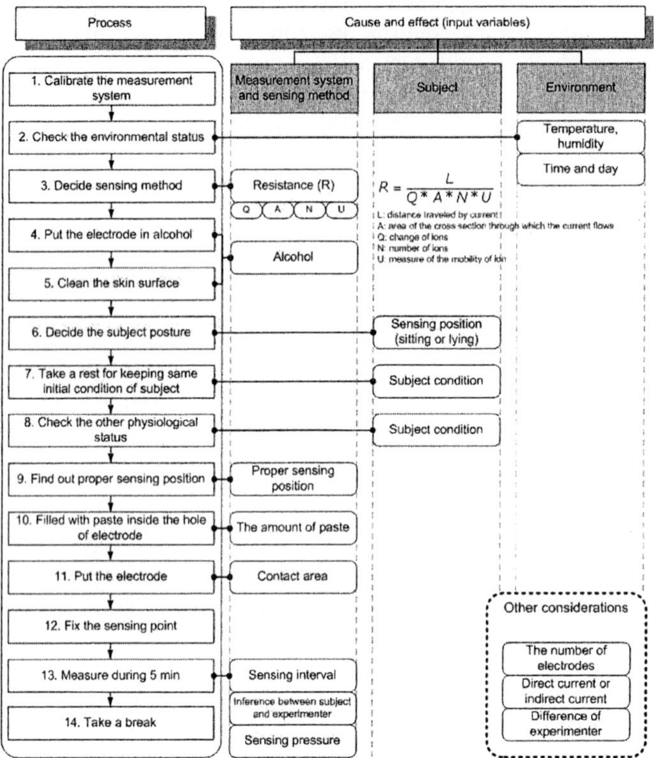

Fig. 1. Process analysis and possible input variables

We analyzed that disinfecting with alcohol, the posture of the subject such as lying or sitting had considerable influences in sensing. In addition, the sensing position like arms or fingers, the amount of paste, sensing pressure, electrical inference between the experimenter and the subject all have potential to affect the experimental results. In section 4, we evaluated whether measurement values had an influence on varying the sensing conditions or not.

2.2 Position Based Physiological Sensing Method

Among other conditions as mentioned in section 2.1, sensing position is one of the important conditions for affective sensing. From previous research, we know that meridians and acupuncture spots have a unique characteristic in that there is a lower resistance than any other point around acupuncture spot 4. Utilizing this, position based emotion recognition consists of four steps: sensing through the electrodes for analyzing skin resistance, preprocessing of noise filtering, computing the correlation of emotion labeled physiological signal and deciding the points responsible. The process is depicted in Fig. 2. The experiment is designed with the 7 by 24 matrix as shown in Fig. 3, covering two heart-related meridians.

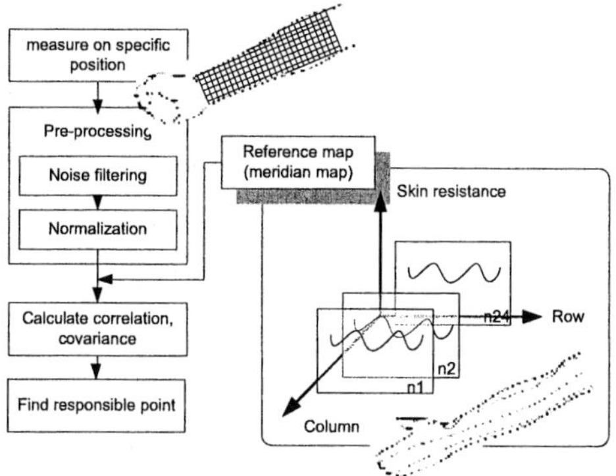

Fig. 2. Steps for finding proper sensing position

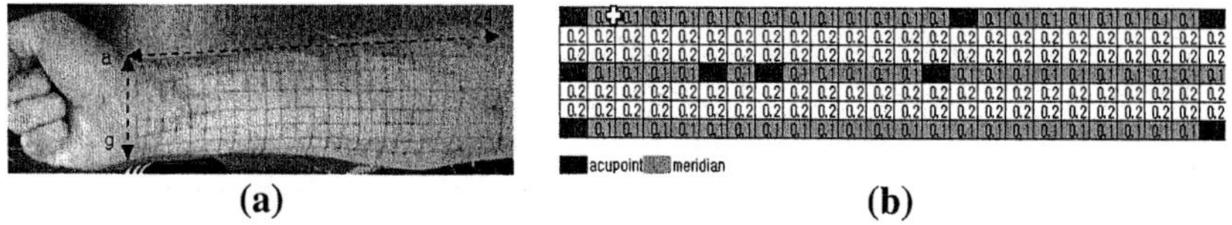

Fig. 3. (a) 7 by 24 matrixes forearm matrix (b) reference map of meridian and acupuncture spots

We measure the resistance at random points of the forearm to find out the acupuncture spots by sensing the current. We check for either low resistance points or lines connecting the low resistance measurements. We select key sensing points by computing the correlation between the expectations of the reference map and the measurements from the same column line. Each element of matrix is filled with expectations based on acupuncture spots. We determine the sensing position to be the junction of two lines: the vertical lines are the highly correlated column lines from among 24 lines and horizontal lines are the two heart-related acupuncture spots.

3 Feature Extraction for Emotion Recognition

Pulse diagnosis is one of the primary diagnostic methods used in oriental medical acupuncture and herbal medicine. Each emotion has a close relationship between the organism and the inner status as referenced by Yin and Yang and five element theories 56. Joy is revealed directly in the heart when the blood circulation is dynamic. Each meridian is inherently followed by the reflection of the status of each organ, and any variance creates a different meaning according to the position and the characteristic of the signal. Depth, frequency, quality or shape, width, strength, length, and rhythm of the pulsation are key characteristics found in diagnosis, providing information which is then used to treat a wide range of disease conditions.

Depth information is extracted by categorizing the sensing position along with pressure into floating pulsation and deep pulsation. We calculate this with two basic variables of period and intensity. Floating pulsation can be measured when the signal has a low intensity and high speed. Deep pulsation is only detectable in the case of high intensity and low speed pulsation. Therefore, the measurement factor is computed by the ratio of speed and intensity of the pulsation.

$$D_i = \frac{I_{norm}}{T_i} \tag{2}$$

where, D_i implies the depth information in i^{th} segment pulsation, and I_{norm} is normalized intensity, T_i means the ith period of the pulsation. Frequency of pulsation is interpreted by the speed of the pulsation. Each pulsation has one peak and one point of inflection. The reverse number of the difference value between the peaks is interpreted as the frequency at a segment of the pulsation. The average frequency during one minute is the heartbeat of the subject. R_i is the relative time when the peak is occurred.

$$F_i = \frac{1}{R_{i+1} - R_i} \tag{3}$$

Strength indicates the intensity or amplitude of the pulsation. Full strength means that the pulsation is wide and strong. Empty strength shows a wide but not strong pulsation. However, the amplitude of pulsation varies with environmental changes and the sensing pressure. Therefore, we use a normalized value to determine the status of pulsation. Rhythm is defined as the regularity of the pulsation. If the variation of the period (RR interval) is large and unstable with rapid speed, we determine the pulsation to be hurried. If the rhythm is rapid and is accompanied with irregularly in the peak to peak interval, we can anticipate that the heart agitated by heat.

$$I_i = \frac{1}{N-1}(R_i R_{i+1} - \overline{RR}) \tag{4}$$

Where, $\overline{RR}$ is an average one minute period in pulsation and N is the total number of peaks in one minute. Quality and shape mean the status such as roughness, smoothness, thickness, and thinness. We define the quality and shape with the standard deviation and time difference between peak point and 50% of the falling point. Skin conductance is one of the diagnosis parameters used in an oriental medical science. In this section, we found the specific sensing points and measured the average of skin conductance. In the case of skin conductance, a lot of difficulties are presented practically. A reciprocal of the resistance must be measured due to the small amount of current. Therefore, we employed a normalized skin conductance value and transition value.

4 Experimental Results and Analysis

We conducted experiments to determine the effective factor prominent under one variable condition which restricted other conditions. We took ten measurements of the conductivity of seven acupuncture spots while varying the sensing conditions such as infection of the skin surface by using alcohol. By exploiting MINITAB simulation tool, we applied the two-sample T analysis method to find out whether the alcohol affects the measurement value or not. Eventually, the difference in conductivity between an acupuncture spot and non-acupuncture spot was found to be dependent on the following conditions; sensing position, sensing pressure, inference between subject and experimenter, experimenter, and sensing interval. We set the experimental condition according to the previous results. As a result, the Gage R&R is 25.33% when control variables are considered and 62.32 % without considering control variables, as shown in Table 1. If the Gage R&R is more than 30%, the system is not accepted as a valid measurement system due to low resolution and large variation 3. This result demonstrated that acupuncture spot sensing should be considered especially carefully with respect to sensing pressure, sensing position, interference from other subjects, and sensing interval, than to other conditions.

Table 1. Total gage R&R result

Source	*StdDev(sd)*	*Study var*
Total Gage R&R	*0.565*	*25.33*
Repeatability	*0.270*	*12.15*
Reproducibility	*0.495*	*22.22*
Variation	*2.23*	*100*

We set one electrode on the arbitrary point of a 7 by 24 matrix on with 1cm square the right forearm. The other is placed on the left fingertip which is used as the ground point. To collect the system-independent signals, we used two kinds of sensing devices, MP-35 and EAV, with different backgrounds. The data was gathered over a period of 10 days from a single male subject who was 25 years old.

We computed the correlation coefficient of same vertical line in pairs of gathered data in order to check the day dependence factor. When we set the threshold coefficients as 0.3, 0.4, and 0.5, the correlated data was found to be 70%, 64%, and 60%, respectively. We determined the threshold of the correlation coefficient to be 0.4 since the number of neglected column vectors was the same as with a 0.5 threshold value. Additionally, when the coefficient was 0.4, we could not use 6, 7, 16, and 17th columns due to a day dependency factor.

The results of correlation between expected values and actual measurements are illustrated in Fig. 4. From these result, we analyzed the measurements from certain positions which exhibited patterns similar to acupuncture spots. In this experiment, six lines, column 1, 6, 8, 14, 15, and 24, were extracted from the acupuncture spot map which included black marked points. Each line was analyzed with an acupuncture spot wave up to two adjunct lines. We found out that column 1 was the outstanding point resulting in an averaging 6.3 correlation coefficient among 78 % of the data. In addition, 4, 6, 7, 15, 17, and 22 revealed useful correlation coefficients in 53 % of the data. We selected the column 1, 4, 15, 20, and 22 as significant points in recognizing a user's internal status. However, the 6, 7, and 17 columns were not reliable to use, due to day dependency.

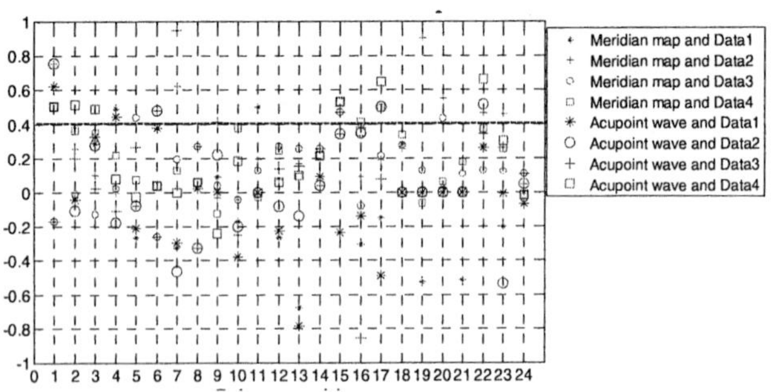

Fig. 4. Correlation between measurements and expectations

For emotion induction, we stimulated the user to a set emotional status with multimodal media like music and image, which were predefined according to the user preference. We used two kinds of stimuli, i.e. positive and negative as a medium to evoke the certain emotion. We adopted the basic five-emotion model followed by Yin and Yang and Five elements theory. The emotional status was divided into the emotional bases of joy, anger, grief, sadness, thoughtfulness, fear, and fright. However, 'sadness' and 'grief' were combined together for sensing. Additionally, the 'fright' basis is not applicable to express the emotion status in daily life. Eventually, for the purpose of this study, we assume the basic emotions to be an individual's common status, joy, anger, and sadness. After gathering the raw signals, we calculated the features based on the proposed method. Then, the feature projection analysis (PCA) was employed to check the reliable three dimensional features. We selected the higher priority features such as rhythm, strength, and quality or shape in Case A, and its linear combination in Case B. In order to figure out whether the selected features were useful or not, neural network classifier were applied for classification of the result, as shown in Table 2.

The ratio of correct recognition rate was comparable with that of previous results. One advantages of the proposed feature set is actually a smaller number of features. In case of four emotion categories, we found that smaller feature set can replace the result of a larger number of feature set while maintaining a comparable recognition rate. It means that, a small number of features, using a PCA based on oriental medical science, can be used efficiently and effectively.

Table 2. Results of classification according to the features (a) irregularity, GSR transition, speed (b) linear combination of 3 features using PCA (c) irregularity, norm GSR, GSR transition

input	*output*	*Hidden node*	*Momen-tum*	*Learning rate*	*Learning error*	*Test error*
3	*4*	*10*	*0.2*	*0.5*	*53%*	*32.50%*
		12	*0.2*	*0.5*	*48%*	*32.50%*
			(a)			
3	*4*	*10*	*0.2*	*0.5*	*62%*	*40.50%*
		12	*0.2*	*0.5*	*52%*	*37.50%*
			(b)			
3	*4*	*10*	*0.2*	*0.5*	*48%*	*36.00%*
		12	*0.2*	*0.5*	*42%*	*25.50%*
			(c)			

5 Conclusion and Future Work

We have proposed a physiological sensing and emotion recognition based on oriental medical science. In physiological sensing, we found that acupuncture spots are more responsible for measuring stimuli than acupuncture spot and random points combined. For feature extraction, the present version uses only a portion of the data recorded from PPG sensor and GSR sensor. We analyzed various ways clinically used for diagnosis in oriental medical science. As a result, we discovered the feasibility that a small number of features can replace the complex and multimodal features currently used. Finally, we concluded the proposed sensing methodology and feature extraction is noteworthy for emotion recognition since the recognition rate was 74.5% under four emotional statuses. Future work includes applying multiple user databases and combining with several user contexts such as time of day and location of person, in order to help determine emotional status.

References

1. Rosalind W. Picard et al, "Toward Machine Emotional Intelligence: Analysis of Affective Physiological Stat,"IEEE Trans on pattern analysis and machine intelligence, vol23, no.10, 2001
2. Daniel Chen and Roel Vertegaal, "Using Mental Load for Managing Interruptions In Physiologically Attentive User Interfaces,"In Extended Abstracts of ACM CHI 2004 Conference on Human Factors in Computing Systems, Vienna, Austria, 2004
3. Automobile Industry Action Group(AIAG), "Measurement system analysis reference manual," 2nd edition. ASQC Quality Press.
4. C.S.Poon, T.T.C.Choy, F.T.Koide, "A Reliable Method for Locating Electroperme-able Points on the Skin Surface", Am J Chin Med., Autumn; 8(3):283-9, 1980
5. Giovanni Maciocia, "Foundations of Chinese Medicine: A Comprehensive Text for Acupuncturists and Herbalists," Churchill livingstone, 1989
6. Marcy Goldstein, "Classical Five-Element Acupuncture," Jacksonville Medicine, 2000.

Human Machine Interaction: The Special Role for Human Unconscious Emotional Information Processing

Maurits van den Noort[1], Kenneth Hugdahl[1], and Peggy Bosch[2]

[1] University of Bergen, Department of Cognitive Neuroscience,
Jonas Lies vei 91,N-5009 Bergen, Norway
{Van den Noort, Hugdahl, Maurits.Noort}@Psybp.uib.no
http://www.mauritsvandennoort.com

[2] University of Bergen, Department of Psychiatry and Clinical Medicine,
Sandviksleitet 1,N-5035 Bergen, Norway
{Bosch, Pbosch}@online.no

Abstract. The nature of (un)conscious human emotional information processing remains a great mystery. On the one hand, classical models view human conscious emotional information processing as computation among the brain's neurons but fail to address its enigmatic features. On the other hand, quantum processes (superposition of states, nonlocality, entanglement,) also remain mysterious, yet are being harnessed in revolutionary information technologies like quantum computation, quantum cryptography, and quantum teleportation. In this paper, we would like to discuss several experiments that suggest a special role for unconscious emotional information processing in the human-computer interaction. What are its consequences and could this be the missing link between quantum information theory and conscious human emotional information processing?

1 Quantum Information Theory

Einstein proposed his revolutionary hypothesis of the light-quantum 100 years ago. Later, Einstein took his light-quantum hypothesis a stage further and he formulated the probability laws governing the emission and absorption of radiation by an atom [6], [13]. Many scientists did not accept Einstein's hypothesis due to several reasons.

From the beginning of quantum mechanics, the concept of measurement and the possible role of consciousness in the solution to the measurement problem have been important issues. Despite of these controversies, quantum theory has further developed and describes the bizarre properties of matter and energy at near-atomic scales. These properties include: 1) quantum coherence, in which individual particles yield identity to a collective, unifying wave function (exemplified in Bose-Einstein condensates). 2) non-local quantum entanglement, in which spatially separated particle states are nonetheless connected or related. 3) quantum superposition, in which particles exist in two or more states or locations simultaneously. 4) quantum state reduction or 'collapse of the wave function', in which superpositioned particles reduce or collapse to specific choices [31].

J. Tao, T. Tan, and R.W. Picard (Eds.): ACII 2005, LNCS 3784, pp. 598 – 605, 2005.

According to some scientists, all four quantum properties can be applied to the seemingly inexplicable features of consciousness. First, quantum coherence (e.g. Bose-Einstein condensation) is a possible physical basis for 'binding' or unity of consciousness [17]. Second, non-local entanglements (e.g. 'Einstein-Podolsky-Rosen correlations') serve as a potential basis for associative memory and non-local emotional interpersonal connection. Third, quantum superposition of information provides a basis for preconscious and subconscious processes, dreams and altered states. Finally, quantum state reduction (quantum computation) serves as a possible physical mechanism for the transition from preconscious processes to consciousness [23], [24].

In the quantum, real time is uncertain and events may run in a non-linear way. Quantum state reductions such as objective reduction events may send quantum information "backwards in time", for example according to the Aharonov "dual vector" theory. Time may simply be indeterminate in the quantum superposition phase [10].

In addition to non-linear information processing, information can exist in quantum superposition, for example, as quantum bits or 'qubits' of both 1 and 0 in contrast to the classical information theories. Qubits interact or compute by entanglement and then reduce or collapse to a solution expressed in classical bits (either 1 or 0).

In the Orch OR model, quantum computation occurs in microtubules within the brain's neurons. Microtubules are polymers of the protein tubulin, which in the Orch OR model transiently exist in quantum superposition of two or more conformational states. Following periods of preconscious quantum computation (e.g. on the order of tens to hundreds of milliseconds) tubulin superpositions reduce or 'self-collapse' at an objective threshold due to a quantum gravity mechanism proposed by Penrose [23], [24]. Microtubule-associated protein (MAP-2) connections provide input during classical phases. Each Orch OR quantum computation determines classical output states of tubulin, which govern neurophysiological events, such as initiating spikes at the axon hillock, regulating synaptic strengths, forming new MAP-2 attachment sites and gap-junction connections, and establishing starting conditions for the next conscious event [9], [11], [25].

However, most cognitive- and neuroscientists are skeptical. How could the human brain process information in a non-linear way? Quantum physics and Neuroscience have nothing to do with each other. Moreover, this is simply against our experiences in daily life, in which time is completely linear! There is a hot debate going on between physicists and cognitive neuroscientists. In this paper, we would like to present two neuroimaging studies on emotions, in which non-linear information processing was found. Moreover, we would like to suggest that the solution in this debate lies in human unconscious information processing. At the higher (conscious) level, information is processed in a linear way. However, at the unconscious level, human information processing is similar to what quantum information theory would predict. As a result, non-linear information processing at this level is possible. Before discussing this more into detail, we would like to briefly discuss some of the main findings of human information processing. The focus will be on emotional information processing, since the neuroimaging studies that we will discuss later in this paper to support our theory are also studies on emotions.

2 Human Information Processing

If we want to understand the human machine interaction with respect to emotional information processing, it is essential to understand normal human emotional information processing. In the late seventies, the cognitive approach to emotions was more or less the only approach [8], [19]. This started to change with the publication of the paper *"Feeling and Thinking: Preferences Need No Inferences"* by Robert Zajonc [31]. He argued, on the basis of logic and clever experiments, that emotion can exist before and without cognition.

Much of contemporary psychology has come to recognize that a great deal of human emotional functioning is rooted in unconscious processes. During the last two decades, a lot of behavioral studies were conducted in this field. These studies, for example, showed that humans pick up the emotional content of facial expressions outside conscious awareness and intent to influence perceptions of the target individual [1], [20], [21], [22]. Other studies showed that humans evaluate objects (as for example "good" or "bad") at an unconscious level [2], [3], [5].

Current theories of emotion suggest that stimuli are first processed via an automatically engaged neural mechanism, which occurs outside conscious awareness. This mechanism operates in conjunction with a slower and more comprehensive process that allows a detailed evaluation of the potentially harmful stimulus [15], [16]. Evidence comes from neuroimaging studies. Event-related potential (ERP) data revealed a double dissociation for the conscious versus unconscious perception of negative stimuli. In the unconscious condition, responses to the perception of negative stimuli were enhanced relative to neutral for the N2 "excitatory" component (a negative potential at +/-200 milliseconds), which is thought to represent orienting and automatic aspects of information processing. By contrast, conscious perception of negative stimuli was associated with relatively enhanced responses for the late P3 "inhibitory" component (a positive potential at +/-300 milliseconds), implicated in the integration of emotional processes [16].

The conclusion can be drawn that unconscious emotional information processing happens all the time and has direct behavioral consequences [27]. Until now, these unconscious processes remain a great mystery. Although we are beginning to understand some of the mechanisms behind unconscious emotional information processing, a lot remains unanswered. For example, do humans process emotional information at the unconscious level in exactly the same way as at the conscious level and what are its implications for the human machine interaction? Moreover, could this perhaps be the missing link between quantum information theory and conscious human emotional information processing? [28]

3 Non-linear Emotional Information Processing

To answer these questions, data will be presented from two neuroimaging studies. It is important to note that both in the fMRI-study and in the ERP-study highly emotional versus more neutral stimuli were used and all stimuli were randomized with replacement. This is important because these results could otherwise be contributed completely to an expectancy effect of the participant.

3.1 FMRI Study

Bierman and Scholte conducted an fMRI-study on emotions [4], [29], [30]. In the experiment, a 1.5 Tesla Siemens system was used. Ten participants (6 male, 4 female) entered the study. The experiment started with an instruction that was given outside the scanner. The participants were instructed to relax while passively looking at the pictures that were randomly presented by a computer connected to a video projector onto a screen. Then, an MPRAGE high resolution scan which lasted for about 20 minutes was conducted. Moreover, a position localizer scan of about 2 minutes was conducted after which the experimental task of about 13 minutes was presented. The participants were able to watch the screen by looking at a mirror inside the scan. They were requested to try to forget any emotional material right after exposure finished so that the next presentation would be influenced as little as possible by the previous one. The stimulus material consisted of a picture pool of 36 emotional (18 erotic, 18 violent) and 48 neutral stimuli. The neutral and violent stimuli were taken from the International Affective Picture System [12] while the erotic material was taken from a previous study on sexuality by Laan [14]. For each stimulus presentation, the stimulus condition was determined randomly with a priori chance of 2 neutral versus 1 emotional. Each stimulus sequence started with the 4.2 second presentation of a fixation point during which the anticipation was measured. After the exposure of the stimulus picture, which also lasted 4.2 seconds, there was a period of 8.4 seconds during which the participant was supposed to recover from the stimulus presentation. Data were analyzed using Brainvoyager. The main hypothesis of the study was, whether a significant prestimulus difference in BOLD signal for the different stimuli could be found [27]. This non-linear information processing would be indirect evidence for quantum information processing in the human brain.

The poststimulus results showed whole visual cortex activation, which could be expected because visual stimuli were used. Interestingly, all the regions of interest resulting from the contrast analysis, showed a response for all stimuli (including the calm pictures). An exception to this was the subcortical region close to the amygdala. Both erotic and violent pictures showed a response there. This is in line with previous findings [7], [15].

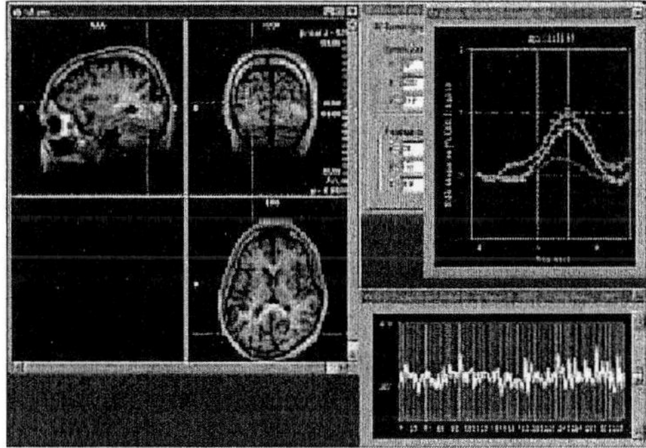

Fig. 1. Results from an fMRI experiment. There is a significant difference in the prestimulus phase between highly emotional (pink curve) and neutral stimuli (blue curve) 4 seconds before stimulus presentation.

The analysis of the prestimulus phase showed a significant prestimulus effect that was widely distributed over many brain regions, including hippocampus, pallidum, amygdala, and caudate nucleum. Most brain regions did not show striking differences in anticipation before emotional and neutral stimuli. However, larger anticipatory activation preceding emotional stimuli compared to neutral stimuli was found in the right amygdala and in the nucleus caudatus. For the male participants, as can be seen in Fig. 1, this appeared before the erotic stimuli while for the female both erotic and violent stimuli produced this prestimulus effect [27], [28]. These results suggest the existence of unconscious non-linear information processing in the human brain, which could be expected according to the quantum information theory.

3.2 ERP Study

However, the temporal resolution of fMRI is not good enough and therefore a replication study was conducted with the same experimental set-up while using ERP [18]. 26 adult participants, 11 males, 15 females, participated in the experiment. Each participant was fitted with an EEG electrode cap according to the International 10-20 system. An additional electrode for recording the electrooculogram (EOG) was placed above the right eye to monitor eye blinks and movement. Data editing was blind to stimulus category (calm or emotional targets). To reduce the possibility of false-positive findings, statistically conservative procedures were chosen for data analysis. Because it controls for autocorrelations inherent in physiologic signals and their underlying non-normal distributions, randomized permutation analysis was used to determine statistical significance of the differences between emotional and calm curves during the prestimulus period. Results for the group as a whole showed a significant difference in ERPs in the prestimulus period for future calm versus emotional pictures at both FP1 (left frontopolar; $t_{sum} = -28.82$, $p < .05$) and FP2 (right frontopolar; $t_{sum} = -27.27$, $p < .05$) EEG sites. The ERPs for a future emotional stimulus were more negative, with the point of maximum negativity occurring slightly before that of the ERPs for the future calm pictures. In addition, there was a positive shift with a steep slope observed approximately 4 seconds before the emotional stimuli. In both locations, this positive shift in the emotional trial ERP occurred approximately a second before the shift occurred in the calm trial ERPs. There was a significant t_{sum} difference between the prestimulus ERPs for calm versus emotional trials at midline EEG site Pz ($t_{\mathrm{sum}} = -13.24$, $p < .05$). Because of the significant findings at FP1 and FP2, an additional RPA of the EOG channel was conducted, which revealed that eye movement artifacts did not contribute to this result [29]. These results are in line with unconscious non-linear emotional information processing in the human brain, which could be expected according to quantum information theory.

4 Human Machine Interaction

In this paper, data was presented that support the quantum information theory of human emotional information processing. Evidence for unconscious non-linear human information processing was found, however, more research on this topic is needed. This is in particular necessary with respect to the direct human computer emotional interaction. So far we do know from studies with random generators, for example, that non-linear information-processing is possible up to longer time distances [30]. In these studies, evidence for consciousness-related anomalies in random physical systems was found [26]. Before, during, and after powerful engaging events, the measurement system was affected. This was, for instance, the case before, during, and after the September 11 attacks. Significant trends in the data were found that can normally not be expected in the data produced by random generators [27]. However, one should be critical with these data since alternative explanations, like methodological problems with the random generators, can not be completely excluded [29]. In addition, it is unknown whether non-linear information processing as observed in random generator data is the same mechanism underlying biological organisms. Therefore, more (brain) research in the direct human computer emotional interaction is needed.

5 General Discussion

The results that were presented in this paper might surprise scientists, who have a more conservative view on quantum physics and cognitive neuroscience. It is obvious that we are only beginning to understand quantum information processing in the human brain and the mechanisms behind human machine interaction. Scientists often do not like the idea that unconscious emotional information processing plays an important role in human beings. We wish to emphasize that we are not saying that consciousness is not important for human beings, on the contrary, it is of great importance, but human consciousness is also restricted. Therefore, for optimal functioning, it is vital that consciousness is only used for some higher mental processes, whereas unconscious information processing is needed when the conscious mind is otherwise occupied.

In physics, nature is normally described in particles, molecules, waves etc., which is very useful from a mathematical point of view, but from a strict physical point of view: it is wrong. In fact particles, molecules, waves etc. do not *exist* but are only used to *describe* nature. It is the opinion of the authors that we can use these concepts in our calculations, but perhaps it is time to redefine nature and describe it not in particles, molecules, waves etc., but as a very large information processor, of which human beings are only a small part. If we describe nature as a very large information processor we can also better describe human computer interaction and understand unconscious non linear emotional information processing. Then, at the unconscious level in sharp contrast to the conscious level people are able to process emotional information in a non-linear way. Since humans process information not only unconsciously but also at a conscious level there seems to be an inconsistency. In reality, however, this is only an illusion. Or to say it in Einstein's words:

"People like us, who believe in physics, know that the distinction between past, present, and future is only a stubbornly persistent illusion." - Albert Einstein

References

1. Baldwin, M.W., Carrell, S.E., Lopez, D.F.: Priming relationship schemas: My advisor and the Pope are watching me from the back of my mind. J. Exp. Soc. Psychol. 26 (1990) 435-454
2. Bargh, J.A., Chaiken, S., Govender, R., Pratto, F.: The generality of the automatic attitude activation effect. J. Pers. Soc. Psychol. 62 (1992) 893-912
3. Bargh, J.A., Chaiken, S., Raymond, P., Hymes, C.: The automatic evaluation effect: Unconditionally automatic attitude activation with a pronunciation task. J. Exp. Soc. Psychol. 32 (1996) 104-128
4. Bierman, D.J., Scholte, H.S.: Anomalous anticipatory brain activation preceding exposure of emotional and neutral pictures. Toward a Science of Consciousness IV, Tucson, USA. (2002)
5. Chen, M., Bargh, J.A.: Nonconscious approach and avoidance behavioral consequences of the automatic evaluation effect. Pers. Soc. Psychol. B. 25 (1999) 215-224
6. Einstein, A.: Quantentheorie der Strahlung. Phys. Z. 18 (1917) 121
7. Everitt, J.W.: Sexual motivation: A neural and behavioral analysis of the mechanisms underlying appetitive and copulatory responses of male rats. Neurosci. Behav. R. 14 (1990) 217-232
8. Fehr, B., Russell, J.A.: Concept of emotion viewed from a prototype perspective. J. Exp. Psychol.: General. 113 (1984) 464-486
9. Hameroff, S.R.: Quantum computation in brain microtubules? The Penrose-Hameroff 'Orch OR' model of consciousness. Philosophical Transactions Royal Society London A. 356 (1998) 1869-1896
10. Hameroff, S.R.: Time, Consciousness and Quantum Events in Fundamental Spacetime Geometry. Proceedings of the nature of time: Physics, geometry and perception NATO advanced research workshop (2003)
11. Hameroff, S.R., Penrose, R.: Conscious events as orchestrated spacetime selections. J. of Consciousness Studies. 3 (1996) 36-53
12. Ito, T.A., Cacioppo, J.T., Lang, P.J.: Eliciting affect using the International Affective Picture System: Bivariate evaluation and ambivalence. Pers. Soc. Psychol. B. 24 (1998) 855-879
13. Klein, M.J.: Einstein and the Wave-particle Duality. The Natural Philosopher. 3 (1963) 3-49
14. Laan, E., Everaerd, W., Bellen, G., Hanewald, G.: Women's sexual and emotional responses to male- and female-produced erotica. Arch. Sex. Behav. 23 (1994) 153-170
15. LeDoux, J.E. (ed.): The emotional brain. Simon & Schuster, New York (1996)
16. Liddell, B.J., Williams, L.M., Rathjen, J., Shevrin, H., Gordon, E.: A Temporal Dissociation of Subliminal versus Supraliminal Fear Perception: An Event-related Potential Study. J. Cognitive Neurosci. 16 (2004) 479-486
17. Marshall, I.N.: Consciousness and Bose-Einstein condensates. New Ideas Psychol. 7 (1989) 73-83
18. McCraty, R., Atkinson, M., Bradley, R.T.: Electrophysiological Evidence of Intuition. The J. Altern. Complement. Med. 10 (2004) 325-336
19. Mesquita, B., Frijda, N.: Cultural variations in emotions: A review. Psychol. B. 112 (1992) 179-204
20. Murphy, S.T., Zajonc, R.B.: Affect cognition, and awareness: Affective priming with optimal and suboptimal stimulus exposures. J. Pers. Soc. Psychol. 64 (1993) 723-739

21. Niedenthal, P.M.: Implicit perception of affective information. J. Exp. Soc. Psychol. 26 (1990) 505-527
22. Niedenthal, P.M., Cantor, N.: Affective responses as guides to category-based influences. Motivation and Emotion. 10 (1986) 217-231
23. Penrose, R. (ed.): The Emperor's New Mind. Oxford University Press, Oxford (1989)
24. Penrose, R. (ed.): Shadows of the Mind: A Search for the Missing Science of Consciousness. Oxford University Press, Oxford (1994)
25. Penrose, R., Hameroff, S.R.: What gaps? Reply to Grush and Churchland. J. of Consciousness Studies. 2 (1995) 98-112
26. Radin, D.I., Nelson, R.D.: Evidence for consciousness-related anomalies in random physical systems. Found. Phys. 19 (1987) 1414-1499
27. Van den Noort, M.W.M.L. (ed.): The Unconscious Brain: The Relative Time and Information Theory of Emotions. Citadel, Oegstgeest (2003)
28. Van den Noort, M.W.M.L.: Unconscious information processing of emotions: Non-linear processing. 10th Annual Meeting of the Organization for Human Brain Mapping, Budapest, Hungary. (2004a)
29. Van den Noort, M.W.M.L.: Unconscious information processing of emotions: Non-linear processing. 28th International Congress of Psychology, Beijing, China. (2004b)
30. Van den Noort, M.W.M.L.: Unconscious information processing of emotions: Non-linear processing. Int. J. Psychol. 39 (2004c) 69-70
31. Woolf, N.J., Hameroff, S.R.: A quantum approach to visual consciousness. Trends in Cognitive Sciences 5 (2001) 472-478
32. Zajonc, R.B.: Feeling and thinking: Preferences need no inferences. Am. Psychol. 35 (1980) 151-175

Affective Computing Model Based on Rough Sets

Chen Yong[1,2] and He Tong[1]

[1] School of Math. and Sys. Sci., Shandong Univ., Jinan 250100, Shandong, China
yong-ch@hotmail.com

[2] School of Sciences, Jinan Univ., Jinan 250022, Shandong, China
hetong229@163.com

Abstract. The paper first builds a novel affective model based on rough sets, presents the static description of affective space. Meanwhile, the paper creatively combines rough sets with Markov chain, gives the dynamic forecast of human affective change. In this affective model, some concepts and states are defined such as affective description precision and so on. It is a fundamental work to more research. Simulations are done using Matlab software, and simulation results show that this affective model can well simulate the human emotion. The results of this paper are innovative. It is a new research direction of affective computing that rough sets and affective computing infiltrate each other.

1 Introduction

Emotion is an important part of psychology actions, psychologists are paying more attention to the research of emotion. So far, there are a lot of affective theories, such as the correlative theory of emotion and economy change, which is provided by James [1]. Thereafter, there are the affective motivation theory, the affective behavior theory, the affective cognizance theory and so on [2]. But there aren't lots of definite quantity researches on emotion. In 1997, Professor Picard punished her monograph 'Affective Computing'[3], in this book she defined 'Affective computing is computing that relates to, arises from, or deliberately influences emotions'. Thus, the conception 'Affective Computing'was put forward. Soon after, the academy paid attention to it and the enterprise was quickly in response to it. The British Telecom had built the expert group of affective computing research. IBM had exploited the 'affective mouse'. At present, the research of endowing the computer with emotion is becoming an important research direction. However, affective computing is a very difficult problem. Emotion is a psychological phenomenon, which has nonlinear character, that is to say, emotion has uncertainty, so affective computing belongs to the research of uncertainty question.

In 1982, Professor Z. Pawlak put forward Rough Sets theory [4], it generalized the classical sets on research uncertainty question and it had showed advantage

J. Tao, T. Tan, and R.W. Picard (Eds.): ACII 2005, LNCS 3784, pp. 606–613, 2005.

and rationality in many fields. This paper analyzes human emotion, builds affective model and makes affective computing by using rough sets theory. We first apply the rough sets theory to the affective research, which is a new research direction of affective computing.

The rest of the paper is organized as follows: Section 2 introduces some terminology and presents preliminary results on psychology. Section 3 is devoted to the static description of emotion by using rough sets theory. In section 4, we combine rough sets and Markov chain to analyze the dynamic change of emotion. Section 5 simulates affective model by using Matlab software and gives some relative analyses. Section 6 describes some concluding remarks.

2 Affective Basic Conception

The human emotion is a quite complicated phenomenon and it has various contents. For the need of our research, we classify the emotion based on psychology theory [5].

Emotions are human's experiences for objective things, they reflect people' needs whether are satisfied or not, they conclude two aspects: (1) Affective process: The process of affective state's change is an important part of the affective process. From characters, affective states can be divided into happy, rage, dread, sad and so on. (2)Affective personality: It concludes needs, desire, motivation, interesting and so on, which are the personality orientation. It also concludes capability, temperament, character, attitudes and so on, which are the personality psychology characters.

In basic affective theory [6], the human emotions have many attribute dimensions, psychologists usually use strong or feeble to describe affective strength degree. For example, sad can be described as pity, despond, sorrow, melancholy, grief and despair; happy can be described as cozy, comfortable, pleasant, bright, cheer and spree, which are increasing in strength degree. Recently, psychologists have put forward more deliberate dimensions to describe emotion. From those, Izard [7] generalized four widely used dimensions, which are pleasant dimension, nervous dimension, impulse dimension and assurance dimension.

The intercourse of the human and the nature usually makes use of eyes, ears, mouth, skins and so on. The information received by the five sense organs is called affective information, viz. vision affective information, hearing affective information, scent affective information, gustatory affective information and feeling affective information. The research on affective information has already made home and abroad [8]. By researching the affective information, we can measure somebody's any emotions at sometime. Throughout the rest of the paper, we supposed the human emotions can be completely measured.

For the convenience of our research, we firstly give some conceptions:

Definition 1. *All of the human emotions constitute* **affective space.**

Definition 2. *All kinds of signals and information to measure emotions are called* **affective information.**

Definition 3. *At sometime, all of the emotions of somebody constitute* ***affective states set.***

Definition 4. *At sometime, the mostly or typical emotions of somebody constitute the* ***leading affective set.***

Generally speaking, the affective states set is the proper subset of the affective space. Affective experience is very complicated, such as 'not know whether to laugh or cry', 'pleasure and sadness are mixed'and so on. In this paper, we supposed several kinds of emotions can exist at the same time, but there are primary and secondary, for example, somebody's leading emotion is 'rage'at a time, but he may has the 'glorious feeling'.

Thus, from the analysis above and according to the literature [8], we regard, among the affective information, emotions and affective states (affective space), there is the following logic connection: *By collecting and disposing, we receive affective information, after analyzing, we can measure one person's emotions, finally, all kinds of emotions constitute affective states set.*

3 The Affective Static Description Based on Rough Sets

In this section we give the static description based on rough sets. The conception 'Affective space', 'Affective states set'have been given above. But we notice that, in actual psychology analysis and computing, we can't discriminate one emotion's ascription, that is to say, there is indiscernibility among emotions. For example, in [6], happy can be described as cozy, comfortable, pleasant, bright, cheer and spree, there are six different grades. It is supposed that somebody's happy emotion is considered as spree, if his happy emotion is stronger than spree, we have to consider that his happy emotion is also spree. That is to say, two different emotions in affective space have to be considered as the same, which embodies the indiscernibility of emotions and induces roughness of affective computing. So, we consider affective modeling based on rough sets and solve the indiscernibility in affective description.

Given affective space U, it is can also be called the affective universe of discourse, thus the human affective states set is a rough set, exact definition is as follows: Based on affective basic conceptions, we divide the affective space into finite affective equivalent class by using the affective class in psychology. Meanwhile, based on the affective attribute dimensions description above, we also can divide the affective space into different finite affective equivalent class. Thus we obtain a group of equivalent relations $\Re$ on U. $\forall R_i \in \Re$, according to the knowledge of rough sets[4], $\cap R_i$ is also an equivalent relation, which is denoted as $ind(R)$, so $U/ind(R)$ is another equivalent class division of affective space. Our affective model just based on this division. Then the human affective states set X is described as $(\underline{R}(X), \overline{R}(X))$, and

$$\underline{R}(X) = \cup\{Y \in U/ind(R) \mid Y \subseteq X\} \tag{1}$$

$$\overline{R}(X) = \cup\{Y \in U/ind(R) \mid Y \cap X \neq \phi\} \tag{2}$$

We notice that the human affective states set on time T is described as a rough set $A^T(X) = (\underline{R}(X), \overline{R}(X))^{(T)}$, then$\underline{R}(X)$ and $\overline{R}(X)$have definite actual meaning. $\underline{R}(X)$means the person's leading affective character on time T, $\overline{R}(X)$means all of the person's affective states on time T .

When we describe the human affective states set as a rough set, we allow the person can have many kinds of different affective states at the same time, so the relation between the number of elementary in the set and its equivalent class can tell us whether one's emotion is various or not. We can conveniently give the definition of the affective variety degree.

Definition 5. *Given the affective universe of discourse U and knowledge base$K = (U, \Re)$, $R \in \Re$ is an equivalent relation, $[x]_R$ is R equivalent class.Let affective states set $A^T(X)$, call $Q(X)$ the* **affective variety degree**, *and*

$$Q(X) = \sum \frac{| A^T(X) \cap [x]_R |}{| [x]_R |} \tag{3}$$

Obviously, variety degree describes how many emotions one person has and the bigger the value is, the more emotions the person has.

Another important thing is how to describe the affective description precision in different conditions. The next definition gives us such convenience that we can control the affective description precision based on the research require.

Definition 6. *Given the affective universe of discourse U and knowledge base$K = (U, \Re)$, $R \in \Re$ is an equivalent relation. Let affective states set $A^T(X)$, Call $\alpha_R(X)$ the* **affective description precision**, *and*

$$\alpha_R(X) = \frac{| \underline{R}(X) |}{| \overline{R}(X) |} \tag{4}$$

Here: $X \neq \phi$, $| A |$ denotes the number of elementary in set A.

In [9], there are two properties of $\alpha_R(X)$:

1. $\forall R \in \Re$ and $X \subseteq U$, there is $0 \leq \alpha_R(X) \leq 1$;
2. Let $R_1, R_2 \in \Re$, if $U/R_1 \subseteq U/R_2$, then $\alpha_{R_2}(X) \leq \alpha_{R_1}(X)$.

For property 2, its affective description meaning is: the finer the affective space is divided, the bigger the affective description precision is, so we can describe the emotion more exactly. That is obviously accord to our common sense. That is to say, our affective modeling based on rough sets and the precision definition are well accord to nature, which in favor of our more research.

4 The Affective Dynamic Description Based on Rough Sets

The simulation of affective states and affective dynamic forecast are the critical contents of affective computing. At present, many scientists[10, 11] simulated the affective dynamic change by using Markov chain. When there is no environment stimulus, affective states mostly behave as a spontaneous transition process, which usually can be simulated by Markov chain.

In affective space, there is one kind of emotion which has special meanings, it is the calm state. We denote it with Φ. When there is no environment stimulus, [5, 6] point that all kinds of human emotions will converge to the calm state. That is to say, it is the main trend of human affective transition that any one kind of emotion will transfer to the calm state. So we can regard the affective transition process as a Markov process and simulate affective transition by using Markov chain. Meanwhile, there is an ordinary return state, which is the calm state.

According to the psychology knowledge, the human affective transition is always a periodic process that from calm state to any other emotions and then back to calm state. This process repeats again and again, but their time intervals are random. Due to space limitations, we will discuss the cycle question of affective transition in another paper. In this paper we creatively combine rough sets and Markov chain to analyze affective dynamic change process.

Given the affective universe of discourse U_1 (nonempty finite set), R_1 is an equivalent relation on U_1, $[x]_{R_1}$ is R_1 equivalent class, $X_1 \subset U_1$. Based on rough sets, the affective states set on time T is $A^T(X_1) = (\underline{R_1}(X_1), \overline{R_1}(X_1))^{(T)}$, and

$$\underline{R_1}(X_1) = \cup[x]_{R_1} = \{x | x \in [x]_{R_1} \subseteq X_1\} \tag{5}$$

$$\overline{R_1}(X_1) = \cup[x]_{R_1} = \{x | x \in [x]_{R_1} \cap X_1 \neq \phi\} \tag{6}$$

For the affective states set$A^T(X_1)$, it is supposed that there are k kinds of affective states sets when it transfer from time T to time $T+1$, denoted as $A^{T+1}(X_1), \cdots, A^{T+1}(X_k)$. Let the transition probabilities of affective states sets are $P_{11}, P_{12}, \cdots, P_{1k}$ separately. Similarly, we can define the transition probability of other $k-1$ kinds of affective states sets $A^T(X_i), i = 2, \cdots, k$, when they transfer from time T to time $T+1$.

Let $a_1(T+1) = (\underline{R_1}(X_1), \overline{R_1}(X_1))^{(T+1)}, \cdots, a_k(T+1) = (\underline{R_k}(X_k), \overline{R_k}(X_k))^{(T+1)}$,

$$P = \begin{pmatrix} P_{11} & P_{12} & \cdots & P_{1k} \\ P_{21} & P_{22} & \cdots & P_{2k} \\ \vdots & \vdots & \vdots & \vdots \\ P_{k1} & P_{k2} & \cdots & P_{kk} \end{pmatrix}, a(T+1) = (a_1(T+1), \cdots, a_k(T+1))$$

Then we have

$$a(T+1) = a(T) \cdot P \tag{7}$$

Supposed a person has n kinds of emotions, which have m kinds of attribute dimensions. So there are l kinds of possible affective states, where

$$l = (C_n^1 + C_n^2 + \cdots + C_n^n)(C_m^1 + C_m^2 + \cdots + C_m^m) + 1 \tag{8}$$

then affective transition probability matrix is$(P_{ij})_{l \times l}$. There are many methods to confirm the transition probability of the transition matrix, generally, statistical method is widely used.

Markov chain contains various contents. Here, we make use of the absorption chain in Markov chain to simulate the process that affective transfer from an arbitrary emotion to the calm state for the first time. We firstly give the basic conception and properties of absorption chain [12].

Definition 7. [12] *The state i is called* **the absorption state**, *if its transition probability $P_{ii} = 1$.*

Definition 8. [12] *A Markov chain is called* **the absorption chain**, *if it at least has one absorption state and any unabsorption state can reach some absorption state by plus probability in finite transition steps.*

Let an absorption chain has r kinds of absorption states and $k - r$ kinds of unabsorption states, then the transition matrix of absorption chain can be written as follow:

$$P = \begin{pmatrix} Q & R \\ 0 & I_{r\times r} \end{pmatrix} \tag{9}$$

Here: Q is $(k-r)$ by $(k-r)$ square matrix and its eigenvalue $|\lambda(Q)| < 1$. I is the unit matrix.

Absorption chain has two properties[12]:

Property 1. In above standard form of P, $(I - Q)$ is reversible, and

$$M = (I - Q)^{-1} = \sum_{s=1}^{\infty} Q^s \tag{10}$$

Let column vector $e = (1, \cdots, 1)^T$, then the ith component of the vector $y = M \cdot e$ is the number of average transition step that from the ith unabsorption state to some absorption state.

Let unabsorption state is i , absorption state is j ,then $f_{ij}(n)$ is actually the probability that i transfer to j by n steps and $f_{ij} = \sum_{n=1}^{\infty} f_{ij}(n)$ is the probability that i transfer to j eventually. Let $F = \{f_{ij}\}_{(k-r)\times r}$, then we have

Property 2. Let P is above standard form, then

$$F = M \cdot R \tag{11}$$

Given affective state sets, supposed there are k kinds of states when emotions transfer from time T to time $T+1$. For the given absorption chain, there are two cases of its transition process: 1. After a period of time (maybe including many transition steps), the above k kinds of states will be absorbed by the calm state. 2. The above k kinds of states will be absorbed by $l (l < k)$ kinds of states. In case 2, the l kinds of states are regarded as the typical affective states. For example, the mental disease sufferer can have any other typical affective states besides calm state, such as sad or ignorant and so on. For the l kinds of states, we can similarly give transition matrix P_{ll} and continue the above steps. Eventually, they will be absorbed by calm state, so we complete the description of an affective transition cycle.

5 Simulation

In this section, we give the simulation of the above process that emotions transfer from an arbitrary emotion to the calm state for the first time.

For the convenience of computing, we only consider three emotions: happy, sad, dread and two attribute dimensions: nervous dimension, impulse dimension. We suppose there is just one emotion at one time, so there are $C_3^1(C_2^1+C_2^2)+1=10$ kinds of affective possible states. Let somebody's affective states set $A^T(s)$ is $\{$(sad, nervous), (dread, not impulse)$\}$ at some time. We give the affective transition matrix by using the following psychology statistical rules: 1. For any affective state, it will keep its own state or transfer to calm state by bigger probability. The shorter the time interval t is, the bigger probability of keeping its own state. 2. The probability of transferring to any other states is relatively little, we suppose they are equal. The longer the time interval t is, the bigger probability of transferring to other state.

Using the above rules,we give a matrix

$$P_{10\times 10}=\begin{pmatrix} 0.17 & 0.0875 & 0.0875 & 0.0875 & 0.0875 & 0.0875 & 0.0875 & 0.0875 & 0.0875 & 0.13 \\ 0.075 & 0.2 & 0.075 & 0.075 & 0.075 & 0.075 & 0.075 & 0.075 & 0.075 & 0.2 \\ 0.0625 & 0.0625 & 0.25 & 0.0625 & 0.0625 & 0.0625 & 0.0625 & 0.0625 & 0.0625 & 0.25 \\ 0.0875 & 0.0875 & 0.0875 & 0.1 & 0.0875 & 0.0875 & 0.0875 & 0.0875 & 0.0875 & 0.2 \\ 0.08 & 0.08 & 0.08 & 0.08 & 0.2 & 0.08 & 0.08 & 0.08 & 0.08 & 0.16 \\ 0.09 & 0.09 & 0.09 & 0.09 & 0.09 & 0.14 & 0.09 & 0.09 & 0.09 & 0.14 \\ 0.08 & 0.08 & 0.08 & 0.08 & 0.08 & 0.08 & 0.16 & 0.08 & 0.08 & 0.16 \\ 0.0875 & 0.0875 & 0.0875 & 0.0875 & 0.0875 & 0.0875 & 0.0875 & 0.2 & 0.0875 & 0.1 \\ 0.075 & 0.075 & 0.075 & 0.075 & 0.075 & 0.075 & 0.075 & 0.075 & 0.2 & 0.2 \\ 0 & 0 & 0 & 0 & 0 & 0 & 0 & 0 & 0 & 1 \end{pmatrix} \tag{12}$$

Here: We supposed the first affective states set is $A^T(s)$, the last one is the calm state, and $P_{ij}(i,j=1,\cdots,10)$ denotes the probability of state i transfer to state j .The matrix satisfies the property of absorption chain, so after computing, we have $M=(I-Q)^{-1}$, and

$$M=\begin{pmatrix} 1.6242 & 0.5602 & 0.6033 & 0.4964 & 0.5571 & 0.5160 & 0.5447 & 0.5523 & 0.5602 \\ 0.4802 & 1.6464 & 0.5423 & 0.4462 & 0.5007 & 0.4638 & 0.4895 & 0.4964 & 0.5035 \\ 0.4310 & 0.4519 & 1.7174 & 0.4004 & 0.4493 & 0.4162 & 0.4393 & 0.4455 & 0.4519 \\ 0.4964 & 0.5205 & 0.5606 & 1.4739 & 0.5176 & 0.4794 & 0.5061 & 0.5132 & 0.5205 \\ 0.5093 & 0.5340 & 0.5751 & 0.4732 & 1.6674 & 0.4919 & 0.5192 & 0.5265 & 0.5340 \\ 0.5307 & 0.5565 & 0.5993 & 0.4931 & 0.5534 & 1.5652 & 0.5411 & 0.5487 & 0.5565 \\ 0.4980 & 0.5222 & 0.5623 & 0.4627 & 0.5192 & 0.4810 & 1.6188 & 0.5148 & 0.5222 \\ 0.5523 & 0.5792 & 0.6237 & 0.5132 & 0.5759 & 0.5334 & 0.5631 & 1.6978 & 0.5792 \\ 0.4802 & 0.5035 & 0.5423 & 0.4462 & 0.5007 & 0.4638 & 0.4895 & 0.4964 & 1.6464 \end{pmatrix} \tag{13}$$

$$y=M\cdot e=\begin{pmatrix} 6.0145 & 5.5689 & 5.2029 & 5.5881 & 5.8307 & 5.9446 & 5.7011 & 6.2178 & 5.5689 \end{pmatrix}^T \tag{14}$$

The simulation shows that the first state will be absorbed by calm state after 7 time intervals. Similarly, we can obtain other states' transition time intervals. And

$$F = M \cdot R = \begin{pmatrix} 1 & 1 & 1 & 1 & 1 & 1 & 1 & 1 & 1 \end{pmatrix}^T \tag{15}$$

This shows the probability that the given affective states eventually transfer to the calm state is 1. All the above results show that our model based on rough sets and Markov chain can well simulate the human affective dynamic change.

6 Concluding Remarks

The paper presents the fundamental work about affective computing. Psychology conceptions are generalized and two hypothesizes are given: 1. A person can have several kinds of affective states at the same time and the human emotion has several attribute dimensions. 2. When there is no environment stimulus, all kinds of human emotions will converge to the calm state. That is to say, the main trend of human affective transition is from any one emotion to calm state. Then we give the static description of emotion based on rough sets theory. Furthermore we combine rough sets and Markov chain to analyze the dynamic change of emotion, which is a new point to more research. At last, we simulate our affective model by using Matlab software and give some relative analyses. When there is environment stimulus the affective change question and the affective transition cycle question, which are our research emphases in future.

References

1. James W.:*Psychology.* Cambridge, MA:Harvard University Press, 1890.
2. Sdorow L.: *Psychology.* WC Brown, US, 1990.
3. Picard R. W. : *Affective Computing* . MIT Press , London , England , 1997.
4. Pawlak Z.: Rough Sets [J]. International Journal of Computer and Information Sciences, **11** (1982) 341-356.
5. Ye Yiqian, He Cundao, Liang Ningjian: *General Psychology.* Shanghai: East China Normal University Press, 1997-08.
6. Meng Zhaolan:*The Human Emotions.* Shanghai People's Publishing House, 1989.
7. Izard C.:*Human Emotion.* New York: Plenum Press, 1977.
8. Mao Xia: Kansei Information Processing. Journal of Telemetry, Tracking and Command, **21(6)** (2000) 58-62.
9. Zhang Wenxiu, Wu Weizhi, Liang Jiye. *Rough sets theories and methods.* Science Press, 2003.
10. Teng Shaodong, Wang Zhiliang: Affective Computing Model Based on Markov Chain. Computer Engineering. **31(5)** (2005) 17-19.
11. Gu Xuejing, Wang Zhiliang: Artificial Psychology Modeling Method Based on HMM. The 1st Chinese Conference on Affective Computing and Intelligent Interaction (ACII'03), 2003-12-08: 31-36.
12. Zhang Zhuokui, Chen Huichan: *Random Process.* Xi Dian University Press, 2003.

The Research of a Teaching Assistant System Based on Artificial Psychology

Xiuyan Meng, Zhiliang Wang, Guojiang Wang, Lin Shi, and Xiaotian Wu

School of Information Engineering, University of Science & Technology Beijing, Beijing 100083, China
Mengxy1976@126.com

Abstract. A humanistic computer teaching system is presented in this paper. The core of this system is the affective interaction between teacher and student. Based on theories in Psychology and the theory of Artificial Psychology, the emotion-learning model is developed. Four basic emotions and four types of learning psychology state are defined according to the Basic Emotion Theory, and two-dimensional emotion space is designed ground on Dimensional Emotion theory. This system could offer the student's psychological state and psychological value to the teacher. Finally, this system was realized by using the recognition method that is based on digital image processing technology.

1 Preface

With the rapid development of computer technology and the prevalence of network, the modern educational form using electronic technology have got more and more attention, such as electronic classroom, distance education, network education. Network teaching systems have been developed for years in foreign country developed countries. In 2000, a plan of "digital learning" was brought forward in the American educational technology forum. The German Research Center for Artificial Intelligence set up a special research center to develop E-learning system. The development of distance education system has been paid great attention to in China, and the "modern E-learning project" has put in practice. Nowadays many kinds of network education systems or distance education systems appeared one by one in China. Electronic teaching method using computer technology has an advantage over the traditional one; because it can offer lively teaching with integration of multimedia data such as letters, images and videos. But presently, compared to the traditional education form, most of electronic education is lack of the affective interactive between the teacher and the students, so the teacher cannot get the response of the students in time, and the existing computer teaching system take the psychology of the learners into little account. Psychologists considered that the emotion and feeling are the especially important factors in learning and they keep close relationship with the progress of cognition and attention. Negative emotion such as tension, dumps and anger can weaken the sense of human and slow the thinking, so it can go against the learning. On the other hand, positive emotion makes the sense better and makes the thinking smart, so it can speed the learning [1]. The research production of brain science indicates that emotion play an important role in human learning [2]. Thus

J. Tao, T. Tan, and R.W. Picard (Eds.): ACII 2005, LNCS 3784, pp. 614–621, 2005.

emotion would greatly affect learning. In modern society the people pay more and more attention on the use of emotion in education. Now with the development of society, electronic education system has entered into individualized development era. It requires the education system can offer humanistic interactive teaching and teaching students in accordance of their aptitude, meanwhile can make intelligent adjustment of teaching according to the interest and emotion of learners. To meet this requirement, this paper presented a humanistic teaching assistant system that focused on the affective interaction based on Artificial Psychology. This system implemented the philosophy of harmonious human-computer interactive.

2 The Introduction of This System

This system is a teaching assistant computer system which is based on the theory of Artificial Psychology and affective computing. We used the method of image processing and pattern recognition, the technology of harmonious human-computer interactive to develop this system. This system obeys the principle of "make the students being center, they are the main body of recognition and the initiative builder of knowledge". The core of this system is the consideration of the student's emotion and psychological state. It can recognizes expression information through the method of facial expression recognition and gesture recognition based on the technology of image processing, and make research in affective modeling based on the theory and method of emotional psychology, cognitive psychology, educational psychology and artificial psychology, and based on all of these present the emotion-learning model.

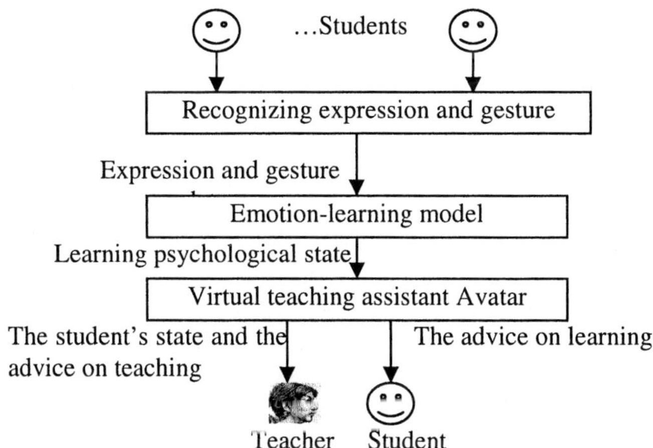

Fig. 1. The functional structure of this system

This system uses the B/S structure and realizes the data transmission using mobile Agent. The Browser end includes one teacher end and many student ends. The hardwares of this system include two servers, many terminals, and one video camera per student terminal. This system includes the module of affective modeling, the recognition module of expression information, and the module of Avatar virtual teaching assistant. The function structure of this system is presented as figure 1.

The student browser can recognize the expression and gesture of students through running the program of expression information recognition in server, transfer the recognized expression information to the emotional model through mobile Agent, gain the learning psychological state by using emotional model to process expression information, and transfer it to the virtual teaching assistant Avatar. In teacher browser Avatar can represent the psychological state of students to the teacher, and bring forward some suggestion for the teacher and students to improve the learning effect. Thus it can realize the interactive between the teacher and learners. Mobile Agent is on duty of all the data transmission in the network.

3 The Design of System's Function Module

3.1 The Design of Emotional Model

The design of emotional model is the emphasis of the research of affective computing and also the core of this system. The system builds the students' emotion-learning module according to the theory of emotional psychology, cognitive psychology and educational psychology. As the opinion of psychology theory [4], emotion, which is a mental process, has special external representation------expression, it includes the expression of face, gesture and tone. Facial expression is the pattern of all facial muscle's change of eyebrow, nose and lips. The expression of gesture is feeling behavior of all the body except the face, the expression of tone happens while the tone, rhythm and velocity are changing. Among the three expressions, facial expression can be used to distinguish different emotions best; furthermore, only facial expression has the pattern for demarcating the special emotion. Then, facial expression is the main symbol of distinguishing the emotions, gesture and tone are accessorial. So, the expressions information to be recognized in this system is facial expression and gesture, the facial expression is the leading data and gesture is accessorial.

There are various definitions about basic emotion. Izard used the method of factor analysis and found 8 - 11 kinds of basic emotions: interest, surprise, pain, disgust, pleasure, anger, dread, sadness, ashamedness, scorn and guiltiness [4]. Ekman sorts the emotion into 6 kinds [5]: joy, anger, disgust, dread, sadness and surprise. In view of the theories, its realizability and applicability, this system defined four types of basic emotion: happiness, sadness, interest and disgust, and build emotion space of two dimensions on the theory of Dimensional Emotion (e.g. emotional model of three dimensions put forward based cognition theory by Blumenthal[6]). As showing on the following figure2, two dimensions of this emotion space are happiness --- unhappiness, attention---refusal. All the normal emotion can be found the corresponding point in the circle which radius is 1 and the x-axis is the dimension of happiness --- unhappiness, y-axis is the dimension of attention----refusal. All points outside of the circle represent abnormal emotion. The point of coordinate represents the emotional statement of neutral, pleasure and sadness are the reverse emotion of each other and they are 1 and -1 on x-axis; interest and disgust are also the reverse emotion of each other, and they are 1 and -1 on y-axis.

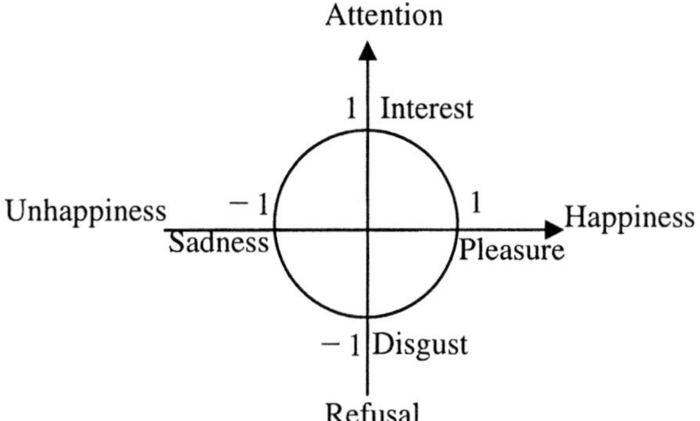

Fig. 2. Two-dimensional emotion space

Every normal emotion could represent with the two-dimensional vector (x, y). The modulus of the vector γ shows the intensity of emotion, its value is in the set of [0, 1]. Beyond this scope, the emotion is abnormal. The angle of the vector θ shows the tendency of emotion to four types of basic emotion. The definition of γ and θ are as follow:

$$\gamma = \sqrt{x^2 + y^2} \tag{1}$$

$$\theta = \begin{cases} \arccos \dfrac{x}{\sqrt{x^2 + y^2}}, & \text{当 } y > 0 \\ \pi + \arccos \dfrac{x}{\sqrt{x^2 + y^2}} & \text{当 } y < 0 \end{cases} \tag{2}$$

Emotion is a compound psychology progress of multi-component, multi-dimension, multi-kind and multi-level, so any definition of basic emotion or dimensional emotion has localization. The emotion space and basic emotion in this system are also a representation of emotion and only suit for this system.

In order to express students' learning state clearly, the system also defined four studying psychology states: favor (i.e. be interesting to the course), boredom (i.e. be not interesting to the course), comprehension (i.e. totally comprehend the course), puzzlement (i.e. not understanding the course). Then according to the relationship between emotion and cognition (positive emotion is good for studying, negative emotion is bad for studying), the mapping between learning state and emotion space is established (see figure3). Grounded on this mapping, we could get the student's psychology state and evaluate whether the students' learning states are suitable to study, furthermore, we are informed the value of the state and the cause of the bad state.

Suppose: one emotion e= (x, y), then the value of x indicates the degree of the understanding of the course, while x= 1, it shows the student understands the course clearly, that means the present psychology state of the student is comprehension; while x = -1, it represents the student doesn't understand the course at all, then the present psychology state is puzzlement. The value of y represents the degree of interest in the course. While y = 1, it says high interesting, the present psychology is favor. While y =-1, it states the student have no interest in the class, the present psychology state is boredom.

The computing formula of value about learning state is:

$$v = \cos(\theta - \frac{\pi}{4}) \times \gamma \tag{3}$$

θ and γ is the angle and modulus of the emotion vector, When $v = 1$, the present psychology state of the student is very suitable for studying. The evaluate value of -1 shows the student is not fit to study at that time.

According to the value of $\frac{|y|}{|x|}$, we can also know why the present state is not fit to study. The system can give some advice to the teacher and student based on the causes. If $\frac{|y|}{|x|}>1$, the cause of bad learning state is the student could not catch the course. The cause is the student have no interesting in the course if $\frac{|y|}{|x|}<1$

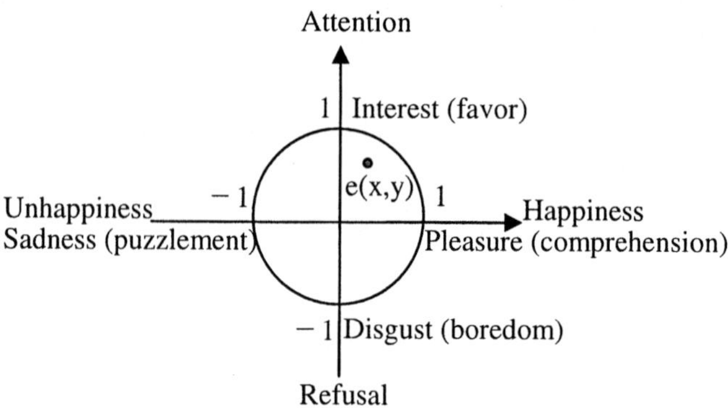

Fig. 3. The mapping between learning state and two-dimensional emotion space

The figure4 is the sketch map of emotion-learning model. Firstly, according to the relationship between expression and emotion in the emotional psychology (the expression include facial expression and gesture expression), this model process the expression data which are recognized with information recognize module, then the emotion of student is given. Secondly, the emotion is quantified and denoted with the two-dimension vector in the two-dimensional emotion space. Thirdly, the students' learning state and evaluation value of state can be got in accordance with the relation between learning state and two-dimension emotion space.

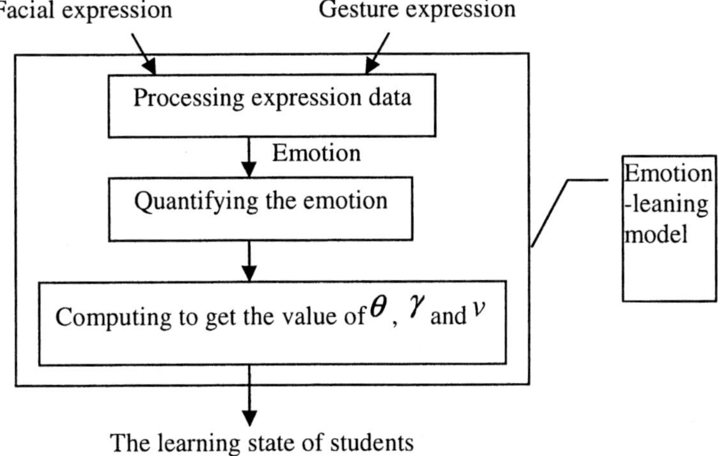

Fig. 4. The sketch map of emotion-learning model

3.2 The Module of Expression Recognition

This module includes facial expression recognition and gesture expression recognition (often named gesture recognition for short). The function of this module is detecting students' facial features and gesture features and identifying the facial expression and gesture expression followed from the features. The facial recognition and gesture recognition have the very similar process and technique, but the data they processed are different. The program of facial expression recognition processes the information of change on the human's face, such as close the eyes, open the mouth, frown and so on. The gesture recognition program processes the change information of gesture, for example the body lean to the front or back, raise the arms. The key part of the system is expression recognition module. The effect of this module influences the quality of the whole system. According to the difference of object to be processed, the current methods of feature extraction include the method of extracting Geometric, statistical, spectral-transform-based, and kinetic features. The recognition methods in common use are linear discriminant, artificial nerve network (ANN), support vector machine (SVM). The functional flow chart of this module is described as figure5. In the particular design of this module, it is required to define the relationship between emotion and expression according to the psychology and the system demands, for example brows and corners of the mouth going upwards show pleasure, and they drooping show disgust.

3.3 The Module of Virtual Teaching Assistant—Avatar

Avatar is a two-dimension cartoon character, it run in the browsers. The output of emotion-learning model is the input of this module. The output of this module is students' learning state and advice, such as the number of the students who are tired of the course and who are interested to it. If the teachers must adapt their teaching to students, Avatar will give some advice. Avatar also advises the student how to improve learning. Furthermore, Avatar can achieve the communication between students and teachers.

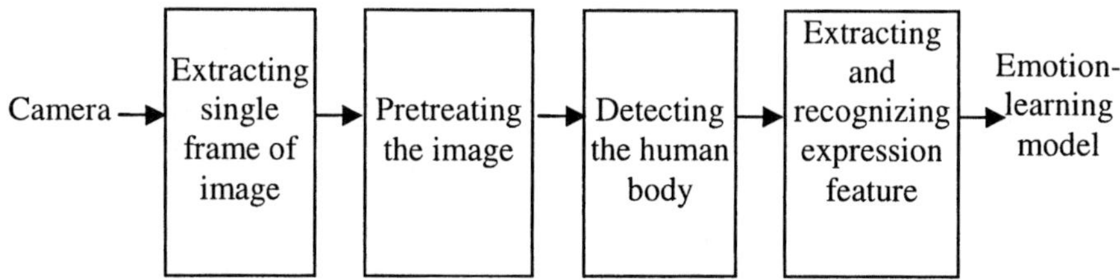

Fig. 5. The module of expression recognition

4 Programming the System

This system was developed with using Microsoft Visual C++ 6.0 and SQL Server. The method of orientation on geometry feature and the complexion model are adopted in the expression recognition module. The function of gesture recognition is realized with the method of distribution on complexion density. The demonstration effect picture of the system is as follow:

Fig. 6. The demonstration effect picture of the system□The left is Avater interface, the right is the effect of facial expression recognition

5 Conclusions

This system can provide the teacher with the emotional information of students in real time, including learning state, the evaluation value of the learning state and the cause of the bad state. And this system can give advices to teachers and students in order to improve the effect of teaching. The emotional interaction between teacher and students has been achieved in this system. The Teaching Assistant System makes up the shortage of the modern electronic education form which is lack of emotional interactive, it is good for improving the efficiency and effect of electronic and network teaching, and though it we really achieve the humanistic computer teaching assistant. This system not only can cooperate with e-learning teaching system, but also can be used for teaching in electronic classroom independently. In future, we will be engaged in in-depth study. We will try to add voice recognize technology, to improve the emotion-teaching model as well as the technology of detection and recognition, and to design more visual virtual teaching assistant. We will make great efforts to develop a more practical, more humanistic teaching system. Our research achievement can be expanded to use in other areas, such as in e-government and e-commerce, we can use it to develop the virtual service officer for e-government and virtual seller assistant for e-commerce.

Acknowledgments

The paper supported by the key lab named Advanced Information Science and Network Technology of Beijing (No. TDXX0503) and the key foundation of USTB.

References

1. Youzhi Wang, Lun Ouyang.: the essence of Psychology——theory and application. Beijing□the Capital University of Economics & Business Press(2003)
2. Decheng Ding, Wei Zhang, Meimei Shi.: Modern Brain Science and Education. Journal of Shaanxi Normal University(Natural Science Edition),Vol.32(2004)
3. Zhiliang Wang.: Artificial Psychology——a most Accessible Science Research to Human Brain. Journal of University of Science and Technology Beijing, VoL22 No.5, (2000)
4. Zhaolan Meng.: General Psychology. Beijing: Peking University Press, 1994,9
5. Ekman,P. :An argument for basic emotions. Cognition and Emotion,6,169-200(1992)
6. Jianglin Wu.: the Generality of Psychology. Guangzhou: Guangdong High Education Press (2003)

Emotion Estimation and Reasoning Based on Affective Textual Interaction

Chunling Ma[1], Helmut Prendinger[2], and Mitsuru Ishizuka[1]

[1] Graduate School of Information Science and Technology, University of Tokyo, 7-3-1 Hongo, Bunkyo-ku, Tokyo 113-8656, Japan
{macl, ishizuka}@miv.t.u-tokyo.ac.jp
[2] National Institute of Informatics, 2-1-2 Hitotsubashi, Chiyoda-ku, Tokyo 101-8430, Japan
helmut@nii.ac.jp

Abstract. This paper presents a novel approach to Emotion Estimation that assesses the affective content from textual messages. Our main goals are to detect emotion from chat or other dialogue messages and to employ animated agents capable of the emotional reasoning based on the textual interaction. In this paper, the emotion estimation module is applied to a chat system, where avatars associated with chat partners act out the assessed emotions of messages through multiple modalities, including synthetic speech and associated affective gestures.

1 Introduction

An important issue in meeting the needs of the spatially distributed knowledge society is to provide natural and intuitive communication tools. In order to improve textual methods such as e-mail, online chat systems and dialog system, some recent systems are based on like-like embodied agents as a new multi-modal communication means [9]. Most prominently, the BodyChat system [2] employs embodied conversational avatars to mimic human-human face-to-face communication. The TelMeA system [12] uses embodied agents to deliver messages in an asynchronous online community system. Other work employs agents as personal representatives to express the user's point of view of (personal) documents [1].

Although avatars may improve the expressivity of online communication, it remains within the responsibility of the user to carefully prepare the affective content of the textual message. Picard [8] provides a suggestive example: " 'How many of you have lost more than a day's work trying to straighten out some confusion over an email note that was received with the wrong tone?' A majority of hands usually go up when I ask an audience this question. Email is an affect-limited form of communication." [8, p. 87]

In order to increase the 'affective bandwidth' of computer-mediated exchange, the internet community typically uses special ASCII symbol combinations, so-called 'emoticons', to express the emotional tone of the message (e.g. ":-)" for "happy"). As a complementary technique, work on 'textual affect sensing' proposes to analyze the textual message itself for affective qualities. In the e-mail composer EmpathyBuddy [5], emotional content of text is processed by an approach based on large-scale

J. Tao, T. Tan, and R.W. Picard (Eds.): ACII 2005, LNCS 3784, pp. 622–628, 2005.

real-world knowledge. The assessed emotion is then attached to the textual message in the form of a caricature face that displays the relevant emotion.

The concept presented in this paper can be conceived as an alternative to the EmpathyBuddy system [5]. Our approach is based on the following methods: (i) the affective content of the textual message is recognized by an advanced keyword spotting technique, (ii) syntactical sentence-level processing is applied for detection of affective meaning, and (iii) animated 2D full-body agents perform the emotional coloring of the message using synthetic affective speech and appropriate gestures.

2 Calculating Emotion Estimation from Text

The approach for providing emotional estimations for natural-language texts is based on a keyword spotting technique, i.e. the system divides a text into words and performs an emotional estimation for each of these words, as well as a sentence-level processing technique, i.e. the relationship among subject, verb and object is extracted to improve emotion estimation.

The initial step of analyzing an emotional scenario is to define the emotions relevant to the application scenario. In our research, we use the six (basic) emotions from Ekman's research [3]: *happiness*, *sadness*, *anger*, *fear*, *surprise* and *disgust*.

2.1 Affective Words

We employ WordNet-Affect Database [13] of ITS-irst (The Center for Scientific and Technological Research of Autonomous Province of Trento, Italy) with WordNet 1.6 [4] to first find synonyms sets of affective words. We select the emotion "seed" words according to these six emotion categories, i.e., "happy", "sad", "angry", "surprise", "fear", "disgusted", then use key words recognition and synonyms to choose related words from WordNet based on the affective words set. The emotional weight of these words is given based on their *sense* that represents a meaning of a word in WordNet database. Normally, a word has several meanings, but not all the meanings of it are emotional. For example, the verb "beat" has 5 emotional senses among 23 senses in WordNet. So the emotional weight of verb "beat" is 0.22, i.e. the proportion of emotional senses among total senses. The range of emotional weight for each emotion category is [0, 1]. The words are categorized with their part of speech (POS) tag. So we have four affective words database according to WordNet database categories --- *verb*, *adjective*, *adverb* and *noun*. For example, both "joy" and "joyful" belong to "happiness" emotion category, but they are existing in two different database, "noun" and "adjective". The noun "joy" has its emotion vector as [1.0 0.0 0.0 0.0 0.0 0.0] while adjective "joyful" has the same emotion vector of [1.0 0.0 0.0 0.0 0.0 0.0]. The examples of affective words extracted from WordNet are shown in Table 1.

2.2 Word-Level Processing

After building the affective lexicon, we use the word spotting technique to estimate emotion of word phrase. The system will calculate the overall emotional estimation for the phrase by summing the extracted estimations. For example, the nouns phrase "a surprise, terrible news" can get the two affective word vectors: "surprise [0.0 0.0 0.0

0.0 1.0 0.0]" and "terrible [0.0 1.0 0.0 0.0 0.0 0.0]", so the final emotion vector will be [0.0 1.0 0.0 0.0 1.0 0.0]. The emotion of this phrase is "surprise" and "sadness".

Table 1. Examples of affective words extracted from WordNet (adjective database)

Word	POS	Emotion Vector
exciting	a	[0.76 0.0 0.0 0.0 0.0 0.0]
fortunate	a	[0.72 0.0 0.0 0.0 0.72 0.0]
happy	a	[1.0 0.0 0.0 0.0 0.0 0.0]
healthy	a	[0.66 0.0 0.0 0.0 0.0 0.0]
shaken	a	[0.0 0.0 0.0 0.0 1.0 0.0]
sad	a	[0.0 1.0 0.0 0.0 0.0 0.0]
tearing	a	[0.0 1.0 0.0 0.0 1.0 0.0]
....	.	...

2.3 Sentence-Level Processing

The word spotting method is too simple to deal with sentences such as "I think that he is happy" or "the lake near my city was very beautiful, but now it is polluted" since here, the speaker is not necessarily happy or the speaker's emotion depends on the semantic of the sentence deeply. We hence perform the following steps on *sentence-level processing*.

2.3.1 Sentence Splitting

In this step, multiple-sentence text is spited into single sentences. Each sentence is estimating the emotion separately.

2.3.2 POS (Part of Speech) Tagging and Sentence Structure Recognition

In this step, the syntactic phrase types are derived out from parse trees that are generated by the parser. The phrase types express the semantic roles in the sentence, for examples, noun phrase (NP), verb phrase (VP) and clause phrase (S or SBAR).

First, we eliminate 'non-emotional' sentences first: (i) Questions, (ii) Clause Phrase beginning with "when" "after" "before" or "if".

Second, we perform the sentence processing. In the top-level of the sentence, the syntactic subject and verb can be derived from noun phrase and verb phrase. Then we recognize some structure patterns of the verb phrase as following types.

- Verb + Adjective Phrase. If the subject is first person pronouns or with the noun terms that are related to the speaker, we calculate the emotion of Adjective Phrase with the word-level method mentioned in 2.2 above. Otherwise, it is treated as non-emotional. For example, "The book I bought yesterday is very good." In the sentence, "The book" is related to the speaker because "I bought yesterday", so the emotion estimation of adjective phrase "very good" can be applied to the subject and treated as the emotion of speaker. Therefore, the emotion of this sentence is "happiness" with the emotion vector [1.0 0.0 0.0 0.0 0.0 0.0].
- Verb + Noun Phrase. If the verb exists in the emotion database, after extracting the emotion estimation of the verb, we analyze the noun phrase of the verb phrase: if the noun terms in the noun phrase are related to the speaker, the emotion

estimation of the verb will apply to the speaker. Otherwise, it is non-emotional for the speaker. If the verb doesn't exist in the emotion database, we search the knowledge database to get the emotion effect of the verb and the emotion will affect to the speaker if the subject is related to the speaker. The knowledge base is extracted from OMCS (Open Mind Common Sense) knowledge base [7], which includes some affective rules, such as "buy something" is a way to "get something", one of the affect of "get good thing" is "being happy". Therefore, the sentence "I bought a very good book yesterday" can be treated as "happiness".

- Verb + Clause Sentence. The rules described above are used to analyze the Clause Sentence and the emotion estimation of the Clause sentence is returned back. Then the rules of "Verb + Noun Phrase" pattern are used again. For example, "I think he is good there", "he is good there" will return non-emotional, so apply to "I" and "think", the final result is non-emotional.

2.3.3 Negation Detection

In this step, we detect 'negation' in sentences. Since negatively prefixed words such as "unhappy" are already included in the emotion database, they do not have to be considered. On the other hand, negative verb forms such as "have not", "was not", "did not" are detected and flip the polarity of the emotion word.

3 Embodied Conversational Messengers

Based on the engine for textual emotion estimation from text, we built a chat system that extracts the emotion from the user's input sentence. In the following, we briefly describe our chat system where animated life-like agents with synthetic speech and gestures serve as user avatars and conversational messengers.

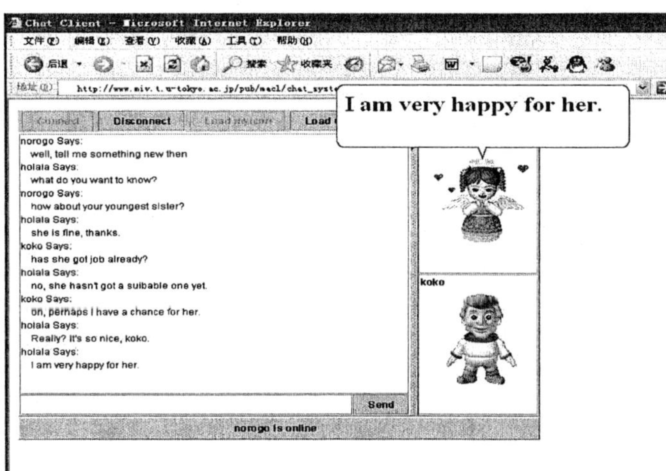

Fig. 1. Chat Client Interface demonstration

Fig. 1 shows an example of a chat client, where three persons are involved in a chatting activity. Among them "norogo" refers to the user as one of the chat clients, the other two (named "holala" and "koko") are displayed by their own avatar characters. The female character is the avatar of "holala"; the male character is the avatar of "koko". In this scenario, the following chatting was processing:

norogo Says(to holala): how about your youngest sister?
holala Says(to norogo): she is fine, thanks.
koko Says(to holala): has she got job already?
holala Says(to koko): no, she has't got a suitable one yet.
koko Says(to holala): oh, perhaps I have a chance for her.
holala Says(to koko): Really? It's so nice, koko.
holala Says(to koko): I am very happy for her.

When the chat partner called "holala" types the message "I am very happy for her", her avatar character expresses the "gladness" emotion. The relevant emotion word in the sentence is the word "happy", which is defined as "gladness" in the emotion database. The words "very" add to the intensity of the emotion conveyed by "happy". The emotional content of the message "I am very happy for her." is expressed through the avatar by synthetic speech and a (exaggerated) non-verbal expression of gladness.

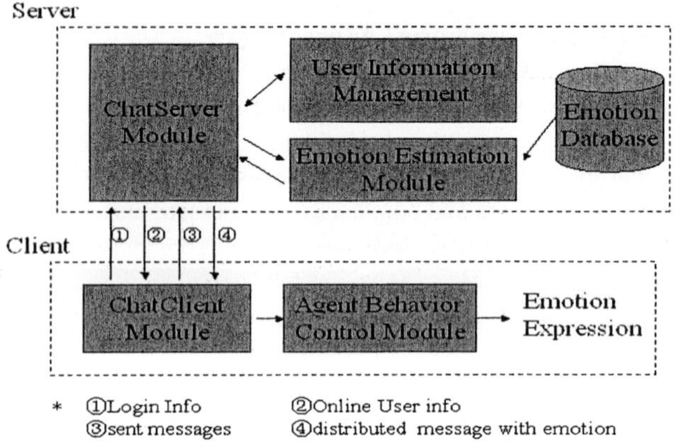

Fig. 2. Architecture of the chat system

The architecture of the chat system is depicted in Fig. 2. On the server side, the ChatServer module is used to listen to the clients' connection and incoming messages. The Emotion Estimation module analyzes the emotion tendency of the incoming messages and returns the result back to the ChatServer Module. In this system, emotion detection is context independent, i.e. we currently do not consider the current mood or emotion of a chat partner. Once the emotion of a message is estimated, the avatar will perform the message with affective expression. The analysis of emotion is based on an emotion database and the algorithm mentioned in Sect. 2. The chat system has been implemented using the Java platform, JavaScript, the Microsoft Agent package [6], and Stanford javaNLP API [10]. The behavior sequence and messages to be spoken out are sent to JavaScript functions as parameters. Currently we use a light client design in the system; i.e. the client side essentially sends connection requests to the server module, and sends or receives messages. When the connection is established, the client will request the server to send its information, e.g. to a particular agent character. The server will update its online list of the clients for each client. Then the user can choose the chat user to talk with in the animated style. After a chat user is chosen, the Agent Behavior Control module is called to generate a behavior expression corresponding to the emotion estimation value. On the server side, we also maintain a user information database.

4 Conclusions and Future Work

This paper presents an Emotion Estimation approach based on textual interaction. In our approach, a word spotting technique and syntactical sentence-level processing are proposed. The issue of emotional reasoning based on affective text has been studied and implemented in different contexts and approaches [5,11,13], which include the use of affect dictionaries, simple natural language processing techniques, and commonsense knowledge of real world. Our approach is based on the affect lexicon and simple rules of commonsense knowledge with sentence-level processing. The difference of our approach to other studies is that our aim is to decide the emotional content of the online textual messages in real time, so that we may trace the relationship between speaker and conversational content. Emotion assessment is based on the role of a verb in a sentence. The emotion reasoning procedure is bottom-up, i.e. the word spotting technique is used to decide the emotion of basic phrase type, and then the distilled emotion category is transferred to the upper layer phrase. This approach allows for more efficient reasoning than approaches based on the real-world knowledge, and we can get better results than by using a simple word spotting approach.

In our future work, we plan to improve the Emotion Estimation module, specifically by combining past emotional states as a parameter for deciding the affective meaning of the user's current message. In addition, the speaker's mood will be associated with the topic of the conversation. In this way, we hope to obtain a better identification of the relation between speaker and topic terms in the sentence.

References

1. Bickmore, T.W., (ed.): Animated autonomous personal representatives. In Proceedings 2nd International Conference on Autonomous Agents (Agent-98), Minneapolis, MN (1998) 8-15
2. Cassell, J., Vilhj´almsson, H.: Fully embodied conversational avatars: Making communicative behaviors autonomous. Autonomous Agents and Multi-Agent Systems (1999) 2:45–64
3. Ekman, P.: Facial Expression and Emotion. American Psychologist (1993) 48, 384-392
4. Fellbaum C.: WordNet: An Electronic Lexical Database. MIT Press. (1982)
5. Liu, H., Lieberman, H., Selker, T.: A model of textual affect sensing using real-world Knowledge. In Proceedings International Conference on Intelligent User Interfaces (IUI-03) (2003) 125–132
6. Microsoft. Developing for Microsoft Agent. Microsoft Press. Redmond, WA (1998)

7. MIT Media Lab: Open Mind Common Sense (2005) URL: http://commonsense.media.mit.edu/
8. Picard., R. W.: Affective Computing. The MIT Press, Cambridge, MA (1997)
9. Prendinger, H., Ishizuka, M.: editors. Life-Like Characters.Tools, Affective Functions, and Applications. Cognitive Technologies. Springer Verlag, Berlin Heidelberg (2004)
10. Stanford NLP Group (2005) URL: http://nlp.stanford.edu
11. Subasic, P. and Huettner, A.: Affect Analysis of text using fuzzy semantic typing. IEEE Transactions on Fuzzy Systems (2001) 9: 483-496
12. 12.Takahashi, T. (ed.): TelMeA—Expressive avatars in asynchronous communications. International Journal of Human-Computer Studies (2005) 62:193–209
13. Valitutti, A., Strapparava, C., Stock, O.: Developing Affective Lexical Resources. PsychNology Journal. (2004) Volume 2, Number 1, 61-83

An Emotion Model of 3D Virtual Characters in Intelligent Virtual Environment

Zhen Liu[1] and Zhi Geng Pan[2]

[1] The Faculty of Information Science and Technology, Ningbo University, 315211, China
liuzhen@nbu.edu.cn
[2] State Key Lab of CAD&CG, Zhejiang University, Hangzhou 310027, China
zgpan@cad.zju.edu.cn

Abstract. Human emotion is related to stimulus and cognitive appraisal. Emotion is very important to entertainment application of virtual reality. Emotion model of 3D virtual characters is a challenging branch of Intelligent Virtual Environment (IVE). A believable 3D character should be provided with emotion and perception. In general, a virtual character is regarded as an autonomous agent with sense, perception, behavior and action. An emotion model of 3D virtual characters on the basis of psychology theory is presented in this paper. Our work is to construct 3D virtual characters that have internal sensor and perception for external stimulus, and express emotion autonomously in real time. Firstly, architecture of a virtual character is set up by cognitive model; Secondly, emotion class is set up by OCC and Plutchik's emotion theory; Thirdly, some new concepts about emotion are presented with a general mathematical model which is relation among emotion, stimulus, motivation variable, personality variable. Fourthly, a perception model of 3D characters by Gibson's theory is introduced. As a result, an emotional animation demo system of 3D virtual character is implemented on PC.

1 Introduction

Emotion is a complex subjective experience by outside stimulus. Emotion is very important to entertainment application of virtual reality. Emotion model of 3D virtual characters is a challenging branch of Intelligent Virtual Environment (IVE)[1]. A 3D virtual character is regarded as an autonomous agent and should be provided with the ability of emotion expression besides perception and behavior. Our research is mainly based on behavior animation [2][3][4], our goal is to construct 3D virtual characters with the ability of emotion self-control in IVE. The emotion model in this paper gives a quantitative description for emotion process.

The remainder of this paper is organized as follows: In the section 2, architecture of virtual character is described by cognitive model. In the section 3, emotion class of virtual characters is introduced. In the section 4, an emotion model of virtual characters is presented, if the intensity of an emotion stimulus is bigger than the resistive intensity of an emotion, an emotion will occur. In the section 5, a new model of

J. Tao, T. Tan, and R.W. Picard (Eds.): ACII 2005, LNCS 3784, pp. 629–636, 2005.

perception of 3D virtual character is presented. In the section6, emotional animation demo system of 3D virtual characters is realized. Finally, conclusion is in Section 7.

2 Architecture of 3D Virtual Characters

A virtual character can be regarded as an agent. An ideal agent is one that always does whatever action is expected to maximize its performance measure, on the basis of perception and built-in knowledge [3].

In this paper, architecture of virtual character is presented in Fig. 1.

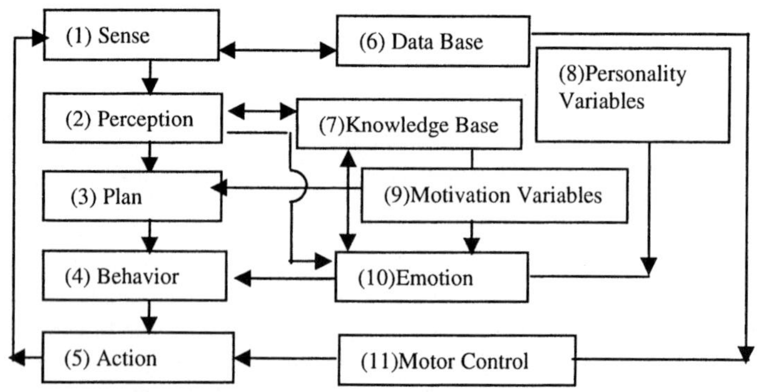

Fig. 1. Architecture of a 3D virtual character by cognitive model

(1) The sense module of character reads the database to the perception module.
(2) The perception module reads the knowledge base, and repairs the default motion plan and updates external stimulus.
(3) The plan module includes the current goals. It reads the knowledge base and makes behavior codes to behavior module.
(4) The behavior module is responsible for plan module and emotion module, and control the action module. Behaviors are expressed by a set of behavior codes, this module convert emotion expression code to behavior code.
(5) The action module uses the motion control module and executes the behavior. It will read motion capture data from database.
(6) The database module includes 3D geometry of virtual environment, original information and current state information, such as, the original location and parameters of virtual character, motion capture data, 3D model and location of objects, default motion plan scripts which record some goal location, and internal state for motivation variables.
(7) The knowledge base module includes some production rules in scripts that express the relations among motivation variable, emotion and behaviors.
(8) Personality variables are some stable psychological traits of a virtual character.
(9) Motivation variables include some physiology parameters of virtual character. For example, tiredness is one of motivation variables. We can set up a value between 0 and 1 to measure it. If the value is equal to 0, the character is not tired,

while if the value is equal to 1, the character is too tired. These two different states will influence emotion variously.

(10) The emotion module receives external information from perception, and reads motivation and personality variables. If an emotion is active, this module will create emotion expression, emotion expression code will be sent to behavior module.

(11) The motion control module includes inverse kinematics arithmetic and motion captures arithmetic.

3 Emotion Class of Virtual Characters

There are some classical research works in emotion model. The theories of emotion in psychology [5] demonstrate that emotion is a cognitive interpretation of those responses to emotional experiences. Emotion associates the environment stimulus with the character personality on the basis of James-Lange theory of emotion and Schachter-Singer theory of emotion, and occurs with motivation simultaneously. In some sense, motivation can intensify emotion, but emotion can also create motivation. Emotion is usually transitory, with a relatively clear beginning and ending, and a short duration. Ortony et al set up an emotion cognitive model that is called OCC model [6]. In the model, emotions are generated in reaction to objects, actions of agents and events. They outlined specifications for 22 emotion types. Picard gave the concept of affective computing for interface between human and computer [7]. In the opinion of Plutchik's emotion classification [8], emotion intensity distributes on a "circle" with eight basic categories of emotion that motivate various kinds of adaptive behavior of character. In the center of "circle", emotion intensity is zero, while in the edge of "circle" emotion intensity is one. In this paper, the simplified Plutchik's emotion classification on face expression is as follows: happiness, surprise, sadness, fear, disgust, and anger.

This paper integrates OCC emotion model and Plutchik's emotion classification together; a virtual character can have 22 types emotion in OCC model, and six basic face expressions. We can set a function from OCC emotion types to six face expressions in table 1.

Table 1. Relation between Plutchik's simplified emotion types and OCC emotion types

Plutchik's types	Emotion types in OCC model
Happiness	Happy-for, Gloating, Joy, Pride, Admiration, Love, Hope, Satisfaction, Relief, Gratification, Gratitude
Disgust	Hate
Anger	Anger, Reproach, Hate
Sadness	Resentment,Pity,Distress,Shame,Disappointment, Remorse
Fear	Fear, Fear-confirmed
Surprise	By context

4 Emotion Model of Virtual Characters

In this section, we give some new definitions for describing emotion process of virtual characters.

Definition 1. For a certain virtual character, ***BE*** is a basic emotion class set, ***BE***= $\{be_1, \ldots, be_N\}$, $i \in [0, N]$, be_i is a basic emotion (such as happy-for).N is the number of basic emotion class.

Definition 2. For a certain virtual character, *t* is time variable, $E(t)$ is emotion variable.

Definition 3. For an emotion variable $E(t)$, $\Theta_i[E(t)]$ is membership function for emotion class be_i, $\Theta_i[E(t)] \in [0,1]$.

If $\Theta_i[E(t)] = 0$, the virtual character has no emotion be_i; If $\Theta_i[E(t)]=1$, the virtual character has emotion be_i with intensity =1.

Definition 4. For a certain virtual character, $O_j(t)$ is an external stimulus, $j \in [0, no]$, *no* is the number of stimulus. $\Theta[O_{ji}(t)]$ is the stimulus intensity function of $O_j(t)$ for emotion class be_i, $\Theta[O_{ji}(t)] \in [0, 1]$.

Definition 5. For a certain external stimulus $O_j(t)$, $d_j(t)$ is distance from virtual character to center of stimulus $O_j(t)$.

In general, $\partial \Theta[O_{ji}(t)] / \partial d_j(t) < 0$, there exist two distance D_{max} and D_{min}, if $d_j(t) > D_{max}$, $\Theta[O_{ji}(t)]=0$; if $d_j(t) < D_{min}$, $\Theta[O_{ji}(t)]=1$.

Definition 6. For a certain virtual character, $C_i(t)$ is the resistive intensity of emotion class be_i, $i \in [0, N]$, The weaker $C_i(t)$ of a virtual character is, the more emotional the virtual character becomes to be with emotion class be_i. $C_i(t) \in [0, 1]$.

Definition 7. For a certain virtual character, $PS_k(t)$ is the personality variable, $\Theta[PS_k(t)]$ is the intensity of $PS_k(t)$, $k \in [1, nps]$, *nps* is the number of personality. $\Theta[PS_k(t)] \in [0, 1]$. In this paper, we use the Five Factor Model Personality [9][10], and PS1(t)=openness, $PS_2(t)$=conscientiousness, $PS_3(t)$=extraversion, $PS_4(t)$=agreeableness, $PS_5(t)$=neuroticism.

Definition 8. For a certain virtual character, $MV_m(t)$ is the motivation variable, m [1,*w*], *w* is the number of motivation variable. $\Theta[MV_m(t)]$ is the intensity of $MV_m(t)$, $\Theta[MV_m(t)] \in [0, 1]$. R_m is the weights of $MV_m(t)$, $R_m \in [0, 1]$, and

$$\sum_{m=1}^{w} R_m = 1 . \quad (1)$$

In this paper, *w* is 5 by Maslow's theory, and $MV_1(t)$=Physiological, $MV_2(t)$=Safety, $MV_3(t)$=Affiliation, $MV_4(t)$=Achievement, $MV_5(t)$=Self-Actualization.

Definition 9. For a certain $C_i(t)$, personality has impact on emotion state, α_{ki} is an impact coefficient from personality $PS_k(t)$ to $C_i(t)$. $NC_{ki}(t)$ is the updating $C_i(t)$ with considering impact from personality $PS_k(t)$, $NC_{ki}(t) = \min[\alpha_{ki} C_i(t), 1]$, $\alpha_{ki} >= 0$.

If $\alpha_{ki}=1$, $NC_{ki}(t)= C_i(t)$, personality has no impact on resistive intensity of emotion. $NC_i(t)$ is the updating $C_i(t)$ with considering impact from all personality variable,

$$NC_i(t)=\sum_{k=1}^{nps} \Theta\,[PS_k(t)]\,NC_{ki}(t) \;\Big/\; \sum_{k=1}^{nps} \Theta\,[PS_k(t)]. \tag{2}$$

Definition 10. For a certain $C_i(t)$, motivation has impact on emotion state, β_{mi} is an impact coefficient from motivation variable $MV_m(t)$ to $C_i(t)$. $MC_{mi}(t)$ is the updating $C_i(t)$ with considering impact from motivation variable $MV_m(t)$, $M\,C_{mi}(t)$=min[β_{mi} $C_i(t)$,1], β_{mi} >=0. If $\beta_{mi}=1$, $M\,C_{mi}(t)= C_i(t)$, motivation variable has no impact on emotion. $MC_i(t)$ is the updating $C_i(t)$ with considering impact from all motivation variable, and so:

$$MC_i(t)=\sum_{m=1}^{w} \Theta\,[MV_m(t)]\,R_m\,MC_{mi}(t) \;\Big/\; \sum_{m=1}^{w} \Theta\,[MV_m(t)]\,R_m. \tag{3}$$

Definition 11. For a certain $C_i(t)$, motivation and personality has impact on emotion state in the same time, $TC_i(t)$ is the updating $C_i(t)$ with considering impact both from personality and motivation. $TC_i(t)$=min($NC_i(t)$, $MC_i(t)$).

Definition 12. For a certain external stimulus $O_j(t)$ and resistive intensity of emotion $TC_i(t)$, the emotion trigger of $O_j(t)$ can be expressed as:

If $\Theta\,[O_{ji}(t)]$ - $TC_i(t)$<0, the emotion class be$_i$ is not active, $\Theta_{ji}[E(t)]$=0; If $\Theta\,[O_{ji}(t)]$ - $TC_i(t)$>0, the emotion class be$_i$ is active with the intensity $\Theta_i[E(t)]$, in this paper, $\Theta_{ji}\,[E(t)]$= [$\Theta\,[O_{ji}(t)]$ - $TC_i(t)$]/[1- $TC_i(t)$].

5 Perception of 3D Virtual Characters

3D Virtual characters should be equipped with visual, tactile and auditory sensors in order to execute the perception. This paper only discusses the visual perception of characters. Synthetic vision is an important method for visual perception [11], which can accurately simulate the vision from view of character. In this paper, each object is assigned a unique color code, to check which objects are visible to virtual character; the scene is rendered from the character's point of view with no texture (only with color by color ID for each object in Fig.2.), There are many characters in a complex IVE, synthetic vision will be costly. Furthermore, this method cannot get the semantic information for objects. Therefore, another method for simulation of visual perception is presented in this paper. Our method is based on the Gibson's theory of affordances[12], affordances are relations among space, time and action. A character can perceive these affordances directly. An affordance is invariance for environment. We set up some semantic information in database for special area or object in the 3D virtual environment. For example, when a character wants to walk across a road, only the zebra crossing is accessible, so that the character will select zebra crossing. Scene octree [11] can be used to simulate the character memory for static object in 3D vir

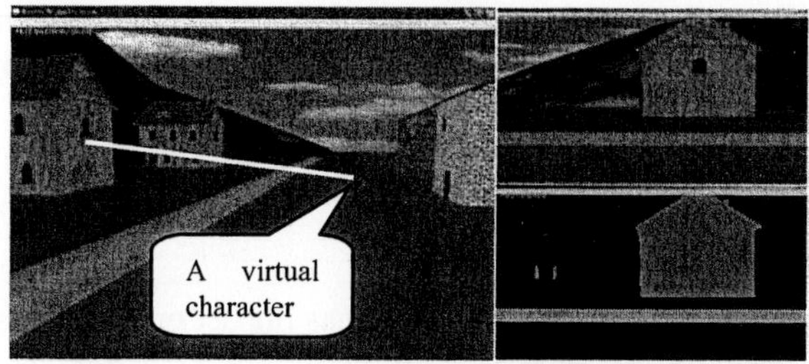

Fig. 2. A virtual character is watching a house on the left part of Fig.2; the right part of Fig.2 is vision image and synthetic vision image (in the bottom right corner)

tual environment in our demo system. With doing so, some navigating points can be set up in a 3D environment, and a character can seek the navigating point that is nearest to him and move to it. Usually, a character moves from one navigating point to another. A default plan is a script file that records default-navigating points of a character. If there is no external stimulus, a character walks by a walking plan. When a character perceives an object or events, he may stop walking and make some actions (such as avoiding object), then he continues walking to the nearest navigating point.

The visual perception of virtual character is limited to a sphere, with a radius of R and angle scope of θ. We adapt the method of Tu et al [2]. The vision sensor is at point O(the midpoint between the two eyes), and sets up local right-handed coordinate system. O is the origin and X axis is along front orientation. To determine if the object P is visible, the first step is to judge whether P is in the vision scope. If P is in the vision scope, the character detects whether other objects occlude it. The second step is to shoot a ray from O to P. If $\|P-O\| < R$ and the angle between the ray and X axis is less than $\theta/2$, the object is visible. In a 3D virtual environment, there are a lot of dynamic objects, on which we set up feature points (such as geometric center). If one feature point is visible, the object is regarded as visible.

6 Experimental Results

A Demo system of 3D virtual characters animation is developed with Visual c++ and Direct3D. Unlike traditional computer animation in 3D animation tool (such as Maya), the character in the demo system is autonomous and behavioral, the virtual character have the ability to sense and perceive virtual environment, the emotion behavior was expressed by the body pose movement and facial expression, users can rove the virtual world and watch the virtual characters from any position. Emotion interactions between two characters are nonverbal, all information of nonverbal emotion interaction will be sent to blackboard (a block of common memory that is used to share communication information among characters), each character will perceive the emotion state of others. Body pose animation and facial expression animation are integrated together by analytical inverse kinematics method and motion captures data, geometry blending is used to create facial expression animation.

In order to simplify perception model of virtual character, attention mechanisms should be integrated in process of perception. Virtual characters need not focus to all objects in virtual environment by attention mechanism of psychology. An attention object list which virtual character could focus to can be set up beforehand for different virtual characters. If an object is in the scope of perception, but is not in attention object list, then the character will not perceive the object. A snapshot of our demo system is shown in Fig. 3.

Fig. 3. John is selling drink, Marry is walking on road, Mike is searching on grass, a forklift is driving to Mike and John, when the forklift is near enough to John (the distance is less that 50m), John will express surprise emotion on face

7 Conclusion and Future Work

The paper can be summarized as follows:

1. Architecture of 3D virtual characters is presented. This model uses the motivation variables and personality variables to express internal physiology and psychology parameters.
2. A visual perception model is presented, some semantic information is set up for special area in virtual environment, and scene octree is used to simulate the character memory for space.

3. Emotion is active from external stimulus. If an intensity of stimulus is bigger than the resistive intensity of emotion, that emotion will occur. A computational model of emotion is presented.
4. A demo of emotional behavior animation is realized on PC.

The process of human emotion is very complex. this paper only gives a outline on stimulus and emotion. There is still much hard work to do. For the emotion model of virtual character in a large complex virtual environment, we hope to add uncertain reasoning models to describe emotion expression, and further study the emotion stimulus. Further more, we want to extend the demo system to construct emotional story and a virtual society of characters.

References

1. Aylett, R., Marc, C. : Intelligent Virtual Environments, A State-of-the art Report. Eurographics 2001, (2001) 87-109
2. Tu, X., Terzopoulos, D.: Artificial fishes: Physics, locomotion, perception, behavior, In Proc. SIGGRAPH'94 Conf, Orlando, FL USA, (1994) 43-50
3. Funge, J., Tu, X., Terzopoulos, D.: Cognitive Modeling: Knowledge, Reasoning and Planning for Intelligent Characters, In Proc. SIGGRAPH'99 Conf, Los Angeles, CA, (1999) 29-38
4. Badler, N., Phillips, C., Webber, B.: Simulating Humans: Computer Graphics Animation and Control, New York: Oxford University Press (1993) 154-159
5. Bernstein, D.A., Stewart, A.C., Roy, E.J., Wickens, C.D.: Psychology (forth edition), New York: Houghton Miffin Company (1997) 360-361
6. Ortony, A., Clore, G.L., Collins, A.: The cognitive structure of emotions. New York: Cambridge University Press (1988)
7. Picard, R.W.: Affective Computing, MIT Press, London, England (1997)
8. Available online: http://www.wikipedia.org/wiki/Emotion
9. Egges, A., Kshirsagar, S., Thalmann, N.M.: Generic personality and emotion simulation for conversational agents, Computer Animation and Virtual Worlds, 15, (2004) 1-13
10. Gratch, J., Marsella, S.: A Domain-independent framework for modeling emotion, Journal of Cognitive Systems Research, 5(4), (2004) 269-306
11. Noser, H., Renault, O., Thalmann.D., Thalmann, N.M.: Navigation for Digital Actors Based on Synthetic Vision, Memory, and Learning, Computer & Graphics, 19(1), (1995) 7-19
12. Gibson, J.J.: The ecological approach to visual perception.NJ:Lawrence Erlbaum Associates, Inc, Hillsdale(1986)

An Adaptive Personality Model for ECAs

He Xiao, Donald Reid, Andrew Marriott, and E.K. Gulland

Curtin University of Technology,
Hayman Rd. Bentley, Western Australia
raytrace@cs.curtin.edu.au

Abstract. Curtin University's Talking Heads (TH) combine an MPEG-4 compliant Facial Animation Engine (FAE), a Text To Emotional Speech Synthesiser (TTES), and a multi-modal Dialogue Manager (DM), that accesses a Knowledge Base (KB) and outputs Virtual Human Markup Language (VHML) text which drives the TTES and FAE. A user enters a question and an animated TH responds with a believable and affective voice and actions. However, this response to the user is normally marked up in VHML by the KB developer to produce the required facial gestures and emotional display. A real person does not react by fixed rules but on personality, beliefs, good and bad previous experiences, and training. This paper reviews personality theories and models relevant to THs, and then discusses the research at Curtin over the last five years in implementing and evaluating personality models. Finally the paper proposes an active, adaptive personality model to unify that work.

1 Introduction

Curtin's THs (or Embodied Conversational Agents (ECAs) [1, 2]), combine an MPEG-4 [3, 4] compliant FAE [5], a TTES [6, 7], a multi-modal DM [8-10], and a VHML [11-15] KB. A typical application uses a client to display one or more THs connected to one or more servers for the TTES and the DM. The use of VHML means that the application client can transparently be a plain text interface, a Web page, voice only, a TH with complex facial gestures, voice and emotion, or an entire Virtual Human with body language. A response from the KB could then simply be displayed, spoken, or enacted by a TH. If the client were a TH newsreader, a VHML news item example from the KB might be:

```
<sad>
  <pitch range="+150%" middle="-10%">
   And here's the latest <pitch middle="-18%">news.</pitch>
   <pause length="short"/> Detectives investigating the
   <emph>brutal</emph> murder of Sarah Payne, <blink/> have
   received 200 fresh calls from the public.
  </pitch><smile/>
</sad>
```

The text from this news report has been marked up by the KB developer, based upon their feeling for how the news should be read: overall a sad voice and posture, a pause after the first sentence for the listener to pay attention, emphasis on the word "brutal", a short blink at the sentence break, and a smile at the end of the second

J. Tao, T. Tan, and R.W. Picard (Eds.): ACII 2005, LNCS 3784, pp. 637 – 645, 2005.

sentence since it probably indicates good news. However, it must be noted that the marking up of this dynamic and constantly changing information by the KB developer is very tedious and time consuming. It would be more appropriate for the TH to deliver the information with its **own** emphasis, gestures, and emotions. That is, the TH would filter this information through its own personality by marking up the plain text with VHML, and this would impart a different "look and sound" to the news. This personality filtering is applicable to any information delivered by a TH. Ultimately, the TH's personality would make the interaction more human and more humane.

2 Personality Theories

It has been proposed that personality, mood and emotion are necessary for building believable ECAs [16-21]. Time duration is the main difference between these three components [20, 22, 23]. Figure 1 (from [20]) shows that emotion is a momentary state and mood is more static than emotion. Personality in contrast, does not change over time. Wilson[22] suggested that these three layers have different priorities for controlling behaviour: emotions have the highest priority whilst personality has the lowest. Moffat [23] also indicated a focus difference between emotion and personality. Emotions are focused on specific events, actions and objects whilst personality is more general. The investigation of relation and interaction among emotion, mood and personality is necessary to build a powerful personality model.

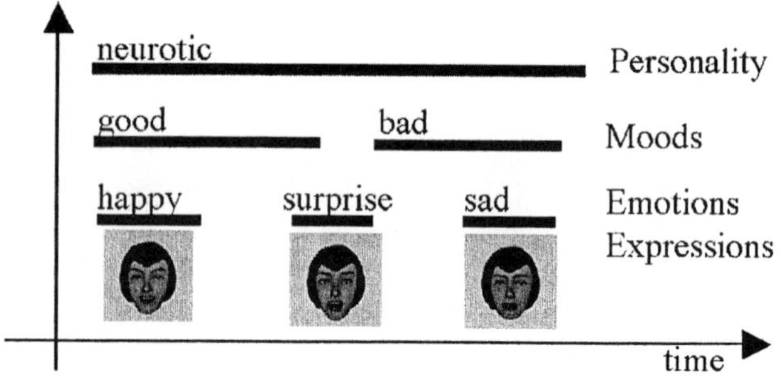

Fig. 1. Personality, Mood and Emotion [20]

Emotion

Emotion is a essential part of a believable ECA that communicates with humans [19, 24, 25]. Computer science researchers concerned with facial, body and vocal expressions, as well as the appraisal of an agent's emotions based on its reactions to objects, events and actions, have developed a number of emotional models (Reilly and Bates' Em [26], Gratch's Émile [27], Vélasquez's Cathexis [25] and Prendinger et al. SCREAM [28]). Many of these employed the cognitive appraisal model of OCC [29]. Emotions in the OCC model are the result of three kinds of appraisals: appraisal of the pleasantness of events with respect to the agent's goals, of the approval of the

Table 1. Basic emotions of the OCC and Ekman models

Model	Emotion types
OCC	Happy-for Resentment Gloating Pity Joy Distress Pride Shame Admiration Reproach Love Hate Satisfaction Fears-confirmed Relief Disappointment Gratification Remorse Gratitude Anger Hope and Fear
Ekman	Happiness Anger Disgust Sadness Surprise and Fear

actions of the agent or another agent with respect to a set of standards for behaviour, and of the liking of objects with respect to the attitudes of the agent [26]. The 22 emotion types modelled in OCC contrasts strongly with the 6 basic emotions of Ekman [30] that are widely used for facial and vocal expressions of an ECA. Table1 shows the emotion types of these models.

Bartneck [19], using OCC, split the emotion process into the following phases:

1. Find what emotional types are affected using the evaluation of an event, action or object based on the ECA's knowledge.
2. Calculate the intensities of the affected emotional types.
3. Interact the emotion value with the ECA's current emotional state.
4. Map the 22 OCC emotion types to a possible lower number of expression emotions available to the ECA. The ECA then renders its emotion through facial, body and vocal expressions.

Additionally, a phase is needed to blend emotion types to one emotion. This phase solves the problem of more than one emotion type being generated at each moment. For example, the ECA may be both happy because of an interesting topic, and disgusted with the user's silly questions.

Mood

Adopting a psychobiological perspective, mood is explained by Vélasquez [25] as a low level of arousal within an emotional system whilst emotion is explained as a high level of arousal. Mood is a necessary bridge which links personality to emotion expression since a personality models' high level descriptions make it difficult to directly control the emotions that are visible on the virtual face [20].

Kshirsagar [20] simply defined mood as one dimensional, going from bad mood to good mood, while Rousseau's social-psychological model [31] divided mood into two categories: agent-oriented moods, and self-oriented moods. The agent-oriented moods are directed toward other individuals whereas the self-oriented moods are not[31]. The distinction between self-oriented and agent-oriented moods can make a character rather happy in general, yet remain angry at a particular individual because of what he/she did to the character [31].

Personality

Personality represents those characteristics of the individual that account for consistent patterns of thinking, feeling and acting[32]. This broad definition of personality also indicates that personality makes people different from one another [33]. The definition can be adopted to describe the personality of an ECA as a relatively stable pattern that affects emotion expression and behaviour, and differentiates it from another ECA. Since psychologists have been interested in personality since the beginning of the last century, many researchers [20, 34, 35] have used the psychology literature for modelling an ECA's personality.

The first comprehensive theory of personality was Freud's psychoanalytical theory that attributed an individual's thoughts and actions to the unconscious in regulating behaviour [36]. Biological theories attempted to explain differences in behaviour in terms of differences in physiology, particularly brain function [33]. Social learning theories explained differences in behaviour in terms of a continuous reciprocal interaction between cognitive, behavioural, and environmental determinants [37]. Gordon Allport[42], Raymond Cattell and Hans Eysenck proposed trait theories that used traits as descriptors to describe personality [33]. Traits are labels given to consistent aspects of personality and are viewed as continuous dimensions [33]. Whether all people possess the same dimensions of personality and differ only in the value is still debated by psychologists. However, most trait theorists assume that all people have a fixed number of basic dimensions of personality: Eysenck and Eysenck's [38] two basic dimensions of personality, Cattell's 16 dimensions and Costa & McCrae's [39] Five Factor Model and so on. These theories are widely recognised, but there are few implemented ECA personality models (see Table 2).

Table 2. Trait theories

Trait theories	Dimensions	Computer Science Cases
Eysenck & Eysenck's 2 basic dimensions	Extraversion Neuroticism	
Five Factor Model	Openness Conscientiousness Extraversion Agreeableness Neuroticism	·Multilayer Personality Model [20] ·Fuzzy Agents with Personality [41] ·André's three lifelike characters project [18]
Interpersonal theory	Dominance Friendliness	·Breese and Ball's emotion/personality model [17] ·Nass et al. computer-based personality [34]

Most of the computational models of personality are based on trait theories because the traits that originate in everyday language are easy to understand, and the conversion from trait dimensions to a computational model is simple.

Rousseau [35] proposed 16 dimensions of personality that are based on the processes that intelligent agents usually perform. These 16 dimensions have been successfully applied in Cybercafé and Bui's ParleE [43]. The modelling of ECA's personality is not limited to trait theories. For example, the personality model of Rousseau and Hayes-Roth [31] adopted the psychology theories of social learning.

Psychologists Byrne et al. [44] indicated that humans prefer to interact with others who are similar in personality to themselves. Following this finding, human computer interaction research by Nass et al. [34] found that users are more satisfied with the interaction when the user and the computer have similar personalities. For example, a submissive user prefers a submissive ECA instead of a dominant one. It follows that an ECA system that allows a user to choose or develop a suitable personality for the ECA they interact with will result in a more satisfying interaction.

3 Curtin's Implemented Personality Applications

Shepherdson [45] focused on specific personality traits that could be modelled in an MPEG-4 compliant TH: dominance, submissiveness, friendliness and unfriendliness which are of their importance in interpersonal communication. The study used facial expressions of emotions, eye behaviour (gaze behaviour, eyelid closure and openness, eyelid blinks), mouth gestures, head movements (head-turning, head-nodding) and gestures (eyebrow raising and lowering) to convey different personality traits. Each of the chosen personality traits was modelled and stored in a personality (PST) file that directed the display and control of facial expressions.

Shepherdson [45] had the three hypotheses - the TH implementing personality will:

1. be able to communicate the spoken information to the user more effectively,
2. correctly exhibit personalities as intended by the author,
3. be perceived by users as a more humane interface.

Only the second hypothesis was proven conclusively although anecdotal evidence indicated some support for the other two. Also, to better differentiate the personalities, a bigger set of gestures is required and to be an effective communicator, a TH requires clear and audible speech from a better speech synthesis. Further, the research concluded that since personality is not just a single value (e.g. dominant), but a continuum of values, future work should allow the blending of personality traits.

Gulland [46] evaluated a case study built on the Five Factor Model. The Idolum framework demonstrated an idle-time behaviour of moods and emotions controlled by a consistent personality. In order to be more believable, Idolum took into account aspects of personality, mood and stimuli elements from psychological models such as a time cycle (winter/summer), the weather, or a manic/depressive cycle that can effect on emotional behaviour (see Figure 2). To avoid predictable and repetitive actions, which can hinder the believability of a character [47], it was seen as important to incorporate a small random factor in the change of emotional levels and the relevant behaviours calculated from these levels.

Another problem considered by Gulland was the action-expression problem [48] where two or more emotions are at similar levels and may compete unnaturally. This was solved by tracking the rate of change in each emotion and/or replacing conflicting emotions within a certain range of each other, with "confused-type" behaviours.

Building on this, Dam and de Souza [49] reported on a TH system that "learnt" the user's opinions about weather conditions so as to mimic the user's likes and dislikes. Although this "mimic personality" research was done in a limited domain, the results supported the research on personality compatibility done by Nass et al [34].

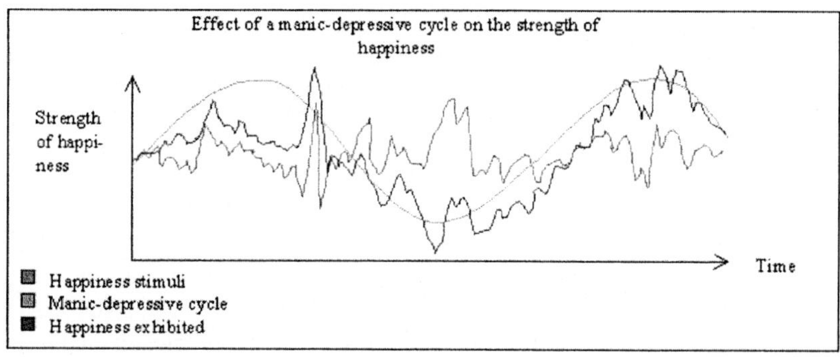

Fig. 2. Contrived example of the effect of a manic/depressive cycle on the strength of "happiness" exhibited (from Gulland [46])

Beard and Reid [50, 51] and Marriott [10] have continued in this research area by addressing the issues of personalities in THs, and the issues of human-TH interaction concerned with personality. For example, a user may be able to determine the personality of a TH through its voice and actions, but the opposite – the TH determining the personality of the user - is not true due to the single-modal input to the TH system from the user – plain text. To this end, the existing DM has been modified to cater for multi-modal input (such as emotion values). Although convoluted, the user can now also include emotion in the dialogue with a TH by manipulating graphical slider values for emotions. These emotions may enable a TH to determine the personality of the user over many interactions.

4 Curtin's Current Personality System

The applications of the previous section did not fully integrate the personality model into the TH – it was always an add-on either to the server or to the client. Current research efforts are concentrating on developing an integrated framework that can be used by both the client and the server, and that enables the displaying and evaluation of different personality theories. Figure 3 is a schematic of the developing system.

The Active Personality Model is Object Oriented code that is loaded and executed at runtime on both the server and client. The network channel will allow both system and user personality models to be used interchangeably, with the model being either sent from the server to the client or vice versa. The ability to create and load client-side user personality models allows for transparent research by disparate groups.

The Active Personality Model will "remember" user interactions through the use of per-user files that contain learnt preferences about how to interact with each user. The user interaction will change over time as the ECA personality changes the per-user file preferences.

This research is ongoing, with the existing ECA framework currently being modified to accommodate the Active Personality Model and its requirement to be used on both the client and the server. Several simple but easily identifiable personalities are currently being modelled for implementation. Evaluation is planned for late 2005.

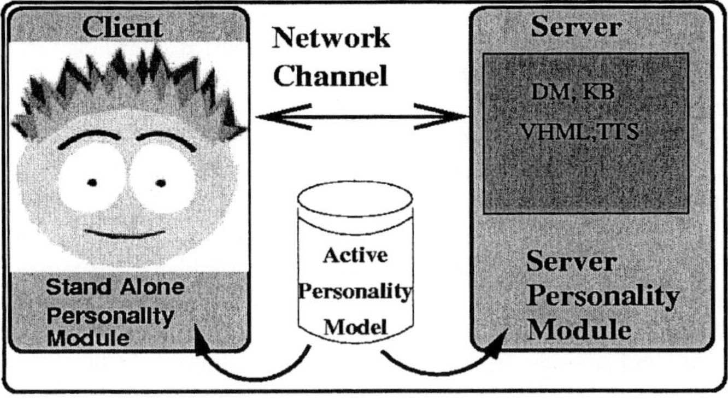

Fig. 3. An Active Personality Model

5 Conclusion

The design, implementation and evaluation of a personality model for an ECA is difficult, due to the "human" nature of personality. Some initial steps have been taken, and the current study, especially the evaluation method and the evaluation results, should be beneficial to other researchers in this relatively new area of ECA construction.

References

1. Cassell, J., et al., eds. Embodied Conversational Agents. 2001, MIT Press: Cambridge, MA, USA. 430.
2. Ruttkay, Z., C. Dormann, and H. Noot. Evaluating ECAs – What and how? in AAMAS Workshop on Embodied conversational agents. 2002. Bologna, Italy.
3. ISO/IEC, Text for ISO/IEC FDIS 14496-1 Systems. Online at http://www.cselt.it/mpeg/working_documents.htm. 1998a, ISO/IEC.
4. Pandzic, I.S. and R. Forchheimer, MPEG-4 Facial Animation - The standard, implementations and applications. 2002, Chichester, UK: John Wiley & sons.
5. Lavagetto, F. and R. Pockaj, The Facial Animation Engine: towards a high-level interface for the design of MPEG-4 compliant animated faces. IEEE Trans. on Circuits and Systems for Video Technology, 1999. 9(2).
6. Stallo, J., Simulating Emotional Speech for a Talking Head, in School of Computing. 2000, Curtin University of Technology: Perth, Australia.
7. Marriott, A., et al., The Face of the Future. Journal of Research and Practice in Information Technology, 2001b. 32(3/4): p. 231-245.
8. Marriott, A., A Facial Animation case study for HCI: the VHML-based Mentor System, in MPEG-4 Facial Animation - The standard, implementations and applications, I. Pandzic and R. Forchheimer, Editors. 2002, John Wiley: New York.
9. Marriott, A. and B. Shortland-Jones, The Mentor System, in "Tutorial Dialogue Systems: With a View Towards the Classroom" Workshop Proceedings of 11th International Conference on Artificial Intelligence in Education. 18 July 2003, AIED2003: Sydney, Australia.

10. Marriott, A. and S. Beard, gUI. Specifying Complete User Interaction, in Life-Like Characters. Tools, Affective Functions and Applications, H. Prendinger and M. Ishizuka, Editors. 2004, Springer-Verlag: Berlin, Germany. p. 111-134.
11. Marriott, A., VHML in Special IST 5th Framework workshop on VHML. 5-6 February 2002, European Union IST: Bruxelles, Belgium.
12. Marriott, A., et al., VHML - Directing a Talking Head in Active Media Technology LNCS 2252 J. Liu, et al., Editors. 2001, Springer: Hong Kong p. 90-100.
13. Gustavsson, C., L. Strindlund, and E. Wiknertz, Verification, Validation and Evaluation of the Virtual Human Markup Language (VHML), in Institutionen för Systemteknik. 2002, LIU: Linkoping.
14. Beard, S. and D. Reid. MetaFace and VHML: A First Implementation of the Virtual Human Markup Language. in AAMAS workshop on Embodied Conversational Agents - let's specify and evaluate them! 2002. Bologna, Italy: AAMAS 2002.
15. Marriott, A. and S. Beard, VHML Standardisation, in Special IST 5th Framework meeting on Representation Formats/Languages. 18 July 2002, European Union IST: Bologna, Italy.
16. Barker, T. The Illusion of Life Revisited. in AAMAS 2003 Workshop on Embodied conversational characters as individuals. 2003. Melbourne, Australia.
17. Breese, J. and G. Ball, Modeling Emotional State and Personality for Conversational Agents, in Technical Report. 1998, Microsoft Corporation.
18. André, E., et al. Integrating Models of Personality and Emotions into Lifelike Characters. in Proceedings of the workshop on Affect in Interactions - Towards a new Generation of Interfaces in conjunction with the 3rd i3 Annual Conference. 1999. Siena, Italy.
19. Bartneck, C. Integrating the OCC Model of Emotions in Embodied Characters. in Workshop on Virtual Conversational Characters: Applications, Methods, and Research Challenges. 2002. Melbourne.
20. Kshirsagar, S. A Multilayer Personality Model. in Proceedings of 2nd International Symposium on Smart Graphics. 2002. Hawthorne, New York.
21. Egges, A. and S. Kshirsagar, Generic Personality and Emotion Simulation for Conversational Agents. Computer Animation and Virtual Worlds, 2004. 15(1): p. 1-13.
22. Wilson, I. The Artificial Emotion Engine TM, Driving Emotional Behavior. in the AAAI 2000 Spring Symposium on Artificial Intelligence and Interactive Entertainment. 1999: AAAI Press.
23. Moffat, D., Personality Parameters and Programs, in Creating Personalities for Synthetic Actors. 1997, Springer Verlag: New York. p. 120-165.
24. Bates, J., The role of emotion in believable agents. Communications of the ACM, 1994. 37(7): p. 122-125.
25. Vélasquez, J.D. Modeling emotions and other motivations in synthetic agent. in Proceedings of the AAAI Conference 1997. 1997: AAAI Press and the MIT Press.
26. Reilly, W.S. and J. Bates, Building Emotional Agents. 1992, School of Computer Science, Carnegie Mellon University: Pittsburgh.
27. Gratch, J. Émile: Marshalling Passions in Training and Education. in Proceedings of the 4th International Conference on Autonomous Agents. 2000. Barcelona, Spain.
28. Prendinger, H., S. Descamps, and M. Ishizuka. Scripting the Bodies and Minds of Life-like Characters. in The 7th Pacific Rim International Conference on Artificial Intelligence,. 2002. Tokyo, Japan.
29. Ortony, A., G. Clore, and A. Collins, The Cognitive Structure of Emotions. 1988, Cambridge: Cambridge University Press.

30. Ekman, P., W.V. Friesen, and P. Ellsworth, Emotion in the Human Face: Guidelines for Research and an Integration of Findings, ed. A.P. Goldstein. 1972, New York: Pergamon Press Inc. 191.
31. Rousseau, D. and B. Hayes-Roth, A Social-Psychological Model for Synthetic Actors. 1997, Knowledge Systems Laboratory, Stanford University.
32. Pervin, L.A. and O.P. John, Personality: Theory and Research. 2001, New York: John Wiley & Sons, Inc. 656.
33. Hewstone, M., F.D. Fincham, and J. Foster, eds. Psychology. 2005, Blackwell: Oxford.
34. Nass, C., et al., Can Computer Personalities Be Human Personalities? International Journal of Human-Computer Studies, 1995. 43(2): p. 223-239.
35. Rousseau, D. Personality in Computer Characters. in Proceedings of the 1996 AAAI Workshop on Entertainment and AI / A-Life. 1996. Portland.
36. Myers, D.G., Psychology. 2004, New York: Worth publishers. 741.
37. Bandura, A., Social Learning Theory. 1977: Prentice-Hall Inc.
38. Eysenck, S.B.G. and H.J. Eysenck, The validity of questionnaire and rating assessments of extraversion and neuroticism, and their factorial stability. British Journal of Psychology, 1963. 54(1): p. 51-62.
39. McCrae, R.R. and O.P. John, An introduction to the five-factor model and its applications. Journal of Personality, 1992. 60: p. 175-215.
40. Acton, G.S., Interpersonal Theory. 1998.
41. Ghasem-Aghaee, N. and T.I. Ören. Towards Fuzzy Agents with Dynamic Personality for Human Behavior Simulation. in Proceedings of the 2003 Summer Computer Simulation Conference. 2003. Montreal, PQ, Canada.
42. Allport, G.W., Personality: A psychological interpretation. 1937, New York: Henry Holt.
43. Bui, T.D., et al. ParleE: An adaptive plan-based event appraisal model of emotions. in Proceedings KI 2002, 25th German Conference on Artificial Intelligence. 2002. Aachen: Springer.
44. Byrne, D., W. Griffitt, and D. Stefaniak, Attraction and Similarity of Personality Characteristics. Journal of Personality and Social Psychology, 1967. 5: p. 82-90.
45. Shepherdson, R.H., The personality of a Talking Head, in School of Computing. 2000, Curtin University of Technology: Perth, Australia.
46. Gulland, E.K., Psychological Modelling of an Asynchronous Idle-Time Personality for a Talking Head, in School of Computing. 2001, Curtin University of Technology: Perth, Australia.
47. Lester, J.C. and B.A. Stone. Increasing Believability in Animated Pedagogical Agents. in First International Conference on Autonomous Agents. 1997: ACM.
48. Petta, P. Principled generation of expressive behavior in an interactive exhibit. in Workshop on Emotion-Based Agent Architectures. 1999. Seattle, USA.
49. Dam, H. and S.d. Souza. Applying Talking Head Technology to a Web based Weather Service. in Virtual Conversational Characters Workshop, Human Factors 2002. 2002. Melbourne.
50. Beard, S., D. Reid, and R. Shepherdson. Believable and Interactive Talking Heads for Websites: MetaFace and MPEG-4. in 6th International Computer Science Conference: Active Media Technology. 2001. Hong Kong.
51. Beard, S., MetaFace: A Virtual Face Framework and Metaphor, in Department of Computer science. 2004, Curtin University of Technology: Perth, Western Australia.

The Effect of Mood on Self-paced Study Time

Yong Niu[1,2] and Xiaolan Fu[1,*]

[1] State Key Laboratory of Brain and Cognitive Science, Institute of Psychology, Chinese Academy of Sciences, Beijing, China 100101
{niuy, fuxl}@psych.ac.cn
[2] Graduate School of the Chinese Academy of Sciences, Beijing, China 100039

Abstract. The present study investigated the effect of mood on self-paced study time. Twenty-eight university students voluntarily participated in the experiment. Half of them listened to positive music and the other half listened to negative music for nine minutes. After self-assessment of mood, they made self-paced study for word-pairs. The results showed that negative and positive mood have not significant effect on self-paced study time.

1 Introduction

Metacognition includes monitoring process and control process [28]. Underlying much of the work on metacognition is a view of the person as an organism that actively monitors and regulates their cognitive processes towards the achievement of particular goals [20]. Allocation of self-paced study time is one of important components in control process [24]. Self-directed learning is central both to everyday memory performance and to achievement in education [5], [17], [29]. There are many factors influence the allocation of self-paced study time, such as the difficulty of item [8], [9], [10], the norm of study [12], [21], [27], the total time available [31], [33], judgments of interest for items [34], and reward benefits [12]. However, there was few research which had been done to investigate the effect of mood on the allocation of self-paced study time.

Mood is often described as diffuse and long-lasting affective states [25]. They are experienced without simultaneous awareness of their causes [4], [6], [9], [30], [35]. According to a recent integrative theory, the mood-behavior model (MBM) [15], moods do not have stable motivational implications, but they can influence behavior through two processes. The relevant process in the present context is the informational mood impact. It means that moods influence evaluative behavior-related judgments and appraisals. Moods can influence these appraisals in terms of mood congruency effects in that people are more optimistic in a positive mood than in a negative mood. These mood-influenced appraisals — which are explicable as the product of an information integration process in which mood, as a piece of information, is integrated with all other available information into a judgment [1], [2], [3], [15] — will result in behavioral adjustments.

The present research deals with the effect of different moods on allocation of self-paced study time. We predicted that negative mood may result the longer time for items because there are higher subjective demand and higher effort-related autonomic activity in negative context than in positive context [16].

* Corresponding author.

J. Tao, T. Tan, and R.W. Picard (Eds.): ACII 2005, LNCS 3784, pp. 646 – 651, 2005.

2 Method

2.1 Participants and Design

Twenty-eight university students with various majors (14 women and 14 men with an average age of 21.43 years) voluntarily attended the study and received a small amount of money. Participants were randomly divided into 2 groups. A 2 (mood valence: negative vs. positive) ×2 (word-pairs difficulty: related vs. unrelated) mixed-model design in which mood valance was between-subject variable and word-pairs was within-subject variable. Both related word-pairs and unrelated word-pairs were used to increase the variability of difficulty across items. The gender was balanced between two mood valence conditions. Dependent variables were self-paced study time and recall performance.

2.2 Materials and Apparatus

Items consisted of 30 paired associates in which 15 were related pairs (e.g., star-sky), and 15 were unrelated (e.g., corn-map). Computers displayed all instructions and controlled all aspects of the word-pairs study procedure. The Computers also recorded participants' responses.

2.3 Procedure

The study was announced as a test about music and words. On arriving at the laboratory, participants were instructed to sit for ten minutes and read newspapers. The purpose was to make them habituate the environment of laboratory and keep calm.

2.3.1 Mood Induction

After the habituation period we introduced the mood introduction procedures. In accordance with the conceptualization of mood as a not object-related state, we did not mention that we were interested in participants' affective reactions and introduced the mood inductions as "tasks" in which we would test their knowledge about the music they would listen. In the music conditions participants received headphones and read "Task 1: Listening to pieces of music." Participants in the music-negative-mood condition listened to a sad China-qin piece (Hu jia shi ba pai, composed by Cai, Wen-ji) for nine minutes. Participants in the music-positive-mood condition listened to 3 easy listening pieces for nine minutes: "Laugh in sea" (composed by Huang Zhan), "Gong and drum for bumper" (composed by Peng Xiuwen & Cai Huiquan), and "Jiu Jiu Yan yang tian" (composed by Gao Ruxing). These pieces of music have been selected by specialists and rated by 30 graduate students.

After the mood inductions, participants received a questionnaire that contained several questions about the music (e.g., "Are you familiar with the pieces of music?" and "What music instruments are the pieces of music played by?"). Embedded into these questions was the mood manipulation check with the Positive Hedonic Tone (happy, joyful, contented, and cheerful) and Negative Hedonic Tone (sad, frustrated, depressed, and dissatisfied) scales of the UWIST Mood Adjective Checklist [23]. Participants rated the extent to which each of the eight adjectives reflected their momentary feeling state ("Right now, I'm feeling …"). Scales ranged from 0 (not at all) to 6 (very much).

2.3.2 Word-Pair Study

Once participants completed the questionnaire, they received instructions which presented on screen of computer:

We will study 30 word-pairs which will be presented on screen in turn. Each word-pair only will be presented once. When you think that you have remembered the word-pair, you can press space key to study the next word-pair. Please study attentively. After you study all of word-pairs, we will present the first word of every word-pair on screen in turn and ask you to write the correspondent word.

After participants understand the instructions, they began self-paced study. When a participant pressed the space key to begin a given trial, the first item was presented. The item remained on the screen until the participant again pressed the space keys, which result in the presentation of the next item. Study time for that item was operationalized as the time between the presentation of an item for study and the following participant-initiated key press.

Presentation of the last item selected for restudy was followed by a 30-s distractor task, which in turn was followed by paired-associate recall. For each recall trial, the cue of an item was presented, and participants were instructed to either write the correct response down on paper and then press the space key or directly press the space key if they felt that they did not remember the answer. Then the cue of the next item was presented on screen. The presentation order of items was randomized anew. After the final item was presented for recall, participants were debriefed and received their payment.

Before mood inductions, participants made a short practice in order to grasp the procedure of self-paced study for word-pairs.

3 Results

3.1 Mood Manipulation Checks

We created mood scores for each participant by summing the Positive Hedonic Tone scale values with the reverse-coded Negative Hedonic Tone scale values of the UWIST Mood Adjective Checklist (Cronbach's $\alpha = .86$). This way, higher values reflect a more positive mood. The mood manipulation procedure was checked by independent samples t-Test of the self-reported mood rating. The mood manipulation procedure was effective as there was significant effect of mood induction $t\ (1, 27) = 4.699$, $p < 0.01$.

3.2 Self-paced Study Time

For each participant, we computed the mean of study time (s) for related word-pairs and unrelated ones separately. Means across individual's mean of study time are reported in the top half of Table 1.

The effect of moods (negative vs. positive) and difficulty of items (related vs. unrelated) on study time were assessed by 2 (moods) × 2 (difficulty of items) analysis of variance (ANOVA). The main effect of moods was not reliable, $F(1, 27) = 0.774$, $MSE = 4084772.71$. The main effect of difficulty of items was reliable, $F(1, 27) = 106.831$, $MSE = 4084772.71$, $p < 0.01$. Study time was reliably greater for unrelated word-pairs than for related word-pairs. The interaction between mood and difficulty of items was not reliable, $F(1, 27) = 0.035$, $MSE = 0.853$.

3.3 Recall Performance

For each participant, the proportion of items that were correctly recalled was calculated separately for each item difficulty condition. Means across individual's proportion of correctly recalled items are reported in Table 1.

Table 1. Self-paced study time (s) and recall performance (%)

	Related word-pairs		Unrelated word-pairs	
	Positive	Negative	Positive	Negative
Self-paced study time	4434 (2747)	3998 (1065)	8980 (3560)	8346 (3852)
Recall performance	86.2 (17.47)	83.8 (14.13)	51.93 (21.2)	60.93 (24.67)

Entries are mean across individual's self-paced study time (s) and the mean across individual's proportion of correct recall performance. Values in parentheses are standard errors of the means.

The effect of moods (negative vs. positive) and difficulty of items (related vs. unrelated) on recall performance were assessed by 2 (moods) × 2 (difficulty of items) analysis of variance (ANOVA). The main effect of mood was not reliable, $F(1, 27) = 0.256$, $MSE = 13.687$. The main effect of difficulty of items was reliable, $F(1, 27) = 49.682$, $MSE = 5.176$, $p < 0.01$. Recall performance was reliably greater for unrelated word-pairs than for related word-pairs. The interaction between mood and difficulty of items was not reliable, $F(1, 27) = 1.987$, $p = 0.17$.

4 Discussion

The present study investigated mood states' impact on self-paced study time. But we did not find any reliable differences between negative and positive mood. There may be two reasons. First, there are great individual differences about the allocation of self-paced study time. We can see that the standard deviations are high. Second, although we use instructions to prevent the participants knowing our experimental goal, some participants may still guess the real purpose of the music, which can reduce mood's informational impact on subsequent self-paced study. This is because when people know the actual source of their moods, mood congruency effects disappear [7], [14], [18], [19], [31], [32]. We will explore the effect of mood on self-paced study time further by using within-design of mood and more strict control.

In additional, from our results we can see the difficulty of items have significant effect on self-paced study time. People spend more time on more difficult items, which is consistent with the previous studies [12], [21], [26].

Acknowledgement

This research was supported in part by grants from 973 Program of Chinese Ministry of Science and Technology (2002CB312103), from the National Natural Science Foundation of China (60433030 and 30270466), and from the Chinese Academy of Sciences (0302037).

References

1. Abele, A., Gendolla, G.H.E., Petzold, P.: Positive mood and ingroup-outgroup differentiation in a minimal group paradigm. Personality and Social Psychology Bulletin. 24 (1998) 1343-1357
2. Abele, A., Petzold, P.: How does mood operate in an impression formation task? An information integration approach. European Journal of Social Psychology. 24 (1994) 173-187
3. Abele, A., Gendolla, G.H.E.: Satisfaction judgments in positive and negative moods: Effects of concurrent assimilation and contrast producing processes. Personality and Social Psychology Bulletin. 25 (1999) 892-905
4. Averill, J.R.: A constructivist view of emotions. In R. Plutchik, H. Kellerman (Eds.), Emotions: Theory, research, and experience (Vol. 1, pp. 305-339), New York: Academic Press (1980)
5. Bjork, R.A.: Memory and metamemory: Considerations in the training of human beings. In: Metcalfe, J., Shimamura, A.P. (Eds.), Metacognition: Knowing About Knowing, MIT Press, Cambridge, MA (1994)
6. Bollonow, O.F.: Das Wesen der Stimmungen [The origin of moods]. Frankfurt, Germany: Klostermann (1956)
7. Clore, G.L.: Cognitive phenomenology: Feelings and the construction of judgment. In L. L. Martin, A. Tesser (Eds.), The construction of social judgment (pp. 133-163), Hillsdale, NJ: Erlbaum (1992)
8. Dufresne, AKobasigawa□A.: Developmental differences in children's spontaneous allocation of study time. The Journal of Generic Psychology. 149 (1988) 87-92
9. Dufresne, A., & Kobasigawa, A.: Children's spontaneous allocation of study time: Differential and sufficient aspects. Journal of Experimental Child Psychology. 47 (1989) 274-296
10. Dunlosky, J., Cornor, L.T.: Age differences in the allocation of study time account for age differences in memory performance. Memory & Cognition. 25 (1997) 691-700
11. Hertzog, C.: Older and younger adults use a functionally identical algorithm to select items for restudy during multitrial learning. Journals of Gerontology: Series B: Psychological Sciences and Social Sciences. 52 (1997) 178-186.
12. Dunlosky, J., Thiede, K.W.: What makes people study more? An evaluation of four factors that affect people's self-paced study. Acta Psychologica. 98 (1998) 37-56
13. Frijda, N.: Moods, emotion episodes, and emotions. In M. Lewis, J. M. Haviland (Eds.), Handbook of emotions (pp. 381-403). New York: Guilford Press (1993)
14. Gasper, K., & Clore, G.L.: The persistent use of negative affect by anxious individuals to estimate risk. Journal of Personality and Social Psychology. 74 (1998) 1350-1363.
15. Gendolla, G.H.E.: On the impact of mood on behavior: An integrative theory and a review. Revieww of General Psychology. 4 (2000) 378-408.
16. Gendolla, G.H.E., Abele, A., Krusken, J.: The informational impact of mood on effort mobilization: A study of cardiovascular and electrodermal responses. Emotion. 1 (2001) 12-24
17. Hertzog, C., Dunlosky, J.: The aging of practical memory: An overview. In: Hermann, D.J., McEvoy, C., Hertzog, C., Hertel, P., Johnson, M. K. (Eds.), Basic and Applied Memory Research: Theory in Context, vol. 1. Lawrence Erlbaum, Hillsdale, NJ (1996)
18. Hirt, E.R., Levine, G.M., McDonald, H.E., Melton, J., Martin, L.L.: The role of mood in quantitative and qualitative aspects of performance: Single or multiple mechanisms. Journal of Experimental Social Psychology. 33 (1997) 602-629.

19. Keltner, D., Lock, K.D., Audrain, P.C.: The influence of attribution on the relevance of negative feelings to personal satisfaction. Personality and Social Psychology Bulletin. 19 (1993) 21-29
20. Koriat, A., Metacognition research: an interim report. In T.J. Perfect, B.L. Schwartz: (Eds.), Applied Metacognition (pp. 39-67). Cambridge University Press (2002)
21. Le Ny, J.F., Denhiere, G., Le Taillanter, D.: Regulation of study-time and interstimulus similarity in self-paced learning conditions. Acta Psychologica. 36 (1972) 280-289
22. Masur, E.F.., McIntyre, C.W., Flavell, J.H.: Developmental changes in apportionment of study time among items in a multitrial free recall task. Journal of Experiemental Child Psychology. 15 (1973) 237-246
23. Matthews, G.., Gaschke, Y,N., Chamberlain, A.G..: Refining the measurement of mood: The UWIST Mood Adjective Checklist. British Journal of Psychology. 81 (1990) 17-42
24. Metcalfe, J., Shimamura, A.P.: Metacognition: Knowing About Knowing. MIT Press, Cambridge, MA (1994)
25. Morris, W.N.: Mood: The frame of Mind. New York: Springer (1989)
26. Nelson, T.O., Dunlosky, J., Graf, A., Narens, L.: Utilization of metacognitive judgments in the allocation of study during multitrial learning. Psychological Science. 5 (1994) 207-213
27. Nelson, T.O., Leonesio, R.J.: Allocation of self-paced study time and the "labor-in-vain effect." Journal of Experimental Psychology: Learning, memory and Cognition. 14 (1988) 676-686
28. Nelson, T.O., Narens, L.: Metamemory: A theoretical framework and new findings. In: Bower, G.H. (Ed.), The Psychology of Learning and Motivation, vol. 26. Academic Press, New York (1990) 125-141
29. Schunk, D.H., Zimmerman, B.J.: Self-regulation of learning and performance. Lawrence Erlbaum, Hillsdale, NJ (1994)
30. Schwarz, N.: Feelings as information: Information and motivational functions of affective states. In E.T. Higgins, R.M. Sorrentino (Eds.): Motivation and cognition: Foundations of social behavior (Vol, 2, pp. 527-561). New York: Guilford Press (1990)
31. Schwarz, N., & Clore, G.L.: Mood, misattribution, and judgments of well-being: Informative and directive functions of affective states. Journal of Personality and Social Psychology. 45 (1983) 513-523
32. Thiede, K.W., Dunlosky, J.: Toward a general model of self-regulated study: an analysis of selection of items for study and self-paced study time. 25 (1999) 1024-1037
33. Sinclair, R.C., Mark, M.M., Clore, G.L.: Mood-related persuasion depends on (mis)attributions. Social Cognition. 12 (1994) 309-326
34. Son, L.K., Metcalfe, J.: Metacognitive and control strategies in study-time allocation. Journal of Experimental Psychology: Learning, memory and Cognition. 26 (2000) 204-221
35. Wyer, R.S., Clore, G.L., Isebell, L.M.: Affect and information processing. In M. P. Zanna (Ed.), Advances in experimental social psychology (Vol. 31, pp. 1-77). New York: Academic Press (1999)

The Effect of Embodied Conversational Agents' Speech Quality on Users' Attention and Emotion

Noël Chateau, Valérie Maffiolo, Nathalie Pican, and Marc Mersiol

France Telecom, R&D Division, Technology Research Center,
2 avenue Pierre-Marzin, 22307, Lannion, France
{noel.chateau, valerie.maffiolo, nathalie.pican, marc.mersiol}@francetelecom.com

Abstract. This study investigates the influence of the speech quality of Embodied Conversational Agents (ECAs) on users' perception, behavior and emotions. Twenty-four subjects interacted in a Wizard of Oz (WOZ) setup with two ECAs in two scenarios of a virtual theater partner application. In both scenarios, each ECA had three different speech qualities: natural, high-quality synthetic and low-quality synthetic. Eye gaze data show that subjects' visual attention was not influenced by ECA's speech quality, but by their look. On the other hand, subjects' self-report of emotions and verbal descriptions of their perceptions were influenced by ECAs' speech quality. Finally, Galvanic Skin Response data were neither influenced by ECAs' look, nor by their speech quality. These results stress the importance of the correct matching of the auditory and visual modalities of ECAs and give methodological insights for the assessment of user's perception, behavior and emotions when interacting with virtual characters.

1 Introduction

Embodied Conversational Agents (ECAs) are synthetic characters that users can communicate with for various purposes, ranging from information delivery to education [2]. A large volume of past research has focused on developing their behavior and personality in order to improve their autonomy [15], while most recent developments have targeted at including emotion management in user-ECA interaction [2, 11, 15]. These efforts aim at improving several aspects in user-ECA interaction that address design, usability, practical usage and user perception questions [11].

Concerning the design question, on the vocal side, the ECA community can benefit from recent progresses achieved by the speech technology community on the development of expressive synthetic speech (e.g., [1, 10]). Integrating expressive synthetic speech may bring significant improvements on four main levels:

- First, users might be more stimulated and engaged in the interaction since it has already been shown that a simple tuning of a speech synthesizer to an extrovert voice style, based on prosody and volume manipulation, can stimulate the engagement of young users in the interaction with ECAs [4].
- Second, as attention to speech is partly driven by prosodic patterns [7], expressive synthetic speech where prosody is finely controlled could probably better capture users' attention, improving their understanding, memorization and

J. Tao, T. Tan, and R.W. Picard (Eds.): ACII 2005, LNCS 3784, pp. 652–659, 2005.

engagement in the conversation. Attention to speech could also influence visual attention to the ECA.

- Third, as affective loops influence the engagement of users in interaction with systems [6], if ECA could express emotions by speech, in return, users could be more engaged in the emotional dimension of the interaction, feeling and expressing their emotions.
- Fourth, as expressivity is highly contributive to the naturalness of synthetic speech which is itself contributive to its global quality [13], expressive synthetic speech could enhance the global perceived quality of ECAs and therefore their credibility [16].

These research hypotheses are quite hard to tackle since little is known about the impact of expressivity, and more generally of quality of synthetic speech on user-ECA interactions. Indeed, as observed by [4], up to now, most design questions of ECAs have addressed the graphics design but not the auditory design.

The goal of the present study is to investigate the impact of ECAs' speech quality on users' perception, behavior and emotions, in the context of a Virtual Theater Partner (VTP) application. This application allows users to play small scenes of theater plays by interacting with a VTP embodied by an ECA. This test was oriented to the analysis of users' reactions and not to the efficacy of the application in terms of performance of learning, so no data were collected regarding this aspect of the application. As the tested application may be adapted in the future to adults or children, adults as well as children participated to the experiments.

2 Test Setup

2.1 The Virtual Theater Partner Application

Subjects interacted with the VTP application in two scenarios. The VTPs were based on two virtual characters developed by France Telecom [12]. In a first scenario (called the Prince scenario), the VTP played the role of the business man and the subject had to play the role of a child. In a second scenario (called the Lesson scenario), the VTP played the role of a female professor and the subject had to play the role of the student.

The interaction was based on the WOZ methodology. Before the test, subjects were told they would interact orally with their VTP, using speech recognition. Therefore, they only had to play their lines and the VTP would play his/hers. During the test, the only peripheral devices used were the screen (including an infrared video camera for eye-tracking), one loudspeaker and a microphone (meant to be connected to the speech recognition engine). In reality, the different lines of the VTP were pre-treated prior to the test and stored as video files on the computer. Located in another room with an audiovisual feedback of the subject, the experimenter launched the appropriate video file after the ending of each line of the subject.

Figure 1 shows a screenshot of the user interface for the Prince scenario. On the left side appears the video frame where was displayed the VTP. On the right side appear the different lines that the subjects had to play. As we suspected that the presence of the lines played by the VTP could influence subjects' eye gaze, only subjects' lines appeared on the interface. They were grouped in three paragraphs that corresponded to three sessions of the test during which the VTP had a different speech quality.

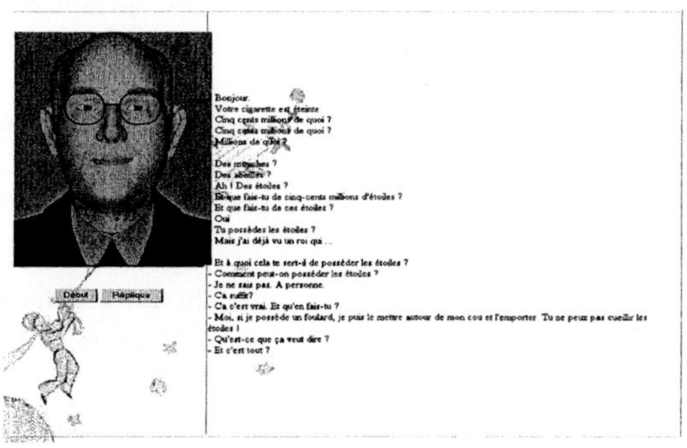

Fig. 1. Screenshot of the application for the Prince scenario

2.2 Test Protocol

Three independent variables were manipulated during the test. The first one was the VTP associated to the scenario: in the Prince scenario, the VTP was a man and in the Lesson scenario, a woman.

The second independent variable was the speech quality. For each scenario, a natural voice and two synthetic voices were used. The natural voices (a male for business man and a female for the professor) were recorded from amateur actors. Synthetic voices were produced by France Telecom's TTS technology. The diphon version of France Telecom's TTS was used. A first quality level used a built-in prosodic pattern and a second one used the prosodic pattern extracted from the analysis of the corresponding natural voice's recordings. Therefore, for each scenario, the main difference in quality between the two synthetic voices came from the naturalness of the prosody: the low-quality (LQ) version had an unspecific prosodic pattern whereas the high-quality (HQ) one had a prosodic pattern specifically tuned for the VTP application.

The third independent variable was the age of the subjects. Seventeen adult subjects (age ranging from 19 to 47, mean = 27,2) and seven children (age ranging from 11 to 14, mean = 12,7) participated to the test.

The three independent variables were manipulated as follows: twelve subjects (nine adults and three children) ran the prince scenario then, after a little break, the lesson scenario, and the twelve others the other way round. Each scenario was split in three sessions. During one session, the VTP had one of the three speech qualities (Natural, HQ Synthetic, LQ Synthetic). In order to counterbalance order effects, the three voices were presented in a 3x3 latin-square to three sub-groups of four subjects each.

In order to assess their emotional reaction during their interaction with the VTP, at the end of each session, subjects had to fill in a PrEmo form by ticking one or several cartoons reflecting their emotional state during the interaction. This form is a static version of the PrEmo questionnaire consisting in eighteen short clips of a cartoon expressing nine positive and nine negative emotions (see details in [5]).

Finally, at the end of the test, subjects had a 30-min interview with the experimenter. During this interview, subjects were asked to freely verbalize their perception and feelings regarding the different aspects of the test (VTP's look, speech, behavior, personality and credibility; easy of use and utility of the application). Each session lasted approximately 90 to 120 sec. A whole scenario lasted approximately 15 min.

During the test, the AMUSE tool was used to record subject's eye gaze and Galvanic Skin Response (GSR) [3]. Table 1 gives the list of dependent variables that were derived from eye gaze and GSR data.

Table 1. Dependent variables derived from eye gaze and GSR data

Variable	Description
PT_VTP[1]	time percentage of the interaction during which users looked at the VTP frame
PT_lines	time percentage of the interaction during which users looked at their lines
PT_other	time percentage of the interaction during which users looked at somewhere else than the VTP or their lines
GSR[2]	mean GSR during the interaction
GSR_VTP[3]	mean GSR when subjects looked at the VTP during the interaction
GSR_lines	mean GSR when subjects looked at their lines during the interaction
GSR_other	mean GSR when subjects looked at somewhere else than the VTP or their lines

3 Results

Adults and children eye gaze and GSR data were analyzed separately and revealed no significant differences between the two groups. However, the small number of children does not allow a powerful and reliable statistical analysis. Consequently, eye gaze and GSR data from the two groups were merged for statistical analysis. Due to glasses or contact lenses, three adults and one child failed the calibration procedure for the eye-tracker. Consequently, the AMUSE tool was not used for them and the data analysis is only based on the data of fourteen adults and six children.

3.1 Eye Gaze and GSR Data

Figure 2 shows the mean percentage of time subjects looked at the three zones defined for the analysis for the two scenarios and the three speech qualities. It can be observed that for the Prince scenario, subjects share their eye gaze between the VTP and their lines around a 50 % - 50 % balance. The influence of voice quality seems to be small and was not found significant on the three dependent variables. In the Lesson scenario, subjects tend to be much more distracted since they spend around 20 to 25 % of the interaction time looking somewhere else than their lines or the VTP.

---

1 Fixation durations shorter than 300 ms were considered as saccadic eye movements and filtered out [14].

2 Individual GSR data were normalized for each subject by subtracting his/her average GSR data on the six sessions.

3 Considering an average latency of 1.4 sec of GSR signals [8], GSR_VTP, GSR_lines and GSR_other signals were taken into account only after a 1.4-sec fixation duration.

Globally, from the Prince to the Lesson scenario, PT_VTP falls of 14 % and PT_lines of 8 %. A significant main effect of scenario was found for the PT_VTP variable (F(1,19) = 4.55, *p<0.05*) and the PT_other variable (F(1,19)=5.32, *p<0.05*). No significant interactions between speech quality and scenario were found for the three variables.

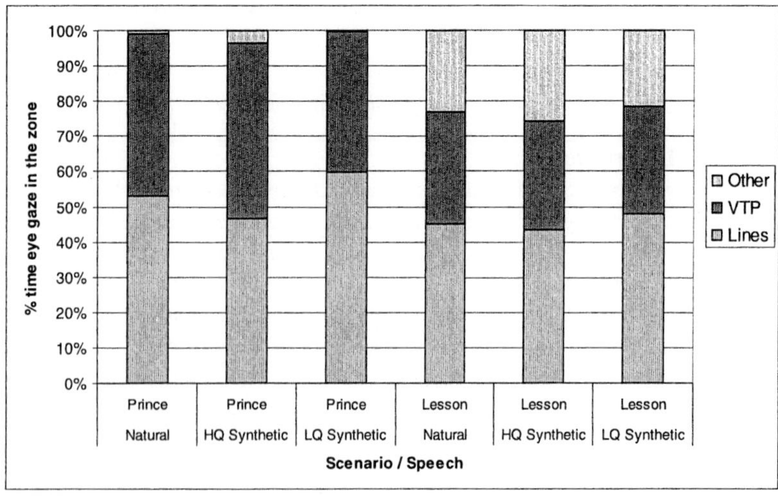

Fig. 2. Mean percentages of time subjects look at their lines (strips), the VTP (bricks) or somewhere else dots) for the two scenarios (Prince or Lesson) and the three speech qualities (Natural, Synthetic High-Quality, Synthetic Low-Quality)

Although the reduction of PT_lines in the Lesson scenario is not significant, the distraction effect occurring in this scenario seems to reveal a *global* inattention phenomenon that is independent on speech quality. Therefore, the modification of the behavior of subjects might result from the professor VTP itself. This hypothesis will be analyzed with verbal and PrEmo data in the following.

An ANOVA was conducted on the variables derived from GSR data. No significant effect was found indicating that subjects' stress and emotional arousal were not influenced by their gaze behavior and by the experimental conditions. Although those conditions differed on a design point of view, they did not highly differ on an interaction point of view, since the WOz protocol was organized in such a way that interaction problems were avoided. Consequently, subjects were not put in a stressful and/or emotional situation intense enough to significantly modify their GSR.

3.2 Final Interview and PrEmo Data

Except for a one particular case, no major differences of verbal description of their perception were found between children and adults. The majority of subjects appreciated the business man's look; some representative verbatim are: "*expressive, lively, well-suited to the character.*" His natural speech was found "*pleasant, lively, natural,*" although a bit "*young*" for a few subjects. His HQ synthetic speech was half described as "*pleasant, appropriate, credible*" but also half as "*too rigid, mechanical, jerky, aggressive.*" Finally, his LQ synthetic speech was mainly described as "*robotic, unpleasant, monotonous.*" The associations between the look and different speech qualities were mainly found "*good, credible*" for the natural speech and the HQ synthetic speech, but "*unpleasant, robotic*" for the LQ synthetic speech.

Concerning the professor's look, it was mainly described as being "*too stereotyped, sad, cold, poorly attractive.*" Her natural speech was unanimously perceived as "*realistic, pleasant, fitted to the lines, soft, warm, dynamic.*" Her HQ and LQ synthetic speeches were unanimously found "*tiresome, too robotic, unattractive, authoritarian.*" The association between the look and the natural speech was found "*fine*" for a few subjects (mainly children in that case) and "*not coherent*" for others, whereas those with the HQ and LQ synthetic speeches were found " *unattractive, no-credible.*"

These verbal data show that the business man of the Prince scenario was rather appreciated and that only his LQ synthetic speech was found to be unpleasant, which had for consequence a poor credibility and pleasantness of the look /speech association for this specific speech quality. On the contrary, the professor of the Lesson scenario was rather not appreciated and both her HQ and LQ synthetic speeches were rejected. Only the association look/ natural speech was found coherent and successful for some subjects, mainly children. This global bad perception of the professor VTP probably explains why subjects were rather inattentive in the Lesson scenario.

Table 2. Number of positive and negative emotions reported by adults and children with the PrEmo sheets, for the two scenarios and the three speech qualities

		Prince Scenario			Lesson Scenario		
		Nat.	Synth. HQ	Synth. LQ	Nat.	Synth. HQ	Synth. LQ
Adults	Pos	13	12	12	6	12	9
	Neg	12	10	10	19	12	13
Children	Pos	7	5	4	7	6	4
	Neg	1	2	4	2	2	4

Table 2 shows the number of positive/negative emotions reported by adults and children for each scenario and speech quality, using the PrEmo sheets. For the Prince scenario, positive emotions are reported only slightly more frequently than negative ones for adults and children, except for the natural speech for children who reported six positive emotions and only one negative. For the Lesson scenario, adults massively reported negative emotions when they interacted with the natural-speech professor. They reported the same number of negative and positive emotions for the HQ synthetic speech, and more negative emotions for the LQ synthetic speech. On the opposite, children reported more positive emotions for the natural and the HQ synthetic speeches and an equivalent number for the LQ synthetic one.

There seems to be a discrepancy between the PrEmo data and the verbal data collected during the final interview. Concerning the business man, the final perception of a poor quality and a poor association with his look for his LQ synthetic speech are not found with PrEmo. Concerning the professor, the positive appreciation of her natural voice observed during the interview is not found for adults with PrEmo. Moreover, synthetic speeches that were rejected during the interview are not so severely judged with PrEmo. These differences probably result from effects of memory and evaluation. When *a posteriori* self-reports of short-term emotions are collected (with PrEMo), subjects do not necessarily integrate comparisons with other recent experiences with other stimuli. They probably restrict their judgments on the emotional experience they had a few seconds ago. Once they have a global perception of the whole set of stimuli, they tend to stabilize their judgments. These judgments are partly based on their past emotional experience, but also on comparisons with other stimuli and probably with internal own references. All these information converge to a double evaluation process leading to an absolute hedonic judgment and a comparative judgment.

4 Conclusion

On the methodological point of view, this study shows the complementarity of the various evaluation methods used to assess and analyze users' perception, behavior and emotions. Behavioral data derived from eye-gaze analysis revealed how users' visual attention were influenced by the ECA they were interacting with. On the other hand, GSR data were not sensitive to the different designs of ECAs. This may probably result from the fact that users always interacted without any difficulty with ECAs, which did not trigger any significant stress or emotional arousal. Verbal data collected during the final interview allowed interpretation of behavioral data, showing that the inattention phenomenon occurring in the Lesson scenario was resulting from a bad perception of the ECA's look. Finally, the PrEmo data revealed interesting differences between adults and children that were not found with other data. As the PrEmo sheets use cartoons easy to understand and appropriate for children, they probably helped them in expressing the specific perception they had with ECAs.

PrEmo and verbal data showed a combined influence of the look and speech quality of ECAs on users' self-report of emotions and their global perception. Natural and HQ synthetic speech of the male ECA were appreciated whereas only the natural speech of the female ECA was appreciated, and mainly by children. The fact that users were less tolerant with the female synthetic speech qualities may probably result from the fact that the female ECA's look was disliked by most of subjects. This result underlines the strength of the interaction between visual and auditory perception of ECAs and that their successful design is based on a careful matching between their look and voices [9].

Acknowledgements

The authors wish to thank Danielle Pelé and Gaspard Breton for furnishing the VTPs and Jean-Jacques Ferré for his help in going through the data.

References

1. Campbell, N.: Specifying Affect and Emotion for Expressive Speech Synthesis. In: Gelbukh, A. (ed.): Computational Linguistics and Intelligent Text Processing, Proc. CICLing-2004. Lecture Notes in Computer Science, Springer-Verlag (2004)

2. Cassell, J. Sullivan, J., Prevost, S., Churchill, E. (eds.): Embodied conversational agents. Cambridge, MA: MIT Press (2000)
3. Chateau, N., Mersiol, M.: AMUSE: A tool for evaluating affective interfaces, Proc. CHI2005, Workshop Innovative approaches to evaluating affective interfaces (2005)
4. Darves, C., Oviatt, S., Coulston, R.: The Impact of Auditory Embodiment on Animated Character Design. In: Proceedings of the International Joint Conference on Autonomous Agents and Multi-Agent Systems, Embodied Agents Workshop (2002)
5. Desmet, P.M.A., Hekkert, P., Jacobs, J.J.: When a car makes you smile: Development and application of an instrument to measure product emotions. In: Hoch, S.J., Meyer, R.J. (eds.), Advances in Consumer Research, 27 (2000) 111-117
6. Höök, K., Sengers, P., Andersson, G.: Sense and Sensibility: Evaluation and Interactive Art Computer Human Interaction, Fort Lauderdale (2003)
7. Jones, M. R., Yee, W.: Attending to auditory events: the role of temporal organization. In: McAdams, S., Bigand, E. (eds.): Thinking in sound: The cognitive psychology of human audition. New York: Oxford University Press, 69-112 (1993)
8. Lockhart, R.: Interrelations between amplitude, latency, rise time and the edelberg recovery measure of the galvanic skin response, Psychophysiology, vol. 9, no. 4 (1967) 437–442
9. Mersiol, M., Chateau, N., Maffiolo, V.: Talking Heads: Which Matching between Faces and Synthetic Voices? Proc. Fourth IEEE International Conference on Multimodal Interfaces (2002) 69-74
10. Narayanan, S., Alwan, A.: Text to Speech Synthesis: New Paradigms and Advances, Prentice Hall PTR, New Jersey (2004)
11. Nijholt, A.: Towards multi-modal emotion display in embodied agents. In: Proceedings of the 5th Biannual Conference on Artificial Neural Networks and Expert Systems, Dunedin, New Zealand (2001)
12. Pelé, D., Breton, G., Panaget, F., Loyson, S.: Let's find a restaurant with Nestor. A 3D embodied conversational agent on the Web. AAMAS Workshop on embodied conversational characters as individuals, Australia (2003)
13. Polkowsky, M., Lewis, J.: Expanding the MOS: Development and psychometric evaluation of the MOS-R and the MOS-X, International Journal of Speech Technology, 6 (2003) 161-182
14. Rayner, K.: Eye movements in reading and information processing: 20 years of research. Psychologica Bulletin, 124 (1998) 372-422
15. Ruttkay, Z., Doorman, C., Noot, H.: Evaluating ECAs - What and how?, Proc. of the AAMAS02 Workshop on 'Embodied conversational agents - let's specify and evaluate them!', Bologna, Italy (2002)
16. Ruttkay, Z., Pelachaud, C. (eds.): From Brows to Trust: Evaluating Embodied Conversational Agents. Kluwer Academic Publishers (2004)

Knowledge Reconfiguration Considering the Distance of Personal Preference

JeongYon Shim

Division of General Studies, Computer Science, Kangnam University,
San 6-2, Kugal-ri, Kihung-up,YongIn Si, KyeongKi Do, Korea
Tel: +82 31 2803 736
mariashim@kangnam.ac.kr

Abstract. For the purpose of processing data efficiently in the huge data environment, a design of intelligent system based on the function of human brain is necessary. This paper describes how to reconstruct the efficient subject memory considering the personal preference from the objective facts. Conceptual modeling of new knowledge reconfiguration based on the common node connection from a different memory is proposed. The well formed structure of knowledge frame with special synonym list was designed for the efficient knowledge reconfiguration, and using this structure Knowledge retrieval mechanism was made to perform extracting the associated data.We applied this mechanism to the supposed virtual knowledge frame and tested.

1 Introduction

Generally it is known that everything is connected with others according to the interactive associations and has a dynamic connectionism in the world. Things are connected to other things according to their basic structure and common sense rules. However living creatures do not take the original form of all the information but select the important factors and information appropriate for surviving in the environment. The selected factors are reconstructed and adjusted in the inner frame. It is a very efficient mechanism for small living things to survive in the complicate circumstance. As they reconstruct the important information and functions very closely according to their individual interests,they can react to stimulus promptly and process the information efficiently in spite of small intellectual part compared to the amount of huge data in the environment. It is guessed that the memory formation of human brain is similar to this mechanism and memory is formed by reconfiguring the selected information from the outside according to the personal preference and characteristics. It is because he has a different memory and a different thinking mechanism that human being has his own thinking way. The structure of knowledge in human brain is not fixed but dynamically changes. New knowledge comes in and is stored and an unimportant data decay and are forgotten. The complexity lies not only in changing but also in many different memory frame. But human brain can always maintain the alive new knowledge in high degree of importance.During forming

J. Tao, T. Tan, and R.W. Picard (Eds.): ACII 2005, LNCS 3784, pp. 660–667, 2005.

knowledge, the new data from the outside are reconstructed by being adjusted to his own knowledge structure. This reconfiguration function is an indispensable element for efficient memory management. It is also an very important function for preventing the redundancy and inconsistency problem of knowledge Base.

Many studies for solving redundancy and inconsistency problem have been made for many years in Database Researching area. But it is limited to standardizing the inconsistent concepts or terminologies[3,7].

Accordingly, in this paper we define Personal distance of knowledge frame and propose memory reconfiguration mechanism based on the personal distance for the efficient knowledge frame management. In this mechanism, an incoming inconsistent knowledge is reconfigured from the common node in the existing knowledge frame. A key point of this study is how to reconstruct the efficient subject memory considering the personal preference from the objective facts.

2 Knowledge Reconfiguration in the Memory

2.1 Knowledge Representation: Actual Distance vs. Personal Distance

The structure of knowledge frame has a logical form of knowledge net according to their associations as shown in figure 1. This figure shows the reconfiguration of personal memory from the different sources. Actual knowledge net is structured by common sense knowledge and rules. But Personal Knowledge net is configured by various factors,i.e,personal preference, personal interest and the degree of stimuli from different Actual knowledge nets or new input cluster of knowledge.

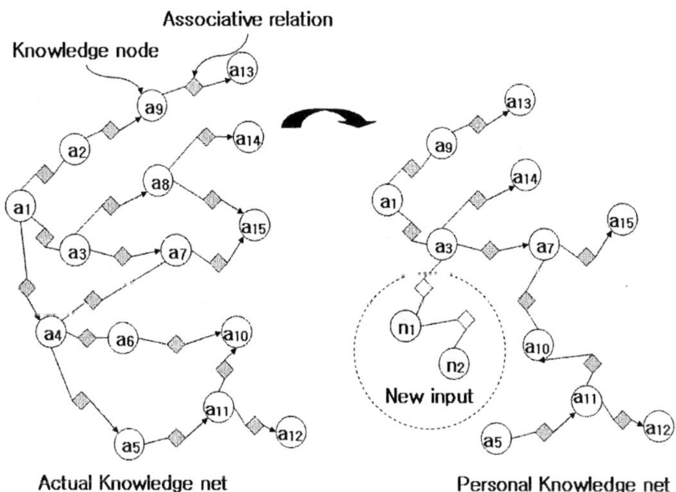

Fig. 1. Actual knowledge net vs. Personal knowledge net

The basic Knowledge net consists of knowledge node and associative relation. Knowledge node has a keyword representing the name of the knowledge. Associative relation includes its associative linguistic relation name,associative degree and distance.

Associative degree W_{ij} is conditional probability from a_1 to a_2 as following equation. It represents an associative strength between two nodes.

$$W_{ij} = P(a_i|a_j) \tag{1}$$

We define the distance between node a_1 and node a_2 in Actual Knowledge net as Actual distance, d_{ij} which has a value of [0,1]. The subjective distance reconfigured in Personal Knowledge net is defined as Personal distance. Personal distance d'_{ij} is calculated by:

$$d'_{ij} = \frac{1}{1+e^{-\gamma}}, \gamma = \delta_{ij} + \Sigma d_{ik} * d_{kj} \tag{2}$$

where δ_{ij} is a value of personal preference, [0,1].

3 Knowledge Reconfiguration Mechanism

As described in the previous section, memory Reconfiguration is a necessary function for maintaining the accurate and substantial knowledge frame. The incoming new knowledge and its associative relation should be estimated in Evaluation module for confidence. In Evaluation module, Confidence factor,C_i is calculated using Importance factor, I_i, and frequency degree,F_i. Knowledge Reconfiguration module decides if it make this incoming new knowledge take part in the reconfiguration process with Confidence factor.

$$F_i = \frac{1}{1+e^{-n}} \tag{3}$$

Where n denotes frequency of access. Confidence factor is calculated by equation 4.

$$C_i = \frac{I_i + F_i}{2} \tag{4}$$

Memory Reconfiguration
Memory reconfiguration mechanism starts to search the common nodes in the existing frame when a new knowledge frame comes in. If the common node is found, reconfiguring process centering around common node is made as shown in figure 2.

However, there are several cases for reconfiguration during searching the correspondent nodes and relation in the existing knowledge frame. Accordingly, five cases are considered as follows.

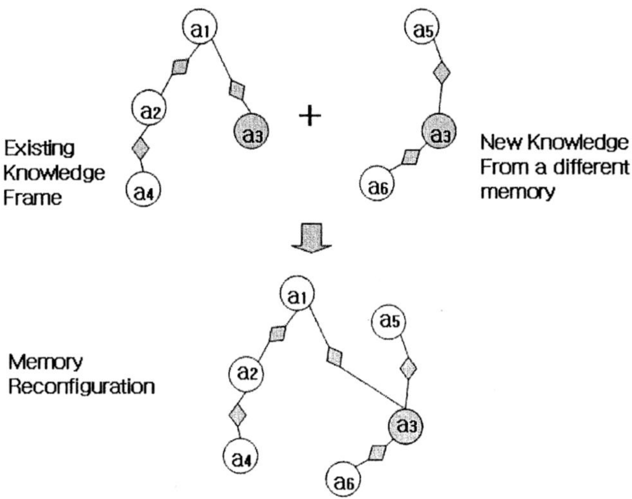

Fig. 2. Knowledge reconfiguration

Case 1 :($a_i = a_{newi}$, $a_j = a_{newj}$, $R_{ij} = R_{newij}$)

In this case the weight of associative relation and Personal distance are adjusted by the equation because all the three terms are correspondent.

$$K = W_{ij} + W_{newij} \tag{5}$$

$$W_{ij} = \frac{1}{1 + e^{-K}} \tag{6}$$

$$d'_{ij} = \frac{1}{1 + e^{-\gamma}}, \gamma = \delta_{ij} + \Sigma d_{ik} * d_{kj} \tag{7}$$

Case 2 :($a_i = a_{newi}$, $a_j = a_{newj}$, $R_{ij} \neq R_{newij}$)

The new associative relation link is created.

Case 3 :($a_i = a_{newi}$, $a_j \neq a_{newj}$, $R_{ij} \neq R_{newij}$)

The new associative relation link and knowledge node are created.

Case 4 :($a_i = a_{newi}$, $a_j \neq a_{newj}$, $R_{ij} = R_{newij}$)

In this case adjusting process is required because there is a conflict between the existing frame and incoming new knowledge frame. If the strength of associative relation between the existing nodes is greater than the strength of new one,the new frame is aborted. Otherwise, the links of the existing frame are deleted , new link is created and the new strength substitutes for the old one.

Case 5 :($a_i \neq a_{newi}$, $a_j \neq a_{newj}$, $R_{ij} \neq R_{newij}$)

A new link is connected to the root node because there is no correspondent frame to the new frame in the existing memory.

When the new knowledge and associative relation selected in evaluation testing are propagated into the knowledge frame, Knowledge reconfiguration mechanism starts according to the following Algorithm 1.

Algorithm 1 : Knowledge Reconfiguration algorithm

(I/O interface)

Step 1 : Input the new knowledge, associative degree and the importance of the knowledge I_i.

(Temporary memory)

Step 2 : Store on Temporary memory.

(Evaluation Module)

Step 3 : Calculate confidence degree.

$$F_i = \frac{1}{1+e^{-n}}$$

$$C_i = \frac{I_i + F_i}{2}$$

Step 4 : If($C_i \geq \epsilon$) & (t $\geq$ T)

Then goto Forgetting module

Else goto Knowledge Reconfiguration module.

Forgetting module :

Move the input knowledge to the forgetting pool and remove it.

Knowledge Reconfiguration module :

Step 4-1 :

Search the representative name in the knowledge node and synonym list.

Step 4-2 :

Case 1: ($a_i = a_{newi}$, $a_j = a_{newj}$, $R_{ij} = R_{newij}$)

Adjust the associative relation degree

$$K = W_{ij} + W_{newij}$$

$$W_{ij} = \frac{1}{1+e^{-K}}$$

$$d'_{ij} = \frac{1}{1+e^{-\gamma}}, \gamma = \delta_{ij} + \Sigma d_{ik} * d_{kj}$$

Case 2: ($a_i = a_{newi}$, $a_j = a_{newj}$, $R_{ij} \neq R_{newij}$)

Create the new associative relation

Case 3: ($a_i = a_{newi}$, $a_j \neq a_{newj}$, $R_{ij} \neq R_{newij}$)

Create the new link and node

Case 4: ($a_i = a_{newi}$, $a_j \neq a_{newj}$, $R_{ij} = R_{newij}$)

the state of confliction

if $W_{ij} \geq W_{newij}$

Then Abort the new knowledge pair

Else Delete the existing link and create the new link.

Case 5: ($a_i \neq a_{newi}$, $a_j \neq a_{newj}$, $R_{ij} \neq R_{newij}$)

Create the associative relation and node connected to Root

Step 5: if knowledge pair = t

Then goto Step 6

Else goto Step 1

Step 6: STOP.

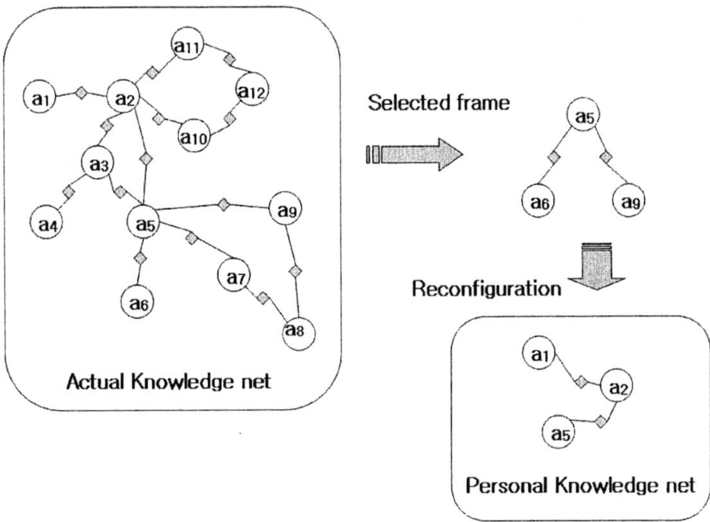

Fig. 3. Example

* Actual Knowledge net

node1	node2	R-ij	W-ij	d-ij
a1	a2	R 1 2	0.89	0.30
a2	a3	R 2 3	0.70	0.30
a2	a5	R 2 5	0.60	0.30
a2	a10	R 2 10	0.20	0.40
a2	a11	R 2 11	0.20	0.30
a3	a4	R 3 4	0.90	0.40
a3	a5	R 3 5	0.40	0.30
a4	Nill	R 4 4	0.00	0.00
a5	a6	R 5 6	0.42	0.30
a5	a7	R 5 7	0.50	0.20
a5	a9	R 5 9	0.60	0.30
a6	Nill	R 6 6	0.00	0.00
a7	a8	R 7 8	0.70	0.30
a8	Nill	R 8 8	0.00	0.00
a9	a8	R 9 8	0.20	0.30
a10	a12	R 10 12	0.10	0.30
a11	a12	R 11 12	0.40	0.30
a12	Nill	R 12 12	0.00	0.00

Fig. 4. Actual Knowledge net

4 Experiments

We tested with the supposed virtual knowledge frame. Figure 3 shows an example used for experiments that test the reconfiguration with the selected knowledge

* Initial state of Personal net

node1	node2	R-ij	W-ij	d-ij	d'-ij
a1	a2	R 1 2	0.89	0.30	0.789045
a2	a5	R 2 5	0.60	0.30	0.987690
a5	Nill	R 5 5	0.00	0.00	0.000000

* Reconfiguration of Personal net

node1	node2	R-ij	W-ij	d-ij	d'-ij
a1	a2	R 1 2	0.89	0.30	0.789045
a2	a5	R 2 5	0.60	0.30	0.987690
a2	a10	R 2 10	0.20	0.40	0.769876
a5	a6	R 5 6	0.42	0.30	0.678590
a5	a9	R 5 9	0.60	0.30	0.876795
a6	Nill	R 6 6	0.00	0.00	0.000000
a9	Nill	R 8 8	0.00	0.00	0.000000

Fig. 5. The list of Personal net after reconfiguration

frame from Actual knowledge net when the structures of actual knowledge net and existing Personal knowledge net are given.

Figure 4 depicts the initial data of node of Actual Knowledge net a_{ij},Relation name R_{ij}, associative degree W_{ij} and actual distance d_{ij}. The changed results by Knowledge Reconfiguration mechanism are shown in Figure 5. It shows the changed list of Personal Knowledge net including personal distance d'_{ij} after reconfiguration.

From the experiment, we can find that it reforms the knowledge frame and extracts the related data using this structure easily. It can solve redundancy and inconsistency problem of DB.

5 Conclusion

We proposed Conceptual model of new knowledge reconfiguration based on the common node connection from a different memory. We defined Personal distance of knowledge frame and propose memory reconfiguration mechanism based on the personal distance for the efficient knowledge frame management. In this mechanism, an incoming inconsistent knowledge is reconfigured from the common node in the existing knowledge frame. A key point of this study is how to reconstruct the efficient subject memory considering the personal preference from the objective facts.

As a result of testing, we could find that it can reform the knowledge frame and extract the related data using this structure easily. It could solve redundancy and inconsistency problem. This mechanism can be applied to construct personal memory structure and personal preference can be calculated by strength of associative relations. Personal preference is a very important information for providing service considering personal characteristics in many areas of E-commerce system, Database management and etc.

References

1. E. Bruce Goldstein Sensation and Perception *BROOKS/COLE.*
2. John R. Anderson Learning and Memory *Prentice Hall.*
3. R.A .Frost Introduction to Knowledge Base Systems *WilliamCollins Sons Co. Ltd..*
4. Jeong-Yon Shim, Chong-Sun Hwang Data Extraction from Associative Matrix based on Selective learning system *IJCNN'99, Washongton D.C.*
5. Jeong-Yon Shim, Chong-Sun Hwang Intelligent Hierarchical Associative Knowledge Learning System with Knowledge acquisition and Extraction , *ICONIP2000, Deajeon, Korea.*
6. Jean-Marc Adamo Data Mining for Association rules and sequential patterns , *Springer.*
7. Adrian A. Hopgood Knowledge based systems for engineers ans Scientist ,*CRC press.*

Emotional Sequencing and Development in Fairy Tales

Cecilia Ovesdotter Alm[1] and Richard Sproat[2]

[1] Dept. of Linguistics, Univ. of Illinois, Urbana, USA
ebbaalm@uiuc.edu
[2] Dept. of Linguistics, Dept. of Electrical Engineering, Univ. of Illinois, Urbana, USA

Abstract. Affect is a transient phenomenon, with emotions tending to blend and interact over time [4]. This paper discusses emotional distributions in child-directed texts. It provides statistical evidence for the relevance of emotional sequencing, and evaluates trends of emotional story development, based on annotation statistics on 22 Grimms' fairy tales which form part of a larger on-going text-annotation project that is also introduced. The study is motivated by the need for exploring features for *text-based emotion prediction* at the sentence-level, for use in expressive text-to-speech synthesis of children's stories.

1 Introduction

This study aims to clarify the relevance of sequential emotion information in text annotation with statistical analysis at the intersentential and text level. In addition, it presents our annotation project and factors that influence the perception of emotions in text.

The study of emotional distributions is motivated by the need for non-lexical features for boosting a classification approach to *text-based emotion prediction*. Predicting emotions in text is useful for subsequent affective text-to-speech synthesis (TTS). We work on child-directed TTS and thus consider fairy tales. Because this genre is schematic, the assumption is that tales have partially predictable *emotional distributions*, e.g. with a NEUTRAL descriptive begin and a HAPPY end. Also, emotions decay, and therefore emotional sentences will most likely be surrounded by NEUTRAL sentences. However, emotions can also be prolonged and even ascend in strength. Intuitively, emotions such as SADNESS appear more likely to span consecutive sentences; while e.g. SURPRISE by nature is more instantaneous. Moreover, the emotional development at the text level can be analyzed from the point of view of the story's emotional trajectory.

In section 2, we present an overview of our on-going text annotation project, and discuss the text-based emotion annotation task based on interannotator agreement measures. Next, we describe the annotated data which was used for statistical analysis in section 3. Then, sections 4 and 5 present statistical analysis of emotional distributions, whereas section 6 concludes with a short discussion and the implications of the study for a learning scenario.

J. Tao, T. Tan, and R.W. Picard (Eds.): ACII 2005, LNCS 3784, pp. 668–674, 2005.

2 Annotation of Emotional Content in Text

Our current text-annotation project targets the annotation of emotional contents in three sets of children's stories, including stories by Beatrix Potter, the Grimms' fairy tales, and tales written by the Danish author H. C. Andersen. The three parts reflect levels of increasing reader maturity. For example, emotions have a notably higher complexity in H. C. Andersen's work, e.g. with embedded emotion assignment where emotions are ascribed to characters by other characters in the story. Eventually, the annotated corpus (approximately 180 stories) will be made publically available.

The annotators are native speakers of US English who attended a literary course on Grimms' Fairy Tales. They mark each sentence in a story with one of 8 primary emotions, listed in table 1, from the point of view of the *feeler* in the sentence, i.e. the emotional target is that perceived by the salient character in the sentence. This helps to focus the annotation task since emotions are often subject to different perspectives.[1] So far, stories have been independently annotated by two people so, as a next step, the annotations produced by each annotator pair are evaluated statistically, and the annotated texts are subsequently post-processed by the first author, who tie-breaks disagreements by choosing the most appropriate of the conflicting labels.

The annotators received a one-hour training session and a manual; however they were not trained together with their eventual pair partner. While such a tandem training scenario may have yielded a higher interannotator score, we did not want to adjust or bias their judgements, but rather get as natural responses as possible, in order to gain more insight into task difficulty and the dynamic nature of emotional targets.

Table 1. Basic emotion categories

Abbreviation	Emotion class
A	ANGRY
D	DISGUSTED
F	FEARFUL
H	HAPPY
Sa	SAD
Su+	POSITIVELY SURPRISED
Su-	NEGATIVELY SURPRISED

Table 2 presents interannotator statistics for a preliminary data set. The two annotators from group A covered a set of 20 Grimms' stories (1357 sentences), whereas group B annotated a different set of 22 Grimms' stories (1581 sentences). We report on the kappa statistics for inter-annotator agreement, as well as the percent overlap between the paired annotators. For the latter measure, classes

[1] Since the narrator may also address the audience directly, the *reader* can also be the *feeler*. Other information is also marked, e.g. emotional intensities, or phrases contributing to emotion assignment.

Table 2. Inter-annotator statistics for 2 groups of paired annotators

	Kappa b	$P(b_{i=j})$	$P(m_{i=j})$	$P(t_{i=j})$
Gr A	0.51	0.64	0.73	0.76
Gr B	0.24	0.45	0.49	0.50

Table 3. Inter-annotation matrix. Group A's a_1 and a_2 and group B's b_1 and b_2 annotated 20 and 22 Grimms' stories, respectively.

a_1/a_2	A	D	F	H	N	Sa	Su+	Su-
A	**87**	0	2	0	4	5	1	8
D	23	2	1	3	7	10	2	8
F	1	0	**56**	2	16	4	2	12
H	3	0	2	**157**	30	1	5	3
N	19	0	16	92	**457**	39	17	41
Sa	6	1	2	2	9	**71**	0	8
Su+	0	2	0	16	14	0	14	4
Su-	8	0	4	5	19	3	5	26

b_1/b_2	A	D	F	H	N	Sa	Su+	Su-
A	*87*	0	6	0	**172**	6	1	4
D	2	1	1	1	**13**	1	0	0
F	3	0	*46*	0	**165**	11	2	4
H	1	0	0	*46*	**192**	1	6	0
N	0	0	4	2	*473*	1	0	0
Sa	1	0	7	3	**137**	*41*	0	7
Su+	0	0	0	3	**65**	1	*10*	1
Su-	4	0	2	0	**41**	1	1	4

were also combined into their semantically intuitive superclasses, where t refers to the top level, i.e. whether a sentence is neutral or non-neutral, m to whether an emotional sentence has neutral, positive or negative valence, and b to the basic level emotion category, e.g. ANGRY, HAPPY, etc., including NEUTRAL.

The kappa scores in table 2 are lower than more straight-forward NLP annotation tasks. This confirms the task difficulty and that emotion annotation is sensitive to factors such as subjective interpretation and annotator personality. Also, it is interesting to note that the degree of percent annotation overlap increases as emotion categories are collapsed into more general classes. This could indicate that task difficulty increases for human annotators at the finer-grained distinctions of affect; however, more research is needed to confirm that this is indeed the case.

Moreover, compared to group A, group B showed a substantially lower kappa score on this partial corpus. To investigate the differences in the annotation patterns of group A and B, confusion matrices for both groups were computed which considered all basic emotion categories. The confusion matrices visualize the degree of annotation agreement versus disagreement for an annotator pair. For group A, the diagonal of the left side of table 3 shows that the most frequently chosen category is the same for both annotators for 5 out of 8 emotion labels.[2] For group B, the NEUTRAL category is the dominant source of confusion, as seen in the right side of table 3. This is due to the annotators' sensitivity towards neutral versus non-neutral contents being located at two extremes; b_1 assigned NEUTRAL to 80% of the sentences, whereas b_2 only assigned it to 30%. This highlights that because emotion perception lacks a clear definition as basis and is subjective, NEUTRAL, i.e. the absence of emotion, suffers from the same problem. Nevertheless, the diagonal shows that, besides the NEUTRAL confusion, group B's annotators still had highest within category annotation counts for 6 of the 8 emotion labels.

[2] The smallest category, DISGUSTED, appears to be problematic. Within the context of emotion recognition in speech, similarly [6] noted concerns with this category.

Table 4. Intra-annotator statistics for 3 annotators after reannotating 4 Grimms' stories

	Kappa (b)	$P(b_{i=i})$	$P(m_{i=i})$	$P(t_{i=i})$
Gr A A1	0.64	0.76	0.80	0.82
Gr B A1	0.60	0.67	0.78	0.82
Gr B A2	0.68	0.87	0.88	0.88

The distinctions in the kappa results between groups A and B lead us to go one step further and measure intra-annotator consistency. We asked 3 annotators to reannotate 4 Grimms' stories and compared these against the original annotations made by the same annotator, cf. table 4. The results of the intra-annotation experiments in table 4 showed that annotators experienced problems with keeping the emotional targets fixed and stable between annotation times. At this point, it is difficult to say what these fluctuations mean, but they could be related to extra-textual factors, such as deviations in the annotator's mood on the different occasions, cf. [4]. At any rate, these results confirm that emotional targets will tend to be interpreted and perceived dynamically, and that there are bounds on the levels of agreement that can be expected. Further research will help determine what those bounds are.

3 Data for Analysis of Emotional Distributions

The fairy tales used for statistical analysis of emotional distributions consisted of a preliminary tie-broken data set of 22 Grimms' fairy tales or 1580 sentences.[3] The distribution across labels in this subcorpus is included in table 5, with NEUTRAL being most frequent. In this part of the study, we were mostly interested in *local* emotional sequencing. Table 6 shows co-occurrence counts between sentential emotions with emotions of the preceding sentences in the left part, versus with emotions of following sentences on the right. B and E characterized a story's first and last sentence, i.e. when no sentence preceded or followed, respectively.

Table 5. Percent of annotated labels

ANGRY (A): 12%	DISGUSTED (D): 1%	FEARFUL (F): 7%	HAPPY (H): 7%
NEUTRAL (N): 60%	SAD (SA): 7%	POS. SURPRISED (SU+): 3%	NEG. SURPRISED (SU.-): 3%

4 Statistical Analysis of Emotional Distrubutions

We statistically analyze the following questions:

1. Do fairy tales more frequently begin NEUTRAL and end HAPPY?
2. Does NEUTRAL dominate emotional sentences' immediate context?
3. Which emotions are more often prolonged, and which are not?

[3] 1 sentence was an editorial comment and was thus removed from the annotated corpus.

Table 6. Preceding S emotion counts vs. **following S** emotion counts

0/-1	A	D	H	F	N	Sa	Su-	Su+	B
A	57	4	8	17	90	14	4	1	0
D	2	6	0	0	5	1	0	0	0
H	7	0	13	3	61	7	4	11	1
F	15	0	6	17	50	11	8	4	0
N	94	3	55	55	636	46	12	25	21
Sa	9	1	5	9	58	28	4	2	0
Su-	6	0	1	5	15	4	8	2	0
Su+	3	0	6	3	27	5	1	4	0

0/+1	A	D	H	F	N	Sa	Su-	Su+	E
A	57	2	7	15	94	9	6	3	2
D	4	6	0	0	3	1	0	0	0
H	8	0	13	6	55	5	1	6	13
F	17	0	3	17	55	9	5	3	2
N	90	5	61	50	636	58	15	27	5
Sa	14	1	7	11	46	28	4	5	0
Su-	4	0	4	8	12	4	8	1	0
Su+	1	0	11	4	25	2	2	4	0

The three above points were statistically evaluated by a one-way significance test for difference between the proportions of time that $emotion_i$ and $emotion_j$ immediately preceded or followed $emotion_k$, using the following equation:

$$Z = \frac{\hat{E}_i - \hat{E}_j}{\sqrt{\hat{E}(1-\hat{E})(\frac{2}{n})}} \tag{1}$$

Where $\hat{E}_i = \frac{E_i}{n}$, i.e. the proportion of assignments of $emotion_i$ in sample n, $\hat{E} = \frac{E_i+E_j}{2n}$, and n is the number of sentences with $emotion_k$. Note that this is a particular case of test for difference between 2 proportions when the samples are of the same size.[4] All significance tests were done at 95% confidence level.

The first question considered the prominence of NEUTRAL and HAPPY at opposite story boundaries. Here $emotion_k$ is the special case of *begin* or *end* of a story. The tests showed that NEUTRAL occurred significantly more frequently in the first sentence and HAPPY in the last sentence, compared to other emotions. This confirms that at story boundaries certain emotions can be expected.

The second question asked, for each emotion, was whether NEUTRAL dominated its adjacent context by testing the difference in proportions between NEUTRAL against other emotions in the preceding and following sentences. For all emotions except DISGUSTED in both contexts and SU- in the following context, NEUTRAL was significantly more frequent compared to other emotions. Thus, for the majority of emotions, NEUTRAL is indeed the most frequent context, which is consistent with the emotional decay factor.

The third question covered emotional prolongation, and was divided into two parts. Given that the above results already demonstrated the dominance of NEUTRAL and the behavior at story boundaries, N, B, and E adjacency counts were excluded.

The first test for emotional prolongation covered whether each emotion was more likely to co-occur with sentences of its own category, as opposed to with other *emotional* categories. Given consecutive sentences, ANGRY and SAD significantly more often preceded and followed themselves compared to other emotions.

[4] Also note that it is only necessary to consider the proportion of an emotion against the proportion of the most frequent one of all other emotions; significance for all smaller proportions follows inductively.

Moreover, DISGUSTED only significantly more often preceded itself. No statistical evidence was found for HAPPY, FEARFUL and the two SURPRISED conditions. This result corroborates the intuition that some emotions, SURPRISE or FEAR, transition more rapidly than others, such as SADNESS and ANGER. Moreover, a HAPPY emotion expresses contentment with the status quo, whereas negative events force action and keep the narrative plot going, which would explain why HAPPY did not show significant prolongation.

In the second test of emotional prolongation, preceding and following emotions were regarded as either positive PE={H, SU+} or negative NE={A, D, F, SA, SU-}. All NE showed statistical significance for immediate adjacency with NE members. For the positive case, only SU+ was significantly more often followed by PE sentences. Note that it makes intuitive sense that POSITIVE SURPRISE is more notably followed, but not preceded, by positive emotions.

5 Emotional Trajectory

Next, we explored if tales reflect a particular emotional trajectory. To increase generalization, emotions were again combined into PE and NE subsets, while N={NEUTRAL} was a singleton class. Each of the 22 stories was divided into fifths and the aggregate frequency counts of PE, NE and N was computed for each fifth over all stories.

Fig. 1 shows that emotional activity in fact corresponded to a wave-shaped pattern. The first fifth is the least emotional level, probably because it descriptively sets the scene of the story. The peak of NE activity in part 2 of the stories could reflect a common pattern in folk tales: due to an event or need early in

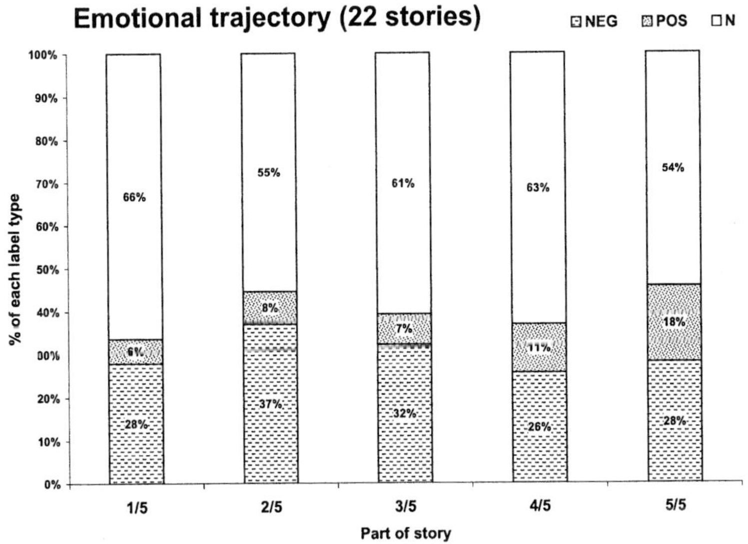

Fig. 1. Emotional trajectory over 5 story portions

the story, the hero/heroine must depart on a quest (cf. [5]), and such an event is likely to involve emotional experience. The peak of PE in the final part probably signifies the 'reward' state, i.e. the happy end. Also note that negative emotion increases slightly in the last fifth; according to Propp's schematic outline of folk tales [5], toward the end the villain is 'exposed' as such and then 'punished', i.e. events likely to call for negative emotions, such as ANGER. In addition, Propp's template does not always apply, and a few stories end on a negative note.

6 Concluding Discussion

This paper discussed emotional distributions in 22 fairy tales in terms of patterns of emotional sequencing and positioning, and also in terms of emotional development, temporally across the story. It additionally provided an overview of the larger on-going annotation project and the issues involved when annotating fairy tale texts for emotional contents.

Although the characteristics and size of the corpus may have influenced the analysis, emotional distributions seem promising as contributing features for *text-based emotion prediction*. In a companion study, we have tentatively observed that annotated sequencing could contribute to slight accuracy improvement of a linear classifier (subject to learner parameters) for bipartite classification of neutral vs. emotional sentences. Naturally, for sequencing to be useful, we must develop automatic inference methods for such features.

Lastly, emotional sequencing could also reflect complex "meta-emotions" [3]. An interesting extension of this work would be to widen the analysis to such cases.

Acknowledgments

This work was funded by NSF under award ITR-#0205731, and data annotation by a UIUC Research Board grant. The authors take sole responsibility for the work.

References

1. Cahn, J.: The Generation of Affect in Synthesized Speech. J. Am. Voice I/O Soc. **8** (1990) 1–19
2. van Santen, J. et al.: Applications of computer generated expressive speech for communication disorders. EUROSPEECH (2003) 1657–1660
3. Liu H., Lieberman H., Selker T.: A model of textual affect sensing using real-world knowledge. Intelligent User Interfaces (2003) 125–132
4. Picard, R.: Affective computing. Massachusetts, MIT Press (1997)
5. Propp, V.: Morphology of the Folktale. Austin, Univ. Texas Press (1968)
6. Scherer, K. R.: Vocal communication of emotion: a review of research paradigms. Speech Communication **40:1-2** (2003) 227–256.

Informal User Interface for Graphical Computing

Zhengxing Sun and Jing Liu

State Key Lab for Novel Software Technology, Nanjing University, 210093, China
szx@nju.edu.cn

Abstract. This paper explores a concept of sketch-based informal user interface for graphic computing, which can be characterized by two properties: stroke-based input and perceptual processing of strokes. A sketch-based graphics input prototype system designed for creative brainstorming in conceptual design is introduced. Two core technologies for implementing such a system, adaptive sketch recognition and dynamic user modeling, are also outlined.

1 Introduction

For over three decades, the graphical user interfaces (GUI) and its associated desktop metaphors have dominated both the marketplace and HCI research. As computers changes in terms of physical size, capacity, usage and ubiquity, peoples interact with them in more informal ways than they used to. The obvious question arises, such as what is the next major generation in the evolution of user interfaces and if there is a paradigm (and its associated technology) that will displace GUI and become the dominant user interface model. There is no shortage of HCI researches collectively called as post-WIMP interfaces [1] or non-command interfaces [2], such as various flavors of immersive environments (virtual, augmented, and mixed reality), tangible interfaces, haptic interfaces and so on. The common goal of them is to make computers more intelligent, more convenient to use, more adaptable to the human-preferred communication mode, and to allow the user to concentrate on the task itself without worrying about commands.

In the domain of graphical computing, people are accustomed to write down their improvisatory ideas. For them, the ability to rapidly deliver their ideas using graphic objects with uncertain types, indefinite sizes, irregular shapes, and inaccurate positions is most important. However, most current drafting tools are formal and computer-oriented, which requires users to select graphic patterns from lots of toolbar buttons or menu items and does not work well for expressing arbitrary graphical ideas or geometric shapes in computers. Users frequently find it inconvenient via too many mouse-clicks. They also complain that they have to memorize the precise position of each toolbar button or menu item since they cannot focus on the design idea itself when utilizing these tools to deliver their bursting creative ideas. Therefore, they cannot finish the design fluently due to too many interruptions.

In this paper, we will explore an informal user interface (IUI) paradigm using sketching for graphical computing and illustrate our experiments on this topic. The remainder of this paper is organized as follows. In section 2, the concept of the sketch-based informal user interface is defined with two properties: stroke-based

J. Tao, T. Tan, and R.W. Picard (Eds.): ACII 2005, LNCS 3784, pp. 675 – 682, 2005.

input and perceptual processing, and some related works are outlined. Section 3 briefly introduces our prototype system, named as Magic-Sketch, embodying the idea of informal user interface. Section 4 discusses two core techniques for implementing informal user interface. Conclusions and future works are given in the final Section.

2 Sketch-Based Informal User Interfaces for Graphic Computing

People have been using pen and paper to express graphical ideas for centuries, which is a preferred choice for creative brainstorming [3]. Even in this high-tech computer era, paper and pencils have still to be designers' preferred choice to quickly sketch bursting ideas. It can help user convey ideas and guide our thought process both by aiding short-term memory and by helping to make abstract problems more concrete. Sketch-based user interface is an informal input modality of increasing interest for human-computer interaction. It embodies a non-command user interface for the graphical applications in that the user can transfer visual ideas into target computers without converting the ideas into a sequence of tedious command operations. The term "informal" is referred to that sketch-based interfaces are tolerant of the user's input and show variability in their output. The tolerance means allowable differences in input function mapping to an internal representation. The variability means that an internal representation can be mapped in a number of ways to an output mechanism without appearing to have a different meaning.

The sketchy shape in its rough state contains more information than the regularized one. But its ambiguity and uncertainty make the deduction of intents very difficult. The regularized shape is better for users to communicate and recall their original intention of this sketch in graphical applications. It will be more helpful for graphic computing if the sketchy shape can be recognized and converted into the user-intended regular shape. Therefore, the manner of sketch-based graphic input is that user can draw their approximate line shapes with pen-based stroking quickly and fluently, while computer must recognize/covert user's inputting strokes to the regular shapes immediately.

Pen-based stroking is usually recognized as a dragging operation in a standard programming environment: it is initiated by "button press" event, followed by a sequence of "mouse move" event, and terminated by "button release" event. The system's reaction is based on the entire trajectory of the pen's movement during the stroking, not just the pen's position at the end. In stroking, the user first imagines the desired stroke shape and then draws the shape on the screen at once, while the user constantly adjusts the cursor position observing the feedback objects during dragging. Through stroke seems to be a primitive unit in sketch user interface at first appearance, the stroke is not a structural and unique constitutive geometric primitive of a shape for human cognition. Therefore, stroke segmentation is the groundwork for realizing sketch-based IUI, which decomposes the inputting strokes into basic geometric primitives, such as lines and curves. As strokes can be segmented in many different ways, the challenge of stroke segmentation is to find out which bumps and bends are intended and which are accident. Sezgin [4] have used both curvature and speed information in a stroke to locate breakpoints, while Saund [5] used more perceptual context, including local features such as curvature and intersections, as well as global features such as closed paths. All of them use empirical thresholds to test the validity of an approximation that ultimately leads to the problem of a threshold being too tight or too loose.

The another important property is its advanced processing of strokes inspired by human perception, which characterizes sketch-based IUI as a non-command user interface and makes sketch-based IUI different from plain pen-based scribbling systems that simply convert the user's pen movement into a painted stroke on the screen without any further processing. We call this advanced processing as "perceptual processing" or "sketch recognition". The idea behind sketch recognition is inspired by the observation that human beings perceive rich information in simple drawings, such as possible geometric relations among line primitives, three-dimensional shapes from two-dimensional silhouettes. Sketch recognition is an attempt to simulate human perception at least in limited domains. The goal of sketch recognition is to allow the user to perform complicated tasks with a minimum amount of explicit control. Sketch-based IUI must free users from detailed command operations by this perceptual processing of freeform strokes and reduces significantly the effort spent on learning commands. A variety of sketch recognition techniques have been proposed, which can be classified into three categories: feature-based methods [6][7], graph-based methods [8] and machine learning methods [9][10]. In addition, several experimental systems for supporting sketch-based informal user interface in limited domain, such as Sim-U-Sketch for mechanical design and simulation [11], DENIM for the early stages of web site design [12], and so on. In summary, while there has been significant progress in sketch recognition, the poor efficiency of the recognition engines is always frustrating, especially for complex sketchy shapes and newly added users. The main challenge in sketch recognition is that a recognizer should be adaptable to a particular user's sketching styles. More importantly, most symbol recognizers do stroke fragmentation and symbol recognition separately. This would apparently result in aimless segmentation of strokes and incorrect recognition of symbols deviating from users' intentions.

3 Magic-Sketch: A Sketch-Based Platform for Graphic Input

3.1 Overview of Magic-Sketch

We have being developed a prototype platform of sketch-based graphic input for conceptual design to support users' creativities, named Magic-Sketch. The framework of Magic-Sketch is outlined in Fig. 1. It is mainly consisted of following components: stroke pre-processing, stroke segmentation and sketch recognition, dynamic user modeling, database management, input and edit interface, and application interfaces.

As a basis of sketch-based graphic input, the *stroke pre-processing* is firstly adopted to eliminate the noise that may come from restriction of input condition or habits [13], such as redundant points reducing, agglomerate points filtering and end points refinement. The candidate breakpoints of strokes are also distinguished, where the pen speed is at a minimum; the ink exhibits high curvature, or the sign of the curvature changes besides the start and end point of each stroke. The *stroke segmentation* and *Sketch recognition* are then used to decompose each stroke into some kinds of primitives and recognize each of individual geometric shapes such as glyphs and symbols and their relationships in the inputting pattern respectively. Several gesture commands are also recognized. To adapt for the arbitrariness and amphibology of inputting, we propose a novel method of sketch recognition, which integrates stroke segmentation with sketch recognition. This will be discussed in next subsection. *Dynamic user modeling* is designed to build user models for each specific user to capture users' habit of drawing styles and to facilitate the sketch recognition in an incremental manner. This will be discussed in the subsection 3.3. In addition, user model can also been updated by user mediation based on relevance feedback techniques, where user can refine/correct the recognition results by interactive feedback based on partial and overall structural similarity between inputting drawing and templates [13].

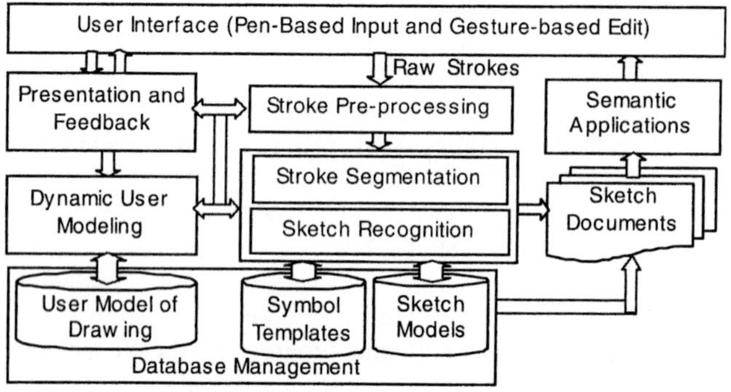

Fig. 1. Framework of Sketch-based Graphics Input Tool

In order to preserve and manage the information during user drawing, two types of data model are designed in our prototype system as shown in Fig. 2. Fig. 2(a) shows the hierarchical structure of Sketch model, which includes backboard, raw strokes, primitives, shapes and semantics from the bottom up. Backboard is a host structural format that sketches are located in. We can use HTML or XHTML as a backboard to define a *sketch document* for sketch model. This will make sketch model more powerful and portable for different domains. Raw stroke refers to ink points that are sampled by input equipment. Primitives and shapes are the geometric and relation information of the tokens extracted from raw strokes. Sketch semantics refers to recognized symbols related to applied domain. User model is also organized in a layered structure, as shown in Fig. 2(b). For a specific user, besides the identifier of user, some of his/her drawing properties of ink points, strokes, symbols and applied domain are defined, such as pen pressure and drawing speed at each of ink points, the temporal sequence of strokes, frequency of intended symbol and so on.

We also design a particular *user interface* to support the freedom and fluency of pen-based drawing and editing. We offer 9 gestures to users, including copying, deleting, dragging, pasting, undo, redo, cleaning panel, finishing and selecting. The interactive editor is provided with the manager of the document. It provides an interactive and visualized interface for document editing. If the input strokes are identified as a visual token, then the new token will be added to the document, together with corresponding modifications of their spatial relations. If the stroke is recognized as a gesture commands, the editor processes them directly, just as common document editors. User interactions are saved in for feedback. The user feedback style indicates two styles. One is the time that the system submits its result. The other is the granularity that the result is presented in. This means that the form of result, which is shown to user, can be different, from regularized strokes to the whole sketch after recognition.

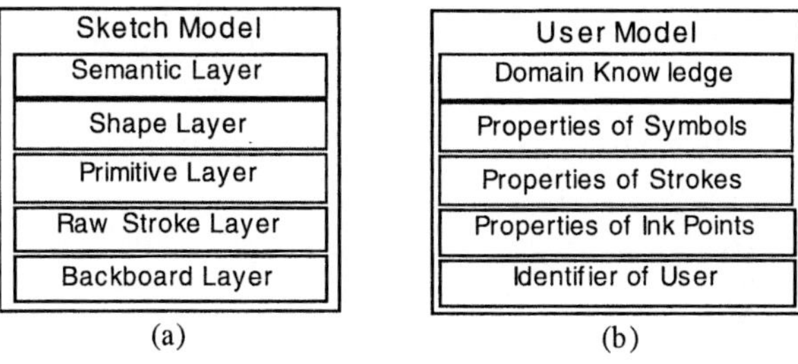

Fig. 2. Conceptual model of data structure in Magic-Sketch

3.2 Adaptive Sketch Recognition Based on Templates

Most of the existing methods treat stroke segmentation and sketch recognition separately. In fact, a user is purposeful with the intended symbol in head when expressing his/her ideas with the particular sketchy shape based on both the current observations and the past experiences, though he/she draws one stroke after another. This is the primary reason for the poor accuracy of recognizers no matter how robust they might. Therefore, it is necessary for sketch recognition to integrate the process of stroke segmentation and sketch recognition, in order to account for the variations inherent in hand-drawn sketches.

To achieve this goal, we propose a novel approach of adaptive sketch recognition by regarding both of stroke segmentation and sketch recognition as a problem of "fitting to a template" with a minimal fitting error between input patterns and the particular domain definition models of the symbol (templates). Fig. 3 shows the flowchart of our strategy, which is designed to work for single isolated symbols. Examples include symbols in conceptual design, analogy electric circuits design, data flow diagrams, algorithmic flowcharts and so on.

In our strategy, stroke segmentation optimizes the combination of breakpoints by calculating the similarity between the primitives of inputting pattern and that of the templates based on the selection of candidate breakpoints in stroke pre-processing. This makes stroke segmentation be well guided by the templates.

Given a sketchy symbol *SM* and a template *T*, *SM* is consisted of a sequence of strokes, each stroke contains a set of the ordered candidate breakpoints; a template *T* is represented as a set of ordered primitives $T\{t(i)\}$, the number of breakpoints needed to be identified is: $k=NT\text{-}NS$(in general, $NS \le NT \le NB\text{-}1$, where, *NT* is the number of primitives for defining a template of symbol, *NS* is the number of strokes and *NB* is the total numbers of ordered candidate breakpoints (NB_i is the number of ordered candidate breakpoints for i^{th} stroke.) respectively for an inputting sketchy symbol. The problem of *stroke segmentation* using templates can then be defined as to select k numbers of breakpoints from the ordered candidate breakpoints to fragment the storke into some segments such that a sketchy shape represented by these segments is fit for some of shape definitions in template library with minimal fitting error.

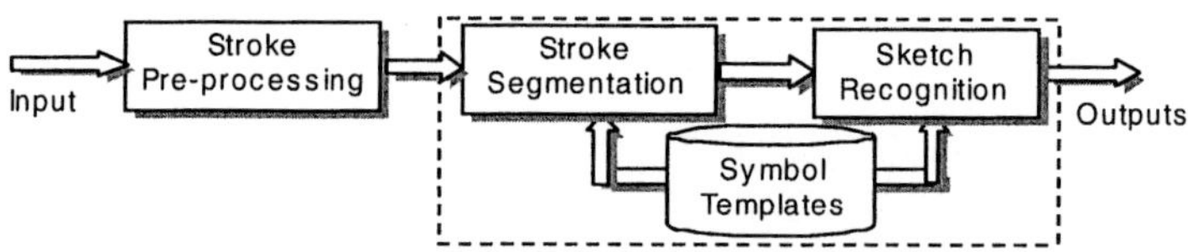

Fig. 3. Flowchart of strategy for adaptive sketch recognition

To find an optimal fragmentation of a set of strokes with template T, one assumes that the optimal solution for fragmenting everything up to the selected breakpoint with a template $T\{t(i)|i=1,2,\ldots,NT-1\}$ has been computed, and the piece from the choice breakpoint to the end is then fit with $T\{t(NT)\}$. A recursive solution is then defined based on above optimal substructure. Let $d(n,m,k,t)$ be a minimal fitting error to approximate every point up to the mth point in the nth stroke with the template t, and let $f(S_n,i,m,t(j))$ be the fitting error, resulting from fitting the segment from the ith point up to the mth point in the nth stroke using $t(j)$. The best fragmentation for a set of strokes with NS strokes using K breakpoints and a template T would thus be $d(NS, NB,K,T)$. The recursive definition of $d(n,m,k,t)$ is expressed as follows:

$$d(n,m,k,t)=\begin{cases}\left[\sum_{i=1}^{n-1} f(S_i,1,NB_i,t(i))\right]+f(S_n,1,m,t(n)), & \text{if } k=0;\\ \min_{k<i<m}\{f(S_n,i,m,t(NT))+d(n,i,k-1,t(j\mid j=1,\cdots,NT-1))\}, & \text{if } n=1,k>0;\\ \min\begin{cases} f(S_n,m,NB_{n-1},t(NT))+d(n-1,i,k,t(j\mid j=1,\cdots,NT-1)) \\ \min_{k<i<m}\{f(S_n,i,m,t(NT))+d(n,i,k-1,t(j\mid j=1,\cdots,NT-1))\}\end{cases}, & \text{if } n>1,k>0.\end{cases} \quad (1)$$

Sketch recognition can then take the results of optimization of stroke segmentation directly as candidate symbols and prune the list of candidate symbols by matching each of primitives and their relationships of drawing shape with the templates. In practice, we design a nested recursive solution by adapting to the technology of dynamic programming. This brings on not only the integration of stroke segmentation and sketch recognition concurrently, but the acceleration of the optimization process also. The contexts of drawing or user model can also be used to reduce the computing complexity. Experiments prove adaptability of this method to both different drawing styles and various shapes with different complexities. Details can be seen in [14].

3.3 Dynamic User Modeling

It is quite difficult and impossible to ask computers to completely understand various sketches. To facilitate the processing of computers, it may be helpful for perceptual processing of strokes that computer can incrementally share the drawing habits and cognitive understanding of humans. Therefore, we propose a dynamic user modeling method to collect and analyze the user's drawings incrementally and establish user model dynamically to assist sketch recognition.

In our work, the term 'user model' mainly means how a user draws a particular sketchy shape or reflects the user's drawing style. For a specific user, a user model is organized as an incremental decision tree, where the root records the user's id and each leaf node records the class label of the inputting graphics, and the branch nodes, that is one part of the integrate graph represented by the leaf node, record the drawing properties of each stroke. All drawing attributes are put together to identify one stroke and used to avoid over-branching of the tree. Each time he/she is drawing, user model is used as an assistance of sketch recognition to predict the "possible shapes" and updated incrementally based on statistical calculation of his/her historical drawing properties. Fig. 4 shows the principle of our strategy of dynamic user modeling.

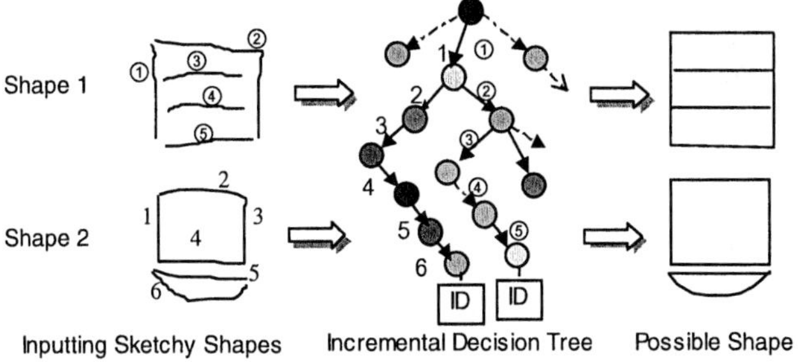

Fig. 4. Illustration of principle of dynamic user modeling

Along with the training process, the decision tree will grow and adjust to the user's styles in stroke sequence and construction of composite shapes. When a composite shape is being sketched in a sequence of strokes, each stroke may be tried to match along the branch. If the matching is successful, the possible composite shape can be predicted or recognized, and, at the same time, the weight of related nodes in the user models are adjusted. Let g' is a weight of the current searching node and *GList* is a list of the candidate objects of the current node, the weight of the candidate objects from this node is "$g' \cdot Glist$. All candidate objects from all surveyed nodes will be ranked by its weight and the objects with less weight will be deleted if there are the same objects classes. When another stroke is input, the direction of this stroke can be calculated as s_1 and s_2, the relation to the last stroke is r_1 and r_2, and the possible shape classes is R_{ij}. Consequently, the weight of the next searching node is: $g = g's_m r_n R_{ij}$, where m, n=1 or 2, and i, j=1,…,14, which is based on our statistic analysis of our experiments. Otherwise, a new branch of the tree is created. Once a composite shape does not exist in the template, the strokes are collected and added to the system after shape regularization. Experimental results prove both effective and efficient of the proposed strategy. Details can be seen in [10] and [13].

4 Conclusion

This paper explores a novel concept of sketch-based informal user interface for graphic computing, Such an interaction mode can be characterized by two properties: pen-based stroking and perceptual processing of strokes, and makes user transfer visual ideas into computer without converting the ideas into a sequence of tedious command operations. This carries through the vision of human-centric computing. A prototype system has embodied some characteristics of informal user interface and two core technologies, adaptive sketch recognition and dynamic user modeling, make it more robust. Obviously, an important task for further researches is to identify an emerging application domain and find a paradigm of interface for that domain.

Acknowledgement

The work described in this paper was supported by grants from National Natural Science Foundation of China (Project No. 69903006 and 60373065) and the Program for New Century Excellent Talents in University of China (2004).

References

1. van Dam A. Post-WIMP user interfaces, Communications of ACM, Vol.40, No.2 (1997).
2. Nielsen J. Non-command user interfaces, Communications of ACM, Vol.36, No.4 (1993).
3. Fish J and S Scrivener, Amplifying the mind's eye: Sketching and visual cognition, Leonardo, Vol. 23, No. 1 (1990) 117-126.
4. Sezgin T. M., Stahovich T., Davis R., Sketch-based interface: early processing for sketch understanding, Proceedings of the 2001 Workshop on PUI, Orlando, Florida, (2001) 1-8.
5. Saund, E, Finding Perceptually Closed Paths in Sketches and Drawings, Transactions on Pattern Analysis and Machine Intelligence. Vol.25, No.4, (2003) 475-491.
6. Rubine Dean, Specifying gestures by example, Computer Graphics, Vol. 25, No. 1 (1991).
7. Fonseca M. J., Pimentel C., Jorge J. A., An online scribble recognizer for calligraphic interfaces. In: AAAI Symposium on Sketch Understanding, AAAI Press (2002) 51-58.
8. Xu X G, Sun Z X, Peng B B, et al, An online composite graphics recognition approach based on matching of spatial relation graphs, IJDAR, Vol. 7, No. 1 (2004) 44-55.
9. Sezgin T. M. and Davis R., HMM-Based Efficient Sketch Recognition, Proceedings of the international conference on Intelligence user interfaces, San Diego, USA, 2005.
10. Sun Z. X., Liu W. Y., et al, User Adaptation for Online Sketchy Shape Recognition. Lecture Notes in Computer Science, Vol. 3088. Springer-Veralg (2004) 303-314.
11. Levent Burak Kara, Thomas F Stahovich, Sim-U-Sketch: A Sketch-Based Interface for Simulink, Proceedings of AVI-2004 (2004) 354-357.
12. Newman M W, James L, Hong J I, et al: DENIM: An informal web site design tool inspired by observations of practice, HCI, Vol. 18 (2003) 259-324.
13. Sun Z X, Wang Q, Yin J F, et al, Incremental Online Sketchy Shape Recognition with Dynamic Modeling and Relevance Feedback, Proceedings of ICMLC2004, Shanghai, China, (2004) 3787-3792.
14. Sun Z X, Yin J F, Yuan B, A novel approach for sketchy shape recognition, Proceedings of GREC2005, Hong Kong, China, (2005).

Building a Believable Character for Real-Time Virtual Environments

Zhigeng Pan, Hongwei Yang, Bing Xu, and Mingmin Zhang

China State Key Lab of CAD&CG,
Zhejiang University, Hangzhou, 310027 P.R. China
{Zgpan, Yanghongwei, Xubin, Zmm}@cad.zju.edu.cn

Abstract. To endow the synthetic characters with autonomous behaviors interests several fields of researchers, especially the experts of computer graphics. In this paper, we propose a believable brain architecture to allow the synthetic character to achieve high level of autonomy. There are three new capabilities. Firstly, this architecture is not a simple stimulation-action model, but adds a layer between stimulation and action called agency that plays a role of extraction and synthesis. Secondly, hierarchy Finite State Machines (FSMs) and fuzzy logic techniques are embedded into the synthetic character's brain. Finally, the ability to integrate the emotion expression model into the brain architecture allows the synthetic characters to express their sensibilities such as happy, angry, sorry, etc., which can inspire the users' passion and fuse them into the virtual world.

1 Believability

Since the enormous classic work on Disney animation (Thomas and Johnson [1]), there have been a number of researches have long wished to build a character that seems to think, feel, live and even share some of our life with it. Thus, there is a need to "endow" the character with believable action. The notion of "believable character" does not mean an honest or reliable character, but one that provides the illusion of life, and thus permits the user's suspension of disbelief. Such characters are, in effect, autonomous agents with their own perceptional, behavioral, and motor mechanisms.

In 1987, Craig Reynolds [2] takes the lead in putting forward a computer model of coordinated animal motion such as bird flocks and fish schools. Tu and Terzopoulos [3] have taken major strides towards creating realistic, self-animating graphical characters through biomechanical modeling and the principles of behavioral animation introduced in the seminal work of Reynolds [2]. Funge [4] develops the cognitive modeling language CML to help build cognitive models. Among the research, synthetic character groups in MIT media lab are focused on developing a practical approach to real-time learning for synthetic characters[5,6]. To enhance the autonomy of virtual humans, Thalmann [7] uses a free flow hierarchy together with a hierarchical classifier system to obtain a virtual human capable to realistically decide by its own (according to its motivations and perceptions) the needed actions in a given environment. Motion synthesis

J. Tao, T. Tan, and R.W. Picard (Eds.): ACII 2005, LNCS 3784, pp. 683–690, 2005.

also plays an important role in realizing the believable character. Kuffner [8] is interested in developing efficient motion planning algorithms and software for simulating and synthesizing motion for complex kinematic and dynamic systems.

Since the true-life humans have a wide variety of expressive actions that react their personalities, emotions, and communicative needs [9,10]. These variations often influence the performance of simpler gestures or facial movements. To make the users suspend disbelief, there is currently considerable research activity on computational models of emotion. For example in the Oz project 'Edge of Intention' where graphically simple creatures called Woggles reflect their emotional responses on a very simple set of features [11]. A further interesting use of this type of emotional/cognitive response system can be seen in a development of the STEVE system. This is an immersive training system which models a US soldier carrying out a peace-keeping mission in Bosnia [12]. Amaya, Bruderlin, and Calvert present a more general method for adding emotion to motions. They derive emotional transforms from motion capture data by quantifying the differences between neutral and emotion-driven actions using the speed of the end-effector and the spatial amplitude of joint angle signals [13]. This increases believability by preventing agents from reacting in the same manner in identical contexts and gives the impression that each agent has distinct emotions and personalities.

In this paper, we present a novel brain architecture for creation of real-time characters with believability. The distinct characteristics from the other works are: we develop finite-sized memory with two parts: storing sensoring information and predicting the dynamic object's state in the memory module. This memory structure can reflect the forgetfulness and persistence that are the fundamental characteristics of human being. To make the synthetic characters bear the human-like behaviors, we adopt fuzzy logic and hierarchical FSMs to implement real-time behaviors in the action planning mechanism. Fuzzy logic used here can deal with imprecise and uncertainty instances such as the human's thinking and perceptions. Hierarchical FSMs can accelerate the processes of action selections to satisfy the real-time requirement. Emotion expression model is also integrated into our system that can augment the character's personality, which moves the users and fuses them into the virtual world. In addition, this system uses any 3D model for characters and other virtual objects and is therefore highly dynamic and configurable.

The paper is structured as follows: in section 2 we present the architecture of the character's brain. The Implementation of believable character for real-time environments is discussed in section 3. The next section presents two illustrative examples generated with the architecture and in the last one we state our conclusions and possible extensions of this system.

2 Brain Architecture

The meaning of autonomous character with believability is to look on the character as autonomous agent. With minimal input from the animator, the character can sense and memory virtual environment by its own brain and select the convincing behavior in terms of its own belief to correspond to the virtual environment. As an autonomous agent, sensoring information, action planning, and motion control functions should be considered in the process of building a cognitive model. According to the three fundamental functions, Figure 1 shows the brain of the believable character in the system.

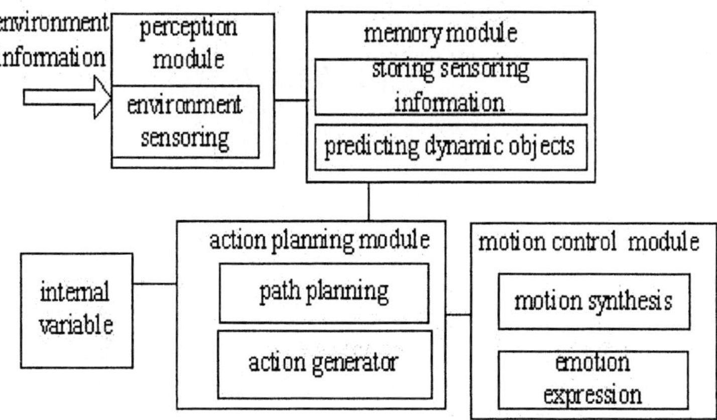

Fig. 1. Brain architecture of the autonomous character

3 Implementation of the Believable Character for Real-Time Environments

3.1 Environmental Sensing

As we stated in the beginning of this chapter, a character's perception model has the ability to simulate, perceive the environment and filter the useless sensoring information. As for the character such as a human or a mammal, vision is the most important and prevalent method to gain sensoring information from virtual environment. In our brain architecture, therefore, perception model basically refers to the vision perception.

Synthetic Vision. In general, a human being's vision sensor is limited to 180 degree spherical angle extending to an effective radius r. The spherical angle and the visual range r define a view volume which objects can be seen. At the same time, occlusion is also modeled in the visual perception of the human being. Therefore, there are two steps to judge which objects can be seen. The first step is to calculate the view volume; the second step is to detect which object in the visual range is occluded. To simplify the computation, one way we adopted is to use each object's cuboid boundary in the calculating of the occlusion. Then the visibility of an object can be estimated by calculating the representative points.

If one of those points can be seen, the object will be perceived. The next step is to consider the object that occluded only by static and rather big objects. An object is "seen" if and only if some part of it enters the visual range (or view volume) and it is not fully occluded behind some other opaque object.

3.2 Action Planning

After the autonomous character achieves the environment information by the perception module, then is to plan the behaviors according to the sensoring information. To realize convincing behaviors for the characters, we integrate internal variable, path planning, and memory into the behavior planning mechanism to implement the convincing behavior. The following parts will give more detailed descriptions of how to implement action planning.

Internal Variable. Internal Variables are used to model character's internal state especially emotion state which can be expressed their values as a continuous value, but they suffer from inadequately or improperly expressing associated with human thinking and perceptions. So a fuzzy logic is developed for internal variables in this paper. In contrast to precise logic, fuzzy logic deals with imprecise and uncertainty information based on the fuzziness measurement of set members.

In the following, we give an example to show how to apply internal variables into behavior rules. Suppose a character wants to talk to someone and the system has some following behavior rules: Rule 1: if not-known the person then pass him; Rule 2: if known the person then talk to him; Rule 3: if known the person well then talk to him.

In the above behavior rules, the system uses the term "KNOWN" to describe the internal variable. Suppose the current value of "KNOWN" is 25. Using the triangle membership, we can convert the current numerical value 25 into 0.75,0.25,0.0. Transferring these membership values to the above behavior rules by using the max-min criterion [14], we can draw the conclusion that he character doesn't know the person and will pass him.

Memory. There are two important characteristics in human being's memory: persistence and oblivion. Persistence means the memory can maintain a model of an object that has been seen before even when the observed object is not directly seen. Oblivion means that the objects that have been seen will fade from the human's memory after a period of time. In this paper, two modules are adopted in the virtual memory: storing sensoring information and predict the dynamic object's state. The sensoring information especially focused on the position in space among the objects is expressed by finite-sized list of events. Each event can drive the action selection module to generate appropriate actions. If the list is full, the memory will forget the old event and displace the oldest event with new events in the list. To understand the function of the second module, we will assume such a phenomenon in the following lines. "A character is walking along the road. Suddenly, he sees a ball coming towards him. He quickly hides behind a tree. To his surprise, the ball doesn't drop. He raises his head and sees the ball hang on the tree".

Now, we analyze how the memory works. When the character sees a moving ball, the memory begins to estimate the ball's next location according to its last observed velocity and some "common sense" knowledge of physics predefined by animator. When the ball fails to drop at the corresponding position calculated by the memory, the memory will send a "surprise" event to the action planning mechanism, which will drive the motion control to express the "surprise" emotion.

Action Generator. Action generator is the process of choosing, at each moment in time, the most appropriate action with regard to all types of perception information.

In general, action can be realized by three ways. The first way is to prepare the action by animators. The second way is to convert the action into animation trees or graphs. The last way is to generate action randomly. In this paper, Finite State Machines (FSMs) is our target representations for characters' plans.

Finite State Machines (FSMs): Are abstract models with a set of "states" that can be traversed. Within these states, the FSMs not only have a special set of outputs but remember the state and can transition to another state, if and only if a set of inputs or premises are met.

Since hierarchical structures has the prominent advantage to deal with the conflict of behaviors or sharing the information between behaviors. This paper builds hierarchical FSMs. The high-level FSMs will be arranged to implement the goal-directed actions, or the compound action. The behaviors generated by the high-level FSMs cannot directly drive the motion system. According to the goal-oriented intention obtained from high-level FSMs, the low-level FSMs will implement the pre-defined actions or direct actions. For example, figure 2 shows the whole process of looking for a toy for a synthetic character. The low-level FSMs also showed in figure 2 will help the character to avoid collision and choose the correct direction at each timestep. The above mentioned behaviors based on the hierarchical FSMs are only an instance. The animator can expand the FSMs to acquire various behaviors. At the same time, the design of multi-level FSMs

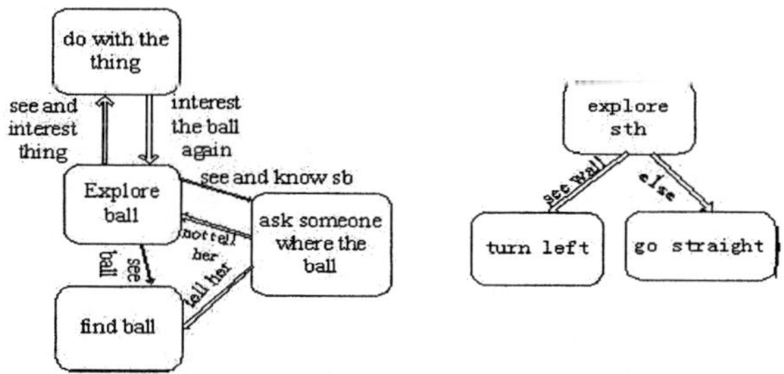

Fig. 2. (a)The high-level behaviors (b)The low-level behaviors

makes the reasoning process more easily and more quickly. Further more, we can achieve rich and colorful behavior animation only by altering the high-level FSMs.

3.3 Motion Control

The last step is to implement motion controller module. Motion controller answers for operating the concrete motion. The detailed technique about the motion controller can be acquired in [15]. In motion controller module, we produce rich emotive behaviors to exhibit contextually appropriate facial expressions and expressive gestures, they could exploit the visual channel to advise, encourage, and empathize with learners. We are currently creating facial animation models by using the tool of Facegen, which based on the theory of geometry distortion to create various expressions. The emotion expression model, integrated into the cognitive system, makes life-like animation, and makes the characters more emotionally engaging, which help the user to suspend disblief.

4 Examples

Example 1: "meimei find the ball" The heroine, meimei is looking for her ball. She sees an unknown girl on the way to ball. She passes her, and goes ahead (see figure 3a). Suddenly, she finds something lying in the front, which inspires her with interest and she decides to see it (see figure 3b). After she knows it is a toy, she decides to find her ball again. Finally, she sees her ball and walks towards it (see figure 3c).

Fig. 3. (a) she sees an unknown girl and passed her (b) she sees an interesting thing and walks towards it (c) she finds her ball and walks towards it

Fig. 4. the facial expression of the boy (a)happy (b)sorry

Example 2: The following screenshot introduce a scene: the boy sees a man walk towards him, he thinks the man want to buy the beer, he is very happy (see figure 4.1); but the man tells him he has not enough money, the boy is very sorry (see figure 4.2).

5 Conclusions and Future Works

In this paper, we have designed a believable brain architecture for the synthetic characters, which can use features such as sensing, memory, planning, emotion expression and motion control to create a human-like brain to achieve their goals. We have designed finite-sized memory with two parts. This structure reflects the forgetfulness and persistence that are the fundamental characteristics of human being. Secondly, fuzzy logic and hierarchical FSMs have been adopted to describe character's actions and illustrate our design by giving examples. Thirdly, Human sensing provides individualized models of the local context that can be combined with internal models of personality and emotion to produce appropriate actions and reactions.

In our current implementation, we have only taken into account the behaviors planned by the animator. There are some works will be investigated in the future. The first is how to increase the characters' abilities to learn automatically. The second is how to exhibit the emotion more accurately and vividly.

Acknowledgements

This research work is supported by 973 project (grant no:2002CB312100), co-supported by China-EU project (ELVIS), and TRAPOYT Program in Higher Education Institution of MOE, PRC. The authors would like to express thanks to Dr. Xu Weiwei, Dr. Liu Zhen who give constructive suggestion to this research work.

References

1. Thomas, F., Johnston, O.: Disney Animation: The Illusion of Life. Abbeville Press, New York (1981)
2. Reynolds, C.W.: Flocks, herds, and schools: A distributed behavioral model. Computer Graphics, (1987) 21(4): 25-34
3. Tu, X., Terzopoulos, D.: Artificial fishes: Physics, locomotion, perception, behavior. Pro-ceedings of SIGGRAPH (1994), 24-29
4. Funge, J., Tu, X., Terzopoulos, D.: Cognitive Modeling: Knowledge, Reasoning and Plan-ning for Intelligent Characters. SIGGRAPH (1999) 11-13
5. Isla, D., Burke, R., Downie, M., Blumberg, B.: A Layered Brain Architecture for Synthetic Creatures. Proceedings of IJCAI, Seattle, WA, August (2001)
6. Blumberg, B., Downie, M., Ivanov, Y., Berlin, M., Johnson, M.P., Tomlinson, B.: Inte-grated Learning for Interactive Synthetic Characters. SIGGRAPH (2002)

7. De Sevin, E., Thalmann, D.: The complexity of testing a motivational model of action selec-tion for virtual humans. Computer Graphics International (CGI), IEEE Computer So-cietyPress, June (2004)
8. Yamane, K., Kuffner, J., Hodgins, J.K.: Synthesizing Animations of Human Manipulation Tasks. SIGGRAPH (2004)
9. Cassell, J., Thorisson, K. R.: The power of a nod and a glance: Envelope vs. emotional feedback in animated conversational agents. Applied Artificial Intelligence (1999) 13:519-538
10. Canamero, D.: Modelling motivations and emotions as a basis for intelligent behaviour. 1st International Conference Autonomous Agents, ACM press (1998) 148-155
11. Bates, J.: The role of emotion in believable agents. Communications of the ACM, (1994) 37(7): 122-125
12. Gratch, J., Rickel, J., Masalla, S.: Tears and Fears. 5Th International Conference on Autonomous Agents, (2001) 113-118
13. Amaya, K., Bruderlin, A., Calvert, T.: Emotion from Motion. In W. A. Davis and R. Bartels (Eds), Graphics Interface '96, 222-229. Canadian Information Processing Society, Canadian Human-Computer Communications Society, May, (1996)
14. Yuan, Y., Zhuang, H.: A Genetic Algorithm for Generating Fuzzy Classification Rules. Fuzzy Sets and Systems, (1996) 84: 1-19
15. Xu, W.: the research of human animation for intelligent virtual environment. Ph.D. Thesis, University of Zhejiang, (2002)

A Wearable Multi-sensor System for Mobile Acquisition of Emotion-Related Physiological Data

Christian Peter[1], Eric Ebert [1,2], and Helmut Beikirch[2]

[1] Fraunhofer Institute for Computer Graphics Rostock, Joachim Jungius Str. 11, 18059 Rostock, Germany
christian.peter@igd-r.fraunhofer.de
[2] University of Rostock, Faculty of Computer Science and Electrical Engineering, Albert-Einstein-Str. 2, 18059 Rostock, Germany
helmut.beikirch@uni-rostock.de

Abstract. Interest in emotion detection is increasing significantly. For research and development in the field of Affective Computing and emotion-aware interaction techniques, reliable and robust technology is needed for detecting emotional signs in users under everyday conditions. In this paper, a novel wearable system for measuring emotion-related physiological parameters is presented. Currently heart rate, skin conductivity, and skin temperature are taken; further sensors can easily be added. The system is very easy to use, robust, and suitable for mobile and long-time logging of data. It has an open architecture and can easily be integrated into other systems or applications. The system is designed for use in emotion research as well as in everyday affective applications.

1 Introduction

Affective Computing and Intelligent Interaction are key technologies to enable computers to observe, understand, and exhibit emotion. Researchers and engineers around the world work on ways to incorporate and exploit emotion in systems and applications, computer scientists investigate the role emotions play in Human-Machine Interaction, and psychologists, sociologists and anthropologists examine potential effects of affective systems on people and their relations to each other, machines, and media (cf. [1, 2, 3, 4, 5]). They all rely heavily on reliable and robust equipment to detect signs of emotions in the human in focus.

There are a number of commercial systems available for measuring emotion-related peripheral physiological parameters like skin conductivity, skin temperature, or heart rate. However, those systems have been developed for medical or psychological studies, which usually take place in fixed lab environments with a wired subject sitting fairly motionless in front of a display, occasionally hitting buttons on a keyboard or computer mouse. For studies on emotion in everyday human-computer interaction in natural settings at home or at work, in the office, the train, or on the aeroplane, the systems available proof to be unsuitable.

The system introduced in this paper has been designed for emotion researchers who want to examine emotional aspects of life outside the lab, for software developers who want to make use of emotion information in their systems without

J. Tao, T. Tan, and R.W. Picard (Eds.): ACII 2005, LNCS 3784, pp. 691 – 698, 2005.

bothering about physiology, measurement artefacts, or filter chains, and of course also for psychologists who want to perform their studies in a natural setting without the irritating and distracting effects of wires on a subject. The system has been designed for use by lay-persons in an everyday environment, mobile or stationary, and without putting restrictions on the user's behaviour. It gives the researcher and programmer the most possible freedom in handling the data, providing the measurements conveniently in engineering units. Developed with the researcher and application developer in mind, the device is fitted with robust and reliable error handling and diagnosis mechanisms, guaranteeing sensible data continuously being available along with reliability information. The system is small, light-weight, functions wirelessly, transmits data immediately and is also able to store data locally. It operates as long as 140 hours with one battery pack. It has an open architecture and sends out the data in an open format, allowing software developers to easily incorporate the device into their systems as emotion sensing input source.

In the next section, requirements are defined for developing sensing devices for emotion-related physiological data to be used in HCI research and affect processing applications. A concept of a system meeting the identified requirements is developed in the subsequent section, followed by the description of a system implementing it. A discussion and outlook concludes the paper.

2 Requirements

Currently available sensor systems such as Thought Technologies' Procomp family, Mindmedia's Nexus device, or BodyMedia's SenseWear system are widely used in emotion research besides traditional medical devices like electrocardiographs (ECG), electroencephalographs (EEG), and electromyographs (EMG) for collecting emotion-related physiological data. Except the SenseWear system, they all use traditional electrodes as sensor elements, which are attached to the subjects with tape or Velcro fastener, the wires being directly connected to the data collecting device. This not only irritates and distracts the subject from the task, but also hinders free and natural movements (confer e.g. [6]). The collected data are either stored locally on the device, or transmitted directly to the processing computer. In either case, the data can only be accessed, viewed and analysed using the manufacturer's software and are not available instantly to other applications. If at all, data can be "exported" after the session for off-line analysis with third-party products.

Affective applications, however, need direct and immediate access to the data to allow for continuous adaptation of the system to an ever-changing user state. There should be no need to use proprietary software. Also, there should always be sensible data available, freeing the programmer from caring about lost connections, transmission errors, badly fitted electrodes, and other technical side aspects. For the same reason, data should be made available to processing applications in engineering units, avoiding inclusion of sensor-specific formulae into applications and eliminating the risk of conversion errors.

The device needs to be very robust. In research experiments, subjects should not need to pay attention to wires or cables while performing tasks. In everyday applications, users won't accept frail hard- or software. Basic sensors should be integrated within the system. There should be no need to fumble about with additional components in order to get sensible data out of the device. At the current state of the art, heart rate and skin conductivity are strong physiological indicators of emotion.

Easy usage and a fixed position of the electrodes are prerequisite for reliable acquisition of physiological data. Difficult handling of loose sensor elements as is usual with currently available systems leads to differently attached electrodes, at different positions, with different pressure, for every individual. This is critical, as tests performed by us proofed that e.g. skin resistance taken at the hand differs by several hundred kilo ohms and sometimes even Mega ohms at positions just 1 cm apart. Also, different electrode pressure causes different temperature flows between electrodes and skin, influencing the value and speed of change of the measured temperature. Hence, usual methods to attach sensor elements with tape or Velcro lead to uncontrolled, different conditions for each subject of a study.

Concerning the number and type of sensors used, it should be possible to easily add further sensors of any manufacturer to the system. An open protocol to allow third-party sensors feeding their data into the system is hence considered a desired feature.

Finally, a small form factor, light weight, and operation over a longer period of time are essential for mobile real-world applications. They increase the willingness of subjects of non-lab and long-time studies to wear the apparatus and are important for the acceptance of everyday applications and system. Operation over a longer period of time is prerequisite for longitudinal research studies, which are very rare in the field of emotion research due to the lack of appropriate equipment. A device that can be used mobile over several days or even weeks will hence open new possibilities for emotion research and will yield new insights into everyday emotional response.

Those requirements are main features identified necessary for a system to be used as emotion-related input device for affective applications and emotion-aware interaction techniques. As mentioned above, existing systems show different severe limitations each. A concept for new devices meeting the identified requirements is worked out in the following section.

3 Concept

For a system to meet the criteria identified above, a distributed architecture with wirelessly connected components seems to be most appropriate. A sensor unit should be placed close to the body of the user, ideally hiding any wires and being comfortable to wear. A base unit takes care of receiving, validating, and storing the data locally, as well as of making them available immediately to processing applications. The base unit should be freely positionable within a sensible range of the sensor unit to allow, for instance, the experimenter to monitor the captured data immediately and out of sight of the subject, or for the office worker to go for a cup of coffee without caring about the experiment he is involved in. Of course, the system should be able to cope with the base unit losing contact with the sensor unit, or multiple sensor units communicating with one or many base units at the same time.

3.1 Sensor Unit

For acquisition of peripheral physiological data, sensor elements need to be in direct contact with the subject's skin. To avoid long wires leading from the electrodes to the data processing electronics, the sensor unit should be close to the actual measuring point. To allow for an easy usage and hence increased acceptance of the system, all the electronics and wires should be invisibly integrated in a device or clothing usually worn by people, for instance a glove, wristband, brassiere, jewellery, or a headband. As has been shown in other studies (e.g. [7]), those integrated devices are quickly accepted and users soon forget about being monitored.

The main task of the sensor unit is to capture the data and to perform basic pre-evaluations on them, like detecting measurement errors or sensor failures. If errors occur, appropriate action could be taken, like re-adjustment of the sensing elements, calibration of circuitry, or notification of the base unit. Before the data can be transmitted, they have to be wrapped in an appropriate transmission protocol, and a checksum has to be generated.

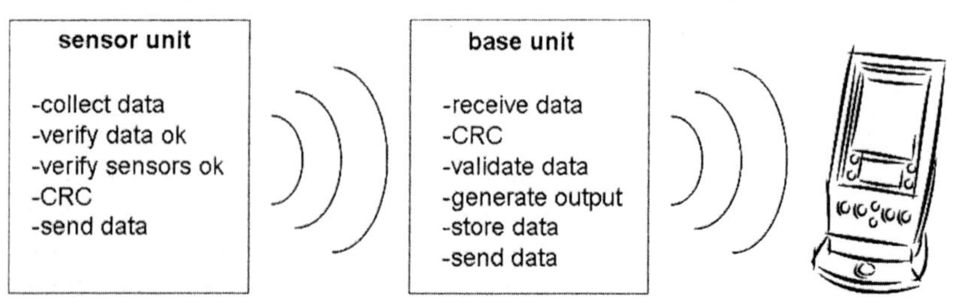

Fig. 1. Block diagram of the system

3.2 Base Unit

The base unit is to receive the data from one or many sensor units. Received data get a time stamp to allow assignment of the data to application events and to make it possible to correlate them with other data. After validating the checksum, data will be evaluated for sensibility, based on stored information on typical values and development characteristics of the data and possibly under consideration of other sensor's results. For instance, when all sensors don't send sensible data, it is likely that the sensor unit is not attached properly to the user. When just one sensor reports unusual data, there might be a problem with that sensor, or a single sensing element might not be properly attached. In case of a sensor error, the sensor unit could, for instance, be reset. In case a bad attachment of the sensor unit is assumed, the user could be notified and asked for assistance.

Based on the evaluation result, output data will be prepared in a next step. Since it is desirable to provide data continuously, missing or bad data have to be treated, for instance by filling gaps with likely data. Where alterations have been performed on the data, this has to be made known to the processing applications. Prepared like this, the data can be sent out continuously to a processing host. For applications with no permanent link to a processing host, the possibility to store the data locally has to be provided.

4 Implementation

A sensor system has been developed [8] at Fraunhofer IGD Rostock which follows the concept above and offers additional, convenient features. Apart from the required measurements of skin conductivity and heart rate, skin temperature and ambient air temperature are measured. The base unit features a display to visualise the current state of the system, or data. Basic user input is possible by buttons, allowing, for instance, setting user events or toggling between visualizations. As a special feature for applications and mobile devices, the base unit can generate events, such as detection of certain physiological states, which are made available through an optical coupler to the outside world. Communication between sensor unit and base unit is done wirelessly using an ISM (Industry, Scientific, and Medical) band transmitter. With the currently used transmitter, the range is 10-30 meters indoors and up to 300 meters outdoors.

The current version of the system uses a glove as garment hosting the sensor unit.

4.1 Sensor Unit

All sensors except for the heart rate are integrated in a glove. This allows for short and hidden wires from the sensing elements for skin temperature and skin conductivity to the circuit board, which is also accommodated by the glove. The used heart rate receiver from Polar is designed for being mounted near the hand and is also integrated in the sensor unit's electronics. As heart rate sensor, a conventional chest belt is used.

The skin conductivity sensor is implemented two-fold. This helps to increase the robustness of the system significantly. Data evaluation checks can be performed more reliably based on those duplicate data. The skin temperature is taken at two different positions as well but integrated in one sensor, leading to higher accuracy and higher resolution.

Also in the sensor unit, the ambient air temperature near the device is measured. This is another important factor for calculating sensor status and data reliability, since skin temperature and skin conductivity vary with changing environmental temperature.

Skin temperature as well as skin conductivity are sampled 20 times per second each. Heart rate data are sent out by the heart rate sensor immediately after a beat has been detected. The collected data are immediately digitized and assessed for sensor failure as described in the data validation section below. Based on the evaluation results, output data are prepared in a next step. In case of bad or temporarily no data from a sensor, previous data are used to estimate the likely current value. In this case, a flag in the transmission protocol is set accordingly. Wrapped into the protocol and fitted with a CRC check sum, the data are sent out permanently by the integrated ISM-band transmitter.

4.2 Base Unit

The base unit receives the data transmitted from the sensor unit. Thanks to the wireless connection, multiple sensor units can be used, provided they have different identifiers. Immediately after they have been received the data get a time stamp. After a positive check sum evaluation, data are validated as described in the data validation section below. The validation results are stored along with the data and their time stamp on a local exchangeable memory card. If desired, they can also be sent out permanently to a host computer using a serial connection like traditional RS232, USB, or Bluetooth.

Also in the base unit, the environmental temperature is taken again. This is an additional indicator on environmental changes the person might be exposed to and complements the according measurement of the sensor unit (while the sun might shine on the hands of the user, resulting in a higher local temperature near the hand, the room might still be chilly).

All data are made available in engineering units. The temperature is represented in degree Celsius with a resolution of 0.01°C. The skin resistance comes in kilo ohms with a resolution of 300 kilo ohms. The heart rate comes in beats per minute with a resolution of 1 bpm. Transmission speed to a processing host is for each of the sensors 5 validated values per second.

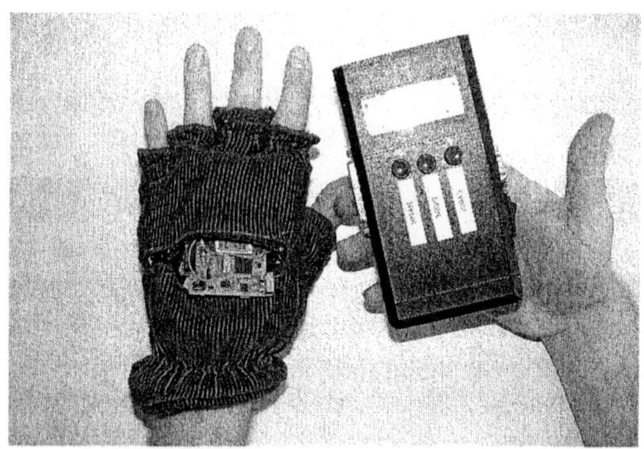

Fig. 2. Prototype of glove with sensor unit, and base unit (right)

4.3 Data Validation

Data are validated throughout the system at two levels: a low-level evaluation is performed on the data in the sensor unit, and a higher level validation is carried out in the base unit with respect to usefulness of the data. Validation is based on the SEVA (Self Validation) standard [9], [10], [11].

Low Level Validation

The sensor unit collects data from several sensors. In the configuration described in this paper there are two skin resistance sensors, one skin temperature sensor, one ambient air temperature sensor, and one heart rate sensor. Except for the air temperature sensor, all sensors need direct connection to the user's body. As the user moves about sensing elements might become temporarily detached. Those cases are handled at the data level by the sensor unit. If no data are received from a sensing element, a "best estimate" is sent instead. A flag in the transmission protocol is set in this case, indicating that the data are estimates. If no data have been received from a sensor for a longer period of time (e.g. for 10 samples), a sensor status flag is set accordingly in the transmission protocol.

High Level Validation

Based on the data and sensor status received from the base unit and on the check sum result, the status of each sensor is analysed by the base unit continuously and validated SEVA data are generated. The following data are produced:

- Validated measurement value (VMV): this corresponds to the actually measured value as long as no problem occurred and the data are in a sensible range. In case of problems, i.e. estimated data have been received or the sensor status being blind, further considerations on the most likely value are made. In case data move out of a predefined range or develop unusual (i.e. heart rate over 200 bpm, jump of skin temperature by 2 °C within 0.2 seconds), a VMV value will be estimated based on previously received data and stored measurand characteristics.
- Validated uncertainty (VU): the VU denotes the likely error of the VMV. It can be seen as an "uncertainty band" enclosing the VMV.
- Measurement value status (MVS): a discrete parameter indicating the reliability of the VMV. According to the SEVA standard, possible values are: clear (valid measurement), blurred (estimated data after known errors have occurred), dazzled (estimated data with uncertain cause of problems), and blind (estimated data of increasing uncertainty).
- Device status (DS): the device status indicates how operational a sensor is. The SEVA standard proposes 6 states: good (no problems), testing (sensor in self-test), suspect (malfunction possible but not yet verified), impaired (malfunction with low impact), bad (serious malfunction diagnosed), and critical (sensor not operational).
- Detailed diagnostics (DD): in case of an error, precise information on the error are provided, e.g. no data, wrong CRC, data out of range.

Those SEVA data are stored in the base unit and communicated to processing applications, along with the data.

5 Discussion and Outlook

A sensor system has been described for nearly unobtrusively collecting emotion-related physiological data. The system is suited for mobile use over a longer period of time, storing the data on an exchangeable memory card or transmitting them immediately to a processing host. A robust data evaluation mechanism allows for continuous data availability and provides information on the reliability of the data and the sensor status. Processing applications can therefore make use of the data without the need of sensor-specific knowledge and without caring about technical side aspects such as badly fitted electrodes or transmission errors.

An open protocol is used to communicate sensor data from sensor units to the base unit which allows integration of third-party products complying to the protocol. Data are made available to processing applications via an open protocol as well. The system is hence best suited as input device for any application processing emotion-related physiological parameters. Fixed positions and constant pressure of sensing elements eliminate uncontrolled sensing conditions in emotion studies.

Further developments of the system include a heart rate sensor without a chest belt, a respiration sensor, and a sensor for blood volume pressure. The communication protocol will be developed further to allow multiple sensor units and multiple base units operating close to each other at the same time. Also, more powerful ISM band transmitters will be evaluated.

References

1. Picard, R.W.: Affective Computing. M.I.T. Press, Cambridge, MA (1997).
2. Arafa Y., Botelho L.M., Bullock A., Figueiredo P., Gebhard P., Höök K., Mamdani E. H., Paiva A., Petta P., Sengers P., Vala M.: Affective Interactions for in Real-time Applications: the SAFIRA Project (2004).
3. Interacting with Computers. Volume 14, Issue 2, (2002).
4. Interacting with Computers. Volume 16, Issue 4, (2004).
5. Reeves B., Nass C.: The Media Equation. Center for the Study of Language and Information (1996).
6. Haag A., Goronzy S., Schaich P., Williams J.: Emotion Recognition Using Bio-sensors: First Steps towards an Automatic System. In: André et al (Eds.): Affective Dialogue Systems. Springer-Verlag Berlin, Heidelberg, New York (2004).
7. Picard, R., Scheirer, J.: The Galvactivator: A Glove that Senses and Communicates Skin Conductivity. 9th Intl. Conference on Human-Computer Interaction, New Orleans (2001)
8. Ebert, E.: Weiterentwicklung und Verifikation eines Messsystem zur Erfassung humanphysiologischer Sensordaten unter Berücksichtigung des SEVA-Konzepts. MsC Thesis, University of Rostock (2005).
9. BS 7986: Industrial process measurement and control – Data quality metrics. Available from BSI Customer Services email: orders@bsi-global.com (2004).
10. Henry M.P.: Self-Validating Sensors – Towards Standards and Products. Automatione e Strumentazione (2001).
11. Zhou, F., Archer, N., Bowles, J., Clarke, D., Henry, M., Peter, C.: A general hardware platform for sensor validation. IEE Colloquium on intelligent and self-validating sensors, Oxford (1999).

The HandWave Bluetooth Skin Conductance Sensor

Marc Strauss[1], Carson Reynolds[1], Stephen Hughes[2], Kyoung Park[3], Gary McDarby[2], and Rosalind W. Picard[1]

[1] MIT Media Laboratory, 20 Ames Street, Cambridge, Massachusetts 02139, USA
{mstrauss, carsonr, picard}@media.mit.edu
[2] Media Lab Europe, Sugar House Lane, Bellevue, Dublin 8, Ireland
{Stephen.Hughes, Gary.McDarby}@mle.ie
[3] Digital Media Lab, 517-10 Dogok-Dong, Gangnam-gu, Seoul, Korea
park@icu.ac.kr

Abstract. HandWave is a small, wireless, networked skin conductance sensor for affective computing applications. It is used to detect information related to emotional, cognitive, and physical arousal of mobile users. Many existing affective computing systems make use of sensors that are inflexible and often physically attached to supporting computers. In contrast, HandWave allows an additional degree of flexibility by providing ad-hoc wireless networking capabilities to a wide variety of Bluetooth devices as well as adaptive biosignal amplification. As a consequence, HandWave is used in a variety of affective computing applications such as games, tutoring systems, experimental data collection, and augmented journaling. This paper describes the novel design attributes of this handheld sensor, its development, and various form factors. Future work includes an extension of this approach to other biometric signals of interest to affective computing researchers.

1 Untethered Affect

Much of the work on ubiquitous and perceptual computing has focused on ways in which individuals can interact with computers in less constrained contexts than typing on a keyboard at a fixed desk. Indeed, affective computing ("computing that relates to, arises from, or deliberately influences emotion" [1]) is motivated in part by the potential for more human-like and natural communication with computers. Ironically, many current affective computing prototypes require that users be tethered in an unnatural, and often cumbersome, manner. The HandWave device provides an example of a noticeably more flexible approach to sensing for affect, viewed from the standpoint of both users and application developers.

1.1 Affect Sensing

An affect sensor is a device that receives an input signal and processes it in order to detect some evidence of emotions. There are many techniques and modalities used to detect affect: physiological sensors, facial expression recognition, speech prosody recognition, and pressure sensors [2] have all been applied to the problem. Affect sensors are often coupled with algorithms that are specifically designed to distinguish and classify patterns associated with emotional states [3]. Among physiological

J. Tao, T. Tan, and R.W. Picard (Eds.): ACII 2005, LNCS 3784, pp. 699 – 706, 2005.

signals, electrodermal activity [4], respiration, eletrokardiogram (EKG), and eyeblink rates have already been investigated by psychophysiology researchers.

1.2 Existing Electrodermal Activity Devices

A variety of devices and circuit designs already exist for detecting electrodermal activity. Three of the designs discussed below require that the user be cabled to a host computer. The last design, which uses Bluetooth, is similar to the HandWave, but is proprietary and closed.

ProComp. Biofeedback data acquisition devices have been used by a number of researchers to capture physiological data for affective computing applications. In addition to skin conductance, the ProComp series from Thought Technology Ltd. [7] is capable of capturing eight other channels that can be configured to collect "EEG, EKG, RMS EMG, ... heart rate, blood volume pulse, respiration, goniometry, force, and voltage input." The device communicates to a host computer using a fiber-optic cable, requiring the user to be tethered.

BioPac. The BioPac MP [8] is a modular system for collecting a variety of physiological signals for research or educational purposes. The system provides a data-acquisition board that can be connected to a host computer by USB or Ethernet cable. A variety of amplifier modules can be purchased for a wide variety of physiological signals including skin conductance.

Galvactivator. The affective computing group at the MIT Media Lab developed "a glove-like wearable device that senses the wearer's skin conductivity and maps its values to a bright LED display" [9]. The galvactivator device also provides a data port from which an analog to digital converter can sample. The sensor is comfortable, but requires that the wearer be cabled to a host computer to transmit EDA data.

Brainquiry. As a maker of "neurofeedback, biofeedback and psychophysiological measuring equipment," Brainquiry [10] sells a compact galvanic skin response sensor which uses Bluetooth to communicate with a host computer. However, little information is provided by the manufacturer about the proprietary design of the biofeedback amplifier.

2 Electrodermal Response

When one becomes mentally, emotionally, or physically aroused, a response is triggered in one's skin. Known as the electrodermal activity (EDA), this response can be used as an indicator of one's level of excitement or relaxation. This phenomenon is known as the sympathetic response, and is commonly referred to as "Fight or Flight." During excitation, in accordance with the sympathetic response, sweat glands in the skin fill with sweat, a weak electrolyte and good conductor. This results in many low-resistance parallel pathways, thereby increasing the conductivity of the skin [5].

EDA consists of two components: tonic and phasic [4]. The tonic component is a low frequency baseline conductivity level, which can oscillate over the course of days. The phasic component rides on top of the tonic component, is of higher frequency, and generally increases when a person is aroused. Problematically, each person has a different tonic conductivity, so in order to infer the arousal level of the subject, the relative changes in EDA must be analyzed over a period of time. Furthermore, skin conductance (measured in units of siemens; formerly mhos) depends on the skin path length between the two electrodes contacts, even for subjects with identical skin conductivity (measured in units of siemens/meter). It is for these reasons that it is crucial to analyze the temporal variations of the EDA signal.

3 HardWare

The core of the HandWave consists of two sandwiched printed circuit boards, one containing amplification circuitry, and one containing the Bluetooth module. The amplifier board provides the power connections and the terminal for the pair of electrodes. The device resides within an injection molded polypropylene housing, which includes an external power switch and electrode connection port.

We have designed the HandWave electronics and periphery in order to facilitate ease of use. For such a technology to become widespread, universality is essential. We decided to use Bluetooth technology and a standard battery size in order to increase the universality of the HandWave. These features allow the HandWave to be an off-the-shelf device, equipped for maximum operation with minimal support.

3.1 Amplifier Board

The amplification circuitry resident on the HandWave is centered around a PIC 16LF88 microcontroller. The PIC collects the EDA data, communicates with the processor embedded in the Bluetooth module, and controls the gain of the amplification circuitry. The analog-to-digital converter on the PIC is used to gather the EDA data. During operation, if the EDA signal approaches the limit of the ADC range, the PIC will adjust the amplification gain accordingly. The HandWave uses this adjustable gain to initially center and continually adjust the gain mode in order to increase EDA data resolution.

The signal amplification on the HandWave has two stages, implemented on a dual-package operational amplifier. The first stage of amplification uses a 0.5 Volt reference to maintain a constant voltage across the skin. In accordance with an inverting amplifier configuration, the voltage gain of this stage is controlled by a resistance ratio. One of these resistances is provided by the subject's skin, as measured between a pair of electrodes. The other is subject to alteration by an analog switch, controlled by the PIC, which provides four different gain modes by switching different resistors into the circuit. The schematic for this first amplification stage is shown in Figure 1. The second amplification stage is used to invert, scale, and shift the EDA signal in order to match the PIC ADC usable voltage range.

The HandWave can measure skin conductance levels between 0 and 40 microsiemens (μS). The four gain modes have ranges of 0-5, 4-10, 8-20, and 16-40 μS. The gain mode information is transferred in parallel with ADC readings so the receiving computer can reconstruct the absolute measured skin conductance level.

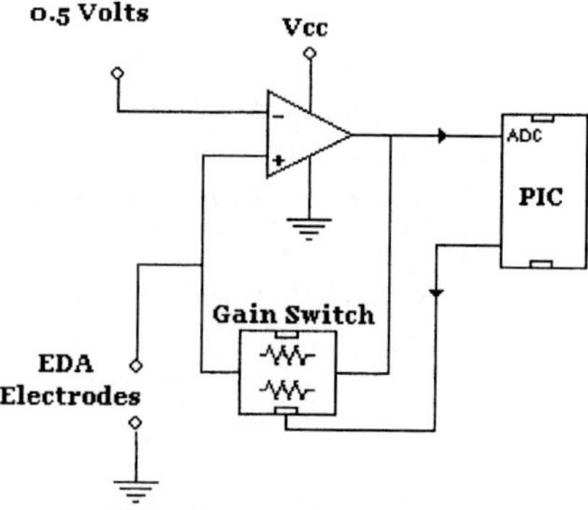

Fig. 1. First EDA signal amplification stage. The PIC can adjust the gain if the signal approaches the limit of the ADC range. Four gain modes are implemented in this way.

The ADC on the PIC has 10-bit resolution. In order to detect EDA up to 20 Hz in frequency and attenuate signal noise to a level less than that which would alter the least significant bit, the PIC ADC samples at 1280 Hz. The PIC software averages every 32 samples, and the averages are sent over the wireless link at a rate of 40 Hz. In actuality, skin conductivity need not be measured at frequencies exceeding 5 Hz [11]. In the final prototype, the EDA signal resolution and sampling speed are high enough that minute changes in skin conductance from individual deep breaths are detected by the HandWave, as shown in Figure 2:

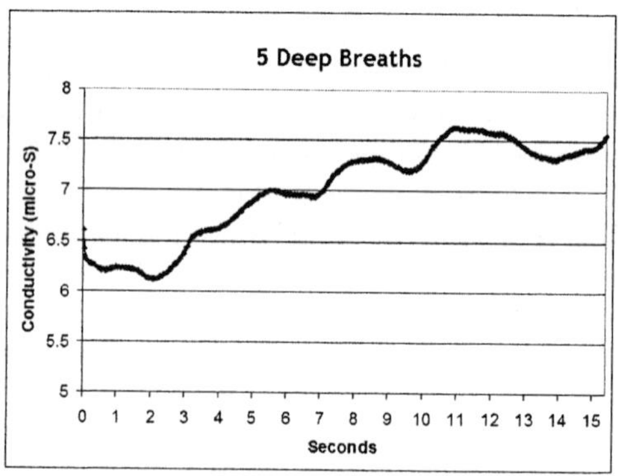

Fig. 2. EDA signal from the HandWave during deep breathing. The breaths can be seen in the fluctuations of the signal, and confirmed through comparison with the time axis.

Many design considerations were combined in order to reduce the size of the HandWave. The geometry of the circuit boards, as well as their dense component arrangement significantly reduces the size of the device. The interface for in-circuit PIC programming consists of solder pads on the surface of the amplification board. Spring-loaded probes in a custom jig make electrical contact with these pads during programming. These design factors help to make the HandWave smaller and thereby less obtrusive to the wearer. The top of the amplifier board is shown in Figure 3:

Fig. 3. HandWave amplification board. The size of the board was reduced by densely arranging the surface-mount components and utilizing solder pads for in-circuit programming.

3.2 Bluetooth Board

The Bluetooth transceiver used for the HandWave is a Mitsumi WML-C20A module. This module is integrated with an antenna and a processor with 512 kB of flash ROM. During normal operation, the module streams the EDA output received from the PIC over the wireless link to a nearby Bluetooth-equipped computer. Being a class-1 module, the WML-C20A is specified to be able to maintain connections at up to 100 meters. The Bluetooth module can also send information received over the wireless link to the PIC, resulting in bi-directional data transfer capabilities.

3.3 Power and Electrodes

The HandWave can be powered by any voltage source between 3.3 and 16 Volts. The device has been measured to draw approximately 70 mA of current during normal operation. The majority of the current is drawn by the Bluetooth module, which is specified to consume up to 150 mA.

Medical-grade electrodes are used in conjunction with conductive gel to provide a reliable electrical connection to the subject's skin. We have used Ag/AgCl electrodes placed either on two adjacent fingers or on opposite sides of the palm. These configurations both provide skin path lengths on the order of four inches.

3.4 Housing

The original form factor for the HandWave was a wristwatch. This allows a sturdy, adjustable fixation to the wrist, in close proximity to the hand where the electrodes are placed. However, the power consumption of the device necessitated replacement of the coin cell batteries after two hours of operation.

We next tested the HandWave in a handheld orb, with only electrodes and a power switch exposed. The orb allowed the use of a larger battery, which only had to be replaced occasionally. However, we found that the subject, while holding the orb, was able to significantly increase his EDA reading by squeezing the orb, thereby improving the fidelity of the electrode connection. These motion artifacts, compounded with the inconvenience of accessing the embedded device for maintenance, prompted the design and manufacture of a dedicated housing for the HandWave sensor.

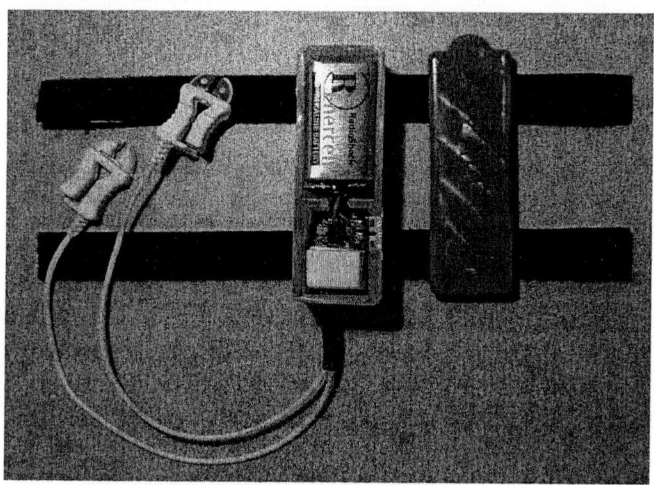

Fig. 4. The HandWave, replete with housing, battery, wrist straps, and electrode leads

The most recent revision of the HandWave housing is shown in Figure 4. It is injection-molded out of polypropylene, and includes one cavity for the HandWave circuit boards, one cavity for a 9V battery, and one cavity for a power switch. There is also a single port on the side of the housing for connecting the electrodes to the amplifier board. The housing can be mounted on the wrist with Velcro straps or clips. The lid attaches to the housing body by means of a snap fit, and the power switch, circuit boards, and battery are press-fit into their respective cavities. The 9V battery provides power for approximately 10 hours of operation, and the press/snap fit assembly allows easy access to the interior elements. Finally, the electrodes are not situated on the housing itself, which prevents the wearer from inducing significant motion artifacts in the EDA signal.

4 Applications

The HandWave device is currently being used in a variety of different applications. This is due in part to the ease with which the device can be integrated into existing systems: the use of Bluetooth technology gives the HandWave universal connectivity, and the standard battery size and easy-access housing make it user-friendly. This allows the HandWave to transmit EDA data to preexisting computers, PDAs, mobile phones, or any other device which is equipped with a Bluetooth transceiver.

Big Gulp. A virtual environment that simulates underwater exploration in a shallow coral reef and along an undersea cliff. The environment is designed to support children engaged in inquiry-based science learning activities. We have developed a visualization of user attention maps in Big Gulp using a HandWave sensor. By stimulating users with startle events, we determined the location and intensity of user attention throughout the environment. Head direction readings reveal the areas of longest dwell time within the virtual world. The degree of attention level at particular regions is measured through EDA and represented by rendered air bubbles. The size of the bubbles represents the amplitude of changes in skin conductance.

Learning Companion. A relational agent that supports different meta-cognitive strategies to help students overcome frustration [12]. The system makes use of a large number of sensors: facial expression recognition, pressure-sensitive mouse and chair, and skin conductance as measured by a HandWave. Information from these sensors is merged to achieve affective mirroring: the agent subtly mimics the user's various aspects of the user's affective expressions.

Collective Calm. A multiplayer biofeedback video game that teaches players how to relax within a competitive environment while learning to cooperate as part of a team. The game is based around a virtual 'tug of war' competition between two teams in which each player gains individual strength by relaxing, and thereby decreasing his or her skin conductance. The team that collectively relaxes the most wins the game. HandWaves are used to measure each of the four players' EDA in real time.

5 Conclusions

We have described a wearable wireless skin conductance sensor, HandWave, and applications. The HandWave's small, unobtrusive form factor and use of wireless data transfer provide an additional degree of flexibility when compared to tethered skin conductance sensors. The use of Bluetooth technology and a standard battery size allows for portability and quick system integration. Future possibilities for the HandWave include creation of similar EKG, pulse rate, respiration, and other biosignal amplifiers for use with Bluetooth wireless data transfer. Furthermore, EDA sensors can be installed in existing handheld devices such as cellular phones, which already possess wireless capabilities.

References

1. Picard R.W. (1997). Affective Computing (MIT Press, Cambridge, MA)
2. Reynolds, C. (2001). The sensing and measurement of frustration with computers. Master's Thesis. Massachusetts Institute of Technology , Cambridge , MA.
3. Qi, Y. and Picard, R.W. (2002). Context-sensitive Bayesian Classifiers and Application to Mouse Pressure Pattern Classification, in Proceedings of International Conference on Pattern Recognition, August 2002, Quebec City, Canada.
4. Boucsein, W. (1992). Electrodermal Activity, Plenum Series in Behavioral Psychophysiology and Medicine, Plenum Press
5. Malmivuo, J. Plonsey, R. "Bioelectromagnetism." The Electrodermal Response. Oxford University Press: New York. 1995.
6. Thought Technology Ltd. (2005). Biofeedback Equipment: ProComp Infiniti Hardware. http://www.thoughttechnology.com/procomp.htm
7. BioPac Systems, Inc. (2005). MP System Features. http://www.biopac.com/mp100_features.htm
8. Picard, R. W. and Scheirer, J. (2001). The Galvactivator: A Glove that Senses and Communicates Skin Conductivity. Proceedings 9th Int. Conf. on HCI, 2001, New Orleans, USA, 2001.

9. Brainquiry, BV. (2005). PET-GSR Wireless. http://www.brainquiry.nl/shop.php?pId=24
10. Geddes L.A., Baker L.E. (1989). Principles of Applied Biomedical Instrumentation, 3rd ed., John Wiley, New York, N.Y.
11. Burleson, W. and R. W. Picard (2004). Affective Agents: Sustaining Motivation to Learn Through Failure and a State of Stuck. Social and Emotional Intelligence in Learning Environments Workshop In conjunction with the 7th International Conference on Intelligent Tutoring Systems, Maceio - Alagoas, Brasil, August 31st, 2004.

Intelligent Expressions of Emotions

Magalie Ochs[1,3], Radosław Niewiadomski[2], Catherine Pelachaud[3], and David Sadek[1]

[1] France Telecom, R&D Division, Technology Center, France
{magalie.ochs, david.sadek}@francetelecom.com
[2] Department of Mathematics and Computer Science, University of Perugia, Italy
radek@dipmat.unipg.it
[3] LINC Lab., IUT of Montreuil, Université Paris VIII, France
c.pelachaud@iut.univ-paris8.fr

Abstract. We propose an architecture of an embodied conversational agent that takes into account two aspects of emotions: the emotions triggered by an event (the felt emotions) and the expressed emotions (the displayed ones), which may differ in real life. In this paper, we present a formalization of emotion eliciting-events based on a model of the agent's mental state composed of beliefs, choices, and uncertainties. This model enables to identify the emotional state of an agent at any time. We also introduce a computational model based on fuzzy logic that computes facial expressions of emotions blending. Finally, examples of facial expressions resulting from the implementation of our model are shown.

1 Introduction and Motivation

A growing interest in using animated characters as interface of computational system has been observed in the recent years. This is motivated by an attempt to enhance human-machine interaction. Animated characters are generally used to embody some roles typically performed by humans, as for example a tutor [9] or an actor [11]. When facing these virtual interlocutors, the user has the propensity to interact in a similar way as when communicating with a human [15]. One of the crucial issues in the creation of animated characters is to enhance them with social intelligence and communicative abilities to give them the capacity to interact with the user in natural way and to display complex and subtle expressions.

Recent researches have highlighted a specific aspect of social intelligence based on emotional abilities, called *emotional intelligence*. It represents the capacity to express, understand and manage one's own emotions, and to perceive and interpret those of others [20]. In interpersonal relationships, the emotional intelligence determines an individual's chances to achieve her aims [6].

Introducing emotional intelligence into an animated character means, first, to give her the ability to express emotions. That requires two types of emotional skills: the knowledge of the circumstances under which emotions are triggered, and how to express them. However, an expressed emotion does not always reveal a felt emotion. A person may decide to express an emotion different from the one she actually felt because she has to follow some socio-cultural norms or she is pursuing some others of her goals. Ekman [4] refers to the former as display rules. We distinguish two kinds of

J. Tao, T. Tan, and R.W. Picard (Eds.): ACII 2005, LNCS 3784, pp. 707–714, 2005.

emotions: the felt emotion named *elicited-emotion* and the expressed one called *expressed-emotion*. The elicited-emotion is triggered by a person's evaluation of a significant event [21]. One can suppress, intensify, de-intensify, mask or replace her own elicited-emotion in order to display an expressed-emotion consistent with some display rules [4]. Most of researches so far have focused on elicited-emotions of animated characters while less attention has been paid to the second type of emotion.

In this paper we propose a model that enables an agent to *intelligently* express emotions. That is, the type and intensity of the elicited- and/or expressed-emotions must be consistent not only with an event that has triggered it, but also with the socio-cultural context of the interaction. To achieve this goal, it is necessary, on the one hand, to distinguish between elicited- and expressed- emotions, and one the other hand, to go beyond the facial expression of basic emotions and to take into account blending of emotions.

2 System Overview

Figure 1 illustrates the agent architecture capable of displaying elicited and expressed emotions. It is composed of a natural dialog engine called *Artimis* [19] which can interact with users in natural language. It is based on a BDI approach. After the occurrence of an event, it computes the mental state of the agent and sends it to the Emotional Module. Depending on the current mental state and the socio-cultural context, the *Emotional Module* identifies the elicited and expressed emotions and their intensities. Finally, the *Facial Expressions of Emotions Blending Module* computes the resulting facial expression. The emotions are then displayed through the facial expressions of embodied conversational agent *Greta* [12].

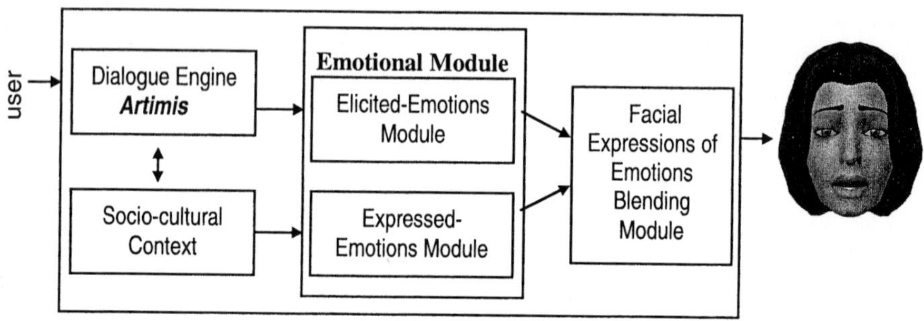

Fig. 1. Architecture for the intelligent expressions of emotions

For the moment, the socio-cultural context is not implemented in our system. In this paper, we focus on two components of the process of emotion displaying: the generation of elicited-emotions (Elicited-Emotions Module) and the computation of facial expressions for blends of emotions (Facial Expressions of Emotions Blending Module).

3 The Elicited-Emotions Module

An agent who expresses emotions should be able to identify the emotional meaning of a situation in order to trigger appropriate emotions. According to cognitive appraisal theories [10, 21], emotions are elicited by the evaluation of an event based on specific set of criteria (called *appraisal variables*). The values of these variables depend both on situational and cultural factors and on particular individual's features (such as goals, preferences, personality traits,...) [21]. In the next section, we present some models that integrate aspects of appraisal theories. Then, we propose a representation and formalization of elicited-emotions based on mental states of a rational agent.

3.1 Computational Models of Elicited-Emotion Generation

In architecture Tok, the module Em provides the emotions triggered by a perceived event and their intensity according to a set of rules [13] based on the well-known OCC theory [10]. In deRosis et *al.*'s model [16], the elicited-emotions are represented by a Dynamic Belief Network and correspond to a particular modification of the agent's beliefs about the achievement or a threat of an agent's goal. Gratch and Marsella [8] have recently developed a complex model of emotions which takes into account coping behaviors.

Most of researches propose to consider specific modules or particular representations of the world to compute the values of appraisal variables in a situation to identify the elicited-emotions.

3.2 An Agent's Mental State

Rational agents with an explicit representation of the notion of mental state (as for example the BDI agents) allow for identifying directly the elicited-emotions through their mental states without adding a specific representation of the world or a module of appraisal variable evaluation. The mental states of BDI agents are composed of mental attitudes such as beliefs, desires and intentions. We use a model of rational agent based on a formal theory of interaction (called *Rational Interaction Theory* [18]), and on a BDI approach. The implementation of this theory has given rise to a rational dialog agent technology (named *Artimis*) that provides a generic framework to instantiate intelligent agents able to engage with both human interlocutors and artificial agents in a rich interaction [19].

In the Rational Interaction Theory, the model of an agent's mental state is based on three primitive attitudes: *belief*, *uncertainty*, and *choice,* formalized with the modal operators B, U, and C as follows (*p* being a closed formula denoted a proposition): $\mathbf{B}_i p$ means "agent *i* thinks that *p* is true", $\mathbf{U}_{i,pr} p$ means "agent *i* thinks that *p* has a probability *pr* to be true". If *pr* equals to 1 then uncertainty is equivalent to belief. $\mathbf{C}_i p$ means "agent *i* desires that *p* be currently true". Several others operators have been introduced to formalize the occurring action, the agent who has achieved it, and temporal relation (for more details see [18, 19]).

3.3 Emotional Mental States

A mental state corresponds to an agent's cognitive representation of the world at a given instant. It includes a representation of the event perceived in the environment.

Accordingly, an occurred emotion eliciting-event is also represented through mental attitudes. We call *emotional mental state* the configuration of mental attitudes corresponding to an emotion elicited-event. According to the appraisal theories, an emotion eliciting-event corresponds to a particular combination of appraisal variable values [21]. Then, an emotional mental state is a representation of these specific values by mental attitudes.

We base our researches on the OCC model of emotions [10] which is particularly adapted to a BDI approach. In the work presented here, we focus on the emotions that differ, according to the OCC model, in their appraisal variable "Desirability of an event": joy, sadness, fear and anger. We consider also the emotion of surprise. The positive (resp. negative) emotions are elicited by a desirable (resp. undesirable) expected or occurred event. An event is desirable (resp. undesirable) if it allows for the increasing (resp. decreasing) of the *achievement degree* of one (or several) agent's goal(s). In terms of primitive mental attitudes, a goal corresponds to the choice (*p*) of an agent (*i*). The achievement degree is expressed by the probability (*pr*) associated with uncertainty ($U_{i,pr}p$). An agent's choice is totally achieved if the achievement degree is equal to 1 (*i.e.*, when it corresponds to an agent's belief), and is partially achieved if it inferior to 1. We distinguish four literal values for the desirability appraisal variable:

(1) ***Present desirability of an event e for a choice p*:** It corresponds to an agent's mental state that involves the belief that an occurred event *e* has enabled to increase the likelihood (*i.e.*, achievement degree) of one of her choice *p*. Let us give an example to illustrate *present desirability*. Suppose that an agent *i* wishes to have received a mail from a friend (choice *p* of *i*: $C_i p$) who has promised to send it. As long as agent *i* has not checked her mailbox, she is uncertain about having received it (*p* is an uncertainty with a probability *pr_past*: $U_{i,\ pr\_past}p$). After having checked her mailbox (event *e*), she realizes that she has received it (i.e. $U_{i,\ pr\_present}p$ with pr_present > pr_past). In this case, the combination of these primitive mental attitudes corresponds to a *present desirability* of event *e* for choice *p*.

(2) ***Future desirability of an event e for a choice p*:** It corresponds to an agent's mental state that involves the belief that an event *e* expected with a certain probability *pr_feasibility* can increase the likelihood of one of agent's choice *p*. In the example above, if agent *i* believes that by checking her mailbox (that it can do with a probability *pr_feasibility)* she will realize that her friend has send her the mail, then her mental state corresponds to *future desirability* of event *e* for choice *p*.

(3) ***Present*** and (4) ***Future undesirability of an event e for a choice p*** corresponds to cases where the likelihood of a choice *p* of an agent decreases because of an (expected/occurred) event *e*.

Each of these literal desirability values is associated with a numerical value called *desirability degree*. It is function of the variation of the achievement degree and the feasibility likelihood (*pr_feasibility*) of an expected event. Accordingly, the more the achievement degree of an agent's choice is increased by an event and the more the event is likely to occur, the more this event is desirable.

From these formalisations of the desirability variable and based on the OCC model [10], we can represent the emotional mental states associated with the emotions with mental attitudes. Joy is elicited by the occurrence of a desirable event. Accordingly, the emotional mental state of joy corresponds to the configuration of mental attitudes of *present desirability* described above. A rational agent generates an elicited-emotion of joy if her mental state contains this emotional mental state. In the example described above, the agent who receives the mail experiences joy. In the same way, given the fact that sadness emotion corresponds to an undesirable occurred event, the associated emotional mental state is equivalent to the configuration of mental attitudes of *present undesirability*. The emotion of anger corresponds to mental state which is composed of the configuration of mental attitudes of *present undesirability* and the agent's belief that another one is responsible of the event occurred. Fear emotions are triggered by an undesirable expected event. Then, the emotional mental states associated correspond to the *future undesirability* configurations of mental attitudes. The intensity of these emotions is function of the desirability degree.

The emotion of surprise corresponds to the mental state which contains the belief of the occurrence of unexpected event. The intensity of this emotion is function of the probability of the feasibility of the event (*pr_feasibility*) before its occurrence.

A rational agent can experience different emotions at the same time. For instance, given the formalisation described, the emotions of anger and sadness can be triggered because of a same event. These elicited-emotions and their intensities are then provided to the Facial Expressions of Emotions Blending Module.

4 The Facial Expressions of Emotions Blending Module

The term *emotion blending* refers to several different phenomena in the literature. In [14], "affect blends" are defined as "multiple simultaneous facial expressions". Indeed, a person may show two or more emotions at any time [4]. Blending appears if two emotions overlap in time [5]. Emotions are usually expressed on different facial areas. One facial area may rarely display expressions which are characteristic for two different emotions. Emotions may also occur in rapid sequences one after the other. Blends may be due by rapid sequences, superposition of two or more emotions or by masking one from another one. Finally, different blending of facial expressions can be distinguished depending both on the type of emotions (elicited or expressed-emotions) and on their apparition in time (sequence, superposition…) [4, 5]. In this section, we propose a model to compute facial expressions of emotions blending based on fuzzy logic.

4.1 Different Approaches for Expressions of Blending

While most of the existing animated characters use facial expressions to show emotions, less attention has been paid to expressions of blending. From a dimensional model of emotions, Tsapatsoulis et *al.* [22] and Albrecht et *al.* [1] applied an interpolation between expression parameters of two emotions to compute the blending expressions. The Emotional Disc model [17] uses a bi-linear interpolation directly between two expressions. Based on Ekman's results, Duy Bui [3] proposes fuzzy logic rules for each possible emotions pair to determine the blending expressions according to emotions intensity.

Instead of basing our model at the level of facial muscle contractions as previous models did, we propose a face partition based model to compute not only the facial expressions resulting from the superposition of two elicited-emotions but also from the masking of an elicited one by another one. This allows our model to differentiate the facial expressions resulting from the blending of elicited and expressed-emotions.

4.2 Computational Model for Emotion Blending

Emotion blending leads to a particular facial expression that may either result from combining the facial components of both emotions. The visual effects of blending depend on both the type and intensity of emotions as well as if they are felt (elicited-emotion) or fake (expressed-emotion). Indeed, the expression of two elicited-emotions can be different from the blending of the same pair of emotions when one is felt and the other one is expressed. Usually, humans are not able to control all their facial muscles efficiently [5]. For example, masking sadness with anger is different from feeling both sadness and anger at the same time [4]. For the moment, we have considered only these two cases of emotion blending: the superposition of two elicited-emotions and the masking of an elicited-emotion by an expressed one (a felt emotion being masked by a fake emotion due to some display rules). The case of the sequence of emotions will be dealt in the future. We have implemented different computational models for each blend type, superposition and masking.

Superposition. Ekman [4, 5] proposed a model of blended expressions by combining the upper part of one expression with the lower part of the other one. We use these findings and we consider two areas in the face: the upper face (noted *U*) and the lower face (noted *L*). Bassili [2] and Gouta [7] found that negative emotions are mainly perceived from the upper part of the face while positive emotions on the lower part. We use the results of this perceptual test to generate facial expression of two emotions to ensure that the resulting expression conveys both emotions. To combine emotions, we introduce the priority operator noted ">" and the equivalence operator "≡". "$E_i > E_j$" means that E_i is expressed through the upper area in the case of blending of E_i and E_j, while "$E_i \equiv E_j$" means there is no predominance for this particular face area. This latter case occurs for instance, when surprise and fear are blended [4].

The fuzzy inference is used to model the combination of the facial expressions of two elicited-emotions. More precisely, the fuzzy rules are based on both: the predominance between emotions introduced by the operators ">","≡" and intensities of emotions. Using fuzzy logic allows us not to consider separately all possible emotion pairs. It takes into account the different types of emotions and all the spectrum of their intensities to generate distinct facial expressions.

Masking. Ekman [4] claims that upper face expression is usually more difficult to control. So we can postulate that usually the upper face region shows felt emotion and the lower region is used to mask it. Moreover, Ekman distinguishes some reliable features of felt emotion like: fear or sadness brows, or glary eyes in case of anger. Such reliable features lack in fake expressions. The masking can be seen as asymmetric emotion-communicative function, whereas superposition is rather symmetric. Indeed, given two emotions *Ei* and *Ej*, the masking of *Ei* by *Ej* leads to a different facial expression than the masking of *Ej* by *Ei* [4], while this is not the case for superposition. Following Ekman's research [4], we have defined the face area that contains the reliable features for each felt emotion. In our model this area displays the elicited-emotion, while the other area shows the masking (i.e. expressed-) emotion (See: Fig. 2c). Doing so enables us to model the asymmetry property of masking.

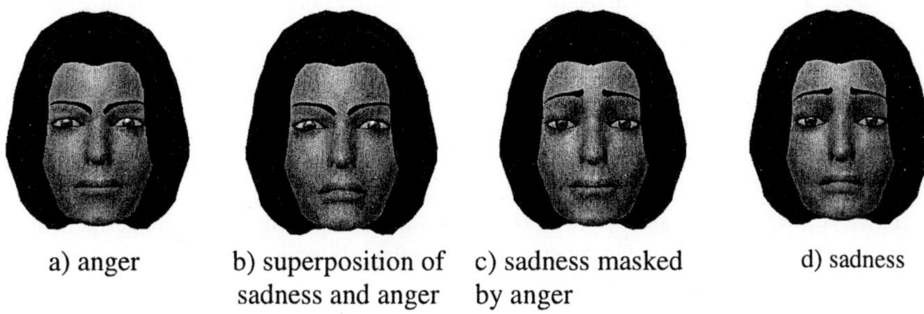

a) anger | b) superposition of sadness and anger | c) sadness masked by anger | d) sadness

Fig. 2. Facial expressions of the ECA Greta [12]

5 Conclusion

In this paper, we have presented a formalization of events triggering emotions as well as a model for the facial expression of blends of emotions. In the near future we aim at evaluating our model, in particular related to the perception of blends of emotions. The next steps consist in adding the abilities to the agent to determine the most appropriate emotion to express according to a socio-cultural context or to achieve specific goals. Future developments are also foreseen to work on a more fine-grained face partition to improve the agent's expressiveness and believability.

Acknowledgement

We are very grateful to Susanne Kaiser for her insight on facial expressions of emotion and to Nédra Mellouli for her help on the fuzzy logic model. We thank also Elisabetta Bevacqua and Maurizio Mancini for implementing the Greta system. Part of this research is supported by the EU FP6 Network of Excellence HUMAINE, IST contract 507422.

References

1. Albrecht I., Schroder M., Haber J., Seidel H.: Mixed feelings: Expression of non-basic emotions in a muscle-based talking head, Special issue of Journal of Virtual Reality on "Language, Speech & Gesture", to appear.
2. Bassili J.N., Emotion recognition: the role of facial movement and the relative importance of upper and lower areas of the face, Jour. Pers. Soc. Psychol., 37 (11), 2049-2058, 1979.
3. Duy Bui T. Creating Emotions And Facial Expressions For Embodied Agents, PhD thesis, University of Twente, Department of Computer Science, Enschede, 2004.
4. Ekman P., Friesen W.V.: Unmasking the Face. A guide to recognizing emotions from facial clues. Prentice-Hall, Inc., Englewood Cliffs, New Jersey, 1975.
5. Ekman P., The Face Revealed, Weidenfeld & Nicolson, London, 2003.

6. Goleman D., *Emotional Intelligence*, Paris, Laffont, 1997.
7. Gouta K, Miyamoto M., Emotion recognition, facial components associated with various emotions, Shinrigaku Kenkyu Aug, 71 (3), 211-8, 2000.
8. Gratch, J. and Marsella, S. A domain-independent Framework for modeling emotion. *Journal of Cognitive Systems Research*, 5 (4), 269-306.2004.
9. Johnson, W.L., Rickel, J.W., and Lester, J.C. Animated pedagogical agents: Face-to-face interaction in interactive learning environments. *International Journal of Artificial Intelligence in Education*, 11, 47-78. 2000.
10. Ortony, A., Clore, G. L. and A., C. *The cognitive structure of emotions*, Cambridge University Press, 1988.
11. Paiva A., Machado I., and Prada R. Heroes, villains, magicians,...: Dramatics personae in a virtual story creation environment. In *Proceedings International Conference on Intelligent User Interfaces, 129-136, 2001.*
12. Pelachaud C. , Bilvi M. Computational Model of Believable Conversational Agents, in *Communication in Multiagent Systems: background, current trends and future*, Marc-Philippe Huget (Ed), Springer-Verlag, 2650, 300-317, 2003.
13. Reilly, S. Believable Social and Emotional Agents, University of Carnegie Mellon, 1996.
14. Richmond V.P., Croskey J.C.: Non Verbal Behavior in Interpersonal relations, Allyn & Bacon Inc. 1999.
15. Reeves B., and Nash C., *The Media Equation: How People Treat Computers*, Televisions and New Media Like Real People and Places. New York: Cambridge Univ. Press, 1996.
16. Rosis, F. d., Pelachaud, C., Poggi, I., Carofiglio, V. and Carolis, B. D. From Greta's mind to her face: modelling the dynamics of affective states in a conversational embodied agent. *International Journal of Human-Computer Studies*, 59(1-2), 81-118.2003.
17. Ruttkay Z., Noot H., ten Hagen P.: Emotion Disc and Emotion Squares: tools to explore the facial expression face, in Computer Graphics Forum, 22 (1), 49-53, 2003.
18. Sadek, D. Attitudes mentales et interaction rationnelle: vers une théorie formelle de la communication. Thèse, informatique, Université de Rennes I, 1991.
19. Sadek, D., Bretier, P. and Panaget, F. ARTIMIS: Natural Dialogue Meets Rational Agency. In: *Proceedings of 15th International Joint Conference on Artificial Intelligence (IJCAI'97)*, Nagoya, Japon, 1030-1035. 1997.
20. Salovey, P., Bedell, B., Detweiler, J., & Mayer, J.D. *Current directions in emotional intelligence research.* In M. Lewis & J.M. Haviland-Jones (Eds.), Handbook of emotions. New York: Guilford Press, 504-520, 2000.
21. Scherer, K. *Emotion.* Introduction to Social Psychology: A European perspective. M. Hewstone and W. Stroebe, Oxford, 151-191. 2000.
22. Tsapatsoulis N., Raouzaiou A., Kollias S., Crowie R., Douglas-Cowie E.: Emotion Recognition and Synthesis Based on MPEG-4 FAPs, in "MPEG-4 Facial Animation", Igor Pandzic, R. Forchheimer (eds), John Wiley & Sons, UK, 2002.

Environment Expression: Expressing Emotions Through Cameras, Lights and Music

Celso de Melo and Ana Paiva

IST-Technical University of Lisbon and INESC-ID,
Avenida Prof. Cavaco Silva – Taguspark,
2780-990 Porto Salvo, Portugal
{celso.de.melo, ana.paiva}@inesc-id.pt

Abstract. Environment expression is about going beyond the usual Human emotion expression channels in virtual worlds. This work proposes an integrated storytelling model – the *environment expression model* – capable of expressing emotions through three channels: cinematography, illumination and music. Stories are organized into prioritized *points of interest* which can be characters or dialogues. Characters synthesize cognitive emotions based on the OCC emotion theory. Dialogues have collective emotional states which reflect the participant's emotional state. During storytelling, at each instant, the highest priority point of interest is focused through the expression channels. The cinematography channel and the illumination channel reflect the point of interest's strongest emotion type and intensity. The music channel reflects the valence of the point of interest's mood. Finally, a study was conducted to evaluate the model. Results confirm the influence of environment expression on emotion perception and reveal moderate success of this work's approach.

1 Introduction

The advent of digital technology has introduced several new ways to tell a story. Storytelling has evolved into a complex process involving sophisticated virtual characters capable of body, facial and voice expression and sophisticated virtual environments capable of cinematography, illumination and music expression.

This work is about virtual environments telling stories and expressing emotions. The idea behind environment expression comes from theatre. Theatre is one of the most complete forms of expression. Dramatic expression, text, sceneries, lights, make-up, sound, music and dance work together to tell a story [1]. With the advent of movies, new expression channels came to be, being the camera the most pervasive one. With the advent of digital technology, yet new channels of expression were created making it easier to break the rules of Nature.

This work proposes an integrated storytelling model – the environment expression model – capable of expressing emotions through three different channels: cinematography, illumination and music. The story is organized according to prioritized points of interest which can be either characters or dialogues. Characters synthesize cognitive emotions based on the OCC emotion theory. Dialogues have collective emotional states which reflect their participants' emotional states. During

J. Tao, T. Tan, and R.W. Picard (Eds.): ACII 2005, LNCS 3784, pp. 715–722, 2005.

storytelling, at each instant of time, the highest priority point of interest is focused differently by each of the environment expression channels.

The rest of this paper is organized as follows. Section 2 overviews the environment expression model. Section 3 describes the OCC based emotion state for both kinds of points of interest. Sections 4 to 6 describe, respectively, the cinematography, illumination and music expression channels. Section 7 describes a study conducted to assess the influence and relevance of environment expression in storytelling, as well as the adequacy of this work's approach. Finally, section 8 draws some conclusions.

2 Environment Expression Model

The *environment expression model* has the following components: (1) the *story module*; (2) the *director*; (3) and the three environment expression channels – *cinematography*, *illumination* and *music*. Fig.1 summarizes this model.

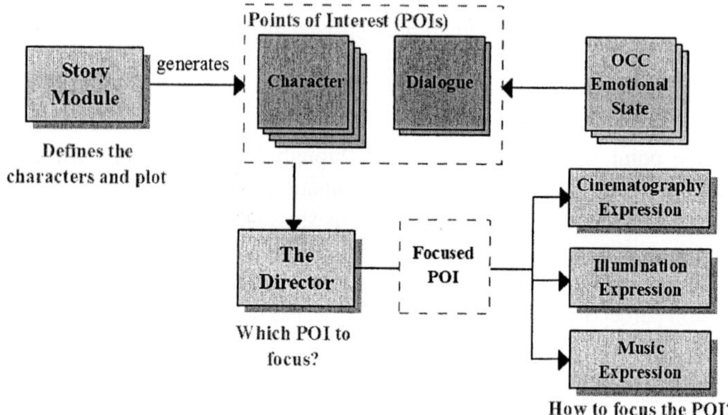

Fig. 1. The environment expression model

The story module essentially defines the story's plot and characters. At any given instant, a story can be defined by a set of *points of interest* which compete for the audience's attention. A point of interest can be a *character* or a *dialogue* between two characters. Furthermore, this module assigns priorities to the points of interest.

Usually in stories, characters perceive, synthesize and express emotions. This work considers cognitively generated emotions and, in this sense, uses the OCC emotion theory. The character's and the dialogue's emotional states are described in section 3.

One principle which is extensively used in theatre, animation and cinema is to focus the audience's attention to a single aspect of the story at a time [1]. This makes the message clearer. Using this principle, from all the generated story points of interest, the director focuses the audience's attention to the highest priority one.

Finally, an environment expression channel is a means by which the focused point of interest is presented to the audience. Besides just making the point of interest accessible to the audience's senses, these channels also express emotions. Each of the three explored channels is described in sections 4 to 6.

3 Emotion Synthesis

In this work characters can synthesize cognitive emotions. Emotion synthesis is based on the OCC emotion theory. Dialogues have collective emotional states which reflect their participants' emotional states. Following, subsection 3.1 overviews the OCC emotion theory, subsection 3.2 presents the character's emotional state model and subsection 3.3 presents the dialogue's emotional state model.

3.1 Background

The Ortony, Clore and Collins (OCC) emotion theory defines emotions as "valenced reactions to events, agents, or objects, with their particular nature being determined by the way in which the eliciting situation is construed". Thus, emotions result from cognitive interpretation of some emotion eliciting situation. The theory proposes 22 different *emotion types*, as well as a set of global and local variables [2]. As a general theory for emotions, however, it is incomplete. Though it proposes a mechanism for converting eliciting situations into cognitive emotions, not much is said on converting eliciting situations into the proposed variables' values or on emotion expression.

3.2 Character's Emotional State

The character's emotional state is based on a full implementation of the OCC theory, including its 22 emotion types, local and global variables. This work also explores emotion issues such as *decay, potential calculation, intensity reinforcement* and the effect of global variables on potentials, all of which are not solved by the OCC theory. As suggested in [2], only emotions whose potential is greater than a threshold are active. As suggested in [3], intensities are constrained to the interval [0; 10].

In Nature, an active emotion does not stay active forever as it decays with time [4]. Thus, for all emotion types, decay is represented by function (1), based on [4], where Δt is the time elapsed since the emotion was last elicited, *d* is the emotion *decay rate* which is empirical, and i_0 is the intensity at the instant it was last elicited:

$$decay(\Delta t, d) = i_0 \times \exp(-0{,}1 \times d \times \Delta t)\ . \tag{1}$$

Potential is a function of local and global variables. The latter shall be addressed below. As suggested in [3], all emotion potentials are constrained to the interval [0; 10] and all local variables values to the interval [-10; 10]. Essentially, potential is a function of the eliciting situation which is defined as the values assigned to the local variables. As this assignment is not defined in the OCC theory, intuition was used. According to the OCC theory, different sets of variables are considered for different emotion types. Thus, to transform these values into a single one representing potential, 22 different functions, which will not be described, were developed.

In Nature, when an active emotion is elicited the effect is not the same as if it were elicited for the first time [4]. This work uses, for all emotion types, function (2), based on [3], where *i* is the intensity, *t* is the emotion's threshold, and *p* is the potential:

$$reinforce(i, t, p) = \log_2(\exp(i + t) + \exp(p))\ . \tag{2}$$

The two global variables focused in this work are *arousal* and *mood.* Arousal is related to the physiological manifestation of emotions. It is characterized as follows: is positive; decays linearly with time; reinforcement occurs with emotion eliciting; increases elicited emotion potential. Mood refers to the longer-term effects of emotions. Moods can last for hours, days, and maybe longer, in contrast to emotions which last few minutes [4]. It is characterized as follows: can be negative or positive; converges to zero linearly with time; reinforcement occurs with emotion eliciting.

3.3 Dialogue's Emotional State

Suppose that, at a certain instant, a dialogue is the story's highest priority point of interest and, thus, is being focused by the expression channels. If each participating character is characterized by a different local emotional state, how is the global dialogue emotional state characterized? This work proposes a simple answer: *the dialogue's emotional state is the average of all the participant characters' emotional states.* In concrete, this corresponds to averaging each of the characters' active emotions intensities and global variables values.

4 Cinematography Expression

Cinematography environment expression is about telling a story through a camera. The section begins by describing some of the cinematography literature's established guidelines relating camera parameters to emotion expression and, then, proceeds to describe their application in this work.

4.1 Background

A *shot* represents a camera configuration of a certain time duration which is not broken up by cuts [7]. A shot can be either static or dynamic. Shots can vary, among others, according to the *distance* and to the *angle* with the point of interest. Regarding distance, the closer the camera is, the higher is the audience's attachment to the point of interest [5][7]. Five distance shots are commonly used [5]: (1) extreme close up, which focuses a particular detail, like the character's eyes; (2) close up, which focuses the character's face; (3) medium shot, which focuses the character from the waist up; (4) full shot, which focuses the whole character; (5) long shot, which films the whole character and also the surrounding environment. These shots need not focus characters, as any other point of interest can be focused as long as the distances are adjusted. Regarding angle, [5] mentions three representative shots: (1) *eye level* – the camera is placed at the height of the point of interest, representing a neutral view; (2) *high angle* – the camera films the point of interest from above creating the impression of smallness and isolation; (3) *low-angle* – the camera films the point of interest from below creating the impression of a powerful point of interest.

4.2 Expression

Cinematography expression reflects the focused point of interest emotional state's strongest emotion as follows:

(1) *If it is anger or pride*, a low-angle shot is chosen (Fig.2-a);
(2) *If it is fear*, a high-angle shot is chosen (Fig.2-b);
(3) *If its potential is on the interval [0; 15[*, the full shot is chosen (Fig.2-c);
(4) *If its potential is in the interval [1.5; 2.5[*, the medium shot is chosen (Fig.2-d);
(5) *If its potential is in the interval [2.5; 4.5[*, a close-up is chosen (Fig.2-e);
(6) *Otherwise*, an extreme close-up of the eyes is chosen (Fig.2-f).

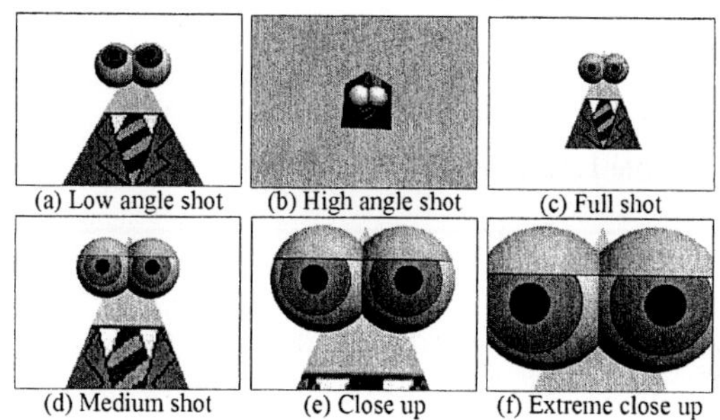

Fig. 2. Cinematography expression shots reflect the character's emotional state. a)-b) Angle shots reflect the character's power. c) –f) Distance shots reflect different emotion intensity.

5 Illumination Expression

Illumination environment expression is about telling a story through lights. The section begins by describing research in illumination and on the relation between color and emotion proceeding, then, to describe its application to this work.

5.1 Background

Regarding placement, the *three-point-lighting* technique is widely used in movies to illuminate characters [7]. It is a configuration composed of the following light "roles": (1) *key light* – which is the main source of light focusing the character; (2) *Fill light* – which is a low-intensity light that fills an area that is otherwise too dark; (3) *Back light* – which is used to separate the character from the background. Regarding light color, color association with emotion is widely documented (see [8] and associated references). For instance, red is normally associated with something exciting or aggressive; yellow with something cheerful; green with nature and, thus, relaxing; blue with quietness; green-yellow with vomit and, thus, displeasing; grey is neutral; among others. Regarding brightness, it is known that well illuminated scenes are happy and cheerful and poorly illuminated scenes are mysterious and sad. [7]

5.2 Expression

Illumination expression uses three-point-lighting to illuminate the focused point of interest. In particular, the key light is a point light placed between the point of interest and the camera. Emotion expression is achieved through key light's parameters manipulation. In concrete, its color is associated to the strongest emotion type according to Table 1. Presently, this work considers 12 out of the 22 OCC emotion types. Finally, brightness varies with the strongest emotion intensity and valence. Variation is implemented through the light's attenuation factor according to equation (3) if the emotion is positive and equation (4) if it is negative.

$$\text{Attenuation}_{\text{positive}} = \min(0.5, 1 - \text{emotionIntensity} / \text{maxEmotionIntensity}) . \tag{3}$$

$$\text{Attenuation}_{\text{negative}} = \max(0.25, \text{emotionIntensity} / \text{maxEmotionIntensity}) . \tag{4}$$

Table 1. Explored OCC emotion types to color mapping

OCC Emotion type	Color (RGB)
anger, reproach	red (255, 0, 0)
disappointment, fears-confirmed	grey (200, 200, 200)
disliking	green-yellow (220, 255, 0)
distress	dark grey (153, 153, 153)
fear, relief, neutral	white (255, 255, 255)
hope, liking, satisfaction	bright yellow (255, 255, 200)
joy	yellow (255, 255, 0)

6 Music Expression

Music environment expression is about telling a story through music. The section begins by describing research relating music and emotion and proceeding, then, to describe its application to this work.

6.1 Background

The relationship between music and emotion can be explored on four dimensions: (1) *Structural features* – which relates the music's structure with emotions; (2) *Performance features* – which refer to the influence of the *interpretation* of the music; (3) *Listener features* – which refer to the influence of the listener's attitudes and cultural influences; (4) *Contextual features* – which refer to aspects of the performance and/or listening situation. Regarding structural features, tempo is one of the most influencing factors affecting emotional expression in music. Fast tempo may be associated with happy/exciting emotions and slow tempo with sad/calmness emotions. There are many others parameters which lie beyond the scope of this work. Regarding performance features, [9] says that the expressive intention of the performer is converted into various cues during the performance. Regarding listener features, they can consist of musical systems that are shared by a culture, inference dispositions based on personality, prior experience, musical talent and valenced memory associations. Finally, contextual features refer to aspects of the context under which the composition is performed and listened to. [9]

6.2 Expression

In this work, music expression reflects the focused point of interest's *mood valence* – positive, neutral and negative. To convey mood valence, music, with the same valence, is randomly selected from a library. To fill in the library, music was selected according to the following simple criteria: (1) Positive songs have fast tempo and, if they have lyrics it should be positively valenced; (2) Neutral songs have medium tempo; (3) Sad songs have slow tempo and, if they have lyrics, it should be negatively valenced. Regarding the association of lyrics emotional valence to the music's valence, if the performer tries to convey the music's mood through cues (subsection 6.1), then it is reasonable to expect that the lyric's mood propagates to the performance's structural features.

7 Study

A study was conducted to assess the influence and relevance of environment expression to the audience's perception of the story characters' emotional state, as well as the adequacy of this work's approach for each expression channel.

The study was based on an application called *dancing solids*. This is a cartoon-like application which tells stories about male and female geometric solids seducing each other through dance. In the end, if the female likes the male they'll simply marry.

The study was organized into four parts: (1) *Subject Profile* – where the subject's profile was assessed; (2) *Emotion Perception* - where the subject was presented with one of seven OCC emotion types – anger, disliking, distress, fear, joy, liking, reproach – or neutral emotion expression with varying configurations of two of the expression channels – cinematography and illumination. The subject was then asked to guess the expressed emotions from a set of options which was provided; (3) *Music emotional valence* – where the subject was asked to classify 12 music compositions according to one of the following mood valences: positive/happy; neutral; negative/sad; (4) *Stories interpretation* – where the subject was presented with two different versions of the same dancing solids story. Stories were assigned randomly a happy – girl marries boy – or unhappy ending – girl doesn't marry boy. Version A had no environment expression, while version B had all three channels active. The subject was then asked which was the preferred version.

The study was presented to 50 students at Technical University of Lisbon. Average age was 23 years. Regarding emotion perception, collected data revealed that: perception of distress, joy, liking, neutral was highly accurate (above 75%) even without environment expression; illumination color expression increased accuracy particularly for anger (from 13% to 43%), disliking (from 13% to 20%) and reproach (from 46% to 60%); the cinematography channel emotion type to camera shot mapping, in general, did not influence accuracy. Regarding music emotion valence, average subject classification matched predictions for 92% of the music. Regarding stories interpretation, when the ending was unhappy both versions were equally enjoyed (60% of the subjects) followed by version B (35%). When the ending was happy version B was preferred (50% of the subjects) followed by version A (33%).

8 Conclusions

This work proposes an integrated architecture for storytelling capable of expression through three channels: cinematography, illumination and music. Stories are organized into prioritized points of interest which can be characters or dialogues. Emotion synthesis is based on the OCC emotion theory. Emotion expression is achieved through the expression channels. At each instant, the highest priority point of interest is focused. The cinematography channel reflects the point of interest's strongest emotion type and intensity. The illumination channel uses three-point-lighting to illuminate the point of interest and the key light's color and brightness vary according to the strongest emotion type and intensity respectively. The music channel expresses the valence of the point of interest's mood by playing music with the same valence. Music selection was based on tempo and lyrics emotional valence.

Evaluation of this work confirmed the relevance of environment expression for emotion perception in storytelling. Regarding the proposed approach, the study revealed that: the emotion type to camera shots mapping in the cinematography channel needs further tuning; illumination color association with the emotion types is effective; mood valenced music selection based on tempo and lyrics emotional valence is sufficient to produce satisfactory results; and, finally, people prefer a version of a story which is told with environment expression than one which does not.

References

1. Solmer, A.: Manual de Teatro. Temas e Debates (2003)
2. Ortony, A., Clore, G., Collins, A.: The Cognitive Structure of Emotions. Cambridge University Press (1988)
3. Paiva, A., Aylett, R., Dias, J., Sobral, D., Louchar, S., Zoll, C., Raimundo, G., Rebelo, F., Otero, N.: VICTEC Deliverable 5.3.1: Final Prototype of Emphatic Synthetic Characters, Chapter 2 (2004)
4. Picard, R.: Affective Computing. The MIT Press (1997)
5. Arijon, D.: Grammar of Film Language. Silman-James Press (1976)
6. Hornung, A.: Autonomous Real-Time Camera Agents in Interactive Narratives and Games - MhD thesis at the Laboratory for Mixed Realities (2003)
7. Birn, J.: [digital] Lighting & Rendering. New Riders (2000)
8. Kaya, N.: Relationship between color and emotion: a study of college students in College Student Journal (2004)
9. Juslin, P., Sloboda, J.: Music and Emotion: theory and research. Oxford University Press (2001)

Dynamic User Modeling in Health Promotion Dialogs

Valeria Carofiglio, Fiorella de Rosis, and Nicole Novielli

Intelligent Interfaces, Department of Informatics, University of Bari,
Via Orabona 4, 70126 Bari, Italy
{carofiglio, derosis, novielli}@di.uniba.it
http://www.di.uniba.it/intint/

Abstract. We describe our experience with the design, implementation and revision of a dynamic user model for adapting health promotion dialogs with ECAs to the 'stage of change' of the users and to their 'social' attitude toward the agent. The user model was built by learning a bayesian network from a corpus of data collected with a Wizard of Oz study. We discuss how uncertainty in the recognition of the user's mental state may be reduced by integrating a simple linguistic parser with knowledge about the interaction context represented in the model.

1 Introduction

Advice giving in the domain of health promotion is generally based on the Prochaska and Di Clemente's Transtheoretical Model of Change [11]. According to this model, plans to apply in persuading subjects to change of attitude in a problem behavior are related to their stage of change in the process of modifying beliefs and intentions about this behavior. On the other hand, persuasion theories state that knowledge of the affective state of the addressee may contribute considerably to select an appropriate persuasion strategy [9,12,13]. Using information about stage of change and affective state of the client enables therapists to adapt their advice giving plans to the positive or negative attitude of the clients towards their problem behavior and towards the therapist herself. We aim at implementing an Embodied Conversational Agent (ECA) which simulates this situation in the domain of healthy eating. In our project, the agent 'observes' the user to infer his stage of change and attitude towards the system, to adapt dynamically its persuasion plan and style to the presumed situation. We leave out of this paper the description of the dialog simulation method we adopt, which maybe found in [2], to focus on description of the method we apply in recognizing and revising dynamically the user's mental state. Integration of several media (speech, physiological parameters, facial expressions and so on) is suggested as an effective method to recognize the affective state of users in human-computer interaction. If, however, text input is the only interaction form enabled to the user, as in our conversational system, this methods is not applicable. In this case, a possibility is to integrate text analysis of individual user 'moves' [7,8] with an interpretation process that considers the context in which the move was entered. In this paper, we describe how we adopted this method for recognizing the stage of change of the user and his attitude towards the ECA. In Section 2, we briefly introduce the theories behind our model.

J. Tao, T. Tan, and R.W. Picard (Eds.): ACII 2005, LNCS 3784, pp. 723 – 730, 2005.

In Section 3 we describe how we identified the two components of the user's mental state in a corpus of advice-giving dialogs collected with a Wizard of Oz study. Section 4 outlines how we learned, from this corpus, structure and parameters of the dynamic belief network which represents the user model. We conclude the paper with a discussion in Section 5.

2 The Theories Behind Our Model

The Transtheoretical model of change [11] identifies five main steps in the progression from a *wrong* behavior to a *correct* one:

- in the *pre-contemplation* stage, subjects believe that their behavior is correct and do not want to change it, now or later;
- in the *contemplation* stage, they doubt that their behavior is acceptable, think about why they follow the bad habit, consider seriously the opportunity of changing it but do not want to commit to change it soon;
- in the *preparation* stage, they believe that their behavior should be changed and intend to do it soon;
- in the *action* stage, they are following a plan to change behavior (from some months);
- in the *maintenance* stage, they are maintaining change from more than 6 months.

Changing from one step to the next one may be more or less fast, depending on how serious is the problem, how persistent is the subject in following the wrong behavior and how persuasive are the arguments employed by the therapist to convince him. As demonstrated by the definitions above, the model suggests that the various stages may be recognized from a *set of signs*: belief that behavior is 'correct' or 'wrong'; intention to change it if wrong; belief that (internal and external) conditions exist to change it; .. and so on. It suggests, as well, actions the therapist may adopt to promote a correct behavior in every stage.

As far as the social attitude of the user towards the system is concerned, after Nass and colleagues demonstrated several forms of 'antropomorphic behavior' of users towards technologies [10], ECAs were proposed as a new paradigm which should enhance sociality of interaction. Among the affective aspects of communication, *interpersonal warmth* appears to be the most relevant in this case: this has been defined as "*the pleasant, contented, intimate feeling that occurs during positive interactions with friends, family, colleagues and romantic partners*" and is displayed by means of verbal expressions such as self-disclosure, emotional expressiveness, verbal immediacy, personal idioms and others (see an extended analysis of research in this domain, in [1]). Although we know that such a kind of intimacy cannot be established in short-term interactions of the kind we consider in our system, we expected to find at least some traces of these expressions as signs of the social attitude of users towards our ECA.

3 The Corpus of Dialogs

The ECA we employ in our advice giving dialogs is a quite realistic agent which takes the appearance of a young woman (see figure 1). It was implemented with a commercial graphical software (Haptek) and text-to-speech synthesizer (Loquendo), after manipulating them to create new affect expressions and enable the agent to pronounce any utterance labelled with an appropriate mark-up language.

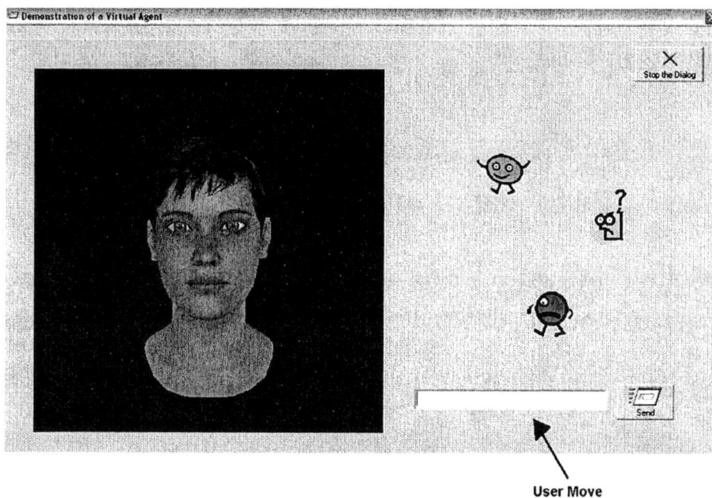

Fig. 1. The Embodied Conversational Agent employed in our Wizard of Oz studies

To test the kind of relationship users establish with our agent and the behavior the agent should show to respond appropriately to the user requirements, we performed a Wizard of Oz (WOZ) study. This study involved 30 subjects between 23 and 30 years of age, equidistributed in gender and background (graduated students in humanities or computer science). In the experiment, subjects interacted with the ECA to discuss their eating habits and received information and suggestions about possible problems discovered during the conversation. A detailed description of the WOZ tool and the experiment conditions may be found in [4]: we here synthesize its major aspects. Subjects involved in the study were initially informed about the aim of the conversational system and compiled a questionnaire assessing their attitude and behavior towards healthy eating. When ready, they asked to start the conversation with the ECA and, like in every WOZ study, thought they were interacting with a working dialog system. They could just answer the agent questions or 'take the initiative' in the dialog, by making comments and raising questions to the agent. When the subject decided to stop the dialog, a final questionnaire was displayed on the video, to collect subjective evaluation (in a Likert scale) of information provided (how much credible, persuasive, etc it was) and of the agent (how much competent, sincere etc it was). Every dialog was stored in a log at the end of interaction. The corpus of 30 dialogs and 712 subject moves was analyzed from both a quantitative and a qualitative viewpoint. We defined two measures of the subject's attitude during the dialog: a) *level of involvement*, as a function of the dialog duration and of the average length (in characters) of the user moves, and b) *degree of initiative*, as a function of the percentage of questions raised by the subject over all the dialog moves. Subjects showed several signs of social emotions (sympathy, appreciation or irritation, disappointment) and of social relationship with the agent of the kind suggested in [1]. They were mostly in the pre-contemplation stage and a few of them changed of stage during the dialog: this is not surprising, considering that young people are interested in this topic and that unhealthy dieting is not a very serious problem. We defined a set of *signs of social attitude* of the subject towards the agent that we could recognize with linguistic analysis of the subject moves and defined a markup language with which three independent raters were asked to annotate the dialogs. Table 1 describes the markup language and shows the main results of annotation in terms of two indices: (i) *majority agreement*, as the percentage of cases in which at least two of the three raters agreed on labelling a move, and (ii) *kappa* [5], a chance-corrected measure of agreement. As the value of kappa depends on how skew is the distribution of the considered variable, given an agreement rate its value depends on the frequency of the sign of interest: this explains why the two measures are not closely correlated.

Table 1. Markup language and agreement among raters for signs of social attitude towards the agent and stage of change

Sign with definition [value]	Majority agreement	Kappa
Friendly self-introduction [Yes/No] Whether the subject introduces himself with a friendly attitude (e.g. by giving his name or by explaining the reasons why he is participating in the dialog	.98	.87
Familiar style [Yes/No] Whether the subject employes a current language, dialectal forms, etc	.33	.16
Talks about self [Yes/No] Whether the subject provides information about self which was not explicitly requested by the agent	.73	.64
Personal questions about the agent [Yes/No] Whether the subject asks private information to the agent or tries to reciprocate suggestions	.70	.56
Humor [Yes/No] Whether the subject makes any kind of verbal joke in his move	.84	.36
Comments on the dialog [Positive/Negative] Whether the subject makes any kind of comment on the agent behavior in the dialog	.82/.86	.42
Friendly farewell [Yes/No] Whether the subject requests to carry-on the dialog or employs any friendly form of leave	.93	.65
Believes behavior wrong [Yes/No]	.91	.46
Intends to change [Yes/No]	.97	.54

The table shows that there were good majority agreements and kappa for friendly self-introduction, talks about self and friendly farewell and a reasonably good value for personal questions about the agent. Familiar style had a quite low rate and kappa, while humor had a high rate but a low kappa. Agreement was quite good for the two signs of stage of change.

4 User Models as Dynamic Belief Networks

We applied results of the corpus analysis to build a model of the user's mental state which includes the dimensions of interest for dialog adaptation. The user modeling procedure integrates two components: (i) a very simple *parsing* of the user moves based on word semantics and salience and (ii) a *dynamic belief network* (DBN) which considers the context in which the the move was uttered, by handling uncertainty in the relationships among the various components. The model is employed to infer how the mental state of the user evolves during the dialog in relation to the dialog history. The dimensions of the user's mental state which are relevant in advice-giving dialogs are, as we said, stage of change and social attitude towards the ECA. These are *hidden* variables which depend on *observable* ones, such as the 'stable' characteristics of the users (their background and gender), the context in which the move was entered (previous agent move) and the linguistic features of the user move recognized by parsing. *Intermediate* variables are the signs of mental state listed in Table 1. We simulate the following situation: at the beginning of interaction, the model is initialized by assigning a value to the stable user characteristics. At every dialog step, knowledge about the context and evidence produced by the parser are entered and propagated in the network: the model revises the probabilities of hidden variables. As the situation gradually evolves from a dialog step to the next one, we represent the model with a DBN [6]. DBNs, also called time-stamped models, are local belief networks (called time slices) expanded over time; time slices are connected through temporal links to constitute a full model. The following is a legenda for the names of variables in figure 2:

- *Stable and known user characteristics*: background in humanities or computer science (*Back*);
- *context*: category of the previous agent move (*Ctext*), and of the current user move (*Mtype*);
- *dynamically evolving, unknown user characteristics*: social attitude towards the ECA (*Psatt*) which may be 'friendly' or 'neutral' and stage of change (*SoC*) which may be 'pre-contemplation', 'contemplation' or 'preparation'; two instances of these variables are included in the network, at times T and T+1, connected by 'temporal links';
- *signs of social attitude and stage of change*: believes behaviour wrong (*Bbw*) and intends to change (*Itc*) for *SoC*; friendly self-introduction (*Fsint*), familiar style (*Fstyl*), talks about self (*Perin*), personal questions to the agent (*Qagt*), comments on the dialog (*Comm*) and friendly farewell (*F-fw*) for the social attitude;
- *results of parsing*: these variables are in direct connection with those in the previous category: their labels start with a P.

Links among variables describe the causal relationships among stable characteristics of the users and their behavior, via intermediate nodes. DBNs, as employed in this paper, are said to be 'strictly repetitive models'. This means that structure and parameters of individual time slices is identical and temporal links between two consecutive time slices are always the same. We use a special kind of strictly repetitive model in which the Markov property holds: *the past has no impact on the future given the present.* In our simulations, every time slice corresponds to a user move, the stable user characteristics not change from time to time (this is why we omitted the node *Back* from the figure) and temporal links are established only between dynamic subject characteristics in two consecutive time slices.

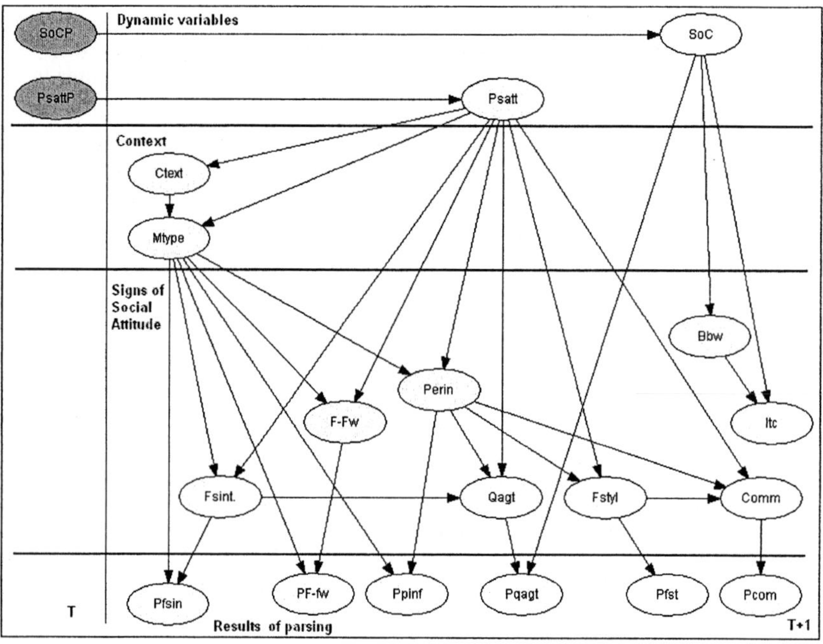

Fig. 2. The dynamic belief network representing the user model

We built the model with a combination of theoretical considerations, learning from the database of cases and subjective estimates. We employed our corpus of WOZ dialogs to train the model with the K2 learning algorithm [3]. This algorithm enables listing the nodes according to a 'search order': in our view, it is particularly appropriate in learning user models, in which links among nodes have a specified meaning and orientation, 'trigger variables' usually correspond to network roots and 'observable' ones to leaf nodes. K2 tries to find the model that fits data best by maximizing the log likelihood but does not care about the use of the resulting model and its predictive ability. We therefore applied the algorithm interactively, by learning automatically both the network structure and its parameters. At every step, we checked the plausibility of learned links, introduced, when needed, other links to avoid problems in evidence propagation due to d-separation properties and checked problems in probability tables due to 'sparse data'. The model shows that a background in humanities implies a higher level of social attitude towards the agent and friendly self introduction in particular. When the level of social attitude is low, self presentation and farewell are sometimes omitted to immediately raise questions to the agent and few comments are made after agent's answers or suggestions. The use of familiar style is associated with talking about self; this is especially included in comments or answers to the agent's questions; personal questions about the agent prevail in the contemplation and the preparation stages of change and often come after friendly self-introduction, ... and so on. The model is employed as follows in the dialog simulation:

- at the beginning of interaction, it is initialized by propagating evidence about the user characteristics;
- after every user move, its linguistic features are analyzed with the parser and these results are introduced and propagated in the network together with evidence about the context;
- the new probabilities of the signs of social attitude and stage of change are read and contribute to formulating the next agent move, while the probabilities of 'dynamic variables' support revising high-level planning of the agent behavior.

The following is an example of simulation of the initial part of a dialog with Giulia, a subject with a background in humanities, that we did in the scope of an 'internal' validation of the predictive value of the model. A stands for 'agent' and U for 'user'; we omit from the example the analysis of SoC. The initial probability that Giulia will establish a social relationship with the ECA is *P(Psatt = Yes) = .61.*

==

A: Hi, My name is Valentina: I'm here to suggest you how to improve your diet.

U: Hi Valentina: my name is Giulia, and I'm happy to interact with you.

Ctext = SelfIntroduction; Parsing(FriendlySelfIntroduction) = Yes; P(Pfsin) = 1; P(Fsint) = .98; P(Psatt = Yes) = .88
** After a friendly self-introduction, the probability of social attitude increases.*

A: OK: let's start, then. What did you eat at breakfast yesterday?

U: Cappuccino and cornetto

Ctext = Question; P(Psatt = Yes) = .71
** After a 'neutral' move, the probability of social attitude decreases, due to the decay effect of the link between PsattP and Psatt.*

A: What did you eat at lunch?

U: I went to a wedding where I eated a lot of fantastic food!!

Ctext = Question; Parsing(Familiar style) = Yes; Parsing(TalksAboutSelf) = Yes P(Pfst) = 1; P(Ppinf) = 1; P(Fstyl) = .75 ; P(Perin) = .69; P(Psatt = Yes) = .88;
** The sensitivity of parsing for familiar style and talks about self is not high: hence the medium values of P(Fstyl) and P(Perin); however, the probability of social attitude after propagating this evidence and information about the context increases again.*

...

==

5 Discussion

Health promotion dialogs are a promising application of affective computing. With the research described in this paper we studied, in particular, how dynamic user models which include an affective component may be built by integrating text analysis of dialog moves with knowledge about context and user characteristics, in a dynamically evolving user model. So far, we performed an internal validation of the predictive value of our model on some of the dialogs in the corpus: as an immediate step further, we plan to extend it to an external validation with new dialogs.

Acknowledgements. This work was financed by HUMAINE, the European Human-Machine Interaction Network of Excellence on Emotion (EC Contract 507422). We thank Berardina De Carolis and Giuseppe Clarizio for cooperating in the implementation of the WOZ tool and Loquendo for providing us their software in the scope of a scientific cooperation.

References

1. Andersen, P.A. and Guerrero, L.K.: The brightside of relational communication: interpersonal warmth as a social emotion. In Andersen, P.A. and Guerrero, L.K.: Handbook of Communication and Emotions. Research, theory, applications and contexts. Academic Press (1998).
2. Cavalluzzi, A., Carofiglio V. and de Rosis, F.: Affective Advice-Giving Dialogs. In E.André, L.Dybkjaer, W.Minker and P.Heisterkamp (Eds): Affective Dialogue Systems. Springer LNAI 3068 (2004).
3. Cooper, G.F. and Herskovitz, E.: A Bayesian method for the induction of probabilistic networks from data. Machine Learning , 9 (1992).
4. de Rosis, F. Cavalluzzi, A. Mazzotta, I. and Novielli, N.: Can embodied conversational agents induce empathy in users? AISB Virtual Social Characters Symposium (2005).
5. Di Eugenio, B. And Glass, M.: The Kappa statistics, a second look. Computational Linguistics, 2004.
6. Jensen, F.V.: Bayesian Networks and Decision Graphs. Springer (2001).
7. Lee, C.M., Narayanan, S.S., Pieraccini, R.: Combining acoustic and language information for emotion recognition. Proc. Of ICSLP (2002).
8. Litman, D., Forbes, K., Silliman, S.: Towards emotion prediction in spoken tutoring dialogues. Proc. of HLT/NAACL} (2003).
9. Miceli, M., de Rosis, F. and Poggi, I.: Emotional and non emotional persuasion. Applied Artificial Intelligence: an International Journal. (in press).
10. 10.Nass, C., Moon, Y, Fogg, B.J. and Dryer, D.C.: Can computer personalities be human personalities? Int J Human-Computer Studies, 43 (1995).
11. 11.Prochaska, J., Di Clemente, C., Norcross, H. In search of how people change: applications to addictive behavior. Americal Psychologist, 47, (1992).
12. Sillince, J.A. and Minors, R.H.: What makes a strong argument? Emotions, highly-placed values and role-playing. Communication and Cognition (1991).
13. Walton, D. The place of emotion in argument. The Pennsylvania State University Press (1992).

Achieving Empathic Engagement Through Affective Interaction with Synthetic Characters

Lynne Hall[1], Sarah Woods[2], Ruth Aylett[3], Lynne Newall[4], and Ana Paiva[5]

[1] School of Computing and Technology, University of Sunderland, Sunderland, SR6 0DD, UK
lynne.hall@sunderland.ac.uk
[2] Adaptive Systems Research Group, University of Hertfordshire, College Lane, Hatfield, Herts, AL10 9AB, UK
s.n.woods@herts.ac.uk
[3] Mathematics and Computer Science, Heriot-Watt University, Edinburgh, EH14 4AS
ruth@macs.hw.ac.uk
[4] Scbool of Informatics, Northumbria University, Newcastle upon Tyne, NE1 8ST, UK
lynne.newall@unn.ac.uk
[5] INESC-ID and IST, Instituto Superior Técnico, Av. Prof. Cavaco Silva, Tagus Park, 2780-990 Porto Salvo, Portugal
ana.paiva@inesc-id.pt

Abstract. This paper considers affective interactions to achieve empathic engagement with synthetic characters in virtual learning environments, in order to support and induce the expression of empathy in children. The paper presents FearNot!, a school based virtual learning environment, populated by synthetic characters used for personal, social and health education, specifically bullying issues in schools. An empirical study of 345 children aged 8-11 years who interacted with FearNot! is outlined. The results identify that affective interactions resulting in the expression of empathy were increased when children had high levels of belief and interest in character conversations and if they believed that their interactions had an impact on the characters' behaviour.

1 Introduction

Affective interaction relates to, arises from, or influences feelings and emotion [18] and generates acts between user and computer that have a reciprocal effect on feelings and emotion. Evoking affect in users has been achieved through a range of approaches and for a variety of motives, including making systems simpler to use [22], affecting the user's physical and mental health [15], reducing stress levels [14] and improving the learning experience [20]. Research has highlighted the potential of affective interaction with synthetic characters in educational drama and story telling applications e.g. Ghostwriter [19], Virtual Puppet Theatre [1, 13]; and personal, social and health education [4, 7, 15].

Empathic engagement is the fostering of emotional involvement intending to create a coherent cognitive and emotional experience which results in empathic relations

J. Tao, T. Tan, and R.W. Picard (Eds.): ACII 2005, LNCS 3784, pp. 731 – 738, 2005.

between a user and a synthetic character. Empathising with characters permits a deeper exploration and understanding of sensitive social and personal issues [5]. Here, we are focusing on affective empathy, that is processes with an affective outcome of a shared affect of two persons [6], or "*An observer reacting emotionally because he perceives that another is experiencing or about to experience an emotion*" [21]. For the user to experience an empathic response to a character, the interaction must affect the user's emotions in one of two ways: by mediation via situation, where a situation is presented that encourages the user to recognise the emotion felt by the target, or by mediation via expression, where the target shows emotional expressions with which the user can identify [16].

The VICTEC (Virtual ICT with Empathic Characters) project [3] applied synthetic characters and emergent narrative to Personal and Health Social Education (PHSE) for children aged 8-12, in the UK, Portugal and Germany, through using 3D self-animating characters to create improvised dramas. The goal in VICTEC was to support affective interaction between the child and the synthetic characters resulting in empathic engagement for the user in a social and emotional learning situation. Our aim was to affect users and evoke empathy and empathic engagement in social and emotional learning for bullying and coping strategies, using mediation via both situation and expression.

In this paper we focus specifically on the evocation of affect and empathy through the child's engagement with the characters and perception of the characters engagement with the user. In section 2 we briefly outline FearNot! (Fun with Empathic Agents to Reach Novel Outcomes in Teaching), the virtual learning environment developed in VICTEC. In section 3 we discuss its use in an empirical study with 345 children. In section 4 we briefly outline our results. Section 5 presents a discussion of these results, followed by some brief conclusions.

2 FearNot!

FearNot! aimed to enable children to explore physical and relational bullying issues, and coping strategies, through affective interaction and empathic engagement with the synthetic characters who populated a virtual school. Interaction with FearNot! was achieved through scenarios in which the main purpose of the communication was to engage in social interaction as opposed to accomplishing a task as efficiently as possible.

A design decision was made to provide FearNot! characters with only crude facial expressions and limited gestures [3] and this was evaluated using a Classroom Discussion Forum [10]. We found that children in the 8-12 age group had relatively little to say about emotions, either their own or those of the characters. However, children clearly understood the characters' expressions having no problems in identifying the emotional state of the characters and found the appearance appropriate. The simple cartoonesque approach supported mediation by expression with children empathizing with the characters, feeling both sympathy and anger.

In a FearNot interaction the child user was asked to take responsibility for the victim, providing support and advice as they would to another child. This interaction enables the user to experience the character's emotions and problems in a distanced way, while being at the same time engaged in and affected by what happens to the characters [3, 7, 15, 16] leading to empathic engagement.

During the interaction with FearNot!, the child user viewed one physical bullying scenario and one relational scenario. Each child initially provided their personal information (name, gender and age) and a unique personal code. After the introduction of the characters, school and situation, children viewed the first bullying episode, followed by the victimised character seeking rescue in the school library, where it started to communicate with the user. Within the initiated dialogue the user selected an advice from a list of coping strategies (shown as a drop down menu). The user also explained his/her selection and what he/she thinks will happen after having implemented the selected strategy, by typing it in (see figure 1).

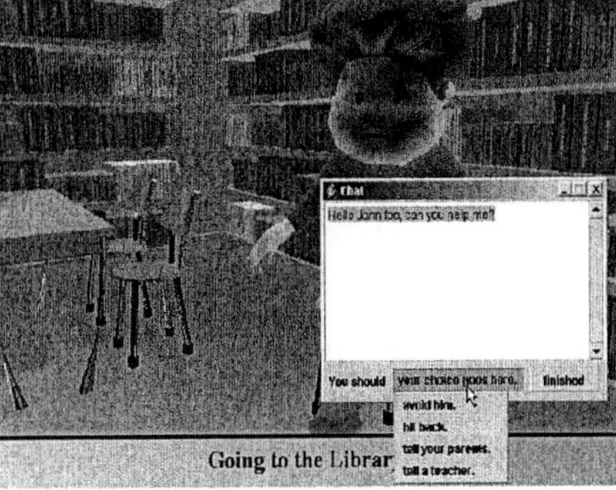

Fig. 1. Interaction with victim

The next episode then began. The content of the final episode depended on the choices made by the user concerning the coping strategies: Paul, the bystander in the physical bullying scenario, might act as a defender for John (the victim), in this case the user had selected a successful strategy, i.e. "telling someone"; or Martina (the bystander) might offer Frances (the victim) help. However, if the user selected an unsuccessful strategy, i.e. "run away", the victim rejected the help in the final episode. At the end of the scenario, a universal educational message was displayed pointing out that "telling someone" is always a good choice.

3 Investigating Affect and Empathy in FearNot!

To investigate the children's empathic engagement and affective reactions to the synthetic characters in FearNot!, we performed a large scale study with a scripted version of the FearNot! prototype [3, 9]. This large scale evaluation event called "Virtually Friends" was held at the University of Hertfordshire, UK, in June 2004.

345 children participated in the event. 172 male (49.9%) and 173 female (50.1%). The sample age range was 8 to 11, mean age of 9.95 (SD: 0.50). The sample comprised of children from a wide range of local primary schools.

3.1 Method

Two classes from different schools participated each day in the study. All children individually interacted with FearNot! on standard PCs.

FearNot! began with a physical bullying scenario comprised of three episodes and children had the role of an advisor to help provide the victim character with coping strategies to try and stop the bullying behaviour. After the physical scenario, children had the opportunity to interact with the relational scenario showing the drama of bullying among four girls.

After the interaction children completed the Character Evaluation Questionnaire (CEQ). This was designed in order to evaluate children's perceptions and views of the characters in FearNot, see table 1. This questionnaire is based on the Trailer Questionnaire [23] that has been used extensively with a non-interactive FearNot! prototype as is reported in [12]. Questions relating to choosing characters were answered by selecting character names (posters of the characters were displayed with both a graphic and the name as an aide memoire). Children's views were predominantly measured according to a 5 point Likert scale.

Table 1. Content of the Character Evaluation Questionnaire

Aspect	Nature of Questions
Character preference	Character liked most and least, most like to be friends with Prime character - who child would choose to be
Character Attributes	Realism and smoothness of movement Clothes appreciation and similarity to own Age
Character conversations	Content believability, interest and similarity to own conversations
Impact	Victims acceptance of advice and how much child had helped
Bullying Storyline	Storyline believability and length
Similarity	Character that looks and behaves most and least like you
Empathy towards characters	Feeling sorry for characters and if yes which character Feeling angry towards the characters and if yes which character Ideomotoric empathy based on expected behaviour

4 Results

Character Conversations

Substantial significant differences were found between feeling sorry for the characters and whether the children found what the characters spoke about believable ($t(306) = 4.10$, $p < .001$). Those children who expressed feeling sorry for the characters in the drama rated the character conversations as being more believable than those children that did not feel sorry for any of the characters (sorry for characters: M conversation believability = 2.08 vs. did not feel sorry for characters: M conversation believability = 2.70). Significant differences emerged between feeling anger towards characters in the drama and character conversation believability (t (293) = 2.27, p = .02), (anger towards characters: M conversation believability = 2.13 vs. did not feel anger towards characters: M conversation believability = 2.45).

Significant differences were also revealed between children's ratings of interest in the character conversations, and feeling sorry and angry towards characters in the dramas (sorry for characters t (307) = 4.62, p < .001), (anger towards characters t (294) = 3.47, p = .001). Children who expressed feeling sorry for the characters in the drama rated the character conversation as significantly more interesting compared to those children who did not feel empathy towards any of the characters (sorry for characters: M conversation interest = 2.35, did not feel sorry for characters: M conversation interest = 3.09). This same pattern of findings was found for anger towards characters, where children who expressed anger towards characters rated the character conversation interest as significantly higher compared to those children who did not express anger (anger towards characters: M conversation interest = 2.33, did not feel anger towards characters: M conversation interest = 2.85).

No significant differences were uncovered between children's ratings of conversation similarity with characters in the drama and expression of feeling sorry or angry towards the characters in the drama.

Character Impact and Empathy

Independent samples t-tests were calculated to determine whether the level of impact children felt their help had on the characters' actions in the virtual learning environment was associated with the amount of empathy expressed towards the characters in the virtual dramas. Overall, a trend was revealed for children feeling sorry for the victim characters in the dramas and whether they felt that the victim characters John and Frances followed their coping strategy advice on how to stop the bullying behaviour (t (316) = 1.83, p = .07) (felt sorry for characters M = 2.18 vs. did not feel sorry for characters M = 2.43). A trend was also found between whether children felt sorry for the victim characters and whether the child felt that they had actually helped John or Frances with the bullying situation (t (307) = 1.62, p = .1) (felt sorry for characters M = 2.19 vs. did not feel sorry for characters M = 2.44).

When these analyses were calculated for boys and girls separately no significant differences emerged with the exception of one finding for the girls. Girls were significantly more likely to express feeling sorry for the victim characters if they believed that their advice had actually helped John and Frances (t (155) = 2.23, p = .03) (felt sorry for characters M = 2.10 vs. did not feel sorry for characters M = 2.71).

5 Discussion

In this paper we have considered the evocation of affect and empathy focusing on engagement with the characters. Gender, perceived similarity to character and character preference all have an impact on empathic engagement and results are reported elsewhere ([9, 17]). Here, we are focusing on the mediation of the situation, considering the child's engagement with the character's conversation and the child's perception of their impact on character's actions.

Supporting earlier findings [23], empathic engagement does not appear to be strongly related to character appearance. Thus, although children were critical of the graphics, animation, lack of voices and character movement in FearNot! [10] this did not appear to impact on levels of affect, engagement and believability. This suggests that children are mediating via situation rather than via expression. The situation is expressed most clearly through the conversation of the characters.

The character conversations and FearNot! scenarios were developed using a drama production methodology by a team of experienced researchers in bullying, teachers, and drama staff. These scenarios were extensively tested to ensure that they had believable and interesting storylines [11], provided key educational messages [8] and that characters had appropriate language and behaviour [2]. Our results highlight that this approach has produced interesting and believable characters that affect and engage most children.

We found that those children who expressed feeling sorry for and angry about the characters in the drama rated the character conversations as being more believable and interesting than those children that did not feel sorry for any of the characters. Affect can clearly be evoked with child users through the use of mediation via situation, evidenced by the users feeling sorrow or anger towards the characters in the situations presented in the drama, and their interest in the conversations between characters. The higher rating of belief and interest in character conversation shows a greater level of engagement with the scenario and the characters leading to increased affect and empathy.

The study presented here used a high fidelity prototype of FearNot that provided a scripted rather than an emergent narrative. In this version, the structure of FearNot! gave little possibility for the child to really influence what happened, with only two possible final episodes. However, a significant number of children believed that their interaction had impacted on the character's behaviour. Further, results indicated that levels of affect and empathic engagement are higher if children felt that their interactions were having an impact on the characters' behaviour.

Children expressed more empathy towards the characters in the drama if they felt that the characters had followed their coping strategy advice, and if they felt like they had actually helped the victim characters. This was particularly significant for girls who were more likely to express feeling sorry for the victim characters if they believed that their advice had actually helped. These results indicate that empathic engagement and the affect of that engagement are increased if the child believes that their presence and interventions has had an impact on the characters.

In the current version of FearNot, the child's impact on the characters is supported using an emergent narrative approach, in which action is driven by the characters themselves. This approach has been used as a natural solution to making the victim responsive to the advice the child gives. This responsiveness is constrained through the need for FearNot to attain pedagogical outcomes, and current work focuses on the extent to which the necessarily somewhat unpredictable outcomes of episodes are in conflict with social and emotional pedagogical objectives. Current work focuses on ensuring that both pedagogical effectiveness and character responsiveness are achieved by FearNot!

6 Conclusions

This paper has considered the use of affective interaction to support and induce the expression of empathy with children. The synthetic characters in FearNot! involved children in empathic engagement, with engagement in believable and interesting situations creating affect, leading to an empathic response. From our results, we can conclude that affect and empathic engagement can be increased if the child believes that their interactions are having an impact on the character's activities.

References

1. André, E., Klesen, M., Gebhard, P., Allen, S., and Rist, T., "Exploiting models of personality and emotions to control the behaviour of animated interface agents," presented at Workshop on Achieving Human-Like Behavior in Interactive Animated Agents, Barcelona, Spain, 2000.
2. Aylett, R. S. and Louchart, S., "Narrative theories and emergent interactive narrative," *IJCEELL journal (special issue on narrative in education)*, vol. 14, pp. 506-518, 2004.
3. Aylett, R. S., Paiva, A., Woods, S., Hall, L., and Zoll, C., "Expressive Characters in Anti-Bullying Education," in *Animating Expressive Characters for Social Interaction*, L. Canamero and R. Aylett, Eds.: John Benjamins, 2005.
4. Bates, J., "The Role of Emotion in Believable Agents," *Communications of the ACM*, vol. 37(7) &P 122-125., 1994.
5. Dautenhahn, K., Bond, A. H., Canamero, L., and Edmonds, B., *Socially intelligent agents: Creating relationships with computers and robots.* Massachusetts, USA: Kluwer Academic Publishers, 2002.
6. Davis, M. H., *Empathy: A social psychological approach.* Dubuque: Brown and Benchmark Publishers, 1994.
7. Gratch, J. and Marsella, S., "Tears and fears: Modeling emotions and emotional behaviors in synthetic agents," presented at Fifth International Conference on Autonomous Agents, 2001.
8. Hall, L., "Virtual Environments in Schools: Teacher's Workshop Report," Centre for Virtual Environments, University of Salford, Salford December 2003.
9. Hall, L. and Woods, S., "Empathic interaction with synthetic characters: the importance of similarity," in *Encyclopaedia of Human Computer Interaction*, C. Ghaoui, Ed.: Idea Group, 2005.
10. Hall, L., Woods, S., and Dautenhahn, K., "FearNot! Designing in the Classroom," presented at British HCI, Leeds, UK, 2004.
11. Hall, L., Woods, S., Dautenhahn, K., and Sobreperez, P., "Guiding Virtual World Design Using Storyboards," presented at Interaction Design with Children, Maryland, 2004.
12. Hall, L., Woods, S., Sobral, D., Paiva, A., Dautenhahn, K., Wolke, D., and Newall, L., "Designing Empathic Agents: Adults vs. Kids," presented at Intelligent Tutoring Systems 7th International Conference, ITS 2004, Maceio, Brazil, 2004.
13. Klesen, M., Szatkowski, J., and Lehmann, N., "The Black Sheep:Interactive improvisation in a 3D Virtual World," presented at i3 Annual Conference 2000, Jönköping, Sweden, 2000.
14. Liu, K. and Picard, R. W., "Embedded Empathy in Continuous, Interactive Health Assessment," presented at CHI Workshop on HCI Challenges in Health Assessment, Portland, Oregon, 2005.

15. Marsella, S., Johnson, W. L., and LaBore, C., "Interactive Pedagogical Drama for Health Interventions," presented at 11th International Conference on Artificial Intelligence in Education, Sydney, Australia, 2003.
16. Paiva, A., Dias, J., Sobral, D., Aylett, R., Sobreperez, P., Woods, S., Zoll, C., and Hall, L., "Caring for Agents and Agents that Care: Building Empathic Relations with Synthetic Agents," presented at AAMAS 2004, New York, 2004.
17. Paiva, A., Dias, J., Sobral, D., Aylett, R., Woods, S., Hall, L., and Zoll, C., "Learning by feeling: Evoking Empathy with Synthetic Characters," *Journal of Applied AI*, in print.
18. Picard, R., *Affective Computing*. Cambridge, MA: MIT Press, 1997.
19. Robertson, J. and Oberlander, J., "Ghostwriter: Educational Drama and Presence in a Virtual Environment," *Journal of Computer Mediated Communication*, vol. 8, 2002.
20. Sampson, D. and Karagiannidis, C., "Personalised learning: Educational, technical and standardisation perspective," *Interactive Educational Multimedia*, vol. 4, pp. 24-39, 2002.
21. Stotland, E., Mathews, K. E., Sherman, S. E., Hannson, R. O., and Richardson, B. Z., *Empathy, fantasy and helping*. Beverly Hills: Sage, 1978.
22. van Vugt, H. C., Hoorn, J. F., and Konijn, E. A., "Digital bonding: Interactive and affective affordances of interface characters," presented at AAMAS 2005, Utrecht, 2005.
23. Woods, S., Hall, L., Sobral, D., Dautenhahn, K., and Wolke, D., "A study into the believability of animated characters in the context of bullying intervention," presented at IVA '03, Kloster Irsee, Germany, 2003.

Real-Life Emotion Representation and Detection in Call Centers Data

Laurence Vidrascu and Laurence Devillers

Department of Human-Machine Communication, LIMSI-CNRS, Orsay, France,
LIMSI-CNRS, BP133, 91 403, Orsay cedex
{vidrascu, devil}@limsi.fr

Abstract.. Since the early studies of human behavior, emotions have attracted the interest of researchers in Neuroscience and Psychology. Recently, it has been a growing field of research in computer science. We are exploring how to represent and automatically detect a subject's emotional state. In contrast with most previous studies conducted on artificial data, this paper addresses some of the challenges faced when studying real-life non-basic emotions. Real-life spoken dialogs from call-center services have revealed the presence of many blended emotions. A soft emotion vector is used to represent emotion mixtures. This representation enables to obtain a much more reliable annotation and to select the part of the corpus without conflictual blended emotions for training models. A correct detection rate of about 80% is obtained between Negative and Neutral emotions and between Fear and Neutral emotions using paralinguistic cues on a corpus of 20 hours of recording.

1 Introduction

Detecting emotions can help orienting the evolution of a human-computer interaction via dynamic modification of the dialog strategy. We focus on real-life corpora which allow the study of complex and natural emotion behavior. Our aim is twofold, to study emotion mixtures in natural data and to achieve high level of performances in real-life emotion detection. Call centers provide interesting solutions for recording people in various natural emotional states since the recordings can be made imperceptibly. Among the natural corpora for emotion detection, we can mention the 'Lifelog' corpus consisting of everyday interactions between a female speaker and her family and friends [1]; the 'Interviews corpus' also known as the Belfast database [2]; the 'EmoTV' corpus - a set of TV interviews in French recorded in the HUMAINE project [3]; and medical dialogs [4]. Obviously, the types of emotions found in the corpus are heavily dependent on the task and situation. A corpus of real agent client dialogs (20 hours) recorded in French, at a Medical Emergency call center, is studied in this paper.

There are many reviews on the representation of emotions. For a recent review, the reader will refer to Cowie & Cornelius [5]. Three types of theories generally used to represent emotions are: abstract dimensions, appraisal dimensions and most commonly verbal categories.

According to Osgood [6], the communication of emotions is conceptualized following several dimensions such as Evaluation, Power and Activation. Other subjective

J. Tao, T. Tan, and R.W. Picard (Eds.): ACII 2005, LNCS 3784, pp. 739 – 746, 2005.

dimensions also include: intensity, control, tension, etc. Instead of naming emotions as discrete categories, they are defined along continuous abstract dimensions. The most widely employed scheme is based on the two perceptive abstract dimensions: Activation-Evaluation and has been employed to annotate several corpora with the Feeltrace tool [7]. However, other dimensions are necessary, for instance, for distinguishing between Fear and Anger.

The appraisal theory [8] provides detailed specification of appraisal dimensions that are assumed to be used in evaluating emotion-antecedent events (novelty, pleasantness, goal relevance, etc). The major methodological problem is that the only reliable way to ensure a correct annotation is to ask the persons themselves to perform it. If done in real-time this can affect the expression of the emotions, but if done a posteriori, it relies on the person's recall of the situation. New abstract dimensions are suggested by appraisal theorists [8], for example the goal conduciveness/obstructiveness of an event, i.e. the individual's potential to cope with the consequences.

Most emotion detection studies have only focused on verbal categories using a minimal set of emotions to be tractable, often basic emotion (anger, fear, etc.). However, it is well-known that linguistic labels are imprecise and capture only a specific aspect of phenomena, i.e. those that are immediately relevant for speakers in a particular context. In this work we make the assumption that it is possible to perceive and to annotate mixtures of emotions. There is no clear typology of the different mixtures of emotions. Blended emotions can be considered as the presence of two or more emotions at the same time, one of which may be considered Major and the others Minor. The Major emotion can be related to the dominant emotion in the brain, with the other perceived emotions in a mixture being secondary. Our philosophy is to represent emotional states with a soft emotion vector combining Major and Minor emotions [3, 10]. The same emotion representation with Major and Minor labels has been used for audiovisual data [10]. A soft vector is obtained after the combination of annotations done by different raters with the Major and Minor emotion annotation. Such soft representation allows a better reliable annotation and also a better knowledge of the emotions mixtures present in the corpus. For detection purposes, this knowledge is used to select appropriate subsets of the corpus in order to obtain better detection performances. Automatic systems can lead to a deeper understanding of the perception of emotion by identifying the relevant cues to emotion detection in natural emotional states. Our detection experiments use prosodic and spectral features, but also some disfluencies (hesitation, pauses) and some non-verbal events such as laughter, inspiration, expiration, which were time-stamped during the transcription phase. We report in this paper our experiments on classification for Negative to Positive classes and for Fear to Neutral classes without taking into account the conflictual emotion mixtures.

Section 2 is devoted to the description of the corpus. Section 3 presents the emotion labeling scheme and the analysis and reliability of our annotations. Section 4 describes the cues and the selection procedure. Models and results are briefly reported in 5.

2 Real-Life Corpus

The studies reported in this paper were done on a corpus of naturally-occurring dialogs recorded in a real-life call center. The corpus contains real agent-client recordings obtained from a convention between a medical emergency call center and the LIMSI-CNRS. The transcribed corpus contains about 20 hours of data. The service center can be reached 24 hours a day, 7 days a week. Its aim is to offer medical advice. An agent follows a precise, predefined strategy during the interaction to efficiently acquire important information. His role is to determine the call topic and to obtain sufficient details about this situation so as to be able to evaluate the call emergency and to take a decision. In the case of emergency calls, the patients often express stress, pain, fear of being sick or even real panic. This study is based on a 20-hour subset comprised of 688 agent-client dialogs (7 different agents, 784 clients). About 10% of speech data is not transcribed since there is heavily overlapping speech. Table 1 summarizes the characteristics of the corpus.

Table 1. Corpus characteristics: 688 agent-client dialogs of around 20 hours (M: male, F: female)

#agents	7 (3M, 4F)
#clients	688 dialogs (271M, 513F)
#turns/dialog	Average: 48
#distinct words	9.2 k
#total words	262 k

The use of these data carefully respected ethical conventions and agreements ensuring the anonymity of the callers, the privacy of personal information and the non-diffusion of the corpus and annotations. The transcription guidelines are similar to those used for spoken dialogs in Amities project (www.dcs.shef.ac.uk/nlp/amities/). Some additional markers have been added to denote named-entities, breath, silence, intelligible speech, laugh, tears, clearing throat and other noises (mouth noise).

3 Emotion Annotation

Our emotion and meta-data annotation scheme and the choice of our labels have been described in [9]. The meta-data are given at the dialog level. The scheme specification at the segment level enables annotation of emotion labels and abstract dimensions with one or two emotion labels for segment, selected from fine-grained and coarse-grained labels as well as some local emotional context cues. The audio signal was further segmented into emotional segments where the annotators felt it was appropriate, so the temporal-grain can be finer than the speaker turn. In order to minimize the annotation time, only the abstract dimensions which are complementary with verbal categories are labeled. The bi-polar Valence (Negative/Positive) is deducted from the fine grained verbal labels. The only ambiguity concerns the class 'Surprise' which can be associated with both positive and negative emotions. Activation (passive, normal, active) is often confused with Intensity (low, middle, high) by non-expert annotators. In these annotations, only intensity is rated on a 5-level scale. Rough labels for the bi-polar Activation (Passive/Active) were extracted from fine-grained verbal labels. We also added a new dimension named Self-Control (not the Power/Control described in [6]). The Self-Control dimension is a meta-annotation describing the perception of the self-control of the person (from controlled to uncontrolled on a 7-level scale). All combinations of categories are possible with only one exception; for the verbal label surprise, which has an ambiguous valence, there must be a minor indicating the valence.

The set of labels is hierarchically organized, from coarse-grained to fine-grained labels in order to deal with the lack of occurrences of fine-grained emotions and to allow for different annotator judgments. A definition and instances for each label were given in the annotation protocol. Because there are few positive occurrences in the corpus, there is only one coarse positive class. The annotation level used to train emotion detection system can be chosen based on the number of segments available.

Table 2. Emotion classes hierarchy: multi-level of granularity

Valence-level	Coarse level (7 classes)	Fine-grained level (20 classes + Neutral)
Negative	Fear	Fear, Anxiety, Stress, Panic, Embarrassment, Dismay
	Anger	Anger, Annoyance, Impatience, ColdAnger, HotAnger
	Sadness	Sadness, Disappointment, Resignation, Despair
	Hurt	Hurt
Negative or Positive	Surprise	Surprise
Positive	Positive	Interest, Compassion, Amusement, Relief
Neutral	Neutral	Neutral

3.1 Annotation Validation

The high subjectivity of human annotation requires the use of rigorous annotation protocols. After deciding the list of labels and the adopted scheme, precise rules for segmentation must be determined along with the number of annotators and the validation procedures. We also have to consider inter-labeler consistency and confidence measures. There are different measures of annotation reliability; for instance, the widely used Kappa inter-coder agreement measure for categorical labels and the Cronbach's alpha measure for continuous variables. For those measures, one label by segment is normally used. When a mixture of emotions is annotated, a solution is to compare only the Major label or to add some rules to improve inter-labeler agreement such as Major/Minor = Minor/Major. We have adopted a self re-annotation procedure of small sets of dialogs at different time (for instance once a month) in order to judge the intra-annotator coherence over time. As shown in

Table 3, the annotations reliability seems to stabilize around 85%. This result is a proof of the difficulty of the task.

Table 3. Labeler inter-reliability in terms of % agreement between two annotations by the same labeler at different times. Dec-Feb means first annotation in December, re-annotation in February (14 dialogs), Jan-Feb First annotation in January, re-annotation in February (11 dialogs), Mar-Apr (16 dialogs), Apr-May (16 dialogs). The two lines for Agent and Client corresponds to the 2 annotations (Labeller1 and Labeller2) (The corpus annotation started in December).

	Dec-Feb	Jan-Feb	Mar-Apr	Apr-May
Agent	76.4 (369 seg.)	82.9 (287 seg.)	86.1 (495 seg.)	85.7 (405 seg.)
	66.5 (369 seg.)	80.8 (279 seg.)	86.8 (499 seg.)	87.6 (412 seg.)
Client	73.9 (356 seg.)	83.9 (255 seg.)	83.4 (499 seg.)	84.2 (442 seg.)
	78.5 (350 seg.)	76.5 (254 seg.)	81.4 (505 seg.)	85.8 (450 seg.)

Since segments were labeled by more than one labeler and also since segments could be assigned one or two labels, it was necessary to create a mapping (i.e. to reduce the multiple labels per segment to one label) for the machine learning experiments. Let us consider each annotation as a vector (Major, Minor). The mapping combines the N (Major, Minor) vectors (for N annotators) in an emotion soft vector. Different weights are given to the emotion annotation, one weight to the Major emotions (wM) and one other to the Minor emotions (wm) [9]. About 50% of the corpus was thus labeled as neutral.

The 5 top classes of the fine-grained emotion labels were Neutral, Anxiety, Stress, Relief and Amusement for clients and Neutral, Interest, Compassion and Surprise for agents. In order to assess the consistency of the selected labels, the inter-annotator agreement was calculated. The Kappa value is 0.55 for clients and 0.35 for agents when only considering Major annotation. The Kappa values are slightly better (0.6 and 0.37, respectively) if a rule allowing common annotation in one of the two annotations Major and Minor is used.

3.2 Blended Emotions

Labeler 1 assigned a Minor label for 31 % of the non neutral segments, whereas labeler 2 for only 17 %. A first rough description of emotions mixture was defined. Mixed emotions within the same coarse-grained label are noted as **Ambiguous**. A labeler perceiving an emotion between annoyance and hotAnger would label it "Annoyance/Hot Anger". A mixture between two different coarse-grained labels is called **Conflictual** if they don't have the same valence, **Non-conflictual** otherwise. The non-conflictual mixtures can be separated into positive and negative. An example of a conflictual emotion would be "Anxiety/Annoyance". When perceived with another emotion, the class 'Surprise' doesn't fit into those categories because its valence is not set, which accounts for a class **Surprise**.

For analysis purposes, the Conflictual and Unconflictual emotions mixtures are manifestly the most interesting data. It is to be noted (see Figure 1) that both annotators have perceived mixtures in those classes and that they appear in different positions in the dialog (i.e. for Agent and Client: when a recurring blended emotion for an agent would be to feel both compassion and annoyance towards a caller, a caller might feel worry coupled with relief from knowing help is on its way…). For detection purposes, we have not considered those mixed emotion segments but improve the performance of the system by choosing non blended and non conflictual emotion segments.

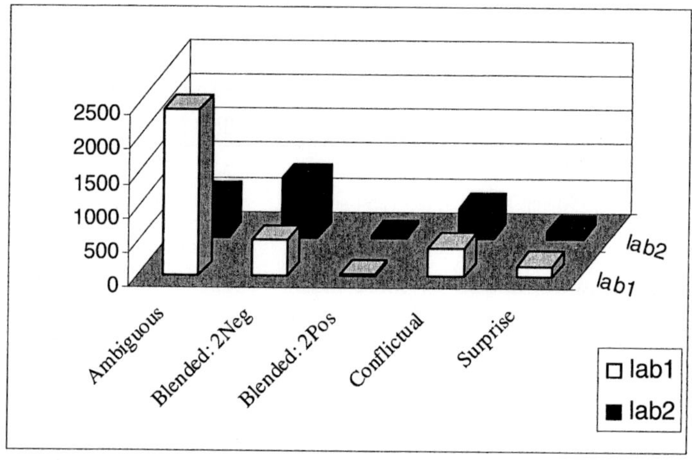

Fig. 1. Repartition of the mixed emotions for each labeler. *Lab1* and *Lab2* are the two labelers; *Blended: 2Pos* means that the two labels are chosen from two different positive coarse grained labels ('Amusement', 'Relief, 'Compassion/Interest'); *Blended: 2Neg* means that the two labels are chosen from two different negative coarse grained labels ('Fear', 'Anger', 'Sadness' and 'Hurt').

4 Features

A crucial problem for all emotion recognition system is the selection of the set of relevant features to be used with the most efficient machine learning algorithm.

In the experiments reported in this paper, we have focused on the extraction of lexical, prosodic, spectral, disfluency and non-verbal events cues. For prosodic (F0 and energy) and spectral cue extraction, the Praat program [11] has been used. About fifty features will be input to a classifier which will select the most relevant ones:

- **F0 and Spectral features** (Log-normalized per speaker): *min*, *max*, *mean*, *standard deviation*, *range* at the turn level, *slope* (mean and max) in the voiced segments, *regression coefficient* and its *mean square error* (performed on the voiced parts as well), *maximum cross-variation of F0* between two adjoining voiced segments (inter-segment) and with each voiced segment(intra-segment), *ratio* of the number of voiced and non-voiced segments, *formants* and their *bandwidth* (first and second): min, max, mean, standard deviation, range..

- **Energy features** (normalized): *min*, *max*, *mean*, *standard deviation* and *range* at the segment level.
- **Duration features**: *speaking rate* (inverse of the average length of the speech voiced parts), number and length of *silences* (unvoiced portions between 200-800 ms).
- **Disfluency features**: number of *pauses and filled pauses* ("euh" in French) per utterance annotated with time-stamps during transcription.
- **Non linguistic event features**: *inspiration*, *expiration*, *mouth noise laughter*, *crying*, and *unintelligible voice*. These features are marked during the transcription phase.

5 Classification

The above set of features are computed for all emotion segments and fed into a classifier. Ongoing experiences are being done on the corpus using Support Vector Machines ([12]: algorithms search an optimal hyperplan to separate the data) As a first study, experiments were only made on broad classes.

For reliability, all experiments were done using jack-knifing with 5 subsets (4 subsets are used for training and one for test, the experiment is repeated 4 times with each subset being used for test). This procedure is repeated 10 times with different subsets.

Table 4. Neutral/Negative detection performances with all features. The number into parenthesis is the standard deviation.

Role in the dialogue	Emotion classification	SVM
Agent	Neutral / Anger	75.0 (2.4)
	Neutral / Negative	73.4 (3.1)
Client	Neutral / Negative	80.2 (2.4)
	Neutral / Fear	83.8 (0.9)

Different performances have been obtained taking into account the role in the dialog. Clients are much clearer than Agents when they express Negative emotions (80% vs 73% of good detection). Experiments selecting non blended emotion for training models have yielded a high level of emotion detection performance (comparable to those already achieved on subsets of the corpus [9]) and hopefully it will improve emotion detection with more classes or with same valence classes such as Anger and-Fear.

6 Discussion and Perspectives

This paper focuses on real-life emotions and shows the complexity of natural emotional behavior expressed in dialogs on a medical call center. Our study of this corpus, using a uni-modal channel (only speech), reveals the presence of mixtures of emotions with conflictual or non-conflictual valences. When selecting the reliable part of the annotated corpus, the performances obtained are around 80% of good detection between Negative and Neutral or Fear and Neutral. Further experiments are to be made on finer classes.

We have not yet used all the corpus annotations such as intensity and control dimensions, and also meta-data annotations. These annotations will be correlated with the soft-vector emotion annotation in future experiments. We also intend to combine linguistic cues and paralinguistic cues as done in previous experiments [9].

Acknowledgements

This work was partially financed by several EC projects: FP6-CHIL and NoE HUMAINE. The authors would like to thank, M. Lesprit and J. Martel for their help with data annotation. The work is conducted in the framework of a convention between the APHP France and the LIMSI-CNRS. The authors would like to thank the Professor P. Carli, the Doctor P. Sauval and their collegues N. Borgne, A. Rouillard and G. Benezit.

References

1. Campbell, N.: Accounting for Voice Quality Variation, Speech Prosody 2004 (2004) 217-220.
2. Douglas-Cowie, E., Campbell, N., Cowie, R. and Roach, R., "Emotional speech; Towards a new generation of databases," Speech Communication, (2003).
3. Abrilian, S., Devillers, L., Buisine, S. and Martin, J.C.: EmoTV1: Annotation of Real-life Emotions for the Specification of Multimodal Affective Interfaces, HCI International (2005)
4. Craggs, R. & Wood, M.M.: A 2-dimensional annotation scheme for emotion in dialogue, Proceedings of AAAI Spring Symposium on Exploring Attitude and Affect in Text: Theories and Applications, Stanford University. (2004).
5. Cowie, R. & Cornelius, R.R: Describing the emotional states expressed in speech, Speech Communication, 40(1-2) (2003) 5-32
6. Osgood, C., May, W.H. & Miron, M.S: Cross-cultural Universals of Affective Meaning. University of Illinois Press, Urbana & al, (1975)
7. Cowie, R.,Douglas-Cowie, E., Tsapatsoulis, N., Votsis, G., Kollias, S., Fellenz, W. & Taylor, J. : Emotion Recognition in Human-Computer Interaction. IEEE Signal Processing Magazine, 18(1) (2001) 32-80.
8. Scherer K.R.: Appraisal Theory. In: Dalgleish, T. Power, M. (Eds), Handbook of Cognition and Emotion. John Wiley, New York, (1999) 637-663.
9. Devillers L., Vidrascu L. & Lamel L.: Challenges in real-life emotion annotation and machine learning based detection, to appear in Journal of Neural Networks 2005.
10. Devillers, L., Abrilian, S., Martin, J.-C.: Representing real life emotions in audiovisual data with non basic emotional patterns and context features.(ACII'2005) (submitted)
11. Boersma, P.: Accurate short-term analysis of the fundamental frequency and the harmonics-to-noise ratio of a sampled sound", Proceedings of the Institute of Phonetic Sciences, (1993) 97-110
12. Vapnik, V.N.: The Nature of Statistical Learning Theory, Springer (1995).

Affective Touch for Robotic Companions

Walter Dan Stiehl and Cynthia Breazeal

Robotic Life Group, MIT Media Lab, Cambridge, MA 02139, USA
wdstiehl@mit.edu, cynthiab@media.mit.edu

Abstract. As robotic platforms are designed for human robot interaction applications, a full body sense of touch, or "sensitive skin," becomes important. The Huggable is a new type of therapeutic robotic companion based upon relational touch interactions. The initial use of neural networks to classify the affective content of touch is described.

1 Introduction

The realm of touch in robotic systems has largely been limited to manipulation. In these platforms, such as the NASA/DARPA Robonaut Hand [1], tactile sensors are only placed on the surface of the robotic hand or gripper, and the remainder of the robot is largely not sensed. Clearly, there are many other applications for tactile sensing in robotics.

Lumelsky, Shur, and Wagner originally proposed the idea of a "sensitive skin" in 2001 [2]. A "sensitive skin" features a large number of sensors of different modalities, such as temperature, pressure, etc., which cover the entire surface of the robot. Biological skin also features a large number of sensors of different modalities for the purpose of encoding the external world through touch [3]. Currently, there exist only a handful of robots which feature a full-body "sensitive skin," such as [4]. In many of these applications, the "skin" is used primarily to protect the robot from damaging itself or a human user. There are a number of other applications for such "skins" which have yet to be addressed.

In this paper, we present the Huggable, a new type of therapeutic robotic companion based upon relational touch interactions. Unlike other robotic companions, such as Sony's AIBO [5], the Huggable features a *full body*, multi-modal, "sensitive skin" for the purpose of sensing the affective content of touch in human-robot interactions. Unlike previous work, which has used a neural approach for object recognition through touch [6], the focus of this approach is to detect the affective content of the social interaction – petting, tickling, etc. A brief description of the design of the Huggable is first presented to provide context for the neural network approach used to classify the affective content of social tactile interactions, the focus of this paper. A more detailed discussion of the design can be found in [7].

2 The Huggable: A Therapeutic Robotic Companion for Relational, Affective Touch

In the full implementation of the Huggable, shown in Fig. 1, it features a full-body sensitive skin, silent back-drivable voice coil actuators [8], an inertial measurement

J. Tao, T. Tan, and R.W. Picard (Eds.): ACII 2005, LNCS 3784, pp. 747 – 754, 2005.

unit [9], and an embedded PC with wireless communication capabilities for behaviors, patient monitoring, and data collection. Vision and auditory processing may be added as well to allow for multi-modal interactions.

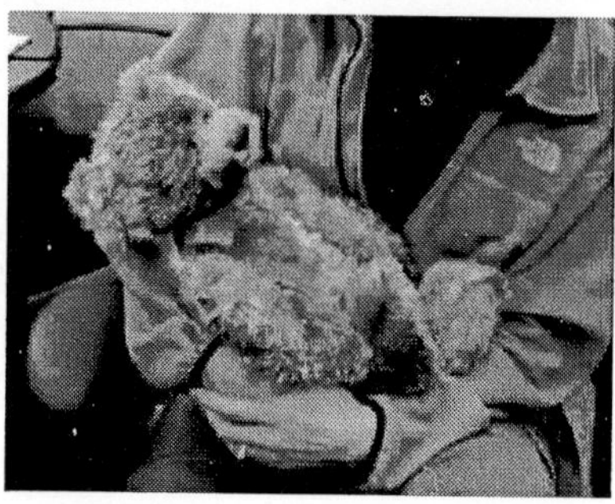

Fig. 1. The Huggable – Currently in Development

The goal of the Huggable project is to deploy these robotic companions to hospitals and nursing homes for robot therapy applications with a wide range of users from the elderly to small children. As such, a series of design decisions were made to develop a robot which invites users of all ages to interact with it. First, the overall weight of the Huggable must be kept below 5 lbs to allow it to be picked up and held in one's arms. The Huggable features a strong, light-weight, ribbed mechanical understructure for this purpose. Second, the Huggable must have a soft feel that is pleasant to touch. Unlike many robotic platforms which have a hard exterior, the Huggable features a soft silicone synthetic skin under the soft furry exterior of Fig. 1.

Third, the Huggable must convey the "illusion of life" through life-like motion. Quiet, smooth, back drivable voice-coil actuators, as opposed to the traditional geared DC motors, are used for all the degrees of freedom of the Huggable. In the current design, the bear features a 3-DOF neck, 2-DOF eyebrow mechanism, 1-DOF ear mechanism, and a 2-DOF "Hug" shoulder mechanism. The neck and shoulders allow for active touch behaviors such as orienting towards touch, nuzzling, and hugging. The ears and eyebrows are used to express the internal state of the robot.

Finally, the Huggable must be able to detect the affective content of the social interaction the user is having with the robot, and respond appropriately. To accomplish this design constraint, the Huggable features a full body "sensitive skin" based upon the ideas of [2], as well as the organization of the somatosensory system in humans and animals [3]. The "sensitive skin" of the Huggable features four modalities of somatic information – pain, temperature, touch, and kinesthetic information. For touch, electric field sensors are used to measure proximity and Quantum Tunneling Composite (QTC) sensors are used to measure force. Temperature is sensed using thermistors. Kinesthetic information is measured by potentiometers. Finally, pain is treated as an intense sensor signal of any one of these stimuli. Due to space constraints, a further discussion of these sensors and the processing used appears in [7].

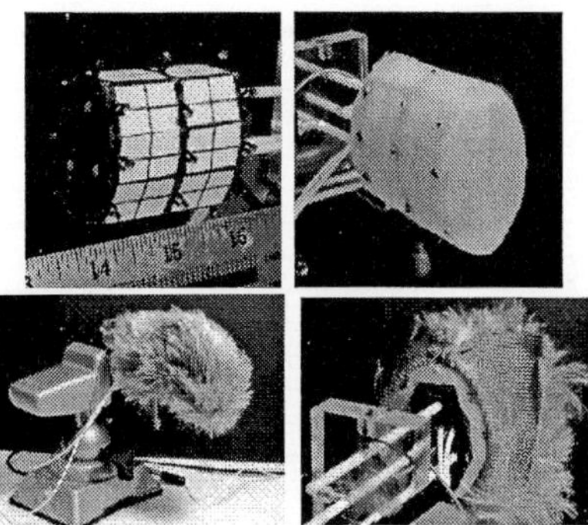

Fig. 2. The Finished Arm Test Section. The upper left shows the sensor layout. Each white rectangle is one QTC sensor. The silver sensors above the surface of the QTC sensors are the thermistors. The electric field sensing electrodes, not shown, are located on the bottom plane of each sensor circuit board. The upper right shows the synthetic silicone skin placed onto the assembly. The holes cut out in the skin allow for the thermistors to pass through the skin for better temperature sensing. The lower left is the finished assembly with the fur arm sleeve attached. The lower right shows the layered structure. All dimensions shown are in inches.

Currently, a single arm section, shown in Fig. 2, has been created. It features a total of 64 QTC sensors, 24 temperature sensors, and 2 electric field sensing electrodes. The finished Huggable will have over 1000 QTC sensors, 400 temperature sensors, and 45 electric field sensing electrodes. This high spatial resolution is necessary to detect the social and affective content of touch.

3 Classifying the Affective Content of Touch

There are many types of touch interactions that convey affective or social content. Handshakes are a form of greeting. Poking is used to get someone's attention. Petting is a calming gesture for both the animal and the person doing the petting. Slaps are a form of punishment. Many more examples exist. The Huggable is designed for therapy applications for people who have limited or no access to companion animals. Thus, the Huggable should be able to classify the numerous types of tactile interactions that people have with companion animals, so as to respond appropriately. This section describes an early experiment conducted with the arm section of Fig. 2 to classify the affective content of touch.

3.1 Experimental Design

The arm section of Fig. 2 was clamped to the top surface of a lab bench. Data from the top and left region of the arm section (half of the arm) was recorded as a baud rate of 57600. This arm section was selected as it corresponded to one electric field electrode. A total of 200 data sets were created from 16 different affective touch interaction types. These interactions were organized into 9 classes and 6 response types as

Table 1. The Data Sets Used for the Classification of Affective Touch

Type	# of Data Sets	Class	Response
Tickle: Softly, Fingers Only	10	Tickle	Tease Pleasant
Tickle: Hard, Fingers Only	10	Tickle	Tease Painful
Poking: Softly	20	Poking	Tease Pleasant
Poking: Hard	20	Poking	Tease Painful
Scratching: One Finger Softly	20	Scratching	Touch Pleasant
Scratching: One Finger Hard	20	Scratching	Touch Painful
Slapping: Fingers Only Softly	10	Slapping	Punishment Light
Slapping: Fingers and Palm Softly	10	Slapping	Punishment Light
Slapping: Fingers Only Hard	10	Slapping	Punishment Painful
Petting: Softly	10	Petting	Touch Pleasant
Petting: Hard	10	Petting	Touch Painful
Patting: Softly	10	Patting	Touch Pleasant
Patting: Hard	10	Patting	Touch Painful
Rubbing	10	Rubbing	Touch Pleasant
Squeezing	10	Squeeze	Touch Painful
Contact	10	Contact	Touch Pleasant

shown in Table 1. The response type is how the Huggable interprets what behavior to perform. For example, a pleasant touch should signify a happy reaction while strong punishment should result in a pain response. In this preliminary study all data sets were created through interaction with the arm section by a single person. Future work will expand upon this with multiple users.

Due to time constraints, the sensor values were not calibrated. Equation 1 was used to normalize each sensor reading to a baseline for each data set of Table 1:

$$NormalizedSensorValue = \frac{SensorValue - baseline}{SensorMaxValue - baseline} \tag{1}$$

The reading of sensor values was not optimized in time. The electric field sensors required a much longer time period to read a single value, 4 ms, compared to the temperature and force sensors, 50 μs. Thus in the current implementation the electric field sensors created a bottleneck as each sensor was read one after another. In future, it will be possible to read from all the temperature and force sensors in a body region while the electric field sensor is being read, thus eliminating this problem.

3.2 Feature Extraction

A set of features are calculated from each data set at each time step. The normalized sensor value of Equation 1 is filtered and negative values are set to zero. The number of active sensor values within a receptive field is calculated and normalized by the number of sensors within that receptive field. For example, if the receptive field consists of the 8 QTC sensors on a single sensor circuit board and all sensors are active then the value of the active sensor count is 1.0. If only 4 of the 8 sensors are active in one receptive field, this value would be 0.5.

The normalized sensor value sum is calculated by dividing the sum of the sensor values in each receptive field by the number of sensors in that field. The normalized sensor value sum is 1.0 if all the sensors in a receptive field are at their maximum value. Thus, this feature calculates the average sensor value for a single receptive field. In contrast, the normalized average sensor value sum is calculated by dividing the sum of the sensor values in each receptive field by the number of active sensors in that field. This feature calculates the average across all active sensors in a field, not the total number. The normalized average sensor value sum is 1.0 if all the active sensors in a receptive field are at their maximum value and the inactive sensors were 0.

The change in sensor value sum between each time step is calculated by subtracting the previous normalized sensor value sum from the current normalized sensor value sum. Two additional binary features are used to indicate the direction of the change. The sensor value increasing feature is true (1) if the sign of the change in normalized sensor value sum is positive. The sensor value decreasing feature is true (1) if the sign is negative.

A set of binary features is calculated to determine the degree of activity within a receptive field. One feature is a 1 if the current sensor was active at the last time step and still is. Another feature is 1 if the sensor was not active at the last time step and still is inactive. Finally, one other feature is 1 only if there was no change in sensor value, i.e., the sensor was inactive and still is, or was active and still is. The number of time steps since there was a change in activity for a sensor is calculated. This value is normalized at 1 if it has been 100 samples or more since there was a change in activity (i.e., changing from active to inactive or vice versa). This feature can encode the periodicity of a signal.

The centroid location and direction of motion within a receptive field are calculated as described in [10]. The direction of motion is then divided into eight 45-degree regions – up, upper left, left, lower left, down, lower right, right, and upper right. A corresponding binary feature for each of the eight directions is 1 if the direction of motion falls within that range and 0 otherwise. Changes in the direction of motion are indicated by another binary feature. Finally, the number of time steps since the last direction change is calculated.

The features described in the section can be calculated for any receptive field. A receptive field could be the entire arm, or simple one sensor processing board within the arm. The receptive field could also consist of all the types of sensors – QTC, temperature, and electric field; or could be one specific sensor type. In this paper features were calculated for each sensor type, with the receptive field being a single sensor circuit board consisting of 8 QTC sensors, 3 temperature, and a shared electric field sensor.

3.3 Neural Network Classification

The 200 trials of Table 1 were randomly assigned into a training and validation data set of approximately equal size. One of the data sets of Table 1 was corrupt, thus there were only 199 data sets used. MATLAB was used for feature extraction as well as training and testing of the neural network offline. A neural network approach was chosen for classification in this preliminary study.

A three layer neural network was trained with 100 inner layer nodes. The number of output nodes was 16 for the type neural network classifier, 9 for the class neural network classifier, and 6 for the response neural network classifier. The "logsig" transfer function was used with the "trainrp" transfer function for all three neural networks. The learning rate was 0.001. The maximum number of epochs was 1000. The error tolerance was 1e-3. The output of each neural network was rounded, so that all probabilities greater than 0.5 were recorded as being classified and those less than

0.5 were not classified. Due to time constraints, only one neural network was trained for each of the type, class, and response classifiers. Table 2 and 3 show the results of the neural network classification for class and response classification. The classification by type is not shown due to space constraints.

There were a large number of "no contact" situations within the data sets. Thus, the usual measurement of accuracy does not reveal much information as the number of true negatives, due to "no contact" or other affective touch situations, dominate the number of true positives in the data set, yielding very high accuracies. Specificity, sensitivity, positive predictive value (ppv), and negative predictive value (npv) are used instead [11]. Specificity, the probability that an interaction will be classified as not occurring when that interaction did occur, is given by Equation 2. Sensitivity, the probability that an interaction will be classified as having occurred when it did occur, is shown in Equation 3. The positive predictive value, Equation 4, and negative predictive value, Equation 5, is the probability that the interaction did or did not occur.

$$Specificity = \frac{TrueNegative}{TrueNegative + FalsePositive} \tag{2}$$

$$Sensitivity = \frac{TruePositive}{TruePositive + FalseNegative} \tag{3}$$

$$ppv = \frac{TruePositive}{TruePositive + FalsePositive} \tag{4}$$

$$npv = \frac{TrueNegative}{TrueNegative + FalseNegative} \tag{5}$$

The classification by class yielded much better results than the classification by type. This was expected due to the fact that the distinction between "soft" and "hard" versions of the same stimuli may not have differed sharply as force was not controlled during data collection. Thus it may have been that the same stimuli could have been labeled as "soft" and "hard." As shown in Table 2, for all cases, except for slap (not shown), the positive predictive value and sensitivity are greater than chance. Slap was not classified well by the neural network indicating an error in the design of the feature detector, or there may have been very few occurrences of labeled slaps in the training set. A slap happens very quickly and only a single time, compared to the other interactions such as scratching or rubbing. In the current implementation, there is a 4 ms delay per cycle as the electric field sensor is read. As such, the amount of slap data on which the neural network could be trained is much less than the other types of interactions.

As shown in Table 3, the performance of touch classification showed the best results. The classification of punishment, light or strong, is not shown in the table due to its very poor classification. As discussed previously, the classification of the slap class yielded very poor results. The punishment response type consists primarily of slaps as shown in Table 1. Thus, it makes sense that the punishment response would be classified very poorly as well. An improvement in the classification of slaps should yield a better classification of the punishment response.

The grouping of classes into response types is done subjectively. Thus there may be a better grouping which yields better results. Another interesting pattern emerges from looking at the grouping of the types into responses shown in Table 14-1. The touch pleasant has five types. The touch painful has four types. The tease pleasant, tease painful, and punishment light each have two types. The punishment strong only has one type. There is a strong relationship between the order of positive predictive value and sensitivity to the number of types within one response. Thus it appears that the amount of data within the training set is having an effect on the classification result. In the future the responses should be better balanced in terms of quantity of data for each response in the training set.

Table 2. The Results of the Neural Network Classification for Class. PPV = positive predictive value, NPV = negative predictive value.

Class	PPV	NPV	Sensitivity	Specificity	Chance
Tickle	0.67	0.94	0.57	0.96	0.11
Poke	0.41	0.95	0.29	0.97	0.11
Scratch	0.67	0.94	0.65	0.94	0.11
Pet	0.58	0.97	0.26	0.99	0.11
Pat	0.23	0.99	0.20	0.99	0.11
Rub	0.72	0.98	0.73	0.98	0.11
Squeeze	0.84	0.97	0.73	0.98	0.11
Contact	0.81	0.98	0.84	0.97	0.11

Table 3. The Results of the Neural Network Classification for Response Type. PPV = positive predictive value, NPV = negative predictive value.

Response	PPV	NPV	Sensitivity	Specificity	Chance
Tease Pleasant	0.40	0.93	0.25	0.97	0.17
Tease Painful	0.66	0.94	0.53	0.96	0.17
Touch Pleasant	0.77	0.90	0.74	0.90	0.17
Touch Painful	0.70	0.91	0.70	0.91	0.17

4 Conclusions and Future Work

The results shown for the classification of affective touch show promise for the creation of such systems for a wide variety of robotic platforms. The initial use of a neural network approach shows that such social affective classes of touch can be separated from one another. The next steps will be to continue to develop the Huggable with the goal of the full body implementation of the "sensitive skin" and to develop other real-time classification methods for the affective content of touch. As the robot is able to process how it is being held and interacted with, it can select the appropriate behaviors and motion to provide a very enriching experience for those who do not have the access to companion animal therapy.

Acknowledgments

The authors wish to thank Professor Chris Moore of MIT Brain and Cognitive Sciences for his help in the understanding of the somatosensory system. Professor Joe

Paradiso of the MIT Media Lab provided help with the implementation of the electric field sensor. Professor Rosalind Picard of the MIT Media Lab provided an introduction to pattern classification techniques through her class. The authors also thank the other members of the Robotic Life Group, specifically Jeff Lieberman, Louis Basel, Levi Lalla, and Mike Wolf who also have contributed to the design and construction of the Huggable. This work is partially supported by a Microsoft iCampus grant, the MIT Media Lab Things that Think and Digital Life Consortia, and the NSF Center for Bits and Atoms Contract No.CCR-0122419.

References

1. Martin, T.B., et al. Tactile Gloves for Autonomous Grasping with the NASA/DARPA Robonaut. in International Conference on Robotics and Automation (ICRA'04). 2004. New Orleans, LA.
2. Lumelsky, V.J., M.S. Shur, and S. Wagner, Sensitive Skin. IEEE Sensors Journal, 2001. 1(1): p. 41-51.
3. Kandel, E.R., J.H. Schwartz, and T.M. Jessell, Principles of Neuroscience, 4th Edition. 4th ed. 2000, New York: McGraw-Hill Health Professions Division. 1414.
4. Iwata, H. and S. Sugano. Whole-body Covering Tactile Interface for Human Robot Coordination. in International Conference on Robotics and Automation. 2002. Washington, DC: IEEE.
5. Sony Product Literature, AIBO ERS-7M2 website: http://www.sonystyle.com/is-bin/INTERSHOP.enfinity/eCS/Store/en/-/USD/LC_BrowseCatalog-Start;sid=5PwkGv1dhiQkIb8nCd8uEbJRgVs-2uQV4R0=?CategoryName=lc_AIBO.
6. Heidemann, G. and M. Schopfer. Dynamic Tactile Sensing for Object Identification. in International Conference on Robotics and Automation (ICRA'04). 2004. New Orleans, LA: IEEE.
7. Stiehl, W.D., et al. Design of a Therapeutic Robotic Companion for Relational, Affective Touch. in IEEE International Workshop on Robot and Human Interactive Communication (RO-MAN 2005) (Currently Under Review). 2005. Nashville, TN.
8. McBean, J. and C. Breazeal. Voice Coil Actuators for Human-Robot Interaction. in IEEE/RSJ International Conference on Intelligent Robots and Systems (IROS04). 2004. Sendai, Japan.
9. Morris, S.J., A Shoe-Integrated Sensor System for Wireless Gait Analysis and Real-Time Therapeutic Feedback, in Health Sciences and Technology Sc.D. Thesis. 2004, MIT: Cambridge.
10. Stiehl, W.D. and C. Breazeal. Applying a "Somatic Alphabet" Approach to Inferring Orientation, Motion, and Direction in Clusters of Force Sensing Resistors. in IEEE/RSJ International Conference on Intelligent Robots and Systems (IROS04). 2004.
11. rapid-diagnostics.org, Accuracy of Diagnostics Tests: http://www.rapid-diagnostics.org/accuracy.htm.

Dynamic Mapping Method Based Speech Driven Face Animation System

Panrong Yin and Jianhua Tao

National Laboratory of Pattern Recognition (NLPR),
Institute of Automation, Chinese Academy of Sciences, Beijing
{pryin, jhtao}@nlpr.ia.ac.cn

Abstract. In the paper, we design and develop a speech driven face animation system based on the dynamic mapping method. The face animation is synthesized by the unit concatenating, and synchronous with the real speech. The units are selected according to the cost functions which correspond to voice spectrum distance between training and target units. Visual distance between two adjacent training units is also used to get better mapping results. Finally, the Viterbi method is used to find out the best face animation sequence. The experimental results show that synthesized lip movement has a good and natural quality.

1 Introduction

Visual speech synthesis has been developed for improving human-machine interface such as virtual announcer, email reader, mobile messenger reader and so on. It also helps hearing-impaired people to communicate with others or those in noisy environment.

According to driven sources, visual speech synthesis can be categorized into text driven face animation and speech driven face animation. Since TTVS [8],[9] depends too much on languages content analysis and can not offer co-articulation information, more and more researchers pay attention to synthesis from real speech [1],[2],[3],[4].

A speech driven face animation system is usually established in four steps as defined in "picture my voice"[1]: label a audio-visual database; give representation of both the auditory and visual speech; find a method to describe the relationship between two representations; synthesize the visible speech given the auditory speech.

A labeled audio-visual database is the base of the whole system. But there are little labeled databases of visual speech and none universal one, so many researchers have to record their own database for training visual speech. Some recorded a stream of dynamic images of interested regions in videos [6],[8],[9],[13], another recorded static facial visemes by 3D laser scans, the other obtained dynamic 3D coordinates of marked-up face through motion capture system [2],[14] or 2D to 3D image reconstruction method [3],[4].

Good feature representations have an important impact on the system performance. For audio features, some researchers used text-dependant language

J. Tao, T. Tan, and R.W. Picard (Eds.): ACII 2005, LNCS 3784, pp. 755–763, 2005.

units to analyze their corresponding static visemes; but in order to reduce manual intervention, many researchers turned to extract acoustic features of speech as audio features. For visual features, many researchers used images [6],[8],[13], visemes[9], FAPs[14], PCs[3],[4], 3D coordinates[14], 3D distance measurements [2],[3], optical flows[13].

The key component of visual speech synthesis is audio-visual mapping. Many methods have been applied in this area: TDNN[1], MLPs[4], KNN[3], HMM[2], GMM, VQ[2], Rule-based[9],[13],[14]. At present, there are mainly two approaches for synthesis: through speech recognition and not through speech recognition. The first approach divides speech signal into language units such as phonemes, syllables, words, then maps the units directly to the lip shapes and concatenates them. Yamamoto E.[2] recognized phonemes through training HMM, and mapped them directly to corresponding lip shapes, through smoothing algorithm, the lip movement sequence is obtained. The second approach analyzes the bimodal data through statistical learning model, and finds out the mapping between the continuous acoustic features and facial control parameters, so as to drive the face animation directly by a novel speech. "Picture my voice"[1] trained an ANN to learn the mapping from LPCs to face animation parameters, they used current frame, 5 backward and 5 forward time steps as the input to model the context.

After getting the FAP streams from audio-visual mapping method, there are two ways to synthesize talking head: model-based animation [3],[4],[11],[14] and image-based animation[6],[8],[9],[13].

Recently, a new approach for audio-visual mapping has arisen [8],[10], which is inspired from speech synthesis [7]. This method means to construct new data stream by concatenating stored data units in training database. It has advantage of that the synthesis result appears very natural and realistic. Our approach considers phonemes as units instead of frames, because frame-by-frame mapping is difficult to take account for phoneme context and may lose some co-articulation information. In our system, model-based animation model is chosen as talking head model, though it appears less reality than image-based model, it requires

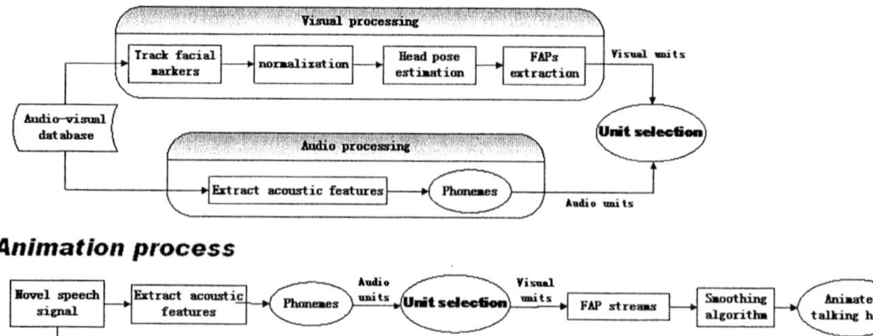

Fig. 1. Speech driven face animation system framework

less computation cost, less training database and can be easily replanted to embedded system such as PDA, mobile phone. In this paper, 3D coordinates of FDPs which are compatible with MPEG-4 standard [5] can be recorded by Motion Capture System, they reflect real facial movements. Since animated talking head is required to be more lifelike and individual, FAPs are extracted as visual features so as to apply our synthesized animation control parameters to different 3D mesh models.

Our talking head system is composed of two processes: training process and animation process (Fig. 1). In the rest of the paper, section 2 introduces the database setup and audio-visual feature extraction, section 3 focuses on the unit selection realization, section 4 gives the experimental result of synthesized talking face, section 5 is the conclusion and future work description.

2 Data Acquisition and Analysis

2.1 Data Acquisition

Since FAPs in MPEG-4 facial animation standard can denote face movement which is speaker independent, a commercially available motion capture system (Motion Analysis) is used to track the FDPs on speaker's face as shown in Fig. 2 and 8 cameras with 75 Hz sampling frequency are employed. According to FDPs defined in MPEG-4, 50 points are selected to encode the face shape. The output of the motion capture system are 3D trajectories of all the 50 markers. During experiment, the rigid head movement is not avoided, so 5 markers on the head are used to compensate the global head movement to get the non-rigid facial deformations.

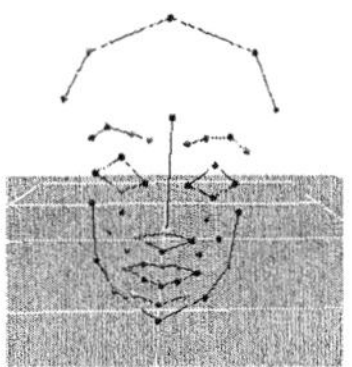

Fig. 2. Placement of markers on neutral face and capture data sample

2.2 FAPs Extraction

In order to extract FAPs correctly, the 3D trajectories of face markers have to be normalized into an upright position in positive XYZ space firstly. And then the least-square based fitting method of two 3D point sets is used to extract the rigid head movements[12], in our case, the two point sets correspond to the 5 points on the head before and after head movement. Their relationship can be described by:

$$q_i = Rp_i + t, \quad i = 1, \ldots, 5. \tag{1}$$

Once rotation R and translation t matrixes are estimated, the global head movements can be eliminated by back projecting Equation.1 to 3D trajectories of rest points.

There are two most popular visual representation standard, one is the Facial Action Coding System[15] developed by Ekman and Friesen, the other is MPEG-4 SNHC [5]. FACS defined 44 AUs to denote the independent facial muscles' action, more than 7000 AU combinations have been observed. 68 FAPs which are defined in MPEG-4 SNHC also can represent the basic facial actions, including two high-level parameters, viseme and expression, and 66 low-level parameters. They are divided into 10 groups according to effect regions. Since AUs can not offer quantitative description for face animation, our approach is to convert 3D FDPs movements into low-level FAPs. FAPs are computed and normalized in terms of FAPUs which are the distances between the main facial feature points. So they can be applied to different face models in a consistent way. In the paper, 15 FAPs (Table. 1) involved in group 2 and group 8 are extracted to represent the lip movement.

Table 1. FAPs for visual representation in our system

Group	FAP name	Group	FAP name
2	Open_jaw	8	Stretch_l_cornerlip_o
2	Trust_jaw	8	Lower_t_lip_lm_o
2	Shift_jaw	8	Lower_t_lip_rm_o
2	Push_b_lip	8	Raise_b_lip_lm_o
2	Push_t_lip	8	Raise_b_lip_rm_o
8	Lower_t_midlip_o	8	Raise_l_cornerlip_o
8	Raise_b_midlip_o	8	Raise_r_cornerlip_o
8	Stretch_r_cornerlip_o		

So the output of motion capture system at t step:

$$d = \{x_1, y_1, z_1, \ldots, x_n, y_n, z_n\}^T \in R^{3n}, \quad n = 45.$$

can be converted into:

$$\bar{v}^t = \{FAP_1^t, FAP_2^t, \ldots, FAP_{15}^t\}^T.$$

So the visual representation for a data sample which contains m frames is:

$$V = \{\bar{v}^1, \bar{v}^2, \ldots, \bar{v}^m\}^T.$$

2.3 Acoustic Feature Vectorization

There are different parameters for representation of acoustic speech, such as LPC, LSF, MFCC, formant and so on. MFCC gives an alternative representation to speech spectra, which contains some audition information. So in our approach, MFCCs in each audio frame are chosen as the audio feature. The speech signal, sampled at 16 kHz, is blocked into frames of 27 ms. In each frame, we computed 16 coefficients. So each t frame of speech can be represented as:

$$\bar{a}^t = \{c_1^t, c_2^t, \ldots, c_{16}^t\}^T.$$

These vectors are then grouped into a matrix in a data sample with m frames:

$$A = \{\bar{a}^1, \bar{a}^2, \ldots, \bar{a}^m\}^T.$$

3 Audio-Visual Dynamic Mapping

In order to synthesize a vivid and realistic talking head, an audio-visual dynamic mapping method which is inspired from the concatenative speech synthesis[7] is employed in our system. The difference is that they select speech units to synthesize a novel concatenative speech, but we select audio-visual units according to a novel speech input to synthesize continuous FAP streams to drive a talking head.

This method is based on two cost functions (Equation. 2):

$$COST = \alpha C^a + (1-\alpha)C^v. \tag{2}$$

where C^a is the voice spectrum distance, C^v is the visual distance between two adjacent units, and the weight α balances the effect of the two cost functions.

It is also much like HMM, the synthesized unit flows are the hidden states, phoneme pieces of speech input are the observable states. Difference stays at the cost functions instead of probabilities[7].

In the unit selection procedures, according to the target phoneme unit of novel speech, we list the candidates which have smaller acoustic distances with them. Because the acoustic parameters MFCCs are related to people's vocal tract, so smaller acoustic spectrum distance reflects smaller visual difference.

The audio content distance measures how close the candidate unit compared with the target unit, it determines whether the most appropriate audio-visual unit have been selected. The voice spectrum distance also accounts for the context of target unit. The context covers the former and latter two phonemes for vowels and the former and latter phoneme for consonants. So the voice spectrum distance is defined by Equation. 3:

$$C_j^a = \sum_{t=1}^{n}\sum^{m} w_m a(t_{t+m}, u_{t+m}), \quad m = [-1, 0, +1] or [-2, -1, 0, +1, +2]. \tag{3}$$

The weights w_m are determined by the method used in[11], the difference is that they computed the linear blending weights in terms of a phoneme's time duration, but we take three or five adjacent phonemes into account. $a(t_{t+m}, u_{t+m})$ is the Eucilidian distance of the acoustic feature of two phonemes. For the sake of reducing the complexity of Viterbi search, we set a limit of candidate number for selection.

Not only we should found out the correct speech signal unit, but also the smooth synthesized face animation should be considered. In training process, we just label the phoneme positions in each sentence without segmenting them, so it will enable the unit selection to find out the smoothest unit following the previous one. The concatenation cost measures how closely the mouth shapes of the adjacent units match. So the FAPs of the last frame of former phoneme unit are compared with that of the first frame of current phoneme unit (Equation. 4).

$$C^v = \sum_{t=2}^{n} v(u_{t-1}, u_t). \tag{4}$$

where $v(u_{t-1}, u_t)$ is the Eucilidian distance of the adjacent visual features of two phonemes.

Once the two cost functions (audio content distance and visual distance) are computed, the graph for unit selection is constructed. Our approach finally aims to find the best path in this graph which generates minimum COST. Just like HMM, Viterbi is a valid search method for this application.

4 Experimental Results

In the paper, a collection of 286 sentences are recorded. For each, four times are used as training data, one time as validation data and another 9 sentences as test data. Fig. 3 indicates the selected synthesized FAP stream results. In order to evaluate the synthesized result, both quantitative evaluation and qualitative observation results are shown. Since the synthesized FAP streams are concatenated by units in training database, so it is impossible to be absolutely same with the recorded FAP stream. Correlation coefficients (Equation. 5) are used to represent the deviation similarity between them, because it is a measure of how well trends in the predicted values follow trends in past actual values. Table. 2 shows the average correlation coefficients for each FAPs on the whole database.

$$CC = \frac{1}{T} \sum_{t=1}^{T} \frac{(\hat{f}(t) - \hat{\mu})(f(t) - \mu)}{\hat{\sigma}\sigma}. \tag{5}$$

where $f(t)$ is the recorded FAP stream, $\hat{f}(t)$ is the synthesis, T is the total number of frames in the database, and μ and σ are corresponding mean and standard deviation.

From Table 2, the synthesized results show a good performance of our method. Although the test sentences show smaller correlation coefficients, they still can synthesize most of FAPs. It is also noticed that the CC of FAP #15 and #60 of validation data are even smaller than those of test data, it may be mainly because of the speaker's habit of that she speaks sentences with randomly shifting mouth corner.

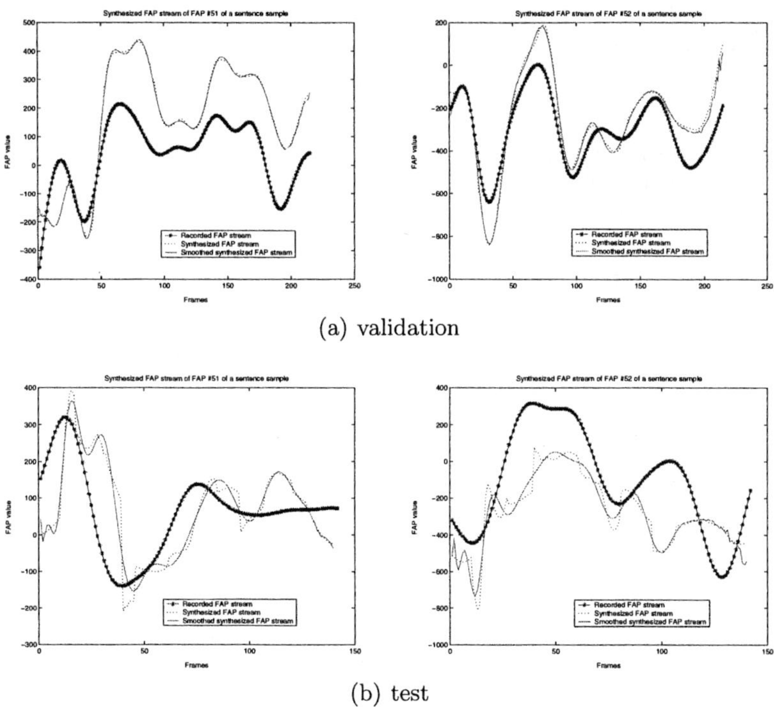

(a) validation

(b) test

Fig. 3. Selected synthesized FAP streams from (a) validation and (b) test sentence

Table 2. The average correlation coefficient for each FAPs on the whole database

Correlation Coefficients		Validation	Test
	#3	0.855	0.622
	#14	0.674	0.656
	#15	0.553	0.761
	#16	0.767	0.677
	#17	0.716	0.788
	#51	0.820	0.732
	#52	0.812	0.741
FAP No.	#53	0.817	0.722
	#54	0.832	0.636
	#55	0.709	0.684
	#56	0.768	0.736
	#57	0.749	0.714
	#58	0.787	0.720
	#59	0.661	0.640
	#60	0.569	0.730

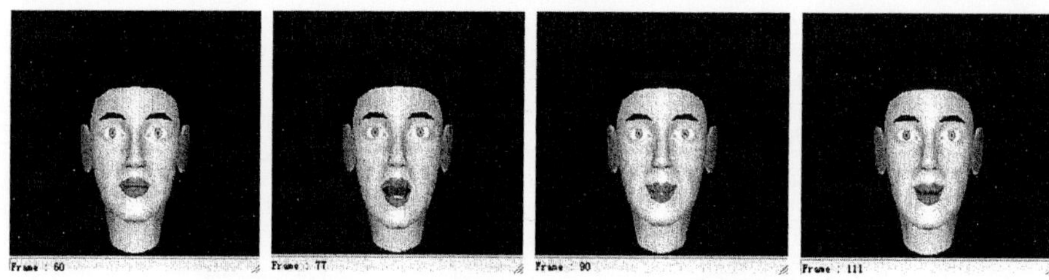

Fig. 4. Some frames of synthesized talking head

At last, a MPEG-4 facial animation engine is used to access our synthesized FAP streams qualitatively. The animation model displays at a frame rate of 75 fps. Fig. 4 shows some frames of synthesized talking head.

While many other researchers used images, optical flows, principal components. etc as stored units, in this paper, FAPs are extracted. It has advantage of small storage, being able to be applied to non-specific model, and also to drive both 3D mesh model and 2D images. The unit selection dynamic mapping method we used is a simplification of HMM, but it appears very good and natural, because the real talker's face movements are treated as the candidate units. Without parameter adjust, under-fitting, over-fitting problems which are involved in learning method like ANN, it is a simple, direct and effective way to synthesize the talking head.

5 Conclusion and Future Work

In the present work, we have presented a speech driven face animation system which is based on the MPEG-4 animation model. The system employs FAPs which are extracted from 3D coordinates of FDPs to represent the visual feature. The acoustic features of real speaker's speech are used to directly drive animation model. It makes the driven source independent from text content and languages. The unit selection method is applied for audio-visual dynamic mapping. Both audio content distance and the visual distance between the adjacent units are taken into account. Finally, we give the quantitative and qualitative evaluation for the synthesized concatenative FAP streams.

For a big training database, our method appears lower speed to find out the corresponding audio-visual units, so we now investigate some statistic methods to cluster the phonemes in training database. As one speaker's speech is tested for the present work, different person' novel speech will be inputs in real application, so in the future work, we can apply some methods of voice conversion to extend our system to different voices.

References

1. Dominic W. Massaro, Jonas Beskow, Michael M. Cohen, Christopher L. Fry, Tony Rodriguez: Picture My Voice: Audio to Visual Speech. Synthesis using Artificial Neural Networks. Proceedings of AVSP'99, pp.133-138. Santa Cruz, CA.(1999).

2. Yamamoto E., Nakamura, S., Shikano, K: Lip movement synthesis from speech based on Hidden Markov Models. Speech Communication, Vol. 26,(1998)105-115.
3. R. Gutierrez-Osuna, P. K. Kakumanu, A. Esposito, O. N. Garcia, A. Bojorquez, J. L. Castillo, I. Rudomin: Speech-Driven Facial Animation With Realistic Dynamics. IEEE Trans on Multimedia, Vol.7, No.1,(2005)
4. Pengyu Hong, Zhen Wen, Thomas S. Huang: Real-time speech-driven face animation with expressions using neural networks. IEEE Trans on Neural Networks, Vol.13, No.4,(2002)
5. A. Murat Tekalp, JoK rn Ostermann: Face and 2-D mesh animation in MPEG-4, Signal Processing: Image Communication Vol.15,(2000)387-421
6. Bregler C., Covell M., Slaney M.: Video Rewrite: Driving Visual Speech with Audio. ACM SIGGRAPH, (1997)
7. Hunt A., Black A.: Unit selection in a concatenative speech synthesis system using a large speech database. ICASSP, vol.1,(1996)373-376
8. Cosatto E, Potamianos G, Graf H P: Audio-visual unit selection for the synthesis of photo-realistic talking-heads. IEEE International Conference on Multimedia and Expo, ICME Vol.2,(2000)619-622
9. T. Ezzat, T. Poggio: MikeTalk: A Talking Facial Display Based on Morphing Visemes. Proc. Computer Animation Conference, Philadelphia, USA, (1998)
10. Ram R. Rao, Tsuhan Chen, Russell M. Mersereau: Audio-to-Visual Conversion for Multi-media Communication. IEEE Trans on Industrial Electronics, Vol.45, No.1,(1998)
11. Jian-Qing Wang, Ka-Ho Wong, Pheng-Ann Pheng, Meng H.M., Tien-Tsin Wong: A real-time Cantonese text-to-audiovisual speech synthesizer. ICASSP '04, Vol.1,(2004)
12. K.S. Arun, T.S. Huang, S.D.Blostein: Least-square fitting of two 3-D point sets. IEEE Trans on Pattern Analysis and Machine Intelligence, vol.9, no.5,(1987)698-700
13. Ashish Verma, L. Venkata Subramaniam, Nitendra Rajput, Chalapathy Neti, Tanveer A. Faruquie: Animating Expressive Faces Across Languages. IEEE Trans on Multimedia, Vol.6, No.6,(2004)
14. S. Kshirsagar, T. Molet, and N.M. Thalmann: Principal Components of expressive speech animation. Proc. Of Computer Graphics International,(2001)
15. P. Ekman and W. V. Friesen: Facial Action Coding System. Palo Alto, Calif: Consulting Psychologists Press,(1978)

Affective Intelligence: A Novel User Interface Paradigm

Barnabas Takacs

Digital Elite Inc., Los Angeles, USA
BTakacs@digitalElite.net
www.digitalElite.net

Abstract. This paper describes an advanced human-computer interface that combines real-time, reactive and high fidelity virtual humans with artificial vision and communicative intelligence to create a closed-loop interaction model and achieve an affective interface. The system, called the Virtual Human Interface (VHI), utilizes a photo-real facial and body model as a virtual agent to convey information beyond speech and actions. Specifically, the VHI uses a dictionary of nonverbal signals including body language, hand gestures and subtle emotional display to support verbal content in a reactive manner. Furthermore, its built in facial tracking and artificial vision system allows the virtual human to maintain eye contact, follow the motion of the user and even recognizing when somebody joins him or her in front of the terminal and act accordingly. Additional sensors allow the virtual agent to react to touch, voice and other modalities of interaction. The system has been tested in a real-world scenario whereas a virtual child reacted to visitors in an exhibition space.

1 Introduction

To mimic the quality of everyday human communication, future computer interfaces must combine the benefits of high visual fidelity with conversational intelligence and — above all— the ability to modulate the emotions of their users. During the past several decades, researchers have conducted countless studies on agents and human animation in order to create a HCI that works by utilizing the natural means of interaction, such as words, gestures, glances and body language instead of traditional computer devices, such as the keyboard and mouse.

To address this problem we have been developing a novel system that uses photo-realistic, high fidelity human representations and a natural model human dialog. Photo-realistic virtual humans due to their similarities to their real-life counterparts make a powerful affective interface and will likely be the primary means of communication between computers and humans in the future.

Our solution builds upon many years of interdisciplinary research to create a closed-loop model of interaction whereas the user's internal state (emotion, level of attention, etc.) is constantly monitored and driven directly by the animated character with the purpose of creating emotional bonding. This emotional bonding then acts as a catalyst to help turn information to knowledge. In other words, our advanced user interface draws on emotions to help its users (most frequently students) in the learning process by intelligently tailoring its workload and constantly adapting its presentation strategies. Hence the name *affective intelligence*.

J. Tao, T. Tan, and R.W. Picard (Eds.): ACII 2005, LNCS 3784, pp. 764–771, 2005.

2 State-of-the-Art

Most research in the field of conversational agents and animated humans thus far employed low resolution (i.e. small polygon count) virtual characters that was rather simple to animate in real time [1]. Many of these animation systems initially addressed purposes other than the needs of human–computer interaction. However, the requirements of facial animation—and especially speech synthesis—demand a different underlying architecture that can effectively model how real faces move and change [2-4]. As a result, research began to focus on creating autonomous agents that could exhibit rich personalities and interact in virtual worlds inhabited by other characters [5,6]. To provide the illusion of a life-like character, researchers have developed detailed emotional and personality models that can control the animation channels as a function of the virtual human's personality, mood, and emotions [7,8]. However, the real-time interaction with these virtual characters posed an extra set of technical challenges in terms of the speed, computational power, and visual quality required to make the user believe that he or she is interacting with a living creature. To achieve this goal, researchers eventually replaced pre-crafted animated actions with intelligent behavior modules that could control speech, locomotion, gaze, blinks, gestures (including various postures), and interaction with the environment. Our VHI system builds on this research by employing photo-realistic virtual humans, providing users with information, learning services, and entertainment in a personalized and adaptive manner [9-11].

3 The Virtual Human Interface (VHI)

The Virtual Human Interface (*VHI*) system we have developed represents a shift in the traditional paradigm of HCI or conversational agents as it places the user in a closed-loop-dialogue situation where affect plays a key role during the interactive process. Specifically, while "traditional" HCI interfaces are designed to provide help on how to do things, the photo-real digital humans and synthetic 3D elements in the *VHI* system serve to engage the user in a process of emotional responses which in turn opens a channel to "engrave" knowledge and modify their behavior. From a practical point of view the *VHI* implements this functionality with the help of high fidelity virtual humans "who" can talk, act, emote and express a wide range of facial expressions as well as body gestures [11]. The underlying affective mechanisms of photo-real digital humans rely on the tremendous power facial information processing in the brain and therefore it works fundamentally differently from stylized humanoids or cartoon characters that base their mechanisms on self-projection. As such the *VHI* provides a novel means to unlock and further utilize the learning capability residing in each and every one of us. By conveying subtle facial signals, as demonstrated in Figure 1., positive reinforcement allows us to access and activate both our *declarative* (i.e. our memory of information and events) and *procedural memory.* (i.e. the knowledge how to ride a bike) while engaging in the process of emotional responses in an entertaining fashion.

Fig. 1. Subtle changes of emotional display of a photo-real virtual humans during interaction with the user

The implementation of the *VHI* system involved many different modules of animation, perception, compositing and creating synthetic environments to place our virtual characters in. Figure 2. Specifically, our intelligent digital human "lives" within the confides of a high-throughput interactive virtual world. To create such an environment one needs to go beyond the traditional methodology of real-time rendering and support a variety input and output devices that facilitate the interaction process and create a fully immersive experience. Examples include a head-mounted display system (HMD), multiple 3&6DOF trackers, a low-cost hand glove, a special purpose eye tracker and standard devices, such as a joystick. In addition to delivering high-end graphics cards to create the highest possible visual realism the *VHI* system also features live video input, real-time image processing, face- and object recognition with tracking capabilities, chroma-key filters, an augmented reality interface and even panoramic 360° backgrounds for full immersion. Finally, beyond the visual experience, the system also supports quadraphonic 3D sound sources with simulated effect of speed and motion as the user moves around in the virtual space. Further details on the architecture and its major elements can be found in [15].

4 Perception and Affective Intelligence

The ability to perceive its environment, both synthetic and the outside world of that of the user, is a key element when attempting to build a truly intelligent virtual agent. We define *VHI*'s input modalities corresponding to *vision*, *touch*, and *hearing* in the context of the communication process and the functionality of the animated character itself. In particular, the three implemented senses connect to information channels that have a direct affect on the animated character's *gaze*, *facial expressions*, *locomotion*, and *body gestures*. The foundation for implementing this functionality and executing these actions hinges partly on the processing of external visual, auditory, and touch-related signals. The *VHI* connects its users to the synthetic human's 3D world by means of *markers*. Markers are invisible dimensionless representations of 3D positions attached to any object in the scene. They carry unique hierarchical labels and we can refer to them by their names in describing a high-level task. We could attach multiple markers to a camera, a table, the floor, or the virtual monitor—a special-purpose object in the virtual environment that is analogous to the computer screen. We map the live video stream directly onto this monitor and assign and display results of the visual processing here —the locations and identities of the people in front of the terminal— using temporally changing markers. One of the major advantages of using the marker-based representation is that it defines and executes at a high level, symbolically, all tasks that the virtual human needs to carry out. This information can then be processed by our cognitive engine based on the *SOAR* [8] architecture or controlled locally. An example of the latter is to direct the gaze of the character by issuing a "look at me" command where "me" is the name of the marker attached to the currently active camera. To carry out these commands, the *VHI* includes advanced target animation and inverse kinematics functions that take into consideration the current constraints on the virtual human's body.

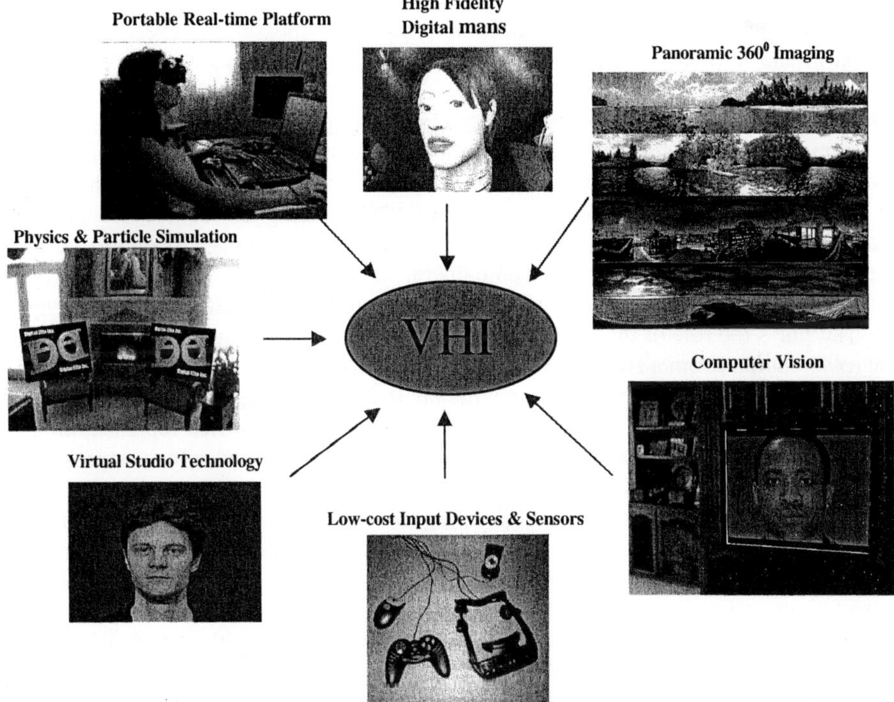

Fig. 2. Key elements of the Virtual Human Interface used to implement our model of Affective Intelligence

5 Closed Loop Model of Communication

The closed loop interaction model of human computer interaction, as implemented in the *VHI* affective intelligence system, combines the power of high fidelity facial animation with advanced computer vision and perception techniques, briefly described in the preceding section, to create a truly bi-directional user interface where the actions and reactions of the person in front of the computer monitor directly affect the behavior of the interactive content delivery system. In particular, we model the interaction process between the user and the system as part of a closed loop dialog taking place between the participants. This dialog, exploits the most important characteristics of a face-to-face communication, including the use of non-verbal gestures and meta-communication signals to control the flow of information. As such, the *Closed Loop Dialog* model draws on the characteristics of human face-to-face communication specifically the gaze behavior that follows well researched patterns and rules of interaction. As an example, this mechanism — known as turn-taking — may appear during the course of a computerized lecture where the role of the listener and the speaker shift periodically [12,14]. The principle idea behind this closed loop system is to treat the problem of recognizing a user's internal state as an *active optimization* problem in contrast to a passive observer method. In this context the goal of the interface is to maximize the user's ability to absorb the information being presented. This goal is achieved by constantly measuring levels of interest, attention and perhaps fatigue. In such a way the interface framework is enabled to consider how the user's most important resource, namely his or her attention is allocated over time. To maximize the gain in knowledge we must minimize the cost of interaction by reducing the overall demand on attention. In other words, the system must be able to "read" the many telltale signs the user is projecting during the course of interaction. These signs — all of us read them during the coarse of our daily interactions with others — can be readily derived from visual cues made available to the training system using a simple web-camera.

The dialog model presented here assumes that while being instructed or informed, the user plays the role of the listener and when active input is required, he or she plays the role a talker. From a HCI point of view we are interested in gathering input to feed symbolic data to the main cognitive engine i.e. the Artificial Intelligence (AI) module that drives the application. With the help of this symbolic, quantified representation of the outside world we a machine understandable layer is created which appropriates actions and strategies suitable for action planning. As an example, paying attention means that the guiding gestures (e.g. pointing to an object) presented by the animated digital human are followed by an appropriate shift of gaze and attention to that region of the screen. Thus, the user's performance can be gauged by forming and creating expectations and comparing the measured reactions with the anticipated responses.

To measure the user's responses we enabled our virtual human with perception, most importantly the ability to *see*. As an example, specialized vision modules are responsible for detecting and recognizing one or multiple people in front of the display and analyzing their facial location, expressions, point of gaze and other telltale signs of their attentive and emotional states. Thus, the built in face recognition and facial information processing module plays a critical role in understanding and appropriately reacting to the user's needs. Maintaining eye contact and the ability to turn away from or look at the user during the course of interaction believably mimics the everyday communication process taking place between real people and thus subliminally signals the user his or her turn. As a result our virtual human's ability to deliver non-verbal communication signals to support information content by means of subtle facial gestures is of critical importance in implementing the closed-loop model.

Our goal was achieved by creating high fidelity digital copies of living people. These virtual face models can talk, act and deliver over 1000 different facial expressions seamlessly integrated into the communication process. Since people rarely express emotions in front of their computer screens — except when reading email — the virtual human interface system attempts to keep track of the user's internal state using psychological models of emotion and learning. We then internally model and adapt to these user states and create a mechanism for the virtual agent to express its own feelings with the purpose of modulating the user's own mood. Finally, body gestures add a further layer to this process. Specifically, the overall direction of the body, hand gestures and beats, transient motions and pointing gestures may be used to indicate action, requested input or direct the user's attention to a particularly important piece of information. As a result the virtual human interface solution is capable of "driving" the user's attention and expect certain reactions in response. When those expectations fail to be realized, it may well be an indication that the user has lost interest or could not follow the instructions the digital human was presenting. In such situations, the system is capable to backtrack and adjust its presentation strategy accordingly.

6 The Power of Face-to-Face Interaction for Affective Interfaces

Face-to-face communication with a digital interactive virtual human is one of the most powerful methods for providing personalized and highly efficient information exchange with a built-in emotional component. As introduced in the preceding section, this dialog very precisely governs the role of the "talker" and the "listener" while these roles — that may periodically shift from time to time as the interaction progresses — adhere to a set of rules that are well documented in the communication literature [12-14]. The rules of this on-going dialog can therefore be used very effectively to limit the possible interpretations of the user's behavior and categorize them as being appropriate or not in a given information exchange scenario. To explain this better let us briefly discuss the "rules" of participating in dialogs. A typical pattern when two people conversing with one another is asymmetrical. It consists of the listener maintaining fairly long gazes at the speaker with short interruptions to glance away, while the speaker looks ate the listener for frequent but much shorter looks. It was estimated that when two people are talking about 60% of the conversation involves gaze and 30% involves mutual gaze, i.e. eye contact [13,14]. People look nearly twice as much (75%) while listening as while speaking (41%), and they tend to look less when there are objects present, especially if they are related to the conversation. These results suggest that eye gaze is a powerful mechanism to help control the flow of turn taking in a human computer interface dialog. Measuring and interpreting gaze behavior of the user in the context of the face-to-face communication process (as opposed to treating it as a generic random variable) therefore has clear advantages. In particular, we can take advantage of the closed-loop nature of the dialog process in that the communication system no longer passively observes the user, but rather - based in its current assessment of his/her state - it subconsciously prompts them in order to gauge their response. These prompts may occur in the form of multi-modal output, including visual or auditory cues. In conclusion we believe that models of face-to-face communication is one of the most important cornerstones of affective computing.

7 Conclusion

In this paper we described a novel affective Human Computer Interface that presents the process of interaction as a continuous and bi-direction dialog taking place between two parties in a closed-loop virtual environment. This two-way communication was implemented by combining interactive photo-real virtual human models made possible by state-of-the art animation, and real-time rendering techniques and advanced computer vision algorithms to process information obtained from the user. This combined solution successfully created a platform that utilizes the advanced capabilities of virtual humans to express subtle and non-verbal facial signals and subsequently modulate verbal content as a function of the user's actions and reactions. We argue, that such a closed loop interface, termed here as *Affective Intelligence*, may serve as the foundation for the next generation of human-centered intelligent devices, interface and agents. These systems will understand what we want from them and act accordingly to provide a wide range of future services.

References

1. Badler, N., M.S. Palmer, and R. Bindiganavale, Animation Control for Real-Time Virtual Humans, *Comm. ACM*, vol. 42, no. 8, 1999.
2. Terzopoulos, D. and K. Waters, Techniques for Realistic Facial Modeling and Animation, *Computer Animation*, M. Thalmann and D. Thalmann, eds., Springer-Verlag, 1991.
3. Pasquariello, S. and C. Pelachaud, Greta: A Simple Facial Animation Engine, *Proc. 6th Online World Conf. Soft Computing in Industrial Applications*, Springer-Verlag, 2001.
4. Morishima, S., Face Analysis and Synthesis, *IEEE Signal Processing*, vol. 18, no. 3, 2001
5. Cassell, J., H. Vilhjlmsson, and T. Bickmore, BEAT: The Behavior Expression Animation Toolkit, *Proc. SIGGRAPH*, ACM Press, 2001.
6. Poggi, I., C. Pelachaud, and F. de Rosis, Eye Communication in a Conversational 3D Synthetic Agent, *J. Artificial Intelligence*, vol. 13, no. 3, 2000.
7. Rickel, J.S. et al., Toward a New Generation of Virtual Humans for Interactive Experiences, *IEEE Intelligent Systems*, vol. 17, no. 4, 2002.
8. Johnson, W.L. , W. Rickel, and J.C. Lester, Animated Pedagogical Agents: Face-to-Face Interaction in Interactive Learning Environments, *Int'l J. Artificial Intelligence in Education*, vol. 11, 2000.
9. Takács, B., B. Kiss, (2003), Virtual Human Interface: a Photo-realistic Real-Time Digital Human with Perceptive and Communicative Intelligence, *IEEE Computer Graphics and Applications, Special Issue on Perceptual Multimodal Interfaces*, September-October, 2003.
10. Takács, B. (2005), Special Education & Rehabilitation: Teaching and Healing with Interactive Graphics, , *IEEE Computer Graphics and Applications, Special Issue on Computer Graphics in Education*, under review.

11. Kiss, B., B. Benedek, G. Szijarto, and B. Takács, (2004), Closed Loop Dialog Model of Face-to-Face Communication with a Photo-Real Virtual Human, *SPIE Electronic Imaging Visual Communications and Image Processing*, San Jose, California, 2004.
12. Short, J., E. Williams, B. Christie, *The Social Psychology of Telecommunications,* Wiley, London, 1976.
13. Argyle, M. *The Psychology of Interpersonal Behavior,* Penguin Books, London, 1967.
14. Argyle, M., M. Cook, *Gaze and Mutual Gaze,* Cambridge University Press, London, 1977.
15. Digital Elite Inc. www.digitalElite.net

Affective Guide with Attitude

Mei Yii Lim, Ruth Aylett, and Christian Martyn Jones

School of Mathematical and Computer Sciences,
Heriot Watt University, Edinburgh, EH14 4AS, Scotland
{myl, ruth, cmj}@macs.hw.ac.uk

Abstract. The Affective Guide System is a mobile context-aware and spatial-aware system, offering the user with an affective multimodal interaction interface. The system takes advantage of the current mobile and wireless technologies. It includes an 'affective guide with attitude' that links its memories and visitor's interest to the spatial location so that stories are relevant to what can be immediately seen. This paper presents a review of related work, the system in detail, challenges and the future work to be carried out.

1 Introduction

The main aim of this research is the creation of an 'affective guide with attitude' to provide adaptive guidance and engaging interaction. Here, the word 'attitude' refers to the guide's perspective and personality. The use of different personality guide agents to narrate the story is due to the fact that there usually exist multiple interpretations of the same historical event, depending on the storyteller's perspective [1]. The guide tells stories based on his or her past experiences taking into consideration the user's interests. The hypothesis here is that an emotional agent with personality can make interaction more realistic and natural as well as present the user with a more engaging and memorable visit by holding attention and helping comprehension of new information.

2 Related Work

Research in the field of Augmented Reality, Mobile and Context-Aware Tour Guide applications is growing. Cyberguide [2] is a series of prototypes of a mobile context-aware tour guide that detects the user's physical location and crude orientation, without taking into consideration the user's interests. HyperAudio [3] and HIPS [4] adopt multimodality to get round the static constraints of the environment and perform user modeling based on the history of interaction, visitor attitude, physical environment and visiting path. MARS [5] is a testbed that allows indoor and outdoor users to access and manage real world spatial information while DEEP MAP [6] project is able to generate personal guided walks through the City of Heidelberg.

While none of the above systems employ a life-like animated character, C-MAP [7], is an early attempt to build a personal mobile life-like assistant that

J. Tao, T. Tan, and R.W. Picard (Eds.): ACII 2005, LNCS 3784, pp. 772–779, 2005.

provides visitors touring museums and open exhibitions with information based on their location and individual interests. PEACH [8] enhanced the appreciation of cultural heritage through the development of a personal guide. [9] attempts to shape dialogue interactions between an interactive gesture-choreographed conversational character and the user in an online virtual exhibition of a XVI century Portugese ship.

[10] proposed storytelling from a virtual guide perspective, constructing stories by improvising. In Geist [11], the history of the City of Heidelberg, Germany and the Thirty Years War is shown in a way that the audience receives an immersive, dramatic and action rich experience with a high factor of enjoyment. The [12] Ghost Project achieved high quality agent-based assistance without demanding visualization requirements. Some other related works are the SAGRES [13], Kyoto·Tour Guide project [14], etc.

All these systems aim to provide user with context-aware information. However, the life-like animated characters employed lack a real affective model. Additionally, affective interaction between the characters and user is missing! According to [15], the individual's interaction with computers is inherently natural and social, hence affective communication is expected by people when they interact with computers. The inclusion of this missing element is the core focus of this research.

There has been a series of efforts for making artifacts with their own emotional structure. The Oz project [16] aimed at producing agents with a broad set of capabilities where individual *Woggles* had specific habits and interests which were shown as different personalities. Cañamero [17] proposed an architecture that relies on both motivations and emotions to perform behavior selection that influences the creatures perception of both the external world and their own body.

Velásquez's robot, *Yuppy* [18] is a biologically plausible computational framework for Emotion-Based Control. Previous emotional experiences form an emotional memory, which affects action selection strategy when it re-encounters similar situations. In *AlphaWolf* [19], the wolves' emotions generate context-specific emotional memories based on the "somatic marker hypothesis" presented by Damasio [20], which affects how they will interact in the future.

The 'Psi' agents [21,22] framework focuses on emotional modulation of perception, action-selection, planning and memory access. [23] integrates a connectionist cognitive model of emotional processing called SESAME [24] with a synthetic force model, SOF-Soar architecture [25] for training in a battlefield simulation.

3 The Affective Guide System

The Affective Guide System integrates the PDA with a Global Positioning System, a speech synthesis system and utilizes wireless communication. Fig. 1 gives an illustration of the system architecture. It consists of two emotional agents with attitude. These guides present users with different versions of the same story about an event or place allowing them to understand an event more deeply, a learning strategy targeted by the UK National Curriculum for History [26].

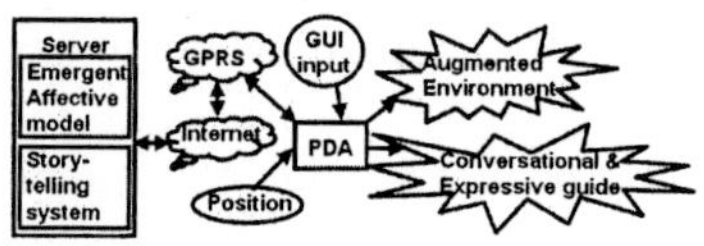

Fig. 1. The Overall System Architecture

A brief ice-breaking session takes place before a tour starts. Based on the user's input, the guide plans a route. On the way to the destination, the guide will draw the users attention to landmarks, and applying a story-telling technique [10] will links the memory and interests of the guide as well as the visitor to the spatial location. The user interacts using the graphical user interface (GUI) and receives responses by means of text, graphics and audio. A server performs the processing and holds the guides emotional memory and memory about facts and sends the information to the PDA on demand.

3.1 Emergent Affective and Personality Model

The Emergent Affective Model, presented in Fig. 2 is designed based on the 'Psi' [21,22] model with the addition of emotional memory. The 'Psi' model is unique in that emotions are not explicitly defined but emerge from the modulation of information processing, action selection, planning and memory access. Flexibility is achieved with the capability of the cognitive processes to adapt appropriately to various circumstances through the interaction of various parameters and built-in motivators.

In this model, motivation is represented by the needs and aims of the user as well as those of the guide; emotions are reflected by the modulating parameters, their causes and influences, while cognition is represented by information processes in GENERATE INTENTION, SELECT INTENTION, RUN INTENTION and PERCEPT as well as in the memory of intentions and other environmental factors.

The guide needs to maintain its level of competence (the degree of capability of coping with differing perspectives) and keeps the user attention high by adjusting its behavior appropriately to the level of uncertainty (the degree of predictability of the environment). The guide receives user inputs, system feedback and the GPS information continuously, then, generates an intention, let's say a story topic. These intentions together with its built-in motivators - level of competence and level of uncertainty are stored in a memory of intentions. The user's response, for example, the degree to which he or she agrees with the guide's argument, contributes to the guide's competence level, while the accuracy of the GPS reading contributes to its level of uncertainty.

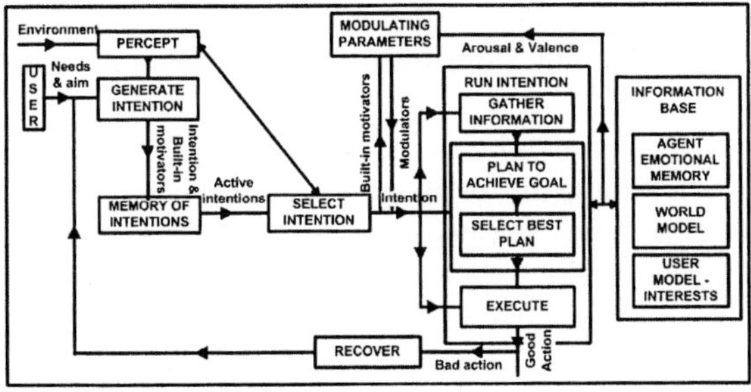

Fig. 2. The Emergent Affective and Personality Model

Next, depending on the importance of the need and the urgency for realization, one of the active intentions is selected. Then, the guide decides autonomously whether to gather information, to design a plan or to run an existing plan. The decision is made based on the value of the built-in motivators and modulators such as arousal level (rate of processing), resolution level (carefulness and attentiveness of behavior) and selection threshold (how easy is it for another motive to take over) or in other words, the agent's current emotional state.

For example, in an uncertain environment (GPS accuracy is low) and a low level of competence (user is in disagreement with the guide's perspective), the guides arousal level and selection threshold will be high while its resolution level should be low in which case, we may diagnose that the guide is experiencing anxiety. In this situation, the agent tends to give a more general story of the current site. On the other hand, when its level of competence is high and the environment is stable, it may experience a high, but not too high level of arousal and selection threshold, with a medium resolution level. This time, the agent may be said to experience pride and hence, it is not easy for another goal to take over. It will perform some planning and provide a more elaborated story on the current subject.

By doing so, it adapts its behavior according to its internal states and the environmental circumstances. Each execution of intention will produce a feedback into the system and recovery will be performed when necessary.

3.2 Emotional Memory

Recent studies in neurology provide evidence that memory files contain not only data or information but emotions as well [27]. It has also long been known that emotionally arousing events are more likely to be later recollected than similar, neutral events [28]. Those memories are part of what makes up our personality, controls our behaviors and often produces our mood.

Taking this view, the guide possesses a long-term memory that is made up of both semantic and emotional memories. Semantic memory includes location-related information and the user profile while emotional memory is memory for previous experiences and will be generated through simulation of past experiences. Additionally, the guide's current memory holds information about recent processing.

Emotional information can be categorised into two dimensions: arousal, that is, how exciting or calming an experience is and valence, that is, whether an experience causes a positive or a negative impact [29]. Consequently, the guide's emotional memory holds an 'arousal' tag and a 'valence' tag. The inclusion of 'arousal' tag is analogous to the *Emotional Tagging* concept, according to which the activation of the amygdala in emotionally arousing events marks the experience as important [30]. The 'valence' tag serves as the basis of the guide's level of competence.

When interacting with the user, the agent will be engaged in meaningful reconstruction of its own past [31], at the same time presenting facts about the place of interest. This recollective experience is related to the evocation of previously experienced emotions through the activation of the emotion tags. These values combine with the built-in motivators values to trigger the arousal level, resolution level and selection threshold, resulting in re-experiencing of emotions, though there might be a slight variation due to the input from the user.

The user's responses form positive and negative stimuli to the agent. The GUI provides user with various degrees of agreeableness in opinion of which he/she can choose from as the guide presents its story. Based on these responses, the guide will make assumptions about the user's interest and take it into consideration in story generation. When the user adopts the guide's perspective by agreeing, the agent's level of competence increases which leads to a more detailed explanation about the subject or related subjects. Similarly, when the user disagrees, the agent's level of competences decreases and the agent tends to focus on only the important points of the subject without much elaboration.

3.3 Personality

Personality plays an important role in this application. Based on a brief survey of real-world tour guides experiences, we found that factors like role, interest, experience, type of tour, guide's belief, guide's personality and visitor group can affect the presentation of information. Most guides tend to incorporate beliefs and past experiences, whether his/her own or that of others while narrating a story. Different guides have different presentation styles and some guides are more chatty than others. Visitors' age, origin, race, group size, etc. also contribute to the type of story told.

Similarly, the virtual guide's personality will reflect the guide's ideology or perspective about a particular historical event. It manifests the guide's personal life experiences. In our model, personality emerges from varying the weight of each modulator which ranges from 0 to 1. Fig. 3 gives an illustration of how variation of the modulators' weight can lead to different personality guides.

The personality of the guide is reflected by the way it tackles interaction circumstances which map nicely to a personality traits model. The modulators are mapped onto the temperament dimensions defined by [32], where 'Psychoticism'

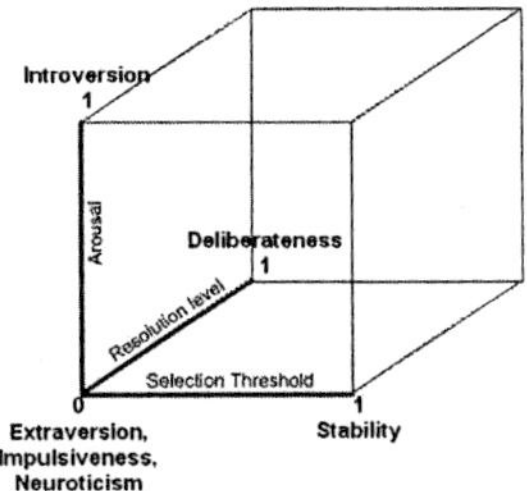

Fig. 3. Personality cube

is replaced by the Impulsivity-Deliberateness dimensions of [33] which better describe the resolution level. If a guide is given a resolution level weight of 0.1, this will mean that the guide is impulsive. It will present the story briefly without much consideration. As the weight increases, it becomes more and more attentive and careful. When the value reaches 1, the agent is deliberate, performs detailed planning and present stories based on the user's interest.

4 Challenges and Future Work

The biggest challenge of this research is retaining high user attention and generating a long-term memory in the user. Next, is determining the relevant set of emotions. Besides that, it is important to match the appearance of the character with its behavioral and interactive potential. Appropriate representations must be established for the agent memories, the world model and the user model. The system must also take into account the special interests of each user to automatically propose an appropriate presentation of fact and story. Technically, accuracy of GPS tracking needs consideration so that the guide is spatially responsive. The limited resources of the PDA requires consideration of visual techniques other than facial animation for emotion expression.

The current focus of this research is the development of the Emergent Affective model. Since the model integrates many components, construction will be performed in a rapid prototyping manner. Evaluation is essential throughout and at the end of development phase to ensure a functional model as well as to allow refinement.

Acknowledgements

Work supported by the European Union's Sixth Framework Programme, in the IST (Information Society Technologies) Thematic Priotity IST-2002-2.3.1.6 Multimodal Interfaces, HUMAINE (Human-Machine Interaction Network on Emotion) [34] (Contract no. 507422). The authors are solely responsible for the content of this publication. It does not represent the opinion of the European Community and the European Community is not responsible for any use that might be made of data appearing therein.

References

1. Tozzi, V.: Past reality and multiple interpretations in historical investigation. Stud Social Political Thought 2 (2000)
2. Abowd, G.D., Atkeson, C.G., Hong, H., Long, S., Kooper, R., Pinkerton, M.: Cyberguide: A mobile context-aware tour guide. Wireless Networks **3** (1997) 421–433
3. Not, E., Petrelli, D., Sarini, M., Stock, O., Strapparava, C., Zancanaro, M.: Hypernavigation in the physical space: adapting presentations to the user and to the situational context. The New Review of Hypermedia and Multimedia **4** (1998) 33–45
4. O'Grady, M.J., O'Rafferty, R.P., O'Hare, G.M.P.: A tourist-centric mechanism for interacting with the environment. In: Proceedings of the First International Workshop on Managing Interactions in Smart Environments, Dublin, Ireland, Springer (1999) 56–67
5. Höllerer, T., Feiner, S., Terauchi, T., Rashid, G., Hallaway, D.: Exploring MARS: developing indoor and outdoor user interfaces to a mobile augmented reality system. Computers and Graphics **23** (1999) 779–785
6. Malaka, R., Zipf, A.: Deep map challenging it research in the framework of a tourist information system. In Buhalis, D., Fesenmaier, D.R., S. Klein, e., eds.: Information and Communication technologies in tourism. Springer-Verlag, New York (2000)
7. Sumi, Y., Etani, T., Fels, S., Simone, N., Kobayashi, K., Mase, K.: C-map: Building a context-aware mobile assistant for exhibition tours. The First Kyoto Meeting on Social Interaction and Communityware (1998)
8. PEACH: Personal experience with active cultural heritage. (2004) http://peach.itc.it/home.htm.
9. Almeida, P., Yokoi, S.: Interactive character as a virtual tour guide to an online museum exhibition. In: Proceeding of Museum and the Web 2003. (2003)
10. Ibanez, J., Aylett, R., Ruiz-Rodarte, R.: Storytelling in virtual environments from a virtual guide perspective. Virtual Reality (2003)
11. Braun, N.: Storytelling & conversation to improve the fun factor in software applications. In Blythe, M.A., Monk, A.F., Overbeeke, K., Wright, P.C., eds.: Funology, From Usability to Enjoyment, Dordrecht, Kluwer Academic Publishers (2003)
12. DELCA: Enter the world of ghosts: New assisting and entertaining virtual agents. Working paper, DELCA Ghost Project, IT University of Copenhagen (2004) http://www.itu.dk/research/delca/papers/delca_ghosts.pdf.
13. Bertolleti, A.C., Moraes, M.C., da Rocha Costa, A.C.: Providing personal assistance in the sagres virtual museum. In: Proceeding of Museum and the Web 2001. (2001)
14. Doyle, P., Isbister, K.: Touring machines: Guide agents for sharing stories about digital places (1999)
15. Nass, C., Steuer, J., Tauber, T.: Computers are social actors. In: CHI'94 Conference Proceedings, ACM (1994) 72–78
16. Bates, J.: The nature of characters in interactive worlds and the oz project (1992)
17. Cañamero, D.: Modeling motivations and emotions as a basis for intelligent behavior. In Johnson, W.L., Hayes-Roth, B., eds.: Proceedings of the 1st International Conference on Autonomous Agents, New York, ACM Press (1997) 148–155
18. Velásquez, J.: A computational framework for emotion-based control. In: Proceeding of the Grounding Emotions in Adaptive Systems Workshop, SAB '98, Zurich, Switzerland (1998)

19. Tomlinson, B., Blumberg, B.: *AlphaWolf*: Social learning, emotion and development in autonomous virtual agents (2002)
20. Damasio, A.R.: Descartes' Error: Emotion, Reason, and the Human Brain. G.P. Putnam, New York (1994)
21. Bartl, C., Dörner, D.: Comparing the behavior of psi with human behavior in the biolab game. In Ritter, F.E., Young, R.M., eds.: Proceedings of the Second International Conference on Cognitive Modeling, Nottingham, Nottingham University Press (1998)
22. Dörner, D.: The mathematics of emotions. In Frank Detje, D.D., Schaub, H., eds.: Proceedings of the Fifth International Conference on Cognitive Modeling, Bamberg, Germany (2003) 75–79
23. Randolph M. Hones, Amy E. Henninger, E.C.: Interfacing emotional behavior moderators with intelligent synthetic forces. In: Proceeding of the 11th CGF-BR Conference, Orlando, FL (2002)
24. Chown, E.: Consolidation and Learning: A Connectionist Model of Human Credit Assignment. PhD thesis, University of Michigan (1993)
25. G. Taylor, F.K., Nielsen, P.: Special operations forces ifors. In: Proceeding of the 10th Conference on Computer Generated Forces and Behavioral Representation, Norfolk, VA (2001) 301–306
26. NHC: History: The level description. (2004) http://www.ncaction.org.uk/subjects/history/levels.htm.
27. Carver, J.M.: Emotional memory management: Positive control over your memory. Burn Survivors Throughout the World Inc. (2005) http://www.burnsurvivorsttw.org/articles/memory.html.
28. Riesberg, D., Heuer, F.: Remembering the details of emotional events. Affect and Accuracy in Recall: Studies of 'Flashbulb' Memories (1992) 162–190
29. Kensinger, E.A., Corkin, S.: Two routes to emotional memory: Distinct neural processes for valence and arousal. PNAS **101** (2004) 3310–3315
30. Richter-Levin, G., Akirav, I.: Emotional tagging of memory formation - in the search for neural mechanisms. Brain Research Reviews **43** (2003) 247–256
31. Dautenhahn, K.: The art of designing socially intelligent agents – science, fiction and the human in the loop (1998)
32. Eysenck, H.J., Eysenck, M.: Personality and Individual Differences: A Natural Science Approach. Plenum Press, New York (1985)
33. Buss, A.H., Plomin, R.: A temperament theory of personality development. Wiley, New York (1975)
34. HUMAINE: Human-machine interaction network on emotion. (2004) http://emotion-research.net.

Detecting Emotions in Conversations Between Driver and In-Car Information Systems

Christian Martyn Jones[1] and Ing-Marie Jonsson[2]

[1] School of Mathematical and Computer Sciences,
Heriot-Watt University, Edinburgh, EH14 4AS, UK
cmj@macs.hw.ac.uk
[2] Department of Communication,
Stanford University, California 94305, USA
ingmarie@csli.stanford.edu

Abstract. Speech interaction with in-car controls is becoming more commonplace as the interaction is considered to be less distracting to the driver. Cars of today are equipped with speech recognition system to dial phone numbers and to control the cockpit environment. Furthermore satellite navigation systems provide the driver with verbal directions to their destination. The paper extends the speech interaction between driver and car to consider automatic recognition of the emotional state of the driver and appropriate responses by the car to improve the driver mood. The emotion of the driver has been found to influence driving performance and by actively responding to the emotional of the driver the car could improve their driving.

1 Introduction

Todays cars are fitting with interactive information systems including high quality audio/video systems, pin-point satellite navigation systems, hands free telephony and control over climate and ride conditions. Current research and attention theory suggests that speech-based interactions would be less detrimental to the driver than would interactions with a visual display [1]. With potentially more devices and more complex devices for the driver to control using speech as an interface is no longer a gimick but a necessity. Introducing speech-based interaction and conversation into the car highlights the potential influence of linguistic and paralinguistic cues. These cues play a critical role in human—human interactions, manifesting among other things, personality and emotion [2]. Previous studies show that alerting drivers to hazards in the road results in a more cautious and safer driving [3]. An in-car voice system was used to give the drivers relevant and timely road information, and thereby providing extra time and distance for them to evaluate the driving situation. Emotion of the car-voice was found to impact on driving performance. Results from a study matching and miss-matching the emotion of the car-voice and the emotion of the driver showed that matched emotions positively impacted driving performance [3]. These results make it interesting to investigate the feasibility of designing the emotionally responsive car.

J. Tao, T. Tan, and R.W. Picard (Eds.): ACII 2005, LNCS 3784, pp. 780 – 787, 2005.

2 An Emotionally Responsive Car

The development of an emotionally responsive car involves a number of technically demanding stages. In practise, the driver and car will converse two-way, where each will listen and respond to the others request for information and their emotional well-being. Systems to understand the requests from the driver and to retrieve and respond with appropriate information are not considered in this paper. Instead we concentrate on recognising the emotional state of the driver so that the car can modify its response both in the words it uses but also the presentation of the message by stressing particular words in the message and speaking in an appropriate emotional state. By the car altering its 'standard' voice response it will be able to empathise with the driver and ultimately improve the wellbeing and driving performance. This paper reports on our continued work to develop the acoustic emotion recognition part of the project and to test the technology within the car environment.

3 Development of Acoustic Emotion Recognition

There is considerable research interest in detecting and recognising human emotions automatically both academically [4],[5] and commercially [6]. Emotional information can be obtained by tracking facial motion, gestures and body language using image capture and processing; monitoring physiological changes using biometric measurements taken from the steering wheel and seat/seat-belt; and also analysing the acoustic cues contained in speech. Currently, video cameras and biometric sensors are not fitted as standard in cars, however speech controlled systems are already commonplace. Voice-controlled satellite navigation, voice-dial mobile phones and voice-controlled multimedia systems exist and drivers are educated and comfortable with their use. Therefore the project can incorporate voice-based emotion recognition without any requirement of additional hardware or changes to the driver's environment.

The acoustic emotion recognition system used in this project has been trained to recognise a range of emotions including boredom, sadness, grief, frustration, extreme anger, happiness and surprise. The system is trained on emotional speech obtained from United Kingdom and North American English speaking drama students at the Royal Scottish Academy of Music and Drama (RSAMD) using personalised and strongly emotive scenarios and constrained and free speech. All examples were validated in a blind listening study using human listeners before inclusion in our emotive speech corpus. The system uses 10 acoustic features including pitch, volume, rate of speech and other spectral coefficients and maps these features to emotions using statistical and neutral network classifiers. Using a test emotive speech data set the overall performance of the emotion recognition system is greater than 70% for 5 emotional groups of boredom, sadness/grief, frustration/extreme anger, happiness and surprise. The emotion recognition can track changes in emotional state over time and present its emotion decisions as a numerical indicator of the degree of emotional cues present in the speech. In addition, and to aid visualisation, the emotional state of the speaker can be displayed as an emotional face image, Table 1.

Table 1. Tracking changes in emotional state over time using an acoustic emotion recognition system. Plot shows speech waveform (top), numerical classification of the emotion state for happiness, surprise, anger/frustration, sadness/grief, the overal decision of the emotion recognition system (2nd bottom) and a graphical representation of the emotion for each second of time.

Speech waveform									
Boredom	1.00	1.00	0.00	0.00	0.00	0.00	0.00	0.00	0.01
Happiness	0.00	0.00	0.90	1.00	0.00	0.00	0.00	0.00	0.00
Surprise	0.00	0.00	0.15	1.00	1.00	0.00	0.00	0.00	0.00
Anger	0.06	0.00	0.00	0.00	0.00	1.00	1.00	0.00	0.00
Sadness	0.31	0.09	0.00	0.00	0.00	0.00	0.00	0.00	0.99
Decision	Bored	Bored	Happy	Not sure	Sur-prise	Anger	Anger	None	Sad
Emotional face images									

4 The Emotive Driver Project

The project builds on our initial research to assess the feasibility of automatically detecting driver emotions using speech [7]. The experiment sets out to record conversations between the car and the driver and to test the accuracy and validity of the automatic acoustic emotion recognition system in detecting, recognising and tracking emotions in the speech. The experiment consisted of an 8 day study at Oxford Brookes University, UK using 60 participants, 29 male and 31 female. Participants operated the STISIM driving simulator [8], Fig. 1, using an accelerator pedal, a brake pedal, and a force-feedback steering wheel, Fig. 2. All participants experienced the same pre-defined route and properties for both driving conditions and the car. The drive lasted approximately 20 minutes for each participant.

Fig. 1. STISIM simulator driving software showing front and rear views together with speedometer and rev counter

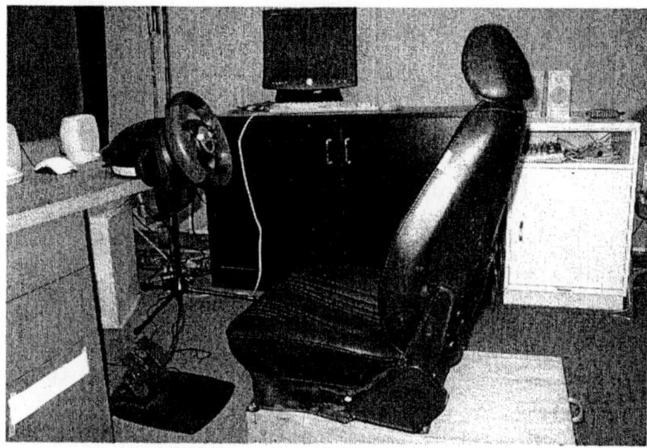

Fig. 2. Simulator driving hardware including pedals for an automatic car, steering wheel and car seat

Engine noise, brake screech, indicators, sirens etc together with verbal information from the car was played through stereo speakers. The information presented included instructions such as:

- This road is very busy during rush hour and traffic is slow
- This road too narrow and windy for cyclists
- The police often use radar here so make sure to keep to the speed limit
- This is a really windy stretch
- Pedestrians cross the road without looking in this school zone
- Some drivers need to pay more attention to the driving
- Parts of this road are under construction
- There is a traffic jam ahead if you turn left you might avoid it
- This road has many construction zones
- There is an accident ahead if you turn left here you might avoid it
- This stretch of road is always slippery
- This road is narrow and windy for slowly vehicles
- This stretch of road often has a problem with the fog

In addition the car attempts to engage the driver in conversation by saying:

- I get stress in traffic almost every day, how often do you get stressed with traffic problems?
- What do think about traffic?
- What do you think about the driving conditions?
- Do you generally like to drive at, above or below the speech limit?
- How do you like the car's performance?
- What types of situations makes you feel stressed whilst driving?
- I like to drive with people who talk to me, what is your favorite person to driver with?
- How do think you are driving?
- I like driving on mountain roads, what's your favorite road to drive on?

- How are you feeling right now?
- What kinds of things do you think about whilst driving?
- Do you find it stressful talking to people whilst driving?
- What do you think about this car?
- I'd love to ride in one of the new minis what is your favorite car to drive?
- I find that driving on narrow roads makes me feel stressed what kinds of roads makes you feel stressed?
- This is miserable, what's your strategy for coping with rain and fog whilst driving?

Speech from the participants was recorded using an Andrea directional bean with 4 microphones placed in front and about 1.5 meters away from the driver and recorded on a Sony Handicam DVD201. This microphone is typical of those used in the cars of today and provided a clean acoustic recording without overly sampling the car noise. The driving sessions were also videotaped from the front left of the driver to show driver hands, arms, upper body, head and eye motion, and facial expressions. Although this study does not consider image processing as a means to recognise driver emotions the video is used to correlate results from the acoustic emotion recognition with the emotions displayed in the faces of the drivers.

5 Results from Listener and Automatic Emotion Recognition Systems

The participants exhibit a range of emotions including boredom, sadness, anger, happiness and surprise, however for most of the drive the participants have a neutral/natural or a downbeat, bored/sad emotional state. When challenged in the drive by obstacles in the road, other drivers, difficult road conditions and pedestrians, we observe strong emotions from the drivers. During these emotional events the acoustic emotion recognition system must detect and recognise the emotional state of the driver.

By listening to the speech recording, a transcript of the drive has been created which includes not only the words of the conversation but also the emotional state of the driver. The same speech recording was processed by the acoustic emotion recognition system and its output classification represented as emotive faces for each second of the drive. The performance of the automatic emotion recognition system was determined by comparing the human emotion transcript against the output from the recognition system. The project is ongoing and we continue to process the speech data from drivers. An example speech and emotion transcript created by the human listener is included as Fig. 3, together with the emotional classification obtained automatically from the emotion recognition system Fig. 4.

There is a correlation between the emotional transcript created by the human listener and the emotion output returned automatically by the acoustic emotion recognition system. However there are occasions where the speech is masked by car noise (such as engine, brakes etc) and times when the driver could be one of two emotions such bored or sad, happiness or surprised. Classifying speech into emotions is challenging and there are occasions when the human listener is confused between sadness and boredom and happiness and surprise, rather like the automatic emotion recognition system. Grouping boredom and sadness together and calling this 'down-beat' may overcome much of these confusions. Similarly grouping happiness and surprise together as 'upbeat' also reduces confusions.

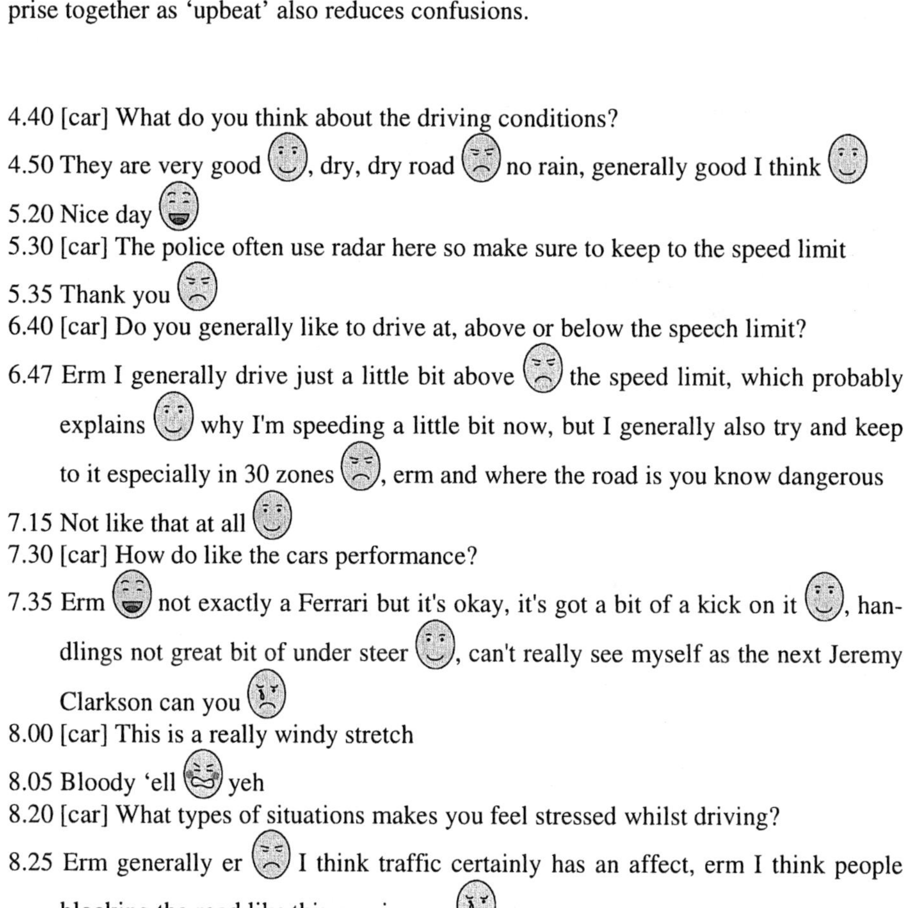

4.40 [car] What do you think about the driving conditions?
4.50 They are very good, dry, dry road no rain, generally good I think
5.20 Nice day
5.30 [car] The police often use radar here so make sure to keep to the speed limit
5.35 Thank you
6.40 [car] Do you generally like to drive at, above or below the speech limit?
6.47 Erm I generally drive just a little bit above the speed limit, which probably explains why I'm speeding a little bit now, but I generally also try and keep to it especially in 30 zones, erm and where the road is you know dangerous
7.15 Not like that at all
7.30 [car] How do like the cars performance?
7.35 Erm not exactly a Ferrari but it's okay, it's got a bit of a kick on it, handlings not great bit of under steer, can't really see myself as the next Jeremy Clarkson can you
8.00 [car] This is a really windy stretch
8.05 Bloody 'ell yeh
8.20 [car] What types of situations makes you feel stressed whilst driving?
8.25 Erm generally er I think traffic certainly has an affect, erm I think people blocking the road like this guy is now

Fig. 3. Transcript of conversation between car and driver including the classification of emotional state of the driver as considered acoustically by the human listener

We have considered the correlation between the emotional transcript of the human listener and the automated emotion recognition system and can report that on average there is 60-75% correlation for the 5 emotional groups. The current range of emotions detected may not be the optimal range of emotions required for the emotionally responsive car and the performance of the emotion recognition can be improved by using the 'downbeat' and 'upbeat' groupings.

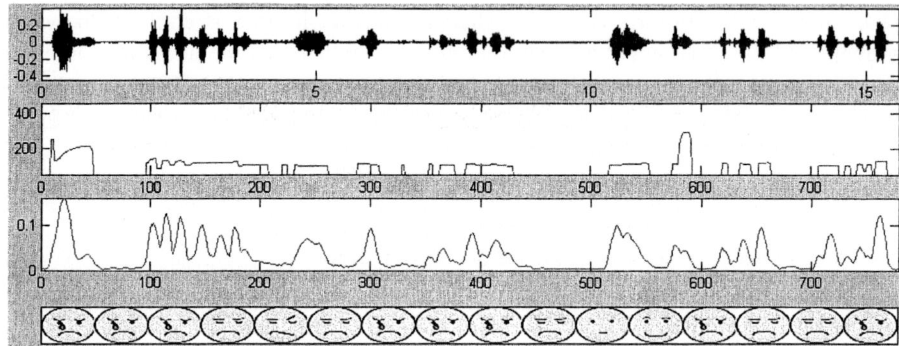

Fig. 4. Automatically generated transcript of the driver's speech using the emotion recognition system. Plots shown are waveform (top), pitch track (2nd), volume track (3rd) and the automatic classification of emotion (bottom) in the voice for a section of speech from 24.13-24.30 minutes. The driver has been asked "What is your favorite car to drive?" and responds by saying "Erm I'd go for an Austin Marin Vanquish and the whole prestige of the car, probably pretend to be James Bond and it's a lovely car". The emotion track shows that the driver is talking in a downbeat, matter-of-fact manner but gets enthusiastic and upbeat when talking about James Bond.

6 Extensions to the Current Research

The research is ongoing and we continue to analyse speech from the drivers and consider improvements for future work [7]. Although the in-car system asks questions of the driver many of the participants did not respond and engage in conversation. 25% of the participants did not converse with the car and thus we were unable to ascertain their emotional state acoustically. Future work will consider why the drivers did not talk with the car. Are they too focused on the task of driving? Do they not feel comfortable talking with the car? Do they not feel the car is listening to them and responding appropriately? We will adapt the conversational interface to help encourage conversation and enable the acoustic emotion recognition to gain insight into the mood of the driver.

Once the car knows the emotional state of the driver how should it adapt? Previous studies have considered varying the paralinguistic cues only [9], however should the content of the response also change, and how? Should the car become less or more talkative depending on the mood of the driver? Should the car alter the telematics, climate, music in the car in response the mood of the driver?

Further research should consider the affect of altering the car response and car environment to driver emotion. One strategy is to exhibit empathy by changing the emotion of the car-voice to match the user. Empathy fosters relationship development, as it communicates support, caring, and concern for the welfare of another. A voice which expresses happiness in situations where the user is happy and sounds subdued or sad in situations where the user is upset would strongly increase the connection between the user and the voice [10].

How fast should the emotion of voice change? Although rapid response to predicted emotion of the user can be effective, there are a number of dangers in this approach. Emotions can change in seconds in the human brain and body [11]. A sad person may momentarily be happy if someone tells a joke, but will fall back into their sad state relatively quickly. Conversely, happy drivers may become frustrated as they must slam on the brakes for a yellow light, but their emotion may quickly switch back to feeling positively. If the voice in the car immediately adapted to the user's emotions, drivers would experience occurrences such as the car-voice changing its emotion in mid-sentence. This would dramatically increase cognitive load constantly activate new emotions in the driver and be perceived as psychotic.

Mood must be taken into account to make the car-voice an effective interaction partner. Moods tend to bias feelings and cognition over longer terms, and while moods can be influenced by emotions, they are more stable and effectively filter events. A person in a good mood tends to view everything in a positive light, while a person in a bad mood does the opposite. Drivers that are in a good mood when entering a car are more likely to experience positive emotion during an interaction with a car-voice than drivers in a bad mood. Therefore it seems that emotion in technology-based voices must balance responsiveness and inertia by orienting to both emotion and mood.

Humans are what they feel: Performance, knowledge, beliefs, and feelings are to a large extent determined by emotions. People are also influences by voice interactions with people and interfaces. This makes it important for designers of speech based systems to work with linguistic and para-linguistic cues, especially emotional cues, to create the desired effect when people interact with the system.

References

1. Lunenfeld, H.: Human Factor Considerations of Motorist Navigation and Information Systems, Proceedings of Vehicle Navigation and Information Systems (1989) 35–42
2. Strayer, D., and Johnston, W.: Driven to Distraction: Dual-Task Studies of Simulated Driving and Conversing on a Cellular Telephone", Psychological Science 12 (2001) 462–466
3. Jonsson et al.: Increasing Safety in Cars by Matching Driver Emotion and Car Voice Emotion, Proceedings of CHI 2005 (2005)
4. Cowie R. et al.: Emotion Recognition in Human-Computer Interaction. IEEE Signal Processing Magazine (Jan 2001) 32-80
5. The Humaine Portal.: Research on Emotion and Human-Machine Interaction, http://www.emotion-research.net/ (2004)
6. Jones C.: Project to Develop Voice-Driven Emotive Technologies, Internal Report for Scottish Executive, Enterprise Transport and Lifelong Learning Department, UK (2004)
7. Jones C. and Jonsson I-M.: Speech Patterns for Older Adults While Driving, Proceedings of HCI International 2005 Las Vegas USA (2005)
8. STISIM Drive System, Systems Technology, Inc. California, http://www.systemstech.com/
9. Isen, A.M.: Positive Affect and Decision Making, in Lewis, M. and Haviland-Jones, J.M. eds. Handbook of Emotions, The Guilford Press (2000) 417-435
10. Brave, S.: Agents That Care: Investigating the Effects of Orientation of Emotion Exhibited by an Embodied Computer Agent, Doctoral Dissertation. Stanford University, CA (2003)
11. Picard, R.W.: Affective Computing. MIT Press, Cambridge, MA (1997)

Human Vibration Environment of Wearable Computer

Zhiqi Huang, Dongyi Chen, and Shiji Xiahou

The mobile computing center of University of Electronic Science and Technology of China, Chengdu, China 610054
{qqzzhh, chenxigt}@hotmail.com
xiahousj@yahoo.com.cn

Abstract. The applied prospect of the wearable computer is very extensive, in order to put wearable computer into practice, one of key technologies to be solved is to improve antivibration capability. The brand-new human-computer interaction mode that the wearable computer offers, determines that the human body is its working environment. The beginning of our research work is to study the vibration environment in which the wearable computer should be working. The vibration that the wearable computer receives can be divided into two kinds, first, by the vibration of the human body transmission from external vibration, second, by the vibration of the human movement. In this paper, two environment that wearable computer often works in have been studied, and it is considered that the vibration caused by human moving is more intensive than the vibration transmitting from external vibration through human body.

1 Introduction

Wearable computer is new-type mobile computing equipment, which can be worn on the user's body. It offers a different human-computer interactive mode from traditional computer. It can afford ability of obtaining, exchanging and managing information whenever and wherever. Its extensive applied prospect gets the concern of all trades, especially in national defense, spaceflight, mining, and so on.

The human-computer interaction of the wearable computer often adopts the following three modes: constancy, augmentation and mediation, showed in Fig. 1[1].

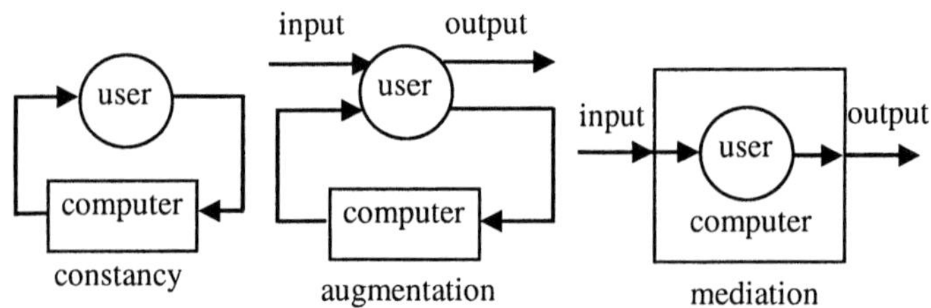

Fig. 1. The human-computer interaction of the wearable computer

J. Tao, T. Tan, and R.W. Picard (Eds.): ACII 2005, LNCS 3784, pp. 788 – 794, 2005.

In the vibration environment, because of fatigue effect of vibration and the resonance phenomenon, behaviors of electricity descended, components and parts invalidated may present in the electrical equipments. The wearable computer is the typical electronic equipment used under the vibration environment for a long time. Wearable computer can't adopt the method of increasing size and weight to increase its week antivibration ability. On the other hand, some occasion require the wearable computer to have strong antivibration ability because of special demands.

2 The Vibration Environment of Wearable Computer

The wearable computer receives the body vibration while being used. The random vibration will badly affect the computer's function and life, so it is necessary to study wearable computer vibration and find out solution to decrease it.

There are two kinds' vibrations: one is people being in vibration environment while using wearable computer, such as sitting or standing in vehicles, the vibration are transmitted from other vibration source via the human body, the human body is the transmit channels in this way; the other is people using wearable computer when walking、 running or jumping, the human body is the source of vibration. The Fig. 2 shows two typical vibration environment of wearable computer.

Fig. 2. Typical vibration environment of wearable computer: the left is people using wearable computer when driving a car; the right is the author using wearable computer when walking

3 The First Type Vibration – Caused by Vehicles

In fact, human body can be considered as a buffer device, which separates the vibration caused by vehicles and wearable computers, when we ride in various kinds of vehicles such as cars, trains, planes, etc. The vibration that computer receives is transmitted from external vibration resource via human body, in this case, the research should be combined with both external vibration situation and the body's transmission of this vibration.

With different vehicles, the user will meet different conditions of vibration with various frequency and intensity. Under different running speeds, orbit conditions and load quantities, vehicles would produce different frequency and amplitude of vibration.

The vibration environment caused by these vehicles is random vibration with medium and low frequency, and the vibration is mainly in vertical direction [2]. Therefore, what we mainly discussed is the external vibration source transmission in the Z axial direction via human body. For non-stable-state random vibrations, we must obtain the ratio and range of the vibration acceleration by measure and calculate.

The manner that the wearable computer worn on user generally adopts the distributed structure, which means that host computer、power supply、input/output equipment etc, are distributed as independent components in every part of body where are easily worn. In the preliminary study of transmissibility in every body part of users, considering the suitable wearable part of human body and the sensitive range of body itself, we choose four typical parts of human body as research parts, they are the upper arm、chest、belly and waist.[3] The testing environment is in rear seat of the car running on city road.

The Tektronix portable digital oscilloscopes, IBM ThinkPad, the environment vibration analysis instrument are used in our test. The environment vibration analysis instrument whose measure scope is 1-80Hz is selected. It can only print out the vibration level of the tested object; can not show the wave-shape and frequency of vibration. In this test, the output of analysis instrument is respectively connected with oscilloscope and ThinkPad via serial port. The value of the vibration acceleration is collected and recorded by ThinkPad; the wave-shape of vibration is displayed on the screen of the oscilloscope. The frame of the test system is shown in Fig. 3.

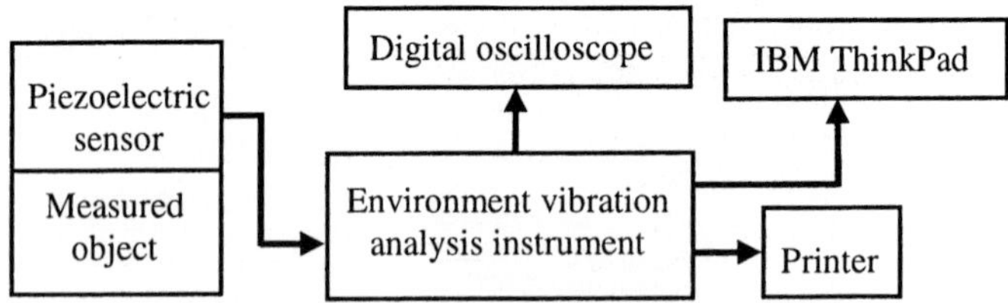

Fig. 3. The vibration tests system: piezoelectric sensor captures the mechanic signal and changes it to the electronic signal; environment vibration analysis instrument processes data; printer prints data; ThinkPad records data; oscilloscope displays waveform

While testing, the car is driven on the city road, and its speed keeps at 40-50 km/h. Because of the situation of the road, the wave-shape of vibration from the car rear seat is very irregular when car is being driven, and the frequency of vibration change great, its scope is from 4 Hz to26 Hz. The data which we record is the VAL, which is value of the vibration acceleration. The value of VAL is dealt by the environment vibration analysis instrument according as equation (1).

$$VAL=20\lg\frac{a}{a_0}(dB) \tag{1}$$

a is the valid value of the vibration acceleration, its unit is m/s^2. a_0 is the reference value of the vibration acceleration, $a_0=10^{-6}$m/s^2. In this test, the tested objects include the rear seat of the car, the experimenter's waist, belly, chest and upper arm.. The tested datum is recorded into ThinkPad every 300 milliseconds via serial port. 1,800 data are recorded from every tested part. Table 1 show these recorded data which has been dealt with statistic [4] (unit: dB).

Table 1. Statistic of test data, including rear seat, waist, belly,chest and upper arm

	rear seat	waist	belly	chest	upper arm
max	122.7	123.1	121.1	120.9	124.0
expectation	113.4	113.5	115.0	115.9	117.6
standard deviation	4.87	3.94	3.00	3.63	3.00
average standard deviation	0.115	0.093	0.071	0.086	0.071
average ratio	—	1.001	1.014	1.022	1.037

The value of expectation in Table 1 is estimated on point; it can only approach the value of expectation which objectively exist in tested data. Now, we estimate the scope of the expectation value which is every tested part, the believed probability $\alpha = 99\%$.

Because of we do not know the distribution and the variance of tested data, its average should be comply with t distribution. For example, we estimate the scope where the expectation value of the rear seat tested data locate. The average of data $\overline{x}=113.4$, The average of standard deviation $S_{\overline{x}}=0.115$ freedom is 1800-1=1799, $\alpha = 99\%$, comply with equation(2)

$$P\left[\left|\frac{\overline{x}-E(x)}{\sqrt{\frac{S^2}{n}}}\right| \le t_\alpha\right] = 1-\alpha \tag{2}$$

Consulting the table about t distribution, we can know $t_{0.01}=2.576$, confidence interval is $\left[\overline{x}-t_\alpha\sqrt{\frac{S^2}{n}}, \overline{x}+t_\alpha\sqrt{\frac{S^2}{n}}\right]$, bring into the data, we get [113.1, 113.7].

To the rear seat's VAL, the scope of expectation value [113.1, 113.7], its possibility is 99%, similarly; to the loin's VAL, the scope of expectation value [113.3, 113.7]; to the belly's VAL, the scope of expectation value [114.8, 115.2]; to the chest's VAL, the scope of expectation value [115.7.1, 116.1]; to the upper arm's VAL, the scope of expectation value [117.4, 117.8].

The almost tested data fall into the respective scope of expectation valuc. The scope is 113dB-118dB,it also is $0.45m/s^2$-$0.79m/s^2$. The waist, belly, chest and upper arm's expectation value divided by the rear seat's expectation value, the respective ratio is100.1%,101.4%,102.2% and 103.7%. Fig. 4 shows the relation of these ratios.

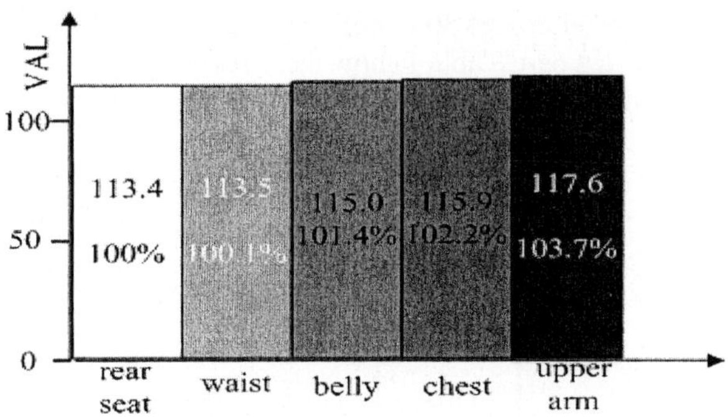

Fig. 4. The relation of vibration acceleration about tested parts

The result of this test indicates these ratios are below 4%. At the same time, we find the vibration acceleration augment one by one in order, the order is waist, belly, chest and upper arm. So we can draw a conclusion, which is the vibration acceleration of body part should be enlarged when the distance from body part to rare seat is enlarged.

4 The Second Type Vibration – Caused by User Moving

We are using the wearable computer when walking, running or jumping, the vibration caused by body's movement is the vibration source of wearable computer, and each part of body generate different vibration during the process of the different movement. In this paper, as the human walking, the Z axial direction vibration generated by several typical wearable parts has been researched preliminarily. The tested parts are upper arm, chest, belly and waist. The vibration test system is the same as before, showed as Fig.3.

During the test, the measured person fixed the piezoelectric sensor on the measured parts as same as wear the wearable computer, in this way, the vibration condition we measured could be considered approximately matches the condition that we use the wearable computer. We have tested ten times for every tested part, and in each test, the vibration waveform is recorded by oscilloscope and the testing data is recorded by ThinkPad, totally obtained 200 test values each time. One group of vibration waveform recorded is shown as follow Fig. 5.

The vibration waveforms have the certain regulation compared with the vibration waveform which we got in previous test, although they are still irregular. I think the main reason include two aspects: one is the form of human walk is a type of periodically reciprocating motion; the other is the exterior influence which walking human suffered smaller than running car.

The vibration waveforms show vibration frequency of these tested parts are very low, scope from 1Hz to 3Hz, moreover, these waveforms are very similar, these characters accord with the characters of human walk. The value of vibration acceleration has been dealt with statistic, showed in Table 2 (unit: dB).

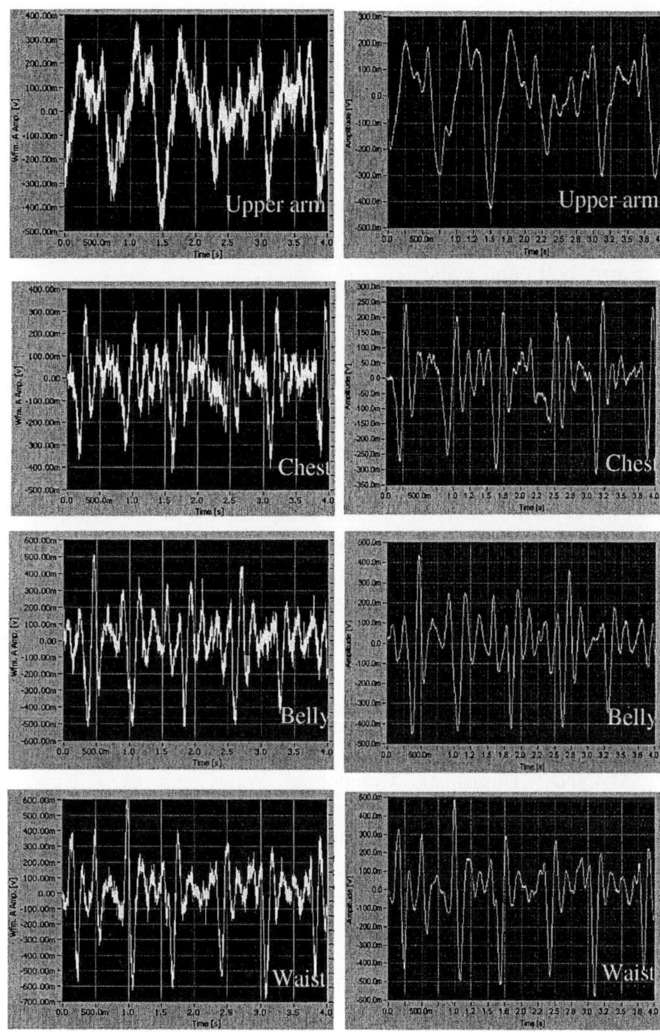

Fig. 5. The left graph shows the original waveform, and the right waveform is processed by a low-pass filter. X-Axis is Amp, its unit is *mV*; Y-Axis is time, its unit is *t*.

Table 2. Statistic of test data, including waist, belly, chest and upper arm

	chest	upper arm	belly	waist
max	121.4	122.3	122.7	123.7
expectation	119.2	119.7	120.7	121.2
standard deviation	1.51	1.54	1.83	3.13
average standard deviation	0.48	0.49	0.58	0.99

According to the analytical method used in previous test, we can estimate: at 99% possibility ,to the chest's VAL, the scope of expectation value [118.0, 120.4]; to the upper arm's VAL, the scope of expectation value [118.4, 121.0]; to the belly's VAL, the scope of expectation value [119.2, 112.2]; to the waist's VAL, the scope of expectation value [118.6, 123.8].

The almost tested data fall into the respective scope of expectation value. The scope is 117dB-124dB, it also is 0.71 $m/s^2 - 1.58m/s^2$. These expectation values in the Table 3 indicate the acceleration amplitude of vibration change from small to large sequencing in chest, upper arm, belly and waist.

5 Conclusion

Comparatively, we use wearable computer when we are moving more than are sitting in running car. The vibration acceleration brought out by human walking is larger than by running car transferring to human body, this verdict is very clear in this paper. And other human movements, such as run and jump should produce more violent vibration than what walk produce. So the vibration environment caused by human movement is more rugged and more research worthy. In the next research work, studying the influence, which the wearable computer suffered when we use it in course of our movements including walk, run and jump, should be our research emphases.

References

1. STEVE MANNN: Humanistic Computing: WearComp as a New Framework and Application for Intelligent Signal. Proceedings of the IEEE, (1998) 86(11):2123-2151.
2. Dunshu Zhao, Mingzhi Liu: the analysis and test about electronic instrument vibration. Publishing house of Southeast University, (1990) 1-5.
3. F. Gemperle, C. Kasabach, J. Stivoric, M. Bauer, R. Martin: Design for Wearability. Proceedings of the Second International Symposium on Wearable Computing, Oct. (1998) 116-122.
4. Ying gu: reliability engineering mathematics. Publishing house of electronics industry, (2004) 127-173

Approximation of Class Unions Based on Dominance-Matrix Within Dominance-Based Rough Set Approach*

Ming Li, Baowei Zhang, Tong Wang, and Li Zhao

School of Computer and Communication,
Lanzhou University of Technology, Lanzhou 730050, P.R. China
bwzh1980@163.com

Abstract. Dominance-based Rough Set Approach (DRSA) is an extension of classical Rough Set Theory (RST). Approximation of class unions is a very important approach in DRSA. Aiming at the disadvantage of the classical method we presented a new methodology for approximation of class unions based on dominance-matrix. It only needs to calculate the dominance-matrix and does not need to consider the preference relations one by one. Thus it greatly simplifies the process. Besides it is intuitive and efficient. The example illustrates its feasibility and efficiency.

1 Introduction

The original rough set approach [1,2] is proved to be very useful in dealing with the inconsistency problems following from information granulation. The original rough set idea is failing, however, when preference-orders of attribute domains (criteria) are to be taken into account. Precisely, it cannot handle inconsistencies following from violation of the dominance principle. This inconsistency is characteristic for preferential information used in Multicriteria Decision Analysis (MCDA) problems, like sorting, choice, or ranking.

In order to deal with this kind of inconsistency a number of methodological changes to the original rough sets theory is necessary. To deal with preference-ordered domains of criteria and preference-ordered decision classes, Greco et al. (1996,1998a, 1999) [3,4,5,6] have proposed an extension of the Rough Set Theory (RST), called Dominance-based Rough Set Approach (DRSA).This innovation is mainly based on substitution of the indiscernibility relation by a dominance relation in the rough approximation of decision classes.

In this paper we wish to concentrate on the approximation of class unions. The previous work within DRSA only proposed relative definitions of the concept including approximation of class unions, but it did not have given any efficient algorithm. So we can only use the original definition to get the approximation of class unions. Thus not only it is very complex but also it requires a considerable amount of comput-

* This paper is partially supported by Natural Science Foundation of Gansu and Foundation of Science Research of Gansu Education Office under grant 0416B-04.

J. Tao, T. Tan, and R.W. Picard (Eds.): ACII 2005, LNCS 3784, pp. 795 – 802, 2005.

ing time. In this paper we analyzed the process of the approximation of class unions, proposed dominance-matrices and presented a new method for the approximation of class unions based on dominance-matrix. It simplified the process of calculation and decreased the computing time.

2 Dominance-Based Rough Set Approach

2.1 Data Representation

Data are often presented as a table, where columns are labeled by *criteria*, rows by *objects,* and entries of the table are *criterion values*. Formally, a decision table is the 4-tuple $S = \langle U, Q, V, f \rangle$, where U is a set of objects, Q is a finite set of criteria, $V = \bigcup_{q \in Q} V_q$, where V_q is the domain of the criteria q, and $f: U \times Q \rightarrow V$ is an information function such that $f(x,q) \in V_q$ for every $(x,q) \in U \times Q$. One of the elements of Q is the pre-defined decision criteria d, while the other plays the role of condition C (set $C \neq \phi$).

It is assumed that the domain of a criteria $q \in Q$ is completely preordered by an outranking relation $\succeq_q$; $x \succeq_q y$ means that x is at least so good as (outranks) y with respect to the criteria q[7].

The decision criteria d, the discrete domain of which will be denoted as $V_d = \{v_d^t, t \in T\}, T = \{1, ..., n\}$, produce a partition $Cl(d) = \{Cl_t, t \in T\}$ of U into a finite number of classed $Cl_t = \{x \in U : f(x,q) = v_d^t\}$. This kind of partitioning is called sorting. Each object $x \in U$ is assigned one and only one class $Cl_t \in Cl(d)$. The classes from $Cl(d)$ are preference-ordered according to an increasing order of class indices, i.e. for all $r, s \in T$, such $r > s$, the objects from Cl_r are strictly preferred to the objects from Cl_s. For this reason, we can consider the upward and downward unions of classed, which are defined as: $Cl_t^{\geq} = \bigcup_{s \geq t} Cl_s$, $Cl_t^{\leq} = \bigcup_{s \leq t} Cl_s, t \in T$. The statement $x \in Cl_t^{\geq}$ means "x belongs to at least class Cl_t", while $x \in Cl_t^{\leq}$ means "x belongs to at most class Cl_t".

2.2 Dominance Relation and Approximation of Class Unions

The dominance relation between objects is defined as follows. For a given decision table S, the object x is said to dominate the object y with respect to a set of criteria $P \subseteq C$, denotation $xD_P y$ if $x \succeq_q y, \forall q \in P$. For each $P \subseteq C$, the dominance relation D_P is reflexive and transitive, i.e. it is partial pre-order.

Given a $P \subseteq C$, the set of objects that dominate x, called P-dominating set, is defined as follows: $D_P^+(x) = \{y \in U : yD_P x\}$, and the set of objects that are dominated by x, called P-dominated set, is defined as follows: $D_P^-(x) = \{y \in U : xD_P y\}$.

The P-lower and the P-upper approximation of $Cl_t^{\geq}, t \in T$, with respect to $P \subseteq C$, are defined, respectively, as:

$\underline{P}(Cl_t^{\geq}) = \{x \in U : D_P^+(x) \subseteq Cl_t^{\geq}\}$, $\overline{P}(Cl_t^{\geq}) = \{x \in U : D_P^-(x) \cap Cl_t^{\geq} \neq \phi\}$.

Analogously, the P-lower and the P-upper approximation of $Cl_t^{\leq}, t \in T$, with respect to $P \subseteq C$, are defined, respectively, as:

$\underline{P}(Cl_t^{\leq}) = \{x \in U : D_P^-(x) \subseteq Cl_t^{\leq}\}$, $\overline{P}(Cl_t^{\leq}) = \{x \in U : D_P^+(x) \cap Cl_t^{\leq} \neq \phi\}$.

Finally, the P-boundaries of $Cl_t^{\geq}$ and $Cl_t^{\leq}$ are defined as:

$Bn(Cl_t^{\geq}) = \overline{P}(Cl_t^{\geq}) - \underline{P}(Cl_t^{\geq})$, $Bn(Cl_t^{\leq}) = \overline{P}(Cl_t^{\leq}) - \underline{P}(Cl_t^{\leq})$.

2.3 Definition of Decision Rules

The decision rules are expression of the form 'if [conditions], then [consequent]' that represent a form of dependency between condition and the decision criterion. Procedures for generating decision rules from a decision table use an inductive learning principle.

We can distinguish three types of rules: Certain, possible and approximate. Certain rules are generated from lower approximations of unions of classes; possible rules are generated from upper approximation of unions of lasses and approximate rules are generated from boundary regions.

1. $D_{\geq}$-decision rules, which have the following form:

$$\text{if } f(x,q_1) \geq r_{q1} \text{ and } f(x,q_2) \geq r_{q2} \text{ and} \cdots f(x,q_p) \geq r_{qp}, \text{ then } x \in Cl_t^{\geq}$$

where $P = \{q_1, q_2, \ldots, q_p\} \subseteq C$, $(r_{q1}, r_{q2}, \cdots, r_{qp}) \in V_{q1} \times V_{q2} \times \cdots \times V_{qp}$ and $t \in T$. We call it "at least" rules. These rules are supported only by objects from the P-lower approximations of the upward unions of classes $Cl_t^{\geq}$.

2. $D_{\leq}$-decision rules, which have the following form:

$$\text{if } f(x,q_1) \leq r_{q1} \text{ and } f(x,q_2) \leq r_{q2} \text{ and} \cdots f(x,q_p) \leq r_{qp}, \text{ then } x \in Cl_t^{\leq}$$

where $P = \{q_1, q_2, \ldots, q_p\} \subseteq C$, $(r_{q1}, r_{q2}, \cdots, r_{qp}) \in V_{q1} \times V_{q2} \times \cdots \times V_{qp}$ and $t \in T$. We call it "at most" rules. These rules are supported only by objects from the P-upper approximations of the downward unions of classes $Cl_t^{\leq}$.

3. $D_{\geq\leq}$-decision rules, which have the following form:

$if\ f(x,q_1)\geq r_{q1}\ and\ f(x,q_2)\geq r_{q2}\ and \cdots f(x,q_k)\geq r_{qk}\ and\ f(x,q_{k+1})\leq r_{qk+1}$ $and \cdots f(x,q_p)\leq r_{qp}, then\ x\in Cl_t \bigcup Cl_{t+1} \bigcup \cdots \bigcup Cl_s$,

where $O'=\{q_1,q_2,\cdots,q_k\}\subseteq C$, $O''=\{q_{k+1},q_{k+2},\cdots,q_p\}\subseteq C$, $P=O'\bigcup O''$, O' and O'' not necessarily disjoint, $(r_{q1},r_{q2},\cdots,r_{qp})\in V_{q1}\times V_{q2}\times\cdots\times V_{qp}$, $s,t\in T\ such\ that\ t<s$; these rules are supported by objects from the P-boundaries of the unions of classes $Cl_t^{\geq}$ and $Cl_t^{\leq}$.

3 Approximation of Class Unions Based on Dominance-Matrix

3.1 Formalization of the Problem

Approximations of class unions are defined as follows:

$$\underline{P}(Cl_t^{\geq})=\{x\in U: D_P^{+}(x)\subseteq Cl_t^{\geq}\}$$
$$\overline{P}(Cl_t^{\geq})=\{x\in U: D_P^{-}(x)\bigcap Cl_t^{\geq}\neq\phi\}=\bigcup_{x\in Cl_t^{\geq}} D_P^{+}(x)$$

$$\underline{P}(Cl_t^{\leq})=\{x\in U: D_P^{-}(x)\subseteq Cl_t^{\leq}\}$$
$$\overline{P}(Cl_t^{\leq})=\{x\in U: D_P^{+}(x)\bigcap Cl_t^{\leq}\neq\phi\}=\bigcup_{x\in Cl_t^{\leq}} D_P^{-}(x)$$

$$Bn(Cl_t^{\geq})=\overline{P}(Cl_t^{\geq})-\underline{P}(Cl_t^{\geq}) \qquad Bn(Cl_t^{\leq})=\overline{P}(Cl_t^{\leq})-\underline{P}(Cl_t^{\leq})$$

Before we can only use the original definition above to get the approximation of class unions. In order to simplify the process of calculation we give the dominance-matrix as in part 3.2.

3.2 Dominance-Matrix

$S=\langle U,Q,V,f\rangle$ is a decision system. Assume that it has n objects and m condition attributes.

$U=\{x_1,x_2,\ldots,x_n\}$, $Q=C\bigcup d$, C represents the condition criteria and d is the decision criteria.

Dominance-matrix is defined as follows.

There are two types of dominance-matrix: one for upward unions $Cl_t^{\geq}$ and the other for downward unions $Cl_t^{\leq}$.

$M(Cl^{\geq}) = [C_{i.j}]_{n \times n}$ is the dominance-matrix for upward unions.

where

$$C_{i,j} = \begin{cases} 1 & x_i D_C x_j \\ 0 & otherwise \end{cases} \quad (1)$$

Let us describe the matrix as: $M(Cl^{\geq}) = [C_{i.j}]_{n \times n} = [b_1, b_2, ..., b_n]$, b_i is the i column of the binary matrix and $b_i = [C_{1,i}, C_{2,i} ..., C_{n,i}]^{\tau}$, where τ represents the transposition of the vector.

Analogously, $M(Cl^{\leq}) = [C'_{i.j}]_{n \times n} = [b'_1, b'_2 ..., b'_n]$ is the dominance-matrix for downward unions.

where

$$C'_{i,j} = \begin{cases} 1 & x_j D_C x_i \\ 0 & otherwise \end{cases} \quad (2)$$

3.3 Approximation of Class Unions Based on Dominance-Matrix

Let us consider binary matrix which we get from the original decision system. For simplicity, here we only discuss the approximation of upward class unions $Cl^{\geq}$. The process of getting the one of downward class unions is analogical.

$M(Cl^{\geq}) = [C_{i.j}]_{n \times n} = [b_1, b_2, ..., b_n]$, for $Cl_t^{\geq}$ first we can find all the objects appearing in $Cl_t^{\geq}$, then setting all the corresponding rows in $M(Cl^{\geq})$ of the objects to zero we will get $M'(Cl^{\geq})$.(e.g. Assuming $Cl_t^{\geq} = \{x_1, x_3, x_5\}$, then we set the first, third and the fifth row of the matrix to zero) If there exist a column vector in $M'(Cl^{\geq})$ equal to zero vector, the corresponding object of the vector must be the member of $\underline{C}(Cl_t^{\geq})$. Finding all the column vectors in $M'(Cl^{\geq})$ equal to zero and their corresponding objects we will get the lower approximation $\underline{C}(Cl_t^{\geq})$. (e.g. The third column is equal to zero vector, then the corresponding object x_3 must be the member of the lower approximation).

In order to obtain the upper approximation of $Cl_t^{\geq}$ first we also need to find all the objects appearing in $Cl_t^{\geq}$ and their corresponding column vectors in the matrix $M(Cl^{\geq})$. Then adding them together we can get a column vector. The next we can find all the element not equal to zero in the column vector thus their corresponding objects are the upper approximation of $Cl_t^{\geq}$.

After obtaining the lower and upper approximation we can easily get the boundary according to the original definition.

4 Example

Now let us apply the example in [6] to analyze the approximation of class unions based on dominance-matrix. It is an example of evaluation in a high school proposed by Grabich (1994) [8]. The example concerns six students described by means of four attributes (see Table 1):

Table 1. Data table with examples for classification

student	A1	A2	A3	A4
S1	good	good	Bad	good
S2	medium	bad	Bad	bad
S3	medium	bad	Bad	good
S4	bad	bad	Bad	bad
S5	medium	good	good	bad
S6	good	bad	good	good

•A1, level in Mathematics •A2, level in Physics
•A3, level in Literature •A4, global evaluation (decision class)

Here we assume “good” is better than “medium” and “medium” is better than “bad”. Since only two classes (class “good”, $Cl_2 = \{S1, S3, S6\}$ and class “bad”, $Cl_1 = \{S2, S4, S5\}$) are considered, we have $Cl_1^{\leq} = Cl_1$ and $Cl_2^{\geq} = Cl_2$. $Cl_1^{\geq}$ and $Cl_2^{\leq}$ are equal to the universe so it is of no concern to consider it. As previously, $C = \{A_1, A_2, A_3\}$ and $D = \{A_4\}$.

Applying the original definition the C-lower approximations, the c-upper approximations and the C-boundaries of classes $Cl_1^{\leq}$ and $Cl_2^{\geq}$ are equal, respectively, to:

$$\underline{C}(Cl_1^{\leq}) = \{S4\},\ \overline{C}(Cl_1^{\leq}) = \{S2, S3, S4, S5\},\ Bn_C(Cl_1^{\leq}) = \{S2, S3, S5\}$$

$$\underline{C}(Cl_2^{\geq}) = \{S1, S6\},\ \overline{C}(Cl_2^{\geq}) = \{S1, S2, S3, S5, S6\},$$

$$Bn_C(Cl_2^{\geq}) = \{S2, S3, S5\}$$

The next we will calculate the C-lower approximations, the C-upper approximations and the C-boundaries based on dominance-matrix. Within our methodology first we can obtain the dominance-matrix. According to the definition in (1) and (2) we get dominance-matrices $M(Cl^{\geq})$ and $M(Cl^{\leq})$ as follows.

$$M(Cl^{\geq}) = \begin{array}{c|cccccc} & S1 & S2 & S3 & S4 & S5 & S6 \\ \hline S1 & 1 & 1 & 1 & 1 & 0 & 0 \\ S2 & 0 & 1 & 1 & 1 & 0 & 0 \\ S3 & 0 & 1 & 1 & 1 & 0 & 0 \\ S4 & 0 & 0 & 0 & 1 & 0 & 0 \\ S5 & 0 & 1 & 1 & 1 & 1 & 0 \\ S6 & 0 & 1 & 1 & 1 & 0 & 0 \end{array}$$

$$M(Cl^{\leq}) = \begin{array}{c|cccccc} & S1 & S2 & S3 & S4 & S5 & S6 \\ \hline S1 & 1 & 0 & 0 & 0 & 0 & 0 \\ S2 & 1 & 1 & 1 & 0 & 1 & 1 \\ S3 & 1 & 1 & 1 & 0 & 1 & 1 \\ S4 & 1 & 1 & 1 & 1 & 1 & 1 \\ S5 & 0 & 0 & 0 & 0 & 1 & 0 \\ S6 & 0 & 0 & 0 & 0 & 0 & 1 \end{array}$$

For $Cl_2^{\geq}$, $Cl_2^{\geq} = \{S1, S3, S6\}$ so setting corresponding row 1st,3rd and 6th row of $M(Cl^{\geq})$ to zero we get $M'(Cl^{\geq})$. Analogously, for $Cl_1^{\leq}$ setting 2nd, 4th and 5th row of $M(Cl^{\leq})$ to zero we get $M'(Cl^{\leq})$.

$$M'(Cl^{\geq}) = \begin{bmatrix} 0 & 0 & 0 & 0 & 0 & 0 \\ 0 & 1 & 1 & 1 & 0 & 0 \\ 0 & 0 & 0 & 0 & 0 & 0 \\ 0 & 0 & 0 & 1 & 0 & 0 \\ 0 & 1 & 1 & 1 & 1 & 0 \\ 0 & 0 & 0 & 0 & 0 & 0 \end{bmatrix} \qquad M'(Cl^{\leq}) = \begin{bmatrix} 1 & 0 & 0 & 0 & 0 & 0 \\ 0 & 0 & 0 & 0 & 0 & 0 \\ 1 & 1 & 1 & 0 & 1 & 1 \\ 0 & 0 & 0 & 0 & 0 & 0 \\ 0 & 0 & 0 & 0 & 0 & 0 \\ 0 & 0 & 0 & 0 & 0 & 1 \end{bmatrix}$$

In $M'(Cl^{\geq})$ the 1st and 2nd row are equal to zero so their corresponding objects S1 and S2 are members of $\underline{C}(Cl_2^{\geq})$. It is $\underline{C}(Cl_2^{\geq}) = \{S1, S6\}$. Analogously, $\underline{C}(Cl_1^{\leq}) = \{S4\}$.

For $Cl_2^{\geq}$, $Cl_2^{\geq} = \{S1, S3, S6\}$ so adding corresponding row 1st ,3rd and 6th row of $M(Cl^{\geq})$ together we get column vector $V = [2 \quad 1 \quad 1 \quad 0 \quad 1 \quad 2]^{\tau}$. The corresponding objects of element not equal to zero in V are S1, S2, S3, S5 and S6. So $\overline{C}(Cl_2^{\geq}) = \{S1, S2, S3, S5, S6\}$. Analogously, $\overline{C}(Cl_1^{\leq}) = \{S2, S3, S4, S5\}$.

According to the lower and upper approximation the C-boundaries can be calculated as $Bn_C(Cl_1^{\leq}) = \{S2, S3, S5\}$ and $Bn_C(Cl_2^{\geq}) = \{S2, S3, S5\}$. It is easy to see that result is the same as the one in [6]. So the approximation of class unions based on dominance-matrix is feasible and effective.

5 Conclusions

The task of approximating the classes unions is a very complex computational job. In this paper we proposed dominance-matrix and presented a new method for approximation of class unions based on dominance-matrix. It only needs to calculate the dominance-matrix and does not need to consider the preference relations one by one. The benefit is a considerable simplification of the process and much faster execution. Besides the calculation is very easy and intuitive. In the future we will try to apply dominance-matrix to obtain reducts and cores of the criteria.

References

1. Pawlak. Z. Rough sets. International Journal of Information & computer science, 11, 341-356,1982.
2. Pawlak. Z., Rough sets. Theoretical Aspects of Reasoning about Data. Kluwer Academic Publishers, Dordrecht, 1991.
3. Greco S., Matarazzo, B and Slowinski,R., Rough approximation of a preference relation by dominance relations. ICS Research report 16/96, Warsaw University of Technology, Warsaw, and 1996 in: European journal of Operational Research 117,62-83 1999.
4. Greco S., Matarazzo, B and Slowinski,R.,A new rough set approach to evaluation of bankrupt risk. In: Zopounidis, C.(ed.), Operational Tools in the management of Financial Risks. Kluwer, Doordrecht, 121-136, 1998.
5. Greco S., Matarazzo, B and Slowinski,R.Rough sets methodology for sorting problems in presence of multiple attributes and criteria. European Journal of Operational Research, 138,247-259, 2002.
6. Greco S., Matarazzo, B and Slowinski,R.,Rough sets theory for multicriteria decision analysis. European Journal of Operational Research,129, 1, 1-47, 2001.
7. Skowron A., Rauszer C., The discernibility matrices and functions in information system. In: Slowinski R. (ed.), Intelligent decision support. Handbook of Applications and Advances of the Rough Set Theory, Kluwer Academic Publishers, Dordrecht 331-362, 1992.
8. Grabish, M., 1994. Fuzzy integral in multicriteria decision making. Fuzzy Sets and System 89,279-298.

An Online Multi-stroke Sketch Recognition Method Integrated with Stroke Segmentation

Jianfeng Yin and Zhengxing Sun

State Key Lab for Novel Software Technology, Nanjing University, 210093, PR China
szx@nju.edu.cn

Abstract. In this paper a novel multi-stroke sketch recognition method is presented. This method integrates the stroke segmentation and sketch recognition into a single approach, in which both stroke segmentation and sketch recognition are uniformed as a problem of "fitting to a template" with a minimal fitting error, and a nesting Dynamic Programming algorithm is designed to accelerate the optimizing approach.

1 Introduction

Pen-based user interface is becoming increasingly significant because it is convenient, fast, and closer to human's t traditional communication way using pen and paper. Sketching is a primary way to use the pen-based user interface. A sketch-based user interface can provide not only the intelligent conceptualization environment for the users, but also an efficient way to edit, store and transport the sketches [1].

There has been a significant amount of research to date in various aspects of sketch-based user interfaces [2]. Obviously, sketch recognition is the most important part, because all of the attractive advantages of pen-based user interface can benefit peoples only after the sketches are recognized. Some of existing methods regard the strokes as the primitives of sketches [3][4][5]. Because the same sketch can be composed by different combination of strokes, this method is difficult to recognize multi-stroke sketches. The others recognize sketches based on stroke segmentation, which segment the strokes into primitives [6]. One of the problems of this kind method is that a small mistake of the stroke segmentation will result in a big error in recognition. Another problem is there's a conflict between the recognition accuracy and the speed. Statistical recognizers [7][8], which can do the recognition fast, don't have an accurate result, while graph recognizers can distinguish similar graphics, but the recognition time is too long to be accepted [9][10].

In this paper we will present a new multi-stroke sketch recognition method, which treats the stroke segmentation and sketch recognition as an optimizing problem and designs a nesting DP approach to combine this two parts into a single approach. To get recognition more accuracy and faster, we predigest the Attributed Relation Graph into an Ordered Topological Relation Chain (*OTRC*), and give out the similarity computing method for *OTRC*. The remainder of this paper is organized as follows. In section 2, the idea of proposed method is outlined Section 3 introduces our method in details. Some experiments are given in section 4and conclusions are made in the final Section.

J. Tao, T. Tan, and R.W. Picard (Eds.): ACII 2005, LNCS 3784, pp. 803 – 810, 2005.

2 Framework of Our Multi-stroke Sketch Recognition

Most of existing sketch recognition methods based on stroke segmentation treat the stroke segmentation and sketch recognition separately [6][10] as shown in **Fig. 1**(a). In this approach the sketch recognition is much dependent on stroke segmentation; a little mistake in stroke segmentation will cause a fatal error in sketch recognition.

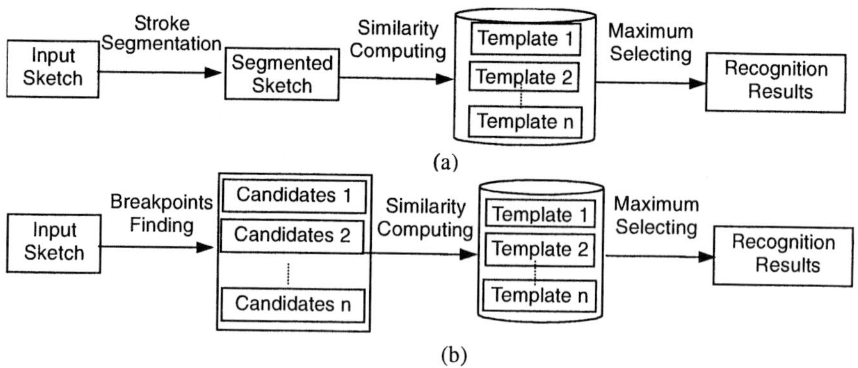

Fig. 1. Flow chart of traditional methods and our method

We believe that stroke segmentation and sketch recognition are dependent each other. A recognition approach needs the stroke be segmented, while the recognition result also can guide the segmentation approach [11]. **Fig. 1**(b) is the flow chart of our method. We do not give the segmentation result directly, but a set of candidate results, which will be calculated the similarity with the templates, and the one with the maximum similarity is the segmentation result, while the corresponding template is the recognition result.

The number of the candidate segmentation results is exponential in the size of candidate breakpoints, which we pick out using the traditional method such as pen speed and curvature. Obviously, an exhaustive search is a poor strategy and not practical for interactive applications. In this paper we present a polynomial time algorithm that is simple and optimal using a Dynamic Programming [12] approach.

3 Sketch Recognition Combining with Stroke Segmentation

3.1 Definition of Ordered Topologic Relation Chain

The best way to describe a graphic is using an Attributed Relation Graph, in which the nodes are the primitives of a graphic; the edges are the relations between two primitives and the length of the edges are the attributes of the relations. However, because matching of two graphs is an NPC problem, it is difficult to develop a time efficient sketch recognition method using *ARG*. We using the temporal information of the sketches and simplify the Attributed Relation Graph to Ordered Topologic Relation Chain. An *OTRC* is a chain that contains the ordered primitives and the topologic relations between two neighbored primitives. Before we define the *OTRC* we give some definitions about the primitives and topologic relations.

***Definition 1*:** Primitive set $\Sigma T=\{T_{Arc}, T_{Line}\}$. There are two types of primitives in our method: arcs (T_{Arc}) and lines (T_{Line}).

Definition 2*:** Attribute set of primitive $\Sigma TA=\{P_{start}, P_{end}, P_{Center}, a, b, delta\}$. P_{start} is the start point of the primitive. P_{end} is the end point of the primitive. P_{Center} is the center point of the primitive. a is the long axis of the ellipse which contains the primitive. b is the short axis of the ellipse which contains the primitive. ***delta is the rotate angle of the primitive in clockwise.

Definition 3: Topologic relation set of primitives $\Sigma R=\{R_{ICt}, R_{T1}, R_{T2r}, R_{ISr}, R_P, R_N\}$. There are 6 kinds of topologic relations in this paper that are shown in **Fig. 2**.

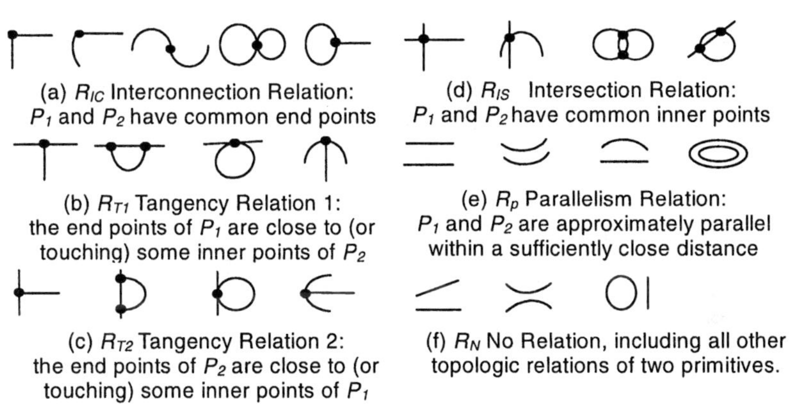

(a) R_{IC} Interconnection Relation: P_1 and P_2 have common end points
(d) R_{IS} Intersection Relation: P_1 and P_2 have common inner points
(b) R_{T1} Tangency Relation 1: the end points of P_1 are close to (or touching) some inner points of P_2
(e) R_p Parallelism Relation: P_1 and P_2 are approximately parallel within a sufficiently close distance
(c) R_{T2} Tangency Relation 2: the end points of P_2 are close to (or touching) some inner points of P_1
(f) R_N No Relation, including all other topologic relations of two primitives.

Fig. 2. Topologic relations of primitives

Definition 4: The set of attributes of relationship are $AR=(AR_{IC}, AR_{T1}, AR_{T2}, AR_{IS}, AR_P, AR_N)$. The attributes AR_{IC}, AR_{T1}, AR_{T2} and AR_{IS} are defined as the angle between the two primitives at the common point in clockwise, as shown in **Fig. 3**(a) and (b). If one of the two primitives is an arc segment, the angle can be calculated in terms of with a tangent line or a local chord at a common point on the arc, as shown in **Fig. 3**(c). The attribute of parallelism relationship AR_P is defined by the ratio of the length of the superposition part of the two primitives to the average length of them as shown in **Fig. 3**(d). The attribute AR_N. is set to null.

Definition 5: Ordered Topologic Relation Chain ***OTRC=(V, TV, AV, R, TR, AR)***. ***V*** is a set of primitives. ***TV*** is a set of primitive types. ***AV*** is a set of primitive attributes. ***R*** is a set of primitive topologic relations. ***TR*** is a set of primitive topologic relation types. ***AR*** is a set of primitive topologic relation attributes.

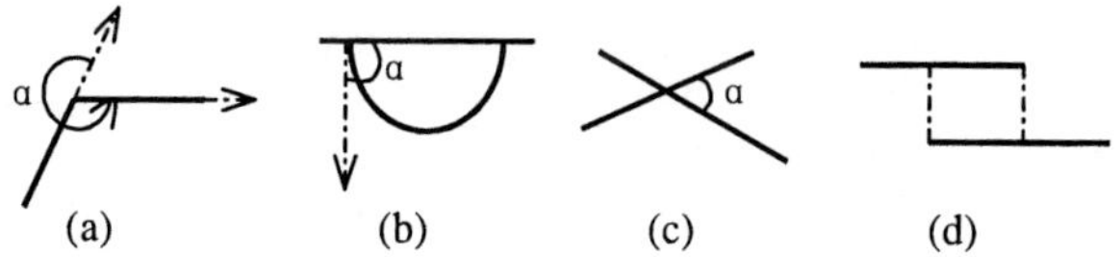

Fig. 3. Definition of attributes of primitives

An *OTRC* is a time ordered primitive list, which contains the types of the primitives and the topologic relations of every two neighboring primitives. The similarity between two *OTRC*s is a summation of the ordered primitive type similarity and primitive topologic relation similarity. The error between two *OTRC*s with the same amount of primitive is calculated like this:

$$f = \sum_{i=1}^{n} f_T(V[i], V'[i]) + \sum_{i=1}^{n-1} f_R(R[i], R'[i]) \qquad (1)$$

When n is the number of primitives, f_T computes the error between two primitive types while f_R computes the error between two topologic relations. We define f_T as fallows:

(i). If $T_{V1}=T_{Line}$, $T_{V2}=T_{Line}$, then $f_T = 0$;

(ii). If $T_{V1}=T_{Line}$, $T_{V2}=T_{Arc}$, then $f_T(V_1,V_2)=\frac{d}{l+d}$, as shown in **Fig. 4**(a).

(iii). If $T_{V1}=T_{Arc}$, $T_{V2}=T_{Arc}$, then $f_T(V_1,V_2)=\frac{|\alpha-\beta|}{\alpha+\beta}$, as shown in **Fig. 4**(b).

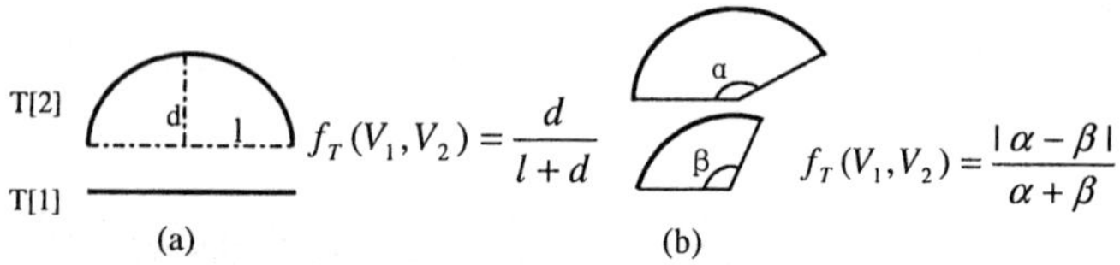

T[2] d l $f_T(V_1,V_2)=\frac{d}{l+d}$ α β $f_T(V_1,V_2)=\frac{|\alpha-\beta|}{\alpha+\beta}$

T[1]

(a) (b)

Fig. 4. Primitive similarity calculating

f_R is defined as fallows:

(i). If $T_{R1} \neq T_{R2}$, then $f_R=1$;

(ii). If $T_{R1}=T_{R2}=R_{IC}$, then $f_R = |(R_1.Angle - R_2.Angle|)/2*\pi$;

(iii). If $T_{R1}=T_{R2}$ and $T_{R1}= R_{T1}, R_{T2}, R_{IC}$ or R_P, then $f_R = |(R_1.Angle - R_2.Angle)| \big/ \frac{\pi}{2}$;

(iv). If $T_{R1}=T_{R2}=R_P$, then
$f_R = |(R_1.\text{superposition} - R_2.\text{superposition})|/(R_1.\text{superposition} + R_2.\text{superposition})$;

(v). If $T_{R1}=T_{R2}=R_N$, then $f_R = \frac{1}{2}$.

3.2 Sketch Based on Ordered Templates Using DP

The problem of stroke segmentation is an optimization problem in which the goal is to minimize the error from fitting a shape with basis elements by identifying an optimal set of breakpoints. And if we replace the fitting error by the product OTRC similarity and approximate similarity, we will get the most similar template to the input sketch that is the recognition result, as well as the segmentation result. Suppose k breakpoints are needed to fragment S into T, a brute force approach would do an exhaustive search on all combinations of k breakpoints. This approach requires testing C_m^k sets of breakpoints, where m is the total number of data points in S. The number of combinations is exponential in the size of m, and therefore this exhaustive search method is a poor strategy and not practical for use in interactive applications. Below, we describe a polynomial time algorithm that is simple and optimal using a DP approach. To simplify the problem we calculate the error between input sketch and the template not the similarity.

Given a sketched symbol S and a template T, find a set of breakpoints in S such that the fitting performed according to T yields the minimum error. The sketched symbol S consists of a sequence of strokes $\{S_1, S_2, \ldots, S_N\}$ and each stroke S_i contains a sequence of timed-ordered candidate breakpoints $\{P_{i1}, P_{i2}, \ldots, P_{iM}\}$, the number of candidate breakpoints in stroke n is Ln. The template T is a string of L's and E's. The number of breakpoints is K=$T.len$-N, where $T.len$ is the number of basis fragments in T, and N is the total number of strokes. The algorithm requires symbols to contain fewer strokes than the number of basis elements to fit.

Let $d(n,m,k,t,j)$ be the minimum fitting error to approximate every point up to the mth point in the nth stroke with the template t, and let $f(S_n, m, l, t[i], j)$ be the error resulting from comparing the segment from P_{nm} to P_{nl} using $t[i]$, and j is the index of primitive I the template used last time. The best fragmentation for S with N strokes using K breakpoints and a template T would thus be $d(1, 1, K, T\square 0)$. $d(n,m,k,t,j)$ is defined as follows.

$$d(n,m,k,t,j)=\begin{cases} [\sum_{i=1}^{n-1} f(S_i,1,Li,t[i])]+f(S_n,1,Ln,t[n]) & k=0 \\ \min\limits_{m<i<Ln-k}\{f(S_n,m,i,t[j+1],j)+d(n,i,k-1,t,j+1)\} & n=1,k>0 \\ \min\begin{Bmatrix} f(S_n,m,Ln,t[j+1],j)+d(n-1,1,k,t,j+1), \\ \min\limits_{m<i<Ln-k}\{f(S_n,m,i,t[j+1],j)+d(n,i,k-1,t,j+1)\} \end{Bmatrix} & n>1,k>0 \end{cases} \quad (2)$$

When k=0, each of the strokes is fit with the corresponding basis in the template and the segment from P_{i0} to P_{im} in the nth stroke is compared with the ith primitive in the template. When n=1 and k>0, a choice has to be made on a point P_{ni} to be the breakpoint and i>k, otherwise the number of breakpoints required would exceed the number of data points available. When n>1 and k>0, in addition to checking the best breakpoint to use in S_n, the following stroke (S_{n+1}) must also be checked because it is possible that the best breakpoint may lie in any of the following strokes. Due to the optimal substructure, the optimal fragmentation for the last point in the following stroke S_{n+1} is all that must be checked.

In the formula we presented last, $f(S_n, m, l, t[j+1], j)$ contains not only the approximating error but also the matching error, when *m, l* are the indexes of candidate breakpoints in stroke, *t[i]* is *i*th primitive in template *t*, *j* is the index of primitive last used. $f(S_n, m, l, t[i], j)$ is defined as follow:

$$f(S_n, m, l, t[i], j) = \begin{cases} f_T(S_n, m, l, t[i]) * f_A(S_n, m, l, t[i]) & j = 0 \\ (f_T(S_n, m, l, t[i]) + f_R(S_n, m, l, R_{i,j})) * f_A(S_n, m, l, t[i]) & j > 0 \end{cases} \quad (3)$$

f_T and f_R are defined in last section and f_A is approximate error. The algorithm has a run time complexity of $O(K \times M^2)$ where *K* is the number of breakpoints and *M* is the total number of data points. The space requirement is $O(K \times M)$ for keeping a table of solutions to the sub-problems.

3.3 Sketch Recognition Based on Unordered Templates Using Nesting DP

If the basis ordering information is not known, the fragmentation problem becomes more complex. In a naïve approach, the algorithm presented in the previous section could be applied to each combination of the basis elements. The combination that yields the least fit error is selected as the optimal fragmentation of the sketched shape. For a template consisting *n* primitives, there are a total of *n!* number of orderings. This number is exponential in the size of n. Using DP, this problem can be solved in polynomial time. This result is more efficient than using DP to solve all *n!* combinations, since the solutions to each of the overlapping sub-problems is only computed once. Follow formal shows a recursive solution based on DP for optimal fragmentation of the set of strokes.

$$d(n, m, k, t, j) =$$

$$\begin{cases} f(S_n, m, Ln, t[1], j) & t.Len = 1, k = 0 \\ \min\limits_{0<u<T.Len+1} \{f(S_n, m, Ln, t[u], j) + d(n+1, 1, k, t - t[u], t[u]index)\} & t.Len > 1, k = 0 \\ \min\limits_{0<u<t.Len+1} \{ \min\limits_{m<v<Ln-k} \{f(S_n, m, v, t[u], j) + d(n, v, k-1, t - t[u], t[u]index)\}\} & n = 1, k > 0 \\ \min\limits_{0<u<t.Len+1} \left\{ \min \begin{Bmatrix} f(S_n, m, Ln, t[u], j) + d(n+1, 1, k, t - t[u], t[u]index) \\ \min\limits_{m<v<Ln-k} \{f(S_n, m, v, t[u], j) + d(n, v, k-1, t - t[u], t[u]index)\} \end{Bmatrix} \right\} & n > 1, k > 0 \end{cases} \quad (4)$$

4 Experiments and Discussion

Our target class of application for this work composes four shapes, which is shown in **Fig. 5**. Shape *a* and *b* are similar to each other, they are used to test the ability of our method to distinguish similar shapes. Shape *c* is a moderate complex shape, which is composed by different kinds of primitives and relations. Shape *d* is a complex shape with 9 primitives. It is used to verify the time efficiencies of our method.

We have implemented our algorithms and tested them on user-sketched symbols collected from 4 users. Each user was asked to sketch 100 examples for each of the 4 shapes. The data set contains a total of 1,600 examples overall and about 400 examples per shape. The template library is consisted by 150 shapes, in which there 20 simple shapes, 96 moderate complex shapes, and 34 complex shapes. The experiment data is got from a PC with a Pentium 2.8G CPU and 512M memory. The result is shown in **Table 1**. The square points marked in input sketches are candidate breakpoints, in which the dark points are the breakpoints found out by our method. We can see that all of the four different target shapes are recognized correctly. The different stroke combination of shape *d* have got different recognition results, that's because we use all of the possible segmentation result to compare with the templates, and different segmentation will get the maximum similarity with different templates.

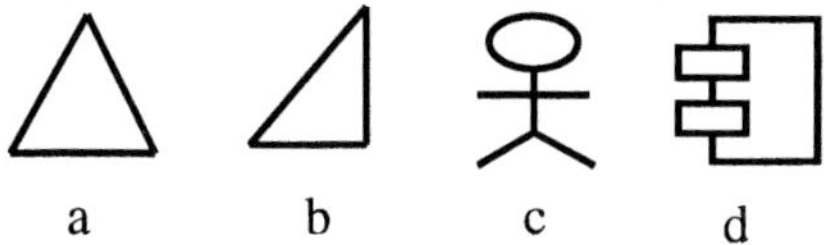

Fig. 5. Four types of shapes for our experiments

Table 1. Recognition result

	Input	Number of strokes, primitives and candidates	Recognition result (ordered by similarity)	Time spent
Simple shapes, less than 3 primitives		1, 3, 2		7.8 ms
		1, 3, 2		7.9 ms
Moderate complex shapes, 4~8 primitves		5, 5, 0		92.5 ms
		4, 5, 3		123.6 ms
Complex shapes, more than 8 primitves		13,13, 0		294.3 ms
		4, 13, 13		466.5 ms

It takes about 10 ms to recognize a simple shape, while moderate complex shape needs about 150ms and complex shape needs less than 500ms. The time spent for reorganization much depends on the number of primitives, and the number of candidate breakpoints, that's why the different stroke combination of the same shape has different recognition time. However, because sketching is more usually used in conceptive design and outline description, one single sketch will hardly be much complex, or the traditional CAD tools maybe more helpful. For shape *a* and *b*, our algorithms achieved 98% accuracy rate. For shape *c* and *d*, the accuracy rate is higher than 95%.

5 Conclusion

Our method treats the stroke segmentation and sketch recognition as an optimizing approach to find the combination of breakpoints and template with the minimum matching error, and uses a DP approach to integrate the two parts into a single approach. Also, DP approach is used to accelerate the optimizing approach. The experiment shows that our algorithm can provide high accurate recognition results as well as acceptable online recognition speed.

Acknowledgement

This paper is supported by the grants from the National Natural Science Foundation of China [Project No. 69903006 and 60373065] and the Program for New Century Excellent Talents in University of China (2004).

References

1. Hearst, M.A., Gross, M.D., Landay, J.A. and Stahovich, T.F. Sketching Intelligent Systems. IEEE Intelligent System, 3 (3). 10-19.
2. Landay, J.A. and Myers, B.A. Sketching Interfaces: Toward More Human Interface Design. IEEE Computer, 34 (3). 56-64.
3. Lee S. W. and Kim Y. J. A New Type of Recurrent Neural Network for Handwritten Character Recognition. Proc. 3rd International Conference on Document Analysis and Recognition, Vol. 1, 1995.
4. Rubine, D. Specifying gestures by example. Computer Graphics 25:329–337, 1991.
5. Kimura, T. D. Apte, A. and Sengupta, S. A graphic diagram editor for pen computers. Software Concepts and Tools 82–95, 1994.
6. Chris Calhoun, Thomas F. Stahovich, Tolga Kurtoglu, et al, Recognizing Multi-Stroke Symbols. AAAI Spring Symposium on Sketch Understanding. AAAI Press (2002).
7. Fonseca, M.J., Pimentel, C. and Jorge, J.A., CALI: An Online Scribble Recognizer for Calligraphic Interfaces. In 2002 AAAI Spring Symposium - Sketch Understanding, (Palo Alto CA, 2002), AAAI Press, 51-58. 24 (7). 643-152.
8. Ulgen, F., Flavell, A. and Akamatsu, N. Recognition of On-Line Handdrawn Geometric Shapes by Fuzzy Filtering and Neural Network Classification. in HCI International '95, (1995) 567-572.
9. Li C., Yang B., and Xie W. On-line Hand-sketched Graphics Recognition Based on Attributed Relation Graph Matching. Proc. 3rd world congress on intelligent control and automation, pp.2549-2553, Hefei, China, 2000.
10. Xu X G, Sun Z X, Peng B B, et al. An online composite graphics recognition approach based on matching of spatial relation graphs. IJDAR (2004).
11. Sun Z X, Yin J F, Yuan B, A novel approach for sketchy shape recognition, Proceedings of GREC2005, Hong Kong, China, (2005).
12. Bellman R.E. Dynamic Programming. Princeton University Press, 1957.

A Model That Simulates the Interplay Between Emotion and Internal Need

Xiaoxiao Wang, Jiwei Liu, and Zhiliang Wang

College of Information and Engineering,
University of Science and Technology of Beijing,
100083 Beijing, China
2004wangxiao@sohu.com

Abstract. This paper proposes an emotion model that simulates the interplay between emotion and internal need of human being which influence human intelligence activities. The model includes emotion, internal need and decision modules. The aim of the model is to explore the role of emotion-like processes in intelligent machines. Simulations are conducted to test the performance of the emotion model.

1 Introduction

It has been generally acknowledged that emotions are essential in human intelligence. A.Damasio's [1] patients who appear to be intelligent, and unusually rational suffer from an impaired ability to make decisions. A.Sloman [2] has for many years argued that intelligent machines will necessarily experience emotion states. Also, importance of emotion for intelligent machines was emphasized by R.Picard [3], [4].

There have been several attempts to model emotion in software agents and other intelligent machines. C.Breazeal [5] proposed robot architectures with a motivational system that associates motivations with both drives and emotions. In the work of T.Fukuda *et al.* [6], [7], an emotional autonomous agent model applied to a virtual autonomous agent. El Jed Mehdi *et al.* [8] developed an emotional model that can be integrated into characters in an interactive virtual reality environment. This model describes the relationship between emotion, mood and personality. Zhehua Wei *et al.*'s [9] work described an emotion model applied to virtual human techniques. Our approach differs from theirs in that it focuses on the interplay between emotion and internal need.

To explore the role of emotion-like processes in intelligent machines, we attempt to construct a model that serves the same useful functions of emotion and internal need in living creatures. Further research is required to integrate the model to autonomous agents to enable them interact with human being in an appropriate and expressive way.

2 Structure of the Model

We agree with some psychologists: emotion is the result of a subjective measurement of the probability of survival of the organism in a given situation [10]. Many

J. Tao, T. Tan, and R.W. Picard (Eds.): ACII 2005, LNCS 3784, pp. 811 – 818, 2005.

researchers believe that each emotion expresses a quantity or magnitude in a positive/negative scale. We consider that emotions are positive when the situation seems to favor organism's survival and they tend to be negative when the situation seems to be unfavorable for its survival.

To give the definition of internal need, we must tell the difference between the concept of emotion and motivation. Emotion and motivation both depend on the relationship between the organism and its environment. In the case of emotion, the emphasis is on the evaluative aspect of this relationship: how the situation makes the person feel; in the case of motivation, it is how the individual acts with respect to the situation that is of interest [11]. We agree with S.Dworkin [12]: need are internal sources of motivation. Hence, we define internal need as some physiological and psychological needs which should be satisfied. In our model, the value of positive emotions increases when internal need is satisfied, while the value of negative emotions decreases. Similarly, the opposite is possible when the internal need is not satisfied.

The internal need is satisfied by executing a series of actions in the model. We agree with some psychologists: people often do things because they anticipate that they will make them feel better in some way [13]. Therefore, the principle of action selecting is to select the action which contributes to increase in satisfaction of internal need.

The model includes emotion, internal need and decision modules. Figure 1. represents the structure of the emotion model.

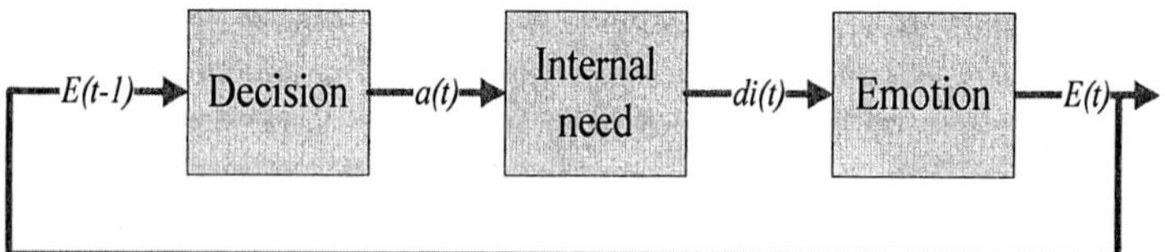

Fig. 1. Structure of the model

The decision module undertakes the selection of actions which change the satisfaction of internal need. $a(t)$ describes the action selected by decision module at moment t. The internal need module computes the satisfaction of internal need according to the output of decision module. $di(t)$ denotes the difference between the satisfaction of internal need at moment t and that at moment $t-1$. The emotion module determines the emotion state $E(t)$. To select the action $a(t)$, $E(t-1)$ is conveyed to decision module. The meaning of some variables mentioned above is explained at some length in the ensuing chapters.

3 Emotion Module

We adopt the emotional categories proposed by R.Plutchik [14]. We use a set of discrete variables to characterize the emotion. These variables are made up of several pairs of opposites. We group joy, acceptance etc into positive emotion variables. The opposites are negative emotion variables. This paper supposes that all sets of variables consist of k values. We define *e(t)* as the emotion value at moment t. *e(t)* is an m-dimensional vector where all m emotion intensities are represented by a value in the interval [0, 1]. $e(t) = [e^1, e^2, ... e^m]$. The intensity of emotion value decrease by the rate of *decr(e)*. We multiply each dimension of emotion value by k and rejects decimal fractions of these outputs. The outcome is defined as emotion state, denoted by *E(t)*. $E(t) = [E^1, E^2, ... E^m]$. All emotion states comprise emotion space. We define $dis(E_i(t), E_j(t))$ as the emotion distance between emotion states $E_i(t)$ and $E_j(t)$.

$$dis(E_i(t), E_j(t)) = \sqrt{(E_i^1 - E_j^1)^2 + (E_i^2 - E_j^2)^2 + ... + (E_i^m - E_j^m)^2} \qquad (1)$$

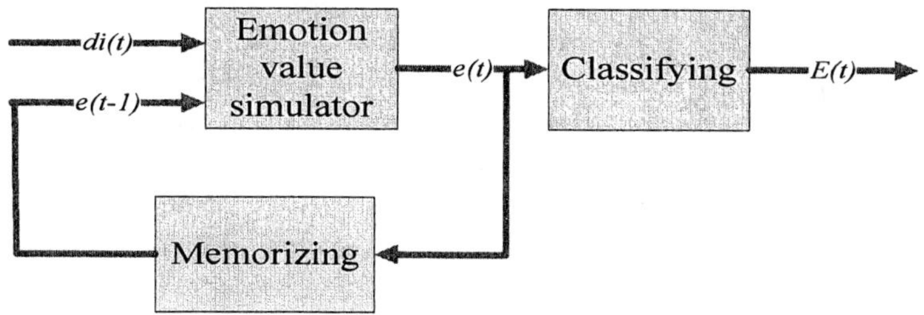

Fig. 2. Structure of the emotion module

In order to describe the influence of the internal needs on the emotion variables, we define a M_{ie} $(n \times m)$ matrix which associates a weight of every internal need with every dimension of the emotion value. The satisfaction of certain internal needs lead to the increase in values of several positive emotion variables. Furthermore, those values which represent the influence of internal need on the opposite emotion variables are opposite numbers. *de(t)* is the difference between *e(t)* and *e(t-1)* caused by *di(t)*. The computation is made according to the following formula:

$$de(t) = di(t) \cdot Mie \qquad (2)$$

e(t) is calculated as follows:

$$e(t) = e(t-1) + de(t) - decr(e) \qquad (3)$$

e(t-1) denotes the emotion value at moment *t-1* which is stored in the memorizing block. As a last step, the intensity vector *e(t)* is passed through a sigmoid function to confine all the elements of emotion value to a value from zero to one. The classifying block realizes the transformation from emotion value to emotion state.

4 Internal Need Module

We represent the satisfaction of internal need at moment t as an n-dimensional vector *i(t)* where n represents the dimensions of the internal need. All the elements in *i(t)* are in the interval [0, 1]. It decreases over time by the rate of *decr(i)*. We define *di(t)* as the difference between *i(t)* and *i(t-1)* caused by *a(t)*. Also, we consider that every dimension of *i(t)* is influenced by action vector *a(t)* produced by decision module. The influence is represented in the $M_{ai}(l \times n)$ matrix by a value in the interval [-1, 1]. If the elements of *e(t)* reached extreme value, the addition (subtraction) operation would stop. *di(t)* and *i(t)* are computed by the following equations:

$$di(t)=a(t)\cdot Mai \tag{4}$$

$$i(t)= i(t-1)+ di(t)-decr(i) \tag{5}$$

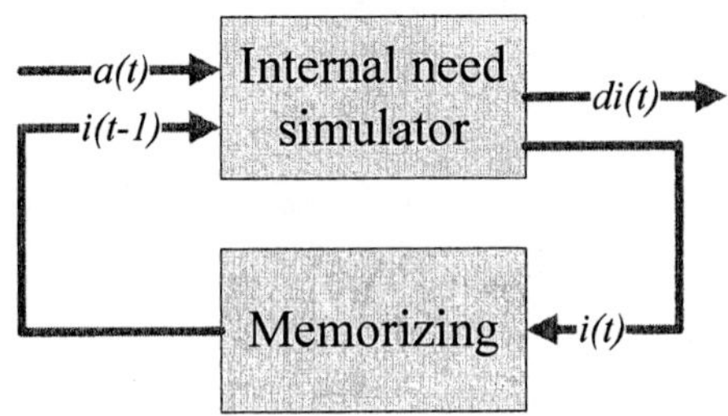

Fig. 3. Structure of the internal need module

5 Decision Module

We define the action taken at moment *t* as an *l*-dimension vector *a(t)*, where each element represents an action. If the decision module chooses an *action* at moment *t*, the value of the corresponding element in *a(t)* is 1 and values of the remainder are all 0. The action selecting block chooses *a(t)* according to *E(t)* and *f*. *f* which means a mapping from *E(t)* to *a(t)* is produced by policy computing block.

To represent the influence of action on internal need, we define reward as the satisfaction of internal need caused by certain action. Consequently the model prefers to select actions which obtain higher reward. Since satisfaction of internal need influences emotion value, emotions may thus serve partly as rewards for selected action.

How to select the action at decision moment? To obtain a lot of reward, the model should prefer actions that it has tried in the past and found to be effective in producing reward. But to discover which actions these are it has to select actions that it has not tried before. Greedy strategy is a simple method of action selecting. When the model visits an emotion state, the decision module selects the action with the highest rewards for that state–action pair. Therefore in the event of that action producing a high immediate reward, the updating mechanism causes the agent to be partial to that action.

However, this can cause considerable trouble in obtaining the most reward because the short-term effect of an action can be misleading. Therefore occasionally the decision module has to divert from its policy of selecting the most preferred action and instead select some other action.

We believe that markov decision process is useful for solving this problem. Markov decision processes are models for sequential decision making under uncertainty, which take into account both immediate and long-term consequences of decisions [15]. Formally, a markov decision process model is a tuple (*T, X, A, P, r*), where: *T* is a set of decision moments; *X* is a set of stochastic state variables; *A* is a set of available actions; *P* is a set of transition probability matrixes; *r* is a reward function. A policy is defined as a procedure for selecting an action in each state. When $c = E(t) \in X$ characterizes the emotion state at moment $t \in T$, selection of action $a \in A$ will result in a transition to state *c'* at moment *t+1* with probability $p(c' | c, a)$.

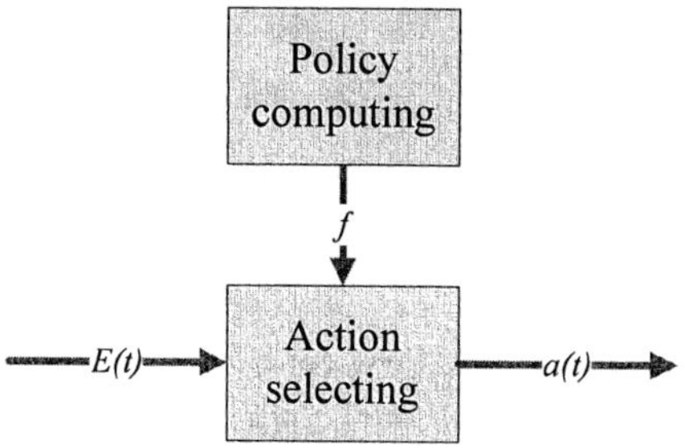

Fig. 4. Structure of decision module

How can we get transition probability matrix *P*? Given the fact as follows:1) Without any influence of action, the intensity of all emotion variables decreases over time.2) At next time, the transition probability of emotion state coming to itself is biggest among other states. Other transition probability is inversely proportional to emotion distance (see Sect. 3.1) between the two states. It is difficult to compute transition probability directly. We try to its approximate solution by numerical method.

We define reward function denoted by *r(E,a)* as a function whose independent variables are *E(t)* and *a(t)*. After we get the transition probability matrix, we can calculate the policy *f*. We adopt infinite-stage average cost model and find the solution of policy by value iteration algorithm [16].

The policy is computed according to the following iteration formula:

$$R^*(i) = \max_{a \in A_i} \left(r(E,a) + \sum_{j \in S} p(j | i, a) R^*(j) \right) \tag{6}$$

$$f(i) \in \arg\max_{a \in A_i} \left\{ r(E,a) + \sum_{j \in S} p(j | i, a) R^*(j) \right\} \tag{7}$$

6 Simulation

6.1 Description of the Simulation

In this section, we describe a simulation to test the proposed emotion model. The proposed model was implemented as a program under the MATLAB development environment. In the experiments, we suppose emotion variables are comprised of joy and sadness. The important consideration is the reduction in computation.

In the simulation, the three actions *sleeping*, *eating*, and *recreating*, can influence the value of the three internal need variables *rest*, *energy*, *entertainment*.

At first, the value of the emotion value joy and sadness are all randomly set in [0, 1]. The action *sleeping* leads to increase in the satisfaction of internal need *rest*, while reduces the value of satisfaction of internal need *entertainment* and *energy*. The action *eating* satisfies the internal need *energy*, while results in some decrease in satisfaction of other internal needs. The action *recreating* contributes to increase in internal need *entertainment* and brings about decrease in satisfaction of other internal needs.

Sampling moment is defined as the time which the model selected one action and updated its emotion state and satisfaction of internal need. The simulation stopped when it reached the 100th sampling moment.

6.2 Result

Figure 5 demonstrates the change of emotion value. The peak figure for emotion value of joy was nearly 0.7 at the first sampling moment of the simulation. Then the figure kept decreasing, reaching a low point around 0.5 at the 19th sampling moment. This shows the fact that the intensity of emotions decreases over time. Then the figure jumped back up to 0.55. It sank back to 0.5 after a few sampling moments. The emotion value fluctuation reflects the influence of action. That is to say, the model selected actions which kept the positive emotion in a relative high value timely. It is also noteworthy that the figure for emotion sadness never exceeded 0.4. This is because the model selected actions which prevented the value of negative emotion from reaching a high level.

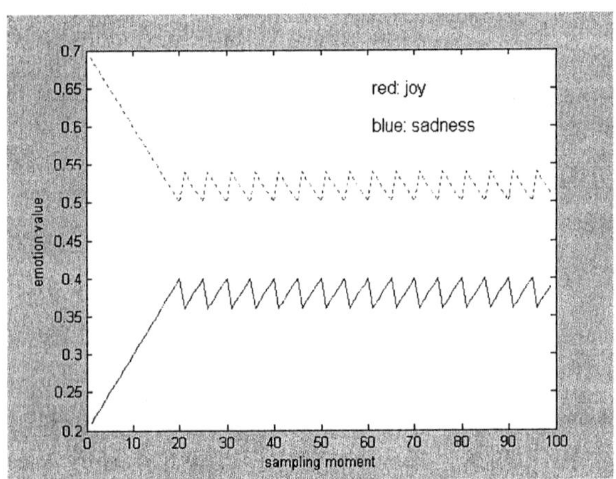

Fig. 5. Horizontal coordinate fixes positions of *sampling moment* and vertical coordinate fixes positions of *emotion value*. There are 100 *sampling moments* in all. The red line represents the intensity of emotion joy, while the blue one represents the intensity of emotion sadness.

Owing to some simplifying assumptions that have been made, the proposed model is rather shallow. Despite its simplicity, the model proves to be capable to provide believable simulations and it is suitable under the circumstances requiring real-time performance.

7 Future Work

Our intent is not to validate the emotional model by itself (so many arbitrary parameters) but to explore the role of emotion-like processes in intelligent machines. Further research is required to investigate extensions to the basic model form proposed here. For instance, the computation of transition probability grows exponentially with the complexity of the model. We plan to compute the probabilities in more efficient exact solution method as well as approximation scheme. Furthermore, the interaction between emotion model and external stimuli are needed to enable the model to be used in autonomous agents. A next step in the current line of research would be to design an autonomous agent that uses the proposed model.

Acknowledgements

The investigations were (partly) supported by the key Lab named Advanced information Science and Network Technology of Beijing (No.TDXX0503) and the key foundation of USTB.

References

1. A. Damasio: Descartes Error: Emotion, Reason, and the Human Brain. New York: G.P. Putnam, 1994.
2. A. Sloman, M. Croucher: "Why robots will have emotions," Proceedings of IJCAI7, pp. 197-202, 1987.
3. R. Picard: Affective Computing. MIT press, 1997.
4. R. Picard: "Affective computing: challenges," Int. J. Human-Computer Studies, vol. 59, pp. 55-64, 2003.
5. C. Breazeal: "Function meets style: insights from emotion theory applied to HRI," Systems, Man and Cybernetics, Part C, IEEE Transactions on, vol. 34, pp. 187-194, 2004.
6. O. Popovici Vlad, T. Fukuda: "Model based emotional status simulation," Robot and Human Interactive Communication, 2002. Proceedings. 11th IEEE International Workshop on, pp. 93-98, 2002.
7. O. Popovici Vlad, G. Vachkov, T. fukuda: "fuzzy emotion interpolation system for emotional autonomous agents," SICE 2002. Proceedings of the 41st SICE Annual Conference, vol. 5, pp. 3157-3162, 2002.
8. El Jed Mehdi *et al*: "Modeling character emotion in an interactive virtual environment," Groupe de Recherche en Ing´enierie Cognitive - Institut de Recherche en Informatique de Toulouse. (available at http://www.irit.fr/GRIC/ER/emo.pdf)
9. Zhehua Wei *et al*: "The research of artificial psychology model," TENCON '02. Proceedings. 2002 IEEE Region 10 Conference on Computers, Communications, Control and Power Engineering, vol. 1, pp. 691-694, 2002.
10. Available at http://www.biopsychology.org/biopsychology/papers/what_is_emotion.htm.

11. Available at http://www.le.ac.uk/psychology/amc/lepsemot.html.
12. S. Dworkin: "Drives, Needs and Awareness," (available at http://people.uncw.edu/dworkins/psy418s05ppt/Chapter08.ppt)
13. R. Thayer *et al*: "Self-regulation of mood: strategies for changing a bad mood, raising energy, and reducing tension," Journal of Personality and Social Psychology, vol. 67, pp. 910-925, 1994.
14. Available at http://library.thinkquest.org/25500/index2.htm.
15. K. Aström: "Optimal control of Markov processes with incomplete state information," Journal of Mathematical Analysis and Applications, vol. 10, pp. 174-205, 1965.
16. A. Gosavi: "Reinforcement learning for long-run average cost," European Journal of Operational Research, vol. 155, pp. 654-674, 2004.

Affective Dialogue Communication System with Emotional Memories for Humanoid Robots

M.S. Ryoo*, Yong-ho Seo, Hye-Won Jung, and H.S. Yang

Artificial Intelligence and Media Laboratory,
Department of Electrical Engineering and Computer Science,
Korea Advanced Institute of Science and Technology,
373-1, Guseong-dong, Yuseong-gu, Daejeon, 305-701, Republic of Korea
{mryoo, yhseo, hwjung, hsyang}@kaist.ac.kr

Abstract. Memories are vital in human interactions. To interact sociably with a human, a robot should not only recognize and express emotions like a human, but also share emotional experience with humans. We present an affective human-robot communication system for a humanoid robot, AMI, which we designed to enable high-level communication with a human through dialogue. AMI communicates with humans by preserving emotional memories of users and topics, and it naturally engages in dialogue with humans. Humans therefore perceive AMI to be more human-like and friendly. Thus, interaction between AMI and humans is enhanced.

1 Introduction

Affective computing is becoming a more important research issue in the area of robotics. Several studies in robotics have been conducted to enable affective interaction between humans and robots [1,2,3]. However, most studies have focused only on primitive interactions, such as facial expressions or body movements. A sociable robot that can naturally interact with humans must be capable of high-level interaction; that is, it must be able to communicate with humans in the form of dialogue. Thus, the robot must be able to synthesize its emotion and express it in a dialogue. Our research enables robots to have high-level dialogue similar to the conversational robot Mel, who attempted to converse with humans [4]. However, Mel ignored the emotions and multimodality of human-robot communication. Our goal is to design and implement a sociable robot that can affectively interact with humans through dialogue.

The major improvement in our framework is the construction of a memory system that stores explicit emotional memories of past events. The literature from cognitive science and neuroscience suggests that emotional memories are vital when the human brain synthesizes emotions [5]. While previous research on sociable robots either ignores the emotional memory or maintains the emotional memory implicitly in high-level interaction, we need to establish explicit memories of emotions, events, and concepts. We have therefore adopted the concept of emotional memory for our

* Current address: CVRC, University of Texas at Austin. mryoo@mail.utexas.edu.

J. Tao, T. Tan, and R.W. Picard (Eds.): ACII 2005, LNCS 3784, pp. 819 – 827, 2005.

humanoid robot. Our memory system maintains explicit memories of previous emotional events. Thus, the emotional system can synthesize emotions on the basis of emotional memories.

In this project, we have developed a general affective dialogue system for a social humanoid robot named AMI. To enable affective dialogue interactions, we constructed an emotional memory system for our framework. The memory system comprises five subsystems: namely, perception, motivation, memory, behavior, and expression. In the perception system, we implemented a bimodal emotion recognizer for recognizing emotions. To ensure AMI can respond appropriately to the emotional status of users and itself, we designed subsystems that use their own drive, emotions, and memory.

2 System Overview

Motivated the human brain structure discovered by cognitive scientist [5], we have designed the framework for our sociable humanoid robot. We designed the affective communication framework to include the five subsystems shown in Fig. 1. Our framework is similar to the creature kernel framework for synthetic characters [6]. The same framework was also applied to the software architecture of Kismet [1]. However, since our goal is to enable dialogue interactions, we improved the framework so that our robot can preserve explicit memories. Thus, our system has two major benefits over older systems.

Memory System. We added a memory system to the referred framework. The memory system enables AMI to represent, and reflect upon, itself and its human partners. It also enhances AMI's social skills and fosters communication with humans. To enable affective interaction between AMI and humans, we enabled AMI to preserve its emotional memory of users and topics.

Dialogue Interaction. Other affective robots, such as Kismet, were based on an infant-caretaker interaction, but our system is based mainly on a dialogue interaction. Accordingly, our internal design and implementation differ from other robots because of our distinct goal of multimodal affective communication.

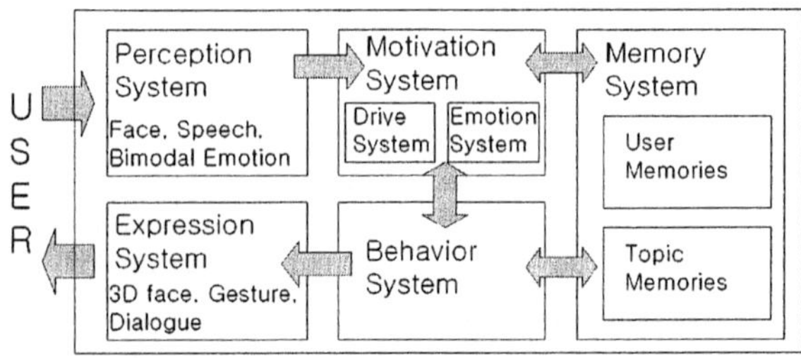

Fig. 1. The figure illustrates the overall framework of the affective system that enables dialogue interactions

The main functions of each subsystem are summarized as follows. The perception system, which mainly extracts information from the outside world, comprises the subsystems of face detection, face recognition, emotion recognition, and motion and color detection. The motivation system is composed of a drive and an emotional system. Drives are motivators; they include endogenous drives and externally induced desires. The emotional system synthesizes AMI's artificial emotions. The memory system, as mentioned above, preserves the emotional memories of users and topics. We improved the subsystems of our previous humanoid robots [7].

3 Perception System

Face Detection and Recognition: The face detection system uses a bottom-up, feature-based approach. The system searches input image for a set of facial features, and groups regions into face candidates based on the geometric relationship of the facial features. Finally, the system decides whether the candidate region is a face by locating eyes in the eye region of a candidate's face. The detected image is sent to the face recognizer and to the emotion recognizer. Face recognizer determines the user's identity from face database. See [7] for more detailed information on implementation.

Bimodal Emotion Recognition: We estimate emotion through facial expression and speech, and then integrate them to enable bimodal emotion recognition. For emotion recognition through facial expression, we normalized the image captured. We then extracted the following two features, which are based on Ekman's facial expression features [8]: One is Facial image of lips, brow and forehead, and the other is edge image of lips, brow and forehead.

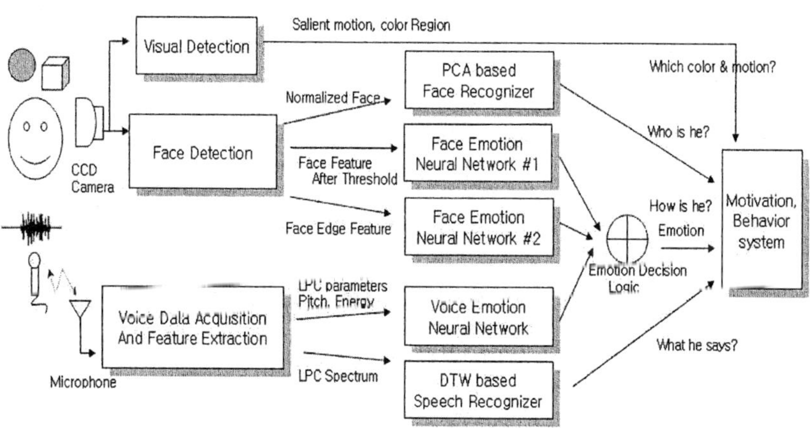

Fig. 2. The figure shows the structure of the perception system

Next, for emotion recognition through speech, we adopted a recognition method similar to the one used in the life-like communication agents MUSE and MIC [9]. Our system extracts two features: a phonetic feature and a prosodic feature. We used a neural network to train each feature vector.

For bimodal emotion recognition, we used decision logic to integrate the two training results. The final result vector of the decision logic (R_{final}) is as follows:

$$R_{final} = (R_{face}W_f + R_{speech}W_s) + R_{final\text{-}1} - \delta t. \tag{1}$$

R_{face} and R_{speech} are the results vector of the emotion recognition through facial expression and speech. W_f and W_s are the weights of the two modalities. $R_{final\text{-}1}$ is the previous emotion result determined by decision logic, and δ is a decay term that eventually restores the emotional status to neutral. The overall correctness of bimodal emotion system recognition was about 80 percent for each of the five testers. By resolving confusion, the bimodal emotion system performed better than facial-only and speech-only systems.

4 Motivation System

4.1 Drive System

Previously, we defined three basic drives for a robot's affective communication with humans: the drive to interact with humans, the drive to ingratiate itself with humans, and the drive to maintain its well-being [7].

The first drive motivates AMI to approach and greet humans. The second drive prompts AMI to make humans feel better. When AMI interacts with humans, it tries to ingratiate itself while considering the human's emotional state. The third drive is related to AMI's maintenance of its own well-being, especially with regard to psychological and physical fatigue. When AMI experiences extreme anger or sadness, or when its battery is too low, it stops interacting with humans.

4.2 Emotional System

Emotions are significant in human behavior, communication and interaction [10]. A synthesized emotion influences the behavior system and the drive system as a control mechanism. To enable AMI to synthesize emotions, we used a model that comprises the three dimensions of emotion [11]. This model characterizes emotions in terms of stance (open/close), valence (negative/positive) and arousal (low/high). Our system always assumes the stance to be open, because AMI is always openly involved in interactions. Therefore, we only consider valence and arousal, implying that only three emotions are possible for AMI: happiness, sadness, and anger.

Arousal factor (CurrentUserArousal): The arousal factor is determined by factors such as whether AMI finds the human, and whether the human responds. Low arousal increases the emotion of sadness.

Valence factor (CurrentUserResponse): The valence factor is determined by whether the human responds appropriately to AMI's requests. A negative response increases the emotion of anger; a positive response increases the emotion of happiness.

The synthesized emotion is also influenced by the drive and the memory system. We used the following equation to compute AMI's emotional status (Ei(t)):

$$\begin{aligned} &\text{If } t = 0, E_i(t) = M_i \quad (t = 0 \text{ when new face appears}) \\ &\text{If } t \neq 0, E_i(t) = A_i(t) + E_i(t-1) + \sum D_i(t) + M_i - \delta t. \end{aligned} \tag{2}$$

E_i is AMI's emotional status; t is time; i is happiness, sadness, or anger; A_i is the emotional status calculated by the mapping function of [Arousal, Valence, Stance] from the current activated behavior; D_i is the emotional status defined by the activation and intensity of the unsatisfied drives in the drive system; M_i is the emotion from the memory system; and δt is a decay term that restores the emotional status to neutral.

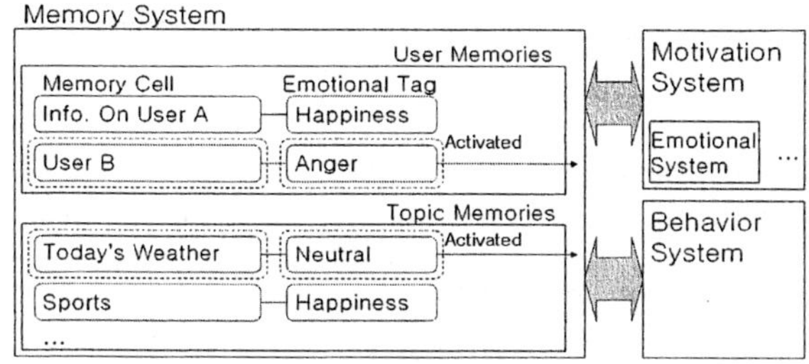

Fig. 3. Activation of memory cells in the memory system

5 Memory System

Our system presents the emotional memories required for more natural and intelligent affective communication with humans. In view of our research objectives, we implemented two memory groups: a user memory, which represents memories of previous interactions with users; and a topic memory, which represents AMI's knowledge of specific topics. When the memory cell is created, AMI's current emotional state is attached to the memory cell as an emotional tag. Later, the memory cells can be activated by AMI's perception system or emotional state. Even though many memory cells can be activated by the perception system or the emotional system, only one memory cell is chosen from AMI's memory group to interact with the other subsystems. The selected memory cell is sent to the behavior system, and the behavior system changes behavior accordingly. Furthermore, the emotional tag is sent to the emotional system as the M_i parameter of the emotional system.

5.1 User Memory

User memories are memories that store information on users. User memories contain data on the user's personality and preference, and this data helps AMI to determine behaviors. Furthermore, as mentioned above, an emotional tag is attached to each memory cell, every time when the memory cell is generated.

After saving data on the user's active and passive responses, AMI uses this data to determine the user's personality. AMI also save the user's preferences, such as likes and dislikes regarding several dialogue topics. This information helps AMI interact appropriately. If AMI recalls this information in the next interaction with the same user, the user thinks AMI is intelligent and the interaction may become more profuse and interesting.

In addition, AMI saves its most frequently occurring emotion, generated by the emotional system mentioned above, as an emotional tag for the latest interaction with the user. These tags subsequently influence AMI's emotional status when it meets the user again. The emotional tags attached to the memory cells are considered AMI's emotional feelings towards the user. Humans often have feelings towards those with whom they communicate. When they meet someone again, they might be influenced by their feelings and memories of the person. The emotional tags in our system are treated similarly: When a memory cell is activated, its emotional tag is passed to the emotional system to help synthesize emotions.

The activation of user memories is represented as follows:

$$U_i(t) = W_{me} \sum E_k(t)\, EU_i(t) + W_{mc}\, C_i. \tag{3}$$

U_i is the activation value of that user memory, t is time, $E_k(t)$ is AMI's current emotion, and $EU_i(t)$ is the emotional tag of the user memory cell. Thus, $\sum E_k(t)\, EU_i(t)$ indicates the extent of the match between AMI's current emotion and the emotion of the user memory. In addition, C_i is 1 if the current user equals the user of memory U_i. Otherwise, C_i is 0. Finally, W_{me} and W_{mc} are the weight factors.

The memory system selects one user memory after considering the activation values from the perception and emotional systems. That memory is then passed to other systems. Because $U_i(t)$ does not always equal C_i, AMI can activate the memory of a different user with whom it is currently interacting, based on its current emotions.

5.2 Topic Memory

Topic memories contain conversational sentences that AMI has learned from users. The topic memories are first created when the perception system recognizes that the frequency of a keyword has exceeded a threshold; that is, when the user has mentioned the same keyword several times. After AMI's behavior system confirms that the user is talking about a particular keyword, the memory system makes a new topic memory cell for that keyword. In the memory cell, the sentences of the user are stored and an emotional tag is attached with respect to AMI's current emotion.

Of all the topic memories, only the one with the highest activation value is selected at time t. We calculated the activation values of the topic memories, $T_i(t)$, as follows:

$$\begin{aligned} &\text{If COMM} = 0,\ T_i(t) = W_{mt} \sum E_k(t)\, ET_i(t) \\ &\text{If COMM} = i,\ T_i(t) = 1. \end{aligned} \tag{4}$$

COMM represents the user's command to retrieve specific topic memory, t is time, $E_k(t)$ is AMI's current emotion, and $ET_i(t)$ is the emotional tag of the topic. Thus, $\sum E_k(t)\, ET_i(t)$ indicates the extent of the match between AMI's current emotion and the emotion of the memory of the topic. Finally, W_{mt} is a weight factor.

6 Behavior System

Previously, we reported that the structure of the behavior system has three levels, which address the three drives of the motivation system [7]. As the system moves down a level, more specific behavior is determined according to the affective relationship between the robot and human.

The first level of the behavior system is called drive selection. The behavior group of this level communicates with the motivation system and determines which of the three basic drives should be addressed. The second level, called high-level behavior selection, decides which high-level behavior should be adopted in relation to the perception and internal information in the determined drive. In the third level, called low-level behavior selection, each low-level type of behavior is composed of dialogue and gestures, and is executed in the expression system. A low-level type of behavior is therefore selected after considering the emotion and memory from other systems.

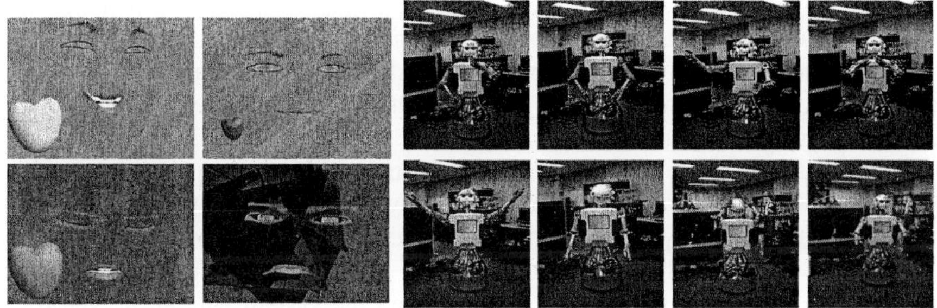

Fig. 4. AMI's facial expressions and gestures

7 Expression System

The expression system, the implementation of which is described in [7], is the intermediate interface between the behavior system and AMI's hardware and it has three subsystems: a dialogue expression system, a 3-D facial expression system, and a gesture expression system.

8 Experimental Results and Conclusions

We first confirmed that each subsystem satisfies its objectives. From our evaluation, we drew the graph in Fig. 5, which shows the subsystem's flow during a sample interaction. The graph also shows the behavior system (finding, greeting, consoling and so on), the motivation system (AMI's drives and emotions), and the perception system (the user's emotional status).

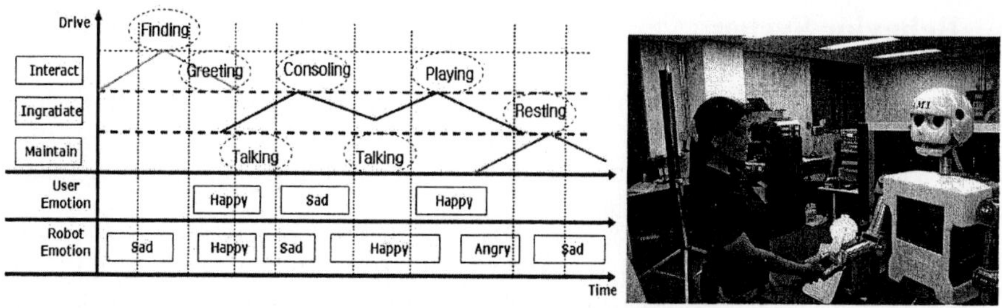

Fig. 5. The work flow of the system

Five users participated in the experiment. We used the procedure of Strack, Martin, and Stepper [12]. The procedure requires participants to hold a pen in their mouths to trigger an emotional response. Each participant was asked to interact with AMI five times while displaying an emotional state of happiness, sadness, or neutrality. For each interaction, all participants evaluated the naturalness of the conversation. They were given three buttons to indicate a negative evaluation: one button indicated an emotional mismatch, another indicated redundancy in the conversation, and the third indicated other errors. If no buttons were pressed, we assumed that particular conversation was natural. Visual input and speech input were given to AMI directly, and all processes were performed on-line.

To evaluate our framework of the emotional memory, we compared three types of systems: one without an emotional or memory system, one with an emotional system but without a memory system, and one with both an emotional and memory system. Table 1 shows the results. The results suggest that the overall performance of the systems with an emotional memory is better than the system without it. The results clearly suggest that emotional memory helps AMI to synthesize more natural emotions and to reduce redundancy in conversational topics.

We have presented an affective communication robot with explicit emotional memories of users and topics. In our system, the emotional memory is the key to improving affective interaction between humans and robots. Other sociable robots have either ignored emotional memories or maintained them implicitly. Our research suggests that explicit emotional memory enhances high-level affective dialogue.

Table 1. Experimental results of interactions

		W/o emotion, w/o memory	With emotion, w/o memory	With emotion, with memory
Natural		54%	70%	76%
Unnatural	Emotion mismatch	19%	10%	5%
	Redundancy	14%	6%	3%
	Other errors	13%	14%	16%

We plan to extend AMI's memory system with a greater variety of memories, including visual objects or high-level concepts. AMI's current memory cells are limited to conversational topics and user-information. In future, AMI will be capable of memorizing information on visual input and word segments, and of making connections between them.

Acknowledgement

This research was partly supported by the Korea Ministry of Science and Technology through the Brain Science Research Center and by the Information Technology Research Center (ITRC) Support Program, the Ministry of Information and Communication.

References

1. Breazeal, C.: Designing Sociable Robots. MIT Press, Cambridge, MA (2002)
2. Arkin, R.C., Fujita, M., Takagi, T., Hasegawa, R.: An Ethological and Emotional Basis for Human-Robot Interaction. Robotics and Autonomous Systems, 42 (2003)
3. Shibata, T. at al.: Emergence of emotional behavior through physical interaction between human and artificial emotional creature. ICRA (2000) 2868-2873
4. Sidner, C.L., Lee, C., Lesh, N.: The Role of Dialog in Human Robot Interaction. International Workshop on Language Understanding and Agents for Real World Interaction (2003)
5. Ledoux, J.: The Emotional brain: the mysterious under pinning of emotional life. New York: Simon & Schuster (1996)
6. Yoon, S.Y., Burke, R.C., Blumberg, B.M., Schneider, G.E.: Interactive Training for Synthetic Characters. AAAI (2000)
7. Jung, H., Seo, Y., Ryoo, M.S., Yang, H.S.: Affective communication system with multimodality for the humanoid robot AMI. Humanoids (2004)
8. Ekman, P., Friesen, W.V.: Facial Action Coding System: Investigator's Guide. Consulting Psychologists Press, Palo Alto, CA (1978)
9. Tosa, N., Nakatsu, R.: Life-like Communication Agent - Emotion Sensing Character "MIC" & Feeling Session Character "MUSE."ICMCS (1996)
10. Armon-Jones, C.: The social functions of emotions. R. Harre (ed.), The Social Construction of Emotions, Basil Blackwell, Oxford (1985)
11. Schlossberg, H.: Three dimensions of emotion. Psychology Review 61 (1954)
12. Strack, F., Martin, L.L., Stepper, S.: Inhibiting and facilitating condition of facial expressions: A non-obtrusive test of the facial feedback hypothesis. Journal of Personality and Social Psychology, 54 (1988) 768 777

Scenario-Based Interactive Intention Understanding in Pen-Based User Interfaces

Xiaochun Wang, Yanyan Qin, Feng Tian, and Guozhong Dai

Institute of Software, Chinese Academy of Sciences, P.R. of China
xiaochun02@iscas.cn

Abstract. Interactive intention understanding is important for Pen-based User Interface (PUI). Many works on this topic are reported, and focus on handwriting or sketching recognition algorithms at the lexical layer. But these algorithms cannot totally solve the problem of intention understanding and can not provide the pen-based software with high usability. Hence, a scenario-based interactive intention understanding framework is presented in this paper, and is used to simulate human cognitive mechanisms and cognitive habits. By providing the understanding environment supporting the framework, we can apply the framework to the practical PUI system. The evaluation of the Scientific Training Management System for the Chinese National Diving Team shows that the framework is effective in improving the usability and enhancing the intention understanding capacity of this system.

1 Introduction

Sketching and writing are natural activities in many situations. Using pen and paper, a person can quickly write down ideas, as well as draw rough pictures and diagrams. Pen-based User Interface[1] simulates this situation. The nature of this kind of interfaces allows people to focus on their task without having to worry about how to user computer.

Since PUI became an important topic, a lot of software have created, such as Windows CE[2], Apple company's NewtonOS[3],DENIM[4], SATIN[5], FlatLand[6]. But the PUI and pen-based systems are not widely used, because these systems mainly utilize the recognition of stroke clusters at the lexical layer and the result of recognition expresses the grade of the precision by probability . As a result, extraction of user intention is not accurate, and understanding errors often happen in pen-based system so that the user cannot naturally interact with these systems.

Compared with related works, user's mediating [7] is a good method to solve the inaccurate reference. The system presents the multiple alternative displays, and then user selects the correct one. Or user iterates what he or she has written when understanding error happened. Both methods impose a larger interactive burden on user so that correcting too many errors will destroy user's passion. Intention understanding [8] may be a way to solve this problem. There are some algorithms for intention extraction. These algorithms[8][9] are very efficient in

J. Tao, T. Tan, and R.W. Picard (Eds.): ACII 2005, LNCS 3784, pp. 828–835, 2005.

small scope, cannot be applied to the system with wider application domain. In fact, intention understanding is related to the specific scenario and the context in physical world. Therefore, scenario can be utilized to solve the inaccurate problem. In this paper, we integrate scenario, intention extraction, domain knowledge, user's mediating and put forward a scenario-based interactive intention understanding framework to raise the understanding capacity of PUI system.

In the rest of this paper, Section 2 discusses related work. Section 3 proposes scenario-based interactive intention understanding framework. Section 4 describes how to build scenario-based understanding environment to support this framework. Then the framework is applied to a practical system which is introduced in Section 5. Section 6 concludes the paper.

2 Related Work

Scenario covers a wide application area ranging from human-computer interaction [10] and requirements engineering [11] to formal specifications [12] and code synthesis [13] Scenarios of human-computer interaction can help us to describe how to use the computer system and imagine more usable computer system[14]. Pen-based user interface development also adopts the scenario-based design method[7].

Different applications of scenario emphasize the different view of point and different goal. We argue that human cognitive activity is based on scenario. Intention understanding always relates to specific scenario, its context, knowledge rule, and depends on them to enhance the capacity of understanding. Hence, we propose a scenario-based interactive intention understanding framework which is applied to pen-based systems to improve their usability.

3 Scenario-Based Interactive Intention Understanding Framework

Based on human cognitive mechanisms and cognitive habits, we designed a scenario-based interactive intention understanding framework, as shown in Fig.1, to support handwriting and sketch understanding.

Users' sketches or handwriting are delivered to PUI system in primitive sequences. Before primitives are passed to perceptual processor, the focus scenario is calculated by the scenario transit manager. There are two methods to determine the focus scenario. The one is that the focus scenario is explicitly directed by the user's command corresponding to the user's intention; the other is that the focus scenario is determined implicitly in interaction and the user is unaware of the transit.

After the scenario transit manager determines the focus scenario, primitive is passed to the perceptual processor in the focus scenario. The perceptual processing is low-level cognition, which collects the basic features of strokes, e.g. the bounding box or local spatial relationships under certain interaction contexts,

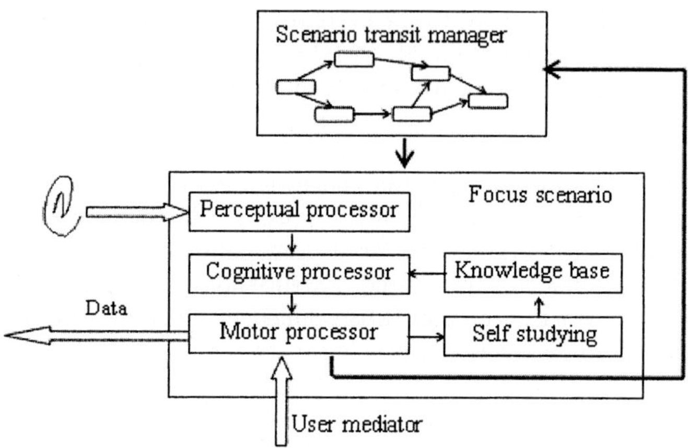

Fig. 1. The Framework of scenario-based interactive intention understanding

e.g. identifying clusters of strokes. Perceptual processing is equivalent to what humans directly perceive from the visual system without thinking.

Cognitive processor accepts the output of the perceptual processor. With the help of domain knowledge in the scenario, the cognitive processor will understand user intention, and rectify the errors that have happened in the perceptual processor. Cognitive processing is equal to the phase humans utilize the knowledge rule to reason and draw the conclusion.

The motor processor in the focus scenario presents understanding results of the cognitive processor to the user. If the result is data, the data will display to the user; if a command, the command will be executed and display its result; if a scenario transit command, the scenario transit management will transit the focus scenario according to the command.

Although the union of the scenario and domain knowledge enhances the capacity of intention recognition, the understanding error is inevitable all the same after the system have utilized all the knowledge to rectify, because the processing is based on the inaccurate reference. Therefore, the system allow user to correct the understanding error by interaction. User's mediating is an effective remedy to the system understanding error, which ensures the system using the inaccurate reference usable, but has an influence on the usability of system. Recognizing-by-example is another method to increase the understanding rate. Providing the capacity of self-studying or direct instruction by user, the system will not take the same mistakes. This method can personalize the knowledge base, and reduce the burden of user's mediating.

4 Scenario-Based Understanding Environment

In order to support the framework, it is necessary to build the understanding environment consisting of scenarios. In fact, the Pen-based application system is a domain-specific intention understanding environment in which the intention is transformed into actions to operate the object by sketching in one scenario and if users cannot finish the task in a scenario, they will go on their task by transiting into anther scenario. Therefore, we define an understanding environment as:

$$U = (S, I, T, S_0, S_E, S_f)$$

S is a set of scenarios in an understanding environment. I is the intention which can be input with pen. T is a transition relation between scenario ($T \subseteq S \times I \times S$). S_0 is the initial scenario($S_0 \in S$). S_E is the goal scenario($S_E \in S$). S_f is the focus scenario ($S_f \in S$). The U also can be regarded as a scenario which composes of all S in U so that the scenario can be nested. The scenario-based intention understanding environment can be built through three steps: the first, determine and design the scenario; the second, design the transit relation between scenarios; finally, model and summarize the knowledge in every scenario.

4.1 Building Scenario

Scenario is the background of intention understanding in this paper. We identify four fundamental elements of scenario for intention understanding. Scenario can be defined as:

$$S = (\boldsymbol{Identifier},\ \boldsymbol{IRange}, \boldsymbol{Object}, \boldsymbol{Knowledge})$$

Identifier is the unique token of the scenario designed by designer. ***IRange*** is the key element of scenario, is the intention sets which can be handled in the scenario. The intention can be classified into two categories. The one is the intention keeping the scenario, and the other is the intention transiting the scenario. ***Object*** is the object operated to implement the intention. ***Knowledge*** is the knowledge rule revising the perceptual result, including constraints such as the order of the intentions accepted by the scenario, rules such as knowledge rectifying the understanding error.

According to the scenario-based pen-based user interface design [7], scenario can be correspondingly created. The intention scope, the object, the knowledge in the scenario can be designed easily according to the scenario design in pen-based user interface. This kind of scenario is explicit scenario, because users have the conception of scenario in their mind, transit between scenarios is controlled by user intention and thinking is broken between scenarios.

In order to further improve the capacity of intention understanding, we put forward implicit scenario. The implicit scenario is defined as an intention understanding scope, and user don't percept the existence of this kind of scenario, and it is not necessary for users to know its existence. According to the action-object interface model[15], user intention can be decomposed into sub-intentions so that the implicit scenario can be created in accordance with these sub-intentions.

4.2 Scenario Transit Design

Transit of scenario can be defined as a 3-tuple: $(S_1, \boldsymbol{i}, S_2)$, where S_1 and S_2 is scenario, $\boldsymbol{i}$ is the intention that make S_1 transit to S_2. Generally, $\boldsymbol{i}$ is tightly related to a scenario. In our Design $\boldsymbol{i}$ = Shape::S::Rule, which indicate that the intention related not only to shape of primitive but also to the scenario and its knowledge rules such space rule, time rule, semantic rule. When user input command or data into the focus scenario , $S_f(P) \in I$ implements the conversion from primitive to intention. Once going into one scenario, all primitives will be handled in this scenario until one of the transit conditions is satisfied. According to scenario transit description, we can build the scenario transit diagram which can describe the whole application context. As a result, all intentions in this understanding environment can utilize this transit network to interpret.

According to the method of building scenario, the scenario transit has two categories. One is the explicit transit corresponding to the explicit scenario. The other is the implicit transit corresponding to the implicit scenario. Since the explicit scenario is designed according to the pen-based user interface design, the transit between Scenarios can be designed according to scenario transit in pen-based user interface. This kind of transit is generally finished by gesture.

Transit between implicit scenarios is implicit, that is to say, there is no break in user's brain when the scenario is transited. Generally, intention of transiting scenario is not gesture, but is data. This kind of data is the critical data. After these data has been processed, another scenario will become the focus scenario.

4.3 Knowledge Modeling in Scenario

Knowledge model is composed of ***right-base***, ***rectify-base***, ***union-base***, ***decomposition-base*** and ***context-base***. ***Right-base*** identifies the correct understanding which is sent from perceptual processor. ***Rectify-base*** corrects the perceptual error which the similarity of shapes leads to. ***Union-base*** analyzes errors which that one whole understanding unit are segmented into multi-parts lead to. ***Decomposition-base*** indicates that the system combines several primitives into one so that understanding error is led to, and this kind of primitive should be decomposed according to heuristic rule. ***Context-base*** will correct the error according to the context.

5 A Practical System Based on the Framework

We demonstrate how to utilize the scenario-based intention understanding framework through Pen-based Scientific Training Management System. Fig. 2 is the scenario a coach is handwriting his training plan for an athlete with a digital pen. The entry cell in the table also can be regarded as a sub-scenario. The coach can switch one cell to another. In every cell, the system uses the implicit scenario transit environment to attain more precise recognition of handwritten plan, and the transit control between these implicit scenarios is taken by the coach's ambiguous intention. We take for example coach's handwriting plan to demonstration how to build the implicit intention understand environment.

The understanding of handwritten plan begins with the system's receiving strokes which express the coach' s intention, then these strokes are delivered to the on-line character segmentation processor and are segmented into primitive

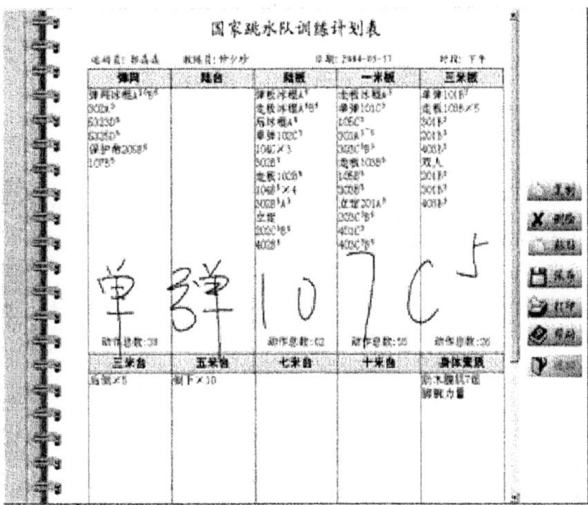

Fig. 2. The Scenario a coach is handwriting training plan for an athlete with digital pen

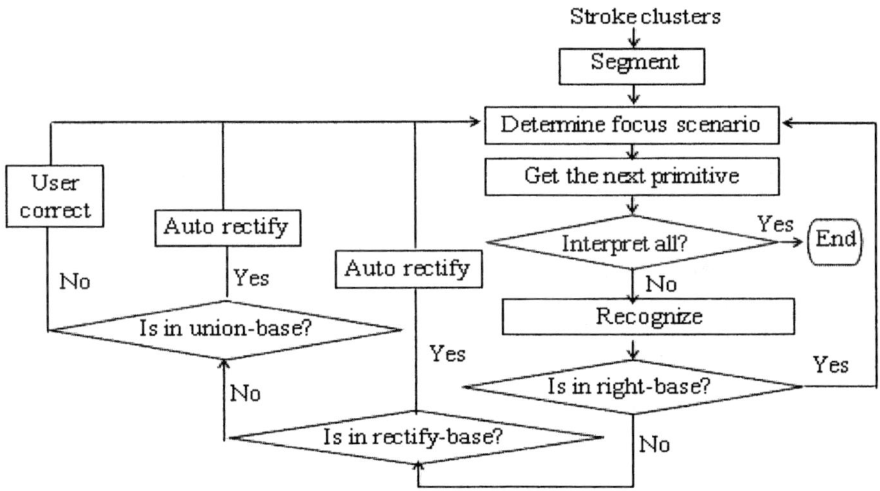

Fig. 3. An instance of thc scenario-based interactive intention understanding framework. This instance is applied to on-line recognition of handwritten training plan.

sequencos(Scc Fig. 3). After determined the focus scenario by the scenario transit manager, the first primitive in time sequence is passed to the recognition processor in focus scenario. Then the recognition result is sent to the ***right-base***. If the ***right-base*** believes that the recognition result matches with the coach's intention, the result is passed to the scenario manager to determine the focus scenario. Otherwise the primitive will be handled by the ***rectify-base***, if the recognition result is in ***rectify-base***, the result will be corrected. In order to handle the separation of left and right part of Chinese character, the ***union-base*** is designed. If the primitive cannot be corrected by ***union-base***, the system will provide a multi-candidate window for user's correction.

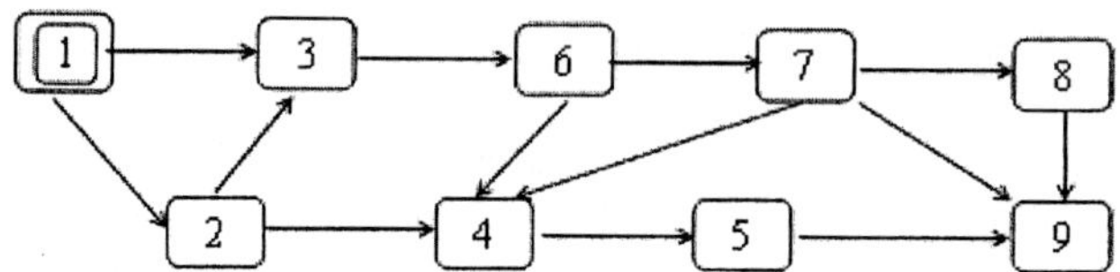

Fig. 4. The scenario transit diagram which is built for the on-line recognition of handwritten training plan. Scenario identifier is $1, 2, \cdots, 9$.

Table 1. Comparison of the recognition rate of PRE and POST. PRE, POST in the table denotes the situation the framework is not used, used respectively.

	Chinese character		Letter		Number		Special character	
	Total num	Error rate	Total num	Error rate	Total num	Error rate	Total num	Error rate
PRE	567	15.34%	3554	11.97%	8761	15.19%	105	8.57%
POST	670	4.33%	3625	1.54%	8943	1.25%	119	3.36%

Providing the scenario-based understanding environment for the framework instance is a matter of primary importance. We analyzed all formats of handwritten plan (such as the formats in Fig. 2) in the design phase, and then nine implicit scenarios were created to describe the process of coaches' handwriting plan (See Fig. 4). In this understanding environment, $S = \{1, 2, \cdots, 9\}, S_0 = 1, S_E = 9, I = \{Chinese, capital, number, \cdots\}$, T ={(1,3,Number),(1,2,character) ,$\cdots$}. Initially, $S_f = 1$.

Creating the scenario is easy. Take the example of the scenario1, *identifier* = 1, *IRange* = {Chinese, number, capital}, *object* = NULL. Collecting knowledge rules is a little complex. Some rules can be acquired at advance, for example, number can only be continuously accepted four times in scenario1. Some knowledge is captured during the course of bug. For example, when "单" follows "弓" in temporal sequence of recognition results, they will be united into "弹". This kind of knowledge effectively remedies the understanding error.

After finishing the system, we conducted a user study to measure the degree to which the system is perceived as easy to use, natural and efficient. Thirteen coaches were asked to handwrite their plan. The initial system didn't use this framework. At a result, the average error rate of handwriting recognition is 14.27%. After using this framework, the average error rate is 1.50% and overall coaches praised our system because this system let them naturally handwrite their training plan for athlete with scarcely any error. The detail information is shown in Table 1.

6 Conclusion

Handwriting or sketch recognition is a key technique for intention understanding. But the accurate understanding cannot be attained only through the recognition at the lexical layer. Therefore, we present a scenario-based interactive intention understanding framework, and provide an understanding environment to support the framework. Then the framework is applied to the Scientific Training Management System. The framework enhances the recognition rate of handwritten plan so that overall coaches in the Chinese National Diving Team praised the system because it let them naturally handwrite their plan with scarcely any error.

Acknowledgements. The project is supported by the National Key Basic Research and Development Program of China under Grant No. 2002CB312103; is also supported by Key Innovation Project from Institute of Software, Chinese Academy of Sciences.

References

1. Dai G, Tian F, Li J, etc., Researches on Pen-based User Interfaces. In: Constantine Stephanidis, ed. Proceedings of the HCI International 2003. Greek: Lawrence Erlbaum Associates (2003) 54-60
2. MSDN Library: Windows CE Documentation. Microsoft, http://msdn.microsoft.com/library/default.asp
3. Apple, Newton Toolkit User's Guide (1996)
4. Mark W. Newman, James Lin, Jason I. Hong, and James A. Landay, DENIM: An Informal Web Site Design Tool Inspired by Observations of Practice. In Human-Computer Interaction, vol. 18, no.3, (2003) 259-324
5. Hong, J.I. and Landay, J.A., SATIN: A Toolkit for Informal Ink-based Applications. In Proceedings of UIST'00 Symposium on User Interface Software and Technology, San Diego, CA, ACM (2000) 63-72
6. Elizabeth D. Mynatt, Takeo Igarashi, W. Keith Edwards, Anthony LaMarca, Flatland: New Dimensions in Office Whiteboards, ACM SIGCHI Conference on Human Factors in Computing Systems, Pittsburgh (1999) 346-353
7. Li jie, Research on Pen-based user interface development method [Ph.D. Thesis], Beijing: Institute of Software, CAS (2004) 55-59
8. Yang Li, Incremental Sketch Understanding for Intention Extraction in Sketch-based User Interface, CS Technical Report, University of California, Berkeley. (2003) UCB//CSD-03-1284
9. Junfeng Li, Xiwen Zhang, Xiang Ao, Guozhong Dai, Sketch Recognition with Continuous Feedback Based On Incremental Intention Extraction, International Conference on Intelligent User Interfaces, San Diego, California, USA (2005)
10. J. Jacko & A. Sears (Eds.), the Human-Computer Interaction Handbook: Fundamentals, Evolving Technologies and Emerging Applications. Lawrence Erlbaum Associates, (2002) 1032-1050
11. Alistair G. Sutcliffe, Neil A. M. Maiden, Shailey Minocha, Darrel Manuel, Supporting Scenario-Based Requirements Engineering. IEEE Trans. Software Eng. vol. 24, no.12, (1998)1072-1088
12. Uchitel, S., Incremental Elaboration of Scenario-Based specifications and Behaviors Models using Implied Scenarios, Ph.D. Thesis, Imperial College (2003)
13. Harel, D. ,From Play-In Scenarios to Code: An achievable Dream. IEEE Software vol. 34, no.1, (2001) 53-60
14. Carroll, J.M., Five Reasons for Scenario-Based Design. In Proceedings of the 32nd Hawai International Conference on System Sciences, IEEE Computer Society Press (1999)
15. Shneiderman, Ben, Designing the User Interface: Strategies for Effective Human-Computer Interaction, Addison Wesley Longman, Inc. (1998)

An Augmented Reality-Based Application for Equipment Maintenance

Changzhi Ke, Bo Kang, Dongyi Chen, and Xinyu Li

Mobile Computing Center & School of Automation Engineering,
University of Electronic and Science Technology of China,
Chengdu, China 610054
kcz1981@163.com, {kangbo, lixy}@uestc.edu.cn,
chenxigt@hotmail.com

Abstract. Augmented Reality (AR) is a technology that merges real-world images with computer-generated virtual objects, superimposes the virtual objects upon the real world, and exhibits them in the view of the users. Mechanical maintenance and repair tasks in industrial environments are prospective domains for AR applications. In this paper a prototype of AR system for training and assisting in maintaining equipment (PC) is presented. The key hardware feature of the system is a binocular video see-through Head Mounted Display (HMD), which presents the augmented reality to the users; the tracking system, which gives the position and orientation of equipment using ARToolKit; and a laptop PC for the platform of the whole application. The design and architecture of this system is described. Experimental results are finally presented.

1 Introduction

Augmented Reality (AR) combines real and virtual objects(such as text,2D images, or 3D models) in a real environment by computer graphic and visualization technology, which can registers real and virtual objects with each other using sensing technology, and makes interactive with each other in real time[1]. AR can increase users visual experience, expand theirs visual system, and help people achieve theirs tasks with a more natural way by the interactivity of real world and the virtual objects. There are potential applications in the areas of medical visualization, engineering design, maintenance and repair, annotation, robot path planning, entertainment, and military aircraft navigation and targeting, more and more prototypes have been successfully built up in these areas so far[1,2].

With the development of technology, the complexity of equipments function has increased and brought more probability of error-arising. When an error happened, we need to display the status of equipments and then do further maintaining and repairing. When repairing workers don't know how to fix, or the fixing problem lasts long, it will cause big lose. In order to put down the lost of equipment failure, we should improve the maintaining efficiency and reduce the repairing time. In the process of repairing, maintenance man has to detect problems and then think the equipment information in the equipment environment. Then they analyze the information from several regard points. On the base of traditional optimum decision making and appreciation method,

J. Tao, T. Tan, and R.W. Picard (Eds.): ACII 2005, LNCS 3784, pp. 836 – 841, 2005.

AR technology can combine the equipment information with graphic information at one vision point in the real world, and then display and feedback the related information to the maintenance man. It is an effective method to solve the problem with man's visualization ideation. Based on the characteristic of equipment maintenance, this paper has set up an equipment maintenance prototype of desktop PC with AR technology, and discussed the application of AR in the equipment maintenance.

2 System Design

2.1 Overall Architecture

The prototype system can make users complete the equipment maintenance in the augmented reality environment. Its main realization process as follows:[3]

Firstly, from the different presetting angles, the camera in the video see-through HMD collects the image of desktop PC in the reality, and then transmits the image information to the graphic system of the laptop PC for disposing.

Secondly, the system immerge the virtual objects into the real environment (desktop PC), with the 3D reconstruction on local scene, the inter-placement of virtual objects, the illumination recovery, shadow generation technology and so on.

Finally, the system transmits the augmented video to the video see-through HMD. From the video see-through HMD, users can make intuitionistic judgment and analyse the encountered problems with the augmented view. Figure 1 is the frame of the system.

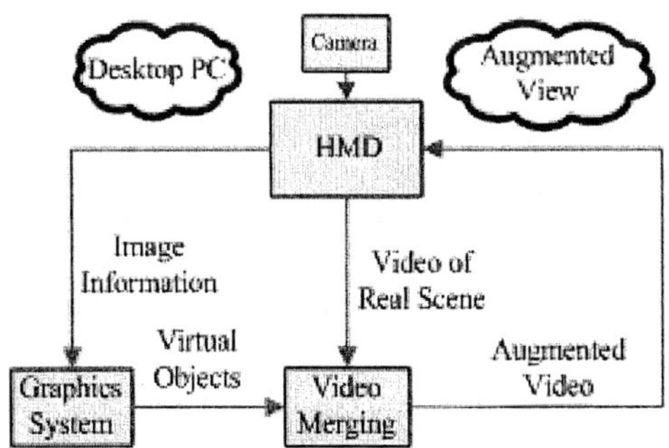

Fig. 1. The frame of the system

Compared with the method based upon the imagination of the expert to judge and analyze, the system provides a more intuitionistic and true method, which reduces the subjectivity and liberty of visual appreciation. It is undoubtedly a more scientific approach for equipment maintaining. The purpose of our research is to find whether it can be more convenient for users to realize the auxiliary function of the equipment maintaining. The laptop is operating under window XP. We use the ARToolKit as Augmented Reality software system.

2.2 ARToolKit

ARToolKit is an open-source software library for building augmented reality applications and has been inspired and implemented by HIT laboratory at University of Washington. It uses computer vision techniques to calculate the real camera position and orientation relative to markers, allowing the programmer to overlay virtual objects onto these markers. The fast, precise tracking library functions provided by ARToolKit enable the rapid development of many new AR applications[4].

A characteristic of the ARToolKit is the virtual object to be tracked wears the marker. The Marker is the black-white squared card with different designs. It has simple shape and can be easily identified by input equipments. The position and orientation of the camera can be calculated by identifying markers in a video stream. More exactly a reference coordinate system is centered at a marker image and the system calculate the camera transformation matrix which is then used for rendering 3D objects. We have designed some markers for our PC maintenance prototype, and three of them are shown in the Table 1.

ARToolkit performs the following steps:[5,6]

1. Turn captured video images into binary images.
2. Search the image for black square regions.
3. For each square capture and match its pattern against templates.
4. Use the known square size and pattern orientation to calculate a camera transformation matrix.
5. Draw the virtual objects.

Table 1. Some markers used in our prototype system

CD ROM	Hard Disk	Power
C	H	

2.3 Hardware Environment

Our setup consists only of off-the-shelf hardware components (see the figure 2).At the core lays a powerful laptop computer equipped with an ATI Mobility Radeon 9000 VGA card and a 1.7GHz Dothan processor. It is carried in a backpack by the user. As a display we deploy a Cy-Visor DH-4400VP video see-through color display which equipped with a web camera for vision tracking, a microphone and an earphone[7].

The main user interface is a Twiddler2. The Twidddler2 provides the same input to your computer as both a conventional keyboard and a mouse that weighs 4 ounces and fits in the palm of your hand. The Twiddler2 is designed to be operated by only one hand. The hand not holding the Twiddler2 is free for other tasks.

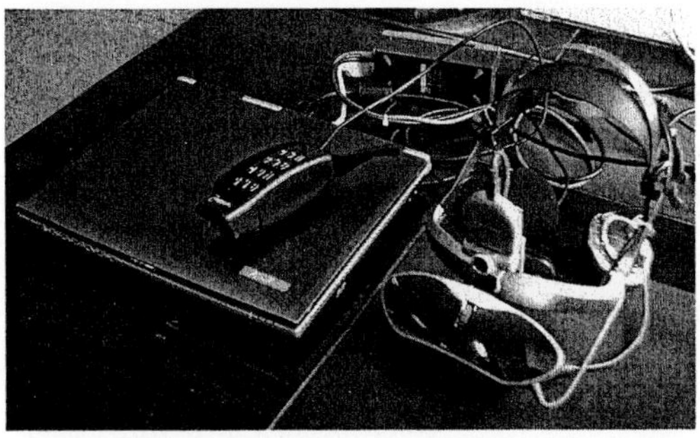

Fig. 2. The components of setup

3 Implementation and Results

We implemented a simple PC maintenance application to demonstrate the viability of our AR system. In the target scenario for this particular application, a user attempts to repair a normal desktop PC, possibly for the first time. The user utilizes augmented reality, ultimately with a see-through head-mounted display, to gain information about the components of PC. The AR system can supply a wide variety of support for the user. Annotations may identify the position of the equipment by highlighting frame, describe its name, or present other important information like maintenance or manufacturing records.

Fig. 3. A user wearing a laptop computer and HMD

Imagine a user is ready to maintain a desktop PC, his/her task is essentially to accurately find and install the components of PC: CD-ROM drive, hard disk and power supply. As shown in Figure 3, a user wearing a laptop computer and HMD is going to work with a desktop PC on the table. When a marker which is corresponding to one of components in PC is identified by AR system, the user can simultaneously see the virtual annotation information that overlay on the markers through HMD. These annotations overlay images are real scene images from the user's viewpoint with three kinds of information shown in Table 2: positional frames, textual annotations, pointing arrows.

Table 2. Kinds of annotations

Virtual Annotation information	Function
Positional frames	Showing the positions of the components which will install to the user
Textual annotations	Showing the names of the components which will install to the user
Pointing arrows	Showing the orientations of the components which will install to the user

When these markers that relate to the virtual annotation information can be placed in right corresponding positions and they could be identified later, the user can depend on the annotated information to successfully complete the tasks by this AR system. Figure 4 shows the annotation overlay images provided to the user.

In Figure 4, the virtual green frame which overlay on the marker shows the position of CD-ROM drive, and the textual annotation and red pointing arrow simultaneously appear around the frame which expresses the name and orientation of the CD-ROM drive respectively. With the same design, the virtual yellow and blue frames integrating with the textual annotations and pointing arrows respectively provide the support information of the power supply and hard disk to the user. Through the virtual annotated information, user can easily realize the basic structure and install technique of components in desktop PC. Therefore, our prototype system is especially suitable for the freshman using computer.

Fig. 4. AR User's view

4 Conclusion

The experimental results have shown that this prototype of AR system is able to satisfy the requirements of AR application. With this AR system, users can get help from the computer-generated virtual objects which interact with the real world through HMD.

According to the different elements in PC, we can increase such virtual objects as pictures and texts.

In the near future, we intend to improve the prototype in various ways. The user interface and interaction methods need enhancement to make manipulation of graphical objects easier, and to reducing the weight of the user equipment and making it completely wireless.

References

1. Azuma, R: A Survey of Augmented Reality. Presence: Teleoperators and Virtual Environments. vol. 6, no. 4, Aug (1997), 355-385.
2. Azuma, R. et al: Recent advances in augmented reality. IEEE Computer Graphics and Applications, Nov (2001), 34-47.
3. Reitmayr,G., Schmalstieg ,D.: Mobile Collaborative Augmented Reality. ISAR, (2001)□3-4.
4. http://www.hitl.washington.edu/artoolkit/.
5. Kato, H., Billinghurst, M., Morinaga, K., Tachibana, K.: The Effect of Spatial Cues in Augmented Reality Video Conferencing. Proceedings of the 9th International Conference on Human-Computer Interaction (HCI), New Orleans, USA, (2001), 1-4.
6. Kato, H., Billinghurst, M., Poupyrev, I., Imamoto, K., Tachibana, K.: Virtual Object Manipulation on a Table-Top AR Environment. In proceedings of the International Symposium on Augmented Reality, ISAR, (2000), 4-5.
7. Reitmayr,G., Schmalstieg, D.: A Wearable 3D Augmented Reality Workspace. Short paper, Proc. ISCW, (2001), 1-2.

Highly Interactive Interface for Virtual Amusement Land Deriving Active Participation of Users

Seongah Chin

#147-2, anyang-8 Dong, Manan-Gu, Anyang-City, Kyunggi-Do, Korea
Division of Multimedia, Sungkyul University
solideo@sungkyul.edu

Abstract. In this paper an interactive 3D virtual amusement land supporting user's interactivity with various virtual contents is presented for increasing reality and immersion of a virtual park. Most existing 2D amusement contents provide less interactivity and reality than the proposed one does. This method enables users to navigate virtual space actively and to experience virtual contents on real-time rendering.

1 Introduction

As Internet users tend to be proliferated to the public, various and broad contents are demanded constantly. Facilitating high-speed network precedes developing and publishing the high quality contents so that Internet users not merely access Web3D contents but also utilize them. Recently broadband network increasingly has extended to Internet users resulting in that various contents are constantly growing. However, currently existing contents do not seem to satisfy users with respect to reality, immersion and participation. The drawbacks can be confined to suitability for characteristics of contents, interest deriving user's participation and representation of reality. Thus various and broad contents conveying real-time 3D rendering are requested in order to boost interactivity as a new way of dynamic communication methods. In particular Web3D contents implemented in VRML and X3D play a key role in providing interactivity for users such as game, entertainment, cyber education, amusement park, exhibition and E-commerce. Such 3D contents bring more utility or fun than 2D and closely working with paying customers to deliver beachhead applications where 3D provides clear benefits in productivity or user experience [1], [2]. Major online retailers or entertainment sites have recently adapted Web3D contents for attracting and holding onto customers for years.

Network based Virtual Reality is closely related to a way of life such as shopping, education, model house, cyber museum and so on. Thus virtual experience should be focused on building Web3D contents helping us to feel and experience contents as real as possible by providing interactivity. The contents should be available to convey feeing of space and dynamic 3D capability. Currently most existing virtual amusement contents are only based on 2D interface. We conducted review on currently

J. Tao, T. Tan, and R.W. Picard (Eds.): ACII 2005, LNCS 3784, pp. 842–849, 2005.

existing contents in order to figure our drawbacks. Disneyland [5] represents 2D interface without interactivity supplying only images and text information. Universal Studio [9] and Seoul Land [8] have partly used interactivity with 2D iconic interface along with movies. Lotte World [7] has provided 2D iconic interface without interactivity. In the conclusion, at first the lack of immersion is detected in mostly existing contents. In other words, it is not suitable for unique purpose of the contents making users experience as well as just view. Secondly, most of them offering 2D interface to users fall short of reality of spacious navigation due to lack of 3D interface.

In this paper, we present an interactive Web3D Virtual amusement land making us capable of experiencing and navigating via 3D interface and interactive events. Customers are able to experience the contents as well as to view them in 3D boosting reality and immersion and deriving user's interest

2 Interactive Virtual Amusement Land

The motivation and interest of the users should be emphasized on developing virtual amusement land since it is a kind of entertainments. Thus emotion should be considered as a key factor in designing an interactive virtual amusement land. Emotional icon is adapted to increase immersion considering location, color and size of the icon and integration as well [6].

Table 1. Comparison between existing Cyber-amusement sites

Comparison	Lotte World	Seoul Land	Disney Land	Universal Studio
Interface	2 D	Captured 3D	2 D	2 D
Interaction	One way	Partial	One way	Partial
Equipment	Image, Text, Movie	Image, Text	Image, Text	Movie

In the Table 1 clearly distinct difference can be detected betweens existing Cyber-amusement sites with respect to usage of interface, interaction and equipment. In short, there exist several limitations of immersion making users bring fun via indirect experience of amusement equipments. Moreover, they still provide just common interface not being able to drawing interests of users.

In addition interviews from users have been performed in order to find out interests, responses, and needs of users about usage of amusement lands. The results have been conveyed into the process of creating simulations such as 3D interface, event-driven animation in cyber-amusement sites and appearance of 3D characters.

Principle of Designing the Content

Prior to development of the contents, we collected user's expectation two times via inquiry. They are requested to answer limit, demands, requirements and information gathered from general amusement land Web sites. Thus, hindrance of usability can be investigated as shown Table 2. At first inquiry, users tend to need easy and quick method for understanding main purpose of the site. In addition, lack of realistic model of playing equipment is pointed out and highly completed interface design as well.

Table 2. Hindrance of usability

1st inquiry	2nd inquiry
•Necessity of summary for the main object of the site •Lack of realistic models for playing equipments • Need high completion of interface design	•Slow loading •Inconvenience to install plug in •Ignorance of user's option •Interactivity

At second inquiry, slow loading and inconvenience to install plug in are mentioned along with short of interactivity. Finally currently existing amusement contents fall short of user's expectation and requirement as shown in Table 3. The comparison points out different representation of methods such as user interface, playing equipment and button.

Table 3. Comparison between existing contents and proposed content

specification	Existing Contents	Proposed Content
•User interface	•Image and Text based site •Movie and board	•Interactivity •3D real-time rendering •3D character
•Playing Equipment	•Image and Text based equipment •Lack of dynamic model	•3D Virtual amusement •3D facial Expression
•Button	•2D image based button	•3D modeling based button

Based on two inquiries and the comparison in Table 3, we design cultural model of the virtual amusement land as shown in Figure 1.

Object Model Optimization Using 2 Stages

At first, loading speed and real time rendering should be considered to be effective and interested. Thus two stages of optimization are highly required such as initial model optimization and post processing optimization. In other others, in modeling stage caricature like models are definitely needed standing for key aspects of the object. We focus on reducing vertex as simple as possible without loss of critical aspect. At second stage post reduction processing should be conducted in order to represent high quality of the object.

User-Centered Interactive Interface and Immersion

How to make objects communicate users?

We adapt events in order to provide interactivity between users and object such as playing equipment, zoom, start, open and menus.

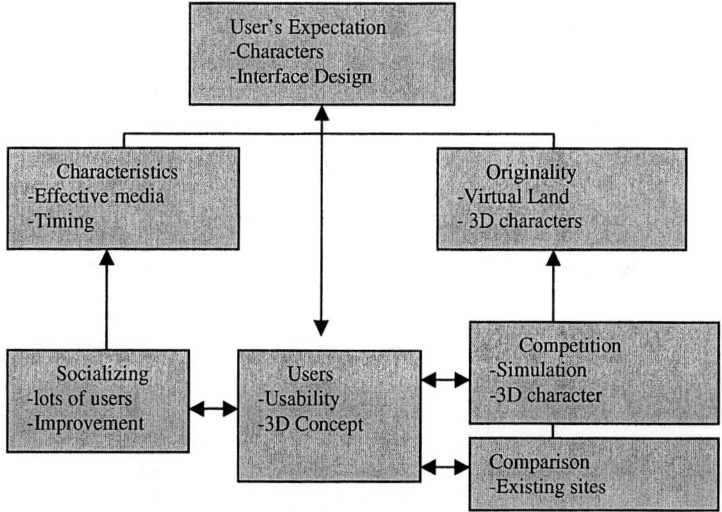

Fig. 1. Cultural model of the proposed content

An eventOut signals a target to properly act by clicking a mouse enabling TouchSensor in VRML whereas an eventIn takes signal. Only manipulating the mouse make use of interactivity. Thus users are capable of rotating the object and simulating equipments, which makes it possible to provide immersion and interactivity. In particular various eventIns are connected to Viewpoint, AudioClip, Materials and so on so that object are able to respond to user's request. Users can freely manipulate objects what they want to handle just by clicking a mouse.

```
ROUTE $70.event_out1 TO $61.toggle
ROUTE $70.event_out1 TO $119.on
ROUTE $37.itemSelected TO $72.nEvent
ROUTE $72.nEventDec TO $74.nEvent
ROUTE $94._fraction_ TO $95.set_fraction
ROUTE $111.event_out3 TO $125.on
ROUTE $111.event_out3 TO $117.bind
```

Fig. 2. Event Signals and Route nodes

In Figure 2 various eventOut and Route nodes are introduced in VRML offering dynamic user interaction. Once an eventOut signal reaches a target object, predefined responses start with activating. Various animations can be connected to one object. In Figure 2, eventOut5 makes Back.toggle work.

In Figure 3 an icon based interactive interface is shown as demonstrating the Gyro-drop. By clicking show menu open, close, start, zoom-in and out and perspective view denoted by dotted ovals are functioning according to almost same process in real.

In clicking Open icon the gyro-drop is ready to open the entrance and leave shown in Figure 3 (b). By clicking the Start icon the gyro-drop starts to move up until it reach the top as shown in (c) and (d). Here we also provide users with several Zooms and perspective view. Bear characters appear as users making us feel friendly and practically.

(a) Image of Gyro-drop

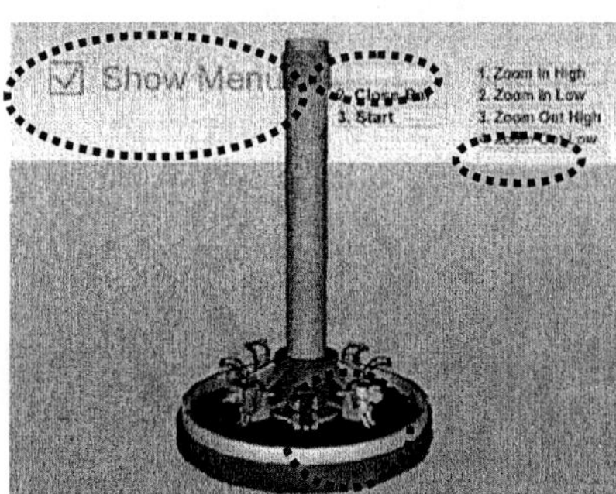

(b) 3D simulation on the initial stage

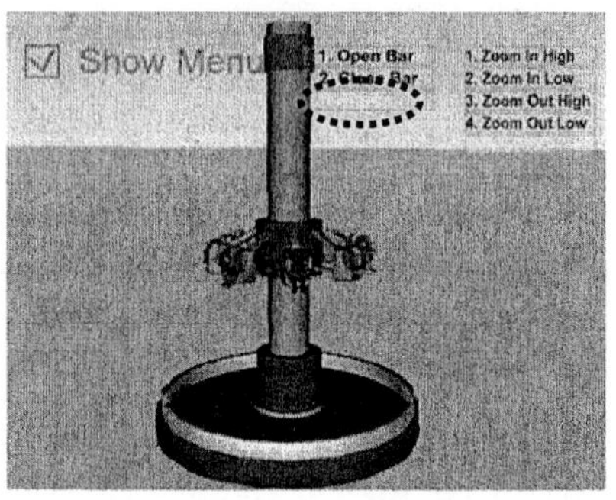

(c) 3D simulation on the medium stage

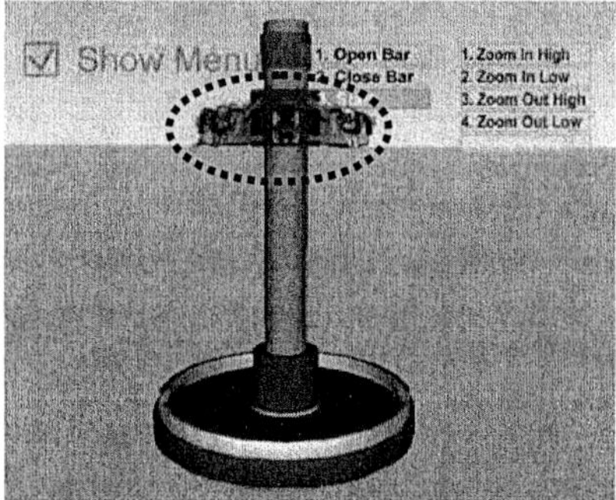

(d) 3D simulation on the top stage

Fig. 3. Gyro-drop simulation and interactivity

Virtual Landscape

The whole landscape and tour can be available making users feel like walking and fly around the virtual land. By providing dynamic overview, users can experience exotic 3D space tour in Web contents including gyro-drop rounded by dotted oval in Figure 4 (b). In virtual restaurant, this method heavily focuses on interactive menu demonstrating food can be looked over in details served by human like characters. In Figure 4 (d) Japanese restaurant shows real-like view and various menus denoted by dotted oval appearing when pressing each menu in the icons.

(a) Virtual landscape in perspective view

(b) Another view of Virtual landscape

(c) Indian restaurant

(d) Japanese restaurant

Fig. 4. Virtual landscape with restaurants

3 Experimental Results and Conclusions

The work has been constructed is a virtual amusement land enabling us to interact with virtual playing equipment, and navigate virtual landscape. Virtual experience should be focused on building Web3D contents helping us to feel and experience contents as real as possible by providing interactivity. The contents should be available to convey feeing of space and dynamic 3D capability. Currently most existing virtual amusement contents are only based on 2D interface. We present an interactive Web3D Virtual amusement land making us capable of experiencing and navigating via 3D interface and interactive events. Customers are able to experience the contents as well as view them in 3D boosting reality and immersion and deriving user's interest. We implemented our Web3D under Windows 2000/XP in VRML, script language and auxiliary graphic tools. In Figure 5, we have shown simulation results created by the principles and functions based on real scene in the amusement lands.

(a) Image of mini-balloon

(b) 3D simulation of mini-balloon

(c) Image of spin-cup

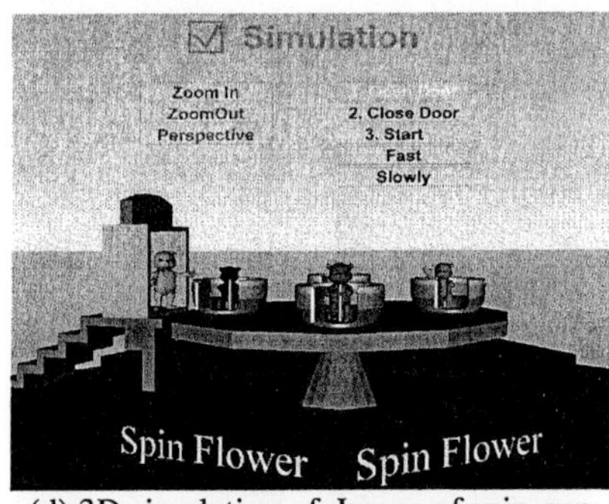

(d) 3D simulation of Image of spin-cup

(e) Image of mono-rail

(f) 3D simulation of mono-rail

Fig. 5. Experimental Results showing real images on the left column corresponding 3D simulation on the right column

Acknowledgments

This work has been partially supported by University Industrial Technology Force (UNITEF). The author would like to thank to Ms. E. Cho and Ms. B. Kim for collecting data and help.

References

1. AARON E. WALSH, Mikael Bourges-Sevenier, Core Web3D, Prentice Hall PTR, 2001
2. Burdea,G. & Coiffet,P, "Virtual reality technology", New York:John Wiley & Sons.1996
3. J. Gratch, J. Rickel, E. Andre, N. Badler, J. Cassel & E. Petajan, "Creating Interative Virtual Humans : Some Assembly Required", IEEE INTELLIGENT SYSTEMS, 2002
4. R. Torre, P. Fua, S. Balcisoy, M. Ponder & Daniel Thalmann, " Interaction Between Real and Virtual Humans : Playing Checkers, Eurographics Workshop on Virtual Environments, June 2000
5. http://disneyland.disney.go.com
6. http://www.leesunho.pe.kr
7. http://www.lotteworld.co.kr
8. http://www.seouland.co.kr
9. http://themeparks.universalstudios.com
10. http://www.web3d.org

The Effects of Interactive Video Printer Technology on Encoding Strategies in Young Children's Episodic Memory

Misuk Kim

Dept. of Child Welfare Study, Chung-Ang University, 221, HeukSeok-dong, Dongjak-gu, Seoul, Korea
Kmisukch@yahoo.co.kr

Abstract. This study was done to explore the effects of video printer technology on young children's episodic memory. Five-year-old children were found to increase their memory of episodic events if they segmented the event into small units by video printer. But, seven-year-old children could not have any benefits of memory by using it. The discussion of these results will given on the topic of developmental differences of encoding strategies and the effects of video printer on memory.

1 Introduction

Script is schema-memory model of an event structure formed by repeated experiences (Schank & Abelson, 1977). With repeated experiences of similar events, general script of the event is established in memory. This can guide attention, retention, and retrieval whenever people experience new events (Mandler, 1984). Children also have event script. These include such as restaurant, campfire, and birthday (Nelson, 1984). Generally it is well known that very young children can remember event scripts established or experienced in their memory. However, they can't remember unfamiliar events. For example, four-year-old children could not remember an episodic event after their first experience of it. They remember the event better after several experiences of similar (or same) events, even though they omitted many details. However, seven-year-old children were found to remember details of the event even after their first experience (Farrar & Goodman, 1990). Even with experiences, four- and five-year-old children can't remember an arbitrary event (Fivush, Kuebli, & Clubb, 1992). These findings suggest that younger children rely on schematic structure, which is called "script," in memory.

There are controversial issues of the developmental differences in regards to younger children remembering information less than older children. Among those, mnemonic strategies are important factors that influence younger children's memory. Mnemonic strategy is conscious-cognitive activity to remember something, and these mnemonic activities keep words (or information) alive in short-term memory and encourage its transfer to long-term memory (Flavell at al., 2002). Mnemonic strategies include encoding, elaboration, rehearsal, and organization (Sigler, 1991). Among these, encoding strategy is known to be an important factor to establish script

J. Tao, T. Tan, and R.W. Picard (Eds.): ACII 2005, LNCS 3784, pp. 850–857, 2005.

knowledge. Generally, a script established as content knowledge can be the tool for remembering. This is possible by using enhanced encoding, which is, encouraging attention to the information that should be remembered (Sigler, 1998, pp. 206). At the same time, encoding also seems to be an important strategy to establish event script. Newtson and his colleagues studied these topics.

Using a button technique, Newtson and his colleagues explored how perception of different units of action influences the interpretation of people's behavior and learning. In the button technique, subjects were given a button to press whenever they think that a meaningful unit of the behavior stream appears on the videotape. Segmenting behavior streams into fine units enhanced the ability to infer an actor's personality traits and problem-solving abilities from the videotape (Newtson, 1973; Newtson & Rinder, 1979). On the other hand, Newtson suggested that if people segmented a stream of behavior into meaningful units, the segmented breakpoints were remembered better than non-breakpoints of the event. Actions of breakpoints were described more accurately than non-breakpoints actions (Newtson & Engquist, 1976). A breakpoint is a pinpoint or spike at which a person's body is reorganized when the person moves (Netwson, 1973). In addition to action units, episodic boundaries are also remembered better. Newtson, Gown, and Patterson (1980) replicated this finding with five-year-old children (Newtson et al., 1987). Rinder (1982) found that adults who segmented events into finer units recognized breakpoints better than non-breakpoints whereas adults who segmented larger units did not show any differences in recognition memory.

Being similar to this button technique, Arnone, Grabowski, and Rynd (1994) studied interactive video technology in order to explore its effectiveness on young children's memory. Interactive video technology is defined as any video program in which the sequence and selection of instructional messages are determined by the user's response to the material (Floyd, 1982). Arnone and his colleague gave first- and second-graders in their study the opportunity to stop and look at videotape whenever they needed to review it in a test trial. The instructional material on the videotape was "A visit to the Museum". The 14 minutes videotape consisted of paintings, sculpture, and ceramics. The videotape showed artwork such as still life, portraits, etc. After seeing the videotape, the children were given achievement test. In the test, children were shown pictures of the artwork that they had been exposed to in the practice, and then they were asked to "remember everything that you know about what you saw." Experimenter also gave advices to encourage the child to stop and think about specific content, to skip a section. Results indicated that first grade children recalled information better when they stopped and reviewed it.

From Newtson's and Arnone and his colleagues' result, it is obvious that young children's self-control and reflection of information at encoding phase helped them to remember events. Thus, if young children are induced to use interactive video technology spontaneously at encoding phase, their memory might improve. Therefore, a hypothesis is made that five-year-old children's event memory might be improved if they have opportunities to segment the events they experience through interactive video printer technology in this study. Video Printer is a machine that produces image-like photographs from a videotape of an event by pressing a button. Specifically, it is assumed that young children's event memory might improve if they make and reflect the event they experience by this video printer. This also leads to a hypothesis about the quality of breakpoints, which might influence on event memory. The better quality of picture might be related to the children's ability of remembering event.

2 Methods

2.1 Subjects

A total of 48 children were sampled from the Amherst Area in Massachusetts. Twenty-four 5-year-old children and twenty-four 7-year-old children served as experimental subjects. The children were randomly assigned to one of two treatment conditions. Twelve children in each age group were assigned to the Video Printer Group, and twelve other children in each age group were assigned to the Video Tape Group.

2.2 Materials

The videotape consisted of six plans of actions. In the videotape, a man, sitting on a chair by a table, demonstrated the way of how to make a Navaho sand pattern. Only his torso and hands doing the action were seen in the videotape. There were two silver plates on the table: The left one was empty while the right one was full of sand. First, the man named a rake, a sieve, a spoon, a funnel, and a cup that were on the table. Then he showed six steps of actions in the order as followings: 1. He scooped three spoonfuls of sand into a cup. 2. He shook a sieve of sand into the plate. 3. He smoothed out the sand with his left hand. 4. He raked the sand and made six crossing lines on it. 5. He poured leftover rocks from the sieve into the funnel on the cup. 6. He poured rocks into the cup all around the plate. There is each main action in each step. Each main action in each step includes (1) putting a spoon of sand in a cup in the first step, (2) Shaving a sieve of sand all around pan in the second step (3) Smoothing sand all around pan with the hand in the third step (4) Raking sand on plate in cross row pattern in the fourth step (5) Pouring rocks in the sieve through funnel in the cup in the fifth step (6) Pouring rocks all around sand plate in the sixth step. There are pre actions and after actions related to each main action.

2.3 Procedure

All of the children were given memory test during the first session. Children in the video printer group were shown their video prints mixed up after they had made six prints from video printer. Then, hey were asked to arrange these prints in the correct sequence as portrayed in the videotape and "tell the story" of the making of the Navaho sand pattern (immediate recall with pictures). Following this, the pictures were removed and the children were once again asked to tell the story (immediate recall without pictures). Each child in the video only group was given video prints that were made by the "yoked control" partner from the video printer group. They were asked to arrange these video prints in the correct sequence. Then they were asked to look at these prints and tell the story of the making of the Navaho sand pattern. Then, they were asked to recall the story without the pictures. One day later, all children were invited back. First, they were asked to recall the story of the Navaho sand pattern without looking at the video prints (delayed recall without pictures).

2.4 Research Design

A factorial design was used in this experiment. They were two ages, two treatment conditions, and three memory measures with repeated measurement used. Ages were between subject groups. Treatment conditions and the three memory measures were taken within subject groups.

2.5 Dependent Variables and Scores

The assessment was used to measure three dependent variables, immediate recall with pictures, immediate recall without pictures and delayed recall without pictures to remember "how to make a Navaho sand pattern" on the videotape. Scores of verbal protocol ranged from 0 to 3. The criteria of accurate description were based on whether an agent of action and names of objects in the action were described. The most accurate description of a main action was score 3. A general description of a main action was scored 1. If main action is detailed but the name of an object or agent was omitted, the description was scored 2. In order to determine the relationship between breakpoint boundary and each memory measure, picture quality was assessed on the breakpoint boundaries of actions that the children made. The quality of each picture the children made was evaluated by an action scheme. If a child makes a photograph of a main action, the child was given a score of 3. If the photograph concerned pre and subsequent action, a score of 1 was given. If no photograph was made of main, pre, or subsequent action in one action category, a score of 0 was given.

3 Results

To measure the effects of the video printer on memory, an analysis of variance with repeated measures was used to analyze a design 2 (age) X 2 (treatment conditions) X 3(three memory measures) for recall. Dependent variables were differences on each of the five scores: immediate recall with pictures, immediate recall without pictures, and delayed recall without pictures. There was no three-way interaction. There was significant two-way interaction between age and treatment conditions for the three measures.

3.1 Recalls

There was two-way interactions for treatment and age (F=.000, P<.05) and main effects for age (F=.000, P<.05) and for treatment (F=.000, P<.05). For the age difference, there were significant mean differences between the Video Printer group and Video Only group only for the five-year-old children. In order to see the interaction effect of age and treatment, Manova was used. There were significant differences of two treatment conditions for each memory measure in five-year-old children (Immediate recall with pictures (F=.000, P<.05), immediate recall without pictures (F=.000, P<.05), and delayed recall without pictures (F=.000, P<.05)). But, there were no significant differences of two treatment conditions for each memory measures in seven-year-old children [immediate recall with pictures (F=.461, P>.05), immediate recall without pictures(F=.579, P>.05), delayed recall without pictures (F=.712, P>.05)]. Thus, the two-way interaction between age and treatment conditions is due to the significant mean differences in each memory measures for five-year-old children. For details of mean differences of three memory measures in each age group, each mean is described in Table 1.

Table 1. Each mean of three memories

	Video Printer	**Video Only**
Immediate Recall with Pictures		
Five-years-old	10.08(2.90)	4.25(2.63)
Seven-years-old	12.33(2.60)	11.60(2.74)
Immediate Recall without Pictures		
Five-years-old	9.75(2.80)	3.50(3.45)
Seven-years-old	12.25(1.86)	11.66(2.74)
Delayed Recall without Pictures		
Five-years-old	8.83(1.94)	2.75(3.49)
Seven-years-old	11.83(2.58)	12.16(1.52)

The five-year-old children obviously benefited from using the video printer, but seven-year-old children did not benefit either because the episodic event used in the present study was too simple to measure the effects or because the video printer itself is a useless tool for helping seven-year-old children to remember. In the following research studies, these issues should be explored.

3.2 Relationship of Picture Quality and Recalls

It was assumed that children's memory would be better if they made good breakpoints of main actions. All Pictures that were made by children were judged to be non-breakpoint or breakpoint. If children made a picture of a main action, the picture was evaluated as a breakpoint. Non-breakpoints of an event consist of pre-actions and subsequent actions. A Spearman Correlation Coefficient was derived for collapsed age. For the Video printer group, there was a significant relationship between the quality of the pictures and immediate recall with pictures in main action 3, 4, and 6. Even though there was no significant correlation between picture quality and immediate recall with pictures in other main actions, it almost reached significant levels. For main action 1, the correlation was distinctly low. For this action, there might be primacy effect. As a result, children might remember these first actions regardless of picture quality. There were no significant relationships between picture quality and immediate and delayed recall without pictures except for the case of main action 3 in immediate recall without pictures and main action 2 in delayed recall without pictures.

Table 2. Spearman correlation between picture quality and each memory

Each memory	Picture Quality
	1 2 3 4 5 6
Imm. with Pic.	
1	r=.1069, P=.741
2	r=.5409, P=.069
3	r=.7127, *P=.009
4	r=.5869, *P=.045
5	r=.5409, P=.0669
6	r=.6606, *P=.019
Imm.without Pic.	
1	r=-.821, *P=.001
2	r=.3786, P=.225
3	r=.6990, *P=.011
4	r=.4868, P=.109
5	r=.4787, P=.115
6	r=.4226, P=.171
Del. Without Pic.	
1	r=-.2342, P=.464
2	r=.6110, *P=.035
3	r=.5410, P=.069
4	r=.3636, P=.245
5	r=.3840, P=.218
6	r=.1429 *P=.658

The relationship between picture quality and memory seems to depend on the nature of pre and sub action. Compared to actions 3, 4, 6, action scheme 2, 5 were complicated. Action schemes 3, 4, 6 consisted of one pre action, one main action, and one subsequent action. In order to achieve plan schemes 2 and 5, there needed to be more than one pre action or subsequent action. For example, action 2, 5, there are several steps to reach the main action in the action scheme, which consist of more actions, objects to remember than other action schemes. This complicated structure of actions might lead to the ineffectiveness of good quality of printers on memory. For the Video Only group, there was no relationship between picture quality and three memories except for immediate recall without pictures in main action 6(r=.7628, *P=.004). Therefore, the picture as a cue for prompting was effective only when children made those by themselves.

4 Discussion

The main purpose of this study was to explore the effects of video printer technology on children's memory. It was predicted that five-year-old children would improve their memory by segmenting and reflecting an event with a video printer. As predicted, five-year-old children who made pictures of the event remembered better than those who only watched the event. While interacting with the video printer, children must be induced to reflect on the event by deciding when to make breakpoints. There need to be an act of deciding which one of scenes indicates best action to tell story during this process. Mnemonic strategies in young children were known to use mnemonic strategies such as categorical organizational strategy, keyword strategy, and mental effort (Carr & Schneider, 1991; Pressley, Borkowski, & Schneider, 1987). In general, five-year-old children were found not to use these strategies spontaneously whereas older children were found to do so (Bjorklund et al., 1977). Five-year-old children were able to use these strategies if given explicit training (Ornstein et al, 1985). Explicit training in these strategies was not found to improve recall in young children (Bjorklund & Harnishfeger, 1987; Carr & Schneider, 1991). But, in present study, five-year-old children used it and improved their memory if young children are induced to use the strategy spontaneously. The use of spontaneous strategy might lead to "conscious control" of information-processing at an encoding phase. This might contribute to the improvement of event memory in five-years-old children. The children also remembered better if they attend to information they need to remember, that are breakpoints of behavior.

References

1. Arnone, M., Grabowski, B., & Rynd, C.: Curiosity as a Personality Variable Influencing Learning in a Learner Controlled Lesson with and without Advisement. Educational Technology and Development 41(1) (1994) 5-20.
2. Bjorklund, D. F., & Harnishfeger, K. K.: Developmental Differences in the Mental Efforts Requirements for the use of an Organizational Strategy in Free Recall. Journal of Experimental Child Psychology 44 (1987) 109-125.
3. Bjorklund, D. F., Ornstein, P. A., J. R.: Developmental Differences in the Mental Effort Requirements for the use of an Organizational Strategy in Free Recall. Journal of Experimental Child Psychology 22 (1977) 109-125
4. Carr, M., & Schneider, W.: Long-Term Maintenance of Organizational Strategies in Kindergarten Children. Contemporary Educational Psychology 16 (1991) 61-75.
5. Farrar, M. J., & Goodman, G. S.: Developmental Differences in the Relation Between Scripts and Episodic Memory: Do they Exist? In Fivush, R., & Hudson, J., Knowing and Remembering in Young Children. Cambridge Univeristy Press (1990) 30-64
6. Fivush, R., Kuebli, J., & Clubb, P. A.: The Structure of Events and Event Representations: A Developmental Analysis. Child Development 63 (1992) 188-202
7. Flavel, J., Miller, P. H., & Miller, S. A.: Cognitive Development. NJ: Prentice Hall (2002)
8. Floyd, S.: Thinking Interactively. In S. Floyd and Floyd (Eds.), Handbook of Interactive Video. White Plains, NY: Knowledge Industry Publication (1982)
9. Mandler, J. M.: Stories, Scripts and Scenes: Aspects of Schema Theory. Hillsdale, NJ: Erlbaum. (1984)

10. Nelson, K.: Event Knowledge and Cognitive Development. In K. Nelson, Event Knowledge: Structure and Function in Development. Hillsdale, NJ: Erlbaum (1986) 2-19
11. Newtson, D.: Attribution and the Unit of Perception of Ongoing Behavior. Journal of Personality and Social Psychology 28 (1973) 28-38
12. Newtson, D., & Engquist, G.: The Perceptual Organization of Ongoing Behavior. Journal of Experimental Social Psychology 12 (1976) 436-450
13. Newtson, D., & Rinder, R. J.: Variation in Behavior Perception and Ability. Journal of Personality and Social Psychology 37(10) (1979) 1847-1858.
14. Newtson, D., Gown, D., & Patterson, C.: The Development of Action Discrimination. Paper Presented at the Meeting of the American Psychological Association, Montreal. Patterson. (1980)
15. Newtson, D., Hairfield, J., Bloomingdale, J., & Cutino, S.: Social Cognition 5(3) (1987) 191-237
16. Rinder, R.: Different Units of Information in the Perception of Behavior. Doctoral Dissertation, University of Virginia. (1982)
17. Ornstein, P. A., & Naus, M. J.: Effects of the Knowledge Base on Children's Memory Strategies. In H. W. Reese(Ed.), Advances in Child Development and Behavior, Vol. 19, New York: Academic Press (1985)
18. Pressley, M., Borkowski, J. G., & Schneider, W.: Cognitive Strategies: Good Strategy Users Coordinate Metacognition and Knowledge. In R. Vesta G. Whitehurst (Eds.), Annals of Child Development (1987)
19. Rinder, R.: Different Units of Information in the Perception of Behavior. Doctoral Dissertation, University of Virginia. (1982)
20. Schank, R. C., & Abelson, R. P.: Scripts, Plans, Goals, and Understanding. Hillsdale, NJ: Erlbaum (1977)
21. Sigler, R: Children's Thinking. NJ: Prentice Hall (1991)
22. Sigler, R: Children's Thinking. NJ: Prentice Hall (1998)

Towards an Expressive Typology in Storytelling: A Perceptive Approach

Véronique Bralé[1], Valérie Maffiolo[1], Ioannis Kanellos[2], and Thierry Moudenc[1]

[1] France Telecom R&D, Technologies Division,
Technopole Anticipa, 2, av. Pierre Marzin, 22307 Lannion, France
{veronique.brale, valerie.maffiolo,
thierry.moudenc}@francetelecom.com
[2] LUSSI, ENST Bretagne, 29238 Brest Cedex, France
ioannis.kanellos@enst-bretagne.fr

Abstract. This paper investigates the perception of expressiveness in storytelling. The aim is to establish a typology by identifying in a first step different perceived expressive forms. Two perceptive tests, a listening and a reading test, have been set up using a free semantic verbalization method. In particular, we focused on the influence of verbal and non verbal information on the perception of expressive types. From a detailed analysis of the listening test answers we distinguished between three situational categories of expressiveness specific to storytelling (emotions, emotional attitudes and means of expression). A comparison of the data collected in both tests has yielded different cues that seem to have been interpreted as expressing surprise, fear and sadness.

1 Introduction

This study is carried out in the framework of research on expressive speech synthesis. Two main communication situations can be distinguished: interactive (human-computer interaction, e-mail reading) vs. non interactive communication situation (book reading). Nonetheless, more expressiveness in synthetic speech is needed in these two practices: some prosodic features can be manually tuned, but current systems are still not able to synthesize expressive speech automatically. In this work, we deal with the non interactive case of expressiveness.

A text can be vocalized in different ways according to the expressiveness the speaker wants to convey. Though current Text To Speech systems produce high quality and intelligible speech, they are still not able to produce such expressiveness. Storytelling constitutes a possible application for TTS synthesis, for example in the case of a virtual storyteller system [1]. As storytelling involves various standard forms of expressive speech, our work focuses on this particular practice and intends to answer the following questions. What are the different expressive types occurring in storytelling and what are their constitutive elements? Our aim is to identify expressive types that are consistent with the three following dimensions. The first one concerns the interpretation process, i.e. the attribution of meaning to a text by a reader-speaker. Several levels are involved in this process: punctuation, lexicon, syntax, thematic relations, cotext (textual context), context (knowledge of a tale) and intertext (relation

J. Tao, T. Tan, and R.W. Picard (Eds.): ACII 2005, LNCS 3784, pp. 858–865, 2005.

of a tale with other texts). The second dimension deals with the vocalization of this text by the speaker, his/her vocal production depending on the particular interpretation he/she has. Finally, the third dimension concerns the perception of this vocal production by a listener. This perception includes a process of attribution of meaning to the vocal production. This paper deals with the perceptive dimension studying more precisely the respective contribution of verbal and non verbal contents to the perception of expressive types. We do not deal with gestures and facial expressions. As there is no broad consensus on the distinction between para and extra-linguistic [2], we focus on non verbal or paralinguistic information [3] as opposed to linguistic information (verbal content) and non or extra-linguistic information (sex, age…).

Expressiveness is used here to refer to voluntary communicative affective expression as opposed to involuntary and direct expression of the speaker's emotional states during his/her speech communication process [4]. Of course, in the specific case of storytelling, we are not interested in the speaker's own emotional states, but either in the expression of the emotions felt by the story characters or in the expression aiming at inducing emotional states to the listener. So we will use the term "emotional attitude" referring to the voluntary communication process aiming at expressing or inducing emotions.

The present paper is organized as follows. Section 2 and 3 present respectively the corpus creation and the tests procedures. Section 4 describes and discusses the results of the tests. Finally, section 5 concludes and suggests possible future work.

2 Corpus

The corpus used in this study is composed of speech sentences taken from several well-known fairy tales by J. & W. Grimm, C. Perrault and H.C. Andersen, such as Cinderella, Little Red Riding Hood or The Ugly Duckling. The corpus language is French. The sentences were read by professional speakers. Fairy tales have been chosen because they obviously contain various forms of expressive speech. Moreover, they are part of everybody's common experience in all communicative positions (reader, speaker or listener). So we considered fairy tales as a common background among the subjects who participated in the perceptive tests.

Having been recorded by actors under studio conditions, this speech corpus is an "in vitro" and "acted" corpus [4]. Nonetheless, it differs from traditional acted emotional speech corpora because the professional speakers were not directly asked to simulate specific emotions and the sentences read were not neutral carrier sentences being held constant.

The spoken corpus used in this study is composed of a selection of 480 speech sentences taken from 13 well-known fairy tales read by one male and three female professional speakers. These particular speech sentences were extracted from larger recordings because of the speech's good acoustic quality (that is, speech being free from any noise). Besides, half of the sentences were selected because they seemed to be expressive or neutral and the others were randomly selected. The written corpus is made of the textual transcripts of the speech sentences.

3 Test Procedures

Two perceptive tests were carried out each with three different groups of 16 subjects. As a whole, 48 male and 48 female subjects took part in the experiments. They were naive listeners between 20 and 62 years old and belonging to various socio-professional categories. The subjects were shared according to their age so that each group was representative of the three following age brackets: 20 to 30, 30 to 40 and more than 40.

Listening Test. During the first test, each group of subjects listened successively to 160 speech sentences. They were told that the sentences were taken from well-known fairy tales. They could listen to each sentence only once. Even if this single listening could influence the tests results, we thought that it was closer to the real situation in which somebody listens to a fairy tale that is being read and interprets what they hear as time goes by. The sound restitution was made by headphones in laboratory conditions. The test lasted two hours maximum. The sentences were presented in a randomized order to each subject. A free semantic verbalization method has been used as our aim was to get very fine grained and various answers. After listening to each sentence, the subjects were asked to answer freely and spontaneously the following question: *"What does the narrator want to express?"*. There was no restriction concerning the type of answer to give: the subjects were free to use their own words and to type in a single word, a phrase or a whole sentence if they wanted. However, they had to give an answer. A training phase with five sentences has been carried out before the test so as to familiarize the subjects with the task and the computer interface that enabled them to type in the answers directly with the computer keyboard. The word "emotion" was deliberately not used in the question because we did not want to influence the subjects' answers by narrowing their attention to the usual but still problematic six emotions (anger, fear, happiness, sadness, surprise and disgust). Yet, the subjects were told that they were not asked to reformulate nor sum up the sentence content.

Reading Test. During the second test, each group of subjects read successively on a computer screen the 160 textual transcripts of the speech sentences. The verbalization task and the question asked to the subjects were the same as in the listening test. This test lasted also two hours maximum. Contrary to the first test, they did not listen to the sentences. The sentences were written and remained displayed on the screen while the answer was being typed in. Consequently, the subjects could take their time to read the sentences whereas the spoken sentences could only be heard once. This procedure was necessary because the reading time differs for each subject whereas the listening time is the same. A training phase had also been carried out before the test.

Perception Test Paradigm. We deliberately chose not to use the widespread perception test paradigm of forced-choice identification in which subjects are prescribed a set of labels and must assign to each stimulus one emotion category label [5]. The first reason is that we did not have this set of labels before the test. Besides, as [6] pointed out, what a speaker wants to express is less important than the meaning being perceived. Thus, we did not reduce the human perception of expressiveness in speech to a simple capacity to recognize previously encoded emotions being evaluated in terms of success or failure. Moreover, as underlined by [7], forced-choice identification tests consist rather in discriminating among several alternatives rather than properly identifying an emotional category.

4 Results and Discussions

4.1 Role of the Context

A first point has to be made about the influence of the context (knowledge of the tale) upon the subjects' answers in both tests. Indeed, the subjects had to interpret isolated sentences separated from their cotext, i.e. from the text that surrounds them. Nonetheless, the knowledge of fairy tales played an important part. A case in point is the sentence *"The following day, dressed like an old pedlar-woman, she went and knocked at the dwarfs' door."* Some subjects gave the answers: revenge, nastiness of the queen, Snow White's kindness, trap, plot. In this sentence, the queen and Snow White are not mentioned but the subjects obviously recognized the story and knew who the characters were. We considered this knowledge as common to all the subjects that participated in the tests. Indeed, one of our working hypotheses was that the context influence was nearly the same in all the answers. Even if the context actually influenced the subjects' answers, it seemed to concern only few answers. Nevertheless, this aspect will be further investigated in a future perceptive test.

4.2 Listening Test Results

The subjective data collected in the listening test were very rich and large: 7680 answers. We think that this richness is partly due to the question asked to the subjects and more precisely, to the fact that the word "emotion" was not directly mentioned. Indeed some answers such as suspense or mystery are not proper emotions, but we consider them as attitudes used to induce or express emotional states. A first stage consisting in the manual cleaning of all the data resulted in 11818 verbatim. We call verbatim, meaningful units in answers. For example, the answer "surprise and joy" contains two verbatim. Then, in order to reduce data redundancy, verbatim such as surprised, astonishment and surprise have been clustered using morphological and synonymic relations. Occurrence frequencies have been calculated for each clustered item. The least significant items were discarded according to the ratio between the number of items occurrences in the answers and the number of different sentences for which these items occurred. Finally, 42 items were derived from the whole data. As the data were quite heterogeneous, we distinguished between three items categories corresponding to the three situational categories mentioned before. The first one deals with emotions such as anger, fear or joy.

Table 1. Most frequent items

	Occurrences in answers	Sentences listened to
Surprise	628	172
Fear	587	184
Sadness	420	143
Happiness	343	126
Anger	151	78

As shown in Table 1, it is interesting to notice that the five most frequent items belonged the traditional "big six" emotions. The high occurrence-sentence ratio for these items reveals a strong inter-subjects agreement. We can also notice that the last one, disgust, also appeared in the answers but it was less frequent and less significant than the five others. The second category refers to emotional attitudes, i.e. ways of inducing emotions to the listener or expressing characters' emotions. For example, nastiness or aggressiveness are items belonging to this category. Finally, the third one contains potential means of expression of these emotional attitudes. They can be various verbal and non verbal information, as order or quickness. Some subjects made even clear the link between emotions, attitudes and their means of expressions when giving for example in the same answer anger, nastiness and quick speech.

4.3 Listening Test vs. Reading Test

Another part of the data analysis consisted in the comparison between the results of the two tests. After closely comparing the listening and reading tests data for each one of the 480 sentences, we separated the four following categories. This is of course a first way of studying the data as the listening and reading test answers cannot be directly associated respectively to non verbal and verbal contents, the influence of verbal and non verbal levels being much more complex.

- Listening and reading tests items were similar. For example, for the sentence *"The door was still ajar when the wolf jumped into the room."*, we got the following items in the listening and reading tests answers: rapidity, surprise and quickness. This type of answers represents 2.5 % of the corpus.
- Listening and reading tests items were different. For the sentence *"I have been looking for you for quite a long time!"*, the items given in the listening test were threat, nastiness and anger. On the opposite, the items given in the reading test were relief, result and end of search. This type represents only 0.2% of the corpus.
- Listening test items were richer than reading test ones. For the sentence *"What big teeth you have got, grandmother!"*, the items given in the listening test were surprise, astonishment whereas the items given in the reading test were surprise, astonishment but also fear and fright. 19.1% of the answers belong to this type.
- Listening and reading tests items were partly similar. For the sentence *"One moment longer, if you please."*, some items were common to the two tests answers, as for request or plea, some were only given in the listening test such as fear, panic and others were only given in the reading test as order. This type represents the majority of the answers (78.2%).

We could also have distinguished another type of answers. Indeed in some sentences, it seemed that the verbal content was perceived as less intensive as the non verbal content. For example, in the sentence *"We got rid of him!"*, the reading test answers were relief, satisfaction and success. The listening test answers were quite similar: *relief, at last... what a satisfaction! and victory!!!* Yet, the punctuation used in the listening test answers can be considered as more expressive, more intensive than in the reading test. In addition, we could say that this notion of intensity also appeared in the use of words expressing different levels of intensity. For example, stupefaction or amazement are more intense than surprise. This aspect has not been closely studied in this work, but still seems of great interest.

4.4 Surprise, Fear and Sadness

Afterwards, the three most frequent items (surprise, fear and sadness) were studied in details. Sentences in which these items occurred only once were discarded. Our aim was to get more precise cues about the respective influence of verbal and non verbal contents in the expression of these three emotions. Table 2 shows the distribution of these cues in the sentences according to the three perceived emotions and the tests (listening and/or reading) in which the answers were given. Some sentences contained several different cues. Among the 113 sentences that were perceived as expressing surprise, 43 were perceived as expressing surprise only during the listening test and 70 during both tests. Nevertheless, this did not necessarily mean that in these two groups of sentences, surprise was respectively conveyed only by the non verbal and verbal contents. Indeed, when looking more closely at each of the sentences perceived as expressing surprise, fear and sadness, it appeared that the emotions were partly conveyed by a combination of several verbal cues at different levels: punctuation, syntax and lexicon.

Table 2. Verbal and non verbal cues in surprise, fear and sadness sentences

Items		Surprise		Fear		Sadness	
Tests		LR	L	LR	L	LR	L
Number of sentences		**70**	**43**	75	38	44	32
Punctuation	!	11	2	0	4	0	1
Syntax	Excl.	19	4	6	9	1	0
	Quest.	8	6	**17**	5	7	4
Lexicon	Interj.	5	1	1	1	4	3
	Emot. word	6	0	12	0	**13**	2
	Sem. theme	25	6	33	10	14	15
Non verbal		0	**29**	0	**14**	0	**10**

For example, 17 sentences that were perceived as expressing fear during the listening and reading tests were questions and 13 sentences that were perceived as expressing sadness during both tests contained an emotional word.

The surprise item distinguishes from the other items because there were 11 exclamative sentences that contained only a punctuation mark as a cue for exclamation. Contrary to the other exclamative sentences, they did not contain both an exclamation mark and a typical exclamative syntactic structure such as *how...*, *what a...* or an interjection as *oh, my God*. We thus supposed that surprise was expressed by the exclamation mark in the reading test and by some prosodic equivalent information in the listening test. For the other exclamative sentences, surprise seems to have been conveyed by the verbal content, i.e. at least by the exclamation mark and an exclamative structure. Concerning the question mark, all the sentences including one had also an interrogative structure, so verbal and non verbal content can both have been interpreted as expressing surprise in the listening test.

As far as the lexicon is concerned, there were several explicit emotional words specific to each emotional state such as *surprised, frightened* or *crying*. As verbal cues, they obviously have strongly influenced the subjects' perception in both tests: the sentences containing an explicit emotional word were perceived as expressing this emotional state in both tests. Other less explicit lexical cues were also contained in the sentences such as words expressing recurring semantic themes directly linked to a specific item. For example, we noticed that some surprise sentences contained words belonging to the following semantic themes: *strangeness*, *discovery*, *suddenness*, *intensity*. Some themes seemed to be specifically associated to an emotion: *nasty character* or *flight* were associated to fear and *loneliness*, *misfortune* or *separation* to sadness, but others were common to several emotions, such as *death* to fear and sadness or *strangeness* to surprise and fear.

Concerning the sentences for which the items surprise, fear and sadness were given only in the listening test, and more precisely those which contained lexical (interjections, semantic themes) and syntactic cues (exclamation or question), two hypotheses can be made to explain the fact that they were not perceived as expressing surprise, fear or sadness by the subjects who participated in the reading test. On the one hand, it can mean that in these sentences the emotional states were only conveyed by the non verbal content. On the other hand, it could be due to chance, i.e. these particular subjects have focused their attention on other semantic themes or cues, but other subjects might have interpreted the sentences differently.

Besides, the case of a few declarative sentences is worth noticing. They have not been perceived as expressing surprise in the reading test whereas similar exclamative sentences have been perceived as expressing surprise: *"My God, how happy you are."* and *"My God, how ugly you are!"*. The final stop in the first sentence seems to have been more important in expressing surprise than the other verbal cues as *my God* and the exclamative structure *how ugly you are*. Indeed, the reading test answers focused on *assertion* and *noticing*. Finally, we pointed out 53 sentences (29 for surprise, 14 for fear and 10 for sadness) for which we can suppose that these emotions were only expressed by means of the non verbal content, i.e. prosodic information, since they did not contain any particular verbal cues.

5 Conclusion and Future Work

This preliminary study aiming at establishing an expressive typology yielded different perceived expressive forms in storytelling. They were separated into three situational categories (emotions, emotional attitudes, means of expression). We identified several verbal and non verbal cues involved in the perception of three specific emotions (surprise, fear and sadness).

As we suppose that the perceived expressive forms partly correspond to different produced expressive forms, non verbal aspects will be dealt with in future work from a production viewpoint. Our interest will focus on the interaction between these aspects and specific verbal cues such as those highlighted in this paper. The role played by the non verbal content in intensifying expressive forms conveyed by the verbal content would notably require further study, checking the assumption made by [8] that some non verbal cues convey *"affective information only in conjunction with specific linguistic features of the text"*, thus rejecting the "parallel channel approach" that considers the non verbal channel meaning as being *"superimposed on the meaning of the text in an essentially additive way"*.

The present study is part of a more general semiotics issue considering verbal and non verbal contents as two semiotic dimensions being either complementary or concurrent or even contradictory. The interpretation may therefore be defined as a selection process, made by the reader-speaker or the listener through different points of view modeling the verbal and non verbal information. In such a process, some cues are emphasized whereas others are discarded. In the specific framework of expressive speech synthesis, our aim is to determine cues correlates contributing to a plurisemiotic model of expressive types that could be used by present TTS synthesizers.

References

1. Theune, M., Meijs, K., Ordelman, R., Akker, R. o. d., and Heylen, D.: Narrative speech for a Virtual Storyteller. Human-Machine Interaction Network on Emotion Workshop: Emotion in Interaction (2005)
2. Lacheret-Dujour, A., Beaugendre, F.: La prosodie du français. CNRS Editions, Paris (1999)
3. Maekawa, K.: Production and perception of 'paralinguistic' information. Speech Prosody (2004) 367-374
4. Aubergé, V., Audibert, N., Rilliard, A.: Why and how to control the authentic emotional speech corpora. Eurospeech (2003) 185-188
5. Schröder, M.: Speech and Emotion Research: An overview of research frameworks and a dimensional approach to emotional speech synthesis. Ph.D., Univ. of Saarland (2004)
6. Léon, P.: Précis de phonostylistique : parole et expressivité. Nathan, Paris (1993)
7. Banse, R., Scherer, K. R.: Acoustic profiles in vocal emotion expression. Journal of Personality and Social Psychology (1996) vol. 70, 614-636
8. Scherer, K. R., Ladd, D. R., Silverman, K. E. A.: Vocal cues to speaker affect: Testing two models. J. Acoust. Soc. Amer. (1984) vol. 76, 1346-1356

Affective-Cognitive Learning and Decision Making: A Motivational Reward Framework for Affective Agents

Hyungil Ahn and Rosalind W. Picard

MIT Media Lab, Cambridge MA 02139, USA
{hiahn, picard}@media.mit.edu

Abstract. In this paper we present a new computational framework of affective-cognitive learning and decision making for affective agents, inspired by human learning and recent neuroscience and psychology. In the proposed framework 'internal reward from cognition and emotion' and 'external reward from the external world' serve as motivation in learning and decision making. We construct this model, integrating affect and cognition, with the aim of enabling machines to make smarter and more human-like decisions for better human-machine interactions.

1 Introduction

Recent affective neuroscience and psychology have reported that human affect and emotional experience play a significant, and useful, role in human learning and decision making. In normal individuals, the covert biases related to previous emotional experience of comparable situations assist the reasoning process and facilitate the efficient processing of knowledge and logic necessary for conscious decisions [3]. It has been argued that positive affect increases intrinsic motivation [6]. Also, the neurotransmitter, dopamine serves as motivational reward and the dopamine (DA) circuit plays an integral part in the reinforcing or reward learning in the emotional brain. The DA circuit is significant in the emotional function of the brain - the basic impulse to search, investigate, and make sense of the environment [8]. Although a model of curiosity for self-motivated development has been researched [11] and a model of intrinsically motivated reinforcement learning based on the options framework has been proposed [2], the extension of cognitive theory to explain and exploit the role of affect in learning is in its infancy [10]. This paper presents a new computational framework of affective-cognitive learning and decision making, inspired by human learning and recent neuroscience and psychology.

2 Affective-Cognitive Learning and Decision Making

2.1 The Affective Agent

For humans or other animals, motivation is essential in their learning and decision making and 'wanting' is directly linked to motivation [4,8]. Also, 'wanting'

J. Tao, T. Tan, and R.W. Picard (Eds.): ACII 2005, LNCS 3784, pp. 866–873, 2005.

can be decomposed into 'implicit incentive salience wanting' and 'cognitive incentive goal-directed wanting' [4]. Inspired by recent affective neuroscience, our approach assumes that an *affective agent* has both cognition and emotion and its motivation can be modeled by reward and that 'internal reward from cognition and emotion' and 'external reward from the external world' can explain motivation in its learning and decision making. Further, we propose a mental or internal simulation loop which computes internal reward for each imagined decision. The internal simulation loop functions as 'expectation or imagination loop' for thinking and 'as-if-body-loop'[5] for feeling in an affective agent. This loop assesses the total weighted internal reward from cognition and emotion in the framework.

For example, the MIT Media Lab's Affective Computing Group in collaboration with Robotic Life Group is building a robotic computer (RoCo) that moves its monitor 'head' and 'neck'. RoCo is an affective agent that is being designed to interact with users in a natural way for applications such as learning, rapport-building, interactive teaching, and posture improvement.

Also, RoCo can learn and decide how to behave to maximize external rewards from the user. In a simulation of RoCo, we adopted a user model where a user tended to give a reward ('show pleasure') under these decisions: RoCo decides to 'track' when the user state is 'attentive', RoCo decides to 'entertain' when the user state is 'distracted', and RoCo decides to 'stretch' when the user state is 'slumped'. From the perspective of RoCo, the user is the external world. We assume that RoCo can perceive the external world (the user) and by means of an *attention model*, can recognize one of a user's five different states - 'attentive', 'distracted', 'slumped', 'showing pleasure' (as a reward for RoCo), 'showing displeasure' (as a punishment for RoCo) - with an accuracy of 90%. A user's state recognized by RoCo can be viewed as part of the *cognitive state* of RoCo, since once it is recognized it is merely a label to RoCo.

We construct RoCo to have two goals in the simulation: to try to make the user 'attentive' or to 'show pleasure'. RoCo's internal cognitive rewards are always given toward encouraging itself to make its goals. Thus, RoCo has a positive internal cognitive reward for decisions that result in the user being 'attentive' or 'showing pleasure'. We call such a state a *'cognitively wanted state'*.

RoCo also has two internal *emotional states* labeled 'feeling good' and 'feeling bad', and we bias RoCo to want to feel good rather than bad. In other words, 'feeling good' is RoCo's *'emotionally wanted state'*. When the user 'shows pleasure' the 'feeling good' state becomes more likely, while when the user 'shows displeasure' RoCo's 'feeling bad' state becomes more probable.

Each of RoCo's decisions – 'tracking', 'entertaining', etc., may be composed of lower-level decisions. Thus, we propose that an affective agent should have a hierarchical network of decisions, and each decision should have an internal affective-cognitive decision-making process that can decide which lower-level decision is appropriate given the current cognitive and emotional states.

2.2 The Hierarchical Network of Affective-Cognitive Decisions

In the previous section we proposed a hierarchical network of decisions for an affective agent. However, we prefer to use a more special and meaningful term *'affective-cognitive decision (ACD)'* rather than to use a general term 'decision'. According to this terminology, an affective agent has a hierarchical network of ACDs (Figure 1) and an ACD is composed of temporally sequential lower-level ACDs or lower-level primitive skills. An *affective-cognitive decision (ACD)* has a certain goal and is able to start (activate) or stop (deactivate) other ACDs for achieving the goal. An *episode* is completed when a cognitive state of the goal is achieved. An ACD is activated when a higher-level ACD sends an activation signal to it, and deactivated when a higher-level ACD sends a deactivation signal to it or it completes an episode.

Our model is framed probabilistically. Let c, e, $\hat{e}$, d, c' and e', respectively, denote the current cognitive state (c), the current emotional state (e), the probability distribution of the current emotional state ($\hat{e}$), the current lower-level ACD (d) being chosen, the next cognitive state (c') after the current lower-level ACD, and the next emotional state (e'). An ACD maintains an attention model, a cognition model $\Pr(c' \mid c, d)$, an emotion model $\Pr(e' \mid c', e)$, a decision-making model $\Pr(d \mid \hat{e}, c)$, a cognitive reward model $Q_{CR}(c, d)$ and an emotional reward model $Q_{ER}(\hat{e}, c, d)$.

Whenever a lower-level ACD d has been made and acted upon, the corresponding *external reward* from the external world can be assessed and be used for updating the models of the ACD with the self-motivating *internal reward.*

An ACD also maintains an *attention model* to extract useful features from the perceived multi-modal external stimuli (from the external world, e.g. recognizing postural and facial features of the user). Each ACD can have its own attention

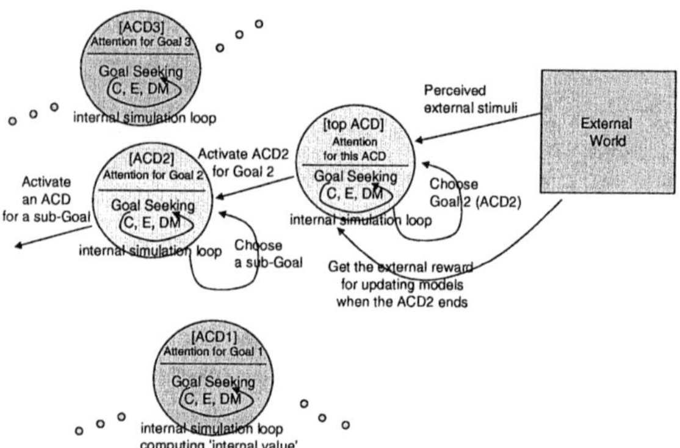

Fig. 1. The hierarchical network of affective-cognitive decisions for affective-cognitive learning and decision making: C, E and DM denote cognition-related models, emotion-related models, and the decision making model, respectively. For example, Goal 2 is chosen in the top ACD and then ACD2 is activated.

model for its goal. Thus, an attention model can lower the dimensionality of the cognitive state space for each ACD. In this paper we are not focusing on how an attention model for an ACD works, rather we assume that each ACD has a given attention model for its goal. A *cognitive state* $c \in C = \{1, \cdots, |C|\}$ for an ACD results from the attention model. In addition, we assume that in each time step or time window an ACD can have only one cognitive state although it might be false in the case that the external world is partially observable. Actually in this case, we think that it might be preferable to extend the framework to employ a probability distribution of cognitive states rather than the cognitive state itself. The *cognition model* $\Pr(c' \mid c, d)$ is a cognitive state transition model or a world simulation model. The cognition model $\Pr(c' \mid c, d)$ together with the *model of the cognitive reward* $R_{CR}(c')$ will allow us to represent a kind of 'cognitive self-motivation' in choosing the ACD d.

An *emotional state* e is modeled as a discrete state in the current framework: $e \in E = \{1, \cdots, |E|\}$. In the current RoCo simulation, E is the simple binary set {'feeling bad', 'feeling good'}. However, in each time step we assume that e is not explicitly known and only the probability distribution $\hat{e}$ of the current emotional state e is known: $\hat{e} = (\hat{e}_1, \cdots, \hat{e}_{|E|})$ where $\hat{e}_j$ is the probability that the current emotional state e is $j \in E = \{1, \cdots, |E|\}$. The *emotion model* $\Pr(e' \mid c', e)$ can be considered as the cognitive appraisal model for emotional states. For instance, Roseman's cognitive appraisal model can give rise to seventeen emotions - surprise, fear, hope, joy, relief, sadness, distress, frustration, disgust, liking, dislike, anger, contempt, pride, regret, guilt, shame - by a small number of appraisals such as unexpectedness, motivational state and situational state, probability, control potential, problem type and agency [9]. By combining the *emotion transition model* $\Pr(e' \mid \hat{e}, c, d) = \sum_{i=1}^{|C|} \Pr(e' \mid c' = i, \hat{e}\,) \Pr(c' = i \mid c, d) = \sum_{i=1}^{|C|} \sum_{k=1}^{|E|} \hat{e}_k \Pr(e' \mid c' = i, e = k) \Pr(c' = i \mid c, d)$ and the *model of the emotional reward* $R_{ER}(e')$, we will construct a form of 'emotional self-motivation' for choosing an ACD d. Moreover, the *decision-making model* $\Pr(d \mid \hat{e}, c)$ can be thought of as a seeking model of sub-goals or lower-level ACDs.

2.3 The Algorithm

Each ACD runs the following algorithm which has two main parts: the actor (choosing a lower-level ACD through the internal simulation loop while the ACD is activated) and the critic (updating models of the ACD whenever the previously chosen lower-level ACD is finished).

In the mental or internal simulation loop the agent can simulate an imagined lower-level ACD according to the decision-making model $\Pr(d \mid \hat{e}, c)$ which results from the Boltzmann selection using the state-ACD value $Q_{DM}(\hat{e}, c, d)$, and obtain an internal cognitive value $v_{int,C}$ and an internal affective value $v_{int,E}$. In order to compute the total internal value v_{int}, the internal cognitive and affective values are weighted by a willpower factor $\lambda_C(d)$ and a feeling factor $\lambda_E(d)$, respectively. Cognition and emotion influence the decision-making process through changing willpower and feeling factors as well as through internal values. The agent simulates different lower-level ACDs until it finds out a lower-level ACD which has positive internal value ($v_{int} > 0$). When such a lower-level ACD is located, the agent actually performs it and receives the external reward r_{ext}.

Whenever the previously chosen lower-level ACD is finished, the reward models and the decision-making model are updated in the reinforcement framework. The computation of the internal cognitive reward and the internal emotional reward suggests that we also construct models related with cognitively wanted states $R_{CR}(c')$ and with emotionally wanted states $R_{ER}(e')$, respectively. The value of $R_{CR}(c')$ models how much the next cognitive state c' is cognitively wanted to achieve the goal of the ACD after acting upon the current lower-level ACD d at the current cognitive state c. Similarly the value of $R_{ER}(e')$ models how much the next emotional state e' is emotionally wanted: for instance, if e' has positive valence, it is more emotionally wanted. The internal cognitive reward and the internal emotional reward, respectively, are used for updating the cognitive reward model $Q_{CR}(c, d)$ and the emotional reward model $Q_{ER}(\hat{e}, c, d)$.

The following is the algorithm for any ACD. However, the top ACD is special and different from other ACDs in that it is always activated.

The Algorithm for Each Affective-Cognitive Decision (ACD)

Loop forever

if (the activation signal is received from a higher-level ACD) Activate this ACD and start a new episode and get the probability distribution of the current emotional state $\hat{e}$ from the higher-level ACD

if (the deactivation signal is received from a higher-level ACD) Send the deactivation signal to current lower-level ACD and deactivate this ACD

if (an episode of this ACD is completed) Send the completion signal to the higher-level ACD and deactivate this ACD

The *Attention model* extracts useful features from the perceived multi-modal external stimuli for the goal of this ACD and outputs the features as a cognitive state $c \in C = \{1, \cdots, |C|\}$.

Update the probability distribution of the current emotional state $\hat{e} = (\hat{e}_1, \cdots, \hat{e}_{|E|})$ where $\hat{e}_j$ is the probability with which the current emotional state $e \in E = \{1, \cdots, |E|\}$ is j: $\hat{e}_{old}$ is the probability distribution of the previous emotional state which comes from the completed previously chosen lower-level ACD and assume that the emotion model $\Pr(e' \mid c', e)$ is given, then

$$
\begin{aligned}
\hat{e}_j = \Pr(e = j|c, \hat{e}_{old}) &= \sum_{k=1}^{|E|} \Pr(e = j, e_{old} = k|c, \hat{e}_{old}) \\
&= \sum_{k=1}^{|E|} \Pr(e = j|e_{old} = k, c, \hat{e}_{old}) \Pr(e_{old} = k|c, \hat{e}_{old}) \\
&= \sum_{k=1}^{|E|} \hat{e}_{old,k} \Pr(e = j|c, e_{old} = k) \qquad \text{for all } j \in E
\end{aligned}
$$

if (the cognitive state c is different from the previous cognitive state) flagCogStateChanged = 1
else flagCognitiveStateChanged = 0

// the actor part
if (this ACD is activated and (previously chosen lower-level ACD is completed or flagCogStateChanged == 1))

α is the discount factor, $0 < \alpha < 1$.

β is the inverse temperature for the Boltzmann selection, γ is the learning rate, $0 < \gamma < 1$.

The number of steps in the internal simulation loop nInternalStep = 0, and the maximum number of steps nMaxInternalStep = 100.

For each lower-level ACD $k \in D = \{1, \cdots, |D|\}$, willpower factor $\lambda_C(k) = 1$, feeling factor $\lambda_E(k) = 1$, the discount factors for willpower and feeling factors are $0 < \varepsilon_C < 1$ and

$0 < \varepsilon_E < 1$.

while ($v_{int} < 0$ and nInternalStep < nMaxInternalStep) // the internal loop

Choose a lower-level ACD $d \in D = \{1, \cdots, |D|\}$ from

$$\Pr(d = k|\hat{e}, c) = \frac{\exp(\beta Q_{DM}(\hat{e}, c, k))}{\sum_{l=1}^{|D|} \exp(\beta Q_{DM}(\hat{e}, c, l))} = \frac{\exp(\beta \sum_{j=1}^{|E|} \hat{e}_j Q_{DM}(e = j, c, k))}{\sum_{l=1}^{|D|} \exp(\beta \sum_{j=1}^{|E|} \hat{e}_j Q_{DM}(e = j, c, l))}$$

Get internal cognitive value $v_{int,C} = Q_{CR}(c, d)$

Get internal affective value $v_{int,E} = Q_{ER}(\hat{e}, c, d) = \sum_{j=1}^{|E|} \hat{e}_j Q_{ER}(j, c, d)$

Get internal value $v_{int} = \lambda_C(d) \times v_{int,C} + \lambda_E(d) \times v_{int,E}$

Update willpower and feeling factors when cognition and emotion conflict with each other (Note: The following is an example model which assumes that factors are exponentially decreasing):

if ($v_{int,C} > 0$ *and* $v_{int,E} < 0$)
  if ($v_{int} > 0$) $\lambda_C(d) = \varepsilon_C \lambda_C(d)$
  else if ($v_{int} < 0$) $\lambda_E(d) = \varepsilon_E \lambda_E(d)$
else if ($v_{int,C} < 0$ *and* $v_{int,E} > 0$)
  if ($v_{int} > 0$) $\lambda_E(d) = \varepsilon_E \lambda_E(d)$
  else if ($v_{int} < 0$) $\lambda_C(d) = \varepsilon_C \lambda_C(d)$

nInternalStep = nInternalStep + 1

end // end of the internal loop

if (flagCogStateChanged == 1) {
  if (the lower-level ACD d is different from the current running lower-level ACD)
    Send the deactivation signal to the current running lower-level ACD and activate the lower-level ACD d
}
Send the activation signal to the lower-level ACD d

end // end of the actor part

// the critic part
if (the completion signal is received from the lower-level ACD d)

Perceive the new cognitive state c_{new} and the new cognitive reward $r_{CR,new}$

Get the external reward r_{ext}

Update the model of the cognitive reward: $R_{CR}(c_{new}) \leftarrow (1 - \gamma) R_{CR}(c_{new}) + \gamma r_{CR,new}$

Update the model of the external reward: $R_{ext}(c, d) \leftarrow (1 - \gamma) R_{ext}(c, d) + \gamma r_{ext}$

Update the cognition model (world simulation model):
$Q_C(c, d, c_{new}) \leftarrow Q_C(c, d, c_{new}) + 1$

$$\Pr(c' = i|c, d) = \frac{Q_C(c,d,c'=i)}{\sum_{k=1}^{|C|} Q_C(c,d,c'=k)} \quad \text{for all } i \in C$$

Update the cognitive reward model:

$$Q_{CR}(c, d) = \sum_{j=1}^{|C|} \left\{ R_{CR}(c' = j) + \alpha \max_{d'} Q_{CR}(j, d') \right\} \Pr(c' = j|c, d)$$

Update the emotional reward model: for all $j \in E$, $Q_{ER}(j, c, d) =$

$$\sum_{k=1}^{|C|} \sum_{l=1}^{|E|} \left\{ R_{ER}(e' = l) + \alpha \max_{d'} Q_{ER}(l, k, d') \right\} \Pr(e' = l|c' = k, e = j) \Pr(c' = k|c, d)$$

(Note: $\Pr(e' = l|c' = k, e = j) \Pr(c' = k|c, d) = \Pr(e' = l, c' = k|e = j, c, d)$)

Update the decision-making model:

$$Q_{DM}(j, c, d) = R_{ext}(c, d) + \sum_{k=1}^{|C|} R_{CR}(c' = k) \Pr(c' = k|c, d)$$
$$+ \sum_{k=1}^{|C|} \sum_{l=1}^{|E|} R_{ER}(e' = l) \Pr(e' = l|c' = k, e = j) \Pr(c' = k|c, d)$$
$$+ \alpha \sum_{k=1}^{|C|} \sum_{l=1}^{|E|} \max_{d'} Q_{DM}(l, k, d') \Pr(e' = l|c' = k, e = j) \Pr(c' = k|c, d) \qquad \text{for all } j \in E$$

end // end of the critic part

2.4 Preliminary Experimental Results

Now we describe preliminary experimental results showing the performance of the algorithm. We applied the algorithm to a simulation of RoCo, a physically animate computer described in Section 2.1. The simulation of RoCo and detailed results can be seen in [1].

RoCo's goals in this simulation are to make the user 'attentive' and to 'show pleasure' (give a reward). We use the top ACD for this joint goal and RoCo has three kinds of lower-level ACDs for the top ACD: D = { 'tracking', 'stretching', 'entertaining' }. RoCo's cognitively wanted states are the user's 'attentive' or 'showing pleasure' states: r_{CR} = 1 for c' = 'attentive (to user's task)' or 'showing pleasure', otherwise r_{CR} = -1. Moreover, we assume that RoCo's emotionally wanted state is 'feeling good': $R_{ER}(e' =$ 'feeling good'$) = 1, R_{ER}(e' =$ 'feeling bad'$) = -1$. RoCo obtains an external reward $r_{ext} = 1$ or -1 whenever the user shows pleasure or displeasure, respectively. We also assume that the 'entertaining' ACD has three kinds of lower-level ACDs: for the 'entertaining' ACD, D = {'ent1', 'ent2', 'ent3'}. The 'entertaining' ACD is assumed to use the same kinds of cognitive states and emotional states as in the top ACD. However, differently from the top ACD, the cognitively wanted state of the 'entertaining' ACD is the user's 'showing pleasure' state only.

For E = {'feeling bad (1)','feeling good (2)'}, we use an emotion model $\Pr(e' \mid c', e)$ as follows. If c' is cognitively wanted, $\Pr(e' = 2 \mid c', e = 1) = 0.8$, $\Pr(e' = 1 \mid c', e = 1) = 0.2$, $\Pr(e' = 2 \mid c', e = 2) = 1.0$, $\Pr(e' = 1 \mid c', e = 2) = 0.0$. If c' is cognitively unwanted, $\Pr(e' = 2 \mid c', e = 1) = 0.0$, $\Pr(e' = 1 \mid c', e = 1) = 1.0$, $\Pr(e' = 2 \mid c', e = 2) = 0.2$, $\Pr(e' = 1 \mid c', e = 2) = 0.8$. If c' is neither cognitively wanted nor unwanted, $\Pr(e' = 2 \mid c', e = 1) = 0.3$, $\Pr(e' = 1 \mid c', e = 1) = 0.7$, $\Pr(e' = 2 \mid c', e = 2) = 0.7$, $\Pr(e' = 1 \mid c', e = 2) = 0.3$. This emotion model functions in such a way that the probability of feeling good increases if c' is cognitively wanted, the probability of feeling bad increases if c' is cognitively unwanted, and the probability of each emotional state goes exponentially to the neutral value (0.5), if c' is neither cognitively wanted nor unwanted.

Given a user's state transition model $\Pr_{user}(c' \mid c, d)$ where the user tends to give rewards ('showing pleasure') when RoCo takes 'tracking' at his or her 'attentive' state, 'ent2' at 'distracted' state, and 'stretching' at 'slumped' state, we confirmed that RoCo learned quite desirable decision-making models for both ACDs to maximize external rewards. Of course, RoCo made very good world simulation models for both ACDs that approximated the user's state transition model very well, in particular, for state-ACD pairs (c, d) related with the optimal policy. We also found out that the internal simulation loop was helpful in fast learning of the user's desire. With the internal rewards from cognition and emotion, the internal simulation loop utilized the trade-off between exploration and exploitation well.

3 Conclusions and Future Work

In this paper, we proposed a new framework of affective-cognitive learning and decision making where 'internal reward from cognition and emotion' and 'external reward from the external world' serve as motivation in learning and decision making. We also described a hierarchical network of ACDs and an algorithm that implements them. Future work includes more careful proofs of the efficacy of the internal simulation loop and internal rewards, detailed models of various factors in the algorithm, an emotion model for cognitive appraisal of emotional states, a model of curiosity as 'the exploratory drive', a model of empathy, and applications of the algorithm for more complex situations. We expect that the framework should ultimately enable affective agents to have much smoother human-computer interaction.

References

1. `http://web.media.mit.edu/~hiahn/roco.html`
2. Singh, S., Barto, A. G., and Chentanez, N. (2004). Intrinsically motivated reinforcement learning. In Advances in Neural Information Processing 18.
3. Bechara, A., Damasio, H., Tranel, D., and Damasio, A. (1997). Deciding Advantageously Before Knowing the Advantageous Strategy. Science. 275, p. 1293-1295.
4. Berridge, KC. and Robinson, TE. (2003). Parsing reward. Trends in Neurosciences. Vol. 26 No. 9.
5. Damasio, A. (1995). Descartes Error. Emotion, Reason and the Human Brain. Quill.
6. Estrada, C., Isen, A.M. and Young, M.J. (1994). Positive Affect Influences Creative Problem Solving Reported Source of Practice Satisfaction in Physicians. Motivation and Emotion, 18, p. 285-299.
7. Mowrer, OH. (1960). Learning and behavior. John Wiley.
8. Panksepp, J. (1998). Affective Neuroscience. Chap 8 and 9. Oxford university press.
9. Picard, R. W. (1997). Affective Computing. MIT Press, Cambridge, MA.
10. Picard, R. W., Papert, S., Bender, W., Blumberg, B., Breazeal, C., Cavallo, D., Machover, D., Resnick, M., Roy, D.and Strohecker, C. (2004). Affective learning - a manifesto. BT Technology Journal, Vol 22 No 4.
11. Schmidhuber, J., Self-Motivated Development Through Rewards for Predictor Errors / Improvements. Developmental Robotics 2005 AAAI Spring Symposium.

A Flexible Intelligent Knowledge Capsule for Efficient Data Mining/Reactive Level Extraction

JeongYon Shim

Division of General Studies, Computer Science, Kangnam University,
San 6-2, Kugal-ri, Kihung-up,YongIn Si, KyeongKi Do, Korea
Tel: +82 31 2803 736
mariashim@kangnam.ac.kr

Abstract. The construction of memory and its mechanism is very important to develop the efficient intelligent system. We designed a flexible Intelligent capsule for efficient data mining. The episode memory and its association are specially designed. The proposed knowledge capsule has a hierarchical structure and many functions of selection, learning,storing and data extraction. Based on this knowledge structure, it has a flexible memory and reactive level extraction mechanism. We constructed event oriented virtual memory and tested learning and associative knowledge retrieval function with virtual memory.

1 Introduction

It is known that the divided areas take part in special functions in brain and according to the functions brain has four memories, i.e Episode memory, Learning memory, Proceeding memory and Priming memory. 'Episode memory' stores the events of our living. In the type of this memory, consciousness takes part in and the information about time and location is memorized. 'Learning memory' stores the logical facts and rules[2]. We are conscious of the two types of Episode memory and Learning memory. These memories get the various information from the surrounding environment,arrange the data and allocate them to many parts in the cortex. For surviving in complex circumstance, maintaining an intelligent frame and mechanism is very important. As the importance of information processing is getting high in huge data surroundings,the development for intelligent system for automatic data acquisition, selection, storing and data extraction is required. Many researches has been studied for making more intelligent system in different various ways.

As an effort for this point, we designed a flexible Intelligent capsule for efficient data mining. The episode memory and its association are specially designed. The proposed knowledge capsule has a hierarchical structure and many functions of selection, learning,storing and data extraction. Based on this knowledge structure, it has a flexible memory and reactive level extraction mechanism. We constructed event oriented virtual memory and tested learning and associative knowledge retrieval function with a virtual memory.

J. Tao, T. Tan, and R.W. Picard (Eds.): ACII 2005, LNCS 3784, pp. 874–881, 2005.

2 A Design of Intelligent Knowledge Capsule

2.1 The Structure

Intelligent knowledge capsule is designed for data acquisition, selection, storing and extraction.

As shown in Fig. 1, This system consists of Learning memory, Rule base, and Episode memory. They are related to the others according to their association. The memory is constructed by information acquisition process. The obtained data from the knowledge environment come into Input Interface and are temporarily stored in Temporary memory. They are selected and distributed by the basic mechanism. For autonomous learning mechanism. Learning engine receives the training data of the special domain and process its learning mechanism. Episode memory stores the event oriented facts with the information of time and location and memorize them according to the flow of events sequentially. Memory Index which composed of Short term memory Index and Long term memory Index is used for efficient knowledge retrieval.

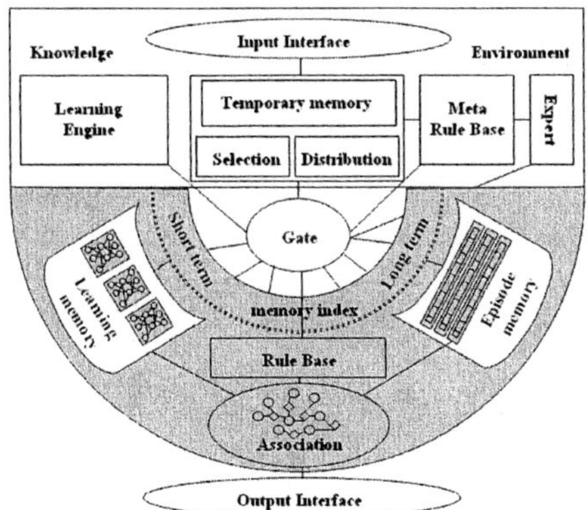

Fig. 1. The structure of Knowledge capsule

2.2 Autonomous Learning Mechanism

Knowledge Learning Frame has the Hierarchical structure and also has KLN (Knowledge Learning Net) module which consists of modular Neural networks representing the domain knowledge for the autonomous learning process as shown in Figure 2[1]. These domains are connected to the corresponding areas in the other layers vertically and related with the associative relation in the association module.The observed mixed input data are selected and distributed to the corresponding NN(Neural Network) in the Selection/Distribution module by filtering function F_i, which is the criteria for determining the state of firing.

$$F_i = P(C_i|e_1, e_2, \ldots, e_n) = \prod_{k=1}^{n} (C_i|e_k) \quad (1)$$

where C_i denotes a hypothesis for disease class and $e_k = e_1, \ldots, e_n$ denotes a sequence of observed data. F_i can be obtained by calculating the belief in C_i. If filtering factor F_i is over the threshold, q_i, $(F_i \geq q_i)$, the corresponding class is fired. The corresponding KLN of the fired class starts the learning or perception mechanism and produces the output. The values of the cells that don't belong to the activated class, are filtered and cleared. The structure of NN is three layered neural network trained by BP learning algorithm[3].

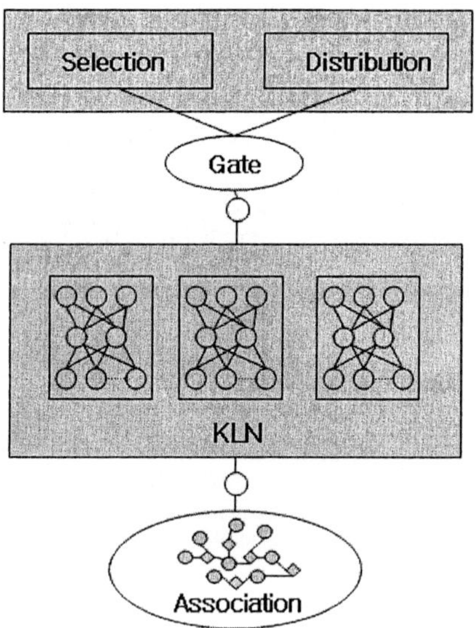

Fig. 2. Knowledge learning frame

2.3 Association

Association level consists of nodes and their relations. These nodes are connected to their neighbors according to their associative relations horizontally and connected to NN of the previous layer vertically. Their relations are represented by the relational graph as shown in Figure 3.

The relational graph is transformed to the forms of AM(Associative Matrix) in order to process the knowledge retrieval mechanism. AM has the values of associative strengths in the matrix form.

For example, the relational graph in Figure 4. can be transferred to the associative matrix A.

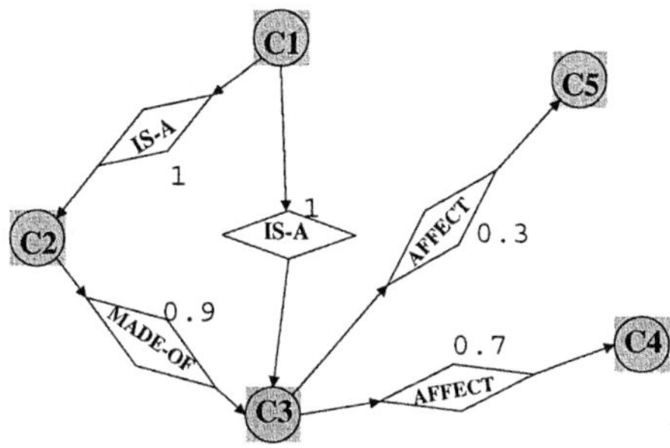

Fig. 3. Figure 3. Relational graph in Association level

The associative matrix,A, is :

$$A = \begin{bmatrix} 1.0 & 1.0 & 1.0 & 0.0 & 0.0 \\ -1.0 & 1.0 & 0.9 & 0.0 & 0.0 \\ -1.0 & -0.9 & 1.0 & 0.7 & 0.3 \\ 0.0 & 0.0 & -0.7 & 1.0 & 0.0 \\ 0.0 & 0.0 & -0.3 & 0.0 & 1.0 \end{bmatrix}$$

The matrix, A, has the form of $A = [R_{ij}]$. The associative strength,R_{ij}, between C_i and C_j is calculated by equation (2).

$$R_{ij} = P(a_i|a_j)D \tag{2}$$

where D is the direction arrow, $D = 1 or -1$, $i = 1, \ldots, n$, $j = 1, \ldots, n$.

3 Reactive Level Extraction

3.1 Adaptable Associative Relation and Controlling Masking Threshold for Data Extraction

Data extraction mechanism can be applied after learning was finished. In the previous section, associative relation and AM are described. using this Associative relation, the data related to keyword can be extracted. During the extraction this system can control the level of data extraction and the strength of Associative relation is be designed to be changed for maintaining the recent information.

There are two factors to decide extraction level. First one is controlling the masking threshold for data extraction. The masking threshold is decided by central part when the process of data extraction is made.

Second one is changing the value of associative relation. The representing way of associative relation value described in the previous section should be changed. The strength of associative relation is represented by two factors,i.e Degree of Importance,I_i and Freshness F_i.

Degree of Importance represents the conditional probability from node a_i to a_j.

$$I_{ij} = P(a_i|a_j) \tag{3}$$

Freshness means how frequently the node is accessed for data extraction and how fresh memory is. In this system, Freshness is measured by checking how many the node was referred in recent time using the following time slot. It has 20 time slots and check the accessing time as a sliding window from the most recent time point to 20 previous steps.

Table 1. Time Slot

Present	—	—	—	—	—	past
Time point	1st	2nd	3rd	4th	...	20th
Referred	1	0	1	1	...	0

If the referred number is r ,the number of Time slot is t, and the weight of slot is s, Freshness is calculated by the following equation.

$$F_{ij} = \frac{r}{t} * s \tag{4}$$

Based on this relational structure, the level of data extraction can be controlled by masking threshold, θ. During the controlling the extraction level, three cases are considered. First is to consider only degree of Importance, second is to consider only Freshness and last one is to consider both values. In last case, it takes the average value,A_i, of two.

$$A_{ij} = \frac{I_{ij} + F_{ij}}{2} \tag{5}$$

The changed associative matrix,A, is :

$$A = \begin{bmatrix} 1.0/1.0 & 1.0/0.9 & 1.0/0.7 & 0.0/0.0 & 0.0/0.0 \\ -1.0/0.0 & 1.0/1.0 & 0.9/0.9 & 0.0/0.0 & 0.0/0.0 \\ -1.0/1.0 & -0.9/0.2 & 1.0/1.0 & 0.7/0.6 & 0.3/0.2 \\ 0.0/0.0 & 0.0/0.0 & -0.7/1.0 & 1.0/1.0 & 0.0/0.0 \\ 0.0/0.0 & 0.0/0.0 & -0.3/1.0 & 0.0/0.0 & 1.0/1.0 \end{bmatrix}$$

When the class,C_i, in the relational graph is assumed to be activated, from the node, C_i, the inferential paths can be extracted using the knowledge retrieval algorithm[1]. The Extracted path, E_i has the following form.

$$E_i = \left[C_i \; (I_{ij}/F_{ij}/A_{ij}) \; C_j \right]$$

Using associative matrix, extracted path can be produced as follows.

E_1 =[C_1 1.0/0.9/0.5 C_2 0.9/0.9/0.9 C_3 0.7/0.6/0.75 C_4]
E_2 =[C_1 1.0/0.9/0.5 C_2 0.9/0.9/0.9]
E_3 =[C_3 0.7/0.7/0.7 C_5]
E_4 =[C_1 1.0/0.7/0.4 C_3 0.7/0.6/0.65 C_4]
E_5 =[C_1 1.0/0.7/0.4 C_3 0.7/0.2/0.45 C_5]

The masking threshold applied to the extracted paths including degree of Importance, Freshness and combined factor in the strength of associative relation. The data which has the value greater than or equal to the threshold,θ are selected from extracted path. For example ,suppose that θ is 0.7 and only Freshness is considered, the following path is selected.

$E_1 = [C_1\ 0.9\ C_2\ 0.9\ C_3]$
$E_1 = [C_1\ 0.9\ C_2\ 0.9\ C_3]$
$E_3 = [C_3\ 0.7\ C_5]$
$E_4 = [C_1\ 0.7\ C_3]$
$E_5 = [C_1\ 0.7\ C_3]$

4 Experiments

This system is applied to the virtual memory. In this paper, we focused on the data extraction mechanism according to reactive level and the experimental results about the other functions as learning, selection, Episode memory concept and memory storing are described in the other papers in detail[1].

Figure 4 shows changed Associative Matrix and the process of data extraction considering reactive level using the Associative Matrix. Figure 5 represents the reactive level according to masking threshold.

$$A = \begin{bmatrix} 1.0/1.0 & 1.0/0.9 & 1.0/0.7 & 0.0/0.0 & 0.0/0.0 \\ -1.0/0.0 & 1.0/1.0 & 0.9/0.9 & 0.0/0.0 & 0.0/0.0 \\ -1.0/1.0 & -0.9/0.2 & 1.0/1.0 & 0.7/0.6 & 0.3/0.2 \\ 0.0/0.0 & 0.0/0.0 & -0.7/1.0 & 1.0/1.0 & 0.0/0.0 \\ 0.0/0.0 & 0.0/0.0 & -0.3/1.0 & 0.0/0.0 & 1.0/1.0 \end{bmatrix}$$

```
... Changed Associative Matrix [I/F]

1.00/1.00 1.00/0.90 1.00/0.90 0.00/0.00 0.00/0.00
-1.00/0.00 1.00/1.00 0.90/0.70 0.00/0.00 0.00/0.00
-1.00/1.00 -0.90/0.80 1.00/1.00 0.70/0.30 0.30/0.60
0.00/0.00 0.00/0.00 -0.70/0.70 1.00/1.00 0.00/0.00
0.00/0.00 0.00/0.00 -0.30/0.50 0.00/0.00 1.00/1.00

... Calculating Average degree A [I/F/A]

1.00/1.00/1.00 1.00/0.90/0.95 1.00/0.90/0.95 0.00/0.00/0.00 0.00/0.00/0.00
-1.00/0.00/-0.50 1.00/1.00/1.00 0.90/0.70/0.80 0.00/0.00/0.00 0.00/0.00/0.00
-1.00/-1.00/-1.00 -0.90/-0.80/-0.85 1.00/1.00/1.00 0.70/0.30/0.50 0.30/0.60/0.45
0.00/0.00/0.00 0.00/0.00/0.00 -0.70/-0.70/-0.70 1.00/1.00/1.00 0.00/0.00/0.00
0.00/0.00/0.00 0.00/0.00/0.00 -0.30/-0.50/-0.40 0.00/0.00/0.00 1.00/1.00/1.00

.. extracted data path

a1 1.00/0.90/0.95 a2 0.90/0.70/0.80 a3 0.70/0.30/0.50 a4
a3 0.30/0.60/0.45 a5
```

Fig. 4. Changed Associative Matrix and Reactive Level Extraction

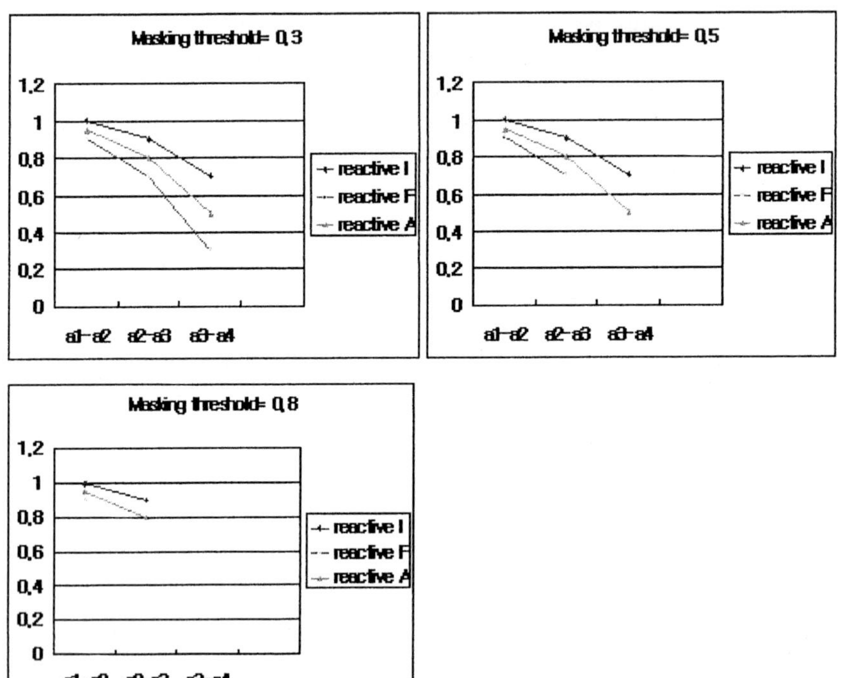

Fig. 5. The change of Reactive Level by Masking threshold

As it is shown in the experiment output, the structure of memory is very flexibly designed and data can be extracted by the reactive level.

5 Conclusion

We proposed knowledge capsule which has a hierarchical structure and many functions of selection, learning,storing and data extraction. Based on this knowledge structure, it has a flexible memory and reactive level extraction mechanism. We constructed event oriented virtual memory and tested learning and associative knowledge retrieval function with virtual memory. As a result of experiments, we could find this system has a flexible memory and can produce the extracted data according to the reactive level. This function is applicable to build the flexible memory in intelligent brain system.

References

1. Jeong-Yon Shim, Knowledge Retrieval Using Bayesian Associative Relation in the Three Dimensional Modular System,pp630-635, *Lecture Notes in Computer Science(3007), 2004.*
2. John R. Anderson Learning and Memory *Prentice Hall.*

3. Laurene Fausett: Fundamentals of Neural Networks,Prentice Hall
4. Simon Haykin: Neural Networks,Prentice Hall
5. Jeong-Yon Shim, Chong-Sun Hwang,Data Extraction from Associative Matrix based on Selective learning system,IJCNN'99, Washongton D.C
6. John R. Anderson,Learning and Memory,Prentice Hall

On/Off Switching Mechanism in Knowledge Structure of Reticular Activating System

JeongYon Shim

Division of General Studies, Computer Science, Kangnam University,
San 6-2, Kugal-ri, Kihung-up,YongIn Si, KyeongKi Do, Korea
Tel: +82 31 2803 736
mariashim@kangnam.ac.kr

Abstract. Reticular Activating system which has a form of small neural networks in the brain is closely related system with the automatic nervous system. It takes charge of the function that distinguishes between memorizing one and the others, accepts the only selected information and discards the unnecessary things.In this paper, we propose Reticular Activating system which has Knowledge acquisition, selection, storing, reconfiguration and retrieving part. In this paper, On/Off Switching mechanism for flexible memory is specially designed and tested.

1 Introduction

It is known that Reticular Activating System of Human brain takes part in discriminating ,selecting the important information to be stored in brain and discarding unnecessary ones. Reticular Activating System has a form of network of neuron cells in brain and is closely related to autonomic nervous system. This function is a very important strategy to survive in external huge information circumstance. As it stores only selected necessary information,it can raise the efficiency.

Due to the development of computer technology and emergence of Internet, we are exposed to very huge information environment. As surroundings are encircled with a flood of information, the requirement of data extraction and efficient mechanism is increasing.

Accordingly in this paper,we design Reticular activating system with selective information processing in the following five viewpoints: First, it has a selecting function. In this mechanism, it makes a decision if it selects the incoming data or not. Second, it has a learning mechanism for knowledge acquisition. In this step, the training data are learned. Third, this system has a knowledge reconfiguration function. It reconstructs the knowledge net in accordance with a purpose of the system. Forth, it has a function of On/Off Switching. On/Off Switching works when there are multiple knowledge net for one keyword. In case of Inference it is reacted by On/Off switching and multiple thinking chains are produced.

This system consists of Knowledge acquisition, selection , storing and retrieving part. Reticular Activating layer is connected to Meta knowledge in the high

J. Tao, T. Tan, and R.W. Picard (Eds.): ACII 2005, LNCS 3784, pp. 882–889, 2005.

level of this system and takes part in Data Selection. We applied this system to the virtual memory and tested the knowledge retrieval process of thinking chain using On/Off switching.

2 Reticular Activating System

In this section Reticular Activating System which can select and store the information was designed. As shown in Fig. 1, this system has a hierarchical structure and it consists of Knowledge acquisition, Selection and Storing to Memory.

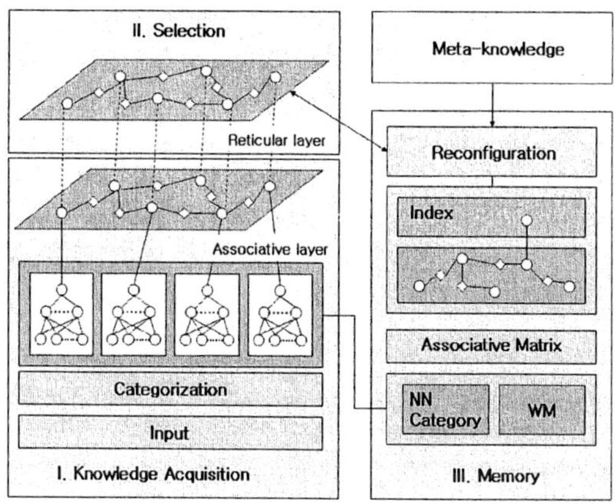

Fig. 1. Associative memory frame

First, Knowledge acquisition part has multi modular NN(neural Network)s and perform the learning process with the training data according to the categories. It uses BP(Back Propagation) algorithm. The output nodes of Modular NN are connected to nodes in Associative layer which has logical network connected by associative relations. Its learning mechanism is described in the paper [1] in detail

Second, Rcticular Activating layer has a knowledge net which consists of nodes and their associative relations. The nodes in knowledge net are connected to the nodes of Associative layer vertically. The importance value is assigned to the connection weight of this vertical relation. Selection module performs selecting process with these values of associative relations and vertical relations using the criteria given by Mcta Knowledge.

Third, Storing to Memory consists of two part of Knowledge Reconfiguration and storing the values for NN. In Reconfiguration, the selected nodes and relations are reconfigured and stored in memory. The knowledge net is performed by attaching nodes centering around common node. After reconfiguration the centering node is connected to index which is used in searching process. In the case of polysemy, the common node is connected by On/Off switching to multiple knowledge net. The another part of memory is storing the values for NN. After finishing the learning process of modular NN, this system stores the values of category, parameters and weight matrix. These stored values are used for perception, inference and knowledge retrieval.

Reticular Activating System performs the functions of Learning, Selection , memory reconfiguration and Knowledge retrieval as these three parts collaborates on a work interactively.

3 On/Off Switching Mechanism in Knowledge Structure

3.1 The Structure of Reticular Activating Layer

In this section ,Selection, Storing and Knowledge Retrieval of Reticular Activating System are described. This system has a same structure of multi modular NN ,learning and functions of Associative layer as explained in the paper [1]. As shown in figure 2, the nodes of reticular layer are connected each other with Associative relation , R_{ij} horizontally and are also connected to the nodes in Associative layer with connection weight R_{ij} vertically.

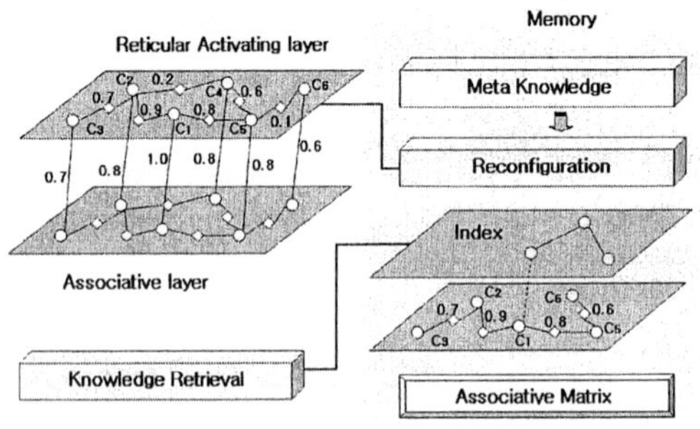

Fig. 2. Reticular Activating Layer

The connection weights R_{ij} and S_{ij} are used for selecting when Meta knowledge gives a criteria.

Storing Criteria:
$V_i \geq 0.5, R_{ij} \geq 0.5$

If Meta knowledge gives a following storing criteria, the nodes and relations satisfying this criteria are selected. The selected nodes and relations are reconfigured by attaching the related nodes centering common node [7]. This centering common node is connected to the index node in Index layer and used for searching as a keyword.

After reconfiguration, new knowledge net is formed and it is transferred to Associative Matrix which is used for knowledge retrieval.

3.2 On/Off Switching Mechanism in Knowledge Structure

As shown in Figure 2, the selected nodes from Reticular Activating Layer are reconstructed by reconfiguration rule. Closely related conceptual nodes starts to be connected to each other according to the strength of importance. Sometimes, the problem of polysemy occurred. Polysemy means that identical terms can be used in very different semantic contexts.

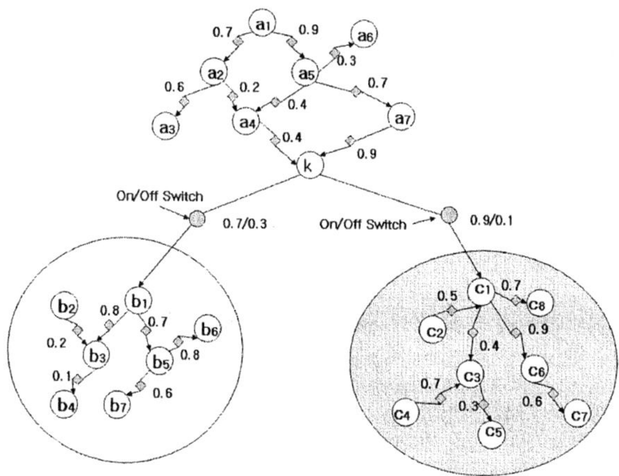

Fig. 3. Reticular Activating Layer

To solve this problem, we designed On/Off Switching for controlling thinking chain. Here, we define the reachable path from the starting point as thinking chain. The common node K is connected to multiple knowledge nets though On/Off Switching in figure 3. The activation for the selected knowledge net is controlled by central signal,c. The degree of activation α is calculated by equation (1) with given connection probability, p.

$$\alpha = cp(1 - c)(1 - p) \tag{1}$$

In the process of Inference and Knowledge retrieval, thinking chain is made according to the activation switching value. So, the form of thinking chain extracted from the structure of reconfigured knowledge depends on the value of On/Off switching.

3.3 Representation of Knowledge Net

The knowledge net is represented by directed graph which consists of nodes and arcs. Their associative relations are represented as list as shown in table1, table2 and table3. Table 1 represents the list of main knowledge net, table 1 represents list of knowledge net1 and table 2 represents list of knowledge net2. The connection probability between main net and net1 is 0.7 and the connection probability between main net and net2 is 0.9.

Table 1. List of associative relation in Knowledge net

node1	node2	Rel	deg
Root	a_1	R_{01}	0.0
a_1	a_2	R_{12}	0.7
a_1	a_5	R_{15}	0.9
a_2	a_3	R_{23}	0.6
a_2	a_4	R_{24}	0.2
a_3	null	R_{33}	0.0
a_4	k	R_{4k}	0.4
a_5	a_4	R_{54}	0.4
a_5	a_6	R_{56}	0.3
a_5	a_7	R_{57}	0.7
a_6	null	R_{66}	0.0
a_7	null	R_{77}	0.0
k	net_1	R_{kn1}	0.7
k	net_2	R_{kn2}	0.9

3.4 Retrieval of Thinking Chain

Thinking chain is defined as a reachable path from the starting point and target point. The extracted thinking chain using reconfigured knowledge net can be used for inference, decision making and data mining scheme.

For example, the thinking chains including k in table1,table2 and table 3 are obtained as follows.

1. From starting point a_1 to node k
a_1 0.7 a_2 0.2 a_4 0.4 k
a_1 0.9 a_5 0.4 a_4 0.4 k
a_1 0.9 a_5 0.7 a_7 0.7 k
2. From k to net_i
k on/off 0.7/0.3 net1 k 0.7/0.3 b_1 0.8 b_3 0.1 b_7 k 0.7/0.3 b_1 0.7 b_5 0.6 b_7 k 0.7/0.3 b_1 0.7 b_5 0.8 b_6
K on/off 0.9/0.1 net2 k 0.9/0.1 c_1 0.4 c_3 0.3 c_5 k 0.9/0.1 c_1 0.8 c_8 k 0.9/0.1 c_1 0.9 c_6 0.6 c_7

Table 2. List of associative relation in Knowledge net: net1

node1	node2	Rel	deg
net_1	b_1	R_{n11}	0.7
b_1	b_3	R_{13}	0.8
b_1	b_5	R_{15}	0.7
b_2	b_3	R_{23}	0.2
b_3	b_4	R_{34}	0.1
b_4	null	R_{44}	0.0
b_5	b_6	R_{56}	0.8
b_5	b_7	R_{57}	0.6
b_6	null	R_{66}	0.0
b_7	*null*	R_{77}	0.0

Table 3. List of associative relation in Knowledge net: net2

node1	node2	Rel	deg
net_2	c_1	R_{n21}	0.9
c_1	c_3	R_{13}	0.4
c_1	c_6	R_{16}	0.9
c_1	c_8	R_{18}	0.7
c_2	c_1	R_{21}	0.5
c_3	c_5	R_{35}	0.3
c_4	c_3	R_{43}	0.7
c_5	*null*	R_{55}	0.0
c_6	c_7	R_{67}	0.6
c_7	*null*	R_{77}	0.0

4 Experiments

In this section, we applied this system to virtual memory and tested knowledge retrieval mechanism using On/Off Switching mechanism in reconfigured knowledge net as following figure 4.

Figure 5 shows the testing results using On/Off switching mechanism. From the experiments,we can find that this system can produce multiple thinking chains according to the degree of On/Off switching. This On/Off switching can be usefully used for making flexible memory in the intelligent system. And Reticular Activating system also has functions of selective reaction, knowledge acquisition (learning), storing and inference. Experiments for this functions are described in previous papers [1,6] in detail.

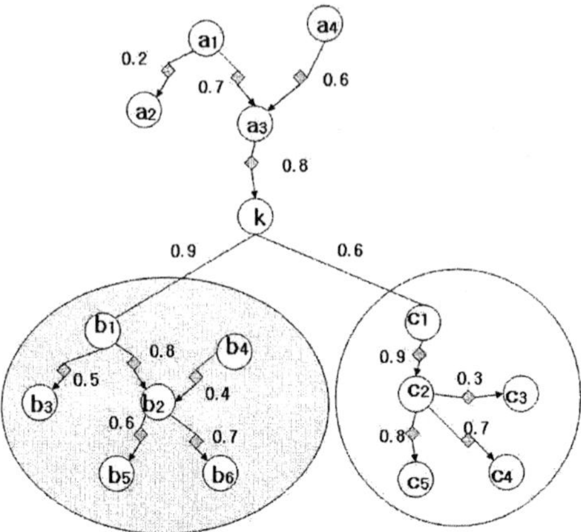

Fig. 4. Reticular Activating Layer

5 Conclusion

In this paper, we propose Reticular Activating system which has functions of selective reaction, learning and inference. This system consists of Knowledge acquisition, selection , storing and retrieving part. Reticular Activating layer is connected to Meta knowledge in the high level of this system and takes part in Data Selection. Reconfiguration and On/Off Switching mechanism in knowledge net are specially designed. We applied this system to the virtual memory and tested On/Off Switching mechanism.

As a result of testing, we could find that it can extract the related thinking chains easily. This system is expected to be applicable to many areas as data mining, pattern recognition and circumspect decision making problem considering associative concepts and prior knowledge.

```
On/Off Switching....

Start...
From a1 - k - switching

Thingking chains...

Input net1 signal (on/off)? on
Input net2 signal (on/off)? off

a1 0.700000 a3 0.800000 k net1 on 0.900000 b1 0.500000 b3
a1 0.700000 a3 0.800000 k net1 on 0.900000 b1 0.800000 b2 0.600000 b5
a1 0.700000 a3 0.800000 k net1 on 0.900000 b1 0.800000 b2 0.700000 b8
a1 0.700000 a3 0.800000 k net2 off 0.400000 c1 0.900000 c2 0.300000 c3
a1 0.700000 a3 0.800000 k net2 off 0.400000 c1 0.900000 c2 0.700000 c4
a1 0.700000 a3 0.800000 k net2 off 0.400000 c1 0.900000 c2 0.800000 c5

end...
```

Fig. 5. Retrieved thinking chain from On/Off Switching

References

1. Jeong-Yon Shim:Knowledge Retrieval Using Bayesian Associative Relation in the Three Dimensional ModularSystem,Lecture Notes in Computer Science, Vol.3007,Springer-Verlag,(2004)630-635
2. E. Bruce Goldstein,Sensation and Perception,BROOKS/COLE
3. Judea Pearl : Probabilistic reasoning in intelligent systems, networks plausible inference,Morgan kaufman Publishers (1988)
4. Laurene Fausett: Fundamentals of Neural Networks,Prentice Hall
5. Simon Haykin: Neural Networks,Prentice Hall
6. Jeong-Yon Shim, Chong-Sun Hwang,Data Extraction from Associative Matrix based on Selective learning system,IJCNN'99, Washongton D.C
7. John R. Anderson,Learning and Memory,Prentice Hall

Uncharted Passions: User Displays of Positive Affect with an Adaptive Affective System

Lesley Axelrod and Kate Hone

Brunel University, School of Information Systems, Computing and Mathematics,
Uxbridge, Middlesex UB8 3PH, UK
+44 (0) 1895 274000
{kate.hone, lesley.axelrod}@brunel.ac.uk

Abstract. Affective technologies have potential to enhance human-computer interaction (HCI). The problem is that much development is technically, rather than user driven, raising many unanswered questions about user preferences and opening new areas for research. People naturally incorporate emotional messages during interpersonal communication with other people, but their use of holistic communication including emotional displays during HCI has not been widely reported. Using Wizard-of-Oz (WOZ) methods, experimental design and methods of sequential analysis from the social sciences, we have recorded, analyzed and compared emotional displays of participants during interaction with an apparently affective system and a standard, non-affective version. During interaction, participants portray extremely varied, sometimes intense, ever-changing displays of emotions and these are rated as significantly more positive in the affective computer condition and as significantly more intense in the told affective condition. We also discuss behavioural responses to the different conditions. These results are relevant to the design of future affective systems.

1 Background

We live in a developing 'experience culture' where our emotional management is of critical importance [5]. Emotions are now recognized as complex human control systems, crucial to decision making, creativity, playing and learning that operate on three systems, biological, neurological, psychological and at three levels, visceral, behavioural and reflective [13, 9,10]. Emotion recognition technology is currently being developed with the aim of improving the quality of human-computer interaction. Affective interfaces may offer commercial advantages and have potential to reduce user stress and enhance the fun and personalization of many applications [10].

Human communication is multimodal, complex and rule based. Meaning is naturally conveyed using all five human senses, including [1]:

- appearance (both fixed aspects such as height or changeable aspects such as use of fashion or architectural artefacts);
- movement (including gestures, postural shifts and facial expressions);
- sound (including speech aspects such as content, pace etc, paralinguistic aspects such as tone of voice and intonation, and non verbal sounds such as affect bursts);

J. Tao, T. Tan, and R.W. Picard (Eds.): ACII 2005, LNCS 3784, pp. 890–897, 2005.

- spatial and temporal use (such as physical positioning for interaction, and timing of responses);
- touch and smell (for example use of hand shaking, or perfume).

People treat new media such as computers as if they are dealing with real people [12]. They modify their communication to suit their perceived conversation partner [14]. New conventions also emerge for technologically mediated communication, such as in internet chat rooms, or telephone text messaging [14, 8].

The concept of 'emotion' is poorly defined. We have borrowed from Picard's terminology and used 'affect' for the spectrum of feelings, moods, sentiments etc. and we distinguish between inner emotional experiences and the outward 'emotional expressions' that people may use to convey messages about their emotional states [11]. Questions about the use of affective systems are not being addressed because of the current state of the technology: affective systems are simply not yet good enough to be implemented in realistic applications. Emerging systems vary in the affective cues they can recognize and in their responsive display mechanisms. Recognition of modalities is constrained. Responses range from adaptive systems that alter pace or content, to avatars reflecting user emotions, to artificial personalities that generate their own emotional displays [11]. As these systems are not yet fully functional, relatively few studies have attempted to study user interactions with affective systems that respond to human emotion.

The research described in this paper takes a user-centred perspective, examining some of the basic assumptions that underlie the development of affective computing applications. We were interested in determining user responses to affective computing interventions. Specifically we were concerned with whether such interventions could lead to more positive experiences of interaction, as indicated by use of positively rated emotional expressions. We were also interested in the degree to which users would emphasize their emotional expressions in situations where they believed that the computer could respond to this.

In order to investigate these issues an experiment was designed in which an affective computing application was simulated through the use of a Wizard of Oz (WOZ) set up (where a hidden human observer controls the computer's 'affective' response). Affective interventions were provided within the context of a game involving problem solving. The design of the experiment was such that in some conditions the system appeared to vary its response on the basis of recognized emotional expressions at the interface, for instance providing clues when the user displayed negative affect. We hypothesized that such interventions would lead to user interaction with more positive emotional expressions. We also varied the conditions according to whether the user was explicitly told in advance that the system might react to their emotional expressions. This design allowed us to separately examine the effects due to the system response itself and those due to users' expectations. We predicted that those anticipating an affective application would show increased positive emotional expression during their interactions.

For this user-centered study, 60 participants played a simple 'word ladder' game under different controlled conditions. Using 2 x 2 factorial design, and a Wizard of Oz scenario, half the participants interacted with a system that adapted on the basis of the user's emotional expression and half were told the system could react to their emotional expressions.

2 Experimental Design

Factorial Design
We used a WOZ approach to simulate the capabilities of future emotion recognition technology [3]. The experiment had a 2 × 2 between-subjects factorial design. The factors were:

Acted affective (with two levels; 'standard' vs. 'system appears affective'). This refers to whether the system appeared to act affectively. In the 'standard' condition clues and messages appeared only in response to the user clicking the 'help' button. In the 'system appears affective' condition, if the participant was observed via the one way mirror to use emotional expressions, the game was controlled so that appropriate clues or messages appeared to them.

Told affective (with two levels; 'expect standard system' vs. 'expect affective system'). This refers to whether the participant expected the system to act affectively. In the 'expect standard system' condition participants were told they would be testing the usability of a word game. In the 'expect affective system' condition they were told that they would be testing the usability of a word game on a prototype system, that might recognize or respond to some of their emotions.

There were therefore four experimental conditions in total, representing the factorial combination of the two factors.

The Game
A 'word-ladder' game was selected for the experiment as the task involves problem solving which is an area where affective interventions may be helpful. An initial word and a target word are given. Individuals have to attempt to transform the initial word into the target word by changing one letter on each of a number of given lines, or 'rungs', in response to clues, as seen in figure 1.

Given words	Clues	Solution
HEAD		HEAD
	To listen	HEAR
	Animal that growls	BEAR
BEER		BEER

Fig. 1. Structure of word-ladder game

The game was designed to trigger episodes of user frustration and satisfaction. It involved the use of a slightly 'sticky' mouse, added time pressure and unexpected system interrupts. Clues during the game involved images and text likely to provoke some emotional responses. Figure 2 shows a screenshot from the application.

Participants
Sixty participants took part in the study (42 male and 18 female); fifteen were allocated to each experimental condition. All were currently living in the UK and most

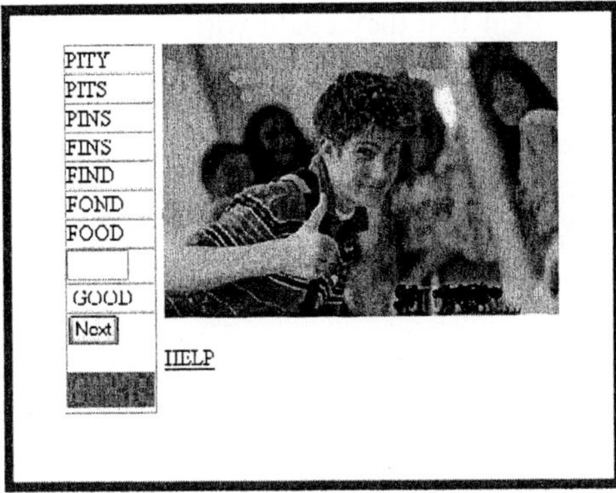

Fig. 2. Screen shot of Word-ladder application

were graduate and undergraduate students. Participants were paid for their participation. The majority of participants were aged between 18 and 25. It was a pre-requisite that they be reasonably fluent in English. An attempt was made to match groups for cultural background and age.

Procedure

Before undertaking the word-ladder task, informed consent was sought and demographic data were collected. The degree of detail given about the purposes of the study was varied according to the experimental condition as described in the design. We were careful to ensure that although details were omitted in some conditions, no participants were given false information about the purposes of the study.

Participants attempted the word-ladder game, in either standard or affective mode depending on their allocation to one of the four experimental conditions. They were given 10 minutes to interact with the system.

In the 'acted affective' conditions WOZ techniques were used to simulate the capabilities of future emotion recognition technology. The experiment took place in a usability laboratory where two adjoining rooms, linked by a one way mirror were used, so the researcher could observe the participant without being seen. One room was reserved for the use of participants in the experiment, containing a standard desktop personal computer (PC) with a PC mounted video camera. The other room was reserved for the researcher and contained a PC with two screens attached. The PCs were linked by an area network so the researcher could view the participant's 'puzzle' screen and the context of the participant's interactive behaviour at all times, as well as the researcher's own 'control' screen. When the system was intended to appear affective, the researcher could monitor and judge the affective state of the participant via the one way mirror, and adapt the game accordingly, so that clues and messages received by the participant were tailored to their emotional displays. All interactions were video-taped for later analysis and logs were collected of user keystrokes and mouse movements.

As half the participants had not been initially informed about the role of affect in the experiment, there were some ethical concerns, so all subjects were fully debriefed at the end of their participation and apologies given for any failure to fully inform beforehand. It was made clear that they could withdraw their data from the trial, if desired.

We have already established that participants performed significantly better and rated themselves as feeling more positive when using the adaptive affective recognition version of the application [4]. Our aim was to see if their use of emotional expressions during interaction reflected this.

3 Analysis

Techniques from the social sciences were borrowed in order to analyze use of emotional expressions during interaction. Based on Bakeman and Gottman's Sequential Interaction Analysis methods, we developed a novel coding system to identify units of emotionally expressive behaviour which, in the domain of affective computing, we chose to call 'affectemes' [2].

1. Data about task performance was captured and logged and participants completed questionnaires giving their demographic data, views on usability issues and their emotional performances.
2. All video recordings were edited to enable a view of the participant's behaviour as well as the graphical user interface showing the game environment.
3. Time sampling was used to reduce the coding load and 2nd and 7th minutes were selected for in-depth analysis.
4. These were imported into Transana (qualitative analysis tool) [16].
5. Units of emotional expression (affectemes) were time stamped and clipped.
6. Each affecteme clip was rated for valence and arousal, using an adapted version of the Self Assessment Manikin [6]. On the 9 point valence rating scale of this tool, positive ratings are low and negative ratings are high. On the 9 point arousal rating scale, high arousal has a low score and low arousal has a high score.
7. Common emotional expressions in this domain were noted and named.
8. Inter coder reliability was established.
9. Data was entered into Statistical Package for the Social Sciences (SPSS) and statistical analysis carried out. The experiment's main research hypotheses were tested using analysis of variance (ANOVA).

4 Results

Valence. We found that when using an apparently affective system, users' affectemes are rated as having significantly more positive valence. ANOVA showed a main effect of system affective response on ratings of valence of user's emotional expressions. $F(1,56)=12.63$, $p<0.01$). Participants showed, on average, use of more positively rated emotional expressions with the affective intervention. Participants were more likely to show positively rated emotional expressions when they had been told that the system was affective. There was also a significant interaction effect with whether the system had provided an affective response ($F(1,56)=12.63$, $p<0.01$). The

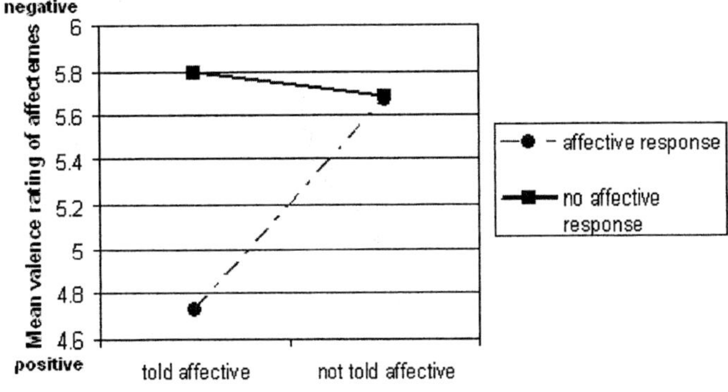

Fig. 3. Interaction plot for ratings of positive valence

most positively rated emotional expressions were from those participants who had been told that the system might respond to their emotional expression, and where the system did in fact act affectively. This interaction effect is shown in the interaction plot in figure 3.

Arousal. We found that when told the system they will be using is an affective system, users' affectemes are rated as having significantly more intense arousal. ANOVA showed a main effect of system affective response on ratings of valence of user's emotional expressions. $F(1,56)=4.74$, $p<0.05$). Participants showed, on average, use of more intensely rated emotional expressions with the told affective intervention. Participants were more likely to show emotional expressions rated as having higher arousal when they had been told that the system was affective.

Behaviours. Data samples show an immensely wide array of emotional expressions during affective HCI, as seen in figure 4, ranging from subtle to intense and using many modalities, in all the experimental conditions. These included grooming behaviours, postural shifts, facial expressions, vocal affect bursts, gestures and speech. A very noticeable behaviour was time spent resting chin or cheek on hands.

Fig. 4. Array of emotions of one participant

5 Discussion

The results described here demonstrate that participants used emotional expressions rated as significantly more positive as a result of adapting an application on the basis of affect recognition and most positive of all when it also acted affectively.

This confirms suggestions that affective computing has the potential to improve human-computer interaction. Previously empirical support for this claim was limited due to the relative immaturity of the technology to enable emotion recognition. In this experiment we were able to simulate (using a Wizard of Oz set up) the proposed capability of future systems to recognize affect from observed user behaviour. The results are notable as they support the importance of ongoing work to enable emotion recognition at the user interface.

The research also considered how users' emotional expressions might vary when they use an affective system. It has been suggested that, in the short term at least, emotion recognition technology will need users to exaggerate or deliberately pose their emotional expressions [7]. We were therefore interested in whether telling a user that the system might respond to their emotions would lead to a greater degree of emotional expression at the interface. We were also interested in whether users might naturally adapt to systems which respond to emotion by displaying more expression, even when not specifically aware that the system might adapt.

We have found some tangible differences in observable behaviour as a result of the experimental manipulations. Participants used emotional expressions rated as having higher arousal in the conditions where they had been told the system would respond to their affect.

The highest ratings for positive emotional expression were from those participants who were expecting an affective response, and where the system did actually adapt. These results suggest that users of an affective system will show more positive affect when they both believe the system is affective and the system acts affectively.

The results from this data are encouraging for the success of affective computing as they suggest that users will show more positive behaviours during HCI.

6 Conclusions and Future Work

We have used a structured method to quantify observed behaviour and rate it for valence and arousal. It seems emotional behaviour is altered when people believe they are interacting with an affective system or when the system demonstrates some affect.

The exact behaviours observed vary between individuals. We observed a number of variables in our participants, including personality type, communication style (both self rated and rated by the researcher), affect susceptibility, and demographics. Data mining may establish links between particular variables and particular behaviours.

We have used a structured rating scale to categorise perceived emotional behaviours, but we made no attempt to link the observed behaviours to inner emotional experiences of participants. However we are experimenting with using an Appraisal Analysis Framework [15] to examine the use of behaviours in context and assess their function. It seems from assessment of the video data that various behaviours are used when a participant is having difficulty in progressing the game. A number of behaviours that are commonly used in human to human communication to manage turn taking, are seen. These include sudden shifts in posture, shaking of the head and negative facial expressions.

We are now carrying out a further experiment to see if these behaviours are increased when the affective system responds specifically to them, or when the participants are trained to use them.

Acknowledgement

This research is supported by the EPSRC, grant reference R81374/01.

References

1. Argyle, M., 1988, *Bodily Communication*, 2nd Edition. New York: Methuen.
2. Axelrod, l., & Hone, K. (2004) Affecteme, Affectic, Affecticon: Measuring Affective Interaction with Standard and Affective Systems in *Proceedings of 18th British HCI Group Annual Conference 2004 'Design for Life' Conference,* Leeds, UK (Sept 2004)
3. Axelrod, L., Hone, K. (2004) Smoke and Mirrors: Gathering User Requirements for Emerging Affective Systems. Proceedings of 26th International Conference on Information Technology Interfaces, ITI 2004.
4. Axelrod, L., Hone, K., 2005, E-motional Advantage: Performance and Satisfaction Gains with Affective Computing. *Proceedings of CHI 2005 'Technology, Community, Safety' Conference on Human Factors in Computer Systems*, Portland, USA
5. Bunting, M., 2004, *Willing Slaves: How The Overwork Culture Is Ruling Our Lives* HarperCollins.
6. Bradley, M.M., Lang P.J. Measuring emotion: the Self-Assessment Manikin and the Semantic Differential. *J Behav Ther Exp Psychiatry* 25,1 (1994) 49-59.
7. Hayes-Roth, B., Ball, G., Lisetti, C., Picard, R. and Stern, A. Panel on affect and emotion in the user interface. *Proc Int. Conf.Intelligent User Interfaces*, 1998, 91-94.
8. Ito Mizuko, A New Set of Social Rules for a Newly Wireless Society *http://www.ojr.org/japan/wireless/1043770650.php*
9. Minsky, M., 2004, *The Emotion Machine* (draft) available at www.media.mit.edu/~minsky/
10. Norman, D. A., 2004, *Emotional Design: Why We Love (or Hate) Everyday Things*. Basic Books
11. Picard, R.W. *Affective Computing*. Cambridge,MA: The MIT Press, 1977.
12. Reeves, B., Nass, C. *The Media Equation: How people treat computers, television and new media like real people and places.* CSLI Publications 1998
13. Scherer, K., Schorr, A., and Johnstone, T. *Appraisal Processes in Emotion.* USA, OUP, 2001.
14. Shechtman, N., Horowitz, L.M. Media Inequality in Conversation: How People Behave Differently when Interacting with Computers and People. *Proceedings of CHI 2003,* Ft Lauderdale, Florida USA.
15. White P. R. R., (2005) *The Appraisal Analysis Website.* http://www.grammatics.com/appraisal/
16. Woods, D. K., Fassnacht, C, 2004 Wisconsin Centre for Education Research, TRANSANA website http://www2.wcer.wisc.edu/Transana

Affective Composites: Autonomy and Proxy in Pedagogical Agent Networks

Eric R. Hamilton

US Air Force Academy, CO 80840-6200, USA
eric.hamilton@usafa.af.mil

Abstract. This paper proposes an alternative paradigm for building affective competencies in embodied conversational agents (ECAs). The key feature of this approach -- and the reason for referring to it as an alternative paradigm -- entails use of hybrid ECAs that are expressive both autonomously and as pass-through proxies for human communications. The context in which this hybrid ECA paradigm is currently under investigation involves animated pedagogical agents. Other domains for which ECAs are under current and envisioned use, however, such as medical interviews, may also be appropriate for their application. One critical research question involves testing the conjecture that human affect shared through an agent reverberates to or scaffolds the empathic credibility, trustworthiness or effectiveness of the agent when it is functioning autonomously.

1 Introduction

This article proposes an alternative paradigm for building affective competencies in embodied conversational agents (ECAs) [1]. The key feature of this approach -- and the reason for referring to it as an alternative paradigm -- entails use of hybrid ECAs that are expressive both autonomously and as pass-through proxies for human communications. The context in which this hybrid ECA paradigm is currently under investigation involves animated pedagogical agents (intelligent, virtual tutors with life-like affective features [2-4]). Other domains for which ECAs are under current and envisioned use, however, may also be appropriate for their application. Within the context of instructional settings that use animated pedagogical agents, this paradigm may help to create the theoretical capacity to induce in group learning settings a form of the individual phenomenon of flow [5, 6], an affectively rich sense of immersion and competence in challenging work or play.

The effort to develop this paradigm entails an international network of research and commercial partners in the US, Canada, China, and Germany. It is supported by the US National Science Foundation and more details about the specific project appears on the NSF website at the location appearing in the Reference section [7]. A class of "ALASKA" instructional platforms – agent and library augmented shared knowledge areas – instantiates this paradigm.

J. Tao, T. Tan, and R.W. Picard (Eds.): ACII 2005, LNCS 3784, pp. 898–906, 2005.

2 Agent and Library Augmented Shared Knowledge Areas (ALASKA)

An ALASKA platform integrates a) pedagogical animated agents, b) shared collaborative workspaces that enable users in a self-contained or distributed classroom environment to remotely view and modify the displays of others; and c) a specialized learning object repository to illustrate, describe or provide visualizations of curriculum concepts. A rich system of social interaction and communication occupies normal classrooms. ALASKA comprises an effort to capitalize on that social interaction system by blending it with animated and intelligent agents over collaborative network structures.

In ALASKA as in other peer [2-4, 8] or cognitive tutor systems [9], learners interact one-on-one with a personal agent in instructional, mentoring, or other types of conversational activities. Adopting content-rich collaborative *networks,* however, theoretically creates the opportunity for a) agents to interact with each other to broker human-peer tutoring relationships; b) for the teacher to direct agents, hybridizing their autonomy; and c) for the teacher to "take over" an agent in order to communicate directly with a learner, thereby hybridizing the identity of the agent and creating the composite affect system this paper proposes. Finally, the accessibility to the agent network, students and teacher of d) a common library of clarifying visualizations, animations or fuller explanations of concepts round out the core features of ALASKA.

A network of students, agents and classroom teacher, amplify the one-on-one social interaction of agent-learner systems with significant new interactive possibilities. In a classroom with n students who each work with an agent, this implies n agent-related dyads. A networked system, however, in which agents interact with each other (n^2-1 dyads), with the teacher (n dyads) and with their respective students (n dyads) theoretically creates $n^2 + 2n - 1$ dyads involving at least one agent. In a classroom of 20 students, for example, the networking features convert 20 agent-related dyads to 439 agent-related dyads. The paper returns to this computation in discussion of interactional bandwidth; the intent here is to suggest numerical considerations of the alternate networking paradigm that ALASKA produces in designing for more interactive pathways. Dyadic count, however, is a gross and preliminary indicator for interactional potential. While it usefully conveys the fundamentally different arithmetic of networking agents, multiplying agent-related dyads has neither value nor intrinsic wisdom in the absence of spurring more profound learning, human performance or human interaction. Creating an expansive system of interactive pathways provides only a necessary but still insufficient part of the context for discussion of composite agent-affect systems (item c above) that rely on networking. To extend this context, the following scenario more holistically attempts to illustrate the four agent-related design features enumerated above, and the overall functionality of a collaborative "what you see is what I see" [10, 11] instructional network design. This scenario is similar to those appearing elsewhere [12, 13].

Scenario. Anna was excited. Barely six weeks into the introductory high school programming course she taught, she felt a strong rapport with her students. Sure, she wished that the distribution of student ability levels was not so great, but she had already discovered with increasing frequency that sometimes the most extraordinary performances came from seemingly ordinary students who became engaged. She also felt so much more equipped for the class. A group of students majoring in computer science from the local college had helped pull together a pool of explanatory applets (in a few cases starting from scratch) to accompany the curriculum. Now in its second year, the program was producing and polishing some very useful applets that had the twin virtues of being both reusable and modifiable to keep up with course changes. She also knew some of the common pitfalls for the class and had a library of electronically prepared "mini-explanations" that she could send out to one or more students when needed, complete with a visualization applet.

Today's Lesson. The lesson was a great topic. The students had learned in the previous days about nested loops and random number generators. This session was one of the payoff days when putting a few ideas together would produce elegant mathematical results while creating some beautiful fractal imagery. The class discussion would be short and revolve around whether the random number generator could be used in an infinite loop to pick one of three functions to modify the x and y coordinates of a point to be plotted on a graphing canvas. Each time the coordinates are modified and plotted, the random decision would repeat the point-plotting using the new coordinates. Anna loved watching the students watch with puzzlement and pleasure as a fractal would unfold before them. She was not going to let on that anything unusual would be taking place. She led the discussion recapping the underlying concepts of random numbers and nested loops. She sent the programming exercise to the class and watched them start.

Some Students Get off to a Quick Start. Her first step was to do a run of thumbnail views of a group of twenty students – she could peer into a subset of their screens with sufficient resolution to see that several of them were off to the races. She touched the personalized "encourage/correct so far" icon on her response palette and then icons for the students. Though they were in different parts of the room, most received a warm and friendly voice from their personal agents who passed along the teacher's personal encouragement. Some had opted out of having an embodied agent and simply received text or audio messages based on their preferences. The students would all finish at different times. Each time they did, their respective agent would send a notification to the teacher's agent who posted a progress tally in the teacher's space. The agents also posed a set of probes for the students who completed early, based on interests the agents had learned about their students. In a friendly tone, some agents asked their students how the fractal would behave if its color parameters changed with each pixel using the same functions that modify the spatial coordinates. The agents were ready both to watch their students develop modifications to answer the follow-up probes and to retrieve a few examples themselves. In these particular cases, the agent would suggest the students write their own routine before they experimented with the applets. Adopting a mentoring voice, some agents were also ready to sketch a few pieces of information about the Collage Theorem on which the exercise was based. Anna was confident that this group of her charges was in good shape.

Others are Proceeding Well. Anna could see the screens of another group of students – it was not a trivial exercise, and they were tentative in their work but seemed to have the right idea. Some were sending questions that simply needed a one or two word answer that she would either shoot back or simply say to them across the room. Some were looking up a text explanation of nested loops and a couple of students were obtaining explanations from their respective agents. Even when she was working with Jason (below) Anna was able to answer quick questions that would have otherwise kept these students from proceeding.

Some are Stuck. She knew from the thumbnails of the workspaces that several students were not able to start the exercise. The students would type or jot any question that needed clarifying and send it to the teacher if she was not immediately available to help them. Anna's screen displayed several similar questions from around the class related to how to connect the random function to the decision about which of the three functions graphed the next circle. She knew this was a conceptual hurdle and had prepared one of her mini-explanations and a nice visual routine that showed how random numbers could be used to drive decisions in a program. She decided whether to break the flow of the class by re-explaining this topic to everyone or sending her mini-explanation and applet to this group. Her mini-explanation was electronically stored as voice and could be rendered directly by an agent, passing along intonations along with the underlying explanation. She sent a message to the students with the five questions. "Thanks for your question – I think that this explanation and applet might help. Take a look at it and let me know if it helps you get started. Your agent may suggest some other avenues but if this doesn't help let me know right away." A few minutes later, Anna was able to thumbnail the screens of all these students and saw that three were progressing. "Mike, Sarah, Tom, that explanation helped? The agents certainly could have done the follow-up, but it seemed easier just for Anna to ask. The three, located around the classroom, nodded without taking their eyes off the screen.

Two aren't Able to Start at All. Jason and Sue were a different story. They seemed lost. Sue had sent an alert that she did not really know where to begin, grateful for the anonymity of messaging. Jason didn't bother with a message, but he knew that his teacher could see from her station that he had not started. Anna decided she would work directly with Jason after Sue's agent sent a discreet query to the agents of the fastest moving students to see if any would volunteer their "student" to help Sue answer some questions to get started. The agents brokered a quick connection. Sue's agent gently asked her if she was willing to get some help and the two students were able to work on the problem together in Sue's workspace even though they weren't sitting together and would not have any other easy way to match up without the agents. Anna was able to help Jason, and Sue also received individualized help from another human, although now, six weeks into the course, almost everyone seemed comfortable and trusting of their personal agents.

Reflection. Anna thought about why the students were comfortable with the agents. The agents certainly helped *her* a lot, but they also seemed to be getting a lot of help themselves. Sometimes it was easier for her simply to take over one or more agents at one time, and sometimes to let the agents work on their own. She appreciated the flexibility of being able to decide at the time. She tried to decide whether her job was harder or easier with this environment. Both, she figured. The days of running around the class and trying to guess who might need her help the most were over. She could see their work from her own station. The days of guessing how many students were actually doing the problem-solving were over, as were the days of re-stating a lot of explanations she had given many times before. She was able to connect students to help one another where it made sense, even if they were not sitting next to each other. But now that she saw a lot more of what was going on in the class, she had to keep track of a lot more information and spend her time on the more challenging work of understanding what her students were thinking. And the students were indeed thinking more. A large number of the students who were stuck or lost would have figured out something else to do with their time while she picked one or two of them to help– so would the four or five who only needed a few minutes to do the exercise. It seemed that the students were spending a much larger fraction of their class time doing real thinking and learning. There was a high performance expectation and high performance kind of resonance in the class. It was both easier and harder she decided, and certainly more complex. But more rewarding.

3 Flexibility in Help Resources and in Agent Proxy and Autonomy

The scenario depicts a flexible system to provide help to a student, who can initiate help requests from this default sequence of help resources:

1) (embodied and intelligent) agents → 2) applets → 3) human peers → 4) teacher. Students can pose questions of their personal agents that can furnish answers based on resident domain expertise. At the next level, they can provide applets or short videos; then, they can broker peer human tutoring relationships; and they can seek assistance from a teacher. Such a cascading sequence provides an intuitively logical order and structure, though classroom social interactions are too complex to constrain to a single path for obtaining help, requiring, instead, what Spiro et al [14] refer to as "random-access" to resources and cognitive flexibility. Such a default sequence of cascading resources can be easily altered if the student seeks help immediately from the teacher, bypassing the agent, or requests peer assistance immediately. Similarly, the teacher can use agents to furnish feedback or assistance, or simply call out students, bypassing default routings. The teacher can initiate peer-assistance episodes. The teacher can examine multiple thumbnail displays of many students at once over the collaborative workspace, or walk about a class interacting with students one at a time.

Such flexibility is essential to the paradigm this paper suggests. It is designed to accommodate the complexities of classroom interactions, and it blurs the task lines between actors that a student relies on in a classroom, including teacher, peer human tutors, pedagogical agent tutors, and other instructional objects. In blurring task lines between actors, some aspects of identity also shift. For example, the agents possess domain expertise and limited intelligence (through parsers, simple learning algorithms, and FAQ databases), but a significant portion of their intelligence is derived from access to a library of electronic objects that they share with other agents and that the teacher or student can access independently or through agent mediation. That is, the agents are intelligent, but their identity as autonomously intelligent has an asterisk: a portion of that intelligence is distributed over the network.

A more important blurring of identity emerges from the teacher taking over the agent to communicate to an individual student. Why might this be useful? Recall the earlier computational exercise: A classroom of 20 students who each possesses a pedagogical agent to work with them on a one-on-one basis entails 20 agent-related dyads. Networking those agents, however, so that agents can communicate not only with their own students but with the agents for the other students and with the teacher, yields 439 agent-related dyads, and an increase in what we term "interactional bandwidth" [6, 15]; such an increase can turn the task of hybridizing agents into an educationally and socially meaningful accomplishment.

By interactional bandwidth, we refer to the capacity of a learning environment to mediate meaningful content and affective representations that are shared by participants in that environment. At first approximation, elevating the number of agent-related dyads from 20 to 439 significantly increases such bandwidth. The end-goal of an agent-rich classroom network also includes enhancing human-human dyads and interactions.

Consider two contrasting images. The first one is of children raising their hands in a classroom waiting for a teacher to call on them. Such a setting has a tiny bandwidth at least relative to learning. Very little exchange of content is taking place – usually there is a lot of guessing by the teacher, but the students are keeping their content representations private until called upon. For a second image, consider a common split-screen newscast, perhaps with two people in a studio, a stock market ticker, sports scores, network logo, and story caption – such a display entails a plethora of multitasking content that requires parallel processing. Humans can process such displays routinely. Yet in classroom settings we often limit actors to the guessing and content-starved traditions of the first image. The parallel processing capacity of humans to absorb data may shed light on why hybridizing agents can be so valuable in taking advantage of increased interactional bandwidth.

ALASKA hybridization occurs when agents are directed by a teacher to pass along affectively attuned and content-rich communication to students. It is instantiated through a "response palette" that features a repertoire of facially- and voice- nuanced responses s/he has available for agent inheritance or pass-through transmission to the student. In the ALASKA shared-workspace environment, the teacher relies on the parallel processing competencies required, for example, to make sense out of the complex newscast display. She can overview the thumbnails of everyone in the class simultaneously, collecting enough information to judge fairly accurately what group of students was starting on track, which needed some simple assistance, and which needed significantly more. She might press the icons, for example, for eight students scattered around the class; then, she selects from a palette a message – which consists both of words and expressions – that she deems appropriate for those eight (e.g., "Nice start! Let me know if you have any questions but you are definitely on the right track.) Pressing on a send button activates the agents at each of those eight stations who pass on this communiqué. She can perform the same operation, say, for another group of five students but have the agents not only send a verbal message but suggest an applet (e.g., "When you are nesting multiple loops, make sure that you are incrementing the index values separately for each loop. Check out this quick animation if you think it might be helpful."). An expert teacher might realistically be able to make such visual judgments and send a set of messages in a relatively short period of time – perhaps one to two minutes, through which thirteen students receive agent-mediated, affect-rich, content-informed feedback from the teacher. It involves only two sends over the network, but the messages are disbursed to thirteen different locations. In theory, this represents a significantly higher number of informed, reasonably personalized, affectively attuned, and empathetic feedbacks to those in the classroom than a conventional setting could allow. **It does so by allowing the teacher to scaffold the work of many agents at once, by originating and sending messages that the agents deliver or mediate.** Interactional bandwidth multiplies significantly as the agents function as teacher proxies.

4 Research Directions and Conclusion

The purpose of this paper is to advance a way of thinking and stimulate conversation about artificial agents that function in networks and that can express both their own communications and that of a teacher in a classroom. Linking the collaborative workspaces, pedagogical ECAs, and digital libraries entails integration of existing technologies; that integration is the current technical phase of this research, and it is a prerequisite to a research agenda that investigates theoretical and practical dimensions of autonomous/proxy agent hybrids. Several directions are posed here. One critical and obvious research question involves testing the conjecture that human affect shared through an agent reverberates to or scaffolds the empathic credibility, trustworthiness or effectiveness of the agent functioning autonomously. The personality of the teacher, frequency of proxy actions, and other proxy parameters are among variables that may elevate or depress any reverberation or scaffolding effects, A technical question involves whether the student is alerted that a proxy action is underway, i.e., that the teacher is communicating through an agent rather than the agent functioning autonomously. If the student is not aware that the agent is in a proxy mode, but only that it *might* be, does that increase or decrease the reverberation or scaffolding effects? Another variation involves whether *dual* agents might more effectively relay inherited affect and autonomous affect separately [16].

The construct of "affective valence" as an informal composite index of how life-like an agent's expressions are may be useful as a means to aggregate independent variables such programmed affective intensity, balance of emotion types, animation and gestural synchronization and dependent variables such as believability and resonance with humans [17]. Creating and testing more formalized metrics for a construct such as affective valence would constitute an important step to comparing the life-likeness of agent models and it may contribute to important work on learner preferences in pedagogical agents [2, 4].

The merits of replacing humans with machines have been an important theme of discourse in educational technology since the advent of computer-assisted instruction. Much of the discussion has been moot or obscured by the instructional awkwardness and ineffectiveness of educational technologies to mimic more complex behaviors and expressions of real teachers. As pedagogical agents become more affectively, cognitively and socially sophisticated, the question inevitably will become more salient and pressing when viewed through an "either/or" lens [18]. We propose, though, means to bypass this way of looking at the instructional or classroom design with agents. This is effected by using a subtle form of "both" real and artificial in the same embodiment through engineering in the embodied agents both anthropomorphic competencies and the capacity to inherit and pass-through the communication of a real person. Migrating agents to pedagogically-astute networks where they join forces with humans can help fulfill a vision whereby *virtual human interactions* can render *real human interactions* more potent and satisfying as the earlier scenario hopefully suggests. Architectures in which agents express affect and intelligence both autonomously and as proxies for humans may hold the counterintuitive promise of real humans rendering virtual humans more effective in fulfilling their core task of engaging students in meaningful and complex learning experiences.

References

1. Cassell, J., et al. *More Than Just a Pretty Face: Affordances of Embodiment.* in *IUI 2000.* 2000. New Orleans, Louisiana.
2. Baylor, A.L. *The Impact of Three Pedagogical Agent Roles.* in *AAMAS '03.* 2003. Melbourne, Australia.
3. Johnson, W.L., J.W. Rickel, and J.C. Lester, *Animated pedagogical agents: Face-to-face interaction in interactive learning environments.* International Journal of Artificial Intelligence in Education, 2000. **11**: p. 47-78.
4. Kim, Y., *Learners' Expectations of the Desirable Characteristics of Virtual Learning Companions.* In submission, 2005.
5. Csikszentmihalyi, M., *Finding Flow: The Psychology of Engagement With Everyday Life.* 2000, New York: Basic Books.
6. Hamilton, E., *Raising Interactional Bandwidth and Approaching Learning Flow through Agent and Library Augmented Shared Knowledge Areas (ALASKA).* in submission, 2005.
7. Hamilton, E., et al. *Agent and Library Augmented Shared Knowledge Areas (ALASKA).* 2004 [cited; Available from: http://www.nsf.gov/awardsearch/showAward.do?AwardNumber=0420310.
8. Baylor, A., *Beyond butlers: Intelligent agents as mentors.* Journal of Educational Computing Research, 2000. **22**(4): p. 373-382.
9. Koedinger, K.R., et al., *Intelligent tutoring goes to school in the big city.* International Journal of Artificial Intelligence in Education, 1997. **8**: p. 30-43.
10. Hamilton, E., *Pen-based and multimedia shared network spaces that increase learning flow and generative learning*, in *Advanced Research in Computers and Communications in Education: New Human Abilities for the Networked Society*, G. Cumming, T. Okamoto, and L. Gomez, Editors. 1999, IOS Press: Tokyo.
11. Prideaux, D., *Implementing Java Based Telecollaboration Groupware.* 2001.

12. Hamilton, E. *Agent and Library Augmented Shared Knowledge Areas (ALASKA).* in *Proceedings of the International Conference on Multimodal Interfaces (ICMI'04).* 2004. State College, PA: ACM.
13. Hamilton, E., et al. *Interactive Pathway Design for Learning through Agent and Library Augmented Shared Knowledge Areas (ALASKA).* in *IEEE-Pervasive Computing*. 2005. Kauai, Hawaii.
14. Spiro, R.J., et al., *Cognitive Flexibility, Constructivism, and Hypertext: Random Access Instruction for Advanced Knowledge.* Educational Technology, 1991: p. 24-33.
15. Hamilton, E. and J. Cherniavsky, *Issues in synchronous versus asynchronous E-learning platforms*, in *Web-Based Learning: Theory, Research and Practice*, H. O'Neill and R. Perez, Editors. 2005 (in press), Lawrence Erlbaum: Mahwah, NJ.
16. Baylor, A.L., *Agent Proxy Ideas: E-Mail Communication, 06/03/05 to E. Hamilton*. 2005.
17. Cowella, A.J., *Manipulation of non-verbal interaction style and demographic embodiment to increase anthropomorphic computer character credibility.* International Journal of Human-Computer Studies, 2005. **2**: p. 281-306.
18. Cole, R., *Creating the Next Generation of Intelligent Animated Conversational Agents.* ITR grant IIS-0086107. 2000: National Science Foundation.

An Affective User Interface Based on Facial Expression Recognition and Eye-Gaze Tracking

Soo-Mi Choi and Yong-Guk Kim

School of Computer Engineering, Sejong University, Seoul, Korea
{smchoi, ykim}@sejong.ac.kr

Abstract. This paper describes a pipeline by which facial expression and eye-gaze of the user are tracked, and then 3D facial animation is synthesized in the remote place based upon timing information of the facial and eye movement information. The system first detects a facial area within the given image and then classifies its facial expression into 7 emotional weightings. Such weighting information, transmitted to the PDA via a mobile network, is used for non-photorealistic facial expression animation. It turns out that facial expression animation using emotional curves is more effective in expressing the timing of an expression comparing to the linear interpolation method. The emotional avatar embedded on a mobile platform has some potential in conveying emotion between peoples via Internet.

1 Introduction

We identify someone by looking at his/her face, since each person typically has unique and distinctive features in the face. Moreover, human face is a great communication device, because the face can evoke diverse facial expressions according to the internal emotions. So one can read someone's emotional state from his/her facial expression and respond to it appropriately. Humans are able to recognize facial expressions of the rendered face on the screen (or paper) as well as of the real face. In fact, researchers in the computer graphics and multimedia areas have been developed a series of face models and their implementations for using in diverse human-computer interaction applications or for animating an avatar in the cyberspace. As an example, the early attempt of unifying the facial expression recognition and facial animation envisioned such virtual face avatar as a future communication media [5]. In fact, such avatar has some advantage compared to the real face since it can be anonymous, friendly, funny and animated in real-time basis [7].

The present study will present a multi-step pipeline: in the first step the facial expressions of the face within the video images are recognized as a time sequence, and eye tracker picks up gaze direction of the user; in the second step the extracted emotional information and eye trajectory are transmitted to a remote client via the mobile network; in the final step the cartoon-like 3D facial expression and eye movements are rendered on a PDA using that information as shown in Fig. 1. To classify the facial expression, it needs to detect the facial area within the given image and then to

J. Tao, T. Tan, and R.W. Picard (Eds.): ACII 2005, LNCS 3784, pp. 907 – 914, 2005.

normalize the selected facial area according to a template. The facial expression information obtained at the first part is transmitted to the next part via the mobile network. The computing platform of the second part is a mobile PDA, which has Internet connection and yet has limited processing power and memory size. We have adopted a non-photorealistic method in rendering a 3D facial expression on the PDA.

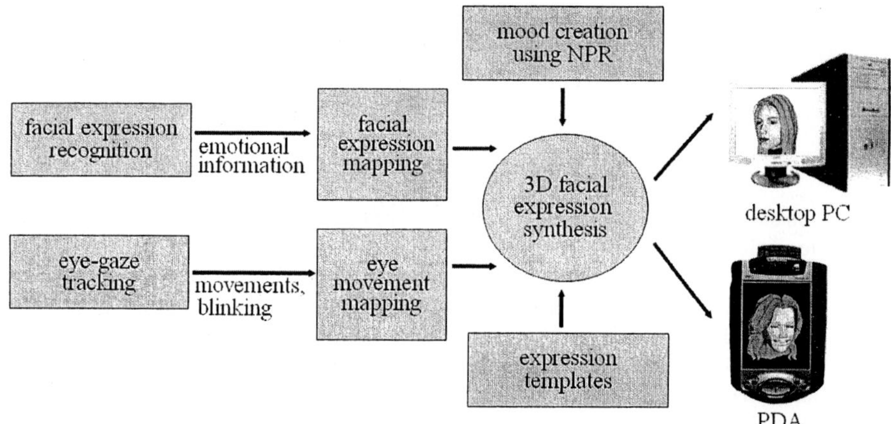

Fig. 1. The schematic diagram of the facial expression recognition-synthesis system

The structure of this paper is as follow. In section 2, we describe the automatic recognition of facial expressions. The non-photorealistic rendering and timing aspect of emotion into animation will be described in section 3. In section 4, we show how to incorporate eye-gaze tracking into the animation. We discuss the result and conclude in section 5.

2 Automatic Facial Expression Recognition

The pipeline proposed in this paper consists of two main parts. The first part classifies its facial expression of the face contained in the video from the camera and the system is operated in the server. The second part is within the client such as a PDA where a 3D face is animated according to the emotion graph transmitted from the server.

In general, the facial expression recognition system consists of three stages: in the first stage, it detects a face area within the given image, called the face detection; in the second stage, the positions of three facial features (i.e. two eyes and mouth) will be located within the detected face for normalizing the face area; the final stage classifies a facial expression of the given face using a classifier.

In our study, Adaboost algorithm is used for the face detection task. In addition, we can train the algorithm to deal with size variation and rotation of the face. In any case, once a face is detected using this machine, the face image needs to be normalized by locating the positions of two eyes and the mouth.

Fig. 2. Cohn-Kanade facial expression database

After the normalization stage, Gabor wavelets are applied to the 20X20 grid drawn over the image, and the convolution output from this operation is forwarded to the next stage to classify the facial expression. For this purpose, we have used the EFM (Enhanced Fisher Discriminant Model), which in fact combines PCA (Principal Component Analysis) with Fisher Discriminant, and it was initially developed for the face perception. Comparative study shows that performance of the system has increased by adding Gabor wavelets at least 10% and the EFM outperforms the PCA. When the Gabor wavelets and the EFM are combined, the recognition rate of the system reaches to 92%.

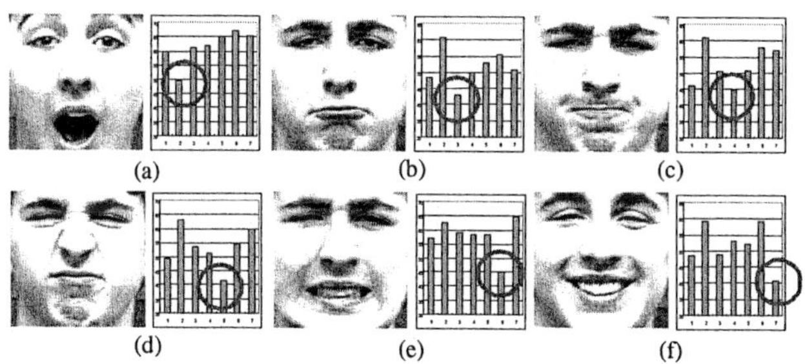

Fig. 3. The results of automatic facial expression recognition

We have used standard Cohn-Kanade database [4] for training and performance measurement of the system as shown in Fig. 2. Fig. 3 shows six basic facial expressions of a subject from the facial expression database, and the corresponding emotional similarity measurements performed by EFM. Each facial image is shown beside a bar graph. In the bar graph, each vertical bar represents the similarity measure to one of the seven emotions from neutral (bar1), surprise (bar2), fear (bar3), sadness (bar4), anger (bar5), disgust (bar6) and happiness (bar7) from the left to the right, respectively. For instance, as Fig. 3(a) is the image for 'surprise', the height of the bar2 is the shortest among seven vertical bars, indicating that the measurement by the system agrees with our visual perception.

3 Facial Animation for an Affective User Interface

We have developed 3D facial animation as an affective communication tool, based on automatic facial expression recognition and real-time eye-gaze tracking. For this purpose, a non-photorealistic rendering technique is applied to the face model to enhance familiarity and uniqueness of the 3D faces.

Although, the widely used technique in animating faces has been a key-frame interpolation, recent study in facial behavior suggests that our facial expressions cannot model properly wopith such simple assumption [2]. For instance, the true intention of a character can be conveyed genuinely, when the timing of the action is properly executed. In fact, it is known that animators normally adopt a discrete interpolation gimmick by inserting an anticipation frame between two key-frames.

In this paper, we present a facial expression recognition-synthesis pipeline in which the emotional curves obtained from the front recognition stage provide the timing information for the facial animation. The seven emotional curves (i.e. neutral, surprise, fear, sadness, anger, disgust, happiness) give weighting information for facial synthesis. The horizontal axis of the emotional curves shows the change of time and the vertical one represents the similarity measure. As the basis for generating non-linear expression synthesis, we use the concepts of weighting information based on emotional curves and blending functions. Each emotion has an emotional curve obtained by automatic facial expression recognition. Each emotional expression also has an associated target set of facial control parameter values. The actual parameter value used at a given animation frame time $F_p(t)$ is determined by blending emotional curves using a weighted average:

$$F_p(t) = \sum_{e=1}^{n} (W_{ep}(t) T_{ep}) / \sum_{e=1}^{n} W_{ep}(t) \qquad (1)$$

where n is the number of recognized expressions and T_{ep} are the target facial control parameter values. W_{ep} is the weight of an emotional expression. For stable animation, two dominant expressions are blended in runtime.

The relationship between the original faces and the corresponding 3D faces obtained by emotional curves is illustrated in Fig. 4. The input face images are in Fig. 4(a). The animation sequence by emotional curves for the 'surprise' is illustrated in Fig. 4(b), while the same sequence is shown using the linear interpolation method in Fig. 4(c). When you compare two sequences, it is possible to observe that the surprise expression is attained suddenly from frame 4 to frame 5 in Fig. 4(b), whereas the same expression is evolved in a linear fashion in Fig. 4(c). As the recent research suggests that human is very sensitive on the timing of facial expression, the facial animation based upon emotional curves reflects faithfully user's emotional state in the animation sequence.

In general, non-photorealistic graphics refers to a set of techniques for creating images where artistic expression is the immediate goal, rather than adherence to photorealism. Silhouette edges are useful in conveying effectively a great deal of information with a very few strokes using non-photorealistic rendering (NPR). In order to add emotional appeal for the real-time rendering, we draw silhouette edges using a depth buffer directly in image space [10]. The only two sets of polygons are needed to compute visible silhouette edges for a given viewpoint. These two sets are the first layer of visible polygons nearest the viewpoint (P_1) and the second layer of

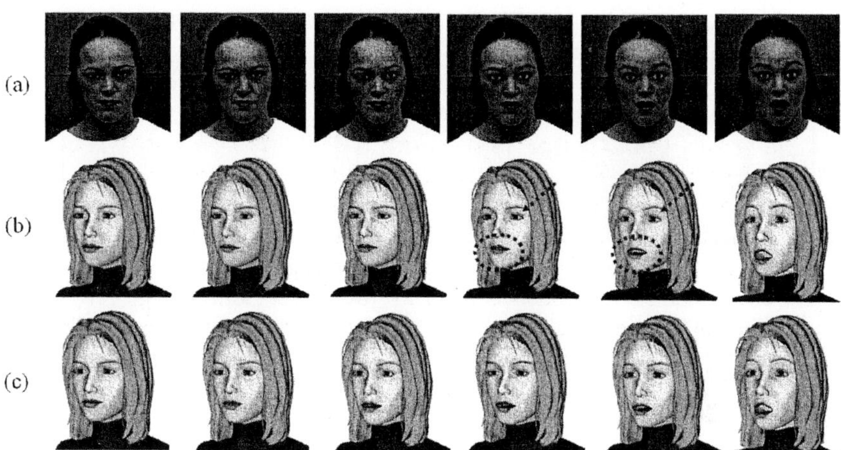

Fig. 4. A comparison of the results of facial animation methods: (a) input face images; (b) facial animation using emotional curves; (c) facial animation using linear interpolation

completely visible or partially visible. P_2 can be computed using the same visibility algorithm after subtracting the polygons in the first layer from the set of all polygons. The intersection of P_1 and P_2 gives the silhouette edges in the object space. To create interesting effects, the silhouette edges with non-uniform widths can be rendered by translating back-facing polygons. The width of the resulting silhouette depends on the orientation of the back-facing polygons and also the orientation of the corresponding occluding front facing polygon. Fig. 5 illustrates the results of the photorealistic as well as the non-photorealistic rendering.

In order to animate humors and subtle emotions, we have also tried the cartoon-like shading [1] as a non-photorealistic rendering technique (See Fig. 6), rather than smoothly interpolating shading across a model. In our system, the diffuse lighting at the vertices is defined by the following lighting equation:

$$C_i = a_g a_m + a_l a_m + (\max\{L \cdot n, 0\}) d_l d_m \quad (2)$$

C_i is the vertex color, a_g is the coefficient of global ambient light, a_l and d_l are the ambient and diffuse coefficients of the light source, and a_m and d_m are the ambient and diffuse coefficients of the object's material. L is the unit vector from the light source to the vertex, and n is the unit normal to the surface at the vertex. Instead of calculating the colors per vertex, a 1D texture map of a minimal number of colors is computed and stored ahead of time (i.e. illuminated main color, shadow color, and highlight color). For the PDA we have developed the software system using Embedded Visual C++ 3.0 and PocketGL™ as a PocketPC 3D graphics library. Considering the limitation of processing speed of the PDA, we have used minimum number of polygons in rendering the 3D face, and have adopted an optimization method for the floating-point operations.

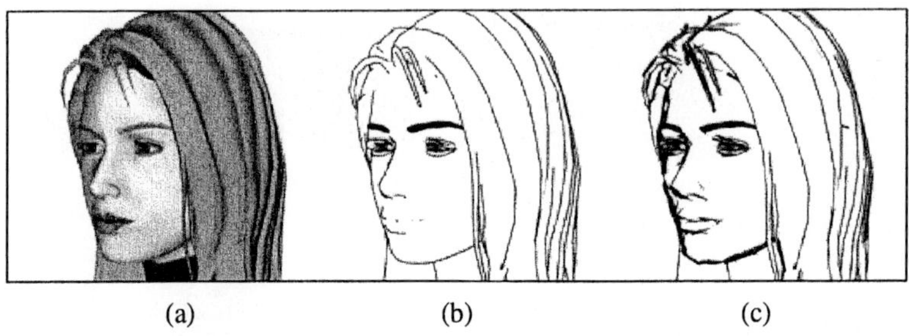

(a) (b) (c)

Fig. 5. A comparison of the results of photorealistic and non-photorealistic rendering: (a) photorealistic rendering; (b) non-photorealistic rendering with uniform silhouette edges; (c) non-photorealistic rendering with non-uniform silhouette edges

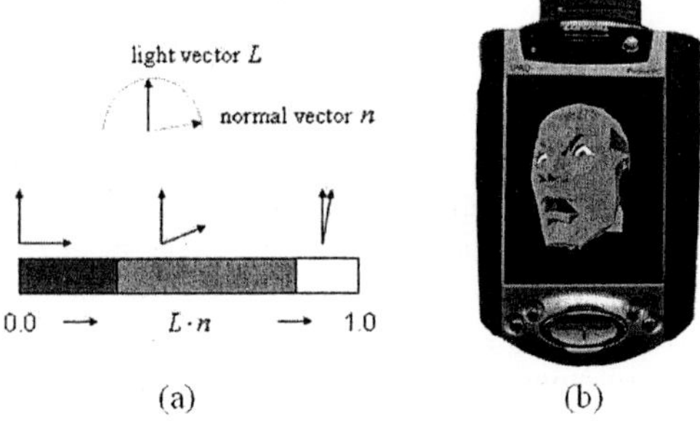

Fig. 6. Cartoon-like shading: (a) 1D texture map; (b) cartoon rendering on the PDA

4 Eye-Gaze Tracking and Animation

Human eye movements play an essential role as a channel of affective communication. Researchers have been tried to embody the eye movements into facial animation for a natural appeal. A line of research on eye movements has focused on empirical models built on information gathered from case studies of people or statistical models of eye-gaze tracking data. The empirical or statistical models of the eyes can be used to generate the attentional behavior for a virtual character to appear natural. Our primary purpose here is to develop a vivid graphical interface that allows the user to transmit emotions in real-time. In this study, we have implemented an eye model directly reflects the eye movements of the user with the aid of an eye-gaze tracker as shown in Fig. 7.

The gaze animation is performed using the eye-gaze tracking data. When the direction of eye-gaze is changed from the vector $\mathbf{v}_0$ to the vector $\mathbf{v}_1$ as shown in Fig. 7(c), the eyeball's rotation can be computed using a quaternion. The quaternion is defined by $\mathbf{Q} = (\mathbf{x}_2, \mathbf{y}_2, \mathbf{z}_2, \mathbf{cos}(\alpha/2))$ where $(\mathbf{x}_2, \mathbf{y}_2, \mathbf{z}_2)$ is the unit rotation vector and α is the angle through which the direction of eye is rotated until it is aligned with the vector $\mathbf{v}_1$.

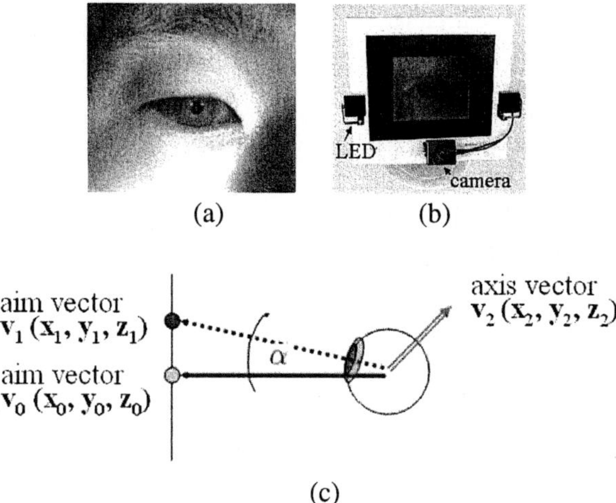

Fig. 7. Eye Tracker and Eye direction vectors; (a) a tracked iris; (b) the eye tracker; (c) eye direction vectors

Fig. 8(a) demonstrates a facial animation sequence where the gaze of the virtual character follows the eye movement trajectory of the user. The dotted lines in Fig. 8(b) indicate how the user moves his eye into several directions. This experiment was prepared to confirm that eye-gaze animation is carried out according to the eye movement trajectory of the user.

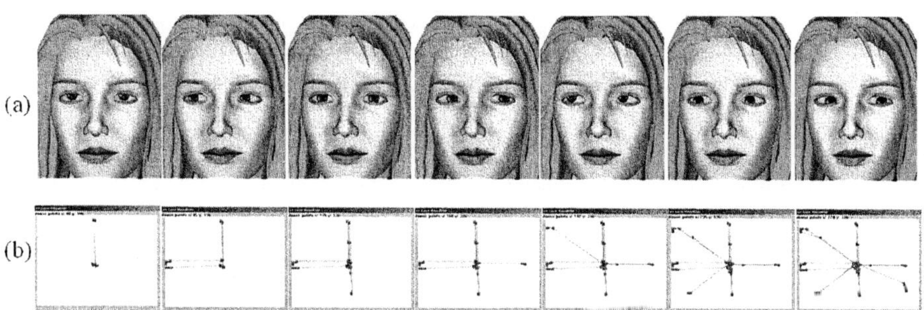

Fig. 8. Eye-gaze animation (a) and eye movement trajectory (b)

5 Discussion and Conclusions

The present study demonstrates a pipeline where the facial expression recognition system is integrated with the 3D facial animation on the PDA via a mobile network. In addition, eye-gaze of the user is also incorporated using the eye tracker. We present a basic framework in which an emotional avatar that attains human emotional states can be generated. In particular, we have found that facial expression synthesis using the emotional curves obtained from the facial expression recognition is more natural in expressing the timing of a facial animation than using the simple linear interpolation method. We have also developed a cartoon shading method as one of the non-photorealistic techniques in rendering an avatar on the PDA without employing extensive polygons. It is known that human gaze information provides an effective way of conveying emotion. The present study combines eye-gaze and facial expression for animating a live 3D facial avatar. We expect that this kind of emotional avatar can be an effective communication mean in the ubiquitous computing environment.

References

1. L. Adam, C. Marshall, M. Harris, and M. Blackstein, "Stylized Rendering Techniques for Scalable Real-Time 3D Animation", In Symposium of Non-Photorealistic Animation and Rendering (NPAR) 2000, pp. 13-20, 2000.
2. J. Cohn *et al.*, "Multimodal Coordination of Facial Action, Head Rotation, and Eye Motion during Spontaneous Smiles", IEEE Conference on Automatic Face and Gesture, Korea, May 2004.
3. P. Ekman and W. Friesen, "Unmasking the Face. A Guide to Recognizing Emotions from Facial Clues", Palo Alto. Consulting Psychologists Press, 1975.
4. T. Kanade, J. Cohn, and Y. Tian, "Comprehensive Database for Facial Expression Analysis", Proc. Int'l Conf. Face and Gesture Recognition, pp. 46-53, 2000.
5. N. Magnenat-Thalmann, P. Kalra, and M. Escher, "Face to Virtual Face", Proceeding of IEEE, pp.870-883, 1998.
6. F.I. Parke and K. Waters, "Computer Facial Animation", A K Peters, 1996.
7. I. Buck, A. Finkelstein, C. Jacobs, et al., "Performance-Driven Hand-Drawn Animation", In Symposium of Non-Photorealistic Animation and Rendering (NPAR) 2000, pp. 101-108, 2000
8. S. Pandzic, "Facial Animation Framework for the Web and Mobile Platforms", Web3D, pp. 24-28, 2002.
9. M. Byun, I. Badler, "Qualitative Parametric Modifiers for Facial Animations", SIGGRAPH, pp. 65-71, 2002.
10. R. Raskar, M. Cohen, "Image Precision Silhouette Edges", Symposium on Interactive 3D Graphics, pp. 135-140, 1999.

Watch and Feel: An Affective Interface in a Virtual Storytelling Environment

Rui Figueiredo and Ana Paiva

GAIPS Grupo de Agentes Inteligentes e Personagens Sintéticas,
INESC-ID and IST, Tagus Park,
Av. Prof. Cavaco Silva, 2780-990 Porto Salvo, Portugal
{rui.figueiredo, ana.paiva}@inesc-id.pt

Abstract. In this paper we describe a study carried out with SenToy: a tangible interface that has the shape of a doll and is used to capture emotions from its user whilst performing specific gestures. SenToy was used with an application named Fearnot!, which is a virtual storytelling environment, where characters act autonomously and in character, so that stories emerge from those autonomous actions. The integration of SenToy in FearNot! was evaluated in two ways: (1) if users were able to manipulate the tangible interface appropriately, even if engaged in storytelling situation and (2) if the emotions expressed by the users with SenToy were the same as the ones reported to have been felt after the session. The results of the study show that Sentoy can be used to understand how the viewers reacted to the stories portrayed, and at the same time that the emotions that were expressed with SenToy (apart from some exceptions, reported in the paper) are indeed similar as the ones reported to have been felt by the users.

Keywords: Affective tangible interface, affective computing, synthetic characters.

1 Introduction

The interaction between humans and computers has evolved significantly over the last few years. Line-driven commands were replaced by sophisticated Graphical User Interfaces, which are most common nowadays. However, alternative approaches have recently been proposed, one of them is the use of Tangible User Interfaces (TUI) [5]. The philosophy behind TUIs is to allow people to interact with computers via familiar tangible objects, therefore taking advantage of the richness of the tactile world allowing the users to interact with the computer in ways that are more intuitive and natural.

In this paper we explore the use of an affective tangible interface as a way to get feedback from users interacting with a virtual storytelling environment. Interactive and Virtual storytelling, in general, allows for users to become emersed in a story, where they can act and thus affect the development of the story. Several approaches have been taken in the way in which the story is affected by the

J. Tao, T. Tan, and R.W. Picard (Eds.): ACII 2005, LNCS 3784, pp. 915–922, 2005.

actions of the users. For example, users may act as "Gods" [4] in the story, as participants (thus having their own characters in the story) or simply as mere audience.

In this paper we show how a tangible interface can be used as a way to gather and thus adapt stories to actions performed by users with a tangible interface. To do that, we have used an affective tangible interface, SenToy [2], which detects a set of emotions that the user may want to transmit through a set of gestures. SenToy was used to collect emotional data from users that were watching a story.

Our goals with this work were: (1) test if users were able to manipulate the tangible interface appropriately, even if engaged in storytelling situation and (2) if the emotions expressed by the users with SenToy were the same as the ones reported to have been felt after the storytelling session.

The results of the study show that SenToy can be used to understand how the viewers reacted to the stories portrayed, and at the same time that the emotions that were expressed with SenToy (apart from some exceptions, reported in the paper) are indeed similar as the ones reported to have been felt by the users.

The paper is organised as follows: first we will give a brief overview of SenToy and of the storytelling application. Then we will describe the experiment done with 9 children and discuss the results obtained.

2 SenToy

SenToy is a tangible interface that has the shape of a doll and has the ability to detect gestures that represent emotions expressed by the user. SenToy is used within a system with two elements, the doll itself which is responsible for acquiring all the information regarding its handling by the user, and the computer that receives the data from the doll and proceeds by doing its processing and interpretation giving as an output an emotion with a certain certainty value. A picture of SenToy is given in figure 1.

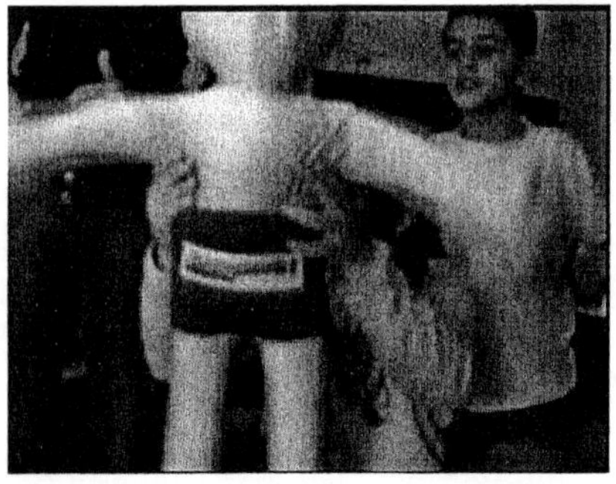

Fig. 1. Picture of *SenToy*

The patterns interpreted as emotions described in table 1. These patterns were decided after some design experiments (using a WoZ methodology) conducted with users (see [2]) and dolls.

Table 1. Patterns associated with emotions

Gesture	Emotion
Move the doll up and down	Happy
Slightly bend the doll's head onward	Sad
Agitate the doll vigorously	Anger
Cover the doll's eyes with it's hands	Fear
Incline the doll's body backwards and making the doll move backwards	Surprise

In the concrete case we are exploring, only four emotions were considered, which were: *Happiness*, *Sadness*, *Anger* and *Fear*. The other two emotions did not make sense for the storytelling application we wanted to consider.

3 FearNot!

Fearnot! is a 3D virtual storytelling application created for an European-funded project named VICTEC which goal was to investigate the technologies required to evoke an empathic responses between users and synthetic characters[6]. The creation of empathy is seen as a way of involving the user emotionally in improvised virtual drama in an area of Personal and Social Education (PSE), and specifically in this project that of anti-bullying education for children aged 8-12. Thus, FearNot! [3] features a virtual world inhabited by synthetic characters (that portray children) that act autonomously according to their goals and roles in the story. The roles can be "bully", "victim", "bystander" or "helper". Bullying episodes are generated by the actions of the characters in the world. The whole story is divided into episodes, "bullying" episodes. The users influence the development of the story by providing advice to the victim on what to do next.

In order to control the experiment, the version of FearNot! used in this research consists of a set of scripted scenarios, that include an introduction, where the characters of the story are presented (John, the victim and Luke the bully), then a bullying episode is shown followed by a phase were questions are asked to the users about the bullying episode. Then, according to the users' answers the path of the story evolves, and in the end an educational message is given to the viewers.

The scripted story used in this research was a story of physical bulling, where a bully (Luke) pushes the victim's (John) books to the flor and mocks him. After this bullying episode the victim asks the user for advice (the victim interacts with the user in a corner of the library) and according to the advice given by the child user a new episode is chosen. The second episode's scenario is a football game where again, the bully attacks John verbally. In this episode a "helper" comes to John's rescue. Finally, in the last episode John is again helped and John thanks for it.

4 Fearnot! with SenToy

The objective of using SenToy in FearNot! was to allow for further interaction of the users with the application. Also, our main research questions were also to test if users were able to manipulate the tangible interface appropriately, even if engaged in storytelling situation. So, in technical terms we had to embed SenToy's components into the FearNot! application. Furthermore, as users were allowed to use SenToy all the results of that interaction needed to saved in a log file containing information about which emotions and in which part of the story those emotions were expressed with SenToy.

As the episodes in FerNot! were defined in script files, some new information had to be added to the script files, so that the logs could record which part of the story was being displayed when the user used SenToy to express an emotion. To do that, changes were made to the ViewManager (an agent in the architecture used to built FearNot!) which is responsible for the parsing of the script files. The architecture of the new system is shown in figure 2.

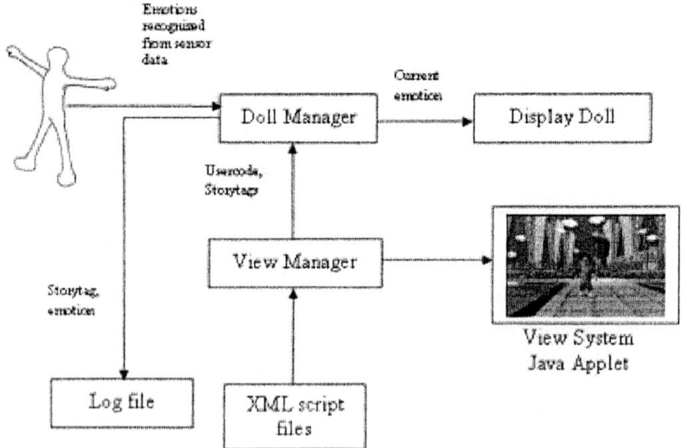

Fig. 2. Functionality added to Fearnot!

In the shown architecture the *ViewManager* is responsible for controlling the scripted story displayed in the *ViewSystem*. The *Doll Manager* is responsible for maintaining a state that describes what emotion was last received from SenToy, which part of the story we are currently in, and creating a log file with this information. The *Doll Manager* is also responsible for sending the current emotion to *Display Doll* which is the component responsible for displaying a cartoon face with emotions in the screen each time a new emotion is detected.

The cartoon faces were used as a way to provide immediate feedback to the child on what emotion she/he was expressing. These were immediate reactions to the gestures made with SenToy. For example, if the user expresses happiness with SenToy a cartoon face which represents that emotion will be displayed in the screen and will change only when the user expresses a different emotion. The cartoon faces were taken from [7] and are shown in figure 3 (a).

(a) Cartoon Facial Expressions used as a feedback to the SenToy gestures

(b) Fearnot! and the window that displays the emotions detected from Sentoy

Fig. 3. Cartoon facial expressions

The cartoon face is displayed at the left corner of the screen as shown in figure 3 (b).

5 Results

In order to evaluate the impact of SenToy within the context of FearNot! we randomly chose eight children aged between eight and eleven years and we let them use FearNot! and SenToy. Before the experience the children were given some time to try out the gestures needed to express emotions.

The experience was carried out individually and in the end the session, each child filled a questionnaire about the characters of the story, the conversations, how much the liked using SenToy and about the easiness of expression of the emotions. Apart from the log files obtained, all the procedure was filmed for further analysis.

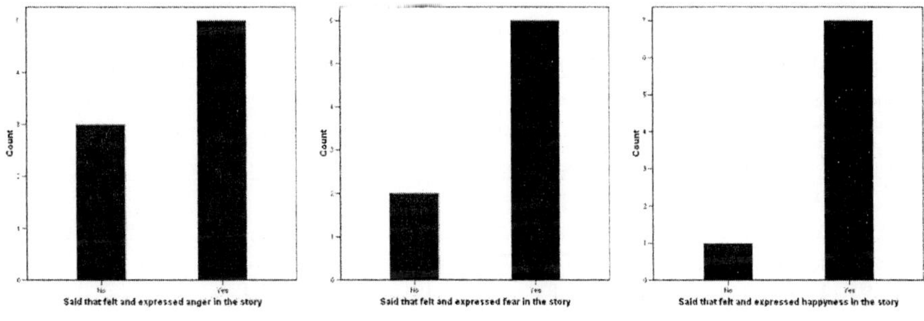

Fig. 4. Discrepancy between the emotions and the answers to the questionnaires

	Child 1	Child 2	Child 3	Child 4	Child 5	Child 6	Child 7	Child 8
The victim is presented				Sad		Happy	Fear Sad	
The victim talks about his problems	Sad		Sad		Sad	Sad Happy	Sad Fear	
The neutral character is presented			Fear	Angry		Happy	Angry	Sad
The victim is studying, the bully is coming close to him						Happy		
The bully throws the victim's books to the floor					Angry Sad	Happy	Angry	
The bully pushes the victim to the floor when the victim was trying to pick up the books		Sad		Sad			Sad	Sad
The bully mocks the victim after throwing him to the floor	Sad	Sad Angry	Happy	Sad	Sad Angry	Sad	Sad Happy	Sad Happy
In the library		Sad	Sad	Sad Happy	Fear	Sad	Sad	Fear
The user is being asked if he can help the victim	Sad Angry Fear	Sad	Sad Fear	Sad	Fear Sad	Sad	Sad	Sad
The football encounter		Happy Sad			Angry	Happy	Happy	
The bully hits the victim because he didn't pass him the ball		Fear Sad		Sad	Angry	Sad	Happy Sad	
The bully mocks the victim after hitting him for not passing the ball		Angry Sad			Sad Happy		Sad Fear	Sad
The neutral character says to the bully that he must leave the victim alone		Angry	Sad		Happy	Sad	Fear	Sad
Going to the library							Fear	
The user is being asked if he can help the victim for the second time		Angry Sad	Sad			Sad	Fear	
The victim faces the bully		Angry Sad	Sad		Sad		Sad Fear	
The neutral character makes an intervention, not allowing the bully to hit the victim again		Happy	Sad Happy			Happy		
The victim tries to hit the bully				Sad	Sad		Fear	Angry
The victim thanks the neutral character	Happy	Happy	Happy					

Fig. 5. Log with emotions

Figure 5 summarizes the analysis made on the video footage and its combination with the captured log files.

From the logs obtained, the results show that the emotion that was expressed more often was sadness. This is in accordance with the contents of the displayed story. Furthermore, as can be seen from the table 5 children did express sadness at the right moments (for example when the bully pushes the victim, or when the victim faces the bully). Indeed, most of the children expressed emotions that were in accordance with what was being displayed in the story. There was one exception in the group of eight children, where the child just considered SenToy as a doll and used it like a toy an not like an emotional interface, thus not paying much attention to the story, and spending most of her time playing with SenToy and making the cartoon face display whatever she wanted.

At the end of the session we asked children what they had experienced during the story and the results were compared with the logs of what they had expressed. Although the results show that in general they are similar, there were some small differences found between what children said they felt and what was in the log. Figure 4 illustrates these differences. The graph about the sad emotion is omitted because every child said and indeed expressed that emotion during the story. In the case of the other three emotions, especially anger, there are several cases where the children expressed it but didn't mention they felt it in the questionnaires. In the case of the fear emotion, there was one case where there was a big discrepancy, as the emotion was expressed fifteen times during the story but the child said she never expressed it, but this child was the exception already mentioned above. Finally, in the case of happiness, there was one disagreing case, where the emotion was expressed three times but the child said she never felt it during the story.

Although the results show that indeed SenToy can be used as a way to capture the emotions, even if users are engaged in a storytelling scenario, these differences detected can have several implications. One explanation is that children may have forgotten that they expressed a particular emotion and their evaluation at the end only reflects what they got at the end of the session. Another explanation is that they may have made a mistake and expressed a wrong emotion instead of the one they originally wanted to express (although this is less likely as the emotions are expressed in very different ways[1] so it is very difficult to an emotion to be wrongly detected).

6 Conclusions

In this paper we have reported an experiment of using SenToy (a tangible affective interface) in the context of a virtual storytelling application. The use of SenToy was very positive not only because it confirmed again that children really liked SenToy but also because it allowed us to gather emotional data about the users of FearNot!.

The data captured, shows that indeed children felt sadness (as expected). Other emotions, such as anger or fear, the results show that there were some differences. Furthermore, the analysis made on the data collected also indicates that this kind of interface can be a distraction, (in this case some of the users were more interested in the interface than in the story).

However, and as a final comment, we believe that further studies should be performed investigating how tangible interfaces can be combined in virtual storytelling.

References

1. Anderson,G. and Höök, K. and Paiva, A., *Using a Wizard of Oz study to inform the design of SenToy.* Designing Interactive Systems DIS', ACM Press, 2002.
2. Paiva, A., et. al. *SenToy: an affective sympathetic interface.* International Journal of Human-Computer Studies, 59, (2003).
3. A. Paiva and J. Dias and D. Sobral and R. Aylett and S. Woods and L. Hall and C. Zoll, *Caring for Agents and Agents that Care: Building Empathic Relations with Synthetic Agents*, AAMAS 2004, ACM Press, 2004.
4. M. Cavazza and O. Martin and F. Charles and S. Mead and X. Marichal, Interacting with Virtual Agents in Mixed Reality Interactive Storytelling, *Intelligent Virtual Agents (IVA 2003)*, Springer, 2003.
5. H. Ishii and B. Ullmer, Tangible Bits: Towards Seamless Interfaces between People, Bits and Atoms, *Proceedings of Conference on Human Factors in Computing Systems (CHI'97)* ACM Press, 1997.
6. Woods, S., at al. *What's Going On? Investigating Bullying using Animated Characters.* Intelligent Virtual Agents, Springer, 2003.
7. Facial Expressions of Emotion, *http://www.dushkin.com/connectext/psy/ch10/facex.mhtml.*

Affective Music Processing: Challenges

Somnuk Phon-Amnuaisuk

Music Informatics Research Group,
Faculty of Information Technology, Multimedia University,
Jln Multimedia, 63100 Cyberjaya, Selangor Darul Ehsan, Malaysia
somnuk.amnuaisuk@mmu.edu.my

Abstract. Our states of mind keep on changing all the time. How do we determine a mapping between our states of mind and music stimulus? In this report, we discuss, from a bird's eye view, the meanings and effects of music which are impressed upon us. We review related literature in musical meanings and computational model, and finally we discuss the impression while listening to the fourth movement of the Pastoral. We point out challenges and suggest plausible computational approches to the affective music computing.

1 Introduction

It is undeniable that music affects us. It has been reported in Sloboda [16] that music is capable of provoking various kinds of responses, for examples: a shiver down the spine, laughter, a lump in the throat, tears, sexual arousal, sweating, etc. It is possible that we should be able to measure the affective phenomena via some kind of measurements. However, this whole process is very complex. The process involves many unknown factors beginning with the processing in our perceptions, the processing in the brain to the emotional outcome. We investigate the music affective processing/computing in this report. We decide to develop the following text based on four questions:

1. Are there meanings in music?
2. Are musical meanings capable of exciting us? What are the underlying mechanisms?
3. Can we compute them? What kind of representation framework is needed?
4. Can we establish the real cause-effect relationships between the stimulus patterns and the observed emotional/physical responses patterns?

Are there meaning in music? We know that when a person says *"I am depressed"* or *"I am very happy"*. The speaker usually mean he/she is depressed or very happy. Is music capable of expressing meanings in a similar manner? Many scholars believe so. Meyer [9] defines common beliefs regarding musical meanings into two different pairs: *absolutist* versus *refferentialist* and *formalist* versus *expressionist*. In brief, absolutist and referentialist differ in whether the musical meanings are only confined within the context of the work or whether

J. Tao, T. Tan, and R.W. Picard (Eds.): ACII 2005, LNCS 3784, pp. 923–930, 2005.

there exists extramusical components, while the formalist and the expressionist differ in whether the musical meanings are capable of exciting feelings and emotions in the listeners.

Are musical meanings capable of exciting us? Our stance belongs to the expressionist perspective. We believe that music is capable of carrying meanings (both *designative* and *embodied* [9, p. 35]), and the music is able to draw some kind of responses in the listeners.

What are the underlying mechanisms? In order to empathise and be moved by music, (a) Is the understanding of the content of music a nessesary factor? Is this a conscious cognitive process? or (b) the music will excite us some how. Meyer suggest that the whole process involves both conscious and unconscious sub-processes.

There are two main theories related to the above question: *the expression theory* and *the arousal theory*. The expression theory argues that the creator of the music with a mental state M would produce the work that expresses M. The arousal theory argues that the music that is supposed to express E would induce the mental state E in the listeners. Unfortunately, these two theories are not sufficient to answer the question above. Upon listening to a piece of music, we may recognise that there are expressions of joy, melancholy, anger, etc. However, it is also possible that we may not feel anything. Given that we do have some emotional responses, it may not be of the same response as the music appears to suggest. This seems to disfavour the position of the arousal theory and suggests that affective experiences are conscious (musical understandings/reasonings is an important ingredient).

However there are pieces of evidence from a brain damage patient who is classified as *amusia* without *aphasia* in neurophychological terms. The patient has a severe deficit in music processing (e.g. music recognition and expressive ability) but is with normal speech comprehension and expression). Nevertheless, the patient can still derive proper emotional interpretation of music (e.g. sad, anger) without an adequate structural analysis of the music [11]. This evidence suggests that it is possible that the processing of emotional content may not require the understnading of the content.

Can we compute them? What kind of representation framework is needed? We lean toward *functionalism* in this issue. It would be possible to see the patterns in both input stimuli and output responses. Examples of input patterns include musical properties such as pitch, duration, chordal quality, tonality, intensity, etc. The relationships among those properties are *measurements* (e.g. similarity and distance measurement) or *propositional relationships* between concepts e.g. perfect5^{th}(c,g), tonic(key(C major),c). Examples of output responses include descriptions of physiological behaviours such as the pulse rate, body temperature, lump in throat, etc; descriptions of musical experiences in terms of cognitive categories such as time, space, light, touch, fire, rain, etc. Various representation schemes could be used to construct a computational model. We shall discuss more of this in section two.

Can we establish the real cause-effect relationships? Last question poses quite a challenge since patterns can only suggest correlations. We should be able to establish clear correlations between patterns but it is probably quite hard to claim for causal relationships (since we may not be able to spell out all the attributes involved in the process and therefore may fail to capture the real picture of the problem).

2 Previous Works in Computational Model of Music

In this section, We focus our discussion in two main parts: the music representation and the inference mechanisms.

2.1 Representing Music

In general, we can see music representations as patterns of music structural units. This is quite natural to the music domain. Some authorities may even remark that music theory is about the studying of musical structures. Majority of the works look at musical properties as patterns of forms, melodies, harmonies and textures. Examples of these patterns are *formal structures, pitch contours, motif, harmonic patterns,* etc. These input patterns may arouse other responses in the listeners (e.g. *changes in pulse rate, emotional states,* etc).

There are many works on how one should represent music [2] [21] [17] [14]. The representation is designed to suit different level of abstractions for different tasks (e.g. music as a wave energy, music as sequences of pitch symbols). Basically we are required to look at patterns and associate them with suitable vocabulary for the domain. Knowledge patterns in terms of *Grammars, Production rules* or other observed *patterns* (e.g. statistical based) are all plausible representation schemes (see ref [1] [13] [18] [20]).

2.2 Inferencing

What is needed in this affective music computing is a theory that explains our affective experiences given a musical stimuli. At the moment, we do not have such a complete theory that offers an explanation to the relationship between input stimuli and output responses. However, we do have chunks of knowledge scattered around the whole domain.

Meyer [9] argues for *tendency* and *expectation* in music. This tendency to respond may be either conscious or unconscious. Its rejection or fulfillment creates different affective experiences. Many works have investigated music from these perspectives e.g. *tonal pitch space [6]; harmony space [8]; implication-realisation model* [10], etc. It is possible to compute expectation levels from these kind of models.

The expectation level may be used to correlate with affective experiences. Correlations in a very crude form between levels of tensions and musical properties (e.g. between changes in tension and in dynamic, pitch register, and tonal stability), are quite well known. In one of Sloboda experiments [16], he discovers that musical features such as *melodic appogiaturas, melodic or harmonic sequence* and *harmony descending cycle of fifths to tonic* appear to arouse *"tears or a lump in throat"* while musical feature such as *new or unprepared melody* and *sudden dynamic or textural change* appear to arouse *"shivers or goose pimples"* There are also other reports regarding the computing of affective responses. Scherer and Zentner [19] suggest that emotional effects may be determined by a multiplicative function consisting of many factors (e.g. structural features, performance features, listener features, contextual features).

However, we have not reached a clear understanding of the whole process yet. The total affective experiences may be attributed to many other factors (e.g. past events, sight, fragrance, places, etc.). Kivy [5] suggests that music can be expressive of emotions in various ways: (a) music resembles the expressive tone of the human voice–the speech theory; (b) musical structures resemble our gestures for a particular expression e.g. sadness is associated with low tone and slow movement, etc.–the contour theory (c) conventional elements (accepted norm vocabulary e.g. minuet is a court dance, horn is hunting, minor is a sad tone etc.), and (d) the contribution of text, titled, e.g. Moonlight sonata.

Based on this line of thought, affective computing involes two main steps:

1. Analysis of input patterns: Infer musical structures (patterns) and/or musical meanings from the input representation.
2. Analysis of responses patterns: Indentify emotional patterns and the correlations among the input/output observed patterns and the emotions.

3 Affective Music Processing

3.1 Challenge: Analysis of Input patterns

Music is described in many ways, for examples, *narration, qualitatively described, quantitatively described,* or *structurally described.* Below are examples of plausible analysis styles. We give these examples to emphasize the challenges of the computation model.

In the narrative style, the music is described as it progresses, the analyst usually describes music material from the start to end. The narration may include extramusical interpretation by suggesting a program content or interpretation of the composers' mental states. Sometimes, music is described using other cognitive modes. Pitch may be described as bright, muddy, sharp, etc. Melody may be described as sweet, hot, etc. Texture may be described as a dense forrest, a flow of water, etc. We say music is qualitatively described here. In the structural descriptive style, music is structurally described. The formal structure, the melody, harmony and the texture of works in different genres portray different patterns (e.g. different formal structures: e.g. *a sonata form, theme and variations, songs, etc*; different melodic styles; different harmonic vocabulary; and different textures). This kind of analysis is very natural to be implemented using

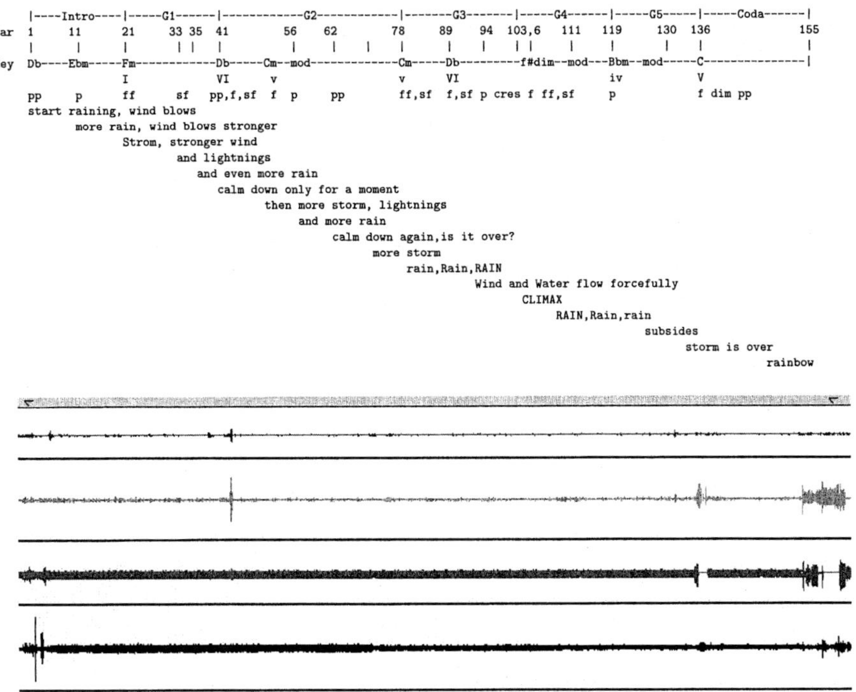

Fig. 1. The high level structure of the 4th movement and the corresponding four EEG signals. All the EEG signals are filtered with the bandpass filter set at 20-110 Hz (from top to bottom are measurements from F4-F3, C4-C3, P4-P3 and Pz-Fz, the electrode names are based on the 10-20 system).

computers. Majority of works in AI-music are based on the ideas of extracting knowledge from patterns then using them to create new pieces (e.g. Cope [4]). Finally, the number of occurrences of structural units is a useful measurement for further inference. Statistical inference is natural to quantitative described units.

3.2 Challenge: Analysis of Response Patterns

This is the most neglected part in traditional music analysis where the focus is always at the music material. However, in recent years, a focus on users' responses has gained more and more interest in cognitive-music community as well as in AI-music. Early works in this area extract information from subjects by interviewing them; asking subjects to express their emotion to the music stimulus in real time. This is useful to extract higher level knowledge. With recent progress in signal processing technology, physiological responses such as *BVP (Blood Volume Pressure), EEG (Electroencephalogram), EMG (Electromyogram)* have gained more popularity as a representation of users responses at a low level [12].

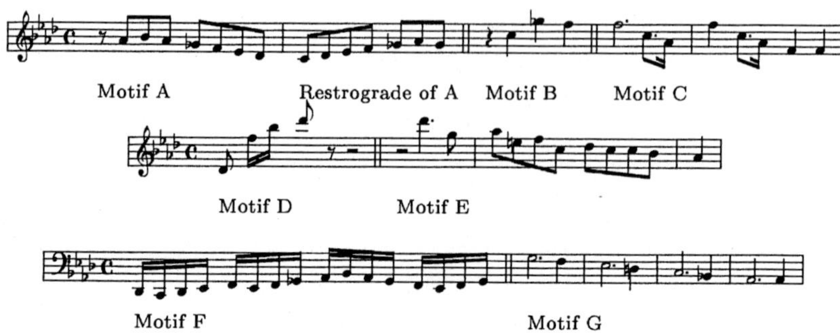

Fig. 2. Basic building blocks

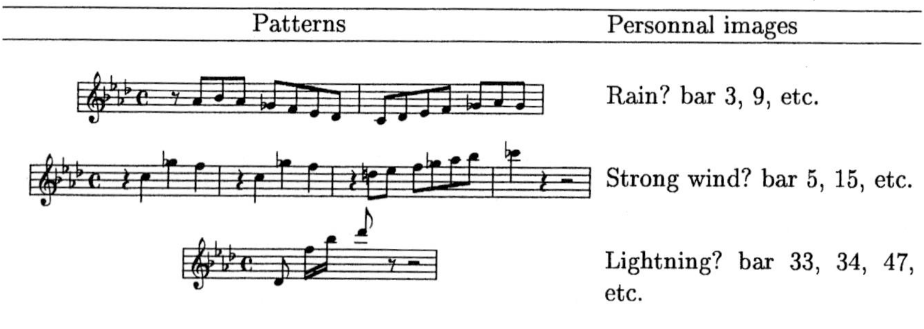

Patterns	Personnal images
	Rain? bar 3, 9, etc.
	Strong wind? bar 5, 15, etc.
	Lightning? bar 33, 34, 47, etc.

Fig. 3. Extramusical interpretations

3.3 Case Study: Beethoven's Pastoral Symphony

Structural Analysis. The structural analysis has been one of the most focused reserach issue in AI-music community since early days. In the diagram in Figure 1, we give information regarding the music material structure (divided into seven groups: intro, G1 to G5, and coda) and the tonal structure. This information Figure 2 shows examples of melodic figures which occur throughout the movement. The main tasks in structural analysis involve extracting *primitive patterns* (e.g. rhythmic, melodic and harmonic patterns), forming higher hierarchical patterns and establishing relationships among those patterns to form new concepts.

Many reserachers have been working to find a way to automate this process. The generative theory of tonal music (GTTM) [7], the implication-realization model [10], the general computational theory of musical structure [15] are examples of works that attempt to come up with computational models that explain the musical structures. However, these works still did not provide a clear answer to the problem of structural analysis. A complete structural analysis should reveal details of musical form, melodic units, harmonic units and their organisation. However, to automate the process as a computer program is not a trivial task.

Extramusical Analysis. This is a much more complex problem than the structural analysis. In the structural analysis, image, sound image and methaphor never come into picture when analysing the structure of the piece. The *flight of the Bumble-bee* is probably a good example of how music can invoke other sound images and result in a mapping in meaning to music. This kind of association is abundant. We list some of these melodic figures in this movement in Figure 3.

Bridging the Gap. Many works in neuroscience and psychophysiology suggest a close relationship between stimuli and the EEG signal. Bertrand and Tallon-Baudry [3] suggests that the information in the γ range (30-100 Hz) could play a useful role in object representation. We have analysed the EEG signal in Figure 1 and also found that high activitis in the γ band (around 40 Hz). We believe this could be a useful area to explore. We might be able to catalogue different patterns of EEG with different musical patterns (as depicted in Figure 2, 3).

4 Conclusion: Affective Music Processing

The path from the music stimuli to affective states is a mysterious one. Many experiemnts suggest that emotional responses to music are common (though not absolutely universal). To find out about this relationship, we need to establish the correlation between stimuli and affective responses.

The correlation between musical stimuli and observed responses may reveal a causal relationship. We may be able to correlate information from stimuli (e.g. changes in musical structures such as form, melody, harmony, texture) to the changes in observed responses (e.g. changes in phisiological responses, changes in reported emotions, etc.). A sucessful establishment of causal relationships between stimuli and affective states would enhance a deep understanding of our knowledge in this area.

References

1. Baroni, M. and Brunetti, R. and Callegari, L. and Jacobni, C.: A grammar for melody: Relationship between melody and harmony. In Baroni, M. and Callegari, L., editors, *Musical grammar and Computer analysis*, pages 201-218. Firenze, 1982.
2. Bernard, B.: Symbolic and sonic representations of sound-object structures. In Balaban, M., Ebcioglu, K. and Laske, O., editors, *Understanding Music with AI: Perspectives on music cognition*, chapter 4, pages 65-109. The AAAI Press/The MIT Press, 1992.
3. Bertrand, O. and Tallon-Baudry, C.: Oscillatory gamma activity in humans: a possible role for object representation. *Psychophysiology*, 38:211-223, 2000.
4. Cope, D.: *Computer and Musical Style.* Oxford University Press, 1991.
5. Kivy, P.: *Introduction to a Philosophy of Music.* New York, Oxford University Press, 2002.
6. Lerdahl, F.: Tonal pitch space. *Music Perception*, 5(3):315-350, 1988.
7. Lerdahl, F. and Jackendoff, R.: *A Generative Theory of Tonal Music.* The MIT Press, 1983.

8. Longuet-Higgins, H.C.: Letter to a musical friend. *The Music Review*, 23:244-248, 1962.
9. Meyer, L.B.: *Emotion and Meaning in Music.* The University of Chicago Press, Chicago and London, 1956.
10. Narmour, E.: *The Analysis and Cognition of Basic Melodic Structure.* The University of Chicago Press, 1990.
11. Peretz, I., Gagnon, L. and Bouchard, B.: Music and emotion: perceptual determinants, immediacy, and isolation after brain damage. *Cognition*, 68:111-141, 1998.
12. Picard, R.W.: *Affective Computing.* The MIT Press, 1997.
13. Phon-Amnuaisuk, S.: Control language for harmonisation process. In Christina Anagnostopoulou, Miguel Ferrand, and Alan Smaill, editors, *Music and Artificial Intelligence, Second International Conference, ICMAI 2002, Edinburgh, Scotland, UK, September 12-14, 2002, Proceedings*, volume 2445 of *Lecture Notes in Computer Science.* Springer, 2002.
14. Phon-Amnuaisuk, S.: Logical representation of musical concepts. In Carlos Agon and Gerard Assayag, editors, *Sound and Music Computing, International Conference, smc'04, Paris, France, October 20-24, 2004, Proceedings*, pages 49-56. IRCAM, 2004.
15. Cambouropoulos, E.: Towards a General Computational Theory of Musical Structure, Faculty of Music and Dept. of Artificial Intelligence, University of Edinburgh, 1998.
16. Sloboda, J.A.: Music structure and empirical response: Some empirical findings. *Psychology of Music*, 19:110-120, 1991.
17. Smaill, A., Wiggins, G., and Miranda, E.: Music representation: Between the musician and the computer. In Smith, M., Wiggins, G. and Smaill, A. editors, *Music education : an artificial intelligence approach; Proceedings of a Workshop held as part of AI-ED 93, World Conference on AI in Education, Edinburgh.* Springer-Verlag, 1993.
18. Steedman, M.: A generative grammar for jazz chord sequences. *Music Perception*, 2:52-77, 1984.
19. Scherer K.R., and Zentner, M.R.: Emotional Effects of Music: Production Rules. In Juslin, P.N. and Sloboda, J.A. editors, *Music and emotion: theory and research*, Oxford; New York: Oxford University Press, 2001.
20. Terrat, R.G.: Logical representation of musical concepts. In Carlos Agon and Gerard Assayag, editors, *Sound and Music Computing, International Conference, smc'04, Paris, France, October 20-24, 2004, Proceedings*, pages 65-70. IRCAM, 2004.
21. West, R., Howell, P. and Cross, I.: Musical structure and knowledge representation. In Howell, P., West, R. and Cross, I. editors, *Representing Musical Structure*, chapter 1, pages 1-30. Academic Press, 1991.

A User-Centered Approach to Affective Interaction

Petra Sundström[1], Anna Ståhl[2], and Kristina Höök[1]

[1] DSV KTH/SU,
Forum 100, 164 40 Kista, Sweden
{petra, kia}@dsv.su.se
[2] SICS,
Box 1263, 164 29 Kista, Sweden
{annas}@sics.se

Abstract. We have built eMoto, a mobile service for sending and receiving affective messages, with the explicit aim of addressing the inner experience of emotions. eMoto is a designed artifact that carries emotional experiences only achieved through interaction. Following on the theories of embodiment, we argue emotional experiences can not be design in only design for. eMoto is the result of a user-centered design approach, realized through a set of initial brainstorming methods, a *persona*, a *Laban-analysis* of body language and a *two-tiered evaluation method.* eMoto is not a system that could have been designed from theory only, but require an iterative engagement with end-users, however, in combination with theoretical work. More specifically, we will show how we have managed to design an *ambiguous* and open system that allows for users' *emotional engagement.*

1 Introduction

Our approach to affective interaction differs somewhat from the goals in affective computing [13]. Instead of inferring information about users' affective state, building computational models of affect and responding accordingly, our approach is *user-centered.* Our aim is to build systems that have users engaged in interaction. We want users to feel they are involved in an intriguing communication with the system and through the system with each other. Therefore, users should be allowed to express their own emotions rather than having their emotions interpreted by the system. To ensure this engagement, we apply iterative design methods involving users continuously in the design cycle. What we build are designed artifacts that embody this user experience, but it is only in interaction with users that we can tell whether we have succeeded [6]. Thus, our approach is user-centered in both aims and methodology.

Research in psychology and neurology shows that both body and mind are involved when experiencing emotions [3,4]. It is common knowledge that emotions influence people's body movements and sometimes emotions become reinforced or even initiated by such bodily signals [5]. Thus, it should be possible to design for stronger affective involvement with artifacts through addressing physical, bodily interaction modalities. Tangible interaction [11], gesture-based interaction [1], and interaction through plush toys and other artifacts [12], are all examples of such physical modalities. We have summarized our design aims into what we name an *affective*

J. Tao, T. Tan, and R.W. Picard (Eds.): ACII 2005, LNCS 3784, pp. 931 – 938, 2005.

loop. In an affective loop, users may consciously express an emotion to a system that they may or may not feel at that point in time, but since they convey the emotion through their physical, bodily, behavior, they will get more and more involved with the experience as such and with their own emotional processes. If the system, in turn, responds through appropriate feedback conveyed in sensual modalities, the user might become even more involved with the expressions. Thus, step by step in the interaction cycle, the user is 'pulling' herself as well as is being 'pulled' into an affective loop.

To design for this intriguing affective loop experience we have taken inspiration from Gaver and colleagues and their work on ambiguity [8]. Most designers would probably see ambiguity as a dilemma for design. However, Gaver and colleagues [8; p. 1] look upon it as:

"[...] a resource for design that can be used to encourage close personal engagement with systems."

They argue that in an ambiguous situation people are forced to get involved and decide upon their own interpretation of what is happening. As affective interaction oftentimes is an invented, on-going process inside ourselves or between partners and close friends, taking on different shades and expressions in each relationship we have with others, ambiguity of the designed expressions will allow for interpretation that is personal to our needs. Ambiguous design is also related to embodiment that regard meaning as arising from social practice and use of systems [6]. An open-ended ambiguous design allow for interpretation and for taking expressions into use based on individual and collective interpretations. Ambiguity in a system will also allow for ambiguity and meaning making. However, there has to be the right level of ambiguity, since too much ambiguity might make it hard to understand the interaction and might make users frustrated [9].

As a research vehicle we have designed, implemented and evaluated a mobile service named *eMoto* (see Figure 1), a system that embodies our design ideas. In here, we will use eMoto to exemplify on our user-centered design approach. We will discuss how we have used a combination of theory and iterative engagement with end-users to design an ambiguous and open system that allows for users' emotional engagement. Before we turn our methodology we will however first present our design in some detail.

2 eMoto

eMoto is built in Personal Java and runs on P800 and P900 mobile phones, two of Sony Ericsson's Symbian phones. Both phones have touch-sensitive screens that the user interacts with through a stylus. In eMoto, the user first writes a text message and then finds a suitable affective graphical expression to add to the background of her text. To find this expression, the user navigates in a circular background of colors, shapes and animations through using a set of affective gestures, see Figure 1. The gestures are done separately from writing the message and require consciously pressuring and shaking the stylus in order to move around in the background circle. The stylus pen has for this purpose been equipped with an accelerometer and a pressure sensor. The original stylus that comes with Sony Ericsson's Symbian phones has the size and shape of a toothpick, which is convenient for the purpose of interacting with the touch screen, however, it does not have the shape that users can be physical with in the way that is intended by our design aims. Thus we looked for a more physical design, but a physical design that in itself is nothing more than an artifact. The shape should not limit the user but instead allow her to express herself in a range of different movements and gestures. We wanted the stylus to fit better in the hand and to be formed in a material that physically would respond back to the user. The final design would also have to fit all the technology that was needed for the extended stylus to act as a wireless sensor network, still; we wanted it to keep its purpose of being suitable for interacting with the touch screen. We did not want to attach the sensors to the mobile phone since that would require users to first interact with the gestures and then look for feedback on the mobile phone, an interaction model that do not fulfill the definition of the affective loop where timing of expressions and feedback are essential.

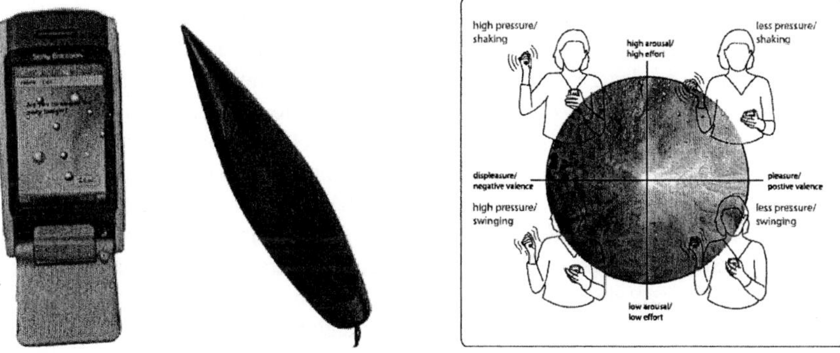

Fig. 1. The left figure shows the extended stylus and eMoto running on a P900 while the right figure shows the interaction design; high pressure makes the user go left on the background circle to more negative emotions while intense shaking takes her to the top to more energetic emotions (the animations can be seen on emoto.sics.se/animations).

2.1 The Affective Expressions

We aim to avoid a labeled or iconic view of emotions; instead we want to design for more of the inner experience of emotional expressions. Both gestures and graphical expressions are designed from an analysis of emotional body language where we have used Laban-notation to extract underlyi : dimensions of emotional gestures [7]. Neither the gestures nor the graphical expressions can nor should be mapped to a specific emotion in a one-to-one relation. The mapping between the gestures and the graphical expressions is, however, a key factor to emotional engagement in an affective loop. It is essential that both gestures and the graphical feedback build on the same inner experience of emotions for users to get more and more involved in the interaction. The aim is ambiguous expressions that blend into each other and open for interpretation. Since it is the inner experience of emotions that is desired, and also, since it is not the gestures that are communicated to the receiver of these messages, the exact three-dimensional shape of the gestures is not important and therefore not captured. Instead the gestures are set up as combinations of pressure and movement. This allows for physical engagement but opens for users' personal body movements. Figure 1 describes the four extreme gestures having those two variables. However, in between those extremes there can be a whole range of combinations of movement and pressure. Ambiguity is also applied on the design of the graphical expressions in the background of messages. The expressions, formed as a circle, are non-symbolic and designed from what is known about the effects of colors, shapes and animations. These graphical expressions are also what is communicated to the receiver and then also aim to convey more of the emotional content through the very narrow channel that a text message otherwise provides.

3 A User-Centered Design Process

Designing an artifact that aims to embody emotional experiences in interaction is extremely hard to create simply theory. Instead, this must be done in interaction with users. Theory and abstract reasoning is not enough when the aim is to say something of how a designed artifact will be used and understood in practice [6].

Regarding the eMoto service, more specifically, we have aimed for ambiguity as one of the means to design for user involvement and emotional experiences. Important is to find the right level of ambiguity for a specific user group and the only way to do this is to involve users in the design process. There are several ways to do this but we have used a *questionnaire*, *the persona method* and a *two-tiered evaluation method.*

The questions of our questionnaire, sent in the beginning of this project to 80 potential users, concerned how well users felt that they could express emotions through SMS. The results revealed a need for richer expressions and also a frustration with current means. For example, some indicated that they made use of smilies, but said the few smilies they actually used had quite many limitations to what they could express. Most of the women said they more often used words to express the emotional expression they wanted to convey but they also said it often was hard to verbalize a complex emotional state.

The questionnaire results were used to create a *persona* [2]. A persona is a precise description of a hypothetical person, which in the design process, is an alternative way to talk about the targeted user group as one user and steer the design process. The persona set up for the eMoto service is named Sandra. In short she is a confident 29 year old woman who likes to spend time with her friends and family. Sandra does not care much of how things work technically, but she likes new cool features and she is very happy with her new mobile phone that has a camera and internet functionalities. Sandra is a smart woman, who also is very open and keen on having the ability to express herself, a woman who stands a high level of ambiguity.

In the design and implementation face we have used a *two-tiered evaluation method* [10], which implies that each part of an affective interaction system must be evaluated on its own and redesigned before combined into an overall design and evaluated against its purpose. It might be that an idea of an affective interaction system is really good but unless the expressions used in each part of that system are understood by the end-user, the overall idea will fail anyway. Therefore it is important with continuous interactions with users during the whole design cycle, and not just when the final design already has been set.

Thus far, two user studies have been conducted on eMoto. First a user study to validate the level of ambiguity in the colors, shapes and animations before they were combined and, in a second study, evaluated together with the affective gestures. For both user studies we have recruited users similar to our persona.

The first graphical expressions study was performed by subjects in pairs in front of a laptop in a lab environment. 6 pairs took part in this user study which was set up as a modification of the classical think aloud technique. Users were set in situations were they had to discuss various parts of the affective background circle.

After some redesign of the graphical expressions a second user study of eMoto was conducted to see if our idea of creating an open and ambiguous interaction model by only capturing the underlying dimensions of emotional gestures and not their exact shape was enough to make users emotionally involved in the sense defined by our affective loop idea. 18 subjects participated in this user study which also was set in a lab environment but this time as individual sessions and with the system running on a P900 mobile phone connected to the extended stylus. The results related to the gestures as such have been published elsewhere [14]. In here we will discuss results that relate to users' emotional engagement achieved by an ambiguous design and use this to argue for our user-centered design approach.

4 Results Related to Our User-Centered Design Approach

To make users involved with their own emotions and with what they want to express to the recipient of their message it is important they are not forced to simplify neither the expressivity of the gestures, nor the expressivity the message they send. To achieve this involvement, the affective loop, we have therefore strived for a somewhat ambiguous design of both gestures and graphical expressions. However, the right level of ambiguity is not found through solely one user study. Instead, we have worked iteratively with user studies and redesign to find this level for our specific system and user group. Let us present some of the results from our user studies illustrating how one can strive for and find the right level of ambiguous expressivity through involving users in the design process. We also discuss how this ambiguity in turn allowed for emotional engagement, but also how this is related to users' personality: this kind of system will not fit for everyone, but mainly for the intended user group – our *persona*.

Ambiguity. Regarding ambiguity of the expressions our design goal was to find a level were the expressions are open for interpretation and personality but still has some generality between subjects so that they can understand each other. In the first user study users interpreted one of the objects in the graphical background circle in a too depictive way. 3 groups out of 6 associated a specific object with a rose and thereby with romance rather than the frustrated expression it was supposed to portray. According to our idea of users engaged in an affective loop, the mapping between the gestures and the graphical background need to be set up in a way were the expressions build on the same inner experience. This would not be the case if we were to have an object resembling a rose in the area a user navigates to with frustrated and angry gestures.

Regarding the second user study and the openness of the gestures, the prototype did not have any sensors for registering the exact shape of gestures, for example, whether users held the stylus above their head, in their lap or down low, but this we found to be a consistent pattern related to different emotions. 14 subjects held the stylus high up in the air for excited emotions and 9 subjects held the stylus lower, often in their lap, for sadness (which can be seen in Figure 2). One subject commented on this:

"Up high for emotions that goes up and low down for emotions that go down. Angry is more straight."[1]

Fig. 2. Subjects involved in the four scenarios (see Table 1); 'the racist doorman', 'the perfect job', 'the ex-boyfriend', and 'the hammock'

Table 1. Scenarios

Scenarios	
The racist doorman	You write to tell a friend that you and your other friend could not get into the bar because of a racist doorman.
The perfect job	You write to tell your boyfriend that you got the job you applied for even though there were over a thousand other applicants.
The ex-boyfriend	You write to tell a friend that your boyfriend who you love so much has dumped you.
The hammock	You write to a friend who is at work telling her that you are relaxing in the hammock.

Our intention is to capture the inner experience of the affective gestures and from that the communicational aspect of the gestures, the shape of them, is not important. The shape of gestures is, however, one aspect of users' personal expressivity and emotional involvement. Our aim has been not to design for anything like a new sign language but instead allow users to add their own personal shapes to the gestures. The results show that users added shape to their gestures and to them it also seemed as if the system was capturing that. Regarding the graphical expressions, however, the communicational aspect is important both for the user to get involved in the affective loop but also for her to be able to express herself. The results show that since users could add their own shape to the gestures they could also more easily resemble characteristics of the graphical expressions which to the users made the mapping more coherent than what we had anticipated in the theoretical parts of our design process.

[1] All citations are translated from Swedish by the authors.

Emotional Engagement. The results also show that capturing the underlying dimensions of movement and pressure was enough for users to get emotionally engaged in the interaction. Moreover, it was obvious that users got more relaxed and enjoyed themselves more when they got to do the gestures in a context, in combination with the graphical feedback and having scenarios, summarized in Table 1, to which it made sense to react emotionally. Users were asked to interact with the extended stylus to find suitable affective expressions to these scenarios. The first picture in Figure 2 shows a subject engaged with 'the racist doorman' scenario. She not only had a stern facial expression and bit her teeth together really hard, but she also uttered:

"Now I'm really pissed and it's night time and we were gonna have fun together and..."

The second picture shows a subject engaged with 'the perfect job' scenario. This subject waved her hand in the air and smiled. In the third picture a subject engaged in 'the ex boyfriend' scenario expressed depression both in her face and in how she just hang her arm down with a very loose grip on the stylus. Finally, in the last picture the subject was neutral and she just held the stylus in her hand for 'the hammock' scenario. A video analysis, based on the authors' interpretation of the subjects' usage, their facial expression and their general appearance, showed that 12 subjects out of the 18 got emotionally engaged with 'the racist doorman', 15 with 'the perfect job', 14 with 'the ex-boyfriend' and 16 with 'the hammock' scenario. For these subjects it was the overall interaction that had them emotionally engaged and not the designed artifact nor the graphical expressions in themselves a notion that could not have been validated without interactions with users.

Personality. The second user study of eMoto, however, indicated that users' personality had an effect on their emotional expressions and experiences of the interaction. In a concluding questionnaire the first question was about using gestures to express emotions. When comparing the answers to this question with the results from the video analysis it became even more apparent that there were two groups of users. 12 subjects of the 18 felt relaxed when using their body language:

"Cool! It really feels like I'm communicating the emotions I've got without being aware of them."

"I think that's really good, especially if you have had a hard time to express yourself in words. It can also be a fun complement to other ways of expressing yourself."

While six subjects were a bit uncomfortable in doing so:

"Hard! Partly because you have so different strength and partly because it's basically hard."

"I think it would be easier to gesticulate in front of a camera and do small movements. That would feel better in an environment with a lot of people."

The video analysis of the subjects' emotional engagement when interacting with the scenarios also showed that these six subjects had a more difficult time than the rest of the subjects to relax and be engaged with the prototype and the scenarios. This can partly be explained as a mismatch between their personality and the targeted user group for eMoto, Sandra. In general, some users might be more open to physical, bodily expressions than others. However, further studies are needed to disentangle whether this is the reason behind this difference.

5 Conclusions

We have presented a user-centered approach to affective interaction, user-centered in both aims and methodology. In here, we have used eMoto, a mobile service for sending and receiving affective messages, as a touchstone to illustrate how a user-centered perspective can help to achieve design aims from an embodied interaction perspective [6]. More specifically, we have discussed how we have used ambiguity in affective expressions to design for openness and emotional engagement. We argue that a user-centered perspective could be used to a greater extent within affective computing to generate ideas that are intuitive to users but which also give them stronger emotional experiences.

References

1. Cassell, J. A Framework for Gesture Generation and Interpretation, In Computer Vision in Human Machine Interaction, R. Cipolla and A. Pentlan, eds. Cambridge University Press, New York, USA, 1998.
2. Cooper, A. The Inmates are Running the Asylum, Sams Publishing, USA, 1999.
3. Damasio, A. R. Descartes' Error: Emotion, Reason and the Human Brain, Grosset/Putnam, New York, 1994.
4. Davidson, R. J., Scherer, K. R., and Goldsmith, H. H., Handbook of Affective Sciences, Oxford, USA, 2003.
5. Davidson, R. J., Pizzagalli, D., Nitschke, J. B., Kalin, N. H. Parsing the subcomponents of emotion and disorders of emotion: perspectives from affective neuroscience", In Handbook of Affective Sciences, Davidson, R. J., Scherer, K. R., Goldsmith, H. H. (eds.), 2003.
6. Dourish, P. Where the action is. The Foundations of embodied Interaction, MIT Press, 2001.
7. Fagerberg, P., Ståhl, A. and Höök, K. Designing gestures for affective input: an analysis of shape, effort and valence, In Proceedings of Mobile Ubiquitous and Multimedia, MUM 2003, Norrköping, Sweden, 2003.
8. Gaver, W., Beaver J. and Benford, S. Ambiguity as a Resource for Design, In Proceedings of the conference on Human factors in computing systems, Pages: 233 – 240, ACM Press, 2003.
9. Höök, K., Sengers, P., and Andersson, G. Sense and Sensibility: Evaluation and Interactive Art, In Proceedings of the conference on Human factors in computing system (CHI'03), Ft. Lauderdale, Florida, USA, 2003.
10. Höök, K. User-Centred Design and Evaluation of Affective Interfaces, In From Brows to Trust: Evaluating Embodied Conversational Agents, Ruttkay, Z., and Pelachaud, C. (eds), Published in the Human-Computer Interaction Series – volume 7, Kluwer, 2004.
11. Ishii, H., and Ullmer, B. Tangible bits: Towards seam-less interfaces between people, bits and atoms, Proceed-ings of the SIGCHI conference on Human factors in computing systems, Pages: 234 – 241, ACM Press, 1997.
12. Paiva, A., Costa, M., Chaves, R., Piedade, M., Mourão, D., Sobral, D., Höök, K., Andersson, G., and Bullock, A. SenToy: an Affective Sympathetic Interface, International Journal of Human Computer Studies, Volume 59, Issues 1-2, July 2003, Pages 227-235, Elsevier.
13. Picard, R. Affective Computing, MIT Press, Cambridge, MA, USA, 1997.
14. Sundström, P., Ståhl, A., and Höök, K. eMoto – Affectively Involving both Body and Mind, In Extended Abstracts CHI'05, Portland, Oregon, USA, 2005.

Designing and Redesigning an Affective Interface for an Adaptive Museum Guide

Dina Goren-Bar, Ilenia Graziola, Cesare Rocchi, Fabio Pianesi, Oliviero Stock, and Massimo Zancanaro

ITC-irst, via Sommarive, 18, 38050 Povo (Trento), Italy
{gorenbar,graziola,rocchi,pianesi,stock,zancana}@itc.it

Abstract. The ideal museum guide should observe the user affective reactions to the presentations and adapt its behavior. In this paper we describe the user-centred design of an adaptive multimedia mobile guide with an affective interface. The novel approach has required a series of redesign cycles. We comment in particular on the last experiments we did with the prototype, users' observations during interviews and more objective considerations based on logs. We show how the last design is better understood by the user, though there is still room for improvements.

1 Introduction

Affective interfaces can have an important role in a museum [7, 5]. In the context of a museum visit guide, we claim that defining user explicit input just as expression of her current affective attitude may be the best way to influence the system's behavior. A day at the museum is a personal experience which involves both cognitive and emotional traits of a person. The affective reaction to the guide is a strong element to be taken into account: the ideal guide should observe these reactions and adapt its behavior continuously.

In order to ensure that each visitor is allowed to interpret the visit according to her personal traits, for example interests or pace, a multimedia adaptive guide should support strong and fine tuned personalization of all the information provided. These are the prerequisites to match visitors' expectations and to stimulate her attention while allowing for both learning and enjoyment, so that the visit can result a meaningful experience.

In the framework of the PEACH project, we have designed, implemented and evaluated a series of prototypes of adaptive multimedia mobile guides. Previous studies on the behavior of visitors in museums state that the visit is a blend of education and entertainment [3] and visitors do not have a precise goal or a task. The ideal adaptive guide should not be intrusive and allow for a simple interaction. It has to be intuitive and the interaction should be minimal and effective [8]. In the context of an adaptive museum guide, the user should delegate the interaction control to the system [6]. The user should just express what exhibit and explanations she liked without taking care of what should be the systems actions or interrupting the normal course of the visit.

J. Tao, T. Tan, and R.W. Picard (Eds.): ACII 2005, LNCS 3784, pp. 939–946, 2005.

We have developed an affective user interface where the visitor can signal its affective attitude during the visit by means of a graphical widget (called the like-o-meter). The system takes into account such a feedback and selects/organizes the content according to users' liking or disliking. The user model incrementally updates the information collected from users' behavior on the interface, and shows it to the visitor through the same widget which thus act as an output as well as an input device. Hopefully, this will increase controllability as well as scrutability [2] of the overall system: the user will be able adjust the user model every time she finds discrepancies or wrong estimates influencing the visitor overall experiencing from using the artifact as well as from the physical visit.

We engaged in iterative prototype design and evaluation cycles until we achieved an interface that can let users to intuitively convey their affective attitudes. The first PEACH User Interface implemented just two buttons: WOW, on the upper right side of the PDA screen, and BASTA! (enough!) on the lower left side of the screen. The results of the pilot study showed that the system performed wrong adaptations because the visitors did not understand the two-button interface (see[4] for details). To study users' perception more in depth, we resort to an action protocol and retrospective-interview qualitative study also reported in [4]. This technique is similar to think-aloud; the main difference is that the user's does not provide comments during the execution of the task, but later on, while the user and the experimenter are watching a video recording of the previous interaction [9]. In particular, we targeted the expression of the affect implemented through the WOW button. In general, they seemed to perceive the WOW button as the key element of the whole interface, often using it to start the interaction (not needed at all) and requesting for another rather than to express their affective attitude. The BASTA! button was interpreted as a 'stop'. The intended meaning of "I don't like this" was not understood leading to incoherent system behavior: given the conceptual model, the system should not allow the user to take any action, but simply to express feelings.

The results encouraged us to continue the redesign and evaluation process until we achieve an interface that successfully promotes visitors to provide their affective attitudes during a guided visit at a museum.

2 First Redesign (Major)

Figure 1 displays the new PEACH affective interface. We call this new widget the like-o-meter. During the presentation, the visitor can express on a scale his degree of interest for the presentation: "I like it" (one or two click on the happy face), or "I don't like it", by pressing once or twice on the sad face on the left (two degrees of disliking). Those are the only User Actions. When the visitor expresses his/her liking about a presentation the system updates the user model and the liking is propagated along the templates' network. If the user signals some degree of "liking", the system activates the main part of the presentation, this way providing more information about the current topic. The overall goal here is to give the visitor a clear indication that his actions do have an effect on the presentation, while avoiding that he could interpret his own actions as a request for more information. Conversely, the expression of disliking prevents deeper explanations and even stops the presentation in case the visitor expresses the greatest dislike.

Interest is computed in terms of explicit or inferred liking of the content of a template. The interest on a template is set when the user adjusts the like-o-meter, during the actual presentation of the information contained in the template. Then, a propagation model on the templates' network allows the system to infer the interest on closer templates. The system also informs the user about its own assessment of his interest on the current presentation, by pre-setting the like-o-meter. Thus, this widget is at the same time an input device and an output device that the system exploits to inform the visitor about the user model. This satisfies the necessity for the users to control the User Model, as pointed out in [6].

The system performs another type of content adaptation with respect to the *history of the interaction*. The UI component keeps track of the users visit, enabling the comparison of the current presentation with the previously seen ones. Users are free to perform a flexible visit according to their preferences, patience, reception capability and time. Their actions are recorded in the UM. If the user goes back to an already seen fresco, the UI component presents the same topics of interest in a different manner, e.g., by establishing comparisons with other seen panels of the fresco.

2.1 Evaluation of the First Version of the *Like-o-Meter*

In this second study, we focused on how well the users are able to recognize and use the like-o-meter widget. In particular, we investigated whether the like-o-meter communicates properly its meaning.

The user study consisted again in an action protocol with retrospection. They were videotaped while using the system and then interviewed while watching their past behavior. It was conducted on two users in a room with the panels reproducing the

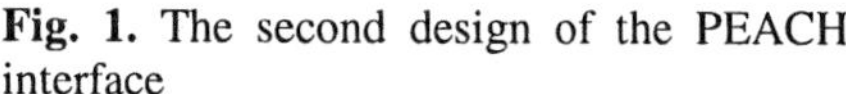

Fig. 1. The second design of the PEACH interface

Fig. 2. The current **design of the PEACH interface**

original fresco exploited in the pervious user study (for more details on the setting see [5]). First, the experimenter presented an introduction of the museum setting and showed a copy of the fresco used in the experiment. Then, she quickly demonstrated the functioning of the system.

The assigned task was to signal interest during the presentation and a slight dislike during the description of the first detail. They had to be enthusiastic about the description of the second detail, and to stop the presentation during the description of the third detail. This task allowed checking the proper understanding of the 'like-o-meter' while assuring that the interaction could be handled by our partial mockup.

The results of this user study were quite encouraging, showing a high degree of understanding and satisfaction by the two users.

From the responses and comments of the participants the following considerations emerged:

The participants were able to communicate their interest to the system using correctly the *like-o-meter*. They recognized that the positions +1 and +2 caused more information to be provided. The relationships between the standard (abstract) and the in-depth presentations (content and follow-up) were clear to the subjects. Given the limitations of this small study, we cannot reliably conclude that they fully realized that their expression of liking on a given current exhibit also affected the presentations to come. The understanding of the meaning of the moderate disliking (i.e. position -1) is somewhat poorer than that of the liking. Apparently, the users come to expect that the expression of a moderate disliking should cause the system to provide less information. Indeed, in our current system, the expression of a moderate dislike only changes the user model and does not affect the current presentation. The users did not expect that the neutral position of the *like-o-meter* could be selected, and expected that a single button press would have moved the slider from -1 to 1. Actually, we realized that the neutral position may have two distinct meanings: according to the first, it communicates a degree of liking which is neither positive nor negative, while according to the second meaning to the neutral position corresponds to a lack of information about the user interest. Both of our users seemed to exploit the second meaning, expecting that only the system would be allowed to use the neutral position.

One participant clearly noticed the feedback of the user model and understood that it was related to her previous behavior. Both participants understood this feedback like a system initiative. Summing up, the participants were able to properly carry out the task with a reasonable understanding the conceptual model of the system. They both agreed that the interface is easy to use and that their expectations about the interest model were fulfilled. The real understanding of the long-term effects of expression of liking did not emerged clearly due to the limitation of the mockup used.

3 Second Redesign (Minor)

The goal of the last redesign was to fix the minor issue emerged with the previous study, in particular, with respect to the neutral position, and to develop a prototype robust enough to be used in an ecological setting.

Figure 3 presents the new interface. From the graphical point of view, the main change is the introduction of a needle that can be moved two steps toward the smile and two steps toward the sad face by clicking on the faces. The system initially set the needle in a middle position but this position cannot be set by the user thus reinforcing that needle in middle means “no information”.

3.1 Evaluation of the Current PEACH *Like-o-Meter* Guide

This user study took place in the realm of Torre Aquila at The Castle of Buonconsiglio, Trento, Italy. Ten subjects were recruited on site among the museums visitors and they were offered a free entrance to the Castle as a reward. A one-page explanation of the system was presented to each subject. There was no training session. Each visit lasted on average twenty minutes and it was followed by a semi-structured interview. All the interactions were video-recorded.

The new prototype covered half of the Cycle of the Months frescos (i.e. two walls of the room). The system included a logging procedure that saves all users’ interactions (clicks, changes of position).

The aim of the interview was to solicit subjects’ opinions about their understanding of the interface and its underlying the model. We were mainly interested in finding out if the visitors understand the like-o-meter as a tool meant to give and receive feedback about their (dis)liking of the presentations and if they do notice the adaptations performed by the system.

Qualitative observations confirm that subjects tend to look mostly at the fresco and are prone to check the PDA screen only at the beginning of a new presentation (see also the results in [1]. This was also confirmed by interviews: the images on the screen are considered useful to identify the details in the fresco but subjects tended to look primarily at the artwork.

Figure 3 summarizes the answers obtained during interviews. All the subjects find useful that the interface provides images that illustrate (parts of) the fresco since they help locating the details presented. All the subjects used the like-o-meter during the visit and found the interface simple to use. Half of the subjects recognize that the system provided follow-up information during the presentation. Most of the subjects did not recognize the system initiative and the propagation of the interest among the topics. Three out of ten subjects considered useful the needle (like-o-meter) as a means of feedback for their clicks. Almost all the subjects found the needle in the position they expected. All the visitors were satisfied of the whole visit.

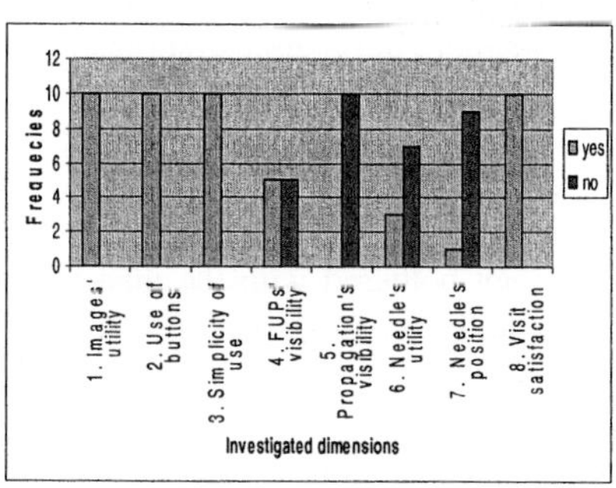

Fig. 3. Summary of subjects’ answers.

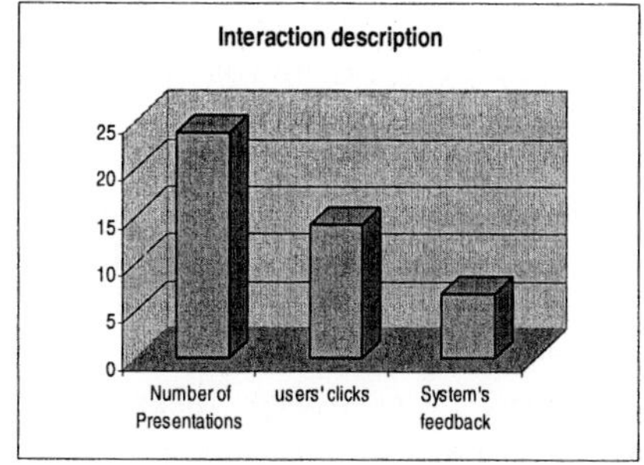

Fig. 4. Description of the interaction

Figure 4 describes the average usage of the system. An average of 23.8 presentations was accessed by the subjects while the like-o-meter was used 14.1 times on average. When a visitor expresses his likening through the like-o-meter, the system provides more information only when available (yet, of course, it always propagates the interests to the other topics). The third column of figure 4 shows how many times the system autonomously sets the like-o-meter.

Considering the amount of usage of the like-o-meter (see Fig. 5), the subjects were quite heterogeneous, encompassing ‘frequent clickers’ (people with a frequent clicking activity, 33 clicks is the maximum) and people who rarely interacted (e.g 5 clicks is the minimum). The most selected value is “moderate liking”, (5.1 frequency), whereas the least selected is ”high liking”.

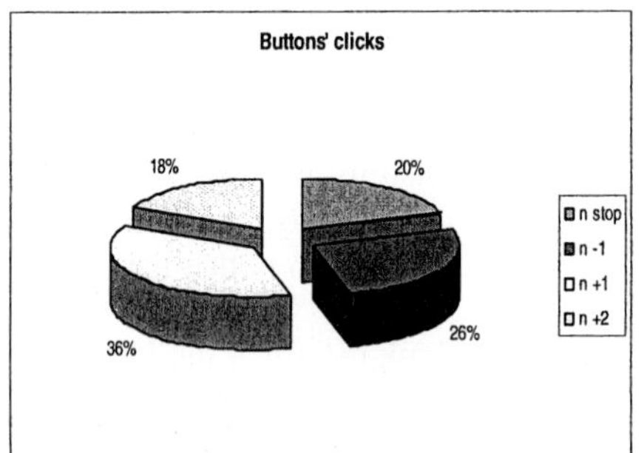

Fig. 5. Distribution of buttons’ clicks

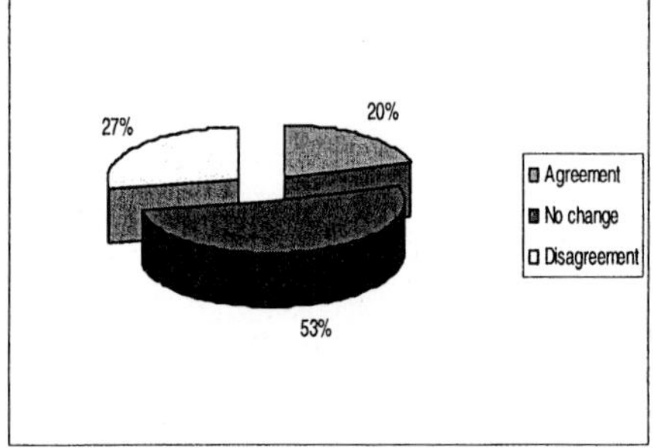

Fig. 6. Efficacy of adaptivity

Figure 6 show the subjects’ behavior when the system autonomously changed the like-o-meter. Since we didn’t want to interrupt the subjects’ interaction, we consider an agreement as the subject reinforcement of the system’s liking estimation. For example, if the system set the like-o-meter on “moderate liking” and the subject during the presentation sets it at “high liking”, an agreement is scored. When the subject corrected the system’s estimation, a disagreement was scored. Of course, in case of no change (which amount 53% of the times), we cannot say whether the subject accepted the estimation or simply she did not see it.

The post-interviews revealed that even if some subjects noticed the adaptation (“I think that the system gave more information on the last detail”, “They system gave more information for some of the topics”) most of them did not realize that the system actually present some information in a deeper way. Also, most of the subjects did not notice the system autonomously setting the like-o-meter (“I never noticed the needle in a different place”) or simply they did not care about it (“The needle could also not been used. It would not have made a big difference”).

The encouraging aspect is that the subjects were not bothered with the idea of expressing their feelings (and some of them explicitly said they like it) even when they thought that the system did not react. When we asked them why they actually used the like-o-meter, their answers range from “Because I liked [disliked] this topic” or “Because I think that this action help me to memorize the arguments”. It is worth noting that similar answers were provided even by the persons that did notice the follow-up.

4 Discussion

The task of re-designing the PEACH affective user interface achieved encouraging results based on the informal evaluation of the last interface that was conducted with ten subjects in a real scenario. The major result is that users provided affective feedback through the *like-o-meter*. Subjects found the like-o-meter widget pretty usable. They used the like-o-meter often and properly (that is, to signal their liking of a presentation topic). All the subjects were able to begin working with the system in few minutes, and to effectively perform the visit. The like-o-meter was understood mainly as an input device, to give feedback to the system, but rarely as an output device, to receive feedback from the system. Subjects did not completely understand the underlying adaptation model. For example, few people noticed that some time the needle position was preset by the system and few noticed they received more information about a given topic. This is not necessarily a negative evidence for the evaluation in particular because adaptation is meant to be "transparent". The guide succeeds to be a companion to the visit without requiring significant cognitive load and explicit attention from the visitor. Although adaptation was not explicitly noticed by the users, the logs confirm that they were able to effectively manage the system. This might indicate that when users perceive their role as merely providing their affective attitudes they probably allow the system to be responsible for all the embedded adaptive behaviors without even being bothered consciously of their results. In this case users can freely experience the visit. This hypothesis might be supported by the fact that the overall experience was very positive since all the participants enjoyed the visit.

Of course, more user studies are still needed to confirm our hypothesis and to gain statistical evidence on the visitors' behavior. Yet, a powerful methodological tool to investigate non-task based interactions, like the museum experience, is needed in order to assess the impact of the interaction-delegation paradigm.

Acknowledgments

This work was conducted in the context of the PEACH project funded by the Autonomous Province of Trento.

References

1. Alfaro I., Nardon M., Pianesi P., Stock O., Zancanaro M. Using Cinematic Techniques on Mobile Devices for Cultural Tourism. In *Information Technology & Tourism*, Vol. 7 Issue 2, 2004.
2. Czarkowski, M and Kay, J. 2002, A scrutable adaptive hypertext, De Bra, P, P Brusilovsky, R Conejo (eds), *Proceedings of AH'2002, Adaptive Hypertext 2002*, Springer, 384 - 387.
3. Dierking, L D. 1992, *The Museum Experience*. Washington, D.C.: American Association of Museums.
4. Goren-Bar D., Graziola I., Kuflik, T. Pianesi F. Rocchi C., Stock O., and Zancanaro M. (2005) I like it – An Affective Interface for a Multimodal Museum Guide. In *Affective Interaction: The computer in the Affective loop* at *Intelligent User Interfaces IUI'05*. San Diego, CA. January 9-13, 2005.

5. Goren-Bar D., Graziola I, Pianesi F., Rocchi C., Stock O., and Zancanaro M. (2005) I like it - Affective Control of Information Flow in a Personalized Mobile Museum Guide, in *Workshop of Innovative Approaches to Evaluating Affective Interfaces (CHI 2005 Workshop)* , Portland, USA
6. Graziola I., Pianesi P., Zancanaro M., Goren-Bar D. 2005, Dimensions of Adaptivity in Mobile Systems: Personality and People's Attitudes. In *Proceedings of Intelligent User Interfaces IUI05*, San Diego, CA. January.
7. Lim,M. Y., Aylett, R. & Jones, Ch.M. 2005, Empathic Interaction with a Virtual Guide, in *Proceedings of the Joint Symposium on Virtual Social Agents*, AISB 2005 Convention, April 12-15. 122-129
8. Proctor,N. and Tellis, C. 2003, The State of the Art in Museum Handhelds in 2003. *In Museum and the Web*, Antenna Audio, United Kingdom and USA.
9. Van Someren M. W. 1994, *Think Aloud Method: A Practical Guide to Modeling Cognitive Processes* Academic Press.

Intelligent Interaction for Linguistic Learning

Vito Leonardo Plantamura, Enrica Gentile, and Anna Angelini

Dipartimento di Informatica, Università degli Studi di Bari,
via Orabona, 4 - 70126 Bari, Italy
{plantamura, gentile, angelini}@di.uniba.it

Abstract. The choice of a friendly interface for learning a foreign language is the fundamental theme of the research illustrated in this paper. Several are the means used in a dialogue among human beings and they essentially require the knowledge of the linguistic terminology, the context where the dialogue is inserted and the final goal. The use of technological tools which emulate the human beings' manners can be useful in the communication processes where the interaction with situations of the every-day life is required. HyperEnglish, the multimedia courseware we are developing, is a prototype for the experimentation and evaluation of the reached hypotheses, where the fundamental goal is the building of an intelligent environment to learn the English language simplifying the communication and allowing to live emotions of the real life.

1 Introduction

The communicative component encourages the interaction activity in the language learning paths, especially through the traditional mailing exchange.

Using formative methodologies of collaborative learning which encourage communication experiences among peers, the interest may be arisen and the student motivated.

The study on the intelligent interfaces and the use of affective-agents in the human–machine interaction is based on the exploitation of all the human "manners" to encourage learning processes otherwise not used. They allow us to individuate collaborative learning solutions adequate to the teaching of a foreign language.

The first component to be studied is the interface which has to draw the student's attention and allow him to learn terms and concepts that will be otherwise abandoned very soon.

Moreover, great relevance must be given to the contextualisation of the learning simulative activities and their insertion in every-day activities in order to avoid lack of motivation and desertion of the formative path.

As in traditional lectures motivation fails after some minutes, in the e-learning environment it must be supported by using several means of communication, inviting the student to use all his/her expressive elements in order to keep his/her attention.

The human-computer interaction takes place both in a traditional way, by using the keyboard or the mouse, and with more natural and human-friendly methods as the voice interaction, the gesture and the face-expressions.

J. Tao, T. Tan, and R.W. Picard (Eds.): ACII 2005, LNCS 3784, pp. 947 – 955, 2005.

The communication tool which better encourages the human-to-human and the human-computer interactions is the spoken language combined with other modalities which answer to usability and efficacy criteria.

However, not always the spoken language is the ideal means of communication to learn every kind of circumstance or skill.

Very often the traditional means of interaction are efficacious because, in teaching a foreign language, together with the spoken jargon, the student must know the written communicative forms and the grammar.

Another aspect to be taken into consideration is the graphic interface [10] which stimulates the students' emotive reaction. As a matter of fact, emotions enrich the spoken communication and sometimes allow associative understanding of the communicative act [4].

2 Learning Paradigm

The traditional language learning methods are essentially based on the passive reception of linguistic structures and terminology without taking into consideration the context which is fundamental in acquiring the meaning.

Table 1. Linguistic Function

Unit	Function
1	Asking for and giving name and nationality
2	Locating people and things
3	Talking about possession
4	Asking far giving personal information
5	Asking and giving info about birth
6	Expressing likes and dislikes
7	Asking and telling the time
8	Describing actions
9	Asking and saying what people do every day
10	Asking and talking about quantity
11	Giving and following order or instructions
12	Offering, accepting, refusing
13	Expressing future intentions
14	Talking about arranged plans
15	Making comparisons (I)
16	Asking and talking about past experiences (I)
17	Making comparisons (II)
18	Expressing, narrating past -time relations
19	Asking and talking about past experiences (II)
20	Expressing ability, possibility, obligation and necessity

Excluding the social context where the language is used, they reduce the student' s learning activity, who, on the contrary, would be stimulated by the use of the language within a personal dialogue experience.

The cognitive and behavioural models are the traditional didactic methods used in teaching the English language.

We combined the cognitive model with some functionalities of the behavioural model in order to teach the spoken behaviour by means of examples.

In the cognitive model the language to be learned is considered as an integrative process of the learning abilities of the student and the potential already acquired in his/her mother tongue. It allows the individuation of active learning processes avoiding passive acquiring of linguistic structures.

The choice of the cognitive model leads to the communicative approach where the student uses the language as a tool for interacting with others. He must develop all the linguistic active and passive activities.

A didactic consequence of this model is the use of the functional-notional method to reach the desired knowledge. This model defines linguistic functions, table 1, which satisfy the users' needs as for example: social functions (salutation, presentation); intellectual functions (accepting or refusing something, describing objects and places); emotional functions (agreeing, disagreeing, expressing desires).

These functions require a specific knowledge of the language to be used. The notions may be based on:

- grammar: pronouns, adjectives, articles;
- time: hour, date, verb tenses;
- prepositions.

The use of intelligent interfaces in dramatisation allows the full exploitation of the means of communication both for the spoken and not-spoken activities.

3 Learning by Dramatisation

HyperEnglish was designed to answer the needs of several users with different level of competence of the English language. It is addressed to people, coming from school or university or from the job market who need to learn the language in order to communicate in general every-day situations and not in specific fields.

In HyperEnglish the student is required to project him/herself in situations created in the virtual world where he/she becomes the principal actor.

He has to interact with others in the scene asking questions and giving answers, so practicing the language.

The courseware does not only require the mechanic repetition of standard sentences in the dialogues, but the student is required to choose one of the actors in the scene and substitute him/her. By using the original vignette as the base, he/she must decide "what to say" and "how to say it", creating a possible dialogue. All the actors of the scenes are designed as intelligent agents able to interact with the student during the substitution phase adapting themselves to the expressions of the dialogues.

The agent does not address to the student by saying "All right!" or "That's wrong!", as in the case of an e-learning courseware, but draws the student's attention on specific aspects of his/her speech. For example, it asks to repeat the word which is not correctly pronounced, giving possible suggestions; otherwise, if everything is well-done, the dialogue goes on without interruptions.

In order to characterize HyperEnglish as a full-immersion courseware, the designers decided to adopt the English language throughout the course. So doing, interferences by the mother tongue are avoided, developing a mental approach to the language which will help the student to think and act in the target language.

At the same time this didactic choice makes the course more general and it may be used by students of different nationalities.

The understanding of a dialogue in a foreign language is essentially based on good pronunciation, so, at the beginning, our work focused on a speech-matching problem.

The algorithm used is based on speech recognition techniques that allow the transforming of the pronounced sentence in a textual representation and its matching with a database where all the sentences of the dialogues are stored [6].

The pronounced sentences are recorded so that the students are allowed to listen to them again and the tutor may evaluate their activity. Particular sentences which the tutor considers "acceptable" will be introduced in the database later, in a dynamic way. So doing, the student plays a very important role in the creation of new elements in the courseware.

4 Intelligent Agent

The first element which makes the e-learning tool attractive is the interaction modality. In particular, interfaces and required modalities of interaction are considered.

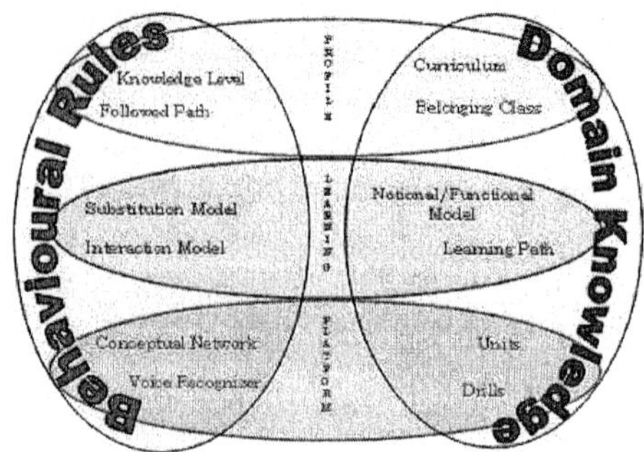

Fig. 1. System Architecture

In designing the agents, figure 1, we have considered a modular architecture composed by behavioural tasks which solve specific problems and interact in order to practice control on them.

The functioning strategy of our intelligent agent may be expressed by two components: perception and interaction.

The **perception** phase includes the voice recognition of the sentences pronounced by the student and their relative assessment. It takes into consideration all the basic aspects referred to the student profile and the followed path. This defines the agent behaviour that **interacts** with the student following the strategies, stimulated by his/her reactions, which are present in the behavioural rules associated to the intelligent agent.

The first element we have considered is the need to know and evaluate the level of attention and interest the student showed during the course. In order to evaluate this

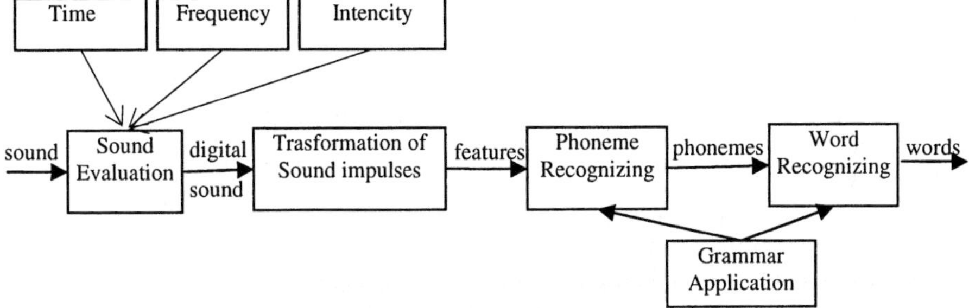

Fig. 2. Voice Recognition

level an analysis of the used vocal system has been done, taking into consideration time, pause frequency and voice intensity parameters, figure 2.

The time parameter compares the total duration of the sentence to be pronounced and the duration of the student expression. This allows the assessment of the knowledge of the pronounced words within a context.

The frequency of the pauses calculates the "no sound" time during the pronouncing activity so evaluating if the student knows how to pronounce each word.

The voice intensity controls if the sentence is pronounced aloud or silently, showing if the student is sure of his/her pronounce during the dialogue.

These characteristics indicate to the agent which interaction modality to adopt with the current student.

As described in the following, the student is required to become protagonist of a situation which aims at teaching the functions described in the previous paragraph.

During this substitution the student interacts with the actors in the scene as in a virtual film. The actors may be more than two, and each one is an intelligent agent able to adapt itself to the student's dialogue.

In particular, the sentence pronounced by the student is evaluated according to three fundamental levels: syntactic, semantic and contextual.

The **syntactic** correction points out words not listed in the English Dictionary which the system does not understand. This mistake essentially shows a pronouncing problem. In this case, for example, the agent reaction is to kindly ask the student to repeat the dialogue:

```
A: Sorry, I didn't hear you, may you repeat, please?
```

The **semantic** correction controls the grammar of the sentence. Each word is included in the English Dictionary, but the system does not understand the sentence due to grammar problems. In this case, for example, the agent interacts with the student asking explanation:

```
A: Sorry, I didn't understand, may you repeat, please?
```

The agent may help the student to exactly formulate the sentence, suggesting correct linguistic structures.

The last correction, the **contextual**, verifies if the pronounced sentence is appropriate to the context. In this case the agent is able to understand the meaning of the sentence and answers referring to the sentence itself. For example:

```
A: What's your name?
S: It's ten o'clock.
A: I didn't ask you "What time is it?" but "What's your
   name?"
```

From the educative point of view, it is important to understand the student reactions to the agent interaction. To follow the dramatization without interruptions is a great source of motivation for the student who is an active participant in the scene. The corrections given through simple interactions produce a good effects on the learning.

The course adapting to the student skills is an innovative aspect in learning paths. The practiced experimentation has given an extraordinary contribution to a learning modality which uses intelligent interfaces which adapt themselves to the situations.

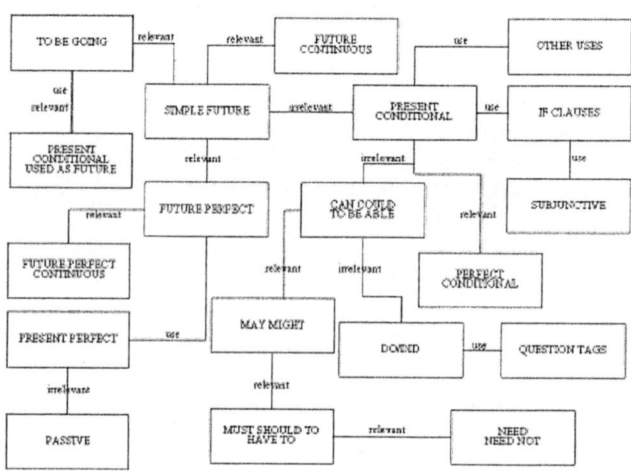

Fig. 3. Conceptual Network

5 Learning Experimentation

The course develops in 20 teaching units organized in order to allow the student to learn each basic communicative function of the language through the handling of determined concepts, table 1. Each teaching unit is composed by a module of Animation/Substitution, and by a module of traditional exercises (Drill). Furthermore, the course is provided with a grammar book hypertextually connected with each single unit.

At the beginning of the course the student is asked to give some general information about him/herself in order to adjust the course-surfing to each student's characteristics. Moreover, there is a brief training phase of the voice-recognizer to enhance its performance. The student is also allowed to choose if he/she wants to attend the course autonomously opting for the lesson he/she intends to attend, or for being "accompanied" during the various lessons along a tailored training path organized by the tutor.

For its hypertextual characteristics, the course is based on a concept network which allows to follow equivalent training paths based on each single student's cognitive skills, figure 3. During his/her performance, if he/she wants to, he/she can re-play the scene, listen again to specific dialogue sentences or phrases pronounced by the agent he/she is replacing and, in the end he/she can re-play the conversation listening to his/her substitution.

As language learning includes the integration of the four main linguistic skills (listening, reading, speaking and writing), it is possible to re-play the sketches together with the balloons containing the written sentences, figure 4. In this way the student can also choose to practise the writing skill by writing in the sketch the text of her/his dialogue instead of pronouncing it.

Fig. 4. Spoken and Written Substitution

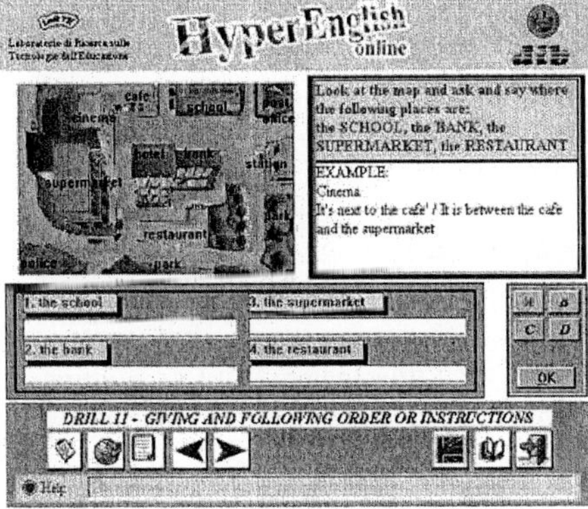

Fig. 5. Drill

The unit is considered complete only when all the possible substitutions, both oral and written, and all the corresponding drills have been practised by the student.

The drill interface widely respects the characteristics of usability and makes the drill execution pleasant and entertaining; as a matter of fact drills are always accompanied by a brief explanation and by an example, Figure 5.

The experimentation results have been quite encouraging, as they have reflected a high satisfaction level of the course, particularly as far as interaction was concerned. This tool worked not only as a learning tool, but also as a practising and perfecting one. In comparison to traditional methods, it offers the student the chance of testing all his/her communicative skills.

Both the initial and the final test results show that there was considerable improvement as for the profit level in all cases, between the beginning and the end of the course.

6 Conclusion

The students who experimented the course were positively impressed and interested in the possibility of virtually entering a familiar situation, because this requires active and continuous involvement, and provides immediate feedback.

Intelligent interfaces will play a leading role for the e-learning development in the next future. As a matter of fact, the advantages discovered during the research for the implementation of this tool have been relevant and will surely open new roads towards the research in the e-learning field.

References

1. Allen, J.F., Ferguson, G., Miller, B., and Ringger, E., Spoken Dialogue and Interactive Planning, Proc. Of the ARPA Spoken Language Technology Workshop, Austin, TX, Jan. (1995)
2. Bernsen, N.O., Dybkjaer, H., and Dybkjaer., L.: What Should Your Speech System Say, IEEE Computer, (1997), 30(12)
3. Burleson, W.: Affective Learning Companions, Doctoral Consortium in conjunction with the 7th International Conference on Intelligent Tutoring Systems, Maceio - Alagoas, Brasil, August 30th, (2004)
4. Bolt, R.A.: "Put-That-There": Voice and Gesture at the Graphics Interface. Computer Graphics, (1980), 14(3):262-270
5. Genesereth, M. R. and Ketchpel, S. P.: Software agents. Communications of the ACM, (1995), 37(2):48-53
6. Gentile, E., Plantamura, P., Plantamura, V.L.: Multimedia Linguistic Learning, Proceedings of IEEE International Conference on Multimedia and Expo (ICME2000), 7-10
7. Jennings, N. R., Varga, L. Z., Aarnts, R. P., Fuchs, J., and Skarek, P.: Transforming standalone expert system into a community of cooperating agents. International Journal of Engineering Applications of Artificial Intelligence, (1993), 6(4):317-331
8. Maes, P.: Social interface agents: Acquiring competence by learning from users and other agent. In Etzioni, O., editor, Software Agents – Papers from the 1994 Spring Symposium (Technical Report SS-94-03), (1994), 71-78, AAAI Press

9. Picard, R. W., Wexelblat R. W. and A.: Future Interfaces: Social and Emotional, CHI, April 20-25, Minneapolis, MN, (2002), 698-699
10. Picard R. W.: Affective Computing, MIT Press, Cambridge, (1997)
11. Shoham, Y.: Time for action: on the relation between time, knowledge and action. In Proceedings of the Eleventh International Joint Conference on Artificial Intelligence (IJCAI-89), 954-959, Detroit, MI

A Three-Layered Architecture for Socially Intelligent Agents: Modeling the Multilevel Process of Emotions

Christine L. Lisetti[1] and Andreas Marpaung[2]

[1] Affective Social Computing Laboratory, Institut Eurecom, , Postfach 10 52 80, 06560 Sophia-Antipolis, France
Lisetti@eurecom.fr
http://www.eurecom.fr/~lisetti
[2] Computer Science Dept., University of Central Florida, Orlando, USA
marpaung@cs.ucf.edu

Abstract. In this article, we propose the design of a three-layered agent architecture inspired from the Multilevel Process Theory of Emotion (Leventhal and Scherer, 1987). Our project aims at modeling emotions on an autonomous embodied robotic agent, expanding upon our previous work (Lisetti, et al., 2004). Our agent is designed to socially interact with humans, navigating in an office suite environment, and engaging people in social interactions. We describe: (1) the psychological theory of emotion which inspired our design, (2) our proposed agent architecture, (3) the needed hardware additions that we implemented on a robot, (3) the robot's multi-modal interface designed especially to engage humans in natural (and hopefully pleasant) social interactions.

1 Introduction

As robots begin to enter our everyday life, an important human-robot interaction issue becomes that of *social interactions*. Because emotions have a crucial evolutionary functional aspect in social intelligence, without which complex intelligent systems with limited resources cannot function efficiently [13], [14] or maintain a satisfactory relationship with their environment [15], we focus our current contribution to the study of emotional social intelligence for robots. Indeed, the recent emergence of affective computing combined with artificial intelligence [16] has made it possible to design computer systems that have "social expertise" in order to be more autonomous and to naturally bring the human – a principally social animal – into the loop of human-computer interaction.

In this article, *social expertise* is considered in terms of (1) internal motivational goal-based abilities and (2) external communicative behavior. Because of the important functional role that emotions play in human decision-making and in human-human communication, we propose a paradigm for modeling some of the functions of emotions in intelligent autonomous artificial agents to enhance both (a) robot autonomy and (b) human-robot interaction. To this end, we developed an autonomous service robot whose functionality has been designed so that it could socially interact with humans on a daily basis in the context of an office suite environment and studied

J. Tao, T. Tan, and R.W. Picard (Eds.): ACII 2005, LNCS 3784, pp. 956–963, 2005.

and evaluated the design *in vivo*. The social robot is furthermore evaluated from a social informatics approach, using workplace ethnography to guide its design *while* it is being developed.

2 A Three-Layered Emotion-Based Architecture

2.1 Related Research

There have been several attempts to model emotions in software agents and robots and to use these models to enhance functionality. El-Nasr [17] uses a fuzzy logic model for simulating emotional behaviors in an animated environment. Contrary to our approach directed toward robots, her research is directed toward HCI and computer simulation.

Velasquez's work [10], [18] is concerned with autonomous agents, particularly robots in which control arises from emotional processing. This work describes an emotion-based control framework and focuses on affect programs which are implemented by integration of circuits from several systems that mediate perception, attention, motivation, emotion, behavior, and motor control. These range from simple reflex-like emotions, to facilitation of attention, to emotional learning. Although the approach is different, its motivation is similar to ours.

Breazeal's work [8], [9] also involves robot architectures with a motivational system that associates motivations with both drives and emotions. Emotions are implemented in a framework very similar to that of Velasquez's work but Breazeal's emphasis is on the function of emotions in social exchanges and learning with a human caretaker. Our approach is different from Breazeal's in that it is currently focused on both social exchanges and the use of emotions to control a single agent.

In Michaud's work [19], [20], emotions *per se* are not represented in the model, but emotion capability is achieved by incorporating it into the control architecture as a global background state. Our approach which chooses to represent the emotional system explicitly (as discussed later) differs from Michaud's in that respect. Although both Michaud and our approach revolve around the notion of emotion as monitoring progress toward goals, our work explicitly represents emotion and corresponds to a formal cognitive model.

Murphy and Lisetti's approach [11] uses the multilevel hierarchy of emotions where emotions both modify active behaviors at the sensory-motor level and change the set of active behaviors at the schematic level for a pair of cooperating heterogeneous robots with interdependent tasks.

Our current approach builds on that work, setting the framework for more elaborate emotion representations while starting to implement simple ones and associating these with expressions (facial and spoken) in order to simultaneously evaluate human perceptions of such social robots so as to guide further design decisions.

2.2 A Multilevel Emotion State Generator (ESG)

The design of our emotion-based architecture is based on the *Multilevel Process Theory of Emotion* (Leventhal and Scherer, 1987) shown in Figure 1. In short, the Multilevel Process Theory of Emotion postulates that the experience of emotion is a product of a hierarchical multi-component processing system.: (1) *Sensory motor level* – generates the primary emotion in response to the basic stimulus features in a non-deliberative manner; (2) *Schematic level* – integrates specific situational perceptions with autonomic, subjective, expressive and instrumental responses in a concrete and patterned script-like memory system; (3) C*onceptual level* – is deliberative and involves reasoning over the past, projecting into the future, and comparing emotional schemata to avoid unsuccessful situations (and is not be treated in our current implementation).

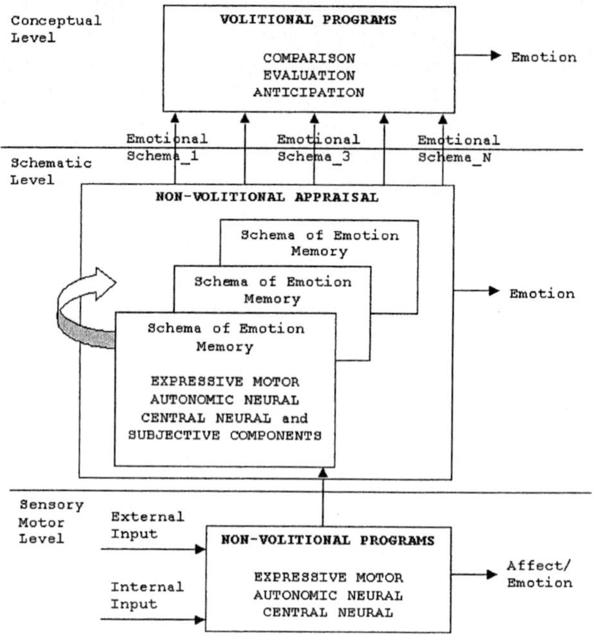

Fig. 1. Multilevel Emotion State Generator (ESG)

2.3 Robotic Platform

Our robotic implementation, a Pioneer PeopleBot from Activmedia shown in Figure 2, is a continuation of our previous project – Cherry the AmigoBot – the little red robot designed to navigate in an office suite, to deliver supplies to offices and to greet people according to their social status via an animated avatar (Lisetti et al., 2004).

The ActivMedia Peoplebots (ActivMedia, 2002) are equipped with twenty-four sonars, one movable camera, one gripper that can be moved up and down, front and back. To meet our goals of enabling human-centered dynamic interactions with our agent, we added hardware to the original PeopleBot: a DesXcape 150 DM touch-screen so that users can easily point-and-click the destination to the robot assistant, a wireless antenna for DesXcape touch screen communication, one floor-level camera for navigation, one eye-level camera for face-recognition, (and one laser for future ability to generate maps instantly).

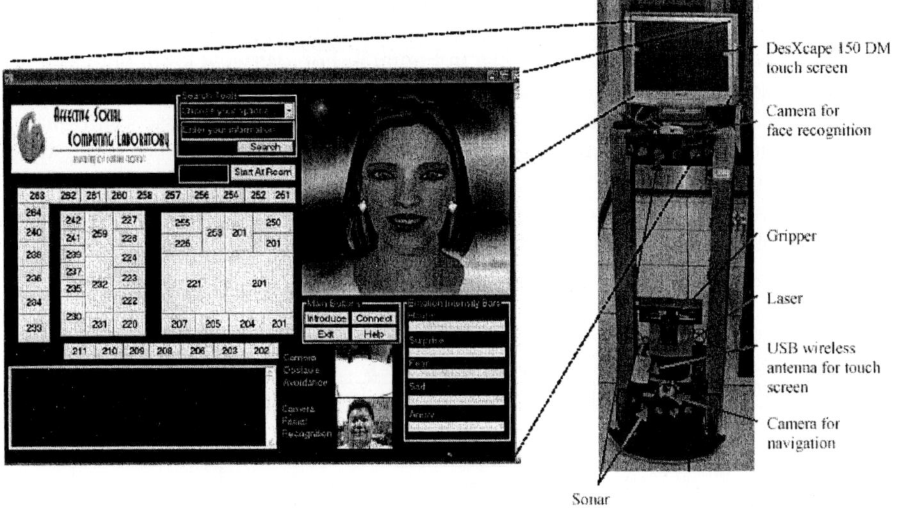

Fig. 2. Our social robot platform

2.4 Multimodal Interface with an Expressive Avatar

Through the on-board computer, we execute the interface that we created and display it through the touch screen wirelessly (Figure 2). The interface, a modified version of Cherry's which was tested as far as its users' acceptance (Lisetti et al., 2004), integrates several components such as an anthropomorphic avatar, a point-and-click map, progress bars showing real-time changes of the robot's emotion-like states, in addition to several help menus, i.e., speech text box, search properties, start-at-room option, and two live-capture video frames – one showing the robot's floor vision, the other its eye-level vision.

In addition, in order to enable our agent to have the ability to communicate its internal emotion-like states, we animate an avatar 's facial expressions. For each emotion-like stage we are modeling (happiness, surprise, fear, sad, and anger), we have designed facial expressions closed to the Facial Action Coding System (FACS) which are shown in Figure 3 (a-c).

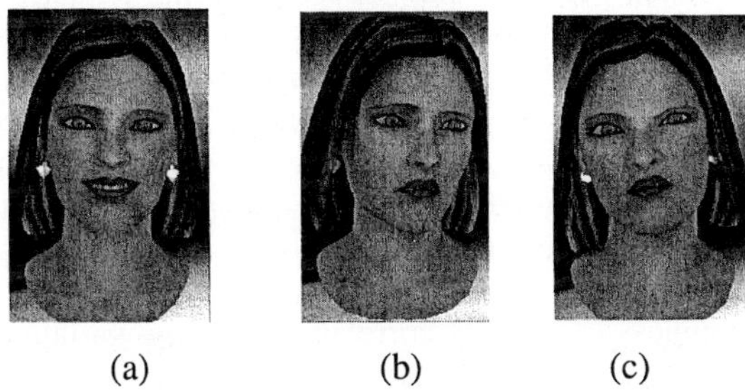

Fig. 3. Facial expressions for the modeled emotions (a) Happy, (b) Sad, (c) Angry

2.5 Using the Architecture for our Robotic Platform

The general agent architecture is shown in Figure 4. For every cycle (in our case, it is 1000 mm travel distance), the Input Sensors send inputs read to the Perceptual System for processing. The Perceptual System is a simple system that abstracts information from the outside world with some interpreted meaning for the robot (e.g., walls, floors, open or closed doors, faces) and sends its outputs (valid sonar readings, vision-navigation interpretation, and person's name) to the Emotion State Generator (ESG) which in turn triggers certain emotion-like states as we will describe later.

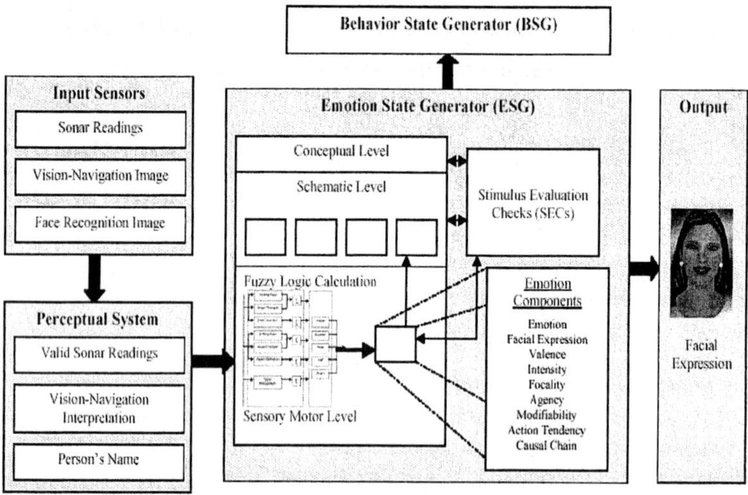

Fig. 4. Petra's Detailed Three-Layered Architecture

In our design, sonar is used in conjunction with vision to navigate around the office suite. A sonar reading is considered invalid if the sum of the left-most and the right-most sonar readings are extremely more or less than the distance between the aisle (1,500 mm for our case). And vice versa, the reading is valid if the sum of both readings is around 1,500 mm. Floor vision is used to perform course correction to center itself between the corridor aisles, and to detect obstacles (e.g. garbage can, boxes, people). Eye-level vision performs face recognition on a database of the facial images of the 25 workers in the office suite.

As shown in Figure 4, the Perceptual System passes these sensory information to the Emotional State Generator (ESG): door detected, object detected, whether a person was recognized, the name of the person recognized. A fuzzy logic model (Takagi, Sugeno, 1985) is further used to deal with the uncertainty of the sensory information and determine the current emotion-like state based on an (currently) ad-hoc OR-mapping.

For example, happiness is strongly correlated with low variations from the sonar reading, recognizing a face, or finding that the office where it was sent is open. Similarly, anger is correlated with finding repetitively closed doors and repetitively not recognizing people.

2.6 Sequential Evaluation Checks

In order to produce emotion for each level, many researchers have hypothesized that specific emotions are triggered through a series of sequential evaluation checks (SECs) of the various stimuli (Scherer, 1984; Scherer, 1986; Weiner, Russell, and Lerman, 1979; Smith and Ellsworth, 1985). We have identified specific SECs we considered particularly useful for the design of artificial agents into an Affective Knowledge of Representation (AKR) (Lisetti, 2002). In AKR, each emotion has many components, e.g., valence, intensity, focality, agency, modifiability, action tendency, and causal chains which we describe below:

Facial Expression: *happy/sad/surprised/angry:* is used to control the avatar's animation.

Valence: *positive/ negative:* is used to describe the pleasant or unpleasant dimension of an affective state.

Intensity: *very high/ high/ medium/ low/ very low:* varies in terms of degree. The intensity of an affective state is relevant to the importance, relevance and urgency of the message that the state carries.

Focality: *event/ object:* is used to indicate whether the emotions are about something: an event (the trigger to surprise) or an object (the object of jealousy).

Agency: *self/ other:* is used to indicate who was responsible for the emotion, the agent itself *self*, or someone else *other.*

Modifiability: *high/ medium/ low/ none:* is used to refer to duration and time perspective, or to the judgment that a course of events is capable of changing.

Action Tendency: identifies the most appropriate (suite of) actions to be taken from that emotional state. For example, happy is associated with generalized readiness, frustration with change current strategy, and discouraged with give up or release expectations.

Causal Chain: identifies the causation of a stimulus event associated with the emotion. For example, happy has these causal chains: (1) Something good happened to me, (2) I wanted this, (3) I do not want other things, and (4) Because of this, I feel good. These can used by the agent to verbally express and explain to humans what emotion-like state it finds itself in.

Emotion components are checked to create a schema of emotion to be stored in the memory. The checking is done by assigning appropriate values to the emotion components based on pleasantness, importance, relevance, urgency, etc.

Table 2 shows a schema when an unexpected moving object suddenly appears in the captured navigation-image, i.e, walking students. In this case, surprise will become the current state. Indeed, the sudden appearance of a person in the navigation image is detected as an obstacle that can slow down the navigation process, due to the course correction that needs to be performed should the person remain in the navigation image on the next cycle. Thus *intensity* component is very high and the *action tendency* is to avoid potential obstacles. Since the face cannot be detected at farther distance, the *valence* is negative, and the *modifiability* is set to its default–medium because the agent has not performed obstacle avoidance to change the course event. In addition, the facial expression component is set to surprise to drive the animation of the facial expressions of the interface avatar.

Table 2. *Surprise* schema

Components	Values
Emotion	SURPRISE
Facial Expression	Surprise
Valence	Negative
Intensity	Very High
Focality	Object – walking student
Agency	Other
Modifiability	Medium
Action Tendency	Avoid
Causal Chain	- Something happened now - I did not think before now that this will happen - If I thought about it, I would have said that this will not happen - Because of this, I feel something bad

3 Conclusion

This work has presented an initial attempt to develop a 3-layered emotion-based architecture for artificial agents based on Scherer and Leventhal's multilevel process theory of emotions. Still much work remains to render this approach complete, and this study will continue to point out the power of emotions in human intelligence (which might be impossible to fully computationalize).

References

ActivMedia. www.activmedia.com, 2002.

Arkin, R. C. *Behavior-Based Robotics*, Cambridge, MA: MIT Press, 1998.

Breazeal, C. and Scassellati, B., "Infant-like Social Interactions Between a Robot and a Human Caretaker". To appear in *Special issue of Adaptive Behavior on Simulation Models of Social Agents*, guest editor Kerstin Dautenhahn. 2000

Breazeal, C. "Emotion and sociable humanoid robots". *International Journal of Human Computer Studies.* Vol. 59. pg. 119 – 155. 2003

Brooks, R and Flynn, A. "Fast, Cheap, and Out of Control", AI Memo 1182, MIT AI Laboratory, 1989.

Brown, S. Lisetti, C. and Marpaung, A. Cherry, the Little Red Robot with a Mission and a Personality. In *Working Notes of the AAAI Fall Symposium Series on Human-Robot Interaction*, Menlo Park, CA: AAAI Press. Cape Cod, MA, November 2002.

Casper, J. "Human-robot interactions during the robot-assisted urban search and rescue response at the World Trade Center." MS Thesis, Computer Science and Engineering, University of South Florida, April 2002.

Casper, J. and Murphy, R. "Workflow study on human-robot interaction in USAR." In *Proceedings of ICRA 2002*, pp. 1997 – 2003. 2002.

Ekman, P and Friesen, W. "The Facial Action Coding System". Consulting Psychologist Press, San Francisco, CA, 1978.

El-Nasr, Magy Seif. Yen, John. Ioerger, Thomas. FLAME - A Fuzzy Logic Adaptive Model of Emotions, *Automous Agents and Multi-agent Systems*, 3, 219-257, 2000.

Identix Inc. www.identix.com, 2002.

Leventhal, H. "A perceptual-motor processing model of emotion." In P. Pilner, K. Blankenstein, & I.M. Spigel (Eds.), *Perception of emotion in self and others. Vol. 5* (pp. 1 – 46). New York: Plenum. 1979

Leventhal, H., "Toward a comprehensive theory of emotion." In L. Berkowitz (Ed.), *Advances in experimental social Psychology. Vol. 13* (pp. 139 – 207). New York: Academic Press, 1980

Leventhal, H. and Scherer, K. "The relationship of emotion to cognition: A functional approach to a semantic controversy." *Cognition and Emotion.* Vol. 1. No. 1. pp. 3 – 28. 1987.

Lisetti, C. Brown, S. Alvarez, K. and Marpaung, A. A Social Informatics Approach to Human-Robot Interaction with an Office Service Robot. *IEEE Transactions on Systems, Man, and Cybernetics - Special Issue on Human Robot Interaction,* Vol. 34(2), May 2004.

Lisetti, C. and Bianchi, N. Modeling Multimodal Expression of User's Affective Subjective Experience. *User Modeling and User-Adapted Interaction, An International Journal,* Vol. 12(1): 49-84. 2002

Marpaung, A. "Social Robots with Emotion State Generator Enhancing Human-Robot Interaction (HRI)". Master's thesis. University of Central Florida. in progress 2004.

Murphy, R. R. Use of Scripts for Coordinating Perception and Action, In *Proceedings of IROS-96* , 1996a.

Murphy, R. R. Biological and Cognitive Foundations of Intelligent Sensor Fusion, *IEEE Transactions on Systems, Man and Cybernetics*, 26 (1), 42-51, 1996b.

Murphy, R. R. Dempster-Shafer Theory for Sensor Fusion in Autonomous Mobile Robots, *IEEE Transactions on Robotics and Automation*, 14 (2), 1998.

Murphy, R. R. *Introduction to AI Robotics.* Cambridge, MA: MIT Press, 2000.

Murphy, R. R., Lisetti, C. L., Irish, L., Tardif, R. and Gage, A., Emotion-Based Control of Cooperating Heterogeneous Mobile Robots, *IEEE Transactions on Robotics and Automation*, Vol. 18, 2002.

Picard, Rosalind W. Affective Computing, Cambridge, Mass.: MIT Press, 1997.

Scherer, K. "Emotion as a multicomponent process: A model and some cross-cultural data." In P. Shaver (Ed.), *Review of personality and social psychology.* Vol. 5. *Emotions, relationships and health* (pp. 37 – 63). Beverly Hills, CA: Sage. 1984

Scherer, K. "Vocal affect expression: A review and a model for future research." *Psychological Bulletin.* 99. pp. 143 – 165. 1986

Smith, C. A., Ellsworth, P.C. "Patterns of cognitive appraisal in emotion." *Journal of Personality and Social Psychology.* 48. pp. 813 – 838. 1985

Simmons, R. Goldberg, D. Goode, A. et al. GRACE An Autonomous Robot for the AAAI Robot Challenge. *AI Magazine.* Vol. 24. No. 2. p. 51 – 72. 2003

Sony. www.us.aibo.com. 2004.

Takagi, H. and Sugeno, M.. "Fuzzy identification of systems and its application to modeling and control". *IEEE Transactions on Systems, Man and Cybernetics*, 15 (1), 1985.

Velasquez, Juan. "Cathexis, A Computational Model for the Generation of Emotions and their Influence in the Behavior of Autonomous Agents". Master's thesis. Massachusetts Institute of Technology. 1996

Velasquez, Juan. "Modeling Emotion-Based Decision Making". *In proceedings of AAAI Fall Symposium Emotional & Intelligent: The Tangled Knot of Cognition.* 1998

Weiner, B., Russell, D., Lerman, D. "The cognition-emotion process in achievement-related contexts. *Journal of Personality and Social Psychology,* 37, pp. 1211 – 1220. 1979.

Multi-stream Confidence Analysis for Audio-Visual Affect Recognition

Zhihong Zeng, Jilin Tu, Ming Liu, and Thomas S. Huang

Beckman Institute for Advanced Science and Technology,
University of Illinois at Urbana-Champaign,
405 N. Mathews Av., Urbana, IL 61801
{zhzeng, jilintu, mingliu1, huang}@ifp.uiuc.edu

Abstract. Changes in a speaker's emotion are a fundamental component in human communication. Some emotions motivate human actions while others add deeper meaning and richness to human interactions. In this paper, we explore the development of a computing algorithm that uses audio and visual sensors to recognize a speaker's affective state. Within the framework of Multi-stream Hidden Markov Model (MHMM), we analyze audio and visual observations to detect 11 cognitive/emotive states. We investigate the use of individual modality confidence measures as a means of estimating weights when combining likelihoods in the audio-visual decision fusion. Person-independent experimental results from 20 subjects in 660 sequences suggest that the use of stream exponents estimated on training data results in classification accuracy improvement of audio-visual affect recognition.

1 Introduction

The traditional Human Computer Interaction (HCI) system is constructed to emphasize the transmission of explicit messages while ignoring implicit information about the user such as changes in emotional states. However, changes in a speaker's emotion are a fundamental component in human communication. Some emotions motivate human actions while others add deeper meaning and richness to human interactions. Consequently, the traditional HCI that ignores a user's emotional states is only making use of a small portion of the data available in an interaction. This fact has inspired the research field of "emotional computing" [5] which aims at enabling computers to express and recognize emotion. The ability to detect and track a user's affect state has the potential of allowing a computing system to initiate communication with a user based on the perceived needs of the user within the context of the user's actions. This enables a computing system to offer relevant information when a user needs help not just when the user requests help. In this way, human computer interaction can become more natural, persuasive, and friendly.

The work in this paper is motivated by the ITR project (itr.beckman.uiuc.edu). The goal of this project is to contribute to the development of multimodal human-computer intelligent interaction environment. An educational learning environment was used as a test-bed to evaluate the ideas and tools resulting from this research. This test-bed focused on using Lego gears to teach math and science concepts to upper elementary and middle school children. The project focuses on using proactive

J. Tao, T. Tan, and R.W. Picard (Eds.): ACII 2005, LNCS 3784, pp. 964–971, 2005.

computing to achieve two ends. First, to help children explore and understand a variety of phenomena ranging from mathematic ratios to advanced concepts of mechanical advantage and least common multiples. The second goal of the project is to support and prolong a student's interest in the activities while also promoting a high level of student engagement. This is accomplished through a multimodal computer learning environment that uses audio-visual sensors to recognize the student's affective states (e.g. interest, boredom, frustration and puzzlement) and to proactively apply appropriate context specific tutoring strategies (e.g. encouragement, transition/guidance, and confirmation). Through these techniques, students explore a variety of math and science concepts in a highly engaged mode of learning.

Multimodal sensory information fusion is a process that enables human ability to assess emotional states robustly and flexibly. To more accurately simulate the human ability to assess affect, an automatic affect recognition system should also make use of multimodal data. In this paper, we present our efforts toward audio-visual affect recognition. Based on the psychological study [9] which indicated people mainly rely on facial expressions and vocal intonations to judge someone's affective states, we focus on the analysis of facial expression in the visual channel, speech prosody in the audio channel, and bimodal fusion.

For integrating audio and visual streams, we applied the multi-stream hidden Markov model (MHMM) [11][12] which can be fused at the parallel architecture. We investigate the use of individual modality confidence measures as a means of estimating weights when combining likelihoods in the audio-visual decision fusion. Our person-independent affect recognition approaches were tested in 660 sequences based on 20 subjects with 11 HCI-related affect states. The experimental results show that the use of stream exponents results in affect classification accuracy improvement of audio-visual affect recognition.

2 Related Work

Researchers from many different disciplines are interested in the possibility of automated affect analysis and recognition. Recent advances in computing power and multimedia technologies are facilitating efforts toward audio-visual affect recognition. According to [1], only four papers reported advances of bimodal affect recognition. In addition, there have been four papers of bimodal emotion recognition recently published in 2004 and 2005

Among these eight papers, four papers did person-independent audio-visual affect recognition [2-4][14]. Compared with the four reports, we in this paper explore the use of individual modality confidence measures as a means of estimating weights when combining likelihoods in the audio-visual decision fusion. [3-4] applied rule-based methods for combining two modalities. [2] applied the single-modal method in a sequential manner for bimodal recognition. [14] simply uses manual setting of weights in audio-visual fusion.

Audio-visual fusion is an instance of the general classifier fusion problem. This paper explores decision fusion method in affect recognition application which combines the single-modality classifier outputs to recognize audio-visual affect. Classifier fusion based on their individual decision about the classes of interest is an active area of research with many applications [10][12]. Combination strategies are different in various aspects, such as the architecture used (parallel, cascade, or hierarchical combination), and information level considered at integration (abstract, rank-order, or measurement level). Although examples of most of these categories can be found in audio-visual Automatic Speech Recognition (AVASR) literature [12], few studies are found audio-visual affect recognition. In addition, most of AVASR studies focus on two-stream combination. This paper explores three-stream fusion problem.

3 Database

The datasets used in previous papers [2-4] were small in the number of subjects, and were not related directly to human computer interaction. To overcome these problems, a large-scale database was collected [13]. This database consists of controlled performances of 7 basic emotions (happiness, sadness, fear, surprise, anger, disgust, and neutral), and 4 cognitive states (interest, boredom, puzzlement and frustration).

The 20 subjects (10 female and 10 males) in our database consist of graduate and undergraduate students from different disciplines. This set of videos contains subjects with a wide variability in physiognomy. Although the subjects displayed affect expressions on request, the subjects chose how to express each state. They were simply asked to display facial expressions and speak appropriate sentences. Each subject was required to repeat each state with speech three times. Therefore, for every affective state, there are 3*20=60 video sequences. And there are totally 60*11=660 sequences for 11 affective states. The time of every sequence ranged from 2-6 seconds.

Speech energy was used to determine start and end points of each emotion expression because they easier to detect than those of facial expressions. Once these segments were defined, corresponding points of facial feature sequences were labeled.

4 Facial Feature Extraction

A tracking algorithm called Piecewise Bezier Volume Deformation (PBVD) tracking [6] is applied to extract facial features in our experiment.

This face tracker uses a 3D facial mesh model which is embedded in multiple Bezier volumes. The shape of the mesh can be changed with the movement of the control points in the Bezier volumes. That guarantees the surface patches to be continuous and smooth. In the first video frame (frontal view of a neutral facial expression), the 3-D facial mesh model is constructed by manual or automatic selection [15] of landmark facial feature points. Once the model was fitted, the tracker can track head motion and local deformations of the facial features by an optical flow method. These deformations are measured in terms of magnitudes of 12 predefined motions of facial features around mouth, eyelids and eyebrows, called Motion Units (MUs), which are shown in Figure 1. A facial expression is represented as a linear combination of the 12 Motion Units (MU) in the following formula

$$V = BDP = B[D_1 D_2 ... D_{12}] \begin{bmatrix} p_1 \\ p_2 \\ ... \\ p_{12} \end{bmatrix} \quad (1)$$

where B is constructed by Bezier basis functions, $D_i (i = 1,...,12)$ is the displacement vector of ith MU, and the $p_i (i = 1,...,12)$ is the magnitude of ith MU deformation. The overall motion of the head and face is represented as

$$R(V_0 + BDP) + T \quad (2)$$

where R is the 3D rotation matrix, T is the 3D translation matrix, and V_0 is the initial neutral face model.

The local deformation output P of the tracker is used as facial affective features for affect recognition. The face tracker outputs 30 frames per second.

We notice that the movements of facial features are related to both affective states and content of speech. Thus, smooth facial features [16] are calculated by averaging facial features at consecutive frames to reduce the influence of speech on facial expression, based on the assumption that the influence of speech on face features is temporary, and the influence of affect is relatively more persistent.

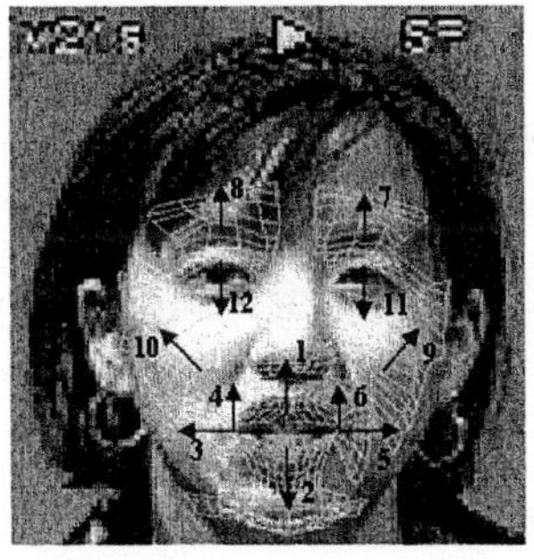

Fig. 1. 12 facial Motion Units

Regarding person-independent affect recognition, facial feature normalization is crucial because every subject has different physiognomy. To express an affect, different subjects will display different magnitudes of 12 MUs. To overcome this difference, the neutral expression for each person has been used as the normalization standard. In detail, for a given subject, the magnitudes of 12 MUs at every frame were normalized by the corresponding feature means of the neutral expression of the same subject.

After the feature vector of each frame is normalized, it is quantized into 19-size codebook by vector quantization (VQ).

5 Audio Feature Extraction

For audio feature extraction, Entropic Signal Processing System named get_f0, a commercial software package, is used. It implements a fundamental frequency estimation algorithm using the normalized cross correlation function and dynamic programming [7]. The program can output the pitch F0 for fundamental frequency estimate, RMS energy for local root mean squared measurements, prob_voice for probability of voicing, and the peak normalized cross-correlation value that was used to determine the output F0. The experimental results in [8] showed pitch and energy are the most important factors in affect classification. Therefore, in our experiment, we only used these two audio features for affect recognition. Some prosody features, like frequency and duration of silence, could have implication in the HMM structure of energy and pitch.

Obviously, the emotional information in the voice depends on the subject and recording condition. The pitch varies widely from person to person. In general, males speak with a lower pitch than females. Thus, for a given subject, the pitch at every frame is normalized by the pitch mean of the neutral expression sequence of the same subject. The same is done for energy features to normalize amplitude change due to the speaker volume and the distance of a speaker for microphone.

Similarly to the visual feature quantization, the energy and pitch are quantized into 19-size codebook by vector quantization respectively.

6 Decision Fusion for Audio-Visual Affect Recognition

The main aim in this paper is to investigate and propose algorithm for the automatic recognition of audio-visual affect recognition. In our case, audio and visual observations are available. Each observation can be used alone to train single-modality statistical classifiers to recognize affective states. However, we hope that combining audio-visual information will give rise to a multi-modal classifier with superior performance to both single-modality ones.

We apply decision fusion method for audio-visual affect recognition which combine the single-modality HMM classifier outputs to recognize audio-visual affect. Specifically, class conditional log-likelihoods from the three classifiers are linearly combined using appropriate weights that explicitly model the reliability of each classifier. Such modeling is very important because discrimination power of the audio and visual streams can vary widely, depending on the acoustic noise in the environment, visual channel degradations, face tracker inaccuracies.

The decision fusion technique for audio-visual affect recognition used in this paper belong to the paradigm of multiple classifier integration using a parallel architecture, adaptive combination weights, and class measurement level information. In our application, the composite facial feature from video, energy and pitch features from audio are treated as three streams, and modeled by three component HMMs. We investigate integration where face-only, energy-only and pitch-only recognizer hypotheses are rescored by the log-likelihood combination of these streams, which allows complete asynchrony among the three HMMs.

Let us denote the audio-visual observation vector which corresponds to an affective expression by $O = \{O^{(s)}\}$ where $s \in \{v, p, e\}$ representing visual, pitch and energy features respectively. The MHMM models its audio-visual likelihoods of the affective states (classes) as the product of the likelihood of its single-stream components, raised to appropriate stream exponents, namely

$$P[O \mid c] = \prod_{s \in \{v,p,e\}} P(O^{(s)} \mid c)^{\lambda_s} \tag{3}$$

where c denotes the affective states, and λ_s denote the stream exponents (weights), that are non-negative adding up to one, and are a function of the modality. The parameters of the MHMM [11] can be estimated using the EM algorithm. In our case, the stream exponents (weights) capture the confidence of the individual classifiers for our database condition, and are estimated by individual stream component performances (i.e. accuracies) on training data.

7 Experimental Results

In our experiment, the composite facial feature from video, energy and pitch features from audio are treated as three streams, and modeled by three component HMMs with 12 hidden states. The person-independent affect recognition algorithm was tested on 20 subjects (10 females and 10 males). For this test, all of the sequences of one subject are used as the test sequences, and the sequences of the remaining 19 subjects are used as training sequences. Among the training data of 19 subjects, we randomly choose the data of 14 subjects to estimate the parameters of the-single stream component HMMs. Then, the remaining training data of 5 subjects are used to estimate the performance of these component HMMs. Their classification accuracies are linearly mapped to stream exponents in (3) of MHMM which are adding to one. Finally, the test data of one subject are used to test the performance of this MHMM. The procedure is repeated 20 times, each time leaving a different person out (leave-one-out cross-validation). For every affective state, there are 3*20=60 expression sequences. Therefore, there are totally 60*11=660 sequences for 11 affective states.

Besides our above-mentioned audio-visual fusion denoted as MHMM 3, we also applied other five methods in our experiment: 1) face-only HMM. 2) pitch-only HMM. 3) energy-only HMM. 4) MHMM 1: each time 14 of 19 persons on training data are used to train single-stream component HMM , and audio-visual likelihoods are combined without stream exponents λ_s in (3) ; 5)MHMM 2: each time all 19 persons on training data are used to train single-stream component HMM , and audio-visual likelihoods are combined without stream exponents λ_s in (3). The affect recognition results in our experiment are summarized in Table 1.

Table 1. Average affect recognition rates in our experiment

	Face	Pitch	Energy	MHMM1	MHMM2	MHMM3
Accuracy	0.39	0.60	0.69	0.70	0.72	0.75

Among the six methods mentioned above, face-only HMM gave the poorest performance. The main reason is that speaking influences facial expressions. Especially, subjects seldom display expressive peaks which are main characteristic for pure facial expressions without speaking. Pitch-only and energy-only HMMs performed better than face-only HMM but worse than MHMM because MHMM combine information of face, pitch and energy which provide complementary information for recognition. Among MHMM methods, MHMM1 gave worst performance because it only used the training data of 14 subjects and does not use stream exponents in the fusion stage. MHMM2 has the better recognition rate than MHMM1 because MHMM2 use more data for training. MHMM3 has the best performance because it uses stream exponents estimated on training data of 5 subjects. That suggests that with the limited training data, it is better to divide the training data for estimating single-stream component HMMs and for estimating stream reliability respectively in decision fusion than using all training data for single-stream component HMMs like MHMM2. It is important in the case where single-stream component HMM performances differ largely.

8 Conclusion

With an automatic affect recognizer, a computer can respond appropriately to the user's affective state rather than simply responding to user commands. In this way, the nature of the computer interactions would become more authentic, persuasive, and meaningful. This type of interaction is the ultimate goal of ITR project where attending to changes in the child's affective states leads to a high level of engagement and knowledge acquisition. To accomplish this end, this paper applies an audio-visual fusion method for person-independent affect recognition.

We investigate the use of single modality confidence measures as a means of estimating weights when combining likelihoods in the audio-visual decision fusion. Person-independent experimental results from 20 subjects in 660 sequences show that the use of stream exponents estimated on training data results in affect classification accuracy improvement in audio-visual affect recognition.

Multimodal recognition of human affective states is a largely unexplored and challenging problem. The elicited nature of the affects performed in our database has the potential to differ from corresponding performances in natural settings. The next stage in the evaluation of this algorithm will be attempting to detect these affect states in human interactions where the states are performed naturally.

Acknowledgement

We like to thank Dr. Lawrence Chen for collecting the valuable data in this paper for audio-visual affect recognition. This work was supported by National Science Foundation (Information Technology Research Grant# 0085980) and Beckman postdoctoral fellowship funding.

References

1. Pantic M., Rothkrantz, L.J.M., Toward an affect-sensitive multimodal human-computer interaction, Proceedings of the IEEE, Vol. 91, No. 9, Sept. 2003, 1370-1390
2. Chen, L. and Huang, T. S., Emotional expressions in audiovisual human computer interaction, Int. Conf. on Multimedia & Expo 2000, 423-426
3. Chen, L., Huang, T. S., Miyasato, T., and Nakatsu, R., Multimodal human emotion/expression recognition, Int. Conf. on Automatic Face & Gesture Recognition 1998, 396-401
4. De Silva, L. C., and Ng, P. C., Bimodal emotion recognition, Int. Conf. on Automatic Face & Gesture Recognition 2000, 332-335
5. Picard, R.W., Affective Computing, MIT Press, Cambridge, 1997.
6. Tao, H. and Huang, T.S., Explanation-based facial motion tracking using a piecewise Bezier volume deformation mode ,CVPR'99, vol.1, pp. 611-617, 1999
7. Talkin, D., A Robust Algorithm for Pitch Tracking, in Speech Coding and Synthesis, Kkeijn, W.B., and Paliwal, K.K., Eds., Amsterdam: Elsevier Science, 1995
8. Kwon, O.W., Chan, K., Hao, J., Lee, T.W, Emotion Recognition by Speech Signals, EUROSPEECH 2003.
9. Mehrabian, A., Communication without words, Psychol. Today, vol.2, no.4, 53-56, 1968
10. Jain, A.J., Duin, R.P.W., and Mao, J., Statistical Pattern Recognition: A Review. IEEE PAMI, 4-37, Vol.22, No.1, January, 2000.
11. Bourlard, H. and Dupont, S., A New ASR Approach Based on Independent Processing And Recombination of Partial Frequency Bands, 1996
12. G. Potamianos, C. Neti, G. Gravier, and A. Garg, Automatic Recognition of audio-visual speech: Recent progress and challenges, Proceedings of the IEEE, vol. 91, no. 9, Sep. 2003
13. Chen, L.S, Joint Processing of Audio-Visual Informa-tion for the Recognition of Emotional Expressions in Human-Computer Interaction, PhD thesis, UIUC, 2000
14. Zeng, Z., Tu, J., Pianfetti, B., Liu, M., Zhang, T., Zhang, Z., Huang, T.S., Levinson, S., Audio-visual Affect Recognition through Multi-stream Fused HMM for HCI, CVPR 2005
15. Tu, J., Zhang, Z., Zeng, Z. and Huang, T.S., Face Localization via Hierarchical Condensation with Fisher Boosting Feature Selection, In Proc. Computer Vision and Pattern Recognition, 2004.
16. Zeng, Z., Tu, J., Liu, M., Zhang, T., Rizzolo, N., Zhang, Z., Huang, T.S., Roth, D., and Levinson, S., Bimodal HCI-related Affect Recognition, ICMI 2004

Investigation of Emotive Expressions of Spoken Sentences

Wenjie Cao[1,2], Chengqing Zong[1], and Bo Xu[1]

[1] National Laboratory of Pattern Recognition, Chinese Academy of Sciences, No. 95, ZhongGuanCun EastRoad, Beijing 100080, China
{wjcao, cqzong, xubo}@nlpr.ia.ac.cn
[2] GETA-CLIPS, IMAG, 385 rue de la Bibliothèque, BP 53, 38041 Grenoble Cedex 9, France

Abstract. When we meet an emotion keyword in a sentence that expresses a kind of emotion, or a word that does not directly express emotion but carries an attitude clue, it could be the case that the speaker is just stating a truth without any affection; it could be an expression of attitudes or emotive states of the agent but using different ways, or it could be other cases. In this case, it seems doubtable to determine the exact communicative emotion function of a sentence just based on the "keywords". This paper endeavors to investigate the collective influence of some factors to the communicative emotion function of a sentence. These factors include emotion keywords, and sentence features such as the mood, negation, etc. we believe that the results will be useful for emotion detection or generation of short sentences.

1 Introduction

Human emotion detecting and emotion generation have been paid much attention in physiological aspects, such as speech, facial expressions, hand gesture, and body movement [1]. Most of the researches are conducted by utilizing physiological features. While not so many efforts have been made to analyze or detect emotions in text. Though we accept the opinion that human could detect or express emotions through sounds, facial expressions, and gestures without using words or expressing meanings, it is also important to find out or to infuse emotion expressions into sentences when there is a meaning transfer. For example, understanding the meaning of sentences in order to grasp the exact emotions or attitudes of speakers (spoken language) or characters (written language); or in another aspect, selecting vocabulary according to the communicative emotive purpose of the speaker in order to generate affective texts.

In traditional natural language processing (NLP), notion of the meaning of text mainly refers to the literal meaning of text which is relatively objective. Accordingly, resources for NLP researches are also built up for such a purpose. Generally, they cannot provide emotive information in lexica and grammars. Or at least, they cannot provide information especially for emotive text processing.

Even for researches on emotive text, as far as known from our available literatures, at least for Chinese processing, most efforts have been made to researches on the emotion detecting methods such as keyword spotting, statistical approaches. However

J. Tao, T. Tan, and R.W. Picard (Eds.): ACII 2005, LNCS 3784, pp. 972–980, 2005.

researches from the more basic angle of view have been neglected. The result is: all the approaches perform quite well for long text, while they are in vain for processing short sentences. Researchers have started to resolve this problem for English text, for example by using an enormous enough commonsense knowledge base [5]. However, we haven't found similar work for Chinese from literatures.

So, no matter whatever we want to do, to detect emotion from text or to generate emotive text, the first thing we want to do is investigate a real emotive corpus.

This paper is to discover in Chinese spoken language, how do words and phrases that are correlated with emotions effect in a sentence? How do moods, negations, semantics of sentence elements influence the communicative emotive function of a sentence? How a human being expresses his subjective affections (including sentiments, attitude towards objects, and so on) through meaningful sentences?

This paper is structured as follows: section two briefly introduces some related theories and work. Section three presents the investigation results of the BTEC corpus. In the fourth section, the paper makes the conclusion.

2 Related Work

2.1 Emotion Models

Several emotion model have been proposed [2][11]. While OCC model (the acronym of Ortony, Clore, and Collins) has established itself as a standard computational emotion model for emotion detection and synthesis [7].

In OCC model, 22 emotion categories in three groups are specified based on the reactions of the agent to situations constructed either as being goal relevant events, as acts of an agent accountable, or as attractive or unattractive objects. The model also offers a structure of variables for emotional computation, such as the determination of the intensity of the emotion types.

The classification of emotions in OCC:

- Consequences of events: 1) positive: happy-for, gloating, hope, joy, satisfaction, relief; 2) negative: resentment, pity, fear, distress, fear-confirmed, disappointment;
- Actions of agents: 1) Positive: pride, admiration; 2) Negative : Shame, reproach;
- consequences of events & actions of agents: 1) Positive: gratification, gratitude; 2)Negative : remorse, anger;
- Aspects of objects: 1) Positive: like; 2) Negative: dislike.

Many studies employ OCC to generate emotions [1][8][10]. In 1996, Reilly W.S.N. produced an Em model. Em model is another computational model based on OCC, but it is more complicated and integrated. In this model, emotions are classified into 25 categories. Three other emotions are: frustration, startle, and other attitude-based emotions. The definition of each emotion is also slightly different from that of OCC; the Em model computes emotions mainly by measuring the fulfillment (or the possibility of the fulfillment) of the goal of an agent, and the importance of the goal to the agent [10].

Theory of Ortony forms the basis of our work. The classification of emotion keywords, as well as the emotional sentences, is based on the theory of Ortony, OCC model. The classification of emotions has been slightly modified according to the word usage status of the corpus. Categories *happy-for*, *joy*, and *gloating* have been merged, categories *satisfaction*, *gratification*, and *relief* have been merged, and distress and pity have been merged into one category. Moreover, *surprise*, and *tension* are added into the emotion list.

2.2 Emotional Word Classification

A classic work on measuring affective meaning in words is Osgood's Theory of Semantic Differentiation [9]. Their semantic differential technique is using several pairs of bipolar adjectives, such as active-passive; good-bad; optimistic-pessimistic; positive-negative; strong-weak; serious-humorous, to scale the responses of agents to words, short phrases, or texts.

Each pair of bipolar adjectives is a factor in the semantic differential technique. As a result, the differential technique can cope with quite a large number of aspects of affective meaning. About the importance of the factors, Osgood et al. [9] gave an surprising answer after extensive empirical tests that most of the variance in judgment could be explained by only three major factors of the affective meaning: the *evaluative* factor (e.g., good–bad); the *potency* factor (e.g., strong–weak); and the *activity* factor (e.g., active–passive). The evaluative factor is the most important. [4]

Kamps J. and Marx M. explores how the structure of the WordNet lexical database might be used to assess affective or emotive meaning, and construct measures based on Osgood's semantic differential technique[4]. The measures could be effective for emotion detecting in long text.

Tao J.H. provided a clear classification of vocabulary [12]. He divides vocabulary into content words and emotion functional words. It is easy to tell the meaning of the two categories as their name imply. The emotion functional words consist of three categories: Emotional keywords, Modifier words, and Metaphor words. Emotional keywords provide the basic emotion value of the input sentence (such as "生气/angry", "快乐/happy", "悲伤/sad"). He uses a reduced set of OCC for tagging emotional keyword. Modifier words are modifiers in the sentence, such as "非常/very", "太/too", etc. They are most probably used to enhance or weaken, or even change (e.g. negation) the emotion. The metaphor words normally have no direct action on the emotion states but do have the latent influence on them. They are further divided by Tao into two types: one is for spontaneous expressing; the others only denote personal character.

For detecting emotion in text, Tao J.H. proposes a unified architecture based on Emotion eStimation Net (ESiN) which seamlessly integrates context dependent probabilistic hierarchical sub-lexical modeling.

In our work, since our investigation is just a qualitative one, which does not involve quantitative analysis such as the intensity of emotions, the emotional keywords are classified into two categories: EmoWord is the emotion word, which directly express emotion; PotEmoWord refers to the potential emotion word, which does not directly express emotion, but potentially carry a positive or negative attitudes of the speaker. We can understand better by using analogies: EmoWords are similar to the emotional keywords defined by Tao; and PotEmoWords are something analogous with the Metaphor words defined by Tao barring the part which signifies the intensity of emotions.

3 Investigation of Emotional Sentences from BTEC

3.1 Overview of the Corpus

BTEC corpus of CSTAR (Consortium for Speech Translation Advanced Research, please refer to http://www.c-star.org/ for more information) is used for providing emotional sentences. 162,320 Chinese-English parallel spoken utterances are involved in the corpus. After preprocessing such as dividing the utterances into sentences, wiping off repeated pairs, segmenting, and annotating with POS, we have finally got about 130,000 Chinese sentences in total.

The BTEC corpus covers utterances and dialogues commonly used in 13 scenarios and domains, including: Restaurant, Airports, Emporium, Drinkery, Bank, Post office, Hospital, Personal services, Transportation, Travel, Hotel, Security and Others. The result of the investigation on the corpus may be influenced by the composition of the corpus, but it is still meaningful within these scenarios and domains.

Generally, sentences bearing emotions could be divided into two categories. The first category includes those sentences with obvious emotional keywords. The emotional keywords consist of EmoWords (e.g. "高兴/happy", "悲伤/sad"), and PotEmoWords (e.g. "贤明/sage", "愚蠢/stupid"). The second category includes those sentences which do not contain obvious emotional keywords, but through them people could still detect emotion delivery by deeply understanding the sentences. For example, "爷爷刚刚去世了/Grandpa has just passed away". Although no word in the sentence bears evident emotions, profound sadness could be detected based on the content and the commonsense that the speaker loves his (or her) grandpa. Sometimes, domain correlated information is also required for emotion detecting. It is not practical for us to handle the second category for the moment, since we lack of commonsense and domain information. This paper tackles the first category of emotional sentences which contains emotional keywords.

The strategy for extracting emotional sentences from BTEC is "two-time filtering".

The first time, a word list coming from the *Chinese thesaurus* [6] is used as the "base" for sentences extracting. The word list contains EmoWord categories and some of the PotEmoWords. About 8000 sentences are drawn out after this filtration.

For fear that some emotional sentences are missed due to the incompletion of the word list, a second time extraction is conducted to extract sentences belonging to the first category that do not consist of distinct emotion words. We assume a supposition that sentences bearing emotions tend to express themselves with exaggerated degree adverbs (e.g. "很/very", "太/too"). So a degree adverbs list is used to "pick out" those words missed in the first step. After this filtration, about 5800 sentences are extracted. Finally we obtain 13849 "emotional" sentences. Considering there are mis-extractions, and redundancies in that we have got the Chinese corpus from bilingual resources and one Chinese sentence may correspond to several English sentences, we remove the redundancy, and got 6683 sentences. These sentences make up of the basic corpus for our emotional investigation. The emotional corpus involves 5433 words.

3.2 Investigation of Emotional Sentences

In this sub-section, firstly, the investigation results of the emotional sentences are presented. Secondly, the influence of moods is given. Thirdly, the influence of domains to the composition of emotions is presented.

Statistical Results of Emotional Sentences

The POS constitution of emotional keywords (including emotion words and potential emotion words) is as table 1. In the 683 keywords, 197 are EmoWords and 486 are PotEmoWords.

Table 1. POS composition of emotional keywords

POS	nouns	adjectives	verbs	adverbs	total keywords
Number of words / frequency	123 / 344	365 / 5864	185 / 2864	10 / 48	683 / 9120
Percent (%)	18.0 / 3.8	53.4 / 64.3	27.1 / 31.4	1.5 / 0.5	100 / 100

From table 1, we can see the main three categories for emotion expression is adjective, verb, and noun. The adjectives are the premier portion, which take more than half of the emotional keywords, while verb takes the second important position. Averagely, per sentence includes *1.36* emotional keywords.

For sentences that contain EmoWords, totally 2881 sentences are detected.

Table 2. Composition of sentences with emotion words

Emotion of keywords	number of sentences	Emotion of keywords	number of sentences
admiration	19	disappoint	19
reproach	6	frustrate	25
gratitude	167	fear	197
anger	24	hope	327
happy-for/joy/gloating	498	pride	17
distress/pity	97	shame	166
like	1058	surprise	86
dislike	44	tension	54
faction/gratification/relief	87		

And totally 3802 sentences are extracted which contains the 486 PotEmoWords.

Some Analysis

Sentence could be viewed as a tool that express specific meanings, perform specific functions or achieve specific goals of the speaker. The real emotive meanings and the communicative functions of the sentences above are unlikely to be accordant with the keywords in the sentences. This paper gives some other factors that influence the emotive meaning of sentences. They are: 1) the moods of the sentences; 2) domain classification.

Before analysis, to differentiate the emotional function of a sentence from the literal meaning of the sentence, it is necessary to explicitly enounce the factors for the function of emotional communication:

- EmoKeywd: the emotion borne by the emotion keyword;
- EmoAgent: the person who generate the emotion;
- EmoObject: the object that arouse the emotion. It could be a thing, a person, an event, or anything. It could be empty if the sentence is just a description of the emotion state of the agent;
- EmoReason: the reason why the agent has the emotion;
- EmoPurSpeaker: the purpose for the speaker to speak the emotive sentence.

With these factors, we could perform the emotional analysis without being affected by other factors such as the syntactic structure of a sentence.

(1) Influence of Mood

Different mood of a sentence has influence on the emotional function of a sentence. The paper notifies different cases, and exemplifies them with some typical sentences.

a) *Imperative* mood is commonly accompanied by an expectation of emotion transition. Phenomena occur in the corpus could be divided into the following two cases.

If the EmoAgent is the interlocutor, the EmoPurSpeaker is to request the interlocutor to change his emotion to EmoKeywd, or not to EmoKeywd (if there is a negation), e.g.

1) 不要骄傲/don't be proud;
2) 放松你自己/relax yourself!.

If the EmoAgent is the speaker himself, the EmoPurSpeaker is to request the interlocutor (to do something) to meet the speaker's demand of changing emotion state, e.g.

1) 请不要让我失望/Please don't let me down.
2) 请给我一个满意的理由/ Please give me a gratifying excuse.

A third possibility is blessing sentences, which normally express the hope of the speaker that wish the interlocutor to be in a good status, e.g.

1) 圣诞快乐！ Merry Christmas!
2) 祝你度过美好的一天！ / Have a nice day!
3) 祝你<旅途/飞行>愉快！ / Wish you have a nice <trip/flight>!

b) The emotional function of *interrogative* sentences is to enquire the emotion factors. Examples of enquiring for the attitude of the EmoAgent to an object:

1) 杰克遇见你很高兴，不是吗?/ Jack was very happy to meet you, wasn't he?
2) 喜欢棒球吗?/ Do you like baseball?
3) 旅行令人愉快吗?/ Was the trip enjoyable?

Enquiring for the emotion state of the EmoAgent:

你高兴吗? / Are you glad?

Enquiring for the EmoObject:

1) 你喜欢吃哪个，苹果还是橙子? / Which one do you like to eat, apple or orange?
2) 应该怪谁? / Who should be blamed?

Enquiring for the EmoReason:

你为什么那么生气? / Why do you get so angry?

Table 3. Distribution of emotional words in different domain

Domain	Sentences number	Nouns Number/freq	adjectives Number/freq	verbs Number/freq
Restaurant	451	5 / 5	45 / 480	21 / 177
Airlines	364	17 / 22	54 / 387	23 / 132
Emporium	553	9 / 16	58 / 404	20 / 292
Drinkery	107	0 / 0	34 / 78	16 / 57
Bank	15	0 / 0	8 / 13	5 / 5
Post office	14	0 / 0	4 / 11	4 / 4
Hospital	799	20 / 56	64 / 940	39 / 96
Personal services	60	1 / 2	12 / 41	8 / 30
Transportation	259	8 / 11	43 / 329	21 / 105
Travel	965	23 / 33	106 / 677	60 / 473
Hotel	390	9 / 14	50 / 337	30 / 177
Security	161	11	143	64
Others	2545	66 / 174	241 / 2023	111 / 1252

And the distribution of EmoWord in some domains is shown in Table 4. We just select the top three categories in each domain.

Table 4. Distribution of EmoWord in some domains

Domain	Emotion of EmoWords	Percent (%)	Total frequency of EmoWord
Restaurant	Shame, satisfaction, like	81.3	283
Airlines	Happy, hope, like	64.3	235
Emporium	Like, shame, hope	93.4	372
Drinkery	Like, happy-for, hope	71.9	64
Hospital	Distress, fear, distress	54.9	91
Transport	Distress, happy-for, like	73.3	217
Travel	Like, happy-for, shame	62.9	536
Hotel	Remorse, happy-for, like	74.7	261
Security	Remorse, tension, surpri	68.4	117

Enquiring for other information:

你找到你喜欢的了吗? / Have you found what do you like?

c) *Exclamatory* mood is relatively safer to detect the attitude of the speaker directly from the EmoKeywd. E.g.

多么美妙的音乐片啊！ / What a wonderful music film!
太吓人了！ / How terrible it is!

(2) Influence of Domain
The distribution of emotional words in different domain is given in Table 3.

From Table 4, we can see that all the analyzed domains are concentrated on specific emotion dimensions, which could show the characteristics of the domains.

4 Conclusion

This paper briefly presents our primary work on emotional analysis of spoken sentences. The classification of emotion and potential emotion words are discussed. The main contribution of the paper is that it opens out the composition of an emotion spoken corpus to researchers in forms of statistical data which shows an overview of the corpus, statistical data, and enumerative examples which describe the composition of the corpus in more details. The results discover the relation between the emotion word categories and some syntactic features of sentences, and the emotional communicative functions of sentences. An emotive feature set is brought forward for computable analysis of the sentences. The feature set is quite simple and primary. But it provides an important idea of representing the emotional function of a sentence in a new level other than the syntactic level or semantic level. This will be significant for building up the computable emotion model, as well as for easily analyzing the relation between structures of different level of representations, the latter of which is really important for emotion detection or generation of short sentences.

5 Acknowledgements

The research work described in this paper has been supported by the natural science foundation of China under the grant number 60375018 and 60121302, the PRA project (No. SI02-05) of the Ministry of Science and Technology of China, and also the Outstanding Overseas Chinese Scholars Fund of the Chinese Academy of Sciences (No. 2003-1-1).

References

1. Bartneck C.: Integrating the OCC Model of Emotions in Embodied Characters. Workshop on Virtual Conversational Characters: Applications, Methods, and Research Challenges. Melbourne (2002)
2. Elliott, C.: The Affective Reasoner: A Process Model of Emotions in a Multi-agent System. PhD thesis, Northwestern University, The Institute for the Learning Sciences, Technical Report No. 32. (1992)

3. Gratch J., Marsella S.: Technical Details of a Domain-independent Framework for Modeling Emotion. Technical Report ICT-TR, University of Southern California, Los Angeles, CA (2004)
4. Kamps J., Marx M.: Words with Attitude. BNAIC, Groningen (2002)
5. Liu H., Lieberman H., Selker T.: A Model of Textual Affect Sensing using Real-World Knowledge. Proceedings of the ACM International Conference on Intelligent User Interfaces, Miami, USA (2003) 125-132
6. Mei J., Zhu Y., et al: Chinese Thesaurus. Shanghai Lexicographical Publishing House (1983)
7. Ortony A., Clore G. L., and Collins A.: The Cognitive Structure of Emotions. Cambridge University Press (1988)
8. Ortony A.: On making believable emotional agents believable. in Trapple, R. P. ed.: Emotions in humans and artifacts, MIT Press, Cambridge, USA (2003)
9. Osgood, Succi G., and Tannenbaum P.: The Measurement of Meaning. University of Illinois Press, Urbana IL (1957)
10. Reilly W.S.N.: Believable Social and Emotional Agents. PhD thesis, CMU USA (1996)
11. Sloman, A.: Motives, mechanisms and emotions. Cognition and Emotion, 1 (1987) 217-234
12. Tao J.H.: Context Based Emotion Detection from Text Input. ICSLP Jeju Island, Korea (2004) 1337-1340

Affective Computing: A Review

Jianhua Tao and Tieniu Tan

National Laboratory of Pattern Recognition (NLPR), Institute of Automation, Chinese Academy of Sciences, P.O.X. 2728, Beijing 100080
{jhtao, tnt}@nlpr.ia.ac.cn

Abstract. Affective computing is currently one of the most active research topics, furthermore, having increasingly intensive attention. This strong interest is driven by a wide spectrum of promising applications in many areas such as virtual reality, smart surveillance, perceptual interface, etc. Affective computing concerns multidisciplinary knowledge background such as psychology, cognitive, physiology and computer sciences. The paper is emphasized on the several issues involved implicitly in the whole interactive feedback loop. Various methods for each issue are discussed in order to examine the state of the art. Finally, some research challenges and future directions are also discussed.

1 Introduction

Affective computing is trying to assign computers the human-like capabilities of observation, interpretation and generation of affect features. It is an important topic for the harmonious human-computer interaction, by increasing the quality of human-computer communication and improving the intelligence of the computer.

The research on affect or emotion can be traced from nowadays to 19 century [2]. Traditionally, "affect" was seldom linked to lifeless machines, and was normally studied by psychologists. It is quite new in the recent years that the affect features were captured and processed by the computer. The affective computing builds an "affect model" based on the various sensors-captured information, and builds a personalized computing system with the capability of perception, interpretation to human's feeling as well as giving us intelligent, sensitive and friendly responses.

To get the impression of state of art of the research in affective computing, the paper briefly summaries some key technologies for the research during last several years, such as emotional speech processing, facial expression, body gesture and movement, multimodal system, affect understanding and generating, etc. A brief discussion will also be made in each topic. Furthermore, the paper also introduces some related projects in the world, which gives the clearer impression on the current/past research work and applications. Based on above summary and analysis, the paper discussed some hot research topics which might be a big challenge to improve the current research work.

The paper is organized as follows. Section 2 describes the recent development of the related key technologies. Section 3 describes some related projects in this area. Section 4 summaries the hot research topics. The final conclusion of the paper will be made in section 5.

J. Tao, T. Tan, and R.W. Picard (Eds.): ACII 2005, LNCS 3784, pp. 981–995, 2005.

2 State of Art of Key Technologies

The standard procedure of affective interaction consists of affect information capture and modeling, affect understanding and expression etc. As we know, people express the affects through a series of action on facial expression, body movements, various gestures, voice behavior, and other physiological signals, such as heart rate and sweat, etc. The following parts will try to review the most active key technologies in these area, such emotional speech processing, facial expression recognition and generating, body gesture and movement, multimodal system, affect understanding and generating, etc.

2.1 Emotional Speech Processing

For emotional speech processing, it is a widely known fact that the emotional speech differs with respect to the acoustic features[43]. Some prosody features, such as pitch variables (F0 level, range, contour and jitter), speaking rate have been analyzed by some researchers [46]. Parameters describing laryngal processes on voice quality were also taken into account in someone's work [42]. Tato [48] made some experiments which showed how "quality features" are used in addition to "prosody features.

The above acoustic features are widely used for the research of emotion recognition with the pattern recognition methods. For instance, Dellaert [45] used prosody features and compared three classifiers: the maximum likelihood Bayes classification, kernel regression, and k-nearest neighbor in emotion recognition for sadness, anger, happiness and fear. Petrushin [46] used vocal parameters and a computer agent for emotion recognition. Lee [47] used liear discriminant classification with Gaussian class-conditional probability distribution and k-nearest neighborhood methods to classify utterances into two basic emotion states, negative and non-negative. Yu [49] used SVMs for emotion detection. A average accuracy of 73% was reported. Nick [40] proposed a perception model of affective speech utterances and shown that there are consistent differences in the acoustic features of same-word utterances that are perceived as having different discourse effects or displaying different affective states. The work proposed that rather than selecting one label to describe each utterance, a vector of activations across a range of features may be more appropriate.

For emotion generating with speech synthesis, Mozziconacci [7] added emotion control parameters on the basis of tune methods resulting in higher performance power of voice composing. Cahn [8], by means of a visualized acoustic parameters editor, achieved the output of emotional speech with manual inferences. Recently, some efforts have been down with the idea of the large corpus. A typical system was finished by Campbell [50], who created an expressive speech synthesis with a five years' large corpus and gave us an impressive synthesis results. Schroeder[51], Eide[44] generated a expressive TTS engine which can be directed, via an extended SSML, to use a variety of expressive styles with about ten hours of "neutral" sentences. Optionally, rules translating certain expressive elements to ToBI markup are manually derived. Chuang[52] and Tao[11] used emotional keywords and emotion trigger words to generate the emotional TTS system. The final emotion state is determined based on the emotion outputs from textual content module.

The results were especially used in the dialogue systems to improve the naturalness/expressiveness of the answering speech.

Till now, most of the researches on emotional speech are still focused on some typical acoustic features analysis in different languages. Some work in emotion classification systems and rule based emotional speech synthesis systems have been done [18], however, the lack on the capture and the analysis of more detailed/reliable physiological features limits the further improvement of the research. The people express the feeling not only by the acoustic features, but also with the content they want to say. Different words, phrases and syntactic structures, etc. can make lots kinds of expression results and styles. Though, some language cognition has been done by some psychologist before [29], lots of work is still needed for the integration of these two research topics.

2.2 Facial Expression

Facial expressions and movements such as a smile or a nod are used either to fulfill a semantic function, to communicate emotions, or as conversational cues. Similar as speech processing, the research of facial expression consists of works on coding, recognition and generation, and have been done for a very long history. For instance, Etcoff [9] parameterized the structure of the chief parts of human's face through 37 lines, which enables people to roughly tell the affect status of faces; Ekman [39] built facial action coding system. They classified human's facial expressions into many action units. With this method, he described facial expressions with six basic emotions, joy, anger, surprise, disgust, fear and sadness. Currently, most of the facial features can be found from the definition of MPEG-4. MPEG-4 allows the user to configure and build systems for many applications by allowing flexibility in the system configurations, by providing various levels of interactivity with audio-visual content [29][30]. In this standard, both mesh model [33] or muscle model are used to create 3-D facial models .

To do the facial expression analysis, most of the facial features were captured by the optical flow or active appearance model. Lyons [54] applied the supervised Fisher linear discriminant analysis(FDA) to learn an adequate linear subspace from class-specified training samples and the samples projected to this subspace can be best separated. Principal component analysis (PCA) [20] and independent component analysis (ICA) [25] have been used to for the expression classification. For facial expression recognition, there are many other methods, such as, Gabor wavelets [54], neural network [53], Hidden Markov Models (HMM) [30], Point Distribute Model (PDM), optical flow, geometrical tracking method, EGM method and so on. Among them, the Gabor representation has been favored by many researchers due to its good performance and not sensitive to the face posture and the lighting background. [54].

The pioneering work on facial animation was done by Frederic I. Parke in the 1970s. In the last decade the quality of facial animations has improved remarkably due to the development of hardware and corresponding software. But in these days, the generating of lifelike animated faces still remains an open issue. Many researchers used methods based on images [34][36], visemes[37], FAPs[43], PCs[31][32], 3D coordinates[37], 3D distance measurements [30][31] or optical flows[38] to generate facial expression. Normally, the face expression should be synchronized with speech when people express their ideas or feeling, it shows the audio-visual mapping is the key component to generate a vivid talking head system. There are mainly two approaches for the synthesis: via speech recognition or driven by speech directly. The first approach divides speech signal into language units such as phonemes, syllables, words, then maps the units directly to the lip shapes and concatenates them. Yamamoto E.[30] recognized phonemes through training HMM, and mapped them directly to corresponding lip shapes, through smoothing algorithm, the lip movement sequence is obtained. The second approach analyzes the bimodal data through statistical learning model, and finds out the mapping between the continuous acoustic features and facial control parameters, so as to drive the face animation directly by a novel speech. Massaro [29] trained ANN to learn the mapping from LPCs to face animation parameters, they used current frame, 5 backward and 5 forward time step as the input to model the context. Many other methods have also been tried, such as, TDNN[29], MLPs[32], KNN[31], HMM[30], GMM, VQ[30], Rule-based [37][38].

Recently, a new approach for audio-visual mapping has arisen [36], which is inspired from speech synthesis [35]. This method means to construct new data stream by concatenating stored data units in training database. It has advantage of that the synthesis result appears very natural and realistic. But even for that, the lip movement is still the focus in most of the research. Full facial expression, especially the correlation between facial expression and more acoustic features, such as prosody, timbre, etc. has seldom been touched. It needs more work in processing the features which we ignored before.

2.3 Body Gesture and Movement

Body gesture and movement is defined by the positions of body arthroses and their changes with time. Currently, the work for gesture processing is more focused on the hand tracking. Hand gestures can convery various and diverse meanings, to enhance the mood or to behave as a sign language. Traditionally, there are two methods, apparentness methods [15] and 3-D modeling methods [17]. The apparentness based method makes out the model by analyzing apparent features of hand gestures from 2-D images, while the 3-D methods do the tracking in real 3D environment. Compared to 3-D methods, the apparentness methods are less complicated, and more easy to be used in real-time computation, however more efforts should be done to adapt the method into high noise background and the real application. Some efforts have been done to adopt mixed modeling methods and describe the features of static hand gesture with multiple features (such as local profile features and overall image matrix features) [16]. It shows the higher and more robust tracking results.

In order to realize body gesture and movement based from image sequences, the key point is how to confirm the positions of body arthroses according to given image information. The existing methods normally require some limitation [17], such as, (a) different dress colours according to different body arthroses; (b) simple moving directions; (c) simple backgrounds; (d) some manual initial markings. With these methods, the profile of the target body is picked up at first, and then virtual framework that is similar to real body framework is taken out through energy function. After that, arthroses positions are determined based on the virtual framework by using anthropotomy knowledge. The energy function can restrain some background noises, and has low requirement for the preciseness of the fetched body profile. In addition, some people enable the computers to more accurately capture data of face and body's rapid movement by some auxiliary equipment like electromagnetic inductor [14] and optical reflection signs [13]. Till now, the work is still a difficult subject in computer vision's area, especially in real application. Concerning the capture of body gesture and movement, in addition to further improvement of the capture accuracy and efficiency of parameters, how to obtain more robust and subtle body-language is still an urgent difficult problem for affective computing.

2.4 Multimodal System

As we can imagine, the direct human to human interaction is, by definition, multimodal interaction in which participants encounter a steady stream of meaningful facial expressions, gestures, body postures, head movements, words, grammatical constructions, and prosodic contours. Multimodal systems are convinced by most of the researchers to improve the results of affect recognition/understand and to generate more vivid expressions in human computer interaction [10][12]. Multimodal systems are able to meet the stringent performance requirements imposed by various applications [10]. Such as, in biometrics recognition systems, Brunelli et al. [55] describe a multimodal biometric system that uses the face and voice traits of an individual for identification. Their system combines the matching scores of five different matchers operating on the voice and face features, to generate a single matching score that is used for identification. Bigun et al. [56]develop a statistical framework based on Bayesian statistics to integrate information presented by the speech (text-dependent) and face data of a user. Kumar et al. [57] combined hand geometry and palmprint biometrics in a verification system. A commercial product called BioID [58] uses voice, lip motion and face features of a user to verify identity. Jain and Ross [59] improved the performance of a multimodal system by learning user-specific parameters. General strategies for combining multiple classifiers have been suggested in [60] and [61]. There is a large amount of literature available on the various combination strategies for fusing multiple modalities using the matching scores (see for example [62]).

In human computer interaction applications, it has been widely used for smart room, virtual reality, etc. Among them, the ubiquitous computing [65] might be the most representative application of this technology, which encompasses a wide range of research topics, including distributed computing, mobile computing, sensor networks, human-computer interaction, and artificial intelligence.

The multimodal technology is just arisen in recent years, most existing system are lack of efficient method to integrate the different channels, the synchronized control modeling for multi-channel information processing are still not well solved. More work should be done in the parameters integrations.

2.5 Affect Understanding and Cognition

The affective understanding module is the next in logical sequence after the recognition module. The affective understanding may contain the functions by absorbing information, remembering the information, modeling the user's current mood, modeling the user's emotional life, applying the user affect model, updating the user affect model, building and maintaining a user-editable taxonomy of user preferences, featuring two-way communication with the system's recognition module, eventually building and maintaining a more complete model of the user's behavior, eventually modeling the user's context, providing a basis for the generation of synthetic system affect, ensure confidentiality and security. [63]

The OCC model [41] might be one of the most successful models from all of the work. It classifies the people's emotions as a result of events, objects and other agents under three categories. People are happy or unhappy with an event, like or dislike an object, approve or disapprove an agent. There are 22 detailed emotions under the three emotion categories. Though the OCC model provides three groups of emotions depending on reactions to external things, it is really hard to do that in real environments, where we get more complicated reactions. Sometimes, some reactions may involve all of the emotions in the three categories. For example, when people see their neighbors beat the child, they may feel distressed and do not wish such an event (beating the child) to happen, and feel it a pity that the child is beaten. They may also reproach their neighbors for violating the human rights and contempt them for beating their child. Finally, they may start to hate their neighbor because of the event. From this process, we can see that people often experience more than one emotion because of complex external environments, instead of just one single emotion state. Therefore, it is difficult for us to understand the emotional experience of sadness and happiness mixed together and surprised happiness.

Affects are closely related to cognition. Psychologists have always been exploring this issue for a long time. In recent years the researchers from computer sciences also hope to verify the relations between affects and cognition through various experiments, for instance, the emotion group of Geneva university designed a set of computer games dealing with questions and answers. Experiment participants experience emotional changes as playing the games. Their facial expressions and sounds emitted during the game are collected as samples to be analyzed. This kind of games triggers emotions that can be used to help researchers study and explore the interaction of emotion triggering and cognition levels. Similar experiments were also conducted by UIUC in their multimodal interaction system.

Though the experiment designs and small samples are preliminary, the experiment shows that the close relation between emotions and cognition are being more valued by emotion researchers. From the preliminary theoretical framework to the current preliminary experiment, human beings are gradually revealing the secrets of their complex brains. With this progress, we are able to go deep into our brains, better control emotions triggered by brains, avoid the damaging behaviors brought about by passive and negative emotions, help mentally and psychologically ill patients overcome emotional shadows and make our psychological world more beautiful.

3 Projects

Although the affective computing is a new concept in recent years, there are already some related projects. We cannot list all of them, but only summarizing some of them according to author's experiences. They are described in the following.

3.1 HUMAINE (EU Project)

HUMAINE (Human-Machine Interaction Network on Emotion) is a Network of Excellence in the EU's Sixth Framework Programme. The project aims to lay the foundations for European development of systems that can register, model and/or influence human emotional and emotion-related states and processes - 'emotion-oriented systems'. Such systems may be central to future interfaces, but their conceptual underpinnings are not sufficiently advanced to be sure of their real potential or the best way to develop them. One of the reasons is that relevant knowledge is dispersed across many disciplines. HUMAINE brings together lots of experts from the key disciplines in a programme designed to achieve intellectual integration. It identifies six thematic areas that cut across traditional groupings and offer a framework for an appropriate division - theory of emotion; signal/sign interfaces; the structure of emotionally coloured interactions; emotion in cognition and action; emotion in communication and persuasion; and usability of emotion-oriented systems. [21]

3.2 Affective-Cognitive Framework for Learning and Decision-Making (MIT Affective Computing Research Group)

The project aims to redress many of the classic problems, that most machine learning and decision-making models, however, are based on old, purely cognitive models, and are slow, brittle, and awkward to adapt, by developing new models that integrate affect with cognition. Ultimately, such improvements will allow machines to make smart and more human-like decisions for better human-machine interactions. [22]

3.3 Oz Project (CMU)

Oz is a computer system that allows authors to create and present interactive dramas. The architecture of the project includes a simulated physical world, several characters, an interactor, a theory of presentation, and a drama manager. A model of each character's body and of the interactor's body are in the physical world. Outside the physical world, a model of mind controls each character's actions. The interactor's actions are controlled by the interactor. Sensory information is passed from the physical world to the interactor through an interface controlled by a theory of presentation. In the project framework, the drama manager influences the characters' minds, the physical world, and the presentation theory. [23]

3.4 Emotion, Stress and Coping in Families with Adolescents: Assessing Personality Factors and Situational Aspects in an Experimental Computer Game (Geneva Emotion Research Group)

The project studies behavioral coping strategies developed by adolescents to face different types of stressful situations, with a specific focus on coping functionality, and complements coping research using questionnaires by controlled studies in the laboratory. Combining intra- and the inter-individual approaches to coping such that both situational and personality variables can be measured. Therefore, coping is studied in an intra-individual setting (one person confronted to different types of situations, at different moments in time), nested within an inter-individual setting (several individuals are compared with regard to their individual coping across different situations). [24]

3.5 The Cognition and Affect Project (University of Birmingham)

The main goal of this project is to understand the types of architectures that are capable of accounting for the whole range of human (and non-human) mental states and processes, including not only intelligent capabilities, such as the ability to learn to find your way in an unfamiliar town and the ability to think about infinite sets, but also moods, emotions, desires, and the like. For instance, they have investigated whether the ability to have emotional states is an accident of animal evolution or an inevitable consequence of design requirements and constraints, for instance in resource-limited intelligent robots. [25]

3.6 BlueEyes (IBM)

The project aims at creating computational devices with the sort of perceptual abilities that people take for granted. BlueEyes uses sensing technology to identify a user's actions and to extract key information. This information is then analyzed to determine the user's physical, emotional, or informational state, which in turn can be used to help make the user more productive by performing expected actions or by providing expected information. For example, a BlueEyes-enabled television could become active when the user makes eye contact, at which point the user could then tell the television to "turn on". [26]

3.7 People and Robot (CMU)

The project is directed at three little-understood aspects of service robots in society: the design and behavior of service robots; the ways that humans and robots interact; how service robots function as members of a work team. The initial domain for this work is elder communities and hospitals, where service robots can do useful but taxing tasks. The research aims at the design of appropriate appearance and interactions of service robots in these contexts. [27]

3.8 Affect Sensitive Human-Robot Collaboration (Vanderbilt University)

The projects involves developing a novel affect-sensitive architecture for human-robot cooperation, where the robot is expected to recognize human psychological states (for instance-stress, panic, fear, engagement in task at hand). This technique involves real-time monitoring of physiological signals of a human subject using wearable sensors. These may include his/her heart rate variability, brainwaves, skin conductance, respiration, muscle tension, blood pressure and temperature. The signals are analyzed in n real-time to infer the emotional states of the human interacting with the robot. The robot controller considers the psychological state in its feedback loop to decide on a course of action. The work exploits recent advances in control theory, signal processing, pattern recognition, and experimental psychology. [28]

3.9 Expressive Visual Speech Synthesis (NLPR, Institute of Automation, Chinese Academy of Sciences)

The project aims to enhance multimodal interfaces by adapting them to users' intentions and behaviours. For this, high-level characteristics of voices and faces are defined that describe a person's expressiveness, as induced by the communicative intention, the current speaker state, the environmental condition, the relationship with his/her interlocutor(s), as well as by the person's identity, as circumscribed by gender, personality characteristics, age, language, and cultural membership. The project aims to make scientific breakthroughs by generating a multiplicity of voices and faces by extracting the features from speech, facial images and videos. The project will render man-machine communication more effective and natural by adding personality and expressiveness to the pure linguistic content that is currently generated by synthetic voices and talking heads, and by reacting to the intention and behaviour of the user.

4 Research Challenges

On the basis of perception, analysis, and modeling of affective features information such as speech and body language. The interrelation among research contents is illustrated in the following sketch:

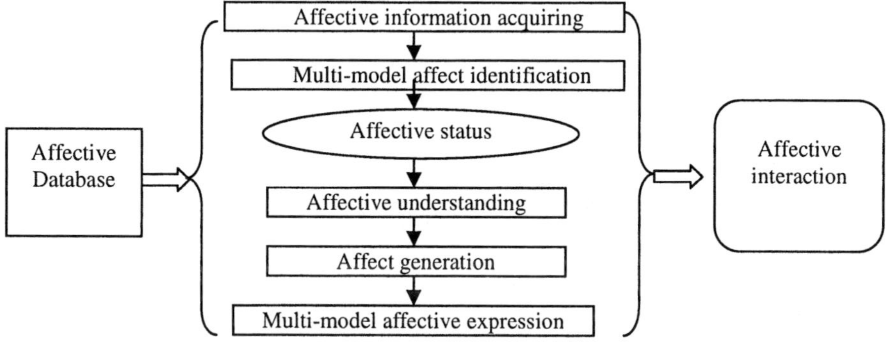

Fig. 1. Research framework

With the analysis above, some challenging research topics might be collected here.

4.1 Affective Understanding and Adaptation

Existing models of emotion use highly stylized stereotypes of personality types and emotional responsiveness, which do not correspond to real behavior in real people. There are lots of arguments in how to define the emotions. Someone might think it is not possible to model affect, and no way for affective understanding. This question has been discussed by Picard in her paper [63]. We know, "with any complex modelling problem, there are ways to handle complexity and contribute to progress in understanding. If we want to model affect at the neuropeptide signalling level, then we are limited indeed, because we know only a small part about how such molecules communicate among the organs in our body and realtime sensing of local molecular activity is not easily accomplished. "[63]

With the affect model, the ultimate purpose of affective computing is to assist the computer properly react after it understands the user's affect and meaning, and then be accustomed to the changes of the user's affect. Currently, there are some work use the man-aided method to evaluate the user's feeling. It is still an important issue on how to analyze the dynamic characteristics of the user's affect and how to make the computer react properly according to the identification result of affective information. Affect is closed associated with personalities, environment, and cultural background, precise affect understanding model can only be realized by combining all these information. Psychological research results indicate that affect could be extended from the past affect states. Moreover, the lack of dynamic affect information mechanism is another important factor restricting current affect models. Therefore, how to define and integrate these information, how to describe/inegrate the dynamic affect information and how to improve the adaptation algorithm to natural scenarios should be the emphasis in the future research. It helps to build a personalized affective interaction system, by specifying the personal information and environment in real application.

4.2 Multi-model Based Affective Information Processing

As analysis in 2.4, the lack of the coordination mechanism of affective parameters under multi-model condition quite limits the affective understanding and the affect prompts. The amalgamation of different channels is not just the combination of them, but to find the mutual relations among all channel information. The mutual relation could make better integration of the different channels during interaction phases for both recognition/understanding and information generation. Figure 2 shows common affective status identification flow.

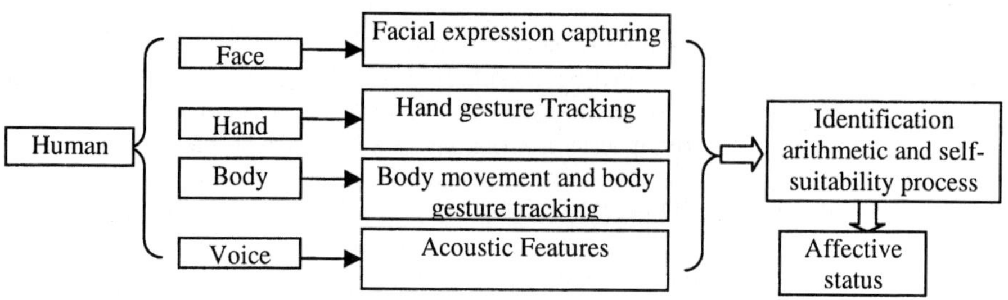

Fig. 2. Multi-model based affective recognition

4.3 Affective Feature Capturing in Real Environments

Most of current affective feature capturing is still limited in labs or studios, which are less complicated and have smaller background noises. The currently available information can only be used in information retrieval and common feature identification, which is too rough to make affective computing for complicated affect changes. Apart from developing high-quality affective interaction, we should emphasize on establishing automatic affective information capture from real environment and getting more reliable and detailed features, especially, for particular facial features' tracking and description, robust hand/body gesture tracking and modeling, more physiological acoustic parameters capture and modeling.

4.4 Affective Interaction in Multi-agent System

The study of agent based systems evolved from the field of Distributed Artificial Intelligence in the early to mid 1980's, with the development of intelligent Multi-Agent systems being given new impetus by the emergence of the World Wide Web and the Internet. Solving the problems associated with, and taking advantage of the opportunities offered by, this inherently distributed and unstructured environment are seen as major application areas for intelligent and Multi-Agent systems. Traditional affective interaction is just based on the single human computer interaction procedures. It is really a challenge work on how to make affective interaction in multi-agent system. In contrast to classical applications in artificial intelligence, the central ideas underlying multi-agent based affective interaction are that:

- the affect of one agent could be influenced by the other agents.
- the system exhibits goal directed behavior
- one agent can interact with and negotiate with other agents (possibly human) in order to achieve their goals
- the whole system can apply intelligence in the way they react to a dynamic and unpredictable environment.

Apart from the implementation of practical and useful systems another main goal in the study of Multi-Agent based affective interaction systems are to understand interaction among intelligent entities whether they are computational, human or both.

4.5 Affective Database

The shortage of affective database is one of the reasons why current study of affective computing is confined. Establishing a database storing a numerous number of affective data, especially multi-model affective data, is necessary to affective computing, and is also prerequisite for deeply studying affect mechanism. Some existing corpus consists of expressive speech [64], facial expression in videos [34][36][37][38], statistic 2D or 3D facial images [31][32], and motion capture data [30][43], etc. Nearly all of them are used for specific research, such as, emotion recognition, facial animation, etc. Due to lack of more detailed cognition experiments, the current database is hard to be used for the research of affective understanding. Further research should be involved in design, collection, marking, search, tool making, and other relative works related to multi-model affective data.

5 Conclusion

Though the concept of affective computing has come out not for a long time, it attracts high and extensive attention from academy and enterprise fields. The study and application of relevant fields are booming. To sum up, the existing researches are mainly limited in the detailed and scattered fields like voice and body language. Because of the lack of large affect data resources, no effective mechanism for multi feature affective computing and relevant learning and controlling algorithms and the insufficiency of adaptation to natural scenarios, computers can not accurately judge and generate a human-like affect status and have real effective affect interaction. As a whole, various theoretical problems concerning affective computing are not well solved. Even for that, there are still some applications, for instances, adding the function of automatic perception to people's mood in information household appliances and intelligent instruments to provide better services to people; making use of the function of affect concept analysis in computer retrieval system to improve the accuracy and efficiency of information retrieval; adding affect factors in the remote education platform may intensify the education effects; utilizing multi-model affect interaction technology in virtual reality application may build intelligent space and virtual scenario closer to real life etc. In addition, affect calculation may also be applied in the related industries like digital entertainment, robots and intelligent toys to realize more personalitive style and build more vivid scenario.

In recent years, the ubiquitous computing and wearable computing, which are closely related to affective computing, have achieved the pervasive attention of scientists. Ubiquitous computing and wearable computing are the necessary products of the combination of mobile computing technology and computer individualization. Concerning design, the computing technology becomes a part of our daily life and is closely tied with computer users. All these bring great conveniences to the real time capture of affect information as well as provide a perfect platform for affective computing. By means of the organic integration with affective computing, a colorful world of computing technology will be built.

References

[1] R.W. Picard, Affective computing. MIT Press, 1997.

[2] W. James, What is emotion? , Mind 9, 188-205, 1884.

[3] A. R. Damasio, Descartes, Error : Emotion, Reason, and the Human Brain, New York, NY: Gosset/Putnam Press, 1994.

[4] P. Ekman, Basic Emotions. Handbook of Cognition and Emotion. New York: John Wiley, 1999.

[5] H. Schlossberg, Three dimensions of emotion, Psychological review, 61, 81-88, 1954.

[6] C.E. Osgood,G.J. Suci,P.H. Tannenbaum, (eds.), The measurements of meaning, University of Illinois Press, 1957.

[7] Sylvie J.L. Mozziconacci and Dik J. Hermes, Expression of emotion and attitude through temporal speech variations, ICSLP2000, Beijing, 2000.

[8] J.E. Cahn, The generation of affect in synthesized speech, Journal of the American Voice I/O Society, vol. 8, July 1990.

[9] N.L. Etcoff, J.J. Magee, Categorical perception of facial expressions, Cognition, 44, 227-240, 1992.

[10] A.Camurri, G.De Poli, M.Leman, G.Volpe, A Multi-layered Conceptual Framework for Expressive Gesture Applications, Proc. Intl MOSART Workshop, Barcelona, Nov. 2001

[11] Jianhua Tao, Emotion Control of Chinese Speech Synthesis in Natural Environment. Eurospeech2003, Geneva, Sep.2003

[12] R. Cowie., Emotion recognition in human-computer interaction. IEEE Signal Processing Magazine, 18(1):32-80, 2001.

[13] A.Azarbayejani, etc., Real-Time 3-D Tracking of the Human Body, IMAGE'COM 96, Bordeaux, France, May 1996

[14] J. F. O'Brien, B. Bodenheimer, G. Brostow, and J. Hodgins, ``Automatic Joint Parameter Estimation from Magnetic Motion Capture Data", Proceedings of Graphics Interface 2000, Montreal, Canada, pp. 53-60, May 2000.

[15] Vladimir I. Pavlovic, Rajeev Sharma, Thomas S. Huang , Visual Interpretation of Hand Gestures for Human-Computer Interaction: A Review, IEEE Transactions on Pattern Analysis and Machine Intelligence, 1997
[16] D. M. Gavrila, The Visual Analysis of Human Movement: A Survey, Computer Vision and Image Understanding, Vol. 73, No.1. January, 1999: 82-98
[17] J. K. Aggarwal, Q. Cai, Human Motion Analysis: A Review, Computer Vision and Image Understanding, Vol. 73, No. 3, 1999
[18] Tsuyoshi Moriyama, Shinji Ozawa, Emotion Recognition and Synthesis System on Speech, IEEE International Conference on Multimedia Computing and Systems, 1999 Florence, Italy
[19] R. Antonio, and Hanna Damasio. Brain and Language. Scientific American September, 1992. 89-95
[20] A. J. Calder, A Principal Component Analysis of Facial Expression. Vision Research, 2001, Vol 41.
[21] http://emotion-research.net/
[22] http://affect.media.mit.edu/
[23] http://www.cs.cmu.edu/afs/cs.cmu.edu/project/oz/web/oz.html
[24] http://www.unige.ch/fapse/emotion/
[25] http://www.cs.bham.ac.uk/%7Eaxs/cogaff.html
[26] http://www.almaden.ibm.com/cs/BlueEyes/index.html
[27] http://www.peopleandrobots.org/
[28] http://robotics.vuse.vanderbilt.edu/affect.htm
[29] Dominic W. Massaro , Jonas Beskow, Michael M. Cohen, Christopher L. Fry, and Tony Rodriguez. Picture My Voice: Audio to Visual Speech Synthesis using Artificial Neural Networks. Proceedings of AVSP'99, pp.133-138. Santa Cruz, CA., August, 1999.
[30] Yamamoto E., Nakamura, S., & Shikano, K. Lip movement synthesis from speech based on Hidden Markov Models. Speech Communication, 26, (1998).105-115
[31] R. Gutierrez-Osuna, P. K. Kakumanu, A. Esposito, O. N. Garcia,A. Bojorquez, J. L. Castillo, and I. Rudomin. Speech-Driven Facial Animation With Realistic Dynamics. IEEE Trans. on Multimedia, Vol. 7, No. 1, Feb, 2005
[32] Pengyu Hong, Zhen Wen, and Thomas S. Huang, Real-time speech-driven face animation with expressions using neural networks. IEEE Trans on Neural Networks, Vol. 13, No. 4, July, 2002.
[33] A. Murat Tekalp, , JoK rn Ostermann,_Face and 2-D mesh animation in MPEG-4, Signal Processing: *Image Communication* 15 (2000) 387-421.
[34] Bregler, C., Covell, M., Slaney, M., Video Rewrite: Driving Visual Speech with Audio, ACM SIGGRAPH, 1997.
[35] Hunt, A., Black, A., Unit selection in a concatenative speech synthesis system using a large speech database, ICASSP, vol. 1, pp. 373-376, 1996.
[36] Cosatto E, Potamianos G, Graf H P. Audio-visual unit selection for the synthesis of photo-realistic talking-heads. In: IEEE International Conference on Multimedia and Expo, ICME 2000. 2: 619~622
[37] T. Ezzat, T. Poggio, MikeTalk: A Talking Facial Display Based on Morphing Visemes, in Proc. Computer Animation Conference, Philadelphia, USA, 1998.
[38] Ashish Verma, L. Venkata Subramaniam, Nitendra Rajput, Chalapathy Neti, Tanveer A Faruquie. Animating Expressive Faces Across Languages. IEEE Trans on Multimedia, Vol. 6, No. 6, Dec, 2004.
[39] P. Ekman and W. V. Friesen, Facial Action Coding System. Palo Alto, Calif: Con

[40] Nick Campbell, "Perception of Affect in Speech - towards an Automatic Processing of Paralinguistic Information in Spoken Conversation", ICSLP2004, Jeju, Oct, 2004.

[41] Andrew Ortony, Gerald L. Clore, Allan Collins, "The Cognitive Structure of Emotions", book

[42] C. Gobl and A. N'ı Chasaide, "The role of voice quality in communicating emotion, mood and attitude," Speech Communication, vol. 40, pp. 189–212, 2003.

[43] Scherer K.R., "Vocal affect expression: A review and a model for future research," Psychological Bulletin, vol. 99, pp. 143–165, 1986.

[44] E. Eide, A. Aaron, R. Bakis, W. Hamza, M. Picheny, and J. Pitrelli, A corpus-based approach to <ahem/> expressive speech synthesis, IEEE speech synthesis workshop, 2002, Santa Monica

[45] Dellaert, F., Polzin, t., and Waibel, A., Recognizing Emotion in Speech", In Proc. Of ICSLP 1996, Philadelphia, PA, pp. 1970-1973, 1996.

[46] Petrushin, V. A., "Emotion Recognition in Speech Signal: Experimental Study, Development and Application." ICSLP 2000, Beijing.

[47] Lee, C.M.; Narayanan, S.; Pieraccini, R., Recognition of Negative Emotion in the Human Speech Signals, Workshop on Auto. Speech Recognition and Understanding, Dec 2001.

[48] Tato, R., Santos, R., Kompe, R., Pardo, J.M., Emotional Space Improves Emotion Recognition, in Proc. Of ICSLP-2002, Denver, Colorado, September 2002.

[49] Yu, F., Chang, E., Xu, Y.Q., and Shum, H.Y., Emotion Detection From Speech To Enrich Multimedia Content, in the second IEEE Pacific-Rim Conference on Multimedia, October 24-26, 2001, Beijing, China.

[50] Nick Campbell, Synthesis Units for Conversational Speech - Using Phrasal Segments, http://feast.atr.jp/nick/refs.html

[51] M. Schröder & S. Breuer. XML Representation Languages as a Way of Interconnecting TTS Modules. Proc. ICSLP'04 Jeju, Korea.

[52] Ze-Jing Chuang and Chung-Hsien Wu "Emotion Recognition from Textual Input using an Emotional Semantic Network," In Proceedings of International Conference on Spoken Language Processing, ICSLP 2002, Denver, 2002.

[53] H. Kobayashi and F. Hara, "Recognition of Six Basic Facial Expressions and Their Strength by Neural Network," *Proc. Int'l Workshop Robot and Human Comm.*, pp. 381-386, 1992.

[54] Michael J. Lyons, Shigeru Akamatsu, Miyuki Kamachi , Jiro Gyoba. Coding Facial Expressions with Gabor Wavelets. *Proceedings, Third IEEE International Conference on Automatic Face and Gesture Recognition,* April 14-16 1998, Nara Japan, IEEE Computer Society, pp. 200-205.

[55] R. Brunelli and D. Falavigna, "Person Identification Using Multiple Cues", *IEEE Trans. On Pattern Analysis and Machine Intelligence*, Vol. 12, No. 10, pp. 955-966, Oct 1995.

[56] E. S. Bigun, J. Bigun, B. Duc, and S. Fischer, "Expert Conciliation for Multimodal Person Authentication Systems using Bayesian Statistics", Proc. *International Conference on Audio and Video-Based Biometric Person Authentication (AVBPA)*, pp. 291-300, Crans-Montana, Switzerland, March 1997.

[57] A. Kumar, D. C. Wong, H. C. Shen, and A. K. Jain, "Personal Verification using Palmprint and Hand Geometry Biometric", *4th International Conference on Audio- and Video-based Biometric Person Authentication*, Guildford, UK, June 9-11, 2003.

[58] R. W. Frischholz and U. Dieckmann, "Bioid: A Multimodal Biometric Identification System", *IEEE Computer*, Vol. 33, No. 2, pp. 64-68, 2000.

[59] A. K. Jain and A. Ross, "Learning User-specific Parameters in a Multibiometric System", Proc. International Conference on Image Processing (ICIP), Rochester, New York, September 22-25, 2002.
[60] T. K. Ho, J. J. Hull, and S. N. Srihari, "Decision Combination in Multiple Classifier Systems", *IEEE Trans. on Pattern Analysis and Machine Intelligence*, Vol. 16, No. 1, pp. 66-75, January 1994.
[61] J. Kittler, M. Hatef, R. P. W. Duin, and J. Matas, "On Combining Classifiers", *IEEE Trans. on Pattern Analysis and Machine Intelligence*, Vol. 20, No. 3, pp. 226-239, Mar 1998.
[62] U. Dieckmann, P. Plankensteiner, and T. Wagner, "Sesam: A Biometric Person Identification System Using Sensor Fusion", *Pattern Recognition Letters*, Vol. 18, No. 9, pp.827-833, 1997.
[63] Picard, RW, Affective Computing: Challenges, Int. Journal of Human-Computer Studies, Vol. 59, Issues 1-2, July 2003, pp. 55-64.
[64] Nick Campbell, Databases of Expressive Speech, COCOSDA 2003, Singapore
[65] http://www.ubiq.com/hypertext/weiser/UbiHome.html

Personalized Facial Animation Based on 3D Model Fitting from Two Orthogonal Face Images

Yonglin Li and Jianhua Tao

National Lab of Pattern and Recognition, Institute of Automation,
Chinese Academic of Sciences, Beijing 100080
{ylli, jhtao} @nlpr.ia.ac.cn

Abstract. In this paper, a personalized MPEG-4 compliant facial animation system in embedded platform is presented. We report a semi-automatic and rapid approach for personalized modeling from two orthogonal face images. The approach is very easy and efficient. With multi-dimension texture mapping, the personalized face model offers a much more lifelike behavior. The system can be used in game, interactive services etc.

1 Introduction

Facial animation has already proved to be impressive in interactive services, like human-machine interactions or virtual reality application or web services. For example, such systems can be used in news reading, help desk, e-cogent, playmail etc [3]. Although the cartoon like characters can play expressive impression, they can not very attractive. If lifelike and personalized characters can be used, the visual quality will become much better.

Facial animation research started in the early 70's by Parke's [11] pioneer work. In the last decade the quality of facial animations has improved remarkably due to the development of hardware and corresponding software. But in these days the generating of lifelike animated faces still remains an open issue. Human were train since birth to recognize faces and scrutinize facial expression. So we are very sensitive to the slightest changes of the synthesized face model [3].

There have been many work focus on creating a personalized face model. One technology which has been used widely is from the 3D rang data [4, 17, 18]. Another technology is from two orthogonal images, one frontal view and one side view [5, 7, 8, 9].Others have make attempt from images or video sequences which contains multiple views of a person [19, 20, 21].

During the animation, many researchers have focused on personalized facial animation from two orthogonal face images, one frontal view and one side view, in this process; they usually extract the 3D position of the facial feather points from the two orthogonal images automatically or by additional manual work. A generic face model is then fitted according the corresponding 3D position of the facial feather points to make global adaption, local deformation are used to make other feather points. After the deformation, texture mapping were applied to ensure the reality.

Another technique is introduced by Takaaki Akimoto [5] etc. In his paper, the 3D generic model is projected according to the orthogonal images after the facial feather

J. Tao, T. Tan, and R.W. Picard (Eds.): ACII 2005, LNCS 3784, pp. 996 – 1003, 2005.

points are extracted. Interpolation method was then used to calculate the displacement of non-feather vertices. Texture mapping is also used from two joint face images. However, he didn't find the transformation during the deformation of the generic model to ensure the accuracy.

Liu [2] has improved the technique by using only one frontal view of the face image by adapting all the computing in 2D space, no 3D transformation or rotation is considered. It makes the process easier and more efficient, however, the frontal view image can only afford limit degree in 3D space during animation, no depth information is considered for the reality of personalized face model.

Unlike liu's work, we expand the method to two orthogonal images, the approach doesn't need to compute the 3D position of the facial feather points. And the transformation matrix of the generic model is computed to ensure the accuracy in deformation. This make the process easier and more efficient since all the computing were restricted in 2D space.

The animation process was made according to MPEG-4 facial animation framework [22, 23]. Currently, MPEG-4 defines facial animation technique depending on the displacement of the facial definition points (FDP) described by facial animation parameters (FAP). For very low bit-rate communication, MPEG-4 defines Synthetic-Natural Hybrid Coding (SNHC), which can achieve the 1kbps condition by using the 68 significant parameters including 2 high level parameters define the viseme and expression and 66 low level parameters define the motion behaviors.

Animation in the embedded platform have attracted more and more researcher [6,10,12], Thomas Di Giacomo[6] had presented an approach that automatically refines or simplifies 3D facial animation, including its transformation to 2D graphics, to be displayed at interactive frame rates on heterogeneous devices. It lucked reality in appearance and was not personalized in behavior since their model is only a generic model with proper material. Our system can show a personalized and lifelike face model in such platform which makes it very attractive in interactive services.

The paper is organized as follows: Section 2 presents our approach in detail. In section 3, we use the model in real application with embedded environment. Section 4, then, makes some discussing of the current and future works.

2 Personalized 3D Face Model Creation

Our approach begins with pre-processing of two orthogonal images, and then the generic face model is projected according to the two view images. After projection, model fitting algorithm is presented for automatic face adaption, while all feather points were fitted, Radial Basis Function (RBF) is used to the transformation result. To ensure the reality, multi-direction texture mapping technique is used. The procedure for personalizing a 3D face model is described next in details.

2.1 Pre-processing

See the fact that the head height of same person should be equal, suppose R= HF/HS, where HF is height of the head in the frontal view image, HS is height of the head in the side view image, the side view image can be scaled through R to make the two images exactly the same in head height.

Then facial feather points have to be extracted for the fitting process. In this step we extract the facial feather points semi-automatically, the eye, mouth corner and nose tip are extracted automatically, manual efforts were used to locate other feather points which can describe the face contour. The feather points were chose mainly based on their importance in the face images. In total 32 feature points in front view image and 20 feature points in side view image are selected.

2.2 3D Model Fitting

The generic model used is based on the IST facial model [24] which is widely used in the SNHC of MPEG-4. The back part of the face model is excluded to improve efficiency in the late rendering process. Fig. 1 shows the generic model from different view.

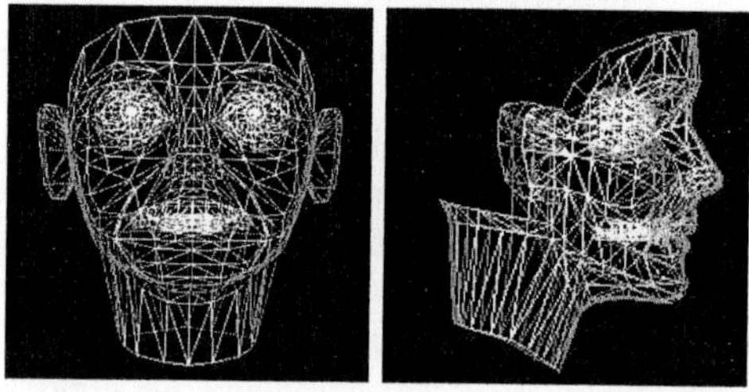

Fig. 1. Generic face model without hair part in different views

The adaptation process is as follows:

1) We project the generic model to XY plan and YZ plan according to the frontal and side view images, and select 32 and 20 corresponding points according to the face images in the generic face model.
2) Then, the 32 corresponding feather points in the XY projection were used. We suppose $P_{Mf} = (X_{Mf}, Y_{Mf})^T$ is the position of the feather points of the model, where $_{Mf}$ denotes the XY projection of the 3D model, $P_{If} = (X_{If}, Y_{If})^T$ is the position of the feather points of the face image, where $_{If}$ denotes the front view face image. s is the scaling factor. R is a $2*2$ rotation matrix, T is the translation vector. Eq.1 gives the sum squared error between the calculated points $\{P_{Mf1}....P_{Mfk}....P_{Mfn}\}$ $(k = 1....32)$ and the corresponding feather points $\{P_{If1}....P_{Ifk}....P_{Ifn}\}$ $(k = 1....32)$.

$$\text{Min } E(s, R, T) = \sum_{\text{points}} (P_{mf} - P_{if}) \tag{1}$$

Where

$$s \cdot R \cdot P_{mf} + T = P_{if} \tag{2}$$

With above results, procrustes [14, 15] analysis were used to compute the value of s, R, T iteratively. In the experiment, like Liu [2]'s result, we also find one iteration is sufficient in most cases.

3) After the 32 corresponding feather points were fitted, Radial Basis Function (RBF) was applied to deform other feather points of the generic model. Details can be found in [16].

4) We use $P_{Ms} = (X_{Ms}, Y_{Ms})^T$ to represent the position of the feature points of the generic model, where $_{MS}$ is the YZ projection of the 3D model, and use $P_{Is} = (X_{Is}, Y_{Is})^T$ to be the position of the feather points of the face image, where $_{Is}$ is the side view face image. Apply the algorithm in step 2 and 3 to fit the side face model. Fig. 2 shows the fitting result. From the experiment result we can see the approach performs very well.

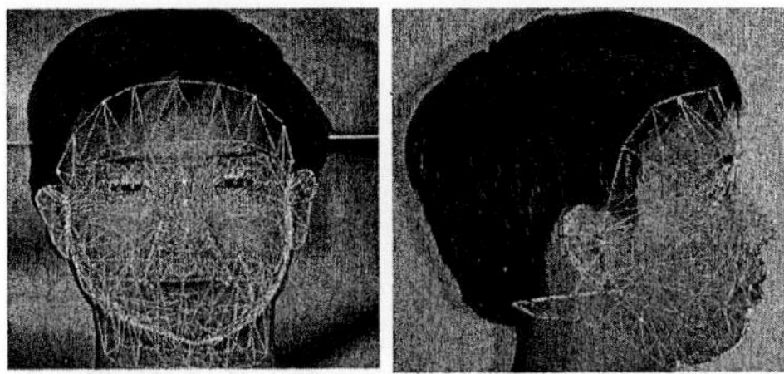

Fig. 2. Fitting result in front view and side view image

5) After that, the personalized face model can be directly reconstructed by combining the above two fitting results in both front view and side view. Let's define a 2D position ($X=X_f, Y=Y_f$) in the model from the front view and ($Z=Z_s$, $Y=Y_s$) from the side view. Then, the position (X, Y, Z) of the 3D face model could be got by:

$$\begin{cases} X=X_f; \\ Y=(Y_f+Y_s)/2; \\ Z=Z_s; \end{cases} \quad (3)$$

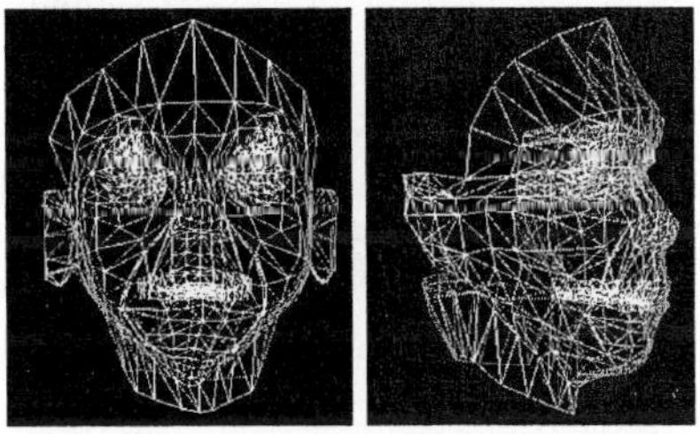

Fig. 3. Personalized model without texture in different views

During the fitting processing, we found that the Y_f and Y_s is quit similar. This partly proved that the algorithm play very well. Fig. 3. shows reconstruction results of personalized 3D face model.

6) Finally, the texture mapping are then applied to the model to ensure the reality, in the experiment multi-direction mapping algorithm were used by simply estimate the angle between the normal vector of the triangles in the model and the Z axis, to determine whether the frontal image or the side image should used. To join the front and side view images smoothly, the system maps a blended image where the texture mapping encounter each other, the blending ratio is according to the location of the personalized face model. This makes the texture mapping process more simple in computation. The result can be seen as follows.

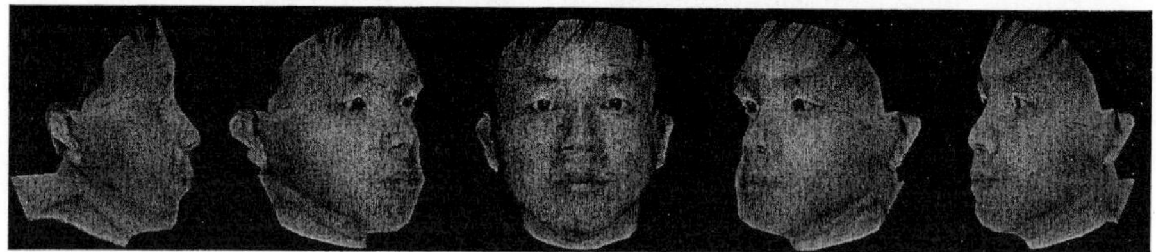

Fig. 4. Personalized face model with texture mapping

3 Real-Time Animation in Embedded Platform

Animation comes directly when the personalized face model has created. But it faces difficulty when the animating process display on embedded platform like mobile phones and personal digital assistant with limit CPU and RAM. So proper computer graphic rendering technology has to be considered.

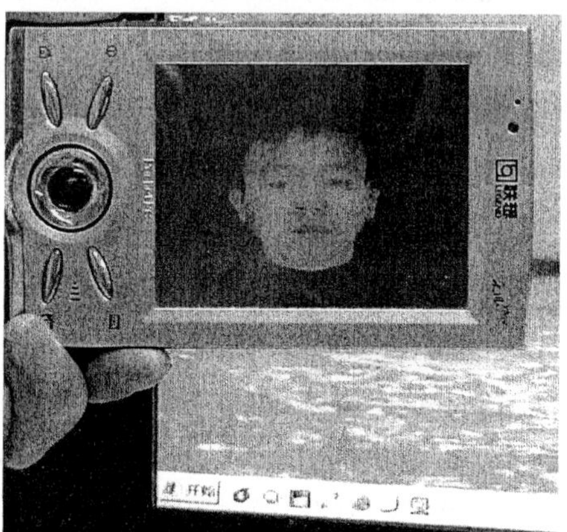

Fig. 5. Personalized facial animation in embedded platform

The animation processing was tested in a personal digital assistant with 206-MHz processor and 64Mbytes main memory. In fact, only 6-8MB was available when the animation process enabled. In the experiment, the mesh vertices were simplified to 780 and 1640 triangle in total; this is suitable for many embedded platforms. The floating-point arithmetic was converted to fixed-point arithmetic also. And Klimt [25] is also used to replay standard OpenGL function. These improvements can make the animation and rendering real-time. As expected. The personalized face model can displayed an expressive result. It can display 10--20 Fps (Frame rates per second) which is enough for real time animation in such platform. Fig. 5 and 6 have showed the animating result.

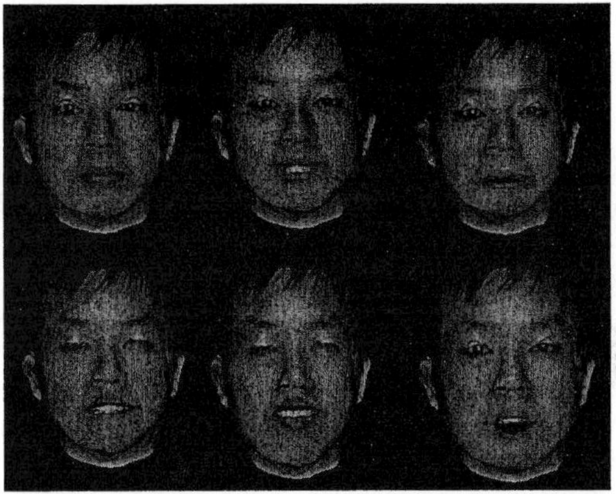

Fig. 6. Generating different expression for the personalized face model

4 Discussion and Future Work

Compared to the original techniques, the system is more efficient and easy, the computation is only applied in two dimension space, and this is different from the original techniques where the computation made in three dimension spaces while fitting the feather points. So our approach shows better quality in computation complexity. This makes the modeling more quickly.

Unlike just interpolating to face model projection, the system use mean square errors regulation and procrustes analysis [14, 15] to compute the fitting matrix. This has ensured the precision during the matching process. These improvements had enhanced the reality of personalized face model compared to original techniques which can be found in Fig.4 and 6. The improvements in computation complexity and reality in personalized face model are showed in Tab.1.

Table 1. Compares with other techniques

Methods / Characteristics	A-Nasser Ansari[9]	Takaaki [5]	Our approach
Computation complexity	high	Low	Low
Reality	Low	Low	High

The system has proved to be real-time in the embedded platform successfully. So it might be able to be used in the application 3G platforms in the future. Further improvements should be focus on the fully automatic extraction of facial feature points and proper computer graphic techniques for enhancing the rending efficiency in embedded platform.

5 Conclusion

In this paper, a semi-automatic and rapid approach for creating a personalized face model from two orthogonal face images is presented. The approach is very easy and efficient compared to original approaches. We also report a real-time MPEG-4 compliant facial animation system in embedded platform. With multi-dimension texture mapping, the personalized face model offers a much more lifelike behavior.

References

1. Jianhua Tao, Tieniu Tan. Emotional Chinese talkinghead system. International Conference on Multimedia Interface,2004
2. Zicheng Liu. A fully automatic system to model faces from a single image. Technical report MSR-TR-2003-55
3. Eric Cosatto, Jorn Ostermann, Hans Peter Graf, Juergen Schroeter. Lifelike Talking faces for interactive services. Proceeding of IEEE special issue on multimedia human computer interaction. September,2003
4. Yuencheng Lee, Demetri Terzopoulos, Keith Waters. Realistic modeling for facial animation. Proceedings of SIGGRAPH 1995
5. Takaaki Akimoto, Yasuhito Suenaga, Richard S.Wallace. Automatic creation of 3D Facial Models. IEEE Computer Graphics& Applications. 1993
6. Thomas Di Giacomo, Hyung-Seok Kim, Stephane Garchery, Nadia Magnenat-Thalmann. Benchmark-Driven automatic transmoding of 3D to 2D talking heads. Workshop on Modelling and Motion Capture Techniques for Virtual Environments, December 2004
7. Nikos Grammalidis, Nikos Sarris, Michael G.Strintzis. Generation of Personalized MPEG-4 compliant talking heads. International Workshop on Digital Communications (IWDC 2002), pp. 185-190, 2002.
8. Shiguang Shan, Wen Gao, Jie Yan, Hongming Zhang, Xilin Chen. Individual 3D face synthesis based on orthogonal photos and speech-driven facial animation. International Conference on Image Processing 2000
9. A-Nasser Ansari and Mohamed Abdel-Mottaleb. 3-D face modeling using two views and a generic face model with application to 3-D face recognition. Proceeding of the IEEE conference on Advanced Video and Signal Based Surveillance. 2003
10. Igor S. Pandzic. Facial animation framework for the web and mobile platforms. ACM Special Interest Group on Computer Graphics and Interactive Techniques 2002
11. F.I. Parke. Computer generated animation of faces. ACM National Conference. ACM, November 1972.
12. Florent Duguet, George Drettakis. Flexible Point-based rendering on mobile devices. IEEE Computer Graphics and Applications number 4 volume 24 July-August 2004
13. Murat Tekalp, Jorn Ostermann. MPEG-4 Facial Animation Project. http://www.cs.technion.ac.il/~gip/projects/s2002/Dmitry_Vadim_MPEG4/index.htm
14. J.R. Hurley and R.B.Cattell. The Procrustes program: Producing a direct rotation to test an hypothesized factor structure Behavior Science.1962, pp258–262
15. AL Yuille, PW Hallinan, DS Cohen. Feature extraction from faces using deformable templates. International Journal of Computer Vision, 1992
16. Floater, M.S., and A. Iske, Multistep Scattered Data Interpolation using Compactly Supported Radial Basis Functions, Journal of Computational and Applied Mathematics vol.73, no.5, pp. 65-78, 1996

17. L.S.Chen, T.S.Huang, J.Ostermann. Animated Talkinghead with Personalized 3D Head Model. IEEE first Workshop on Multimedia Signal Processing,1997.
18. V.Blanz and T.Vetter. A Morphable Model for the Synthesis of 3D faces. In Proc. SIGGRAPH99,1999.
19. Frederic Pighin, Richad Szeliski, David H.Salesin. Modeling and Animating Realistic Faces from Images. International Journal of Computer Vision 50(2),143-169,2002.
20. Z.Liu, Z.Zhang, G.Jacobs and M.Cohen. Rapid modeling of animated faces from video. Journal of Visualization and Computer Animation, 12(4):227-240,Sep,2001.
21. M Dimitrijevic, S Ilic, P Fua. Accurate Face Models from Uncalibrated and Ill-Lit Video Sequences. Conference on Computer Vision and Pattern Recognition 2004
22. ISO/IEC IS 14496-2 Viusal, 1999
23. A.Murat Tekalp, Jorn Ostermann. Face and 2-D mesh animation in MPEG-4. Signal Processing: Image Communication, 15 (2000) 387~421
24. Gabriel Antunes Abrantes, Fernando Pereira. MPEG-4 Facial Animation Technology: Survey, Implementation, and Result. IEEE Transactions on Circuits and Systems for Video Technology, Vol. 9,NO.2,March,1999
25. Klimt- the open source 3D Graphics Library for Mobile Devices http://studierstube.org/klimt/

Author Index

Lecture Notes in Computer Science

For information about Vols. 1–3678

please contact your bookseller or Springer

Vol. 3785: K.-K. Lau, R. Banach (Eds.), Formal Methods and Software Engineering. XIV, 496 pages. 2005.

Vol. 3784: J. Tao, T. Tan, R.W. Picard (Eds.), Affective Computing and Intelligent Interaction. XIX, 1008 pages. 2005.

Vol. 3781: S.Z. Li, Z. Sun, T. Tan, S. Pankanti, G. Chollet, D. Zhang (Eds.), Advances in Biometric Person Authentication. XI, 250 pages. 2005.

Vol. 3780: K. Yi (Ed.), Programming Languages and Systems. XI, 435 pages. 2005.

Vol. 3777: O.B. Lupanov, O.M. Kasim-Zade, A.V. Chaskin, K. Steinhöfel (Eds.), Stochastic Algorithms: Foundations and Applications. VIII, 239 pages. 2005.

Vol. 3775: J. Schoenwaelder, J. Serrat (Eds.), Ambient Networks. XIII, 281 pages. 2005.

Vol. 3772: M. Consens, G. Navarro (Eds.), String Processing and Information Retrieval. XIV, 406 pages. 2005.

Vol. 3770: J. Akoka, S.W. Liddle, I.-Y. Song, M. Bertolotto, I. Comyn-Wattiau, W.-J.v.d. Heuvel, M. Kolp, J. Trujillo, C. Kop, H.C. Mayr (Eds.), Perspectives in Conceptual Modeling. XXII, 476 pages. 2005.

Vol. 3766: N. Sebe, M.S. Lew, T.S. Huang (Eds.), Computer Vision in Human-Computer Interaction. X, 231 pages. 2005.

Vol. 3765: Y. Liu, T. Jiang, C. Zhang (Eds.), Computer Vision for Biomedical Image Applications. X, 563 pages. 2005.

Vol. 3762: R. Meersman, Z. Tari, P. Herrero (Eds.), On the Move to Meaningful Internet Systems 2005: OTM Workshops. XXXI, 1228 pages. 2005.

Vol. 3761: R. Meersman, Z. Tari (Eds.), On the Move to Meaningful Internet Systems 2005: CoopIS, DOA, and ODBASE, Part II. XXVII, 653 pages. 2005.

Vol. 3760: R. Meersman, Z. Tari (Eds.), On the Move to Meaningful Internet Systems 2005: CoopIS, DOA, and ODBASE, Part I. XXVII, 921 pages. 2005.

Vol. 3759: G. Chen, Y. Pan, M. Guo, J. Lu (Eds.), Parallel and Distributed Processing and Applications - ISPA 2005 Workshops. XIII, 669 pages. 2005.

Vol. 3758: Y. Pan, D. Chen, M. Guo, J. Cao, J. Dongarra (Eds.), Parallel and Distributed Processing and Applications. XXIII, 1162 pages. 2005.

Vol. 3756: J. Cao, W. Nejdl, M. Xu (Eds.), Advanced Parallel Processing Technologies. XIV, 526 pages. 2005.

Vol. 3754: J. Dalmau Royo, G. Hasegawa (Eds.), Management of Multimedia Networks and Services. XII, 384 pages. 2005.

Vol. 3752: N. Paragios, O. Faugeras, T. Chan, C. Schnoerr (Eds.), Variational, Geometric, and Level Set Methods in Computer Vision. XI, 369 pages. 2005.

Vol. 3751: T. Magedanz, E.R. M. Madeira, P. Dini (Eds.), Operations and Management in IP-Based Networks. X, 213 pages. 2005.

Vol. 3750: J.S. Duncan, G. Gerig (Eds.), Medical Image Computing and Computer-Assisted Intervention – MICCAI 2005, Part II. XL, 1018 pages. 2005.

Vol. 3749: J.S. Duncan, G. Gerig (Eds.), Medical Image Computing and Computer-Assisted Intervention – MICCAI 2005, Part I. XXXIX, 942 pages. 2005.

Vol. 3747: C.A. Maziero, J.G. Silva, A.M.S. Andrade, F.M.d. Assis Silva (Eds.), Dependable Computing. XV, 267 pages. 2005.

Vol. 3746: P. Bozanis, E.N. Houstis (Eds.), Advances in Informatics. XIX, 879 pages. 2005.

Vol. 3745: J.L. Oliveira, V. Maojo, F. Martin-Sanchez, A.S. Pereira (Eds.), Biological and Medical Data Analysis. XII, 422 pages. 2005. (Subseries LNBI).

Vol. 3744: T. Magedanz, A. Karmouch, S. Pierre, I. Venieris (Eds.), Mobility Aware Technologies and Applications. XIV, 418 pages. 2005.

Vol. 3740: T. Srikanthan, J. Xue, C.-H. Chang (Eds.), Advances in Computer Systems Architecture. XVII, 833 pages. 2005.

Vol. 3739: W. Fan, Z. Wu, J. Yang (Eds.), Advances in Web-Age Information Management. XXIV, 930 pages. 2005.

Vol. 3738: V.R. Syrotiuk, E. Chávez (Eds.), Ad-Hoc, Mobile, and Wireless Networks. XI, 360 pages. 2005.

Vol. 3735: A. Hoffmann, H. Motoda, T. Scheffer (Eds.), Discovery Science. XVI, 400 pages. 2005. (Subseries LNAI).

Vol. 3734: S. Jain, H.U. Simon, E. Tomita (Eds.), Algorithmic Learning Theory. XII, 490 pages. 2005. (Subseries LNAI).

Vol. 3733: P. Yolum, T. Güngör, F. Gürgen, C. Özturan (Eds.), Computer and Information Sciences - ISCIS 2005. XXI, 973 pages. 2005.

Vol. 3731: F. Wang (Ed.), Formal Techniques for Networked and Distributed Systems - FORTE 2005. XII, 558 pages. 2005.

Vol. 3728: V. Paliouras, J. Vounckx, D. Verkest (Eds.), Integrated Circuit and System Design. XV, 753 pages. 2005.

Vol. 3726: L.T. Yang, O.F. Rana, B. Di Martino, J. Dongarra (Eds.), High Performance Computing and Communcations. XXVI, 1116 pages. 2005.

Vol. 3725: D. Borrione, W. Paul (Eds.), Correct Hardware Design and Verification Methods. XII, 412 pages. 2005.

Vol. 3724: P. Fraigniaud (Ed.), Distributed Computing. XIV, 520 pages. 2005.

Vol. 3723: W. Zhao, S. Gong, X. Tang (Eds.), Analysis and Modelling of Faces and Gestures. XI, 4234 pages. 2005.

Vol. 3722: D. Van Hung, M. Wirsing (Eds.), Theoretical Aspects of Computing – ICTAC 2005. XIV, 614 pages. 2005.

Vol. 3721: A. Jorge, L. Torgo, P. Brazdil, R. Camacho, J. Gama (Eds.), Knowledge Discovery in Databases: PKDD 2005. XXIII, 719 pages. 2005. (Subseries LNAI).

Vol. 3720: J. Gama, R. Camacho, P. Brazdil, A. Jorge, L. Torgo (Eds.), Machine Learning: ECML 2005. XXIII, 769 pages. 2005. (Subseries LNAI).

Vol. 3719: M. Hobbs, A.M. Goscinski, W. Zhou (Eds.), Distributed and Parallel Computing. XI, 448 pages. 2005.

Vol. 3718: V.G. Ganzha, E.W. Mayr, E.V. Vorozhtsov (Eds.), Computer Algebra in Scientific Computing. XII, 502 pages. 2005.

Vol. 3717: B. Gramlich (Ed.), Frontiers of Combining Systems. X, 321 pages. 2005. (Subseries LNAI).

Vol. 3716: L. Delcambre, C. Kop, H.C. Mayr, J. Mylopoulos, O. Pastor (Eds.), Conceptual Modeling – ER 2005. XVI, 498 pages. 2005.

Vol. 3715: E. Dawson, S. Vaudenay (Eds.), Progress in Cryptology – Mycrypt 2005. XI, 329 pages. 2005.

Vol. 3714: H. Obbink, K. Pohl (Eds.), Software Product Lines. XIII, 235 pages. 2005.

Vol. 3713: L. Briand, C. Williams (Eds.), Model Driven Engineering Languages and Systems. XV, 722 pages. 2005.

Vol. 3712: R. Reussner, J. Mayer, J.A. Stafford, S. Overhage, S. Becker, P.J. Schroeder (Eds.), Quality of Software Architectures and Software Quality. XIII, 289 pages. 2005.

Vol. 3711: F. Kishino, Y. Kitamura, H. Kato, N. Nagata (Eds.), Entertainment Computing - ICEC 2005. XXIV, 540 pages. 2005.

Vol. 3710: M. Barni, I. Cox, T. Kalker, H.J. Kim (Eds.), Digital Watermarking. XII, 485 pages. 2005.

Vol. 3709: P. van Beek (Ed.), Principles and Practice of Constraint Programming - CP 2005. XX, 887 pages. 2005.

Vol. 3708: J. Blanc-Talon, W. Philips, D.C. Popescu, P. Scheunders (Eds.), Advanced Concepts for Intelligent Vision Systems. XXII, 725 pages. 2005.

Vol. 3707: D.A. Peled, Y.-K. Tsay (Eds.), Automated Technology for Verification and Analysis. XII, 506 pages. 2005.

Vol. 3706: H. Fuks, S. Lukosch, A.C. Salgado (Eds.), Groupware: Design, Implementation, and Use. XII, 378 pages. 2005.

Vol. 3704: M. De Gregorio, V. Di Maio, M. Frucci, C. Musio (Eds.), Brain, Vision, and Artificial Intelligence. XV, 556 pages. 2005.

Vol. 3703: F. Fages, S. Soliman (Eds.), Principles and Practice of Semantic Web Reasoning. VIII, 163 pages. 2005.

Vol. 3702: B. Beckert (Ed.), Automated Reasoning with Analytic Tableaux and Related Methods. XIII, 343 pages. 2005. (Subseries LNAI).

Vol. 3701: M. Coppo, E. Lodi, G. M. Pinna (Eds.), Theoretical Computer Science. XI, 411 pages. 2005.

Vol. 3699: C.S. Calude, M.J. Dinneen, G. Păun, M. J. Pérez-Jiménez, G. Rozenberg (Eds.), Unconventional Computation. XI, 267 pages. 2005.

Vol. 3698: U. Furbach (Ed.), KI 2005: Advances in Artificial Intelligence. XIII, 409 pages. 2005. (Subseries LNAI).

Vol. 3697: W. Duch, J. Kacprzyk, E. Oja, S. Zadrożny (Eds.), Artificial Neural Networks: Formal Models and Their Applications – ICANN 2005, Part II. XXXII, 1045 pages. 2005.

Vol. 3696: W. Duch, J. Kacprzyk, E. Oja, S. Zadrożny (Eds.), Artificial Neural Networks: Biological Inspirations – ICANN 2005, Part I. XXXI, 703 pages. 2005.

Vol. 3695: M.R. Berthold, R. Glen, K. Diederichs, O. Kohlbacher, I. Fischer (Eds.), Computational Life Sciences. XI, 277 pages. 2005. (Subseries LNBI).

Vol. 3694: M. Malek, E. Nett, N. Suri (Eds.), Service Availability. VIII, 213 pages. 2005.

Vol. 3693: A.G. Cohn, D.M. Mark (Eds.), Spatial Information Theory. XII, 493 pages. 2005.

Vol. 3692: R. Casadio, G. Myers (Eds.), Algorithms in Bioinformatics. X, 436 pages. 2005. (Subseries LNBI).

Vol. 3691: A. Gagalowicz, W. Philips (Eds.), Computer Analysis of Images and Patterns. XIX, 865 pages. 2005.

Vol. 3690: M. Pěchouček, P. Petta, L.Z. Varga (Eds.), Multi-Agent Systems and Applications IV. XVII, 667 pages. 2005. (Subseries LNAI).

Vol. 3689: G.G. Lee, A. Yamada, H. Meng, S.H. Myaeng (Eds.), Information Retrieval Technology. XVII, 735 pages. 2005.

Vol. 3688: R. Winther, B.A. Gran, G. Dahll (Eds.), Computer Safety, Reliability, and Security. XI, 405 pages. 2005.

Vol. 3687: S. Singh, M. Singh, C. Apte, P. Perner (Eds.), Pattern Recognition and Image Analysis, Part II. XXV, 809 pages. 2005.

Vol. 3686: S. Singh, M. Singh, C. Apte, P. Perner (Eds.), Pattern Recognition and Data Mining, Part I. XXVI, 689 pages. 2005.

Vol. 3685: V. Gorodetsky, I. Kotenko, V. Skormin (Eds.), Computer Network Security. XIV, 480 pages. 2005.

Vol. 3684: R. Khosla, R.J. Howlett, L.C. Jain (Eds.), Knowledge-Based Intelligent Information and Engineering Systems, Part IV. LXXIX, 933 pages. 2005. (Subseries LNAI).

Vol. 3683: R. Khosla, R.J. Howlett, L.C. Jain (Eds.), Knowledge-Based Intelligent Information and Engineering Systems, Part III. LXXX, 1397 pages. 2005. (Subseries LNAI).

Vol. 3682: R. Khosla, R.J. Howlett, L.C. Jain (Eds.), Knowledge-Based Intelligent Information and Engineering Systems, Part II. LXXIX, 1371 pages. 2005. (Subseries LNAI).

Vol. 3681: R. Khosla, R.J. Howlett, L.C. Jain (Eds.), Knowledge-Based Intelligent Information and Engineering Systems, Part I. LXXX, 1319 pages. 2005. (Subseries LNAI).

Vol. 3680: C. Priami, A. Zelikovsky (Eds.), Transactions on Computational Systems Biology II. IX, 153 pages. 2005. (Subseries LNBI).

Vol. 3679: S.d.C. di Vimercati, P. Syverson, D. Gollmann (Eds.), Computer Security – ESORICS 2005. XI, 509 pages. 2005.